COMMERCIAL REPORTS

AREA STUDIES SERIES

EDITORIAL DIRECTOR Professor J J O'Meara
RESEARCH UNIT DIRECTOR T F Turley
ASSISTANT DIRECTOR S Cashman

CHIEF EDITORIAL ADVISERS

P Ford
Professor Emeritus, Southampton University
Mrs G Ford

SPECIAL EDITORIAL CONSULTANT FOR
THE UNITED STATES PAPERS

H C Allen
Commonwealth Fund Professor of American History, University College, London
Director of the London University Institute of United States Studies

RESEARCH EDITORS
Johann A Norstedt
Marilyn Evers Norstedt

This Series is published with the active co-operation of
SOUTHAMPTON UNIVERSITY

IRISH UNIVERSITY PRESS AREA STUDIES SERIES

BRITISH PARLIAMENTARY PAPERS

UNITED STATES OF AMERICA

38

Embassy and consular
commercial reports
1895-96

IRISH UNIVERSITY PRESS
Shannon   Ireland

PUBLISHER'S NOTE

The documents in this series are selected from the nineteenth-century British House of Commons *sessional and command papers*. All of the original papers relating to the United States of America are included with the exception of two kinds of very brief and unimportant papers. Omitted are (1) random statistical trade returns which are included in the larger and complete yearly trade figures and (2) returns relating to postal services, which are irregularly presented, of tangential USA relevance, and easily available in other sources.

The original documents have been reproduced by photo-lithography and are unabridged even to the extent of retaining the first printers' imprints. Imperfections in the original printing are sometimes unavoidably reproduced.

This reprint is an enlargement from the original octavo format.

© 1971 Irish University Press Shannon Ireland

Microfilm, microfiche and other forms of micro-publishing
© *Irish University Microforms Shannon Ireland*

ISBN 0 7165 1538 5

Printed and published by
Irish University Press Shannon Ireland
DUBLIN CORK BELFAST LONDON NEW YORK
T M MacGlinchey *Publisher* Robert Hogg *Printer*

Oversize
HC
103
.I72
v.38

Contents

IUP Page Number

For ease of reference IUP editors have assigned a continuous pagination which appears on the top outer margin of each page.

Commercial Reports

F.O. annual series no. 1512: report on Baltimore, 1894
1895 [C.7581–52] CI 9

F.O. annual series no. 1517: report on Charleston, 1894
1895 [C.7581–57] CI 31

F.O. annual series no. 1536: report on Boston, 1894
1895 [C.7581–76] CI 77

F.O. annual series no. 1541: report on the agriculture of the
Boston district, 1894
1895 [C.7581–81] CI 97

F.O. annual series no. 1542: report on the agriculture of the
New Orleans district, 1894
1895 [C.7581–82] CI 111

F.O. annual series no. 1543: report on Chicago, 1894
1895 [C.7581–83] CI 131

F.O. annual series no. 1551: report on New Orleans, 1894
1895 [C.7581–91] CI 189

F.O. annual series no. 1561: report on New York, 1894
1895 [C.7581–101] CI 237

F.O. annual series no. 1568: report on Galveston, 1894
1895 [C.7581–108] CI 265

F.O. annual series no. 1576: report on San Francisco, 1894
1895 [C.7581–116] CI 329

F.O. annual series no. 1590: report on the agriculture of
New York, New Jersey, Connecticut, Delaware, Rhode Island, 1894
1895 [C.7828–7] CI 451

F.O. annual series no. 1687: report on Galveston, 1895
1896 [C.7919–55] LXXXIX 465

F.O. annual series no. 1688: report on New Orleans, 1895
1896 [C.7919–56] LXXXIX 511

F.O. annual series no. 1701: report on Boston, 1895
1896 [C.7919–69] LXXXIX 543

F.O. annual series no. 1711: report on Charleston, 1895
1896 [C.7919–79] LXXXIX 567

F.O. annual series no. 1712: report on Baltimore, 1895
1896 [C.7919–80] LXXXIX 609

F.O. annual series no. 1725: report on Chicago, 1895
1896 [C.7919–93] LXXXIX 623

F.O. annual series no. 1734: report on Portland, Oregon, 1895
1896 [C.7919–102] LXXXIX 769

F.O. annual series no. 1750: report on San Francisco, 1895
1896 [C.7919–118] LXXXIX 827

F.O. annual series no. 1767: report on New York, 1895
1896 [C.7919–135] LXXXIX 879

As most commercial reports are extracted from larger papers, the reader should note that a particular report may lack a proper title page.

YOUNGSTOWN STATE UNIVERSITY
LIBRARY

FOREIGN OFFICE.
1895.
ANNUAL SERIES.

No. 1512.

DIPLOMATIC AND CONSULAR REPORTS ON TRADE AND FINANCE.

UNITED STATES.

REPORT FOR THE YEAR 1894

ON THE

TRADE OF THE CONSULAR DISTRICT OF BALTIMORE.

REFERENCE TO PREVIOUS REPORT, Annual Series No. 1340.

Presented to both Houses of Parliament by Command of Her Majesty,
APRIL, 1895.

LONDON:
PRINTED FOR HER MAJESTY'S STATIONERY OFFICE,
BY HARRISON AND SONS, ST. MARTIN'S LANE,
PRINTERS IN ORDINARY TO HER MAJESTY.

And to be purchased, either directly or through any Bookseller, from
EYRE & SPOTTISWOODE, EAST HARDING STREET, FLEET STREET, E.C., and
32, ABINGDON STREET, WESTMINSTER, S.W.; or
JOHN MENZIES & Co., 12, HANOVER STREET, EDINBURGH, and
90, WEST NILE STREET, GLASGOW; or
HODGES, FIGGIS, & Co., Limited, 104, GRAFTON STREET, DUBLIN.

1895.

[C. 7581—52.] *Price Three Halfpence.*

New Series of Reports.

Reports of the Annual Series have been issued from Her Majesty's Diplomatic and Consular Officers at the following places, and may be obtained from the sources indicated on the title-page:—

No.		Price
1390.	New Orleans	2½d.
1391.	Manila	2d.
1392.	Foochow	1d.
1393.	Ningpo	1d.
1394.	Chinkiang	1d.
1395.	Tamsui	1d.
1396.	Chungking	1½d.
1397.	Philadelphia	3½d.
1398.	Bilbao	2½d.
1399.	Dunkirk	1d.
1400.	Amoy	1½d.
1401.	Tainan	1d.
1402.	Ichang	1d.
1403.	Aleppo	1d.
1404.	Madrid	1d.
1405.	Newchwang	1d.
1406.	Wênchow	½d.
1407.	Pakhoi	1½d.
1408.	Hankow	1d.
1409.	Amsterdam	1d.
1410.	Copenhagen	½d.
1411.	Damascus	1d.
1412.	Chefoo	3d.
1413.	Swatow	1d.
1414.	Mannheim	1½d.
1415.	Fiume	2d.
1416.	Athens	6d.
1417.	Söul	1½d.
1418.	Beyrout	1d.
1419.	Berlin	1½d.
1420.	Nice	3d.
1421.	Yokohama	1½d.
1422.	Maracaibo	1d.
1423.	Tunis	1½d.
1424.	Baghdad and Bussorah	1d.
1425.	Rio Grande do Sul	7d.
1426.	Erzeroum	1d.
1427.	Christiania	5½d.
1428.	Charleston	5½d.
1429.	Meshed	1d.
1430.	Copenhagen	½d.
1431.	Galveston	2½d.
1432.	Hamburg	2½d.
1433.	Brindisi	2½d.
1434.	Gothenburg	2d.
1435.	Kiungchow	1d.
1436.	St. Petersburg	½d.
1437.	Malaga	1d.
1438.	Chicago	2½d.
1439.	Odessa	2d.
1440.	Tabreez	½d.
1441.	Tahiti	½d.
1442.	Shanghai	2d.
1443.	Nagasaki	1d.
1444.	Madrid	2½d.
1445.	Malaga	2½d.
1446.	Rotterdam	1d.
1447.	Port Said	1d.
1448.	Sofia	2½d.
1449.	Warsaw	1½d.
1450.	Africa (Congo)	2d.

No.		Price
1451.	Jeddah	1½d.
1452.	San Francisco	5½d.
1453.	Oporto	2d.
1454.	Barcelona	2d.
1455.	New Caledonia	½d.
1456.	Smyrna	1d.
1457.	Macao	1d.
1458.	Samoa	1d.
1459.	Hiogo and Osaka	3d.
1460.	Lisbon	2d.
1461.	Pekin	2d.
1462.	Corunna	2d.
1463.	Mozambique	15d.
1464.	Munich	1½d.
1465.	St. Petersburg	3d.
1466.	Naples	1d.
1467.	Montevideo	2½d.
1468.	Aden	1d.
1469.	Tokio	1½d.
1470.	Dantzig	5d.
1471.	Guayaquil	1d.
1472.	Canton	1½d.
1473.	Dar-al-Baida	3d.
1474.	Teheran	2d.
1475.	Bushire	2d.
1476.	Tangier	2d.
1477.	Rome	2d.
1478.	Hamburg	4d.
1479.	The Hague	1½d.
1480.	Belgrade	2d.
1481.	Batoum	1½d.
1482.	Teneriffe	½d.
1483.	Lisbon	2½d.
1484.	Buda-Pesth	½d.
1485.	Rome	5½d.
1486.	Para	1d.
1487.	Odessa	1d.
1488.	Hakodate	1d.
1489.	Beira	1½d.
1490.	Berne	1½d.
1491.	Copenhagen	1d.
1492.	Stettin	2½d.
1493.	Rio Grande do Sul	1½d.
1494.	Serajevo	1d.
1495.	Buenos Ayres	9d.
1496.	Florence	2d.
1497.	Lisbon	1½d.
1498.	Paris	2d.
1499.	Bolivia	1½d.
1500.	Patras	1½d.
1501.	Bordeaux	3d.
1502.	Madrid	2d.
1503.	Amsterdam	1d.
1504.	Suakin	1d.
1505.	Angora	1d.
1506.	Havre	2½d.
1507.	Algiers	11d.
1508.	La Rochelle	3d.
1509.	Vera Cruz	2d.
1510.	Puerto Cortes	1d.
1511.	Taganrog	1d.

No. 1512.

Reference to previous Report, Annual Series No. 1340.

UNITED STATES.

BALTIMORE.

Consul Segrave to the Earl of Kimberley.

My Lord,   Baltimore, March 13, 1895.

I HAVE the honour to transmit to your Lordship, Reports on the Trade and Commerce of Baltimore, Norfolk, and Richmond, for the year 1894.

I have, &c.
(Signed)   W. F. SEGRAVE.

Report on the Trade and Commerce of the Consular District of Baltimore for the Year 1894.

Abstract of Contents.

	Page
Baltimore trade report	1
Depression of trade	2
Causes of	2
Remedies suggested	2
Baltimore trade	3
Railway strike: its effects	4
Ship canal	4
Shipping	5
Aluminium boats	5
Progress of Baltimore	5
Labour	6
Local finance	7
Immigration	7
Grain trade	7
Cotton	8
Other foreign trade	8
Tables	10
Norfolk trade report	13
Richmond trade report	17

In periods of depression in trade those whom it affects most are constantly speculating on its causes.

It may not be, therefore, out of place to note the various and divergent opinions which are expressed as to the approximate causes of the present collapse of business in this country.

(1914)

UNITED STATES.

Depression, causes of.

The past year closed with very gloomy prospects. The gold reserve was being constantly depleted, and the metal was being exported by every steamer.

Trade was abnormally dull, and the prices of grain and cotton unprecedently low.

It was felt, however, that if the cause of the depression could be ascertained a considerable advance would have been made towards discovering a remedy for it.

On the one hand it was confidently asserted that the depression primarily arose from the purchase of silver by the Government, so the Act of 1891, commonly known as "the Sherman Act," was repealed.

Then, that it was occasioned by the financial panic of 1893; but that soon passed away.

Again, it was attributed to scarcity of money; now, money is cheap, and there is plenty of it—of a sort.

Later on, the Tariff Bill was blamed, but the best and worst of that is now known.

The foregoing assigned causes for the depression have all disappeared, but the depression itself remains.

Remedy for.

At the present time, the generally received and probably the most accurate opinion formed is that the collapse of trade, the withdrawals of foreign capital, and the low prices of securities and products is due to mistrust of the finances of the country, and that wise, prudent, and, above all, prompt legislation is absolutely necessary to restore impaired confidence.

The discussion of the currency question by the legislature has demonstrated the utter absurdity of hoping to patch up a bank currency without first setting the national finances in order, and it is declared with confidence that the real and only remedy towards attaining the desirable end, is to call in and cancel the 500,000,000 dol. of United States legal tender gold demand notes, as in the present condition of things it is above all necessary to demonstrate to the world at large that this country is not only able, but resolved to maintain its currency on a parity with gold, the sure and only means by which confidence can be restored.

In a recent message to Congress the President has summed up the situation in forcible and graphic language. He has pointed out to them their duty, and has called upon them, in vigorous language, to act and to act promptly.

For years the people have ignored the danger lurking in their inflated paper money (locally "rag" money), but have continually gone on putting in circulation blocks of treasury notes and silver certificates, which are practically, at the present day, fictitious currency.

The attempt to counteract this evil, and overcome the consequent and natural mistrust by selling bonds for gold, has proved to be an utter failure. The bullion paid into the treasury with the right hand has been withdrawn with the left, and the only apparent result is that the country has made an addition of some 20,000,000*l.* to its debt, and that without helping its credit in the least.

The President says justly that to offer the creditor silver worth less than half its former price in gold is to cheat him out of half what is due to him.

He points out the dangers to which tampering with the currency has brought the country, not only for bankers and money-dealers, but for every man as well who lives by his daily labour.

The President recommends the issue of a new gold loan in 50 years 3 per cent. bonds, the proceeds to be applied to withdrawing and cancelling the paper money, so long the plague and danger of the country.

As an alternative he recommends that the new bonds be used by national banks as security for their own note circulation.

If such a proposal were coupled with the restriction of the bank note to a minimum value of 10 dol., it would no doubt, in the end, counteract the danger of excessive paper money from which this country has so long suffered.

Trade of Baltimore

As a natural consequence of the dismal situation of the country the trade of Baltimore during the past year shows considerable diminution, as well in volume as in value.

Few have escaped from the malignant influence of that depression which has signalised 1894 as the worst year in the last quarter of a century in the commercial annals of the city. Although Baltimore was not smitten by any financial panic like that which passed over the country in 1893, yet we are still suffering from its effects in the paralysis of industry and enterprise.

That the collapse of trade has not proved more fatal than the subjoined details demonstrate goes far to prove that business in Baltimore is based upon a more secure foundation than in other more pretentious centres in this country.

The watch-word for all business men during the past year was "Caution."

The rival parties in the federal legislature were involved in a long drawn out debate, over changes in the fiscal policy, having for its object the reduction of the tariff, approximating to a basis for revenue purposes alone.

In the meantime no business venture could be prudently undertaken, or so long as the commercial policy of the country was undetermined.

Twice in the year the Federal Government was forced to purchase gold in order to maintain the 100,000,000 dol. reserve, and it is now conceded by most business men, in this part of the country at least, that it is impracticable to restore financial confidence unless, of two things, either the Congress legislates towards the cancelling of the United States legal tender bonds or notes, or some policy is adopted whereby the gold reserve may be maintained in such volume as will satisfy the public, as well at home as abroad, that the country is able to maintain its notes on a parity with gold.

(1914)

Yet in spite of all the opposing influences which have been at work, in opposition to a restoration of confidence, it is satisfactory to note that Baltimore has held its own during the year in a truly gratifying manner.

There have been no failures of any importance, and the banks and financial institutions have maintained that reputation for prudence and strength which has enabled them to promulgate, with marked effect, their plan for reforming the National Bank currency, now universally known in the country as "The Baltimore plan."

Railway strike, its effects. The great railway strike which during a month in the past year paralysed the trade of the Western States, and practically cut this city off from Chicago, did not prove an altogether unmitigated evil for the farmers in the State.

Like almost all large cities on the Atlantic seaboard, Baltimore depends to a great extent on Chicago for its supply of meat.

When the strike was at its most acute stage, beef rose in price here from 3d. to 4d. per lb.

The farmers in the adjacent country took prompt advantage of the occasion, and were so enabled to dispose of their stock at an enhanced value.

Ship canal. The construction of the proposed Maryland and Delaware Ship Canal which has been so long before the public was advocated with renewed persistency and no little ability during the past year. Not only was it contended that, by cutting the canal through the Delaware Peninsula, the foreign and coasting trade of Baltimore would derive immense impulse and benefit, but that in time of possible war it would add considerably to the defence of the coast.

It was contended that the proposed canal would shorten the voyage from Baltimore to all northern European ports by some 24 hours, obviating the tedious and difficult navigation of Chesapeake Bay.

The Baltimore Chamber of Commerce, representing the shipping and mercantile interests of the city, has, however, in a recent report, exposed the fallacy of these pretensions, and pronounced strongly in opposition to the canal.

They declare that the very suggestion of such a canal is objectionable to the shipowner owing to the increased danger of navigation, and that, if underwriters did not demand a higher rate of premium on vessels using it, they would be sure to require exemption from the consequences of groundings, collisions, &c., as has already been done in the cases of the Suez and Manchester Canals.

They draw attention to the enormous expense which would be caused, not only in excavating a canal 54 miles in length, but also in dredging the approaches to a depth of 28 to 30 feet, as well as to the risk of ice in winter.

Finally they assert that no time would be gained by using the canal, as a ship would require 17 hours to steam through it from Baltimore to Delaware Bay under the most favourable conditions, and assuming it to be lighted, whereas at the present time a steamer can leave Baltimore at any hour of daylight and reach the open sea at the Capes in 16 hours.

The annexed shipping returns show large decreases in tonnage over those of 1893.

<small>Shipping.</small>

There was a falling-off of the total tonnage cleared of 264,490 tons, and of which 229,640 tons represented British shipping alone.

During the year seven steamships and nine sailing vessels were built, having an aggregate tonnage of 2,007 tons, and there are at present 1,140 vessels, with a net tonnage of 108,718 tons, owned and registered at this port.

Reports of 67 marine disasters were received at the custom-house, involving a loss of 34 human lives, and 25,000*l.* in shipping and 1,800*l.* in cargo property.

Tests of the aluminium boats recently constructed by a Baltimore firm have been made under the supervision of the Naval Department, and are reported to have proved singularly successful.

<small>Aluminium boats.</small>

The first boat which was experimented upon was 18 feet long, 4 feet beam, and 2 feet deep amidships, and weighed 350 lbs. It was placed empty in the water, when a man tried, unsuccessfully, to capsize it, by sitting on the gunwale. It was then heavily laden, yet remained $4\frac{1}{2}$ inches above water amidships. The boat was subsequently unloaded and the air-tight compartments tested by capsizing it, yet it was found impossible to get it more than half full of water, as the air-tight compartments held it so high as to act on the principle of a self-bailer. The boat was then taken alongside a wharf and filled with water until the gunwale was flush with the surface, when a man got on each end over the air-tight compartment. Even then the boat did not sink, but so soon as cast loose it heeled over, emptied one-half of the water, and then righted itself.

The naval officials are said to have been much impressed by the success of these experiments, and to have reported favourably on them as ship's lifeboats, and for other life-saving purposes. Their great drawback lies in the extreme susceptibility of aluminium to the corrosive action of salt water.

Few cities in this country have equalled the progress made by Baltimore within the past two or three years.

<small>Progress of Baltimore.</small>

The population is now over 500,000, and is annually increasing at the rate of about 20,000.

It is fast becoming one of the chief manufacturing centres of the country, mainly owing to its singular local advantages, which enable it, through its water and railway communications, to obtain raw material to any extent at the cheapest rates.

According to the latest census, that of 1890, there were within the limits of the city and its adjacent suburbs 5,265 factories, having a capital of 92,500,000 dol., giving employment to 84,000 hands, whose wages for the year aggregated 36,000,000 dol., and the value of whose product was 135,000,000 dol.

(1914)

UNITED STATES.

Since then manufactures have largely extended, a probable addition of some 20,000,000 dol. being invested in them, and now giving employment to 100,000 hands, with wages amounting to 42,000,000 dol.

Some idea may be formed of the value of Baltimore factories in comparing them with those of the other States in this consular district, as is shown below:—

Locality.	Capital Invested.	Number of Hands.	Wages.	Product.
	Millions of Dollars.		Millions of Dollars.	Millions of Dollars.
Baltimore	92½	84,000	93	135
Virginia	63½	59,591	19¾	88½
West Virginia	28	21,969	8½	38¾
Kentucky	80	65,759	27¾	126¾

Labour.

It is believed that, under the normal condition of labour at Baltimore, there are 5,000 hands constantly out of employment. In December, 1893, it was estimated that that number had doubled. An exhaustive enquiry made in the early part of 1894 placed the estimate of unemployed working hands at 33 per cent. In many trades, however, the proportion is even larger. Thus it was reported of the ironmoulders that 70 per cent. were out of work, of the painters 75 per cent., shoe lasters 50 per cent. In point of fact, out of 13 trades, giving employment to 11,795 persons, it was reported that 4,482, or nearly 38 per cent., were idle.

It is supposed that one-fifth of the population of the city is engaged in productive work as distinguished from professional avocations, thus making the working population amount to about 100,000 souls. As it is known that in 13 leading trades 38 per cent. of the workmen are unemployed, it may reasonably be concluded that the same condition exists in an equally large proportion of the entire body of working men; and this is, moreover, the more probable as the unskilled labourer's employment depends more or less on that of the skilled hands.

It would thus appear that there were upwards of 34,000 persons unemployed, or more than one-third of the entire labouring population, at the commencement of the past year, and the present condition of labour is practically identical.

The depressed condition of labour would no doubt have been much more acute had it not been for the large public works undertaken by the municipality and other bodies in beautifying and improving the communications of the city. Nine miles of improved pavement were laid during the year, and when it is considered that a pavior is paid at the rate of 16s. 6d. a day, and that a large amount of unskilled labour is engaged in the work, there can be small doubt that it has done much to ease the strain for the necessitous classes.

BALTIMORE.

Local finance. The bank clearances for 1894 showed, as compared with those of 1893, a falling-off of over 32,000,000 dol. This decrease, however, must be attributed to the general depression of business which prevailed. It is, however, to be noted that the decrease in Baltimore was not so great as in other cities in the country.

There have been no failures during the year. The banks have stood intact the heavy strain which was placed upon them, and which was specially severe in the early part of the year.

The savings banks appear to be even stronger than in 1893, as during the past year they received an excess of deposits over payments amounting to 875,000 dol., as against an excess of payments over receipts in 1893 of 1,500,000 dol.

Immigration. Hard times and repressive immigration laws are telling seriously on arrivals of immigrants at the port.

During the past year 7,670 immigrants arrived at Baltimore, being 13,516 fewer in number than during the preceding year. They were of the following nationalities:—

Country.	Number of Immigrants.
England 30	
Scotland 2	
Ireland 6	
Colonies 11	
	49
Austria	1,123
Belgium	3
Brazil	6
Cuba	2
Denmark	8
France	1
Germany	5,017
Netherlands	4
Sweden-Norway	20
Roumania	1
Russia	1,435
Switzerland	1

Of which there were—

	Number of Immigrants.
Males	3,790
Females	3,880

Grain trade. The grain market in 1894 showed great depression as compared with the previous year. This is mainly to be attributed to the ruinously low prices which prevailed in consequence of the general financial insecurity, not only here, but in foreign lands as well.

The farmers in the great wheat and maize producing countries in the west could not meet their expenses at current market rates. Some, who could afford, held their grain. The great majority, however, found it more profitable to give it to their stock.

It is asserted that 33 lbs. of wheat comes much nearer to the standard for fattening cattle than an equal quantity of maize hitherto in use for that purpose. Wheat is decided to be better than maize both for young growing cattle and for fattening beasts. It is, however, preferable to feed with equal parts of wheat and maize. The farmer declares that, when wheat and maize are at the same price, it is more profitable to feed wheat and sell maize, first, because wheat is 7 lbs. heavier per bushel than maize; and, second, because the manure from wheat-fed stock is much more valuable than that from stock fed on maize.

Flour. The civil war in Brazil is in the main accountable for the serious falling-off in this staple. Baltimore has, however, maintained its position as second port in the United States for the export of grain and flour.

Cotton. The last year has been remarkable for a long continued period of stagnation in the cotton trade. The time consumed by Congress in amending the Tariff Bill placed manufacturers and consumers in such a position that they were afraid to do any business except such as was absolutely necessary, being in serious doubt as to how the industry would be affected when the Bill was finally passed.

The various causes had the effect of lowering prices, which were $7\frac{3}{4}$ c. in January to $5\frac{3}{8}$ c. in November, since which, after various fluctuations, the price has advanced to $5\frac{3}{4}$ c.

The cotton mills in this neighbourhood used about 60,000 bales, and 220,600 bales were exported.

The estimate of the total yield of the crop varied from 9,000,000 to 10,500,000 bales.

The over production of cotton was one of the very serious problems which engaged the attention of growers during the past year, and which, moreover, had a most serious effect on the trade of Baltimore with the Southern States.

It is evident that the low price of cotton was not caused by slackness of demand, as more was consumed than in previous years, though no doubt the tightness of money may have depressed values.

Cotton growers have been discussing all manner of plans as a remedy for the present condition of the trade, and the result of which will probably be that the output will be reduced in the future.

A plan was adopted at a recent convention of cotton growers in Mississippi providing for a reduction of 25 per cent. in the cotton acreage in the present year.

Tobacco. The crop of Maryland tobacco which was marketed during the past year amounted to 38,292 hogsheads, being the heaviest grown in the State for the past 10 years.

It was, moreover, of a better quality and a lighter character than that of previous years, although failing in colour. The better quality was scarce, and "medium" not plentiful, and for both of these there was a brisk demand at remunerative prices.

The common quality was, however, very plentiful, and gradually declined in price during the season.

The French régie contracted for 14,000 hogsheads, the largest quantity taken for years.

The crop of Ohio tobacco was also larger than for many years, 11,000 hogsheads having been received.

France contracted for about 3,000 hogsheads, but in the open market the demand was light, and there was left on hand a stock of about 6,000 hogsheads.

The total stock on hand at the close of the year from all sources was 16,000 hogsheads.

Canned goods.

In consequence of failure in the peach crop throughout Maryland and the adjacent States, there was a heavy reduction in the quantity of fruit which was canned. On the other hand, there was excess in the pack of vegetables, and a consequent fall of about 25 per cent. in prices, chiefly of maize and tomatoes.

As a result of moderate weather in the early part of the oyster season the supply was large and prices low, and of this the packers took due advantage.

The supply of pine-apples from the Bahamas was large, and the fruit, like the peach, is gradually being looked upon more as a necessary than, as heretofore, a luxury.

Timber.

The lumber business has been largely affected by the unsettled condition of business, and sales have been tight. The export trade has, therefore, not been so satisfactory as in former years.

Coffee.

The past year has been a quiet one in the coffee trade. Prices gradually declined from the opening of the year until November when they reached 4 c. per 1 lb. A sharp advance of $1\frac{1}{2}$ c. then took place, and this was the only symptom of activity shown in the market during the entire year.

The abrogation of the reciprocity treaty with Brazil has naturally affected the trade, and its advocates feel by no means secure as to the future. This country depends almost entirely on Brazil for its supply of coffee, of which it takes 66 per cent. of the produce, whilst on its part Brazil is said to produce 60 per cent. of the entire supply of the world.

Earthenware.

For nearly half the past year, owing to slackness in the trade, over 90 per cent. of the potteries in this country were closed. In Baltimore, however, they were in work during the entire year, and the value of the output and the number of hands employed, remained practically the same as in previous years.

During the autumn it is said that there was some activity in the factories, attributable to the fact that during the tedious tariff discussion no one would buy anything, and when that was, for the time, over, supplies were short, and there ensued a consequent demand. The foreign trade was unable to supply this demand promptly, and buyers had to fall back on domestic ware. The demand was, however, artificial, and of very short duration.

The prospect for the present year is gloomy in the extreme. The reduction in the tariff and cheap European labour will crush out the industry in this country. Competition is impracticable unless

Fruit.

the cost of labour is largely reduced. Maryland manufacturers assert that they pay nearly 100 per cent. more for labour than it costs in Europe, whilst the import duty has been reduced from 60 per cent. to 30 per cent.

Of all the tropical fruit now imported into this country the banana comes in the largest quantities, as may be seen on referring to the annexed return.

Its cultivation for the foreign market in Jamaica only dates back about 20 years, and it is from that colony that fully 85 per cent. of those consumed in the Atlantic States now come. There are at present four steamships exclusively employed in the banana trade with this port, and which can land their fruit from Port Antonio in a little over 5 days, and almost as fresh and green as when cut. A proportion of each cargo is disposed of in this city, but the largest part is transferred to heated or refrigerator cars, according to season, and sent by rail as far west as Chicago.

It is reported that the crop of oranges in Florida, the chief source of supply for the eastern States, has been completely destroyed by recent severe weather, and that the growers in that State are actually buying oranges in California in order to meet their engagements.

Annex A.—RETURN of all Shipping at the Port of Baltimore during the Year 1894.

ENTERED.

Nationality.	Sailing.		Steam.		Total.	
	Number of Vessels.	Tons.	Number of Vessels.	Tons.	Number of Vessels.	Tons.
British	19	3,971	368	634,880	387	638,851
American, foreign	110	37,285	10	4,085	120	41,370
German	...	...	105	368,441	105	368,441
Italian	20	16,461	...	...	20	16,461
Swedish and Norwegian	1	378	53	26,073	54	26,451
All others	3	468	11	6,484	14	6,952

CLEARED.

Nationality.	Sailing.		Steam.		Total.	
	Number of Vessels.	Tons.	Number of Vessels.	Tons.	Number of Vessels.	Tons.
British	19	3,971	371	635,172	390	639,143
American, foreign	132	52,453	3	2,902	135	55,355
German	...	...	105	368,441	105	368,441
Italian	21	17,289	...	...	21	17,289
Swedish and Norwegian	1	378	53	26,073	54	26,451
All others	3	468	11	6,484	14	6,952

BALTIMORE.

Annex B.—RETURN of Principal Articles of Export from Baltimore during the Years 1894-93.

Articles.		1894. Quantity.	1894. Value.	1893. Quantity.	1893. Value.
			£		£
Grain, bread stuffs—					
Wheat	Quarters	1,041,918	...	1,630,956	...
Flour	Tons	297,104	...	328,274	...
Corn—					
Maize	Cwts.	3,812,476	...	3,544,757	...
Meal	Tons	2,093	...	2,173	...
Oatmeal	,,	1,094	...	...	...
Provisions—					
Cattle	Head	58,204	...	36,896	...
Sheep	,,	32,709	...	...	...
Beef, various	Tons	13,014	...	12,856	...
Pork, ham, bacon	,,	9,672	...	1,205	...
Canned goods	Cases	58,757	...	122,864	...
Lard, tallow	Tons	41,177	...	22,500	...
Oils—					
Illuminating	Barrels	1,015,200	...	567,525	...
Vegetable and animal	,,	55,950	...	63,075	...
Oil ake	Tons	19,567	...	20,491	...
Minerals—					
Copper	,,	21,155	...	19,781	...
Coals	,,	124,273	...	170,583	...
Tin, scrap	,,	1,476	...	...	...
Timber—					
Lumber	1,000 feet	33,095	...	30,260	...
Staves	1,000	1,616	...	1,244	...
Various—					
Bark	Bags	45,093	...	51,824	...
,, extract	Barrels	10,522	...	16,941	...
Cotton	Bales	220,600	...	198,619	...
Hay	Tons	2,016	...	2,958	...
Horse-hair	Bales	4,199	...	...	...
Oleomargarine	Tons	9,306	...	9,635	...
Rosin	Barrels	100,149	...	53,370	...
Seeds	Tons	4,854	...	5,214	...
Starch	,,	1,998	...	3,511	...
Tobacco	Hogsheads	65,835	...	55,514	...
Wax	Tons	1,346	...	1,216	...
Whisky	Barrels	65,098	...	58,436	...
Total ... Dollars		...	63,961,279	...	73,153,482
Equivalent in Sterling £		...	13,185,830	...	15,983,171

12 UNITED STATES.

Annex C.—RETURN of Principal Articles of Import into Baltimore during the Years 1894–93.

Articles.		1894. Quantity.	1894. Value. £	1893. Quantity.	1893. Value. £
Minerals, metals—					
Iron ore	Tons	79,985	...	296,639	...
,, manganese	,,	1,360	...	32,576	...
,, speigle	,,	303	...	8,283	...
Purple ore	,,	1,613	...	3,318	...
Iron, various	,,	2,051	...	2,817	...
Steel, various	,,	431	...	1,918	...
Tin-plate	Boxes	956,959	...	921,124	...
Chemicals and fertilisers—					
Salt, manure	Bags	114,367	...	38,830	...
,, cake	Casks	258	...	2,863	...
Soda, ash	,,	2,713	...	23,834	...
,, caustic	,,	...	...	2,686	...
Sulphur	Tons	16,786	...	13,726	...
Guano and fertilisers, others	Bags	303,271	...	258,688	...
Clay—				8,259	...
Clay, various	Tons	6,502	...		
Cement	Casks	241,558	...	216,030	...
Earthenware	Crates	19,120	...	21,722	...
Liquor—					
Beer	Barrels	1,317	...	2,567	...
Mineral waters	Cases	6,018	...	11,723	...
Whisky	Barrels	14,023	...	6,606	...
Wines and liqueurs	Cases	8,426	...	15,133	...
Fruit—					
Bananas	Bunches	999,838	...	1,179,414	...
Coconuts	1,000	1,891	...	1,656	...
Pine-apples	Dozens	424,609	...	287,492	...
Lemons and oranges	Boxes	22,392	...	18,161	...
Fruit, dried	Packages	6,855	...	12,846	...
Various—					
Coffee	Tons	51,394	...	58,215	...
Fish, salt	Barrels	14,949	...	15,197	...
Hides	Bales	3,972	...	18,559	...
Paints	Tubs	5,153	...	5,188	...
Pickles and preserves	Cases	610	...	968	...
Pepper and spices	Bags	3,982	...	2,218	...
Rice	Tons	8,522	...	10,285	...
Salt	,,	9,835	...	7,308	...
Sugar	,,	3,055	...	...	...
Liquorice	Bales	33,649	...	...	...
Total Dollars	...	...	11,749,927	...	...
Equivalent in Sterling £	...	...	2,422,455	...	3,057,603

Annex D.—TABLE showing Total Value of all Articles Exported from or Imported into Baltimore during the Years 1894–93.

Country.	Exports. 1894. £	Exports. 1893. £	Imports. 1894. £	Imports. 1893. £
Great Britain	7,950,000	10,471,923	955,000	1,147,301
Belgium	650,000	550,000	120,000	130,000
Brazil	145,000	275,000	145,000	133,000
Cuba and Spain	35,000	148,234	75,000	110,000
France	425,000	650,000	15,000	25,000
Germany	2,750,000	2,875,014	600,000	863,302
Netherlands	850,000	812,000	370,000	434,000
Mexico	120,000	..	15,000	..
Italy	..	..	..	55,000
Other countries	260,000	190,000	125,000	160,000
Total	13,185,000	15,983,171	2,420,000	3,057,603

NORFOLK.

Mr. Vice-Consul Myers reports as follows:—

The business of Norfolk during the year 1894 has to some extent sympathised with the condition general in this country; it has been further depressed by partial failure of crops through the tributary country, and the low prices of cotton and other farm products. There have been some failures of mercantile houses; but the statements appended hereto on the whole show that Norfolk continues to grow at a pace, accelerating each year; while the concentration of capital here, and the development and extension of railroads centering here, now aggregating about 18,000 miles, insure this becoming one of the most important seaports on the Atlantic.

This being the deep water terminus of railroads penetrating the southern and south-western States to the Gulf of Mexico and the Mississippi River, the development of the mineral and other material resources of those States indicates such a consequent development at Norfolk as was caused at New York, Philadelphia, and Baltimore by the development of the Western States tributary to those ports. The several steamship lines plying between this port and Boston, Providence, New York, Philadelphia, Baltimore, Washington, Richmond, Savannah, and other southern ports, are constantly improving the character of their steamers, and increasing the volume of business handled.

The direct trade with Europe employs a number of "tramps," mostly British vessels, and has this year received an impetus from the establishment of direct lines to Liverpool; one from Newport News, under the auspices of the Chesapeake and Ohio Railway Company, and one from Norfolk, by the North American Transport Company.

The following is a list of the transport lines connecting Norfolk with all parts of the United States:—

Railroads.—The Norfolk and Western; the Seaboard Air Line; the Norfolk and Carolina; the Chesapeake and Ohio; the Atlantic and Danville; the Norfolk and Southern; the New York, Philadelphia, and Norfolk; the Norfolk, Albemarle, and Atlantic; the Ocean View; the Port Norfolk.

Steamship Lines.—The North American Transport Company; the Old Dominion; the Merchants and Miners; the Clyde; the Washington Steamers; the Bay Line; the James River Line.

Besides these are steamboat lines connecting with the Sound section of North Carolina, and the Nansemond, York, and Rappahannock Rivers.

The manufacturing interests of Norfolk are increasing in value and importance; the distributing facilities offered by her many railway and steamboat lines, the equable climate, and her proximity to raw materials, all contributing to make this one of the most favourable points for manufacturing in the United States.

The rates of wages paid in Norfolk for clerical work and to artisans, mechanics, and labourers are as follows:—

Class of Labour.		Amount Paid.	
		From—	To—
		Dollars.	Dollars.
Printers..	Per 58 hours..	15	18
Binders..	59 ,, ..	9	15
Pressmen	58 ,, ..	5	15
Bakers..	60 ,, ..	8	12
Carpenters	58 ,, ..	12	15
Machinists	58 ,, ..	12	21
Painters..	58 ,, ..	10	15
Masons..	58 ,, ..	24	30
Hod carriers	58 ,, ..	9	10
Tailors..	58 ,, ..	12	18
Cotton screwmen	week ..	18	24
Moulders	,, ..	10	15
Servants..	month ..	7	18
Salesmen	,, ..	35	100
Bookkeepers	,, ..	40	125
Factory help	week ..	3	8

The cotton business for 1894 amounted to 14,833,354 dol., its grocery business to 14,000,000 dol., lumber business to 12,000,000 dol., its coal trade to 6,600,000 dol., and its vegetables to 6,200,000 dol.

Here are only five branches of trade that aggregate a money value of 53,633,345 dol., while the entire business of Norfolk in 1884 only reached 48,007,500 dol.

This year the total business of the port amounted to over 91,000,000 dol., a remarkable exhibit in a year of widespread depression, and indicative of the progress made in 10 years.

	Amount.
	Dollars.
The grain trade of Norfolk last year reached ..	3,000,000
Flour, meal, &c.	1,435,000
The pea-nut trade amounted to	1,080,000

In the latter, Norfolk holds her own as the greatest market in America.

	Amount.
	Dollars.
The oyster business in 1894 amounted to	2,000,000
Fish and game	1,000,000
The estimate of the tobacco and cigar business during the year 1894 is..	1,300,000
Liquors (not malt)..	2,500,000
The drugs, paints, and oils	800,000
Brick and stonework	750,000
Ship chandlery, railroad and steamboat supplies	525,000
Crockery and chinaware	350,000
Stoves and tinware	500,000
Hardware	750,000
Manufactured knit goods..	1,000,000
Barrels and cooperage	1,000,000
Agricultural implements	450,000
Building materials	1,500,000
Fertilizers	2,000,000
Carriages, waggons, and harness..	350,000
Foundries and ironworks	3,000,000
Creosoting works	125,000
Livestock (cattle and sheep)	810,000
Horses and mules..	1,000,000

Ten years ago the business in both of these lines only reached 400,000 dol., and this was considered a full estimate, whereas it will be noticed that the aggregate value of these two lines for the year 1894 amounted to 1,810,000 dol., an increase in 10 years of 1,410,000 dol.

	Amount.
	Dollars.
The dry goods trade last year is estimated at	3,000,000
Boots, shoes, and clothing	3,000,000
Hats and caps..	350,000

There is a great opening in Norfolk for large wholesale houses of this character.

The increase of the postal receipts of Norfolk is one of the best proofs of the city's growth and development. Attention is called to the following statement of postal receipts for the past 10 years:—

	Amount.
	Dol. c.
Year ending January 30, 1885	43,260 27
,, ,, 1886	45,915 85
,, ,, 1887	47,055 71
,, ,, 1888	50,023 86
,, ,, 1889	54,588 78
,, ,, 1890	56,476 60
,, ,, 1891	68,419 82
,, ,, 1892	74,360 20
,, December 31, 1893	78,000 0
,, ,, 1894	83,309 46

The total value of buildings erected in Norfolk during the past 10 years amounted to 4,641,003 dol., as follows:—

Year.	Amount.
	Dollars.
1885	211,875
1886	285,795
1887	428,000
1888	425,000
1889	437,235
1890	375,000
1891	492,000
1892	425,000
1893	550,000
1894	951,858

The increase in value of buildings erected for the year 1894 is very noticeable, considering the general depression of business existing throughout the country. I enclose herewith statements showing the number and tonnage of vessels entered and cleared at this port for the past year; also the principal articles of import and export, and the value thereof.

TABLE showing the Movement of Shipping at this Port (not including the Coasting Trade in American Vessels), representing the Entries and Clearances to and from Foreign Ports only.

ENTERED.

Nationality.	Sailing. Number of Vessels.	Sailing. Tons.	Steam. Number of Vessels.	Steam. Tons.	Total. Number of Vessels.	Total. Tons.
British	6	4,066	367	563,835	373	567,901
Spanish	...	...	32	51,107	32	51,107
German	...	...	6	11,446	6	11,446
Norwegian	...	...	21	11,701	21	11,701
American	17	10,810	...	...	17	10,810
Italian	5	2,510	...	...	5	2,510
Total	28	17,386	426	638,089	454	655,475

CLEARED.

Nationality.	Sailing. Number of Vessels.	Sailing. Tons.	Steam. Number of Vessels.	Steam. Tons.	Total. Number of Vessels.	Total. Tons.
British	3	1,060	384	570,750	387	571,810
Spanish	...	...	32	51,107	32	51,107
German	...	...	9	16,137	9	16,137
Norwegian	...	...	22	12,842	22	12,842
American	49	26,425	...	...	49	26,425
Italian	4	1,670	...	...	4	1,670
Total	56	29,155	447	650,836	503	679,991

BALTIMORE.

TABLE showing Principal Articles of Export and Import at this Port during the past Year, Value calculated at 5 dol. to the 1l.

EXPORTS.

Articles.		Quantity.	Value.
			£
Cotton	Bales..	85,960	..
Corn	Bushels	951,701	..
Coal	Tons ..	112,487	..
Flour	Barrels	27,025	..
Tobacco	Lbs. ..	223,995	..
Cattle	Head ..	5,780	..
Staves	..	..	36,135
Cotton-seed meal	..	..	36,610
Cotton waste	..	..	7,110
Logs and lumber	..	..	94,125
Pea-nuts	..	..	505
Wheat	..	..	5,108
Bark	..	..	2,975
Painters' oil-colours	..	..	11,650
Miscellaneous	..	..	19,148
Total	..	..	1,650,888

IMPORTS.

Articles.		Quantity.	Value.
			£
Muriate potash	Tons ..	475	..
Kanit	„ ..	3,210	..
Nitrate of soda	Bags ..	7,160	..
Salt	Tons ..	1,273	..
Miscellaneous	..	..	2,575
Total	..	..	20,034

RICHMOND.

The volume of trade of the year 1894, as compared with several years preceding the disturbance which commenced in the year 1893, shows a depreciation which, in some lines, amounts to almost a stagnation. *General trade.*

The past 12 months has been a season of gradual reduction, of inflation, of economy, and of weeding out. Business conditions have reached "rock bottom," and are slowly but surely building upon that foundation.

The banking situation and experience constitute the best index to the healthfulness of business and the outlook. The banking capital of Richmond was increased during the year 1894 by 33,463 dol. 50 c., making a present total capital of 3,245,577 dol. 50 c. In 1894 a decrease is shown of 1,629,322 dol. 66 c. *Banks.*

in bank clearances; but while the exhibit for the first 6 months of 1893 was better than that for the first 6 months of 1894, a comparison of the last 6 months of the 2 years shows a reversal of the conditions, and therefore affords proof of a steady revival of business.

Jobbing trade. The exhibit for the jobbing trade for the year may be analysed as follows:—

The total annual sales for the year 1894 amounted to 29,213,880 dol., a decrease as compared with the year 1893 of 3,512,050 dol.

The number of failures in Richmond for the year 1893 was 57, representing assets to the amount of 525,850 dol., and liabilities to the amount of 799,100 dol. For the year 1894 the number of failures was 45, with assets to the amount of 82,800 dol., and liabilities to the amount of 109,000 dol.

Tobacco. The most noticeable feature of the tobacco trade for the year 1894 is the large increase in loose sales, being 29 per cent. over last year, requiring largely increased warehouse facilities. Dark tobaccos of all grades are lower than last year's annual report by 50 c. to 1 dol. per cwt.

Old dark shipping and export trade has been well maintained. Foreign markets have offered the least encouragement to shippers, who, besides this, had many older and higher priced stocks in the declining scale and dull markets to contend with; besides all this, there was a large western crop to compete with.

Our export manufacturing demand has been good, preference given to Virginia and North Carolina tobacco, which ruled so low as to accommodate itself to the low prices of western tobacco.

As generally computed the bright tobacco crop for the year 1894 is about three-fourths of the average. The very good prices paid to planters for the 1894 crop, and the low prices of cotton, it is feared will over-stimulate planting in 1895, to the disadvantage of producers and manufacturers.

James River improvement. The work on the James River being carried on by the United States Government, has been steadily prosecuted during the year. Contracts have been let, terminating in a year, which will make the channel from the city limits across Richmond Bar at least 100 feet wide, and will have a depth of 18 feet at mean low water all the way to Hampton Roads.

From the following tables, giving the statistics of the port for the past year, it will be noticed, by reference to tables A and D, that there is an increase of foreign vessels entering and clearing, and an increase of export, which is principally in cotton, which large increase is practically the result of the reorganisation of the Richmond and Danville Railroad into the Southern Railway Company, which seems to have infused new life and blood into its traffic facilities.

The increase in imports (table C), as compared with the year 1893, is attributable to two reasons, viz., the establishment of the Chesapeake and Ohio Steamship Company, running between Newport News and Liverpool and London, and the creation of a bonded warehouse in the city of Richmond.

Tables giving the statistics of the port for the past year are attached herewith.

Table A.—RETURN of Vessels Entered and Cleared from the Port of Richmond, Va., and its Sub-Port of West Point during the Year 1894 (not including the Coasting Trade of American Vessels).

ENTERED.

Nationality.	Steam.		Sailing.	
	Number of Vessels.	Tons.	Number of Vessels.	Tons.
British ..	19	30,770	1	236
Norwegian	..	..	1	320
United States ..	..	..	2	761
Total ..	19	30,770	4	1,317

CLEARED.

Nationality.	Steam.		Sailing.	
	Number of Vessels.	Tons.	Number of Vessels.	Tons.
British ..	18	29,263	1	236
Norwegian	..	..	1	320
United States ..	..	..	1	292
Total ..	18	29,263	3	848

Table B.—RETURN showing Exports from the Port of Richmond, Va., during the Year 1894.

Articles.		Quantity.	Value.
			Dollars.
Cotton ..	Bales..	124,070	4,121,230
Cotton-seed cake	Sacks..	3,380	6,904
Flour ..	Barrels	4,536	13,699
Shuttle blocks ..	Cases..	2,797	12,394
Staves ..		42,675	3,083
Oak timber	Feet ..	160,515	3,059
Bark ..	Bags ..	2,715	2,58
Walnut logs ..		46	920
Ploughs..	Cases..	4	35
Total		..	4,163,909

UNITED STATES.

Table C.—SPECIFICATIONS of Articles Imported into Richmond, Va., during the Year 1894.

Articles.	Value.
	Dollars.
Guano	31,300
Farm and garden seeds	16,141
Tin-plate	16,037
China and earthenware	3,108
Wines and spirits	3,798
Salt	3,350
Tobacco and cigars	2,574
Block marble	1,503
Cement and plaster	1,498
Oil paintings	1,165
Cut glass	944
Olive oil	398
Miscellaneous	2,748
Total	84,564

Table D.—RETURN showing the Value of Articles Exported from or Imported into Richmond, during the Year 1894.

Country.	Exports.	Imports.
	Dollars.	Dollars.
Great Britain	2,604,461	29,840*
Germany	999,926	6,419
Belgium	542,729	..
France	..	12,311
Canada	3,059	885
Brazil	13,734	..
Orchilla, W.I.	..	31,300
Cuba		2,574
Denmark		604
Italy		361
Japan	..	156
Bermuda	..	88
China	..	26
Total	4,163,909	84,564

Does not include leaf tobacco returned unsold from England, value 13,070 dol.

LONDON:
Printed for Her Majesty's Stationery Office,
By HARRISON AND SONS,
Printers in Ordinary to Her Majesty.
(75 5 | 95—H & S 1914)

FOREIGN OFFICE.
1895.
ANNUAL SERIES.

N⁰· 1517.

DIPLOMATIC AND CONSULAR REPORTS ON TRADE AND FINANCE.

UNITED STATES.

REPORT FOR THE YEAR 1894
ON THE
TRADE OF THE CONSULAR DISTRICT OF CHARLESTON.

REFERENCE TO PREVIOUS REPORT, Annual Series No. 1428.

Presented to both Houses of Parliament by Command of Her Majesty,
APRIL, 1895.

LONDON:
PRINTED FOR HER MAJESTY'S STATIONERY OFFICE,
BY HARRISON AND SONS, ST. MARTIN'S LANE,
PRINTERS IN ORDINARY TO HER MAJESTY.

And to be purchased, either directly or through any Bookseller, from
EYRE & SPOTTISWOODE, EAST HARDING STREET, FLEET STREET, E.C., and
32, ABINGDON STREET, WESTMINSTER, S.W.; or
JOHN MENZIES & Co., 12, HANOVER STREET, EDINBURGH, and
90, WEST NILE STREET, GLASGOW; or
HODGES, FIGGIS, & Co., Limited, 104, GRAFTON STREET, DUBLIN.

1895.

[C. 7581—57.] *Price Twopence Halfpenny.*

New Series of Reports.

Reports of the Annual Series have been issued from Her Majesty's Diplomatic and Consular Officers at the following places, and may be obtained from the sources indicated on the title-page:—

No.		Price.	No.		Price.
1399.	Dunkirk	1d.	1458.	Samoa	1d.
1400.	Amoy	1½d.	1459.	Hiogo and Osaka	3d.
1401.	Tainan	1d.	1460.	Lisbon	2d.
1402.	Ichang	1d.	1461.	Pekin	2d.
1403.	Aleppo	1d.	1462.	Corunna	2d.
1404.	Madrid	1d.	1463.	Mozambique	15d.
1405.	Newchwang	1d.	1464.	Munich	1½d.
1406.	Wenchow	½d.	1465.	St. Petersburg	3d.
1407.	Pakhoi	1½d.	1466.	Naples	1d.
1408.	Hankow	1d.	1467.	Montevideo	2½d.
1409.	Amsterdam	1d.	1468.	Aden	1d.
1410.	Copenhagen	½d.	1469.	Tokio	1½d.
1411.	Damascus	1d.	1470.	Dantzig	5d.
1412.	Chefoo	3d.	1471.	Guayaquil	1d.
1413.	Swatow	1d.	1472.	Canton	1½d.
1414.	Mannheim	1½d.	1473.	Dar-al-Baida	3d.
1415.	Fiume	2d.	1474.	Teheran	2d.
1416.	Athens	6d.	1475.	Bushire	2d.
1417.	Sŏul	1½d.	1476.	Tangier	2d.
1418.	Beyrout	1d.	1477.	Rome	2d.
1419.	Berlin	1½d.	1478.	Hamburg	4d.
1420.	Nice	3d.	1479.	The Hague	1½d.
1421.	Yokohama	1½d.	1480.	Belgrade	2d.
1422.	Maracaibo	1d.	1481.	Batoum	1½d.
1423.	Tunis	1½d.	1482.	Teneriffe	½d.
1424.	Baghdad and Bussorah	1d.	1483.	Lisbon	2½d.
1425.	Rio Grande do Sul	7d.	1484.	Buda-Pesth	½d.
1426.	Erzeroum	1d.	1485.	Rome	5½d.
1427.	Christiania	5½d.	1486.	Fara	1d.
1428.	Charleston	5½d.	1487.	Odessa	1d.
1429.	Meshed	1d.	1488.	Hakodate	1d.
1430.	Copenhagen	½d.	1489.	Beira	1½d.
1431.	Galveston	2½d.	1490.	Berne	1½d.
1432.	Hamburg	2½d.	1491.	Copenhagen	1d.
1433.	Brindisi	2½d.	1492.	Stettin	2½d.
1434.	Gothenburg	2d.	1493.	Rio Grande do Sul	1½d.
1435.	Kiungchow	1d.	1494.	Serajevo	1d.
1436.	St. Petersburg	½d.	1495.	Buenos Ayres	9d.
1437.	Malaga	1d.	1496.	Florence	2d.
1438.	Chicago	2½d.	1497.	Lisbon	1½d.
1439.	Odessa	2d.	1498.	Paris	2d.
1440.	Tabreez	½d.	1499.	Bolivia	1½d.
1441.	Tahiti	½d.	1500.	Patras	1½d.
1442.	Shanghai	2d.	1501.	Bordeaux	2d.
1443.	Nagasaki	1d.	1502.	Madrid	2d.
1444.	Madrid	2½d.	1503.	Amsterdam	1d.
1445.	Malaga	2½d.	1504.	Suakin	1d.
1446.	Rotterdam	1d.	1505.	Angora	1d.
1447.	Port Said	1d.	1506.	Havre	2½d.
1448.	Sofia	2½d.	1507.	Algiers	11d.
1449.	Warsaw	1½d.	1508.	La Rochelle	3d.
1450.	Africa (Congo)	2d.	1509.	Vera Cruz	2d.
1451.	Jeddah	1½d.	1510.	Puerto Cortes	1d.
1452.	San Francisco	5½d.	1511.	Taganrog	1d.
1453.	Oporto	2d.	1512.	Baltimore	1½d.
1454.	Barcelona	2d.	1513.	Mexico	1½d.
1455.	New Caledonia	2d.	1514.	Zaila	1d.
1456.	Smyrna	1d.	1515.	Zomba	3½d.
1457.	Macao	1d.	1516.	Valparaiso	2½d.

No. 1517.

Reference to previous Report, Annual Series No. 1428.

UNITED STATES.

CHARLESTON.

Consul Rawson-Walker to the Earl of Kimberley.

My Lord,   *Charleston, March 5, 1895.*

I HAVE the honour to transmit, herewith enclosed, my Annual Trade Report for Charleston, S.C., and District for the past year of 1894, including also Reports from the Vice-Consuls at Savannah and Brunswick.

                              I have, &c.
                  (Signed)   E. H. RAWSON-WALKER.

Report on the Trade and Commerce of the Consular District of Charleston for the Year 1894.

ABSTRACT of Contents.

	PAGE
General trade	1
Cotton	10
Phosphates and fertilisers	19
Rice trade	26
Naval stores and lumber	29
Shipping and navigation	33
Miscellaneous	37
Cotton seed oil	38
Savannah Vice-Consulate	39
Brunswick Vice-Consulate	44

General Trade.

General trade.

The two principal features that have characterised the general trade of the Port of Charleston during the past year of 1894 were enormous cotton production and low prices; at the close of the year it is estimated by high authority that the cotton crop now being marketed for the current season of 1894–95 will likely reach or possibly exceed 9,400,000 bales of that staple, thus exceeding by

(1915)

over 400,000 bales the highest previously reported crop on record, that of the season of 1891-92, when 9,038.707 bales were produced. The closing prices quoted for middling cotton at Charleston on the last day of 1894 were 5⅛ c. per lb. compared with 7⅜ c. for the same grade on the corresponding date of the year before, showing a decline during the year of about 2¼ c. per lb. or about 33 per cent. decrease in the selling value of this season's crop as compared with last year's; notwithstanding, however, that low prices prevail for nearly all staple articles as well as cotton, and that money is generally tight, provisions have been more plentifully raised than heretofore, and the supply of labour is abundant, and as a rule the condition of the working people will compare favourably with that of previous years, the exceptions being confined to parts of the State where exceptionally bad local conditions prevail.

A series of interesting special reports from the principal sections of the State of South Carolina were prepared at the close of 1894, and, taken as a whole, these reports go to show that throughout the State there is plenty of corn, bacon, sorghum syrup, and sweet potatoes, and that larger quantities of wheat and oats will be grown and hogs reared next season than during the last one. The banks also are solvent, and although bankers and merchants are less disposed to grant credit to farmers than in former years, the position of the farmers now is such that they require it less.

Manufacturing industries are reported to be in a satisfactory and even flourishing condition, and in parts of the State where certain new crops have been tried as experiments last year (as was notably the case in the trial of tobacco growing made in Darlington and Florence counties) results proved most encouraging.

South Carolina raises annually about 500,000 bales of cotton, and in 1893 she raised in addition about 12,500,000 bushels of corn; but in 1894 the production of corn increased to 18,728,000 bushels, a gain of 6,228,000 bushels or 50 per cent. increase over the crop of the previous year. But the people's energies were by no means confined to agricultural pursuits exclusively, for it is not improbable that, in the course of a few years, this will be considered a manufacturing as well as an agricultural State, owing to the rapidly increasing growth of the cotton manufacturing industry and the establishment of many new enterprises for the manufacture of various articles from hard woods, of which there is a practically unlimited supply of raw material in the swamps and forests of the State. In 1880 the total number of cotton spindles in all the southern States of the American Union were 660,000 and the looms numbered 14.300. In the spring of 1894 (and several mills have been added since) South Carolina alone had 569,033 spindles and 16,960 looms, as many spindles and looms as were in the entire south 14 years ago. At the present time it is officially stated that there are in the Southern States 2,167,242 spindles and 14,300 looms with an annual consumption of 723,329 bales of cotton; South Carolina thus having more than one-fourth the spindles, a little less than one-third the looms, and consumes about one-third of the cotton used, say 250,000 bales.

If natural facilities are likely to prove an inducement for keeping up the rapid progress of industrial development, it seems reasonable to expect that South Carolina will continue to lead in her various lines of manufacturing enterprise. In that part of her territory north of the lower line of the hills in what is called the Piedmont section it is estimated that there are more than 1,000,000 horse-power of available water-power, varying in size from 30 to 30,000 horse-power, a force sufficient to work all the cotton, grist, flour, and saw mills now worked by water-power throughout the United States.

South Carolina has about 200 miles of sea coast with broad plains extending from the sea to the blue peaks of the mountains, from the level of the ocean to 2,500 feet above, and embracing within a stretch of 200 miles most varied conditions of climate and topography. The gateway to this State is Charleston, situated about 7 miles from the ocean, having an excellent harbour where shipping finds safe and ample accommodation for anchorage, berthing, &c.; there being about 12 square miles of water in front of the town alone with a depth of water of from 40 to 60 feet. There are $2\frac{1}{2}$ miles of water front on both sides of the town, the East Shore and West Shore Terminal Companies respectively running their railway tracks down to the wharves for the transfer of freights from ships to cars.

20 years ago it was possible for a man to walk over certain parts of Charleston Bar at low water, but this state of affairs has now been so greatly improved by reason of the system of jetty works undertaken and carried forward by the United States Government, that in November last the British steamer "Darwin," drawing 22 feet and 3 inches of water, passed safely over the bar up to the city docks and landed her cargo, and during the same month two steamships, each loaded with over 10,000 bales of cotton, went out to sea without difficulty with plenty of water under their keels. It may also be mentioned as an event worthy of notice in the history of the port that during the past autumn the British steamship "Martin," of 2,460 net tons register and 360 feet long, the largest vessel that ever entered this harbour, came to her dock, took a cotton cargo and proceeded to sea without any lightering or experiencing any trouble whatever. The total tonnage of the port in 1885 was 460,000 tons, and in 1894 it was nearly 800,000 tons. The average depth of the deepest draught vessel crossing Charleston Bar in 1892 was 17 feet, and for the past 12 months of 1894 the average was 20 feet, from this it would appear that the jetties are accomplishing the work for which they were designed, and that the vast sums spent upon these works and the consummate engineering skill that planned and executed them have not been wasted. Originally there were four channels across the bar, the deepest having about 17 feet at high water; the united waters are now

(1915)

made to flow with accelerated velocity, by means of the jetties, between parallel lines of stones, one line stretching from the shore of Morris Island, and the other from the shore of Sullivan's Island, rising above the low water sea-level 3 miles out to sea. The result has been a 23 foot channel now obtained with a reasonable prospect that, eventually, a 26 foot high water channel will be secured, as at first planned. The first sum of money appropriated by Congress for the jetty work here was 200,000 dol. on June 18, 1878, since which time the total appropriations for this purpose have amounted to 3,527,000 dol., and with the estimated expenditure of 753,000 dol. more it is expected that the project will be completed, and Charleston will be one of the deepest water ports on the South Atlantic Coast. The situation of the town is in several other respects also favourable, it being 500 miles from Chicago, 1,000 from Topeka, Kansas, 850 from Kansas City, 500 from Louisville, and 300 from Knoxville, making it possible for her to become the export point at some future day for the great granaries of the West. Charleston is directly connected by her inland waterways, not only with the coast and islands, but also with the interior for 200 or 300 miles.

There are 2,400 miles of navigable rivers, including creeks and inlets of the sea, penetrating the State, and many more hundreds of miles of available waters could be made navigable by the expenditure of a comparatively small amount of money. The waters of most of these means of transportation are connected by canals, cuts, &c., with Charleston Harbour, and from these sources she now receives a considerable amount of commerce which the building up of the State's industries will greatly augment.

Within the past few months a line of steamers has been established between Charleston and Philadelphia, and projected railway combinations promise to place her in more direct communication with the West than heretofore. During last year Charleston manufactured products valued at 11,350,000 dol., had a wholesale and retail trade of 30,600,000 dol., made 4,750,000 dol. worth of fertilisers, mined 1,700,000 dol. worth of phosphate rock, and shipped 2,300,000 dol. worth of fruit and vegetables, 14,000,000 dol. worth of cotton and other items, making the total figures about 71,000,000 dol., equivalent to, say, 14,000,000*l.*

The exports of cotton alone amounted to 407,000 bales, compared with 306,000 bales for the previous year; and the various chemicals used in the manufacture of phosphate fertilisers that were imported amounted to 540,400 dol.; there being also made 325,000 tons of sulphuric acid, and 325,000 tons of fertilisers, which was about one-fourth the total product of the country, the whole fertiliser product of the United States amounting to 1,500,000 tons. There were mined in 1892-93 about 618,000 tons of phosphate rock, which, however, decreased in 1893-94 to 475,000 tons, the falling-off being due to the disastrous hurricane that ravaged the Carolina coast during August of 1893, and which disabled all the river mining companies for over 6 months after; the land mining companies, however, were able to continue operations, and they produced 340,000 tons of land rock in 1894, compared with 316,000 tons during the season before.

One of the most profitable and fast-increasing of Charleston's industries is the raising of early fruits and vegetables, or, as it is generally called here, truck farming for shipment to the northern and western markets, and, notwithstanding the frost of last April that destroyed the fruit and vegetable crops so generally over a large part of the country, there were produced here 100,000 dol. worth of strawberries, 250,000 dol. of potatoes, and 1,850,000 dol. of other early vegetables.

The total assessed values of Charleston's real estate and personal property during the 3 years of 1891-93 were as follows:— in 1891, 21,433,031 dol.; in 1892, 21,987,122 dol.; and in 1893, 23,652,744 dol., showing that there had been a gain of 2,219,713 dol. in the course of 2 years.

The Street Department expended during the year 110,000 dol. on improvements, and there are now 16 miles of streets paved with Belgian blocks, 8 miles with cobble stone pavement, and ¾ mile of asphalt roadway, together with about 2 miles laid with pyrites cinders, and an appropriation of 20,000 dol. was made recently for commencing work on the new Shone sewerage system which is to replace the old tidal drain with which the town is now provided; the Shone system is worked by pressure, the sewage being forced through pipes to a main station where it undergoes a kind of filtering process, the liquid running into the river and the solid residue matter remaining being burnt.

Important changes were also made during the past year at the quarantine station, the charges heretofore made for fumigation and disinfection being removed, only the inspection charge of 15 dol. is now levied from vessels arriving at quarantine, and, with this exception, ships enter, free of quarantine expenses.

A Bill has also been recently passed by the State Legislature making some modifications in the pilotage charges which, while not so much as was hoped for by shipping interests, are nevertheless a step in the right direction, and may lead to still further reduction of pilot rates in the future. The above-mentioned decreases in quarantine and pilot charges at this port are the result of a very general agitation of the question of reducing port charges which was brought before the public last summer at nearly all the American cotton ports, with a view to developing the interests and trade of the ports by cutting down expenses and thus encouraging arrivals of shipping. Similar reductions in quarantine expenses have been made at Savannah; and the other cotton ports in this consular district, namely, Port Royal, Wilmington, and Brunswick have either made lower port rates already, or contemplate taking steps of this kind shortly. *Quarantine charges.*

The wholesale trade last year was, perhaps, the dullest and least profitable ever experienced throughout the country at large, and Charleston shared in the general depression, and there were some failures and falling-off in various lines of trade, but fortunately no labour troubles or riots, that proved so disastrous in some other places, occurred here, the relations of employer and employed remained undisturbed, and when reductions of wages were rendered necessary by reason of business dulness, they were accepted with philosophical resignation on the ground that half a loaf is better than no bread. In examining the details of the different branches of trade, as given further on, it will be seen that the falling-off in the amount of sales given in a number of instances is due rather to decreased prices than to the volume of business done.

Charleston's chief manufacturing industry is in making commercial fertilisers from phosphate rock, and this industry was somewhat disturbed last season by the failure of the Royal Fertiliser Company. The large stock which that concern had on hand at the time of its suspension had an unfavourable effect upon the market and kept prices down; most of the other mills increased their output somewhat, but the average price for acid, phosphate, and standard ammoniated goods were about 1 dol. per ton less than last year, making the product of all the mills, including the stock of the Royal Company, about 47,000 dol. lower than the figures for the previous season; the retirement of the Atlantic Company from the field, and its absorption by the Chicora Company took place too late in the commercial season to materially affect prices or figures.

The Charleston Cotton Mill also worked steadily all through the past year, and the output of both cloths and yarns was greater than for the year before, low prices for raw material used were, however, somewhat off-set by lower selling prices for manufactured goods, making the value of the whole annual production only a trifle more than last year. The bag factories did fairly well, but lower prices about balanced larger production, as was the case with the cotton mill; but the bagging company had better prices, quotations averaging about $1\frac{1}{2}$ c. per lb. higher for bagging than last year, making the value of the year's output 400,000 dol., compared with 350,000 dol. during 1893; the quantity produced being nearly the same in both years. The Mutual Oil Refinery did a good business and increased the value of its annual product from 300,000 to 325,000 dol.; 2 years ago the figures for the year were 140,000 dol.

The Palmetto Brewing Company had a prosperous year owing to the fact that under the South Carolina Liquor Law, generally called the Dispensary Law, the brewery was allowed to sell beer through the dispensaries of the State upon payment of a royalty; in this way the brewery was enabled to maintain the value of its annual product to the same figures as for the year before, which were 300,000 dol.

The veneer and basket works proved an important addition to the list of Charleston's manufacturing industries during the past season, the company having 75,000 dol. invested in a thoroughly modern plant, and is reported to be doing well; the envelope and box company, however, were obliged to suspend operations, so far as the manufacture of envelopes were concerned, early in the year owing to the great competition of the large envelope manufactories and trusts of the north, and now the Charleston Company is devoting itself to the making of all varieties of paper boxes, and the enterprise now appears to be on a safe and paying basis.

The commercial year, strictly speaking, at this port ends on August 31 of each year, and trade returns and statistics are annually made up for the 12 months ending on that date, for convenience in the compilation of figures and tables, therefore, the course that has usually been pursued heretofore in these trade reports will be adhered to, viz., of first giving facts and figures for the commercial year, as above stated, and then adding in a supplementary form such statistics and items of trade as have taken place during the last 4 months of the year—that is to say it is proposed to cover the business in two divisions—the first being for the 12 months ending August 31, 1894, and the second for the 4 months ending December 31, 1894.

At the close of the past commercial year, as was expected, it was found that there had been considerable falling-off in several departments of Charleston's trade compared with the year before, owing to the panic and trade depression through which the country had passed, combined with two or three great natural calamities in the shape of hurricanes and storms with which this town has been afflicted; but in spite of all adverse conditions when the new business year opened on September 1, 1894, it found the port's credit unimpaired, and, all things considered, her commercial importance comparing favourably with that of other southern ports.

There was a decrease of 300,000 dol. in the Sea Island cotton trade at this place last year caused by the general inundation of the islands and great damage to crops, owing to the hurricane of 1893; the problem indeed being not so much the saving of the growing cotton as the saving of the islands themselves from being washed out to sea. The resin and turpentine business also decreased about 200,000 dol., caused partly by the destructive effects on the pine trees of the above-mentioned storm, and also in part by the natural decrease of this business owing to the gradual and steady exhaustion of the pine forest in the section of country tributary to Charleston.

In the phosphate rock business there was a falling off of something like 100,000 dol., which however was hardly avoidable as every river mining plant in the State was wrecked by the storm. In the liquor trade the decrease reported amounted to 2,000,000 dol., which is attributable to some extent to the generally bad financial condition of the country and also in part to unfavourable State legislation, which it is said has driven many thousands of dollars of capital out of South Carolina into neighbouring States and counties, thus working injury to many establishments that have heretofore contributed in a considerable measure to the volume of the trade here. There was a decrease in Charleston's rice trade of 700,000 dol., planters having found it impossible to save their crops as the sea had covered the rice fields to the depth of several feet during the August storm.

As an offset, however, to the above-named losses in last year's trade the figures show that Charleston had an increase of nearly 2,000,000 dol. in her cotton trade, and in the cotton goods business there was a gain of 1,000,000 dol., and on the opening of the new business year on September 1, 1894, the general condition of the people of the State was, as already intimated, materially improved in several respects, there being notably less debt to face and larger food supplies on hand than was the case a year ago. The local conditions in Charleston also are somewhat improved, the South Carolina Railway Company, Charleston's principal commercial feeder, was sold after being in litigation in the courts for a number of years, and that property is now in the hands of a few wealthy capitalists who, it is believed, will be able to establish relations with one of the leading western railway systems and operate the line in future in a manner conducive to their own interests and not inimical to those of Charleston.

Before closing these preliminary remarks it may be well to point out what appears to be a most excellent opportunity Charleston now has, in addition to her other advantages, of making this a port of call for orders and a coaling point for British and other foreign vessels. With the deepening of the bar channel to 23 feet it may almost be said that, as a serious obstruction to the growth of commerce, Charleston Bar has practically ceased to exist. Nothing seems to stand in the way of the development of this class of business at the present time but port charges, which are still too high to compete with Norfolk and Port Royal, notwithstanding the fact that considerable reductions were made at this port both in pilot and quarantine expenses during the last 6 months.

A vessel calling now for orders at Norfolk pays only half regular pilot rates, receives her orders and goes wherever she is instructed for her cargo. At Port Royal, South Carolina, where coaling facilities are being established, vessels calling for coal are to be charged the same pilot fees as at Norfolk, and the State levies a quarantine inspection fee of but 3 dol., while at Charleston the quarantine officer is authorised to collect 15 dol. from each vessel arriving for inspection fee, and regular pilot rates are exacted from all vessels alike, whether calling for orders, coal, or cargoes. The feasibility of making this a port of call for many ships that now go elsewhere, provided port charges could be placed at a figure that would compete with other ports, and the prospective depth of 26 feet in the bar channel could be attained, would appear to be shown by the following case.

On December 24 last the steamship "Glenloig" arrived here having previously made arrangements that her orders relative to loading port and charter should be delivered to the master by the pilot boat on duty on the arrival of the vessel off Charleston Bar, and the arrangement was carried out without difficulty, the steamer paying the usual pilot rates therefor.

Instead of isolated cases like that of the steamer "Glenloig" occurring at wide intervals of time, as at present, it seems only reasonable to suppose that, if satisfactory port rates could be established, many other vessels would find it convenient and to their interest to call at this port for orders and coal, each arrival of this nature contributing something to the importance and business of the port which would otherwise be lost. About 20 years ago some of the enterprising citizens of Savannah conceived the idea of making Tybee, at the mouth of the Savannah river, a port of call, and Tybee was connected with Savannah by a short telegraph line which enabled shipmasters who came to Tybee to get orders and put themselves in communication with owners and charterers in any part of the world. The great convenience of the arrangement was at once seen and appreciated by shipping interests, and the large number of vessels now calling for orders at the last named place have added materially to the commercial interests of Savannah.

At Charleston a similar telegraph station might easily be established at some suitable point on Sullivan's Island, which is only about 4 miles from town, and such a station would doubtless be very useful in many cases to shipmasters whose vessels might be anchored inside or even outside the jetty bar entrance, say, for instance, in the position occupied by the United States cruiser "Baltimore" some years ago when she lay for several days off this port drawing too much water to come in at that time.

Attention might also be called to the development of the tobacco-growing industry which during the past year has assumed proportions that has attracted much public interest, not so much on account of the actual quantity of tobacco grown last season in South Carolina as for the promise it gives that the growth and manufacture of this plant may eventually become one of the staple productions of the State.

Last year about 1,000,000 lbs. of tobacco was grown and marketed in Darlington county, and the coming season it is expected that the acreage devoted to tobacco will be increased from 400 to 600 per cent., and it is thought that the next crop will amount to at least 5,000,000 lbs. weight. The average price paid last season for the Darlington grown tobacco was 12 c. per 1 lb., but a considerable part of the more select qualities brought a much higher price, but taking the crop produced as a whole the average was, as stated, 12 c.

10 years ago South Carolina did not produce 1 lb. of tobacco for market; here and there stray patches of this plant were grown in different parts of the State, and it is not improbable that in some of the upper counties a few persons may have produced small quantities of a rather inferior quality in order to supply a strictly local demand, but tobacco growing as a money-

making industry was practically unknown in the State. The possible future importance of the industry, however, is shown by the fact that in Darlington county the acreage cultivated with tobacco was less than 5 per cent. of that devoted to cotton growing last season, yet the value of the tobacco product was 10 per cent. of that of all the cotton raised in the county, the money value of the tobacco crop being placed at 120,000 dol. For many years the opinion prevailed very generally that tobacco could not be successfully cultivated in South Carolina, the impression being that the soil was unsuitable, labour too inefficient, and that the tobacco worm would prove destructive even if the plant could be grown, but the success of last year's experiment seems to have upset these opinions, and has established what appears to be good grounds for the belief that tobacco culture will in future bring about a material change in the condition of the people in the Pee Dee River section of the State.

The details of Charleston's principal branches of trade for the season now under review are given in the following pages, containing figures and statistics under their respective headings, such as cotton, fertilisers, rice, naval stores, lumber, &c.

Cotton.

Cotton.

The total receipts of cotton of all classes at the port of Charleston during the commercial year ending August 31, 1894, were 407,843 bales, compared with 306,419 bales for the preceding year, showing an increase in favour of last season of 101,424 bales. The gratifying increase in receipts for the year just closed is, perhaps, mainly attributable to the improved facilities which now exist at this port for handling this the most important branch of trade done here. The deepening of the harbour entrance is now an accomplished fact, and ships of considerably larger tonnage than have heretofore been possible are now able to enter the port, take cargoes, and depart with safety and despatch, with good prospects of further improvement in this respect when the jetty works, now approaching completion, are finally finished.

Shipments of cotton also from interior points to Charleston, which were formerly much hampered by delays, &c., occasioned by having to break bulk at the various railway station yards, are now delivered at ships' sides direct, avoiding unnecessary drayage and transfer charges, and delays incidental thereto, while the proximity of the port to the ocean ensures despatch in getting to sea after loading cargo, and enables brokers and merchants chartering vessels to rely with a greater degree of certainty than was the case before as to dates of clearance. These facts will doubtless benefit the business of the port when they become more generally known to the shipping world, and the experience of each new arrival will tend to make the matter more widely known.

The above stated advantages have already had the effect of

attracting several new firms, which will cause an increased cotton export business, and their example it is thought will likely be followed by others in the not very remote future. The cotton business last year of Charleston, together with that of the other South Atlantic ports, was much injured by reason of railway freight rate discriminations made by the Southern Railroad and Steamship Association against these ports and in favour of Norfolk. The discriminations referred to have been maintained in spite of earnest protests made by both Charleston and Savannah, but it is hoped that relief will sooner or later be obtained, if not otherwise, by some combination of railway and other interests, which will have the effect of making Charleston an important terminal port for the products of the West, and a more successful competitor than now for the business of the neighbouring States.

At the close of the cotton year reports received from all sections of country growing this staple went to show that the condition of the crop then maturing was very favourable, the indications being that the largest crop on record would be made and marketed next year. An abundant provision crop was also assured, both cotton and corn having been produced at less cost than during any preceding season. Estimates were freely made that the new crop would reach or exceed 9,000,000 bales, which meant that the farmer would in all probability have to face the problem of selling cotton at 6 c. or less per 1 lb., and the question was seriously raised, can cotton producers afford to grow cotton at that price without going into debt? Two years ago the same question had been asked when middling cotton was quoted at 7 c. per 1 lb. with a total crop of 7,500,000 bales, and the question was well worth asking again in view of the disturbed condition of the industrial world, and the uncertainty of the State and national political outlook which at the time baffled some of the best minds of the country. Notwithstanding these disadvantages, however, the cotton farmer of the South appears to have demonstrated that, by judicious economy and raising liberally of necessary household supplies, and making of cotton a secondary or subordinate crop, it was possible for him to keep free from debt, and to live independent of all adverse surroundings, and to be master of the situation, no matter whether the crop produced be 9,000,000 or only 7,000,000 bales.

Receipts.

Receipts. The receipts of cotton at this port for the last season of 1893–94 were 407,843 bales, compared with 306,349 bales the previous season, and 511,309 for the year before, these figures showing that last year's receipts, while 101,454 bales in excess of the previous year, were, nevertheless, 103,466 bales less than for the season of 1891–92. The receipts, however, of 2 years ago were the lowest recorded since 1871–72, when they only amounted to 282,086 bales. The largest receipts of cotton at Charleston in the history of the port occurred in 1880–81, when 628,187 bales came to this market. The next best year was in 1882–83, when the receipts reached 568,207 bales, since which time the highest figure reached for any one year was for the exceptionally large cotton crop season of 1890–91, when this port received 557,744 bales out of the total American cotton crop produced that year of 9,000,000 bales.

At the other cotton ports in this consular district, which embraces all of what are known as the South Atlantic cotton ports (including Charleston) the receipts last year were as follows:—At Savannah, 902,342 bales; Wilmington, 189,834 bales; Brunswick, 99,320 bales; and Port Royal, 77,860 bales.

The comparative exports of upland cotton from the port of Charleston from September 1, 1893, to August 31, 1894, and for the same period in 1892–93, both dates inclusive in each case, were:—

Comparative Exports.

Foreign Exports.

To—	Quantity.	
	1893–94.	1892–93.
	Bales.	Bales.
Liverpool	151,907	83,410
Havre	16,206	7,537
Continental ports	155,964	122,956
Total	324,077	213,903

Coastwise Exports, &c.

Place.	Quantity.	
	1893–94.	1892–93.
	Bales.	Bales.
New York	70,206	72,201
Interior points, by rail	900	3,854
Total	71,106	76,055

CHARLESTON.

GRAND TOTAL.

	Quantity.	
	1893-94.	1892-93.
	Bales.	Bales.
Grand total, foreign and coastwise	395,183	289,958

The following is a statement of the amount of upland cotton received at Charleston, exported therefrom, consumed by the city cotton mill, and also of the stock on hand for the year ending August 31, 1894:—

	Quantity.
	Bales.
Stock on hand, September 1, 1893 ..	12,513
Uplands received during the year ..	405,272
Total	417,785

EXPORTS.

	Quantity.
	Bales.
Exports, foreign and domestic	395,183
Consumed by city cotton mill	11,325
Stock on hand, August 31, 1894.. ..	11,277
Total	417,785

Prices.

Prices for middling upland cotton at Charleston during the past year opened on September 1, 1893, with quotations at $7\frac{1}{2}$ c. for this grade of the staple, which by October 1 had advanced to $7\frac{15}{16}$ c., quotations reaching their highest point for the year on October 20, when $8\frac{1}{16}$ c. was asked.

During November values receded slightly, at the end of which month middlings were $7\frac{5}{8}$ c. per 1 lb., and at the end of December, 1893, they had still further declined to $7\frac{1}{8}$ c. In January, February, March, and April there were moderate fluctuations, prices as a rule continuing in the neighbourhood of a trifle over 7 c. per 1 lb., but in May of 1894, there was a decrease to $6\frac{7}{8}$ c., followed however by a re-action of $7\frac{1}{8}$ c. in June, prices being maintained at 7 to $7\frac{1}{8}$ c. throughout June and July, but early in the month of August another decline

Prices.

occurred, and on September 1, 1894, when the new cotton season of 1894–95 opened, middlings were 6⅜ c., and continued with comparatively few fluctuations and re-actions to steadily decline until the close of the year, quotations on December 31, 1894, being 5⅛ c. for middlings.

Sea Island Cotton.

Sea Island cotton.

Owing to the destruction of the greater part of the Carolina crop of Sea Islands caused by the great storm of August, 1893, and the fears entertained that serious injury had also been done to the Georgia and Florida crops, the market opened with firmness on September 1, 1893, for the better qualities, fine Floridas being quoted at 20 c. per 1 lb., in the latter part of September, and medium fine Carolinas in October sold for 30 c. per 1 lb. for bright, and 25 c. per 1 lb. for "off colour" grades of this class of cotton.

The crop of extra fine Carolinas was almost entirely destroyed, only a few bags of each of the well-known brands being produced of which the quality was much injured. Sales of a few bales of extra fine were made in October at 58 to 60 c. for Carolinas, but later on in the season prices declined to 43 c., and some lots of unusually poor quality sold at even lower figures. Floridas also gradually declined in price until fine Floridas brought only 16½ c. per 1 lb.

East Floridas opened at 24 to 25 c. for the best grades, and were in good demand, being used to some extent as a substitute in place of the deficient supply of the better grade of Carolinas.

At the end of August, 1894, accounts received as to the condition of the growing crop, then nearly matured, were very favourable, and all indications went to show that, in the event of good weather continuing throughout September, there was every reason to expect that next year's crop would be, perhaps, the largest produced since the American civil war. There were, however, some reports received of too much rain from certain sections, but these reports were by no means so numerous or so serious as for many seasons past; the Carolina crop was expected to be moderate, and that the excess should be looked for in the yield of Georgia and Florida.

Receipts and Exports of Sea Islands.

Receipts and exports of Sea Islands.

The receipts, exports, and stock of South Carolina, Georgia, and Florida Sea Island cotton during the cotton year ending September 1, 1894, that is the regular cotton season of 1893–94, as compared with the previous season of 1892–93, were as follows:—

CHARLESTON.

Receipts.

	Quantity.	
	1893-94.	1892-93.
	Bales.	Bales.
Receipts of islands..	2,556	5,824
Georgias and Floridas	15	6
Stock on hand, Sept. 1	422	119
Total	2,993	5,949

Exports.

	Quantity.	
	1893-94.	1892-93.
	Bales.	Bales.
Exports of islands..	2,530	5,527
Stock of islands	463	416
Georgias and Floridas	..	6
Total	2,993	5,949

Comparative Exports.

Comparative exports of Sea Island cotton from the port of Charleston from September 1, 1893, to August 31, 1894, and for the same period during the season of 1892-93, were:—

To—	Quantity.	
	1893-94.	1892-93.
	Bales.	Bales.
Liverpool	1,019	3,219
Havre	267	352
Continental ports..	17	80
Total foreign ports	1,303	3,651
To New York	1,227	1,876
Grand total	2,530	5,527

Total Crop of Sea Islands.

The following comparative statement shows the total extent of the American crop of Sea Island produced in 1893-94 as compared with the previous season of 1892-93, also the total exports and destination, as well as the total stock on hand at Charleston and Savannah:—

South Carolina.

Receipts at—	Quantity.	
	1893–94.	1892–93.
	Bales.	Bales.
Charleston	2,556	5,824
Savannah	67	1,375
Total	2,623	7,199

Georgia and Florida.

Receipts at—	Quantity.	
	1893–94.	1892–93.
	Bales.	Bales.
Charleston	15	6
Savannah	54,192	34,404
Fernandina	145	2,525
Jacksonville	3,910	121
Brunswick	174	726
Total	58,436	37,782

Grand Total.

	Quantity.	
	1893–94.	1892–93.
	Bales.	Bales.
Grand total crop	61,059	44,981

Exports.

The exports of Sea Islands last year amounted to a total from the ports of 61,605 bales of which 2,530 went from Charleston, 1,019 going to Great Britain, 284 to the Continent, and 1,227 to coastwise American ports. The exports from Savannah were 54,840 bales, of which 32,217 went to Great Britain, 4,352 to the Continent, and the remainder to coastwise ports. The rest of the Sea Islands exported were as follows:—From Jacksonville, 3,010 bales; from Brunswick, 174 bales, and from Fernandina, 145 bales—all of the exports from the last three mentioned ports going to coastwise American ports with the exception of 149 bales of Brunswick's shipments which went to Great Britain.

Supplementary.

The figures for the cotton business of Charleston, &c., from September 1 to December 31, which form the first 4 months of the next commercial year of 1894-95, and will be included in next year's annual trade report are given herewith.

The total receipts of all classes of cotton at Charleston from September 1, 1894, to December 31, 1894, amounted to 307,686 bales compared with 329,967 bales for the corresponding period of 1 year ago, showing a falling off for the last season of 22,281 bales; receipts at Savannah for the same time were 675,942 bales last year and 728,002 bales the year before, a decrease of 52,060 bales; Wilmington received 195,547 bales last year in comparison with 195,117 bales the previous season, showing a gain last year of 430 bales, not a very large gain in itself but somewhat surprising in view of the fact that with the exception of Port Royal and West Point, Wilmington is the only cotton port on the Atlantic coast showing an increased number of bales to its credit during the last 4 months of the past year, the other leading Atlantic ports—Norfolk, Charleston, and Savannah all showing a marked falling off. For a good many years Port Royal was not considered a cotton port, and her cotton trade was not included in the official statistics sent out from New York last season, but nevertheless there has been a noticeable development in cotton trade at Port Royal within the past year, and it is reported that 77,192 bales of cotton have been received at that place during the last 4 months of the year, which show an exceedingly large increase in comparison with receipts for 1893.

Charleston struggled hard to maintain her last year's record in the matter of cotton receipts, and up to the latter part of November she succeeded in doing so, but during the last 5 or 6 weeks of the year there was a steady falling backward until the deficit had amounted to over 22,000 bales, and it is not likely that any material change will take place hereafter as the season is now so far advanced.

The Gulf cotton ports took the lead at the opening of the season and have kept it without losing ground, ever since, indeed, the increase in their receipts have been so unusually large that cotton men have regarded them as almost phenomenal.

(1915)

UNITED STATES.

Exports of Uplands and Sea Islands from September 1 to December 31, 1894.

Foreign.

To—	1894.		1893.	
	Sea Islands.	Uplands.	Sea Islands.	Uplands.
	Bales.	Bales.	Bales.	Bales.
Liverpool	1,627	85,170	166	92,002
Havre	53	2,100	..	11,175
Continental ports	..	114,894	..	101,904
Total	1,680	202,164	166	205,081

Coastwise.

To—	1894.		1893.	
	Sea Islands.	Uplands.	Sea Islands.	Uplands.
	Bales.	Bales.	Bales.	Bales.
New York	1,939	36,546	1,077	50,352
Philadelphia	..	642	..	..
Total coastwise ports	1,939	37,188	1,077	50,352

Grand Total.

	1894.		1893.	
	Sea Islands.	Uplands.	Sea Islands.	Uplands.
	Bales.	Bales.	Bales.	Bales.
Grand total, foreign and coastwise	3,619	239,352	1,243	255,433

Closing Prices December 31, 1894.

Closing prices. The cotton market at Charleston on the last day of the year closed moderately firm with reported sales for the day of 250 bales, on a basis of the following quotations posted on the Cotton Exchange official bulletins:—

For—	Per Lb.	
	From—	To—
	Cents.	Cents.
Stained cotton	$4\frac{1}{8}$	$4\frac{3}{4}$
Tinged „	$4\frac{7}{8}$	$5\frac{1}{8}$
Ordinary cotton	..	$4\frac{1}{8}$
Good ordinary cotton	..	$4\frac{5}{16}$
Full „	..	$4\frac{9}{16}$
Low middling „	..	$4\frac{13}{16}$
Middling cotton	..	$5\frac{1}{8}$
Good to full middling cotton ..	$5\frac{3}{8}$	$5\frac{1}{2}$

Sea Islands.

The total receipts of Sea Island cotton from September 1 to December 31, 1894, were 4,791 bales, as compared with 1,243 bales for the same period of the previous year, and 5,192 bales the year before, and the stock left on hand here on the last day of 1894 was 1,635 bales, inclusive of cotton on shipboard, compared with 1,026 bales a year ago, and 1,575 bales for the corresponding date of the preceding year. The market closed quiet for Sea Islands, the sales for the last day of the year being 180 bales, at quotations of 17 to 18 c. for medium fine, 22 to 24 c. for fine, and 28 to 35 c. for extra fine.

Phosphates and Fertilisers.

From the year 1867 to 1880 South Carolina held almost undisputed control of the phosphate business. She made prices and regulated the trade, the land mining companies supplying domestic and the river companies the foreign demand for phosphate rock, without serious opposition from any quarter; but during this period, however, Germany, England, France, Africa, Canada, Mexico, Belgium, Russia, the West Indies, and the Redonda Islands have all become producers, some of large and some of small annual quantities of phosphates. The principal part of the guano used in the United States came from the Chincha Islands, but the present shipments of this article have now become quite small. Kainit came from Russia, nitrate of soda from South America, and slag from the steel works of Russia and Germany.

In 1889 Florida came forward as a competitive producer of phosphates, and has since gone steadily ahead with a yearly increasing output, and now it is said that South Carolina and Florida together mine more phosphate rock than the rest of the world combined, much of the product being of the best known grades, the estimated yearly output being placed at 1,000,000 tons of South Carolina and Florida rock, in comparison with

(1915)

UNITED STATES.

1,890,000 tons supplied by all other countries. The following table will show what countries contribute to make up the full supply of mineral phosphates known and annually consumed in this branch of commerce :—

Country.	Quantity.
	Tons.
Africa, Algiers, and Tunis	7,000
Belgium	220,000
Canada	10,000
England	20,000
France	400,000
Germany	50,000
Norway	5,000
Mexico	5,000
South Carolina	600,000
Florida	500,000
Spain	25,000
West Indies	50,000
Total	1,892,000

Of all the above-mentioned phosphates the two most popular and sought-after varieties are those classed as 75 and 80 per cent. rock—that is to say, the hard rock from Florida and the river rock from South Carolina. Of the former it is said that it is without question one of the most satisfactory materials for the manufacture of fertilisers known to commerce.

South Carolina rock has been used in all quarters since the year 1867, and its good qualities are equally well known to scientists and to manufacturers, as it grinds easily, dries quickly after being treated with acid, works up readily in combination with other fertilising materials, and, in fact, is now a standard article. The river mining industry received its greatest check from the injury done by the hurricane of last August a year ago, which, together with the set-back given to the trade by the States revoking the Coosaw Company's grant, proved so serious that neither the trade nor the State has yet entirely recovered from its injurious effects. But, notwithstanding all adverse conditions, the companies that mined river rock started to work last summer with commendable promptness and energy, and many changes for the better have been made in their plant and working arrangements, among which perhaps the most important improvement has been the establishment of better terminal points for phosphate shipments, where deeper water facilities are available.

On September 1, 1894, the Beaufort and Farmer's Companies were both at work again with full force and time; the Coosaw Company had in operation four rock dredges, and were repairing their other dredges and improving their plant extensively; the Carolina Company were also at the same time repairing the Brotherhood dredge, making it better than ever, and expected soon to be at work again. In addition to the foregoing Messrs.

W. Y. Fripp, James O'Hara, and James Reid had resumed their river mining operations, and all seemed determined to retain the supremacy of this State in phosphate mining.

The land companies were able to keep regularly at work last season, and a number of them made large and expensive improvements with a view of washing and drying rock more economically than heretofore; the Charleston Mining and Manufacturing Company, the pioneer in this line of business, spent particularly large amounts of money in order to keep their company in the front rank, and good results are anticipated for the coming season.

The Rose Mining Company changed hands last season and added considerable improvements to their plant, the Bolton mines added a second land dredge to their works, and have connected themselves with the Charleston and Savannah Railway, the Pon-Pon mines also extended their work by a railway built across the Edisto River into Colleton county.

Up to about 3 years ago most of the phosphate mining schemes for working Florida rock were of a merely speculative character got up to float stock, but most of these concerns have now given place to companies who have gone into the business of mining rock in that State for the legitimate profit there is in the business, and now Florida is the most serious competitor that South Carolina has, the comparative figures for the output of the two States last year being as already mentioned 600.000 tons of rock for South Carolina, and 500,000 tons for Florida, the next largest world's producer being France with an output of 400,000 tons. These figures show at a glance the relative importance of the phosphate industries in the two States named, and the consequent influence which the Florida product must now have, not only on South Carolina phosphate industries, but also upon all the other countries producing this article. The bulk of the Florida phosphate rock is shipped from Punta Gorda, Port Tampa, Fernandina, Brunswick, and Savannah, the last two named places being in this consular district, the shipments of Florida rock last season from Brunswick were about 44,000 tons, and from Savannah, 23,000 tons.

The shipments go principally to Spain, Italy, Sweden, and Denmark which countries take most of the cargoes of hard rock while most of the soft rock goes to the Sandwich Islands.

Tennessee Phosphates.

Much attention has been given to Tennessee rock during the past year, and many scientific persons have gone recently to the Tennessee beds where deposits of phosphate rock have been found. These deposits lie for the most part in Hickman, Wayne, and Perry counties, but some deposits have also been found in Lewis, Bradley, Maury, Servier, Henry, and Dickson counties, situated west of Nashville, and between that city and the Tennessee River, 115 miles east of Memphis, 100 miles west of

(1915)

Chattanooga, and near the little town of Lawrensburg on the Louisville and Nashville Railway, and also near White Bluff, Mount Pleasant, and Hampshire, and in some of the valleys of the State. Colonel Allison, the Commissioner of the State for Agriculture, says that only in certain valleys has rock enough been found to be of any great value, and that the deposits vary from 4 inches to 4 feet in thickness. The State geologist, Mr. Stafford, says that the rock lies in two strata, one above the other, containing phosphate material in sufficient proportion to be of commercial value and economical importance.

The rock is of dark hues, blue, black, yellow, gray, and brown, and is both fine and coarse grain; it also is heavy and apparently requires no washing, and will have to be mined just as coal is— that is by shaft or drift; the phosphate deposits are overlaid by slate and are underlaid by limestone, and, from present appearances, it does not seem probable that it can be mined in large quantities anywhere except as above stated. Most of the Tennessee phosphate contains fluorine and much of it also contains sulphur, and while the deposits are found to be distributed over a wide area, it is only in a comparatively few places that it is rich and thick enough to be profitably mined. There are, however, large areas in which as yet no proper prospecting has been done, there being indications that good rock may be found in Hickman and Wayne counties, but unfortunately it is situated a considerable distance from railway stations and navigable streams, the country being of a hilly character and the rock lying deep.

Small shipments of this rock were made last year to Montgomery and Atlanta, the National Fertiliser Company has also used it, and they speak favourably of its qualities, but there are, however, other parties who, while they admit that it can be used in this country, are, nevertheless, of opinion that it is unsuitable for export to foreign countries. Further particulars and details in regard to the subject of Tennessee phosphate deposits will be found in a special report that was transmitted to the Foreign Office, under date of May 18, 1894, and afterwards published in the Board of Trade Journal for public information.

Phosphate Rock Shipments.

Phosphate rock shipments.

The shipments of phosphate rock mined in South Carolina from September 1, 1893, to August 31, 1894, shipped from the ports of Charleston and Beaufort (Port Royal being included in the latter place) were as follows:—

	Quantity.	
From—	To Foreign Ports.	To Domestic Ports.
	Tons.	Tons.
Charleston	12,417	120,951
Beaufort	82,558	29,450

Prices for rock at the mines near Charleston on September 1 were:—

	Per Ton.	
For—	River Rock.	Land Rock.
	Dol. c.	Dol. c.
Crude rock	3 50	4 0
Hot-air dried rock	4 0	4 75
Hot-air dried, 60 per cent. guaranteed	4 75	4 75

At the close of the year, December 31, 1894, the quotations for rock were:—for crude, f.o.b., 4 dol. per ton; ground rock, also f.o.b., 7 dol. per ton, packed in bags. There were no shipments of phosphate rock reported from Charleston to foreign countries during the last 4 months of the year—that is to say from September 1, 1894, to December 31, 1894, but during this period there were shipped to coastwise ports of the United States 26,576 tons of crude and 715 tons of ground.

Fertilisers.

There are few persons outside the trade who have any idea of the immense amount of money required to conduct the fertiliser business, and many even in the trade know but little of the capital, labour, and material required to carry on the manufacturing of commercial manures in this country and the importance of the interests represented by this industry abroad. 6,000,000 tons of fertilisers are now used by the world, so far as known, and manufacturing this vast quantity of stuff gives employment to many branches of industry, calls to its aid the scientist, chemist, mechanist, and engineer, and brings into use an immense amount of labour and capital, and distributes benefits in the most remote countries. The following table will show where commercial manures are used and the extent of consumption in each country:—

Fertilisers.

Country.	Quantity.
	Tons.
Austria	100,000
Belgium	300,000
France	1,100,000
Germany	1,500,000
Holland	150,000
Italy	100,000
Norway and Sweden	100,000
Great Britain	1,000,000
Spain	100,000
United States	1,550,000
Total	6,000,000

Of the 1,550,000 tons of fertilisers used in the United States, it may be interesting to know that the largest consumer is Georgia, which State takes 280,000 tons annually; the next on the list is South Carolina, 200,000 tons; then Pennsylvania, 150,000 tons; North Carolina, 145,000 tons; and Virginia, 140,000 tons; the remainder being distributed in the various other Eastern and Western States of the Union in different quantities ranging from 90,000 tons for New Jersey down to 10,000 tons taken by Louisiana.

The foregoing figures have been taken from a carefully prepared statement by Professor Charles U. Shepard, one of the best authorities on the subject of phosphates in the State of South Carolina.

The principal products made from phosphate rock as a basis are acidulated bone, bone phosphates, and acid phosphates, and of these articles it is estimated that there are annually made throughout the world about 2,500,000 tons; commercial manures being now used in almost every variety of crop grown; but the cotton crop of the United States probably consumes more than any one agricultural product, although there are numerous sections of country in America where cotton is still raised without the aid of commercial fertilisers.

The nearest approach to a fertiliser factory is a cotton-seed oil mill, it being a comparatively easy matter to quickly convert a cotton mill into an establishment for making phosphate commercial manures, oil mills having at hand ammonia, potash, phosphate acid, and nitrogen. At the present time there are 258 cotton-seed oil mills in the United States, 94 of them being in Texas, 36 in Georgia, 30 in South Carolina, 18 in Tennessee, 10 in North Carolina, 18 in Louisiana, 20 in Alabama, the rest being distributed in the other cotton States, but principally in Arkansas and Mississippi.

There were a good many changes last year in the fertiliser companies; some of them increased their capacity, others bought outright existing companies, putting them under one management. As a rule the profits have been good in the business—

ranging from 10 to 45 per cent.; interior mills appear to have done well, this applying to both the fertiliser and cotton-seed oil mills, the latter being now more numerous than the former. These companies give large numbers of the masses employment, and much capital is also profitably worked in carrying them on, some of the enterprises for manufacturing fertilisers being on a large and imposing scale.

Fertiliser Shipments.

There are practically no fertilisers or commercial manures in a manufactured condition shipped to foreign countries from the port of Charleston, the large annual product of the different establishments at this place either being consumed here or shipped to domestic ports or interior places in this country.

Fertiliser shipments.

The shipments of fertilisers from Charleston from September 1, 1893, to August 31, 1894, amounted to 316,611 tons, of which 142,372 tons went by the South Carolina Railway, 66,534 tons by the North Eastern Railway, 102,261 tons by the Charleston and Savannah Railway, and the remainder by steamer to New York, Boston, Baltimore, and other northern ports.

During the same period the shipments of fertilisers from Savannah were 116,000 tons, and from Port Royal 28,000 tons; and the comparative sales at the three above-mentioned ports during the same time, compared with the previous year, were as follows:—

SALES of Fertilisers.

Place.	Quantity.	
	1893.	1894.
	Tons.	Tons.
Charleston	335,658	316,611
Port Royal	31,000	28,000
Savannah	120,000	116,000
Total	486,658	460,611

Chemicals.

The following comparative table will show in detail the quantities of chemicals imported into Charleston during the last two seasons, and the extent to which they are used in the manufacture of commercial manures, together, also, with the comparative value of the same:—

Chemicals, &c.

| | 1892-93. | | 1893-94. | |
Articles.	Quantity.	Value.	Quantity.	Value.
	Tons.	Dollars.	Tons.	Dollars.
Kainit	6,909	45,042	19,483	140,019
Sulphur	4,490	18,518	14,605	53,306
Muriate potash	1,594	58,231	4,214	157,594
Pyrites	14,192	40,927	12,064	29,033
Nitrate soda	..	..	876	26,575
Manure salt	50	1,163	50	1,164
Phosphates	450	2,467	..	..
Guano	4,050	4,180	..	..
Brimstone	4,050	97,153	9,436	130,305
Sulphate potash	75	3,395	51	2,363
Total	35,835	271,076	59,979	540,409

Fertilisers, September 1, 1894, *to December* 31, 1894, *from Charleston.*

Fertilisers from Charleston.

The amount of fertilisers shipped from the port of Charleston during the last 4 months of the year 1894 were 27,844 tons, all of which went by railway or steamer to domestic ports and interior points in the United States, no shipments of manufactured fertilisers to foreign countries having taken place; indeed Charleston never has been a shipper of fertilisers abroad, as other countries using phosphate commercial manures generally import the rock in its crude or dried condition, and manufacture the fertilisers for themselves.

Rice.

Rice.

The oldest rice planters have never had any experience of a harvest season so disastrous as that of the autumn of 1893; the hurricane of August 27-28 having laid waste most of the rice-planting sections, leaving the planters on the rivers between Charleston and the Georgia line (the Savannah River) in almost a ruined condition, the ravages of the storm not extending in anything like the same degree in its hurtful effects to what is known as the Georgetown section of the State, lying to the northward of Charleston. The hopes at first indulged in, that a considerable portion of the coast had at least in some measure escaped from the effects of the storm above-mentioned, soon proved to be illusive, as a second storm of great violence occurred early in October, which, while not of such extreme severity as the preceding August gale, nevertheless did great damage, causing considerable loss of life, wrecking many plantations, and destroying the bulk of the ungathered crops. After the August storm, incessant rains prevailed for several weeks, keeping the fields under water, preventing labourers from working, and causing

CHARLESTON.

the destruction of much rice that otherwise might have been saved, though, perhaps, in a more or less damaged condition. In many cases the injury resulting from the long continued rains was more harmful than that caused by the violence of the tempest, hence there was a great reduction both as to the quantity and quality of the rice crop produced last season along the entire Atlantic coast.

The total crop last year for the season from September 1, 1893, to August 31, 1894, for the rice-growing sections along the coasts of Carolina and Georgia, usually called the Atlantic coast crop, was only 868,489 bushels, while that of the previous year of 1892-93 was 1,237,479 bushels of rough rice, a decrease for the past year of 1,171,855 bushels.

At the South Carolina mills the receipts of rice last year were 426,629 bushels of rough rice, as compared with 1,237,479 bushels received during the 12 months ending August 31, 1893.

The total rice crop of the United States last year, for the season ending August 31, 1894, was 4,754,549 bushels, compared with 10,132,128 bushels the season before, showing a falling-off last year in the American crop of 5,377,579 bushels, which excessively large decrease is attributable to the fact that the Gulf rice-producing States also suffered severely during the hurricane of 1893, from the same causes that made so serious a curtailment in the Atlantic coast crop.

Shipments in Carolina and Georgia from the rice plantations were greatly retarded, and indeed they did not become general until the middle of October, most of the rice coming to market showing unmistakable evidences of the injury received from the storm and the rain. Not only did the quality of the rice prove inferior, but during the cleaning process, under the action of the pestle, the quantity of middling and small rice from each lot was unusually large and out of all relative proportion, in numerous cases being actually greater than the amount of whole rice produced, resulting in great loss to planters, who, not infrequently, were unable to realise cost of production of the grain.

Owing to these causes high grades of rice became very scarce, and throughout the year such fine qualities as could be offered met a steadily good demand and renunerative prices, ranging from $4\frac{1}{2}$ to $5\frac{3}{4}$ c. per pound. There was no stock on hand at the close of the business year—August 31, 1894; but the new crop of 1894-95, then nearly ready for harvesting, was progressing well, and reports were encouraging for a good yield, although the acreage planted in rice was considerably less than last year. Up to that time the weather had been generally good throughout the State, and while no new crop rice had been brought yet to market, several cargoes were expected to arrive early in September from the first harvestings of the new season.

Rice Crop of Milled or Cleaned Rice.—Season of 1893-94.

The following table shows the extent of the total rice crop

Rice crop of milled or cleaned rice.

produced in the United States last season, with the relative proportions of the South Carolina, Georgia, and Louisiana yield, which go to make up the sum total, the figures given herewith being barrels of milled rice, having an average net weight of 300 lbs. per barrel.

Rice Crop of—	Quantity.	
	Barrels.	Barrels.
SOUTH CAROLINA.		
Milled at Charleston	23,394	
„ Georgetown	12,809	
		36,103
NORTH CAROLINA.		
Milled at Wilmington, Washington, and Newberne	..	12,500
GEORGIA.		
Milled at Savannah	..	27,581

TOTALS.

	Quantity.
	Barrels.
Total Atlantic coast crop	76,184
Total Louisiana crop	329,966
Total for the United States	406,150

Exports of Rice from Charleston and Home Consumption during the past 2 years.

Exports of rice from Charleston and home consumption during the past two years.

The following table shows the exports and home consumption at this port during the past season of 1893-94, in comparison with the previous year:—

To—	Quantity.	
	1893-94.	1892-93.
	Barrels.	Barrels.
New York	19,002	28,367
Interior points by rail	6,601	39,965
Total	25,603	68,332

The quantity of rice received at Charleston from September 1, 1893, to August 31, 1894, expressed in barrels of cleaned rice, was 35,603, compared with 94,332 barrels the previous year, showing a decrease in last year's receipts of 58,729 barrels. During the same time there was consumed at Charleston 10,000 barrels last year, and 26,000 the previous year, which left no stock on hand September 1, 1894, when the new rice season of 1894–95 opened.

Supplementary.

The receipts of rice at Charleston from September 1 to December 31, 1894, were 25,156 barrels of cleaned rice compared with 14,900 barrels for the same 4 months during the previous year. The total exports from September 1 to December 31, 1894, were 14,711 barrels compared with 8,429 barrels for the corresponding time of the year before, and the stock on hand and seaboard on the last day of 1894 amounted to 7,745 barrels, in comparison with 4,533 barrels on the same date 1 year ago. Of the 14,711 barrels exported, as above stated, there were no foreign exports, 10,023 barrels went to interior points by rail, and the rest, 4,688 barrels, going to New York.

[margin: Rice trade from September 1 to December 31, 1894.]

The rice market at the close of the year, 1894, was quiet, with closing quotations of 5 c. to 5¼ c. per lb. for prime grades, 4 c. to 4½ c. for good, and 3 c. to 3¾ c. for fair and nominal prices for common.

From the opening of the new rice season on September 1 to the end of the year the tone of the market was almost uniformly steady with a good demand, receipts as shown by the foregoing figures were very much larger throughout the months of September, October, November, and December of 1894, than during the corresponding months of the previous year, and prices kept up well showing no decline in December quotations compared with those of September, notwithstanding the increased receipts, indeed, if anything, the closing prices were about the best of the season.

Naval Stores and Lumber.

There was a reduction in the receipts of naval stores last year, although, on the whole, prices remained fairly good. The reduction in receipts of resin, turpentine, &c., as pointed out in previous consular trade reports, have been steadily going on for a number of years, owing to the gradual exhaustion of the pine forests in the two Carolinas which has had a tendency to remove the turpentine farms each year further from Charleston into the more profitable virgin pine regions of Georgia, Florida, and Alabama. 25 years ago the principal naval stores market in the United States was Wilmington, North Carolina, but now Savannah, Georgia, has become the first naval stores market in this country,

[margin: Naval stores and lumber.]

and prices for the products of the pine tree are now regulated by that port. At Charleston last year there was not only the natural decrease in the trade to be expected from the gradual thinning out of the pines in the territory tributary to this place, but there was also great havoc done to the trees still in this section by the storm of August, 1893, which added considerably to the ratio of decrease in last year's business; besides, it should be considered that there is really no available new territory into which Charleston can reach out, under present railway conditions, for new business when the sources from whence she draws her naval stores trade become exhausted or temporarily fail.

The receipts of naval stores at Charleston, with the stock on hand, from September 1, 1893, to September 1, 1894, and for the previous year were as follows:—

	1893-94.		1892-93.	
	Spirits of Turpentine.	Resin.	Spirits of Turpentine.	Resin.
	Casks.	Barrels.	Casks.	Barrels.
Stock on hand	2,941	9,497	1,443	15,982
Receipts	14,415	71,392	22,542	121,624
Total	17,356	80,889	23,985	137,606

The exports during the year ending September 1, 1894, were, to coastwise and domestic points, 9,785 casks of spirits of turpentine and 19,755 barrels resin, and to foreign countries 4,886 casks of spirits and 50,895 barrels resin, compared with the previous year's exports of 8,967 casks of spirits and 26,060 barrels of resin, coastwise, and 12,077 casks of spirits, and 102,049 barrels of resin to foreign countries. Of the 4,886 casks of spirits exported foreign last year, 4,484 went to Great Britain and 402 to Genoa, and of the 50,895 barrels of resin, Great Britain took 16,982 barrels; Germany, 14,744; Austria, 3,310; Russia, 3,321; and the remainder went to other continental ports of Europe.

The quotations for the leading grades of resin and for spirits of turpentine, September 1, 1894, were:—for spirits, 25½ c. per gallon, and for resin—"C," 95 c. per barrel; "F," 1 dol. 5 c.; "G," 1 dol. 15 c.; "H," 1 dol. 20 c.; "I," 1 dol. 60 c.; "K," 1 dol. 90 c.; "M," 1 dol. 95 c.; "N," 2 dol. 10 c.

The naval stores business done at Charleston from September 1, to December 31, 1894, is included in the following statement which covers a period from April 1 to December 31, 1894, exact tabulated figures for the last 4 months of the year not being obtainable for the reason that the naval stores year commences April 1, and not September 1 as is the case with other branches of trade at this port.

The total receipts from April 1 to December 31, 1894, were 12,578 casks of turpentine, 52,613 barrels of resin, compared with

18,900 casks of turpentine and 70,170 barrels of resin for the corresponding time of the year before. The exports last season during the same period were 12,987 casks of turpentine and 52,034 barrels of resin, compared with 20,707 casks of turpentine and 89,126 barrels of resin the year before, leaving a stock on hand on the last day of 1894 of 565 casks of turpentine and 4,540 barrels of resin in comparison with 1,603 casks of turpentine and 9,615 barrels of resin on the same date a year ago.

The closing quotations on the last day of 1894 for spirits of turpentine were 24½ c. per gallon, and for resin as follows:— "C," resin, 1 dol. per barrel; "F," 1 dol. 10 c.; "G," 1 dol. 20 c.; "H," 1 dol. 50 c.; "I," 1 dol. 85 c.; "K," 2 dol. 25 c.; "M," 2 dol. 50 c.; "N," 2 dol. 75 c.; "WG" (window glass resin), 2 dol. 90 c.; and "WW" (water white), 3 dol. 15 c. In addition to the foregoing the quotations for "crude turpentine" were given as follows:—Virgin, 1 dol. 75 c. per barrel; yellow dip, 1 dol. 40 c.; and strap, 90 c.

Lumber.

The lumber trade at Charleston during the business year ending August 31, 1894, was in its main features but little different from that of the previous year; prices generally were low, and although the margin of profit was close, yet the shipments compare, as a rule, very favourably with former seasons. The local consumption of lumber has been stimulated by the erection last year of quite a number of elegant and useful buildings in various parts of the town, the building of comfortable homes by persons in moderate circumstances who, in a great many instances, have been enabled to do so through the assistance of the building associations, and the growing preference on the part of many persons for wood rather than brick dwellings since the destructive effects of the earthquake of 1886 on the brick structures; all of which has tended to give an increased local demand for lumber, notwithstanding the general trade depression which has otherwise prevailed in most branches of trade throughout the year. In this connection it may perhaps be well to mention as a noteworthy feature in the lumber business here, that an important change has taken place in the last few years in the sources from which most of the lumber material used now comes; formerly the city mills supplied the demand, but now the principal supplies come from interior points by means of the waterways and railways which enable sellers to offer lumber at prices considerably lower than city mill prices, thus placing the port in a more favourable position for competing for export business with other ports shipping lumber.

The necessity arising from lower prices last year, and the improved facilities now enjoyed for receiving supplies of timber on the rivers more conveniently than heretofore, has induced many persons interested in the business to give greater care to the economical and practicable use of the pine forests, and has also brought about the manufacture of many useful articles of trade that are now made from products of the pine, formerly wasted or neglected. What appears to be most wanted now is the establishment of a variety of manufactories for making wooden wares which would utilise increased quantities of lumber in a profitable way, and would give employment to the labouring classes, besides these industries would contribute to the general trade, and add to the importance of the port.

Exports of Lumber.

Exports of lumber.

The comparative exports of lumber, timber, and cross-ties (railway sleepers) from the port of Charleston from September 1, 1893, to August 31, 1894, as well as for the same period in 1892-93, will be found in the following table:—

COASTWISE EXPORTS.

To—	Quantity. 1893-94.	1892-93.
	Feet.	Feet.
New York	45,356,453	44,922,989
Boston	2,170,000	1,768,000
Philadelphia	4,377,000	5,505,202
Baltimore	941,000	1,800,000
Other American ports	4,775,000	3,953,000
Total	57,619,453	58,009,281

FOREIGN EXPORTS.

To—	Quantity. 1893-94.	1892-93.
	Feet.	Feet.
West Indies	2,570,000	..
South America	..	2,584,063
Other foreign ports	725,000	500,000
Total	3,295,000	3,084,063

CHARLESTON.

GRAND TOTAL.

	Quantity.	
	1893-94.	1892-93.
	Feet.	Feet.
Grand total of both foreign and coastwise	60,914,453	61,093,344

In reviewing the total shipments of lumber yearly from the port of Charleston the business would appear to be a steadily growing one, as is shown by the following figures, which have been taken from the official records of the port of the past 20 years:—In 1875 the lumber exports amounted to only 5,242,238 feet; in 1880 they were 15,437,907 feet; in 1885 they had increased to 30,033,961 feet; in 1890 and 1891 to 51,226,827 feet; and for the last season of 1893-94, as above stated, they were 60,914,453 feet. From September 1 to December 31 in the past year of 1894 the total exports of lumber from this port were 15,321,144 feet, compared with 21,264,872 feet for the same 4 months of the previous year; of the shipments last year 13,951,144 feet were sent coastwise, 1,095,000 feet to the West Indies, and the remainder, 275,000 feet, to other foreign countries.

The lumber market closed at the end of last year with a light demand for well manufactured stock and a fairly good export trade, and quotations were as follows:—For merchantable city sawed lumber, 14 to 16 dol. per 1,000 feet; for railroad lumber, 12 to 14 dol.; for square and sound, 9 to 13 dol.; 8 to 11 dol. for raft; 4 dol. 50 c. to 6 dol. 50 c. for dock timber; and 5 to 7 dol. per 1,000 for shingles.

Shipping and Navigation.

The proportion of Charleston's shipping trade of the past year of 1894 will be seen by referring to the "Annual Return of British Shipping" accompanying this report, which, taken together with the shipping and tonnage of vessels of other nationalities, also given herewith, make up the total of the year's shipping business, the figures including all vessels arriving of 100 tons and over, it not being customary at this port to include in the yearly shipping statistics vessels of smaller size than 100 tons.

Most of the foreign steamers that came here last year carried the British flag, but the bulk of the foreign trade in sailing vessels was done in ships of other nationalities than British, most of the sailing ships being Italian, Spanish, and Norwegian barques and brigs of moderate tonnage, with an occasional arrival of a German, Austrian, or Russian ship; but for the past two or three years the French flag has practically disappeared from the harbour of Charleston on merchant vessels, a French war vessel having been the last ship arriving of any importance flying the tricolour of France several years ago in these waters. Twenty years ago a British steamer's arrival was the exception and not the rule, most of the British arrivals being sailing vessels, the majority of which hailed from Nova Scotia. The change from sailing vessels to steamers has apparently brought about a marked improvement, as there is now far less trouble to adjust differences between masters and their crews than formerly, and fewer desertions take place, which latter fact, however, may be partly accounted for by the wholesome effect which the new treaty with reference to the arrest of deserting seamen which is now in force between the Governments of Great Britain and the United States. Occasional trouble among the crews of British steamers has now and then to be dealt with, but, taken as a whole, out of every 50 or 100 vessels coming to Charleston, the number of instances where trouble occurs among the crews (of anything more than trivial in its nature) is of comparatively rare occurrence, and bears no relative proportion to what it formerly was.

The steamer service between Charleston, New York, and Jacksonville is performed by the Clyde line of American steamships, there being six vessels on the line built for this service, having light draught, large carrying capacity, and good accommodation for passengers, many of whom avail themselves of this route in their winter journeys between the north and the milder climate of Florida. Messrs. W. P. Clyde and Co., the well known owners of the New York Line, have also established during the past autumn, a line of small steamers between Charleston and Philadelphia, and regular service is now maintained between the two ports, the two ships on the Philadelphia line being the "Winyah" and the "Delaware."

The coastwise trade is in the hands of American vessels exclusively, inasmuch as the United States laws prohibit vessels of foreign nationality from engaging in the coastwise trade between United States ports, their privileges being limited to the foreign carrying trade.

During the commercial year ending August 31, 1894, according to figures made up to that time, the total number of vessels, over 100 tons each, arriving at this port were 748, of which 627 were of American nationality and 121 foreign, having a total net tonnage of 844,911 tons, compared with 790 arrivals for the year previous, with a tonnage of 814,761, showing that while there was a numerical decrease in the number of ships in the last commercial year, there was nevertheless an increase in the tonnage.

In addition to the foregoing the following figures have been obtained from a special statement prepared by the harbour-master, giving the arrivals of shipping and the tonnage from

January 1, 1894, to December 31, 1894. The total arrivals at Charleston during 1894 were 753 vessels of all nationalities, with a tonnage of 808,174 tons, compared with 774 arrivals in 1893, having a tonnage of 799,211 tons, showing an increase last year of 8,963 in the tonnage of the port, although there was an actual decrease in the arrivals of 24 vessels. Of the 753 arrivals last year 649 were American, with 685,497 tons; 60 British, of 88,493 tons; 20 Spanish, of 11,770 tons; 10 Norwegian, of 10,374 tons; 19 Italian, of 9,381 tons; 3 German, of 1,397 tons; 1 Austrian, of 667 tons; and 1 Danish, of 595 tons.

UNITED STATES.

RETURN of British Shipping at the Port of Charleston, S.C., in the Year 1894.

Direct Trade in British Vessels from and to Great Britain and British Colonies.

Entered.

Total Number of Vessels.			Total Tonnage.			Total Number of Crews.	Total Value of Cargoes.
With Cargoes.	In Ballast.	Total.	With Cargoes.	In Ballast.	Total.		£
2	21	23	2,155	35,561	37,716	568	1,030

Cleared.

Total Number of Vessels.			Total Tonnage.			Total Number of Crews.	Total Value of Cargoes.
With Cargoes.	In Ballast.	Total.	With Cargoes.	In Ballast.	Total.		£
19	1	20	31,062	14	31,076	481	1,565,450

Indirect or Carrying Trade in British Vessels from and to other Countries.

Entered.

Countries whence Arrived.	Number of Vessels.			Tonnage.			Number of Crews.	Value of Cargoes.
	With Cargoes.	In Ballast.	Total.	With Cargoes.	In Ballast.	Total.		£
Belgium	...	1	1	...	1,598	1,598	22	...
Chile	2	...	2	2,228	...	2,228	39	5,400
France	...	1	1	...	195	195	6	...
Germany	8	1	9	12,949	2,018	14,967	222	50,000
Holland	...	1	1	...	1,728	1,728	26	...
Italy	1	...	1	1,537	...	1,537	23	2,500
Portugal	7	...	7	8,568	...	8,568	169	16,950
Spain	5	1	6	6,446	1,457	7,903	130	13,200
America	...	9	9	...	12,053	12,053	205	...
Total	23	14	37	31,728	19,049	50,777	842	88,050

Cleared.

Countries to which Departed.	Number of Vessels.			Tonnage.			Number of Crews.	Value of Cargoes.
	With Cargoes.	In Ballast.	Total.	With Cargoes.	In Ballast.	Total.		£
France	3	...	3	4,226	...	4,226	66	91,400
Germany	11	...	11	18,654	...	18,654	274	541,000
Italy	2	...	2	2,370	...	2,370	49	4,300
Norway and Sweden	1	...	1	1,271	...	1,271	25	28,000
Russia	1	...	1	1,820	...	1,820	28	41,000
Spain	5	1	6	7,758	1,125	8,883	148	204,000
America	...	13	13	...	17,680	17,680	283	...
Total	23	14	37	36,099	18,805	54,904	878	909,700

Miscellaneous.

The United States Government have recently made public some interesting statistics with reference to the coal produced in the States of Georgia and North Carolina last year, the figures in question having been prepared at the close of the year by the division of mining statistics of the Geographical Survey Department; and from the statement given it appears that in 1894 the total coal product of Georgia amounted to 254,111 short tons of 2,000 lbs. each, compared with 272,740 tons in 1893, a falling-off last year of 18,629 tons, or, say, about 5 per cent. decrease, the decline in value being somewhat sharper, the total valuation of last year's product was placed at 365,972 dol. in 1893, and only 299,290 dol. in 1894, owing to the average price per ton for coal at the mine having fallen from 98 c. to 84½ c., a decline during the year of 13½ c. per ton.

In North Carolina the coal product last year was 13,150 short tons for the whole State, worth at the mines 20,300 dol. Extensive improvements were made during the season at the coal mines situated at Egypt depôt, Chatham County, North Carolina, and in consequence of these improvements the production was somewhat reduced; but a new mine was opened in Moore County that commenced shipping coal last year.

There are no statistics compiled as yet with reference to the number of heat-units per 1 lb. in the different varieties of coal produced in the coal-producing States of the South, which are Virginia, North Carolina, Georgia, Alabama, and Tennessee, and the qualities of the Southern coal as compared with the Northern article, but the census shows that an analysis of coal obtained from the flat top coal fields of Virginia and West Virginia in comparison with that of the Connellsville coal fields of Pennsylvania established the fact that the Southern coal was desirable for coke and other purposes, and British shipmasters speak highly of the Pochahontas coal for steamer's use as it burns well with little ash.

It appears, however, from the reports that the proportion of the total cost of manufacturing expended for coal varies according to the character of the industry and the nature of the finished product, it being shown from statistics covering the operations of textile manufacture during the year 1890, the last reported on, that in manufacturing cotton goods in the Southern States the cost of coal amounted to 1 dol. 45 c. per cent. of the total cost of materials, while the cost of other kinds of fuel was 41 c. per cent., and that in the New England States the cost of coal was 3 dol. 2 c. per cent., and other fuel 6 c. per cent.

It was also shown that of the total cost of materials in wool manufacture in the Southern States, coal constituted 1 dol. 38 c. per cent. and other fuel 45 c. per cent., and that in the New England States coal formed 2 dol. 16 c. per cent., and other fuel 17 c. per cent. of the total cost.

Cotton Seed Oil Industry.

Cotton seed oil industry.

The cotton seed oil industry is a business that has grown from almost nothing just after the close of the American civil war to its present proportions, which have now become of vast importance to the agricultural interests of the cotton producing sections of the country. In 1867 there were only 4 cotton seed oil mills in the United States, while at the present time there are 253 mills throughout the country, 27 of them being situated in South Carolina.

It is somewhat noteworthy that throughout the development of the business there was a constant feeling of apprehension on the part of those most interested that it would be overdone, but each year seems but to add greater stability to the industry and lower prices appear to be off-set by a steadily increasing demand and a wider range of markets for the various products of the cotton seed; the refined oil is rapidly coming into favour for cooking uses both in its natural condition and compounded with other preparations now on the market. The oil itself is a sweet, wholesome, and pure vegetable oil, and is regarded as far preferable by many persons to hogs' grease for kitchen use. In the early history of the oil business prices were 50 to 60 c. per gallon, and sales have been made at a maximum of 60 c. per gallon within the past 2 or 3 years, but, on the other hand, since that time prices have gone as low as 20 c. per gallon. The 27 mills now in operation in South Carolina have a capital of over 1,000,000 dol., and the quantity of seed crushed by them last year was about 75,000 tons valued at 800,000 dol., producing 60,000 barrels of oil, 26,000 tons of cotton seed meal, 5,000 bales of linters, and 25,000 tons of hulls.

The oil is sold in the Northern and Western markets, and is largely used in the manufacture of compound lard and other food products. Several years ago part of the cotton seed meal produced in this State was exported to foreign countries, but during the last 2 years it has all been consumed at home, much of it being used by farmers as a manure, either by direct application of the meal to the land or by composting it with phosphates; the fertiliser companies also consume a certain proportion, and in addition considerable quantities are used as a food for fattening cattle and stock for which it has been found to be well suited when mixed with the cotton seed hulls. The hulls were formerly used for fuel, but the increasing demand for them for cattle food has made them too valuable to be used any longer in that way, and there is now little or no consumption for fuel purposes.

The prices for cotton seed oil at the close of last season was low, quotations being reported at only 20 c. for oil per gallon, the price of seed varies in proportion to the value of oil, indeed, it is regulated by it, and the mills have uniformly paid for seed a fair price such as would be justified by the market value of the product. It has been estimated that the average price paid for seed last year added nearly 1 c. per 1 lb. to the total value of the cotton crop produced in the United States.

Taken altogether the condition of the cotton oil mill industry in South Carolina at the close of the year is healthy, the mills have conducted their affairs on sound business principles, and they have been well supported by the farmers who have derived almost as much benefit from them as the stockholders.

SAVANNAH.

Mr. Vice-Consul Robertson reports as follows:—

Trade and commerce. The trade and commerce of the port for the year 1894 has, on the whole, been generally satisfactory. The great depression all over the country was felt here as well as elsewhere, but, I am glad to say, with no very great severity. Notwithstanding the very low price of cotton and the particularly tight money market not one financial disaster took place at this port. Naturally the very close scrutiny that both factors and merchants were compelled to use in all classes of business, curtailed a large portion of trade that Savannah would have received in more prosperous times, this loss, however, is one that can well be spared at such times of depression.

The general advantages for controlling trade are steadily increasing, and with the return of the former prosperous times Savannah will be well able to hold her own with any of the southern ports of the United States.

Cotton. The season opened under the most unfavourable conditions, money was scarce, and the weather bad for early harvesting the crop. The price at the opening of the season was low, and as the indications were for a large crop the price steadily declined.

Savannah however received her full share of the crop amounting to 915,171 bales of Upland cotton and 54,259 bales Sea Island.

Railroads. The railroads now centering in Savannah are the Central and Southern, the South Bound, Central of Georgia, Savannah Americus and Montgomery, Savannah Florida and Western, and Florida Central and Peninsular. There are also two railroads under construction, viz., the Macon and Atlantic, and the Macon and Dublin, this gives Savannah an almost unlimited territory to draw from in the South and West for her great export trade, and it has already shown good results by bringing large quantities of freight from Florida that would have had to have gone from other ports but for these facilities. These avenues of commerce bring to Savannah the cotton, lumber, naval stores, and farm and mineral products of large portions of the States of Georgia, South Carolina, Florida, Alabama and Tennessee.

Phosphates. In consequence of the increase of territory gathered in by the railroads before mentioned, there are now coming to this port large quantities of Florida phosphate, a thing hitherto unknown here, and has proved a great benefit to shippers from the fact that better results can be obtained by vessels taking part cargoes of this commodity and part cotton, it also proves of advantage to the vessels carrying these cargoes, as it gives them greater stability at sea. While the prices for phosphate is not so lucrative as it was, it has finally resolved itself to a solid basis, and large quantities will continue to be shipped from this port.

Cotton-seed. — The exportation of this commodity has not increased to any appreciable extent since my last report.

Lumber and timber. — The financial depression has been felt most keenly by the dealers in this commodity, and very little business has been done, the South American and West Indian markets being in such a state as to warrant only very guarded investments, and a consequent falling-off in this trade is reported. The shipments to the home markets north, however, are being steadily made, and bring fair prices.

Naval stores. — The trade generally in this commodity was satisfactory, especially as regards resin, which brought a fair price throughout the year. All spirits sold realised prices as high as was reasonable to expect, though in endeavouring to hold out for prices there was a large accumulation of stock at the end of the year. For many reasons great complaints were received from abroad of false packed resin and irregularities in the gauging of spirits of turpentine. This year action was taken by the Board of Trade by appointing a supervising inspector, whose duty it is to see that all laws regarding weighing, gauging, cooperage, and sampling are carried out justly.

This will prevent to a great degree the many disputes between buyers and sellers.

During the year 268,629 casks of spirits of turpentine and 1,000,735 barrels of resin were received.

Rice. — The planting of rice in this district was virtually abandoned this year, owing to the continued heavy losses sustained by the planters through storms, bad harvests, and the heavy receipts from Louisiana.

River and harbour improvements. — The improvements in the Savannah River are being carried on, and under an appropriation of the United States Government, July, 1893, the amount of 2,831,250 dol. (566,250*l.*) was further added to the amounts previously allowed for the continuation of this work. Of this amount, I am informed by Captain O. M. Carter, who has charge as engineer for the United States Government, only about two-thirds has been used up to the present time, and has resulted in increasing the depth of water in the channel of the Savannah River to 26 feet, and a further amount (estimated) at 1,831,250 dol. (366,250*l.*) is asked for to complete the existing project of deepening the river to a mean depth of 30 feet, which it is confidently believed will be granted, and under the same conditions as heretofore existing, it is hoped that by 1896 this most desirable result will be obtained.

Casualties. — The casualties of the past year would have been no more than

CHARLESTON.

usual but for the fact that the merchants while endeavouring to make lower rates in the charges for stevedoring at this port, came into conflict with the labour, and, as a result, on November 6 last, about the opening of the cotton season, nine British steamships were set on fire. More or less cotton was, of course, destroyed, but the damage to the steamships themselves was, after all, but nominal, the expense devolving itself into the detention suffered by those vessels which had to discharge and reload.

These charges have been somewhat reduced by the fact that the quarantine charges have been taken off the vessels arriving here, and are now assumed by the City Government and State Board of Health, thus making the tax on vessels arriving here somewhat less. In consequence of the rivalry existing between this port, Port Royal and Charleston, other reductions will no doubt soon be made by the local government reducing the wharfage and harbour-master's fees, &c., thus I hope shortly to report that this will be one of the cheapest ports for vessels to load at. *Port charges.*

The port has held her own during the year, and it is gratifying to note that out of 310,105 registered tons of foreign vessels, 152,589 registered tons have been under the British flag, or nearly one half. *Shipping.*

Real estate sympathised during the year with all other classes of business. Dulness was the distinguishing feature. While there were spasmodic "spurts," the continuity of demand which makes a market and results in transactions were lacking; investors, while admitting their preference for realty, held off and waited for some time in the future in which to come to the market. As the consequence of this condition no large deals took place. *Real estate.*

However, I still reiterate the statement made in my last report that Savannah offers the best inducements for foreign investments of this class.

The imports show a slight decrease, and the annexed table shows the different articles, amounts, and valuations. *Imports.*

The table of exports, showing the different articles, amounts, and valuations is hereby annexed. *Exports.*

The return of British shipping though showing a large amount of tonnage, it will be noticed that the values have decreased. *Return of British shipping.*

RETURN of Vessels Entered and Cleared at the Port of Savannah during the Year 1894.

ENTERED.

Nationality.	Sailing.		Steam.		Total.	
	Number of Vessels.	Tons.	Number of Vessels.	Tons.	Number of Vessels.	Tons.
American	6	3,878	...	...	6	3,878
British	14	5,957	98	140,741	112	146,698
Norwegian	104	70,935	2	1,833	106	72,768
German	19	16,781	1	1,676	20	18,547
Spanish	3	2,010	6	1,261	9	14,171
Other countries	50	29,580	6	10,631	56	40,211
Total	196	102,231	113	167,042	309	296,273

UNITED STATES.

CLEARED.

Nationality.	Sailing. Number of Vessels.	Sailing. Tons.	Steam. Number of Vessels.	Steam. Tons.	Total Number of Vessels.	Total Tons.
American	4	1,555	...	...	4	1,555
British	16	7,540	98	145,049	114	152,589
Norwegian	103	71,926	2	1,871	105	73,797
German	20	15,712	...	...	20	15,712
Spanish	3	1,032	6	11,541	9	12,573
Other countries	64	37,553	9	16,326	73	53,879
Total	210	135,318	115	174,787	325	310,105

RETURN of Principal Articles of Export from Savannah, Georgia, during the Year 1894.

Articles.		Quantity.	Value. £
Cotton	Lbs.	255,879,520	3,831,392
Cotton seed	„	2,580,557	4,595
Lumber and timber	Feet	9,256,000	22,313
Spirits, turpentine	Gallons	8,849,655	469,407
Resin	„	1,027,200	319,676
All other articles	„	..	77,535
Total	..	..	4,274,918

RETURN of Principal Articles of Import to Savannah, Georgia, during the Year 1894.

Articles.		Quantity.	Value. £
Fertilisers	Tons	6,056	8,134
Muriate of potash	Lbs.	3,196,529	8,924
Sulphate of potash	„	112,560	396
Brimstone	Tons	6,215	19,130
Fruit and nuts	..	..	7,376
Cement	Lbs.	12,069,633	6,704
Salt	„	8,510,024	2,076
Wine and spirits	Gallons	5,520	1,224
Molasses	„	78,367	1,922
Bags and bagging	..	..	4,900
Tin plates	Lbs.	1,103,454	5,316
Dyes	..	..	1,346
Nitrate of soda	Tons	1,087	6,792
All other articles	..	..	6,657
Total	..	..	80,897

RETURN of British Shipping at the Port of Savannah, Georgia, during the Year 1894.

Direct Trade in British Vessels from and to Great Britain and British Colonies.

Entered.

Total Number of Vessels.			Total Tonnage.			Total Number of Crews.	Total Value of Cargoes.
With Cargoes.	In Ballast.	Total.	With Cargoes.	In Ballast.	Total.		£
2	36	38	2,438	52,606	55,044	836	5,590

Cleared.

Total Number of Vessels.			Total Tonnage.			Total Number of Crews.	Total Value of Cargoes.
With Cargoes.	In Ballast.	Total.	With Cargoes.	In Ballast.	Total.		£
36	...	36	52,584	...	52,584	794	1,056,248

Indirect or Carrying Trade in British Vessels from and to other Countries.

Entered.

Countries whence Arrived.	Number of Vessels.			Tonnage.			Number of Crews.	Value of Cargoes.
	With Cargoes.	In Ballast.	Total.	With Cargoes.	In Ballast.	Total.		£
United States	...	39	39	...	53,871	53,871	920	...
Brazil	...	2	2	...	1,790	1,790	20	...
Belgium	...	1	1	...	1,994	1,994	26	...
France	...	13	13	...	12,949	12,949	248	...
Germany	1	1	2	2,630	1,994	4,624	57	4,067
Portugal	...	5	5	...	8,034	8,034	128	...
Spain	1	2	3	168	2,984	3,152	41	1,922
Peru	1	...	1	1,725	...	1,725	16	6,792
Nicaragua	8	...	8	2,505	...	2,505	89	4,000
Total	11	63	74	7,028	84,616	91,644	1,545	16,787

Cleared.

Countries to which Departed.	Number of Vessels.			Tonnage.			Number of Crews.	Value of Cargoes.
	With Cargoes.	In Ballast.	Total.	With Cargoes.	In Ballast.	Total.		£
Argentine Republic	1	...	1	946	...	946	16	20,812
Brazil	2	...	2	867	...	867	31	19,094
France	6	...	6	9,984	...	9,984	107	219,648
Germany	23	...	23	35,900	...	35,900	540	789,800
Italy	9	...	9	14,387	...	14,387	178	316,514
Netherlands	2	...	2	3,260	...	3,260	40	71,720
Russia	9	...	9	10,400	...	10,400	207	228,800
Sweden	1	...	1	800	...	800	26	17,600
Spain	14	...	14	10,670	...	10,670	260	23,470
Uruguay	1	...	1	1,164	...	1,164	16	25,608
United States	...	10	10	...	11,627	11,627	209	255,794
Total	68	10	78	88,378	11,627	100,005	1,630	1,988,860

UNITED STATES.

BRUNSWICK.

Mr. Vice-Consul Torras reports as follows:—

Since my last annual report, I beg to say that the conditions of this port remain about the same, probably owing to the epidemic of yellow fever occurring during the summer of 1893, together with the general lack of business. The trade for the past 12 months, both coastwise and foreign, has been exceedingly dull in all its branches; such few enterprises as were inaugurated during the year 1893 and previous to that year have suffered greatly, and in some cases have been abandoned, thus creating a lack of work and causing some complaint in all classes.

Work on St. Simon's Bar.

The work of deepening the St. Simon's Bar by means of explosions of dynamite is still being pursued, and the good results that have been obtained are expected to be permanent.

Health.

The health of this city during the past year has been very good, in fact the physicians claim that there has been less sickness and deaths reported than any year previous; this they attribute to the new system of sewerage which was commenced the early part of the year, and partially completed before the summer months began. The system is now completed, and the public hopes to keep in future the good record of last year. The local quarantine being operated by the National Government since the appearance of the epidemic of yellow fever, has probably added considerably to the good results obtained in the general health of this city; the station has been furnished with the latest appliances for fumigating and disinfecting vessels. All vessels entering this port subject to quarantine, receive thorough and speedy fumigation free of cost.

Exports for 1894.

Month.	Bales of Cotton. Number.	Barrels of Resin. Number.	Gallons of Spirits, Turpentine. Number.	Value, Total Exports. Dollars.	Remarks.
January	12,607	18,324	133,167	660,485	Of this have been shipped to Great Britain 65,040 bales of cotton valued at 2,300,000 dol.; and to the colonies, 51,900 dol., chiefly for railroad materials exported to Jamaica.
February	3,570	4,120	...	226,944	
March	9,251	18,203	23,490	515,679	
April	9,600	7,694	...	486,688	
May	3,250	14,519	293,344	304,871	
June	1,550	10,759	324,557	270,431	
July	...	14,967	355,753	233,938	
August	...	19,033	102,617	170,216	
September	350	...	...	84,123	
October	18,634	6,830	460,224	776,467	
November	13,222	12,865	342,073	561,078	
December	32,802	2,600	66,437	930,988	
Total	104,836	129,914	2,101,662	5,221,908	

FOREIGN OFFICE.
1895.
ANNUAL SERIES.

No. 1536.

DIPLOMATIC AND CONSULAR REPORTS ON TRADE AND FINANCE.

UNITED STATES.

REPORT FOR THE YEAR 1894
ON THE
TRADE OF THE CONSULAR DISTRICT OF BOSTON.

REFERENCE TO PREVIOUS REPORT, Annual Series No. 1339.

Presented to both Houses of Parliament by Command of Her Majesty,
MAY, 1895.

LONDON:
PRINTED FOR HER MAJESTY'S STATIONERY OFFICE,
BY HARRISON AND SONS, ST. MARTIN'S LANE,
PRINTERS IN ORDINARY TO HER MAJESTY.

And to be purchased, either directly or through any Bookseller, from
EYRE & SPOTTISWOODE, East Harding Street, Fleet Street, E.C., and
32, Abingdon Street, Westminster, S.W.; or
JOHN MENZIES & Co., 12, Hanover Street, Edinburgh, and
90, West Nile Street, Glasgow; or
HODGES, FIGGIS, & Co., Limited, 104, Grafton Street, Dublin.

1895.

[C. 7581—76.] *Price Three Halfpence.*

New Series of Reports.

Reports of the Annual Series have been issued from Her Majesty's Diplomatic and Consular Officers at the following places, and may be obtained from the sources indicated on the title-page:—

No.		Price.	No.		Price.
1418.	Beyrout	1d.	1477.	Rome	2d.
1419.	Berlin	1½d.	1478.	Hamburg	4d.
1420.	Nice	3d.	1479.	The Hague	1½d.
1421.	Yokohama	1½d.	1480.	Belgrade	2d.
1422.	Maracaibo	1d.	1481.	Batoum	1½d.
1423.	Tunis	1½d.	1482.	Teneriffe	½d.
1424.	Baghdad and Bussorah	1d.	1483.	Lisbon	2½d.
1425.	Rio Grande do Sul	7d.	1484.	Buda-Pesth	½d.
1426.	Erzeroum	1d.	1485.	Rome	5½d.
1427.	Christiania	5½d.	1486.	Para	1d.
1428.	Charleston	5½d.	1487.	Odessa	1d.
1429.	Meshed	1d.	1488.	Hakodate	1d.
1430.	Copenhagen	½d.	1489.	Beira	1½d.
1431.	Galveston	2½d.	1490.	Berne	1½d.
1432.	Hamburg	2½d.	1491.	Copenhagen	1d.
1433.	Brindisi	2½d.	1492.	Stettin	2½d.
1434.	Gothenburg	2d.	1493.	Rio Grande do Sul	1½d.
1435.	Kiungchow	1d.	1494.	Serajevo	1d.
1436.	St. Petersburg	½d.	1495.	Buenos Ayres	9d.
1437.	Malaga	1d.	1496.	Florence	2d.
1438.	Chicago	2½d.	1497.	Lisbon	1½d.
1439.	Odessa	2d.	1498.	Paris	2d.
1440.	Tabreez	½d.	1499.	Bolivia	1½d.
1441.	Tahiti	½d.	1500.	Patras	1½d.
1442.	Shanghai	2d.	1501.	Bordeaux	3d.
1443.	Nagasaki	1d.	1502.	Madrid	2d.
1444.	Madrid	2½d.	1503.	Amsterdam	1d.
1445.	Malaga	2½d.	1504.	Suakin	1d.
1446.	Rotterdam	1d.	1505.	Angora	1d.
1447.	Port Said	1d.	1506.	Havre	2½d.
1448.	Sofia	2½d.	1507.	Algiers	11d.
1449.	Warsaw	1½d.	1508.	La Rochelle	3d.
1450.	Africa (Congo)	2d.	1509.	Vera Cruz	2d.
1451.	Jeddah	1½d.	1510.	Puerto Cortes	1d.
1452.	San Francisco	5½d.	1511.	Taganrog	1d.
1453.	Oporto	2d.	1512.	Baltimore	1½d.
1454.	Barcelona	2d.	1513.	Mexico	1½d.
1455.	New Caledonia	½d.	1514.	Zaila	1d.
1456.	Smyrna	1d.	1515.	Zomba	3½d.
1457.	Macao	1d.	1516.	Valparaiso	2½d.
1458.	Samoa	1d.	1517.	Charleston	2½d.
1459.	Hiogo and Osaka	3d.	1518.	Serajevo	1d.
1460.	Lisbon	2d.	1519.	Saigon	1d.
1461.	Pekin	2d.	1520.	Bangkok	2d.
1462.	Corunna	2d.	1521.	Tripoli	1d.
1463.	Mozambique	15d.	1522.	Batavia	1½d.
1464.	Munich	1½d.	1523.	Dakar	½d.
1465.	St. Petersburg	3d.	1524.	Havana	2d.
1466.	Naples	1d.	1525.	Riga	2d.
1467.	Montevideo	2½d.	1526.	Trebizond	1½d.
1468.	Aden	1d.	1527.	Piræus	2½d.
1469.	Tokio	1½d.	1528.	Guayaquil	1½d.
1470.	Dantzig	5d.	1529.	Marseilles	1½d.
1471.	Guayaquil	1d.	1530.	Wuhu	1½d.
1472.	Canton	1½d.	1531.	Rio de Janeiro	2½d.
1473.	Dar-al-Baida	3d.	1532.	Trieste	2d.
1474.	Teheran	2d.	1533.	Brest	1½d.
1475.	Bushire	2d.	1534.	Stockholm	2d.
1476.	Tangier	2d.	1535.	Warsaw	1d.

No. 1536.

Reference to previous Report, Annual Series No. 1339

UNITED STATES.

BOSTON.

Consul Yeats-Brown to the Earl of Kimberley.

My Lord,   *Boston, March* 28, 1895.

I HAVE the honour to enclose my Annual Commercial Report for the year 1894.

I have, &c.
(Signed)   M. YEATS-BROWN.

Report on the Trade and Commerce of Boston for the Year 1894.

ABSTRACT of Contents.

	Page
Introductory remarks	1
Money market	2
Exchange	3
State debts	3
Industries	4
Unemployed	7
Textile industries	7
Fish and fisheries	8
Imports and exports	10
Shipping	11
Immigration	12
Public works	13
Strikes	14
Conclusion	15

Introductory Remarks.

Dulness has been the prevailing feature of the year 1894 in this district. There have been no great commercial disasters to record—fewer failures than in the previous year, money only too abundant; and the export trade business in Boston has been active. But on the whole the year has passed away without any realisation of the hopeful views which were somewhat generally entertained at the commencement of the year.

The long delay in passing the Tariff Bill, and the utter uncertainty prevailing to the last as to what modifications might be insisted upon before it could pass the Senate, of course contributed greatly to defer the time when merchants could undertake contracts, or venture on purchases with any reasonable security; and since the passing of that measure, the financial position of the country, and the constant drain of gold still in progress, is far from encouraging to sound business. No one in this part of the country doubts either the ability or the intention of the United States to fulfil the pledge repeatedly and emphatically given by her present Chief Magistrate, come what may, to redeem her paper in gold; but in other parts of the country there is plenty of noisy talk about the "absolute duty" of the Secretary of the Treasury to use his option as to "coin," and to pay out a silver dollar worth about 47 c., in lieu of a gold dollar worth 100 c. for such paper as is not, on the face of it, marked payable in gold. Unfortunately, as is often the case, the voice of the noisy few makes itself heard as distinctly as that of the far greater mass, who feel aright what the honour, and even the eventual interest, of their country demands; and the consequence is, especially abroad, detrimental to that confidence which is the very life blood of commerce, and especially of international trade.

Money market.

The opening of the year found this market with an overabundance of money and constant accumulation in the hands of bankers. The uncertainty of the action taken by Congress, both with regard to the tariff and the Government loan, which it was evident had to be issued, naturally impeded business. Call loans were at 1½ to 2 per cent.; short time loans 3 to 3½ per cent.; and manufacturing paper 3 per cent., at 6 months. Clearing-house rate was at 1 per cent. all through the month of January. This was the first full month of 1 per cent. ever recorded in Boston; though this rate repeated itself no less than seven times in the 12 months of this year.

In February, Congress having failed to authorise a 3 per cent. issue, a loan of 50,000,000 dol., at 5 per cent. for 10 years, was issued (at a basis of about 3 per cent.), and removed one of the causes of uncertainty and stagnation—at any rate temporarily. The same operation, however, had to be renewed in November, when the second loan of a similar amount was issued; this time, however, at a basis of 2⅞ per cent.

From March business continued to be very slack, and in the summer reached a point of stagnation very rarely experienced in this market. The contrast between this period in 1893 and in 1894 was remarkable, the panic being in full force in July and August of the previous year; whereas in 1894 Boston was only suffering from a plethora of unusable money. In September the clearing-house rate rose to 2 per cent., at which it remained until November.

In the last two months of the year a revival of business was much talked of, but development was slow, and the position remains much the same to the time of writing this report.

Exchange on London for sight bills has been as follows during the year 1894:—

Exchange.

Month.	Lowest.		Highest.	
	Dol.	c.	Dol.	c.
January	4	84	4	86
February	4	85	4	87¼
March	4	87½	4	88
April	4	87½	4	88½
May	4	88	4	88½
June	4	87	4	88½
July	4	87½	4	88½
August	4	86	4	84½
September	4	85	4	87
October	4	86	4	88
November	4	86½	4	87¼
December	4	87¼	4	88

The finances of the four States comprised in this consular district are in a highly satisfactory condition, Massachusetts, far the richest of the four, being the only one which has for years created any new bonded debt; those of New Hampshire and Maine being in course of rapid repayment, and the debt of Vermont being already entirely discharged.

State debts.

Some particulars may be of interest, especially as a good deal of English capital has at one time or another been invested in these securities.

The Massachusetts State debt on December 31, 1894, amounted to 5,813,850*l*., against which there are sinking funds amounting to 3,394,980*l*., leaving the net debt 2,418,872*l*., compared with 2,587,442*l*. the year before. The debt of the State is now due on matters wholly distinct from the results of the war, being in fact entirely for buildings, road improvements, sewerage, and similar expenditure of direct benefit to the State.

Massachusetts.

Every loan which now falls due prior to 1901 has more than sufficient sinking fund for its cancellation. The surplus is therefore being transferred to other more distant loans, whose sinking funds are smaller. The debt, therefore, though large, is in a satisfactory condition, and although new loans will have to be raised for the large expenditures contemplated in the next few years, the State will be able to bear them, and to provide not only for the regular payments of interest, but for the gradual extinction of the capital indebtedness.

The State debt of New Hampshire at the breaking out of the war amounted to 26,234*l*. The debt incurred during the war ran the amount up at the end of 1867 to 749,555*l*., which was, however, reduced in the next year to 697,496*l*. The high water-mark of the State indebtedness was reached in 1872, when it amounted to 827,625*l*., which, however, was then steadily reduced until, on

New Hampshire.

(1913)

UNITED STATES.

June 1, 1894, it stood at 407.308*l.*, and has since been further reduced by 19,044*l.* All the bonds issued in 1872 which have matured have been paid from proceeds of direct taxation, and those which are still outstanding will be extinguished in the same way. In addition to paying off this large amount of debt, the State has erected, without the issue of bonds, an agricultural college, State library, normal school and soldiers' home, and has also made improvements upon its asylum and industrial school. The State has no sinking fund.

Maine. The State of Maine incurred a debt as the result of the war amounting to nearly 800,000*l.*, which was a large sum in proportion to the resources of that State. In 1868, in order to provide for the debt which matured in 1889, a sinking fund was established, and by 1889, when the bonded debt (amounting to 793,480*l.*) matured, the sinking fund realised 247,135*l.* The old debt bore interest at the rate of 6 per cent., but after paying out the proceeds of the sinking fund the remaining debt was funded at 3 per cent., and the bonds were sold at an average rate of 103. These bonds fall due at various dates in amounts varying from 10,000*l.* to 13,000*l.* per annum up to the year 1929, but, by the arrangements made, the whole indebtedness will practically be liquidated with the help of sums raised by taxes by 1922, although it is probable that a special fund will be created for the investment of the income required for the State college and the asylum.

Vermont. Previous to the war the State debt of Vermont only amounted to about 23,000*l.*

The war expenses resulted in a State debt of 330,000*l.*, independently of the very large sums which were paid by direct taxation. This debt was bonded in 6 per cent. issues falling due at various dates from 1871 to 1878. At the close of 1865, however, it was determined to raise 30,000*l.* annually, in addition to the regular sinking fund, for the purpose of paying off the debt more rapidly, and by 1872 180,000*l.* had been paid off. The other loans were largely anticipated and paid before maturity, with the exception of the Agricultural College Bond, which had been, and is to remain, invested.

The Treasurer's report for the year ending June, 1894, shows cash assets amounting to 136,660*l.*, while the liabilities are only 39,729*l.*, showing a cash balance of 97,931*l.*, a very creditable showing for any State, and truly remarkable for a purely agricultural State such as is Vermont.

Industries.

The Bureau of Statistics of Labour for the State of Massachusetts publishes an annual report, which contains a mass of interesting information; but the report for 1894 will not appear for some months. From the volume lately issued for 1893 I extract the following items referring to the years 1892 and 1893.

BOSTON.

The statistical tables in this volume are based upon returns from 4,397 establishments, in 75 classified industries, which sent in reports in 1892 and 1893, and though they do not give aggregates of all the work done in Massachusetts, they do furnish a basis for comparing one year with the other, and may be relied upon as accurately reflecting the industrial conditions prevailing in those two years.

The disastrous influence of the financial crisis for 1893 upon industry is brought out in strong relief by these tables.

The amount of capital invested in these 4,397 establishments was:—

Year.	Amount.
	£
In 1892	87,803,052
1893	88,896,055
Increase	1,093,003

Whereas the total value of stock used was:—

Year.	Amount.
	£
In 1892	75,310,875
1893	69,798,381
Decrease	5,512,494

And the value of goods made was:—

Year.	Amount.
	£
In 1892	127,827,480
1893	117,468,710
Decrease	10,358,770

The following table shows the value of the goods made in each of the 2 years in the nine leading industries of this State:—

(1913)

Industries.	Number of Establishments Considered.	Value of Goods Made.	
		1892.	1893.
		Dollars.	Dollars.
Boots and shoes	712	103,878,098	92,740,686
Carpetings	11	8,214,540	7,427,385
Cotton goods	149	90,811,928	88,189,618
Leather	148	18,644,270	15,548,822
Machines and machinery	335	29,960,988	27,975,359
Metals and metal goods	341	26,259,252	22,878,245
Paper and paper goods	98	26,029,658	22,746,104
Woollen goods	125	34,074,848	28,061,654
Worsted goods	20	17,328,062	15,528,227
Other industries	2,458	283,935,758	266,247,450
Total	4,397	639,137,402	587,343,550

Showing a decrease in the value of the goods produced in 1893, as compared with 1892, of 51,793,852 dol. (10,358,770*l.*), of which the largest actual falling-off is in boots and shoes, although the largest percentage is in woollen goods.

The next table serves to show the average number of persons employed in these leading industries, respectively, in the two years:—

Industries.	Number of Establishments Considered.	Average number of Persons Employed during the Year.		Increase or Decrease in 1893.	
		1892.	1893.	Number.	Percentage.
Boots and shoes	712	48,859	45,339	− 3,470	− 7·10
Carpetings	11	4,703	4,335	− 368	− 7·82
Cotton goods	149	73,748	73,540	− 208	− 0·28
Leather	148	5,918	5,602	− 316	− 5·34
Machines and machinery	335	17,979	17,495	− 484	− 2·69
Metal and metallic goods	341	14,356	13,313	− 1,043	− 7·27
Paper and paper goods	98	10,085	9,658	− 427	− 4·23
Woollen goods	125	17,100	15,857	− 1,243	− 7·27
Worsted goods	20	8,996	9,025	+ 29	+ 0·32
Other industries	2,458	104,459	98,955	− 5,504	− 5·27
Total	4,397	306,203	293,169	13,034	− 4·26

All the leading industries, therefore, except worsted goods, show a decrease in the average number of hands employed in 1893 as compared with the previous year, the largest numerical decrease being in woollen goods; the largest percentage in carpetings. As to the proportion of the sexes employed, there appears to have been practically no variation at all, the percentage being in 1892: males, 66·30; females, 33·70; and in 1893: males, 66·31; females, 33·69.

As to wages and earnings, the following are the figures given in 1892:—Total paid in wages, 27,594,500*l.*, against (in 1893) 25,457,291*l.*, or a decrease of 2,137,221*l.*, the falling-off in wages being more or less in the various trades, but shared in some degree by all, the greatest actual falling-off being in the boot and shoe trade, but the highest percentage in worsted goods, woollen goods, and carpetings.

Unemployed. The number of the unemployed in 1893 was very considerable during a great part of the year. The number given for the month of August, in the manufacturing industries alone, is 55,914, rising to 71,414 in September, and continuing at about 48,000 during October, November, and December; and this statement leaves out of consideration the unemployed in all other occupations, such as trade, transportation, &c., which in Massachusetts suffer when manufacturing is depressed, and are prosperous when manufacturing prospers.

During the winter of 1893-94 much money was subscribed for the purpose of relieving this distress. Many cities and towns endeavoured to meet the entirely exceptional conditions which existed by efforts to provide temporary employment through committees of citizens. In Boston alone such a committee disbursed subscriptions amounting to 27,314*l*, and in the aggregate about 10,000 men and women were thereby provided with relief work. The committee in Boston, as elsewhere, found itself facing unusual conditions requiring immediate action, without previous experience in similar junctures. Considering the circumstances under which it was obliged to act, the various theories regarding such work which prevail here, the large number of persons who applied for relief, and the comparatively small amount of money available, its work was well done, and the money was not spent recklessly or without painstaking investigation into the individual cases.

On this and many other subjects connected with industry and labour, especially with reference to the year 1893, the report of the Labour Bureau gives copious information, and is well worthy of being referred to by anyone who needs details on the subject.

Textile industries. With regard to the textile industries, some interesting statistics are published in a recently printed textile directory. From this it appears that in 1894, in the cotton manufactories of the United States, there was a total of 17,126,418 spindles; of this amount 7,160,480 spindles, or 41 per cent. of the whole, were in the State of Massachusetts. In the other New England States there were 5,440,625 spindles, thus giving to New England about 70 per cent. of the spindles of the entire country. Between the years 1892 and 1894 a gain of 840,319 spindles was made, of which 312,736, or 37 per cent. of the entire increase, was in the State of Massachusetts.

In the wool manufacturing business the ascendency of the New England States is not so conspicuous. There were in 1894 8,111 sets of wool cards, of which 1,811, or about 22 per cent., were in the State of Massachusetts—a larger amount than in any other State; the next in importance being in New York with 1,478 sets, followed by Pennsylvania with 1,478 sets. From 1892 to 1894 there was a decrease of 21 sets of wool cards, of which 16 belonged to Massachusetts. Out of 1,148 worsted combs in operation in the United States, 319, or 28 per cent., were in Massachusetts in 1894. In this instance there was a gain of 51 combs during the 2 years, and of these 17, or 37 per cent., were in this State.

The rivalry of the southern States in textile manufactures is of late actively on the increase, and is keenly watched in New England. It appears, moreover, probable that some of the cotton mills in Massachusetts may seek to profit by the cheaper labour and fuel of the south, and set up branch establishments in those districts, the idea apparently being not to remove the headquarters of the firms from the north, but to make the lower grades of yarns in the south, and continue the further manufacture as well as the sale of the goods from the existing establishments in New England.

Fish and Fisheries.

The annual report of the Boston Fish Bureau states that, taking into consideration the dulness which prevailed in the various lines of industry during the year 1894, the fish business, both salt and fresh, has been fair. The mackerel business, however, has been curtailed, owing to a falling-off in the catch in every country from which supplies are received at Boston.

1894 was a year of great activity in the curing of iced cod, haddock, hake, &c., the over-production of the market fleet. The amount of this fish cured has been nearly equal to the entire catch of cured fish by the New England fleet on Grand and Western Banks.

Salt mackerel.—The year 1894 has been what might be called an up-hill year in the values of new salt mackerel. In the month of February old numbers 1, 2, and 3 sold at 11 dol. to 11 dol. 50 c. per barrel; Irish mackerel sold at 11 dol. to 11 dol. 50 c. per barrel in February, declining in March to from 8 dol. to 9 dol. per barrel. In May all the old mackerel were sold out except the Irish.

The first new mackerel from Cape Shore arrived June 1, and sold at 5 dol. 50 c. per barrel. From this price they advanced in 6 weeks to 11 dol. per barrel.

On June 8 the first new Irish and also the first new Nova Scotia arrived. The Nova Scotia mackerel were packed and rimmed, and sold at 5 dol. 75 c. per barrel. The Irish mackerel were about the same kind of fish as those from Nova Scotia, but the shippers refused to sell at the same prices.

A few barrels of Prince Edward's Island mackerel arrived July 26, and sold at 13 dol. per barrel.

In October a few Norway mackerel arrived, and sold from 15 dol. to 28 dol. per barrel, according to size and quality. They ran smaller than usual, counting from 130 to 135 fish extra, and 170 to 190 No. 1's.

The Irish mackerel received ran small, counting about 300 fish to the barrel, and was the most desirable size for the trade. Irish mackerel advanced in November to 16 dol. per barrel.

Nova Scotia mackerel sold in November at 13 dol. per barrel for plain, and 14 dol. per barrel for rimmed 3's.

The following table shows the imports of salt mackerel into Boston for 1894 as compared with 1893 from England and British North American provinces:—

	1894.	1893.
	Barrels.	Barrels.
England	10,820	8,029
Nova Scotia, Cape Breton, and Prince Edward's Isles	35,099	26,210
Total	45,919	34,339

Under the head of England are included Irish, Norway, French and Scotch mackerel, all being shipped viâ England. The fish, however, are nearly all from Ireland.

Salt codfish. The feature of the codfish market this year has been the scarcity of large dry bank codfish. This scarcity was partly supplied by French fish from Saint Pierre, Miquelon, the receipts from which place have been larger than ever before, amounting to 3,560,000 lbs.

Frozen mackerel. Frozen mackerel are coming into favour more and more each year. They are placed in the refrigerator in the fall of the year, and supply the late trade mackerel.

Smelts. The receipts of smelts during the season which ended March 15 were 40,813 boxes, of which 39,613 boxes were from Canada.

Sardines. The season for packing sardines closed December 15 with a shortage in the pack as compared with 1893 of 55,000 cases. Sardines sold in Boston in January at 3·90 dol. per case, and from this price they sold down as low as 2·90 dol. per case.

Canned lobsters. Trade in canned lobsters was very good from August up to the last of October. The European market was high, and as a result all the good lots of canned lobsters went abroad.

They sold as high as 1·85 dol. per dozen, and even higher for extra fine grades, some of the poorer grades sold as low as 1·25 dol.

Tariff charges. The new tariff on fish came into force in August, and thereby the duty on salt mackerel was reduced from 2 dol. to 1·50 dol. per barrel. Canned lobsters are admitted free of duty. The duty on anchovies and sardines remains the same.

Losses. The heavy gales of January and February destroyed an immense amount of property, and the year's record of vessels lost is the heaviest of this generation. Six vessels went down with every man on board. The New England losses in the year amount to 38 vessels, for a value of 2,139,000 dol., and with the loss of no less than 146 lives, the port of Gloucester alone losing 33 vessels and 137 men.

Banded mackerel. As a matter of curiosity I think it worth mentioning that in the last few years mackerel have been caught in four separate instances with an indiarubber band round them, one was caught about 2 years ago off Boon Island, another at Annisguam, one was caught this season in a trap at Provincetown, another on the coast of Maine, the bands are of the same, or nearly of the same size and appearance, and are put on just behind the pectoral fins, and cover the ventral fins, and in two cases had been on long enough to lose all elasticity, and had worn a groove in the flesh the size of the band.

It would be interesting to know by whom these bands were put on, and when, and for what purpose.

Imports and Exports.

Exports. The total value of the exports of merchandise (exclusive of coin and bullion) from the port of Boston, as given by the Chamber of Commerce, is as follows for the last five years:—

Year.	Value.		
	Home Produce.	Foreign Re-exports.	Total.
	£	£	£
1890	14,428,318	69,503	14,497,821
1891	16,203,685	84,239	16,287,924
1892	17,648,306	112,734	17,761,040
1893	16,425,784	282,204	16,707,988
1894	16,824,905	86,422	16,911,327

Imports. The value of the imports of foreign merchandise (exclusive of coin and bullion) is given as follows:—

Year.	Value.		
	Free Goods.	Dutiable Goods.	Total.
	£	£	£
1890	3,605,000	9,608,000	13,213,000
1891	6,631,737	7,529,187	14,160,924
1892	7,572,598	7,546,115	15,118,713
1893	7,402,113	6,421,629	13,823,742
1894	6,297,758	4,381,768	10,679,526

Coin. The movement of coin and bullion from this port is always comparatively unimportant. There was an export of 431,415*l.* from Boston in 1894, but the export and import of coin and bullion, as a business, is conducted almost entirely through the ports of New York and San Francisco, and by Paso-del-Norte, on the Mexican frontier.

The decrease in the declared value of the imports, as will be observed, is very considerable, but I do not consider it as in any way indicating a permanent decrease in the importance of the commerce of this port, but attribute it entirely to the financial crisis of 1893, and the unsatisfactory condition of affairs resulting from tardy legislation both with regard to the tariff and finance.

Exports.

The declared value of the exports has increased in 1894 as above stated, and but for the abnormally low prices prevailing in all trades the contrast between the two years would have been more apparent as will be seen by the following table, which gives the quantities exported, during the last 4 years, of foodstuffs, live cattle, and hay, which are the principal articles of export from Boston:—

Foodstuffs.

Articles.		1891.	1892.	1893.	1894.
Flour	Barrels	329,801	346,088	374,416	411,964
,,	Sacks	1,992,675	2,574,957	2,298,195	2,569,143
Wheat	Bushels	2,860,564	7,403,935	5,088,230	6,011,826
Corn	,,	4,032,380	2,714,832	5,362,169	3,894,159
Oats	,,	298,383	1,338,308	487,217	57,126
Butter	Lbs.	979,712	1,007,247	636,569	1,072,190
Cheese	,,	11,753,293	11,298,726	10,887,528	12,924,472
Apples	Barrels	229,576	291,684	54,456	459,154
Lard	Lbs.	63,709,418	73,272,807	66,038,239	76,677,826
Bacon	Boxes	340,638	394,809	313,770	376,679
Fresh beef	Quarters	365,370	387,761	337,109	425,922
Cattle	Head	107,671	133,072	95,388	133,711
Hay	Bales	...	...	558,000	690,420

It will be seen that with the exception of Indian corn and oats the export of all foodstuffs has been unusually large.

The hay exported is not the produce of this country, but Canadian hay which comes through in bond owing to the difficulty of finding freight in the Saint Lawrence waters.

Imports.

It is difficult to obtain any detailed information as to imports at this port as the Chamber of Commerce, which keeps accurate record of the export trade, does not interest itself on the subject of imports, which are both less in aggregate amount and consist of an infinitely greater variety of goods.

As I have said above, the diminished import is easily accounted for, and is not to be looked upon as symptomatic of any permanent decrease in the foreign commerce of this port.

Shipping.

The number and tonnage of vessels of all nationalities which entered the port of Boston from foreign ports, according to the custom-house returns, was as follows during the last 5 years:—

Year.	Number of Vessels.	Tons.
1890	2,335	1,464,797
1891	2,342	1,553,600
1892	2,396	1,705,492
1893	2,218	1,650,531
1894	2,079	1,739,640

UNITED STATES.

British shipping.

The total arrivals of British shipping for the same period as shown by the registers kept at the Consulate have been as follows:—

Year.	Number of Vessels.	Tons.
1890	1,827	1,169,732
1891	1,848	1,237,702
1892	1,933	1,377,327
1893	1,785	1,347,406
1894	1,620	1,479,739

These figures show the constantly increasing tendency to the use of larger tonnage and confirm the preponderance of the trade under the British flag.

Freights.

Freights to Liverpool on the principal articles of export have varied during the year as follows:—

Merchandise.		Lowest.	Highest.
		£ s. d.	£ s. d.
Grain	Per bushel..	0 0 0½	0 0 2⅜
Provisions	Per ton	0 3 6	1 1 3
Flour	Per ton	0 3 6	0 12 6
Cotton	Per lb.	0 0 0$\frac{1}{16}$	0 0 0$\frac{11}{64}$
Cattle	Per head	1 10 0	2 10 0
Apples	Per barrel..	0 1 6	0 2 6
Finished leather	Per ton	0 9 0	1 2 6
Sole leather	Per ton	0 9 0	1 15 0
Hay	Per ton	0 7 6	1 17 6

The variations having been extreme during the year, and outward freights from the United Kingdom as usual very poor.

Immigration.

The returns of immigrants are made up in each year to September 30. The number of alien immigrants who arrived at Boston from transatlantic ports in each of the last 5 official years was as follows:—

Year.	Number.
1890	30,802
1891	31,556
1892	31,234
1893	28,143
1894	17,128

The nationality of the 17,128 who arrived in 1894 was as follows:—

Country.	Number.
Ireland	6,553
England and Wales	4,391
Scotland	1,046
Germany	905
Norway	610
Russia and Finland	1,202
Sweden	1,758
All other countries	663
Total	17,128

This does not take into account the immigration from Canada. The number of these is given as 18,598 in the year ending September, 1894, as against 28,314 in the previous year. It is, however, almost impossible to keep an accurate account of the immigrants from British North American provinces, of whom a number naturally come and go across the frontier without anyone knowing whether they are immigrants or merely travellers. The very great decrease in immigration may be looked upon as a universal blessing both to this country and to the immigrants themselves; for though prosperity will undoubtedly return to this country sooner or later, the present certainly is not a favourable moment for new comers.

Public Works.

A great variety of public works have been in progress during 1894; principal among which may be mentioned the extension of the park system and the building of the Public Library. The extension of the park system has made a continuous and beautiful drive from the city itself to Franklin Park and the Arnold Arboretum, which latter stands in the same relation to Boston as Kew Gardens to London, and has the advantage of being far more easily accessible. The Public Library which has cost about 8,000,000 dol., whatever may be said of it externally is fine internally, and most ingeniously fitted with all manner of mechanical appliances for assisting the staff to supply the reading public with the books asked for. It is built to hold 2,500,000 books, and has just been opened to the public at the time of writing this report. Besides these works, many other public works have been in progress during the year, and the amount of building on private account has also been very great, and so much is projected in the immediate future that work is assured for some time to come in the building trade and all branches of industry allied thereto. Iron enters so largely into the composition of the huge constructions now put up for business purposes that quite a lift has been given to the ironworks which supply this district.

UNITED STATES.

All these are signs of the prosperity which undoubtedly exists in spite of the business troubles of 1893, but still I would urgently advise that no one should come here in search of immediate employment.

Discourage immigration. There are still crowds of unemployed hands in all branches of unskilled labour, and it stands to reason that as long as that is the case, work is given by preference to the natives of the country; and I therefore repeat emphatically the warning I gave last year, that it is not a favourable time for intending immigrants to come to this country.

Strikes. There have been several severe and prolonged strikes in the year; the most important of which were those of the cotton industries in Fall River and New Bedford.

The strike at Fall River began August 23 and finished October 30, 1894, and may more properly be called a "shut down" on the part of the manufacturers; though the position was brought about by the action of the weavers who voted a "vacation" of 4 weeks as against the proposal of the Manufacturers' Association of an all round reduction of wages. About 23,000 hands were thrown out of work altogether, and 40,000,000 dol. worth of plant kept idle. There were partial resumptions of work at some of the mills from time to time; but about 8,000 hands were still out on October 29, the day before the final collapse of the strike. It is calculated that the operatives lost 1,500,000 dol. in wages, while the loss of the mills was not great owing to the depressed condition of the market at that time. This strike was marked by ill-feeling between spinners and weavers caused by divergent interests, though all joined in the strike, and all suffered by it.

The New Bedford strike began August 20 and finished October 11, 1894. The strike was against a proposed reduction of 10 per cent., and terminated in a resumption of work at a reduction of 5 per cent. This strike also entailed great privation and suffering on the families of the working hands.

There was also a strike of "garment workers" in Boston in September, but it only lasted a few days. About 4,000 men were out, and they struck against the system of piece-work which had been brought into force about 9 months previously. The men gained the day, and the masters, after trying to get their contract work done in New York, had to come to terms; and, it is said, the hands are gaining from 20 to 40 per cent. more than before the strike.

The strike of the shoeworkers at Haverhill, Mass., began on January 1, 1895, and is not yet terminated at the time of writing this report. This strike aims chiefly at doing away with the so-called contract system, under which certain firms require their hands to deposit a sum which is forfeited if they break their contract of service extending generally over a year. The hands seem strongly to resent this check upon their liberty, although the interest allowed on these deposits is far beyond what they would get from any bank, amounting, I am told, generally to 7 per cent.

No rioting or serious disturbance of the public peace occurred at any of these places, which is immensely to the credit of the working population, since, especially at Fall River and New Bedford, the strikers were reduced to very great straits before they returned to work.

From what I have seen of strikes in this district they appear to me lightly undertaken as compared to strikes at home, and with little organisation and resources; but far better information than I am competent to give will now be available, since in the course of last year Mr. John Burns, from England, and Sir Henry Wrixon, from Australia, both visited this district as well as other parts of the country, and strikes as well as other features of the working class problem were investigated by them.

Conclusion.

Congress has closed without passing any measure tending to clear the financial position, and the prospects of improvement in business remain, therefore, clouded, as they have been for some months past. The price paid for the new loan has caused a good deal of grumbling among business men.

No one who knows this country can doubt that the United States will pull through the present financial difficulties, and that prosperity will return sooner or later; but, on the other hand, there are few signs of any immediate resumption of commercial or industrial activity. The dulness which has characterised business in this district is the prevailing feature in most of the large centres of trade, and the position is even worse in the agricultural sections of the country, where want of reserve funds is added to the unprecedented shrinkage in the value of produce.

Here, as I have before said, it is not capital but confidence that is wanting, for the accumulation of idle capital is probably greater than at any previous period. All this money is awaiting better times, earning hardly any interest for the capitalists who, however, prefer 1 or 2 per cent. with safety, to venturing into their accustomed field of operations until the country is assured that no risky experiments are to be tried with the currency.

In this district not only all the leading men but the whole population are "sound money" men, and a feeling is growing up that the present issue is so important that normal party lines should not be allowed to divide men who think alike on this so-called "silver question," which is after all one of the two most important factors in the present trouble, the other being that the balance of receipts and expenditures has of late been the wrong way. This latter point, however, is of comparatively slight moment, as, independently of the fact that the income tax, now coming into force, will do much to restore the equilibrium, far the heaviest charge on the national income is the pension list, which,

(1913)

in the nature of things, will henceforward be annually reduced, and will eventually die out altogether.

One is apt to forget what an enormous proportion of the annual revenue is given up to this pension list, which was deliberately put on its present basis as a means of getting rid of surplus income which the country had no use for only a few years ago. The pension list for 1894 amounted to 28,235,457$l.$, out of a total ordinary expenditure of 73,549,373$l.$ The interest on the public debt being only 5,568,281$l.$

The one thing that business men in this district fear is rash legislation. They are tolerably satisfied with the currency as it stands, and consider that the essential point is that no theorists should be allowed to try experiments. Their chief desire is to see the confidence that they themselves feel on the subject of sound money extend throughout the country and to the nations with whom they have commercial dealings. Opinions may differ as to the exact course to be taken, but their belief is strong that when the country is aroused to a true appreciation of the position it will put down the projects of the silver men with a firm hand, and make it clear once for all that national as well as personal debts are to be paid in gold.

The theory of bimetalism is not in any way involved in this position, for even the bimetalists admit that this country cannot stand alone in the matter, and that even should the commercial world become converted to bimetalism, many years must elapse before such conversion can become effective. They hold, therefore, that what is immediately urgent is to restore confidence in the determination of this country to meet its engagements in the only coin which, under present circumstances, honestly cancels debts which have been incurred.

Annex A.—RETURN of Shipping in the Foreign Trade at Boston as given by the Custom-House for the Year 1894.

ENTERED.

Nationality.	Sailing.		Steam.		Total.	
	Number of Vessels.	Tons.	Number of Vessels.	Tons.	Number of Vessels.	Tons.
British and other foreign	925	144,569	881	1,413,713	1,806	1,558,282
American	203	102,568	70	78,790	273	181,358
Total	1,128	247,137	951	1,492,503	2,079	1,739,640
,, for the year preceding	1,333	290,801	885	1,359,760	2,218	1,650,561

BOSTON.

CLEARED.

Nationality.	Sailing.		Steam.		Total.	
	Number of Vessels.	Tons.	Number of Vessels.	Tons.	Number of Vessels.	Tons.
British and other foreign	934	132,554	734	1,178,408	1,668	1,310,962
American	212	82,535	68	73,587	280	156,122
Total	1,146	215,089	802	1,251,995	1,948	1,467,084
,, for the year preceding	1,383	256,549	702	1,067,154	2,085	1,323,703

Annex B.—RETURN of the Principal Articles of Export from and Imports into the Port of Boston during the Fiscal Years ending June 30, 1894-93.

EXPORTS.

Articles.	Value.	
	1894.	1893.
	£	£
Meat and dairy products	6,706,400	4,083,162
Horned cattle	2,125,940	1,892,389
Corn, flour, and other breadstuffs	2,879,300	2,977,140
Raw cotton	2,088,400	2,044,640
Leather and manufactures of	1,137,200	898,432
Cotton manufactures	154,200	156,358
Tobacco in leaf and manufactured	96,200	79,676
Iron, steel, and manufactures of	187,200	218,125
All other home produce	1,193,429	4,569,109
Total export of home produce and manufactures	16,568,269	16,919,031
Export of foreign merchandise	226,223	173,053
Total all merchandise	16,794,492	17,092,084
Coin and bullion	430,000	450,050
Grand total	17,224,492	17,542,134

UNITED STATES.

Imports.

Articles.	Value. 1894.	Value. 1893.
	£	£
Sugar and molasses	2,668,900	2,629,733
Chemicals, drugs, &c.	720,000	1,132,640
Iron, steel, and manufactures of, and machinery	526,300	1,048,818
Hides, skins, &c.	483,200	1,076,322
Wool and hair of animals	522,800	2,182,500
Woollen goods	180,200	373,730
Flax, hemp, and manufactures of	416,200	627,841
Cotton goods	184,480	277,745
Fish	251,600	188,185
All other goods	4,108,182	6,334,017
Total	10,061,862	15,871,531
Import of coin and bullion	90,150	5,841
Grand total	10,152,012	15,877,372

NOTE.—These tables do not coincide with the value of imports and exports in the body of the report, which are for the calendar years, whereas these tables are taken from the annual returns issued by the United States Government, which are made up to June 30 in each year.

LONDON:
Printed for Her Majesty's Stationery Office,
BY HARRISON AND SONS,
Printers in Ordinary to Her Majesty.

(75 5 | 95—H & S 1913)

FOREIGN OFFICE.
1895.
ANNUAL SERIES.

No. 1541.

DIPLOMATIC AND CONSULAR REPORTS ON TRADE AND FINANCE.

UNITED STATES.

REPORT FOR THE YEAR 1894

ON THE

AGRICULTURAL CONDITION OF THE BOSTON CONSULAR DISTRICT.

REFERENCE TO PREVIOUS REPORT, Annual Series No. 1379.

Presented to both Houses of Parliament by Command of Her Majesty,
MAY, 1895.

LONDON:
PRINTED FOR HER MAJESTY'S STATIONERY OFFICE,
BY HARRISON AND SONS, ST. MARTIN'S LANE,
PRINTERS IN ORDINARY TO HER MAJESTY.

And to be purchased, either directly or through any Bookseller, from
EYRE & SPOTTISWOODE, EAST HARDING STREET, FLEET STREET, E.C., and
32, ABINGDON STREET, WESTMINSTER, S.W.; or
JOHN MENZIES & Co., 12, HANOVER STREET, EDINBURGH, and
90, WEST NILE STREET, GLASGOW; or
HODGES, FIGGIS, & Co., Limited, 104, GRAFTON STREET, DUBLIN.

1895.

[C. 7581—81.] *Price One Penny.*

New Series of Reports.

Reports of the Annual Series have been issued from Her Majesty's Diplomatic and Consular Officers at the following places, and may be obtained from the sources indicated on the title-page:—

No.		Price.	No.		Price.
1421.	Yokohama	1½d.	1481.	Batoum	1½d.
1422.	Maracaibo	1d.	1482.	Teneriffe	½d.
1423.	Tunis	1½d.	1483.	Lisbon	2½d.
1424.	Baghdad and Bussorah	1d.	1484.	Buda-Pesth	½d.
1425.	Rio Grande do Sul	7d.	1485.	Rome	5½d.
1426.	Erzeroum	1d.	1486.	Para	1d.
1427.	Christiania	5½d.	1487.	Odessa	1d.
1428.	Charleston	5½d.	1488.	Hakodate	1d.
1429.	Meshed	1d.	1489.	Beira	1½d.
1430.	Copenhagen	½d.	1490.	Berne	1½d.
1431.	Galveston	2½d.	1491.	Copenhagen	1d.
1432.	Hamburg	2½d.	1492.	Stettin	2½d.
1433.	Brindisi	2½d.	1493.	Rio Grande do Sul	1½d.
1434.	Gothenburg	2d.	1494.	Serajevo	1d.
1435.	Kiungchow	1d.	1495.	Buenos Ayres	9d.
1436.	St. Petersburg	½d.	1496.	Florence	2d.
1437.	Malaga	1d.	1497.	Lisbon	1½d.
1438.	Chicago	2½d.	1498.	Paris	2d.
1439.	Odessa	2d.	1499.	Bolivia	1½d.
1440.	Tabreez	½d.	1500.	Patras	1½d.
1441.	Tahiti	½d.	1501.	Bordeaux	3d.
1442.	Shanghai	2d.	1502.	Madrid	2d.
1443.	Nagasaki	1d.	1503.	Amsterdam	1d.
1444.	Madrid	2½d.	1504.	Suakin	1d.
1445.	Malaga	2½d.	1505.	Angora	1d.
1446.	Rotterdam	1d.	1506.	Havre	2½d.
1447.	Port Said	1d.	1507.	Algiers	11d.
1448.	Sofia	2½d.	1508.	La Rochelle	3d.
1449.	Warsaw	1½d.	1509.	Vera Cruz	2d.
1450.	Africa (Congo)	2d.	1510.	Puerto Cortes	1d.
1451.	Jeddah	1½d.	1511.	Taganrog	1d.
1452.	San Francisco	5½d.	1512.	Baltimore	1½d.
1453.	Oporto	2d.	1513.	Mexico	1½d.
1454.	Barcelona	2d.	1514.	Zaila	1d.
1455.	New Caledonia	½d.	1515.	Zomba	3½d.
1456.	Smyrna	1d.	1516.	Valparaiso	2½d.
1457.	Macao	1d.	1517.	Charleston	2½d.
1458.	Samoa	1d.	1518.	Serajevo	1d.
1459.	Hiogo and Osaka	3d.	1519.	Saigon	1d.
1460.	Lisbon	2d.	1520.	Bangkok	2d.
1461.	Pekin	2d.	1521.	Tripoli	1d.
1462.	Corunna	2d.	1522.	Batavia	1½d.
1463.	Mozambique	15d.	1523.	Dakar	½d.
1464.	Munich	1½d.	1524.	Havana	2d.
1465.	St. Petersburg	3d.	1525.	Riga	2d.
1466.	Naples	1d.	1526.	Trebizond	1½d.
1467.	Montevideo	2½d.	1527.	Piræus	2½d.
1468.	Aden	1d.	1528.	Guayaquil	1½d.
1469.	Tokio	1½d.	1529.	Marseilles	1½d.
1470.	Dantzig	5d.	1530.	Wuhu	1½d.
1471.	Guayaquil	1d.	1531.	Rio de Janeiro	2½d.
1472.	Canton	1½d.	1532.	Trieste	2d.
1473.	Dar-al-Baida	3d.	1533.	Brest	1½d.
1474.	Teheran	2d.	1534.	Stockholm	2d.
1475.	Bushire	2d.	1535.	Warsaw	1d.
1476.	Tangier	2d.	1536.	Boston	1½d.
1477.	Rome	2d.	1537.	Mozambique	2½d.
1478.	Hamburg	4d.	1538.	Callao	1d.
1479.	The Hague	1½d.	1539.	Aleppo	1½d.
1480.	Belgrade	2d.	1540.	Jaffa	½d.

No. 1541.

Reference to previous Report, Annual Series No. 1379.

UNITED STATES.

BOSTON.

Consul Yeats-Brown to the Earl of Kimberley.

My Lord, Boston, April 16, 1895.

I HAVE the honour to enclose my Annual Agricultural Report for the year 1894.

I have, &c.
(Signed) M. YEATS-BROWN.

Report on the Agriculture of Boston for the Year 1894.

ABSTRACT of Contents.

	PAGE
Weather	1
Crops—	
Apples	2
Hay	3
Corn	4
Oats	4
Potatoes	4
Onions	4
Tobacco	5
Horses	5
Sheep	5
Dairying	6
Farm hands	6
Tuberculosis	7
Conclusion	9

The season opened from 10 days to a fortnight earlier than usual, but the dry weather of April and the first half of May, and the cold storms and frosts following brought conditions to about the average by the first days of June. *Weather.*

The weather during the winter of 1893–94 in New England had been generally favourable for grass and winter grains, and for fruits, except peaches. December, as a month, was cold, though the last half was warmer than usual, and Christmas Day, 1893, was the warmest for very many years. January, 1894, was mild in all southern sections but very cold in the extreme north, the temperature having fallen on the 10th and 11th to 40 degrees below zero in northern Maine, but there was a fairly good covering of snow, so that little injury was done. In southern New England the the ground was more bare but the cold was less intense.

February was the winter month of the year, and gave much stormy cold weather. At Provincetown, on Cape Cod, the temperature fell to a degree below zero on the 24th, and on that day the warmest temperature anywhere in New England were from 5 to 12 degrees above zero, while in western Mass., New Hampshire, and Vermont the highest temperatures registered were from 4 to 11 degrees below zero.

March was extremely warm and dry; only with a sharp wave of cold on the 27th, which did great damage in the central and southern part of the United States, but did no serious harm in New England.

April was generally favourable for farm work and the growth of crops, and by the end of the month rain was badly wanted in many parts of this district.

Light showers fell in Maine in the first days of May, and by the 6th rain had become quite general and pushed the crops wonderfully well. High winds, however, did some damage later in the month and dried the ground, except in parts of New Hampshire, where more rain fell than was needed. In June operations were retarded by wet in the above sections and in Maine, but in Massachusetts the season was fine, and by the end of the month the weather was warm throughout New England.

July opened with wet, but became very hot towards the close of the month, and in some sections the drought became serious. A great thunder shower passed over Boston on the 20th, giving $\frac{1}{2}$ inch of rain in 5 minutes and 2·10 inches in 4 hours.

In August and September the drought was pretty severely felt in some sections, but by the end of September enough rain had fallen in most parts of New England. Before the end of September there were sharp frosts in some parts of Maine, New Hampshire, and Vermont, but, on the whole, the crops were secured in good condition. October was fine, but in the very first days of November winter set in, and though temperatures have not been excessive, the winter has been one of almost unbroken frost, which, however, will not have damaged the country owing to the ground having been well covered by snow.

Crops.

Apples. The crop of early apples was abundant, and those put on the market very early sold for fair prices, but as the bulk of the crop came forward prices fell so much as hardly to pay for the cost of gathering and packing.

The crop of late autumn and winter apples was very large in

New England, especially in Massachusetts; whereas the crop of the whole country is reported as only 44 per cent. of a full crop. I may here observe that the export of apples from Boston in 1894 reached a total of 459,154 barrels, as against 53,456 barrels in 1893 and 291,684 barrels in 1892.

I find the following remarks in the report of the fruit crop by the "Pomologist" of the Board of Agriculture of Massachusetts, which I think worth quoting, as they seem applicable to England as well as any other country:—

"The good quality of our crop is much in favour of a large consumption, as the more good fruit the people have the more they want. Should the business interests of the country revive, we may hope for better prices by holding our winter fruit in cold storage or in good fruit cellars. If, however, one has not good facilities for storing, it will be best to dispose of the crop as harvested, if fair prices are offered. A good honest article, whether made in the factory or the farm, will command a fair price and lead to the largest possible consumption, and in the competition of fruit growing every one must make an effort to produce the best possible crop at the lowest possible cost; and those who succeed in reducing expenses, and at the same time improve the product, are sure of some profit, as in all other businesses. More brain work and better business management is what most of us farmers need. The waste products of many business concerns can be made a source of income, and in fruit growing the lower grades of fruit, which would injure the sales of our main crop, should be utilised in every possible way.

"Thousands upon thousands of bushels of early fall apples go to waste every year, which, if taken in time and dried, would yield a large income. One bushel of ordinary apples, that would not sell for more than 10 to 25 c. per bushel, with the added labour of paring and evaporating, would be worth 75 c. at the present prices of the evaporated product; and cheap home-made evaporators can be made by anyone skilled in the use of tools.

"If the product is not large enough to warrant the use of an evaporator, all waste fruit should be fed to stock. It has been shown by repeated analyses that apples contain a food value, for cows and horses, of from 10 to 20 c. per bushel: and the cost of gathering as they fall can be but little.

"In addition to the value of the fallen apples for food, the fact that many insects are destroyed when they are thus utilised is of great importance, reducing the number of insects for the next season, and, consequently, the cost of production of succeeding crops."

The hay crop has been abundant in New England generally, the exceptions being only in those parts of Massachusetts and New Hampshire which were specially affected by the drought, and the hay was of extra good quality and gathered in exceptionally good condition; a marked contrast to the results in the Western and Central States, where the crop is both short and of poor quality. Hay is one of the most important crops in the district but is not

Hay.

exported, the large quantities of hay which go to England from Boston being Canadian hay shipped here in transit owing to the difficulty of obtaining freightage in the St. Lawrence River.

The reduction in the duty on hay, from 4 to 2 dol. per ton, is not expected to have much effect. The only import that takes place is from the provinces of Ontario and Quebec, and it is thought that, unless in some very exceptional year, it will always suit those provinces better to send their surplus produce to Europe rather than to attempt to place it here, even now that the duty has been reduced one half.

Corn. The main corn pack in 1894 only amounted to 9,000,000 cases, against 14,000,000 cases in 1893 and 16,000,000 cases in 1892. The acreage of corn planted last season was small, but the yield was excellent. Sweet corn, which is a special feature of Maine agriculture, was favoured with good weather, and, while the acreage was less than for several years, the financial results were satisfactory.

Oats. There were 60 packing factories operating as against 84 in 1893.

For a number of years the price of oats has been, relatively, much higher than that of wheat. Throughout the past summer oats sold higher pound for pound than wheat. Crops during the last 3 years have been fair, but at no time was there any such burdensome surplus as in wheat. The price has been so high that exports have fallen off considerably. During the first 8 months of 1894 they amounted to barely 38,000 bushels compared with 3,320,000 bushels in the corresponding period in 1893. The home consumption is apparently on the increase, and farmers are being advised to consider whether it is not wise to increase their acreage of oats, or drop wheat altogether, in view of the deplorably low price which it now fetches.

Potatoes. From the "Homestead's" potato report it appears that the total crop of potatoes in the United States was 164,000,000 bushels against 183,000,000 bushels in the previous year.

The crop in Maine was 7,700,000 bushels in 1894 against 6,230,000 bushels in 1893.

In New Hampshire it was 2,750,000 bushels against 2,600,000 bushels.

In Vermont 3,350,000 bushels against 3,371,000 bushels, and in Massachusetts 3,500,000 bushels against 3,490,000 bushels.

The quality in all these four States was good to fair, and the prices also good as compared to most States in the Union.

Sweet potatoes were a larger crop than was expected in the early part of the year. They have, of late, considerably risen in favour, and when Irish or ordinary potatoes are dear the consumption steadily increases.

Onions. The yield of onions in New England was the smallest known for years, being at least 30 per cent. less than in either of the two preceding years. In consequence there has been a considerable importation of Spanish onions, and consignments have been received from points as distant as Egypt.

The tobacco crop in Massachusetts was very successful. From some farms the report is that it is the best crop in the last ten years, and on all hands it is admitted to be a good crop, of fine quality and colour.

In Vermont the crop was also good, and in New Hampshire, though in some parts the growth was poor, the crop is reported on the whole as average in quantity and of good quality.

Horses have considerably fallen in value. The New York and Philadelphia markets being glutted, a great number of Western horses have been sent into Boston for sale, and the common grades have had to be sold at low prices. Good horses, however, are scarce and in demand.

With the exception of Vermont, and perhaps some few localities in one or two other States, New England is a consumer of horses rather than a producer. Vermont is full of colts sired by trotting blood, which are almost worthless for ordinary purposes. Good 2 and 3 year olds are selling for from 35 dol. to 45 dol. Good roadsters, carriage horses, and single drivers are not plentiful, and will sell readily.

The horses brought into Maine from the West do not readily become acclimatised, and more useful heavy animals, and less small trotting-bred colts are needed there. The introduction of electric street cars has not injured the business of breeding as much as in other parts of the country.

Many New Hampshire farmers sold their horses at a sacrifice in the autumn rather than face the expense of keeping them through the winter.

In Massachusetts many farmers have stopped breeding horses entirely, finding the business no longer profitable, as, owing to the competition of the West, it no longer pays to breed low-class horses; and though good horses sell readily, and pay if brought into the market at maturity, this business is of a far more speculative nature than dealing with lower class stock.

It is, however, a fact that of late years the imported sires have been of a higher class than formerly.

A competent judge says with regard to sheep farming:—"The price of wool is lower than ever before, 40 c. per pound being the average price ten years ago, whereas now it is 15 c. Notwithstanding this great decline, however, with the exception of the dairy, sheep have paid better than any other product of the farm. I am confident that, while the dairy should be the base of farming in this district, the second string to the bow should be sheep."

The mutton, too, raised in New England is excellent for the table, and in the season lambs are in great demand.

It is a very encouraging fact, also, for sheep farmers in this country that there is an increasing export of live sheep to Europe from hence, the total number of live sheep exported from the United States during the first seven months of 1894 having been 117,400, as against 20,400 in the corresponding period in 1893.

(1962)

Dairying.

The cheese market of 1894 was fairly steady, though with no special activity. Owing to the slackness of trade in other branches of industry, hundreds of thousands of working men have been partially if not wholly out of employment, and these are the largest consumers of dairy produce. Yet, from the reports in the "Homestead," it appears that there has been a steady though not rapid movement in the cheese market, and that fair prices have been paid during the season. An interesting comment that I note in the agricultural papers is that the prices paid for the best and for the poorest produce bear the same relation to each other in hard times as in prosperous ones. There does not seem to be any greater demand for inferior butter and cheese in times when money is scarce. Poor and inferior butter and cheese have never, because sold low, proved to be the poor man's want.

The butter trade is also described as "slow" during the year, and prices ruled a few cents lower than in 1893. There was, however, a considerable increase in the quantity made, especially in the first five months of the year. The export of butter from Boston amounted to 1,072,190 lbs., as against 639,569 lbs. in 1893.

I notice an article in the "New England Farmer," by a well-known authority, who says that, in his opinion, when dairies are properly conducted there is no industry that gives so large a return as the dairy farm. If dairies do not pay the fault is in the man who manages them. Dairying should, however, be made the chief industry of the farm to be successful, and the man should have natural ability and aptitude for his business. He must watch each cow, anticipate her wants, and give her all comforts. Feed alone cannot control the quality of milk: the cow has an individuality of her own. The quality, though not the quantity of the milk is born in her, and no feeding will change it.

From Maine the reports say that dairy cows are increasing in every part of the State where creameries have been established; while in the districts remote from creameries there is a notable falling-off in cows, especially in Arostook country, where farmers are depending more each year on chemicals for fertility.

Farm hands.

The general depression in trade and industry during the last two years has not had the effect of increasing the number of applicants for farm work. Tramps, it is true, are very numerous, and some of them will take odd jobs at a dollar to a dollar and a half a day, but are not to be depended upon from one day to the other. In some places where the relief agents in townships offer these men bread and water gratis, or a good "square meal" in return for a light task of wood sawing, 90 per cent. take the bread and water rather than do even the lightest work. The farmers' complaint throughout the country is the utter scarcity of real farm hands—men who can drive a team, plough and hoe, and who take an interest in their work. This class of farm hand has almost entirely disappeared, having been absorbed by the greater attraction of town life.

A very determined effort is being made in Massachusetts to stamp out tuberculosis among cattle. The subject is one of very great interest, not only to this State and country, but to the world in general, as Massachusetts has always been in the van of progress in matters of this sort, and may be relied upon to carry out the experiment it has undertaken without stint in regard to expense, and with a judicious mingling of energy on the part of those charged with carrying out the regulations, and regard for the interests of those affected by the provisions of the law. The Act under which the experiment is being made only came into force on the 20th June last, and the first report of the Board of Cattle Commissioners acting under it has just come out, and I have forwarded copies of it to the Foreign Office, where no doubt it will be made available to the public or to those interested in the subject.*

I think, however, that a short notice of it will not be out of place in the present report.

Previous to the passing of the above-mentioned Act, although cattle inspectors existed throughout the State, their duties were somewhat vague, and more of a permissive than an obligatory nature. From the passing of the Act, however, the law compels all cities and townships to provide inspectors, and these are put under the control of the Board of Cattle Commissioners, whose number is increased from three to five members, and who have considerable powers and very arduous if interesting duties. The inspectors are 394 in number, and are under the control of the Board, though appointed and paid by the cities or townships. Their duties are to inspect all animals, and quarantine those that appear to them affected with any contagious disease. They have also other duties connected with the inspection of all butchered cattle, but these need not here be specified. They have no authority to remove a quarantine once imposed, that power being reserved to the Cattle Commission. Prior to October 4 the existence of contagious disease in animals was determined by the Commissioners by physical examination, but since that date the Commission has adopted the uniform rule of subjecting all animals suspected of being affected with tuberculosis to the tuberculin test. This test is not applied by the inspectors, but by the Commissioners themselves, or their own direct agents and assistants, of whom, up to December 15, 33 had been appointed.

The test is applied as follows:—A sufficient number of preliminary examinations are made with the clinical thermometer to ascertain accurately the normal temperature; these examinations being made at, as nearly as possible, the same time of day in all cases. The normal temperature having been ascertained and recorded, the injection of tuberculin is made in the evening. Eleven hours after the injection the trial temperatures are taken and recorded. These are taken every two hours until the test is finished. The time required to properly complete this part of the test varies considerably; it may be roughly stated at from 6 to 30 hours, with an average of about 12 hours. The Commis-

Tuberculosis.

* Forwarded to Board of Agriculture, May 3.—ED.

sioners, in their report, state that the reaction caused by the tuberculin is so plainly marked in most cases, under the usual conditions, that the animal may be condemned or released with absolute certainty, provided that the necessary care has been observed in making up the tables of temperatures. The animals which pass the examination are branded as sound. Those condemned are, in all cases, dissected and further examined, as, under the Act of 1894, the owner receives full value as compensation should dissection not confirm the diagnosis arrived at by the tuberculin test; whereas if correct, he receives "one half the value thereof at the time of slaughter for food or milk purposes, and without taking into consideration the existence of disease."

Provided always, however, that the animal has been within the State continuously six months prior to its being killed.

This question of compensation gave rise to very great discussion when the Act passed, and has been still more hotly debated since. Previous to June 20, 1894, no compensation whatever was paid for an animal slaughtered in consequence of having been found to be affected with any contagious disease; now, on the contrary, the views of the Legislature have so far altered that, not content with the compensation allowed by the Act of 1894, a fresh Bill has been brought in, and at the time of writing this report has passed through almost all its stages, which contemplates paying no longer the half, but the entire value of animals slaughtered under this Act. Under the old law of 1893, the Commission slaughtered, as tuberculous, 529 animals, for which no compensation at all was paid. Since the passing of the Act to the end of 1894, the new Board of Commissioners have sanctioned payment for 810 cattle, condemned and destroyed as tuberculous, in a total sum of 15,280 dol. 15 c. (about 3,050l.), or on an average at the rate of 3l. 15s. 2d. each; that being half the estimated value of the animals at the time they were killed, "for beef or milk purposes."

It may here be interesting to note the practice in regard to compensation in the other States comprised in this consular district.

Maine relies upon the owners reporting cases of tuberculosis, and does not make any systematic inspection of the animals in the State, but under an Act passed in 1893 the Cattle Commissioners are authorised to destroy animals found affected by infectious or contagious diseases, and to pay the owners "one half of their value, as determined upon the basis of health before infection." With a proviso, however, that no compensation is allowed if the beast has been exposed to infection outside the State, or has been brought into the State within three years previous to its showing evidence of such disease.

The law in New Hampshire is the same except that instead of 3 years the limit of time is 3 months.

In Vermont a new law was passed as lately as November 27, 1894, which fixes the compensation to be paid, as in the other two States, at one half the value "on a health basis," and the limit of previous residence at 6 months, but has this curious limitation with regard to using a tuberculin test, namely, that it may not be used without the owner's consent in the case of any animal owned and resident in the State, but it may freely be used on cattle imported from outside the State if quarantined on suspicion of disease.

Returning to the powers and duties of the Cattle Commissioners in Massachusetts: the system established by the Board meeting, held on October 4 last, embraced the following points:—

1. The test, with tuberculin, of all suspected cases reported by the local inspectors.

2. The regulation of the importation of all neat stock into the State.

3. The quarantine of all imported animals until tested with tuberculin, and either condemned or certified as sound.

4. The establishment of regular quarantine stations.

5. The forbidding of all importations of neat stock, unless delivered at these stations.

6. The branding of all animals that pass the tuberculin test.

7. A systematic examination, by the use of tuberculin, of all animals within the State—beginning with the three southernmost counties.

These resolutions only came into full effect on November 25 last, and the amount of work got through with since is little short of marvellous.

I may mention that the inoculation is entrusted exclusively to veterinary surgeons; the inspectors, as above stated, having nothing, as such, to do with the tuberculin test.

The tuberculin used is exclusively prepared at the United States Laboratory at Washington.

These few notes may serve to show the scope of the work being done by the Massachusetts Board of Cattle Commissioners, but I strongly recommend those interested in the matter to refer to the report itself, of which, as I have said, I have sent some copies to the Foreign Office, and could obtain more if required through the courtesy of the Chairman of the Commission.

Conclusion.

In conclusion, after another year's residence in New England, I see no reason to change the opinion I expressed in my last year's report: that farming can be, and is made to pay in New England, and I therefore repeat the query why should it not be at least an equally good business at home, where both climate and soil are better, and where we have an enormous market at the farmer's very door? If it were a question of cattle and sheep in which they beat us, one might say that these, more or less, look after themselves, and that the rent of the land is so low as to explain their success, but as a matter of fact New England cannot compete with the Western States of America, and does not

Conclusion.

attempt to send us cattle; and what it does send us, in large and increasing quantities, are just the things we surely ought to be able to produce at home, such as fruit, dairy produce, bacon, and lard. No less than 459,000 barrels of apples were exported from Boston alone in 1894, almost all to England, and 1,000,000 lbs. of butter, 13,000,000 lbs. of cheese, and 76,000,000 lbs. of lard !

I again earnestly call attention to the facts, and point out that it is not here a question of vast farms like those in the west, but of farms resembling our own, both as to size and nature of husbandry, and that as neither soil or climate are better than on our side of the water, it looks as if the fault must lie with us if we cannot supply our own markets and keep command of them. No doubt land is generally held far cheaper here than at home, but that does not account for the facts, as there are farmers in England who own their land, and others who are certainly not paying high rents, and yet do not manage to make both ends meet, whereas here it is an undoubted fact, in spite of all grumblers, that farming is a paying profession, and that where a man has ability as well as grit in his composition, he may make far more than a mere competence.

I may cite a case in point of a man who died this last year. He was born on a New England farm, the son of a very small farmer; as a young man he set up for himself on a farm of about 160 acres, which he bought at 2,000*l.* (not therefore any very small sum), having to borrow on mortgage all but a few hundred dollars. In 11 years he had paid off his mortgage, and at the time of his death he left a fortune of about 10,000*l.*, and he had brought up, meanwhile, a large family in comfort, and had educated at least one of his sons at the Agricultural College at Amherst.

This is only one instance of many that I have heard of, and read of in the papers, during the last two years, and the money, I am assured, is not made by speculation, or lucky ventures, but by steady hard work, and above all, by study and intelligence.

Having spent all my life abroad, I have little knowledge of the state of education among our farmers, and would not wish to say anything slighting of them, but I am much struck with the technical knowledge of these New England men, and suspect that their greater quickness of appreciating the necessity of educating themselves, as well as the greater facilities afforded them for cheap education, has better fitted them for the battle of life.

In these days of competition no one can afford to stand still—not any more a farmer than a manufacturer, or a merchant. In my younger days I often remember having advised makers of special goods to study the market more and adapt their make to the requirements of their customers, and at that time they could still afford to answer that they only made their goods one way, and found they had demand enough for all they could turn out. That sort of answer would hardly be given now, and I think the argument applies to farming as well as to manufacturing. Cheap freights have made the world all one country, and no one can go sleepily along the old lines and yet succeed.

I will conclude with a quotation from an article in one of the agricultural papers written by a practical working farmer, just one of these educated, self-made men, who make farming a success. His idea is that not only a man must educate himself as much as he can to be a farmer, but that he must specialize and take up one particular branch of farming if he means to have real success.

"No man has the ability to conduct mixed husbandry with success; no ordinary farmer, with the help usually kept in our farms, has either the physical or the mental ability to succeed by the method now in practice. To succeed he must follow out some one line of work to its greatest perfection. Market gardening as a speciality has become a profitable industry; the ordinary farmer cannot compete, and should not raise more than enough for home consumption. The raising of milk can only be successful as one adopts his crops to this line, and selects the animals best adapted to the production of milk so as to obtain the best results at the least cost. Hundreds of thousands of dollars have been spent in New Hampshire in purchasing fruit trees, and it is safe to say that nine-tenths of the money has been a dead loss. Why? Because the farmer had not any time to give to their proper cultivation, and was not specially educated for fruit culture. To make farming a success more depends upon the man than the industry. He must be a live, wide awake, earnest man. He must be abreast with the times. All his labours, all the products of his hands are the reflections of the man within. I do not mean that we can carry on our farms by brain power alone.

"He that by the plough would thrive
Himself must either hold or drive.

"If he commits both to other hands he will need to be more successful in obtaining 'help' than most of us are. We must not flatter ourselves that the road to success is any other than earnest, diligent, persistent labour."

How far this correspondent's view of specialist farming need be insisted upon I know not, but the general principles are excellent, and I thought the article worth making extracts from as being from the hand of a typical New England farmer.

LONDON:
Printed for Her Majesty's Stationery Office,
By HARRISON AND SONS,
Printers in Ordinary to Her Majesty.
(75 5 | 95—H & S 1962)

FOREIGN OFFICE.
1895.
ANNUAL SERIES.

No. 1542.

DIPLOMATIC AND CONSULAR REPORTS ON TRADE AND FINANCE.

UNITED STATES.

REPORT FOR THE YEAR 1894
ON THE
AGRICULTURE OF NEW ORLEANS AND DISTRICT.

REFERENCE TO PREVIOUS REPORT, Annual Series No. 1390.

Presented to both Houses of Parliament by Command of Her Majesty,
MAY, 1895.

LONDON:
PRINTED FOR HER MAJESTY'S STATIONERY OFFICE,
BY HARRISON AND SONS, ST. MARTIN'S LANE,
PRINTERS IN ORDINARY TO HER MAJESTY.

And to be purchased, either directly or through any Bookseller, from
EYRE & SPOTTISWOODE, EAST HARDING STREET, FLEET STREET, E.C., and
32, ABINGDON STREET, WESTMINSTER, S.W.; or
JOHN MENZIES & Co., 12, HANOVER STREET, EDINBURGH, and
90, WEST NILE STREET, GLASGOW: or
HODGES, FIGGIS, & Co., Limited, 104, GRAFTON STREET, DUBLIN.

1895.
[C. 7581—82.]   *Price Three Halfpence.*

New Series of Reports.

Reports of the Annual Series have been issued from Her Majesty's Diplomatic and Consular Officers at the following places, and may be obtained from the sources indicated on the title-page:—

No.		Price.	No.		Price.
1424.	Baghdad and Bussorah	1d.	1483.	Lisbon	2½d.
1425.	Rio Grande do Sul	7d.	1484.	Buda-Pesth	½d.
1426.	Erzeroum	1d.	1485.	Rome	5½d.
1427.	Christiania	5½d.	1486.	Para	1d.
1428.	Charleston	5½d.	1487.	Odessa	1d.
1429.	Meshed	1d.	1488.	Hakodate	1d.
1430.	Copenhagen	½d.	1489.	Beira	1½d.
1431.	Galveston	2½d.	1490.	Berne	1½d.
1432.	Hamburg	2½d.	1491.	Copenhagen	1d.
1433.	Brindisi	2½d.	1492.	Stettin	2½d.
1434.	Gothenburg	2d.	1493.	Rio Grande do Sul	1½d.
1435.	Kiungchow	1d.	1494.	Serajevo	1d.
1436.	St. Petersburg	½d.	1495.	Buenos Ayres	9d.
1437.	Malaga	1d.	1496.	Florence	2d.
1438.	Chicago	2½d.	1497.	Lisbon	1½d.
1439.	Odessa	2d.	1498.	Paris	2d.
1440.	Tabreez	½d.	1499.	Bolivia	1½d.
1441.	Tahiti	½d.	1500.	Patras	1½d.
1442.	Shanghai	2d.	1501.	Bordeaux	3d.
1443.	Nagasaki	1d.	1502.	Madrid	2d.
1444.	Madrid	2½d.	1503.	Amsterdam	1d.
1445.	Malaga	2½d.	1504.	Suakin	1d.
1446.	Rotterdam	1d.	1505.	Angora	1d.
1447.	Port Said	1d.	1506.	Havre	2½d.
1448.	Sofia	2½d.	1507.	Algiers	11d.
1449.	Warsaw	1½d.	1508.	La Rochelle	3d.
1450.	Africa (Congo)	2d.	1509.	Vera Cruz	2d.
1451.	Jeddah	1½d.	1510.	Puerto Cortes	1d.
1452.	San Francisco	5½d.	1511.	Taganrog	1d.
1453.	Oporto	2d.	1512.	Baltimore	1½d.
1454.	Barcelona	2d.	1513.	Mexico	1½d.
1455.	New Caledonia	½d.	1514.	Zaila	1d.
1456.	Smyrna	1d.	1515.	Zomba	3½d.
1457.	Macao	1d.	1516.	Valparaiso	2½d.
1458.	Samoa	1d.	1517.	Charleston	2½d.
1459.	Hiogo and Osaka	3d.	1518.	Serajevo	1d.
1460.	Lisbon	2d.	1519.	Saigon	1d.
1461.	Pekin	2d.	1520.	Bangkok	2d.
1462.	Corunna	2d.	1521.	Tripoli	1d.
1463.	Mozambique	15d.	1522.	Batavia	1½d.
1464.	Munich	1½d.	1523.	Dakar	½d.
1465.	St. Petersburg	3d.	1524.	Havana	2d.
1466.	Naples	1d.	1525.	Riga	2d.
1467.	Montevideo	2½d.	1526.	Trebizond	1½d.
1468.	Aden	1d.	1527.	Piræus	2½d.
1469.	Tokio	1½d.	1528.	Guayaquil	1½d.
1470.	Dantzig	5d.	1529.	Marseilles	1½d.
1471.	Guayaquil	1d.	1530.	Wuhu	1½d.
1472.	Canton	1½d.	1531.	Rio de Janeiro	2½d.
1473.	Dar-al-Baida	3d.	1532.	Trieste	2d.
1474.	Teheran	2d.	1533.	Brest	1½d.
1475.	Bushire	2d.	1534.	Stockholm	2d.
1476.	Tangier	2d.	1535.	Warsaw	1d.
1477.	Rome	2d.	1536.	Boston	1½d.
1478.	Hamburg	4d.	1537.	Mozambique	2½d.
1479.	The Hague	1½d.	1538.	Callao	1d.
1480.	Belgrade	2d.	1539.	Aleppo	1½d.
1481.	Batoum	1½d.	1540.	Jaffa	½d.
1482.	Teneriffe	½d.	1541.	Boston	1d.

No. 1542.

Reference to previous Report, Annual Series No. 1390.

UNITED STATES.

NEW ORLEANS.

Consul St. John to the Earl of Kimberley.

My Lord,   New Orleans, April 20, 1895.

I HAVE the honour to transmit Agricultural Reports from New Orleans, Pensacola, and Mobile for the year 1894.

           I have, &c.
       (Signed)   C. L. ST. JOHN.

Report on Agriculture of the Consular District of New Orleans for the Year 1894.

ABSTRACT of Contents.

	PAGE
New Orleans—	
Crops	2
Agriculture of Louisiana	
Condition of crops	3
Maize	4
Rice	4
Sugar-cane	4
Potatoes	4
Fertilisers	4
Sweet potatoes	4
Cotton cultivation	5
Contribution of cotton by the South	5
Exhaustion of cotton lands	5
Method of cotton cultivation	5
Labour system	6
Credit system	7
Excessive cotton production	7
Deficiency of food crops	7
Tobacco	8
Ramie	8
Machines	10

(1969)

UNITED STATES.

ABSTRACT of Contents—continued.

	PAGE
Pensacola—	
Agriculture	11
Orange industry	11
Other fruit	11
Agricultural statistics	12
Information and cautionary advice for British agriculturists and perspective emigrants to Florida	16
Mobile—	
Agriculture	17
Live stock	17
Cotton	17
Corn	17
Truck farming	18
Oranges	18
Roots	18
Land, prices, &c.	18
Inducements, &c	18

Crops.

The season has been an exceptionally variable one, the weather changing from hot to cold, with many phenomenal freezes and alternations of droughts and rainy spells. At one time it looked as though there would be a magnificent crop. Then came meteorological disturbances that seem to threaten ruin, and again a good spell followed by a bad one. The cold spell in March of 1894, for instance, caused the greatest damage. It ruined the fruit crop, which, as mentioned in the trade report for New Orleans, may be regarded as a complete failure. The outlook, therefore, during the earlier portion of the season, was bad. Unfavourable weather ruined much cotton; but this, as it subsequently proved, was a blessing, for the farmers in the centre of the cotton belt, being unable to procure enough seed, planted maize instead, which turned out one of the finest crops of its kind ever grown. As maize and its products, pork, &c., are ranging high, it will prove far more beneficial than if half a million more bales of cotton had been raised.

From June, however, there was a general improvement in the weather. In most of the States the crops recovered. Usually the best promises and the highest anticipations of yield are made in June and July, after which the outlook becomes a little worse. This season, however, it has been different. With rare exceptions the condition averages improved from the middle of June to September, and the success of the year has been maize: one of the largest crops ever grown in the South. Wheat and oats have produced unfavourably, and are the only crops, except fruit, of which there can be much complaint. Oats seem to have suffered more than other grain. Sugar, confined largely to Louisiana, was in splendid condition, and the promise was for a larger yield than the magnificent crop of last year, the best on record. Farmers, in general, did not do very well, owing to the losses they sustained by the March frosts. It looked as if there would be a complete failure; but the farmers went energetically to work, saved a great deal of their crop, planted more, and succeeded in getting out of their trouble better than was expected.

The report of labour appears to have been good, and there was enough work to give employment to all.

Cotton farmers throughout the South have held meetings to consider the situation, and take such steps as may be necessary to reduce the acreage, and thus improve the price of cotton.

The several meetings agreed that a reduction in cotton acreage was necessary, recommending 20 per cent., and some farmers signed pledges to reduce their acreage 40 or 50 per cent. The question now is, will these pledges be kept? And, if so, will others, who have not pledged themselves, take advantage and increase their acreage?

Large crops of cotton, sugar, and rice were made, but prices fell below the unprecedentedly low figures of last year, and many of the farmers—as well as planters—have lost money. This country is in close agricultural competition with all the world. The cotton of Egypt and India competes with that of the southern States, and so do rice and sugar of the world compete with that made here.

Louisiana has nearly 45,000 square miles of territory, containing some 25,000,000 acres. Of this amount, 13,000,000 is of alluvial origin, and the rest good upland. The alluvial region is now only cultivated along the banks of rivers, and rivers protected mostly by public and private banks, or levees, as they are called here. The uplands are almost all susceptible of cultivation. *Agricultural interests of Louisiana.*

The geological position of Louisiana forbids the existence of mineral products, save salt and sulphur, and the general low topography furnishes no water power for wheels of manufactories. Louisiana must, therefore, remain for a long time a purely agricultural State. Of her 25,000,000 acres not quite 3,500,000 are in cultivation. Upon these acres were grown last year products valued at some 15,000,000*l*. distributed as follows:—

Products.	Value.
	£
Sugar	7,000,000
Cotton	4,200,000
Rice	600,000
Fruits and vegetables	400,000
Maize, oats, and hay	2,000,000
Oranges	200,000
Live stock and other products	600,000
Total	15,000,000

The season of 1894 was quite different from that of the previous year. The months of February and March were excessively rainy. Very little ploughing could be done, and scarcely any planting. The land remained cold and wet almost up to May 1; consequently all crops were from 2 to 3 weeks later than in 1893. Good stands of cotton, maize, and cane were general, and the weather was favourable for cultivation. *Condition of crops.*

UNITED STATES.

Cotton. Returns from cotton correspondents indicated that about 85 per cent. of the crop was planted up to April 20 and 25. It was estimated that the acreage planted was 90 per cent. of that planted the previous year at the same date. The stand and condition of the crop were generally good, though there were complaints of cotton dying from low temperature nights and mornings, and from high winds prevailing at that time of year.

Maize. The acreage planted was placed at 1 per cent. greater than the former season. The stand was good, and the plant vigorous and growing; but about 20 days late. An increased acreage of 10 per cent. of last year was anticipated.

Rice. The acreage was estimated at 90 per cent. of the previous year; and the stand and condition 14 per cent. below. The reason assigned was unfavourable planting season. The rains were frequent and too heavy; when they stopped the lands became too dry and hard for germination. The stand, in some instances, was so imperfect that planters were contemplating ploughing the fields and trying other crops.

Sugar-cane. The acreage was estimated at 3 per cent. above that of the former year for the whole State; but 7 to 10 per cent. only comprising the sugar-growing district.

Potatoes. This crop was estimated at 90 per cent., with a condition of 85 per cent.

Fertilisers. Returns indicated decrease in the use of fertilisers under all field crops except sugar-cane. The depressed condition of finance, the low price of cotton, and the great desire to make farms self-supporting, were the reasons attributed for this reduction.

Sweet potatoes. A larger crop of sweet potatoes was made this year than for many years past. Farmers now appear to have awakened to the necessity of the occasion, and are preparing for the production of cotton and other monied crops only after all necessaries have been made. A large crop of cotton, with everything else to buy— especially when the market is glutted—is no longer profitable: while a farmer who has all domestic supplies, and a few bales of cotton to defray wearing apparel, other necessaries which he cannot produce, and a few luxuries, is quite independent. This ought to be a lesson to farmers of every country. The price of cotton this year, 1895, is lower than it has ever been known, and, consequently, farmers who have depended entirely on cotton will be left not only unprovided with the necessaries for their families, but also in debt. Extravagance, low prices, and little knowledge of agricultural economy have been known to ruin farmers in other countries; this has lately been pointed out to those resident in the cotton districts of the southern States.

Owing to the over-production of cotton in the southern States having so lowered the price of that article, meetings are being held to finally determine whether or not farmers are prepared to agree to a 25 per cent. reduction in acreage.

Whether the organised movement be a success or not, there is not the least reason to doubt that the acreage will be considerably reduced. The poor financial results of the last crop have deprived farmers of the means of planting as freely as hitherto. The merchants also will not advance to anything like the extent they formerly did, and that fact alone will force the farmers to devote a good portion of their land to food crops.

There is, therefore, every reason to believe that the area devoted to cotton will be much smaller in 1895, whether the farmers adopt the uniform reduction agreement or not. Absolute necessity will compel a reduction, even if common prudence and good business foresight do not teach such a course.

Professor Maxwell, of New Orleans, and Mr. Otken, of McComb City, Mississippi, are authors on essays relative to the "Agricultural Crisis in the South," "Effects of a limited Circulation," "Bad Labour System," and "Too much Credit," &c. I am indebted to the writings of these gentlemen for much of the information contained in this report bearing on the above subjects. *Cultivation of cotton.*

As cotton is pre-eminently the agricultural product of the South, it deserves our first consideration in a report like the present. The world's supply of cotton is chiefly furnished by the United States, India, China, Africa—particularly Egypt—and Brazil, of which the United States contribute about 56 per cent., though according to official statistics it is estimated that no less than 70 per cent. is supplied by this country. *Contribution of the South to the world's production of cotton.*

It would be misleading to compare the yields per acre for every year, as they fluctuate considerably. This year, for instance, the estimated crops were 190 lbs. per acre, while last year, at the same time, the estimate was 148·8 lbs. per acre. A term of 20 years is therefore covered, that is to say, from 1870 to 1889 inclusive, which is divided into two periods, as follows:— *Exhaustion of the cotton lands.*

Periods.	Average Number of Acres Grown.	Average Yield Per Acre.	Average Price per Acre to the Farmer.
		Lbs.	Cents.
1870–79	10,427,842	191	12·8
1880–89	17,731,172	167·7	8·8

The above figures show that the average production of the lands in cotton during the 10 years of the later period was 167·7 lbs. per acre, which is 23·3 lbs., or 12·2 per cent., less than the average yield of the preceding period; showing that the volume of cotton produced by 10,427,842 acres during 1870–1879 period required 11,822,900 during the second period. No less than 1,395,058 acres more had to be cultivated to furnish the same weight of cotton; and to-day upon 20,000,000 acres this excess of acreage required 2,500,000 acres, showing a considerable falling off in prices and reduction in produce per acre.

The figures shown in the above table show that the producing *Method of cultivation of the cotton crop.*

(1969)

power of the cotton lands has declined under the modes of farming followed, especially during the decade ended 1890. Also with the falling prices and declining yield a vast expansion of acreage took place, producing a decreasing crop per acre. This tendency to increase the acreage, Professor Maxwell says in his essay, reproduced in the "Times Democrat," is radically wrong, for it is the direct opposite of the tendency in other branches of intensive agriculture, and in all other industries where we see capital and labour to be concentrated. The advice given is to let poor land drop out of cotton and be planted with green crops for grazing, or be allowed to lie fallow until nature slowly revives it. It may cost less to pick an acre of 100 lbs. than of 300 lbs., but who will compare the expense of picking those 300 lbs. from 1 acre with the cost of gathering the same weight from 3 acres.

Diversification of crops. Further advice, applicable to farmers of all countries, is given to diversify crops, so as to provide, first and foremost, food that the planter, his cattle, and his community require. The farmer must live within himself, and in addition furnish all of the farm products for which there is a ready local market. If, then, the cotton crop is small, or money scarce from low prices, the planter and his family are at all events temporarily provided for, and he has time to look about him. In countries where one staple product has been the rule for a number of years, and where, consequently, no other industry has been practised—such as in sugar-growing colonies—a fall in the price has been followed by almost starvation.

Labour system. Mr. Otken in his essay states that an inefficient labour system is a large element in the agricultural situation in the South, though there is no injustice made to the negroes in such a statement. For many years to come, he says, the interest of the negroes and the interest of the white people must fall or rise together.

That the negro is the best farm labourer for the South there can be no doubt, whatever may be said to the contrary. No white man could replace him in such a climate. Let us see what the negro now does in comparison to the amount of labour performed by him before his emancipation.

In 1860 he produced on an average 5 bales of cotton, 150 bushels of corn (maize), 75 bushels of sweet potatoes, besides field peas, fodder and pumpkins. He helped to raise pigs and so made the meat supply. From the time the crop was gathered he was employed to prepare the farm for the next year, splitting rails, repairing fences, and doing other needed work.

In 1894 the average negro produced 3 bales of cotton and 50 bushels of corn. He raises nothing else. From December to March he does nothing, nor will he under any condition accept work during that period; which goes far to prove that he is a contented man.

To express the efficiency of this labour of 1860 in terms of money, according to present prices, it may be stated thus:—value of 5 bales of cotton, 125 dol. (say 25*l.*); corn, 75 dol. (15*l.*);

peas, fodder, &c., 25 dol. (5l.); pigs raised, 50 dol. (10l.); work in January and February, 20 dol. (4l.); total, 295 dol. (59l.). The value of the produce of the labourer in 1894: cotton, 75 dol. (15l.); corn, 25 dol. (5l.); total 100 dol. (20l.). Though it is shown that the negro is, or ought to be, a contented man in 1895, he can never under such management be a prosperous one, for whether there are two or ten in a family, the work of one man must support the whole family.

A second factor in the situation, says Mr. Otken, is the mode of obtaining annual supplies. A ruinous credit business was begun in 1865, such as formerly was carried on among the peasantry in Roumania by the Jews and with very much the same result, that is to say utter ruin to all concerned, white and negro farmers. *Credit system.*

There can be no doubt that an excessive cotton production has caused the present ruinously low prices; for the law of supply and demand must ever rule the market. Were the planters out of debt they could control the crop without difficulty; but, that not being the case, their hands are tied, though, as stated in another part of this report, an attempt is being made to reduce the acreage. *Excessive cotton production.*

Though the world's demand for cotton grown in this country were 10,000,000 bales, such a supply would be too large when compared to the deficiency of food products. The very credit system of the South has reduced the consumption of cotton goods.

Deficiency of food crops and pigs in the Southern States has caused the present unsatisfactory condition of the farmer. If 150,000,000 bushels of corn (maize) are produced on the soil, a large quantity can be raised by an increase of acreage. If 10,000,000 hogs are raised in seven States, 20,000,000 can be raised. The time, care, and labour now given to several million bales of cotton in excess of the demand, would make the southern States independent as regards food—a more necessary article than unsaleable cotton, except at a loss. *Deficiency of food crops.*

These are the principal causes that underlie the present agricultural crisis. The compensating power of negro labour, as already shown, is reduced fully 150 per cent. The high prices and extravagant purchases, due to the credit system, have squandered a sum equal to the value of all the farm lands in the southern States during a little over a quarter of a century. Vast tracts of land, as a necessary consequence, have passed out of the possession of the original owners. Over-production of cotton has reduced the purchasing power of the staple to half its value. Scanty food crops compel the planter to expend half his cotton to provide those necessaries of life that could be raised at home. Such, or nearly such, is the situation.

UNITED STATES.

Report of Experiments with Tobacco in Louisiana supplied by Professor Stubbs.

Cultivation of tobacco. The seed bed. The utmost care should be exercised in the selection and preparation of the seed bed. Selections should be made, if possible, in new land with a south-western exposure to the morning sun, and timber protection on north and west against cold. (This applies to Louisiana.) When cleared of all vegetation and rubbish pile upon it logs, poles, and brush, which burn continuously for several hours until the entire surface is thoroughly baked to a depth of ½ inch. All coals and trash are raked off, the ashes remaining as fertilisers, and the soil is then thoroughly mulched and pulverised to a depth of 2 or 3 inches. Seed beds can be sown from January to February according to climate. Mix thoroughly one heaping tea-spoonful of seed with many times that quantity of ashes, to prevent too thick sowing, and sow uniformly over 10 feet square of bed, which will supply sufficient to plant 1 acre of land. Tobacco seed are so small they need no "raking in," simply firming the soil by passing a light roller over, or by placing a plank and stamping on it is sufficient. The beds should be trenched around to carry off surplus water.

Preparation of soil. The land should be deeply ploughed in January or February. In March or April it should be cross-ploughed, harrowed, and rows marked off 3½ feet apart. In this furrow the fertiliser should be scattered.

Transplanting. Topping. Pull only strong, vigorous plants showing three or four leaves.

Topping the tobacco should begin when many of the plants show the seed-button. No specific rule can be laid down as to how many leaves should remain on the stalk. Individual judgment must decide. If a plant is strong, vigorous, and large from 14 to 25 leaves may be left, otherwise 9 to 14. Suckering, or the putting out of new growth in the axils of the leaves, will begin soon after topping. These suckers must be removed weekly, and not be permitted to grow over 2 or three inches long.

Curing. There are many ways of curing tobacco. It may be sun-cured, air-cured, charcoal-cured, and flue-cured. The Louisiana experimental station recommends flue-curing.

NEW ORLEANS.

Fertiliser Experiments.

Number of Experiment.	Kind of Fertiliser Used per Acre.	Lbs. Green Tobacco per Acre.	Lbs. Cured Tobacco per Acre.	Percentage of Loss in Curing.
1	160 lbs. nitrate soda	7,428	860	88
2	160 ,, nitrate soda 160 ,, acid phosphate	5,260	960	81
3	160 ,, nitrate soda 160 ,, acid phosphate 60 ,, muriate potash	4,380	1,040	78
4	160 ,, nitrate soda 160 ,, acid phosphate 240 ,, kainite	4,960	960	80
5	160 ,, nitrate soda 160 ,, acid phosphate 140 ,, cotton seed hull ashes	4,580	960	79
6	No manure	2,640	440	83
7	160 lbs. nitrate soda 160 ,, acid phosphate 60 ,, sulphate potash	4,240	920	78
8	120 ,, sulphate ammonia 160 ,, acid phosphate 60 ,, sulphate potash	4,580	1,000	78
9	190 ,, dried blood 160 ,, acid phosphate 60 ,, sulphate potash	4,840	820	83
10	340 ,, cotton seed meal 160 ,, acid phosphate 60 ,, sulphate potash	4,900	980	80

Experiment No. 3 leads, followed closely by No. 8, No. 2, Nos. 4, 5, and 10. The average of all is 890 lbs. Experiment No. 1 is most economical, and while it shows more green tobacco, the percentage of loss is greater, showing excessive sap. Even with tobacco potash does not show much gain. The excess of all potashes over Nos. 1 and 2 is only 38 lbs., while 2 over 1 is 100 lbs. Nitrogen is first needed, phosphate second in lesser quantity, and potash but little if any.

Ramie.

Great interest has lately been manifested at New Orleans in the growth of this plant. Its fibre is beautiful, long, silky, and strong. It rivals silk in lustre and strength, and can be used with it as an adulterant or entirely substitute it in manufactures.

There is a great demand for the properly prepared fibre. It is specially adapted to this soil and climate. Two to four crops may be cut during the season, yielding 8 to 15 tons of green unstripped stalks per acre. It is a perennial plant, and one planting will give continuous crops for many years if properly cultivated.

It has not been generally grown in this country by reason of the absence of efficient machines. However, there is at last a machine now offered the public that may answer the purpose.

The following taken from a Report on the Fibre Production in America answers the question.

Ramie.

What is ramie?

Ramie is a plant belonging to the nettle family (Urticaceæ), which from time immemorial has been cultivated in China, and known to botanists by the name "Boehmeria nivea," frequently called the stingless nettle. It is known as "China grass" and "rhea."

When fully grown the plant attains a height of 4 to 8 feet. It is of rapid growth, and produces from two to four, or even five crops a year without replanting. In Europe the fibre has been woven into a great variety of fabrics, as lace, lace curtains, handkerchiefs, cloth or white goods resembling fine linen, &c., and has been used in connection with cotton, wool, and silk. It likewise produces superior paper. In short, the uses to which it may be put are almost endless, and when the economical extraction of fibre by machinery is successfully accomplished it will become one of the most valuable commercial products of the vegetable kingdom.

The plant is propagated by seeds, by cuttings, or by layers, and by division of the roots. This plant is very sensitive to cold, and the least frost destroys it to the ground.

For further particulars respecting the cultivation of this plant application may be made to this consulate.

Machines. There are machines specially adapted to working ramie green, and others for working it dry, while a few claim to work either green or dry.

In January, 1894, the experiment station of Louisiana, of which Dr. W. C. Stubbs is director, received a proposition from the Textile Syndicate of London to furnish a machine for public trial if the station would grow and furnish the necessary ramie. At the same time preparations were made by the station for a public trial of all machines that would enter.

Two machines were entered for trial, one by the Textile Syndicate of London for green decortication, and the other by Samuel B. Allison, of New Orleans, for dry decortication, Mr. Allison being the inventor and patentee.

These trials, the details of which would here take up too much space, were continued at intervals. They were far from perfect, but at every new trial some difficulty or defect was overcome. The large Allison machine, of which one has now been purchased in Jamaica, delivers its fibre in good condition and better cleaned, but its size and the power that it takes to run it preclude the possibility of its being used in the field upon small experiments.

The smaller Textile Syndicate machine is considerably reduced in size, without destroying its efficiency, but, though great progress has been made, neither of these machines are yet ready for successful operation on a small scale by farmers and planters, according to the opinion of the committee, although the outlook is certainly promising, and there can be no doubt that before long a perfect machine will be turned out.

For further particulars respecting the working of Allison's patent apply to this consulate.

PENSACOLA.

Mr. Vice-Consul Howe reports as follows on agricultural matters:—

The lands at and around Pensacola are planted in vegetables yearly, as the seasons arrive, by the regular market gardeners for sale, as well as by families for their own household use. Fruits are also cultivated here to some extent. The soil is mostly sandy, but it yields very well in some things. Many of the vegetables for table use are grown here, and this truck-farming, so called, is quite an industry, yielding much money to many of those engaged in the business, and who entirely devote their attention to this means of yearly income.

Agriculture. Cultivation of the lands.

Yield.

The immense orange trade of Florida is from the more southern and middle parts of the State. At Pensacola and around here there are some of these trees, but oranges are not cultivated in this part of Florida for the fruit trade. Extreme cold, which is sometimes experienced at Pensacola during the winter months, has from time to time seriously damaged the orange trees at Pensacola and its surroundings.

Orange industry.

Just at the close of the year 1894 a "cold wave" passed over Florida, which it is said has been the coldest weather here since 1835. A record of the thermometer on that occasion showed Pensacola 14 degrees; at other places in Florida 10 degrees. The destruction to the Florida orange crop by this cold weather is reported to have affected not less than 2,000,000 boxes of oranges, or more than half the present crop, which were frozen on the trees.

Large portion of crop frozen lately.

Peaches, and some other of the leading fruits, such as pears, figs, grapes, melons, &c., do well at Pensacola and its surroundings. Peaches, however, are only of moderate size here as a rule, not attaining to the size of the several species of this fruit grown in the more northern latitudes.

Peaches and other fruit.

As regards pears, much attention is being paid to the cultivation of this fruit, and larger tracts of land have been, more particularly of late, planted out in pear orchards, the sandy soil here being apparently most favourable to the growth of the pear tree.

Pears.

The Le Conte pear is the species of this fruit which is now being mostly cultivated. During the year 1894 large shipments of these pears were made to the western markets of the United States, with fair results.

Large shipments.

One-year old Le Conte pear-trees, secured from nurseries, according to the "Southern Cultivator," are the best for orchard planting. "They are trained in the nursery to one stem, are about 2 inches in circumference at the collar, and about 5 feet high; 3 feet of the top should be cut off before or at planting; in other words, the tree should be cut back to 4 feet from the ground.

Orchard planting.

"The trees will thrive without pruning, but they assume an ungainly shape. Some of their branches will run up too high, the fruit on them will be inaccessible, and liable to be whipped off by the hard winds. The Le Conte pear bears phenomenal crops of fruit, and should, therefore, be stacky, with large sturdy limbs,

Quotation about pruning, &c.

and have a well-balanced head, so that the fruit will not be beaten off by storms, and be convenient for gathering.

"Subsequent pruning consists in annually cutting back the leader and the longer branches, and removing the inside branches. A Le Conte tree should at five years be about 15 inches in girth above the collar, 15 to 18 feet high, 8 or 10 feet across the branches at the widest part, and of symmetrical cone-shape. There should be a leader in the centre, and the limbs beginning 2 feet from the ground, and diverge at intervals to the top. If the limbs, including the leader, are annually cut back, leaving the leader somewhat the longest, and the useless buds and limbs removed, the tree naturally assumes the shape before described. At three to four years old the tree commences to form fruit buds, and will require but little pruning thereafter. The weight of the fruit causes the branches to spread, and the tendency to grow small measurably ceases, though the rapid growth of the tree continues for years."

LECONTE PEAR ORCHARD. FIVE YEARS OLD. (FROM PHOTOGRAPH.)

Agricultural statistics. I now go beyond my immediate post, and give some of the latest published agricultural statistics of the State of Florida, which will be information as regards such average things yearly, as presented by the Commissioner of Agriculture to the Governor of the State, and by the latter referred to in his message to the legislature of Florida at its last regular session in the year 1893.

Quotation from the Governor's late remarks. On the agricultural condition of Florida the Governor remarked:— "While it is seldom that an average crop can be had in all parts of the State every year, it is a fact, perhaps not generally recognised, but nevertheless true, that Florida enjoys such a great diversity of climate, soil and production, that a total failure has never yet occurred, and in all probability never will; to this extent we are blessed beyond the people of any other country under the sun, for no other country has a physical conformation so peculiarly its own, of such vast capabilities, of such great diversity of soil and production, and the grandest climate mankind has ever known.

"The cotton crop of last year was very much below that of 1891, a reduction which extended throughout the entire cotton-producing States, and which had the effect of increasing the price of that staple about 60 per cent. over the price obtained for it in 1891. Following up this principle, a further reduction would seem to be desirable, if not necessary, to greater success and profit. It may not be that the difference in receipts was made up by the difference in price, but that discrepancy has in reality been more than replaced by the production of the necessities of life, and other crops that are far more remunerative and better adapted to successful cultivation in the several portions of the State. The yields of corn, potatoes, hogs, sheep, and live-stock generally have been largely increased; tobacco of fine Cuban varieties has been to a great extent substituted as a money crop for cotton. Certainly these crops so much increased more than make up for the loss of the surplus cotton, for the increase in the value of the crops for the last year over the previous year is nearly 3,000,000 dol.

"The tobacco raised in the counties of Gadsden, Leon, Jefferson, and Holmes has been pronounced by experts and manufactories of hand-made cigars, as being almost equal to the best Cuba tobacco for cigar wrappers, which class of tobacco is worth more and is in greater demand than any other, and owing to this fact the growing of Cuba tobacco will, in a short time, be one of the most valuable crops of the State.

"The condition of the fruit crops in all parts of the State has been generally good, having had no cold weather to do any material damage, while the increased yield has met with ready sale at remunerative prices. The orange crop has, on the whole, brought good returns; while the pineapple crop has exceeded the most sanguine expectations, both as to size of crop and favourable prices; the value of the crop 2 years ago was only 147,000 dol., and in 1 year increased to over 600,000 dol. The orange crop exceeds in value any other crop in the State. The planting of fruit orchards suitable to the middle and western parts of the State have progressed rapidly, and many of them are yielding the growers profitable returns on the investment.

"It has been said that there is great depression in agricultural affairs; perhaps this is to some extent true, but undoubtedly the matter has been greatly exaggerated. If there is a depression it is caused mainly by the one-crop idea, for it is reasonable to expect that when the whole farming element of a country is directed toward the production of one particular crop, that increased prices will not prevail; the very opposite is apt to be the result, and the losses will fall invariably upon the farmer, the one who can least afford it.

"We see that in diversity of crop production alone there is wealth to the farmer, and having a land of inexhaustible resources, let us strive, then, by increasing our knowledge of the science of agriculture, to add to the material greatness of our State, till she stands at the very head of all that goes to make up every element of prosperity and happiness."

The following are the tables referred to by me above as giving information respecting the yearly average crops, &c., &c., of Florida, as connected with agricultural matters of the State:—

RETURN of the Field Crops of Florida (Products of 45 Counties) for the Year 1891.

Articles.	Acres.	Quantity.	Classifier.	Value.
				Dollars.
Corn	353,679	3,411,134	Bushels	2,438,112
Rice	3,115	38,818	,,	43,740
Field peas	15,984	136,020	,,	164,134
Pea-nuts	31,296	483,369	,,	458,407
Oats	79,518	442,838	,,	321,538
Sweet potatoes	15,861	1,708,451	,,	811,061
Hay	6,692	9,016	Tons	120,832
Millet	93	470	,,	3,086
Cotton (Upland)	126,247	36,778	Bales	1,213,571
,, (Sea Island)	59,253	13,647	Bags	638,156
Tobacco	1,331	504,208	Pounds	146,130
Sugar-cane, sugar	} 6,881 {	1,503,650	,,	65,706
,, syrup		47,273	Barrels	524,172

RETURN of Vegetables and Garden Products of Florida (Products of 45 Counties) for the Year 1891.

Articles.	Acres.	Quantity.	Classifier.	Value.
				Dollars.
Egg plant	101	5,168	Barrels	15,983
Squashes	219	13,270	,,	20,533
Cabbages	2,582	219,388	,,	210,320
Beans	977	80,616	Crates	112,823
Cucumbers	798	56,339	,,	63,739
English peas	123	5,576	,,	6,950
Beets	114	10,865	,,	8,533
Water melons	2,897	1,895	Car loads	136,569
Tomatoes	4,098	421,746	Boxes	325,226
Irish potatoes	710	45,020	Bushels	62,149

RETURN of the Fruit Crop of Florida (Products of 45 Counties) for the Year 1891.

Articles.	Bearing Trees.	Quantity.	Classifier.	Value.
				Dollars.
Oranges	2,422,489	3,585,564	Boxes	3,838,517
Lemons	32,431	31,586	,,	50,348
Limes	16,694	9,375	,,	5,536
Peaches	226,739	74,725	Bushels	83,465
Figs	..	3,714	,,	4,146
Plums	..	5,817	,,	8,948
Sugar apples	4,555	2,783	Barrels	7,824
Pears	199,176	25,366	,,	58,254
Grape fruit	12,123	8,744	,,	18,627
Bananas	..	50,822	Bunches	22,189
Strawberries	..	1,054,717	Quarts	163,212
Pineapples	..	8,240,180	Apples	612,780
Cocoanuts	55,468	41,910	Nuts	1,702

RETURN of the Live-stock of Florida for the Year 1891.

Description.	Number.	Value.
		Dollars.
Horses	32,944	2,219,089
Mules	8,678	794,594
Jacks and jennets	78	3,393
Stock cattle	449,599	2,525,000
Sheep	113,974	195,203
Goats	15,768	11,770
Hogs	229,145	381,395

RETURN of the Poultry of Florida for the Year 1891.

Description.	Number.	Value.
		Dollars.
Fowls	857,619	249,893
Ducks	5,959	3,136
Geese	23,393	13,435
Turkeys	19,583	17,829
Eggs	1,772,013	325,407

RETURN of the Dairy Products of Florida for the Year 1891.

Description.	Quantity.	Classifier.	Value.
			Dollars.
Milch cows	41,633	..	642,381
Milk	2,843,070	Gallons	891,864
Butter	491,766	Lbs.	131,306
Cheese	1,646	,,	54,100

(1969)

UNITED STATES.

RETURN of Miscellaneous Products of Florida for the Year 1891

Description.	Quantity.	Classifier.	Value.
			Dollars.
Wool	257,635	Lbs.	58,726
Honey	291,946	,,	28,249
Avocado pears	542	Barrels	1,605
Wine	17,688	Gallons	21,282
Grape vines	1,081	Acres	232,085

TABLE showing Total Value of all Products in connection with the above Tables.

Description.	Value.
	Dollars.
Field crops	6,948,645
Vegetable and garden products	962,825
Fruit crops	4,875,348
Live-stock	6,130,444
Poultry	609,700
Dairy products	1,719,651
Miscellaneous products	341,947
Total	21,588,560

TABLE showing Total Acreage in connection with the above Tables.

Description.	Acres.
Field crops	699,950
Vegetable and garden products	13,459
Total	713,409

Information. — In giving the foregoing tables showing the various products of the State of Florida, it will be understood that I have very much in view that this information will be of value to our people in the British possessions where the climates are like the climate of Florida. It will be seen by the tables how many things are grown in Florida that really can be grown in our tropical and semi-tropical places. In fact, many of the products referred to are now cultivated in the British West India Islands, but not by any means to such extent, and on such business principles, as carried out in Florida, and which mode of cultivation can alone lead to such money results as are obtained in Florida in such agricultural pursuits.

Words of advice to would-be emigrants. — For the information of those persons in England and the British possessions looking toward Florida, by reason of the representation of agents of immigration, or of landed proprietors who wish to dispose of their lands here, I have before remarked in these reports on the subject of immigration to Florida, that the utmost caution is to be observed in taking such steps.

It is true that persons with enough money to purchase

already well-established farms in Florida might in the end do very well. But they should be beyond the risk of all their means being absorbed in the event of failure of crops, &c.

It must be understood that the results in agricultural pursuits in Florida, as shown by the tables above given, are brought about by persons who are of the soil, or at least who have had sufficient practical experience with the cultivation of the lands in Florida.

As written above, my chief aim in giving the foregoing tables about the products of Florida is for the benefit of agriculturists in the British possessions where things such as Florida's productions can be grown and made industries of, and to stimulate those agriculturists toward increased energy in the like industries already carried on in those places of our dominions. *Chief aim.*

Mobile.

Mr. Vice-Consul Barnewall reports as follows:—

The agricultural condition of this part of the South has many hopeful features, which cannot but claim the attention of other countries; especially the greatly-increased area devoted to cereals and roots, and general diversified farming throughout the rural districts. Live-stock is claiming the interest of the farmers, and thereby giving a supply of fertilisers which heretofore have been largely artificial, thus lessening the cost of production, and giving a new and paying industry to the agriculturist. *Agriculture.*

While the stringency of the money market has had disastrous effects on the prices of nearly everything grown by the farmer, it has made but little difference in the price of meats, especially the southern products. Cattle, sheep, and hogs are in demand, and the supply is not equal as yet to the consumption. This will still further encourage the farmers to go more extensively into the raising of such stock, as they always command cash in the market, and owing to the excellent climate and plenty of the requisite foods are continually ready for sale. *Live-stock.*

Cotton has been produced in such quantities throughout the South, as well as in Alabama, that prices have gone lower than at any previous time in the history of cotton production, yet the uncertainty of the money markets throughout the year, with general depression of business, all tended to lower the prices. The planters appeared to be in haste to sell, while, had they been able to hold their crop, a price in some measure commensurate with the value of the cotton could have been obtained. The cotton was made at a less cost than ever before, as the planters did not rely upon their cotton yield alone, but had gone more largely than heretofore into diversified farming, and were thus enabled to obtain their supplies at first cost, the only expensive article being the fertilisers which they were compelled to purchase. But less of this is being required yearly as stock increases. *Cotton.*

Corn was produced largely in almost every part of the State, with favourable weather for its growth, and less is being required from other States for home consumption than ever before. Larger yields have been the rule this year, and 30, 40, 50, *Corn.*

and even 75 bushels per acre have been common. During the time of growth there was a sufficiency of precipitation and warmth, while the dry warm weather during the latter part of the season made a plump grain.

Truck farming. The light sandy soil of the section near the Gulf of Mexico is not suited for wheat growth, yet the counties through the centre and north of this State and Mississippi, with their heavy clay soils, show good yields of wheat which, when mixed with the harder northern wheats, make a good grade of flour. The southern portion is adapted more to fruit culture and truck farming, or gardening on a large scale. The past season, however, was most unfavourable for a good yield, owing to a heavy frost in March which nipped the buds and destroyed the plants, and as a result the replanting made the yield too late to supply the early markets, and these farmers made but little profit from their crops.

Oranges. The orange crop of the extreme southern portion was very good, with a yield much larger for this section than for many years, yet a killing frost during the last days of December has had a disastrous effect on the orange trees and similar tender trees. The quality of the food was excellent, as the weather was perfect for ripening it. Pears and peaches were a small crop owing to the spring frost nipping the buds, yet some of the later varieties had almost an average yield.

Roots. Roots, such as potatoes, Irish and sweet, gave a good yield when properly cultivated, but prices were so low they were not a paying crop. Turnips, which are being grown more extensively for stock feeding, did well on the proper ground, and farmers are beginning to learn that in this they have a sure supply of good food for their stock, and as they may be grown on the same ground from which other crops have been harvested, they are grown with but little cost to the farmer, and besides they give him a late green crop when several varieties of grasses are out of season. A much larger area will be in roots in 1895.

Lands; prices, &c. During the past year there has been more demand for land than at any time since 1861, and prices have taken quite an advance, but yet lands of excellent quality and well located may be purchased from 1 dol. (4s. 3d.) per acre and upwards. These lands, when properly cultivated, may be made to produce every kind of crops in abundance which can be grown in the same latitude elsewhere, and the semi-tropical and temperate zones have their products in perfection in the Gulf counties.

Inducements, &c. There are better opportunities for the industrious practical farmer here than in any other section of this vast country, while educational and other facilities are second to none. Railways now permeate every section, and with the superior waterway system of Alabama, through her rivers, every portion is within easy distance of transportation. A line of steamers, carrying freight and passengers between Mobile and Liverpool, or some other British port, would be of great advantage to those who desire to get good homes on this side of the Atlantic, and would be mutually beneficial.

FOREIGN OFFICE.
1895.
ANNUAL SERIES.

Nº 1543.

DIPLOMATIC AND CONSULAR REPORTS ON TRADE AND FINANCE.

UNITED STATES.

REPORT FOR THE YEAR 1894
ON THE
TRADE OF THE CONSULAR DISTRICT OF CHICAGO.

REFERENCE TO PREVIOUS REPORT, Annual Series No. 1438.

Presented to both Houses of Parliament by Command of Her Majesty,
MAY, 1895.

LONDON:
PRINTED FOR HER MAJESTY'S STATIONERY OFFICE,
BY HARRISON AND SONS, ST. MARTIN'S LANE,
PRINTERS IN ORDINARY TO HER MAJESTY.

And to be purchased, either directly or through any Bookseller, from
EYRE & SPOTTISWOODE, EAST HARDING STREET, FLEET STREET, E.C., and
32, ABINGDON STREET, WESTMINSTER, S.W.; or
JOHN MENZIES & Co., 12, HANOVER STREET, EDINBURGH, and
90, WEST NILE STREET, GLASGOW; or
HODGES, FIGGIS, & Co., Limited, 104, GRAFTON STREET, DUBLIN.

1895.

[C. 7581—83.]   *Price Threepence.*

New Series of Reports.

Reports of the Annual Series have been issued from Her Majesty's Diplomatic and Consular Officers at the following places, and may be obtained from the sources indicated on the title-page:—

No.		Price.	No.		Price.
1425.	Rio Grande do Sul	7d.	1484.	Buda-Pesth	½d.
1426.	Erzeroum	1d.	1485.	Rome	5½d.
1427.	Christiania	5½d.	1486.	Para	1d.
1428.	Charleston	5½d.	1487.	Odessa	1d.
1429.	Meshed	1d.	1488.	Hakodate	1d.
1430.	Copenhagen	½d.	1489.	Beira	1½d.
1431.	Galveston	2½d.	1490.	Berne	1½d.
1432.	Hamburg	2½d.	1491.	Copenhagen	1d.
1433.	Brindisi	2½d.	1492.	Stettin	2½d.
1434.	Gothenburg	2d.	1493.	Rio Grande do Sul	1½d.
1435.	Kiungchow	1d.	1494.	Serajevo	1d.
1436.	St. Petersburg	½d.	1495.	Buenos Ayres	9d.
1437.	Malaga	1d.	1496.	Florence	2d.
1438.	Chicago	2½d.	1497.	Lisbon	1½d.
1439.	Odessa	2d.	1498.	Paris	2d.
1440.	Tabreez	½d.	1499.	Bolivia	1½d.
1441.	Tahiti	½d.	1500.	Patras	1½d.
1442.	Shanghai	2d.	1501.	Bordeaux	3d.
1443.	Nagasaki	1d.	1502.	Madrid	2d.
1444.	Madrid	2½d.	1503.	Amsterdam	1d.
1445.	Malaga	2½d.	1504.	Suakin	1d.
1446.	Rotterdam	1d.	1505.	Angora	1d.
1447.	Port Said	1d.	1506.	Havre	2½d.
1448.	Sofia	2½d.	1507.	Algiers	11d.
1449.	Warsaw	1½d.	1508.	La Rochelle	3d.
1450.	Africa (Congo)	2d.	1509.	Vera Cruz	2d.
1451.	Jeddah	1½d.	1510.	Puerto Cortes	1d.
1452.	San Francisco	5½d.	1511.	Taganrog	1d.
1453.	Oporto	2d.	1512.	Baltimore	1½d.
1454.	Barcelona	2d.	1513.	Mexico	1½d.
1455.	New Caledonia	½d.	1514.	Zaila	1d.
1456.	Smyrna	1d.	1515.	Zomba	3½d.
1457.	Macao	1d.	1516.	Valparaiso	2½d.
1458.	Samoa	1d.	1517.	Charleston	2½d.
1459.	Hiogo and Osaka	3d.	1518.	Serajevo	1d.
1460.	Lisbon	2d.	1519.	Saigon	1d.
1461.	Pekin	2d.	1520.	Bangkok	2d.
1462.	Corunna	2d.	1521.	Tripoli	1d.
1463.	Mozambique	15d.	1522.	Batavia	1½d.
1464.	Munich	1½d.	1523.	Dakar	½d.
1465.	St. Petersburg	3d.	1524.	Havana	2d.
1466.	Naples	1d.	1525.	Riga	2d.
1467.	Montevideo	2½d.	1526.	Trebizond	1½d.
1468.	Aden	1d.	1527.	Piræus	2½d.
1469.	Tokio	1½d.	1528.	Guayaquil	1½d.
1470.	Dantzig	5d.	1529.	Marseilles	1½d.
1471.	Guayaquil	1d.	1530.	Wuhu	1½d.
1472.	Canton	1½d.	1531.	Rio de Janeiro	2½d.
1473.	Dar-al-Baida	3d.	1532.	Trieste	2d.
1474.	Teheran	2d.	1533.	Brest	1½d.
1475.	Bushire	2d.	1534.	Stockholm	2d.
1476.	Tangier	2d.	1535.	Warsaw	1d.
1477.	Rome	2d.	1536.	Boston	1½d.
1478.	Hamburg	4d.	1537.	Mozambique	2½d.
1479.	The Hague	1½d.	1538.	Callao	1d.
1480.	Belgrade	2d.	1539.	Aleppo	1½d.
1481.	Batoum	1½d.	1540.	Jaffa	½d.
1482.	Teneriffe	½d.	1541.	Boston	1d.
1483.	Lisbon	2½d.	1542.	New Orleans	1½d.

No. 1543.

Reference to previous Report, Annual Series No. 1438.

UNITED STATES.

CHICAGO.

Consul Hayes-Sadler to the Earl of Kimberley.

My Lord, Chicago, *April* 16, 1895.

I HAVE the honour to transmit herewith a Report on the Trade and Commerce of Chicago during the year 1894, together with the Reports of the British Vice-Consuls at St. Louis, St. Paul, Denver, and Kansas City.

I have, &c.
(Signed) J. HAYES-SADLER.

Report on the Trade and Commerce of the Consular District of Chicago for the Year 1894.

ABSTRACT of Contents.

	PAGE
Chicago—	
Introductory	1
Trade of	2
Produce trade	3
Wholesale trade	5
Manufactures	5
Shipping and freights	7
Imports	7
Miscellaneous	8
The condition of labour	8
St. Louis	16
St. Paul	31
Denver	35
Kansas city	43

NOTE.—Exchange is taken at the rate of 4 dol. 85 c. to the 1*l.*

Introductory.

During the past year general depression has prevailed throughout the whole of this district, checking the prosperity and the natural increase of trade and commerce which had, until 1893,

(1965)

been so marked a feature in the records of each successive year. Some reaction from the inflation caused by the abnormal activity brought about by the World's Columbian Exposition could easily have been foreseen, and a fall in prices as a result of over-production after the successful operations of a series of prosperous years might have been expected, but the depressed condition must be mainly attributed to other causes. The financial panic in the summer of 1893 caused some diminution in the trade returns of that year, but its effect was then far from exhausted, and a further considerable reduction in those of 1894 demonstrates the severity of the crisis, while other influences aggravated the position and retarded any rapid recovery. The partial failure of the crops in some localities, especially in the arid districts, from drought, together with the low price of cereals, told severely on farming interests and curtailed the purchasing power of the agricultural portion of the community; the repeal of the silver law and the suspension of free coinage in India tended to alter monetary conditions, mining interests in the West were greatly depressed, and for a time the silver mining interest was almost wholly suspended; uncertainty with regard to the tariff pervaded the commercial community, and in conjunction with tightness of money checked mercantile enterprise, while strikes and the actions of labour unions hampered many industrial operations. Signs of recovery were not lacking towards the close of the year, business is now gradually improving and better times are confidently looked for, but a great deal of money is still shut up or unprofitable, prices of almost all commodities are lower than at any previous period in these parts, and trade has scarcely yet resumed its usual activity. The depression has been the cause of much disturbance in the labour market and of considerable distress in most parts of the country, wages have fallen where not maintained by the artificial methods resorted to by the unions, and employment of any kind for unskilled and non-union workmen has been difficult to obtain, even at very low rates.

The Trade of Chicago.

The record of trade at Chicago in 1894 shows a considerable falling off in nearly all departments of commerce and manufacture. Owing to the causes already stated, comparative dulness ruled in every branch of industry with but few exceptions, and a further reduction in the returns for the year ensued. The stagnation in business lasted almost throughout the year, but a revival seems to have now set in, and the pause in the great prosperity of this city will no doubt prove to have been only temporary.

Bank clearings.
The bank clearings show a reduction of 74,540,053*l.* compared with those of 1893, and of 169,140,310*l.* compared with those of 1892. They amounted in 1894 to 889,781,590*l.*; in 1893 to 964,321,643*l.*, and in 1892 to 1,058,921,900*l.*

CHICAGO.

Real estate. The transactions in real estate experienced a decline and were less than in any one of the 5 preceding years; the value of transfers amounted in 1894 to 25,195,321*l.*, whereas in 1890 they amounted to 46,474,227*l.*, but the latter was the year in which the exhibition was proposed.

Building trade. In the building trade there was some activity, for the city is ever increasing in size, and the population is now estimated at about 1,750,000. There were 9,736 building permits granted for a total frontage of 221,000 feet at an aggregate contract cost of 6,970,000*l.*, against 8,359 permits for a total frontage of 216,893 feet and an aggregate price of 6,400,000*l.* in 1893. Building operations, though not conducted on so extended a scale as during the 3 years preceding the exhibition, nearly doubled the amount of work done in any year before the exhibition was proposed. The largest building constructed was the Marquette office building, which covers 25,000 square feet, and is finished with the finest quality of mahogany, marble and mosaics.

The total trade, as calculated by the best authority, exclusive of speculative transactions and those in real estate and stocks, amounted to 263,835,000*l.* in value, or 32,065,000*l.* less than in 1893, and 53,265,000*l.* less than in 1892. In round figures the produce trade shows a decrease in value of 9,400,000*l.* compared with that of 1893, and is estimated at 88,098,000*l.*; the wholesale trade, valued at 95,670,000*l.*, shows a decrease of 11,430,000*l.*, and the manufacturing trade fell from 117,300,000*l.* to 103,335,000*l.* From the total value arrived at by adding these separate departments must be deducted about 23,268,000*l.* to allow for where they may overlap each other, particularly as the product of factories is sold wholesale by the manufacturer. This plan of calculation has been always adopted in the estimates made of the total trade of each year.

Produce Trade.

The movement of produce compared with that in 1893 will be seen in the following table:—

(1965)

UNITED STATES.

Principal Articles.		1894. Received.	1894. Shipped.	1893. Received.	1893. Shipped.
Flour	Barrels	4,223,182	3,714,007	4,664,424	4,105,117
Wheat	Bushels	25,665,902	18,213,443	35,355,101	24,715,738
Corn	,,	64,951,815	54,528,482	91,255,154	78,919,781
Oats	,,	63,144,885	50,376,089	84,289,886	67,129,119
Rye	,,	1,368,157	1,100,558	1,707,072	1,320,013
Barley	,,	13,418,392	7,707,218	13,345,845	8,233,268
Grass seeds	Lbs.	47,524,961	66,207,092	52,540,522	72,138,909
Flax seed	Bushels	5,092,668	2,353,757	8,101,992	7,730,641
Cured meats	Lbs.	139,003,374	570,276,662	119,599,941	548,451,386
Canned meats	Cases	64,631	1,159,746	44,666	1,240,900
Dressed beef	Lbs.	136,476,783	1,080,053,993	177,782,265	1,257,581,873
Pork	Barrels	5,999	222,878	6,527	210,092
Lard	Lbs.	63,177,799	409,211,467	47,741,901	367,894,172
Cheese	,,	60,424,190	56,460,940	59,303,480	51,101,900
Butter	,,	167,446,400	151,002,475	150,742,420	145,796,180
Live hogs	Number	7,483,228	2,465,058	6,057,278	2,149,410
Cattle	,,	2,974,393	950,738	3,133,406	900,183
Sheep	,,	3,099,725	333,397	3,031,174	442,865
Calves	,,	160,949	11,888	210,577	13,832
Horses	,,	97,415	90,441	82,492	70,011
Hides	Lbs.	91,640,992	200,652,329	88,002,681	206,813,490
Wool	,,	51,544,381	69,101,205	28,451,708	36,502,734
Lumber	Met. feet.	1,562,577	632,069	1,600,677	719,254
Potatoes	Bushels	4,114,899	1,051,594	4,565,573	959,446
Eggs	Cases	2,106,680	1,221,355	1,728,906	951,600

Wheat and flour. The receipts of wheat and flour show a considerable diminution, wheat falling-off one-third in quantity compared with that in the preceding year. The average price of wheat during the year was 2s. 4d., against an average price of 2s. 9½d. a bushel in 1893, 3s. 3¼d. in 1892, and 3s. 11½d. a bushel in 1891. At one time the price was 2s. a bushel, the lowest figure ever reached in this country. The report that wheat was being used for feeding purposes attracted much attention during the latter part of the year, and it appears that, owing to its comparative cheapness, it was to some extent so used instead of corn in certain parts of this district.

Corn. The receipts of corn also fell short of those in 1893 by nearly one-third—from 91,225,154 to 64,951,815 bushels. The price, on the other hand, rose from an average of 1s. 7½d. a bushel in 1893 to 1s. 9d. in 1894, and in the autumn reached the figure of 2s. 5d. a bushel, at one time selling higher than wheat.

Oats. The average price of oats per bushel was 1s. 3½d., against 1s. 2d. in 1893. During the railway strike in June it rose as high as 2s. 0½d. a bushel.

Rye. There were no great fluctuations in rye, the average price being about 1s. 7½d., the same as in the preceding year.

Barley. The receipts of barley slightly exceeded those of 1893. The crop was excellent, and prices were well maintained.

Flaxseed. Flaxseed rose in price from an average of 4s. 5½d. in 1893 to 5s. 7¼d. in 1894.

Provisions. The provision market was quiet, and prices were comparatively low, mess pork selling at an average price of 2l. 11s. 6d., and prime steam lard at 1l. 9s. 7d. per 100 lbs.

Live stock. The receipts of cattle, though slightly less than in 1893, amounted to nearly 3,000,000 head, while the number of hogs

CHICAGO.

received was 1,500,000 in excess of the number in the preceding year, and prices were, consequently, low. A large number of horses (97,415) were received, but prices were low, local demand being affected by the very general employment of electricity instead of horse-power for street railways in almost all towns, and in some measure by the greatly increased use of bicycles.

Wholesale Trade.

The following table gives the estimated value of business done in the wholesale trade during the last 5 years, from which the inflation caused by the exhibition in many branches will be observed. Retail business in the city suffered also a reaction from the activity of 2 years ago, as well as from uncertainty as to the tariff and tightness in money.

Articles.	1890. £	1891. £	1892. £	1893. £	1894. £
Dry goods and carpets	19,326,000	20,202,000	21,175,000	19,588,000	15,464,000
Groceries	11,691,000	11,691,000	12,860,000	13,000,000	12,990,000
Lumber	7,601,000	8,041,000	8,866,000	7,216,000	7,110,000
Manufactured iron	3,202,000	3,504,000	4,115,000	3,093,000	2,454,000
Clothing	4,433,000	4,742,000	5,366,000	4,021,000	3,918,000
Boots and shoes	5,340,000	5,670,000	6,237,000	5,680,000	6,186,000
Drugs and chemicals	1,464,000	1,567,000	1,711,000	1,645,000	1,546,000
Crockery and glassware	1,132,000	1,237,000	1,340,000	1,340,000	1,237,000
Hats and caps	1,443,000	1,650,000	1,814,000	1,645,000	1,600,000
Millinery	1,443,000	1,443,000	1,568,000	1,445,000	1,031,000
Tobacco and cigars	2,237,000	2,371,000	2,608,000	2,742,000	2,784,000
Fish of all kinds	1,126,000	1,134,000	1,247,000	1,340,000	1,392,000
Oils	825,000	928,000	1,030,000	1,134,000	1,000,000
Dried fruits	887,000	887,000	969,000	1,083,000	979,000
Building materials	919,000	928,000	1,670,000	979,000	825,000
Furs	309,000	361,000	449,000	567,000	753,000
Carriages	382,000	413,000	474,000	412,000	361,000
Pianos and musical instruments	1,485,000	1,608,000	1,850,000	1,495,000	1,670,000
Music books and sheet music	119,000	129,000	148,000	144,000	103,000
Books, stationery, and wall paper	4,536,000	4,536,000	5,155,000	5,361,000	5,052,000
Pig-iron	4,131,000	4,227,000	4,804,000	2,887,000	2,629,000
Coal	5,170,000	5,361,000	6,185,000	4,742,000	3,300,000
Hardware, cutlery	3,608,000	3,984,000	4,536,000	4,227,000	4,126,000
Wooden, willow ware	652,000	722,000	783,000	794,000	804,000
Liquors	2,845,000	3,093,000	3,492,000	3,771,000	3,093,000
Jewellery, watches, and diamonds	4,206,000	5,155,000	5,928,000	5,928,000	4,124,000
Leather	520,000	567,000	619,000	619,000	721,000
Pig-lead and copper	1,168,000	1,237,000	1,312,000	1,186,000	928,000
Paper	...	...	6,186,000	6,186,000	5,155,000
Miscellaneous	8,172,000	9,152,000	3,994,000	2,804,000	2,335,000
Total	100,372,000	106,631,000	118,351,000	107,074,000	95,670,000

Manufacturing Trade.

In almost all branches of manufacture the value of product shows a decrease compared with the value in 1893, the whole loss being estimated at 11·8 per cent. The number of manufacturing firms increased during the year from 3,405 to 3,458

UNITED STATES.

per cent., and the capital employed from 51,387,629*l.* to 52,760,825*l.*; but the number of employés fell-off from 171,000 to 158,000, the wages paid approximately from 20,453,000*l.* to 18,484,000*l.*, and the value of the total product from 117,275,000*l.* to 103,335,000*l.* The price of manufactured goods has almost universally fallen, and the rates of wages has in many cases been reduced, but as a general rule where disputes have arisen the power of labour unions has been able to maintain the rates paid for skilled labour.

Packing business. The total product of the different packing industries fell off about 10 per cent. in value, and is approximately reckoned at 19,691,000*l.* against an estimated value of 22,062,000*l.* in 1893, 24,478,000*l.* in 1892 and 28,304,000*l.* in 1891. The total wages paid are said to have increased from 2,588,000*l.* to 2,887,000*l.* The export of dressed beef and canned goods to foreign countries continues to be an increasing trade.

Iron and steel. The estimated value of the production of iron and steel fell off about 20 per cent., while there was a similar fall in prices realised and in the total amount of wages paid. The total value of production in 1894 is estimated at about 10,794,000*l.* and the wages paid at 2,217,000*l.* The number of rolling mills and foundries remains the same as in 1893, but 28 new factories in different other branches of the iron and steel industry were established last year. The trade is much depressed and prices have never been so low as at present. The demand for rails has been practically nil. Though 147 new miles of railway were constructed in Illinois, very little was done during the year in the way of increasing the railway mileage of the country. The Illinois steel company, which has a capital of nearly 4,000,000*l.*, made a net profit of only 6,000*l.*, but this was an improvement on the deficit of 70,000*l.* shown in 1893. This company has lately constructed a plant at the works at South Chicago for the manufacture of steel plates for shipbuilding, boilers and tanks, but no merchantable product has yet been turned out by the new machinery.

Brass and copper. In brass and copper industries there was increase of 10 in the number of manufacturing firms, but the total value of manufacturing firms, but the total value of product declined from 12,954,000*l.* to 10,793,000*l.*, and the sum of wages paid from 2,144,300*l.* to 1,804,100*l.*

Iron and wood. The whole manufacturing trade in iron and wood combined is estimated to have produced a value of 8,061,800*l.*, or 1,195,800*l.* less than in 1893. Agricultural implements were greatly affected by the financial condition of the country, and the inability of farmers to purchase in consequence of the partial failure and low price of cereals; the reduction in the estimated value of production in this branch of manufacture was 25 per cent.

Wood. In manufactures of wood there was a falling-off in the value of product of about 15 per cent., comparative dulness prevailing in nearly every branch except in the manufacture of pianos and organs.

CHICAGO.

With regard to other manufacturing industries than those above mentioned a general falling-off occurred in the value of product, and prices have been lower than ever known in these parts, the demand, especially in textile fabrics, having been greatly in low-priced goods.

Other industries.

Shipping and Freights.

The following is a return of shipping entered and cleared in the customs district of Chicago, which includes the two small ports of South Chicago and Michigan City:—

Nationality.	Entered. Number of Vessels.	Entered. Tons.	Cleared. Number of Vessels.	Cleared. Tons.	Total. Number of Vessels.	Total. Tons.
Coasting trade	8,230	5,170,292	8,178	5,108,758	16,408	10,279,050
Foreign trade—						
Canadian	12	3,376	12	3,376	24	6,752
American	17	7,592	139	99,026	156	106,618
Total, 1894	8,259	5,181,260	8,329	5,211,160	16,588	10,392,420
,, 1893	8,754	5,456,637	8,789	5,449,470	17,543	10,906,107
,, 1892	10,556	5,966,626	10,567	5,968,337	21,128	11,934,963
,, 1891	10,224	5,524,832	10,394	5,506,700	20,618	11,021,552
,, 1890	10,507	5,136,253	10,547	5,150,615	21,054	10,286,868

Lake freights were unusually low, and except in the case of some of the larger vessels unprofitable. The average rate for the year for corn from Chicago to Buffalo was scarcely $\frac{6}{10}d.$, while in July the average was below $\frac{1}{2}d.$ per bushel. There was a considerable decrease in the movement of grain in lake vessels.

Imports.

The following table gives the nature and value of some of the principal articles of merchandise imported direct to Chicago for the last 5 years:—

Articles.	Value. 1890.	1891.	1892.	1893.	1894.
	£	£	£	£	£
Free goods	702,121	672,462	827,816	798,002	890,111
China, glassware	115,710	171,765	173,445	203,351	135,015
Cigars, tobacco, manufactured	136,744	61,842	62,695	46,015	39,856
Cutlery	4,967	4,880	6,808	9,875	12,956
Diamonds, precious stones	74,486	25,853	51,906	40,687	22,035
Dry goods	991,231	832,262	1,101,031	1,120,787	650,813
Fish of all kinds	31,371	48,501	54,919	37,711	61,746
Iron manufactures, wire	37,961	78,605	127,796	86,810	72,375
Leaf tobacco	34,326	42,298	79,739	124,104	176,310
Millinery goods	18,284	18,801	23,166	15,615	12,118
Tin-plate	336,599	328,094	270,042	240,092	195,944
Wines, liquors	76,178	88,567	106,057	109,253	91,091
Other articles	614,639	742,723	699,837	1,017,648	475,776
Total	3,174,617	3,116,653	3,585,257	3,849,950	2,836,146
Duties	1,069,582	1,233,730	1,544,035	1,711,180	1,091,804

Though the importation of free goods, and of a few dutiable goods such as cutlery, fish, and leaf tobacco has increased, the falling-off in almost all other imported goods has been very heavy, and must be attributed to the depression arising from causes already stated. The stock remaining on hand from the abnormally large quantity of such articles as dry goods, china, glassware, &c., imported to meet the demand during the period of the exhibition, contributed to reduce the price of imported goods, and consequently to diminish occasion for any considerable replenishment. The value of the imports of tin-plate shows a continued decrease, not only arising from the low price, but from increasing manufacture of plates in this country.

Miscellaneous.

Public works. — Considerable work has been done on the drainage canal, and nearly 42 per cent. of the construction of the channel is now completed. The expenditure on construction last year was about 1,000,000*l*., and since the commencement the total expenditure, including right of way and engineering, has amounted to 2,366,792*l*. It is calculated that the total cost of the drainage canal will exceed 5,750,000*l*.

Health. — Notwithstanding an outbreak of small-pox, owing to neglected vaccination, which amounted almost to an epidemic and was the cause of 1,029 deaths, the rate of mortality at Chicago in 1894 was only 15·1 per 1,000. The calculation of this percentage is based on a population estimated from school census figures at 1,749,584. The prevalence of small-pox is now checked. During the year more than 250,000 employés in shops and factories were examined, and those found unprotected were vaccinated.

The Condition of Labour.

Strikes. — The past year has been a remarkable one with respect to strikes and labour troubles, and the action taken during its course by union organisations led to riots which approached the point of endangering public safety. The most disturbed period was from April to August. In April the strike among coal miners, in which about 125,000 men were engaged in different States, was severely felt in Chicago and the whole neighbourhood, where at one time scarcely sufficient coal remained on hand for the partial working of the railway system. The coal mines in Illinois in 1893 turned out 19,949,564 tons, valued at about 4*s.* 3*d.* a ton, for which the price of mining by hand was 2*s.* 11*d.* The price of coal had then fallen nearly 50 per cent. in 12 years, and the average number of running days was only 174. Last year the price of coal sustained a further fall, the demand fell off, and a reduction in the rate of labour was made. These conditions, combined with the system of contracts which bind the men to the terms of the employer or work is denied, the system of company tenement houses, the truck system, and the plan of compulsory insurance adopted by some operators, were the causes of grievance among the miners. The strike lasted about two months, and terminated in mutual concessions, the men gaining rather more advantage than the owners.

About the same time the dissatisfaction felt by a portion of the labouring classes throughout this part of the country at the impossibility of getting work, and at the low rate of wages offered, developed into the organisation of bodies of discontented men, several hundred strong, banded together for the purpose of proceeding to Washington to lay their grievances before the Government, and to demand that an opportunity should be given them of obtaining employment. Only one of these bands ever reached its destination, and only then to fail in its object. The other bands, starting from different points in this district, were unable to proceed far, and gradually dissolved, but the condition which resulted in this public form of expression was such as to enlist some sympathy, and had not their procedure been marred by the seizure of trains and other lawless acts, a wider feeling of compassion might have been aroused for the undoubted distress which existed among the unemployed.

In June occurred the notable strike among the employés at the Pullman car factory; their chief grievance appears to have been that, while their scale of wages was reduced 33 per cent. and regular employment not provided, the heavy rent they were obliged to pay for the rooms they occupied in the Pullman village was not reduced, and that they consequently had not the means of supporting themselves and their families. The American Railway Union soon took part in the dispute by refusing to handle the cars of the Pullman Company, and then a general railway strike followed in sympathy with the Pullman strikers, which for several days practically suspended railway transportation. Riots ensued, a large amount of railway property was destroyed, and safety was only insured by the presence of a large body of United States troops, sent by the Government to protect the mail service and prevent violation of the inter-state commerce law. In this trouble the strikers gained nothing. Many new hands were taken on in the place of those on strike, and the President of the American Railway Union and some others were sentenced to terms of imprisonment for contempt of court. On the other hand, the loss to the railroad companies by property destroyed was heavy, and traffic receipts fell off considerably.

There were several strikes in the building trade early in the year, which resulted in the men gaining the day, contractors being compelled to accede to the demands of the unions from inability otherwise to complete their contracts. The differences, particularly in this trade, arose in almost every case not on the question of wages, though the maintenance of the scale fixed each year at the meeting of delegates and representatives of building societies was consistently demanded, but on the insistence of the unions that no non-union man at all should be employed, and in consequence of the number of unemployed many attempts were made to get work done at a lower rate than that insisted on by the unions. The pretentions of these organisations went even so far as to refuse to work with men of another union which was not amalgamated with their own. An apparent result of this continued disturbance in the labour market, and the great difficulty so many unemployed have found in staving off the pangs of hunger, has been a wave of crime with increased lawlessness in this district, shown by the crowded state of prisons and other institutions, which have in many cases been found of inadequate dimension to meet the number of convictions. The population of this city has enormously increased, but there has been no proportionate development in the capabilities of institutions, certainly to meet conditions such as have existed during the last two years. Hospital and poor-house accommodation, and the resources of relief societies, have been over-taxed, and many a labouring man, impoverished through failure to obtain employment not from his own fault, has found himself in a position of great distress. Men with families have been able to obtain some temporary assistance from relief and aid societies, and much general relief has been afforded by charitable people where cases came to their knowledge, but the suffering which has existed during the last 18 months among the unemployed has been great, and has no doubt led to the increase of crime.

Condition of the labour market.
In every branch of employment more men were required during the period of the exhibition than would have been needed to meet any naturally increased demand, and a greater number were attracted to this city than were even then required, so that at the termination of that period a large surplus population remained for which there was no work; the panic, occurring at the same time, aggravated the congested condition of the labour market, and from this there was, up to the end of last year, no great recovery.

Notwithstanding these hard times, union wages at Chicago and in most parts of the country were maintained at a rate which could afford little ground for complaint, though there was much loss of time from irregularity of work and enforced idleness, but the rate for unskilled labour fell considerably, and non-union men found the greatest difficulty in obtaining any employment. Owing to the despotic character of the various labour organisations, which have not carried their pretentions to a successful issue without violence, a working man, unless he be affiliated to some union, has little chance of employment at the rate paid in the trade. The exercise of individual freedom being so far limited, and there being a constant influx of immigrants from countries where labour is cheap, competition for any description of work has greatly increased, and the position of a working man, whether skilled or unskilled, seeking employment in this part of the country, is one of considerable hardship. Taking into consideration the wear and tear from the nature of work and climate, the cost of lodging and many necessaries, and the higher scale of living and lack of economy which seem incidental if not inseparable from conditions here, the higher wages paid, apparently so attractive, do not afford to the English working man the advantages which at first glance might be supposed or which they seem to offer. The situation has no doubt lately been abnormal owing to the numbers out of work, but it may be safely said that at present few strangers have a chance by honest work of realising the hope of bettering their condition, or of doing more than make both ends meet, even if they succeed in procuring tolerably regular employment, which is by no means the rule.

Women workers at Chicago.

The class of employment which still continues to offer the best chance of saving is domestic service. It is not a popular service with the American born, from a feeling of independence, but wages, though lower than two years ago, are still high ; there is no loss of time except such as may arise from sickness or their own fault, nor expense of board and lodging. An ordinary cook now receives from 1*l*. to 1*l*. 5*s*. per week, and a house or parlour maid from 16*s*. to 1*l*. per week with all found. An exhaustive report published two years ago on working women in Chicago, shows that the numerous branches of industry and occupation in which women are engaged were extending, and that there was an apparent slight rise in the rate paid. It was calculated that in 1888 the average weekly earnings of employées of all kinds were 1*l*. 3*s*. 8*d*.; the average earnings in 1892 for all employées are stated to have been 1*l*. 5*s*. 8*d*. per week, namely, 1*l*. 4*s*. 5*d*. for the working force, and 1*l*. 19*s*. 4*d*. for administrative and office employment. Taking all employées it was found that their average yearly earnings were 63*l*. 11*s*. 10*d*., and their yearly expenses, 61*l*. 10*s*., including cost of rooms and boarding, clothing, and dressmaking, sickness, assistance to others, and incidental expenses. Office employées earned on an average 90*l*. 11*s*. and expended 85*l*. 1*s*. in the year, and operatives earned an average of 61*l*. 1*s*. 7*d*. and expended 59*l*. 5*s*. 3*d*. in the year. The yearly sum paid by all employées for rooms and boarding averaged 35*l*. 16*s*. 5*d*.; office employées paid an average of 46*l*. 8*s*., and operatives an average of 34*l*. 5*s*. 2*d*. Scarcely 1 per cent. of the number of working women who furnished information on which the statistics were based, reported a deficit at the end of the year.

Overcrowding in cities.

The drift of population and immigration towards cities and towns, with a comparative decrease in rural population, have for some years been marked features in all the States of this district more or less. This movement, which has lately been accentuated by the financial crisis and the condition of the labour and produce markets, is attributed to modern inventions, the establishment of new industries in cities, and to the greater inducement to energy and the greater chances of advancement there offered than on the farm. This fancy for city life, together with the depression of agricultural interests, has led to the overcrowding of large cities

UNITED STATES.

particularly in their poorer quarters. Notwithstanding the great increase of population in the State of Illinois, the rural population decreased by 114,000 from 1880 to 1890, even counting small towns of 200 inhabitants in that denomination, while the urban population during the same decade increased 862,529, or more than 66 per cent. As in each successive year there is less public land remaining in the west for occupation, the competition for employment in the cities becomes greater, and this may eventually lead to a lower standard of wages; labour unions may have, up to the present time, been able to maintain the scale for their own members, but it is doubtful whether the tendency is not towards a general fall, which they may be powerless to control, unless a change should occur in prospective conditions.

Labour in Iowa.
In Iowa, where the increase of population from 1880 to 1890 was 287,281, or 17·68 per cent., the increase of the urban population during that period was 261,187, or 50·68 per cent., while the rural population increased only 26,094, or 2·35 per cent. The total population in the State is now nearly 2,000,000.

In this State the rate of wages paid in the principal occupations in the cities was as follows, with the average yearly earnings:—

Trade.	Average Wages per Day.	Average Yearly Earnings.
	s. d.	£ s. d.
Bakers..	7 9	112 8 3
Blacksmiths ..	8 0	117 9 5
Bookkeepers ..	8 1½	121 0 11
Bricklayers ..	16 4	134 14 9
Carpenters ..	9 3	88 1 3
Clerks..	6 1	92 15 8
Coal miners ..	7 8	79 15 11
Painters ..	9 0	125 16 3
Engineers ..	7 10	119 7 8
Wood workers ..	6 3	96 9 8
Unskilled labour ..	4 9	54 15 2

The greater part of the time during which these returns were compiled was before the financial crisis in 1893 threw many employés out of work, and it will be seen from the annual earnings what a number of days were lost in each branch of employment. With regard to women workers the average number of days in the year in which employment was obtained was about 275, and the wages earned varied from 9s. 8d. per week for common domestic servants to 1l. 15s. for stenographers, the average being 1l. 0s. 8d. per week. In this State the average interest on farm mortgages in 1893 was 7·36 per cent. The total mortgage indebtedness on farms was 20,834,211l., or 272l. on each encumbered estate, about one-third of its estimated value.

In Wisconsin.
The State of Wisconsin suffered less from disturbance in the labour market, and from those lawless manifestations which

characterised the distress resulting from industrial stagnation, than almost any other State. According to the report of last year, the per capita wages—that is, the result arrived at by dividing the aggregate wages by the total number of operatives in each industry—paid in 1893, in the principal industries, vary somewhat from those paid in 1889, as will be seen from the following comparison:—

Industry.	Per Capita Wages Paid.	
	1889.	1893.
	£ s. d.	£ s. d.
Lumber, lath, shingles	69 0 10	70 5 9
Machine shops, iron and brass foundries	98 9 7	86 14 9
Railway shops	104 19 4	110 11 6
Beer and malt	110 5 3	117 9 6
Sash, door, blinds; planing mills	76 18 8	79 16 9
Furniture (not including chairs)	52 12 4	67 17 2
Agricultural implements and machinery	88 3 2	133 17 8
Leather	90 19 3	89 5 1
Wagons and carriages	75 10 6	73 1 11
Printing, publishing, bookbinding	106 16 5	98 6 3
Boots and shoes	97 12 7	104 2 1
Rolling mills	113 19 2	137 15 5
Paper and pulp	83 6 5	83 14 3
Chairs and chair stock	61 15 11	61 7 9
Clothing	110 19 3	77 12 4
Flour and feed	135 8 1	96 19 0
Textiles	64 15 5	57 1 11
Beef and pork packing	109 12 10	90 6 11

In almost all industries the majority of operatives receive from 5s. to 8s. a day. In the factories about 6 per cent. receive 12s. a day or upwards, and about 6 per cent. more receive 10s. a day. In the building trade 25 per cent. receive 1s. an hour and upwards, and very few labourers get more than 7d. an hour. The standard wages paid to skilled workmen in Milwaukee in the several branches of the building trade in 1893 were 1s. 2½d. an hour, or 9s. 11d. per day. This is rather higher than the rate paid in Missouri, but not so high as farther west, in the States of Colorado, Nebraska, or Montana.

The general depression in the State of Nebraska has been greatly aggravated by partial failure of the crops in 1893 through drought, especially in the western portion, and their total destruction in a large portion of the State in 1894 from the same cause. A condition of distress thus arose which called for urgent appeals for help, and many car-loads of provisions and coals were forwarded as donations from other States this last winter for the relief of the half starving people, railroads giving free transportation. Western Nebraska lies in the arid belt; it is fertile, and has yielded abundant harvests, but until irrigation, yet in its infancy, has been more widely established, and the right to use water from the streams more carefully safeguarded, it will be

In Nebraska.

subject to similar agricultural disaster. In this State, under the bounties offered in 1889 and 1890 for the production of sugar, the beet industry seemed for a time to hold out excellent prospects, but these bounties being withdrawn, one of the two State factories established there was closed last year, and there is a doubt if the other can continue operations. The losses on grain-growing in the last 2 years have been very heavy; the total cost of the production of wheat, including rent, in 1893, was 1*l.* 18*s.* per acre, and of corn 2*l.* 5*s.* per acre. The Russian cactus or thistle (Salsola Kali L. var. tragus D.C.) has spread rapidly in this and the adjoining States of Dakota, and has become a most pernicious pest. This weed, which is allied to the native tumble weed (Amaranthus albus, L.) appears to have been unknown in these parts a few years ago.

The number and value of farms in Nebraska, as well as the quantity of live-stock had increased since 1880 in a remarkable manner. In 1880 there were 63,387 farms, valued, including buildings and fences, at 34,210,833*l.*, and in 1890 the number of farms was 113,608, valued at 82,960,000*l.*, or an increase of 79·2 per cent. in number, and 27·98 per cent. in value. It appears that, in 1893, 72·99 per cent. of farm families owned, and 27·1 per cent. hired, the farms they cultivated; the percentage of families owning their own land, which was encumbered, was 51·99 per cent., and those who owned free of encumbrance, 48·01 per cent.; so that 27 per cent. hired their farms, 38 per cent. owned their farms with encumbrance, and 35 per cent. owned their farms without encumbrance. On the owned farms the liens amounted to 9,830,553*l.*, or 39·32 per cent. of their value, the average rate of interest paid for which was 8·22 per cent. The average value of the owned and encumbered farms was 600*l.*, and of the mortgage debt 224*l.* With regard to the homes in this State, 59·09 per cent. of home families hired and 43·91 per cent. owned their homes, while of the home-owning families 63·75 per cent. owned free from encumbrance. The encumbered homes were on the average mortgaged to 32·19 per cent. of their value, and the average debt of each encumbered home was 217*l.*, bearing 8·13 per cent. interest. In the largest city, Omaha, 74·06 per cent. of the homes are hired.

In North Dakota.

The result of investigation into farm and home proprietorship in the State of North Dakota shows that with regard to farms 9·90 per cent. of farm families hire, and 90·10 per cent. own the farms they cultivate, and that 48·67 per cent. of farm-owning families own subject to encumbrance, and 51 per cent. free from encumbrance. Thus about 10 per cent. hire, 44 per cent. own with encumbrance, and 46 per cent. without encumbrance. The liens on owned farms amount to 2,302,858*l.*, or 36·30 per cent. of their value, and the debt bears an average interest of 9·54 per cent. There were last year 30,023 farms of an aggregate acreage of 7,448,887 acres, of which 4,520,246 acres were cultivated. With regard to homes 54·70 per cent. hire, and 43·30 per cent. own their homes, and of the latter nearly three-fourths own free of encumbrance; the aggregate debt on those homes which are encumbered is 204,283*l*., or 37·64 per cent. of their value, bearing interest at the average rate of 9·42 per cent.

The crops suffered greatly last year from drought. The acreage of wheat in this State does not largely increase, but during the last 4 years the acreage planted with rye has increased more than 500 per cent., and with barley 150 per cent.

The demonetisation of silver was a great blow to the chief industry of the State of Montana. Many of the largest mines were closed last year, a large amount of capital invested in costly machinery was tied up, and a vast number of men were thrown out of employment. A few of the mines which produce exceptionally high grade ores continued operations on a reduced scale, but silver mining, the great industry of the State, has been deprived for the present of its former prosperity. On the other hand, more attention was turned to gold mining, which in a measure relieved the acuteness of other depressing influences. This industry has largely increased during the last 2 years, and, from the present low price of silver, is likely to reach higher proportions. The crops of 1894 were excellent, the sheep and wool industries in this State were unusually depressed, while there was practically no market for horses. Wages have been reduced in agricultural and pastoral, and to some extent in other occupations, and much distress prevailed amongst those who were forcedly thrown out of employment at the mines. Conditions have now improved, but employment has scarcely resumed its normal proportions. The law enacted in 1887 providing for arbitration and conciliation in settling disputes between capital and labour, and for appointing boards to carry its provisions into effect, has been a failure. The following table gives the average yearly earnings, time lost, cost of living, and wages of persons (exclusive of foremen) employed in certain avocations in the principal employing counties of Montana during the year ended June 30, 1894:—

In Montana.

Avocation.		Average Wages.	Average Number of Days Lost.	Average Yearly Earnings.	Average Cost for Single Person of Board and Lodging per Month.
		£ s. d.		£ s. d.	£ s. d.
Blacksmiths	Per day	0 15 3½	74	173 17 0	5 17 10
Carpenters	,,	0 16 10	126·5	150 18 0	6 1 2
Calciners	,,	0 9 7	82	137 17 0	5 7 1
Clerks and salesmen	Per month	15 3 6	40·7	144 6 0	6 6 8
Coal miners	Per day	0 12 7	114	100 9 0	5 2 10
Engineers, stationary	,,	0 14 11	64·5	214 0 0	6 0 6
Labourers	,,	0 10 6	143	80 19 0	5 1 6
Machinists	,,	0 16 3½	64	212 0 0	6 7 6
Quartz miners	,,	0 15 6	114	117 16 0	6 3 5

The time lost is a serious matter, as from climatic conditions many branches of business, particularly that of construction, are periodically interrupted, and mechanics and artisans ordinarily expect to maintain themselves and their families by following exclusively the trade in which they are skilled. The days lost are almost entirely from no work. The average time lost by bricklayers was 206 days, and of stonemasons 168. The cost of board and lodging is heavy; taking the whole State the average cost for a single male employé is 1*l.* a month for room rent, and 4*l.* for board, or 5*l.* a month for board and lodging.

St. Louis.

Mr. Vice-Consul Western Bascome reports as follows:—

Trade and Commerce.

The year 1894 has been one of general commercial depression throughout the country.

While St. Louis has suffered severely in some departments of trade, such as flour, wheat, corn and rye, cattle, sheep, lumber, sugar, rice, coffee, coal, and potatoes, it has more than held its trade in oats, barley, cotton, bagging, hay, tobacco, lead, hog products, hogs, horses and mules, wool, hides, molasses including glucose, nails, and salt.

Since the panic of 1893 strenuous efforts to reduce expenses of all departments has been going on with the evident purposes to secure net profits from impairment.

The volume of business is less in 1894 when compared with 1893.

Tonnage. The tonnage handled by rail and river shows a decrease of 1,759,181 tons; about 12 per cent.

Receipts. The loss in receipts of all kinds of freight amounted to 911,024 tons, deducting the decrease in coal receipts, 539,979 tons, a loss of 371,045 tons of general freight is shown for the whole year.

Shipments. In outbound freight the decrease was 848,157 tons, and deducting coal shipments, 179,033 tons, a loss of 669,124 tons in shipment of general freight is shown, and in both receipts and shipments a loss of 1,040,169 tons is shown, which is not very unfavourable for a year of general depression, augmented somewhat by the great railroad strike, which paralysed transportation for a short period.

Grain Trade.

Grain trade. The past year has been a phenomenal one in the grain trade, for with very low prices for breadstuffs, lower than ever before, there has been very little foreign demand, and business has been stagnant, the amount handled here, as well as in other centres, has been less than for some years past, and the large stocks in public elevators have not been drawn on to any great extent.

Some attribute this loss of trade to the competition in Russian, Brazilian, and Argentine cereals, and others attribute prevailing low prices to the appreciation in gold purchasing power over that of silver, the commercial value of which will buy as much of such staple products of wheat and cotton as it did when it was on a commercial parity with gold. *Competition. Value in silver.*

Production seems to be going on without restriction, and lower prices must obtain in the future, the home market having narrowed very much as well as the foreign demand.

The Foreign Grain Trade.

The direct exportation of grain viâ the Mississippi river and New Orleans, which has been an important factor in the trade of St. Louis heretofore, was for the year 1894 of small proportions. *Foreign grain trade.*

The free transportation of grain from St. Louis depends largely on the crops in the Trans-Mississippi States, which were deficient in the States of Kansas, Nebraska, Iowa, and Missouri, particularly in the corn crop, and prices ruled too high for export.

The low water in the river which prevailed for nearly 5 months added to the difficulties, and deterred shippers from shipping by this route.

The shipments of wheat and corn amounted to 2,345,503 bushels from St. Louis, and 208,145 bushels of wheat, and 1,175 bushels of corn were shipped by St. Louis parties from Belmont, Mo., viâ the river route. In addition to the above shipments, 406,776 bushels of wheat, and 1,943,595 bushels of corn were exported viâ Atlantic ports. *Shipments.*

Plans are in progress for dredging the channel another season by the Mississippi River Commission, which it is expected will allow continuous shipping throughout the year, while the river is free from ice.

Flour Trade.

The flour trade for the year 1894, while about equal in value to previous seasons, was disappointing in results to city millers. *Flour.*

During the first half of the year all business was paralysed by the coal strike, followed by the railway strike in June, and the flour trade suffered, in common with other industries. The second half of the year, with a bountiful harvest of wheat at very low prices, the millers had a solid basis for a large, safe, and profitable business; but the repeal of the reciprocity features of the tariff practically restored former prohibitive duties levied by Spain on American products to Cuba and other Spanish islands, and cut off the large volume of trade in that direction. The immense crops of cheaper wheat from Argentine, India, and Russia, has enabled foreign mills to make very cheap flour, with which the higher wages of St. Louis will not allow St. Louis flour to compete.

(1965)

UNITED STATES.

Export.

The export for the year was 634,862 barrels, a slight decrease from 1893. Values show a constant decline.

Financial.

Bank clearings.

Our bank clearings, which are considered as an index of the volume of trade, have fallen-off about 1 per cent. from those of 1893, viz., from 227,922,858*l*. in 1893 to 225,540,581*l*. in 1894, while the balances increased from 27,992,529*l*. in 1893 to 34,589,153*l*. in 1894, the latter indicating a return of confidence in the conservatism and stability of our banks.

There was no bank failure here during the panic of 1893, and none since the year 1886.

Resources.

The official returns show the banks to be in a very flourishing condition. The capital stock is 3,190,000*l*.; the surplus and net profits, 1,720,000*l*.; and the deposits and due banks, 13,560,240*l*.; loans and bonds, 12,592,104*l*.; cash and deposits in other banks, 5,460,454*l*.; ratio of cash to deposits, 40¼ per cent.

The increase in deposits since October, 1893, is 1,800,000*l*. Confidence at that time and since has been greatly restored; the loans and cash on hand have increased, and the resources of the banks have increased 3,177,989*l*.

At present there is a large amount seeking investment, which the partial stagnation in general business prevents being used.

A New York financial journal said, in a recent issue:—"St. Louis will this year, 1895, do the largest business in the history of the city. The activity of the business men, the busy look of the streets, the large accounts in banks, all indicate great prosperity there.

"The people live economically, and the merchants are pushing sales of goods at such low prices into the surrounding States, that country merchants do not come further east to buy. It is cheerful, to say the least, to look away from some eastern cities to this bright spot in the west."

While this is in a measure true, yet I do not look for any full realisation until the great questions of the finances of the country are settled upon some sound basis by an increase of the redemption money of the country, and the remonetisation of silver upon a basis that shall be agreed to by the leading commercial countries of the world.

St. Louis is making a good financial showing, mainly from its conservatism and economy. Few new industries are being organised, and the old ones are retrenching and cutting off all experimental expenditures.

The Shoe Trade.

Shoes and boots.

During 1894 a demand for cheap shoes was experienced. The panic of 1893 had closed factories, and driven down wages everywhere to the lowest point. Men were out of work, or earning hardly enough to live on. The result was a widespread call for low-priced footwear. This worked against St. Louis manufactories, as their product was a higher priced commodity. It was therefore necessary to do a heavier business in cases to bring it up to the years 1892 and 1893. This was done, and 1894 actually shows a cash gain over 1893.

During 1894 there were received 783,793 cases from outside points, which varied in size from 12 to 60 pairs, at an average value of 5*l.* per case. This shows 3,918,925*l.* worth received in 1894, against 3,746,090*l.* in 1893, a gain of 172,835*l.* {Receipts.}

Shipments exceeded those of 1893.

The product of the factories for 1894 was estimated at 5,250,000 pairs of all kinds. The average price of this output was lower in 1894 than in previous years, which was from 7*s.* 6*d.* to 7*s.* 9*d.*, down to 6*s.* 7½*d.*; and the output represented a value of 1,732,500*l.* of manufactured goods. This is a gain of 22,500*l.* over the output of 1893, but was below that of 1892, low prices being the main cause of shrinkage. {Product of factories.}

The shipments from Boston, the leading shoe market, to the following large cities was as follows:— {St. Louis second only to Boston.}

City.	Quantity.
	Cases.
St. Louis	609,469
Chicago	461,680
New York	289,277
Baltimore	177,267
Philadelphia	156,567
Cincinnati	114,418

These figures place St. Louis next to Boston as the distributing centre of boots and shoes in the United States.

Groceries.

The year 1894 showed a marked increase in volume of sales in St. Louis over 1893, although many commodities have been very low in price, viz., sugar reached the lowest price ever known in the history of the trade; canned goods, particularly Californian fruits, were more than 25 per cent. less than in 1893. {Groceries.}

The "Interstate Grocer" estimates the increased volume to have been a net average of 7 per cent. over 1893, and during the year there was not a single failure of a wholesale grocery in St. Louis. {No failures.}

The passage of the increased sugar tariff of 40 per cent. was expected to increase the cost of sugar, but owing to the large crop and purchases prior to the date the tariff took effect, buyers loaded themselves up with an invisible supply, the result being great demoralisation in prices, carrying the price lower even {Sugar.}

than before; it being the evident intention of refiners, even at a loss to themselves, to prevent foreign refined sugars from gaining a foothold by lowering the price.

The average price of raw centrifugals from January 1, 1894, to August 31, 1894, was ·0308 c. per lb., and of granulated for the same time ·0408 c. per lb., leaving a difference of 1 c. per lb. for refining. From September 1 to December 31, 1894, the average of raw sugar was ·0354 c. per lb. and granulated ·0418 c. per lb., a difference for refining of only ·0064 c. per lb. The average difference in 1893 between raw and refined being ·0116 c. per lb. The heavy beet sugar crop in Europe caused the great depression in the last 4 months of 1894, and indications seem to point to continued low prices for sugar.

Coffee. The receipts of coffee in 1894 was 246,612 bags, and shipments 309,497 bags. The disparity between the receipts and shipments is accounted for by the receipts being all green coffees about 132 lbs. to the bag, while the shipments are of roasted coffee weighing from 50 to 100 lbs. per bag. During 1894 the demand has greatly increased for roasted coffees, the change from green to roasted being attributed to the inferiority of Brazilian coffees.

The market during the year has been steady, the total decline during the year being 3 c. per lb.

Rice. The receipts of rice were 65,576 barrels in 1894, and 87,959 barrels in 1893, a decrease of 22,383 barrels; the shipments were 70,254 barrels in 1894 and 66,335 barrels in 1893, an increase of 3,919 barrels, being made out of surplus stock of 1893. Many sections in the rice-growing regions report the new crop short. The demand is fully up to the supply warranting better prices in 1895.

Tea. The sales for 1894 have been heavier than usual, and prices have ruled firm. Certain grades of China green tea remained high. Charges were made that St. Louis was sending out adulterated teas, but custom-house inspection of the tea houses failed to find a single package of adulterated teas.

Furniture.

Furniture. The year has not been one of marked prosperity. The spring trade was spasmodic. The large crops of the south-west were marketed at very low prices, causing a diminution in trade which under former prices would have been maintained. The year's business is estimated at 3,000,000*l.*, the manufactured product being about 950,000*l.*

Chairs. There have been additions to the productive facilities, especially in the chair line. One large factory that was idle for several years has resumed work upon a large scale. The street car furniture industry, which was in its infancy a year ago, increased materially in 1894, and steam car seats are shipped from here to all parts of the world. There are seventy firms engaged in the furniture business. No local strikes of any importance have occurred, the 3,500 employés having been kept at work steadily the year through, though a reduction in wages has been made, but the wages are not reduced in proportion to the reduced prices obtainable.

Birch is being largely used as one of the popular woods, mahogany, cherry, and sycamore are greatly in demand, while walnut is mostly used for export business to Mexico and other foreign markets. Inquiries for opening trade relations have been received from Turkey, the Philippian Islands, Cuba, Argentine Confederation, Brazil, Honduras and Columbia. *Materials.*

In hardware the volume of business has been maintained in comparison with 1893, while prices are generally lower. The hardware business has been extended from the eastern boundaries of Indiana, taking in the Gulf States and those west of the Mississippi river, to the Pacific coast extending through Minnesota to the Dominion line. *Hardware.*

The value of the business is placed at 2,900,000*l.*, approximately near that of 1893, but in volume is 15 per cent. larger, the difference in prices averaging about the difference in volume.

The bicycle industry has more than doubled, representing now nearly 200,000*l.*

A careful estimate of sales of cooking stoves, heaters, and ranges, aggregates 225,000*l.*, a reduction of about 22 per cent. from last year, while the business of the entire country shows a falling off of about 30 per cent. *Stoves.*

There has been an increased output of steel ranges for which the outlook continues favourable. Furnaces show increased sales in 1894, 1,200 being reported in 1893 and 1,400 in 1894. *Ranges.*

More farm machinery and implements were sold in 1894 than in 1893; some estimate the increase at 45 per cent., the total sales aggregating 2,900,000*l.* for the year just closed. There has been a large increase in the sale of vehicles (about 2,000,000*l.*), as compared with 1,400,000*l.* in 1893—an increase of 30 per cent. *Farm implements.*

St. Louis holds an important position in the varied appliances of electrical work. *Electric industries.*

The arc lighting of St. Louis is done by four companies, who operate about 4,500 lights of a nominal capacity of 2,000 candles each.

The incandescent lighting is done by three companies, which have about 175,000 lights.

The electrical equipment of these several stations aggregate 20,000 horse-power. The service extends over the entire city, and into the suburbs. The business has suffered somewhat from the business depression of 1894, but the growth has by no means ceased. The year 1895 promises extensive enlargements in plants and distribution system. The most important advancement to be expected in the immediate future is the placing of the major part of the wiring underground within the next 12 months.

The distribution of electricity for power purposes is done by three companies, who aggregate about 4,000-horse power *Power.*

Railways.

throughout the city. It has replaced steam in hundreds of small manufactories and elevator service in tall buildings. It is in connection with street railways that it has accomplished its greatest work. There are nine companies, capitalised at about 3,400,000*l.*, operating 275 miles of single track, running 500 motor cars, with 20,000 horse-power of electrical equipment, and 600 trailers. There are eight power-houses, with a total electrical equipment of about 23,000 horse-power. These lines carried 65,000,000 passengers in 1894, a gain of about 8 per cent. over 1893.

There has been added during the year steam and electrical apparatus of 8,500 horse-power, valued at 160,000*l.*, and have built 33 miles of single track.

The electrical railways employ about 4,000 men regularly.

In electrical manufactories St. Louis has always been a centre of carbon industry. The manufacture of incandescent lamps has grown to be important. Recently the manufacture of alternating current motors, fans, and converters, has been taken up, and is being actively pushed.

Five large supply houses furnish electrical material and equipment. The capital invested is about 25,000*l.*, and the business aggregated about 100,000*l.* in 1894.

Other interests allied to electricity also rank high. Four large street car manufactories are now in full operation, the greater part of the product going to electric railways.

The Iron Trade.

Iron.

Prices have declined almost steadily from the opening to the close of the year for iron and steel.

No. 1 foundry pig-iron declined in price from 2*l.* 9*s.* per ton at the opening to 2*l.* 2*s.* at the close of 1894. No. 2 shows a decline of 6*s.* per ton, and No. 3 foundry a decline of 5*s.* per ton, and grey forge iron at 4*s.* per ton. The consumption of pig-iron has shown an increase of 10 per cent. over 1893, and the situation is brighter than the general conditions would seem to indicate. Common bar-iron has declined materially. Railway supplies are lower than ever before. Splice bars, 1*l.* 12*s.* per ton lower; spikes, 1*l.* 4*s.* per ton lower; links and pins, 1*l.* 8*s.* per ton lower.

Cotton.

Cotton.

The cotton business for the year ending August 31, 1894, shows a marked increase over 1893, although less than 1892, the gross receipts being 625,421 bales, of which 462,032 bales were through shipments, and 163,389 bales local receipts, but this does not indicate the business done by St. Louis factors and buyers, for the reason that a portion of the through shipments were billed directly through for St. Louis account to the seaboard or to Europe, to obtain favourable freight rates.

The question of erecting a large cotton mill in St. Louis is receiving much attention. The advantages in saving transportation in receipts of raw material and distribution of manufactured product is apparent.

Shipments for export to England, 171,205 bales; Germany, 5,907 bales; France, 603 bales; Belgium, 924 bales; Holland, 100 bales; Canada, 28,944 bales; Eastern States for consumption, 401,223 bales.

Tobacco.

The conditions of the market for leaf tobacco were not materially changed in 1894. The estimated crop of burley was 4,000 hogsheads.

The receipts of leaf tobacco were in 1894 43,294 hogsheads and the shipments were 4,226 hogsheads.

St. Louis still holds the first place in the manufacture of tobacco among all the cities of the United States.

The total manufacture for the whole country for the year ending January, 1895, was 235,451,805 lbs., St. Louis output being 53,318,136 lbs.

Live Stock.

In common with most other markets, cattle receipts were less in 1894. The Texas and Indian territory cattle furnish the larger part of the business.

The best prices for fed cattle in January, 1894, was 17s. per 100 lbs. In June the prices ranged from 14s. to 17s. per 100 lbs., the prices obtainable in December.

During the grass season prices ranged from 8s. to 12s., th grass steers selling at 10s. to 12s. per 100 lbs.

During 1894 the hog trade was satisfactory, receipts increase 384,748 head, and sales were comparatively higher than othe classes of stock, prices ranging from 1l. per 100 lbs. in Januar to 1l. 6s. 6d. in September, the highest price during the year.

The receipts of sheep were less in 1894 than in 1893. The prices averaged low, the bulk selling for 9s. 7d. to 12s., in April 16s. to 1l. 3s. was obtained.

Rates of Freight.

From St. Louis by river to New Orleans and steamship Liverpool was 11·60 c. (about 6d.).

From St. Louis by railway from New York and steamship to Liverpool was 18·71 c. (about 9½d.).

24. UNITED STATES.

RETURN of Foreign Shipments of Flour and Grain on through Bills of Lading from St. Louis during the Year 1894, by Rail.

Destination.	Quantity.			
	Flour.	Wheat.	Corn.	Oats.
	Barrels.	Bushels.	Bushels.	Bushels.
England	194,478	177,280	792,769	..
Scotland	108,535	..	..	..
Ireland	66,900	..	..	..
Wales	140	..	..	..
Nova Scotia	600	..	..	..
Newfoundland	19,670	..	..	..
Canada	1,890	..	2,532	..
Germany	4,909	..	..	..
Finland	315	..	..	..
West Indies	125	..	..	..
Denmark	2,016	..	..	..
Norway	46,395	..	..	..
Holland	12,039	421	..	1,570
Belgium	23,981	..	440	..
Spain	350	..	..	..
Cuba	129,991	..	430,385	33,092
Sweden	2,145	..	..	..
Central America	7,760	..	..	..
South America	5,923	..	..	..
Porto Rico	1,154	..	..	..
Seaboard for export	13,108	229,496	715,470	..
Total, by rail	634,682	407,197	1,942,596	34,662
„ river	..	1,042,197	1,236,310	40,000
Grand total	634,682	1,449,394	3,178,906	74,662

Municipal Affairs.

Municipal affairs. The balance in the Treasury at the close of the fiscal year was 433,977*l.*, deducting the liabilities chargeable against this amount, there remains unappropriated 52,249*l.* 10*s.*

Bonded debt. The bonded debt at the close of the fiscal year was 4,239,942*l.* showing a reduction of 35,861*l.* 18*s.* Of the bonds maturing during the year 286,000*l.*, 35,861*l.* 18*s.* was redeemed at maturity out of the sinking fund and 250,000*l.* out of proceeds of the sale of new bonds, being 4 per cent. 20 years renewal, sterling bonds, taken by public subscription in London to the amount of 257,000*l.* by Messrs. Coates, Son and Co., of London, principal and interest payable at the National Bank of Scotland, Limited, London.

Bonds maturing. The bonds maturing during the current fiscal year amount to 434,000*l.*, of this amount 400,000*l.* will be provided for by renewal bonds and 34,500*l.* will be redeemed out of revenue of sinking fund.

The estimated resources of the sinking fund for the current year are 43,000*l.*, of which amount 34,500*l.* will be required to meet maturing bonds.

CHICAGO.

The assessed value of taxable property for 1894 amounts to 62,068,370*l.* an increase of 5,216,212*l.* over the preceding year.

The rates of taxation for city purposes for 1894 remains the same as 1893, viz.:—

Taxation.

Old Limits City Tax.	State.	School.	Per Cent.
1·40	0·25	0·40	2·05
New Limits.			
1·00	0·25	0·42	1·67

The population of the city in 1893 was by directory estimate 574,569, and by the same rule in 1894, 596,157.

Population.

The value of new buildings erected in 1894 was:—

New buildings.

	Value.
	£
New brick buildings	2,178,340
,, frame ,,	90,740
Additions	99,860
Total	2,368,940

The total alarms of fire during 1894 were 1,513, an increase of 78 over 1893. The business in 1894 was considered prosperous in net results, the companies generally making money in 1894, while the losses and expenses in 1893 exceeded the premiums of that year.

Fires.

The losses paid by the companies in 1894 amounted to 238,821*l.* 4*s.*, the amount of insurance involved was 841,217*l.* 1*s.* or 28·38 per cent. of loss to insurance involved.

The most notable event was the completion of the New Union Railway Station, which was formally opened to the public September 1, 1894. It is not only in point of size the largest in the world, but in all its appointments abreast of the times, with equipments the most modern and complete in all respects. The station proper with the connecting train sheds covers an area of 11 acres.

Terminal railway improvements.

30 tracks with a total length of nearly 4 miles are under roof.

Union station.

	Dimensions.
	Square Feet.
The grand waiting room	8,806
Ladies' waiting room, main floor	9,362
Gentlemen's waiting room, main floor	5,187
Dining room, main floor	4,800
General concourse, track floor	8,791
Carriage ,, ,,	6,716
Emigrants' waiting room, track floor	3,132
Lunch room, track floor	3,725
Main track floor	2,904

UNITED STATES.

The "Railway Age" gives the dimensions of train sheds of the largest stations in the world, as follows:—

Comparison with Largest Stations in the World.

	Width.	Length.	Number of Tracks.	Number of Companies.
	Feet.	Feet.		
St. Louis, United States	600	630	30	21
Frankfort-on-the-Main	552	600	18	..
Boston, United States..	460	500	23	2
Philadelphia, Pennsylvania Railway	300	647	16	1
Philadelphia and Reading	200	800	14	1
Jersey City, Pennsylvania Railway	256	653	12	1
Grand Central, New York..	200	..	..	..
Grand Central, Chicago	150	600	6	4

The terminal freight and passenger station in the northern part of the city was opened March 4, 1894, the companies' new bridge across the Missouri River, a few miles north of the city, affords a connection between this line and the St. Louis, Keokuk and North-Western Railway being now completed. The Missouri, Kansas, and Texas Railway occupies a portion of these terminal facilities, completing its independant line from Texas to St. Louis.

Coal. The receipts of bituminous coal decreased during 1894, the receipts were 74,644,375 bushels, and in 1893 they were 88,143,851 bushels. There was 186,494 tons of anthracite coal received in 1894 and 173,653 tons in 1893.

The receipts of coke were 6,365,900 bushels of 40 lbs. in 1894 and 7,807,000 bushels in 1893.

State finances

Financial Statement of Missouri.

	Amount.
	£
The total assessed valuation of real and personal property for 1894 was ..	184,859,210
Railway, bridge, and telegraph	14,058,747
Total	198,917,957

The rate of taxation for State purposes was ¼ of 1 per cent.

CHICAGO.

	Amount.
	£
The balance in the Treasury, January 1, 1894	89,462
Receipts for 1894	711,084
Total	800,546
Amount disbursed during 1894	656,599
Balance in Treasury, December 31, 1894	143,947

The coal mined in the State during 1894 was 2,383,332 tons from 365 mines, the average value was about 5s. 6d. per ton. The number of tons mined in 1893 was 3,190,440 tons at an average value of 5s. per ton, an excess of 807,110 tons mined in 1893 over 1894.

The lead ore product in 1894 was 52,003 tons against 49,626 tons in 1893.

The zinc ore product was 89,150 tons in 1894, against 131,487 tons in 1893.

Value of lead product in 1894 was 389,913*l*., zinc product 267,582*l*.

The number of men employed in the coal mines in 1894 was 7,643, and in lead and zinc mines 5,065.

The surplus products of the State marketed in 1894 have not been published, if collated, and it is impossible to give them as I would like to do.

UNITED STATES.

COMPARATIVE Business in Leading Articles at St. Louis for the Years 1893 and 1894.

Articles.		1893.	1894.
Flour, amount, manufactured	Barrels	1,669,048	1,261,309
,, handled	,,	4,733,838	4,717,954
Wheat, total receipts	Bushels	14,442,999	10,003,242
Corn ,,	,,	33,809,405	23,546,945
Oats ,,	,,	10,056,225	10,196,605
Rye ,,	,,	583,799	140,285
Barley ,,	,,	1,986,746	2,083,438
All grain received (including flour reduced to wheat)	,,	66,348,786	51,646,405
Cotton, receipts	Bales	638,400	812,705
Bagging, manufactured	Yards	12,000,000	13,000,000
Hay, receipts	Tons	141,238	159,969
Tobacco, receipts	Hogsheads	39,587	43,264
Lead, receipts	In 80-lb. pigs	1,348,544	1,463,229
Hog product, total shipments	Lbs.	285,323,741	345,481,499
Cattle, receipts	Head	903,257	773,571
Sheep ,,	,,	397,725	359,895
Hogs ,,	,,	1,105,108	1,489,856
Horses and mules, receipts	,,	46,834	59,832
Lumber and logs ,,	Feet	855,297,730	730,174,856
Shingles	Pieces	148,589,900	106.782,000
Lath	,,	27,621,750	31,354,350
Wool, total receipts	Lbs.	15,024,436	24,861,455
Hides ,,	,,	45,011,866	46,456,970
Sugar, received	,,	273,331,736	198,869,450
Molasses (including glucose)	Gallons	4,274,080	5,765,901
Coffee, received	Bags	248,347	246,612
Rice, receipts	Packages	87,959	66,576
Coal ,,	Bushels	87,769,375	74,644,375
Nails ,,	Kegs	415,416	522,673
Potatoes, receipts	Bushels	1,644,314	1,392,522
Salt, receipts	Barrels	241,189	248,830
,,	Sacks	80,198	60,737
,,	Bushels in bulk	364,020	620,500
Butter	Lbs.	12,575,298	14,138,544
Tons of freight of all kinds received and shipped		16,519,881	15,239,765

CHICAGO.

Custom-house Transactions for 1894.—Condensed Classification Imported into St. Louis during the Year 1894, showing Value and Duty Paid.

Commodities.	Value.	Duty.
	£ s.	£ s.
Ale and stout	4,979 12	1,585 0
Anvils	2,677 0	899 17
Art works	330 12	55 3
Books and printed matter	618 4	154 12
Bricks and tiles	1,793 16	547 8
Barley	1,976 16	1,242 9
Brushes	1,099 8	414 12
Bone and horn, manufacture of	42 4	10 11
Carpets and carpeting	528 8	216 18
Cement	3,368 8	689 15
Coffee	11 8	0 13
Chemicals and drugs	33,214 12	7,775 13
China and earthenware	28,750 12	11,555 2
Cork and manufacture of cork	8,827 8	2,317 2
Cutlery	12,874 12	7,145 4
Diamonds and precious stones	3,582 12	358 5
Fancy goods	4,057 16	1,612 11
Fish	8,454 0	1,184 3
Free goods	59,862 16	..
Glassware	8,376 8	3,060 15
Guns and firearms	13,043 0	3,681 10
Hops	16,030 4	3,938 10
Jewellery	5,176 8	1,387 19
Lead	2,649 0	1,644 2
Marble	2,121 16	952 18
Manufacture of cotton	40,436 4	21,931 7
,, linen	12,630 8	5,053 16
,, iron	8,177 12	4,306 2
,, leather	1,009 16	268 11
,, metal	9,995 8	4,131 19
,, paper	2,501 12	732 12
,, silk	3,839 16	2,070 15
,, wood	2,264 0	670 17
,, wool	5,757 12	4,898 4
Musical instruments	1,626 16	161 3
Nuts and fruits	1,284 4	327 12
Oil	314 4	93 3
Paints and colours	2,096 12	475 16
Rice	22,991 4	4,258 12
Seeds	559 8	70 12
Steel wire	22,581 0	11,000 18
Tin-plate and turn-plate	7,186 8	1,491 7
Tobacco, cigars, &c.	32,016 12	37,324 10
Vegetables	7,633 0	2,080 14
Wines, sparkling, &c.	19,451 4	10,788 19
Window glass	21,614 16	5,771 7
Woollen dress goods	1,010 12	876 18
Spirituous liquors	2,639 0	3,361 19
Skins, dressed	1,125 8	225 2
Miscellaneous merchandise	2,573 8	858 19
Collections from all other sources	..	20,951 1
Total	455,960 16	196,601 14

UNITED STATES.

TRANSACTIONS at the Custom-house for 1894.—Merchandise brought to St. Louis in Bond from following Ports of Entry, showing Foreign Value and Duties.

Ports.	Value.	Duty.
	£ s.	£ s.
Baltimore	42,082 16	13,887 7
Boston	8,572 12	2,828 19
Detroit	589 4	194 9
Montreal	231 16	76 10
New York	197,604 4	65,209 7
Newport News	81,228 12	26,807 9
New Orleans	25,402 0	8,383 13
Philadelphia	72,843 8	49,220 18
Port Huron	5,037 8	1,212 7
Portal, N.D.	837 4	276 10
San Francisco	13,811 8	4,557 15
Tacoma	2,500 8	825 0
Direct to St. Louis	6,218 0	2,052 7
Total	456,959 0	175,532 11
In warehouse December 31, 1894	33,087 8	37,385 2

COMPARATIVE Statement of Receipts at the St. Louis Post Office during the Years 1893 and 1894.

	Value. 1894.	Value. 1893.	Increase or Decrease.
	£ s.	£ s.	£ s.
Postage stamps	297,259 16	285,195 4	+ 12,064 12
Rents, &c.	601 10	704 14	− 103 4
Total	297,861 6	285,899 18	11,961 8

RETURN of Mail Matter, in Pounds, passing Post Office during the Years 1894 and 1893.

	Quantity. 1694.	Quantity. 1893.	Increase or Decrease.
	Pieces.	Pieces.	Pieces.
Originating in St. Louis	22,079,871	18,665,551	+ 3,414,320
Received from other post offices	198,250	288,800	− 90,550
Total	22,278,121	18,954,351	2,463,770
" number of pieces handled	129,101,364	117,746,776	11,354,588

CHICAGO.

UNITED STATES Internal Revenue collected in St. Louis in the Year 1894 compared with 1893.

Description.	Amount. 1893.	Amount. 1894.
	£ s.	£ s.
Lists (penalties, &c.)	3,814 1	1,142 13
Spirit stamps	401,108 3	400,824 18
Tobacco stamps	605,587 15	685,169 7
Cigar stamps	32,292 5	30,969 5
Snuff „	329 12	321 14
Beer „	383,293 6	364,160 0
Special tax	33,934 19	29,669 17
Playing cards	..	1,386 2
Total	1,460,360 1	1,513,643 16
Increase in 1894, all in tobacco	..	53,283 15

CLEARING-HOUSE Statements of Banks.—Comparative Statements for the Years 1893 and 1894.

Month.	Clearings. 1893.	Clearings. 1894.	Balances. 1893.	Balances. 1894.
	£	£	£	£
January	22,944,363	21,054,947	2,844,312	3,660,847
February	18,703,938	16,604,807	2,284,239	2,461,316
March	21,674,394	18,250,272	2,341,532	2,184,914
April	21,552,215	17,719,718	2,855,788	2,194,030
May	21,830,253	19,599,106	2,485,967	3,243,156
June	19,164,246	18,256,391	2,181,523	3,013,185
July	16,519,286	17,506,129	1,709,140	2,434,760
August	13,748,315	18,033,712	1,502,341	3,186,475
September	15,087,541	17,651,205	1,996,133	2,918,117
October	17,287,930	20,226,092	2,108,328	2,781,596
November	19,234,892	19,824,433	2,952,162	2,534,990
December	20,154,975	20,813,764	2,731,258	3,147,763
Total	227,905,348	225,540,576	27,992,723	33,791,149
Decrease	..	2,364,772	..	..
Increase	..	..	..	5,798,426

ST. PAUL.

Mr. Vice-Consul Morphy reports as follows:—

During the past 7 years St. Paul has developed from an overgrown village into a well-built city.

The nebulous and ill-balanced conditions of the boom of 1887 and 1888 have been solved into a solid body.

The development of St. Paul.

Since 1887 prices of all kinds, and notably prices in real estate have declined. But while the decline in prices of real estate has been going on, essential values have steadily increased, and St. Paul has grown into a fine substantial city.

The railroads centering here have been extended and thousands of square miles of new tributary opened up for settlement. Rapid transit within the city has been supplied and close communication established with Minneapolis, the system of electric street railways of St. Paul and Minneapolis, commonly known as "the Twin Cities." being the most perfect and best equipped in the country.

But if not the greatest, the most evident and visible change that has come upon St. Paul since 1887 is in the character of the buildings. Street after street has been built up with lofty handsome business blocks of modern construction, ranging in cost from 150,000 to 850,000 dol. Scattered over the city, outside the business district, which is now spread out half-a-mile beyond the limits of 1887, are new apartment blocks of splendid construction, with all the modern appliances, and all well filled with tenants. The new Court House has been completed, two splendid new theatres have been built, and a score of new school buildings have been erected. Many handsome new church buildings have gone up and handsome residences by the score and hundred have been built on all the beautiful avenues.

All streets are well graded, and wherever the amount of travel makes it necessary, excellent paving has been done, the tendency being to lay asphalte on all streets where there is no heavy draying.

Parks have been improved and developed, tree-planting and boulevarding has been done on an extensive scale, adding greatly to the improvement of the city.

Railroads centering in St. Paul. Centering in St. Paul are the terminals of many railroads which span the continent from the Atlantic to the Pacific. Running eastward, the great "Soo" line (Minneapolis, St. Paul, and Sault Ste. Marie Railway) stretches to the Sault Ste. Marie, in whose locks the whole shipping trade of the upper lakes is condensed; thence into Canada to the principal cities of the Dominion, and then once more entering the United States, running on to Boston and connecting with the Atlantic steamers.

The railroads running to the large cities lying to the east and south-east of St. Paul are the Chicago, St. Paul, Minneapolis, and Omaha Railway, which, by its connections with the Union Pacific gives St. Paul a fourth trans-continental route, the Chicago, Milwaukee, and St. Paul Railway; the Burlington, Cedar Rapids, and Northern Railway; the Chicago Great Western Railway; the Wisconsin Central Railway, and the Minneapolis and St. Louis Railway, all of which have their branches in the agricultural sections of Minnesota and some in the Dakotas, and afford ample connections with eastern and southern lines.

The roads to the head of Lake Superior. Running to the north to the head of the great lakes are 3 lines of road. The Omaha, on its way east, passes through

Duluth and West Superior; the St. Paul and Duluth Railway, and the Eastern Minnesota Railway, this latter being a branch of the Great Northern Railway.

These 3 lines give St. Paul easy access to Lake Superior, bridging the 150 miles of intervening territory in 5 hours, and placing merchants of St. Paul in such a commanding commercial position that they can bring their goods from the factories of the east, or from Europe, and lay them down in this city at less cost for freight and shipment than can Chicago, St. Paul's once overbearing competitor. These roads also place St. Paul in direct and rapid communication with the immense iron ranges of the Mesaba and Vermillion district and the other rich mineral deposits in the north-eastern section of Minnesota. They also penetrate the vast pineries and lumber regions of that district.

Trans-continental roads. To the west the country between St. Paul and the Pacific Ocean is traversed by the Northern Pacific and the Great Northern railroads. These railroads pass through the great agricultural fields of Minnesota and the two Dakotas, through the State of Montana with its great mining and ranching industries, through the State of Washington, with its wonderful fruit-raising capacity, its mineral wealth, its immense forests and fine cattle ranges, to Puget Sound, where the railroads connect with the lines of steamships plying between China, Japan, and Australasian ports, and the ports of Oregon and California. The products of the Orient are carried over these 2 railroads in vast quantities. Each road has many branches stretching north and south touching Idaho, Northern Oregon, and the British possessions. Both roads have direct lines between St. Paul and Winnipeg, Manitoba, where they connect with the Canadian Pacific, affording another trans-continental route.

The "Soo" road also has a direct line running to a point on the Canadian Pacific Railway several hundred miles west of Winnipeg, affording the most direct and shortest route between St. Paul and Vancouver, British Columbia, viâ the Canadian Pacific Railway.

St. Paul the link between the east and west, north and south. St. Paul is the connecting link between the east and the west, the north and the south.

400 miles north of St. Paul is the international boundary line, and 700 miles north of that extend the British possessions, which are rapidly becoming settled.

St. Paul does not stand at the edge of the great north-west, but with 1,100 miles of territory to the north, and 2,000 miles to the west, she holds the key.

Collection of imports. The total collections on imports in this district for 1888 amounted to 206,248 dol. 96 c., while last year they were 247,950 dol. 75 c., being an increase of 41,701 dol. 79 c. This increase signifies little, for 2 years ago the collections amounted to about 500,000 dol., which shows that collections are decreasing. So it is with internal revenue collected, as the following figures will show:—In 1889 there was collected 2,804,859 dol. 28 c.; 1890, 2,704,553 dol. 77 c.; 1891, 2,680,237 dol. 90 c.; 1892,

(1965)

2,634,781 dol. 42 c.; 1893, 2,336,279 dol. 56 c.; 1894, approximated, 2,129,000 dol. These fallings-off are due to decreased values, more home manufacturing, and less extravagant living. The decrease is proportionately distributed among all lines of imports and articles subject to duty, to the latter of which was added, last fall, playing cards.

Comparison of valuations from 1882 to 1894.

Comparison of valuations, City of St. Paul, 1882-94. Also comparisons of values in business district same year:—

	1882.	
	City of St. Paul.	Business District.
	Dollars.	Dollars.
Real estate	20,451,156	6,397,715
Improvements	7,234,475	2,615,400
Exempt	2,718,485	1,013,060
Total	30,404,116	10,026,175

	1888.	
	City of St. Paul.	Business District.
	Dollars.	Dollars.
Real estate	80,562,750	24,948,574
Improvements	18,828,205	8,026,580
Exempt	7,112,240	3,767,640
Total	106,503,195	36,742,794

	1894.	
	City of St. Paul.	Business District.
	Dollars.	Dollars.
Real estate	83,544,669	26,810,665
Improvements	25,597,430	9,682,900
Exempt	9,952,762	4,584,000
Total	119,094,861	41,077,565

State of the banks of St. Paul.

The state of the St. Paul banks at the close of 1894 is a matter of congratulation. The capital stock has been increased since 1883 by 3,300,000 dol., and the deposits by about 8,000,000 dol. The loans and discounts show a large increase up to 1887, and in 1893-94 there is a considerable shrinkage, owing to the contraction of credit and the financial stringency. The following totals for the State and national banks of the city give an idea of their condition for the periods ending 1883, 1887, and 1894:—

	Amount.		
	1883.	1887.	1894.
	Dollars.	Dollars.	Dollars.
Capital stock	5,200,000	7,125,000	8,527,615
Deposits	8,990,002	14,416,274	16,660,378
Loans and discounts	13,383,187	20,835,124	14,794,374

The bank clearances for 1894 were 183,856,875 dol. 90 c. *Bank clearances for 1894.*
Of course this city, Minneapolis and Duluth, the other principal cities of this State, have suffered greatly during the past year from the effects of the awful panic of 1893.

I am pleased to report a general revival of business in all branches, and to report a renewal of confidence. Liquidation is about over, and business will be on a firm basis hereafter. This western country has great recuperative powers. The outlook is bright, and there is every indication we will have an excellent crop. *A general revival of business and a renewal of confidence.*

The biennial session of the State Legislature has been held here for the past few weeks, and will close in a short time. No Acts of any great importance have been introduced. There is at present a measure pending before the House which has passed the Senate, providing that in case of the death intestate of foreigners residing here and leaving property, and the widow or next-of-kin being unsuitable or neglecting for 30 days thereafter to apply for administration, or to request administration be granted to some other person, the same may be granted to the Consul or other representative of the kingdom or country of which the deceased was a native. *Minnesota legislature. Act respecting estates of foreigners dying intestate.*

This Act was introduced at the instance of the several Vice-Consuls residing here, and in order to prevent injustice to the next-of-kin of intestates residing abroad. There is no serious opposition to the Act, and I am assured by the honourable member in whose charge it is that the measure will become law.

DENVER.

Mr. Vice-Consul Pearce reports as follows:—

That the City of Denver and the State of Colorado has not been exempt from the effects of the general depression which has prevailed throughout the whole country during the year 1894 will be apparent from the following report, which I have the honour to submit:—

(1965)

UNITED STATES.

Value of new buildings.
The number of building permits issued by the building inspector of the city for 1894 was 539, the valuation being 152,596*l.*; this shows a decrease of 479 in permits and 447,404*l.* in valuation. The building operations were confined principally to the residence portions of the city.

Real estate.
The transactions in real estate for the year were 2,942,016*l.*, showing a decrease of 3,485,387*l.* from the transactions of the previous year.

Recorded mortgages.
There were 535 mortgages recorded with the clerk of Arapahoe County, in which Denver is situated, with a total value of 2,090,071*l.*, an increase of 613,554*l.* over 1893. The average rate of interest was 7½ per cent.

Loans.
3,447 loans were made on landed and other properties in Denver and Arapahoe County during the year, the total amount loaned being 1,404,432*l.*, a decrease from 1893 of 2,549,238*l.* The rates of interest ranged from 5 to 12 per cent.

Clearing house.
The records of the clearing house for the year show a total of 27,362,104*l.*, a decrease of 9,770,800*l.* from 1893.

Banks.
During the year four of the national banks were consolidated into two, and Denver has now seven national banks. The condition of these banks at the close of the year is shown as follows:—

	Amount.
	£
Total resources	4,769,008
„ loans and discounts	2,657,709
„ capital and surplus	1,256,665
„ deposits	3,510,280

Manufacturing.
The value of the manufactured products of the city of Denver shows a falling-off for the year of 2,262,891*l.*

CHICAGO.

TABLE showing Status of the Industrial Trades.

Description.	Number of Employés.	Wages.	Product.
		£	£
Awnings and tents	40	4,000	30,000
Breweries	280	53,000	270,000
Brooms	65	6,000	20,000
Boilers	50	6,500	31,000
Boxes	34	2,700	6,800
Bicycles	6	800	1,700
Confectionery	100	6,800	25,000
Cotton mills	300	18,000	90,000
Cigars	160	20,000	53,000
Clay products	255	21,800	92,500
Chemicals	17	2,300	12,000
Crackers	80	10,000	70,000
Canning	600	18,400	40,000
Electric supplies	72	7,200	20,000
„ lighting	150	27,000	..
Engraving	15	2,160	4,000
Flour	90	8,300	74,000
Flowers	250	22,000	70,000
Hardware	80	8,320	22,000
Ice	100	8,000	22,500
Lapidaries	16	2,500	8,000
Lead and paints	42	6,000	66,000
Machinery	325	64,000	125,000
Maccaroni	7	500	2,000
Overalls	40	2,600	8,000
Photographic supplies and views	27	4,120	30,000
Plumbers' supplies	100	8,400	46,000
Paper manufacture	200	34,000	98,000
Printing and binding	350	34,000	70,000
Packing houses	160	22,000	590,000
Railroads	1,800	247,000	..
Spice	16	2,000	22,000
Soap	60	7,500	70,000
Stained glass	15	1,900	5,600
Steam laundries	215	21,600	..
Smelters	1,100	165,212	3,598,052
Sheet iron and stamping	154	18,000	83,000
Shirts	75	6,300	15,000
Street railroads	750	107,600	..
Stone and marble	187	38,000	80,000
Saddlery	50	9,400	32,000
Tannery	23	3,100	18,000
Trunks	23	3,700	9,550
Taxidermists	6	800	..
Upholstery	24	3,600	21,000
Wagons	60	7,600	45,000
Total	8,569	1,074,712	5,996,702

During the year the Department of Public Works of the city expended the sum of 159,000*l.* in street paving and sewer construction, and Denver has now 14 miles of paved streets and 173 miles of sewers. *Paving and sewers.*

The records of the Health Department of the city show the *Health.*

death rate in the city for the past nine years to have been as follows:—

Year.	Estimated Population.	Total Deaths.	Rate per 1,000.
1886	73,000	1,119	15·33
1887	80,000	1,525	19·06
1888	85,000	1,729	20·34
1889	96,000	1,808	18·83
1890	106,713	2,530	23·71
1891	113,874	2,118	18·51
1892	120,000	1,713	14·48
1893	125,000	1,578	12·70
1894	140,000	1,663	11·88

Value of taxable property. The total valuation of assessed property in the States for 1894 was 41,781,056*l.*, showing a decrease of 5,953,024*l.* from 1893.

According to returns from the county assessors for the year, there are 9,000,617 acres of grazing lands, valued at 2,207,360*l.*; 3,900,454 acres of agricultural lands, valued at 4,830,157*l.*; 127,305 acres of coal lands, valued at 344,044*l.*

Government lands. Reports received from the 11 land offices in the State go to show that during the year 547,488 acres of Government lands were filed upon and patented; this is a decrease of 198,512 acres from 1893.

Agriculture About 2,000,000 acres of land in Colorado are under cultivation, covered by irrigating ditches. The value of the product from these cultivated lands for 1894 is carefully estimated as follows:—

Articles.		Quantity.	Value.
			£
Wheat	Bushels ..	5,000,000	500,000
Alfalfa	Tons	1,000,000	800,000
Clover and timothy	,, ...	250,000	200,000
Native grass	,, ...	500,000	300,000
Corn, oats, barley, &c... ..	..	..	1,200,000
Vegetables and garden products	..	..	800,000
Potatoes..	Bushels ..	3,600,000	259,200
Fruit	..	..	350,000
Total		..	4,409,200

Live-stock. The estimated number and value of live-stock in Colorado for the year is given by the State Veterinary Surgeon as follows:—

Description.	Number.	Value.
		£
Cattle	900,000	2,160,000
Horses	200,000	800,000
Sheep	1,500,000	600,000
Hogs	60,000	40,000
Mules	10,000	40,000
Total	2,670,000	3,640,000

The market value of live-stock sold from Colorado during the year is estimated at 700,000*l*., the bulk of the shipments going to Kansas City, Omaha, and Chicago.

65 miles of new railroads were constructed in Colorado during the year, making a total of 5,335 miles now in existence. Railroads.

This new railroad construction consists of two short lines connecting the Colorado Midland Railway and the Denver and Rio Grande Railway with the Cripple Creek gold-mining district.

The total assessed valuation of railway property in Colorado for 1894 is 6,047,019*l*.

The output of coal in 1894 was, in a great measure, affected by the strike of the coal miners, which lasted nearly three months. There was a decrease for the year of 927,278 tons, as compared with the production of 1893. The outside demand, on account of the general depression and railroad strikes, was less. Fully 25 per cent. of the product is shipped to neighbouring States and territories, and the prevailing dulness kept the export trade down as well as the home consumption. Coal.

UNITED STATES.

Table showing the Coal Output, by Counties, for the Years 1893 and 1894.

Counties.	Quantity. 1893.	Quantity. 1894.
	Tons of 2,000 lbs.	Tons of 2,000 lbs.
Arapahoe	633	604
Boulder	610,583	335,807
Dolores	1,250	..
El Paso	29,318	64,558
Fremont	468,334	275,033
Gunnison	240,749	190,650
Garfield	195,367	82,226
Huerfano	503,912	414,884
Jefferson	12,348	39,359
Las Animas	1,543,410	1,181,005
La Plata	109,336	92,822
Mesa	20,000	35,990
Montezuma	1,600	..
Park	99,908	97,118
Pitkin	25,500	43,486
Weld	82,433	39,456
Small Mines	3,625	125,000
Total	3,948,306	3,021,028

Table showing Coke Production for the Years 1893–94.

Countries.	Quantity. 1893.	Quantity. 1894.
	Tons of 2,000 lbs.	Tons of 2,000 lbs.
Gunnison	49,955	37,570
Las Animas	232,090	191,762
La Plata	8,000	5,000
Mesa	100	400
Pitkin	56,184	49,213
Total	346,329	283,945

TABLE showing the Output of Coal for the Past 20 Years.

Year.	Quantity.
	Tons of 2,000 lbs.
1875	98,838
1876	117,666
1877	169,000
1878	200,639
1879	322,732
1880	375,000
1881	706,744
1882	1,061,479
1883	1,220,593
1884	1,130,024
1885	1,398,796
1886	1,436,211
1887	1,791,735
1888	2,185,477
1889	2,400,629
1890	3,075,781
1891	3,152.632
1892	3,771,234
1893	3,948.306
1894	3,021,028

Iron industry.

The Colorado Fuel and Iron Company, which mines about all of the iron ore extracted in Colorado, reports a remarkable increase in its iron and steel business during the year. There were 351,873,270 lbs. of iron ore produced in comparison with 168,775,130 lbs. in 1893, and 102,486,400 lbs. in 1892. The net product from the iron ore mined is as follows:—

PIG IRON.

Year.	Quantity.
	Lbs.
1892..	69,957,199
1893..	96,426,539
1894..	158,952,993

The following figures will show the increase in this company's steel rail branch of its business:—

Year.	Quantity.
	Lbs.
1892..	54,621,172
1893..	89,662,068
1894..	149,228,579

Oil.

The output of oil from the Florence wells for the year was about the same as stated in my report for 1893.

42   UNITED STATES.

Mining.   The following is the estimated value of the output from the mines in Colorado for the year 1894:—

Articles.	Value.
	£
Gold	2,123,293
Silver	2,992,248
Lead	653,723
Copper	153,484
Total	5,922,748

Gold increase, 464,287*l.*; silver decrease, 904,683*l.*; lead decrease, 24,025*l.*; copper increase, 50,822*l.*; net decrease, 413,599*l.* The average price of silver for the year was 63 c. per oz., as against 77 c. in 1893.

It will be seen from the above figures, showing the value of the gold and silver produced in the State, that whilst there is a falling-off in the value of the silver there is a large increase in the value of the gold.

This increase in gold is mainly due to the larger output of ore from the mines of Gilpin County, Leadville, and Cripple Creek.

Since the heavy decline in silver, which started in 1893, increased attention has been given to gold mining, which has resulted in a number of new discoveries, which have proved of immense value to the State. The Leadville district, which has been celebrated for its enormous yield of silver and lead ever since its discovery in 1877, has, within the past year, shown a remarkable record as a gold producer, under conditions and in localities where there was formerly no suspicion even of its existence in paying quantities, and it is reasonable to assume from recent developments, that the gold bearing area is very large, and that the output will be considerably increased.

Cripple Creek is now in direct communication with the smelting centres by two distinct lines of railroad, and new discoveries of gold are being made in this new camp. The developments, so far as they have gone, indicate a large gold-producing area, and its future stability as a gold district is now established beyond question. It has been credited with an output of gold during 1894 to the value of nearly 600,000*l.*, and were it not for the prolonged miners' strike which caused a suspension of operations for some months, the yield would have been materially greater.

CHICAGO.

STATEMENT of Values of Imports from Great Britain Entered at the Port of Denver during the Year 1894.

Articles.	Value.
	£ s.
Antiquities and curios	23 8
Tea	329 16
Books and other printed matter	13 0
Carpets	11 12
Earthenware, china, porcelain, &c.	145 12
Leather, manufactures of	26 0
Metals, manufactures of—	
Bedsteads	321 16
Sheep-shears	125 12
Other	193 0
Miscellaneous articles	82 4
Personal effects	112 8
Cotton, manufactures of clothing	2 4
Spirits, distilled—	
Brandy	16 4
Whisky	312 12
Tin-plates and terne-plates	2,934 8
Wines	119 16
Wool, manufactures of—	
Clothing	45 16
Cloths	168 16
Total	4,984 4

RECORD of Imports from Great Britain for the Past 8 Years.

Year.	Value.
	£ s.
1887	5,043 12
1888	8,109 12
1889	17,585 7
1890	32,512 4
1891	26,008 16
1892	9,357 4
1893	6,603 16
1894	4,984 4

KANSAS CITY.

Mr. Vice-Consul Burrough reports as follows :—

The population of Kansas City at its last census was 194,000, and is to-day one of the healthiest cities of North America; one reason being because it is built upon a large number of hills sloping down into the Missouri and Kansas rivers, thus forming a natural sewerage system. The city does not enjoy as good a sewerage system as it demands on account of its rapid growth

UNITED STATES.

and financial depression of real estate in the past few years; but at present an effort is being made to effect a modern sewerage system for the city.

Water. — The water of the city is supplied by waterworks owned by the city, and is taken from the Missouri river, 5 miles above the city, and is pronounced by eminent chemists to be very healthful.

Death rate. — Kansas City is termed one of the healthiest cities on this continent, the death rate for 1894 being 10·59 per 1,000.

Labour. — There has been but little change in the past year in labour, especially for common and mechanical employment; but for clerical work there has been less demand, and in all instances, wages smaller. The outlook for 1895 is better, for great improvements throughout the city are contemplated. During January and February, 1895 more building permits were taken out than during the entire year of 1894.

A short time ago fire destroyed the packing house of Reid Brothers (Main House, Belfast, Ireland), at a loss of about 240,000*l*. The plant is to be rebuilt in 1895, at a cost of about 500,000*l*. New buildings will be erected all over the city, and several packing houses contemplate large additions during the year.

Government buildings. — Work is being pushed at present on the new Government building, which when completed will cost not less than 625,000*l*., and will be used by all Government officials and offices for the district.

Public library building. — There is now being erected here a public library building, which will cost, including the grounds, 45,000*l*., and is under the control of the Board of Education.

Public schools. — Great praise has been given Kansas City for her public school system, which consists of 37 school houses (valued at 327,000*l*.), 342 school-rooms, and 346 teachers; salaries paid in 1894, 54,000*l*.; enrolment, 52,809 pupils.

Live-stock trade. — Live-stock industry in the far west is fast becoming the leading feature. More and more every year we find that the farmer is preparing to fatten and grow more live-stock, for it is far more profitable than selling the grain. It is predicted by many that if the growing European trade continues in cattle, hogs, sheep, horses, mules, and packing house products, it will be but a short time when the bulk of grain for export will be limited from the west; for it can be fed with much more profitable results, and find a much better and satisfactory market. Owing to the drought in some of the western States, which caused early marketing of unripe cattle and hogs, the export will not be as large for 1895 as was first reported; and furthermore, the acreage of range land is becoming more limited every year, which has a tendency also to reduce receipts.

Kansas City stock yards. — I am pleased to report the fast increasing trade of the stock yards, which are the second largest yards in the world.

The Stock Yards Company expended in 1894 330,000*l*. for land and pens, and in 1895 will extend the Exchange Building, making it 190 offices larger at an expense of 15,000*l*.

CHICAGO.

This market is first in the world for handling Texas cattle, first in handling live-stock from all territory west of the Mississippi river, and first in handling feeders and stockers.

The stock yards are located on both sides of the Kansas river, which affords excellent sewerage, and the yards are entered by the entire system of railroads centering in the city. The valuation of stock handled at the yards during 1894 was 22,000,000*l*.; and the total valuation for the past 20 years, 180,000,000*l*. The following statistics will prove valuable to those interested in the live-stock and provision trade.

Official Receipts.

Market.	Cattle and Calves.	Hogs.	Sheep.	Horses and Mules.	Cars.
Kansas City, 1894	1,772,545	2,547,077	589,555	44,237	107,494
„ 1893	1,746,828	1,948,373	565,587	35,097	99,755
Increase, 1894	25,717*	599,704*	20,038*	9,140*	7,739*

* Kansas City had increased in receipts of all classes of live-stock in 1894.

Kansas City Comparative Receipts and Sales, Per Cent. for 1893-94.

Description.	1893. Received.	1893. Sold at Kansas City.	1893. Per Cent. Sold.	1894. Received.	1894. Sold at Kansas City.	1894. Per Cent. Sold.
Cattle	1,660,807	1,539,183	92·67	1,689,193	1,610,338	95·33
Calves	86,021	81,656	94·92	83,352	80,672	96·78
Cattle and Calves	1,746,828	1,620,839	92·78	1,772,545	1,691,010	95·40
Hogs	1,948,373	1,932,772	99·19	2,574,077	2,534,039	99·48
Sheep	569,517	457,675	80·36	589,555	480,967	81·58
Horses and mules	35,097	9,025	25·71	44,237	11,692	26·43
Total	4,299,815	4,020,311	93·49	4,953,414	4,717,708	95·24

UNITED STATES.

United States Department of Agriculture.—Estimate of Animals on Ranches and Farms, January 1, 1895.

	Cattle.	Hogs.	Sheep.	Horses and Mules.
Maine	306,932	79,195	284,435	115,428
New Hampshire	207,593	54,757	106,233	57,308
Vermont	399,977	77,031	226,938	93,877
Massachusetts	261,100	63,256	49,383	65,760
Rhode Island	36,609	13,616	11,279	10,234
Connecticut	211,624	52,172	37,934	43,478
New York	2,259,434	658,605	1,096,560	700,612
New Jersey	241,597	175,515	50,662	93,034
Pennsylvania	1,624,647	1,012,847	1,178,795	683,172
Delaware	60,380	52,167	12,873	35,603
Maryland	261,296	332,019	138,174	149,672
Virginia	668,417	957,037	449,357	292,290
North Carolina	653,528	1,441,763	357,494	249,660
South Carolina	289,439	851,948	78,384	156,709
Georgia	867,260	1,934,892	402,946	268,248
Florida	486,553	376,432	110,627	42,252
Alabama	963,112	1,680,816	326,640	249,336
Mississippi	819,656	1,687,613	390,904	321,680
Louisiana	549,116	838,415	178,745	221,753
Texas	6,881,044	2,734,341	3,738,117	1,457,188
Arkansas	941,810	1,547,689	212,328	359,446
Tennessee	890,915	1,930,049	493,782	544,593
West Virginia	510,012	378,830	635,535	177,445
Kentucky	870,749	1,758,952	1,046,788	582,274
Ohio	1,554,197	2,585,922	3,577,419	858,715
Michigan	936,310	727,974	1,961,946	486,654
Indiana	1,518,253	1,779,325	836,217	800,942
Illinois	2,551,045	3,148.658	857,370	1,399,356
Wisconsin	1,559,067	911,623	1,474,414	471,186
Minnestoa	1,346,437	578,306	489,192	513,029
Iowa	3,767,290	5,516,485	627,930	1,134,426
Missouri	2,548,117	3,561,136	860,820	1,247,400
Kansas	2,481,996	1,822,268	274,883	1,006,649
Nebraska	1,756,098	1,316,047	183,448	711,011
South Dakota	704,262	173,983	323,482	300,608
North Dakota	404,411	108,210	367,171	174,531
Montana	1,117,424	45,690	2,808,717	199,478
Wyoming	785,899	15,834	1,222,538	84,029
Colorado	1,004,206	26,021	1,305,989	194,157
New Mexico	998,589	28,897	3,008,824	90,203
Arizona	664,380	20,904	746,546	55,605
Utah	415,320	54,443	2,039,226	71,592
Nevada	277,274	11,590	544,077	57,397
Idaho	429,053	64,598	919,865	138,457
Washington	542,670	211,870	748,857	201,449
Oregon	917,149	229,714	2,529,759	241,789
California	1,255,354	487,943	3,526,341	576,669
Oklahoma	172,140	48,316	22,778	41,045
Total, United States	50,868,845	44,165,716	42,294,064	18,226,426

CHICAGO.

Number of Live-stock in the United States on January 1, of Each Year.

Year.	Cattle.	Hogs.	Sheep.
1878	30,523,400	32,262,500	35,740,500
1879	33,234,500	34,766,200	38,123,800
1880	33,258,000	34,034,100	40,765,900
1881	33,306,385	36,227,603	43,576,899
1882	35,891,870	44,122,200	45,016,224
1883	41,171,762	43,270,086	49,237,291
1884	42,547,307	44,200,893	50,626,626
1885	43,771,295	45,142,657	50,360,243
1886	45,510,630	46,092,043	48,422,331
1887	48,033,833	44,612,836	44,759,314
1888	49,334,777	44,345,525	43,544,755
1889	50,331,142	50,301,592	42,599,079
1890	52,801,907	51,602,780	44,336,072
1891	52,895,239	50,625,106	43,431,136
1892	54,067,590	52,398,019	44,938,365
1893	52,378,583	46,094,807	47,273,553
1894	53,095,568	45,206,498	45,048,017
1895	50,868,845	44,165,716	42,294,064

Imports of Live-stock into the United States during the Years 1894–93.

	1894.	1893.	Increase.	Decrease.
Cattle	6,051	66	5,985	..
Horses	1,158	2,050	..	892
Sheep	1,344	4,206	..	2,862

Exports of Cattle and Sheep from the United States during the Years 1894–93.

	1894.	1893.	Increase.
Cattle to United Kingdom	385,794	244,110	141,684
Germany	9,505	..	9,505
France	14,540	351	14,189
Other Europe	5,860	635	5,225
Mexico	2,150	663	1,487
West Indies and Bermuda	1,851	1,749	102
Other countries	1,135	776	359
Total	420,835	248,284	172,551
Sheep to United Kingdom	209,566	..	209,566
British North America	50,467	32,557	17,910
Mexico	5,538	1,261	4,277
West Indies and Bermuda	3,078	2,942	136
South America	1,591	1,328	263
Other countries	3,893	46	3,847
Total	274,133	38,134	235,999

UNITED STATES.

EXPORTS of Live-stock Products from the United States to all Countries during the Years 1894-93.

	1894.	1893.	Increase.	Decrease.
	Lbs.	Lbs.	Lbs.	Lbs.
Beef, canned	59,524,794	63,710,539	..	4,185,745
,, fresh	204,314,960	172,897,488	31,417,472	..
,, salted or pickled	65,360,094	54,307,218	11,052,876	..
Tallow	34,683,618	62,233,139	..	27,549,521
Oleomargarine	118,195,049	118,543,327	..	348,278
Total, beef, &c...	482,078,515	471,691,711	10,346,804	..
Mutton	2,423,513	148,897	2,274,616	..
Bacon	440,514,068	347,636,890	92,877,178	..
Hams	95,945,141	81,775,512	14,169,629	..
Pork, fresh	842,942	518,603	324,339	..
,, pickled	63,675,407	50,564,673	13,080,734	..
Lard	479,705,479	341,834,808	137,970,671	..
Total, hog products	1,565,185,065	1,294,201,074	270,983,991	..
Butter	10,088,152	6,944,310	3,143,842	..
Cheese	69,306,654	69,375,702	..	69,048
Total, dairy products	79,394,806	76,320,012	3,074,794	..

CHICAGO.

EXPORTS of Live-stock Products to Europe during the Years 1894–93.

	1894. Quantity. Lbs.	1894. Value. Dollars.	1893. Quantity. Lbs.
UNITED KINGDOM.			
Beef, canned	36,131,456	3,136,779	48,447,996
„ fresh..	203,492,515	17,342,383	172,509,464
„ salted or pickled	28,307,788	1,635,274	24,153,837
Tallow	9,434,491	460,194	23,546,362
Oleomargarine	8,982,455	872,115	7,852,893
	286,348,705	23,446,745	276,510,552
Bacon	342,606,950	29,599,284	296,943,650
Hams	81,815,526	8,588,840	69,362,541
Pork, salted or pickled	15,424,573	1,164,916	10,206,136
Lard	160,132,123	13,153,864	132,188,415
	599,979,172	52,506,904	508,700,742
GERMANY.			
Beef, canned	5,682,463	486,860	6,527,934
„ salted or pickled	8,273,352	505,897	5,590,579
Tallow	3,155,419	153,334	4,676,136
Oleomargarine	28,403,990	2,629,875	26,072,638
	46,515,224	3,775,966	42,867,287
Bacon	13,425,610	1,054,867	4,958,640
Hams	1,607,575	180,270	671,332
Pork, pickled, &c..	2,666,525	197,552	783,100
Lard	107,024,301	8,707,398	59,322,415
	124,724,011	10,140,087	65,735,487
FRANCE.			
Beef, canned	7,019,579	578,733	1,232,808
„ salted or pickled	743,800	42,949	439,700
Tallow	1,329,490	67,163	10,145,199
Oleomargarine	..	..	1,471,785
	9,092,869	688,845	13,287,492
Bacon	4,549,521	395,464	..
Hams	375,713	43,814	28,651
Pork, salted, &c.	214,650	15,866	35,100
Lard	33,914,883	2,785,603	16,618,449
	39,054,767	3,204,747	16,672,200

(1965)

UNITED STATES.

EXPORTS of Live-stock Products to Europe during the Years 1894–93—continued.

	1894.		1893.
	Quantity.	Value.	Quantity.
	Lbs.	Dollars.	Lbs.
OTHER EUROPE.			
Beef, canned	3,465,243	304,205	3,214,973
„ salted or pickled	5,137,265	282,352	4,536,058
Tallow	12,992,133	659,345	15,691,649
Oleomargarine	75,672,233	7,175,805	78,730,760
	97,266,874	8,421,707	102,173,440
Bacon	43,950,699	3,556,477	26,381,369
Hams	2,073,121	232,975	1,594,116
Pork, pickled, &c.	1,118,300	85,830	628,200
Lard	89,783,975	7,449,058	59,755,642
	136,926,095	11,324,340	88,359,327
TOTAL EUROPE.			
United Kingdom	886,327,877	75,953,649	785,211,294
Germany	171,239,235	13,916,053	108,602,774
France	48,147,636	3,929,692	29,959,692
Other Europe	234,192,969	19,746,047	190,532,767
Total products, except mutton	1,339,907,717	113,545,461	1,114,306,527

LIVE-STOCK, United States, January 1, 1894 and 1895 respectively. (Extract Report, United States Department of Agriculture, February 13, 1895.)

	Number.		Increase or Decrease.
	1895.	1894.	
Horses	15,893,318	16,081,139	− 187,821
Mules	2,333,108	2,352,231	− 19,123
Milch cows	16,504,629	16,487,400	+ 17,229
Oxen and other cattle	34,364,216	36,608,168	− 2,243,952
Sheep	42,294,064	45,048,017	− 2,753,953
Hogs	44,165,716	45,206,498	− 1,040,782

NOTE.—Horses have declined in value 24·1 per cent., mules 23·5 per cent., milch cows have increased in value 1 per cent., oxen and other cattle have decreased in value 4·1 per cent., sheep have declined 20·2 per cent., and hogs 16·9 per cent. Kansas City receipts to January 1, 1895, as compared with previous year: Cattle, 1,772,545; increase, 25,717. Hogs, 2,547,077; increase, 598,704. Sheep, 589,555; increase, 20,038. Horses and mules, 44,237; increase, 9,140.

This city ranks tenth in North America for bank clearings; in 1893 same amounted to 97,870,675*l.*, and in 1894, 99,910,580*l.*, showing a favourable increase. *Bank clearings.*

Wholesale trade of Kansas City has held its own for 1894, and has showed increase in some branches of business. The opening of the Oklahoma territory has proved a great help to business men of this city; this being the nearest wholesale market. *Wholesale trade.*

The business failures for 1893 were 107; for 1894, 124; which was not as great as expected, when considering the results of the financial crisis of 1893. *Business failures.*

The sales of postage stamps for 1893 were 112,000*l.*; for 1894, 113,710*l.*, showing a decided improvement. *Post office receipts.*

Kansas City enjoys the facilities of 14 systems of railways, with 28 lines of rails, running into the city, making it the only city in the world with so many. Two lines, namely, M. K. and T. will be constructed to St. Louis, Mo. the coming year; and the K. C. P. and G. Railway to Shreveport, La. Three new lines are contemplated, and if built, will add materially to the city's welfare. *Railway centre.*

The grain trade of 1894 was very unsatisfactory for many reasons: shortage and total failure of crops, hot winds in various localities, causing very light receipts. The grain that was marketed brought small prices on account of over-supply throughout the world. This market did not enjoy any of the export trade which it had heretofore. The receipts were small, amounting to: —Wheat, 10,177,645 bushels; corn, 11,060,366 bushels; oats, 3,911,852 bushels; rye, 76,633 bushels. Total, 25,238,596 bushels. *Grain trade.*

This is the largest packing centre in the world, except Chicago, and the packing trade is rapidly increasing. Six large houses, namely: Armour Packing Co.; Fowler, Son, and Co. (Limited); Swift and Co.; Reid Bros. Packing Company (Limited); Schwartzschild and Sulzberger, and Jacob Dold Packing Company. *Packing house products.*

The above-named houses purchased and packed during 1894—

	Number.
Cattle	909,090
Calves	45,572
Sheep	366,743
Hogs	2,098,512
Total	3,419,917

Showing an increase of 1,320,291 over 1893.

	1893.		1894.	
	Amount.	Number.	Amount.	Number.
	£		£	
Amount of capital invested	3,300,000	..	3,700,000	..
Output	12,000,000	..	13,700,000	..
Total number of men employed	..	7,000	..	8,600

Horse and mule market. This market has increased wonderfully during the last 15 years. Several orders for foreign countries have been filled during the past year, and from present inquiries it looks as though the export trade will continue.

Number of horses and mules received during 1893, 35,697, and 1894, 44,237, showing an increase of 9,140 for 1894.

The largest individual firm of dealers in horses and mules in the world is located at this point.

Kansas hard wheat flour. The grain known throughout the breadstuff world as Kansas hard wheat, and the flour made of it, has advanced greatly in price and commercial importance during recent years. This is due mainly to two causes. First, from it is produced a sharp, granular flour, that is rich in gluten; it absorbs a great deal of water, and makes a strong, sweet bread. Both the British and Continental European demands for Kansas hard wheat flour have more than doubled in the past 2 years on this account. For the same reason the American demand, especially at the south and east, has expanded remarkably. The other reason for the growing popularity of this grain is, that it is of a hardy nature. It stands more drought and freezing weather than any other wheat grown in the south-western winter wheat region of the United States. It was originally introduced into Kansas by Russian emigrants; but has spread over the State, until at least two-thirds of the wheat area of that commonwealth is annually seeded with this grade of wheat.

The western one-third of Missouri, and the southern one-third of Nebraska, also produce a large amount of what is known in the market as Kansas hard wheat. Oklahoma and the Indian territory likewise devote at least one-half the wheat area within their borders to this grade of wheat. The present outlook in the south-west is not so promising as at this time a year ago; but while this includes the whole breadth of the south-western wheat acreage, it does not so directly apply to the Kansas hard winter wheat acreage, as nearly all of the extensively damaged fields were sown in soft winter wheat, or that known generally in the market as Red Western winter wheat. The acreage seeded to Kansas hard winter wheat last autumn in the States and territories mentioned is probably 10 per cent. larger than that of the preceding year; while the whole wheat acreage in this same region is, according to latest advices, about 8 per cent. less than the acreage of the year previous; the increased hard wheat acreage being made at the expense of restricted Red Winter wheat area.

The use of bicycles in this district is increasing yearly fully 100 per cent. There are over 3,000 in use in this city. A great many English-made wheels are in use, and a large trade could be done in exporting them. The only two objections to them being in case of brakes—it takes so long to secure repairs or parts; the second objection—they are a little too heavy. Thousands of farmers are using them instead of riding horseback. *Bicycle transportation.*

The old-fashioned street railways of this city have disappeared, and the city now enjoys a system of cable railways, with a total mileage of 156 miles; one system controls 66 miles. It has been demonstrated that cable transportation is the proper method of carrying passengers where cities are built on hills, as in Kansas City. *Cable railways.*

A great many farmers are experimenting at present in sub-soiling; several sub-soil ploughs, newly patented, are being pushed on the market. *Sub-soiling.*

This is the largest agricultural implement market and re-shipping point in the world. Sales for 1892, 4,000,000*l.*; 1893, 3,572,000*l.*; 1894, 3,272,000*l.* The reason for the decrease in 1893 was attributed to the financial panic and poor cereal crops. The decrease for 1894 was due to the hot winds and drought in the far west, and to restricted purchases by retailers, on account of less inclination to offer credit by jobbers and manufacturers. The present country stock is the lightest ever known, and promise of heavy trade the coming year. I also wish to add that none of the implements handled are manufactured here; all are shipped from States east of Missouri. *Agricultural implement trade.*

Never until last August has cotton-seed meal been used in this part of America for fattening cattle; it has been used in Great Britain and Continental Europe for some years for fattening and fertilising purposes; but owing to the non-export trade of this article, it was forced into this district, and has proved more than a success, for the climate is agreeable to the feed. Some choice cattle on this feed gained 2½ lbs. of flesh per day on a 90 days' full feed for market. Thousands of cars have been handled this season by merchants here for heavy cattle feeders. They are only beginning to recognise that they have in it the most concentrated, nutritious, and cheapest of feeds, and the most easily applied; it is clean, nutritious, concentrated, and convenient to store and handle; it is a home product, free from adulteration, reliable, and always at a fair valuation. These are facts worthy of consideration, and in support of them the following tables of many American feeding materials are offered, as compiled in Bulletin No. 11 of United States Department of Agriculture, as follows:— *Cotton-seed meal for fattening cattle.*

Mill Products.	Protein.	Fat.	Total.
Pure cotton seed meal	50·81	18·01	68·82
„ linseed, O.P. meal	32·90	7·90	40·80
Buckwheat feed	28·90	7·10	36·00
Grano gluten feed	29·40	6·30	35·70
Gluten meal, Al.	29·41	6·26	35·67
Fresh dried brewers' grains	19·90	5·60	25·50
Clean malt sprouts	23·20	1·70	24·90
Oat feed	16·00	7·10	23·10
Winter wheat bran	16·00	4·00	20·00
Medium fine wheat middlings	15·60	4·00	19·60
Clean standard wheat bran	15·40	4·00	19·40
Standard hominy feed	9·80	8·30	18·10
Germ meal	9·80	7·40	17·20
Clean coarse wheat bran	12·90	3·50	16·40
Clean wheat screenings	12·50	3·00	15·50
„ barley „	12·30	2·80	15·10
Corn and oat chop, No. 1, straight	9·60	4·40	14·00
Fancy heavy wheat middlings	10·48	2·07	12.55
Corn meal	9·17	3·17	12·34
Rye feed	10·39	1·71	12·10
Winter wheat middlings	10·68	1·22	11·90
Clean corn bran	6·94	3·97	10·91
Cotton seed hulls	4·76	3·80	8·56
Fresh wet brewers' grains	5·40	1·60	7·00

Protein is the nitrogen containing albumen-like substance of plants, similar in composition and character to the white of an egg. It is the most costly form of food, and, generally speaking, has for its functions the formation of flesh and muscle.

Fat is the fat or oil of the material, and its office is the production of fat and heat on the animal system.

From the above, it is seen that cotton-seed is not only far ahead as a flesh and milk producer, but it is equal to anything as a combined fat and flesh producer, both numbers being added together.

Analyses by an eminent State assayer show that 100 lbs. of cotton-seed meal contains:—

	Per Cent.
Moisture	7·72
Oil	13·91
Albumenoids, or flesh and milk-producing properties	45·47
Gum, starch, &c.	18·58
Fibre	9·72
Ash	5·60
	100·00

CHICAGO.

By an eminent chemist we have the following :—

	Nitrogen.	Phosphoric Acid.	Potash.
	Lbs.	Lbs.	Lbs.
2,000 lbs. wheat bran contains	47$\frac{4}{10}$	60$\frac{2}{10}$	32
,, corn meal ,,	29	12$\frac{8}{10}$	8
,, linseed oil meal contains	106	38$\frac{8}{10}$	20$\frac{2}{10}$
,, cotton seed meal ,,	134$\frac{6}{10}$	60$\frac{6}{10}$	35$\frac{8}{10}$

(1965)

LONDON:
Printed for Her Majesty's Stationery Office,
BY HARRISON AND SONS,
Printers in Ordinary to Her Majesty.
(75 5 | 95—H & S 1965)

FOREIGN OFFICE.
1895.
ANNUAL SERIES.

No. 1551.

DIPLOMATIC AND CONSULAR REPORTS ON TRADE AND FINANCE.

UNITED STATES.

REPORT FOR THE YEAR 1894
ON THE
TRADE OF THE CONSULAR DISTRICT OF NEW ORLEANS.

REFERENCE TO PREVIOUS REPORT, Annual Series No. 1367.

Presented to both Houses of Parliament by Command of Her Majesty,
MAY, 1895.

LONDON:
PRINTED FOR HER MAJESTY'S STATIONERY OFFICE,
BY HARRISON AND SONS, ST. MARTIN'S LANE,
PRINTERS IN ORDINARY TO HER MAJESTY.

And to be purchased, either directly or through any Bookseller, from
EYRE & SPOTTISWOODE, EAST HARDING STREET, FLEET STREET, E.C., and
32, ABINGDON STREET, WESTMINSTER, S.W.; or
JOHN MENZIES & Co., 12, HANOVER STREET, EDINBURGH, and
90, WEST NILE STREET, GLASGOW; or
HODGES, FIGGIS, & Co., Limited, 104, GRAFTON STREET, DUBLIN.

1895.

[C. 7581—91.] *Price Twopence Halfpenny.*

New Series of Reports.

Reports of the Annual Series have been issued from Her Majesty's Diplomatic and Consular Officers at the following places, and may be obtained from the sources indicated on the title-page:—

No.		Price.
1431.	Galveston	2½d.
1432.	Hamburg	2½d.
1433.	Brindisi	2½d.
1434.	Gothenburg	2d.
1435.	Kiungchow	1d.
1436.	St. Petersburg	½d.
1437.	Malaga	1d.
1438.	Chicago	2½d.
1439.	Odessa	2d.
1440.	Tabreez	½d.
1441.	Tahiti	½d.
1442.	Shanghai	2d.
1443.	Nagasaki	1d.
1444.	Madrid	2½d.
1445.	Malaga	2½d.
1446.	Rotterdam	1d.
1447.	Port Said	1d.
1448.	Sofia	2½d.
1449.	Warsaw	1½d.
1450.	Africa (Congo)	2d.
1451.	Jeddah	1½d.
1452.	San Francisco	5½d.
1453.	Oporto	2d.
1454.	Barcelona	2d.
1455.	New Caledonia	½d.
1456.	Smyrna	1d.
1457.	Macao	1d.
1458.	Samoa	1d.
1459.	Hiogo and Osaka	3d.
1460.	Lisbon	2d.
1461.	Pekin	2d.
1462.	Corunna	2d.
1463.	ozambique	15d.
1464.	Munich	1½d.
1465.	St. Petersburg	3d.
1466.	Naples	1d.
1467.	Montevideo	2½d.
1468.	Aden	1d.
1469.	Tokio	1½d.
1470.	Dantzig	5d.
1471.	Guayaquil	1d.
1472.	Canton	1½d.
1473.	Dar-al-Baida	3d.
1474.	Teheran	2d.
1475.	Bushire	2d.
1476.	Tangier	2d.
1477.	Rome	2d.
1478.	Hamburg	4d.
1479.	The Hague	1½d.
1480.	Belgrade	2d.
1481.	Batoum	1½d.
1482.	Teneriffe	½d.
1483.	Lisbon	2½d.
1484.	Buda-Pesth	½d.
1485.	Rome	5½d.
1486.	Para	1d.
1487.	Odessa	1d.
1488.	Hakodate	1d.
1489.	Beira	1½d.
1490.	Berne	1½d.
1491.	Copenhagen	1d.
1492.	Stettin	2½d.
1493.	Rio Grande do Sul	1½d.
1494.	Serajevo	1d.
1495.	Buenos Ayres	9d.
1496.	Florence	2d.
1497.	Lisbon	1½d.
1498.	Paris	2d.
1499.	Bolivia	1½d.
1500.	Patras	1½d.
1501.	Bordeaux	3d.
1502.	Madrid	2d.
1503.	Amsterdam	1d.
1504.	Suakin	1d.
1505.	Angora	1d.
1506.	Havre	2½d.
1507.	Algiers	11d.
1508.	La Rochelle	3d.
1509.	Vera Cruz	2d.
1510.	Puerto Cortes	1d.
1511.	Taganrog	1d.
1512.	Baltimore	1½d.
1513.	Mexico	1½d.
1514.	Zaila	1d.
1515.	Zomba	3½d.
1516.	Valparaiso	2½d.
1517.	Charleston	2½d.
1518.	Serajevo	1d.
1519.	Saigon	1d.
1520.	Bangkok	2d.
1521.	Tripoli	1d.
1522.	Batavia	1½d.
1523.	Dakar	½d.
1524.	Havana	2d.
1525.	Riga	2d.
1526.	Trebizond	1½d.
1527.	Piræus	2½d.
1528.	Guayaquil	1½d.
1529.	Marseilles	1½d.
1530.	Wuhu	1½d.
1531.	Rio de Janeiro	2½d.
1532.	Trieste	2d.
1533.	Brest	1½d.
1534.	Stockholm	2d.
1535.	Warsaw	1d.
1536.	Boston	1½d.
1537.	Mozambique	2½d.
1538.	Callao	1d.
1539.	Aleppo	1½d.
1540.	Jaffa	½d.
1541.	Boston	1d.
1542.	New Orleans	1½d.
1543.	Chicago	3d.
1544.	Palermo	2½d.
1545.	Bengazi	1½d.
1546.	Cagliari	1d.
1547.	Pernambuco	7½d.
1548.	Madrid	1½d.
1549.	Corunna	5d.
1550.	Leghorn	2d.

No. 1551

Reference to previous Report, Annual Series No. 1367.

UNITED STATES.

NEW ORLEANS.

Consul St. John to the Earl of Kimberley.

My Lord,   New Orleans, March 21, 1895.

I HAVE the honour to transmit herewith my Annual Trade Report for 1894, as well as those from Mr. Howe, Her Majesty's Vice-Consul at Pensacola, and Mr. Barnewall, British Vice-Consul at Mobile.

I have &c.
(Signed)   C. L. ST. JOHN.

Report on the Trade and Commerce of the Consular District of New Orleans for the Year 1894.

Abstract of Contents.

	Page
New Orleans—	
Trade and business	2
Cotton	3
„ consumption	3
„ mills	5
„ spindles	6
„ baling	7
Sugar	7
„ bounty	8
„ production	8
Rice	9
Grain shipments	10
Fruits	10
Oranges	11
Tobacco	12
Lumber	13
Baling stuffs—	
Jute	13
Ties	13
Horses and mules	13

(1936)

UNITED STATES.

ABSTRACT of Contents—continued.

	PAGE
New Orleans—continued.	
Wines and liquors	13
Brewing	13
Oak staves	13
Liverpool salt	14
Oyster fishing	14
Labour troubles—	
Fires incidental to	15
Harm done to port by reason of	17
Attention of shipowners drawn to	17
City drainage	17
Rapid transit	17
City debt	17
„ finances	18
Public health	19
Health statistics	19
British Benevolent Society	20
Convict labour	21
Census of five States of district	21
The wharves	21
Lighthouse burnt and rebuilt	22
Exports in British ships	22
British shipping returns	22
Annexes—	
A.—Return of shipping	23
B.— „ exports	24
B.— „ imports	25
C.— „ exports and imports by countries	26
Pensacola—	
Timber trade	26
Coal trade	26
Phosphate	27
Imports	27
Shipping and navigation	28
Ports of Florida	29
Fish industry	31
Population and industries	31
Convict labour	32
General remarks	33
Mobile—	
Cotton	37
Lumber	37
Shipments	38
Timber	39
Hardwoods	39
Staves	40
Wool	40
Naval stores	40
Coal trade	41
Greater facilities	41
Fruit trade and vegetables	42
Bay and harbour improvements	43
Shipping	43

Trade and business of New Orleans. The condition of trade generally throughout the country has been dull and uncertain. Until the tariff question was settled business drooped; but a revival followed in the autumn, and the present outlook is better than for months past. The South did not suffer as much as the North from the financial crisis.

There was a very material decrease in the foreign trade of the city, both in exports and imports. The exports show the lowest figures ever reached. As usual, cotton and its products, amounting to 63,440,246 dol. (13,082,645*l.*), constituted the principal articles of export. Deducting this from the total value of exports, 72,466,186 dol. (14,943,975*l.*), shows the value of all other articles of export as 9,025,940 dol. (1,861,330*l.*).

Cotton trade.

Compared with preceding years the total exports were—

Year.	Value.	
	Currency.	Sterling.
	Dollars.	£
1894	72,466,186	14,943,975
1893	80,005,179	16,495,900
1892	128,507,038	26,496,275
1891	109,029,979	22,480,380

The grain trade has also suffered, especially in wheat, the export of which was only 2,925,541 bushels; wheat and corn combined only 8,366,976 bushels, as against 19,403,067 in 1893 and 21,588,161 in 1892.

Grain trade.

Next in order to cotton and grain as exports come staves, tobacco and manufactures of tobacco, and flour.

In the value of imports coffee easily leads, sugar next, and fruits—principally bananas, lemons, and oranges—occupy the third place. The total value of imports for the year just ended is officially stated at 15,152,520 dol. (3,124,230*l.*).

Annexed will be found certain returns of the principal articles of exports and imports, their quantities and values, and the countries to which sent or received from.

Annexes B and C.

In exports New Orleans holds the second place, and in imports the seventh, as follows:—

	Value.	
	Currency.	Sterling.
	Dollars.	£
Exports	72,466,186	14,941,480
Imports	15,152,520	3,124,230

A falling-off from 1893 respectively of 2,132,777*l.* and 1,146,052*l.*

The receipts of domestic produce show a total of 160,580,893 dol. (33,109,425*l.*) against 150,321,781 dol. (30,064,338*l.*) in 1893, which was the worst shown for many years, and was a decrease of more than 10,000,000*l.* from 1892.

The total value of the commerce of New Orleans during the year ended September 30, 1894, is compared below with that of the preceding year:—

UNITED STATES.

Year.	Value.	
	Currency.	Sterling.
	Dollars.	£
1894	483,507,065	99,692,100
1893	479,819,877	98,932,000

Annex A.

The total arrivals of vessels during the year 1894 were, not counting coastwise American, 919 vessels of all nationalities, equalling 1,059,239 tons, as shown in Table A, annexed.

Local business has been poorer than for some time past, primarily due to the financial crisis.

The bank clearances show a large decrease as compared with 1892-93, which, however, was an exceptionally good season. The banks, it is said, are in a healthier condition.

Bank clearances.

The bank clearances for the last 5 years have been as follows:—

Year.	Currency.
	Dollars.
1893-94	445,200,278
1892-93	527,830,632
1891-92	496,465,741
1890-91	531,764,118
1889-90	521,484,618

Cotton.

The cotton crop of the season of 1893-94 was officially declared by the Secretary of the Cotton Exchange of this city to be 7,549,817 bales, against 6,700,365 bales in 1892-93 and 9,035,379 bales in 1891-92, a gain this season, as compared with that of the preceding one, of 849,452 bales, or 13 per cent.

The mills throughout the country have decreased their consumption, the northern ones particularly; the falling-off in the southern mills being barely 5 per cent. as against 37 per cent. in the northern, so that, comparatively, the South has done remarkably well. The southern mills now do nearly half as much business as the rest of the country, whereas 4 years ago they did but one fourth. 718,515 bales were used, as against 743,848 bales in 1893.

There has been a general, though not heavy, reduction in cotton acreage which, however, will not reduce the crop of 1894-95, which promises to be the largest for years, estimated at about 9,500,000 bales. In North-west Louisiana the prospects are particularly good.

The lower prices obtained for this season's cotton is shown by comparison with that of 1892-93, which, as already stated, was less by 849,452 bales, yet actually yielded 1,632,000 dol. (336,495*l.*) more. With an increased yield of 13 per cent. the money result is 283,118,000 dol. (58,374,790*l.*) against that of

1892–93, 284,750,000 dol. (58,711,285*l*.), showed a diminution of 0·57 per cent., partly compensated for, however, by the crop having been raised on probably less credit and with greater economy, as was natural that the low prices forced the planters to do. The season has been one of low prices, and few years have shown so great a variance between report as to growth and final results.

The price of cotton of season 1894–95 had steadily declined for months, and had reached the lowest figure ever known, 4⅞ c. spots, but the turning point was found, and now the tendency is an upward one.

I give below, in round numbers, the commercial crop for the past 3 years of the States in my district :—

State.	Quantity.		
	1893–94.	1892–93.	1891–92.
	Bales.	Bales.	Bales.
Alabama	925,000	740,000	1,075,000
Arkansas	625,000	535,000	800,000
Florida	50,000	45,000	65,000
Louisiana	400,000	340,000	635,000
Mississippi	916,000	755,000	1,250,000

This commercial crop includes: (1) post receipts ; (2) overland to mills ; (3) Southern consumption ; but takes no account of cotton left over in interior towns.

The following table shows the export of cotton during the season of 1893–94 from seaports in this consular district :—

State.	Great Britain.	France.	Continent and Channel.	Total.
	Bales.	Bales.	Bales.	Bales.
New Orleans	781,922	411,949	442,940	1,636,811
Mobile and Pensacola	33,574	500	1,086	35,160
Total	815,496	412,449	444,026	1,671,971

As shown above, the total export amounted to 1,671,971 bales ; in 1892–93, 1,382,696 bales ; in 1891–92, 2,200,725 bales.

While, as has already been stated, the cotton consumption of the South has done fairly well as compared with the North, a decrease of 25,333 bales is reported, the figures being :— **Cotton mills.**

Year.	Quantity.
	Bales.
For 1892–93	743,848
1893–94	718,515

(1936)

UNITED STATES.

There was a gain in Alabama and Arkansas of 4,803 bales, and a loss in Louisiana and Mississippi of 2,133 bales, so that, in this district, at least, there has been no decrease, but an actual gain.

New mills, with 93,788 spindles, worked up 20,209 bales; deducting this from 743,848 bales consumed by the old mills, would show the decrease to have been 45,542 bales.

The following tables show total of mills, looms, spindles, and consumption by States in this consular district:—

MILLS.

State.	In operation. Old.	In operation. New.	Idle.	New, not completed.	Total.
	Number.	Number.	Number.	Number.	Number.
Alabama	20	3	3	2	28
Arkansas	2	..	1	..	3
Louisiana	4	1	..	..	5
Mississippi	7	1	3	..	11
Total	33	5	..	..	47

SPINDLES.

State.	Old.*	New.	Idle.	New, not completed.	Total.
	Number.	Number.	Number.	Number.	Number.
Alabama	155,617	18,876	3,920	6,448	184,861
Arkansas	6,164	..	2,800	..	8,964
Louisiana	55,500	..	..	..	55,500
Mississippi	54,994	..	4,500	..	59,494
Total	272,275	18,876	11,220	6,448	308,819

* Includes additions to old mills less spindles thrown out.

The spindles now in operation (September, 1894) are 2,282,496 as against 2,171,147 last year, of which—

State.	Mills.	Looms.	Spindles.	Consumed.	Against in 1893.
				Bales.	Bales.
Alabama	23	3,270	174,493	54,592	50,222
Arkansas	2	210	6,164	1,198	765
Louisiana	5	1,496	55,500	13,569	14,408
Mississippi	8	1,800	54,994	14,161	15,955

RETURN showing Weight of Bales during the Year 1893-94.

State.	Number of Bales.	Average Weight.	Quantity.
			Lbs.
Louisiana	1,893,094	501·96	950,257,464
Alabama	199,083	500·80	100,001,246
Florida and Georgia	1,089,703	489·51	553,464,371

Cotton baling. The subject of the inferior baling of cotton in this country, as compared with that of India and Egypt, has again come to the front, owing to a report that a great improvement is about to be made all through the Southern States in the wrapping and compressing of the staple. Whether there is any truth in this promised improvement remains to be seen; but there can be no doubt that unless some means is adopted to guard the cotton from fire, other than that which is in use at present, the insurance companies will materially raise their rates. The recent losses of cotton fires, either while on wharves or on board, have been so heavy that the insurance companies have been dropping money fast; and it stands to reason that this state of things cannot go on much longer. It is in a great measure to the wretched packing of the American cotton that its frequent destruction by fire is due. Photographs were recently taken of 3 bales, respectively American, Indian, and Egyptian, in the condition in which they reached the mill. The Indian bale of 400 lbs. measured 10 cubic feet; it was wholly covered and was fastened with 12 ties. The Egyptian bale of 700 lbs. occupied 15 cubic feet, was completely covered and secured with 11 ties. The American bale of 475 lbs. was said to occupy 22 cubic feet, for it was too shapeless a mass to be accurately measured. The "Times-Democrat" newspaper of New Orleans, from which the information is extracted, goes on to remark "that it is really extraordinary that Americans, usually so alert to pick up a hint, should still go on wrapping, pressing, and baling the staple in the same slovenly and unsafe fashion in which they have been doing for half a century."

Sugar. The production of cane and beet sugar has increased during the past 10 years about 40 per cent. At the last campaign it very closely reached a total of 6,000,000 tons, of which 56 per cent. was beet sugar. The consumption of sugar per capita is regarded as one of the sure tests of the prosperity of a country. While in one light it is a necessity, in another it is a luxury; for the poorer classes feel that they can do without it, and do not use it to any great extent, except in periods of great prosperity. It has been remarked that as the world grows richer, the consumption of sugar increases, and that the amount used to each person in European countries is an excellent test of the social and financial conditions of those several lands. England, it is said, leads in the per capita consumption, but this country will soon equal it. For this reason an effort is being made to raise enough of that

UNITED STATES.

commodity to supply the home consumption, instead of depending on other lands. It is doubtful, however, whether with such an increasing population sufficient sugar could ever be grown to supply the demand; especially when it is considered how much cheaper it can be cultivated and manufactured in tropical climates. The very fact of the necessity for a bounty to sugar producers shows the futility for this country to compete with those situated in more suitable climates. At the beginning of this year, that is to say in February, we had no less than 20 degrees below freezing-point in Louisiana. No sugar stubble can stand such a temperature.

Bounty on sugar.

In my report of last year mention was made of the bounty on sugar provided by the law of 1891, and an impression that existed, as it turned out not without good reason, that Congress purposed to withdraw the promised bounty. The question was mooted and threshed out in Congress, and on March 2, 1895, the appropriation was adopted by the House of Representatives by a vote of 134 to 125.

The action of Congress means a great deal to Louisiana. It means the salvation of the sugar industry, and consequently the revival of many lines of business dependent on that industry. It will enable the producers to pay all the obligations contracted on the last crop, and will place them in a position to continue the production of sugar on a basis compatible with another order of things, that is to say, no bounty to fall back upon.

The bounty promised by Congress was in the nature of a contract made with each and all persons who would engage in the production of cane, beet or sorghum sugar of certain saccharine strength. The amount promised was 2 c. per 1 lb. The amount now appropriated, 1,000,000*l.*, gives eight-tenths of 1 c. per 1 lb. consequently 60 per cent. less than what was expected. On the principle that half a loaf is better than no bread, this unexpected windfall has been most thankfully accepted.

Sugar crop.

The sugar crop of 1893-94 is shown by the Sugar Bureau of this district to be as follows:—

	Quantity.
	Lbs
Open kettle sugar	70,698,087
Vacuum pan sugar..	526,157,557
Total	596,855,644

The following table exhibits the acreage and yield of canes in tons, the yield of sugar and molasses, and the averages in both processes:—

Canes.			Sugar.				Molasses.		
Acres.	Yield, Tons of—	Processes.	Total Yield of in Pounds.	Averages—Pounds of Sugar.		Total Yield of in Gallons.	Averages—Gallons of Molasses.	
				Per Ton of Canes.	Per Acre of Canes.		Per Acre of Canes.	Per Ton of Canes.
35,053	723,903	Open kettle	70,698,087	97·65	1,946·16	4,675,278	6·45	128·55
169,737	3,351,911	Vacuum pan	526,157,557	157·00	3,129·01	13,794,251	4·06	80·92
204,790	4,075,814	...	596,855,644	...	...	18,469,529	...	...

These figures demonstrate the superiority of the vacuum pan over the open kettle process, the former averaging 3,129 lbs. of sugar and 80·92 gallons of molasses to the acre, the latter only 1,946 lbs. of sugar and 128·55 gallons of molasses.

There were 499 sugar houses in operation, a decrease of 19 from 1892-93, this decrease being due to small planters finding it more advantageous to sell their canes by the ton to larger factories.

Of the factories, 482 used steam and 17 horse power; 92 have open kettles, 183 open strike pans, and 224 vacuum strike pans.

The average yield of cane per acre was 19·93 tons, against 18 tons last year.

Rice. The Louisiana rice industry has probably suffered more during the past two years, from a combination of unfavourable circumstances, than any other agricultural interest in the South. Last year the rapid remarketing of an immense crop, twice the amount of any previous yield, forced the prices down to ruinously low figures, while this season there has been a severe loss to the producers from a diminished yield owing to unfavourable weather during the growing season. The best authorities, early in the year, were convinced that the crop would not be more than 1,000,000 bags, or half the crop of the preceding year. Every evidence has borne out the correctness of this estimate. Few persons are aware of the increased consumption of rice in this country. There can be no doubt but that fully 250,000,000 lbs. are now required. The time has nearly arrived when this country will produce all the rice needed for home consumption, and have a surplus for export.

There is a marked falling-off reported in the acreage, but it is believed that the reduction stands for better culture. The present conditions are encouraging, as the crop is being made with less expense owing to plentiful labour, and consequently lower wages, planters generally being independent of banks and merchants.

The following are the imports of rice from August 1, 1893, to July 31, 1894:—

	Quantity.	Value.	Duty Per Lb.
	Lbs.	£	Cents.
Cleaned rice	1,395,261	5,335	2
Paddy	120,151	340	¾
Granulated rice	299,318	860	¼
Total	1,814,730	6,535	

Grain shipments.

The grain shipments from this port have very rapidly decreased during the year, and the falling-off is partly owing to the generally depressed condition of trade and crops in the three States from which New Orleans draws the bulk of her grain trade (namely, Iowa, Kansas, and Nebraska; while the production of North Texas, Indian territory, Oklahoma, and all that region, finds its way to St. Louis, then to New York); partly, it is alleged, to the discriminating by railroads on freight rates, so that the eastern ports would be the chief gainers; and partly to the prolonged drought killing the corn (which was the smallest crop for 13 years), though wheat has done well. Prices for this latter article went lower than for corn, a thing unprecedented before in the agricultural history of this country. A large crop of corn is expected in 1894.

Fruits.

The disastrous storm of 1893 destroyed almost the entire orange crop about the time that it was ready for market, that is to say, on October 3 of the above year (much greater damage however, has since been caused by the very severe weather of February, 1895), when the thermometer, all over this country, fell to 20 degrees below freezing point. The actual damage done to the trees will be ascertained during the season of 1895 and 1896.

The Florida crop of 1893 was a heavy one, and owing to the scarcity of apples, the result to the growers was highly satisfactory. In the matter of peach and pear the crop was almost an entire failure, Louisiana being dependent on Texas and California for a supply. As a matter of fact, peaches, apples, and pears are not a success in these latitudes, where the blossoms are being continually destroyed by frost. It is surprising that attempts are still being made to cultivate fruits to which the climate is not suited.

The banana shipping business suffered a series of extraordinary losses during the railroad strikes. The importation of bananas, lemons, and oranges from foreign ports was not as large as the previous year, hence the volume of trade fell far short of the average. In the instance of bananas this was caused by the appearance of Mobile in the list of banana-importing markets.

Prices of bananas showed the usual fluctuations as guided by receipts, shipping demand, and condition of cargo on arrival.

The foreign lemon and orange trade was considerably less in volume than previous years.

The prices of some of the principal fruits were as follows:—

Articles.		Amount.	
		From—	To—
		s. d	£ s.
Apples	Per barrel ..	8 0	1 12
Louisiana oranges	,, ..	8 0	0 17
Lemons	Per box ..	5 0	2 0
Bananas	,, bunch ..	6 0	0 9
Pineapples	,, dozen ..	5 0	0 14

Oranges. On December 28, 1894, the outlook in Florida was very bright. The orange groves had fruited more generously than usual. Already the growers had marketed about 3,000,000 boxes of oranges at remunerative prices. There were still on the trees 2,500,000 boxes of oranges. But when the morning of December 29 dawned, all this had been swept away; for the mercury had fallen to freezing point, and the oranges were found frozen hard. In a few hours fruit worth several millions of dollars had been turned to ice.

Developments during January, however, seem to confirm the assertion of orange-growers that the December frost had not materially injured the old trees. The weather that followed the Christmas blizzard was exceptionally favourable, and soon it was reported that the trees were shedding the leaves that had been blighted, and were putting forth new growth.

On February 7 everything seemed to point to a good crop. But this cheerful prospect was destined to be succeeded by a condition of hopeless despair; for the mercury, as was mentioned elsewhere in this report, fell to 20 degrees below freezing point. The opinion prevailing is that the last frost was fatal to the trees, and that it will be years before they can recover. No full crop can be expected before 1897. Many of the trees have been split to the ground. Several weeks have elapsed since the cold wave—weeks of the most favourable weather—and no signs of life have been shown by the great majority of the groves. To judge by their appearance the trees are only fit for firewood.

Tobacco. The financial depression of the past 12 months has naturally affected the tobacco business to a certain extent. It is reported that there has been an average shrinking in the manufacture of cigars in the United States of about 20 per cent. during the past year; but the shrinkage at New Orleans has not reached that amount, showing the business to be more prosperous here than elsewhere.

The consumption of cigarettes has increased, and that of chewing tobacco fallen off.

The internal revenue at this port have furnished the following statistics for 1893–94 :—

Description.		Quantity.	Value.
			£
Cigars	Number	69,053,429	414,320
Cigarettes	"	156,567,610	59,499
Manufactured tobacco	Lbs.	922,581	59,645
Perique	"	225,437	22,546
Total			556,010

There are in Louisiana 145 cigar manufactories, 5 snuff, and 41 perique.

In former times New Orleans was a tobacco market of importance, but of late years changes in transportation facilities have delivered this business to other points.

Lumber.

The only industry in the South that has greatly suffered from the financial crisis of 1893, and the stagnation which followed, is the lumber one. It had grown to immense proportions during the past few years, but prices have fallen very low, inflicting a serious set back and causing the suspension of many mills. It is believed that this depression will pass over and the industry resume its former activity. With the many advantages of the South in having such a magnificent area of the finest and most diversified timber, even the "free" entry of timber favoured by the tariff will not operate much as a hindrance. In the States of this district the progress, in values, can easily be shown by comparison with the figures of 10 years ago, viz. :—

States.	Number of Sawmills.	Employés.	Value.	Value 10 Years ago.
			£	£
Alabama	437	6,123	1,675,480	546,300
Arkansas	523	6,712	1,814,430	369,855
Florida	202	4,239	1,118,400	630,980
Louisiana	122	3,091	1,154,580	363,710
Mississippi	338	4,434	1,169,220	395,910

The statistics for the planing mills are even more satisfactory :—

States.	Output in—	
	1890.	1880.
Alabama	1,228,287	161,900
Arkansas	1,761,392	33,100
Florida	270,205	57,000
Louisiana	1,405,576	721,482
Mississippi	136,450	101,200

All jute bagging used to cover is manufactured in this country. The consumption of bagging for the season 1893-94 equalled about 8,000,000 yards, at an average price of about 5¼ c. per yard for 2 lbs. These low prices were due to the financial panic. The market opened at 6⅛ c. per yard, and advanced to 7 c. per yard. *Jute.*

Ties opened at 65 c. per 45 lbs. and 70 c. per 50 lbs. and then advanced about 10 c. per bundle. *Ties.*

Owing to the flattering condition of the growing cotton crop, and the consequent large demand for ties, 45 lbs. were quoted at 75 to 77½ c. and 50 lbs. at 83 to 85 c. Both the above ties are now made of steel at a cheaper rate than in England, and the 45 lb. is taken largely in preference to the old standard 50 lb. tie. There was no importation of ties at that season.

Less of both classes of mules were sold during the past year. Horses were in good demand, and good ones brought good prices. The average prices for 1893-94 were as follows:— *Horses and mules.*

Description.	Prices.	
	From—	To—
	£	£
City mules	40	50
Sugar „	32	40
Rice „	26	35
Cotton „	18	28
Saddle and harness horses	40	70
Heavy draft horses	50	70
Common horses	15	30

With the exception of vermouth, absinthe, and benedictine, very little imported goods have been received here. This was due to the uncertainty of duties to be adopted by the Wilson Tariff Bill. *Wines and liquors.*

Champagne importations have fallen off considerably. This wine seems to decline in popularity, due to irksome and exorbitant charges and the financial straits.

Shippers from San Francisco are furnishing a good claret at a low price. The consumption in this market is on the increase. This is explained by consumers being able to buy from their grocer a gallon of good table claret for 1s. *California wines.*

In fine, sweet, and white wines and brandy the sales have been limited.

257,488 barrels of lager beer were manufactured here during the year ended June 30, 1894. There are now eight breweries in operation at New Orleans, with a capital estimated at about 1,600,000l. *Brewing.*

The total exports of oak staves from New Orleans to foreign and domestic ports were as follows:— *Oak staves.*

Country.	Quantity.	Value.
	Pieces.	£
United Kingdom	1,089,674	..
France	556,390	..
Spain	2,957,728	..
Portugal	1,445,026	..
Germany and Holland	344,781	..
Belgium	4,810	..
Italy	145,550	..
Domestic ports, mostly destined for re-shipment to foreign ports	388,356	..
Total	6,932,315	200,000

The receipts at New Orleans being estimated at about 8,000,000 pieces.

Liverpool salt. The total receipts of all foreign salt were but 102,000 sacks, the smallest annual imports on record for this port. The reduction of rate of duty on all salt imported, should and likely will tend to material increase in the receipts during the coming season; but whether the demand will be improved sufficiently to keep pace with the anticipated increase in imports is, as yet, an open question. During the entire season the demand was very light, though prices were very close to cost of importation, and sometimes less than cost was realised. The trade was small and unsatisfactory. Ample stocks are held in store.

The following figures show the annual receipts and stock of salt for the past 3 years:—

		Quantity.		
		1894.	1893.	1892.
Liverpool	Sacks	102,000	141,000	150,000
Stocks, August 31—				
Liverpool	,,	39,000	57,000	72,000
Turk's Island	Bushels	5,000	6,500	9,000

Turk's Island salt. There were no receipts during the season. The small stock now on hand is ample for any anticipated demand, the latter being small and mostly local.

Minor Industries.

Oyster fishing. One of the minor industries of Louisiana (if it may be dignified with that term, considering the primitive methods of cultivation, or fishing and forwarding to market) has been the oyster fishing.

Prior to the great storm of October, 1893, by which so many

hundreds of people—principally Austrians engaged in this trade—lost their lives, the usual practice was for these fishermen to "squat" in small colonies on any available shore, and either to "plant" his beds or else fish the natural oyster. The extent of the oyster territory was vast, the supply abundant and cheap, while little labour and capital were required. The storm, however, destroyed the natural reefs, in some places burying them under 2 feet of deposit, and necessitated the "planting" of oyster-beds, a long and laborious task.

On these natural reefs any person could fish for oysters, but there was a tacit understanding amongst the fishermen that each man should alone be entitled to fish on any reefs he might plant. This understanding has been broken by some "pirates" as they are termed, men who did not plant, but bided their time, and as soon as the season opened swooped down on the beds planted. Naturally this conduct of the trespassers caused considerable dissension.

Labour Troubles.

Late in October an event occurred which might have had very serious results, the outcome of a strike of white labourers (cotton screwmen) against the employment of coloured men in the loading of cotton on ocean-going ships. Hitherto this had been done by both races in apparent harmony, but it is said the coloured men, having gradually increased in numbers, led the whites to believe that eventually they would find their occupation gone. It would appear that the white labourers are not able alone to undertake the whole of the work in loading ships, yet seem determined that the coloured men are to be driven from the field, a course which would necessarily involve great detention to vessels.

Several masked or disguised men boarded certain British vessels at night and, by force of arms and threats, rifled the vessels of the tools and appliances belonging to, and used by, the coloured screwmen employed in loading these ships, and threw these tools overboard.

Next day it was repeated, this time during working hours, when the coloured men were driven away.

The mayor of this city was applied to by this consulate for protection from such acts on board these vessels and from mob interference in their loading.

No arrests were made though several acts of violence are reported to have occurred.

Early in November several serious cotton fires broke out which were believed not to be accidental; this opinion gaining ground, the Cotton Exchange Board offered 2,000 dol., the "Times-Democrat," a leading newspaper of this city, offered 1,000 dol., and the City offered 250 dol., amounting in all 3,250 dol. about (670l.) for arrest and conviction.

The first fire was that which destroyed the premises of the Fires, incidental

West Indian and Pacific Steamship Company of Liverpool, a corporation whose ships have been coming as regular traders to this port for many years. This was one of the firms which took the initiative in employing coloured labour to effect a reduction in the cost of loading their ships, rates for which had been enormously high, 6 to 7 dol. per day per man, with a limit of bales to be stowed not exceeding 75 bales. The loss by this fire was estimated at, for the wharf premises destroyed, 10,000 dol., and 3,896 bales of cotton, valued at 125,000 dol., which were all ready for shipment.

Another large fire occurred at Westwego on the night of November 12; this, too, was supposed to have been incendiary; altogether 27,691 bales of cotton, valued at about 830,000 dol., have been destroyed by fire.

The disturbed state of affairs has continued to prevail though in a lesser degree. The commerce of the city was seriously menaced, as a withdrawal of shipping would naturally affect it.

No claims in connection with the strike have been made for vessels' detention. An appeal to the Federal Courts for an injunction to restrain these men from interference was obtained by the steamship line already referred to.

Other steamship lines have followed the lead, and now employ any and all who present themselves for employment. This naturally does not smooth matters.

The Board of Arbitrators, consisting of the Governor of the State, the Secretary of the New Orleans Cotton Exchange, and three others have the whole matter under advisement, and it is to be hoped that arrangements will be agreed upon by which all classes, whether employers or labourers, will receive a fair return or recompense.

Again, on February 7, the screwmen and longshoremen working on the British ship "Cayo Mono," knocked off without giving reason or explanation. On the following day the master of the vessel began to take in cargo, which he had received on the wharf and for which he had signed, with his crew. Upon this a police officer notified the master that he had received instructions from the chief of police to prevent the crew from working, as it was against the laws of the State of Louisiana, and warned him that he and his crew were liable to arrest and imprisonment.

The master applied for an injunction against the mayor and chief of police in the United States Court. The application was granted, and the mayor and chief of police were called for trial.

The judge issued a restraining order prohibiting the defendants from interfering with the crew in loading their ship, at the same time expressing an opinion that the State law was unconstitutional. The crew thereupon continued to load.

The struggle between white and coloured screwmen is still going on. The former wish to retain the monopoly at their own exorbitant rate of wages, namely, 50 c. per bale, whereas the coloured screwmen are ready to do the work at 40 c. per bale. This naturally led to a conflict and an attempt to prevent the negroes working on any ship. Several cases have occurred of late where coloured loaders have been interfered with and driven away by out-of-work white men. In every instance the United States Court has been appealed to for protection by the agents of our regular liners, and the loading continued in the presence of United States marshals.

This state of things is doing the port of New Orleans a great deal of harm by driving the carrying trade to more peaceful and cheaper localities. Loaders at this port are receiving no less than 6 dol. a day, and, when able to do 1½ days' work, 9 dol. (1*l.* 17*s.*). {Harm done to port by reason of.}

This is an opportune moment to draw the attention of our great shipowners in England carrying on a large and regular trade with New Orleans, to the fact that the fight against the exorbitant and ruinous charges of the screwmen and longshoremen must be met by concerted action on their part. One or two of the agents have taken the initiative, at a considerable expense, by appealing to the United States Court for protection (which hitherto has never been refused) to load their ships at a reasonable rate; but others have hung back, trusting that the more enterprising would pave the way for their benefit. {Attention of shipowners drawn.}

Signs of a split among union screwmen and others connected with loading of ships are observable, and, before long, if the ship agents would only hold out and work together, a stop might be put to such pretensions; for the United States Courts, with the approval of all business men at New Orleans, are ready to afford all necessary protection with the view to foreigners being allowed to make what terms they can with those willing to load their ships irrespective of colour.

The question of better drainage for the city is, and has been for some time past, engaging the attention of the committee appointed for the purpose. Up to the present time (March) nothing definite—that is as regards the length, width, and depth of the various proposed canals for the different sections, the capacity of the pumping stations, or the cost of the plan—has been determined on. The city is very flat, and being several feet below the level of the Mississippi River, which partly encircles it, the natural outfall for its drainage is towards its rear portion. {City drainage.}

A partial survey of Bayou Bienvenu has enabled the city engineer to reach the conclusion that in capacity and efficiency as an outfall this creek contains the necessary requirements.

In my last report I stated that only one electric car line was running in this city. At the present time (March, 1895) nearly all of the mule car systems have been superseded by electric cars, the advantages of which are many and much appreciated. The cars are commodious, clean, and comfortable, the time consumed in going from one part of the city to another is very much shortened, this latter fact alone tending much to improve the outlying districts, where many houses are rapidly being built. The condition of the streets, however, in these districts needs vast improvement, and this is especially noticeable in the rainy season. {Rapid transit.}

Early in September the Board of Liquidation of the City Debt {City debt.}

placed 4,500,000 dol. (927,830*l.*) of 4 per cent. constitutional city bonds for sale, the Bill authorising the Board to issue these bonds having been passed by the last Legislature in 1892.

These bonds have a life of 40 years. They are intended to replace nearly the entire amount of the city bonds which were outstanding, whether matured or subject to call, the only bonds not thus provided for in the above-named amount being 348,000 dol. (71,740*l.*) of 7 per cents., maturing June, 1895.

This issue placed the city indebtedness upon an equal basis, reducing the amount paid every year in interest to bondholders, principally 6 per cents., and effecting an annual saving of about 150,000 dol. (31,000*l.*) besides greatly simplifying the bonded debt.

The whole issue was taken by the Louisiana National Bank, the Board paying a commission of 3¾ per cent.

The sale might be considered a success, and the city debt in a very satisfactory condition.

The total bonded indebtedness of the city is placed at about 15,284,811 dol. (3,151,500*l.*) as follows:—

Description.	Amount.
	Dollars.
Constitutional bonds	4,140,000
Premium bonds	6,021,380
Extended 6 per cents.	4,503,100
Miscellaneous	620,331

City finances.
The receipts during the half year ended June 30 amounted to 1,781,383 dol. (367,285*l.*), the expenditures to 1,992,523 dol. (428,785*l.*).

The following items comprise the above-named receipts:—

Description.	Amount.
	Dollars.
Taxes of 1893	267,876
„ 1894	637,923
Licences „	296,593
Markets „	110,950
Railroad franchises	96,494
Other items	371,547

The comptroller's report for the 6 months ended December, is at present in the printer's hands, and not available.

The valuation of real estate, &c., and ratio of taxation for 1894:—

Description	Amount.
	Dollars.
Valuation of real estate	95,047,560
„ personal property	41,920,097
Total	136,967,657
Equivalent in sterling (about) £	28,250,750

Ratio of taxation on every 100 dol.

Description.	Amount.
	Dol. c.
City expense tax	1 0
Interest and redemption city bonds	1 0
Total	2 0

Public health. It is gratifying to know from the Board of Health that the mortality of New Orleans is decreasing. The death rate for 1894 was only 24·88, the lowest, with one exception (1889) for a quarter of a century. This means the saving of 313 lives as compared with last year, 656 as compared with the previous one, and 680 as compared with 1883, the worst year New Orleans has known since its day of epidemics.

If we confine our statistics to the white population, who live with some regard to the ordinary rules of health and sanitation, the showing is still more satisfactory. The death rate among the whites for 1894 was only 21·91 per 1,000. It should be even better than this, and would be but for the drainage, which increases the deaths from pneumonia, bronchitis, and kindred diseases.

As the death-rate for 1894 was only 24·88 per 1,000, a rate of 27·42 for the previous 10 years, if New Orleans can but keep up this improvement it will have nothing to complain of. The most important items in this connection are good water, good drainage, and cleanliness, of which there is a lack.

Health statistics. The estimated population of the city is now, according to the Board of Health, 275,000. The total number of deaths in 1894 was 6,843, an average death rate of 24·88. Taking, however, the death rate of the white population separately from the coloured, it is found as follows:—

Description.	Number of Deaths.	Rate per 1,000.
		Per cent.
White	4,272	21·91
Coloured	2,571	52·12

UNITED STATES.

The cause of the greater death rate (more than double) of the coloured population being, no doubt, their lack of sanitary knowledge and their inferior surroundings.

The principal causes of death were—

Description.	Number of Deaths.
Phthisis pulmonalis	835
Pneumonia	364
Bright's disease	277
Malarial fevers	292
Senile debility	282
Cholera infantum	189
Dysentery	111
Enteritis	421
Cancer	168
Meningitis	129
Bronchitis	180
Influenza	50
Diphtheria	125
Typhoid	78
Infantile debility	96
General ,,	40
All other causes	3,206
Total	6,843

Only 2 deaths from small-pox and 4 from measles are recorded.

1,143 deaths occurred in hospitals, asylums, and other public institutions.

There were 567 still births, which are not recorded amongst the deaths.

The highest mortality was in December, 755, and the lowest in August, 471.

The report of the Board of Health is only published biennially, early in 1894.

British Benevolent Society.

The British Benevolent Society of New Orleans, supported by resident British subjects, was incorporated on April 1, 1892, in accordance with the laws of Louisiana. An account of the working of the society is here given.

During the past year (1894) there have been relieved 481 cases, all British subjects, who had received 1,470 meals, 671 lodgings, and in cash for travelling expenses, &c., 29l. The total value of relief amounted to 100l.

This society, in relieving distressed British subjects, helps many who would otherwise have to be taken care of at the police stations or prisons, as under the city ordinance, No. 5,046, all persons found loitering about New Orleans without a fixed abode or means of subsistence are arrested by the police and fined 25 dol. (5l.), or in default condemned to 30 days' imprisonment as vagrants. Cases have occurred where British subjects have been arrested, imprisoned, and fined without sufficient cause, and, therefore, illegally. This has lately been admitted by some of the city officials, who have expressed their opinion that the ordinance ought to be modified, and the police instructed to use more discretion; otherwise, the authorities may some day be called upon to pay heavy damages.

The society also, in a great measure, prevents business men from being constantly annoyed by persons calling at their offices for relief.

During the winter months there is a considerable immigration of British subjects from the North, by stress of weather or scarcity of work, and it is hard for these to be so treated because they are not able to find employment, though a considerable number, it must be confessed, are professional tramps, and it is often a difficult matter for the police and the relieving officer of the British Benevolent Society to distinguish one from the other.

The lease system, that is, the system of leasing convicts out for private enterprise, has lately undergone an almost thorough reform. It had been in use in all the five States comprising this consular district. In Louisiana and in Florida it is still maintained, but no doubt it will be abolished, at least in Louisiana, where, as stated in my last, there is a profound and growing opposition to it, at the next sessions of the Legislature. *Convict labour.*

By Act of February 14, 1893, a sweeping change in the whole prison system of the State of Alabama was effected. In March, 1893, Arkansas abolished the lease system, and later in the year legislation was adopted in the State of Mississippi to put an end to leases after January 1, 1895, and is, therefore, now in force.

By the census returns of the two last decades the population of the five States of this consular district is given below:— *Census.*

States.	Population. 1880.	Population. 1890.	Gain Per Cent.
Louisiana	939,946	1,118,587	19
Florida	269,493	391,422	45·24
Alabama	1,262,505	1,513,017	19·84
Mississippi	1,131,597	1,289,600	13·96
Arkansas	802,525	1,128,179	40·57

The wharfage and other dues levied upon vessels loading with their cargoes in this harbour are so heavy—particularly in comparison with dues levied in neighbouring rival ports—that the business is every day leaving New Orleans and going where it finds better treatment. *The wharves.*

The Chamber of Commerce, therefore, has taken up the subject, and passed a resolution that will at least receive a careful consideration of all business men of New Orleans.

The Chamber of Commerce adopted the following resolution:—
"That the Chairman appoint a special committee, whose duty it shall be to consider the subject of free wharfage."

UNITED STATES.

The purport of this action is that there may be free wharfage, as in the majority of commercial towns; and that, with the view to attaining this end, this port should acquire the wharf lease from the lessees without any delay, as the fruit trade and other lines of traffic are leaving New Orleans and going to neighbouring ports, where the charges are less by 350 dol. (70*l.*) than they are here. The scheme, however, could only be carried out on condition that the lessees be bought out on reasonable and equitable terms, which is very much doubted.

Lighthouse. On May 22, 1894, the South-west Pass light station, on the west side of South-west Pass entrance to the Mississippi river, Louisiana, was destroyed by fire. About a month later, the damage having been repaired, the fixed white light was re-established.

RETURN of the Principal Exports Carried in British Ships during the Year 1894.

Articles.		Quantity.
Cotton	Bales	1,380,454
„ seed	Sacks	3,312
„ „ oil	Barrels	21,672
„ „ cake	Sacks	151,628
„ „ meal	„	395,264
„ „ soap stock	Barrels	10,162
Corn	Bushels	4,519,503
Wheat	„	1,985,009
Flour	Sacks	6,653
Staves	Pieces	3,758,457
Timber	Logs	1,092
„	Pieces	683
Lumber	„	41,631
„	Logs	54
„	Feet	2,360,093
Lead	Bars	3,297
Copper ore	Sacks	6,338
Silver ore	Bars	310
Rice polish	Sacks	1,249
Molasses	Barrels	21,351
Hay	Tons	4,345

British shipping returns. As compared with last year, 1893, British Shipping Returns for 1894 show an improvement.

ENTERED.

Year.	Sailing.		Steam.		Total.	
	Number of Vessels.	Tons.	Number of Vessels.	Tons.	Number of Vessels.	Tons.
1894	6	3,445	329	601,449	335	604,894
1893	13	1,339	348	584,997	361	586,336

NEW ORLEANS.

Cleared.

Year.	Sailing. Number of Vessels.	Tons.	Steam. Number of Vessels.	Tons.	Total. Number of Vessels.	Tons.
1894	5	1,874	309	558,319	314	560,193
1893	13	1,339	363	598,424	376	599,763

Annex A.—RETURN of all Shipping at the Port of New Orleans during the Year 1894.

Entered.

Nationality.	Sailing. Number of Vessels.	Tons.	Steam. Number of Vessels.	Tons.	Total. Number of Vessels.	Tons.
British	6	3,445	329	601,449	335	604,894
American	28	9,172	208	140,809	236	149,981
Norwegian	2	2,548	183	81,477	185	84,025
Spanish	7	4,756	44	95,628	51	100,384
German	7	7,455	26	45,538	33	53,013
Italian	13	7,310	16	12,426	29	19,736
French	...	...	14	26,782	14	26,782
Danish	...	...	10	3,180	10	3,180
Mexican	...	...	5	1,328	5	1,328
Dutch	...	...	4	9,211	4	9,211
Portuguese	15	4,744	1	1,049	16	5,793
Russian	1	912	...	...	1	912
Total	...	...	...	...	919	1,059,239
,, for the year preceding	...	...	...	...	987	1,082,859

Cleared.

Nationality.	Sailing. Number of Vessels.	Tons.	Steam. Number of Vessels.	Tons.	Total. Number of Vessels.	Tons.
British	5	1,874	309	558,319	314	560,193
American	4	1,591	190	118,759	194	120,350
Nowegian	2	2,548	182	80,553	184	83,101
Spanish	9	6,194	52	100,726	61	106,920
German	7	7,455	24	42,403	31	49,858
Italian	15	8,847	14	11,833	29	20,680
French	1	1,148	14	27,134	15	28,282
Danish	...	...	10	3,170	10	3,170
Mexican	...	...	5	1,328	5	1,328
Dutch	...	...	4	9,181	4	9,181
Portuguese	9	4,744	2	2,694	11	7,438
Russian	...	...	1	912	1	912
Total	...	...	...	...	859	991,413
,, for the year preceding	...	...	...	...	954	1,068,511

UNITED STATES.

Annex B.—RETURN of Principal Articles of Export from New Orleans during the Year 1894.

Articles.		Quantity.	Value.
			£
Cotton	Bales..	1,873,807	12,375,680
Cotton-seed oil	Gallons	5,041,493	382,885
Cotton-seed meal and cake	Lbs.	161,178,146	324,080
Corn	Bushels	5,441,435	536,415
Wheat	,,	2,925,541	398,435
Flour	Barrels	133,075	87,665
Staves			347,165
Lumber			38,865
Tobacco and manufactures of			158,990
Syrup and molasses	Gallons	1,124,888	20,845
Malt liquors			10,525
Leather manufactures			7,220
Iron and steel ,,			13,555
Cotton manufactures			12,155
Copper ore			2,225
Other copper			5,960
Other breadstuffs and manufactures of			4,995
Cotton-seed			940
Lead			240
All other articles			215,135
Total			14,943,975

RETURN of Principal Articles of Import to New Orleans during the Year 1894.

Articles.		Quantity.	Value
			£
Asphaltum, crude	Tons	3,064	810
Potash, caustic	Lbs.	874,533	1,030
Sulphur, crude	Tons	2,557	7,410
Coffee	Lbs.	42,258,173	1,484,150
Fertilisers			6,000
Sisal grass and hemp	Tons	1,051	13,210
Burlap bags for grain			45,370
Burlaps			39,130
Indiarubber, crude	Lbs.	477,176	32,000
Salt	,,	20,360,800	7,150
Spices, all kinds			9,420
Mineral waters	Gallons	78,250	4,170
Wood, mahogany, logs and other			2,670
Breadstuffs			4,390
Cement	Lbs.	82,424,551	52,700
Soda caustic	,,	1,148,799	4,730
,, sal	,,	190,045	230
,, ash	,,	499,481	1,130
All other chemicals			5,890
Cotton, manufactures of			34,500
Bricks and tiles			2,500
Chinaware and crockery			30,720
Flax, manufactures of			22,410
Jute ,, ,,			20,220
Fish – sardines, cod, &c.			18,820
Fruits—			
Bananas			267,000
Lemons and oranges			100,000
All other fruits			15,560
Cocoanuts and other			12,730
Glass and glassware			10,360
Machinery, and manufactures of iron and steel			11,380
Tin plates	Lbs.	3,388,176	18,030
Malt liquors	Gallons	63,590	13,030
Oils of all kinds			14,250
Provisions			18,270
Rice	Lbs.	3,619,279	12,030
Silks, manufactures of			3,340
Brandy	Gallons	12,132	3,480
Cordials	,,	43,105	8,910
Sugar, of cane	Lbs.	99,907,212	575,240
,, of beet	,,	280,000	1,880
Tobacco and cigars, &c.			36,150
Vegetables, dried, prepared			18,260
Wines—			
Champagne	Dozens		11,960
Still wine, in casks	Gallons		9,400
,, bottles	Dozens		13,800
Wood, manufactures of			11,660
Wool ,, ,,			7,870
All other articles			77,280
Total			3,124,230

UNITED STATES.

Annex C.—TABLE showing Total Value of all Articles Exported from and Imported to New Orleans, to and from Foreign Countries during the Year 1894.

Country.	Exports.	Imports.
	£	£
Great Britain and Ireland	6,303,900	248,995
British Possessions	21,915	89,005
France	3,210,645	107,220
Germany	2,551,695	90,215
Spain	940,045	3.125
Possessions (Cuba)	32,020	680,485
Italy	793,540	139,960
Netherlands and Possessions	409,500	15,485
Russia on the Baltic	155,170	..
Denmark	110,780	40
Austria and Hungary	76,530	3,590
Belgium	75,250	14,165
Portugal	64,275	310
United States of Colombia	32,495	56,245
Central American States	154,750	225,450
Sweden and Norway	9,590	940
Mexico	180	634,300
Switzerland	..	1,645
Brazil	..	859,490
Other places	1,695	3,565
Total	14,943,975	3,124,230

PENSACOLA.

Mr. Vice-Consul Howe reports as follows:—

Trade exports. The trade of Pensacola for the year 1894 was very good. Among the tables hereto annexed will be found statements giving the quantities, destination, and value of pitch-pine shipments during the year.

Pitch-pine shipments abroad.

I again repeat, as stated in some of my former reports, that the export of pitch-pine timber and lumber from Pensacola to foreign markets appears to go steadily on, the occasional depreciation in values of this wood abroad hardly making any difference in the extensive yearly shipping business.

To markets in the United States. The tables above referred to will also show that many northern markets of the United States take a large supply of pitch-pine from Pensacola by sea. Quantities of pitch-pine lumber are also yearly sent hence to the western markets of this country by railroad, the figures for which cannot be obtained for these reports.

Pensacola's prosperous condition. The port of Pensacola was especially referred to in the last message of the Governor of the State of Florida to the Legislature as being in a prosperous condition, with its large fleet of vessels in port from time to time loading pitch-pine wood.

Coal. The next article of export from Pensacola, which is assuming large proportions, is coal. This coal, as before explained in these reports, is the product of the adjacent State of Alabama, but Pensacola benefits largely by its transit through her port to the various ports to which the coal is shipped. A table giving the shipments of coal from Pensacola during the past year will be found annexed to this report. The quantity exported would no doubt have been largely increased during the year had not strikes intervened at the coal mines, as well as a disastrous fire been experienced, burning down the coal wharf at Pensacola, both of which events stopped shipments for some time from this port.

In connection with the export of coal from Pensacola it may be again observed that British steamers have had quite a good share of this carrying trade. *Shipped in British steamers.*

Although the export of this great article of trade—phosphate—is not from the port of Pensacola, but from other ports in Florida, adjacent to where it is mined, still I may refer to these shipments as of interest to readers of reports on Florida trade. *Phosphate.*

By British shipowners particularly is the carrying trade of Florida phosphate looked into, as it is sent abroad mostly in British steamers. *British ships carry quantities.*

In the Governor's last message to the Legislature he referred to the phosphate of the State as being a source of great wealth to the people of Florida; and these shipments were especially touched upon and given for the year ending December 31, 1892, as follows:—

Description.	Quantity.
	Tons
Hard rock ..	202,019
Land pebble	17,795
River pebble	126,172
Soft phosphate (including home consumption)	8,341
Total	354,327

Of that amount 249,069 tons went to foreign markets, and 105,258 tons to domestic markets.

I mentioned in one of my former reports that an extensive phosphate (steam) preparing establishment has been built in Pensacola's suburbs. This concern is managed in the interests of some of the principal proprietors in Dublin, Ireland, and the phosphate above referred to is to some extent prepared at those works for extensive use in this country. *Phosphate works at Pensacola. Proprietorship in Dublin.*

Pensacola is not much of an importing market from abroad. Nearly all the chief articles of trade are received here from the large northern and western markets of the United States, and amount to several millions of dollars yearly. Some shipments of salt come here yearly from Liverpool. Iron and copper ore is brought here—a few shipments yearly—from Spain and Portugal, which go forward to foundries and smelting works in some places *Imports.*

UNITED STATES.

of these southern States. A British steamer brought 1 of these cargoes during the year.

British goods. Of course there are many things of British manufacture among the mercantile stocks kept at Pensacola, but all of these goods are brought here from the northern markets of the United States.

I am confident that the storekeepers in this section of the United States would be glad to see their way clear to deal directly with the large manufacturing and exporting houses of the United Kingdom for such articles of British manufacture as are desired, and must be had by the people here, and which are now secured from the northern markets, if the practicability of such a business could be seen by overcoming the two most difficult questions which now block this direct trade; that is to say, the present high tariff, and the ways and means for establishing this direct business—the latter, and chief question, never having been looked into by both sides, is the obstacle mostly apparent, I think.

Many articles suited to this market. By the many trade circulars and price lists which I receive continually from England I see many articles suited to the trade here about, and which I believe dealers would be glad to secure direct from first hands, could arrangements to such end be made. This subject, however, has been touched upon by me in these reports before, and commented upon at home, without any actual action on the question having been taken. It may be that this direct trade will yet be inaugurated, to the benefit of both sides.

Shipping. It will be seen by the tables on shipping annexed to this report for the year 1894, that British tonnage not only held its average of late preceding years in vessels and number of tons, but that in volume it exceeded all former years so far as steamships were concerned. The number of British steamers and their tonnage during the year 1894 went beyond any year since the regular opening of steam freight at Pensacola. I think that in this connection my opinion, as given in former reports, to the effect that steamers would eventually take the place of sailing vessels in the carrying trade of Pensacola, is being carried out each recurring year lately.

British tonnage.

While writing upon shipping—to the British public, England's shipowners and the world generally, an important subject—I wish particularly to dwell upon the great advantages of steamers in the carrying trade, as shown by careful and official comparison at this port. Especially in the carrying trade of pitch-pine wood—dangerous cargoes as they are—are steamers best adapted.

Official return as regards steamers. By a recent number of the "Times," I see that a Board of Trade return lately issued shows that during the year 1893, "16 vessels belonging to the United Kingdom and to British possessions abroad, and laden with timber, either were reported missing or are known to have foundered. 44 lives were lost as the result of these disasters. All the 16 ships were sailing vessels. Miscellaneous casualties happened to 8 timber-laden sailing ships and caused the loss of 16 lives. No casualties of any kind are reported to have happened during 1893 to steamships laden with timber."

Such an official statement, and given to the world as it is through such high medium, ought to cause serious reflection upon this important subject. And not only do I believe that lives are far less jeopardised, in fact danger very much minimised in steam vessels carrying timber, than in sailing wooden vessels; but generally in steamers, in my official experience, all things seem to be better in relation to the safety and comfort of the seamen thereon engaged.

Were I to go through the records and notes of this office, and give details here, it would be shown that since the coming of steamers to this port, largely in place of the old plying sailing vessels, not only have complaints of seamen considerably ceased to be brought before me, but also have desertions been far less frequent. Seamen on steamers.

It has appeared to me that the masters and officers of steamers fulfil their position with more dignity and with more consideration for their men than has been my experience in dealing with sailing vessels. Again, the seamen appear to feel more lifted up, as it were, on a steamer than on a sailing vessel, and conduct themselves accordingly. Better satisfied.

The crimp appears to have far less weight on the seaman of a steamer than he has on the sailor of the sailing vessel. The appointments and routine on board of a steamer, to my idea, give a more homelike aspect to affairs. Also, the average steamer enters, loads up, and is gone from this port in 12 to 15 days. The average sailing vessel hangs on in port from 30 to 50 days, and, meantime, if not at the very coming in of the long staying sailing vessel, the seaman is anxious to change his quarters, and deserts, or, at least, leaves the ship in some way, with loss of his hard earned wages. Crimps have less chances. Steamer's short stay in port. Sailing ships stay much longer.

The steamer, as a rule, has no ballast to discharge on entering port before commencing to load. The sailing vessel has, invariably, a large quantity of ballast to be discharged before taking in cargo, which hard work, generally beyond the daily duties of a seaman, he is induced to get rid of, even by desertion and loss of wages.

The steamer then, in almost every respect, is more to be desired in the carrying trade, especially in the timber carrying trade, than the sailing vessel, all things considered.

The tonnage of British vessels cleared at Pensacola during the year 1894 was equal to over one half of the tonnage of all other foreign vessels clearing at the port, and the amount of cargo in tons taken by British vessels was equal to over one-third of the tons of cargo carried by all of the vessels of other foreign flags loading here. An average British steamer carries about 1¾ tons of cargo or over to her ton measurement. An average sailing vessel takes about 1½ tons of cargo or less to each ton measurement. British tonnage compared. Carried out more cargo.

I give as follows, which may be interesting, as showing the average shipping visiting the ports of Florida, as a whole, a statement for the year ending June, 1894, culled from a report by a supervising special agent of the Treasury Department of the United States:— Ports of Florida.

Apalachicola.—Foreign vessels entered, 78; foreign vessels cleared, 56; coastwise vessels entered, 30; coastwise vessels cleared, 46; entries of foreign merchandise, 2; documents issued to vessels, 83; duties and tonnage tax collected, 1,743 dol.; total receipts, 2,343 dol.; value of domestic goods exported, 263,666 dol.; expense of collection, 3,246 dol.

Fernandina.—Foreign vessels entered, 74; foreign vessels cleared, 99; domestic vessels entered, 165; domestic vessels cleared, 149. There were no entries of foreign merchandise. Documents issued to vessels, 51; duties and tonnage tax, 2,659 dol.; aggregate receipts, 3,590 dol.; value of domestic products exported, 1,571,892 dol.; expense of collection, 2,243 dol.

Key West.—Foreign vessels entered, 290; foreign vessels cleared, 305; domestic vessels entered, 219; domestic vessels cleared, 191; entries of merchandise, 4,277; documents issued to vessels, 234; duties and tonnage tax, 550,655 dol.; aggregate receipts, 560,268 dol.; value of foreign goods, exports, 7,146 dol.; value of domestic goods exported, 1,324,973 dol.; expense of collection, 38,988 dol.

Pensacola.—Foreign vessels entered, 439; foreign vessels cleared, 432; domestic vessels entered, 162; domestic vessels cleared, 152; entries of foreign merchandise, 98; documents issued to vessels, 242; duties and tonnage tax, 19,502 dol.; aggregate receipts, 22,648 dol.; domestic goods exported, 4,035,599 dol.; expense of collection, 14,503 dol.

St. Augustine.—Foreign vessels entered, 13; foreign vessels cleared, 13; domestic vessels entered, 1; domestic vessels cleared, 1; entries of foreign merchandise, 18; documents issued to vessels, 43; duties and tonnage tax, 4,591 dol.; aggregate receipts, 4,638 dol.; value of domestic goods exported, 1,147 dol.; expense of collection, 1,803 dol.

St. John's (Jacksonville).—Foreign vessels entered, 31; foreign vessels cleared, 42; domestic vessels entered, 344; domestic vessels cleared, 222; entries of foreign merchandise, 78; documents issued to vessels, 115; duties and tonnage tax, 32,309 dol.; aggregate receipts, 32,656 dol.; value of foreign goods exported, 167 dol.; value of domestic goods exported, 102,929 dol.; expense of collection, 4,666 dol.

St. Mark's (Cedar Keys).—No foreign or coastwise vessels entered; 1 foreign vessel cleared; documents issued to vessels, 29; no duties or tonnage tax collected; aggregate receipts, 3 dol.; value of domestic goods exported, 3,800 dol.; expense of collections, 1,849 dol.

Tampa.—Foreign vessels entered, 62; foreign vessels cleared, 54; domestic vessels entered, 255; domestic vessels cleared, 242; entries of merchandise, 1,830; documents issued to vessels, 104; duties and tonnage tax, 403,220 dol.; aggregate receipts, 407,909 dol.; value of domestic goods exported, 977,655 dol.; expense of collection, 21,304 dol.

Many seaports. It will be seen by the statement that the State of Florida has, I think, the largest number of ports of entry, or out-to-sea ports, of any State in the Southern States of America, perhaps the largest number of seaports in any State of the United States.

Of course, of the foreign vessels, as shown by the statement, British vessels (other than Pensacola's large proportion) were in good number, carrying timber and phosphate from the Florida ports, at which some of such cargoes are always being loaded. *British vessels in good number at the ports.*

It will be seen that the domestic goods exported from Key West and Fernandina were the largest, next to Pensacola, for the period given. From Key West the exports may be put down as having comprised cigars and sponges, by far the largest value being in cigars. A number of persons from the Island of Cuba have settled at Key West, and the manufacture of cigars by them is an immense industry at that port, and the cigars made there are said to be very good, ranking very near to Havana cigars, and commanding large export orders. Most of the tobacco used at Key West for these cigars is from the Island of Cuba. *Large exports from some of these ports.*

The fish industry of Pensacola is very large and keeps quite a number of persons in employment. There are several firms here engaged in this lucrative business. Each firm has a fleet of small vessels which fish on the fishing banks off the Florida coast, returning to Pensacola at certain intervals with their catches of fish. Quantities of ice are taken out for preserving the fish. There are wells in the smacks, and as many of the fish as possible are brought in alive in the wells. Markets far and near are supplied with fish from Pensacola. *Fish.*

The taking of any of the food fishes of the State of Florida for the fish roe by non-residents of the State is frequently complained of, I am informed, and it is recommended that if the law is not now sufficient to prohibit this practice, that a more stringent statute be passed. And the recommendation came before the last Legislature of Florida, that the law in relation to the catching of fish in the fresh waters of the State of Florida, lakes, rivers, creeks and ponds, be so amended as to prohibit the catching of fish of all kinds, except shad, in any of the said fresh waters, by seine, cast-net, drag-net, gill-net, or any other kind of net, and that the penalty for the violation of the law be such as will secure the benefits intended thereby, and that when a fine is imposed by any of the courts for the violation of the law, one half of such fine be paid to the party giving information that leads to the conviction of the parties proceeded against for violating the law. *Taking of fish prohibited by law.*

The Governor in his last message to the Legislature remarked that the State of Florida was in a prosperous condition, and that within the last few years the population had largely increased, and that the resources and prosperity of the State had attracted foreign capital. *Population and industries.*

The railroad mileage of Florida was put at 2,475 miles in 1893, with various other roads in completion. *Railroads.*

(1936)

UNITED STATES.

Some of Principal Articles of Export from the State of Florida during the Year 1892.

Articles.		Quantity.	Value.
			Dollars.
Pitch-pine lumber	Super. feet	286,075,866	3,575,948
„ sawn timber	Cub. feet	23,356,807	3,503,521
„ hewn „	„	42,908,648	53,635
Cedar	„	17,820	4,448
Oak	„	7,732	881
Shingles	Bundles	1,781,770	301,797
Crossties	Number	661,238	198,371
Naval stores (turpentine and resin)	Barrels	17,168	85,840
Cedar	Cases	1,467	7,335
Phosphate	Tons	284,871	2,848,710
Tobacco	Bales	18,847	1,130,820
Total			12,211,306

Employment of population. The population of Florida is mostly engaged in agricultural pursuits in the interior places. At and near the sea port towns the timber and lumber business is the leading industry, with good wages to the people engaged in the latter work.

The hewing of the timber in the pitch-pine forests is an immense industry for some of the people of Florida who live in the timber regions.

Unskilled labour. Plenty of work. Good wages. At Pensacola the industrial class in unskilled labour is mostly supported by the timber trade, working on board ships in stowing the cargoes of timber exported. Also there is plenty of work for this class of labourers in the coal export business from Pensacola. Both classes of labourers, in timber and coal, work at very remunerative wages, ranging according to their positions in the stowing of these cargoes. Wages to these people range from 3 to 6 dol. per day.

Skilled labour. Kept fairly employed. Skilled labour is well paid for at Pensacola also, and among these people, as well as the stevedores, there is always enough work, I think, to keep them fairly employed. The wages for these mechanics range very well. Pensacola's scale of wages, graded by the various labour societies connected with skilled and unskilled labour, always keep well up.

Hiring out of convicts. Quotation from the Governor's remarks on the subject. While writing about the employment of the people, and the rate of wages, I might refer to the apparently strange custom of hiring out prisoners in Florida who have been convicted and imprisoned. The Governor, in his last message to the Legislature, took up this question and remarked that, "The system of leasing convicts, which the State, through circumstances, has been forced to adopt, is very much to be deprecated; but this seems unavoidable at present, because the State has no money with which to erect a State prison for the safe keeping of convicts, and the erection of workshops and other buildings necessary for their profitable employment.

"In leasing the convicts, the State authorities should always take into consideration the character of the lessee as a humane and just man, and see that he treats the convicts with every degree of kindness consistent with their safe keeping and employment.

"I doubt the propriety of allowing the lessee to sublet the convicts, and certainly this should be prohibited, except upon the consent of the State authorities, who should be allowed an opportunity to inquire into the character of the party to whom any convicts may be let. The minors at the convict camp, if possible, should be kept separate and apart from the adults. The lessee should be required by law to have religious service held at the convict camp on every Sabbath day, and he should pay for such services. The law at present requires the State to pay the prison chaplain, but there is no good reason for this. It is recommended that the law be changed so as to meet the ends suggested. Every safeguard should be thrown around the convicts by law, and it is recommended that the State employ some discreet and humane man, as agent, whose duty it shall be to reside at or near the convict camp, to watch over the care and treatment of the convicts, to see that no convict is cruelly or unnecessarily punished, to see that they are comfortably clothed, properly fed and quartered, and that they receive proper medical treatment. Such agent should be a physician of high standing, personally and professionally. He should be required to report from time to time to the Commissioners of State Institutions, and be under their direction."

It appears that the original lessee of the convicts, and who sublets some of them, pays 22½ dol. per annum for each convict, and that the State, by this arrangement, receives over 10,000 dol. per annum for these prisoners. *Amount of hire per annum paid by the lessee of the convicts.*

The population of Pensacola is about 13,000, of the entire State about 391,000 inhabitants.

Pensacola has been blessed for some time past as regards her freedom from yellow fever epidemics. During the year 1894 the town was comparatively healthy. *Health.*

Now follow the tables in connection with, and referred to in this report:—

UNITED STATES.

RETURN of Principal Articles of Export from Pensacola during the Years 1894-93.

Articles.		1894.		1893.	
		Quantity.	Value.	Quantity.	Value.
			£ s. d.		£ s. d.
Pitch pine lumber	Super. feet	148,310,000	370,775 0 0	142,256,000	355,640 0 0
Sawn pitch pine timber	Cubic feet	11,080,277	277,006 18 6	10,208,460	255,211 10 0
Hewn ,, ,,	,,	325,912	7,468 16 4	384,251	8,805 15 0
Cedar	,,	3,716	270 19 2	2,212	161 5 10
Cotton	Bales	300	2,500 0 0	500	5,208 6 8
Coal	Tons	116,591	97,159 3 4	83,292	56,395 12 6
Flour	Sacks	98,425	82,020 16 8	91,392	76,160 0 0
Corn	Bushels	408,798	42,583 2 6	491,000	51,145 16 8
Bran	,,	35,202	2,933 10 0	39,330	3,277 10 0
Oats	,,	26,084	2,173 13 4	59,375	4,947 6 8
Hay	Bales	19,354	4,032 1 8	8,945	1,863 10 10
Resin	Barrels	2,176	1,360 0 0	2,989	1,868 2 6
Shooks	Bundles	4,332	3,610 0 0	5,600	4,583 6 8
Wire fencing	Reels	10,158	6,348 15 10	5,760	3,600 0 0
Pig-iron	Tons	3,718	7,745 16 8	60	125 0 0
Bar-iron	,,	550	3,850 0 0	125	875 0 0
Iron piping	,,	130	1,083 15 0	125	1,041 13 4
Coffins	Boxes	15	156 5 0	140	1,450 16 8
Agricultural implements	,,	75	390 12 6	300	1,562 10 0
Iron safes		104	2,166 13 8	14	291 13 4
Stoves		32	100 0 0	...	..
Lard	Tierces	1,341	8,982 1 8	...	...
Other articles	...	...	2,000 0 0	...	1,200 0 0
Total	...	...	926,718 1 10	...	836,289 16 8

NOTE.—The following as regards the above table of exports is descriptive of the quantities, values, weights, and measures, the conversion of money into sterling being at the rate of 4 dol. 80 c. per 1*l*.; lumber at average of 12 dol. (2*l*. 10s.) per 1,000 superficial feet, board measure; sawn timber at an average of 12 c. (6d.) per cubic foot, basis 40 feet average; hewn timber at an average of 11 c. (5½d.) per cubic foot, basis 100 feet average; cotton at an average of 10 c. (5d.) per lb., in bales of 500 lbs. average weight each bale; coal (1894), 4 dol. (16s. 8d.) per ton; cedar at 35 c. (1s. 5½d.) per cubic foot; flour at 4 dol. (16s. 8d.) per sack of 200 lbs.; corn at 50 c. (2s. 1d.) per bushel; oats at 40 c. (1s. 8d.) per bushel; bran at 40 c. (1s. 8d.) per bushel; hay at 1 dol. (4s. 2d.) per bale of 100 lbs.; resin at 3 dol. (12s. 6d.) per barrel; shooks at 4 dol. (16s. 8d.) per bundle; wire fencing at 3 dol. (12s. 6d.) per reel; pig-iron at 10 dol. (2*l*. 1s. 8d.) per ton; bar-iron at 33 dol. 60 c. (7*l*.) per ton; iron piping, 40 dol. (8*l*. 6s. 8d.) per ton; coffins at 50 dol. (10*l*. 8s. 4d.) each nest; agricultural implements at 25 dol. (5*l*. 4s. 2d.) per box; iron safes at 100 dol. (20*l*. 16s. 8d.) each; stoves at 15 dol. (3*l*. 2s. 6d.) each; lard, 32 dol. (6*l*. 13s. 4d.) per tierce.

RETURN of Principal Articles of Import to Pensacola during the Years 1894-93.

Articles.	Value.	
	1894.	1893.
Chief articles	..	.
Sugar (from Cuba)	58,980	10,500
Other articles	6,950	9,412

NOTE.—As stated elsewhere in this report, the value of chief articles brought to Pensacola yearly amounts to several millions of dollars.

NEW ORLEANS.

TABLE showing the Total Value of all Articles Exported from and Imported to Pensacola from and to Foreign Countries during the Years 1894-93.

	Exports. 1894.	Exports. 1893.	Imports. 1894.	Imports. 1893.
	£ s. d.	£ s. d.	£	£
United Kingdom	252,090 11 8	205,376 6 0	1,650	4,676
British possessions	4,257 0 0	6,957 5 0	300	...
Spain and colonies	197,076 2 8	184,137 5 0	58,980	10,989
Netherlands	54,913 0 0	47,177 0 0	...	...
France	52,351 0 0	53,969 0 0	...	...
Italy	47,786 0 0	53,687 2 0	...	...
Argentine Republic	42,870 0 0	46,295 5 0	...	...
Brazil	33,842 0 0	36,685 1 0	...	...
Mexico	28,071 17 6	29,890 0 0	...	...
Belgium	26,544 0 0	39,979 0 0	...	...
Germany	17,899 0 0	24,633 0 0	5,000	4,247
Uruguay	14,320 0 0	7,542 2 6	...	...
Portugal	10,578 0 0	1,962 0 0	...	...
Austria	7,590 0 0	7,867 2 6	...	...
Egypt, Alexandria	5,476 0 0	9,049 1 6	...	...
Central America	4,644 10 0	3,283 0 0	...	...
Turkey	835 0 0	...	...	...
Norway	...	1,769 0 0	...	...
Total to foreign countries	801,144 1 10	754,278 16 8	...	...
„ to ports in the United States	125,574 0 0	82,011 0 0	...	...
Total	926,718 1 10	836,289 16 8	65,930	19,912

(1936)

UNITED STATES.

TABLE showing Articles, Destination, and Value of Exports from Pensacola during the Year 1894.

Country.	Timber. Sawn.	Timber. Hewn.	Lumber.	Cedar.	Cotton.	Coal.	Pig-iron.	General Cargo.	Value.
	Cub. feet.	Cub. feet.	Super. feet.	Cub. feet.	Bales.	Tons.	Tons.	Tons.	£ s. d.
United Kingdom	7,634,000	34,035	28,077,000	3,328	..	..	100	..	252,090 11 8
British possessions	54,000	..	1,163,000	..	..	..	..	..	4,257 0 0
United States	..	..	21,870,000	..	..	76,325	3,493	..	125,574 6 0
Cuba	..	..	5,906,000	..	..	1,117	125	28,000	187,431 2 8
Netherlands	959,750	58,345	11,879,000	..	..	..	..	..	54,913 0 0
France	501,250	117,938	14,847,000	..	..	..	..	..	52,351 0 0
Italy	938,166	44,498	9,314,000	388	..	..	..	..	47,786 0 0
Argentine Republic	33,000	..	16,818,000	..	..	..	..	..	42,870 0 0
Brazil	48,500	..	12,583,000	..	..	1,400	..	..	33,842 0 0
Mexico	..	..	..	..	..	33,685	..	..	28,071 17 6
Belgium	72,166	23,527	9,896,000	..	..	..	..	..	26,544 0 0
Germany	160,333	24,341	5,341,000	..	300	..	..	..	17,899 0 0
Portugal	237,000	..	638,000	..	..	..	..	..	10,578 0 0
Uruguay	..	..	5,728,000	..	..	..	..	..	14,320 0 0
Spain	253,000	..	1,328,000	..	..	..	..	..	9,645 0 0
Austria	166,946	22,480	1,161,000	..	..	..	..	..	7,590 0 0
Egypt (Alexandria)	22,166	5,748	1,916,000	..	..	..	..	..	5,476 0 0
Central America	..	..	511,000	..	..	4,064	..	..	4,644 10 0
Turkey	..	..	334,000	..	..	..	..	..	835 0 0
Total	11,080,277	325,912	148,310,000	3,716	300	116,591	3,718	28,000	926,718 1 10
,, for the year preceding	10,208,460	384,251	142,256,000	2,212	500	83,272	..	20,637	836,289 16 8

NEW ORLEANS.

RETURN of all Shipping at the Port of Pensacola during the Year 1894.

ENTERED.

Nationality.	Sailing. Number of Vessels.	Sailing. Tons.	Steam. Number of Vessels.	Steam. Tons.	Total. Number of Vessels.	Total. Tons.
British	27	18,987	71	106,244	98	125,231
American	196	110,208	9	4,551	205	114,759
Swedish and Norwegian	115	108,192	10	7,021	125	115,213
Italian	71	48,594	...	...	71	48,594
Russian	49	36,338	...	...	49	36,338
Spanish	1	1,368	6	9,599	7	10,967
German	8	6,955	1	1,703	9	8,658
Austrian	11	7,845	...	...	11	7,845
Netherlands	5	4,869	...	...	5	4,869
Danish	4	2,622	...	...	4	2,622
French	2	2,592	...	...	2	2,592
Portuguese	1	601	...	...	1	601
Greek	1	439	...	...	1	439
Total	491	349,610	97	129,118	588	468,728
,, for the year preceding	488	361,556	77	95,255	565	476,811

CLEARED.

Nationality.	Sailing. Number of Vessels.	Sailing. Tons.	Steam. Number of Vessels.	Steam. Tons.	Total. Number of Vessels.	Total. Tons.
British	32	23,809	71	106,244	103	129,053
American	199	112,324	9	4,551	208	116,875
Swedish and Norwegian	136	127,540	10	7,021	146	134,561
Italian	65	44,250	...	...	65	44,250
Russian	48	36,396	...	...	48	36,396
Spanish	1	1,368	6	9,599	7	10,967
German	6	5,861	1	1,702	7	7,563
Austrian	9	6,224	...	...	9	6,224
Netherlands	5	5,254	...	...	5	5,254
Danish	4	2,622	...	...	4	2,622
French	2	2,592	...	...	2	2,592
Portuguese	2	1,201	...	...	2	1,201
Greek	1	439	...	...	1	439
Total	510	369,880	97	129,117	607	497,997
,, for the year preceding	476	346,288	76	94,025	552	440,313

MOBILE, ALABAMA.

Mr. Vice-Consul Barnewall reports as follows:—

The commercial year commences on September 1, 1893, and ends on August 31, 1894.

Cotton receipts were 215,116 bales, valued at 7,982,955 dol., against 182,884 bales, valued at 7,626,776 dol. 22 c. of the year previous; average price per lb., 7·41 c., against 8·30 c. the previous year. — *Cotton. Receipts and prices.*

There has been a decrease in the direct exports to Liverpool of 2,512 bales. — *Exports.*

When the conditions which prevailed during the past year are — *Lumber.*

(1936)

UNITED STATES.

considered Mobile may be well satisfied with the showing she has made in the lumber trade.

It must be borne in mind that no interest was more adversely affected by the business depression of 1893 than the lumber trade. When general business is bad, construction of buildings, railroad cars, and general repairs stop, and the millmen continue sawing, hoping that the market will improve, but finally they face the inevitable, and shut down their mills. This is a true picture of the experiences of the lumber-men of this country in the past 12 months. Fortunately for Mobile we are not altogether confined to the domestic market.

Shipments. The figures given below show that we have done a very good business with Cuba, and the showing of the trade with Mexico is also satisfactory. The greatest decline in the year's lumber business has been in coastwise shipments. In the year previous shipments amounted to over 30,000,000 feet to various American ports on the Atlantic—Boston, New York, Philadelphia, &c.; this year we have shipped to New York and Boston only 9,000,000 feet. Foreign shipments show the greatest falling-off in the direction of the United Kingdom, the gain to the West Indies, however, making the foreign account about equal. Values, however, have declined and the trade, as a whole, has been unsatisfactory.

The total foreign and coastwise shipments of lumber show a net decline of 21,000,000 feet. The following is in detail the amount shipped, and the destination:—

Destination.	Quantity.
	Feet.
FOREIGN.	
United Kingdom	8,260,390
France	833,270
Spain	308,571
Germany	476,459
Belgium	903,571
Holland	1,627,137
Nicaragua, U.S. Colombia	1,682,546
Mexico	4,896,437
Cuba	19,577,218
Jamaica	2,199,683
Trinidad	833,787
Africa	939,276
Hayti	1,211,195
Various	14,396,787
Total	58,146,327
COASTWISE.	
New York	5,862,024
Boston	3,201,846
Grand total	67,210,197

NEW ORLEANS.

Timber. The timber market has been in a wretched condition for over a year. Aside from the dulness in all lines of trade in foreign countries, there has been a special stumbling-block in the way, and that is the overloaded Liverpool market.

The timber business has made such rapid and ever-increasing strides in the past 8 years that it is to be regretted that any back-set is to be noted; but it is not reasonable to expect that we should go on increasing and never have a back-set.

Shipments. The following table shows the destination and amount of the shipments during the year just closed:—

Country.	Hewn. Quantity.	Hewn. Value.	Sawn. Quantity.	Sawn. Value.
		Dollars.		Dollars
United Kingdom	780,168	..	2,520,789	..
France	150,639	..	135,487	..
Holland	180,483	..	106,830	..
Africa	..	..	83,345	..
Belgium	..	..	45,457	..
Various	23,784	..	20,834	..
Total	1,135,074	124,858·14	2,912,742	334,966·36

Summary.

The following summary of lumber and timber business done in this port shows the standing of 1893–94 as compared with 1892–93. The timber is reduced to superficial feet for the sake of comparison.

Description.	Quantity. 1893–94.	Quantity. 1892–93.
	Super. feet.	Super. feet.
Lumber, total foreign and coastwise	67,210,197	79,304,565
„ railroads	5,650,800	8,000,000
„ towed to Ship Island	..	60,000
„ local or river	5,000,000	7,500,000
Timber, direct in vessels—		
Hewn	13,620,888	30,082,044
Sawn	34,953,012	34,442,064
Timber towed to Ship Island—		
Hewn	100,000	1,108,029
Sawn	150,000	2,170,267
Total	126,684,897	162,666,969
Decrease	35,982,072	..

Hard woods. Hard woods felt the prevailing influences as severely, if not more so, than pine, consequently the record is not up to that of the previous year:—

UNITED STATES.

Articles.	Quantity.	
	1893-94.	1892-93.
	Cub. feet.	Cub. feet.
Oak, hewn	64,597	354,493
Cedar "	59,889	
Poplar "	61,455	} 966,233
Ash "	37,251	
Total	223,192	1,320,726
Decrease	1,097,534	..

Shipments.

Article.	1893-94.		1892-93.	
	Quantity.	Value.	Quantity.	Value.
		Dol. c.		Dollars.
Staves	319,262	33,673 12	190,000	25,000

Wool:

Prices.

Prices at the close of last season ruled at 12 to 13 c.; the average price during the year just closed was about 13½ c. per lb.

Receipts.

The receipts are heavy for the past season; the receipts in bags this season foot up 12,277 bags, against 5,592 bags last season.

Year.	Quantity.	Value.
	Lbs.	Dollars.
1893-94	1,534,625	184,155
1892-93	575,000	86,250

Naval Stores.

Receipts.

Year.	Quantity.	
	Resin.	Turpentine.
	Barrels.	Barrels.
1893-94	85,619	24,091
1892-93	69,120	18,110
Increase	16,499	5,981

Mobile's Coal Trade.

A steady increase during the past year, with the brightest prospects ahead. There are 29 coal-producing States in the Union, and among these Alabama ranks fifth. Of the southern coal-producing States it is by far the largest, Tennessee coming next with an output of about one-third as compared with that of this State. This entire great mineral basin of the south is open to water transportation direct to Mobile through the Tombigbee, Warrior, Alabama, Cahaba, Coosa, and Tallapoosa, and Mobile is nearer to it by from 91 to 193 miles than any other Atlantic port. The three great coal basins of the State are the Warrior, Cahaba, and Coosa, which include eight coal-producing counties—Bibb, Jefferson, St. Clair, Shelby, Tenkaloosa, Walker, and Winton, with small mines in other counties. These in 1893 produced 5,136,935 tons of coal, at a total value of 5,096,792 dol., a decrease from the production of 1892, which exceeded that of 1893 by 392,377 tons, or 7 per cent. in quantity. This was mainly due to the shutting down of furnaces in the two largest producing counties, thus cutting off an important outlet for the mines. Otherwise the State has shown continuous increase in production each year since 1886 until 1893.

The coal business of Mobile has rapidly increased during the past year; this is more specially noted in steam coal, owing to the proportions obtained by the importation of fruit.

More steamers entered this port last year than during the previous one; the records of the harbour master shows the number to be 225, an increase of 105. These steamers use at least 2,500 tons of coal a month, or 30,000 tons per year, and home consumption to a little over 6,000 tons.

The total receipts during the year 1893–94 were 111,660 tons, against 86,293 tons during 1892–93; this applies to Alabama coal alone.

The export and coastwise business was good and would have been more so but for the long strike which paralyzed this branch of trade. To Mexico alone 10,964 tons of coal, and 2,000 tons of coke were shipped by one firm, the others uniting in sending over the bar to Galveston, and to Cuban and Mexican ports 12,575 tons, making a total of 23,539 tons which went southward by water from Mobile during the year 1893–94. The foreign ports to which these shipments were made were Havana, Cardenas, Tampico, Lagunas, Progresso, Vera Cruz, and Bluefields.

The range of prices in Mobile for retail lots has been as follows:— Alabama, 4 dol. to 6 dol. 50 c.; anthracite, 7 dol. to 7 dol. 50 c. per ton; export coal, cargo lots, 2 dol. 15 c. to 2 dol. 25 c. per ton of 2,000 lbs., f.o.b. vessels at dock; tug coal, 2 dol. 75 c. in bunkers; bunker coal for steamers, 2 dol. 50 c., placed in vessel's bunkers and trimmed; coke, carload lots on cars, 4 dol. 50 c. per ton, retail delivered, 6 dol. 50 c. per ton.

In connection with the coal trade of Mobile, an important fact

UNITED STATES.

is the progress being made in the improvements of the Warrior river, extending 14¾ miles from Tuscaloosa to Daniel's creek in the very heart of the Warrior coalfield. The locks are completed, and the abutments for the dam nearly so. The gates are in position, and one dam is in course of construction. Barring any unforeseen accident, the work will be completed inside of twelve months. This would enable barges to be floated down from the coalfields to Mobile at mean high water, even prior to the completion of the improvements in the lower Warrior and the Bigbee, for which plans have been submitted to the department at Washington. In the figures given above no estimate is made of the coal consumed by tugs and railroads.

Our Fruit Trade.

Fruit trade. As a natural and inevitable result of deep water and increased water front facilities, with port charges, &c., which compare favourably with other competing ports of entry, there has been developed a business in the handling of tropical fruits which five years ago no one would have anticipated.

Receipts. The following are the receipts for two years past, compiled from vessels' manifests on file in the United States custom-house:

Articles.		Quantity.	
		1893-94.	1892-93.
Bananas..		1,539,344	365,610
Cocoanuts		5,018,150	2,936,415
Pineapples		104,810	87,399
Oranges..	Loose..	613,385	163,750
,,	Boxes	62,718	48,725
,,	Barrels	819	160
Lemons..		27,500	2,278
Plantains		169,175	75,000

Vegetables. Owing to continued unfavourable weather, there has been a large falling off in the production of vegetables during the past year as shown by figures below:—

Shipments.

Year.	Cabbages.		Potatoes.	
	Quantity.	Value.	Quantity.	Value.
	Crates.	Dollars.	Barrels.	Dollars.
1894	71,218	89,022	25,079	43,890
1893	136,799	187,943	73,325	112,187

Mobile Bay and Harbour.

The work of improvements in the dredged channel of Mobile river and bay has been prosecuted with marked results during the past year. Five powerful dredges have been continuously engaged night and day, widening and deepening the excavated channel leading to our wharves, and its condition is excellent, as evidenced by the increased number of vessels that have proceeded without detention to the lower anchorage, or directly to the Gulf of Mexico. These vessels have drawn from 20 feet to 22 feet 7 inches, and several vessels went over the bar drawing 23 feet 11 inches. To realize the magnitude of this work it will suffice to state that the channel is 33·09 miles in length, and that 6,000,000 cubic yards of material, consisting of soft blue clay and sand, have been removed during the past year, and 9,135,000 cubic yards of the same since the beginning of contracts covering the completion of the present project. The width of the channel is from 240 feet to 120 feet, the latter being only at one place. Its contemplated width will be 280 feet. By a natural process of scouring, caused by the discharge accumulated from the drainage of 40,000 square miles in extent, the water over the bar is yearly deepening. In 1771 it was 10 feet; in 1820, 17 feet; in 1856, 21·5 feet; in 1889, 23·5 feet; and to-day it is 24 feet. The eastern and western walls, forming a natural jetty, are contracting from Fort Morgan to the bar, giving additional scouring force to the waters discharging into the gulf. These results have proved very gratifying indeed, inspiring thorough confidence in the ultimate result of this vast undertaking, and giving us an unrivalled outlet to the gulf. Constantly increasing lines of swift steamers to various home and foreign ports, and especially the sudden development of a large trade in tropical fruits, have made our port a scene of maritime activity, which it is agreeable to record as a manifest testimonial of the importance of our geographical situation, commanding every day great recognition from the commercial world.

Harbourmaster's Report.

The following statement shows the number of vessels that have arrived and departed from this port, beginning September 1, 1893, and ending August 31, 1894. These vessels being of the larger class of sea-going vessels of their respective rigs, and showing the maximum draft of water as drawn by them going up and down the channel :—

Description.	Drawing up to and including		Number.	
	Up.	Down.	Up.	Down.
	Ft. in.	Ft. in.		
Steamships	16 0	21 6	225	228
Ships and barks	17 0	22 7	130	134
Brigs	13 0	15 6	16	16
Schooners	15 0	17 0	189	191
Total	..	..	560	569
,, up and down	..	..	1,129	

As against the corresponding time for the year beginning September 1, 1892, and ending August 31, 1893:—

	Number.
Total vessels up channel	484
,, down channel	497
Grand total	981
Difference in favour of 1893–94	147

While we fell off in the number of sailing vessels we increased in steamships, 105. Referring to the above report, these vessels have, with their respective drafts, passed up and down the channel without material detention.

Several ships have loaded to a draft of 23 feet 11 inches, and passed out over Mobile bar without touching, and that when there was some little swell on the bar.

NEW ORLEANS.

Annex A.—RETURN of all Shipping at the Port of Mobile during the Year 1894.

ENTERED.

Nationality.	Sailing. Number of Vessels.	Sailing. Tons.	Steam. Number of Vessels.	Steam. Tons.	Total. Number of Vessels.	Total. Tons.
British	95	22,567	35	42,749	130	65,316
Norwegian	72	67,180	154	59,340	226	126,520
Russian	17	10,299	8	5,192	25	15,491
Swedish	4	2,909	...	...	4	2,909
Italian	10	6,588	...	...	10	6,588
German	5	4,490	5	2,956	10	7,446
Danish	1	713	3	965	4	1,678
French	1	550	...	...	1	550
Spanish	1	349	2	3,310	3	3,659
Hondurian	2	222	...	...	2	222
American	62	23,134	1	242	63	23,376
Austrian	1	439	...	...	1	439
Columbian	5	315	...	...	5	315
Total	276	139,755	208	114,754	484	254,509
Coastwise	...	...	...	...	81	38,695
Total	...	...	...	...	565	293,204
,, for the year preceding	...	...	...	...	471	261,603

CLEARED.

Nationality.	Sailing. Number of Vessels.	Sailing. Tons.	Steam. Number of Vessels.	Steam. Tons.	Total. Number of Vessels.	Total. Tons.
British	101	28,185	33	39,273	134	67,458
Norwegian	77	71,139	147	57,052	224	128,191
Russian	12	6,943	9	5,841	21	12,784
Swedish	2	1,128	...	...	2	1,128
Italian	8	4,593	...	...	8	4,593
German	6	5,675	5	2,956	11	8,631
Danish	1	713	3	965	4	1,678
French	1	550	...	...	1	550
Spanish	1	349	...	...	1	349
Hondurian	2	222	...	...	2	222
American	80	30,527	1	242	81	30,769
Austrian	1	439	...	...	1	439
Columbian	5	315	...	...	5	315
Total	297	150,778	198	106,329	495	257,107
Coastwise	...	...	...	...	69	28,162
Total	...	...	...	...	564	285,269
,, for the year preceding	...	...	...	...	513	286,555

LONDON :
Printed for Her Majesty's Stationery Office,
By HARRISON AND SONS,
Printers in Ordinary to Her Majesty.
(75   5 | 95—H & S   1936)

FOREIGN OFFICE.
1895.
ANNUAL SERIES.

No. 1561.

DIPLOMATIC AND CONSULAR REPORTS ON TRADE AND FINANCE.

UNITED STATES.

REPORT FOR THE YEAR 1894
ON THE
TRADE OF THE DISTRICT OF THE CONSULATE-GENERAL OF NEW YORK.

REFERENCE TO PREVIOUS REPORT, Annual Series No. 1381.

Presented to both Houses of Parliament by Command of Her Majesty,
JUNE, 1895.

LONDON:
PRINTED FOR HER MAJESTY'S STATIONERY OFFICE,
BY HARRISON AND SONS, ST. MARTIN'S LANE,
PRINTERS IN ORDINARY TO HER MAJESTY.

And to be purchased, either directly or through any Bookseller, from
EYRE & SPOTTISWOODE, EAST HARDING STREET, FLEET STREET, E.C., and
32, ABINGDON STREET, WESTMINSTER, S.W.; or
JOHN MENZIES & Co., 12, HANOVER STREET, EDINBURGH, and
90, WEST NILE STREET, GLASGOW; or
HODGES, FIGGIS, & Co., Limited, 104, GRAFTON STREET, DUBLIN.

1895.

[C. 7581—101.]   *Price Twopence.*

New Series of Reports.

Reports of the Annual Series have been issued from Her Majesty's Diplomatic and Consular Officers at the following places, and may be obtained from the sources indicated on the title-page:—

No.		Price.	No.		Price.
1441.	Tahiti	½d.	1501.	Bordeaux	3d.
1442.	Shanghai	2d.	1502.	Madrid	2d.
1443.	Nagasaki	1d.	1503.	Amsterdam	1d.
1444.	Madrid	2½d.	1504.	Suakin	1d.
1445.	Malaga	2½d.	1505.	Angora	1d.
1446.	Rotterdam	1d.	1506.	Havre	2½d.
1447.	Port Said	1d.	1507.	Algiers	11d.
1448.	Sofia	2½d.	1508.	La Rochelle	3d.
1449.	Warsaw	1½d.	1509.	Vera Cruz	2d.
1450.	Africa (Congo)	2d.	1510.	Puerto Cortes	1d.
1451.	Jeddah	1½d.	1511.	Taganrog	1d.
1452.	San Francisco	5½d.	1512.	Baltimore	1½d.
1453.	Oporto	2d.	1513.	Mexico	1½d.
1454.	Barcelona	2d.	1514.	Zaila	1d.
1455.	New Caledonia	½d.	1515.	Zomba	3½d.
1456.	Smyrna	1d.	1516.	Valparaiso	2½d.
1457.	Macao	1d.	1517.	Charleston	2½d.
1458.	Samoa	1d.	1518.	Serajevo	1d.
1459.	Hiogo and Osaka	3d.	1519.	Saigon	1d.
1460.	Lisbon	2d.	1520.	Bangkok	2d.
1461.	Pekin	2d.	1521.	Tripoli	1d.
1462.	Corunna	2d.	1522.	Batavia	1½d.
1463.	Mozambique	15d.	1523.	Dakar	½d.
1464.	Munich	1½d.	1524.	Havana	2d.
1465.	St. Petersburg	3d.	1525.	Riga	2d.
1466.	Naples	1d.	1526.	Trebizond	1½d.
1467.	Montevideo	2½d.	1527.	Piræus	2½d.
1468.	Aden	1d.	1528.	Guayaquil	1½d.
1469.	Tokio	1½d.	1529.	Marseilles	1½d.
1470.	Dantzig	5d.	1530.	Wuhu	1½d.
1471.	Guayaquil	1d.	1531.	Rio de Janeiro	2½d.
1472.	Canton	1½d.	1532.	Trieste	2d.
1473.	Dar-al-Baida	3d.	1533.	Brest	1½d.
1474.	Teheran	2d.	1534.	Stockholm	2d.
1475.	Bushire	2d.	1535.	Warsaw	1d.
1476.	Tangier	2d.	1536.	Boston	1½d.
1477.	Rome	2d.	1537.	Mozambique	2½d.
1478.	Hamburg	4d.	1538.	Callao	1d.
1479.	The Hague	1½d.	1539.	Aleppo	1½d.
1480.	Belgrade	2d.	1540.	Jaffa	½d.
1481.	Batoum	1½d.	1541.	Boston	1d.
1482.	Teneriffe	½d.	1542.	New Orleans	1½d.
1483.	Lisbon	2½d.	1543.	Chicago	3d.
1484.	Buda-Pesth	½d.	1544.	Palermo	2½d.
1485.	Rome	5½d.	1545.	Bengazi	1½d.
1486.	Para	1d.	1546.	Cagliari	1d.
1487.	Odessa	1d.	1547.	Pernambuco	7½d.
1488.	Hakodate	1d.	1548.	Madrid	1½d.
1489.	Beira	1½d.	1549.	Corunna	5d.
1490.	Berne	1½d.	1550.	Leghorn	2d.
1491.	Copenhagen	1d.	1551.	New Orleans	2½d.
1492.	Stettin	2½d.	1552.	Syra	1½d.
1493.	Rio Grande do Sul	1½d.	1553.	Genoa	9d.
1494.	Serajevo	1d.	1554.	Berlin	2½d.
1495.	Buenos Ayres	9d.	1555.	Tainan	1d.
1496.	Florence	2d.	1556.	Zanzibar	4d.
1497.	Lisbon	1½d.	1557.	Dunkirk	1d.
1498.	Paris	2d.	1558.	Ningpo	1d.
1499.	Bolivia	1½d.	1559.	Pakhoi	1d.
1500.	Patras	1½d.	1560.	Chinkiang	1d.

No. 1561.

Reference to previous Report, Annual Series No. 1381.

UNITED STATES.

NEW YORK.

Consul-General Sanderson to the Earl of Kimberley.

My Lord,   New York, April 30, 1895.

I HAVE the honour to forward my Annual Report on the Trade and Commerce of the Consular District of New York, together with a Report of a similar character which I have received from Mr. Vice-Consul Stockwell respecting Providence, Rhode Island.

I have, &c.
(Signed)   PERCY SANDERSON.

Report on the Trade and Commerce of the Consular District of New York for the Year 1894.

ABSTRACT of Contents.

	Page
General remarks..	2
General review of trade	2
Extraordinary depression	2
Railroads..	3
Agricultural products..	3
Imports and exports	3
Money market	4
Position of New York Clearing House Banks	4
New York Clearing House returns	5
Exchange on London	5
Methods of quoting sterling exchange	5
Stock Exchange..	6
Produce Exchange	7
Failures..	7
State banks of deposit and discount	7
Debt of New York State	8
New York city debt	8
Valuations	8

(1974)

UNITED STATES.

ABSTRACT of Contents—continued.

	PAGE
Trade and commerce—	
Dry goods	8
Cottons	9
Woollens	9
Domestic wool	10
Foreign ,,	10
Carpet wools	10
Prospects of woollen industries	10
Silks	10
Ocean freights—	
Grain	10
General merchandise	10
Cattle	11
Cotton	11
Coal	11
Timber	11
Immigration	11
Sugar	11
Sailing vessels	11
Petroleum	11
General merchandise to Brazil and River Plate	11
Public works	12
Canals	12
Railroad traffic	13
Vital statistics	14
Immigration statistics	14
Return of shipping	16
Principal articles of export	17
,, ,, import	18
Specie—exports and imports	18
Table showing grain shipments	19
Return of seamen	20
Providence, Rhode Island—	
General remarks	21
Money market	21
Custom-house statistics	21
Labour	22
Jewellery business	22
The wool market	22
The cotton market	23
Machinery	23
Lumber	23
Public improvements	23
Public health	24
Return of shipping	24
Imports and exports	25

General Review of Trade.

Extraordinary depression. The expectation that the year 1894 would show decided signs of recovery after the extreme depression of 1893 was not realised. From time to time there appeared to be a tendency towards a revival of business activity, but fresh obstacles presented themselves at every turn, and the year will be noted as one of extraordinary depression in trade and industry, although unmarked by a record of failures such as usually accompanies such conditions.

Contributing causes. Amongst the contributing causes may be mentioned the state of the national finances. With a declining and deficient revenue, and at the same time an obligation to maintain the position of silver and legal tender notes as convertible with gold, the Government found it necessary to issue bonds. Two such issues were made during the year, one in February, the other in November, in each case for a nominal amount of 50,000,000 dol. These bonds were made "payable in coin," and although the practice hitherto has been to pay in gold, attention was directed to the efforts of the silver party in Congress. Amongst other matters a bill was passed to coin the seignorage on silver, and was only prevented from becoming law by the veto of the President. A feeling of insecurity arose as to the policy which might be adopted at some future time, and this feeling became stronger towards the close of the year. While it is estimated that the excess of exports of merchandise and silver during the 12 months amounted to about 38,000,000*l.*, the net exports of gold amounted during the same period to over 16,000,000*l.*, and then did not represent the total amount of gold withdrawn from the Treasury during that period. The export remained unchecked and showed a tendency rather to increase than decrease at the beginning of 1895.

Another cause may be found in the tariff legislation, which formed the subject of a conflict between the two houses of Congress, and dragged on till the month of August, when it was passed somewhat abruptly.

To these may be added, strikes, of which the most notable were those of the bituminous coal miners, which lasted from April 21 to June 18, and caused a lack of fuel which affected industrial establishments and railways; and the general strike of railroad men in July; floods, which interrupted the railway communication on some lines for a fortnight; and extensive forest fires.

Railroads. The condition of the railroads was very unsatisfactory, the falling-off in the gross receipts of the United States railroads in the first 6 months of the year was estimated at 100,000,000 dol., or over 20,000,000*l.*, and that of the net receipts at about half that sum during the same period. As a result reductions in and suspensions of dividend were numerous.

Agricultural products. As regards agricultural products, the crop of Indian corn throughout the United States was estimated at 1,212,000,000 bushels, as compared with 1,619,000,000 bushels in 1893, and 2,060,000,000 bushels in 1894. In some of the States this crop was almost a total failure. The wheat crop was a fair average, estimated at about 460,000,000 bushels, against 396,000,000 bushels in 1893. Oats, 632,000,000 bushels, as compared with 639,000,000 bushels in 1893. In cotton the aggregate yield was very large but the price was extremely low, the average being estimated at under 5 c., or about 2½*d.* a pound.

Imports and Exports.

Imports and exports. As might be expected under such conditions the value of both imports and exports fell off very considerably as compared with

(1974)

UNITED STATES.

immediately preceding years, the former in view of the necessity for curtailing expenses, and the latter in consequence of the low prices ruling. The total imports of merchandise into the United States showed a decrease of about 100,000,000 dol. in 1894, as compared with 1893, and were the smallest since 1886; the value of the exports was about 50,000,000 dol. less than in 1893, and the smallest since 1888.

The excess of silver exports over the imports of the same metal are returned at about 36,500,000 dol., as against 28,000,000 dol. in 1893, and of gold at about 81,000,000 dol., as compared with about 7,000,000 dol. in 1893.

Money Market.

New York money market.

In the money market the contraction of the volume of trade led to an accumulation of currency in the banks, and to very low rates for loans of all descriptions.

On February 3, 1894, the surplus reserve of the New York clearing-house banks stood as high as 111,623,000 dol., or over 22,000,000*l*., at the close of the year the surplus had been reduced to 35,269,000 dol. (7,054,000*l*.), but the rates for loans remained about the same. The discount rates for good commercial 60 to 90 day bills ranged between 2½ and 3¾ per cent.

The following table shows the position of the New York clearing-house banks at different periods of the year, the rate of conversion being 5 dol. to the 1*l*. sterling:—

TABLE showing Position of New York Clearing-house Banks during the Year 1894.

Week Ending—	Loans.	Deposits.	Specie.	Legal Tenders.	Reserve to Deposits.	Surplus Reserve.
	£	£	£	£	Per cent.	£
January 6	83,761,500	103,704,900	22,214,700	20,470,900	41·16	16,759,300
February 3	83,906,100	110,361,700	25,911,800	24,003,200	45·20	22,324,600
March 3	87,860,700	106,348,200	19,505,300	22,237,600	39·25	15,155,800
April 7	90,085,300	110,899,400	19,924,600	23,960,000	39·56	16,159,600
May 5	93,032,400	115,738,800	20,016,400	25,480,000	39·30	16,561,600
June 2	92,998,700	114,427,700	19,803,700	24,396,200	38·62	15,593,100
July 7	96,750,700	117,719,700	18,244,600	25,612,300	37·39	14,426,900
August 4	96,460,900	116,311,200	18,109,400	24,779,200	36·87	13,810,700
September 1	97,976,000	117,194,800	18,237,600	24,225,300	36·23	13,164,200
October 6	100,055,400	117,908,300	18,443,000	22,924,200	35·08	11,890,200
November 3	100,164,400	119,021,000	18,751,100	23,645,000	35·02	12,640,800
December 1	99,892,000	115,967,100	15,305,500	24,130,400	34	10,444,200
,, 2	98,529,400	109,858,300	14,752,200	19,766,200	31·42	7,153,800

The surplus reserve represents the excess over 25 per cent. of the deposits, and the returns give the averages of each week, not the results on the day mentioned.

In 1893 the maximum of deposits was 101,287,600*l*. and the minimum 74,060,500*l*.; the maximum of the surplus reserve 16,163,000*l*., and the minimum a deficiency of 3,309,800*l*.

New York clearing-house returns.

The New York clearing-house returns are the smallest of any year since 1878. Those of 1893 showed a decrease of

NEW YORK.

14·7 per cent., as compared with 1892, but in 1894 there was a still further decrease of 22 per cent., as compared with 1893. The actual figures for the two years are 24,387,807,020 dol. in 1894, and 31,261,037,730 dol. in 1893, or if the rough computation of 5 dol. to the 1*l.* sterling be admitted for purposes of comparison, 4,877,561,404*l.* in 1894, as compared with 6,252,207,546*l.* in 1893. The small extent of stock exchange business, and the fact that many such transactions are now cleared independently will account in some measure for this decrease, but financial transactions and enterprise in general seem to have been checked, and low prices of agricultural products and other articles tended largely in the same direction.

The decrease was most marked in the first quarter of the year, during the last 3 months there was a slight increase as compared with 1893, as will appear from the following table:—

Year.	1st Quarter.	2nd Quarter.	3rd Quarter.	4th Quarter.	Total.
	In Thousands.				
1894	Dollars. 5,938,415	Dollars. 6,010,084	Dollars. 5,580,000	Dollars. 6,859,298	Dollars. 24,387,807
	£ 1,187,683	£ 1,202,017	£ 1,116,000	£ 1,371,860	£ 4,877,560
1893	Dollars. 9,879,033	Dollars. 8,487,726	Dollars. 6,192,642	Dollars. 6,701,637	Dollars. 31,261,038
	£ 1,975,807	£ 1,697,545	£ 1,238,528	£ 1,340,347	£ 6,252,207

The following taken from the "Financial Review, 1895," may be of interest:—

Exchange on London.

"The methods of quoting sterling exchange have varied widely in the past. In the early history of the country the 1*l.* sterling was valued at 4 dol. 44$\frac{4}{9}$ c., based on the value of the Spanish dollar, then current as a standard. Exchange was then quoted at its real value, the dollar being worth almost exactly 4*s.* 6*d.* English money.

Methods of quoting sterling exchange.

"From 1792 to 1834 the American gold coin was of the same standard as the 1*l.* sterling, viz., 22 carats or 916$\frac{2}{3}$ parts in 1,000, and its legal weight of 27 grains the 1 dol. was worth about 97$\frac{1}{3}$ c., and the 1*l.* sterling in American money about 4 dol. 56$\frac{1}{2}$ c.

"In 1834 there was a material reduction in the value of the American gold coin, so that the 1 dol. was worth only about 91$\frac{1}{4}$ c., and the 1*l.* sterling about 4 dol. 87 c. In 1837 another slight change made the 1 dol. worth about 91$\frac{1}{3}$ c., and the 1*l.* about 4 dol. 86$\frac{2}{3}$ c. In 1834 the custom-house valuation of the sovereign was put at 4 dol. 84 c., and it so remained till January 1, 1874. During the changes from 1834 to January 1, 1874, the London Stock Exchange continued to reckon the 1 dol. at 4*s.* 6*d.* (about 9 to 9$\frac{1}{2}$ per cent. too high) involving the practice of quoting American securities about 8$\frac{2}{3}$ per cent. below their actual value. To correspond with the English custom, bankers in New York from 1834 to 1874 quoted sterling exchange at 109-45$\frac{5}{8}$ as par.

(1974)

UNITED STATES.

"By the law of Congress of March 3, 1873, the custom-house valuation of the 1*l.* sterling was placed at its true value of 4·8665 dol., and from January 1, 1874, has been quoted accordingly, the quotation when at par being 4·8665 dol. The London Stock Exchange also made a change in their method of quoting early in 1874, but valued the 1 **dol.** at 4*s.*, or about 97⅓ c.

Sterling exchange in 1894.

"This valuation being about 2⅔ c. below par is equal to a quotable premium of about 2¾ per cent., and accordingly the present London quotation of American securities are about 2¾ per cent. above their actual value, a bond worth 100 in America being quoted in London at 102¾.

"The following table shows the posted rates of sterling exchange, highest and lowest during the different months of 1894, these are as a rule fractionally higher than the rates at which the bulk of transactions are made:—

TABLE showing the Posted Rates of Sterling Exchange for the Year 1894.

Month.		At 60 Days.	At Sight.
January	lowest	4·84	4·86½
	highest	4·86	4·88
February	lowest	4·85	4·87½
	highest	4·87½	4·89½
March	lowest	4·87½	4·89
	highest	4·88	4·89½
April	lowest	4·87½	4·89
	highest	4·88	4·89½
May	lowest	4·88	4·89½
	highest	4·88½	4·90
June	lowest	4·87½	4·89
	highest	4·88½	4·90
July	lowest	4·87½	4·89
	highest	4·88½	4·89½
August	lowest	4·86	4·87½
	highest	4·88½	4·89½
September	lowest	4·85	4·86½
	highest	4·87	4·88
October	lowest	4·86	4·87
	highest	4·88	4·89
November	lowest	4·86½	4·88
	highest	4·87½	4·89
December	lowest	4·87	4·88½
	highest	4·89	4·90

"Under ordinary circumstances the rate for bills payable on demand which admits of the export of gold from New York to London is about 4 dol. 88 c. for bars, and 4 dol. 89 c. for coin, and the rate at which gold can be imported without loss is 4 dol. 83½ c."

Rate adopted in this report.

The rate of exchange which has been adopted throughout this report for converting dollars into pounds sterling is the London Stock Exchange rate of 5 dol. to the 1*l*.

NEW YORK.

Stock exchange. The dealings on the stock exchange were smaller than for many years past, the months of March and August and the beginning of December being the only exception to the general inactivity.

Produce exchange. On the produce exchange the sales were slightly larger than in 1893 but below those of other recent years.

Failures. The following, taken from tables prepared by Messrs. R. G. Dun and Co., shows the number of commercial failures in this consular district in 1894 as compared with 1893:—

	Number of Failures.		Amount of Liabilities.	
	1894.	1893.	1894. £	1893. £
New York	1,976	1,916	7,371,645	16,984,750
Connecticut	253	234	364,230	619,030
New Jersey	212	322	670,350	956,760
Rhode Island	187	181	296,120	206,930
Delaware	61	35	187,360	129,100
Whole of United States	13,885	15,242	38,598,600	69,356,000

State banks of deposit and discount. In his report for the fiscal year, ended September 30, 1894, the Superintendent of Banks for the State of New York mentions that 3 banks were closed for insolvency and 1 bank and 1 individual banker went into voluntary liquidation; that 10 new banks had been closed during the year, and that the 207 banks and 4 individual bankers were in a flourishing condition as a whole. The total capital amounted to about 6,500,000*l.*, showing a slight decrease for the year, and the resources and liabilities were about 54,300,000*l.* In his report the Superintendent recommends that the law should be amended so as to provide that the whole capital stock of a bank shall be paid in before the bank is authorised to commence business. As the law stands at present at least 50 per cent. of the capital stock must be paid in before the bank commences business, and the remainder in instalments of 10 per cent. at the end of each succeeding month. Further, that no officer or employé of a bank be permitted to borrow any of its funds without first applying to the directors and obtaining the favourable opinion of a quorum of the board; that every bank whose surplus does not amount to 20 per cent. of its capital shall be required to set apart at least 10 per cent. of its profits till this proportion is reached; that a uniform method of original entry of deposits should be made compulsory; that the practice of a bank lending money on the security of its own capital should be prohibited; and that institutions receiving money on deposits from sailors, immigrants, and people of this class should be subjected to some reasonable regulation and examination. Two further recommendations are added in respect of the currency, namely, to authorise the Secretary of the Treasury to issue $2\frac{1}{2}$ per cent. bonds, payable in, say 30 years, and with the proceeds retire the legal

UNITED STATES.

tender and Treasury notes, thus creating a bond issue at a very low rate of interest, to be used to secure the circulation to be taken out by the bonds on a par basis; and to repeal the National Banking Act in all respects, except the provisions relating to the issue of the currency and the re-issuing the same, so that all banks shall become State banks and subject to State supervision.

Debt of New York State. The State of New York has been completely out of debt since the close of the fiscal year, which ended on September 30, 1894. The tax rate for the present year is 2 dol. 18 c. per 1,000 as compared with 2 dol. 58 c. last year.

New York City debt. The position of the funded and temporary debts of the city of New York on December 31, 1894, as compared with the same date in 1893, is shown below:—

	December 31, 1893.		December 31, 1894.	
	Currency.	Sterling.	Currency.	Sterling.
	Dollars.	£	Dollars.	£
Funded debt	166,470,849	..	173,991,081	..
Sinking fund	65,708,442	..	69,912,260	..
Net funded debt	100,762,407	20,152,481	104,078,820	20,815,764
Temporary debt	666,074	133,215	1,699,034	339,807

Valuations. The valuations for the year 1894 were:—Real estate, 1,613,057,735 dol.; personal estate, residents, 268,108,047 dol.; non-residents, 33,947,478 dol.; shareholders of banks, 88,218,780 dol.; a total of 2,003,352,037 dol. (400,670,000*l*.). The total taxes for 1894 were 35,659,000 dol. (7,132,000*l*.), levied by a tax of 1·79 per cent. on the assessed valuations of real and personal estate, and 1·585 per cent. on the assessed valuation of the personal estate of such corporations, &c., as were subject to local taxation thereon.

Trade and Commerce.

Dry goods. The business depression and panic which first became apparent about July, 1893, lasted 12 months, and has, consequently, affected the trade of 1894 as well as that of 1893. The profits made in the first half of 1893 were more than swept away during the last 6 months of that year, while it was not till July, 1894, that any real change for the better became manifest. There had been an expectation that there would be no tariff legislation, and the passage of the Bill caused heavy losses to holders of woollen and other classes of dress goods, but by July of 1894 the prices of dry goods, and especially woollens, had fallen so low that there was far less danger in handling and carrying stocks than there had been during the two previous half years.

The financial questions of the day have had their influence on this trade and great caution has been exercised, but it is estimated that most houses during the last 6 months of 1894 more than covered the losses made in the earlier part of the year, and it would appear that the decline in values has reached its lowest point. The present difficulty appears to be how to increase sales in the same ratio as the decrease in values, as a much larger quantity of goods must be handled to produce the same profit as in the past.

Manufacturers of cotton goods have been favoured by the low price of the raw material, but have had to deal with heavy competition. The export trade with China has been seriously affected by the war between that country and Japan; that with South America and Africa, although below an average, has served partially to counterbalance this loss. Low prices have tended to increase the volume of sales, yet the tendency seems to be towards overproduction, judging from the fact that, notwithstanding mills being closed down for weeks, and sometimes months, 27,000 packages placed upon the market by a large corporation were sold at auction for what are described as ruinously low prices.   *Cottons.*

The passing of the free wool tariff by Congress in August, 1894, was a most important event in the history of the wool trade, and the following remarks are taken from a report prepared for the chamber of commerce by a well-known wool merchant.   *Woollens.*

The culmination of protection came with the McKinley Bill of 1890, and its repeal quickly followed. The experiment of free wool and moderate duties on goods had to be faced, and the result seems to be in favour of the contention that free wool is of immense advantage to the American manufacturer as well as to the American consumer.

With an almost prohibitory duty upon foreign wool the American article was alone freely available to the American manufacturers and had to be made the best of, even when unsuitable for the desired results. Foreign manufacturers could select the most suitable wools for every purpose at abnormally low prices owing to the absence of American competition, and could thus successfully fight a high tariff upon goods. The change has given the American manufacturer the choice of the wools of the world, and, although he is in some measure handicapped by the higher rate of wages ruling, this is compensated by the 40 per cent. protection. The course of the trade since the new tariff has thoroughly sustained the prediction of the advocates of free wool. The manufacturers had 4 months given them before the reduced duties upon goods came into force, and they utilised this in meeting, upon a free trade basis for their wool, the active demand which had long been in abeyance owing to tariff agitation. When January 1, 1895, was reached, American products were offered fully as cheap as foreign, and were given the preference, even at a slightly higher price, being better known and of a better quality. No mills have been closed but more machinery has been started, and the natural apprehension of the millowners has given way to great confidence as to the future. They do not claim that profits are large or even reasonable, but they maintain that they can hold their own and do more when they have had time to adapt

Domestic wool.

themselves better to the novel conditions and when the country resumes its normal prosperity.

During the long discussion in Congress the price of wool steadily declined, the stock of domestic wools of a medium to a medium fine grade was larger at the end of the year, in fact, only slightly less than at the close of 1893, the panic year, and there seems no prospect of any immediate rise.

Foreign wools.

Foreign wools have not found so large a market as had been anticipated with the advent of the new tariff, owing to the large domestic supply. A moderate amount of Australian combing has been introduced, but the importations of River Plate, Cape of Good Hope, and skin and scoured wools have been small, and so unremunerative as to deter further operations for the moment.

Carpet wools.

Carpet wools have declined nearly 20 per cent. during the year owing to bad trade, idle machinery, large stocks accumulated during the previous year, and uncertainty as to tariff legislation. Heavy importations were made in the spring in anticipation of free wool, and since the change was made sales have only been possible at reduced prices.

Prospects of woollen industries.

The prospects are looked upon as favourable, inasmuch as with better trade, broader markets and greater experience, more of the fine wools of the world are likely to find an outlet in America, while the stock of goods is small and with a revival of general business an active trade may reasonably be expected.

Silks.

During the year 1893 the silk trade had to contend with strikes of work people in addition to the adverse influence affecting trade in general, and the result has been that the output of many mills has been governed in 1894 entirely by the firm orders received, those making goods for stock restricting their operations as much as possible. With rare exceptions there was no accumulation of stock at the end of the year.

The value of the imports of silk manufactures at the port of New York in the year 1894 amounted to about 4,557,000*l*. as compared with an average of about 6,800,000*l*. for the previous 5 years. The value of the raw material, namely, raw silk, waste, pierced cocoons, and nails imported at all ports in the United States was over 5,000,000*l*., a considerable increase over 1893, and much the same as in 1891.

Review of the Freight Market.

Ocean freights. Steamers.

The carrying trade from America has been, with few exceptions, of an unsatisfactory nature, there has been little attractive business, and the conditions have been unfavourable for vessels belonging to the regular lines. At the commencement of the year freights were fairly active and rates to most ports were well maintained, but as the year advanced there was a great diminution in the export of grain to Europe, notwithstanding the low prices ruling.

Grain.

General merchandise.

There was a fair volume of general merchandise, but not offering in sufficiently large quantities to counteract the weak tendency of grain freights. It would seem that the establishing of freight lines has placed vertu freights upon a lower basis.

The movement of cattle has been rather more extensive than usual, amounting to over 160,000 head from New York. This was divided among the different steamship companies customarily employed in this trade, and gave employment besides to a good many outside vessels. Satisfactory rates were obtained for a considerable time, but latterly this traffic was interfered with by the prohibition by some of the European Governments of the import of American cattle. *Cattle.*

The shipments of cotton have been very heavy, and on the whole the season may be considered a satisfactory one for owners of vessels employed in this trade. Charterers were at first inclined to hold out for lower rates than shipowners were prepared to accept, but the rates finally conceded left a fair margin of profit and they were well maintained. The compressing of the cotton shipped from all the ports has been most unsatisfactory during the greater part of the season, and this is generally attributed to the carelessness of the compressors in the interior, and to their inability to meet the pressure of business which was thrust upon them. *Cotton.*

The coal trade with the West Indies and Central America continues to increase, and the rates of freight obtained compare favourably with those ruling from British ports. *Coal.*

Steam tonnage has found fair employment in the timber trade, in view of the gradual disappearance of sailing vessels, and it is likely to maintain its position in the future. *Timber.*

The imports have been interfered with by the protracted discussion over the tariff legislation.

Vessels of regular lines, with their obligation to sail at fixed dates as advertised, have been great sufferers for want of sufficient cargoes to American ports, and they have had at the same time to contend with a steady and serious diminution of steerage passengers, the immigration having fallen off to a very remarkable extent. *Immigration.*

Some of the best freights obtained during the year were for sugar from the Cuban ports. The uncertainty as to the duty to be imposed under the new tariff created a continuous demand for ready tonnage, and vessels in the right position were enabled to secure good rates of freight. *Sugar.*

The business of sailing vessels has, on the whole, been unsatisfactory. They are continually being encroached upon by steamers, it is difficult for them to obtain remunerative rates, and their number is fast diminishing. *Sailing vessels.*

The export of petroleum in barrels is almost entirely in the hands of the Standard Oil Company, who can practically dictate what rates of freight they will pay. During the summer months freights improved somewhat, but later in the year a reaction took place, and there was a steady decline. *Petroleum.*

During the months of September and October there was a brisk demand for tonnage to carry oil in cases, lumber, and general merchandise to Brazil and the River Plate, in anticipation of a *General merchandise to Brazil and River Plate.*

considerable increase in the customs duties in those countries, to take effect on January 1, 1895, but this demand having been satisfied trade in that direction became dull, and rates declined.

Public Works.

Canals.

The report of the Superintendent of Public Works shows that 3,882,570 tons (of 2,000 lbs.) passed through the canals in 1894, being a reduction of nearly 450,000 tons as compared with 1893, and about 400,000 tons as compared with 1892. This tonnage was distributed as follows:—

	Quantity.
	Tons.
Erie Canal	3,144,144
Champlain Canal	550,279
Black River	56,024
Oswego River	98,843
Cayuga and Seneca	33,270

showing a diminution in each case, the most serious being that of the Champlain Canal, nearly 300,000 tons.

It was composed mainly of the following articles:—

	Quantity.
	Tons.
Products of the forests	872,601
„ „ agriculture	1,412,142
Merchandise	352,741
Manufactures	87,241
Anthracite coal	532,584
Bituminous „	76,784
Stone, lime, and clay	432,370
Domestic salt	66,868
Iron ore	37,641

There was an increase in the quantities of merchandise, manufactures, and domestic salt, but a more than corresponding decrease in the other articles.

As regards the delivery of flour and grain at New York, the figures from January 1 to November 30, 1894, are 114,468,184 bushels, of which 42,608,700 bushels came by canal, equal to about 37 per cent., as compared with 39½ per cent. in 1893, and 23 per cent. in 1892.

In this report it is pointed out that this is the smallest tonnage that has been transported on the canal during any year since 1859, and is the result of various causes, the principal ones being the general stagnation of business during the past year, and the inadequacy of the canals to compete successfully with the railroads for this carrying trade. In connection with this latter cause the Superintendent makes observations to the following effect:—

"While the railways are continually being perfected for this carrying trade, and all other routes are continually being improved for a similar object, the canals have been but little improved in the past quarter of a century. The national Government has made a channel of the depth of 20 feet through the great lakes of Buffalo; they are deepening the Hudson River to a depth of 12 feet to Albany and to Troy. The Canadian Government is making preparations to enlarge its canal of 12 feet to one of 20 feet, so that vessels drawing nearly 20 feet of water may pass direct from Chicago to Montreal; but the Erie and Oswego Canals have only 7 feet of water, the Champlain Canal but 5 feet, and no provision is made by the State of New York for canal improvements to meet this competition.

"A reference is made to section 8 of Article 7 of the Constitution of the State of New York, which provides that 'the Erie Canal, the Champlain Canal, the Oswego Canal, the Black River Canal, and the Cayuga and Seneca Canals shall not be sold, leased, or otherwise disposed of, but shall remain the property of the State, and under its management for ever;' and the report concludes with a recommendation that the Legislature provide the means for the construction of the largest possible canal, intended for boats of such construction as will be able to navigate the inland waters of the State, discharging and receiving their cargoes at Buffalo and New York, or other intermediate points, bearing in mind the necessity for a full and free supply of water, a careful research for the damage that may possibly occur to adjacent property in consequence of such enlargement, and with a view to the most economical method by which such a waterway can be constructed."

Railroads.

During the year 1894 the total tonnage of all classes of merchandise sent westward from New York city by rail was 1,335,926 tons, of 2,000 lbs.; that received amounted to 3,571,318 tons. *Railroad traffic.*

The railroads carrying these goods are New York Central and Hudson River; New York, Lake Erie, and Western; Pennsylvania; Baltimore and Ohio; West Shore; Delaware, Lackawanna, and Western; Lehigh Valley; New York, Ontario, and Western.

The amounts show a reduction as compared with 1893, when the figures were 1,414,736 tons westward, and 4,264,654 tons eastward, while in 1892 they ran still higher, viz., 1,576,239 tons westward, and 5,402,998 tons eastward.

UNITED STATES.

Vital Statistics of New York City for the Years 1894–93.

	Number.	
	1894.	1893.
Births	55,636	51,529
Marriages	17,388	16,144
Deaths	41,175	44,486

Of the deaths reported 17,549 were under 5 years of age. Of that number 10,824 were under 1 year.

Principal Causes of Deaths.	Number.	
	1894.	1893.
Phthisis	4,658	5,124
Pneumonia	4,725	6,487
Bronchitis	1,329	1,577
Diphtheria	2,359	1,970
Croup	511	588
Measles	584	393
Scarlet fever	541	551
Cerebro-spinal meningitis	213	469
Diarrhœal diseases	2,996	3,310
Heart diseases	2,170	2,379
Brights disease	2,479	2,071
Typhoid fever	326	381
Typhus ,,	..	..
Small-pox	154	102
Violence	1,780	1,968

Death rate for 1894, 21·05 per 1,000; for 1893, 23·52 per 1,000.

Immigration.

Immigration statistics. The immigration returns show a great diminution in the number of immigrants landing at New York, the figures being 167,655 in 1894, as compared with 352,885 in 1893, or rather less than one-half. The countries from which they came and their destination are noted below.

NEW YORK.

Country.	Male.	Female.	Total. 1894.	Total. 1893.
	Number.	Number.	Number.	Number.
Great Britain	8,476	4,863	13,339	19,985
Ireland	8,284	12,192	20,476	30,236
Austria-Hungary	11,391	7,663	19,054	57,149
Belgium	380	260	640	2,008
Denmark	2,097	1,564	3,661	7,019
France	1,186	888	2,074	3,644
Germany	13,821	11,997	25,818	55,981
Greece	1,005	30	1,035	1,331
Italy	27,441	9,282	36,723	69,074
Netherlands	717	418	1,135	5,273
Norway	3,158	2,266	5,424	12,862
Portugal	530	643	1,173	3,398
Roumania	208	174	382	..
Russia	11,326	10,233	21,559	48,124
Spain	120	28	148	80
Sweden	4,797	5,570	10,367	28,965
Switzerland	1,383	824	2,207	4,018
Turkey	1,478	684	2,162	1,554
Other countries	233	55	288	2,184
Total	98,031	69,634	167,665	352,885

	Number.
North Atlantic States	123,960
South ,, ,,	2,185
North Central ,,	33,140
South ,, ,,	3,272
Western and Pacific States	5,108

In addition to the above, 1,516 immigrants were refused, 798 of these as being paupers, or likely to become a public charge, and 712 as contract labourers.

(1974)

UNITED STATES.

Return of all Shipping at the Port of New York during the Year 1894.

Entered.

Country.	Steam. Number of Vessels.	Steam. Tons.	Sailing. Number of Vessels.	Sailing. Tons.	Total. Number of Vessels.	Total. Tons.
Great Britain and Colonies	1,632	3,078,653	830	386,846	2,462	3,465,499
United States	327	735,191	733	375,197	1,060	1,110,388
Germany	448	1,223,360	45	52,838	493	1,276,198
France	94	307,848	4	1,990	98	309,838
Sweden and Norway	154	86,379	39	31,039	193	117,418
Belgium	78	251,748	...	...	78	251,748
Italy	13	17,184	74	58,339	87	75,523
Mexico	...	...	...	...	...	...
Netherlands	139	298,568	7	7,279	146	305,847
Austria	1	2,004	4	3,426	5	5,430
Spain	55	89,353	3	1,992	58	91,345
Denmark	31	59,217	1	391	32	59,608
Other European countries	25	42,652	5	3,187	30	45,839
South America	...	...	2	881	2	881
Central America	...	...	...	...	...	...
Other countries	...	...	5	1,556	5	1,556
Total	2,997	6,192,157	1,752	924,961	4,749	7,117,118

Cleared.

Country.	Steam. Number of Vessels.	Steam. Tons.	Sailing. Number of Vessels.	Sailing. Tons.	Total. Number of Vessels.	Total. Tons.
Great Britain and Colonies	1,596	3,067,022	799	382,020	2,395	3,449,042
United States	330	739,264	606	328,532	936	1,067,796
Germany	411	1,114,533	45	52,627	456	1,167,160
France	93	307,236	6	3,958	99	311,194
Sweden and Norway	151	84,523	43	32,192	194	116,715
Belgium	73	242,229	...	...	73	242,229
Italy	13	17,184	57	46,699	70	63,883
Mexico	...	...	...	...	...	...
Netherlands	138	296,446	8	9,210	146	305,656
Austria	1	2,031	6	4,988	7	7,019
Spain	53	84,489	3	951	56	85,440
Denmark	33	61,818	3	869	36	62,687
Other European countries	25	42,252	5	3,174	30	45,426
South America	...	...	3	1,393	3	1,393
Central America	...	...	...	...	...	...
Other countries	...	...	2	1,131	2	1,131
Total	2,917	6,059,027	1,586	867,744	4,503	6,926,771

RETURN of Principal Articles of Export from New York during the Year 1894.

Articles.		Quantity.	Value.
			£
Agricultural implements	..	..	869,498
Bacon and ham	Tons ..	107,469	4,273,145
Beef (fresh)	,, ..	4,858	1,785,518
,, (canned)	,, ..	14,658	494,889
,, (cured and salted)	,, ..	18,157	471,756
Butter	,, ..	3,548	266,213
Cattle (live)	Number	160,694	3,129,404
Cheese	Tons ..	23,431	1,009,404
Copper	,, ..	57,542	2,395,474
Cotton (raw)	,, ..	179,057	5,917,275
,, (cloths)	Yards	172,705,834	2,039,147
Flour	Barrels	6,292,106	4,629,909
Hops	Tons ..	5,724	377,743
Indian corn	,, ..	4,912	1,081,229
Lard	,, ..	134,458	4,868,600
Leather	,, ..	16,540	1,100,092
Machinery	..	..	1,511,189
Oil (illuminating)	Gallons	475,094,530	4,206,985
,, (lubricating)	,,	28,320,462	834,594
Oilcake and meal	Tons ..	70,732	397,730
Pork	,, ..	21,019	717,140
Sewing machines	..	..	366,292
Specie and bullion	..	..	3,142,162
The oil	Tons ..	38,666	1,630,087
Tobacco (leaf)	,, ..	69,449	2,694,618
Wheat	Bushels (of 60 lbs.)	22,913,945	2,930,037

(1974)

RETURN of Principal Articles of Import into New York during the Year 1894.

Articles.		Quantity.	Value.
			£
FREE.			
Coffee	Tons	215,996	14,861,377
Fruits		..	604,079
Indiarubber	Tons	14,755	3,041,721
Skins		91,544,221	2,671,223
Silk	Tons	1,612	1,853,071
Sugar	,,	847,519	9,898,858
Tea	,,	30,153	1,859,222
Wool	,,	1,409	600,000
DUTIABLE.			
Dry Goods—			
Cotton (manufactured)		..	3,894,942
Silk ,,		..	4,655,671
Woollen ,,		..	3,192,262
Fish		..	415,143
Fruits, almonds, and nuts		..	1,463,416
Furs (manufactured)		..	1,091,915
Glass		..	944,592
Gloves and manufactured leather		..	1,329,814
Iron (raw)	Tons	20,909	207,132
,, (manufactured)		..	577,675
Jewellery and precious stones		..	1,305,574
Lead		..	691,489
Specie and bullion		..	4,134,247
Tin-plates	Tons	86,473	949,866
Tobacco (leaf)	,,	7,314	2,205,708
Wines and spirits		..	1,321,034

Port of New York.

TABLE showing Countries to and from which Specie was Imported and Exported in the Year 1894.

Country.	Imports.		Exports.	
	Currency.	Sterling.	Currency.	Sterling.
	Dollars.	£	Dollars.	£
Great Britain	2,726,027	545,205	1,258,075	251,615
France	6,333,127	1,266,626	1,978,500	395,700
Germany	1,591,739	318,348	7,000	1,400
Cuba	4,127,937	825,587	11,766,596	2,353,319
Mexico	2,989,775	597,955	49,155	9,831
Other countries	2,902,631	580,526	651,485	130,297
Total	20,671,236	4,134,247	15,710,811	3,142,162

NOTE.—Exchange calculated at the rate of 5 dol. to the 1*l*.

NEW YORK.

TABLE showing the Grain Shipments from this Port to Great Britain and the Continent of Europe, with the Nationality of the Vessels engaged in the Transport.

Country.	1894. Number of Vessels.	1894. Number of Bushels.	1893. Number of Vessels.	1893. Number of Bushels.
Great Britain	494	21,007,461	606	34,383,778
Belgium	40	2,620,121	76	5,240,242
Netherlands	83	3,272,307	92	4,651,111
Germany	95	2,678,221	130	4,356,399
France	22	1,200,269	43	2,400,269
Portugal	22	1,530,196	29	2,213,108
Denmark	13	494,326	24	988,652
Italy	8	416,758	13	813,516
Spain	4	122,323	6	597,149
Norway	..	..	6	597,149
Russia	1	42,970	..	..

No sailing ships carried grain during 1894.
The grain shipments consisted of the following :—

Articles.	Quantity. 1894.	Quantity. 1893.
	Bushels.	Bushels.
Wheat	24,085,167	37,140,391
Maize	8,959,959	11,302,010
Rye	20,625	384,857
Oats	1,060	4,315,715
Barley	23,237	254,073
Buckwheat	173,057	245,146
Flaxseed	6,185	1,890,683
Peas	115,662	235,851

UNITED STATES.

RETURN of the Number of Seamen who have been Engaged, Discharged, Left Behind, Reported Dead, or Deserted, or who have been relieved at the British Consulate-General, New York, and showing the Total Number of British and Foreign Sailors who were Engaged, Discharged, &c., from British Ships, with the Amount of Wages paid at the Consulate to Seamen on discharge from their Ships and from Hospital or Jail; and also showing the Number of New Agreements entered into during the Year 1894.

Seamen.											Wages.			Agreements.
Engaged.	Discharged.	Left Behind.			Dead.			Deserted.	Relieved.	Nationality.		Total Number of Seamen.	Paid on Discharge from Vessels.	Paid on Discharge from Hospital or Jail.	Total Wages Paid.	Number Opened.
		In Hospital.	In Jail.	Total.	At Sea.	On Shore.	Total.			British.	Foreign.					
9,662	9,075	263	21	284	30	29	59	1,973	162	10,982	11,233	22,215	Dol. c. 367,959 72	Dol. c. 3,565 64	Dol. c. 371,525 36	152

PROVIDENCE, RHODE ISLAND.

Mr. Vice-Consul Stockwell reports as follows:—

The depression in trade and commerce in 1893 extended into 1894, into the very heart of it. In the fall, business began to revive and appeared to have some life left. Some confidence perhaps came from the fact that the tariff, or the official discussion of it (the great disturbing factor of late in American commerce) would not be brought up for two years at least; not till Congress, in another administration, perhaps, undertook to amuse itself at the expense of the people, and the people's trade and trading.

In the money market the rates of discount were the lowest known, the average for the year being 4·60 in the leading banks, while the average for 1893 was 6·23. Bonds were in good demand, but there was a better demand in 1893, but less than in 1892. The bank clearings in 1894 amounted to 244,445,400 dol.; in 1893, 276,538,900 dol.; in 1892, 290,908,500 dol., total shrinkage since 1892, 78,556,600 dol. *Money market.*

In addition to goods imported originally into other ports, thence transported by railway to this port, the following merchandise was brought direct to Providence in vessels during the year 1894:—

CUSTOM-HOUSE Statistics for the Year 1894.

Articles.		Quantity.
Salt	Lbs.	4,878,833
Piling	Pieces	27,392
Lumber	Feet	257,507
Scantlings		231,450
Logwood	Lbs.	2,485,898
Dye-woods	,,	598,456
Laths		11,293
Fustic	Lbs.	101,472
Wool	,,	63,500
Brimstone	Tons	700
Pickets	Pieces	11,835
Timber, squared	Feet	5,000
Lime	Lbs.	1,283,340
Boards	Feet	870,170
Shingles		21,557,450
Plank	Feet	554,431

The value of foreign merchandise entered for immediate consumption and withdrawn from warehouse was 540,960 dol. The duties (not included in the foregoing) collected during the year amounted to 205,805·02 dol. (See Annexes B and C.)

The total number of vessels arriving at the port of Providence during the year from foreign countries was 77, of which 24 were *Tonnage of the port.*

UNITED STATES.

American. Tonnage of vessels hailing from this port :—Sail, 72, tonnage, 7,917; steam, 37, tonnage, 24,774.

Labour. In the cotton industry, wages were reduced during the year 10 per cent., while in the woollen industry the reduction amounted to 13½ per cent. In the different trades there was no change in wages. In the trades, business was dull, but what labour was required was paid for at the old prices.

The jewellery business in Providence is one of large interest, the largest in the country except that at Newark, N.J., and is represented by about 200 establishments. The business of the manufacturing jeweller feels the pulse of the times quickly, more so than most others; naturally in the reduction of living expenses jewellery is the first commodity to be dispensed with. In the *The jewellery business.* year 1893, disasters (failures) and no trade made most of the record. Early in 1894 there was a slight increase in the demand for jewellery. The flurry was over, and the people having more confidence, and the old wages (in some cases at least), began to give some attention to personal adornment. Hence, the jewellery business woke up, and while it has been much less in volume than in previous years, yet it was more than in 1893, and the prospect is in favour, apparently, of a return, gradual though it may be, to old time prosperity.

The wool and woollen goods market and manufacture. The stock of wool on hand in Providence on January 1, 1894, was 500,000 bales. The sales were larger than in 1893, but the finer grades steadily declined in price, as shown in the following table:—

	1893.		1894.	
	From—	To—	From—	To—
	Cents.	Cents.	Cents.	Cents.
Ohio XX and above	23	24	..	18
Michigan X	19	20	16	16½
Fine unwashed	12	18	10	14
½, ⅜, ¼, washed, combed	25	26	21	22
„ unwashed, combed	19	20	16	17
Texas, 12 months	11	14	10	12
„ 6 to 8 months	11	13	10	12
Fine Montana	12	13	9	11
„ medium, Wyo. and Utah	11	13	10	12
North Spring (free), California	15	16	12	13
East Oregon (average)	10	11	11½	12
A, super. choice, brushed	28	30	30	33
B „ „	25	28	26	28
Australian combing and clothing—				
General prices	29	33	17	22
Carpet wools—				
Aleppo	13	14	9¼	10½
Bagdads (colours)	20	22	..	15
„ (white)	22	23	17	18
Autumn (Donskoi)	18	19	..	14
Angora (white)	..	15	11	11½
Camel-hair	14	15	11	12½

The Providence wool market is only a reflection of the Boston market which is the chief wool market of this country. The total sales in Boston during the year 1894 amounted to 139,833,785 lbs., against 122,065,000 lbs. in 1893; the total sales in New York for the same time amounted to 39,875,600 lbs. The total receipts in Boston for the year amounted to 561,531 bales domestic and 100,596 bales foreign, showing an increase in receipts as compared with 1893 of 82,334 bales domestic, and 24.066 bales foreign.

In woollen and worsted manufacture there was general dissatisfaction in 1894. In New England, probably, not more than 25 per cent. of the woollen machinery was in operation all the time during the year. In Rhode Island, at least, only the larger establishments were kept running continuously throughout the year. The tariff is held responsible for a part of the inactivity.

The cotton goods market. — The cotton goods industry had its ups and downs, especially downs during the year. Cotton was plentiful and cheap. If it had been less so, less plentiful and more costly, the mills might not have produced goods at all, or if they had, at such a cut in wages as would have stopped manufacturing. Owing to the low price of cotton, the production in many cases was in excess of the demand. It was an eventful year for the print cloth market. The price of 64 squares at the beginning of the year was $2\frac{3}{4}$ c. and at the close it was $2\frac{11}{16}$ c. During the year the market dropped to $2\frac{9}{16}$ c., the lowest price ever known in Providence.

The manufacture of machinery. — The machinery product of Rhode Island finds its way into every part of the manufacturing world. During the year 1894 most of the shops were running full time, and some of the larger ones were obliged to keep in operation both night and day. The demand for Providence built machinery is so wide that while trade depression may have its effect in lower prices, lower wages, and slow payments, yet the business continues to thrive for the benefit of the operators and the operatives.

Lumber. — The demand for lumber during the year was much less than in 1893. Nearly all the vessels from the provinces bring lumber. In 1893 there were 77 arrivals of British ships from the provinces bringing lumber; in 1894 there were only 46 arrivals.

New buildings. — During the year 1894 675 new buildings were erected in Providence at a cost of 2,544,155 dol.; in 1893 the number of new buildings was 619.

Public improvements. — The improvement of "terminal facilities" for railways, referred to in this report for the last 9 years, is in a state of progression probably, although there appears to be little to prove it. Some time Providence may have, what is predicted will be, the best railway station and approaches in New England. As given in the previous report, the State of Rhode Island issued bonds to the amount of 1,500,000 dol. to build a new State House in the city of Providence. Ground for the new structure has not yet been broken, but may be during the year 1895.

One side of the city of Providence (the Providence River divides the city in its centre) has been provided with improved

Public health.

sewerage with outlet and precipitation tanks at the harbour line. The east side of the city is to have a similar system of sewers. The city drinking water is now subject to suspicion, and it is proposed to introduce a costly filtration plant, and to cleanse the water before it enters the service pipes.

In Rhode Island, as in all New England States, especially Massachusetts, as well as in other parts of the country, attention is now directed to the source of milk supply and the fresh meat supply. The prevalence of the disease known as tuberculosis (identical with consumption in man) among cattle has led to the adoption of extreme measures in several States. During the year in Rhode Island, 401 tuberculous animals were killed by order of the State Board of Agriculture. The State appropriation for this purpose in 1893 was 15,000 dol.; the appropriation for the year will be, probably, 25,000 dol. The State proposes to destroy every tuberculous animal within the State, and the work is now in progress, and a similar work is going on in other New England States, notably in Massachusetts, Vermont, and New Hampshire.

Annex A.—RETURN of Shipping at the Port of Providence during the Year 1894.

ENTERED.

Nationality.	Sailing. Number of Vessels.	Tons.
British	48	4,660
American	24	5,178
Danish	1	381
Italian	2	1,258
Total	75	16,477
„ 1893	112	16,479

CLEARED.

Nationality.	Sailing. Number of Vessels.	Tons.
British	39	3,539
American	11	2,734
Total	50	6,273
„ 1893	78	11,026

Annex B.—RETURN of Principal Articles of Export from Providence during the Year 1894.

Articles.	Quantity.
	£
Coal	32
Iron	1,313
Provisions	584
All others	4
Total	1,897

RETURN of Principal Articles of Import into Providence during the Years 1894–93.

Articles.	Value. 1894.	Value. 1893.
	£	£
Dry goods	29,702	44,594
Chemicals	19,313	11,683
Metals (manufactures of)	13,545	21,567
Rubber	..	146,795
All others	48,748	28,666
Total	111,308	253,305

UNITED STATES.

Annex C.—TABLE showing Total Value of all Articles Exported from and Imported into Providence from and to all Countries during the Years 1894-93.

Country.	Exports. 1894.	Exports. 1893.	Imports. 1894.	Imports. 1893.
	£	£	£	£
Austria ..	..	..	..	7,012
Belgium	..	..	4,565	..
Brazil ..	..	..	.	117,284
British West Indies ..	548	..	7,123	7,750
Canada ..	1,349	..	8,731	8,657
Canary Isles ..	..	..	..	22
Cuba ..	..	..	2,723	2,376
Dutch West Indies	..	..	542	270
England	..	..	47,215	49,504
France ..	..	..	8,241	19,227
Germany	..	..	11,476	14,863
Hayti ..	..	..	5,241	2,702
Ireland ..	..	..	..	31
Italy ..	..	..	7,269	4,378
Japan ..	..	..	134	1,142
Netherlands ..	..	..	4,975	2,645
Portugal	..	..	72	..
Scotland	..	..	1,860	2,711
Spain ..	..	..	..	2,448
Sweden ..	..	..	..	471
Switzerland	..	..	..	7,868
Turkey ..	..	..	..	49
Total ..	1,897	..	110,167	253,305

LONDON:
Printed for Her Majesty's Stationery Office,
By HARRISON AND SONS,
Printers in Ordinary to Her Majesty.
(75 6 | 95— H & S 1974)

FOREIGN OFFICE.
1895.
ANNUAL SERIES.

No. 1568.

DIPLOMATIC AND CONSULAR REPORTS ON TRADE AND FINANCE.

UNITED STATES.

REPORT FOR THE YEAR 1894
ON THE
TRADE OF THE CONSULAR DISTRICT OF GALVESTON.

REFERENCE TO PREVIOUS REPORT, Annual Series No. 1336.

Presented to both Houses of Parliament by Command of Her Majesty,
JUNE, 1895.

LONDON:
PRINTED FOR HER MAJESTY'S STATIONERY OFFICE,
BY HARRISON AND SONS, ST. MARTIN'S LANE,
PRINTERS IN ORDINARY TO HER MAJESTY.

And to be purchased, either directly or through any Bookseller, from
EYRE & SPOTTISWOODE, EAST HARDING STREET, FLEET STREET, E.C., and
32, ABINGDON STREET, WESTMINSTER, S.W.; or
JOHN MENZIES & Co., 12, HANOVER STREET, EDINBURGH, and
90, WEST NILE STREET, GLASGOW; or
HODGES, FIGGIS, & Co., Limited. 104, GRAFTON STREET, DUBLIN.

1895.

[C. 7581—108.] *Price Sevenpence Halfpenny.*

New Series of Reports.

Reports of the Annual Series have been issued from Her Majesty's Diplomatic and Consular Officers at the following places, and may be obtained from the sources indicated on the title-page:—

No.		Price.	No.		Price.
1450.	Africa (Congo)	2d.	1509.	Vera Cruz	2d.
1451.	Jeddah	1½d.	1510.	Puerto Cortes	1d.
1452.	San Francisco	5½d.	1511.	Taganrog	1d.
1453.	Oporto	2d	1512.	Baltimore	1½d.
1454.	Barcelona	2d.	1513.	Mexico	1½d.
1455.	New Caledonia	½d.	1514.	Zaila	1d.
1456.	Smyrna	1d.	1515.	Zomba	3½d.
1457.	Macao	1d.	1516.	Valparaiso	2½d.
1458.	Samoa	1d.	1517.	Charleston	2½d.
1459.	Hiogo and Osaka	3d.	1518.	Serajevo	1d.
1460.	Lisbon	2d.	1519.	Saigon	1d.
1461.	Pekin	2d.	1520.	Bangkok	2d.
1462.	Corunna	2d.	1521.	Tripoli	1d.
1463.	Mozambique	15d.	1522.	Batavia	1½d.
1464.	Munich	1½d.	1523.	Dakar	½d.
1465.	St. Petersburg	3d.	1524.	Havana	2d.
1466.	Naples	1d.	1525.	Riga	2d.
1467.	Montevideo	2½d.	1526.	Trebizond	1½d.
1468.	Aden	1d.	1527.	Piræus	2½d.
1469.	Tokio	1½d.	1528.	Guayaquil	1½d.
1470.	Dantzig	5d.	1529.	Marseilles	1½d.
1471.	Guayaquil	1d.	1530.	Wuhu	1½d.
1472.	Canton	1½d.	1531.	Rio de Janeiro	2½d.
1473.	Dar-al-Baida	3d.	1532.	Trieste	2d.
1474.	Teheran	2d.	1533.	Brest	1½d.
1475.	Bushire	2d.	1534.	Stockholm	2d.
1476.	Tangier	2d.	1535.	Warsaw	1d.
1477.	Rome	2d.	1536.	Boston	1½d.
1478.	Hamburg	4d.	1537.	Mozambique	2½d.
1479.	The Hague	1½d.	1538.	Callao	1d.
1480.	Belgrade	2d.	1539.	Aleppo	1½d.
1481.	Batoum	1½d.	1540.	Jaffa	½d.
1482.	Teneriffe	½d.	1541.	Boston	1d.
1483.	Lisbon	2½d.	1542.	New Orleans	1½d.
1484.	Buda-Pesth	½d.	1543.	Chicago	3d.
1485.	Rome	5½d.	1544.	Palermo	2½d.
1486.	Para	1d.	1545.	Bengazi	1½d.
1487.	Odessa	1d.	1546.	Cagliari	1d.
1488.	Hakodate	1d.	1547.	Pernambuco	7½d.
1489.	Beira	1½d.	1548.	Madrid	1½d.
1490.	Berne	1½d.	1549.	Corunna	5d.
1491.	Copenhagen	1d.	1550.	Leghorn	2d.
1492.	Stettin	2½d.	1551.	New Orleans	2½d.
1493.	Rio Grande do Sul	1½d.	1552.	Syra	1½d.
1494.	Serajevo	1d.	1553.	Genoa	9d.
1495.	Buenos Ayres	9d.	1554.	Berlin	2½d.
1496.	Florence	2d.	1555.	Tainan	1d.
1497.	Lisbon	1½d	1556.	Zanzibar	4d.
1498.	Paris	2d.	1557.	Dunkirk	1d.
1499.	Bolivia	1½d.	1558.	Ningpo	1d.
1500.	Patras	1½d.	1559.	Pakhoi	1d.
1501.	Bordeaux	3d.	1560.	Chinkiang	1d.
1502.	Madrid	2d.	1561.	New York	2d.
1503.	Amsterdam	1d.	1562.	Batoum	11½d.
1504.	Suakin	1d.	1563.	Naples	2d.
1505.	Angora	1d.	1564.	Resht	4½d.
1506.	Havre	2½d.	1565.	Copenhagen	1½d.
1507.	Algiers	11d.	1566.	Porto Rico	1½d.
1508.	La Rochelle	3d.	1567.	Malaga	3d.

No. 1568.

Reference to previous Report, Annual Series No. 1336.

UNITED STATES.

GALVESTON.

Consul Nugent to the Earl of Kimberley.

My Lord, Galveston, March 27, 1895.

I HAVE the honour to forward, herewith enclosed, my Annual Report on the Trade and Commerce, &c., of my Consular District for the year 1894.

I have, &c.
(Signed) HORACE D. NUGENT.

Report on the Trade and Commerce of the Consular District of Galveston for the Year 1894.

ABSTRACT of Contents.

	PAGE
Texas—	
Introductory remarks	3
Low prices of 1894	3
Speculation subsided	3
Immigration; ranching	3
Most memorable year for Galveston	3
Second cotton port in the world	3
Bright prospects as a port	4
General foreign trade	4
Total volume of trade	4
Imports—	
Direct imports	4
Imports free of duty	4
Sugar	4
Imports from Great Britain	5
Cement; dead oil; crockery; burlaps; tin; ale; salt; machinery; coal; soda; jute	5
Imports from France	5
" Belgium	5
Exports—	
Total value of exports, largest ever recorded	5
Cotton	6
Value of cotton exported	6
Cotton seed, oilcake, and meal	6

(1960)

UNITED STATES.

Abstract of Contents—continued.

	PAGE
Texas—continued—	
Exports—continued—	
Cotton seed oil	6
Wheat	6
Wheat flour	6
Logs; lumber	6
Trade of Velasco	6
Export trade to Great Britain	7
„ Germany	7
„ France	7
Exports to other countries	8
Shipping—	
Large increase of shipping	8
Total number of vessels in 1894	8
Coasting trade	8
British shipping largest ever recorded	8
Gradual increase of British shipping since 1889	8
British shipping at Velasco and Sabine Pass	9
Percentage of British shipping at Galveston	9
Freights	9
Railroads—	
New mileage laid down	10
Differential on cotton	10
Development of new lines of trade in Galveston	11
Trade with West Indies	11
Improvements at Galveston	11
Enlargement of terminal facilities	11
New sheds for cotton	12
New water supply	12
Bank clearances	12
Cotton crop of 1893-94—	
Crop of the United States, 1893-94	13
Prices; commercial value	13
Texas crop; details of Texas crop; percentage of crops by groups	13
Total crops for four years, and how disposed of	14
Deliveries by groups	15
Crops by States	15
Galveston receipts and exports	16
Receipts at, and exports from, all United States ports	16
Cotton crop of 1894-95—	
Huge crop estimated	18
Estimate in detail, 1894-95	18
Galveston receipts; largest ever known	18
Standing of Galveston	20
Receipts and exports, 1894-95, at all United States ports and at Galveston	20
Cotton prices	21
Proposed reduction of area in cotton	21
Texas cotton mills	25
Cotton baling—	
Dissatisfaction at baling of cotton from Galveston	26
Causes of the evil	27
Action of Galveston Cotton Exchange	27
„ Cotton Convention at New Orleans	28
Cotton fires, 1894	28
Cotton Exhibition	29
Mortality at Galveston	29
Harbour works at Galveston—	
Advantage of Galveston's situation as a port	30
Probable results of deep water	31
Major Miller's report	32
Latest survey	34
18-foot channel over the bar	34
Progress of works in 1894	35

GALVESTON.

Abstract of Contents.

	PAGE
Texas—continued—	
Harbour works at Galveston—continued—	
Present position of work	36
Recapitulation	36
Other harbour works—	
Ship canal, Galveston Bay	37
Improvements of Buffalo Bayou	38
New Mexico—	
Review of 1894—	
General progress of New Mexico	38
Increase of population	39
Land titles—	
United States Court of Land Claims	40
Taxable property—	
Estimated value of property in 1894	40
Assessments	40
Property by counties	40
Territorial debt—	
Revenue and expenditure	41
Railways	41
Mining—	
Maxwell grant	42
Cochiti mines	42
Alum	43

Introductory Remarks.

Low prices of 1894. The year 1894 will be chiefly remembered in Texas as being one in which two of the leading staples, cotton and maize, fell lower in price than at any other time within the memory of the present generation.

Speculation subsided. The almost universal mania for speculation began to subside in Texas about 4 years ago, and in the interval between then and now, most of the resulting debts have been in one way or another adjusted, so that commercial enterprises are now on a better footing.

Immigration. Immigration, chiefly from the northern and western States, was active, and so, in consequence, were sales in land. The ranchmen and stockmen too had a better year in 1894 than for many years past.

Ranching. On the whole, though still somewhat depressed, business throughout the State has been steady, though perhaps rather duller at the close of the year owing to the low price of cotton.

1894 a most memorable year for Galveston. As regards Galveston itself, 1894 has been in many ways the most remarkable year in her commercial history. Notwithstanding the unprecedented fall in the price of cotton, Galveston has held her own in general business, and in the cotton exporting and shipping business she has made a most flattering and memorable record. **Second cotton port in the world.** She has reached the place of second cotton port in the world from that of fifth in the seventies, and she soon bids fair to be a strong competitor for first place. Her receipts of cotton were 50 per cent. greater than ever before known here, and for the first time in her history over 1,000,000 bales were exported in one year to foreign shores. Galveston was the sixth exporting

UNITED STATES.

Bright prospects as a port.

port, as regards totals, in the United States in 1894. Whilst the cotton season has been an unsatisfactory one to producers, the carriers, both by land and sea, the shipbrokers, stevedores and other labourers have been benefited largely by the increased receipts of cotton at this port.

In short, despite hard times and the shrinkage of money values, the progress of Galveston, especially as one of the most important entrepôts in this country, has been steady and unchecked, and the prospects before her are of the brightest.

General Foreign Trade.

Total volume of trade.

The total value of the foreign trade to and from Galveston and district during the year 1894 amounted to 36,840,091 dol., as compared with 36,823,438 dol. in 1893, a very slight gain. The actual volume of trade was, however, by far the largest ever done in the district, but owing to shrinkage in prices the values do not show material gain.

Imports.

Direct imports.

The total value of the direct imports from foreign countries into Galveston decreased considerably last year, being 677,636 dol., as against 928,343 dol. in 1893. Of this amount of 677,636 dol., 425,428 dol. represents the value of merchandise imported free of duty, the remainder, 152,208 dol., being the value of goods paying duty. As long as the present tariff regulations remain in force and the bar of Galveston harbour prevents the entry of deeply laden vessels, so long it may probably be expected that the foreign trade of Galveston will remain as it is now, an almost purely export one, and that the disproportion between the values of imports and exports will continue to increase as it has done of late years.

Imports free of duty.

The imports of goods free of duty were valued at 425,428 dol., as compared with 701,138 dol. in 1893; whilst those paying duty were 152,208 dol., as against 227,205 dol. in 1893, a falling-off in both cases.

Sugar.

Cuba heads the list in the total value of merchandise imported, sugar, to the amount of 11,299,992 lbs. coming thence, valued at 349,206 dol. This sum, however, shows a great falling-off when compared with 621,186 dol. in 1893.

The only other country from which goods were imported to the value of over 100,000 dol. was Great Britain. The total imports from thence were valued at 152,231 dol., as against 201,961 dol. in 1893; 109,745 dol. representing the value of dutiable articles, and 42,486 dol. that of those free, as against 175,612 dol. and 26,399 dol. respectively in 1893.

TABLES showing Increase or Decrease of Dutiable Imports from Great Britain.

DECREASE.

Articles.	Value.	
	1893.	1894.
	Dollars.	Dollars.
Cement	43,072	10,390
Dead oil creosote	14,720	7,513
Crockery	20,524	14,519
Burlaps	12,790	10,414
Tin and terne plates	25,481	11,298
Ale and porter	18,590	9,825
Salt	10,489	1,942
Machinery	7,857	6,692

INCREASE.

Articles.	Value.	
	1893.	1894.
	Dollars.	Dollars.
Coal	2,114	8,427
Caustic soda	2,274	6,416
Manufactures of jute	1,304	8,121

As regards goods free of duty, the chief items from Great Britain were salt (free since August, 1894), 14,172 dol., and anthracite coal, 7,668 dol.

The imports from France were 11,292 dol. in value, chiefly preserved fruits, and from Belgium, 20,353 dol., nearly all cement. Tables of the imports are annexed.

Imports from France. Imports from Belgium.

Exports.

The total value of exports from the customs district of Galveston in 1894 was the largest ever recorded in one year, amounting to 36,162,455 dol., as against 35,895,195 dol., in 1893. Of this sum, 885,949 dol. represents the value of goods exported from Velasco, and 70,669 dol. that of those from Sabine Pass, as compared with 2,155,903 dol. and 22,757 dol. respectively in 1893. A great portion of the export trade of Velasco it will be seen has this year come to Galveston.

Total value of exports; largest ever recorded.

The export trade of the port of Galveston proper thus shows an increase of nearly 1,500,000 dol. over 1893, the figures being 35,205,837 dol., as against 33,716,535 dol. This represents by far the largest volume of export business ever done by the port.

UNITED STATES.

Cotton.

Value of cotton exported.

Cotton was as usual the leading commodity exported. For the first time in the history of Galveston, over 1,000,000 bales were exported from this port, the total number being 1,072,634 bales, valued at 33,476,858 dol., as compared with 742,532 bales, value 30,842,753 dol. in 1893. Owing to the extremely low price of cotton during the present season of 1894-95, the average value per bale exported fell from 41·50 dol. in 1893 to 31·20 dol. in 1894. Had the average value of past years been maintained, the value of the cotton leaving Galveston would have been over 40,000,000 dol.

Other cotton crop products, such as cotton-seed oil-cake and meal, and cotton-seed oil, figure prominently in the exports from Galveston district.

Cotton-seed oil-cake and meal.

Cotton-seed oil-cake and meal were exported from Galveston to the amount of 60,513 tons, value 1,382,757 dol., as compared with 62,582 tons, value 1,399,872 dol. in 1893, a slight falling-off.

Cotton-seed oil.

Cotton-seed oil itself was exported from Galveston only to the extent of 8,415 gallons in 1894, valued at 2,685 dol., as against 68,800 gallons, value 28,300 dol. in 1893, the greater bulk of the oil from Texas leaving by way of Velasco.

Wheat.

Outside of cotton and its products, the chief commodities exported from this district of Galveston are wheat, wheat flour, logs, and lumber.

Wheat was exported to the amount of 135,137 bushels, value 77,459 dol. in 1894. This shows an immense falling-off since 1893, when 1,308,950 bushels left Galveston, value 934,269 dol. Owing to the lack of water on the bar it has been found impossible to load vessels with grain cargoes, and what trade in wheat there was last year has been transferred to other ports. When, however, another 3 feet of water has been gained there is no doubt that Galveston, with her facilities for loading grain and her position and railway accommodations, will become a leading grain exporting port.

Wheat flour.

The exports of wheat flour in 1894 show an increase over 1893, being 59,859 barrels, value 214,792 dol., as compared with 49,057 barrels, value 198,825 dol.

Logs.

The value of logs exported was 34,885 dol. in 1894, as against 74,694 dol. in 1893, a material decrease in this branch of trade.

Lumber.

Lumber exported from this district all goes from Sabine Pass. There was a large increase in foreign exports of this nature, the figures showing 5,909 feet, value 70,154 dol. in 1894, as against 1,477 feet, value 17,689 dol. in 1893. There are several British schooners now engaged in the business.

Trade of Velasco.

The foreign trade of the new port of Velasco, at the mouth of the Brazos River, is included in the tables annexed to this report, and as will be seen therefrom is chiefly export trade.

The amount of cotton exported from Velasco in 1894 was 1,342 bales, value 46,306 dol., as against 15,061 bales, value 691,842 dol. in 1893. Oilcake was exported to the amount of 60,513 tons, value 748,786 dol., as against 57,648 tons, value

1,343,042 dol. in 1893, and cotton-seed oil to the amount of 209,947 gallons, value 75,980 dol., as compared with 249,620 gallons, value 96,220 dol. in 1893.

The total export trade of Velasco shows a decrease of 1,265,954 dol., being 885,949 dol. in 1894, and 2,151,903 dol. in 1893. This decrease in value has partly resulted from the transfer of business to Galveston and partly from lower prices.

As regards the countries to which merchandise was exported from Galveston customs district, Great Britain stands first as in the value of imports.

Export trade. The total value of goods exported to Great Britain was 20,723,332 dol. from Galveston, and 52,680 dol. from Velasco, as compared with 21,200,496 dol. and 559,242 dol. in 1893, whilst the volume of trade was actually much greater than in 1893, yet owing to the low prices of cotton in 1894, the value of the exports shows a decrease.

647,372 bales of cotton valued at 20,255,300 dol. were exported to Great Britain in 1894, as against 497,478 bales, value 20,508,401 dol. in 1893. A large increase in actual exports, but slight decrease in value. Oilcake and meal to the amount of 21,803 tons, value 477,840 dol., also was sent to Great Britain. In 1893 the figures were 35,426 tons, value 900,920 dol. In this branch of export trade there was a decided falling off as regards Great Britain.

Export trade to Germany. The exports to Germany stand second in value, being 8,132,298 dol. in 1894, as compared with 7,564,326 dol. in 1893, a material increase. Of this amount of 8,132,298 dol., 7,423,306 dol. was from Galveston, and 708,992 dol. was from Velasco, comparing with 6,422,511 dol. and 1,131,815 dol. respectively in 1893. The exports of cotton to Germany show a large increase in amount, being 214,971 bales, as against 136,748 bales in 1893. The values of course do not show such a marked advance, being 6,650,976 dol. in 1894, as compared with 5,783,037 dol. in 1893. All but 1,342 bales of cotton for Germany left Galveston in 1894.

Oilcake and meal was exported to Germany in 1894 from Galveston to the amount of 34,268 tons, value 787,476 dol., and from Velasco 27,093 tons, value 588,659 dol.

The totals show 61,361 tons, value 1,376,135 dol. in 1894, as compared with 62,703 tons, value 1,509,528 dol. in 1893.

In 1893, 27,913 tons, value 697,488 dol., left Galveston for Germany, and 34,790 tons, value 812,040 dol., were forwarded from Velasco.

The only other important item of export to Germany in 1894 was 164,138 gallons of cotton-seed oil from Velasco, valued at 60,000 dol. The figures in 1893 were 68,800 gallons, value 28,300 dol.

Export trade to France. The exports to France show a marked increase in 1894 over 1893, being 5,732,851 dol., as against 4,760,050 dol. The exports of cotton were 182,832 bales, value 5,722,551 dol., as against 108,668 bales, value 4,632,214 dol. in 1893. Cotton formed the bulk of exports to France.

UNITED STATES.

Exports to other countries.

Exports to other countries besides Great Britain, Germany and France were comparatively small and unimportant in 1894, the chief being 21,250 bales of cotton, value 646,613 dol., to Russia, and 53,271 barrels of flour, value 189,678 dol., to Cuba, an increase in both cases over 1893.

Tables showing the exports in detail are annexed.

Shipping.

Large increase of shipping.

As might be readily imagined, the shipping movement of the port of Galveston during the year 1894 showed a large increase owing to the huge cotton crop. Apart even from this, more cotton in proportion came by way of Galveston than ever before, and had the Texas crop been only an average one there is yet no doubt that the shipping movement would have shown an increase. Year by year, as the water on the bar deepens and chances of loading a full cotton cargo at the wharf increase, foreign shipping, especially British, is more and more attracted to this port.

Total number of vessels during 1894.

From returns furnished by the United States custom-house, it was shown that 489 vessels visited Galveston in 1894. This number does not include the foreign shipping coming coastwise— *i.e.*, that having touched at some United States port prior to arrival here. No less than 49 British vessels are thus not accounted for by the custom-house officials, and probably some few foreign. The total entries of shipping into Galveston may thus be put down as being in the neighbourhood of 550 in 1894 —an increase of some 75 vessels over 1893. The method of computing registered tonnage in the United States custom-house differs from that which obtains in the United Kingdom, and the tonnage figures are given without comment.

Coasting trade.

Of the above estimated number of vessels entering the port 309 were American coasting craft, tonnage 306,388, these figures including the bi-weekly service of the Mallory line from New York. Of the remainder, 187 were British, 15 Norwegian, and 15 Spanish.

British shipping; largest ever recorded.

The British shipping movement was the greatest ever recorded in one year from this port. From the return annexed to this report it will be seen that 187 British vessels entered this port in 1894, their combined registered tonnage being 292,382 tons, and the total number of their crews 4,391. This shows an increase over 1893 of 17 vessels, 37,186 tons, and 520 men.

The clearances of British vessels were 169 in number; tonnage 259,586, and total crews 3,959, showing an increase of 8 vessels cleared, 24,401 tonnage, and 253 men in number of crews over 1893.

It is somewhat interesting to see the gradual rise of Galveston as a cotton shipping port in the last few years, as instanced by the steady increase of British shipping.

Gradual increase of

The following table of the clearances of British vessels in the last six years shows not only the gradual increase of numbers, but especially of tonnage, the tonnage of vessels cleared in 1894 being just double that of those cleared in 1889:—

British shipping since 1889.

Year.	Number of British Vessels Cleared.	Tonnage.	Average Tonnage per Vessel.
1889	112	129,272	1,153
1890	120	149,943	1,249
1891	163	220,265	1,351
1892	156	228,799	1,467
1893	161	235,185	1,461
1894	169	259,586	1,536

TABLE showing the Arrivals of British Shipping during the Cotton Season (September to March) in each of the Four last Seasons.

Month.	Number.			
	1891-92.	1892-93.	1893-94.	1894-95.
September	23	23	17	21
October..	38	35	28	39
November	41	29	36	40
December	28	18	21	49
January..	17	19	17	27
February	10	12	9	12
March	7	6	1	10*
Total	164	142	129	198

* Estimated.

It must be noted that 1891–92 was a season in which the crop of cotton was almost as great as in the present season, and was the year marking the first great advance of British shipping at Galveston.

Of the 187 British vessels entering this port, only 17 brought cargoes—a still further decrease from 1893, when there were 24.

The British shipping in the district (excluding Galveston) decreased, there being only 11 vessels at Velasco, as against 25 in 1893, and 6 at Sabine Pass, as against 3 in 1893.

British shipping at Velasco and Sabine Pass.

The percentage of British shipping to the total shipping of the port was about 33 per cent. in number, and about 45 per cent. in tonnage.

Percentage of British shipping at Galveston.

Freights.

Cotton freights, when the year 1894 opened, were 19/64d., and 5 per cent.; cotton-seed cake, 20s. per ton, and small parcels of wheat 3s. 6d. per quarter. In February cotton freights declined to 9/32d. and 5 per cent., and 17/64d. and 5 per cent., at which figures rates remained until the close of the season. Rates on cotton seed cake were then about 22s.

When the season opened again in September rates on cotton to all ports ranged from 7/32d. and 5 per cent. to ¼d. and 5 per cent., owing to excess of tonnage over supplies of cotton.

There was no improvement till the end of October, when rates went up to 9/32d. and 5 per cent., which was about the highest figure they touched during the balance of the year. They fell again to 17/64d. and 5 per cent., and ¼d. and 5 per cent. in November, with an occasional spurt to 9/32d. and 5 per cent. in December; when the year ended they were about ¼d. and 5 per cent.

The average rate on cotton-seed cake from September to January was 20s. There was not sufficient wheat exported to form a basis on.

Railroad.

New mileage laid down. But little was done during the year 1894 in the way of railway construction in Texas. The total amount of new line laid down is given by the "Railway Age" as something over 88 miles, making a total of 10,361 miles in the State.

Differential on cotton. As regards Galveston, however, a question of considerable importance connected with railroads has caused much feeling and dissatisfaction—viz., the lack of fair adjustment of freight rates on cotton into this port. The Railroad Commission of Texas, whilst admitting that the discriminations against Galveston are justifiable neither by law nor equity, have as yet done nothing to relieve this port from such discriminations, and their want of action has led to much feeling here. As the commission recently refused to revise their ruling regarding these differential rates, which work so to the prejudice of Galveston, the question has been taken to the courts; it is the avowed intention of Galveston as a community to carry the fight to the Supreme Court of the United States if necessary.

The first steps have already been taken in the matter, and the case is now before the courts of Texas, and a decision shortly looked for.

The following extract from the report of the chairman of the Transportation Committee of the Galveston Cotton Exchange shows how keenly that and other commercial bodies here feel on this question:—

"We cannot reasonably expect the railroad interests to voluntarily overturn a rate adjustment which they have been so long and carefully creating. We have been making appeals to them for years past, but the wrongs still exist. We must eventually make the fight alone and single-handed, as a business community, and carry our grievances to a tribunal above and beyond the reach of private and corporate interest.

"We have justice on our side, and must eventually secure our rights, but it means a long, hard fight, and the expenditure of considerable money. Every day the contest is delayed but adds to the strength of our adversaries, because they are constantly fattening on the trade wrongfully taken from us. This committee, therefore, appeals to you as individuals and as members of this exchange to do everything you can, individually and collectively, to strengthen and support the freight bureau which we have created to undertake this fight for our commercial emancipation.

"Your committee is informed that it is the purpose of the bureau to immediately file a complaint with the Interstate Commerce Commission, setting forth in detail our grievances under the present freight rate adjustment, and we should carry the fight to the Supreme Court of the United States if necessary to secure justice. As numerous favourable decisions have already been rendered in cases similar to ours, we feel confident of ultimate victory if this community will stand together in the fight. What the rectification of these wrongs, by the removal of the discrimination against us, will mean to Galveston your committee need not consume your time in elaborating, except to state if we had 30 feet of water on our bar to-day, while it would increase and facilitate our ocean commerce, it would in no essential particular affect the present inland freight rate adjustment. The ocean rates will adjust themselves, but discriminations against us will certainly continue just as long as we submit to them. Respectfully submitted,

"WM. F. LADD,
"Chairman."

Development of New Lines of Trade in Galveston.

During 1894, outside of the usual export trade in cotton and cotton-seed cake, a marked development took place in the trade between this port and the West Indies. A regular business has been made of shipping wheat flour from Galveston to Cuba and Porto Rico. The return cargo has consisted of bananas and other tropical fruit, and it has been found possible, owing to the excellent railway service from here, to deliver the fruit at eastern points much more quickly than the fruit landed at New Orleans could be delivered at the same points. *Trade with the West Indies.*

This trade with the West Indies has good prospects apparently, and will probably become important.

Improvements at Galveston.

As regards the improvement and enlargement of terminal facilities at Galveston during 1894 much has been done. Several new piers on the wharf front have been completed, and the land around them has been filled in, thus adding many acres to the *Enlargement of terminal facilities.*

New sheds for cotton.

ground available for the cheap, safe, and quick handling of cotton. A large modern compress and warehouse has been erected at a cost of over 150,000 dol., whilst extensive sheds for cotton have been built on some of the piers, thus greatly improving the facilities of the port for loading that article. Additional shed room is also contemplated on the wharf front, so that by next season Galveston probably may claim to afford better protection to merchandise than any other southern port. The railroad terminal facilities have also been kept up to the mark. There are now 75 miles of terminal lines within the city limits, of which 35 miles are on the wharfs, and specially constructed with a view to the quick handling of cotton. As the result of these improvements Galveston has been able to do the largest business in her history without the slightest friction, in fact with greater ease than when her exports were much less.

New water supply.

Another notable improvement here is the new system of supplying the town of Galveston with water. Hitherto the supply of drinking water has been chiefly drawn from cisterns of rainwater, whilst Artesian water, somewhat brackish in nature, has been used for washing and other purposes. By the early summer, however, it is hoped Galveston will have an adequate supply of good spring water brought from Alta Loma, some 18 miles away, and conveyed under the bay in large pipes. The water is said to be of excellent quality, and the supply will be quite equal to the wants of the town.

Bank Clearances.

The bank clearances at Galveston during the year 1894 were 255,537,260 dol., as against 290,773,555 dol. in 1893.

TABLE showing Monthly Clearances during the Year 1894.

Month.	Amount.
	Dollars.
1894—	
January	24,593,485
February	17,328,175
March	17,250,140
April	15,780,870
May	17,345,695
June	15,475,665
July	14,601,715
August	14,943,075
September	20,320,710
October	31,537,585
November	33,257,740
December	33,102,405
Total	255,537,200

GALVESTON.

Cotton Crop of 1893-94.

According to the Annual Report of the Secretary of the New Orleans Cotton Exchange the cotton crop of the United States for the year ending August 31, 1894, amounted to 7,549,817 bales, an increase over the crop of 1892-93 of 849,452 bales, and a decrease under that of 1891-92 of 1,485,562 bales. The largest gain over 1892-93 was in the Atlantic States, consisting of Alabama, Georgia, Florida, and the Carolinas, these having contributed 548,000 bales of the increase, whilst the group of Gulf States, i.e., Arkansas, Louisiana, Mississippi, and Tennessee, increased by 351,000 bales, and Texas fell off 49,000 bales. *[Crop of the United States in 1893-94.]*

The bulk of this crop was marketed at over $7\frac{1}{2}$ c. for middling, and few violent fluctuations in price were witnessed. Hence, while the season closed at $6\frac{1}{2}$ c. for middling, or about 2 c. per pound under the price of 1892-93, yet it is estimated that more than two-thirds of the crop brought 7·60 c., and the average price per 1 lb. for the year was 7·50 c., or a loss of 1 c. per 1 lb. on the crop, or, in round figures, 5 dol. per bale. *[Prices.]*

The average commercial value of the crop was 37 dol. 50 c. per bale, against 42 dol. 50 c. in 1892-93 and 37 dol. 50 c. in 1891-92, and the total value 283,118,000 dol., against 284,750,000 dol. and 338,812,000 dol. in 1892-93 and 1891-92 respectively. *[Commercial value.]*

Thus whilst the output was 849,452 bales in excess over 1892-93, the value was 1,632,000 dol. less.

During the season of 1893-94 the Texas crop claimed unusual attention by reason of widely varying opinions as to its extent. The season's results showed a total commercial crop for Texas (including Indian territory) of 2,059,060 bales, as against 2,108,523 bales in 1892-93, a decrease of 49,463 bales. The following figures give the Texas commercial crops of 1893-94 and 1892-93 in detail, i.e., the actual amounts moved by railways and other means of transportation:— *[Texas crop.]*

Details of Texas Crop.

	Quantity.	
	1893-94.	1892-93.
	Bales.	Bales.
Receipts at Texas seaboard	1,029,766	1,065,779
Shipped inland to Mexico and points west of Mississippi River	44,988	41,077
Shipped by rail viâ St. Louis and Cairo	316,652	235,990
Receipts at New Orleans (exclusive of Galveston)	638,688	547,845
Receipts at points on Mississippi River north of St. Louis, bound eastward	83,966	217,832
Total	2,059,060	2,108,523

UNITED STATES.

Percentages of crops by groups.

The following table sets forth the percentages of the crops of 1889-90 to 1893-94 that have been delivered from the three groups of cotton-producing States. It shows the great and continued increase of Texas, and also that the Atlantic States have held their own much better than was supposed:—

PERCENTAGES of Total Cotton Crops (Commercial) Delivered from each of the three Groups of the Cotton Belt.

	Percentages.				
	1893-94.	1892-93.	1891-92.	1890-91.	1889-90.
Texas and Indian territory	27	31	26·5	24	20·5
Other Gulf States	29·5	28	33·5	31	36·5
Atlantic States	43·5	41	40	45	43
	100	100	100	100	100

Total crops for 4 years and how disposed of.

The following table shows the total crop of the United States for 4 years, and the disposition of the crop in detail:—

AMERICAN Cotton Crop for 4 Years (Year ending Close of August).

	Quantity.			
	1893-94.	1892-93.	1891-92.	1890-91.
	Bales.	Bales.	Bales.	Bales.
Port receipts	5,940,092	5,088,392	7,137,900	6,976,380
Overland to mills	931,706	912,146	1,253,560	1,110,925
Southern consumption	718,515	743,848	686,080	604,661
	7,590,313	6,744,386	9,077,540	8,691,976
Less taken by southern mills from ports	40,496	44,021	42,162	39,379
Total	7,549,817	6,700,365	9,035,379	8,652,597

GALVESTON.

EXPORTS.

	Quantity.			
	1893-94.	1892-93.	1891-92.	1890-91.
	Bales.	Bales.	Bales.	Bales.
Great Britain	2,859,114	2,307,489	3,315,202	3,329,432
France	587,299	555,239	691,134	559,099
Continent and Channel	1,775,784	1,523,639	1,850,541	1,890,291
Canada, overland	65,690	58,971	76,560	68,369
Total	5,287,887	4,445,338	5,933,437	5,847,191
Stock at close of year	183,787	242,631	419,221	227,624
Northern mills' takings	1,601,173	1,687,286	2,190,766	2,027,362

During these four seasons the proportion of deliveries from the various groups of the cotton-growing States was as follows:—

DELIVERIES from the Cotton States.

	In Thousands of Bales.			
	1893-94.	1892-93.	1891-92.	1890-91.
Texas and Indian territory	2,059	2,108	2,400	2,100
Other Gulf States	2,216	1,865	3,035	2,666
Atlantic States	3,275	2,725	3,600	3,887
Total	7,550	6,700	9,035	8,653

Based on the foregoing, the following indicates about the division of the commercial crop by States in thousands of bales for the past 3 years:—

CROP BY STATES.

	Thousands of Bales.		
	1893-94.	1892-93.	1891-92.
Alabama	925	740	1,075
Arkansas	625	535	800
Florida	50	45	65
Georgia	1,125	940	1,200
Louisiana	400	340	635
Mississippi	916	755	1,250
North Carolina	425	367	480
South Carolina	750	635	780
Tennessee, &c.	275	235	350
Texas and Indian territory	2,059	2,108	2,400
Total	7,550	6,700	9,035

(1960)

UNITED STATES.

Galveston receipts and exports.

Below are given tables of the net receipts of cotton at the various United States ports during the seasons of 1893-94 and 1892-93, and also the exports for the same seasons from these ports. From the figures it will be seen that the Galveston receipts fell off slightly in 1893-94, but her exports, in spite of this, increased. In point of receipt, Galveston occupied the second place in 1893-94, being the only port besides New Orleans to receive over 1,000,000 bales. As regards foreign exports she stood third, both New Orleans and New York surpassing her. It must be, however, remembered that a great deal of cotton shipped via New York arrives there from Galveston by the bi-weekly Mallory boats from here.

NET Receipts of Cotton at United States Ports (as per Form in use by the Cotton Exchanges).

	Quantity.	
	1893-94.	1892-93.
	Bales.	Bales.
New Orleans	1,893,094	1,602,079
Galveston	1,021,724	1,047,910
Mobile and Pensacola	215,616*	190,494
Savannah	969,430	791,211
Charleston	340,603	289,216
Wilmington	189,840	160,098
Norfolk	502,194	297,301
Baltimore	63,673	66,893
New York	108,387	107,068
Boston	101,854	123,751
Philadelphia	50,702	64,371
West Point	239,352	196,148
Newport News	45,668†	12,303
Brunswick	67,058	80,603
Port Royal	77,867	..
El Paso, Texas	1,650	1,140
Laredo, Texas	20,261	25,274
Eagle Pass, Texas	9,075	7,396
Velasco, Texas	8,042	17,869
Other minor points	14,002	7,267
Total	5,940,092	5,088,392

* Including Pensacola, 15,933 bales this year, and 18,909 bales last year.
† Exclusive of 18,521 bales from Norfolk by rail, and 227 bales from West Point via Clyde Line, counted previously in net at both places.
Exclusive of 1,498 bales received from Norfolk.
Exclusive of 4,553 bales received from Savannah and Mobile.

TABLE showing Exports from United States Ports for 1893–94.

From—	Great Britain.	France.	Continent and Channel.	Total.	Total, 1892–93.
	Bales.	Bales.	Bales.	Bales.	Bales.
New Orleans	781,922	411,949	442,940	1,636,811	1,388,600
Galveston	557,346	98,361	118,217	773,924	762,291
Mobile and Pensacola	33,574	500	1,086	35,160	44,096
Savannah	111,791	32,647	371,884	516,322	365,718
Charleston	152,106	16,206	156,056	324,368	217,550
Wilmington	65,028	...	102,376	167,404	131,995
Norfolk	156,590	350	17,070	174,010	139,125
Baltimore	46,612	6,080	154,124	206,816	218,517
New York	457,605	18,606	310,295	786,506	713,537
Boston	231,061	...	10	231,071	230,404
Philadelphia	25,347	...	5,816	31,163	20,791
West Point	76,544	...	19,467	96,011	59,936
Newport News	47,166	...	...	47,166	11,259
Brunswick	38,555	2,600	30,155	71,310	80,603
Port Royal	77,867	...	...	77,867	...
El Paso, &c.	...	...	1,981	1,981	1,406
Laredo	...	...	20,261	20,261	25,274
Eagle Pass	...	...	9,075	9,075	7,396
Velasco	...	...	8,042	8,042	...
San Francisco	...	...	6,929	6,929	17,869
Total	2,307,114	587,299	1,775,784	5,222,197	4,386,367
Last year	2,307,489	555,239	1,523,639	4,386,367	...
Year before	3,315,202	691,134	1,850,541	5,856,877	...

Cotton Crop of 1894–95.

Early in 1894 it was foreseen that, given good weather, the crop of 1894–95 would be a huge one, rivalling even the famous crop of 1891–92. These expectations have been, as far as Texas is concerned, verified, and the prediction that this State would produce a commercial crop of nearly 3,000,000 bales is meeting with fulfilment as far as can be judged at present.

<small>Huge crop estimated.</small>

The following is the estimate of the crop of 1894–95 issued by the Department of Agriculture, and based on returns from September 1 to February 1. From these figures it will be seen that the proportion of the crop forwarded to market, up to February 1 last, was 89·9 per cent., leaving 10·1 per cent. still in the hands of producers or local merchants:—

18 UNITED STATES.

Estimate in Detail, Crop of 1894-95.

States.	Railway and Water Movement.	Remaining on Plantations and Interior Towns.	Bought by Mills.	Total Crop.
	Bales.	Bales.	Bales.	Bales.
North Carolina..	227,172	105,282	104,993	442,447
South Carolina..	488,591	116,874	182,343	788,808
Georgia .	757,020	283,493	110,942	151,460
Florida ..	39,771	5,866	..	45,687
Alabama	530,571	268,158	27,017	825,746
Mississippi	847,228	170,376	9,656	1,127,260
Louisiana	568,405	151,334	6,119	725,858
Texas ..	2,246,043	611,966	3,641	2,861,653
Arkansas	468,332	196,294	636	665,217
Tennessee	250,389	42,342	11,183	303,914
Indian Territory and Okla ..	89,591	22,790	..	112,381
Missouri	20,142	5,728	..	25,770
Virginia	10,872	253	..	11,125
Kentucky	1,657	..	..	1,657
Kansas ..	44	23	..	67
Total	6,545,728	2,080,739	461,533	9,088,000

Galveston receipts, largest ever known.

As can be readily understood, with such a phenomenal crop in Texas, the receipts at Galveston were far beyond the normal, and the cotton-exporting business done here, rendered the season of 1894-95 a most momentous and marked one for this port. The 1,000,000 bale mark was reached on December 12, 1894, nearly a month before the same mark in the season of 1893-94, and 2 months earlier than in that of 1891-92. The enormous number of 1,500,000 bales was reached on February 23 last. This places Galveston far in the lead of all United States cotton ports except New Orleans, and makes her a dangerous rival for that place to face ere long.

Comparative Table showing the Receipts at Galveston each Year since 1885, from the Beginning of the Season up to February 22, together with the Total Receipts at Galveston for the Season and the Texas Crop for the Year.

Year.	Receipts to Date.	Receipts, Season.	Texas Crop.
	Bales.	Bales.	Bales.
1884-85	439,511	463,463	842,660
1885-86	629,620	715,662	1,369,208
1886-87	670,712	725,163	1,345,185
1887-88	616,201	669,109	1,381,523
1888-89	597,714	689,421	1,377,772
1889-90	795,404	860,112	1,748,320
1890-91	881,286	1,023,599	2,111,090
1891-92	1,024,465	1,154,208	2,406,108
1892-93	947,253	1,047,910	2,025,060
1893-94	930,233	1,021,724	1,824,922
1894-95	1,500,672	..	..

GALVESTON.

The receipts at Galveston, from September 1, 1894, to February 23, 1895, inclusive, were 1,500,972 bales, against 933,566 bales for the same period last season. The receipts for a little less than half of the present are not only more for the whole of any previous season, but are 33 per cent. more than the entire receipts for the season of 1891-92, the largest previously recorded.

The receipts at Galveston thus far this season, and the receipts for the same period in 1893-94, are compared with the receipts for the same periods at New Orleans, Savannah, and Charleston, with the percentage of increase as shown:—

	Galveston.	New Orleans.	Savannah.	Charleston.
	Bales.	Bales.	Bales.	Bales.
Receipts to February 23, 1894	933,566	1,614,424	857,668	317,437
Receipts to February 23, 1895	1,500,972	2,131,039	812,303	377,951
Percentage increase	60	32	5	16

Another significant fact in connection with this increase of receipts is that the amount received thus far this season is more than double what had been received on November 15, 1894, the average day for half receipts for the season.

On November 18, 1891, 574,308 bales had been received, half of the receipts for the season; on November 15, 1892, the season's half receipts were 522,374 bales, and on November 20, 1893, there were 509,375 bales. On November 15, 1894, 705,793 bales had been received, and though we have remaining more than half of the season, the amount has already been more than doubled.

Receipts, Exports, and Stocks.

The following table gives the receipts, exports (foreign and coastwise), and stocks from the beginning of the cotton season on September 1, up to and including February 22 of each year. It will be seen that the direct foreign exports from Galveston, thus far this season, exceed the receipts of any former year for the entire season, the largest receipts in any former entire season being 1,154,208 bales in 1891-92:—

UNITED STATES.

Year.	Receipts, Net.	Exports—Foreign.	Exports—Coastwise.	Stock, February 22.
	Bales.	Bales.	Bales.	Bales.
1874	298,434	131,253	62,640	109,430
1875	290,254	159,208	68,894	71,210
1876	390,215	176,680	161,301	60,733
1877	453,890	210,516	178,910	72,759
1878	373,614	158,537	152,750	68,986
1879	481,299	271,232	156,237	62,599
1880	402,899	199,108	141,344	71,757
1881	368,209	182,690	151,475	108,744
1882	525,706	294,793	140,297	71,189
1883	651,098	377,760	208,152	83,025
1884	537,166	320,506	200,358	48,800
1885	439,511	208,157	211,213	30,655
1886	629,620	285,259	283,539	65,944
1887	672,012	348,817	275,970	60,743
1888	616,201	304,929	293,714	28,722
1889	597,714	268,383	304,902	34,450
1890	795,404	726,945	343,031	39,337
1891	881,286	552,198	285,990	61,427
1892	1,024,465	710,042	244,881	85,594
1893	947,253	681,230	201,227	87,783
1894	930,233	710,061	148,544	85,958
1895	1,500,972	1,165,168	196,653	145,067

Standing of Galveston. The following tables show the standing of Galveston among the ports of the United States up to the date of writing, March 6, and also the exports of cotton, in detail, up to the same date:—

Receipts at all United States Ports.

Ports.	This Season.	Last Season.
	Bales.	Bales.
Galveston	1,530,300	943,898
New Orleans	2,207,889	1,654,271
Mobile	255,459	195,427
Savannah	836,593	871,662
Charleston	293,670	320,558
Wilmington	227,089	186,434
Norfolk	403,202	425,260
Baltimore	96,045	49,711
New York	158,775	98,189
Boston	232,979	84,569
Philadelphia	64,467	42,878
West Point	256,335	218,293
Newport News	30,812	37,913
Brunswick	92,317	47,455
Laredo	8,970	..
Eagle Pass	4,284	..
Port Royal	129,423	60,486
Velasco	592	8,192
Other ports	1,150	..
Total	6,900,888	5,245,323
Last year	5,245,323	..
Difference	1,655,562	..

GALVESTON.

TABLE of Receipts and Exports at Galveston, 1894–95, up to March 6, 1895.

	This Season. Bales.	Last Season. Bales.
RECEIPTS.		
Net	1,530,300	943,898
Gross	1,530,300	943,898
EXPORTS.		
Great Britain	733,332	537,448
France	198,467	98,361
Continent	294,412	93,811
Channel	..	6,400
Total foreign	1,226,211	736,020
New York	209,540	155,976
Morgan City	883	520
Other domestic ports	7,041	..
North by rail	52	153
Total coastwise	217,516	156,649
Local consumption	2,662	2,583
Total exports	1,446,389	895,252

Cotton Prices.

On January 1, 1894, the price of middling cotton at Galveston was $7\frac{7}{16}$ c. The price did not fall below 7 c. until May, when it touched $6\frac{15}{16}$ c. During May and June the price remained fairly steady between $6\frac{15}{16}$ c. and $7\frac{1}{16}$ c. There was a further decline in July and August to $6\frac{5}{8}$ c.

The season of 1894–95 opened on September 1 with middling cotton at $6\frac{1}{2}$ c. By September 19 it had fallen to $5\frac{3}{8}$ c. On October 31 the price was $5\frac{1}{4}$ c., and on November 12 it touched the lowest point, 5 c.

Prices recovered a little by the end of the month, when $5\frac{3}{8}$ c. was recorded. On December 22 there was a slight drop to $5\frac{1}{16}$ c., since which date there has been a gradual recovery, $5\frac{3}{16}$ c. being the average price in January and February, while $5\frac{7}{16}$ c. was recorded to-day (March 9).

On the whole, prices have been about 2 c. lower per 1 lb. than during the season of 1893–94.

Proposed Reduction of the Area in Cotton.

The undoubted over-production of cotton in the southern States, as shown in the huge crop of the present season of

1894-95, has caused a widespread alarm, and there is no doubt that southern agriculture is confronted with the most important crisis that has been known for many years. It is alleged that the vast production of cotton in this State is in a great measure responsible for the low prices which have affected the cotton industry in this and other States. On the one hand the detractors of Texas allege that the ambition to convert this State into the greatest cotton State in the Union, has caused a mania for planting cotton indiscriminately and without reference to the adaptability of the soil or the profit to be made, and that the result of this has been to flood the market, and run prices down, whilst on the other side, the upholders of this State declare that the natural increase of farming, owing to immigration, and the cheapness of growing cotton, no fertilisers being required as compared with other States, are largely accountable for the ever-increasing Texas crop.

There is, no doubt, a great deal to be said on both sides. It must be borne in mind, however, that from the reasons above stated, and owing to the vast area of uncultivated land at the disposal of the immigrant and would-be farmer, it is almost a certainty that the Texas cotton area will continue to increase, notwithstanding every precaution to the contrary. At present cotton is the only crop here upon which money can be raised, and profit or no profit, cotton will he, the farmer, plant. The outcome may be that Texas will under-sell the other States; but it is very doubtful if successful measures can be taken to bind all the farmers to reduce their cotton area, and diversify their crops, unless immigration be stopped, and cash advances made on other produce besides cotton—two very improbable things, as matters are now. In the meantime experts declare that the cotton at 5 c. has no purchasing power, and no profit for the planter. It is their opinion, further, that cotton cannot be grown even in this State, where fertilisers are not required, for 5 c., and that 6 c. was the lowest profitable price.

This estimate of 6 c., as the average cost of production, is taken in a section of the cotton belt, where the most fertile land is to be found, and where the conditions are favourable for economic farming.

Taxes are light in Texas; good land is cheap; the majority of planters own their own farms; the tenant class is much smaller than in Mississippi, Alabama, and the Carolinas, and the merchants do not advance as much money to planters as elsewhere in the cotton belt. With the soil rich enough to yield a good crop without the use of commercial manures, and with the farmers released to a great degree from dependence on banks and merchants, the cost of the Texas crop ought to be and is lower than in any other southern State. In spite of this, expert opinion here declares most emphatically that cotton-planting in Texas is unprofitable under existing conditions, and that the cost of production cannot be materially reduced. A reduction of cotton acreage and systematic diversification of crops has been strongly recommended, but with little confidence in the capacity of Texas farmers to take the proffered advice. In short, if the weather be favourable, next season's crop in Texas will, it is thought, be as large as that of 1894. Whilst many planters would lessen their production if all would do so, the fear that the unscrupulous among them would not keep their word, and plant less, but on the contrary—more, and the certainty of immigration, and consequent planting of new areas, combine to maintain the industry here on its present footing.

The following extract from an article on the subject of over-production of cotton, which appeared in a New York daily paper, will be found interesting as giving the reasons for the estimated reduction in the crop (and the consequent enhancing of the value of cotton) in the near future in all other States except Texas:—

"While there may not be any material reduction of cotton-planting in Texas, as the immediate effect of exceptionally low prices, there will undoubtedly be a shrinkage of production in the cotton belt east of the Mississippi. That is the opinion of the majority of merchants in the exchanges of Charleston, Atlanta, Savannah, Montgomery, Memphis, New Orleans, and Galveston. Southern merchants and planters do not believe that the next season's crop will be as large as that of 1894, and consequently they expect that the price will rise. Their reasons may be briefly summarised:—

"1. Experience has shown that an exceptionally large crop, with a fall in price, is invariably followed by a smaller crop the next year. This is the natural result of over-production. An agricultural business that is over-done one year is under-done the next season. The effect of over-production ought to be more noticeable when the decline in price has been sharper than has ever before been known. The production of cotton was doubled between 1850 and 1860, yet the price of the staple declined only 1 c. per lb. During the last decade there has been a drop of 8 or 10 c. The fall in price during the last year can hardly fail to reduce cotton acreage on a large scale.

"2. Production will be curtailed through less intensive cultivation of the cotton fields. The use of phosphates and commercial fertilisers will be discontinued by thousands of tenant farmers, who are not in a position to contract guano debts, and who will try to make a crop with a scant supply of farm manures. This process of 'skinning the land' will not be adopted by educated planters, but it will be the last resource of 'poor white trash' farmers and shiftless negro tenants. The purchase of fertilisers has been one of the largest elements of the cost of producing cotton. Under existing conditions of unprofitable agriculture, retrenchment will begin with disuse of phosphates. Already a falling-off of 40 per cent. in the sale of commercial fertilisers is reported from South Carolina, where planters who have usually purchased 10 car loads are now buying three. Competent judges in that State affirm that the new crop will be raised with less fertiliser that has been employed at any time in 20 years. With the same 'skinning process' in other cotton States, the crop can hardly fail to be materially reduced.

"3. There will be an inevitable re-adjustment and curtailment of credits in the cotton belt. A large proportion of tenant farmers and planters, owning their own land, has been dependent upon the merchants, who have made advances early in the season with a lien upon the crop. With cotton averaging $4\frac{1}{2}$ c. to the producer, there has been no margin of profit in the last season's operations. Rents are unpaid, and bad debts have been incurred; and the planters have not the same resources of borrowing money which they had a year ago. The losses have fallen mainly upon the producers, for the merchant's liens were liquidated when the cotton was marketed. But the merchants will not make advances on the same terms another season, and they will be more careful in lending money than they have been for many years. The shiftless planter will find out that his credit is exhausted, and there will be a general shrinkage of credits, tending materially to reduce the acreage of cotton-planting. While there may not be many mercantile failures as the result of unprofitable cotton crop, the volume of bad debts has been increased, and many planters will find it impracticable to borrow money on any terms. The continuance of these conditions will reduce cotton planting to an economic struggle, culminating in the survival of the fittest. These operations which are held by the most influential members of the cotton exchanges of New Orleans, Savannah, and other southern cities, point to a reduction of the next season's crop.

"4. Systematic efforts are being made in various southern States to reduce the production of cotton, as the only means of restoring prices to a compensating basis. Conventions of cotton growers have been held in Jackson, Miss., Shreveport, La., and other cities, and resolutions have been adopted recommending a curtailment of 25 per cent. in the acreage of cotton for 1895. While it is impracticable for planters' associations to enforce this policy, they have established a rule of practice which will be generally followed in many localities. With the co-operation of the cotton exchanges it may be feasible to organise public opinion throughout the southern States, and not only to diminish cotton production, but also to establish a national planters' association which will provide some satisfactory method of estimating the crop. Agents of Liverpool houses now undertake to forecast the crop before a bale has been sent to market, and it is upon reckless guesswork of this kind in the interest of English purchasers that bear movements are systematically conducted. If the planters can not only reduce the acreage, but also supply some effective means of ascertaining approximately the volume of the crop, and thereby of diminishing gambling in this great staple, they will adopt important measures of self-defence.

"5. The diversification of crops is generally organised as the chief remedy for the evils of over-production of cotton. A reduction of 25 per cent. of the cotton acreage implies the substitution of other crops and the production of home supplies.

This has not been the merchants' policy in prosperous cotton years. They have refused to advance money to planters on any crop except cotton, and they have sold most of the supplies required for the maintenance of life. When cotton was bringing 12 c. a pound the planter was willing to buy corn for his mules and meat for his labourers; and the merchant made money alike out of the crop and out of the plantation supplies. Low prices for cotton have rendered it impracticable for the planter to produce selling crops alone and to buy his supplies. Hay, corn, oats, bacon, and meat, which were formerly sold by the merchant, are now raised by every planter who has learned the philosophy of 5-cent cotton. The development of these industries, now regarded as indispensable, tends to reduce cotton-planting at present prices.

"It was not until 1880 that the cotton crop of the southern States exceeded that of 1860, but in 1890 the gain over the high-water mark of slavery times was over 2,000,000 bales, and in the next year the production ran up to 9,035,000 bales, another gain of over 1,600,000. But the planters were already diversifying their crops with astonishing results. They had increased their corn crop nearly 200,000,000 bushels since 1860; their oat crop over 50,000,000 bushels; their butter product over 15,000,000 cwts.; and their hay crop over 5,000,000 tons. Every year's decline in the price of cotton has forced southern planters to depend more closely upon their own resources for food supplies. There was an increase of 48,000,000 bushels of corn in the southern States last year, and, unless all signs fail, the cotton belt will be almost wholly dependent upon its own supplies of food this year."

Texas Cotton Mills.

The financial depression and the uncertainties regarding tariff legislation seem to have exerted their full influence on cotton consumption in the season of 1893-94. This depression of trade was general, and affected a majority of the southern mills, those in Texas being no exception.

The total cotton consumption in all southern mills in 1893-94 was 718,515 bales, as against 743,848 bales for 1892-93, and 686,080 bales for 1891-92.

The total number of mills in Texas in 1893-94 was 7, of which 4 were running and 3 idle. In these there are 61,800 spindles, of which 35,576 were in operation in 1893-94, and 26,224 idle. The number of bales consumed was 10,122, as against 12,396 in 1892-93. The weight in pounds was 5,171,970, against 6,478,066.

From the above figures it will be seen that Texas as yet makes but a small showing in the matter of local consumption of cotton as compared with the Atlantic States.

The proposed movement of mills to the south is, however, attracting considerable attention, and in this respect the following

Proposed movement of cotton mills to the south.

quotation from an article on the point, which lately appeared in a local journal, is of timely interest:—

"There is a great deal of talk of northern cotton mills moving to the south just at present, and there are those who seem to think that these removals, if made, will enhance the value of the staple. That under certain conditions it will benefit the agricultural classes cannot be disputed, but if farmers continue to devote their attention to cotton, to the neglect of all other crops, it will offer no relief from low prices for the staple. The manufacturer will profit by the over-production; and if the granaries, corn-cribs, meat and canned goods packeries, to feed the mill operatives, are to be located in the north and west, as in the past, those sections will benefit at the expense of the cotton-raisers. There is no better country on earth for producing almost every description of food used by the human race than Texas and the south, and it can be produced with less labour and at less cost than in most other sections. With diversification of crops, the production of its own meat, fruits, and vegetables, the south can feed the mill operatives cheaper than any other section. When the people here make up their minds to raise food crops in preference to cotton, and bring the cost of living to the working people below the cost in other sections, they will offer greater inducements to northern manufacturers to locate than any that have yet been advanced. The time to begin this diversification of crops is the present season. That cotton does not pay at present prices is disputed by no practical farmer, and that even a 7,000,000 bale crop next year will bring prices to a paying basis is doubtful. The large crop of the present year has gone out of sight and into the hands of consumers to a great extent, but it does not follow that it has been consumed. The present low prices have caused the mills to stock up largely, and sales of nearly 100,000 bales to the trade of Liverpool last week indicate that the stocking up is still going on over there. By the time the stock is disposed of the mills will be loaded, and will show little disposition to purchase—even if the crop is short—at greatly enhanced prices, but will prefer to exhaust their stocks and live on a hand-to-mouth policy until another big crop year comes and knocks the price down to a non-paying basis again. In the meantime, if the agriculturists diversify their crops and make the cost of living in the south as cheap for food as it is now comparatively for clothing, they will offer irresistible inducements for manufacturers to locate among them and furnish them a profitable market for fruits and vegetables, and make them independent of cotton as the sole money crop."

Cotton Baling.

Dissatisfaction in baling of Galveston cotton.

The alleged poor baling and consequent loss of much of the American cotton received at Liverpool, has caused a smouldering discontent for years past. This season the dissatisfaction has broken out into action, and a numerously attended and influential meeting of the Liverpool Cotton Exchange was held to discuss the matter, and the attention of American shippers of cotton, especially at Galveston, called to the growing evil and loss attendant on the extremely poor baling of the cotton coming through this port.

Causes of the evil. The evil complained of no doubt arises from the poor covering of the bales used in the interior of Texas, and more especially from the practice which obtains here of chartering a vessel for a lump sum, when the stevedore and his men, in order to get the fullest carrying power out of the vessel and thus make money for the charterer, pull to pieces, mutilate and break hundreds of bales in the attempt to load the vessel to her utmost capacity. It is a serious question for Galveston and the shipbrokers here, for if the present bad condition of bales on arrival at destination continues, cotton will seek other points of shipment.

Action of Galveston Cotton Exchange. Early in the present year the Galveston Cotton Exchange took steps to correct the evil complained of, and issued a memorial to all commercial and financial bodies interested in cotton, reviewing the situation, and closing with the following resolution of the Directors:—

" Whereas the insufficient covering of American cotton by material of inferior quality is notorious, and the ragged condition of bales, when landed at ports of discharge and at mill points, has become a constant source of loss and inconvenience to shippers and consignees, be it

" Resolved, that from and after September 1, 1895, all bales of the new crop covered with less than 6 yards of 44-inch bagging of a lighter weight than $2\frac{1}{4}$ lbs. minimum per yard, shall be declared unmerchantable, unless recovered properly at the expense of seller.

" Resolved, further, that this rule be brought to the attention of all bagging manufacturers of the country with the request and recommendations that for the ensuing year that they manufacture cotton bagging of above standard weight of fibre only, woven sufficiently close, and calendered to such a degree as to permit of the clear and distinct marking of the bales.

" Resolved, further, that the attention of the manufacturers be directed to the importance of making steel ties and buckles out of the best material only, and not lighter than 45 lbs. per bundle of 30 ties of 11 to $11\frac{1}{2}$ feet in length.

" Resolved, further, that a copy of these resolutions and memorial be mailed to every ginner in Texas, and the Press be requested to give them the widest possible publicity among farmers.

" It is also recommended to all ginners, to adopt a uniform box for baling cotton of 60 inches in length and 28 inches in width, which dimensions experience has proved to be the most suitable for compressing of the bales, as well as for their transportation in railroad cars and stowage by vessels. The present irregularity of the gin boxes is the cause of much of the poor compressing and loss of space to the carrier, resulting in higher freights to the detriment of the farmer, and serves as an excuse, although totally unwarranted, for the plucking and cutting of bales by stevedores of vessels.

"JULIUS RUNGE, President.
"S. O. YOUNG, Secretary."

Action of Cotton Convention at New Orleans. This question of baling and compressing cotton was subsequently brought before the Cotton and Maritime Convention at New Orleans, and the resolutions given above were discussed.

Resolutions were passed to the effect that a standard bale of cotton on and after September 1, 1895, should not measure over 28 inches wide, nor 58 inches long, box measure, to be covered with bagging in its entirety including sampling holes with a quality of bagging weighing not less than $2\frac{1}{4}$ lbs. or 44 inches wide, and to be compressed at a minimum density of 25 lbs. per cubic foot. All ocean freights after that date are to be based on such a bale; otherwise, extra freight will be charged, and while the Conference did not and could not, in the nature of things, undertake to pass these resolutions into an obligatory law, still the prevailing opinion was, that the shipbrokers at the various ports represented will insist that future engagements of cotton adhere to this given standard, or else they will charge an extra rate for bale not in conformity therewith. All modern compresses can easily compress cotton to the required density as indicated above, and inasmuch as they charge not more than 50 c. for compressing, which fee is also exacted by the inferior and almost obsolete compresses, it is no more than equitable that compresses not able to compress to the above standard should either reduce their price for compressing, or be subject to the payment of the cost of such re-compressing as may be found necessary, when the cotton is about to be delivered to the ship.

The previous standard of density has been $22\frac{1}{2}$ lbs. per cubic foot, and it will be seen that the density has been raised 10 per cent., which, in the long run, means that ocean freight rates will be reduced to that extent, 10 per cent., inasmuch as competition between ship agents where they find a vessel can carry 10 per cent. more cargo, will immediately accept a correspondingly less freight rate.

Cotton Fires.

These have been but few in 1894, and only one of them of importance, viz., that on the steamship "Masonic" in December, when 2,600 bales were damaged by fire and water. The increased shed accommodation and the more careful inspection have born fruit, and this port may be considered fortunate in the matter of cotton fires when compared with New Orleans and Savannah.

GALVESTON.

Cotton Exhibition.

An exhibition of cotton and other domestic products was held in the autumn of 1894 at Waco, in Texas. One of the most noteworthy exhibits was that of cotton itself, not only from Texas, but from every cotton-producing country in the world, including Smyrna, Cyprus, Egypt, Tahiti, Fiji, Peru, Brazil, and India. Though on a comparatively small scale, and not to be compared with the shortly forthcoming exhibition at Atlanta, Georgia, yet the "cotton palace," as it was called, was very successful, and was visited by many persons not only from Texas, but from surrounding States.

TABLE showing Mortality at Galveston during the Year 1894.

Causes.	Number of Deaths.
Accidents	58
Asthenia	11
Asphyxia	2
Apoplexy	6
Brain inflammation	19
Bright's disease	25
Bowel diseases	54
Consumption	79
Cancer	15
Colitis	1
Congestion	8
Convulsions	15
Cirrhosis	3
Exhaustion	5
Fever, typhoid	22
Embolism	13
Heart failure	62
Inanition	20
Liver diseases	12
La grippe	4
Marasmus	11
Meningitis	25
Natural causes	5
Paralysis	9
Pneumonia	33
Poisoning	8
Septicæmia	25
Senility	24
Throat diseases	14
Tetanus	24
Total	612

Description.	Number of Deaths.
Number of deaths in Sealy Hospital	81
" St. Mary's Hospital, as per mortuary record	21
Number of premature births and still-born	59

UNITED STATES.

Age at Time of Death.

Year	Number of Deaths
Under 1	89
1 to 5	58
5 10	18
10 20	44
20 30	57
30 40	74
40 50	71
50 60	71
60 70	41
Above 70	75
Total	612

Race.

Description	Number of Deaths
White	485
Coloured	127

Sex.

Description	Number of Deaths
Male	361
Female	251

NOTE.—The death rate was a little over 12 per 1,000 on an estimated population of 50,000.

Harbour Works at Galveston.

Advantages of Galveston's situation as a port.

In my report for 1893 allusion was made at some length to the commanding situation of Galveston as a port, both naturally and artificially. There is no necessity to go deeply again into the question, but it must be apparent to every unbiassed person that, granted the fact that haulage by water is cheaper than that by land, the position of Galveston, so much nearer as she is to vast cotton and grain-producing areas, must in the event of a reasonable depth of water being obtained over the present bar—say, 18 to 20 feet in the long run—attract an enormously increased quantity of produce for export, and that not only from new areas, but also from districts now sending their produce to other ports such as New Orleans. It is true that at the present time discrimination in railway rates exists, and militates largely against this port; but these are matters that must sooner or later adjust themselves, however hard vested interests and railway corporations may fight, and once given deep water the very railways that now convey so much Texas cotton to New Orleans will probably be knocking at the gates of Galveston for entrance.

As it is even now, year by year more and more cotton is attracted here, and in consequence more and more shipping. It is true that the cotton crop of the present season has been huge, but, even allowing for this fact, more charters in proportion than ever before were made for vessels to load at this port, the shipping agents here have counted on deeper water than that previously obtained. In this hope they were somewhat disappointed, as the increase if depth was not so great as had been looked for, but as the jetties approach completion the results wished for appear more certain, and the work of the dredger (already ordered at an outlay of 100,000 dol.), which it is hoped will be in operation by July or August, is relied upon by those capable of judging to give a channel of 18 to 20 feet at least by the commencement of the next cotton season in September.

The result of such a depth of water would give an incalculable impetus to the trade of Galveston, which would then certainly become, if not a great town, at least an enormous entrepôt. As regards cotton, vessels would then be enabled to take a full cargo at the wharf or in the stream, and proceed directly to sea, thus saving the time and great expense of loading the last portion of their cargoes from lighters, as is now the case. Cotton would thus be loaded here as easily, and even more cheaply, than at New Orleans; the 100 miles river passage necessary there would be avoided, pilotage and other dues would be lessened, and in consequence that large portion of the Texas crop which now finds its way to New Orleans would come to its natural outlet, Galveston. *Probable results of deep water.*

Again, with 20 feet of water a large grain trade would be done, and the existing facilities for such a business in the shape of elevators, &c., find full employment, whilst the direct importation of general merchandise, which of late years has greatly fallen off, would receive much impetus.

These are briefly a few of the many and important benefits that Galveston may hope for in obtaining the long-looked for deep water. She has such a truly magnificent country upon which to draw for exports of domestic produce, that once given an unrestricted passage to the sea her future as a port of the first importance, rivalling even New Orleans, is practically assured. During the year 1894 it must be noted that most abnormal conditions prevailed in all the Gulf ports as regards water. The sea seemed in every place to be drawn away from bays and harbours into the open. Galveston was no exception, and there was, in fact, in spite of the further completion of the jetties, actually less water on the bar than in either 1893 or 1892. At one time there were no less than 15 cotton laden vessels waiting at the bar to cross and proceed to sea.

With regard to the actual work done on the gigantic jetties

(1960)

being built here by the United States Government, I have been favoured by Major Miller, U.S.A., the able officer in charge of the work, with a copy of his last report for the financial year ended June 30, 1894. From this interesting report I extract the following information:—

"The project for this improvement (that of the entrance to Galveston Harbour) was adopted in 1874, modified in 1880, and again modified in 1886, the object being to deepen the channel so as to admit of sea-going vessels of the deepest draught to enter the harbour.

"The projects of 1874 and 1880 contemplated construction of two jetties to extend into the Gulf of Mexico to concentrate ebb-flow upon the outer bar in the Gulf, and also to effect deepening on the inner bar at the entrance to Galveston Channel; these jetties to have their origins, respectively at Bolivar Point and Fort Point.

"More or less work was done under these projects. Under that of 1881 a jetty was built from Fort Point to the crest of the outer bar, but it was not fully completed.

"The project of 1886 (that now in progress of execution) also consists in the construction of jetties to extend into the Gulf, one, the south jetty, starting from the east end of Galveston Island, and the other, the north jetty, to start from Bolivar Point, opposite; or, to be more exact, the south jetty was to start from Fort Point, but in 1888 it was decided to connect the inner end of that jetty with the relatively high ground upon which the city of Galveston is built by a stone dyke, known as the shore branch.

"The jetties were to be of stone, to be built to an elevation of 5 feet above mean low tide, and to extend, if necessary, to the contour of 30 feet depth in the Gulf, their sea ends to be 7,000 feet apart, the action of the jetties to be supplemented, if need be, by dredging, the south jetty to follow the line of the jetty of 1881.

"The natural depth upon the outer bar was 12 feet, and that upon the inner bar 13 feet at mean low tide. The general plan of the work is shown upon the accompanying map.

"At the close of the fiscal year ending June 30, 1893, the progress made in the construction of the jetties was as follows:—

"The south jetty had been completed for a distance of 32,000 feet, and an apron, 839 feet long, was constructed at the sea end to prevent scour. This jetty having reached the outer crest of the bar, its further extension was suspended for the present.

"The north jetty, commenced in April, 1893, had been completed for a distance of 1,500 feet, in addition to which 21,100 feet had been partially constructed.

"The effect of this work was plainly shown on the bars, the inner one having entirely disappeared, and the depth on the outer one having increased from 12 to 14 feet, a gain of 2 feet.

"The construction of the north jetty was continued during the present fiscal year, and good progress was made, it having been completed for a distance of 10,000 feet, an advance of 8,500 feet since last year, in addition to which 6,200 feet was partially constructed. The sea end of this jetty is now within 5,000 feet of the outer crest of the bar.

"The total length of the jetties constructed since work was begun in 1887 is—

Description.		Length.
		Linear feet.
South jetty {	Completed ..	32,000
{	Uncompleted ..	829
North jetty {	Completed ..	10,000
{	Uncompleted ..	6,200
Total, June 30, 1894	..	49,029

"The usual annual survey of the bar and channel, as well as of the harbour generally, was made in May and June, 1894. The soundings show a channel depth of $14\frac{1}{2}$ feet on the outer bar. The effect of the north jetty is now beginning to manifest itself. The bar is being worn away, and is very irregular in contour, showing many holes and lumps; the 12-foot contour has moved northward, and embraces a much less area on the bar.

"Galveston Channel has deepened, and now has a maximum depth of $41\frac{1}{2}$ feet. The depth of the inner bar is $24\frac{1}{4}$ feet, an increase of $1\frac{1}{4}$ feet since last year. The 24-foot curve now connects Galveston and Bolivar Channels.

"The 18-foot curve inside the bar advanced 3,200 feet toward the same curve outside. The 12-foot curve on the bar advanced about 500 feet, and the same curve south of south jetty receded about 300 feet. The 18-foot and 24-foot curves outside the bar advanced about 500 feet and 400 feet respectively.

"The amounts expended were as follows:—

Description.	Amount.
	Dollars.
Amount expended under all projects to June 30, 1893	3,359,639
Amount expended during fiscal year ended June 30, 1894	1,008,824
Total expended to June 30, 1894 ..	4,368,463

"The weather and sea were more or less favourable during the year ended June 30, 1894, and protection was afforded by the south jetty for the prosecution of the work on the north jetty, but the lack of protection previously afforded by the south jetty as the work advanced towards the Gulf, and the increased strength of tidal currents caused a discontinuance of pile-driving, and increased the difficulties of construction.

"The amount of stone used in the construction of the north jetty during the year ending June 30, 1894, was 337,159 tons, of which 235,197 tons was rip-rap, and 101,962 tons granite."

As can be readily imagined, a considerable change has taken place in the contours of water, and in the bar itself, since the drawing up of Major Miller's report in last September.

Last survey. The last official survey was made on March 3, 1895, and it was then found that the distance from the inner 18-foot curve to the outer 18-foot curve was only 400 feet, showing that these curves had approached one another 3,200 feet since June, 1894.

Through the kindness of Major Miller, I am enabled to annex a map of the entrance to Galveston harbour, showing the result of this survey of March 3.

18-foot channel over bar. On March 9, 1895, it was officially announced by the Galveston Board of Pilots that there was a clear channel of 18 feet over the bar, and that the results claimed for the jetty plan have been practically attained. As I remarked elsewhere in this report, the result of this deepening over the bar of Galveston harbour is fraught with incalculable benefits to this port.

GALVESTON.

TABLE showing in Detail the Progress of the Work on the North Jetty during the Year 1894.

Month.	Sandstone Placed.	Granite Placed.	Trestle Constructed.	Trestle Complete.	Riprap Apron.	Riprap to Mean Low Tide.	Riprap to Full Height.	Incomplete Granite Covering.	Complete.	Advance of Completed Work during Month.
	Tons.	Tons.	Feet.	Feet.	Feet.	Feet.	Feet.	Feet.	Feet.	Feet.
Conditions at beginning of year	..	..	..	11,500	11,500	9,500	7,200	8,100	7,100	..
Condition at end of each month—										
January	25,623·08	8,653·58	1,000	12,500	12,500	11,100	8,200	8,570	7,650	550
February	10,739·08	9,472·00	..	12,500	12,500	11,500	9,100	10,400	7,930	280
March	10,420·40	7,239·43	200	12,700	12,500	11,900	9,100	11,400	8,075	145
April	19,705·49	10,404·33	800	13,500	13,800	12,000	9,300	11,500	8,600	525
May	21,358·72	9,017·66	1,400	14,900	14,900	12,000	11,700	11,700	9,400	800
June	30,087·62	10,702·53	1,293	16,193	16,200	12,500	12,000	12,500	10,000	600
July	27,935·17	9,602·64	707	16,900	16,900	13,500	12,800	13,100	10,400	400
August	14,906·25	13,936·70	500	17,400	17,500	14,500	13,000	14,300	11,260	860
September	29,375·79	5,214·75	1,600	19,000	19,100	14,800	13,000	14,700	11,685	425
October	27,933·24	8,531·01	1,500	20,500	20,500	15,500	13,000	15,800	12,200	515
November	27,881·32	8,982·47	1,100	21,600	21,500	15,500	15,100	15,800	12,515	315
December	25,124·32	8,316·61	..	21,600	22,000	16,700	15,600	16,100	13,075	560
Total progress	271,090·31	110,071·71	10,100	10,100	10,500	7,200	8,400	8,000	5,975	5,975

Present position of work.

From the figures it will be seen that the completed work advanced from 7,100 to 13,075 feet, a gain of 5,975 feet, whilst the incompleted portion was pushed as far out as 16,700 feet. 271,090 tons of granite were placed in position, and 110,071 tons of rip rap stone used.

At the present time (March 7) the incompleted portion of the north jetty has reached the 16,800-foot mark, and the completed part is 13,800 feet. The trestle work is completed to the 22,018-foot mark, which is beyond the bar in the 18-foot curve of water. When the north jetty is completed to the 22,018-foot mark it is the intention of the engineers to advance both jetties simultaneously, probably until the 30-foot curve of water is encountered.

The Government dredger is not expected before July, but it is quite possible that the dredging by private enterprise may be commenced very shortly.

RECAPITULATION.

	Amount.		Length.	Quantity.
	Dol.	c.	Feet.	Tons.
Total cost of work from the beginning of the jetty system, including past and present contracts, estimated	8,478,000	0	..	..
Total cost of present contract, estimated	6,200,000	0	..	..
Paid on the south jetty under the present contract	1,062,178	0	..	..
Paid on the north jetty to Feb. 28	1,786,255	44	..	..
Total length of south jetty to 30 ft. curve	..		37,000	..
Length of south jetty complete to 18 ft. curve	..		32,000	..
Total length of north jetty to 30 ft. curve	..		27,000	..
Length of north jetty complete to Feb. 28	..		13,800	..
Distance between shore end of jetties	..		12,000	..
Distance between sea end of jetties complete	..		7,000	..
Total number of tons of stone for whole system complete, estimated	..		..	2,002,000
Tons of granite used to Feb. 28	..		..	348,255
Tons of riprap used to Feb. 28	..		..	661,480

At 20 tons to the car the total number of cars of stone for the complete work would be about 100,000 or 5,000 trains of 20 cars each, or a total car length, at 40 feet to the car, or 4,000,000 feet, or nearly 760 miles.

GALVESTON.

Other Harbour Works.

Besides the works at the entrance to Galveston harbour, there are other important Government improvements going on in this vicinity, also under the supervision of Major Miller. They are as follows:—Ship channel in Galveston Bay, channel in West Galveston Bay, Trinity River, Cedar Bayou and Buffalo Bayou improvements.

Of these the first and last named are the most important.

The following are extracts from Major Miller's last report concerning these improvements:—

"The project for this improvement was adopted in 1871, modified in 1877, and again modified in 1892. This latter modification became necessary owing to the acquisition by the United States of the Morgan Cut and Canal. The object of the improvement is to excavate and maintain a channel, 100 feet wide at the bottom, and 12 feet deep, from Bolivar Channel to the San Jacinto River, a distance of 24·33 miles, thereby giving an outlet to the commerce of Buffalo Bayou, of San Jacinto River, of Trinity River, and of Cedar Bayou.

"A channel, having a width of at least 100 feet and a depth of 12 feet, was excavated from Bolivar Channel to Morgan Cut in 1888–89, but as no dredging was done from then to June 30, 1893, the channel had shoaled again to an average depth of 8 feet. The amount expended on this improvement up to that time was 557,315 dol. 80 c.

"The sum of 40,332 dol. 78 c. was expended on this improvement during the fiscal year ending June 30, 1894, and was applied to deepening and widening the channel from the Morgan Canal to the Morgan Beacon, a distance of 4·8 miles. The amount of material dredged was 153,376 cubic yards, the depth in the channel being increased from 8 to 9·5 feet, a gain of 1·5 feet for navigation. There is now an average depth of 9·5 feet from Bolivar Channel to the Morgan Canal.

"This project is not capable of permanent completion, as the shifting sands in the bay cause the channel to shoal considerably when work is suspended. It is estimated that the sum of 100,000 dol. will be required annually to maintain the channel after it has been excavated to the required width and depth.

"It is not practicable to give the statistics of the commerce of the ship channel. Almost the entire floating commerce of Buffalo Bayou, Trinity River, and Cedar Bayou, is carried through this channel, and the commercial statistics are given in the reports for those works. The number of vessels passing through Morgan Canal during the year was 1,979, of which 1,109 were north bound and 870 were south bound.

"It is believed by many of the best informed men of Houston that the advantage to be derived from enabling sea-going ships to reach Houston by way of the ship channel and Buffalo Bayou will be vastly greater than the cost of making and maintaining the channel. The annual report of Buffalo Bayou gives as full statistics of the freight carried upon that stream as could be obtained. It is carried in barges drawing 5 feet when full loaded, and towed by tugs drawing 7 feet and less. These cross Galveston Bay, but the depth of water is already sufficient for them. A large portion of this freight would be loaded directly upon sea-going vessels if they visited Houston. One item of shipment by water down Buffalo Bayou from Houston during the past fiscal year was 275,378 bales of cotton.

<small>Improvement of Buffalo Bayou.</small>

"Buffalo Bayou is a tide-water stream, emptying into San Jacinto River at Lynchburg, about 25 miles below Houston, and about 8 miles above the junction of the San Jacinto with Galveston Bay. White Oak and Simms bayous are tributaries, the former entering at Houston and the latter at a point about 11 miles below.

"A survey of the bayou, with a view to its improvement, was made in 1871, and a subsequent examination between White Oak and Simms bayous was made in 1880. The estimated cost of obtaining a channel 100 feet wide and 12 feet deep in this stream, as stated in the report on the examination, was 385,299 dol. 75 c.

"The object of the improvement is to secure for Buffalo Bayou a channel having the same dimensions (100 feet wide and 12 feet deep) as the one contemplated for Galveston Bay, the aim being to admit sea-going ships to Houston. These dimensions of channel exist naturally in Buffalo Bayou below Simms Bayou and in the San Jacinto River, though it is reported that a small bar exists in San Jacinto River near Morgan Canal.

"The trade of the bayou is practically carried on by the Houston Direct Navigation Company with tugs and barges. Large shipments of cotton are made from Houston to Galveston by water, to be loaded on sea-going vessels at the latter place. The number of bales shipped down the bayou during the present fiscal year was 275,378. The vessels using the bayou during the fiscal year ending June 30, 1894, were as follows:—10 steam, 28 barges, and 62 sailing; tonnage, 2 to 358 tons. Trips during the year, 3,000. Total tonnage, 307,819 tons."

New Mexico.

<small>Review of 1894.</small>

The following extract from the report of the Governor of New Mexico to the United States Secretary of the Interior for the year ended June 30, 1894, gives concisely the history of the territory during that period. Governor Thornton says:—

<small>General progress of New Mexico.</small>

"New Mexico has suffered from the general depression which has affected the entire country during the past 12 months, probably not so seriously as that portion of the country which has been less bountifully blessed by the abundant rains which have fallen throughout this territory and given to our people an unprecedented crop year, all classes of cereals and grasses being at their maximum. It is doubted if the territory ever had more abundant crops than have been raised throughout its length and breadth. There has been no material change in our population; but a healthy growth has set in of a very desirable class of immigration in almost every county in the territory, especially in the agricultural portions thereof. Irrigation enterprises begun within the last two or three years have succeeded admirably, bringing under cultivation large areas of desert land. In more than half the counties of the territory enterprises of importance have been begun which will add largely in the near future to the productiveness and prosperity of our people. Among the fruit-growers in the Mesilla Valley, upon the Rio Grande, many new settlers have purchased and planted large orchards and vineyards. This industry is rapidly growing, and is one of great importance in that locality, as well as in the counties of Colfax, Santa Fé, Bernalilo, Eddy Chaves, and San Juan, all of which localities are destined, in the near future, to become large shippers.

"The increase of population has been of a character calculated to increase the prosperity of this community in a greater degree than would be expected from its numbers. In the south-eastern counties—Eddy, Chaves, and Lincoln—this influx of new settlers has been more widely noted than in any other section. The people who have made new homes there were from the old States of the East; each family that cast its lot there brought in a considerable sum of money, generally about 2,000 dol., but some of them were persons of wealth. It necessarily follows that in an irrigated country the settlement will be of this class. In San Juan County, in the north-west, the same thing has been noted, but as this county lies off of the railroad but little has been heard of the steady development that goes on there. In Colfax and Union counties a steady growth has been observed. This goes on quietly and unheralded, but is no less certain and productive of good order and the advance of the people. The attraction to these sections is the choice irrigated land that is offered the settler at reasonable figures. The most notable influx of settlement, however, was that which followed the discovery of the precious minerals in that section of Bernalillo County known as the Cochiti Mountains. The immigration here was of the hardiest class of miners and prospectors, and a remarkable thing to note is the fact that during the life of the camp there has been only one quarrel in which firearms or deadly weapons were used. That several thousand men bent on the search for wealth should live in the hills for a year, and although under no apparent rules of law, should live peaceably and in good order far surpassing that of any organised town in the United States, or in the world for that matter, is a high and singular commentary on the class of immigration that has blessed New Mexico during the past year. The addition to our population from this one source may be approximately stated at 2,000 persons."

Increase of population.

UNITED STATES.

Land Titles.

United States Court of Land Claims.
The work of the United States Court of Private Land Claims, which advanced so rapidly during the first year of its existence, continued to progress with equal rapidity during 1894.

The work performed was most important, and has apparently been well done. Title to many large tracts of land has been finally determined, many of them in favour of the claimant, others in favour of the Government. In either case, however, the question of title has been settled, thus giving to the owners fresh courage to improve and develop the grants confirmed, or else giving to the public thousands of acres wrongfully claimed.

The number of cases filed in the court was 262. Thirty claims were settled by the court during the year ending June 30, 1894, involving claims to 1,558,875 acres.

Taxable Property.

Estimated value of property in 1894.
The estimated value of the real estate, live stock, merchandise and miscellaneous property in the Territory shows a slight increase, being 43,620,244 dol., as against 41,602,198 dol. in 1893.

Assessments.
The rates of assessment thereon for the year 1894 were as follows:—

For—	Mills on the Dollar.
Territorial purposes	6
Casual deficit bonds	25
Territorial institutions	1·50
Cattle indemnity fund	½
Public schools	2

Property by counties.
The following table shows the value of taxable property by counties: of the total of 43,630,244 dol., 12,780,909 dol. is the estimated value of lands; 5,969,048 dol. of houses and improvements; and 8,057,589 dol. of live stock:—

Counties.	Value.	
	Dollars	c.
Bernalillo	6,377,277	0
Chaves	1,446,002	0
Colfax	3,834,620	0
Donna Ana	2,733,563	0
Eddy	1,992,095	70
Grant	4,129,468	34
Guadaloupe	1,166,120	0
Lincoln	1,546,588	67
Mora	1,427,476	94
Rio Arriba	1,027,277	0
San Juan	520,844	69
Santa Fé	2,631,898	0
San Miguel	5,954,079	0
Sierra	1,380,097	52
Socorro	2,935,968	0
Taos	688,335	0
Valencia	1,783,133	95
	41,574,844	81
Add exemptions to heads of family, under Sec. 1 cap. 6, laws of 1893, on total valuation	2,055,400	0
Total	43,630,244	81

Territorial Debt.

The revenue of New Mexico for the year ended June 30, 1894, was 258,198 dol., whilst the expenditure during the same period was 260,520 dol.

Revenue and expenditure.

The financial condition of the Treasury at the close of that period was as follows:—

	Amount.
	Dollars.
Bonded debt	925,000
Floating debt	21,891
Total	946,891

The cash balance on hand on June 30, 1894, was 139,899 dol.
On the whole the financial status of the territory appears excellent.

Railways.

During 1894 railway building was almost at a standstill in New Mexico. The only extension made was that of the Pecos Valley system, from Eddy to Roswell, in Chaves County, a distance of nearly 100 miles.

Railways.

Mining.

Mining. Mining in New Mexico has suffered greatly from the depression of late years, especially from the low price of lead and silver, the two minerals most largely produced. Notwithstanding this, the prospects of mining are extremely bright, owing to the recent discovery and development of new mining districts, rich in gold, silver, and copper. There are four districts where mining has greatly increased, resulting in an output of paying mineral in large quantities. These are Hillsboro', Pinos Altos, White Oaks, and in the Organ Mountains. The first three are gold camps, the last silver.

It is noteworthy that New Mexico, under favourable circumstances, could annually produce from 20,000,000 dol. to 30,000,000 dol. from her mines, so it is estimated, and in the event of silver ever being re-monevtized at the old ratio of 16 to 1 and accepted as the money of the world, this result would probably be attained.

Maxwell grant. In the northern portion of the territory a good deal of prospecting has been done on the Maxwell Grant. The Moreno Valley, which lies on this grant, has produced steadily for more than a generation, while the Aztec gold mine, the oldest and best in the district, is still a large producer.

Cochiti mines. Public interest has been largely concentrated in 1894 on the newly discovered gold fields of the Cochiti region.

These Cochiti mines lie on the eastern slope of the Irmez Mountains, a Sierra, now commonly called the Cochiti Mountains. The mines take their name from the "Pueblos" of Quarez Indians, that are found among them; they are situated 30 miles due west of Santa Fé. The point of present development is in the heart of an igneous formation 20 miles wide and about 40 long.

At Bland City, a camp in the Pinos Cañyon, both gold and silver are found. It is hard to give an accurate description of this great mineral out-crop. Beginning right under the volcanic ash cap, the porphyry is riven with great wedges of white marble, inoculated with a grayish blue mineral stain. Gold Hill, the mountain on which this crop is most apparent, is between Peno and Cotto Cañyons. These great ledges or reefs of quartz can be traced from the cañyon bed to the top of the mountain—some 900 feet. The quartz is about 20 to 40 feet from one porphyry wall to the other. It is all mineralised, and yields from 40 dol. to 500 dol. per ton in gold and silver. The mineral belt is estimated to extend north and south about 5 miles, and east and west about 1 mile, or 1½ miles.

Alum.

A large deposit of alum has been opened on the Gila River. It is reported to be of great commercial value, and is now being worked with proper railway facilities. These alum beds, as well as those of gypsum and soda nearly, would probably become almost the most productive properties in New Mexico.

Alum.

Annex A.—Statement of Imports Subject to Duty at the Port of Galveston, Texas, for the Year ending December 31, 1894.

Commodities.		Quantity.	Germany. Dollars.	Great Britain. Dollars.	France. Dollars.	Netherlands. Dollars.	Mexico. Dollars.	Porto Rico. Dollars.	Turkey. Dollars.	Spain. Dollars.
Cement, barrels, 400 lbs. gross, each	Lbs.	11,344,371	...	10,390	...	...	...	...	...	...
Coal, bituminous	Tons	3,755	...	8,427	...	...	...	...	...	...
Chemicals—										
Caustic soda	Lbs.	283,801	...	6,416	...	...	...	...	...	...
Sheep dip			...	3,080	...	...	...	...	...	...
Dead oil creosote			...	7,513	...	...	...	...	...	...
Cotton, manufactures of, laces and embroideries			...	384	...	...	...	...	...	...
Earthenware—										
Plain and decorated crockery			...	14,519	...	...	...	...	...	...
Firebrick and tiles			...	496	...	...	...	...	...	...
Flax and hemp, manufactures of—										
Jute	Tons	174	...	...	...	...	...	...	...	...
Burlaps			...	8,121	...	...	...	...	...	...
Fruits and nuts, green and ripe			...	10,414	...	...	...	430	687	...
Fish in oil, sardines in ¼ boxes			...	...	1,624	...	...	...	...	...
Fruits, preserved			...	193	6,336	...	...	...	...	...
Glass, all kinds			74	198	1,295	...	...	...	...	...
Tin and terne plate	Lbs.	310,070	...	11,298	...	...	...	...	...	...
Malt liquor, ale and porter in bottles	Gallons	9,036	...	9,825	282	...	...	...	...	...
Spirits, distilled	,,	396	158	239	680	...	...	...	...	487
Wines, still	Lbs.	987,521	...	93	...	...	...	...	...	...
Salt, January 1 to August 28, 1894 (free after)			...	1,942	...	...	...	...	...	...
Machinery, all kinds (including manufactures of iron)			...	6,692	575	...	...	...	...	...
Vegetables (preserved and prepared)			...	3,126	...	...	...	...	...	...
Olive oil			...	...	...	...	...	...	...	...
Provisions			...	...	...	...	...	...	...	...
Cheese	Lbs.	1,039	...	...	...	...	...	...	...	...
Honey	Gallons	14,060	...	...	...	...	3,449	...	...	...
Breadstuffs, maccaroni and vermicelli			...	...	...	...	...	...	...	...
Sugar, beet (above 16 D.S.)	Lbs.	122,560	3,738	...	...	...	...	...	...	...
Wood, manufactures of			39	139	...	...	...	...	...	...
Wool	,,		...	213	...	...	...	...	...	...
Gelatine			...	957	219	...	...	...	...	...
Chocolate			...	...	...	...	...	...	...	...
Coke	Tons	1,020	...	3,435	...	...	...	...	...	...
Miscellaneous, all other dutiable articles			274	1,635	...	...	9	...	...	...
Subject to duty for 1894			4,283	109,745	11,011	...	3,888	687	...	487
Free of duty for 1894			3,626	42,486	281	631	3,369	2,981	673*	...
Grand total for 1894			7,909	152,231	11,292	631	7,257	3,668	673*	487
,, 1893			9,023	201,961	7,093	4,072	6,599	3,180	...	...
,, 1892			11,318	304,314	13,144	27,304	5,604	11,629	355	...
,, 1891			77,438	394,483	18,023	42,148	44,637	163,403†	899	99

* Japan.   † Nicaragua.

GALVESTON.

STATEMENT of Imports Subject to Duty at the Port of Galveston, Texas, for the Year ending December 31, 1894—continued.

Commodities.	Italy.	Brazil.	British West Indies.	Cuba.	British East India.	Belgium.	Austria-Hungary.	Total, 1894.	Total, 1893.
	Dollars.	Dollars.	Dollars.	Dollars.	Dollars.	Dollars.	Dollars.	Dollars.	Dollars.
Cement, barrels, 400 lbs. gross, each	...	...	...	...	...	...	...	30,624	79,083
Coal, bituminous	...	...	...	...	...	...	...	8,427	2,114
Chemicals—									
Caustic soda	...	...	...	...	...	...	...	6,416	2,274
Sheep dip	...	...	...	...	...	...	...	3,080	2,375
Dead oil creosote	...	...	...	...	228	...	...	7,513	14,720
Cotton, manufactures of, laces and embroideries	...	...	...	...	...	...	...	612	1,068
Earthenware—									
Plain and decorated crockery	...	...	...	...	...	...	...	14,519	20,601
Firebrick and tiles	...	...	...	...	...	...	...	496	2,046
Flax and hemp, manufactures of—									
Jute	...	...	...	...	...	...	...	8,121	1,304
Burlaps	...	...	113	...	...	...	...	10,414	12,790
Fruit and nuts, green and ripe	...	...	...	...	...	...	...	1,230	264
Fish in oil, sardines in ¼ boxes	...	...	...	...	...	...	...	1,624	1,825
Fruits, preserved	...	...	...	...	...	...	...	6,529	773
Glass, all kinds	...	...	...	...	...	...	...	1,567	3,265
Tin and terne plate	...	...	...	...	...	...	...	11,298	25,481
Malt liquor, ale and porter in bottles	...	...	...	...	...	...	...	9,825	18,590
Spirits, distilled	363	...	...	...	...	...	...	521	812
Wines, still	...	...	...	...	...	...	...	1,781	3,195
Salt, January 1 to August 28, 1894 (free after)	...	...	...	...	...	...	...	1,942	10,489
Machinery, all kinds (including manufactures of iron)	16	...	...	...	...	...	50	6,692	7,857
Vegetables, preserved and prepared	639	...	...	...	...	...	...	3,717	1,522
Olive oil	...	...	...	...	...	...	...	689	1,091
Provisions—									
Cheese	31	...	...	...	...	...	...	150	...
Honey	...	...	...	...	...	119	...	3,449	...
Breadstuffs, maccaroni and vermicelli	248	...	...	...	...	...	...	248	...
Sugar beet (above 16 D.S.)	...	...	...	...	...	...	...	3,738	865
Wood, manufactures of	...	...	...	...	...	...	...	178	254
Wool	...	...	...	...	...	...	...	213	...
Gelatine	...	...	...	...	...	...	...	957	...
Chocolate	...	...	...	...	...	...	...	219	...
Coke	22	...	...	...	44	...	...	3,435	3,083
Miscellaneous, all other dutiable articles	...	...	...	...	...	...	...	1,984	...
Subject to duty for 1894	1,319	...769*	113	364,592	272	20,353	50	152,208	...
Free of duty for 1894	...	...	3,695	...	...	...	2,325†	425,428	...
Grand total for 1894	1,319	769*	3,808	364,592	272	20,353	50‡	677,636	...
„ 1893	968	439,723	3,097	621,786	12,315	31,823	2,325†	928,343	...
„ 1892	1,218	329,442	432§	16,275	...	...	123	863,981	...
„ 1891	75	...	...	1,452	10,120†	...	...	1,082,151	...

* Honduras. † British Columbia. ‡ Austria. § Japan.

UNITED STATES.

Annex B.—STATEMENT of Imports Free of Duty at the Port of Galveston, Texas, for the Year ending December 31, 1894.

Articles.	Quantity.	Germany.	Great Britain.	France.	Netherlands.	Mexico.	Porto Rico.	Turkey.	Spain.
		Dollars.	Dollars.	Dollars.	Dollars.	Dollars.	Dollars.	Dollars.	Dollars.
Coffee	Lbs. 24,085	..	..	..	..	95	2,981	..	..
Sugar (centrifugal below No. 16, D.S.)	11,299,992	..	..	..	..	..	..	..	..
Jute butts	..	..	..	..	..	205	..	..	..
Fruits and nuts, green and ripe	..	..	..	..	..	..	..	..	..
American manufactures re-imported	..	2,832	14,575	..	..	..	..	..	..
Household and personal effects and books	..	794	4,272	281	..	..	..	..	..
Coal, anthracite	..	..	7,668	..	..	153	..	..	..
Dye-wood, fustic	..	..	..	..	..	..	..	..	..
Mineral water, natural	..	..	..	..	631	..	..	..	..
Cedar, in logs	44,450	..	..	..	..	1,083	..	..	..
Pepper, black, unground	..	..	1,799	..	..	..	..	..	..
Salt (free of duty since August, 1894)	12,477,304	..	14,172	..	..	..	..	..	..
Miscellaneous, all other free goods	..	..	..	..	..	1,833	..	673*	..
Total free for 1894	..	3,626	42,486	281	631	3,369	2,981	673*	..
,, 1893	..	1,616	26,349	100	522	6,055	3,180	..	..
,, 1892	..	2,003	52,875	725	4,730	3,477	10,867	..	..
,, 1891	..	..	..	..	..	..	..	..	..

* Japan.

GALVESTON.

STATEMENT of Imports Free of Duty at the Port of Galveston, Texas, for the Year ending December 31, 1894—continued.

Articles.	Quantity.	Italy.	Brazil.	British West Indies.	Cuba.	British East India.	Belgium.	Austria-Hungary.	Total, 1894.	Total, 1893.
		Dollars.	Dollars.	Dollars.	Dollars.	Dollars.	Dollars.	Dollars.	Dollars.	Dollars.
Coffee	Lbs. 24,085	..	..	..	954	..	..	..	4,030	3,129
Sugar (centrifugal below No. 16, D.S.)	11,299,992	..	..	..	349,206	..	..	..	349,206	621,186
Jute butts	..	..	..	..	..	41,903	..	..	41,903	41,903
Fruits and nuts, green and ripe	..	..	769*	3,695	14,432	..	..	2,325†	21,426	404
American manufactures re-imported	..	..	..	..	..	..	..	..	17,407	12,450
Household and personal effects and books	..	..	..	..	..	..	..	..	5,347	9,061
Coal, anthracite	..	..	..	..	..	..	..	..	7,668	5,059
Dye-wood, fustic	..	..	..	..	..	..	..	..	153	879
Mineral water, natural	..	..	..	..	..	..	..	..	631	540
Cedar, in logs	44,450	..	..	..	..	..	..	..	1,083	4,074
Pepper, black, unground	..	..	..	..	..	..	..	..	1,799	..
Salt (free of duty since August, 1894)	12,477,304	..	..	..	..	..	..	..	14,172	..
Miscellaneous, all other free goods	..	..	..	..	..	..	..	..	2,506	1,797
Total free for 1894	..	..	769*	3,695	364,592	41,903	..	2,325†	425,428	..
,, 1893	..	..	..	..	621,186	..	227	..	701,138	..
,, 1892	..	158	439,723	2,578	45,743	..	..	..	562,869	..
,, 1891	..	..	..	..	..	..	..	..	557,981	..

* Honduras. † British Columbia.

Annex C.—STATEMENT of Exports of Commodities of Domestic Manufacture and Growth from the Customs District of Galveston for the Year ending December 31, 1894.

Destination.	Cotton. Quantity. Bales.	Cotton. Value. Dollars.	Oilcake and Meal. Quantity. Tons (of 2,240 lbs.)	Oilcake and Meal. Value. Dollars.	Wheat. Quantity. Bushels.	Wheat. Value. Dollars.	Corn. Quantity. Bushels.	Corn. Value. Dollars.
Belgium—								
From Port of Galveston	7,550	244,724	..	..	..	..	..	..
Denmark—								
From Port of Galveston	..	..	2,500	70,000	..	..	..	..
France—								
From Port of Galveston	182,832	5,722,551	210	4,206	2,082	1,249	..	..
Germany—								
From Port of Galveston	213,629	6,604,670	34,268	787,476	16,000	9,000	..	..
,, ,, Velasco	1,342	46,306	27,093	588,659	..	..	..	..
Netherlands—								
From Port of Galveston	..	..	4,367	95,815	70,055	39,010	..	..
,, ,, Velasco	..	..	4,887	107,547	..	..	..	..
Russia—								
From Port of Galveston	21,250	646,613	.	..	..	..	..	..
Great Britain—								
From Port of Galveston	647,373	20,255,300	19,168	425,160	47,000	28,200	..	..
,, ,, Velasco	..	..	2,635	52,680	..	..	..	..
Central America—								
From Port of Galveston	..	..	..	..	..	..	..	..
Mexico—								
From Port of Galveston	..	..	..	..	..	..	..	..
,, Sabine Pass	..	..	..	..	..	..	..	..
British West Indies—								
From Port of Sabine Pass	..	..	..	..	..	..	..	..

GALVESTON.

Statement of Exports of Commodities of Domestic Manufacture and Growth from the Customs District of Galveston for the Year ending December 31, 1894—continued.

Destination.	Cotton. Quantity. Bales.	Cotton. Value. Dollars.	Oilcake and Meal. Quantity. Tons (of 2,240 lbs.)	Oilcake and Meal. Value. Dollars.	Wheat. Quantity. Bushels.	Wheat. Value. Dollars.	Corn. Quantity. Bushels.	Corn. Value. Dollars.
Cuba— From Port of Galveston	..	..	..	..	..	..	5,412	2,597
,, ,, Sabine Pass	..	..	..	..	..	..	..	..
Puerto Rico— From Port of Galveston	..	..	..	..	..	..	..	..
Total for 1894	1,073,976	33,520,164	95,128	2,131,543	135,137	77,459	5,412	2,597
,, 1893	757,593	31,534,595	118,230	2,942,914	1,308,950	934,269	98,509	50,710
,, 1892	808,628	32,610,901	79,088	1,867,441	377,985	335,240	144,775	95,925
,, 1891	774,826	34,217,492	43,196	1,008,541	587,395	588,058	12,741	7,251
,, 1890	499,189	26,303,400	53,484	1,202,779	..	..	35,246	11,989

(1960)

50   UNITED STATES.

STATEMENT of Exports of Commodities of Domestic Manufacture and Growth from the Customs District of Galveston for the Year ending December 31, 1894—continued.

Destination.	Wheat Flour. Quantity. Barrels.	Wheat Flour. Value. Dollars.	Lumber. Quantity. M. feet.	Lumber. Value. Dollars.	Cotton-seed Oil. Quantity. Gallons.	Cotton-seed Oil. Value. Dollars.	Logs. Value. Dollars.	Sundries. Value. Dollars.	Total. Value. Dollars.
Belgium—									
From Port of Galveston	..	..	..	..	..	..	..	185	244,909
Denmark—									
From Port of Galveston	..	..	..	..	..	..	..	..	70,000
France—									
From Port of Galveston	..	..	..	..	8,415	2,685	..	2,160	5,732,851
Germany—									
From Port of Galveston	2	9	48	2,150	..	..	19,937	64	7,423,306
,, ,, Velasco	..	..	..	..	164,138	60,000	12,826	1,201	708,992
Netherlands—									
From Port of Galveston	..	..	..	..	..	..	..	..	134,825
,, ,, Velasco	..	..	..	..	45,809	15,980	750	..	124,277
Russia—									
From Port of Galveston	..	..	..	..	..	..	..	..	646,613
Great Britain—									
From Port of Galveston	368	1,470	..	..	..	..	280	12,922	20,723,382
,, ,, Velasco	..	..	..	..	..	..	..	..	52,680
Central America—									
From Port of Galveston	300	1,058	..	..	..	..	..	359	1,417
Mexico—									
From Port of Galveston	..	..	..	..	..	..	..	70	70
,, ,, Sabine Pass	..	..	3,709	39,296	..	..	1,092	1,338	41,726
British West Indies—									
From Port of Sabine Pass	..	..	725	7,646	..	..	..	235	7,881

GALVESTON.

STATEMENT of Exports of Commodities of Domestic Manufacture and Growth from the Customs District of Galveston for the Year ending December 31, 1894—continued.

Destination.	Wheat Flour. Quantity. Barrels.	Wheat Flour. Value. Dollars.	Lumber. Quantity. M. feet.	Lumber. Value. Dollars.	Cotton-seed Oil. Quantity. Gallons.	Cotton-seed Oil. Value. Dollars.	Logs. Value. Dollars.	Sundries. Value. Dollars.	Total. Value. Dollars.
Cuba—									
From Port of Galveston	53,271	189,678	..	..	..	..	..	13,662	205,937
,, Sabine Pass	..	..	1,427	21,062	..	..	..	..	21,062
Puerto Rico—									
From Port of Galveston	5,918	22,577	..	..	..	..	..	..	22,577
Total for 1894	59,859	214,792	5,909	70,154	218,362	78,665	34,885	32,916	36,162,455
,, 1893	49,057	198,925	1,477	17,689	303,170	116,040	74,694	25,359	35,895,195
,, 1892	21,296	98,226	1,334	16,726	41,263	15,639	47,000	9,904	35,097,002
,, 1891	11,929	51,320	..	16,893	..	2,250	..	..	35,964,460
,, 1890	19,481	30,511	..	200,600	..	..	..	..	27,853,480

(1960)

UNITED STATES.

Annex D.—STATEMENT of Vessels engaged in the Foreign Trade in the District of Galveston during the Year ending December 31, 1894.

ENTERED.

Nationality.	Galveston.				Velasco.				Sabine Pass.			
	In Ballast.		With Cargo.		In Ballast.		With Cargo.		In Ballast.		With Cargo.	
	Number of Vessels.	Tons.	Number of Vessels.	Tons.	Number of Vessels.	Tons.	Number of Vessels.	Tons.	Number of Vessels.	Tons.	Number of Vessels.	Tons.
American	1	165	7	3,647	..	..	..	..	8	3,452	..	..
British	125	233,580	13	28,312	11	15,304	..	..	6	2,676	..	..
German	..	..	..	..	..	..	..	..	..	..	..	..
Mexican	..	..	1	89	..	..	..	..	1	89	..	..
Norwegian	6	5,650	9	3,889	1	1,351	..	..	..	..	..	..
Spanish	13	19,623	2	2,746	..	..	..	..	..	..	..	..
Greek	3	5,239	..	..	..	..	..	..	..	..	..	..
Total for 1894	148	264,257	32	38,683	12	16,655	..	..	15	6,217	..	..
,, 1893	133	188,366	38	31,518	19	24,543	..	..	3	841	..	..
,, 1892	117	167,090	41	42,595	9	11,497	1	116	2	645	..	..
,, 1891	148	169,010	75	63,892	..	..	..	..	..	..	..	..
,, 1890	149	112,514	72	57,795	..	..	..	..	..	..	..	..

GALVESTON

STATEMENT of Vessels engaged in the Foreign Trade in the District of Galveston during the Year ending December 31, 1894—continued.

CLEARED.

Nationality.	Galveston. In Ballast. Number of Vessels.	Galveston. In Ballast. Tons.	Galveston. With Cargo. Number of Vessels.	Galveston. With Cargo. Tons.	Velasco. In Ballast. Number of Vessels.	Velasco. In Ballast. Tons.	Velasco. With Cargo. Number of Vessels.	Velasco. With Cargo. Tons.	Sabine Pass. In Ballast. Number of Vessels.	Sabine Pass. In Ballast. Tons.	Sabine Pass. With Cargo. Number of Vessels.	Sabine Pass. With Cargo. Tons.
American	6	9,419	1	54	..	..	..	..	..	..	16	5,292
British	..	..	163	261,225	..	..	12	16,761	..	..	5	2,230
German	..	..	..	..	..	..	..	..	..	..	..	..
Mexican	1	28	..	..	..	..	1	1,351	..	..	2	178
Norwegian	..	..	15	8,770	..	..	..	..	..	..	..	..
Spanish	..	..	18	26,983	..	..	..	..	..	..	..	..
Greek	..	..	2	3,496	..	..	..	..	..	..	..	..
Total for 1894	7	9,447	199	300,558	..	..	13	18,112	..	..	23	7,700
,, 1893	2	477	194	268,354	..	..	25	33,138	..	..	17	3,710
,, 1892	7	3,493	182	246,517	..	..	10	11,355	3	1,078	2	801
,, 1891	12	4,432	232	250,671	..	..	..	..	..	..	..	..
,, 1890	3	332	219	183,358	..	..	..	..	..	..	..	..

(1960)

Annex E.—RETURN of British Shipping at the Port of Galveston in the Year 1894.

Direct Trade in British Vessels from and to Great Britain and British Colonies.

Entered.

Total Number of Vessels.			Total Tonnage.			Total Number of Crews.	Total Value of Cargoes.
With Cargoes.	In Ballast.	Total.	With Cargoes.	In Ballast.	Total.		£
11	83	94	17,201	136,163	153,364	2,230	...

Cleared.

Total Number of Vessels.			Total Tonnage.			Total Number of Crews.	Total Value of Cargoes.
With Cargoes.	In Ballast.	Total.	With Cargoes.	In Ballast.	Total.		£
90	...	90	142,800	...	142,800	2,131	...

Indirect or Carrying Trade in British Vessels from and to other Countries.

Entered.

Countries whence Arrived.	Number of Vessels.			Tonnage.			Number of Crews.	Value of Cargoes.
	With Cargoes.	In Ballast.	Total.	With Cargoes.	In Ballast.	Total.		£
United States	...	21	21	...	32,781	32,781	496	...
Cape Verdes	...	18	18	...	28,502	28,502	443	...
Mexico	...	17	17	...	25,130	25,130	385	...
Spain	...	6	6	...	10,186	10,186	152	...
Portugal	...	4	4	...	6,065	6,065	91	...
Cuba	2	4	6	587	6,488	7,075	116	...
Belgium	3	1	4	4,774	1,564	6,338	108	...
Brazil	...	4	4	...	5,036	5,036	87	...
Azores	...	2	2	...	1,604	1,604	30	...
Uruguay	...	2	2	...	3,209	3,209	44	...
Germany	...	2	2	...	3,296	3,296	47	...
Honduras	1	...	1	62	...	62	6	...
West Indies	...	1	1	...	1,351	1,351	23	...
Madeira	...	1	1	...	1,540	1,540	23	...
Other countries	...	4	4	...	6,843	6,843	110	...
Total	6	87	93	5,423	133,595	139,018	2,161	...

Cleared.

Countries to which Departed.	Number of Vessels.			Tonnage.			Number of Crews.	Value of Cargoes.
	With Cargoes.	In Ballast.	Total.	With Cargoes.	In Ballast.	Total.		£
United States	...	2	2	...	587	587	20	...
Germany	43	...	43	66,771	...	66,771	1,019	...
France	26	...	26	39,872	...	39,872	622	...
Holland	2	...	2	2,650	...	2,650	46	...
Belgium	2	...	2	2,872	...	2,872	46	...
Russia	2	...	2	2,665	...	2,665	46	...
Denmark	1	...	1	1,307	...	1,307	23	...
Mexico	1	...	1	62	...	62	6	...
Total	77	2	79	116,199	587	116,786	1,828	...

GALVESTON.

Annex F.—STATEMENT of Vessels engaged in the Coasting Trade of Galveston during the undermentioned Years.

Year.	Entered. Nationality.	Number of Vessels.	Tons.	Cleared. Nationality.	Number of Vessels.	Tons.
1894	American	309	306,388	American	267	282,752
1893	American	257	287,071	American	196	252,055
1892	American	240	302,325	American	147	25',358

Consul Nugent to the Earl of Kimberley.

My Lord, Galveston, May 16, 1895.

WITH reference to my Despatch of March 27, I have the honour to transmit herewith enclosed a short Supplementary Report on the Export Trade of Galveston during the season of 1894–95, a season now practically ended.

I venture to think that the recent extraordinary advance of Galveston as a port, as shown in the facts and figures given by me, renders this Report of timely interest to British shipowners and merchants.

I have, &c.
(Signed) HORACE D. NUGENT.

Supplementary Report on the Export Trade of Galveston for the Season 1894–95.

ABSTRACT of Contents.

	PAGE
Introductory remarks	56
Greatest volume of exports ever recorded in one season	56
Value of foreign exports	56
„ coastwise exports	56
Total value of all exports	56
Value of exports in British vessels	56
„ „ foreign vessels	56
Cargoes of British vessels	56
„ foreign vessels	56
Total exports of cotton	56
„ cotton-seed oil-cake	56
„ „ meal	56
Cotton exports to Great Britain	57
„ France	57
„ Continent	57
Review of British shipping	57
Bright outlook for Galveston	57
Tables—	
Receipts and exports of cotton at Galveston	57–58
„ of cotton at all United States ports	59
Exports in British vessels	60
„ foreign vessels	61

UNITED STATES

Introductory remarks.

April 30 in every year may be considered to mark the close of the cotton season at Galveston.

This season begins on September 1 in each year, and it is during the period of September to April that the greater portion of the trade, foreign and domestic, of this port is done.

Galveston, as a port, may be said only to do an export business, the imports being ridiculously out of proportion to the exports.

It is for this reason that this report will deal with the export business alone.

The season just ended has been a most phenomenal one for this port, and such being the case I have thought it advisable to send this short report supplementary to my annual report (which only deals with that part of the past season up to January 1), in order that the latest information may be at the disposal of persons wishing for particulars of the export trade of Texas, and this the more, as, owing to the recent successful efforts to do away with the bar of Galveston harbour, the eyes of many, both here and in England, are turning towards this port as the eventual outlet for the vast cotton and grain products of the south-western States.

Greatest volume of exports ever recorded in one season. Value of foreign exports. Total value of all exports.

A phenomenal cotton crop, the largest ever grown in this State, has resulted in the greatest volume of export trade ever recorded in one season passing through Galveston.

The total volume of this trade going to foreign countries from September 1, 1894, to April 30, 1895, was estimated at 40,494,360 dol., or a little over 9,000,000l. If to this foreign trade be added the coastwise, the total volume of trade leaving the port of Galveston during the season of 1894-95 would approach 50,000,000 dol., or over 10,000,000l.

Value of exports in British vessels. Value of exports in foreign vessels. Cargoes of British vessels. Cargoes of foreign vessels. Total exports of cotton.

From the tables annexed to this report it will be seen that of the total amount of 40,494,360 dol. representing the value of exports to foreign countries, no less than 36,352,009 dol. was the value of exports conveyed in British vessels, only 4,142,351 dol. leaving in vessels other than British.

The cargoes of the British vessels comprised 1,193,011 bales of cotton, 250,558 sacks of cotton-seed oil-cake, and 818,285 sacks of cotton-seed meal, besides sundries.

Foreign vessels carried away 124,172 bales of cotton, 46,240 sacks of cotton-seed cake, 132,126 sacks of cotton-seed meal, and other merchandise, including 20,253 barrels of flour.

The total amount of cotton leaving for foreign ports was 1,317,183 bales, as compared with 762,135 bales in the similar period during 1893-94.

Total exports of cotton-seed oil-cake and cotton-seed meal.

The total amount of cotton-seed cake exported in the season was 296,798 bags, and of cotton-seed meal 940,411 bags.

The figures for last season I have been unable to obtain, but undoubtedly there has been a large increase.

Two tables are also annexed showing the receipts and exports of cotton at Galveston from September 1, 1894, to April 30, 1895, and the receipts at all United States cotton ports during the same period.

GALVESTON.

The standing of Galveston as a cotton port and the marked advance made this season are clearly shown in these tables.

Cotton exports to Great Britain. It will also be seen that 788,136 bales of cotton went to Great Britain, as compared with 549,062 bales in the season of 1893-94.

Cotton exports to France and to the Continent. France took 212,413 bales, as against 98,361 bales, and the Continent, chiefly Germany, 322,107 bales, as against 108,312 bales.

Review of British shipping. It is gratifying to note the supremacy of the British shipping at Galveston. Out of 242 vessels clearing for foreign ports during the period of September 1, 1894, and April 30, 1895, no less than 208 were British.

The British shipping has steadily increased of late years.

In the season of 1892-93, 149 vessels cleared, tonnage (approximately) 218,136; in 1893-94, 134, tonnage 200,232; whilst the past season shows 208, tonnage 324,480.

Bright outlook for Galveston. In conclusion, I may note that the jetty works are proving successful, the bar is disappearing, 18 feet at mean low tide, equal to 19 feet 6 inches at high tide, having been officially announced recently, and the outlook for Galveston as a port is of the brightest.

TABLE of Receipts and Exports of Cotton at and from Galveston for the Seasons of 1893-94 and 1894-95. (September 1, 1894, to April 30, 1895.)

RECEIPTS.

	Quantity.	
	1893-94.	1894-95.
	Bales.	Bales.
Total receipts	987,167	1,634,799

FOREIGN EXPORTS.

Destination.	Quantity.	
	1893-94.	1894-95.
	Bales.	Bales.
Great Britain	549,062	788,186
France	98,361	212,413
Continent (i.e. Germany and Russia)..	108,312	322,107
Channel ..	6,400	..
Total	762,135	1,322,706

UNITED STATES.

Coastwise Exports.

Destination.	Quantity. 1893-94.	Quantity. 1894-95.
	Bales.	Bales.
New York	195,551	276,241
Morgan City	565	1,215
Other domestic ports	..	7,041
North by rail	174	52
Total	196,290	284,549

Summary of Exports.

	Quantity. 1893-94.	Quantity. 1894-95.
	Bales.	Bales.
Total foreign	762,135	1,322,706
„ coastwise	196,290	284,549
	958,425	1,607,255
Local consumption	3,694	3,376
	962,119	1,610,631
Stock in port	25,048	24,168
May 1, 1895	987,167	1,634,799

GALVESTON.

TABLE showing Receipts of Cotton at all United States Ports for the Seasons of 1893–94 and 1894–95. (September 1, 1894, to April 30, 1895.)

Ports.	1893–94.	1894–95.
	Bales.	Bales.
Galveston	987,167	1,634,531
New Orleans	1,804,023	2,501,538
Mobile	210,676	245,525
Savannah	925,492	915,866
Charleston	333,768	422,989
Wilmington	191,247	237,944
Norfolk	463,911	455,934
Baltimore	58,632	111,516
New York	111,360	182,814
Boston	94,885	297,960
Philadelphia	52,410	103,393
West Point	235,400	282,352
Newport News	48,356	32,984
Brunswick	60,630	100,025
Laredo	..	8,970
Eagle Pass	..	4,824
Port Royal	70,142	149,066
Velasco	8,292	592
Other ports	..	1,150
Total	5,656,391	7,689,973
„ last season	..	5,656,391
Difference	..	2,033,582

UNITED STATES.

Export Trade from Galveston in British Ships from September 1, 1894, to April 30, 1895, shown by Months.

Month.	Number of Vessels Cleared.	Cotton. Bales.	Oil-cake. Sacks.	Cotton-seed Meal. Sacks.	Miscellaneous. Quantity.	Description.	Value of Cargoes. Dollars.
September	8	45,680	918	6,720	38,055 24,781 16,349 217	Sacks of wheat Oak staves Pieces of lumber Bags of sugar	1,544,130
October	36	231,099	44,955	59,727	29,907 500 49	Oak staves Barrels, soap stock Sacks of wool	7,090,933
November	39	231,816	38,219	146,626	4,385 23,035	Oak staves Pieces of lumber	6,972,376
December	45	265,389	45,048	115,865	10,860 525 108 26,857 1,092	Oak staves Barrels of flour Bars of copper Oak staves Cedar logs	8,025,285
January	44	261,008	19,555	119,736	214 21 8 4,002 3,782 20 50	Bars of copper Sacks, cotton-seed Cases, pampas plumes Barrels of flour Sacks, copper matté Sheep Oxen	7,567,550
February	15	84,387	12,291	52,327	23,539 4 2,212	Oak staves Cases of lard Logs	2,447,861
March	12	40,578	22,286	215,033	1,100 1,500	Bales of linters Walnut logs	1,572,447
April	9	33,054	67,286	102,251	1,181 500	Logs and sundries Logs Barrels of linters	1,131,427
Total	208	1,193,011	250,558	818,285			36,352,009

GALVESTON.

Export Trade from Galveston in Foreign Ships from September 1, 1894, to April 30, 1895.

Ships.		Cotton.	Oil-cake.	Cotton-seed Meal.	Miscellaneous.		Value of Cargoes.
Name.	Nationality.				Quantity.	Description.	
		Bales.	Sacks.	Sacks.			Dollars.
Maria	Spanish	6,100	..	..	..	..	227,247
Gyller	Norwegian	..	..	..	5,365	Barrels of flour	18,944
Rita	Spanish	4,000	8,118	3,003	..	..	162,251
Vivina	,,	8,514	..	..	..	..	264,710
Paulina	,,	3,810	4,073	5,600	16,915	Staves	117,756
Niceto	,,	5,175	3,662	8,065	..	..	165,750
St. Andrews	Norwegian	8,375	..	..	..	..	229,898
Palantino	Spanish	5,987	..	1,120	4,814	Oak staves	161,262
Gyller	Norwegian	..	..	..	1,200	Barrels of flour	20,187
					5,170	Sacks of flour	
Georgias Michaelina	Greek	8,731	..	..	..	..	239,728
Maria	Spanish	5,375	..	..	..	..	145,125
Transit	Norwegian	..	..	40,320	..	..	46,800
Embiricos	Greek	6,200	..	..	..	..	199,392
Gyller	Norwegian	..	..	..	6,645	Barrels of flour	19,900
Rita	Spanish	5,631	..	..	..	..	164,143
Taurus	Norwegian	500	5,241	47,040	..	..	82,502
Vivina	Spanish	8,020	..	..	..	..	222,580
Paulina	,,	4,330	3,140	..	..	..	134,205
Arbutus	Norwegian	..	4,939	13,538	..	..	42,481

UNITED STATES.

Export Trade from Galveston in Foreign Ships from September 1, 1894, to April 30, 1895—continued.

Ships. Name.	Nationality.	Cotton. Bales	Oil-cake. Sacks.	Cotton-seed Meal. Sacks.	Miscellaneous. Quantity.	Miscellaneous. Description.	Value of Cargoes. Dollars.
Gyller	Norwegian	..	..	..	500	Barrels of flour	21,060
					4,800	Sacks of flour	
A. B. Ball	American bark	..	3,660	..	..	..	10,902
Hoiraag	Norwegian	..	3,195	2,240	..	..	11,362
Hilda	Swedish	1,100	..	..	..	..	32,500
Carolina	Spanish	3,662	3,370	..	800	Copper matté	184,956
Cortez	Norwegian bark	987	..	..	..	..	51,657
Saline	Russian schooner	852	..	..	..	..	25,531
Gyller	Norwegian	..	..	..	6,643	Barrels of flour	23,400
					5	,, beef	
Gracia	Spanish	8,493	2,504	..	..	..	225,000
Stanbo	Norwegian bark	1,008	..	..	..	..	29,188
Francesca	Spanish	5,520	3,061	11,200	..	..	176,147
Pedro	,,	7,400	1,277	..	376	Bags of copper	225,983
Rita	,,	5,876	..	..	..	..	178,646
Vivina	,,	8,526	..	..	..	..	282,058
Total		124,172	46,240	132,126	..	..	4,142,351

(75 6 | 95—H & S 1960)

FOREIGN OFFICE.
1895.
ANNUAL SERIES.

N⁰. 1576.

DIPLOMATIC AND CONSULAR REPORTS ON TRADE AND FINANCE.

UNITED STATES.

REPORT FOR THE YEAR 1894
ON THE
TRADE, &c., OF THE CONSULAR DISTRICT OF SAN FRANCISCO.

REFERENCE TO PREVIOUS REPORT, Annual Series No. 1452.

Presented to both Houses of Parliament by Command of Her Majesty,
JULY, 1895.

LONDON:
PRINTED FOR HER MAJESTY'S STATIONERY OFFICE,
BY HARRISON AND SONS, ST. MARTIN'S LANE,
PRINTERS IN ORDINARY TO HER MAJESTY.

And to be purchased, either directly or through any Bookseller, from
EYRE & SPOTTISWOODE, EAST HARDING STREET, FLEET STREET, E.C., and
32, ABINGDON STREET, WESTMINSTER, S.W.; or
JOHN MENZIES & Co., 12, HANOVER STREET, EDINBURGH, and
90, WEST NILE STREET, GLASGOW; or
HODGES, FIGGIS, & Co., Limited, 104, GRAFTON STREET, DUBLIN.

1895.

[C. 7581—116.]   *Price Sixpence.*

New Series of Reports.

Reports of the Annual Series have been issued from Her Majesty's Diplomatic and Consular Officers at the following places, and may be obtained from the sources indicated on the title-page:—

No.		Price.	No.		Price.
1454.	Barcelona	2d.	1515.	Zomba	3½d.
1455.	New Caledonia	½d.	1516.	Valparaiso	2½d.
1456.	Smyrna	1d.	1517.	Charleston	2½d.
1457.	Macao	1d.	1518.	Serajevo	1d.
1458.	Samoa	1d.	1519.	Saigon	1d.
1459.	Hiogo and Osaka	3d.	1520.	Bangkok	2d.
1460.	Lisbon	2d.	1521.	Tripoli	1d.
1461.	Pekin	2d.	1522.	Batavia	1½d.
1462.	Corunna	2d.	1523.	Dakar	½d.
1463.	Mozambique	15d.	1524.	Havana	2d.
1464.	Munich	1½d.	1525.	Riga	2d.
1465.	St. Petersburg	3d.	1526.	Trebizond	1½d.
1466.	Naples	1d.	1527.	Piræus	2½d.
1467.	Montevideo	2½d.	1528.	Guayaquil	1½d.
1468.	Aden	1d.	1529.	Marseilles	1½d.
1469.	Tokio	1¼d.	1530.	Wuhu	1½d.
1470.	Dantzig	5d.	1531.	Rio de Janeiro	2½d.
1471.	Guayaquil	1d.	1532.	Trieste	2d.
1472.	Canton	1½d.	1533.	Brest	1½d.
1473.	Dar-al-Baida	3d.	1534.	Stockholm	2d.
1474.	Teheran	2d.	1535.	Warsaw	1d.
1475.	Bushire	2d.	1536.	Boston	1½d.
1476.	Tangier	2d.	1537.	Mozambique	2½d.
1477.	Rome	2d.	1538.	Callao	1d.
1478.	Hamburg	4d.	1539.	Aleppo	1½d.
1479.	The Hague	1½d.	1540.	Jaffa	½d.
1480.	Belgrade	2d.	1541.	Boston	1d.
1481.	Batoum	1½d.	1542.	New Orleans	1½d.
1482.	Teneriffe	½d.	1543.	Chicago	3d.
1483.	Lisbon	2½d.	1544.	Palermo	2½d.
1484.	Buda-Pesth	½d.	1545.	Bengazi	1½d.
1485.	Rome	5½d.	1546.	Cagliari	1d.
1486.	Para	1d.	1547.	Pernambuco	7½d.
1487.	Odessa	1d.	1548.	Madrid	1½d.
1488.	Hakodate	1d.	1549.	Corunna	5d.
1489.	Beira	1½d.	1550.	Leghorn	2d.
1490.	Berne	1½d.	1551.	New Orleans	2½d.
1491.	Copenhagen	1d.	1552.	Syra	1½d.
1492.	Stettin	2½d.	1553.	Genoa	9d
1493.	Rio Grande do Sul	1½d.	1554.	Berlin	2½d
1494.	Serajevo	1d.	1555.	Tainan	1d.
1495.	Buenos Ayres	9d.	1556.	Zanzibar	4d.
1496.	Florence	2d.	1557.	Dunkirk	1d.
1497.	Lisbon	1½d.	1558.	Ningpo	1d.
1498.	Paris	2d.	1559.	Pakhoi	1d.
1499.	Bolivia	1½d.	1560.	Chinkiang	1d.
1500.	Patras	1½d.	1561.	New York	2d.
1501.	Bordeaux	3d.	1562.	Batoum	11½d.
1502.	Madrid	2d.	1563.	Naples	2d.
1503.	Amsterdam	1d.	1564.	Resht	4½d.
1504.	Suakin	1d.	1565.	Copenhagen	1½d.
1505.	Angora	1d.	1566.	Porto Rico	1½d.
1506.	Havre	2½d.	1567.	Malaga	3d.
1507.	Algiers	11d.	1568.	Galveston	7½d.
1508.	La Rochelle	3d.	1569.	Tabreez	½d.
1509.	Vera Cruz	2d.	1570.	Fiji	¼d.
1510.	Puerto Cortes	1d.	1571.	Athens	2½d.
1511.	Taganrog	1d.	1572.	Bilbao	3½d.
1512.	Baltimore	1½d.	1573.	Barcelona	3d.
1513.	Mexico	1½d.	1574.	Fiume	2d.
1514.	Zaila	1d.	1575.	Tahiti	1d.

No. 1576.

Reference to previous Report, Annual Series No. 1452.

UNITED STATES.

SAN FRANCISCO.

Acting-Consul Moore to the Earl of Kimberley.

My Lord,   San Francisco, April 30, 1895.

I HAVE the honour to enclose herewith Annual Reports on the Trade, Commerce, and Agriculture of San Francisco, Portland, Astoria, Tacoma, Port Townsend, Los Angeles, and San Diego, for the year 1894.

I have, &c.
(Signed)   WELLESLEY MOORE.

Report on the Trade, Commerce, and Agriculture of the Consular District of San Francisco for the Year 1894.

ABSTRACT of Contents.

	PAGE
San Francisco Consulate—	
General remarks	3
Shipping and navigation; tables of entrances and clearances of vessels..	4
Charters; seamen's wages; shipbuilding	6
Trade and commerce; table of exports and imports	7
Exports; wheat; flour; salmon; barley	8
Tinned fruits and vegetables; brandy; wine; &c.	9
Imports; raw silk; sugar; coal; coffee; rice	11
Tea; tin-plates; cement; &c.	13
Value of articles exported and imported, table of	14
Production of precious metals; mines and mining	14
Clearing-house; commercial and savings banks	17
Diseases; population; real estate	18
Rainfall and temperature; business failures	19
Railway progress	20
Rights of aliens	20
Labour; railway strikes; labour market	22
Agriculture; wheat; barley; produce	23
Viticulture; phylloxera; resistant vines	25
Fruit crop; oranges; cherries; prunes	26
Other kinds of fruit; new fruit plant	28
Low prices for fruit; danger of over-production	29
Co-operative movements; new system of transportation	30
Advice to settlers; beetroot; wool	31

(1984)

UNITED STATES.

Abstract of Contents—continued.

	PAGE
Portland Vice-Consulate—	
Introductory remarks; shipping and navigation	32
Tables of entrances and clearances of vessels	32
Freights; sailors; pilotage; aids to navigation	33
Trade and commerce; table of exports and imports	34
Wheat; flour; other cereals; hop trade	35
Fruit trade; wool; timber; fisheries	36
Salmon; sturgeon; import trade	36
Glass; cement; coal; tin-plates; bags	37
Table of total value of exports and imports	38
Financial; clearing-house; bonds; exchange	38
Population and industries; buildings	39
Manufactures; gold; labour	40
Warning to clerks; health; death rate	40
Public works; waterworks; Government works	40
Jetty; river bars; harbours	41
Agriculture; farming unprofitable	42
Wheat; cost of production; oats; barley	42
Orchards and fruits; prunes; cost of growing	44
Cattle and sheep; general remarks	44
Taxation; city finances; real estate	45
Astoria Vice-Consulate—	
General remarks	46
Shipping and navigation; pilot service	46
Table of entrances and clearances of vessels	48
Table of exports and imports; trade and commerce	48
Salmon fishing and canning; other fishing	49
Logging; lumber; industries	50
Government works; lighthouse	51
Table of total value of exports and imports	52
Tacoma Vice-Consulate—	
General remarks on state; health; marriages	52
Cattle diseases; weather and climate	52
Industries; timber; railways; coal	53
Fisheries	54
Agriculture; grain; wheat	56
Dairying	59
Horticulture	59
Hops; flax; sugar beets	60
Public lands; population and assessment	61
Business failures; aids to commerce and navigation	63
Coxey movement; railway strike	63
State fair; interstate fair; tests of coal	65
General outlook; general remarks on Tacoma	66
Table of entrances and clearances of vessels	67
Trade and commerce; table of exports and imports	68
Increase of exports and imports; trade with China	69
Timber trade; dry dock; smelter	71
Population; health; diseases; industries	72
Public works; education; post-office	73
Financial condition	75
Seattle—	
General remarks	76
Table of shipping; trade and commerce	76
„ exports and imports; timber; fish	77
„ total value of exports and imports	78
Population; health; diseases; climate	79
Education; industries; iron; hides	80
Fisheries; public works; street improvements	80
Fire department; post-office; financial condition	81
Failures; United States land office	81
Port Townsend Vice-Consulate—	
Lumber; freights; quarantine	82
Shipbuilding; steamer lines; dry dock	83

SAN FRANCISCO.

ABSTRACT of Contents—continued.

	Page
Port Townsend Vice-Consulate—continued.	
Pilotage; coal; cement; manufactures	84
Lightship; rocks and shoals; casualties	85
Fur sealing; fishing; real estate; health	85
Table of entrances and clearances of vessels	86
" exports and imports	87
" total value of exports and imports	88
Los Angeles Vice-Consulate—	
Introductory remarks; investments	88
British capital; bonds; mortgages	89
Emigrants	91
Farm pupils; religious matters; education	93
Shipping and navigation	94
Table of entrances and clearances of vessels	94
Trade and commerce; wine; fruit; oranges	95
Prospects of trade with Great Britain	95
Imports; cement; window glass; coal	96
Lumber; hardware; tin-plates; crockery	97
Groceries and provisions; exports; oranges	98
Fruits; dried fruits; honey; vegetables	101
Grain; wool; table of exports and imports	102
Population and industries; divorces	103
Beet sugar; oil; liquor traffic	104
Public works; railways; agriculture	105
Oranges; fruit sent to England; pests	106
Vine diseases; olive oil; railway strike	109
Irrigation	111
San Diego Vice-Consulate—	
Trade and commerce; trade depression	113
General business; wheat and barley	113
Table of imports and exports	114
" total value of exports and imports	114
Shipping and navigation	115
Table of entrances and clearances of vessels	115
Population and industry; country settling up	116
Building; water companies; mineral products	117
Agriculture; dairies; honey; fruits	117
Canaigre root; land values	118
Public works; jetty	118
Railways	119

General Remarks.

The year 1894 will long be remembered for its great business depression, not only in California, but throughout the whole of the United States.

The great decline which has taken place in the value of almost all articles of commerce has been severely felt by the mercantile interests on this coast, and particularly in San Francisco, whose merchants supply the wants of the central portion of the State and consequently are the chief losers through the restricted purchasing power of the agricultural classes.

The California grain growers and dealers have had the most unsatisfactory season during the past twelve months that has ever been experienced in the history of the State. Prices have reached the lowest point on record, and both the domestic and foreign demands show a large falling-off.

The fruit and wine industries suffered severely from the low prices of their products, and the railroad strike, which began at the end of June, threatened to seriously injure the former

(1984)

industry. Happily it occurred at the beginning of the shipping season and was of short duration, and thus only affected the growers of early varieties of fruit.

It is satisfactory to note that the mining industries of the State are beginning to improve. The unexampled depression in silver has turned the attention of miners and capitalists to the gold-mining industry, and the result is that many mines that were abandoned have been re-opened and new properties are in great demand.

An important change was made in the Constitution of the State of California last November which may affect the rights of aliens as to the acquisition and inheritance of real estate and other property in this State. It particularly affects British subjects as so much British capital is invested here. I refer to this subject more fully in another part of this report.

A new railroad to run from the Bay of San Francisco to Kern County, through the San Joaquin Valley, has been projected, the company incorporated, and work will shortly be commenced. Great benefits are expected from this enterprise, as the State has long suffered from want of competition in the movement of its products.

Signs of improvement in business are visible at the time of closing this report. The bank clearing house returns show an increase as compared with the first few months of last year, and the railway companies are hauling more freight. The enthusiasm over the new line of railroad has also had some effect, and has produced a better feeling among business men.

Remarks relating to the various subjects connected with shipping, trade, population and agriculture will be found in this report under the following heads, viz. :—

Shipping and Navigation.

The following table shows the number and nationality of vessels which entered and cleared at this port during the past year :—

SAN FRANCISCO.

Annex A.—RETURN of all Shipping at the Port of San Francisco during the Year 1894.

ENTERED.

Nationality.	Sailing. Number of Vessels.	Sailing. Tons.	Steam. Number of Vessels.	Steam. Tons.	Total. Number of Vessels.	Total. Tons.
British	149	261,440	56	107,475	205	368,915
American, from foreign countries	326	272,586	222	384,639	548	657,225
American, from Atlantic ports of Union	32	56,160	...	...	32	56,160
Hawaiian	14	16,596	17	17,892	31	34,488
Nicaraguan	6	6,194	20	23,852	26	30,046
German	13	18,146	...	...	13	18,146
Italian	8	12,080	...	...	8	12,080
Norwegian	7	11,354	...	...	7	11,354
Others	3	456	1	272	4	728
Total	558	655 012	316	534,130	874	1,189,142
,, for the year preceding	549	644,909	324	525,408	873	1,170,317

CLEARED.

Nationality.	Sailing. Number of Vessels.	Sailing. Tons.	Steam. Number of Vessels.	Steam. Tons.	Total. Number of Vessels.	Total. Tons.
British	140	197,925	56	103,658	196	301,583
American, to foreign countries	325	279,484	216	388,373	541	667,857
American, to Atlantic ports of Union	10	19,082	...	...	10	19,082
Nicaraguan	6	5,290	22	25,903	28	31,193
Hawaiian	10	9,113	20	20,559	30	29,672
German	15	19,820	...	...	15	19,820
Italian	7	10,371	...	...	7	10,371
Norwegian	2	3,024	...	...	2	3,024
Others	2	897	1	272	3	1,169
Total	517	545,006	315	538,765	832	1,083,771
,, for the year preceding	540	592,097	327	529,236	867	1,121,333

NOTE.—The entrances and clearances of American ships do not include the coasting trade, whaling, or fishing voyages.

The number of British vessels entering the port during the year was 23 less than in 1893. The clearances show a decided falling-off, being 69 less than the year preceding. 31 British vessels left here in ballast for other American ports of the Union to load.

The American vessels trading with foreign countries show an increase of 63 entries and 73 clearances over the returns of 1893. The trade done by American ships to and from the Atlantic ports of the Union, however, shows a considerable falling-off due no doubt to cheaper freights overland.

Freights ruled low during the year as will be seen from the following table which is based on prices paid for spot ships to Cork for orders :— Charters.

(1984)

UNITED STATES.

Month.	From—	To—
	£ s. d.	£ s. d.
January	1 5 0	1 6 6
February	..	1 6 3
March	1 5 0	1 6 9
April	1 3 9	1 5 0
May	..	..
June	..	1 5 0
July	1 5 0	1 6 3
August	1 5 0	1 6 0
September	1 5 0	1 6 3
October	1 5 0	1 6 3
November	..	1 7 6
December	1 6 3	1 8 0

Prices.

Seamen's wages. Seamen's wages ruled about 3*l*. per month during the greater part of the year, but were advanced by the boarding master's association to 4*l*. in the autumn. They have now gone back to 3*l*. per month. The high rate of wages formerly paid here was one of the crimps' chief arguments in inducing seamen to desert their vessels.

Steamer lines to New York viâ Panama. Freights between this port and New York viâ Panama have been advanced somewhat, through the discontinuance of the North American Navigation Company's line of steamers, but they have not gone back to the old figures.

The Panama Railway Company and the Pacific Mail Steamship Company are both running steamers to this port, but under an agreement between the two companies the former is restricted to carrying through freight to New York, while the latter attends to that offering at the Central American ports.

Ferry buildings. Part of the foundation of the new ferry buildings has been finished, but it will be some time before the depôt will be erected. The work has been done in a very substantial manner, the whole foundations being arched over with concrete.

Shipbuilding. Shipbuilding was very inactive in 1894, the only vessel of any size launched being a ferry boat of 1,766 tons intended to run on the Bay of San Francisco. The other vessels turned out were small steamers or schooners, many of them measuring under 100 tons.

Nicaragua Canal. Increased interest is being manifested in this enterprise, and memorials have been forwarded to Congress by various organisations on this coast with a view of urging upon that body the necessity of taking action to secure the construction of this waterway at the earliest possible period.

Pilot chart. A monthly pilot chart of the North Pacific Ocean is now published, and the co-operation of the masters of all ships with the Hydrographic Office here is requested, as it is only by their voluntary observations and reports that the work can be made completely successful.

SAN FRANCISCO.

Owing to the railroad strike of 1894 public attention was called to the condition of the rivers of the State, and they are now said to be in a condition more nearly approaching safe navigation than has been the case for years past. *River navigation.*

The following is the catch of the Arctic whaling fleet reported at San Francisco during the last two years:— *Catch of the whaling fleet.*

Year.	Quantity.		
	Oil.	Bone.	Ivory.
	Barrels.	Lbs.	Lbs.
1893	6,952	315,249	8,565
1894	8,119	274,579	7,367

The Seamen's Institute continues to do good work among sailors and apprentices at this port. It is partly supported by contributions from British shipowners and partly by local subscriptions, and is presided over by the Rev. J. Fell, M.A., who came out from Liverpool to establish the undertaking. *Seamen's institute.*

Trade and Commerce.

The following tables show the exports and imports for the past two years:—

Annex B.—RETURN of Principal Articles of Export from San Francisco during the Years 1894–93.

Articles.		1894.		1893.	
		Quantity.	Value.	Quantity.	Value.
			£		£
Wheat and flour	Centals	9,563,187	1,804,021	13,523,008	3,182,182
Tinned salmon	Cases	388,207	352,717	132,020	141,319
Barley	Centals	1,012,926	201,980	2,556,501	485,735
Tinned fruit and vegetables	Cases	164,955	122,567	471,427	377,141
Timber	Feet	17,530,939	66,784	14,166,957	55,563
Brandy	Gallons	300,193	60,563	103,605	18,343
Wine	,,	561,348	56,267	533,502	62,471
Quicksilver	Flasks	7,228	52,042	10,121	73,981
Other articles	...	...	1,811,684	...	1,426,774
Total merchandise	...	...	4,528,625	...	5,823,509
Treasure	...	...	2,795,774	...	2,610,588
Grand total	...	...	7,324,399	...	8,434,097

UNITED STATES.

RETURN of Principal Articles of Import to San Francisco during the Years 1894-93.

Articles.		1894. Quantity.	1894. Value.	1893. Quantity.	1893. Value.
			£		£
Raw silk	Lbs.	4,194,038	2,203,967	2,371,173	1,567,803
Sugar	Tons	148,807	1,841,286	175,976	2,209,389
Coal	,,	894,900	984,390	812,300	913,887
Coffee	Lbs.	27,139,209	823,833	17,038,869	526,296
Rice	Tons	20,494	155,573	15,675	235,125
Tea	Lbs.	5,419,466	142,040	6,080,311	184,919
Tin-plates	Boxes	124,659	134,319	386,093	270,265
Cement	Barrels	306,824	80,656	264,110	79,233
Pig iron	Tons	1,422	3,764	3,538	15,284
Scrap iron	,,	Nil.	Nil.	305	1,220
Other articles	...	...	1,333,109	...	1,877,584
Total merchandise	...	...	7,702,937	...	7,881,005
Treasure	...	...	714,484	...	901,303
Grand total	...	...	8,417,421	...	8,782,308

Exports.

Decrease of exports. The exports of merchandise show a falling-off of 1,294,884*l*. as compared with 1893, but the combined exports of merchandise and treasure only show a decrease of 1,109,698*l*., on account of the exports of treasure in 1894 having been larger than those of the previous year.

Our exports of merchandise show a tremendous shrinkage in value since 1891, being less than half what they were that year. The difference is principally accounted for by the decrease in the quantity and value of wheat and flour.

Wheat. The exports of wheat and flour, expressed as wheat, as in the above table, were the smallest since the early days of our wheat trade. Prices were even lower than last year, opening at 4s. 0⅝d. to 4s. 1¼d. per cental for No. 1 wheat and dropping in October to 3s. 0⅝d. to 3s. 1¼d., the lowest figure at which this quality of the cereal ever sold in the market of San Francisco. At the end of the year prices recovered somewhat, the quotations being 3s. 5⅝d. to 3s. 6¼d. per cental.

Flour. The exports of flour amounted to 787,457 barrels in 1894, against 882,580 barrels in 1893 showing a decrease of 95,123 barrels. No flour was sent to Great Britain during the year, that flourishing trade having entirely disappeared owing to the fact that it cannot be shipped cheaply enough to compete with the home-made article. 417,114 barrels were sent to China, a small increase over last year. Shipments to that quarter were very heavy towards the close of the year, and since the war began between China and Japan. A considerable quantity is shipped to Central America, the Hawaiian Islands, Japan, and Russian Possessions in Asia.

Tinned salmon. The receipts of canned salmon at San Francisco during the past year are given as 860,294 cases, of which only 2,053 cases

SAN FRANCISCO.

are Californian the rest coming from Oregon, Alaska, and British Columbia.

The exports for the year show a large increase over those of 1893, and there was also a shipment of 251,956 cases by sea to New York, making the total amount sent away in this manner 640,163 cases, against 203,316 cases in 1893. Of the amount exported in 1894 Great Britain took 341,846 cases and Australasia 33,907 cases.

The shipments by rail from California amounted to—

	Quantity.
	Lbs.
From San Francisco, canned	21,468,000
,, pickled	4,212,000
Interior, canned	1,442,000
Total	27,122,000

The shipments by rail in 1893 were 21,668,000 lbs.

The total pack of salmon on the Pacific Coast for 1894 is given as follows:—

	Quantity.
	Cases.
Columbia River	511,000
Sacramento River	29,000
Klamath River	3,000
Oregon Fall	100,340
Alaska	678,500
Frazer River	363,967
Northern rivers	130,404
Point Roberts	68,000
Total	1,884,211

Note.—A case consists of 48 1-lb. tins.

The total pack for 1893 was 1,683,761 cases. The pack for 1894 is the greatest pack the coast has ever had. Every year the talk is of reducing the output, but each year with few exceptions, it seems to increase. Prices were lower than last year at the opening of the season, but advanced as the year wore on. The stock carried forward is probably the lightest in some years.

Barley. The exports of this cereal show a heavy decline as compared with 1893, which is attributed to the crop having been more or less stained. Great Britain continues to be our best customer taking 816,835 centals, and the Hawaiian Islands coming next with 143,064 centals. Prices were better than in 1893.

Tinned fruit and vegetables. The exports were much smaller than last year. The railroad strike seriously affected the canning business for a time, as it retarded the shipment of supplies to canneries that depended on railroad points. Shipments to the Eastern States were large being given as 97,106,000 lbs., against 50,014,000 lbs. in 1893. These figures do not represent the total movement, as the railroad company has not made returns for the southern section of the State. Prices ruled low excepting perhaps apricots, which held their own fairly. The canners, however, obtained their fruit at comparatively low prices and were enabled to sell to the eastern trade at reasonable rates.

The following is an estimate of the pack of 1894 by a leading packer:—

Articles.	Quantity.
	Cases.
Apples	5,000
Apricots	275,000
Asparagus	20,000
Cherries, white	105,000
„ black	20,000
Currants	10,000
Gooseberries	5,000
Nectarines	3,000
Pears	180,000
Peas	15,000
Peaches	275,000
Plums	40,000
Grapes	5,000
Raspberries	5,000
Strawberries	5,000
Total	978,000
Miscellaneous—	
Pie fruits	50,000
Tomatoes	200,000
Jams and jellies	15,000
Total	265,000
Grand total	1,243,000

Timber. The receipts at San Francisco were considerably smaller than in 1893, but the exports show an increase over that year. Great Britain was the largest purchaser, taking 7,280,563 feet, which amount, however, includes 2,418,100 feet of dunnage used in stowing grain cargoes. Central America, Australia, and Mexico also took large quantities. Shipments of California redwood to England started up again during the year. Prices ruled low, but an association was formed in the spring which put them up slightly.

Brandy. The exports of brandy show a very large increase over those of 1893, almost all of which was sent to Europe. The quantity taken by Great Britain is stated to be 1,495 gallons in 1894, against 31,011 gallons in 1893.

The amount shipped by rail and sea is given as follows:—

SAN FRANCISCO.

	Quantity.
	Gallons.
By sea from San Francisco	357,881
Rail from the State	433,800
Total	791,681

The exports of wine show a moderate increase over last year, but the shipments to the Eastern States by rail show a very marked increase, making the amount sent out of the State larger than for any previous year.

The shipments are given as follows:—

	Quantity.
	Gallons.
By sea from San Francisco	2,468,792
Rail from the State	11,094,200
Total	13,562,992

Wine.

Shipments by sea have fallen away materially, owing to cheaper railroad freights to New York, as merchants prefer to send their goods overland to eastern ports and from thence by sea to Europe instead of patronising the Cape Horn route with its four months of delay.

The amount of wine sent to Great Britain was 29,261 gallons, against 63,650 gallons in 1893.

The exports of quicksilver show a falling-off, but there were 10,300 flasks sent to New York by sea and 11,356 flasks sent east by rail, bringing up the total shipment to 28,884 flasks, a slight increase over 1893.

Quicksilver.

Other articles in regard to wheat, barley, fruit, brandy, and wine will be found under the head of agriculture.

Imports.

The imports of merchandise show a decrease of 178,068*l.*, as compared with last year, and a decrease of 364,887*l.* of merchandise and treasure combined.

Decrease of imports.

Our imports of merchandise also show a marked decrease since 1891, being 2,962,259*l.* less than they were in that year.

The imports of raw silk show a heavy increase, almost double the amount of the importation of 1893. The whole of this comes from China and Japan, the greater part last year having been supplied by the latter country. It is all sent away overland, a good part of it finding its way to Europe viâ New York.

Raw silk.

UNITED STATES.

Sugar. The imports were considerably less than last year. Our principal supply came from the Hawaiian Islands which sent us 137,014 tons. China sent 10,673 tons, and the remainder came from Central America and other sources. The bulk of the sugar that arrives here is refined in this city and then distributed all over the Pacific Coast and the States and territories as far as the Rocky Mountains. The beet sugar industry of this State received a set-back by the abolition of the bounty paid by the Federal Government, and it is doubtful what the result may be. The sugar market has been the lowest for some years.

Coal. The imports of foreign coal were as follows:—

	Quantity.
	Tons.
From British Columbia	487,600
Australia	177,200
Great Britain	174,000
Other places	56,100
Total	894,000

Besides the above we received 434,200 tons from Seattle, Tacoma, and the Eastern States, bringing our total receipts up to 1,329,100 tons.

The following remarks are taken from the annual circular of a leading coal broker:—

"The uniformity of quotations for cargo lots existing during the year is unprecedented in the former history of the coal trade, as there was no apparent change at all for the first seven months; and the maximum and minimum values will not show a variance of 5 per cent. until the tariff reduction of 35 c. per ton on bituminous grades, causing a decline equal to the exact amount of the tariff change. Our large fuel consumers cannot complain of the prices they have had to pay this year, as they have been the lowest ever known. Our consumption should have been largely increased on that account, were it not for the stagnancy of trade among our principal manufactories. With the seasonable rainfall we have had locally, the exceedingly low prices of pig-iron and coal now ruling, and the gradual return of confidence now visible everywhere, these combined should lead to a revulsion of trade in the near future. In fact the ear-marks are already visible. There is every indication pointing to a possible 20 per cent. increase of fuel to be consumed in 1895 over and above the quantity burnt up this year, and there is no article which so forcibly betokens prosperity as an increased coal demand."

Coffee. The imports of coffee show an increase of over 10,000,000 lbs. above those of 1893. The great bulk of our supply comes from Central America. Our overland shipments show a very large increase, being 8,648,000 lbs., against 2,976,000 lbs. in 1893. Prices ruled lower than the year preceding on account of the large supply.

Rice. The importation of rice shows an increase over last year. Our principal supply comes from China, but we also get a considerable quantity from the Hawaiian Islands and Japan. The shipment of rice from the Southern States to this market has almost entirely ceased.

Tea. The imports of tea have been the smallest in a series of years. This is partly due to the fact that we had a good stock on hand from the year preceding, and partly due to the dull times. Most of our supply comes from Japan.

Tin-plates. The importations have been the smallest since 1885, being only about one-third of those for 1893. This was partly due to the large supply carried over at the end of that year, and partly to the tariff agitation. The consumption during the year was very heavy on account of the activity in the canning business not to speak of other uses to which tin-plate is applied. The stock on hand at the close of 1894 was very small. The market for coke tin-plate opened at 1*l.* 2*s.* It did not fluctuate much until the duty was taken off, when the price went down to 18*s.* It went up to 18*s.* 10*d.* before the close of the year.

Cement. Imports have been the largest since 1891 and the year closed with a heavy stock on hand. The bulk of our importations come from Great Britain, but Belgium and Germany also help to supply our market. Prices were very low all the year, but towards the close they improved somewhat. There is likely to be a good demand from public works, which will help to keep prices firm. Portland is quoted at 8*s.* to 10*s.* per barrel, according to brand.

Pig-iron and scrap-iron. The imports of pig-iron were less than half of what they were in 1893, and the imports of scrap-iron ceased altogether last year. Owing to the reduction of overland freights the domestic iron from the Eastern States can be laid down here at lower prices than have ever before been heard of in this market. Over 12,000 tons of American pig-iron were received here in 1894 with a promising outlook for the coming year. A dullness overspread nearly everything connected with the foundry business in 1894, and our rolling mills and foundries have not experienced the prosperity that they ought to have had considering the low price of iron and coal.

Other articles imported from Great Britain. Considerable quantities of coke, chemicals, cotton cloth, cotton laces, earthenware, linen, pig-tin, wire rods, wire and wire rope, malt liquors, caustic soda, salt, and woollen cloths, besides other articles, are also imported from Great Britain.

The following table shows the volume of trade with each country:—

UNITED STATES.

Annex C.—TABLE showing Total Value of all Articles Exported from and Imported to San Francisco from and to Foreign Countries during the Years 1894-93.

Country.	Exports. 1894.	Exports. 1893.	Imports. 1894.	Imports. 1893.
	£	£	£	£
Great Britain	1,931,332	3,251,786	534,433	853,688
Hawaiian Islands	602,839	597,066	1,774,489	1,568,510
Central America	498,694	413,018	692,227	663,430
China	481,801	511,846	1,205,438	1,026,711
Japan	264,438	110,895	1,854,237	1,408,698
Mexico	226,176	251,771	174,155	199,152
Australasia	175,007	131,874	117,535	181,691
Canada	90,710	142,961	414,856	413,326
Pacific Islands	76,855	90,900	63,309	87,565
Germany	65,700	37,615	123,156	149,737
Asiatic Russia	32,165	28,550	88,202	71,082
South America	22,786	55,726	78,260	83,481
France	20,085	84,875	133,402	174,701
East Indies	9,370	11,179	249,490	377,354
Belgium	788	20,005	96,868	128,704
Italy	..	..	34,048	34,854
Other countries	29,879	83,442	68,832	458,321
Total merchandise	4,528,625	5,823,509	7,702,937	7,881,005
Treasure	2,795,774	2,610,588	714,484	901,303
Grand Total	7,324,399	8,434,097	8,417,421	8,782,308

The exports to Great Britain show a very heavy falling-off. The imports also have shrunk considerably as compared with 1893. The majority of wheat-laden vessels clear for Cork for orders, and the value of their cargoes is included in the exports to Great Britain. A number of them, however, receive orders at Cork to proceed to continental ports to discharge, so that the actual value of the exports to Great Britain are probably considerably less than the amount that appears in the above table.

Metal product.

Messrs. Wells, Fargo, and Co.'s annual statement of the precious metals produced in the States and territories west of the Missouri River (excluding British Columbia and Mexico) gives the production for the last two years as follows:—

Year.	Gold.	Silver.	Copper.	Lead.	Total.
	£	£	£	£	£
1894	9,124,658	5,744,203	4,455,259	1,644,703	20,968,823
1893	6,789,745	7,698,304	4,726,268	1,551,208	20,765,525

The production of gold and silver in the following States and territories comprising this consular district is given as follows for the last two years:—

SAN FRANCISCO.

States and Territories.	Gold. 1894.	Gold. 1893.	Silver. 1894.	Silver. 1893.
	£	£	£	£
California	2,508,129	2,234,407	36,661	51,401
Nevada	289,263	283,721	151,173	247,374
Oregon	320,644	230,395	21,689	22,332
Washington	58,103	54,911	30,610	25,770
Idaho	375,800	329,000	471,800	296,395
Utah	105,938	75,470	247,691	208,223
Arizona	312,257	261,470	39,456	44,954
Total	3,970,134	3,469,374	999,080	896,449

Product of this consular district.

Including base bullion, the total product of this consular district was 8,323,801*l.*

It will be noticed that each of the above States and territories show an increase in the production of gold during the past year, while only three of them show an increase in the production of silver. On account of the very low price of silver many mines have been closed down, as it was found to be impossible to operate them at a profit.

The exports of silver from this port for China and Japan, &c., during the past year amounted to 2,504,136*l.*, against 2,348,332*l.* in 1893.

Gold mining.

The State mineralogist, in his last biennial report, calls attention to the very marked increase of interest which has taken place in gold mining during the past two years. On account of the great decrease in the value of silver, and the political vicissitudes of that metal, the attention of miners has been turned to the gold mining industry. The success attending their investment of capital in such properties has encouraged others to follow their example, and mines which were abandoned some years ago, when conditions were different, have been re-opened, and are now among the largest gold-producing properties of the State. Our annual gold product is largely from the quartz mines. Within recent years there have been so many improvements in the methods and systems of treating the ore that the cost of both mining and milling has been greatly reduced. As a consequence, gold mines are now worked at a profit, which 10 years ago could not be operated under conditions then existing. The gold mines of California are to-day in great demand, but this demand is more for developed properties than for mere "prospects" which may or may not become mines. With the revived interest in this branch of mining the annual gold product of California is expected to materially increase.

Silver mining.

The product of silver mining in California is comparatively small, but the ores of the principal camp (Calico, San Bernardino county) can be worked more cheaply, it is stated, than any other silver ores on the Pacific coast, so that some of the mines there

(1984)

have continued working notwithstanding the fact that silver recently declined to the lowest point of value ever reached.

Hydraulic mining. The second annual report of the California Debris Commission was presented to Congress in December, 1894, and contains some interesting information on this subject. Hydraulic mining was practically stopped in 1884, on account of the damage done to the streams and rivers by the vast amount of mud and gravel washed into them, but since the organisation of the said Commission a gradual resumption has taken place, and 80 applications to mine have been received, of which number 52 have been given permits. The total amount of material mined under permits from October 1, 1893, to October 1, 1894, is estimated at 1,500,000 cubic yards. The available storage provided at present, and partially and wholly completed for future operations is estimated at 8,500,000 cubic yards. Comparing these figures with 38,000,000 cubic yards estimated to have been mined in 1880, it will be seen that the present system provides for only a small percentage of that possible under unrestricted mining. However, there are undoubtedly many mines which have not yet made application to the Commission for which there is available storage as feasible as that prescribed by the Commission for other mines that are working under permits. The requirements of the Commission in respect to storage of detritus vary with many conditions, such as the character of the material, the size and position of the mine, the flow of water, &c. In some cases dams of brush or timber have been approved, but in most cases dams of a more permanent nature are required.

Borax. The production of borax has been reduced of late, owing to the decreased demand, which may be attributed to the prevailing depression in all branches of industry.

Chromic iron. This substance is mined in several counties in this State, but the industry is not very flourishing, owing to the facility with which it can be imported into the eastern States from Asia Minor. Our local product is sent to Baltimore and Philadelphia, but constitutes only about one-fourth of the total consumption there. Ores producing less than 50 per cent. cannot be handled and shipped to compete with the foreign article.

Bituminous rock. Bituminous rock deposits are found and worked in many counties in California, and in some years the product has reached 60,000 tons. Its use as a paving material is constantly on the increase, the bulk of the product coming from the counties of Santa Barbara, Santa Cruz, and San Louis Obispo. Deposits of asphaltum are also found in various parts of the State.

Petroleum. It is stated that California now takes the place of fourth in rank among the States in the production of petroleum, and it is certainly becoming of increased importance among the mineral resources of our State. The petroleum industry has already assumed large proportions in Los Angeles and Ventura counties, and it is prosecuted to a less extent in Santa Clara, Kern, and other counties.

Quicksilver. The production of quicksilver during the year was 30,183

SAN FRANCISCO.

flasks, against 30,402 flasks in 1893. Prices ruled low during the year, the average price per flask being 7l. 4s.

The annual report of the San Francisco clearing-house gives the following figures:—

Clearing-house.

	Amount
	£
Clearings for 1894..	131,705,361
„ 1893..	139,857,155
Decrease ..	8,151,794

These figures are an indication of the great depression in business which has existed in this city since the middle of the year 1893. The average daily clearing in 1894 was 434,671l., against 460,056l. in 1893.

From the Bank Commissioner's report, made up to June 30, 1894, I find the number of banks in this State to be as follows:—

Number of banks in the State.

	Number of Banks.
State savings banks	60
„ commercial banks ..	166
Agencies of foreign banks..	5
National banks	35
Private banks	17
Total	283

The following figures show the condition of the 16 San Francisco commercial banks on June 30, 1894:—

Commercial banks.

RESOURCES.

	Amount.
	£
Bank premises	224,581
Other real estate	239,221
Invested in stocks, bonds, and warrants..	627,102
Loans on real estate	870,926
„ stocks, bonds, and warrants ..	1,879,548
„ other security ..	670,477
„ personal security	4,274,058
Money on hand	2,999,709
Due from banks and bankers	1,840,805
Other assets	526,854
Total	14,153,281

(1984)

UNITED STATES.

LIABILITIES.

	Amount.
	£
Capital paid up	4,802,992
Reserve fund, profit, and loss	2,210,234
Due depositors	5,997,692
Due banks and bankers	951,516
Other liabilities	190,847
Total	14,153,281

Savings banks.

The condition of the 11 San Francisco savings banks on June 30, 1894, was as follows:—

RESOURCES.

	Amount.
	£
Bank premises	418,346
Other real estate	253,082
Invested in stocks and bonds	2,813,526
Loans and real estate	16,402,009
Loans on stocks and bonds	1,149,009
,, other securities	6,244
,, personal security	9,000
Money on hand	726,521
Due from banks and bankers	308,502
Other assets	26,641
Total	22,112,880

LIABILITIES.

	Amount.
	£
Capital paid up	937,000
Reserve fund, &c.	841,023
Due depositors	20,166,615
Other liabilities	168,242
Total	22,112,880

Population and Industry.

Diseases.

The Health Officer's last report, which is made up to June 30, 1894, classifies the deaths in this city as follows:—

SAN FRANCISCO.

Description.	Number of Deaths.
Zymotic diseases	564
Constitutional diseases	1,294
Local diseases	3,220
Developmental diseases	606
Violent deaths	376
Unascertained	..
Total	6,060

This table shows a decrease of one death over the figures of the previous year.

Death rate. The percentage of deaths is given as 18·36 per 1,000 on an estimated population of 330,000.

Population. The white population of San Francisco is estimated at 312,000, and the Chinese at 18,000.

The number of marriages which took place during said year are stated to have been 3,200, and the number of births registered 3,894.

Real estate. The year 1894 was a dull one in real estate the number of sales being 3,404 valued at 2,845,410*l*., against 4,117 sales in 1893 valued at 2,724,298*l*.

Passenger movement. The arrivals and departures for the past 3 years compare as follows:—

Year.	Number.	
	Arrived.	Departed.
1892	94,808	66,962
1893	98,687	78,572
1894	67,182	60,740

The figures for 1894 only represent 9 months of the year as the reports of the Southern Pacific Company were discontinued after September last. There was a large falling-off in the movement of passengers during the time of the railroad strike.

Rainfall and temperature. The following table shows the monthly rainfall and mean temperature at San Francisco for the year ending June, 1894:—

(1984)

	Rainfall.	Temperature.
1893.		
July	·02	56·6
August	·00	56·6
September	·21	59·3
October	·16	57·6
November	4·18	55·6
December	2·25	52·4
1894.		
January	2·61	47·7
February	2·69	48·4
March	·60	50·6
April	·50	55·2
May	1·31	55·4
June	·56	55·9

The total rainfall for the above-mentioned year was 15·09 inches and the mean annual temperature 54·3.

Business failures. The local branch of the Bradstreet Mercantile Agency reports 1,084 failures last year in the Pacific Coast States and territories with liabilities amounting to 1,907,906*l.* as compared with 1,048 failures with liabilities of 2,845,327*l.* in 1893.

Efforts to increase the population. An organisation has lately been formed here called the Half Million Club, the object of which is to increase the population of San Francisco to that number by the year 1900. It will endeavour to unite all the interests of the city in advancing the prosperity of San Francisco and with it the general prosperity of the State.

Railway progress. A company has lately been incorporated under the name of the San Francisco and San Joaquin Valley Railroad to build a line from this city to Bakersfield, in Kern County, about 350 miles long, the line will run through the San Joaquin Valley, but the route it will take has not yet been decided upon. Its present terminus will be at Stockton, but it will eventually be extended to this city and terminal facilities here have been already arranged for. This valley is one of the richest in California, and the farmers located there hail the advent of a competing road with great delight. The towns along the possible line of the road are taking a vast amount of interest in the undertaking, and are making offers to the directors of the company to induce them to build in their direction. A great many large subscriptions for stock were secured in this city, and some of our most prominent business men are among the directors. It is particularly gratifying to Californians to see this road built, as it may eventually be connected with a transcontinental line, and thus afford them relief from the monopoly they have so long suffered under.

Rights of aliens. The people of the State of California at the last election (held in November, 1894) ratified by a majority of their votes an amendment to the State Constitution touching the ownership of land and other property by resident foreigners, which had been previously adopted by the legislative branch of the State Government. The amendment is therefore now a part of the organic law of the State. It reads as follows:—

"Section 17, Art. 1. Foreigners of the white race, or of African descent, eligible to become citizens of the United States under the naturalisation laws thereof, while bona fide residents of this State, shall have the same rights in respect to the acquisition, possession, enjoyment, transmission, and inheritance of all property, other than real estate, as native born citizens; provided, that such aliens owning real estate at the time of the adoption of this amendment may remain such owners; and provided further, that the Legislature may, by statute, provide for the disposition of real estate which shall hereafter be acquired by such aliens by descent or devise."

Legal opinions differ as to the effects of this amendment. Some lawyers hold that the true purport of said amendment is that no non-resident alien can hereafter legally acquire, possess, enjoy, transmit or inherit any real estate or personal property within this State. That non-resident aliens who acquired land or personal property prior to this enactment, can now no longer possess and enjoy the same. That resident aliens, who are eligible to become United States citizens, may possess and enjoy such real estate as they may have owned prior to the adoption of this amendment, but that they cannot in future acquire, possess or enjoy, except by comity of nations, any real estate other than that acquired by them prior to the adoption of the amendment.

Other lawyers hold that the effect of the recent amendment is that resident and non-resident foreigners stand upon exactly the same footing as citizens of the State; that no change has been effected by the adoption of the amendment to the Constitution in the status hitherto existing, and that the only difference made in the law by the amendment is that whereas, previously, the Legislature could not legislate with reference to the rights of resident foreigners as such in real estate held by them, it may now say that both resident and non-resident foreigners shall hereafter hold, transmit or inherit lands upon such terms as it may by law impose. In other words, they hold that until the Legislature shall ordain otherwise the right of holding, transmitting and inheriting real estate is open equally to both resident and non-resident aliens, with every privilege and right which they would have were they citizens.

The State Legislature recently adjourned without having taken any action in this matter. It is therefore impossible to say which view of the effect of the amendment is correct until a case has been passed upon by the Courts. The State Legislature does not meet again until January, 1897.

(1984)

22 UNITED STATES.

Labour.

Railway strike.

California suffered considerably from the great railroad strike of last year which involved more or less almost the entire railway system of the United States. The railway employés on this coast were perhaps among the best paid men of their class to be found anywhere, and appear to have been fairly treated by the companies that employed them. They struck solely out of sympathy with their eastern brethren, and they have received much adverse criticism on this account as it is considered they were not justified in taking a course which so seriously affected the business of the country, not to say anything about the sufferings of their families, without having had some radical grievance of their own that required redressing. The primary cause of the strike was the reduction of wages at the works of the Pullman Palace Car Company at Pullman in the State of Illinois. This was resented by the operatives who through their union ordered a strike. The officers of the American Railway Union took the matter up and ordered a general strike of railroad employés throughout the country. The branch of this society in California was appealed to and it responded by taking similar action here. The striking trainmen of the Southern Pacific Company refused to handle, or allow others to handle, any train in which Pullman palace cars were coupled. The result of this movement was the complete stoppage of all railroad traffic, the paralyzing of the mail service and unavoidably a great loss to all business interests. On the side of the South Pacific Company it was maintained that the company was powerless to comply with the demands of the strikers, owing to the existence of contracts which provided for the running of the cars manufactured by the Pullman Company under penalty of heavy forfeits in case of failure. The most active scenes of the strike were at Sacramento, Los Angeles, and Oakland, but much damage and danger resulted from lawless behaviour at various other places throughout the State. The strike commenced here on June 29 and on July 2 the State militia was called out to protect life and property and to guard and conduct trains in transit. It was followed later by United States regular troops from the garrison at San Francisco and a draft of sailors and marines from the United States war vessels at Mare Island. When the strikers found that the Federal Government intended to protect and convey mail trains at all hazards they became disheartened and by July 26 trains were again running over the Southern Pacific Company's lines in all directions, and the strike was at an end having lasted 28 days. The loss sustained by the fruit interests of the State has been remarked upon elsewhere in this report. The railroads were of course heavy losers as were also the men and their families, particularly the relatives of those who were not reinstated on account of having damaged railroad property. All business interests suffered greatly as we were completely shut off from our eastern communication for some time.

The following figures give some idea of the number of railroad men affected by the strike.

Southern Pacific System.

	Number.
Number of men employed before the strike in California	11,045
,, ,, ,, outside of State	3,446
,, engaged in the strike in California	4,635
,, ,, outside of State	433
,, involved (involuntarily idle) in California	4,813
,, ,, ,, outside of State	1,661

The Southern California Railway Company had 1,058 employés before the strike, of whom 616 went on the strike. 197 of their employés were thrown out of employment by the strike. The strike in this system commenced on June 26 and traffic was fully resumed on July 14.

Manufactories. Owing to the high price of labour and coal on this coast our manufacturing interests continue to languish. The manufacturers of the Eastern States have increased their facilities for producing goods and can deliver them in San Francisco at prices far below what can be afforded by our home factories. In some instances the labour alone on an article manufactured here equals or exceeds the price of a similar article made in the east and freighted here.

Labour market. On account of the great depression in trade there have been large numbers of unemployed in this city throughout the past year. I should strongly dissuade any skilled artisan or labouring man from coming to San Francisco or, in fact, the Pacific Coast, in the hope of obtaining employment. There are more men here now than can get steady work, and even domestic servants find it difficult to get places, and the employment offices are thronged with women and girls seeking work.

No opening for clerks. There is absolutely no opening for clerks, and many young men who come out here, without making any enquiries, are bitterly disappointed on arrival at their inability to secure employment and have to take menial work, if they are lucky enough to find it, or send to their friends for sufficient means to enable them to return to their homes. During the past year a large number of corporations and firms have been reducing their staffs and cutting down salaries and expenses in all directions. This has thrown a great number of clerks out of employment and has glutted the market for this kind of work.

Agriculture.

Wheat. Early in the year there were hopes of an abundant harvest and for a long time it was generally held that the wheat crop was perhaps larger than that of 1893, but the stock-taking of December 1 last, though it was doubtless defective, gave results that effectually dispelled that illusion. The figures then given would not allow of a crop to exceed 750,000 short tons, probably much less, as some people estimate it not to exceed 700,000 tons. Then this sold at prices lower than ever before known. There was therefore much less money to distribute amongst the people and consequently a great restriction of trade. As wheat is the great staple of the State the price of this cereal, as well as the quantity produced, is always associated with the prosperity or depression of the times. There were some hopes early in 1894 that prices would revive. It was thought that the low figures everywhere were due to abnormal conditions of the trade, which would soon pass away, but it looks as if low prices were, except in years of general drought or great wars, to be a recognised feature of the market. The speculators who engineered a "deal" in 1893 ran the price of wheat up in May, and are said to be still holding a large quantity which at present prices would show a loss approximating to 500,000*l.* As soon as this excitement was over the market declined again and October saw the lowest figure at which this cereal ever sold in the market of San Francisco. Prices improved somewhat at the close of the year.

The stock of wheat in California on December 1, 1894, according to estimates prepared by the San Francisco Produce Exchange approximated 650,000 short tons, being 60,000 tons less than at the same time in 1893. Of this amount it is safe to say, that from 250,000 to 300,000 tons are owned by speculators who purchased a good deal of it in 1893 and have since been holding it. The remaining portion is in the hands of farmers, most of whom are financially independent and able to hold for a better market than the present affords.

The present extremely low prices are attributed to several causes. The phenomenal yields of wheat produced in the United States during the years 1891 and 1892 had to be disposed of in addition to the average surplus for export, and although at the present time it is pretty nearly obliterated through consumption or shipment, its influence as a depressing factor has been of tremendous importance. The large amount shipped from the Argentine Republic was no inconsiderable factor, and this country is likely to be a serious competitor of California as both land and labour are so much cheaper there, and it is more favourably situated to lay down its products in the markets of Europe.

Barley. The receipts of barley at San Francisco were only about one half of those of 1893, which were the largest ever known in San Francisco. This, as well as the stock taken in December, shows that our crop was light. The year was a dull one in this cereal, though for a while feed was held high and a good deal was attracted from the States of Washington and Oregon.

Receipts of produce at San Francisco. The following table gives the receipts of various articles of produce at San Francisco in 1894:—

SAN FRANCISCO.

Articles.		Quantity.
Oats	Centals	682,116
Hops	Bales	11,528
Indian corn	Sacks	338,414
Rye	,,	38,562
Beans	,,	518,791
Potatoes	,,	999,838
Onions	,,	125,875
Honey	Cases	3,190

Hops. The crop of the Pacific Coast is said to have reached over 160,000 bales, the largest on record. The quality on an average was disappointing on account of climatic and other influences. The movement was quick but without any attending advance in price. The surplus is still large, and as brewers are well supplied an improvement in the near future is doubtful.

Honey. The crop of honey was very light for 1894. It is said not to have been more than one-eighth of that of 1893 and the lightest for 12 years. The cause is attributed to lack of rain as the bees did well in irrigated districts. Prices remained about the same during the whole year except for fancy grades which ranged high and stock scarce.

Dairy produce. The receipts of dairy produce at San Francisco in 1894 were as follows:—

Sources.	Quantity.		
	Butter.	Cheese.	Eggs.
	Lbs.	Lbs.	Dozens.
California	16,335,700	5,105,400	2,906,815
Oregon	596,800	624,300	72,420
Eastern	324,600	969,920	1,902,140
Total	17,257,100	6,699,620	4,881,375

Viticulture. Viticulture has been much depressed during the last two years, and has probably reached the lowest point ever touched since it was first established in this State. Many people attribute this condition of affairs to the amount of wine produced, which they claim is more than the present market will take, while others think it is due to competition among the wine-dealers. At any rate prices went down to a point where production was conducted at a steady loss to the wine farmer.

A corporation has lately been formed to remedy this state of affairs, which will control the sale of all wine produced by its members, and thus endeavour to raise prices. One of its objects is to improve the quality of the wine sold by compelling its members to distil inferior grades into spirits. This corporation is said to control ten-twelfths of the entire output and prices have shown a material advance since its formation.

The grape crop of 1894 was an exceptionally small one owing to frosts, coulure, hot weather, and early rain. The amount of wine made will not exceed 60 per cent. of that made in 1893, being estimated at 12,600,000 gallons against 21,000,000 gallons for that year. Notwithstanding this fact prices ruled very low and the business was run at a loss to both producers and merchants.

The receipts of Californian wine and brandy at San Francisco in 1893 and 1894 were as follows:—

Description.	Quantity.	
	1894.	1893.
	Gallons.	Gallons.
Wine	11,801,698	11,974,484
Brandy	594,300	782,355

Phylloxera. The phylloxera is still spreading and has obtained a foothold in Alameda, Santa Clara, and San Mateo Counties. As no new vineyards are being planted it will be the cause of a great decrease in the output of wine during the next few years.

Resistant vines. Experiments are being tried to test the resistant properties of the so-called resistant vines to phylloxera. Plants and cuttings have been obtained from France and elsewhere and plots have been planted in different vineyards. The resistant properties of the different varieties cannot be determined for several years.

Fruit growers injured by the strike. The railroad strike seriously interfered with the shipping of Californian fruit for about 3 weeks in July at a time when heavy shipments should have been made. The crop then ripening consisted of plums, early peaches, apricots, and Bartlett pears. The growers of these varieties all suffered more or less loss as their fruit could not be moved, and had to be allowed to rot on the trees or in the warehouse. The local canneries were, as a rule, compelled to reject the loads of the farmer, not having the capacity to use them. Fruit suitable for drying purposes was so disposed of, and such varieties will not prove a total loss.

Fruit crop. Although in many localities certain varieties have suffered from climatic or other causes, taking the State as a whole the fruit crop may be said to have been generally large in yield, while the quality was above the average. Prunes are about the only fruit that produced a light crop, but the large area of new orchards which are coming into bearing will bring up the amount considerably.

Oranges. The great bulk of this fruit grows south of the Tehachapi Range of Mountains. Extensive tracts along the entire foothill belt of the Sierra Nevada Range, aligning both the San Joaquin and Sacramento Valleys, are now being devoted to oranges, lemons, and other citrus fruits, and in the next few years the "Northern Citrus Belt" is expected to become a sharp competitor with the south for the "Eastern Citrus Market." Already extensive eastern shipments have been made from this locality. The absence of frost in many of these sections has given a strong impetus to the industry. The market in this city was very dull

Cherries. The season opened with rare promise, but the heavy rains which fell during May and in the early part of June did a great deal of damage, although the output of fruit was still large. Rain fell during the picking season which hindered the gathering of the crop, and much of the fruit had to be left until it was over ripe and unfit for market. The keeping qualities were impaired by the moisture, and much of the crop that found its way to market was either spoiled or in a very inferior condition. As a result prices were very low, dropping to 1*d*. per 1 lb., and many growers realised but little more than the cost of picking their fruit. Some of the later fruit came through in better condition, and prices advanced.

Apricots. This fruit yielded phenomenally well this season, and prices generally were satisfactory. While the output was large the size of the fruit did not reach the usual average. The amount of fruit dried was extremely large and greatly in excess of that of any previous year, being estimated at from 8,000 to 10,000 tons. This increase is largely due to the strike which shut off the eastern market, and compelled growers to make other disposition of their crops.

Prunes. The crop is estimated to be from 25 to 30 per cent. below that of 1893. There were limited districts where a full crop was reported, but in the principal prune sections, from which the bulk of the crop is derived, the fruit set very light. The favourable growing weather, and the thinning out of the fruit have somewhat increased the size of that remaining, but this increase in size is not sufficient to make up the deficiency. The many new orchards, however, which added their yield to the total bulk, very largely helped to bring up the amount. The total product of prunes will probably foot up from 35,000,000 to 37,000,000 lbs.

The average consumption of prunes in the United States is stated to be now 70,000,000 lbs., and in a year or two with a full average crop our local product is likely to entirely force the foreign article from the market.

This brings us face to face with the important question of a future market for our prune crop. Oregon, Washington, Idaho, and Arizona are producing prunes to some extent. In our own State there are large areas of young orchards yet to come into bearing, and of those already bearing many have not yet reached their full capacity. When these all contribute their full quota to the annual output, California's yield will be doubled. In view of these facts the outlook for prune growers is not very encouraging unless something can be done to encourage a more general use of the fruit in households in the Eastern States. There is practically no possibility of exporting at present. Planting has recently been curtailed, and the low prices ruling are stimulating consumption.

Pears.—Pears have yielded an unusually heavy crop, the Bartlett variety ranging at least 10 per cent. above the average, and all the other varieties being well up. In the early season reports from many pear sections were to the effect that fruit was dropping badly, and it was feared that a shortage would prevail in some sections. This fear, however, was not realised, as the dropping stopped before the fruit had been more than sufficiently thinned to ensure its quality. What had therefore appeared an evil proved to be a benefit to the grower, and an unusually large crop of fine fruit was the result.

When pears came upon the market the strike had nearly run its course, and while the earlier pickings were somewhat affected by it, the greater part of the crop was not interfered with, and found its usual outlet in the Eastern States.

Peaches.—There was a very large crop, but the strike interfered seriously with the marketing of the earlier varieties, and growers who did not have the usual outlet in the Eastern States were compelled to dry their product. The later varieties found a good market, the eastern crop being very light owing to frost there in the peach sections.

Apples.—Upon our upper foothill and mountain lands the apple produces abundantly and of fair quality. It also grows in the warmer valleys, but although of good size and fair to look upon it is too often faulty in both texture and flavour. In many of the coast counties where the temperature is not too high, and in some of the foothill regions of the Sierra Nevada Mountains and coast range, apples are the standard fruit crop.

Olives.—Considerable attention is being paid to the cultivation of olives and the manufacture of olive oil and pickles.

Figs.—In the warmest parts of the State fig culture is carried on very successfully. Owing to the introduction of finer varieties and improved methods of handling the product it promises soon to take a more prominent position among our fruit exports.

Nuts.—The area of walnut culture is spreading rapidly over portions of the State, where it finds a congenial home. Pecans, peanuts, chestnuts, and hazelnuts are also grown. Almonds have been largely planted, and some new varieties have been obtained from experiments which produce excellent results.

Berries.—All kinds of berries, such as strawberries, raspberries, blackberries, cranberries, gooseberries, and currants, besides many other varieties, are largely grown in this State. Strawberries can be obtained in San Francisco at reasonable figures for about 8 months in the year.

Raisins.—The output of raisins was very large in 1894 being estimated at 3,500,000 boxes, an increase of 500,000 boxes over the product of 1893. Prices have ruled very low for the past two seasons, which the packers attribute not so much to over-production as to the manner of placing the goods on the market, and to the fact that many of the growers had pawned their products to money-lenders who were indifferent as to the price obtained so long as they secured the amounts they had advanced.

Returns received from 21 counties show an increased acreage of fruit planted in the spring of 1894 of 17,000 acres. The above figures will cover over half the principal fruit sections of the State, and an estimate of 35,000 acres of new land to all kinds of fruit planted in the present season will probably be as nearly accurate an estimate as could be made. *New fruit planted for 1894.*

Owing to a number of causes, such as glutting of the market, hard times, unsatisfactory service, and the railroad strike, the prices realised for California green fruits in the Eastern States ruled very low this year. On account of the almost total failure of the crop there the year 1894 should have been a prosperous one for the California fruit grower, who, so to speak, had the great market of the east largely to himself. As a rule, however, the markets of the east were kept constantly glutted, and the prices to the grower thereby made ruinously low. *Low prices.*

Such having been the case in 1894, with a probable shipment of 7,000 cars, and with the eastern crop almost a total failure, what is likely to be the result when the California fruit crop will aggregate many more than 7,000 car-loads, as it surely will, within the next few years, and when the eastern crop shall be a normal one, or an unusually large one. The answer is self-evident. There can be but one result, and that result one of disaster to the army of fruit growers in our State, and a serious crippling of the entire green fruit industry of California. *Danger of over-production.*

The danger is fully appreciated by the growers who point out that somewhat similar conditions existed in 1885–86, with this difference that in those years 1,000 car-loads glutted the markets of the east. The difference between the amount at present shipped represents the growth in the volume of our shipments, which growth is largely the result of opening the Atlantic seaboard markets and many interior markets, by the introduction of the auction plan of selling fruits, a system first introduced in connection with the sale of California fruits in 1887.

In the earlier years of the auction sale system it was comparatively easy to regulate the distribution of our fruits in the east from the fact that over 90 per cent. of the shipments made, were made through two mediums, which made it possible to regulate its distribution. Within the past year or two, new conditions have arisen. In place of the great bulk of the fruit passing chiefly through two hands, a large number of co-operative companies, brokers, commission men and others, have entered the field, and have been making indiscriminate shipments to the various eastern markets, resulting in disaster all round. Each shipper has naturally endeavoured to hide his movements from all others, and the result has been that all have worked in the dark, and the forwarding of fruit has been almost entirely a matter of guess-work. With a view of distributing the fruits more intelligently, and thus preventing a glutting of the eastern markets, a Bureau of Information has been established, which will be supported by all persons engaged in the fruit business. This bureau will issue daily bulletins to all subscribers, keeping them fully posted as to the conditions of the eastern markets, so that they can intelligently determine where their fruit is required, and can be disposed of to the best advantage. It has been decided to have only one auction room in each city.

Fruit sent to England.

The shipment of fresh deciduous fruit direct to London, which was tried as an experiment two years since, and suspended in 1893, was resumed again this season. On August 5 a train consisting of 11 refrigerator cars was despatched to New York, and the fruit was there transferred to fast steamers. The time occupied on the journey was $12\frac{1}{2}$ days, and the fruit is said to have arrived in good condition. This shipment was followed by others, but the expenses are very heavy, and unless the fruit can be laid down at a smaller cost for transportation, and with a smaller percentage of loss, it is not likely that the English market will prove a profitable field to work.

Co-operative movements.

The unsatisfactory prices which growers have received from the commission men and jobbers have encouraged the growth of co-operation in the marketing of orchard products. The success of the Southern California Fruit Exchanges, in the handling of citrus fruit, and the Campbell Fruit Union of Santa Clara County, for the manipulation of cured fruits, has largely brought about this result. Various local exchanges sprung up throughout the State, and they have now affected a central organisation, known as the California Fruit Exchange, situated in this city.

These exchanges handle all the product of their members, which is sent to them direct from the orchards. It is then graded by machinery, and the grower obtains a receipt specifying the variety and weight of each grade. From this time its identity is lost, all being put together or dried together, as the case may be, sold by the association, and the proceeds distributed after deducting the necessary charges. The results attained are said to be far more satisfactory than when each grower marketed his own fruit. The association is able to make better terms with the purchasers, handle the product with less expense, and prevent too much fruit being thrown on the market at one time, thus realising better prices than were obtainable under the old method.

New system of transporting fruit.

Experiments of shipping fruit to the Eastern States by the Perkin's system have been tried and have proved very successful. The principle is very simple. Attached to the locomotive is an air-compressor, in which the pressure of air reaches over 80 lbs. to the square inch. Air compressed to such an extent becomes heated to such a degree that the germinal life it contains is destroyed. The sterilized air is passed into a receiver, where it is cooled and then forced into an air-tight car into which the fruit is placed. The germ-laden air is in turn forced out of the car, and the fruit is carried to its destination in perfectly pure air. With but little loss of power to the engine this process is kept up the entire journey. Where only pure air reaches the fruit the process of decomposition is arrested for a long time. There is also a great saving effected by dispensing with the ice in the car, thus saving the cost of same, and allowing more room for fruit.

Beneficial insects. The importation of beneficial insects from Australia to destroy pests that affected the fruit trees of California is said to have proved very successful, some of the pests, such as cottony cushion scale and the black scale having disappeared in many orchards.

Advice to intending settlers. I reiterate the advice given to intending settlers in former reports not to invest in land until they have been out here for one or two years and acquired some knowledge of the country and of the methods of doing business here. Under the present condition of things many people consider it impossible to make a fruit orchard or farm pay. At all events, a man must be favourably situated to do so, and if he buys land without a full knowledge of what he is about, he is very apt to regret his bargain before he has been long in the country. Many new settlers fail through buying too much land, and not keeping enough working capital in hand. Others buy orchards stocked with poor varieties of fruit trees, or badly arranged, and can never arrive at satisfactory results, no matter what capital and labour be expended upon them. There is no difficulty in renting or leasing land in any part of the State, and thus ascertaining if they have an aptitude for the business of fruit-growing or farming before sinking their capital in an undertaking from which they will find it almost impossible to withdraw; certainly not without heavy loss.

Canaigre. Experiments have been made in growing this plant in California. It is a species of rumex or dock, which is successfully cultivated in New Mexico, where an extract factory has been established. Its roots contain a large percentage of tannin, and it is thought that the climate and soil of many parts of California are adapted to its growth.

Beetroot. The production of beetroot sugar in California in 1894 is estimated as follows:—

	Quantity.
	Tons.
At Alvarado	3,000
Watsonville	10,000
Chino	10,000
Total	23,000

It is doubtful at present what effect on this industry the withdrawal of the bounty will have. If the production can be kept up it will be an excellent thing for California and the whole Pacific Coast.

(1984)

UNITED STATES.

Wool.

The total clip of California wool amounted to 36,968,400 lbs., against 33,169,375 lbs. in 1893.

The shipments from San Francisco amounted to 26,640,444 lbs.

Prices ruled low and unprofitable during the year, and the new season does not offer much encouragement. No one specific reason can be furnished as an explanation of the decline in the value of wool, although the new tariff bill is popularly supposed to be the cause. The abundant winter rains, however, will give the farmers and stockmen a bountiful supply of grain and grass, and mutton particularly will be strong in the market throughout the year.

All the values in the foregoing report are calculated at the rate of 5 dol. to the 1*l*. sterling.

PORTLAND, OREGON.

Mr. Vice-Consul Laidlaw reports as follows:—

Introductory remarks.

Business generally throughout this State and district improved very little during 1894. Prices of all produce were very low, and values of imports and exports were even lower than in 1893. The average rates of freight were higher than those of the previous year and comparatively better than in most markets of the world. There is, however, a decided tendency towards a better and more healthy condition of trade.

Shipping and Navigation.

From the following table it will be seen that 91 per cent. of all the tonnage employed in the foreign trade was British, which is a higher average than last year. The average size of vessels was much larger, some of them being over 2,400 tons register.

Annex A.—RETURN of all Shipping at the Port of Portland, Oregon, during the Year 1894.

ENTERED.

Nationality.	Sailing. Number of Vessels.	Sailing. Tons.	Steam. Number of Vessels.	Steam. Tons.	Total. Number of Vessels.	Total. Tons.
British	66	112,656	3	1,192	69	113,848
American, from foreign countries	3	4,301	15	5,880	18	10,181
American, from Atlantic ports	3	4,142	...	...	3	4,142
American, coasting	44	13,853	146	155,408	190	169,261
German	3	4,056	...	...	3	4,056
Norwegian	3	5,233	...	...	3	5,233
Hawaiian	1	2,027	...	...	1	2,027
Danish	1	1,091	...	...	1	1,091
French	1	1,148	...	...	1	1,148
Total	125	148,507	164	162,480	289	310,987
,, for the year preceding	97	127,835	190	168,991	287	296,826

SAN FRANCISCO.

CLEARED.

Nationality.	Sailing. Number of Vessels.	Sailing. Tons.	Steam. Number of Vessels.	Steam. Tons.	Total. Number of Vessels.	Total. Tons.
British	65	108,699	3	1,192	68	109,891
American, to foreign countries	2	2,288	12	5,5 7	14	7,825
American, to Atlantic ports	3	4,956	...	...	3	4,956
American, coasting	51	17,555	154	166,724	205	184,279
German	2	4,056	...	...	2	4,056
Norwegian	1	1,432	...	...	1	1,432
Danish	1	1,091	...	...	1	1,091
French	1	1,148	...	...	1	1,148
Total	126	141,225	169	173,453	295	314,678
,, for the year preceding	98	130,685	172	163,942	270	294,627

Freights.
The average rate of freight during the year for iron and steel vessels loading grain cargoes was 1*l*. 13*s*. 6*d*. to the United Kingdom for orders, including Havre, Antwerp, or Dunkirk, and in some cases Hamburg, at the same rates. The highest rate paid was 1*l*. 16*s*. 3*d*., and the lowest 1*l*. 11*s*. 3*d*. Only one wooden ship loaded grain for the United Kingdom at 1*l*. 7*s*. 6*d*.

The direct option was generally at one-third less, but in quite a large number of charters no deduction was given. Three vessels were towed up from San Francisco to load, charterers paying towage, pilotage, and extra expenses.

Shipping engagements.
The following were the tonnage engagements for sailing vessels during the last 2 years, exclusive of coasting voyages:—

Cargoes.	Tons Register. 1894.	Tons Register. 1893.
Grain and flour	129,055	115,660
Salmon and general	..	1,400
Timber	1,764	8,605
Miscellaneous	5,808	2,957
Total	136,627	128,622

Sailors.
Crimps have not given much trouble during the past year, and all legislation has been in the direction of granting additional protection to sailors. I regret, however, to report that in numerous instances a bonus of 2*l*. per man has been paid by shipmasters for crews. With a little firmness on their part this might be avoided. Wages of A.B. seamen have generally been 4*l*.

The number and changes in crews of British ships entering this port have been as under:—

(1984)

UNITED STATES.

	Number.
Total number of crews	1,761
Deserted	257
Discharged	63
Engaged	333
Reported dead	5
Hospital permits	26

Pilotage and towage. There has been no change in rates of pilotage and towage given in my last report.

Lighterage. Only a few of the larger vessels have found it necessary to lighter a small portion of their cargoes.

Aids to navigation. The attention of shipmasters is called to many changes in buoys at Willapa or Shoalwater, as vessels often drift there in mistake for the Columbia River entrance. A whistling buoy was established off the bar at Tillamook Bay.

Columbia River outside bar whistling buoy (black and white perpendicular stripes, marked C in white), moved April 21, is now in 105 feet of water about $1\frac{1}{4}$ miles outside of the bar. North Head W., Tangent N. by E. $\frac{1}{4}$ E.; Cape Disappointment Lighthouse, N.E. by N.; Point Adams Lighthouse, E., $\frac{5}{8}$ N.; Columbia River Light Vessel, S., $\frac{1}{8}$ W., $3\frac{3}{8}$ miles.

Changes have also been made in position of the "Wreck of the William H. Besse" buoy, Middle Sands buoy, bar buoy, inner bar buoy, Peacock Spit buoy, and Clatsop Spit buoys. Changes were also made during the year in the buoys at Coos Bay and Tillamook, and lighthouses at Heceta Head (Suislaw River) and Umpqua River were put in operation.

It has been decided to transfer the first order light now on Cape Disappointment to a new station to be established on North Head, and to put a fourth order light on Cape Disappointment, and the Point Adams light may eventually be discontinued. Notice will be given of these changes when effected.

Trade and Commerce.

The following tables give the exports and imports during the past 2 years:—

Annex B—RETURN of Principal Articles of Export from Portland, Oregon, during the Years 1894–93.

Articles.		1894 Quantity.	1894 Value.	1893 Quantity.	1893 Value.
			£		£
Wheat	Quarters	752,039	596,810	660,596	697,070
,, flour	Sacks	212,721	144,731	251,626	222,327
Timber	Feet	502,000	891	2,027,000	4,744
Barley	Bushels	90,838	9,045	13,110	1,730
Other articles	...	...	6,343	...	8,052
Total	...	...	757,820	...	933,923

SAN FRANCISCO.

RETURN of Principal Articles of Import to Portland, Oregon, during the Years 1894-93.

Articles.		1894.		1893.	
		Quantity.	Value.	Quantity.	Value.
			£		£
Coals and coke	Tons	9,903	4,628	11,672	6,404
Tin and tin-plate	Lbs.	849,423	4,441	2,167,891	12,248
Rice	,,	2,737,086	15,765	2,134,923	7,393
Earthenware and glass		...	4,685	...	11,146
Salt	Lbs.	5,541,709	3,261	5,643,248	3,593
Cement	Barrels	228,762	34,551	73,395	18,949
Tea	Lbs.	345,930	9,559	290,521	9,238
Hemp and jute	Tons	833	13,265	1,308	31,150
Window glass	Lbs.	357,400	1,203	481,962	1,991
Bags and bagging		...	6,703	...	11,479
Sugar	Lbs.	1,830,994	13,483	2,129,551	16,595
Coffee	,,	206,127	7,346	101,231	4,498
All other articles		...	33,171	...	59,095
Total		...	152,061	...	193,779

NOTE.—The above returns do not include coastwise trade.

The imports from foreign countries show a considerable diminution in value, the only articles in which there is an increase, being rice, cement, tea, and coffee.

The total value of exports coastwise and to foreign countries was about 13 per cent. less than last year. The value of all produce shipped by sea to domestic ports, including three cargoes of wheat and barley shipped to New York, was 674,940*l*., against 631,156*l*. in 1893.

The average quality of the season's wheat is better than last *Wheat.* year, and while the quantity exported was greater, the values were lower. Owing to the burning of the grain elevator here, ships chartered for barley to New York were filled up with wheat, 15,640 quarters were shipped by this route. The shipments to San Francisco were 209,943 quarters, and the total shipments of this cereal from the Columbia River were 977,622 quarters. Total value, 748,743*l*., being an average of 15s. 4d. per quarter. Average last year was 19s. 11d.

There was a continual decline in market prices till October, when the lowest point ever known was touched, and Oregon Valley wheat sold at 14s. 6d., and Walla Walla at 13s. During November and December there was some improvement, and at the close of the year quotations were 15s. 6d. and 14s. respectively, f.o.b.

The exports of flour were less in quantity as well as in value, *Flour.* and prices were lower in proportion than wheat. Shipments to China and Japan were equal to 81,773 sacks of 280 lbs. Total shipments, foreign and coastwise, 324,638 sacks, valued at 222,716*l*. or 21 per cent. less in quantity and 45 per cent. less in value than last year. Average value per sack, 13s. 9d. In January, patent roller extras were quotable at 15s. 8d., and superfines at 12s. 10d. At the close of the year quotations were 13s. 8d. and 11s. 5d. per sack, f.o.b.

(1984)

UNITED STATES.

Other grains. It would appear from the shipments that there was a largely increased harvest of barley, oats, and flaxseed, but prices of both barley and oats were considerably lower than in 1893, while flaxseed was higher.

Barley. Two port cargoes, 43,162 centals were shipped to Bristol and 270,079 centals to San Francisco, also 70,250 centals to New York; average price for the year, 75 c. (3s. 1½d.) per cental for malting and 65 c. (2s. 8½d.) for feed.

Oats. Shipments were more than three times greater than last year, but prices fell after harvest, closing nearly 30 per cent. lower than at the opening of the year.

Flaxseed. The exports were greater than any year since 1889, being about 5½ times greater than in 1893. Prices were very steady.

Hop trade. From the best information at my disposal the yield of Oregon hops was about 53,000 bales, against 38,500 bales last year. The quality was good, but prices were extraordinarily low, dropping from 11½ c. (5¾d.) in January, to 5½ c. (2¾d.) in December, an actual loss to growers.

Fruit trade. Fruit growing was more profitable than other branches of agriculture, and growers found a good market in the middle Western States. During the year there was shipped 22,564,000 lbs. of green fruit and 39,534,000 lbs. of dried.

Wool trade. The wool trade is in a deplorable condition, and prices were remarkably steady during the year, but ruinously low, averaging as follows for unwashed wools:—

| | Per Pound. ||
	From—	To—
	s.　d.	s.　d.
Eastern Oregon	0　2½	0　4½
Willamette Valley	0　4	0　5¼
Umpqua Valley	0　4½	0　5½

Clip of Eastern Oregon was about 16,000,000 lbs.; Valley, 900,000 lbs.; and Umpqua, 225,000 lbs. Nearly all was shipped by rail East. The shipments by sea were 4,115,700 lbs. Local mills consumed about 1,250,000 lbs.

Timber trade. The timber trade was also in a depressed condition and many mills idle. Shipments coastwise, by sea, were 33,040,000 feet sawn timber, valued at 60,309l.

The foreign trade in this article was very small.

Fisheries.
Salmon. As reported by the "Oregon Fish and Game Protector" the salmon pack of the Columbia River was 323,232 cases, and of other bays and rivers in Oregon, 78,324 cases. Each case represents 48 lbs. of salmon.

These are graded as follows:—

	Cases.
Chinook	203,319
Blueback	41,814
Silverside	112,047
Steelheads	40,582
Chinook, whitefish..	3,794
Total	401,556

The market price of tinned salmon varied very little from that of last year.

Shipments. There were no direct shipments to England, 70,094 cases of the Columbia River pack were shipped to San Francisco. No statistics have been published of rail shipments, but the most of the salmon is now marketed in the Eastern States.

Sturgeon. There is quite a trade in sturgeon, which is sent East in "refrigerator cars."

Import trade. As has always been more or less the case, the most of the import trade was done by sail and rail viâ San Francisco and from the Eastern States.

The records of the custom-house show an increase in imports of rice, cement, tea, and coffee, but a considerable decrease in the total value of imports. The trade with Belgium continues to increase.

Window glass. The only imports were from Belgium, which apparently monopolises the trade now.

Cement. After testing the different cements offered, both the United States Engineers and the Water Commission decided in favour of the Belgian article, and a large quantity was bought for the Cascade Locks and Water Reservoirs.

Of the total imports, 60 per cent. came from Belgium. Prices continued low, standard brands selling at 9s. 7d. per barrel. Less known brands sold even below 8s. per barrel. The consumption was larger than usual.

Coal. Wood for fuel was plentiful and cheap, which lessened the consumption of coal. Imports of foreign were even smaller than last year. A cargo was received from Japan, and this coal is in favour for gas-making purposes. Receipts were:—From Australia, 9,903 tons; Japan, 1,754 tons; British Columbia, 600 tons; Great Britain, 370 tons. From coast mines, by rail, about 45,000 tons; from Atlantic ports, by sea, 1,481 tons. Australian sold at about 1l. duty paid. Duty reduced to 40 c.

Tin-plates. Receipts were not much more than one third of the 1893 importation and standard weight B.V. Grades of coke sold at an average of about 1l. 2s. 8d. per box. There is a large steady consumption.

Bags and bagging. Consumption was considerably greater than last year, but prices were less, averaging about 3½d., duty paid, during the first part of the year. After the duty of 1¼ c. was abolished, prices fell to about 2¾d.

(1934)

UNITED STATES.

Hemp and jute.

Besides the direct imports, a large proportion of the demand was supplied from San Francisco.

The consumption of the rope manufactory here was much smaller than last year, and imports of raw hemp and jute declined materially.

The value of all exports and imports by countries is given in the following table :—

Annex C.—TABLE showing Total Value of all Articles Exported from and Imported to Portland, Oregon, from and to Foreign Countries during the Years 1894–93.

Country.	Exports. 1894.	Exports. 1893.	Imports. 1894.	Imports. 1893.
	£	£	£	£
Great Britain	679,783	845,875	35,476	67,197
Belgium	10,000	..	27,032	10,339
British Columbia	10,020	18,412	2,157	6,694
China and Japan	51,997	56,136	39,480	48,477
,, ,, in transit	..	..	..	..
Australia	..	..	3,178	4,351
France	..	13,500	1,177	1,560
Cuba	..	..	532	2,743
Philippine Islands	2,250	..	8,178	24,954
India	..	..	19,817	20,122
Germany	..	..	1,954	2,456
Hawaiian Islands	..	..	12,645	..
All other countries	3,770	..	435	5,377
Total	757,820	933,923	152,061	194,270

Financial.

Failures and suspensions were numerous during the past year, and the shrinkage in property values has been great.

One savings bank and one national bank have permanently closed their doors. The policy of the banks has been to grant any reasonable assistance to their customers, and many firms have thus been tided over the recent crisis in commercial affairs.

Strength has been given to some of the banks by increase of capital during the year. There is, however, no money available for enterprises that are of a speculative nature. Foreclosures of mortgages have been numerous.

Clearing-house.

Transactions of the clearing-house for the last 3 years were as follows :—

	Amount. 1894.	Amount. 1893.	Amount. 1892.
	£	£	£
Exchanges	11,316,504	15,312,951	21,900,719
Balances	2,534,606	3,031,088	4,334,711

The credit of the city continues good, if the premium realised on 30-year 5 per cent. water bonds is any criterion. The following were issued during the year:— **Bonds.**

Date.	Amount.	
	£	
January 18	10,000	At 2½ per cent discount
April 26	50,000	8·625 per cent. premium
June 1	50,000	9·56 per cent. premium
August 15	40,000	9·89 per cent. premium
September 15	60,000	9·89 per cent. premium
October 15	80,000	10·52 per cent. premium

During most of the year exchange was steady and high, and the average for 60 days' sight bills on London was 4 dol. 87 c. per 1l. for Bank, and 4 dol. 85½ c. for Commercial. **Exchange.**

Population and Industries.—Health.

Very few new buildings were erected during the year, and those not of a pretentious character. **Buildings.**

The new city hall, which has cost 103,967l., was completed. This is a very handsome building of grey sandstone, built in the Italian renaissance style. It is 200 feet long, width in the centre 119 feet, and in the wings 142 feet, and is 4 stories in height. A double row of 30 polished granite columns surrounds the outside of the vestibule. The main hallway is paved with red and white marble, and its dimensions are 50 by 68 feet. **City hall.**

Although Oregon cannot be properly called a manufacturing State, nor Portland lay claim to be a city of factories, there are several large plants in operation in and around this city. At Oregon city there is one of the largest electric power plants in the United States, from which all the electric lights here are run, and numerous workshops. The power is furnished by the Falls of the Willamette. **Manufactures. Electric plant.**

There is also a large pulp and paper mill, employing 250 hands, and which has been running steadily manufacturing straw and manilla papers and pulp from cotton-wood and spruce. **Pulp and paper mill.**

The woollen mills have also been running steadily, giving employment to 300 hands. **Woollen mills.**

Two large flour mills are also located at Oregon city, and the large Portland flour mills below this city. **Flour mills.**

At Oswego are the furnaces of the Oregon Iron and Steel Company, which, however, have been practically closed during most of the year, smelting only 548 tons of pig-iron. The product of their pipe foundry was 6,800 tons of water pipes. **Ironworks.**

At Troutdale there is a very large and complete meat packing plant, with a cold storage warehouse here. It is owned and operated by the Union Meat Company, which also largely supplies the city with fresh meats. This company slaughtered during the **Meat packing.**

year 14,000 cattle, 7,000 calves, 48,000 sheep, and 25,000 hogs. The value of its product in hams, lard, meats, &c., was 50,000*l.*

Saw mills. Foundries. — Some of the saw-mills and foundries were closed, and others were very slack.

Factories. Workshops. — The cordage factory and linseed oil works worked only part time, and workshops generally employed fewer hands than usual.

Mining. Silver. — There is no improvement in silver mining, and very few of the Cœur d'Alene mines were worked. Being low grade mines they cannot be worked to a profit at present prices for silver and lead, and the miners' unions will not consent to a reduction of wages, and oppose non-union men doing so.

Gold. — The production of gold has increased very considerably, and it is estimated that in Baker and Union Counties the yield last year was not less than 280,000*l.*

Wells, Fargo, and Co. give the shipments of the precious metals from Oregon last year as—gold, 320,643*l.*; silver, 21,689*l.*

Labour. — The demand for labour during the year has not been good, and but for the large number employed on the new waterworks and at the Government works at the Cascades Locks the position would have been very much worse. There has, however, been less prominent distress amongst the labouring classes than last year. I have to repeat my usual warning to clerks, salesmen, and persons who have no particular avocation, against coming here expecting to secure prompt employment. Unless such persons have some funds on hand they are sure to become distressed.

Health. — The usual summer flood was last year exceptionally great, and the most of the business districts were flooded. It was anticipated that there would be much sickness after the water subsided in July, but owing to the precautions taken by the city authorities such was not the case, and the health of the city has been very good, and the death rate lower than last year.

Death rate. — The total number of deaths reported was 836, which is at the rate of about 10·45 per 100.

Public Works.

Waterworks. — The new waterworks have been completed, and Portland has now an ample supply of probably the purest water on the face of the globe. The work was commenced in 1893, and the capacity of the pipe now laid is 25,000,000 gallons per day. The water is taken from Bull Run River, a clear mountain stream which flows from a lake near the base of Mount Hood. Precautions were taken by reserving the land at the head waters to prevent the contamination of the stream. The elevation at the head works is 710 feet above low water mark of the Willamette River at Portland, and the discharge of the Bull Run River there is about 150,000,000 gallons per day, thus ensuring an ample supply for all time. The water is brought in a pipe 24 miles long to a reservoir on the east side of the river near Portland, 400 feet above low water. From thence it is carried across the river through a submerged pipe to a reservoir in the City Park, 6 miles distant, at an elevation of 290 feet above the base of the city grades. These high service reservoirs on the east and west sides of the river are connected with low service reservoirs, and the water can be supplied direct to the city mains without passing through the reservoirs. The four reservoirs have a capacity of 67,500,000 gallons. The total cost of the waterworks has been 610,870*l*.

A new steel bridge over the Willamette River was opened to the public during the year, the total cost of which was 57,500*l*. Bridge.

During the year the improvement of the Columbia and Willamette Rivers has been continued under the charge of United States engineer Major J. C. Post. Government works.

Congress appropriated sufficient money to finish the great jetty at the mouth of the Columbia River, making 405,130*l*. in all since its inception in 1894, which is only a little over one half of the original estimate. During the year 10,000 feet of the outer end has been raised to the completed height. Since the commencement of the work, in 1885, about 750,000 tons of rock has beeen used, and 120,000 tons more will be required to bring the entire jetty to the required height. The great middle sands have been removed by the erosive action of the waters, and this has left a straight out and in channel, with a depth of 31 feet at mean low water. The old north and south channels have been closed, and the engineers believe that the permanency of the improvement is now assured, and that the depth of water in the channel at the entrance will never be less than it now is. Mouth of Columbia jetty.

The operations last year were confined to dredging on the various bars between Portland and Astoria. The usual summer floods, on June 7, reached the unprecedented height of 33·11 feet above low water (the highest previous record being 28·4 feet), causing an unusual deposit of silt, yet the channels have been kept fairly well open, causing little trouble to shipping. The original estimate in 1891 for a 25-feet channel from Portland to Astoria was 154,493*l*., of which has been expended 82,267*l*. by the port of Portland, and 30,000*l*. by the United States Government. The engineers are now working on an unexpended appropriation of 10,000*l*., made on August 17, and the total amount appropriated by the United States Government, since 1866, when the first work was done on the rivers, is 216,073*l*. River bars.

The following is extracted from the report of Captain T. W. Symons, United States Engineer-in-charge, for the fiscal year ended June 30:— Minor harbours.

"The north jetty tramway is 9,520 feet long, and its enrockment well advanced. The channel has greatly improved, there being now a least depth of 20 feet at mean low water. The amount expended during the year ending June 30, 1894, was 23,207*l*. Coos Bay.

"The amount expended prior to June 30, 1892, was 120,170*l*. As a result, the condition of the entrance was very satisfactory, there being a minimum depth over the bar of 14 feet at low water. Yaquina Bay.

UNITED STATES.

Trouble was threatened, however, by the formation of a bar inside the entrance. The amount expended during the year ended June 30, 1894, was 5,079*l*. The results are practically the same as before. The inner bar disappeared during 1893, but has reformed. It has not yet become an actual obstruction, but threatens to be one."

Siuslaw, Willapa, &c.

Work was also done under Captain Symons' superintendence at Siuslaw, Willapa, Tillamook, and other bays and rivers, and also on the upper reaches of the Columbia and Snake rivers, but these possess little interest except locally.

Cascades canal.

Lieutenant Harry Taylor was in charge of the Government canal and locks at the Cascades of the Columbia River, and a large amount of masonry and concrete was laid, besides excavation. The extraordinary high water of last year may cause a change in the plan, so as to give the top of the work additional height. The river attained a height of 80 feet above low water mark below the cascades and 50 feet above the rapids.

Agriculture.

Farming unprofitable.

Although the year 1893 was considered the most unprofitable one farmers had ever experienced, last year was even more so. The crops generally were bountiful, and harvested in good condition, but prices were in many cases below the cost of production.

Wheat. Cost of production.

Statistics and prices are given under another head in this report, but it may be of interest to give the cost of raising wheat in Eastern Oregon or Washington. Mr. Samuel Turner, of Weston, Umatilla County, makes the following calculations, based on a yield of 20 bushels to the acre on a tract of 300 acres:—

	Per Acre. Currency. Dol. c.	Per Acre. Sterling. £ s. d.
Ploughing once	1 50	0 6 0
Harrowing twice	0 40	0 1 7·20
Seed, vitrioled	0 42	0 1 8·16
Seeding with drill	0 25	0 1 0
Heading	1 63	0 6 6·24
Threshing at 6½ c. per bushel per acre of 20 bushels	1 30	0 5 2·40
Sacks, per 20 bushels	0 75	0 3 0
Hauling 1½ miles to station	0 30	0 1 2·40
Total	6 55	1 6 2·40
Value, 20 bushels at 30 c.	6 0	1 5 0
Loss, 1894	0 55	0 1 2·40

Mr. Walter F. Burrell, owner of a large tract in Whitman County, Washington, makes the following exhaustive statement of the cost of raising and marketing a 30-bushel crop of wheat:—

	Per Acre.	
	Currency.	Sterling.
	Dol. c.	£ s. d.
Ploughing	1 25	0 5 0
Harrowing twice	0 40	0 1 7·20
Seed, including fanning and vitriolating	0 50	0 2 0
Drilling, 40 c.; poisoning squirrels, 12 c.	0 52	0 2 0·96
Heading and stacking	1 50	0 6 0
Threshing at 6 c. per bushel	1 80	0 7 2·40
Sacks and twine	1 12	0 4 5·76
Hauling sacks, 2 c.; hauling wheat, 60 c.	0 62	0 2 5·76
Warehouse forwarding charges 25 c. per ton	0 225	0 0 10·80
Taxes and sundries	0 50	0 2 0
Repairs to fencing	0 10	0 0 4·80
Total	8 535	1 14 1·68

Mr. Burrell also adds the following:—

	Cents.		
Fire insurance on crop in field	6		
Travelling expenses	6		
Superintendence	50		
Harrowing after seeding	20		
Rolling after grain is up	20		
		1 02	0 4 0·96
Making the total disbursements		9 555	1 18 2·64
Value, 30 bushels at 25 c., f.o.b. train		7 50	1 10 0
Loss per acre		2 055	0 8 2·64

The crop harvested in 1894 was the heaviest ever produced, being estimated at 14,000,000 bushels. Two-thirds of the wheat is now raised in Eastern Oregon. Although the Willamette Valley wheat is not so strong as Eastern Oregon or Walla Walla, it commands higher prices abroad.

Oats are a staple crop of this State, averaging 40 to 75 bushels per acre. Last year's harvest was a large one, and shipments coastwise were 135,709 centals, the average value of choice being only 3s. 9d. (95 c.) per cental. *Oats.*

Barley was also a larger crop than usual, but unremunerative to the grower. Values and shipments are given elsewhere in this report. *Barley.*

Flaxseed is an excellent crop to rotate with wheat, and was largely grown last year. Shipments were 3,946,250 centals, and the average price here was 9s. (2 dol. 25 c.) per cental, about the only agricultural product which was higher than last year. *Flaxseed.*

There was a large crop of potatoes, but the prices averaged only 2s. 1¼d. (52½ c.) per cental, about 50 per cent. less than in 1893. *Potatoes.*

Most growers of hops refused to sell early, and as prices dropped to a most unremunerative basis, growers lost money. The crop was the largest ever gathered. *Hops.*

The last 7 or 8 years have wrought great changes in the *Orchards and fruits.*

horticulture of this State, and Oregon fruits are now well known for their excellent quality. At the Columbian Exposition Oregon fruits gained 17 medals, more than any other State in the Union. The trees bear very young and the fruits bear shipment well, and are largely shipped both green and dried to the Middle, Western, and even Eastern States. Reliable statistics give 4,000 acres of prune orchards 6 years old and over, 3,100 acres 5 years old, and 3,000 acres 4 years old within the borders of the State. It is estimated that 6-year old orchards yield 2,000 lbs. of cured prunes per acre, 5-year old 1,000 lbs., and 4-year old 300 lbs. per acre.

Prunes.

Cost of growing.

Growers' estimates of cost of prune cultivation vary considerably, and I select from several before me, one which includes cost of trees, 108 to the acre, planting, ploughing, harrowing, hoeing, interest on land and expenses, which gives the following result:—

	Amount.	
	Currency.	Sterling.
	Dol. c.	£ s. d.
First year	20 0	4 0 0
Second year	14 0	2 16 0
Third year	16 30	3 5 2·40
Fourth year	18 40	3 13 7·20
Fifth year	20 27	4 1 0·96
Total	88 97	17 15 10·56

Another grower says that after trees are 4 years old they will leave a profit to the grower, and that his prunes 12 years old averaged 280 lbs. to the tree. Peach plums same age 326 lbs., apples same age 490 lbs., and in his experience apples paid better than prunes. There is no doubt that there was more money in growing the larger fruits last year than in other branches of agriculture.

Small fruits. Small fruits did not do so well, as being more perishable the consumption must naturally be more local.

Cattle and Sheep.

The assessors' returns show a considerable diminution in numbers of domestic animals within the State, and stock raisers have suffered very much during the past 2 years, particularly horse breeders and sheep owners.

Horses. There is hardly any demand for horses, and owners have no outlet for their stock.

Cattle. Prices. Cattle sold much lower than last year, the average price paid here for steers being 5*l.* 12*s.* (28 dol.), equal to about 4*l.* on the range. Calves 1*l.*

SAN FRANCISCO.

Prices of wool were ruinously low, and sheep sold here at an average of 8s. 6d. (2 dol. 15 c.) per head. — Sheep.

There was more money in swine, which sold at an average of 2l. per head. — Swine.

General Remarks.

The assessed value of all property subject to taxation within the State was, in 1893, 354,498l.; and in 1894, 319,080l. Property within the city was assessed in 1893, 10,866,500l.; and in 1894, 953,785l. Real estate is usually assessed at about 40 per cent. of its market value. — Assessment.

Taxes were levied at the following rates:— — Rate of taxation.

	Per Cent.
State taxes	0·80
County taxes	0·55
City taxes	1·00
Bridge taxes	0·10
District school	0·20
Port of Portland	0·06
Total	2·71

Payable in 1895.

There are 176·89 miles of streets within the city limits, and 76·6 miles of sewers. — Streets. Sewers.

The total revenue of the city, including balances carried over from 1893, was 142,376l., and the total expenditure 121,360l., including 4,000l. of bonds redeemed, 26,555l. expended by fire department, and 20,436l. expended by police department. In addition there was collected from owners of contiguous property the expenditure of 14,111l. on street improvement, 20,403l. on sewers, and but 171l. on street extensions. — City finances.

The revenue from the water works, not included in the above figures, was 42,035l., and the expenditure of the operating department 11,034l. — Water revenue.

Interest on water bonds, 21,500l.

Neither the revenue nor expenditures of the water, bridge and port of Portland commissions are included in the above figures.

The bonded indebtedness of the city, exclusive of water bonds, is now 101,300l. 6 per cent., and 765,000l. 5 per cent. — Bonded debt.

There has been but little business transacted in real estate, and those who have been compelled to sell had to accept about 50 per cent. of the estimated value. — Real estate.

The following is a comparative table of transfers and sales of real estate in the county of Multnomah during the last 4 years:—

Year.					Amount.
					£
1894	..	..	..	..	922,127
1893	..	..	..	..	1,317,142
1892	..	..	..	..	2,297,290
1891	..	..	..	..	2,129,749

NOTE.—All values given in this report are reduced to sterling at the exchange of 5 dol. to the 1*l.*

High water of 1894.

During the months of May and June there is always a flood in the Willamette River caused by the melting snow in the region of the Upper Columbia and Snake rivers bringing down such a volume of water as to impede the outflow of the Willamette into the Columbia, thus backing up its waters. It sometimes overflows into the streets of the city, and until last year the flood of 1876 was the highest known, but in 1894 the water slowly rose until on June 7 it reached 33 feet 11 inches above low water mark, and 5 feet 7 inches higher than in 1876. In some streets the water was nearly 8 feet deep, and most of the business streets of the city became veritable canals navigated by boats, steam launches and freight barges. After reaching its maximum height the river gradually fell, and in a few weeks had retired within its banks. The damage done in some parts of the city was very considerable.

ASTORIA, OREGON.

Mr. Vice-Consul Cherry reports as follows:—

General remarks.

The prosperity of this district has been much improved during the past year, owing altogether to the larger quantity of salmon caught and canned in the town and vicinity, which I estimate to be fully 40 per cent. greater than the year before, of which I give figures under its proper head.

This has stimulated all trading except the transfer of land.

The average income of every head of a family has been estimated to be not less than 180*l.* (900 dol.) per annum. This is directly taken from raw products, lumber, and fish.

Bankers inform me that at the close of last season a larger proportion of the earnings of the fishermen was deposited than in any previous year, showing that the community is debt free.

Shipping and navigation.

There is a notable increase in the amount of shipping in the foreign trade; also that the average tonnage exceeds by over 200 tons per ship that of last year. The increase in number is partly owing to the fact that the price of grain was so low as to prohibit shipments by steamer to San Francisco to be exported from thence, resulting in several vessels coming up from San Francisco on charter.

The increase in size is caused by the permanency of the improvement on the bar by the construction of the jetty, giving confidence that the larger class of vessels can leave the river fully laden without the detention so common formerly, and again by the employment of a much better tug boat both in size and power.

Disasters to shipping.

Fortunately there are no disasters to shipping to record for the past year.

But I regret to have to report the arrival of two British vessels from Acapulco, Mexico, with Mexican coast fever, one of which, the "Marion Ballantyne," had all of her crew but two down with the fever, and losing three lives from the effects. The second vessel, the "Comliebank," had ten cases left here, and two or three in Portland.

It would seem that some effort should be made by masters in preventing the disease, by boiling the water procured in that port, or allowing no water to be drunk, except in the form of tea or coffee. As inquiries made by me confirm my opinion that those who used the water most freely had the fever in its worst form.

Pilot service.

There is no change to report; the same rate has held good for the past year, viz., 1*l.* (5 dol.) per foot draft, and 1*d.* (2 c.) per registered ton.

The pilot boat has remained out on the pilot grounds during the past shipping year.

Complaint has been made by the pilots of the poorness of their pilot boat, but she seems to come out of some very heavy weather seemingly none the worse.

Desertions of seamen.

Desertions of seamen have steadily fallen off, and I am quite sure compare most favourably with any port on the coast. The comparison for the year before is as follows:—

Year.	Number.	Number.
For 1893	56	Out of—1,642
1894	12	1,844

The following table shows the number and nationality of vessels entering and clearing during the past year:—

UNITED STATES.

Annex A.—Return of all Shipping at the Port of Astoria, Oregon, U.S.A., during the Year 1894.

Entered.

Nationality.	Sailing. Number of Vessels.	Sailing. Tons.	Steam. Number of Vessels.	Steam. Tons.	Total. Number of Vessels.	Total. Tons.
British	75	129,678	4	1,355	79	131,033
American, coasting	54	28,902	400	331,482	454	360,384
,, foreign	5	5,144	4	1,401	9	6,545
Danish	1	1,090	...	...	1	1,090
Norwegian	3	5,233	...	...	3	5,233
Hawaiian	1	2,027	...	...	1	2,027
German	3	4,056	...	...	3	4,056
French	1	1,125	...	...	1	1,125
Total	143	177,255	408	334,238	551	511,493
,, for the year preceding	131	138,234	410	332,346	541	470,580

Cleared.

Nationality.	Sailing. Number of Vessels.	Sailing. Tons.	Steam. Number of Vessels.	Steam. Tons.	Total. Number of Vessels.	Total. Tons.
British	73	127,921	3	877	76	128,798
American, coasting	68	30,453	349	326,609	417	367,162
,, foreign	2	2,053	8	3,683	10	5,741
Danish	1	1,090	...	...	1	1,090
Norwegian	3	5,233	...	...	3	5,233
Hawaiian	1	2,027	...	...	1	2,027
German	3	4,056	...	...	3	4,056
French	1	1,124	...	...	1	1,124
Total	152	173,957	360	331,169	512	515,231
,, for the year preceding	392	388,734	60	46,002	452	434,736

Annex B.—Return of Principal Articles of Export from Astoria, Oregon, during the Years 1894–93.

Articles.		1894. Quantity.	1894. Value. £	1893. Quantity.	1893. Value. £
Salmon	Cases	7,800	10,033	11,725	13,880
Wheat	Bushels	58,575	5,589	64,688	10,248
Flour	Barrels	..	..	..	..
Lumber	M. feet	739	1,363	592	1,153
Sundries	..	..	340	..	956
Total	..	..	17,325	..	26,237

RETURN of Principal Articles of Import to Astoria, Oregon, during the Years 1894–93.

Articles.		1894.		1893.	
		Quantity.	Value.	Quantity.	Value.
			£		£
Tin-plates	Boxes	20,755	12,257	40,739	24,548
Salt	Lbs.	112,000	66	..	..
Coal	Tons	910	593	2,781	1,623
Sundries	..	..	3,142	..	1,460
Total	..	..	16,058	..	27,631

Trade and commerce.

The very much greater pack of salmon in this town and vicinity does not show in the returns of imports and exports of tin-plates, as the increase was not anticipated in time to effect the direct shipments of tin-plates. The greater quantity coming by steamer from San Francisco, where the importation was made, and a small quantity from Chicago, the duty for which was paid in Portland.

Of the exports the same may be said, the coasting steamers taking the greater quantity of salmon to San Francisco for shipment thence, and some wheat and flour.

A small shipment of salmon went by rail to New York, and from thence to Liverpool by steamer.

Population.

I cannot find that there has been any material increase in the permanent population of the town, though the increase in the country is steady. Quite a number of the fishermen having taken up holdings on the small tributary rivers and creeks at the lower end of the Columbia River.

The stagnation in the logging trade has, no doubt, sent a number to the mines in southern Oregon and Alaska.

Industries: salmon fishing.

Salmon fishing, owing to the stagnation in the lumber trade, is more and more prominently brought forward as the leading industry, indeed, in making an estimate of the income of the district, I find that salmon fishing brings in at least 80 per cent. of the total income.

The price of raw fish remains the same as the year before, viz., 5 c. (2½d.) per lb. for the Chinook, and 3 c. (1½d.) per lb. for fall fish.

The above prices are for Columbia River fish; this for Chinook fish would be equal to 5s. 6d. per fish. The fish were exceptionally large and fine, being quite firm to the very end of the season.

Salmon canning.

The total pack was far greater than that of the year 1893, and of a far better quality, and owing to the extraordinary spring flood of the Columbia River stopping operations in the upper river canneries, the output of the lower canneries, of which eight are in Astoria, was increased by fully 40 per cent.

Notwithstanding the fall in the price of all other food products canned salmon has held its own, the price of canned kept up with that of the year before.

Owing to larger output the profit to the canner was far greater. About 38,000 cases were shipped to Great Britain, nearly all viâ San Francisco, the United States market taking a very great proportion.

The total pack of the Columbia River was:—

	Cases.
	Number.
Spring catch	485,000
Fall catch	60,000
On the coast south of the Columbia River (about)	40,000
On the coast north of the Columbia River (about)	30,000

Of the 485,000 cases of spring catch a larger proportion than for some years has been Chinook salmon, as against steelheads and blue backs.

This amount of canned salmon uses up about 70,000 boxes of tin-plates.

Sturgeon fishing. — I can procure but little information about this industry. Parties claim that the lower Columbia River is practically fished out, but I notice that sturgeon are being caught on the middle Columbia 200 miles from the ocean.

Smelt and shad. — Both these fish are caught in large quantities for consumption in the towns on the Columbia and its tributaries. I can find no statistics of the catch or prices.

Logging. — As before, the market for sawn lumber directly affects the price, which is now very low.

Another large raft of piling and logs was made up this time in the Columbia River for towing to San Francisco. However, owing to the lateness of the completion of the raft, the weathea was against the enterprise, and shortly after the raft left the Columbia a heavy sea and gale was encountered, and in 3 days the raft was in pieces, nothing being left attached to the tug but the 60 tons of chains and wire rope, which had to be cut adrift. The contents of the raft measured 4,000,000 feet, board measure, the length being 430 feet, and drawing 22 feet of water.

Sawn lumber. — A little more was shipped from this port during the past year, California taking all of the output. Three cargoes left Gray's Harbour (to the north of this) for South America, Australia, and Tonquin.

Box making. — This particular branch of the saw-milling industry continues to expand. After supplying the requirements of the lower Columbia River canneries all the output goes to San Francisco to supply the demand of the canned fruit and meat trade, as well as the fresh fruit shipments from California. Spruce lumber is steadily appreciating in value in consequence, as the wood is practically odourless and light.

I am informed by the manager of the local works that the output of cans was most satisfactory. The cannerymen seem to rely on the Can Company more and more for their supplies, and during the latter part of the season more was taken from the Can Company than was made by the canners themselves. I do not hear of any American tin-plates being used, all plates coming from Great Britain. {Can making.}

The local tannery is still doing a good business, but as far as I can learn the total output is absorbed by California, to be returned in harness and shoes. {Leather tanning.}

Tanning works are still in operation at South Bend. {Tanning works.}

This industry, judging by the increased number of score loads of the product, is doing a profitable business. I notice some of the pulp is going up river to Portland for local consumption. California, however, still takes the bulk. {Wood-pulp.}

The town has been badly in need of a better supply of water, the present waterworks being too small, and of too low a level to provide for the town, which, in fact, has outgrown its supply. {Local enterprises: waterworks.}

The matter after much agitation was finally brought to a head by the purchase of a suitable site at an elevation of 400 feet, and the placing of about 200,000 dol. (40,000*l*.) bonds for supplying the town beyond its present needs.

This town is reputed to be the largest town in the United States without railroad communication with the rest of the country. The citizens of the town and vicinity determined that sufficient inducement should be offered to counteract the opposition of the citizens of places further up the river, subscribed 20 per cent. of the real estate of the town and vicinity as a bonus to the builders of a railway to a trans-continental connection. This subsidy is now in the hands of energetic railroad men, who will doubtless be able to do something. {Railway communication.}

The work on the jetty at the mouth of the Columbia River is nearing completion. This year will finish the work. So far it has done an immense and increasing amount of good to the entrance of the river, giving it a deep and perfectly straight channel for over 6 miles from the ocean with a uniform and wide channel. The old bar is entirely washed away, the water now being nearly 40 feet deep at high water on the shoalest place. {Government works.}

A new first order light is to be erected 2 miles to the north-west of Cape Disappointment light, which will give a larger arc of visibility over 180 degrees, all the sea horizon, as against 140 degrees at Cape Disappointment. It will be of great aid to vessels coming down from the north. {Lighthouse}

The following table shows the value of all imports and exports of this port during the past year:—

(1984)

UNITED STATES.

Annex C.—TABLE showing Total Value of all Articles Exported from and Imported to the Port of Astoria, Oregon, from and to Foreign Countries during the Years 1894–93.

Country.	Exports. 1894.	Exports. 1893.	Imports. 1894.	Imports. 1893.
	£	£	£	£
Great Britain	15,713	23,052	12,272	24,584
British Colonies	21	136	591	1,623
Other countries	1,565	3,050	3,109	1,460
Total	17,299	26,238	15,972	27,667

Health. The health of the district has been excellent; not a single case of any serious disease has shown itself.

TACOMA.

Mr. Vice-Consul Alexander reports as follows:—

General remarks relative to the State. The State of Washington is still feeling the effects of the general depression in business and uneasiness in financial affairs which retarded its growth and progress during the previous year.

Health, births, and deaths. The health of the State has been generally good, there having been no epidemic diseases during the year. The whole number of deaths reported was 1,673. Of those from contagious diseases, there were 7 of scarlet fever, 14 of influenza, 21 of diphtheria and none of small-pox or measles. The whole number of births reported was 3,723 and of marriages 1,775. These figures show a gratifying increase over those of the previous year. The Legislature of 1895 enacted laws making compulsory the reports of births and deaths; also a law giving the State Board of Health complete authority over the disposal of cases of contagious diseases in animals. Glanders was reported from Thurston, Chehalis, and Mason Counties and a member of the State Board of Health, while attending a meeting of the board in the eastern section of the county, reports that he found several cases among horses in Adams County in the neighbourhood of Ritzville. In three cases he had the animals destroyed, and it was his opinion that a good many horses in this section were afflicted with the disease. As no further action was taken in the matter and no cases were reported, it is reasonable to suppose that the disease was exterminated or turned out to be something else. These reports from Eastern Washington stated that many horses, hundreds, had died and were dying of some epidemic disease. Complete investigation has pretty well satisfied this board that the disease is strictly endemic and due to a shrub or plant growing

Marriages.

Cattle disease.

in that portion of the country and which flourished especially during the dry season.

Weather and climate. The weather conditions which prevailed in the State during the year 1894 were furnished to the central office at Seattle from the monthly reports made by 8 regular and 19 voluntary observers of the weather bureau. The mean temperature for the year, as deduced from the reports of 50 stations, was 48·4 degrees, and the mean monthly precipitation 3·62 inches. During the year 1894 the total rainfall in Western Washington (average from 30 stations west of the Cascades) was 61·81 inches, which was 7·86 inches above the 5-year normal, *i.e.*, it was 15 per cent. in excess. The months during which the rainfall was in excess were January, February, March, April, June, September, October, and November. In May, July, August, and December there was a deficiency. August was the month of greatest scarcity, it being the driest August on record. December was the driest month on record of late years. The mean annual temperature in 1894 was 48·6 degrees, or 0·7 below the normal. None of the months departed notably from the normal temperature except December, the coldest on record, averaging 37·1 degrees. It was, however, an exceptionally pleasant month at its close, owing to the unusual number of clear days. The fore part of it was stormy, a low area storm, which will long be remembered for its great severity, prevailed over the coast and Puget Sound regions from the 5th to the 11th. During this storm the barometer touched the lowest point in recent years, heavy rain fell and high gales occurred, doing great damage to shipping. The warmest days of the year were July 13 and 16 when the thermometer reached 96 degrees at Olympia and Ferry respectively. The coldest day was February 21; at Chehalis and Quartermaster the thermometer went down to 9 degrees.

The average total rainfall (from 20 stations east of the Cascades) was 16·91 inches or 1·04 above the 5 year normal, equal to 7 per cent. excess. January, March, April, September, October, and November had an excess of precipitation; February, May, June, July, August, and December had a deficiency. The greatest precipitation occurred in January, the least in August. The summer was an unusually dry one. The mean annual temperature 48·1 degrees was 0·8 below the normal. In August, in which the mean temperature 71·3 degrees was slightly above the normal, the very high temperature of 112 degrees was reached at Sulphur, Franklin County, on the 23rd. The lowest temperature of the year, 17 degrees below zero, occurred at Pullman, Whitman County, on February 22.

Industries: timber. There seem to be no very satisfactory statistics available showing the results of the timber industry during the past year, and no account appears to have been kept of the cargo shipments from the State. The railway shipments to eastern points, viâ the Northern Pacific, Great Northern and Canadian Pacific Railways, amounted to 4,279 truck loads of timber and 12,295 of shingles, as compared with 5,365 truck loads of timber and 7,073 of shingles in 1893. Thus showing a decrease in the timber and a very large increase in the shingles.

Timber cargo freights from Puget Sound were about as follows:— Valparaiso, 1*l.* 17*s.* 6*d.*; Sydney, 1*l.* 12*s.* 6*d.*; Melbourne, 2*l.* 0*s.* 3*d.*; Port Pirie, 1*l.* 18*s.* 9*d.*; United Kingdom, 3*l.* 5*s.*; Shanghai, 2*l.* 10*s.*; Tientsin, 2*l.* 15*s.*; and Africa, 3*l.*

There are 234 shingle mills in operation in this State, with a daily capacity of 16,515,000 shingles. The prices during the year were exceedingly low, ranging from about 3*s.* 6*d.* to 4*s.* 6*d.* per thousand. Notwithstanding the general stagnation in trade, the shipments in shingles show an increase as compared with 1893. The shipments per the Northern Pacific Railway to November 1 being 972,440,000 against 803,740,000 during the same period in 1893 and including those shipped by other railways the increase cannot fall far short of 200,000,000. This industry has been the support of a large number of persons who otherwise would have had great difficulty in getting a livelihood.

Railways. Very little railway building has been done during the past year in this State, not more than 9 miles of new road having been constructed. Almost every road in the State is now in the hands of receivers, thus securing the most economical operation possible.

Coal. From the annual report of the State coal mine inspectors for the year 1894 it appears that 1,163,432 tons were mined. The mines in King County produced in the neighbourhood 500,000 tons, those of Pierce County 410,000 tons, and those of Kittitas County 250,000 tons. The remainder being chiefly taken from the mines in Whatcom, Skagit, Thurston, and Cowlitz Counties. Most of this coal is bituminous in character. The number of men employed in the mines during the year was 4,380, and there were 54 deaths from accidents.

Fisheries. From information kindly furnished by the State Fish Commissioner it appears that there are 10 salmon canneries in operation on the Washington side of the Columbia River and at least half of the salmon tinned on the Columbia River was caught by residents of Washington. The total number of cases of salmon packed by the several canneries amounted to 167,862 being over 100,000 cases more than in 1893. It is estimated that this amount would have been greatly increased had it not been for the floods which occurred during the months of May and June. The price received by the fishermen ranged from 1½*d.* to 2½*d.* per lb., and it is estimated that they received for salmon delivered at the canneries over 105,000*l.* Five canneries on the Columbia River have packed autumn or silver side salmon, one of which is on the Washington side of the river. It is on this side of the river that nearly all of the silver-side salmon are caught, as the conditions are here more favourable for traps and seines than on the Oregon side. The fishermen received 2*d.* per lb. for the autumn salmon. About 15,000*l.* (75,000 dol.) worth of fresh salmon was sold to the fish dealers and shippers and it is estimated that the total amount received by the fishermen of Washington for salmon during the past year reaches, in round numbers, about 165,254*l.* (826,268 dol.). These fishermen have property valued at 97,448*l.* (487,240 dol.), which includes various kinds of nets, such as pound, gill and set nets and seines, besides boats and fishing wheels. The catch of sturgeon on the Columbia River was very small, owing to the indiscriminate slaughter of the young and parent fish, amounting to about 650,000 lbs., for which the fishermen were paid 1½*d.* per lb. 25,000 lbs. of caviare were made, for which 5*d.* per lb. was paid, making a total of 4,400*l.* (22,000 dol.) for sturgeon and caviare. Shad, Columbia River smelt, carp, catfish, and salmon trout were also taken in in considerable quantities, amounting probably in the aggregate to 1,500*l.* The Gray's Harbour district furnished 33,457 cases of tinned salmon, valued at about 4,000*l.* (20,000 dol.).

In the Puget Sound district one new cannery has been constructed and operated, and the Alaska Packers' Association has purchased the Point Roberts and Semialmoo canneries. The floods of May and June, and later the railway strikes interfered considerably with the shipment of fresh salmon to the east. There is one firm in this district engaged in drying and packing codfish, the fish comparing very favourably with the codfish of the Atlantic coast. One schooner load of fresh halibut was sent to San Francisco as an experiment, and no difficulty was found in disposing of the cargo at a fair price.

The following table gives the amount of fresh fish caught in the Puget Sound district during the past year :—

Species.	Quantity.	Average Price. From—	Average Price. To—	Value.
	Lbs.	s. d.	s. d.	£
Salmon, 860,000 caught	..	0 4	1 3*	15,600
Halibut..	1,500,000	..	0 0½†	9,000
Smelt	500,000	..	0 1	2,000
Cod	120,000	..	0 1	570
Herring..	750,000	..	0 0¾	2,340
Other fish	830,000	..	..	2,300
Total	..	..	..	31,810

* Each.
† Per lb.
NOTE.—This does not include the salmon or codfish tinned or cured.

The total amount of salmon tinned at the four canneries in this district was 100,300 cases, valued at 72,000*l.* (360,000 dol.). The work of canning salmon is performed almost throughout the State by Chinese.

The oyster catch in this district for this year was much less than the amount reported for the previous year, as the increased demand has caused the fishermen to place as many as possible on the market, in consequence of which most of the principal beds are now denuded and almost worthless. The acreage of the oyster beds is 1,185, producing about 335 sacks per week. The total amount of oysters taken during the year is 11,400 sacks, for which the oystermen receive 9s. (2·25 dol.) per sack. There were 15,000 sacks of clams taken, averaging 4s. per sack to the digger. The catch of oysters from the Willapa Harbour, just north of the Columbia River, was more than that of 1893. The price, however, was lower, being only 6s. (1·50 dol.) per sack. It is estimated that 40,000 sacks were sold, valued at 12,000*l.* (60,000 dol.), in addition to 200*l.* worth of clams and crabs shipped.

Attention has been given lately to the transplanting of oysters from the Eastern States, and it is believed that there is enough available ground in this harbour to plant 2,000 acres. In the latter part of October the State Fish Commissioner received a supply of oysters from the United States Fish Commissioner for this purpose. 80 barrels of six varieties of eastern oysters were planted and distributed over an area of about 5 acres, the fishermen of the district promising to see that no poaching is done, and that during the spawning season every effort shall be made to provide material for the spawn to catch on. It is hoped that this experiment may prove successful and remunerative. In some waters of this State eastern fish have been placed, and are doing nicely, and it is expected that this experiment also will prove a success.

The laws relative to fish licenses have been amended, and the total amount received for licenses issued during the year was 2,172*l.* (10,860 dol.), which have been paid into what is known as the "Fish Commissioner's Fund," now amounting to 2,566*l.* (12,830 dol.). The number of arrests made was 17 with 13 convictions, the amount paid into the Fish Commissioner's Fund being 90*l.* (450 dol.). The laws for the protection of fish and fishermen are still defective, but it is hoped that at the next session of the Legislature, during the coming year, these may be amended.

Steps are being taken by the Commissioner for the artificial propagation of salmon in the State, the question arising whether salmon could be caught near the mouth of the Columbia River, transported in floats to some fresh-water stream and kept until the spawn should ripen. The experiments made by the Commissioner showed that this result can be successfully achieved, and the State has appropriated 400*l.* (2,000 dol.) for building and maintaining salmon hatcheries.

Agriculture.

Grain, wheat.

A very wet spring prevented the farmers of this State from putting in their crops as early as could have been desired by some. March was the wettest month for many years past, some rain having fallen in both sections of the State almost every day for the first 19 days of the month. The excessive rainfall and snowfall of January presented conditions which were rather unfavourable to the agriculturist. A period of warm spring-like weather set in soon after the last rain of March 19 which lasted but a few days. The season was backward, but not so much so as the preceding one. At the end of March the land was thoroughly soaked. The heavy snowfall in the mountains insured a good supply of moisture to those counties dependent on this source for carrying the crops through the heated and dry periods. Ploughing and pruning of hops were begun in earnest in the central regions of Western Washington about the end of March. The month of April was generally cooler than usual in all parts of the State, very wet in the coast districts and south-eastern counties.

The weather conditions during this month were, on the whole, favourable to crops. There were several light and harmless frosts in both sections of the State. Crops made excellent progress during the month. Oats were well along in most counties on uplands, and fruit trees were covered with blossoms. In some favoured localities of Klickitat County wheat was nearly 2 feet above ground by the end of the month. April was one of the busiest months of the season. Farmers made up for lost time, and farm work of every description was pushed with great activity. During May the temperature was slightly cooler than usual with a deficiency of rainfall in all districts, except a portion of Clallam County where the rainfall was excessive. Much snow was melted on the mountains during May, and the result was great and disastrous freshets in some of the rivers in the north-western and north-eastern parts of the State. In some of the exposed farming districts in Western Washington crops were almost entirely destroyed by water. Good growing weather predominated, and crops were in fine condition at the end of the month, with the exception of prunes and cherries which were injured by frost in some of the western counties. June was a month of low temperatures, excessive cloudiness and frequent showers, especially in Western Washington; the rainfall in the eastern part of the State having been below the average. The grain crops did tolerably well this month. The cold rains injured the fruit crops of Western Washington, particularly apples, cherries, and plums. In other sections of the State, fruit was in good condition. About this time great damage was done to some of the grain crops in Garfield and Douglass Counties by numbers of squirrels. Spring wheat was a little late in most counties, but like autumn wheat was looking well. Haying did not begin as soon as could have been desired, owing to the frequent showers of June, but the crops were in good condition. So far there were no hot winds in Eastern Washington. July brought some very warm and dry weather, which was highly beneficial to all crops. With a few exceptions in the eastern part of the State, where rust appeared on the wheat, the wheat crops made splendid progress during July. Green aphis appeared in some of the

Eastern Washington wheat fields about this time, but the damage was not material. The month was remarkable for the absence of hot burning winds which sometimes blow in Eastern Washington during July. Fruit and garden crops suffered somewhat from lack of moisture in some localities, but not to any great extent. Hops did well wherever the vines were properly looked after. Haying operations were begun in some localities by the end of July. During August the weather was, if anything, even drier than in July, and the temperature was decidedly above the normal in all sections. All crops were greatly benefited, although in a few localities rain was needed for certain crops. During the first 2 or 3 days of the month the thermometer went up to 100 degrees in the south-eastern part of the State, and during the period from the 20th to the 23rd the temperature rose to 108 degrees in the south-eastern counties. The grain crops were beyond any harmful effects of this hot wave however, and no damage resulted. This was the hottest period of the season. The hay crop was all gathered by the end of the month and in excellent condition in all districts. The grain harvest was about half over in some of the counties in the extreme southern portion of the State by the end of August, and in other sections harvesting was well under way. Fruit looked splendid in all counties. Pear trees were heavily loaded in some portions of Kitsap County. About the end of August lice began to increase in the hopyards of Western Washington to an alarming extent, and spraying had to be kept up incessantly to fight the pests successfully. September weather was a little cooler than usual in most sections of the State, and the month was one of the wettest on record, particularly in the western half of the State. The result was that harvesting operations were delayed considerably in some counties west of the Cascades. In the eastern part of the State the grain crops were nearly all gathered by the end of the month. The rainy conditions of September were decidedly injurious to the hop interests of Western Washington, delaying picking which did not begin until about the 15th, at least hop-picking had not become general until about that time. Killing frosts were reported from places in the extreme north-eastern part of the State, which destroyed all tender vegetation. The early autumn rains had the effect of hurrying the work of cutting and threshing the grain crops. Hop-picking was delayed considerably, and was not completed in many yards until after the first week in October.

To summarise: The grain crops of the State have been up to the average in most counties. Barley and oats did better than wheat and were fair crops. The season has been a good one for fruit with the exception of apples, cherries, and plums in some localities. Small berries were remarkably abundant everywhere, the strawberry crop having been unusually large and of good quality. There never was a better hay crop raised in the State than was raised this season. It was gathered in the finest condition desirable. The absolute necessity of careful and intelligent spraying of hops has been thoroughly demonstrated this season. When picking time arrived, the hop-growers found that in every instance where the vines had been properly sprayed throughout the entire season, or soon after the first lice appeared, and in those instances only the hops were in excellent condition and fully up to the average. But this was the case in only a few yards here and there in Western Washington, for on the whole the hop crop of this part of the State was below the average, and in many yards the hops were not picked at all. The rainy weather completed the work of destruction begun by the lice and mould. In the eastern part of the State carefully sprayed hops did very well, and there was not so much damage done from mould as in some of the Western Washington yards. In conclusion it may be said that the crop-growing season of 1894 was a satisfactory one in many respects.

Dairying can be carried on very cheaply and successfully in this State. The climate is particularly favourable and the soil seems well fitted for growing grass, both wild and cultivated, also the roots most needed to produce large quantities of milk and butter. The fodder used in Eastern Washington is timothy, clover, alfalfa, and blue grass, while in Western Washington clover, timothy, and oats are chiefly given. The warm even temperature and green pastures throughout the whole year, particularly in Western Washington, make it most suitable for stock-raising and dairying, especially so for winter dairying which yields almost double profits to that of summer. This industry has been making rapid progress during the past two years. In 1891 there were 3 small creameries in the State, now there are 50 in successful operation, the produce for the past year being valued at 140,000*l*. (700,000 dol.). The supply is very inadequate to the demand, not only for home consumption but for shipment, as very large quantities of butter and condensed milk are shipped through Puget Sound ports to the Orient from Eastern States, all of which supply might be produced in the home State of Washington. These facts show that dairy produce could be made one of the chief and most lucrative industries of the State and should command the attention of agriculturists. It is expected that laws will be passed by the coming Legislature prohibiting the adulteration of foods, more particularly of dairy products. *Dairying.*

There are about 50,000 acres in this State planted with fruit trees, about equally divided on each side of the mountains. In Western Washington the trees are planted in small tracts of from 5 to 10 acres, while in Eastern Washington not so many small tracts are found, but larger farms of from 100 to 300 acres. The varieties of fruit mostly being planted at the present time are winter apples, prunes, peaches, pears, cherries, and apricots. About 10,000 acres were in bearing last year. It is estimated that 1,400,000 lbs. of dried and evaporated fruits have been put up during the season of 1894, of which over 1,000,000 were prunes. These prunes were of remarkable size, averaging 40 to the 1 lb. and were principally of the Italian variety. 45 fruit *Horticulture.*

driers are now in operation in this State. The acreage of small fruits such as gooseberries, strawberries, and currants is about 1,000 acres in the district immediately adjacent to Tacoma and Seattle markets alone. The peaches, apricots, and grapes are grown for the most part in the irrigated districts of South-eastern Washington. There are about 25 nurseries in the State covering in all over 900 acres.

Reports from the fruit sections of the State show that the yield of the different varieties has been about as follows as compared with average crops:—Apples, about three-quarters; prunes, nearly a full crop; cherries, about two-thirds; peaches, a full crop; plums, nearly a full crop; pears, about three-quarters; strawberries, about three-quarters; other small fruits and berries, nearly full crops. During early spring the intervening cold rains intermingled with days of clear sunshine caused many of the leaf lice (green aphis), also the woolly aphis, to hatch out, but they were then washed to the ground by the rains and destroyed, so that, in general, trees, plants, and hop vines were attacked by the insect pests in much smaller numbers than usual, though the woolly aphis increased considerably during the summer season. The markets for other small fruits were limited for the crop of last season, many growers not being able to dispose of their fruits at remunerative prices.

Prices were very low indeed for the early kinds of fruit. This was occasioned by over-production and the careless methods employed in sorting and packing the fruit, supplemented by the general depression in business and also the strike on the railways which, occurring during the height of the fruit season, prevented the fruit reaching markets in first class condition. Winter apples are in great demand and for first class fruit higher prices will be realised than for many other varieties. It is gratifying to note that of all rural industries in the State, horticulture, where proper attention was given, has averaged better results than any other kind of farming in the State of Washington the past season. Lessons will have to be learned that more prompt picking and neater packing must be resorted to. From the enormous quantities of fruit and vegetables going to waste each season in the State it would seem reasonable that steps should be taken towards the establishment of factories for making preserves, jams, pickles, and tinned vegetables. There is no doubt that in the hands of experienced persons, possessing the necessary capital, such factories could be made to pay a very handsome dividend. The only drawback there seems to be is the cost of jars of glass or stone, which at present are imported, should it be found necessary to use them.

Hops. The hop crop for the year 1894 is estimated at 44,500 bales, 16,500 being grown in Yakima County, 9,000 in King County, and about the same number in Pierce County. Owing to mildew, dampness, and the low price given for hops the entire crop was not gathered. The price per 1 lb. was almost 50 per cent. less than in 1893, on account of the over-production. Choice hops brought 3*d*. per 1 lb. and extra quality 4*d*. A still larger area will be planted with hops for the year 1895.

An appropriation of 160*l*. (800 dol.) was made to assist in Flax. the experimental cultivation of flax in this State. The investigations were carried on chiefly in Whatcom County, with thick seeding for the purpose of securing fine quality of fibre regardless of the yield of seed. It was found that 2¾ to 4 tons of straw per acre yields 1,375 to 2,000 lbs. of clean fibre per acre, which will dress 962 to 1,400 lbs. of "line" worth 8½*d*., and 9 to 17 bushels of seed worth about 5*s*., thus averaging from 40*l*. to 50*l*. per acre. It is understood that farmers in the Big Bend and Yakima districts, in addition to those of Whatcom County, will plant a large quantity of flax during the coming year and carry on further experiments.

The division of chemistry of the United States Department Sugar beets. of Agriculture at Washington City, has published the experiments made with sugar beets during the year 1893, from which it appears that 250 packages of best imported seed were sent to persons in this State. Accompanying each package was a pamphlet containing detailed instructions for the preparation of the land, planting the seed and cultivating the beet. Almost every person who received seed complied with the request of the Department and sent one or more beets to be analysed, to determine the amount of sugar in each and its purity. The results showed that as high grade sugar beets can be grown in Washington as in any State of the Union. This is further borne out by the experiments lately conducted by the State Agricultural College at Pullman in Eastern Washington. Seed was furnished gratis by the authorities to over 1,000 persons with specified directions for cultivation. When the beets began to mature each person was requested to send samples for analysis. In response to this request beets were received from 372 farmers in 101 different towns. The following table gives the very satisfactory results of these analyses:—

			Eastern Washington.	Western Washington.
Number of towns	Number		56	45
„ analyses	„		1,188	360
Average weight of beet	Ounces		21	24
„ per cent. of sugar	Per cent.		15·5	14·9
„ purity	„		83·8	83·8

It is intended to carry on further experiments this year (1895) with special reference to the yield per acre and the cost of production, and seed will be again distributed free to all applicants.

From information furnished by the Commissioner of Public The State's Lands it appears that the whole number of acres granted to the public lands. State was 622,000; the number of acres selected in Eastern

Washington was 279,049; the number of acres selected in Western Washington was 156,667; leaving the number of 186,283 to be selected. The value of land in Eastern Washington is estimated at 331,882*l*. (1,659,409 dol.), and the value of timber 171,089*l*. (855,444 dol.), making the total value of land and timber about 502,971*l*. (2,514,853 dol.), averaging 1*l*. 16*s*. per acre. The value of land in Western Washington is estimated at 90,857*l*. (454,284 dol.), and the value of timber at 242,878*l*. (1,214,388 dol.), making the total value of land and timber about 333,735*l*. (1,668,672 dol.), averaging 2*l*. 3*s*. per acre. The lands selected have been apportioned to the several State charitable, educational, penal and reformatory institutions.

Population and Assessment.

The population of the State for 1894 is estimated at 410,000. The following statements taken from the report of the State Board of Equalisation, show that the total number of acres of land, exclusive of town lots, is 14,067,758; the total number of acres of improved land is 2,170,729; the valuation of lands, exclusive of improvements, is 16,220,419*l*. (81,102,096 dol.)., the valuation of improvements is 1,560,349*l*. (7,801,749 dol.); of town property exclusive of improvements, 14,022,512*l*. (70,112,561 dol.); valuation of improvements, 4,933,393*l*. (24,666,966 dol.); the aggregate value of all real property, including improvements, except railway lines, is 36,736,674*l*. (183,683,372 dol.). The returns also show that there are in the State 162,933 horses, mules, and asses, valued at 728,695*l*. (3,643,474 dol.); 190,472 cattle, valued at 438,034*l*. (2,190,168 dol.); 286,487 sheep, valued at 71,621*l*. (358,107 dol.); 67,782 swine, valued at 33,898*l*. (169,491 dol.); and the aggregate of taxable personal property amounted to 5,749,428*l*. (28,747,139 dol.); for the 34 counties of the State.

The length of miles of rails laid in the State by the several railroad companies is over 2,826, valued at 2,762,934*l*. (13,814,671 dol.).

The total value of real and personal property, including railroad lines, is 45,249,036*l*. (226,245,182 dol.); and the total amount of State tax to be paid is 129,774*l*. (648,870 dol.), making the rate of taxation for general State purposes for the year 1894, 2·75 mills on the dollar.

The amount of State taxes collected from the whole State for the year ending October 31, 1894, was 118,939*l*. (594,698 dol.).

The property of the State is valued at 490,798*l*. (2,453,989 dol.) comprised in various institutions, such as a penitentiary, two hospitals for the insane, State university, agricultural college, soldier's home, schools, State capitol, &c. The approximate State debt to October 31, 1894, was 261,464*l*. (1,307,322 dol.).

The total balance on hand in the several funds of the State, according to the report of the State Treasurer for the year ending October 31, 1894, was 55,178*l*. (275,890 dol.), of which 29,469*l*. (147,348 dol.) belonging to the permanent school fund, and 1,649*l*. 8,246 dol.) to the current school fund and comprised the balance of cash in the said funds remaining undistributed to the public schools of the State. These sums are held in trust by the State, and are therefore not available for the payment of current State expenses.

From Bradstreet's report the number of failures in the State during the year 1894 was 154, against 170 in 1893; assets in 1894, 367,021*l*. (1,835,103 dol.), against 450,109*l*. (2,250,547 dol.) in 1893, and liabilities in 1894, 562,647*l*. (2,813,238 dol.), against 503,489*l*. (2,517,444 dol.) in 1893. {Business failures.}

Aids to Commerce and Navigation.

The United States Government has continued the coast survey during the past year and good progress has been made.

The changes made in the lights, buoys, &c., during this same period on the coast of Washington have been very numerous, more particularly in the bays and channels of the inland waters of Puget Sound, thus materially assisting the navigation of vessels engaged in the domestic trade. As due notices are published immediately on the making of these changes, and no effort is spared by the local officer to notify mariners of the same, it is unnecessary to make any further mention of them in this report. However, one or two changes which will affect foreign vessels more particularly are worthy of note.

The fog signal projected last year, to be placed on Marrowstone Point, in Admiralty inlet, will be put in operation this season.

The light vessel and fog signal off Umatilla Reef, south of Cape Flattery, has been authorised by Congress, and the lighthouse board engineer recommends the removal of Starr rock, in Bellingham Bay, off New Whatcom.

The Pilot chart of the North Pacific Ocean, referred to in last year's report as contemplated, provided Congress should make the necessary appropriation, has been issued from the hydrographic office each month, beginning with September, there having been previous issues of January and July. It has been received with great favour by mariners, and is being continually improved. A feature of the last issue was the indication of the best fishing localities in the North Pacific, and a table giving the position, extent, principal varieties of fish found, and the characteristics, &c., of each bank

The spirit of unrest and dissatisfaction which early in the year took shape in Ohio as the "Coxey movement," soon afterwards manifested itself here in Washington, particularly at Spokane, Seattle, and Tacoma, where "armies of the unemployed" were organised in the latter part of April and early in May, 1894, for the purpose of marching to the city of Washington, and there presenting to the Congress of the United States their complaints and requests for relief. That many entered into this "commonweal movement" with good motives, and in honest hope of, in {Coxey movement.}

(1984)

some unknown way, bettering their condition, although the scheme was wild, visionary, and impracticable is probably true. It is also as true that the movement was made an excuse by many of the idle and vicious for a jaunt across the country at the expense of the railroad companies and the communities through which they might pass, to exist in idleness, and by power of numbers levy the tribute of a subsistence upon the people around them.

The "armies" from Seattle and Tacoma, closely watched by deputy United States' marshals, united at Puyallup, about 10 miles from Tacoma, from which point, after several days' camp, and finding their efforts futile to compel the railroad company to furnish them free transportation, they broke up into squads, to make their way as best they could to Spokane, in the extreme eastern part of the State, where they expected to unite with the contingent there, and continue their journey eastward. Numbers having climbed the Cascade mountains, congregated at Ellensburg and North Yakima, at which places some slight tumults occurred, when the United States' marshal, with his force of deputies, in guarding and protecting the property of the railroad company and of private citizens, repelled the attempts of the " army " to appropriate to their own use the property of others.

Many of the mob were arrested for violation of law, and punished. Similar troubles were experienced at Spokane, until finally the stragglers from the west united with the Spokane " division," and the "army," decimated and disintegrating under the surveillance of the officers of the law, straggled out of the State and soon dwindled away and dissolved, though many of its members have since wandered back.

The movement here was similar in its aims to those of the middle States and California, and it is unnecessary to enter into any discussion of the causes which produced them. While they lasted the effect was injurious to both capital and labour, hurtful to the communities upon which these men quartered themselves, and contributed to a continuance of the period of financial depression which rested upon the land.

Railway strike. Following this came the troubles of the great railway strike, which, originating at Pullman, Illinois, widened and spread until it affected a large portion of the railways of the West, extending along the Northern Pacific Railroad into this State. This strike has been the subject of so much attention and discussion by the Press of the country that it is needless to enter into any detailed report of it. The same troubles were experienced here, only in much milder form, as were experienced in the middle West. The receivers of the Northern Pacific Railroad, under direction of the court, and with its aid, through its executive arm the United States' marshal, and later under protection by the federal troops, continued to operate the road with temporarily decreased service, which, however, they were able gradually to restore to full efficiency. In Eastern Washington the trouble was more serious than here in the western part of the State, but on both sides of the mountains outside "agitators" urged on and encouraged meddlesome idlers in their attempts to injure the property of the company, and in malicious attacks on those who entered the service of the receivers in their efforts to keep trains in motion and the road in operation. These occasional acts of violence were disapproved of by many of the strikers, but could not be prevented; a force had been exerted which having started they could not control. The baneful effects of this strike extended to all classes of people. Farm products and fruits could not be shipped, and were lost to the farmers. Shipments were delayed while on the way, scarcity of commodities increased the price thereof, and the general effects of this "tie up" reached all classes of men. The result to the strikers also was in the end disastrous, and many men who ceased work found themselves out of occupation, out of money, and compelled to search in other parts of the country for the means of procuring a reduced livelihood.

In this State there was little or no destruction of property, thanks to the efficient protection given by the officers of the law, municipal, State, and federal, although many schemes were set on foot to injure railway property and cripple its service. As the Northern Pacific was in the hands of receivers appointed by the United States court, numbers were arrested for interfering with railway property, brought before that court, and when their guilt was clear punished for contempt by various terms of imprisonment. In its results this strike, too, injuriously affected the masses of the people, and was too remote from the original cause to be justified by public opinion; it was a sympathetic strike, joined in by railway men and others, not because they themselves were unfairly treated, or sought to remedy grievances of their own, but because the workmen at Pullman were striking for higher pay, and out of encouragement, aid and sympathy for them, the strike extended to those railways upon which Pullman cars were run.

The first agricultural show in the State, for which an appropriation of 2,000*l.* (10,000 dol.) has been made by the Legislature, was held at North Yakima, in Eastern Washington. Unfortunately for any good results that might have accrued therefrom, almost the whole of this appropriation was expended in levelling and improving the grounds, the most noticeable feature of which was a race-course. The benefits derived from the exhibitions of stock, poultry, dairy products, and fruits, seemed to have been left out of consideration altogether, as horse-racing was the chief attraction. Consequently the show cannot be said to have been a great success from an agricultural point of view. Few persons outside of the immediate neighbourhood appear to have taken much interest in these exhibitions, and they were scarcely commented on in the press. It is hoped better results will be obtained at the show contemplated this coming year, and more interest taken by the people. A few shows of more or less merit have been held in other towns of this State,

State Fair.

embracing agriculture, poultry and fruits, and have been fairly successful; and when we consider that these shows were due to the efforts of local farmers, and take into consideration the difficulties to be encountered from the undeveloped state of the country, and the want of facilities for transportation, due credit must be given for the spirit of enterprise shown in this new country. Flower shows, under the auspices of the State Horticultural Society, are contemplated during the coming year.

Interstate Fair. An exhibition similar to the World's Fair of Chicago and the Mid-winter Fair of San Francisco was held in this town for 6 weeks during the autumn, in which the North-Western States and the province of British Columbia, Canada, were represented. Following so closely on the two greater exhibitions and owing to the depressed state of the country, this one did not have the success which its promoters anticipated. Special days during this period were set apart for certain towns in the district, hoping by this means to attract the people from the different places. The exhibits consisted chiefly of horticultural products and a few of the manufacturing industries, together with some exhibits from Chicago and San Francisco, chiefly made by the Italians, who hoped by this means to get rid of the remainder of their goods originally brought over to this country, in which they were not disappointed.

Tests of Washington coal. Owing to criticisms appearing in the local press during the past year on the use by the United States war ships of coal taken from the mines of British Columbia in preference to domestic coal, while cruising in these waters and patrolling the Behring Sea, the Secretary of the Navy ordered that tests should be made of Washington coal on a man-of-war designated for that purpose. Opportunity was given to all owners of coal mines throughout the State, to deliver, at their own expense, at the vessel's side, not less than 30 tons of each variety of coal which they desired to have tested. As these tests are still being made, no definite results can be arrived at as to the comparative value of the different coals. At the present time the warships get their coal supply from the Blue Cañon coal mine in Whatcom County next to British Columbia.

General outlook. The prospects for trade for the State generally, and in Tacoma and Seattle especially, for the present year are not much more encouraging than last year. The crop prospects are fairly good, there has been no loss of stock due to the winter which has been an unusual mild one, as can be seen from the above remarks on climate. Labour has been abundant, and many persons have had a difficulty in procuring employment; some, who were able, embraced the opportunity of visiting again their homes in the East and in Europe, thus relieving the number of those seeking employment, expecting to return when prospects are brighter.

Too much importance cannot be attached to the ill-advised and injurious practice of sending out young men to this country to "better themselves," as, being inexperienced in the ways of the country, what little money and clothes may have been brought with them, soon goes, and they become destitute and discouraged, and, in one or two cases, find themselves behind the prison bars without friends.

The following is a more detailed report of the trade, commerce, and other matters of interest of Tacoma and Seattle separately.

Valuable information and assistance for this report have been afforded by Lieutenant H. T. Mayo, U.S.N., at Port Townsend; Mr. G. N. Salisbury, Observer of the State Weather Bureau; Dr. G. S. Armstrong, Secretary of the State Board of Health; Mr. C. A. Tonneson, Secretary of the State Board of Horticulture; Mr. James Crawford, State Fish Commissioner; Mr. L. R. Grimes, State Auditor; Mr. W. O. Chapman, and by several other officials and gentlemen of these two towns.

General Remarks.

Tacoma, the second largest town in the State, but the chief export one, has, like all other towns, been affected by the universal stagnation of business. It is, however, encouraging to notice that during the year there has been an increase in the exports, and the imports have increased very largely. The low prices which have prevailed have mainly been the cause of the low values, as the quantity shipped was greatly in excess of the year 1893. This increase in the exports and imports may be attributed to the still further developing of the trade with China and Japan; probably the war between these two countries is the cause of the large shipment of flour, both inward and outward steamers being loaded to their fullest capacity. The wheat crop has turned out fairly well, but the price has reached a lower figure than ever before, realising to the farmer an average of 1s. 1d. (27½ c.) per bushel, and 1s. 8d. (40 c.) at the terminal point.

[Margin: General remarks. Tacoma.]

Shipping and Navigation.

The following table shows the number and nationalities of vessels which entered and cleared during the past year:—

Annex A.—RETURN of all Shipping at the Port of Tacoma during the Year 1894.

ENTERED.

Nationality.	Sailing. Number of Vessels.	Sailing. Tons.	Steam. Number of Vessels.	Steam. Tons.	Total. Number of Vessels.	Total. Tons.
British	25	50,669	24	28,561	49	79,230
American	4	6,748	6	2,585	10	9,333
Nicaraguan	1	1,256	...	...	1	1,256
Total	30	58,673	30	31,146	60	89,819
" for the year preceding	27	48,260	30	27,507	57	75,767

UNITED STATES.

CLEARED.

Nationality.	Sailing.		Steam.		Total.	
	Number of Vessels.	Tons.	Number of Vessels.	Tons.	Number of Vessels.	Tons.
British	34	69,280	24	29,423	58	98,703
American	22	20,156	13	16,361	35	36,517
Norwegian	1	2,654	...	...	1	2,654
Nicaraguan	1	1,255	...	...	1	1,255
Total	58	93,345	37	45,784	95	139,129
,, for the year preceding	52	79,415	32	32,771	84	112,186

The Annexes "A," "B," and "C" in this report have been obtained from the custom-house records at this sub-port through the courtesy of J. C. Saunders, Esq., collector of customs for this Puget Sound district, and represent distinctly the foreign business only, no domestic trade being taken account of.

Increase in entrances and clearances.

The number of British vessels entering the port was six more than in 1893, and clearances show three vessels more than in that year. It will be noticed also there is a very great increase in the registered tonnage of vessels.

Increase of imports and exports.

The harbour master reports that during the year 1894, 359 vessels with a total of 514,286 registered tons, entered the sub-port of Tacoma. The inward cargo tonnage was 73,735 and the outward 611,062. This does not include the local vessels which ply up and down Puget Sound.

Trade and Commerce.

The following tables show the exports and imports for the past 2 years:—

Annex B.—RETURN of Principal Articles of Export from Tacoma during the Years 1894-93.

Articles.		1894.		1893.	
		Quantity.	Value.	Quantity.	Value.
			£		£
Wheat	Bushels	4,083,045	390,457	3,481,629	448,308
Flour	Barrels	285,496	139,466	163,235	104,402
Fish, tinned	...	...	52,950	...	39,648
Timber	Feet	15,713,000	27,974	11,500,000	25,268
Other articles	...	...	66,793	...	14,350
Total	...	...	667,640	...	631,976

RETURN of Principal Articles of Import to Tacoma during the Years 1894–93.

Articles.		1894.		1893.	
		Quantity.	Value.	Quantity.	Value.
			£		£
Free—					
Tea	Lbs.	509,818	11,030	57,484	1,232
Jute	,,	1,484,000	9,151	...	...
Rice	,,	90,000	720	...	...
Sugar	Barrels	112,000	584	3,012	93
Household effects	...	...	1,143	...	83
Ore	...	...	1,538	...	...
Other articles	...	...	8,568	...	757
Total	...	...	32,734	...	2,165
Dutiable—					
Sugar	Lbs.	6,309,000	41,345	728,000	5,504
Rice	,,	602,000	2,092	170,550	399
Silk	...	...	35,422	...	...
Cement	Lbs.	10,557,000	5,401	...	2,159
Coal	Tons	1,140	653	...	...
Hemp, flax	,,	33	379	294	294
Other articles	...	...	12,838	...	992
Total	...	...	98,130	...	9,348
,, free and dutiable	...	...	130,864	...	11,513

NOTE.—Exchange has been figured at 5 dol. to the 1*l*.

Among the "other articles" in the export table are included chiefly the articles to Chinese and Japanese ports, consisting of condensed milk, tinned meats, and fruits, butterine, beer, ginseng, oil, machinery, and cotton.

The bulk of the merchandise landed here from oriental ports comes through "in bond" for immediate shipment to eastern points, this port receiving no credit for such shipments, and consequently no estimate can be made of it, as the duty on such merchandise is paid at the port of destination.

The exports show an increase of 45,664*l*. as compared with 1893, while the imports show a large increase of 119,351*l*. The exports of wheat and flour both show a considerable increase in quantity as compared with 1893, there being 602,416 bushels of wheat and 122,261 barrels of flour more than in that year, but the low prices have had a very serious effect on the valuation of the wheat, which shows 57,851*l*. less than in the previous year. With the exception of two cargoes going to the United Kingdom and a small shipment to Canada, all the flour was carried by steamship to China and Japan. *[Increase of exports and imports.]*

"The west coast trade," according to its statement, shows that during the year 1894 there were 5,843,361 bushels of wheat shipped of the approximate value of 566,609*l*. (2,833,045 dol.), of which 1,648,863 bushels, of the approximate value 166,036*l*. (830,177 dol.), went to domestic ports; there were 294,365 barrels of flour, valued approximately at 147,175*l*. (735,873 dol.); the amount of timber shipped was over 57,000,000 feet, estimated value 118,534*l*. (592,668 dol.); the coal shipments amounted to 286,561 tons, with an estimated value of 188,170*l*. (940,853 dol.);

(1984)

the value of tinned salmon was 52,950*l*. (264,751 dol.). Large quantities of local merchandise passed over the wharves of which no account is taken.

Trade with China and Japan.

The line of steamers running between Tacoma, Japan, and Hong-Kong, and operated by the Northern Pacific Steamship Company, has greatly added to the commerce of the port of Tacoma. The steamers "Victoria," "Tacoma," and "Sikh" have, during the past year, performed a monthly service between this port and the Orient, and the indications point to one or more additional steamers being placed upon the line in the early part of the coming year 1895.

The prompt service of this line in the delivery of goods has made it popular with shippers and receivers of freights, which has resulted in an increase of business. The inward cargoes have been of like character as those of previous years, being mainly tea, silk, sugar, rice, matting, and curios, the bulk of which is destined for eastern cities. The outward cargoes, however, have changed somewhat from those reported for 1893, in that during the past year, besides a large amount of flour having gone to Hong-Kong, this trade with Japan has largely increased, and owing probably to the war between Japan and China, large quantities of tinned meats and condensed milk have been carried to Yokohama and Kobe. There have also been taken to Japan by these steamers extensive shipments of raw cotton, lubricating oils, electric and other machinery, besides which there have been several shipments of wheat, and it is most likely that the export of this cereal will amount to considerable proportions in the future, as the Japanese wheat is so much inferior to that grown in the Pacific north-west, and it will be used by them in mixing, for the manufacture of flour for making bread and biscuits. Owing to the regular and efficient mail service performed by the Northern Pacific Steamship Company, the postal authorities have complimented the corporation, and have used it largely in forwarding their mails viâ this port. Arrangements have been made to add another steamship in January, making four in all. With this addition it is expected that mails will be despatched to the Orient every 18 days. This steamship company is the ocean-carrier for the Northern Pacific Railroad Company, working in conjunction with it, Tacoma being the terminal point. Merchandise is at once transferred from the steamships into the trains, which are immediately despatched to their destination. As the business has increased so rapidly during the last year, it is reasonable to believe that this railway company must have received a large proportion of trade, which it justly deserves, as being the first railway in this State, and the opening up and development of the country has in a great measure been due to its efforts. Inducements have been offered to intending settlers by the sale of its lands and other privileges have been granted. During the past year there seems to have been a general reduction, more or less, in the freight rates of all commodities eastward and westward, although still further reductions on some articles are hoped for.

SAN FRANCISCO.

The company has kept its line during this period in first-class operation, when we take into account the difficulties it has had to contend with, such as snow storms in the mountains, floods in the valleys, land-slips, and the general strike.

Timber. The timber trade is represented by 14 saw and shingle mills, which were in operation during the year 1894. The output of these mills was 84,615,000 feet of timber, 16,759,000 feet of lath, and 136,514,000 shingles. Ninety-five cargoes to various points, foreign and domestic, carried away of this amount 55,159,000 feet of timber, and 10,560,000 feet of lath, the estimated value being 106,978*l.* (534,888 dol.). There has been considerable decrease in the rail shipments as compared with the previous year.

Dry dock. The Puget Sound Dry Dock Company, with their floating dock at Quartermaster Harbour, have had 41 vessels, aggregating 28,256 tons, in dock during the year, being 26 steamships, with 10,852 tons gross register, and 15 sailing vessels, with 17,404 tons net register. A fuller account of this dock has been published in the report for last year.

Tacoma smelter. The Tacoma Smelting and Refining Company produced during the past year 34,800 bars of bullion, weighing 3,612,805 lbs.; of this, 14,209 ozs. were gold, 280,204 ozs. were silver, 3,592,438 lbs. were lead; the total value being about 116,316*l.* (581,583 dol.). The average silver quotation for the year was 2*s.* 6*d.* (62⅓ c.). The effect of the continual decrease in the price of silver, and the consequent impetus given to gold mining, is shown by comparison of the ratio of gold smelted to that of silver during the past few years:—

Year.	Gold.	Silver.
	Ounce.	Ounces.
1891	1	63
1892	1	39
1893	1	27
1894	1	20

The ore purchased during the past year by this company was from—

From—	Gross Weight.	Gold.	Silver.	Lead.	Copper.
	Lbs.	Ozs.	Ozs.	Ozs.	Lbs.
Alaska	407,128	649·72	6,478·84	32,811	...
California	22,955	13·57	524·33	...	...
Idaho	9,946,419	903·73	135,431·87	5,003,557	...
Montana	13,685,065	6,222·86	239,552·10	1,380,122	...
Oregon	526,616	1,193·32	2,452·90	2,597	...
Washington	123,714	33·36	1,721·63	12,467	...
British colonies	3,734,262	2,894·19	18,944·33	116,030	71,538
Total	28,446,159	11,910·75	405,106·00	6,547,584	71,538

The following table shows the value of all exports and imports:—

UNITED STATES.

Annex C.—TABLE showing Total Value of all Articles Exported from and Imported to Tacoma to and from Foreign Countries during the Years 1894–93.

Country.	Exports. 1894.	Exports. 1893.	Imports. 1894.	Imports. 1893.
	£	£	£	£
Great Britain	375,439	430,002	5,657	2,500
Hong-Kong	105,611	..	..	..
Japan	74,508	..	14,468	..
Belgium	62,054	9,000	..	..
Germany	16,600	..	..	..
Australia	11,642	5,950	..	..
France	10,483	66,190	..	..
Mexico	7,955	12,859	..	..
Africa	3,901	..	..	..
China	2,629	..	99,119	..
Holland	2,500	..	..	..
Canada	2,257	1,619	7,262	3,095
India	..	..	3,114	..
Hawaiian Islands	..	..	733	..
Other countries	2,061	106,356	511	5,918
Total	677,640	631,976	130,864	11,513

NOTE.—The domestic trade and goods for immediate transportation are not included in this table.

Great Britain is credited with the value of the wheat cargoes contained in the large number of vessels which clear for Queenstown or Falmouth for orders; many of them, however, receive orders at these ports of call to proceed to continental ports to discharge, so the actual value of the exports to Great Britain will probably be very largely reduced. Next to Great Britain in the value of wheat exports is Belgium. The largest export value of timber was made to Australia, and the largest amount of general cargo, both in tonnage and value, to Hong-Kong.

Population and Industries.

Population. Tacoma has an estimated population of 45,000, and at the last registration there were 7,997 names recorded having legal votes, being a decrease from the previous year.

Births. There were 588 births reported, 306 being males, and 282 females. These returns are still very incomplete.

Death rate. The total number of deaths, including 24 premature births, occurring during the past year was 325: 216 males, 109 females. The death rate is very low, being about 6·1 per 1,000.

Diseases. The diseases which caused the greatest number of deaths were:—Consumption, 33; heart disease, 31; pneumonia, 18; and cholera infantum, 21. There were no cases of small-pox or cholera during the past year, and only three of scarlet fever, and one of typhoid fever, which proved fatal.

SAN FRANCISCO.

The last year has been anything but a profitable one from a business point of view. It has been deemed advisable to place many of the large firms doing business in this town in the hands of receivers, and others have consolidated or gone out of business. The close of the year marked a very slight revival of trade, but scarcely worth mentioning, and the prospects for the coming year, from a conservative point, seem very little better. *Industries.*

The policy pursued by the Board of Public Works during the past year has been one of strict economy, in fact, this policy has been pursued in almost every department of the town council, and only that requiring immediate attention has been undertaken, such as repairing streets, sewers, &c. A new bridge to connect a portion of land to be sold by the Federal Government for the benefit of the Puyallup Indians with the town proper, for which the contract had been previously given, marks one of the exceptions. This bridge is however not yet completed. *Public works.*

The total school population from 5 to 21 years of age, for the school year ending June, 1894, was, males, 3,812; females, 3,962; total, 7,774. The enrollment was 5,174, the average membership 4,105, and the average daily attendance 3,971, making the percentage of attendance 96·73. The percentage of punctuality was 99·97. There were 115 teachers and 3 supervisors employed during this period. *Education. Public schools.*

The district now owns 15 school buildings and sites. The cost of these buildings has been 83,560*l.* (417,800 dol.), and of the sites 13,081*l.* (65,405 dol.), making a total cost of 96,641*l.* (483,205 dol.). The present value of this property, by the increased value of the ground, is about 142,509*l.* (712,544 dol.), and of apparatus, furniture, and books 7,147*l.* (35,936 dol.). With this provision for school accommodations it will probably not be necessary to erect any new buildings for some years to come.

The total receipts for the year ending June, 1894, were 40,582*l.* (202,912 dol.), of which amount 26,762*l.* (133,809 dol.) were from taxes, 12,569*l.* (62,849 dol.) from sale of bonds, 1,231*l.* (6,153 dol.) proportion of State funds apportioned by the county superintendent, and 20*l.* (100 dol.) were from other sources. The total disbursements for the year were 42,749*l.* (213,743 dol.), of which 13,163*l.* (65,815 dol.) was expended on permanent property, 19,852*l.* (99,259 dol.) on salaries, 4,591*l.* interest, and 5,143*l.* contingent expenses.

Manual training was introduced into the schools in connection with the High School nearly 2 years ago. In this department instruction is given in industrial drawing and the use of tools.

The past year shows no material decrease in revenue. The domestic and local business remained about the same as the year previous. The Registry Department showed an increase in business, the aggregate amounting to 35,924 pieces handled during the year. The Money Order Department makes a very good record of business transacted, both as to increase in number of orders issued and amount involved, being far in excess of any previous year, and is as follows:— *Post office.*

UNITED STATES.

ISSUED.

Description.	Quantity.	Amount. Currency.	Amount. Sterling.
	Number.	Dollars.	£
Domestic	21,069	171,317	34,263
Postal notes	1,780	3,105	621
International	2,015	33,929	6,786
Total	24,864	208,351	41,670
Fees on same	..	1,840	368
Total amount received..	..	210,191	42,038

PAID.

Description.	Quantity.	Amount. Currency.	Amount. Sterling.
	Number.	Dollars.	£
Domestic	16,929	197,788	39,558
Postal notes	1,370	2,451	490
International	1,258	24,691	4,938
Total	19,557	224,930	44,986
Amount paid in excess of amount received	..	..	2,948

NOTE.—Postal notes were discontinued June 30, 1894.

The most important feature of the office is the rapid increase of foreign exchange with Japan, China, and the Orient. Mails continue to be sent and received by the Northern Pacific Steamship line of steamships, and orders have recently been issued by the Post Office Department at Washington, D.C., that all pouches from the Middle and Atlantic States labelled "Trans-Pacific, Foreign" will be forwarded by the steamship first sailing, whether from San Francisco or Tacoma. Tacoma has the advantage of being one day nearer Yokohama than San Francisco, and the same distance from New York or Chicago. Yokohama mails can be despatched viâ Tacoma and New York, and arrive in London 12 to 15 days in advance of those sent viâ the Suez Canal. On January 12, 1895, a steamship was scheduled to sail from Yokohama to London, and carry the British mails. She was to arrive in London on February 23. On January 13 the steamship "Sikh" of the Northern Pacific Steamship Company's line left Yokohama with 9 sacks of closed mail for Great Britain. The mail arrived in Tacoma on January 27, at 7 A.M.; New York on February 2, at 9.30 A.M., and was despatched by the steamship "Etruria," sailing on the 2nd, and arrived in Liverpool on the 8th, 15 days in advance of mail that left Yokohama one day in advance—a saving of 16 days in transit. This steamship line is not subsidised, and the vessels being of British register receive about one-fourth "sea-postage" on letters and post-cards, and one-half "sea-postage" on other articles. The following is a statement of weight in grammes of mail during the last year:—

Destination.	Letters.	Prints.
	Grammes.	Grammes.
Japan, Corea and Siberia	409,005	3,449,713
Shanghai and North China	69,403	1,339,039
Hong-Kong, East Indies, Straits Settlements, &c.	88,142	888,281
Total	566,550	5,677,033

Financial condition. There is a total of 14 banks in the town, 4 National, 4 State, 4 Savings, and 2 branches of foreign banks. On account of the still unsettled state of business deposits have decreased still further during the past year, and the bank clearances, according to Bradstreet's, during this time have been 5,806,420*l.* (29,032,103 dol.), as against 7,124,492*l.* in 1893, a decrease of about 16·4 per cent.

The valuation of lands in Pierce County, according to the county assessment rolls for 1894, was 1,047,973*l.* (5,239,863 dol.); of improvements on lands, 180,441*l.* (902,205 dol.), and the aggregate valuation of all real property, including improvements, except railroad track, was 5,711,142*l.* (28,555,712 dol.). The State tax levied for general State purposes in Pierce County was 22,098*l.* (110,489 dol.). The tax levy within the town for 1894 was 13·5 mills on the dollar, and outside the town limits 17·2 mills; there was also a special school tax of 5·9 mills. The assessed valuation of the town property for 1894, according to official statement, is 5,290,562*l.* (26,452,812 dol.), as compared with 8,310,668*l.* (41,554,440 dol.) for 1893. The tax levy for 1894, now in course of collection, is 13·5 mills, against 10 mills on the dollar for 1893. This levy includes 4·5 mills to pay interest on the city's bonded indebtedness. This has not been done before. The assessment roll for 1895 is 71,422*l.* (357,113 dol.). The indebtedness of the city at the present date is about 778,494*l.* (3,892,469 dol.), and the estimated credits 273,835*l.* (1,369,175 dol.). The receipts from January to December, 1894, inclusive, from tax levy, liquor and other licenses, pound fees, police court and harbour dues, &c., amount to 53,178*l.* (265,389 dol.). The warrants issued on the general expense and salary funds in payment of all expenses, general and extraordinary, during this period amounted to 51,118*l.* (255,593 dol.).

SEATTLE.

General Remarks.

General remarks.

Seattle, the most important town in the State of Washington, is situated in King County, on the east side of Puget Sound. As descriptions of this town have been given in previous reports it is not necessary to reiterate them again in this report. This town has maintained a steady business growth, although slight, during the past year, and some improvement is expected as the coming year advances.

Shipping and Navigation.

The following table shows the number and nationalities of vessels which entered and cleared during the past year:—

Annex A.—RETURN of all Shipping at the Port of Seattle during the Year 1894.

ENTERED.

Nationality.	Sailing. Number of Vessels.	Sailing. Tons.	Steam. Number of Vessels.	Steam. Tons.	Total. Number of Vessels.	Total. Tons.
British	8	9,589	2	956	10	10,545
American	18	3,883	89	104,300	107	108,183
Total	26	13,472	91	105,256	117	118,728
,, for the year preceding	31	20,825	100	123,600	131	144,425

CLEARED.

Nationality.	Sailing. Number of Vessels.	Sailing. Tons.	Steam. Number of Vessels.	Steam. Tons.	Total. Number of Vessels.	Total. Tons.
British	3	4,761	2	956	5	5,717
American	34	18,636	85	33,028	119	51,664
Total	37	23,397	87	33,984	124	57,381
,, for the year preceding	28	15,359	55	22,566	83	37,925

NOTE.—The entrances and clearances of American vessels do not include the domestic trade.

The annexes "A," "B," and "C" in this report have been obtained from the custom-house records at this sub-port through the courtesy of J. C. Saunders, Esq., collector of customs for this Puget Sound district, and represent the foreign business only no domestic trade being taken account of.

SAN FRANCISCO.

The number of vessels entering this port is less than in 1893, while the clearances show an increase, chiefly in American vessels.

Improvements in harbour facilities during the past year have been undertaken, such as the extension of wharves, docks, &c., and other improvements are contemplated.

Trade and Commerce.

The following tables show the exports and imports for the past 2 years:—

Annex B.—RETURN of Principal Articles of Export from Seattle during the Years 1894–93.

Articles.		1894. Quantity.	1894. Value.	1893. Quantity.	1893. Value.
			£		£
Timber	Feet	12,763,600	22,900	5,280,000	9,000
Wheat	Bushels	178,330	19,000	272,300	32,000
Other articles	..	..	1,700	..	5,327
Total	..	..	43,600	..	46,327

RETURN of Principal Articles of Import to Seattle during the Years 1894–93.

Articles.		1894. Quantity.	1894. Value.	1893. Quantity.	1893. Value.
			£		£
FREE.					
Tea	Lbs.	17,920	480	2,741	133
Other articles	..	..	725	..	1,740
Total	..	..	1,205	..	1,873
DUTIABLE.					
Sugar	Lbs.	2,118,000	14,974	4,156,000	15,000
Rice	,,	1,378,400	3,956	667,000	1,800
Cement	,,	..	1,843	3,440,000	2,050
Wines, liquors	..	..	1,300	..	..
Coal	Tons	686	492	..	..
Other articles	..	..	2,301	..	10,000
Total	..	..	24,866	..	28,850
Total free and dutiable	..	..	26,071	..	30,723

UNITED STATES.

Decrease of exports and imports.

No account in these tables is taken of the goods and merchandise shipped through in bond for immediate transportation.

The exports show a falling off of 2,637*l.* as compared with 1893, and the imports a decrease of 4,652*l.*

Wheat.

The exports of wheat show a large decrease in both quantity and value as compared with 1893.

Timber.

The exports of timber have more than doubled, and exceeded those of 1893 in value by 13,900*l.*

Fish.

Large quantities of fish, salmon and halibut chiefly, were shipped from this town to eastern markets by rail, of which no estimate can be obtained.

The following table shows the value of all exports and imports :—

Annex C.—TABLE showing Total Value of all Articles Exported from and Imported to Seattle from and to Foreign Countries during the Years 1894–93.

Country.	Exports. 1894.	Exports. 1893.	Imports. 1894.	Imports. 1893.
	£	£	£	£
Great Britain	22,130	32,000	2,359	7,600
Canada	..	5,327	2,027	2,523
Japan	..	1,903	1,903	..
Hong-Kong	..	..	1,198	..
Viâ Victoria, B.C.	..	..	18,273	..
Australia	8,333	4,000	..	..
China	4,633	..	..	..
Chile	2,594	..	..	..
Africa (Cape Colony)	1,689	1,000	..	..
New Caledonia	1,412	..	..	..
Sandwich Islands	1,067	2,000	..	..
Other countries	1,712	2,000	311	20,600
Total	43,600	46,327	26,071	30,723

In comparing the past year 1894 with 1893 it will be seen that the bulk of the export trade still goes to Great Britain, although there is a decrease of about 10,000*l.* The exports to Australia have more than doubled; and there has been a slight increase in the trade with Cape Colony and Chile. There has been a general falling-off in the imports of every commodity. The large amount of goods coming in viâ Victoria, British Columbia, consists of merchandise and other articles transported over the Canadian Pacific Railway and their steamers from countries in Europe and Asia. It is impossible to get any accurate figures of the domestic trade of this port as no record is obtainable. Seattle's trade covers a very large amount of country. The business houses are able to compete with San Francisco and

Portland where conditions are equal, and their comparative nearness to Alaska, whose trade with Seattle has been growing steadily for some time, gives them an advantage in time and cost of transportation. Two steamship lines make regular semi-monthly trips between this town and Alaskan ports. The trade with all of the Puget Sound region to the north of Seattle is entirely in the hands of Seattle, as well as the chief part of the remainder of the Sound trade, no less than 33 steamers plying regularly between Seattle and Sound ports, touching at each town on the mainland, and also on the islands in the San Juan Archipelago. Much of the richest and best developed farming land of this section of the State is situated on these islands, and these steamers bring the products of the farm, the garden, and the orchard to be exchanged for groceries, clothing, furniture, and other domestic necessities, as well as implements used for agricultural purposes. What the steamers do for the towns situated along the shores the several railways coming to this town do for those of the interior, reaching to the borders of British Columbia and Idaho, the Canadian Pacific, the Great Northern, the Northern Pacific, and the Oregon Short Line, all running their trains and goods waggons into this town.

Population and Industry.

Population. Seattle's population has remained about the same as last year, estimated at 60,000, and at the last registration there were 10,839 names recorded having legal votes.

Health. Births and deaths. There were 610 birth reports, of which 321 were males, 288 females, and one sex not stated. There were 63 still-births reported. These returns are still very incomplete.

The total number of deaths from all causes during the year was 467, as against 485 in 1893. Of these, 273 were males, and 194 females; the death rate being 7·78 per 1,000, as against 8·08 in 1893.

Diseases. There were no cases of small-pox, but 66 of scarlatina, mostly of mild form, with 2 deaths. The health officer recommends the building of a hospital for infectious diseases. There were 15 cases of whooping-cough, with 3 deaths; 60 of typhoid fever, with 19 deaths; and 20 of diphtheria, with 6 deaths. The other causes of death were chiefly constitutional diseases. 18 cases of suicide were reported, and 4 of murder.

The health officer makes inspection of the sewers, plumbing, and general sanitary conditions of the city. During his various visits to markets and commission houses large quantities of garden produce, consisting of fruits and vegetables, were condemned; also 353 gallons of milk, thus showing the importance of having regular inspections.

Several improvements have been made in the legislation, relative to food adulteration, although it is still very difficult to

(1984)

get convictions. The sanitary condition of the schools proved to be, on the whole, good.

The matter of responsibility relative to the care of the indigent sick seems to be still unsettled. The county appears to take care of the majority, all who are known as "out-patients," while the city takes care of most of the accidents, giving them immediate hospital attention. There were only eight patients admitted to the hospital at the city's expense during last year.

Climate. — The mean annual temperature for the Seattle station has been 50·4 degrees, the highest being 88 degrees and the lowest 21 degrees. The total precipitation for the year was 41·08, and the snowfall 16·6.

The mean maximum temperature for the year was 56·9, and the mean minimum 43·9, the relative humidity being 78 per cent. For the same period the mean monthly rainfall was 3·42.

Education. Public schools. — The number of children enrolled in the 12 public schools for the year ending 1894 was 6,036, the actual attendance being 5,450, and there were 144 teachers employed.

Industry. Iron. — The iron industries now in operation in Seattle consist of four general foundries, two stove foundries, one brass foundry, and six boiler-making establishments. In some of these the largest castings on the coast have been turned out. There are 10 large machine shops and several smaller ones, in addition to the repair shops of the railways terminating in Seattle. Most of these manufacturing establishments commenced as simple repair shops. Much of the boiler castings and machinery used in this district is now finished in this town, thus saving to consumers the difference between low freight rates on manufactured iron and steel and the high freights on the finished articles. The shops and the foundries are fitted up with the most modern tools and the latest appliances. It is estimated that there are 150,000*l.* (750,000 dol.) invested in iron industries in this town, employing about 250 men.

Hide, fur, and leather trade. — The leather industries of Puget Sound are growing in importance and extent. A large quantity of fine furs and skins from the game regions of Alaska, British Columbia, Montana, Idaho, and the north-western regions generally, as well as the catches of the seal hunters, are marketed either in Victoria, British Columbia, or Seattle, and are then exported direct to London. Nearly all the hides and skins taken off in this district are shipped to hide buying houses here, whence they are sent direct to the tanneries, or are converted into leather. Principally rough leather is tanned on this coast at present; but one firm has turned out a very good quality of leather for gloves and linings. The supply of hemlock bark from the forests of Western Washington is almost unlimited, and can be delivered at manufacturing points at a very trifling cost. A very fine extract for tanning is also produced from this bark.

Fisheries. — The salmon cannery established in this town has had a very fair season, during which time 1,494,167 lbs. weight of salmon were taken and put up into 20,300 cases. This cannery employed 127 men and 218 fishermen, and 3 steamers were chartered for carrying the fish to the cannery.

It is estimated that Seattle has about 300 different establishments for manufacturing purposes, giving employment to from 3,500 to 4,000 persons.

Public Works.

During the year several buildings have been erected, the chief of which was the State University, the letting of the contract and the commencement of the erection of which began last May. The building is still unfinished and is to cost, when completed, 25,000*l*. (124,000 dol.). Another large building for business purposes, still under construction, is to be four stories in height, and to cost 20,000*l*. (100,000 dol.). The total estimated cost of the work done is about 93,216*l*. (466,000 dol.). Public works. Buildings and street improvements, &c.

Seattle has about 750 miles of platted streets, of which 105 miles are improved; about 27 miles are totally or partially covered with fir planking. No permanent pavement has been laid except in one or two cases where a few yards have been put down for experimental purposes, chiefly vitrified brick. During the year 1894 7 or 8 miles were graded and sidewalks added at a cost of 20,000*l*. (100,000 dols.).

The town has about 30 miles of sewers, 26 miles being vitrified pipe and 4 miles brick. Continual improvements are being made, necessitating the expenditure of a very large sum of money. This is partly borne by the public and partly by the districts where the improvements are made, according to the nature of the work done.

There were 155 calls in 1894, as against 197 in 1893. The total estimated damage being 17,391*l*. (86,955 dol.). On the property involved there was an insurance of 150,700*l*. (753,500 dol.). The largest loss of property during the year amounted to 5,470*l*. (27,350 dol.). 18 lives were lost during the year, of which 16 perished at one fire. Fire department.

The post-office receipts during the year amounted to 17,206*l*. (86,030 dol.), of which 1,757*l*. (8,789 dol.) was derived from stamps, 1,044*l*. (5,221 dol.) was collected from box rent, and 4*l*. (20 dol.) from sale of waste paper. The salaries paid amounted to about 8,298*l*. (41,490 dol.). The rent of the office was 540*l*. (2,700 dol.). Post-office.

There are now 14 banks in this town, of which 7 are National, 3 State, 3 Savings, and 1 a branch of a foreign bank. Their aggregate resources, exclusive of the foreign bank, at the dates of their last statements were about 1,520,000*l*. (7,600,000 dol.), and their capital, 600,000*l* (3,000,000 dol.). Their deposits are stated at 800,000*l*. (4,000,000 dol.). Financial condition.

Bradstreet reports that the bank failures during the year were 5,396,328*l*. (26,981,639 dol.) in the State of Washington, as against 8,324,761*l*. (41,623,805 dol.) in the preceding year, showing a decrease of 35·2 per cent. Business failures.

From the records of the United States Land Office at Seattle United States Land Office.

(1984)

it appears that there were 7,501,560 acres in this land district, and that 2,876,706 acres were disposed of, 705,601 acres reserved from settlement, leaving about 4,554,289 acres unappropriated and unreserved, of which 173,196 acres are surveyed and 4,381,093 acres are unsurveyed. During the year there were 3,974·56 acres in 42 commuted homesteads. The total purchase price received was over 1,058*l.* (5,294 dol.); 5,090·27 acres in 42 timber lands realising 2,645*l.* (13,226 dol.); about 9,000 acres in pre-emptions, mineral, coal, and other entries, realising over 10,000*l.* (51,600 dol.). Fees and commissions amounted to 2,028*l.* (10,138 dol.).

PORT TOWNSEND.

Lumber. The outlook for lumber shipments from Puget Sound is much brighter this spring than a year ago; in fact, the demand and general shipments show a decided improvement. The Australian demand is much larger and firmer than at any time previous in 3 or 4 years. The markets along the west coast of South America are steadily increasing their orders, which indicates a healthy demand for Puget Sound timber. Several cargoes were shipped to South Africa and brought good prices. Central America and Mexico, on the Pacific slope, have increased their demand over the preceding year. Lumbermen are anticipating a big export trade to China and Japan as soon as peace is declared between the two countries. Already agents have been sent over there to negotiate sales, and the indications at this time are that a brisk trade between Puget Sound and the Orient will spring up this season. Lumber shipments to domestic coastwise ports have been greatly interfered with since the enactment of the present tariff law, which permits the importation of lumber from British Columbia free of duty. Mill owners in Burrard Inlet, British Columbia, have taken advantage of the law, and are shipping many cargoes of rough lumber to California, thus far in American vessels, which, however, is not compulsory. Last year several cargoes of lumber were sent to Europe. To the United Kingdom over 3,000,000 feet, and to other European countries the demand was fairly good.

Freights. Lumber freights from Puget Sound ports to foreign countries do not show any marked improvement over last year, though the present indications point decidedly to an upward tendency.

Rates of Freight.

To—	Per 1,000 Feet.	
	Highest.	Lowest.
	£ s. d.	£ s. d.
Sydney	1 18 6	1 8 9
Melbourne, Port Pirie, and Adelaide..	2 0 0	1 17 6
Calcutta	2 5 0	2 5 0
China	2 2 6	1 17 6
Africa, East London	3 0 0	2 15 0
West Coast South America	1 17 6	1 12 6
Mexico	2 0 0	1 17 6
Honolulu, H.I.	1 5 0	1 4 0
Buenos Ayres	2 6 0	2 4 0
Alexandria..	3 10 0	3 10 0
United Kingdom	3 2 6	2 15 0

Failing to secure the installation of a time ball service here, this office has been furnished with a standard meantime chronometer, and has telegraphic wires running to an instrument in the office by which time signals are secured from the United States Observatory, at Mare Island Navy Yard, San Francisco. This office can, therefore, now furnish comparisons for chronometer errors at any time, and rates for such instruments as are left in the chronometer room for that purpose. This is taken advantage of by most shipmasters, and especially by those who load lumber, on account of much of the lumber being large and awkward to handle and often giving the vessels a good shaking up in loading, which of course does the chronometers no good if left on board during that time. The pilot chart of the North Pacific Ocean has been issued monthly since September, 1894, there having been previously issued special numbers for January and July of the same year. It has been received with great favour by shipmasters and shipping men generally, and is being constantly improved upon. A feature of last issue was an indication of the best fishing banks along the North Pacific coast, with a table showing positions, extent, principal varieties of fish found, characteristics, &c., of each bank. *Hydrographic office.*

The quarantine station referred to in the last report has been completed at Diamond Point, and is now in full operation. A plant also has been established there to disinfect and properly fumigate vessels. The Government has placed a competent surgeon in charge of the station. Vessels from foreign ports are required to call at Port Townsend for quarantine examination. The Government, however, now rigidly requires of vessels arriving from foreign ports a United States consular bill of health; several vessels have recently arrived without bills of health, and were severely fined by the custom-house authorities here. *Quarantine.*

Since the last report one steel and several large wooden *Shipbuilding.*

84   UNITED STATES.

vessels have been built. The whaleback steamer "City of Everett," 2,550 tons, has just returned from making her maiden voyage to San Francisco with 4,000 tons of Vancouver Island coal. The voyage was a success. It appears quite probable that the same company will commence the construction of one or two other whaleback steamers this or next season. The shipyards at Port Blakely last year turned out three or four small schooners.

Steamship lines.
The Northern Pacific, Puget Sound, and Oriental Steamship Line, running British vessels, are doing a profitable business, the trade seems to be steadily increasing. An effort has been made by two rival companies to place opposition steamers on the Puget Sound and Alaska route to compete with the Pacific Coast Steamship Company's regular line of steamers. The result has been to lower freight and passenger rates over 400 per cent. Many hundreds of miners and adventurers have taken advantage of the low rates to rush into the Yukon (Alaska) gold mines, where the short season limits mining to four months in the year. More than 1,200 persons wintered there this season. It is believed that much suffering and privation will result next autumn and winter from this wild rush.

Dry dock.
The Government made a large appropriation this year for the naval dry dock at Port Orchard, and it will doubtless be completed by next winter. Work on the local dock by private parties has been suspended for lack of necessary funds.

Fortifications.
The Government has done nothing as yet towards establishing fortifications at the entrance of Puget Sound, which at present is wholly unprotected save for the occasional presence of a man-of-war. A movement, however, is on foot to locate a large army post near Seattle or Tacoma, and a board of engineers has been appointed to select a site. The military post near this city, Fort Townsend, was recently destroyed by fire, and the troops were withdrawn and sent to Vancouver.

Pilotage.
A measure was defeated in the Legislature lately to pass a law enforcing compulsory pilotage. At present it is optional with the shipmasters to employ pilots, it being generally unnecessary, the open navigation being free from marine dangers and obstacles.

Coal.
Prospecting for coal in this vicinity continues unabated. Several drills have gone down upwards of 1,000 feet, the results being jealously guarded by the prospectors. A large amount of capital is being invested in these borings, and geological indications of the continuation of the Vancouver Island coal veins seem very probable.

Cement.
Two cargoes of cement were imported last year, being mostly used by the Government at Port Orchard in constructing the navy dry dock. The demand otherwise is very light owing to the general suspension of building enterprises.

Cotton.
Large exportations of cotton have been shipped to Japan this season, and the shipments seem to be increasing.

Smuggling.
To prevent the smuggling of Chinese and opium from British Columbia into the United States the Government is building two

fleet and powerful steam launches at this port for patrol service. The recent tariff law reducing the duty on opium from 12 to 6 dol. per 1 lb., and the new rule of registering and numbering Chinese has largely decreased the smuggling business on Puget Sound.

Manufactures. The continued monetary and trade depression throughout the north-west necessitated most of the factories working on about half-time. This applies particularly to the nail and paper works at Everett, and the wire nail factory at Port Townsend. Many of the lumber mills operate on half-time. The flouring mills did much better, most of the product going to the Orient.

Marine hospital. The Government is building a large brick hospital at this port capable of accommodating 300 patients. The building will be ready for occupancy about next September, to replace the old wooden building destroyed by fire last year.

Lightship. The Government has authorised the establishment of a lightship at Umatilla Reef, near Cape Flattery, and it will probably be located there some time in 1896.

Rocks and shoals. A Board of United States Engineers has recommended the removal of Star Rock in Bellingham Bay.

Light and fog signals. The fixed white light at Point Wilson entrance to Port Townsend Harbour has been changed to a steady white light with a red flash. On Marrowstone Point, above Point Wilson, the Government this summer will construct a fog whistle.

French commercial agency. The French commercial agency of this district has just been abolished and France is now unrepresented.

Coast casualties. No British vessels entering the port last year have been wrecked in this district. One ship, the "Scottish Dale," came into port partly dismasted, repaired and proceeded to the Columbia River for a cargo of grain.

Fur sealing. Fur sealing continues to be quite an industry along this coast. Vessels inward bound this season report seeing large numbers migrating northward. During this year two schooners have been built and fitted out from this place. The total catch last season of vessels belonging to this district was 4,613 skins; but this does not show the exact number of skins taken by American owners of schooners, as many owners have their vessels sailing under the British flag and registered out of Victoria, British Columbia. The total catch of British Columbia vessels in 1894 was 95,048 skins, averaging about 1,700 skins to the vessel. The highest number taken by any schooner was 4,560 skins. This season, when the white hunters may be expected to have become more proficient in the use of the spears, the catch will doubtless reach 110,000 skins. The big catch of skins this year has reduced the price of skins considerably, and many owners claimed to have operated their vessels at a loss; consequently in fitting out the vessels this spring wages of sealers were greatly reduced.

Fishing. Several new fishing schooners have been added to the Puget Sound fleet this year, and they seem to have done a profitable business. Most of the fish is shipped east by rail. A new

(1984)

departure is being experimented in this year by fitting schooners out with gasoline benzine; one has already been built and another is about finished. These vessels are intended to go to Alaska, where the halibuts are very plentiful, and, after receiving a cargo, return here and ship the fish to eastern cities in refrigerator cars.

The import trade shows an increase of 16,909*l.* as compared with last year.

The export trade shows a decrease of 12,856*l.* as compared with last year.

On account of the poor times no transfers of real estate have taken place during the past year.

The health of the city has been good, with no infectious or contagious diseases.

The vicinity of Port Townsend being devoid of agricultural resources, the depression in shipping was felt all the more. Many people are in straitened circumstances but no cases of actual suffering have been reported. Nearly all of the outstanding mortgages have been foreclosed, and it is impossible for property holders to negotiate new loans. However, should shipping revive, this city will readily feel the improvement. The actual public indebtedness of this county, city, and school district is about 120,000*l.* drawing interest at the rate of 8 per cent. per annum.

I append the several annexes marked "A," "B," and "C," to show the commerce and trade in this collection district.

Annex A.—RETURN of all Shipping at the Port of Port Townsend during the Year 1894.

ENTERED.

Nationality.	Sailing. Number of Vessels.	Sailing. Tons.	Steam. Number of Vessels.	Steam. Tons.	Total. Number of Vessels.	Total. Tons.
British	25	42,806	11	1,820	36	44,626
American	61	15,175	1,195	595,736	1,256	610,911
Norwegian	3	4,618	...	...	3	4,618
Chilian	10	9,098	...	...	10	9,098
German	2	3,272	...	...	2	3,272
Nicaraguan	2	2,510	...	...	2	2,510
Hawaiian	3	4,272	...	...	3	4,272
Total	106	81,751	1,206	597,556	1,312	679,307
„ for the year preceding	83	76,780	806	499,565	943	576,345

SAN FRANCISCO.

Cleared.

Nationality.	Sailing. Number of Vessels.	Sailing. Tons.	Steam. Number of Vessels.	Steam. Tons.	Total. Number of Vessels.	Total. Tons.
British	14	24,183	11	1,329	25	25,512
American	87	53,354	1,214	658,674	1,301	712,028
Norwegian	1	630	...	...	1	630
Chilian	10	9,098	...	...	10	9,098
German	2	3,272	...	...	2	3,272
Nicuraguan	2	2,510	...	...	2	2,510
Hawaiian	2	3,493	...	...	2	3,493
Total	118	96,540	1,225	660,003	1,341	756,543
,, for the year preceding	96	76,222	845	480,114	941	556,336

Annex B.—Return of Principal Articles of Export from Port Townsend during the Years 1894–93.

Articles.		1894. Quantity.	1894. Value.	1893. Quantity.	1893. Value.
			£		£
Flour	Barrels	...	1,516	...	...
Timber	Feet	55,035,234	113,426	74,374,000	124,732
Iron, and manufactures of iron	...	...	12,300	...	23,261
Oils	...	...	8,200	...	12,125
Furs and hides	...	...	43,350	...	11,911
Provisions, meats	...	...	25,100	...	19,022
Cattle	...	...	19,100	...	21,960
Liquors and wines	...	...	2,275	...	1,316
Wool, and manufactures of wool	...	...	6,660	...	4,001
Cotton	...	...	24,300	...	5,412
Fish	...	...	400	...	1,134
Tinned fruits and vegetables	...	...	2,900	...	9,164
Other articles	...	...	45,494	...	83,839
Total	...	...	305,021	...	317,877

Return of Principal Articles of Import to Port Townsend during the Years 1894–93.

Articles.		1894. Quantity.	1894. Value.	1893. Quantity.	1893. Value.
			£		£
Cement	Tons	...	1,238	6,206	14,292
Coal	,,	287	216	3,468	2,286
Iron, and manufactures of iron	...	...	3,153	...	1,530
Steel wire rods	Tons	...	5,892	1,510	7,701
Tin-plates	...	...	2,495	...	1,980
Lead	...	...	2,100	...	230
Zinc	...	...	150	...	600
Jute	...	...	1,470	...	4,587
Sugar	...	...	1,870	...	37,681
Rice	...	...	22,800	...	2,520
Tea	...	...	4,969	...	1,100
Silk	...	...	2,490	...	2,312
Fish	...	...	78,000	...	...
Other articles	...	...	9,579	...	42,694
Total	...	...	136,422	...	119,513

Annex C.—TABLE showing Total Value of all Articles Exported from and Imported to Port Townsend from and to Foreign Countries during the Years 1894-93.

Country.	Exports. 1894.	Exports. 1893.	Imports. 1894.	Imports. 1893.
	£	£	£	£
Great Britain	1,567	2,340	3,846	17,413
British Columbia and Canada	136,723	186,667	103,785	54,082
Australia	37,055	19,176	..	..
France	..	..	..	281
Belgium	1,005	1,337	5,300	10,944
Hawaiian Islands	24,161	17,745	4,870	1,366
Chili	29,680	33,458	..	126
China	12,837	4,556	11,132	10,165
Peru	9,100	15,525	..	..
Mexico	1,325	11,999	..	..
Japan	900	609	2,156	12,945
Africa	8,311	5,913	..	..
Germany	3,020	2,009	280	214
India	..	2,733	2,484	11,247
Netherlands	2,133	..	..	..
Guatemala	2,723	1,486	..	..
New Caledonia	..	3,430	..	..
Argentine Republic	2,100	1,675	..	..
Fiji Islands	2,320	1,482	480	..
Other countries	61	5,732	2,089	730
Total	305,021	317,877	136,422	119,513

LOS ANGELES.

Mr. Vice-Consul Mortimer reports as follows:—

Introductory remarks. The general depression in business complained of throughout the United States has been less felt in this city and district than elsewhere on the Pacific coast. Compared with the stagnation and decrease in business elsewhere, the activity here has been truly remarkable. The following figures, although they do not show any great volume of business, serve, with other similar returns, to indicate an increase, which is in marked contrast to the decrease in the corresponding figures in nearly all the cities in this country. The superintendent of buildings reports the issue of building permits in this city as follows:—1893, 330,000*l.*; 1894, 470,000*l.* The Los Angeles clearing-house reports clearings (in round numbers) as follows:—

Year.	Value.
	£
1892	7,700,000
1893	8,900,000
1894	9,400,000

These figures do not represent the volume of business done here, as there are several banks which are not members of the clearing-house. The period of prosperity and development in the State of Texas, which commenced with the financial panic in New York in 1873 and lasted until prosperity became general throughout the country in 1879, was ascribed to the fact that many persons in the east, in order to escape the "hard times," or to retrieve their fallen fortunes, realised what they could for their possessions, moved west, and settled in Texas. It appears probable that Southern California is now profiting from a like immigration from the east, induced by like causes. Be that as it may, the facts that the orange crop is a good one, that owing to the destruction of a large part of the Florida orange crop by frost the crop here is being marketed at good prices, that owing to the destruction of a large number of the Florida orange trees by frost prices for California oranges will probably be high for several years; that other crops generally are good here, and that a very large amount of money is being expended here in the development of this city and district, justify me in expressing the opinion that the prosperity of the last 2 years will be maintained, and probably increased. On the other hand, the action of the people in voting in November last in favour of an amendment to the Constitution, by which the right of aliens to own real property in California has been taken away, will delay the settlement of unoccupied lands, and deal a severe blow to the prosperity of the State.

The construction of a good harbour for Los Angeles by the United Sates Government, the completion of the Nicaragua Canal, and the construction of a railway from Los Angeles to Salt Lake City, are undertakings which, as I stated in my last report, are of the utmost importance to this city and district. Although little has been done in these matters in the past year it is, I think, probable that they will all be carried to completion in the not distant future.

I have from time to time pointed out that English investments in this district by syndicates and companies, with the exception of one mortgage company, have been uniformly unsuccessful, and that this want of success is due to swindling promoters in London, and other preventible causes. The "Los Angeles Daily Times" of December 15, 1894, contains an article on British investments here, which is in substance the advice I have given British capitalists in my annual reports for a number of years.

The following is the article in question:—

"British Capital.

"An English gentleman residing in Los Angeles, who is engaged in developing a large irrigation system for an English company, recently showed a 'Times' representative a letter from a prominent and wealthy member of the London Stock

Exchange, in which the latter stated that the recent financial collapse of the Bear Valley Company, and the failure of a large English irrigation company in Utah had made the British investing public so nervous in regard to such enterprises in this section that it was almost impossible to obtain capital for such purposes just now. This leads to some reflections upon the lack of judgment which is displayed by English investors in taking hold of enterprises in this country. When one considers the extraordinary and unbusinesslike manner in which they generally go to work, the wonder is not that they often lose money, but that they ever make any out of their investments in this country.

"When a proposition for the investment of money is brought to the attention of English capitalists, instead of sending out a man who is thoroughly well informed upon the subject at issue, whether it be mining or water development, or the planting of a vineyard, or the manufacturing of wine, in nine cases out of ten they select some person who, while usually very much of a gentleman, and quite a pleasant fellow, understands no more about the business than the Ameer of Afghanistan. He is often a retired army officer, and generally a distant and rather impecunious relative of one of the leading investors. The first thing that he generally does is to erect a very handsome and commodious residence for himself as superintendent. In one case, in the northern part of the State, 100,000 dol. was expended on the house and grounds of the superintendent of an English mining company and 200,000 dol. on a mill before it was discovered that they had no ore. Any one who has resided a few years in Southern California can point to a dozen cases in which failure is directly attributable to such causes, whether it is in the line of of orange growing, wine making, tin mining, the manufacture of paper from yucca, the development of water for irrigation, or any of the other lines of enterprise in which British capital has sought investment in this section.

" Then, again, when the enterprise may be more or less well managed it is often impossible for it to pay a fair rate of interest on the exaggerated amount of money which the investors have paid for it—not paid to the original owners of the property, but to the middlemen. The English system of 'promoters' is one which would put the average American real estate agent of boom times to the blush. These promoters are not satisfied with the modest commission of 5, 10, or even 20 per cent. on a transaction which may run into the millions. About half of the 'swag' is their figure for handling an enterprise and placing it on the market. Then, on the London Stock Exchange, there is a regular system of what is known as 'underwriting,' by which a syndicate of responsible men agree to insure investors from loss for a certain consideration, which is a very heavy consideration, so that by the time the property comes into the hands of the stockholders it is not unlikely to cost them three times the amount that is received by the owner in California.

"This state of affairs is bad, not only for the British investor, but for the California property owner, who needs British money with which to develop his capital. Great Britain has an enormous amount of cheap money; California has an immense area of fertile but at present unproductive land. By bringing these two things together great things may be accomplished, and they may be accomplished with large profit both to the capitalist and the landowner. It is the desire of all who are interested in the permanent welfare of this section that our British friends should do well on their investments here, and no one who is a real friend of Southern California will aid anyone to secure British capital under false pretences. But, as already stated, in nine cases out of ten it is the Britishers themselves who are to blame. A good method to facilitate the investment of some of this idle British money in California is that which is now being pursued by a financial institution in San Francisco, which issues gold bonds bearing 5 per cent. interest secured upon land mortgages, the ample security of which it guarantees. A considerable amount of money has already been obtained from England under this system, some of which has been invested in Los Angeles county. 5 per cent. is considered very good interest in England, while here 12 per cent. may be made with perfect safety in subdividing and selling land. If the investors of Great Britain could only be inspired with confidence in the natural resources and stability of this section, and in the character of the men they deal with, it would be an easy thing to obtain sufficient British capital to subdivide and improve every acre of available land south of the Tehachepi within the next 5 years."

If the services of questionable promoters cannot be dispensed with in the formation of English companies, and if some small modicum of business sense cannot be injected into the management of such companies, when formed, English people will be wise to confine their investments here to lending money on mortgage or the purchase of municipal or school bonds. Seven per cent. net can be obtained on the best first mortgage security, and 4 to 5 per cent. on good gold bonds. Lazard Brothers are the London correspondents of the principal financial house here; the Farmers' and Merchants' Bank, and other banks have London agents. Arrangements can easily be made through these banks for the purchase of bonds, or investments on mortgage.

Bonds. This city is now arranging to issue bonds to the amount of 80,000*l.* at 4½ per cent. to take up bonds bearing a higher rate of interest. They will be dated May 1, 1895, will be for 200*l.* each, and will be sold some time in May next. The objection to them, from an English standpoint, is that one-fortieth of the principal is payable annually.

Mortgages. About 2,500,000*l.* was invested here on mortgage in 1894, of which not less than 1,000,000*l.* represented unpaid purchase money on transfers of real property.

Emigrants. The "Los Angeles Daily Times," in its issue of April 3, 1894, taking for its text the arrest for vagrancy of the son of a Scotch earl—there is no such earldom as the one named in the article, however—points out in a very sensible way the almost certain failure which awaits well-educated young Englishmen of the better classes who, without any business training, come out here to make their fortunes. The writer, after tracing the career of such an one down to the point when he has to pawn his clothes for bread, proceeds as follows :—

"This is a critical time for our young Britisher. In the case of an American boy, who has been brought up to rough it and take his chances in the world, it would simply be a case of being 'gone broke,' but to the young Britisher it is a much more serious affair. In many cases he has never followed any regular occupation in his life except hunting and playing tennis and cricket. He has little or no conception of the hard facts which go to make up the business world, and thus finds himself very much in the condition of a fish out of water. Moreover, having been accustomed all his life to be surrounded by comfort and luxury, and to be always dressed in good taste, when he gets thus down in the world he feels a sense of degradation which an American can scarcely understand. After a few attempts to obtain work, for which he is altogether unfit, it is not surprising that in many cases he 'loses his grip' entirely, and schools himself into the idea that he has a right to be at war with a society which is so strange and unsympathetic to him.

"In other cases, where young men who have been what is known as 'wild' at home, are sent out to California to reform them, the descent in life after they reach this State is naturally far more rapid."

The sons of professional men, retired officers, and all that large class of English gentlemen who have received a fairly good education, but have not been trained to any profession or occupation, rarely succeed, and should not be encouraged to come here. Most of the Englishmen who come here are attracted by the highly-coloured descriptions of emigration agents, picturing the attractions of "the pleasant out-door life of a fruit farmer," where lawn tennis is happily blended with agricultural operations. This class of settlers, who, it is needless to say, always lose their money, will not in future have an opportunity to invest their capital in real property until, after 5 years' residence here, they have become American citizens, as, under the recent amendment to the Constitution, aliens cannot now own real property in California. As far as my experience extends, the most successful English emigrants are those who come here without any capital, and work in subordinate positions until they have saved sufficient capital to purchase land, or go into business on their own account. I have always advised new comers to rent land for at least a year before purchasing, and I am satisfied that the amendment to the Constitution, which, in effect, makes it necessary for aliens to rent land for at least 5 years before purchasing, will be a great boon to embryo fruit farmers. As it is at least doubtful whether aliens who have sufficient capital to purchase land will wait 5 years, and become American citizens, for the privilege of doing so, I am inclined to think that the large landowners who are trying to sell their land will be heavy losers by this new law.

Complaint has again been made to me of a swindle perpe- Farm pupils. trated on a number of young Englishmen. They paid 100 guineas each to an agent in London to be taught farming here, and, as usual in such cases, they did not get what they paid for. Some of them did not receive any value at all for their money, as they found, on arriving here, that the "farmer" to whom they were consigned had absconded. This swindle was first exposed as to this district in "Truth" (London) of August 14, 1884, and I have constantly referred to it since that date in my annual reports. As I stated in my report for 1891, "the qualities which will ensure success here are conspicuously absent in young men who are willing to pay premiums to be taught farming."

I have received numerous inquiries from clergymen of the Religious Established Church about this district, and in response to some of matters. these inquiries I make the following remark:—The Episcopal Church is not strong here from a financial standpoint, some of the clergy, I am informed, receiving as little as 60*l.* per annum.

The public library in this city now contains upwards of Public library. 42,000 books, and is free to all residents of the city, who can borrow books for use in their own houses without charge. It is maintained at a cost to the city of about 4,000*l.* per annum. The record of books taken out for home use during the year 1894 shows the following results:—

	Volumes.
Fiction and periodicals	269,903
All other books	59,502
Total	329,405

A record is kept of all books taken out for home use, and from this record it appears that the following authors are the most popular:—Charles King, Rosa Nouchette Carey, and Clara Louisa Burnham. About one-fourth of the population of this city take advantage of the facilities for self-improvement afforded by this library.

There are 40 free schools in this city, attended by upwards Education. of 11,000 pupils. The estimated value of the school property is 160,000*l.* A large number of the pupils are the children of extremely poor persons, and many people here are becoming a little doubtful as to the wisdom of giving these children an education which will unfit them for the callings in life which are open to them. They argue that if the money expended in giving a lot of poor boys "book learning," which will be practically useless to them, were expended in teaching them a trade or occupation, by the exercise of which they could make a comfortable living, the results would be much more satisfactory to the boys and to the community.

UNITED STATES.

Shipping and Navigation.

The Collector of Customs for this district resides at this city, and deputy collectors reside at the ports (San Pedro, 20 miles south; Redondo, 22 miles south-west; and Port Los Angeles, 16 miles west). As I have stated in previous reports, efforts are being made to secure a large appropriation from Congress for the construction of a breakwater, at a cost of about 1,000,000*l.*, at San Pedro, or Port Los Angeles. The Southern Pacific Company has constructed a wharf at Port Los Angeles, at a cost of 200,000*l.*, and is opposing an appropriation for improvements at San Pedro, claiming that Port Los Angeles is the better site for a harbour. In consequence of these conflicting interests, nothing has been done by Congress, and it does not now appear probable that any considerable appropriation for a harbour will be made for some time to come. An English ship landed a cargo of coal at Port Los Angeles recently, and cleared for Australia in ballast for another cargo; her master told me that his cargo was discharged in a shorter time and with less expense than at any port he has ever been at.

Casualties. — The British steamship, "Crown of England," while engaged in the coal trade between British Columbia and Port Los Angeles, was wrecked on the Santa Barbara Islands in a dense fog, and became a total loss. The crew landed at Port Los Angeles without loss of life.

I am indebted to the Collector of Customs for the following returns of shipping. It does not include the coast trade:—

Annex A.—RETURN of all Shipping at the Ports for Los Angeles, California, during the Year 1894.

ENTERED.

Nationality.	Sailing. Number of Vessels.	Tons.	Steam. Number of Vessels.	Tons.	Total. Number of Vessels.	Tons.
British	3	6,124	6	8,230	9	14,354
American	13	18,200	11	20,812	24	39,012
Other countries	...	...	13	25,038	13	25,038
Total	...	...	...	...	46	78,404

CLEARED.

Nationality.	Sailing. Number of Vessels.	Tons.	Steam. Number of Vessels.	Tons.	Total. Number of Vessels.	Tons.
British	3	6,124	6	8,230	9	14,354
American	13	18,200	11	20,812	24	39,012
Other countries	...	...	13	25,038	13	25,038
Total	...	...	...	...	46	78,404

SAN FRANCISCO.

Trade and Commerce.

Wine-producers here have combined and have succeeded in raising prices about 80 per cent. Prices are still so low, however, that the growers make only a bare living at the increased price; an attempt is being made to eliminate the middle man; whether this is possible, however, has yet to be proved. *Wine.*

The wines and brandies produced in this district are pure and wholesome, and the producers deserve better success than they have hitherto experienced.

The manager of the Southern California Packing Company writes me that his company packed 2,160,000 cans, of 2½ lbs. each, in 1894, and that the total pack of this district was about 5,900,000 cans. He adds, "We have no trouble selling our pack, but owing to the state of trade, and the disreputable competition we have to meet in many places, the margin of profit is sometimes very small. The prospect for a large crop of deciduous fruit is good this year, unless we have a heavy rainstorm when the blossoms are dropping." *Canned fruit.*

The shipment of oranges from this district for the past 3 years has been as follows:— *Oranges.*

Year.	Quantity.
	Tons.
1892	40,000
1893	67,910
1894	49,770

The shipments this season will, it is estimated, reach 80,000 tons. The marked decrease in shipment in 1894 was due to heavy losses by frost and windstorms. The question of over-production is referred to elsewhere in this report.

The trans-continental railways write me that 16,700 tons of vegetables were shipped from this district in 1894. *Vegetables.*

Salt is found in unlimited quantities at Salton, a station on the Colorado Desert, in Riverside County, about 100 miles east of this city. The manager of the New Liverpool Salt Company, of Salton, writes me as follows:—"We have been doing very little in the way of producing for the past 2 years, having a large stock on hand." *Salt.*

I wrote to Mr. Menzies, editor of "The Commercial Bulletin," of this city, asking his views on openings for British trade here. His reply covers the ground so thoroughly that I give it in full as follows:— *Prospects of trade with Great Britain.*

"Southern California has undergone an extremely varied experience during the past 12 months. In the early portion of that period conditions were decidedly adverse, but they afterwards changed materially for the better; so that on the whole we are able to report a year of moderate prosperity. At first we had to

(1984)

go through an industrial agitation started by the suffering unemployed, which culminated in the well-remembered march to Washington. In the month of April we had, on the other hand, the first celebration in this city of 'La Fiesta,' a week of holiday processions and demonstrations, promoted by the Merchants' Association, chiefly for the entertainment of winter visitors, which proved very successful, and will be repeated annually. Presently we found ourselves traversing a dry season, with more or less failure of the grain, hay, and other non-irrigated crops. The railroad strike paralysed business during the first 3 weeks of July; but fortunately, owing to the resolute attitude of the United States district Judge, and to the presence of the United States troops, there was little violence attempted here. The prolonged tariff struggle in Congress restricted trade throughout the Union, and diminished the demand for California products; and free wool, one of the eventual provisions, inflicted a serious blow upon our sheepowners. This, however, about exhausted the run of ill-luck. Since then very promising discoveries of petroleum have been made within about half-a-mile of the centre of Los Angeles, liberal rains have fallen, ensuring abundant crops in the coming season; and frosts in Florida and Valencia have cleared the market for our orange crop.

"Building and other improvements in the city continue without intermission. Two new wholesale grocery houses have been opened or extended, and an additional wholesale clothing firm has been established, besides other trading developments. A rolling mill has been constructed for the conversion of scrap iron into sheets, and is being successfully operated. The condensed milk factory at Buena Park, 20 miles south-east of Los Angeles, which has been closed for a year or two, has changed hands recently, and will be re-opened. New pickle and preserve factories have been started, and other manufacturing developments are continually in progress. The clearing-house returns show a steady increase, in part due, no doubt, to larger transactions in real estate. The only important failures have been those of two firms at Tehachepi, due chiefly to the collapse of the wool-growing industry, the losses from which have fallen for the most part upon San Francisco. Bearing in mind the natural tendency to excessive competition in such an attractive place of residence, present commercial conditions may be described as fairly good, though there are still a great many unemployed, as well as considerable numbers of respectable people that only secure a living with much struggle.

Imports. "Imports have been facilitated by the new reduced tariff, and may be still further, to a slight extent, by the advance in overland rates of freight from the eastern States. There have been hopes of an increase of foreign trade by the new Tehuantepec railroad, and coasting steamers in connection; but as yet, owing to harbour difficulties at the Isthmus, yet to be overcome, this route has not been opened, and the steamers between Panama and San Francisco do not in the meantime touch at any of our local ports.

"Cement is the most staple import from Great Britain, and there is at present a vessel on the way from London loaded chiefly or entirely with it. This article also comes here from Belgium, in specially chartered vessels, along with window-glass, coke, and patent fuel. It is, besides, manufactured at Colton, 60 miles east of Los Angeles, from which points shipments have recently been made for work on the new Prescott and Phœnix Railroad in Arizona, though importers here are, as yet, scarcely sensible of this competition. *Cement.*

"The import duty is considerably lower than last year, and prices have been reduced in conformity; but we are not aware of any alteration in the direction of the trade. Indeed, there is now a vessel at Redondo, one of our local ports, with a supply from Antwerp, the second importation from there, we believe, at the reduced tariff. *Window glass.*

"Nearly all steam and power raisers here now burn local oil, except the gas and electric lighting company, which uses Australian coal. The Southern Pacific Company also imports from that source. The Santa Fé draw their supplies from Gallup, in New Mexico. For domestic purposes the British Columbia product is used here to some extent. *Coal.*

"Chemicals and drugs are without any new feature. Caustic soda for soap-making comes from England, as well as some other staples.

"Lumber is now admitted free into the United States, a change which has caused some annoyance to importers here, who have their own milling plants in the State of Washington. Owing, it is said, to the Chinese and Japanese labour employed in cutting and preparing it, British Columbia pine can be imported here at a cost of 1 dol. (say 4s. 2d.) per 1,000 feet less than that of the domestic article; yet, owing to the uncertainty connected with tariff matters, arrangements cannot be made to permanently utilise this saving. There is as yet, too, some variety of opinion concerning the advantage of the apparent economy, some contending that the Canadian article is just so much inferior, while others attribute any such difference more to the lack of experience and knowledge of the selection suited to our market. In freight there is so far no saving, owing to a combination of carrying interests. Two or more firms here are in the meantime proving by actual experiment what can be done by a diversion of the trade to British Columbia. *Lumber.*

"American prices are so low that there appears to be no opening for an increase of foreign importations, and the same is apparently true of metals generally. *Hardware.*

"Consumption here is small, fruit packers and other users preferring to purchase their cans ready-made in San Francisco. *Tin-plates.*

"Trade here is unaffected by the new tariff, American manufacturers having reduced their prices to meet it. *Crockery and glassware.*

"Dry goods from abroad do not come direct here, but through New York and San Francisco importers. The reduced tariff has made a saving of 5 dol. each in gentlemen's suits of imported *Dry goods.*

(1984)

cloths, and there is also a saving in woollen dress materials from the same cause; but all domestic woollen goods are also cheaper, in consequence of the free admission of competing raw material from abroad. Silks, we understand, are but slightly affected by the new tariff. With the exception of some very superior goods from the South of France, they are chiefly of domestic manufacture. Linen, on the other hand, comes mainly from the North of Ireland, and has within the last 18 months fallen in price from 15 to 20 per cent., mainly owing to the reduction of the import duty, with a corresponding gratifying increase of consumption. A short time ago a representative from a Belfast firm paid a visit here—his first trip across the rocky mountains—and was so well satisfied with the openings presented, that he will in future return annually.

Tea. "The Japanese article is that chiefly preferred by the Americans, though the Chinese is also in use. The Indian and Ceylon varieties are preferred by the British residents, and their consumption is increasing.

Coffee. "Coffee comes chiefly from Central America, by way of San Francisco. Mocha and Java are used to a limited extent for the best trade. The former of these however is scarce, and a substitute for it is badly wanted. Brazilian, roasted and sent here in paper packages from the east, supplies a low class demand.

Sugar. "Sugar imported from the Hawaiian Islands free of duty and refined in San Francisco supplies the bulk of the demand, as a small amount of refined granulated still, however, comes here from Hong-Kong, viâ San Francisco, in spite of the import duty of 40 per cent. ad valorem and $\frac{1}{16}$ of a penny per lb. The beet factory at Chino, 40 miles from here, had a very short season last summer, on account of the drought. It turned out quite a superior refined, granulated sugar, which, however, sells slowly and at a somewhat lower price than the San Francisco article, though that no doubt contains a proportion of beet sugar from the northern factories. The Chino beet product has been found quite satisfactory for table use, but not for preserving purposes. It possesses unfortunately when newly manufactured an objectionable odour, which disappears most quickly when stored in sacks, and these consequently have all been disposed of while several hundred barrels of last season's product are yet on hand, though they also will be sold ere long. The wholesale price is $2\frac{3}{8}d.$ per lb. net cash; while that of the San Francisco article being $2\frac{9}{16}d.$, and the Hong-Kong intermediate. The Chino factory will operate again this year, but it is feared that this may be its last season, if the bounty is not renewed.

Provisions. "Hog products, until quite recently largely imported from the eastern States, now come from there only to a very limited extent. Hogs are now extensively raised all over the State, and the bulk of our supply is obtained from the Cudahy packing house here, and from a similar concern in San Francisco. They are even now canning beef at Cudahy's, though the bulk of that used still comes from the east.

Butter. "Until last year considerable quantities of this came from the east in the late summer and autumn, but there is now a sufficiency on the Pacific coast all the year round, and in certain seasons a surplus. A good deal is produced locally, and the balance is obtained from the northern part of the State. The price of the best quality varies from 7½d. to 1s. 3d. per lb.

Cheese. "Cheese is also for the most part produced locally, though certain varieties are brought here from the north and east and from Europe.

Poultry. "Poultry are somewhat difficult to raise in this warm climate. They do best near the sea coast. The consumption here has of late been largely supplied by eastern importations in cold storage.

Eggs. "Eggs are abundant and cheap in spring and summer but dear at other times, and are then imported largely from the east, chiefly from Kansas. The price varies from 6d. to 1s. 6d. per dozen.

Hay. "Hay, owing to the drought, has been dear here the past season, and a few imports have come from Arizona. The bulk of the supply, however, has been produced locally, or procured from the central and northern portions of the State. Alfalfa, wheat, barley, and oats are the varieties in use, and vary in price, baled with wire, from 2l. to 3l. per ton of 2,000 lbs.

Exports.

Oranges. "Just about a year ago, that is towards the end of March, 1894, a better demand sprang up for this fruit and continued pretty well till the close of the season in June. The shipments reached 4,000 carloads, each of 300 70-lb. boxes. In its issue of June 2, 1894, the 'Commercial Bulletin' said: 'The unfavourable condition of trade throughout the United States has of course been a serious damper upon the orange business; still good prices would have been realised for the limited supply of fruit from this State but for the ruinous interference of the growers' combinations in the marketing of it. As it is, though a few of the shippers have done fairly well, the season has been on the whole a disastrous one for growers and shippers alike.'

"Allusion was there made to the auction sales held by the growers' combinations at leading cities of the United States and Canada, which yielded ruinous prices and completely demoralised the market. This year the sales have been limited so far to San Francisco, but even there have been sufficient to utterly ruin the trade with the whole Pacific coast. The prices realised are always far under the parity of the f.o.b. quotations, and it is presumed that these sales are continued with no other object than to ruin the market of such of the independent growers, outside of the combinations, as have been in the habit of consigning their fruit for sale to commission houses in San Francisco, and

(1984)

thus to force them into the combinations. At the beginning of the present season, besides the auction sales at San Francisco, shippers from Southern California had to meet the competition in the coast trade of a moderate amount of fruit, estimated at 200 cars, from Central and Northern California, where the crops ripen somewhat earlier than here, owing to the great summer heat; and in the east there was absolutely no prospect, until the great freezes, that took place in Florida, put out of the way some 2,000,000 or 2,500,000 boxes that would have supplied eastern markets for some months at prices with which, quality considered, our fruit could not compete. Since then competition has been mostly confined to European and Mexican fruit, and the freeze in Valencia soon restricted the former to shipments from Sicily, a second stroke of good luck for the Southern Californian producers, and although Sicily is sending in enormous and unprecedented supplies, the demand from here has been also quite heavy, and encourages the hope that the entire crop of some 6,500 cars, except that portion sacrificed at the producers' auctions, will be disposed of at prices ranging from 4s. to 10s. per box f.o.b., from which prices, however, a deduction of 1s. 6d. to 2s. per box must be made in order to arrive at the net prices obtained by the grower on the tree. This business is one that is full of hazard and subject to many contingencies, in the variations of the seasons and of the markets here and elsewhere, and from extremes of temperature in transit, from excessive cold and excessive heat, both alike destructive to the fruit, as well as from rejections and claims by eastern receivers. Southern Californian growers are to be congratulated on the fact that the damage to the trees in Florida is so heavy as to cripple the competition of that State for years to come; otherwise it is hard to say what should have become of them, so much apparently was the industry 'boomed' and overdone.

Lemons. "The production of this fruit is steadily increasing, while imports from Sicily are as steadily falling off. Very few Sicilian lemons now come to this coast, and a good sale for our product is obtained in the season in the North-Western States. This industry must also profit by the havoc wrought by the frosts in the groves of Florida, though what the extent of this benefit may be it is at present very difficult to say, since the demand here will not show much activity until after the advent of hot weather. Prices at present are very low, ranging from 2s. for uncured, to 5s. 2d. for cured, per box of 72 lbs., f.o.b.

Fresh deciduous fruits. "Trade in these is for the most part local, and with the adjoining territories, since Northern and Central California are apparently better situated for shipping to the Eastern States. The earliest grapes in the State, however, are raised at Palm Springs, Riverside County, on the margin of the desert. They are of a variety called the Thompson seedless, and are usually shipped with good results to Chicago and other eastern cities. This year, however, they were just ready when the railroad strike occurred; and by the time that was over, northern crops were in

"The production of dried apricots and peaches was very heavy this year; but owing to the drought much of the fruit was unusually small, and prices have been on the average very low, except just at the opening of the season, ranging for the most part between 2*d*. and 3*d*. per lb. in sacks from first hands. Sun-drying is all but universal in this part of the State. Of prunes there was also a good crop, though much of this fruit was also small. Prices have ranged from 1*d*. to 2½*d*. per lb., competition from France having been specially severe. Prospects for the coming season are for a good crop of all descriptions of dried fruits in Southern California, though in the north some damage by frost has been reported. *Dried fruits.*

"Owing to the dryness of the season the crop was small and of medium quality. Layers were scarce and fetched fair prices, say 4*s*. 2*d*. to 8*s*. 4*d*. per 20-lb. box. Loose muscatels in sacks sold for ¾*d*. to 1½*d*. per lb., for the most part, from first hand. *Raisins.*

"The production of pickled olives is rapidly increasing, while the quality also is improving and restricting the sale of the European article here. The value at first hand is fully 2*s*. 6*d*. per gallon. The quality of the oil is very fine, but, so far, it is quite a fancy article being held for nearly twice the price of Crosse and Blackwell's. Plantations are being rapidly extended especially in the neighbourhood of Pomona. *Olives and olive oil.*

"The walnut crop of Southern California last season amounted to about 300 car loads, and would have been a perfect success in respect of quality, but for two very scorching days in the latter part of August, which did it serious injury. This was specially unfortunate, as owing to the failure of the French crop the opportunity was a good one for extending our market and for favourably impressing consumers, while, in fact, a contrary effect has been in many cases produced. Prices varied from 2*d*. to 3½*d*. per lb., according to size and quality. The peanut crop, owing to the drought, was small, and there have been considerable importations of Virginia peanuts to this locality. Prices at first hand were 1½*d*. to 2*d*. per lb. Almonds are beginning to appear here from neighbouring districts, though the local consumption is still for the most part supplied from the northern part of the State. *Nuts.*

"The yield was of course a poor one, and it is estimated that, owing to the drought and consequent shortness of food, one-half of the bees have since died of starvation. Extracted honey has advanced as high as 3½*d*. per lb. for the best; but the sale has been slow, and it has since relapsed to 2½*d*. from the first hand. Comb honey has been very scarce, and our local consumption has been latterly supplied from the northern portion of the State. The description gathered from the white sage in Southern California is very fine, but there is also much of medium quality from other sources. Beeswax is scarce and firm at about 1*s*. to 1*s*. 3*d*. per lb. from first hand. *Honey.*

(1984)

Vegetables.

"The Winningstadt cabbage grown in this neighbourhood is highly esteemed, and is largely shipped to the Eastern States in winter and spring, as also cauliflower and celery. Potatoes are raised on a large scale for shipment in spring and early summer. The cultivators are almost exclusively Chinese, and the profits of the industry are small and precarious. In the winter season green peas and tomatoes are produced in favourable situations by white men for local consumption and shipment to San Francisco. Green peas have never been successfully shipped east, unless in very minute quantities.

Dried beans.

"Dried beans are an important crop in Los Angeles, Ventura, and Santa Barbara Counties, but the product last season was very short. There was a better yield, however, further north, and on the Sacramento River, so that prices have not risen to a high level. The supply is now falling short, but the new season promises to be a very successful one, and in the autumn prices will probably range as usual for the leading varieties from 1d. to 2d. per lb. in sacks.

Grain.

"The wheat raised in this section is mostly grown in the San Fernando Valley. Last year's crop was not half an average; but local requirements have been met by a heavy carry over from the harvest of 1893. The barley crop was rather better, and will be sufficient for local consumption, that is for animal food. This year we shall probably have heavy grain crops, with a large surplus of both wheat and barley for shipment. The maize raised here is used locally and shipped to San Francisco.

Wool.

"The quality raised here is inferior, and sells in the rough, that is unwashed, at 2d. to 2½d. per lb. It is shipped to eastern manufacturing centres.

Hides and pelts.

"Hides and pelts are shipped to San Francisco, there being no tannery here on account of the cost of bringing the bark from the north."

I am indebted to the Collector of Customs for the following returns showing the articles of export and import, and the value of same.

Annex B.—RETURN of Principal Articles of Export from Los Angeles, California, during the Years 1893–94.

Articles.	1893.		1894.	
	Quantity.	Value.	Quantity.	Value.
	Nil.		Nil.	

RETURN of Principal Articles of Import to Los Angeles, California, during the Years 1893-94.

Articles.		1893.		1894.	
		Quantity.	Value.	Quantity.	Value.
			£		£
Coal	Tons	123,965	83,105	131,655	91,568
Pig-iron	,,	..	..	..	..
Cement	Barrels	..	..	14,200	3,594
Other articles	,,	..	40,787	..	..
Total	..	..	123,892	..	95,162

Annex C.—TABLE showing Total Value of all Articles Exported from and Imported to Los Angeles from and to Foreign Countries during the Years 1893-94.

Country.	Exports.		Imports.	
	1893.	1894.	1893.	1894.
			£	£
Great Britain	Nil.		43,093	101,408
Total	..	..	43,093	101,408

Population and Industries.

The population of this city has increased from 51,000 in 1890 to about 85,000.

Decrees of divorce were granted by the Superior Court of Los Angeles County in the past 3 years as follows:—

Year.	Number.
1892	180
1893	209
1894	285

Very few of these divorces were obtained for adultery, nearly all having been granted to wives on account of desertion, failure to provide the necessaries of life, cruelty, and similar causes, and it would therefore appear that the increase in divorce is not due to immorality, but rather to the fact that the legislature, in its desire to protect women, has rendered it too easy for them to obtain divorces from husbands who treat them with less consideration than they think they are entitled to.

Beet sugar.

A very large amount of beet sugar is manufactured at the Chino factory in this district, and, owing to the increase in the duty on raw and refined sugars to 40 per cent. and upwards, the business is so profitable that more land is being planted in sugar beets by tenant farmers of, and purchasers from the Chino Ranch Company, and factories will be erected at Anaheim and other places in this district. If there was any certainty that the present tariff would be maintained for several years, the manufacture of beet sugar would be a most promising field for the investment of money.

I am indebted to Mr. Holabird, manager of the Chino Ranch Company for some statistics, taken from the report of the Commissioner of Internal Revenue, which show the beets raised at Chino contain from 40 to 100 per cent. more sugar, per ton of beets, than any other district in the United States.

Mr. Holabird has also given me the following figures:—

	Quantity.
	Tons.
Product of sugar at Chino in 1894	7,532
„ „ in the United States in 1894	332,431

Oil.

In January and February, 1894, boring for oil was commenced in the western part of this city, and a good deposit of oil, suitable for fuel, was discovered. Upwards of 150 wells have now been sunk within three quarters of a mile of the centre of this city, and many of them are producing more than 40 barrels of oil per day. The oil is found comparatively near the surface, the wells being only 600 to 1,200 feet in depth. Mr. E. L. Doheny, who bored the first well, writes me as follows:—"The output of petroleum in the State of California during the year 1894 approximated 450,000 barrels of 42 gallons each. About two-fifths of the above amount was produced during the first half of the year. The output of the wells in the city of Los Angeles during the year was, approximately, 85,000 barrels, 90 per cent. of which was produced during the last half of the year. Your third question, as to the increase for 1894 over 1893, I am sorry to be unable to answer accurately, but would say the production was at least 20 per cent. greater during 1894. Los Angeles now produces more oil than all the remainder of the State together. And will, perhaps, increase the production to more than twice the amount of 1894, during the coming year."

The discovery of oil in this city has reduced the price from 7s. to 3s. per barrel, and even at 3s. some difficulty is found in marketing the output. The factories in this city consume about 800 barrels per day, and the Chino sugar factory takes 700 more. As soon as it is reasonably certain, however, that the supply is derived from an extensive deposit of oil, it is probable that sufficient factories will be established here to use the output. Three and three-quarter barrels of oil are equal to 1 ton of coal, if therefore the supply be continuous the question of cheap fuel for this district appears to be solved. The railways have been experimenting with a view to using oil in place of coal for fuel. The Southern Pacific Company writes me as to this as follows: "We do not at present contemplate using oil instead of coal as locomotive fuel. We may very likely use oil for kindling fire in locomotives at engine-houses, instead of wood, that, however, may not be done this year." "The Railway Age," "The Railway Review," and other papers interested in railways are discussing the question of the use of oil on locomotives, and, while admitting that it is very successfully used in Russia, the opinion appears to be general that unless the supply increases and the price decreases it cannot be generally used on the railways in this country.

Liquor traffic. Public-houses, here called saloons, pay a monthly license to the city authorities of 10*l.* each. In 1893 there were 165 in this city, there are now 170.

Land agents. An Englishman who thinks of settling here wrote me some months ago to ascertain if he would have any difficulty in finding a suitable piece of land for sale, and concluded his letter by asking if there were any land agents in this city. Land agents, here called "real estate agents," are quite numerous here; they pay a license of 2*l.* 8*s.* per annum, and the city clerk writes me that there are now 224 real estate agents paying this license.

Free hospital. T. Davidson, M.D., C.M., a Scotch physician practising in this city, is, in conjuction with other physicians, endeavouring to establish a free hospital. In reply to a letter I wrote him on the subject he writes me as follows: "In reply to yours of the 18th instant, I may state that we have incorporated under the California laws as the Los Angeles Polyclinic, for the free treatment of the sick poor, to afford facilities for post graduate instruction, and eventually to found a free hospital. The matter will soon be largely before the public. Our rooms, four in number, are located at 337, North Main Street."

Public Works.

Railway to Salt Lake City. For some years past I have from time to time referred to the proposed railway to connect Los Angeles with Salt Lake City, Utah. This railway will be of such importance to Los Angeles, and will so directly affect many British interests that I venture to repeat statements I have made in previous reports. The Union Pacific constructed from Salt Lake City to Milford, about 250 miles, in 1889, and in 1890 graded the line from Milford to Pioche Nevada, another 100 miles. Since 1890 nothing further has been done at the Salt Lake end of the proposed line. In 1893-94 the Nevada Southern Railway, which was incorporated to construct this line, constructed from Blake, a station on the Southern California Railway about 120 miles north-east of Los Angeles, to Vanderbilt, a mining camp about 30 miles north of the point of commencement. This road became involved financially, and is now in the hands of the Atchison, Topeka, and Santa Fé Railway. If the reports I have received as to the fertility and mineral wealth of the country between Blake and Pioche (about 300 miles) be true, or even half true, it is astonishing that capital has not been found in this country to complete the road. Apart from the local traffic it is alleged that there are no heavy grades, and it will shorten the distance from Los Angeles to Chicago by upwards of 400 miles. Several companies have been incorporated here in the past year to build the railway, I am not aware that they have done anything, however, except to incorporate and try to sell bonds in England. I think the road will be a prosperous one; were I sure of it, however, I would not advise English people to buy railway bonds when the whole cost of construction is to be met by the sale of such bonds. I have been assured by several well-informed railway men that this road will never be built until the Union Pacific Railway decides to build it, and I regret to say that it now seems probable that this is the case. It is estimated that about 2,000,000*l.* is required to complete the work of construction. If the communities to be benefited would subscribe half this amount, bonds for the remainder could no doubt be negotiated.

Railway to San Francisco. The Southern Pacific Railway is constructing a railway along the coast from San Francisco to Los Angeles, in addition to their present line through the San Joaquin Valley. The assistant general manager writes me as follows: "Work on the coast line, so-called, between San Luis Obispo and Santa Barbara is being carried along steadily. The line is now completed to a point $24\frac{3}{4}$ miles south of San Luis Obispo. It is impossible to now say when the line will be completed." This line is in operation from Los Angeles to Santa Barbara, and from San Luis Obispo to San Francisco.

Agriculture.

Oranges. In my report for 1893 I commented at some length on the question of over-production of oranges. Owing to the heavy losses sustained this winter by the Florida orange growers, by frost, there is a good demand for California oranges at remunerative prices, and if, as it is stated, a large proportion of the orange trees in Florida have been killed, the orange growers here will probably have several prosperous seasons. The secretary of the Florida Fruit Exchange writes me as follows: "The orange crop of this State for the season 1893–94 was 202,000 tons. The crop of 1894–95 was estimated to be at least 220,000 tons, of which about one half was marketed before the frost. The average net price realised is 4s. per box." As no mention is made of the extent of the injury to the trees, I apprehend that the statements that they are nearly all killed may be approximately true. Mr. Cayley, an Englishman, who is engaged in orange growing at Riverside has kindly written me at some length on the orange industry, and I give his letter in full as follows: "I will endeavour to answer your questions about the orange industry in this section. First as to the profit of the last three years. With few exceptions, though there are exceptions, it is generally allowed by growers that owing to frost, low prices, and a difficulty in marketing the fruit, there has been no profit, taking the last three years together. This year oranges are selling at a very remunerative price though it is not so high as in some previous years. I attribute the present satisfactory price entirely to the fact that so much of the Florida fruit has been destroyed by frost. There has been undoubted over-production in orange growing, and we should have found great difficulty in marketing this year's crop if we had had the enormous Florida crop to compete with. The expenses of irrigating and cultivating are so great here, and our distance from a market so great that competition with Florida becomes very difficult. Now I think that for the next 5 or 6 years we need not fear over-production. The frost in Florida appears to have killed all the young groves, and many of the old ones. How many of them will be replanted it is difficult to say, but as young trees do not begin to bear to any extent till they are 6 years old we shall at any rate have some years of prosperity. Of course much fresh land will be planted in California, but every acre planted is bringing us so much nearer to over-production again, so that it is not for the benefit of the orange industry for more capital to be expended in planting fresh lands. As to the profits of orange growing it is very difficult to collect reliable data. Riverside, which is the chief centre of the orange industry, will this year ship about 2,500 cars of 300 boxes each. The present price of navel oranges is 8s. 8d. f.o.b., which nets the grower about 6s. 8d. I think that if the grower receives over 4s. net for his fruit (navels) he is getting a fair return on his capital, valuing the land at present prices. Seedlings are proportionally less, so that selling oranges at the present price it is impossible for the grower to make a profit if he loses a crop every 2 or 3 years through frost or some other cause. There is some land which is practically free from damaging frosts but it is limited, and any Englishman coming out would do well to spend at least one winter in the locality he thinks of buying in, and make all the enquiries he can and notice whether the fruit is frosted or not. To make a profit three things are absolutely necessary. First, an undoubted supply of water for irrigation; secondly, land where there is no danger of a severe frost; and thirdly, sufficient capital to enable the grower to purchase his grove outright and not have to mortgage it at the high rates of interest charged in California. No grower can expect to make a living and a profit if he is paying 12 per cent. interest on a mortgage. Many places have plenty of water for irrigation in an ordinary year but it behoves the intending purchaser to satisfy himself that the supply is ample in the event of 1 or 2 dry years such as we have just passed through. Riverside is one of the very few places in Southern California where there was no shortage of water last summer. As to frosts, parts of Riverside are practically free from frost and parts are liable to it every year. Anyone with sufficient capital buying a ranch free from frost and with a good water supply will undoubtedly do well for the next few years, buying it at present prices which are much lower than they have ever been. Should the Florida groves be replanted to any great extent, we may have to contend with that bugbear, over-production, as soon as they come into bearing again. I should strongly advise any Englishman coming out now to either buy a ranch in full bearing or at least 3 or 4 years old. Otherwise he might plant out land and find that, by the time he was beginning to get a return for his outlay, there was no market for his fruit at a remunerative price. We have quite a large colony of English here of the better class most of whom are engaged in orange growing. The expenses of a grove are very heavy. Labour is high, though perhaps lower than formerly, and it is absolutely necessary to fertilise so that a man must have a certain amount of capital behind him in addition to his ranch. I have not gone much into figures as they are very deceptive, and two ranches close together often receive very different returns. The whole question seems to be frost and no frost, and the only way to invest profitably is to make sure of buying a ranch practically free from frost as some of them are." On the question of over-production of oranges I beg to refer to my report of 1893, also to articles in "The Investors' Review," London, for July, August, and October, 1894. Since writing the foregoing I see it stated in the press that upwards of 20,000 tons of foreign oranges have been landed in the Eastern States, and in consequence the shipments from Southern California have fallen from 1,200 tons to 200 tons per day.

California fruit in England.

The reports of the State Board of Horticulture are most valuable and interesting, and should be read by everyone interested in California fruits. One of the subjects treated in the last report is the attempt to ship fresh fruits to England. After giving the results of the attempt heretofore made, the report proceeds as follows: "Until such time as we can evolve a better system of shipment of our fruits to England, including cheaper and better transportation, which may be effected by the abolition of heavy refrigerating cars, with their enormous dead weight and their expensive iceing, the English market can be little else than a last resort into which we may be compelled to send our surplus fruit when our home market cannot consume it."

Scale bugs.

The red scale is still doing a good deal of damage in the

orange groves here, and experiments are constantly being made to discover some parasite which will prey on it, Mr. Craw, quarantine officer and entomologist, reports to the State Board of Horticulture as follows: "I visited the Kercheval orange orchard at Los Angeles, on June 25, and investigated the condition of the steel-blue ladybird (orcus chalybæus). While this beetle has spread and done fairly good work against the red scale (aspidiotus aurantii) I would still advise that they be not distributed for the present. In a recent letter from Mr. Koebele (now in Queensland collecting beneficial insects for the Hawaiian Government), he informs me that he has discovered an internal chalcid parasite preying upon the red scale in that country, and that he will endeavour to introduce them into California. I have to report receipt of several small packages of ladybirds, and other beneficial insects, from Mr. Koebele, that have been liberated upon scale infested trees."

Purple scale. In former reports I have described the process of destroying scale bugs by constructing a tent over infested trees, and generating hydrocyanic acid gas in the tent. Mr. Craw reports the destruction of purple scale at Rivera in this county, by this method as follows: "I visited several orange orchards near Rivera, where the trees were treated with hydrocyanic acid gas last fall and winter for the destruction of the Florida 'purple scale' referred to in my last report. Some of the most seriously infested trees were cut back and the stems and branches scrubbed and the adjoining trees were treated with the gas. Most of the infested orchards had a second treatment of gas. The result is that after a day's search I failed to find a single live 'purple scale,' or any that had eggs."

Scale bugs. Mr. Scott, who has been the Horticultural Commissioner for Los Angeles County for a number of years writes me as follows: "The fruit trees in Southern California are in better condition now than at any time since I have been Commissioner. The red scale is doing considerable damage in some districts where fumigation has not been resorted to. It is certainly the worst pest on citrus trees that we have to contend with. It does not attack deciduous trees."

Vine disease The disease which attacked the vines in this district 10 years ago, known here as the "California vine disease," and which up to 1891 destroyed 20,000 acres of vines, has now almost disappeared. Professor Newton B. Pierce, an agent of the Department of Agriculture who is now stationed in Southern California conducting experiments on plant diseases, writes me as to this disease, and as to the phylloxera as follows: "Slight indications of the 'California vine disease' still remain in some vineyards. In some instances this may be traced to the planting of the vineyards with cuttings from infected districts, others appear to be perfectly healthy, except as above the vineyards of the Santa Ana Valley appear to be in a healthy growing condition, no report has been received of any phylloxera appearing in any vineyard except that in which it was found $2\frac{1}{2}$ years ago. It is

Olive oil.

hoped that it has been stamped out there. The above replies to your queries apply to the condition of affairs last fall. It is yet too early to gather data for this season."

The production of olives and olive oil is increasing rapidly, as far as I can learn, however, there is as yet no danger of over-production, and, if the people can be induced to use olive oil for cooking purposes in place of the cotton seed oil and lard mixture or even butter, over-production will be out of the question. It is easier of digestion than the animal oil in butter, and there is no danger of such diseases as are engendered by butter obtained from diseased cows. The "New York Sun," commenting on the production of olives in this district, remarks as follows:— "California hopes to supply the entire American market with olives within the next few years. The production of the olive in the United States will, it is thought, give a new impetus to the use of its oil here. California olive oil is gaining in favour in the East already, although from the nature of things, the increase is not rapid. The pure oils bottled by the producers, under distinctive labels, continue to bring better prices in San Francisco than the best foreign oils. Olive oil is here used chiefly for salads, though its superior excellence in cookery for many purposes is gradually becoming recognised. The oil may be heated to a much higher degree than butter, which is one of its claims to the consideration of housekeepers."

Mr. Elwood Cooper, of Santa Barbara, who planted the first large olive grove in Southern California, is a recognised authority on all matters pertaining to olive culture. I wrote to him for some statistical information about the industry, and received the following reply:—"On account of the railroad strike in July last year no Olive Growers' Convention was held, and no reports of the crop have been made. Such news as I have received would indicate a very small crop, notwithstanding it was the year to expect a full crop. In young orchards there were was a fair crop. But on all the older trees almost no fruit, owing to the lack of rain, it being practically a dry year. I should average it at about one half that of 1893. Olive oil producers are still suffering from the adulterations and substitutions that are sold on the market under false labels at reduced prices. The financial panic has very much retarded the growing increase that was developing amongst intelligent people to demand and use only pure goods. Owing to the limited make, all the supplies will be exhausted before the next crop can be put on the market. A much larger portion of the olives have been pickled, as there is a great demand for them, which cannot be supplied. The price of the oil in bottles has remained without change, sold wholesale at 4s. per bottle. About 1l. 2s. per gallon in bulk would be about 18s. per gallon. We hope to hold another convention in July next, when correct statistics will be compiled."

Scale on olive trees.

Mr. Craw, quarantine officer and entomologist, in his last report to the State Board of Horticulture states as follows:— "Mr. John Scott, County Commissioner of Los Angeles, made a most opportune find in his county last February. This was a new and very serious scale pest, pollinia costæ, of the olive. It is a small light-coloured scale that clusters in thick patches over the large branches and twigs of the olive. From the appearance of the specimens sent me I consider this the most serious pest that could possibly be disseminated through the olive orchards of the State. The trees upon which it was found were purchased in Italy 6 years ago, and in that time were so seriously affected that but few leaves remained and the trees made little or no new growth. The twigs were covered with fungus, under which the scales congregated. The trees were cut down and the branches burned. A close watch will be kept to see that it has not spread. A careful examination should be made of all olive trees that have been introduced from Europe, to see that they are not infested with this scale. The spread of this pest at a time when we have a good prospect of having perfectly clean olive trees in the near future by the good work of the rhizobius ventralis, would be an event to be deplored."

Railway strike, effect of on fruit growers. The strike on the trans-continental railways last summer happened most inopportunely for the fruit growers in this district. No trains were allowed to cross the continent for two weeks, and a vast amount of fruit was allowed to rot on the cars and on the trees. Mr. Lelong, Secretary of the State Board of Horticulture, in his last report, comments as follows on the strike :—" When the apricots and early peaches were ready for shipment, the great strike, which tied up all the trans-continental lines, had been inaugurated, and our growers found themselves with large crops of fine fruit on hand and no means of reaching the market. As a result, the losses to our orchardists were very heavy, and, while it is not possible to obtain an accurate account of the amount, conservative estimates are to the effect that 1,000,000 dol. would not make the fruit growers of California whole from the effects of the strike. The complete tying-up of all trains, and the uncertainty of moving freight, stopped all fruit traffic from the latter part of June to the end of July. It was not until the last few days of July that regular movements of fruit trains were resumed, and in the meantime a very large and important part of the fruit season had passed. The early fruit sections were especially the sufferers by the blockade, as the market for early fruits was practically closed before the blockade was raised."

Irrigation. The rainy season here commences in November and lasts until May. The rainfall in this city since official records have been kept has been as follows :—

UNITED STATES.

Season of—	Number of Inches.
1878–79	11·35
1879–80	20·34
1880–81	13·13
1881–82	10·40
1882–83	12·11
1883–84	38·22
1884–85	9·25
1885–86	22·38
1886–87	13·76
1887–88	14·01
1888–89	19·25
1889–90	34·84
1890–91	13·36
1891–92	11·85
1892–93	26·28
1893–94	6·40

It will be seen from the foregoing table that the rainfall last year was less than in any previous year. In consequence, the crops were very light, the grain in many places not being worth harvesting.

Irrigation Act.

The Irrigation Act, referred to at some length in my last report, is not working very satisfactorily. Several irrigation districts have disincorporated, and others are about to do so. Many persons and companies lending money on mortgage refuse to lend on land included in the limits of an irrigation district, and some mortgage companies provide in their mortgages that if the land mortgaged be included in an irrigation district the money secured by the mortgage shall immediately become due and payable. Persons who think of investing in irrigation bonds should wait until the Supreme Court of the United States has passed on the constitutionality of the Act under which such bonds are issued.

Kern county.

The system of irrigation in Kern County, which is the most extensive in this State, was developed by private enterprise, and not under the Act referred to. The Kern County Land Company maintain an office in London for the sale of these lands, and 200 or 300 English people have purchased land and settled in that county. I have been informed that a large percentage of these people have been unsuccessful, that many of them have left the county, and that many more would do so could they succeed in selling their property. In reply to an inquiry I addressed to the company, I have received the following letter, dated March 20, 1895:—

"In reply to your letter of the 1st inst. requesting information about Kern County which would be of interest to English capitalists or settlers, we beg to submit the following:—The greater portion of the arable land of Kern County is now, and has been for a period of 20 years, owned by the late firm of Miller and Lux and this company. During this period these parties have developed the large irrigating system which now covers these lands. Up to 1890 these lands were used exclusively for stock ranches, and nothing was cultivated except alfalfa. Since that time, however, thousands of acres have been planted to vines and deciduous fruit trees of all kinds by the settlers purchasing these lands, and it has been demonstrated that the soil and climate cannot be excelled in the State for viticulture, horticulture, and alfalfa. Since the spring of 1889 this company has sold over 18,000 acres, a good portion of which was sold to English settlers. Many of them have succeeded; others, less fortunate, have had unnecessary difficulties caused by bad advice at the start, both as regards cropping and the yielding profit. There are two English colonies out here, one at Rosedale and the other at Greenfields; these colonies are divided into 20-acre tracts, prices of which vary from 12*l.* to 16*l.* per acre, according to the location. The terms of payment are one-fourth cash, balance in 3, 4, or 5 years, with interest on deferred payments at 7 per cent. per annum. There are very good opportunities here for young men who are familiar with farming, who know what hard work is, and who realise that success can only be achieved through diligence and industry. In conclusion, we would say to the prospective English settler we have to offer a soil and climate, with abundance of water for irrigation, which cannot be excelled for the culture of deciduous fruits, nuts, hay, grain, and alfalfa, at comparatively low prices and liberal terms. To English capitalists we have to offer the same soil and climate in large tracts at cheaper rates and same terms, either for investment or for colonising purposes."

The great drawback to settlement in this county is the intense heat in summer. As, however, Englishmen cannot now purchase land in California until, after 5 years' residence, they have become citizens, newcomers will have plenty of time to make up their minds when they will settle.

In this report dollars have been converted into sterling at the rate of 5 dol. per 1*l.*

San Diego.

Trade and Commerce.

The past year has been one of depression, and San Diego has suffered in common with other places. There is very little prospect of improvement in the near future. *Trade depressed.*

The value of grain shipments during the year was 34,390*l.* Larger quantities of raisins, fish, hay, honey, hides, wool, cement, and general produce were exported than in the year previous. The revenues collected for the fiscal year ending June 30, 1894, amounted to 19,005*l.* *General business.*

Most of the imports, with the exception of coal and cement, were received by sail and rail from the Eastern States. *Import trade.*

(1984)

UNITED STATES.

Wheat and barley.

No wheat or barley have been exported to the United Kingdom during the past year, although freight rates have ruled low.

The following tables show the exports and imports for the past 2 years:—

RETURN of Principal Articles of Export from San Diego during the Years 1893–94.

Articles.		1893. Quantity.	1893. Value.	1894. Quantity.	1894. Value.
			£ s. d.		£ s. d.
Barley	Bushels	374,966	24,103 8 0	150,382	10,614 16 0
Wheat	,,	86,428	10,501 0 0	138,792	17,114 16 0
Agricultural implements	...	...	305 0 0	...	145 8 0
Fruits and nuts	...	...	239 8 0	...	124 16 0
Manufactures, iron and steel	...	...	2,281 4 0	...	1,682 0 0
Wine	...	...	156 16 0	...	50 16 0
Powder and explosives	...	...	191 8 0	...	188 4 0
Lumber	...	...	701 4 0	...	1,075 12 0
Lime and cement	...	...	24 0 0	...	48 12 0
Coals	...	...	8 4 0	...	3 4 0
Other articles	...	...	8,570 16 0	...	8,064 12 0
Total	...	...	47,082 8 0	...	39,112 16 0

RETURN of Principal Articles of Import to San Diego during the Years 1893–94.

Articles.		1893. Quantity.	1893. Value.	1894. Quantity.	1894. Value.
			£ s. d.		£ s. d.
Coal	Tons	86,098	51,334 8 0	86,594	49,435 6 6
Cement	,,	33,826	9,029 12 0	55,925	14,750 16 6
Other articles	...	...	17,767 16 0	...	24,293 18 0
Total	...	...	78,131 16 0	...	88,480 2 0

TABLE showing Total Value of all Articles Exported from and Imported to San Diego from and to Foreign Countries during the Years 1893–94.

Country.	Exports. 1893.	Exports. 1894.	Imports. 1893.	Imports. 1894.
	£ s.	£ s.	£ s.	£ s.
Great Britain and British possessions	26,359 0	27,326 16	67,303 0	65,392 8
Mexico	20,532 12	11,786 0	10,614 16	23,028 14
Not classified	190 16	..	214 0	59 0
Total	47,082 8	39,112 16	78,131 16	88,480 2

SAN FRANCISCO.

Shipping and Navigation.

The following official figures, furnished by the customs office for 1893–94, will give some idea of the business of the port.

The number of vessels arriving was 322, classified as follows :—

Nationality.	Number of Vessels.	Total Net Tonnage.
American	218	..
British	26	..
Nicaraguan	72	..
Mexican	1	..
German	3	..
Hawaiian	1	..
Chinese	1	..
Total	322	241,035

The value of dutiable imports was 61,583*l.*, and of free imports, 10,585*l.*; receipts of lumber, 17,724,000 feet; coal, value 47,053*l.*; cement, value 9,034*l.*

The following table shows the number and nationalities of vessels which entered and cleared during the year :—

RETURN of all Shipping at the Port of San Diego during the Year 1894.

ENTERED.

Nationality.	Sailing. Number of Vessels.	Sailing. Tons.	Steam. Number of Vessels.	Steam. Tons.	Total. Number of Vessels.	Total. Tons.
British	23	39,889	8	13,264	31	53,153
American	68	7,853	128	124,037	196	131,890
Other countries	2	2,065	70	7,763	72	9,828
Total	93	49,807	206	145,064	299	194,871
,, for the year preceding	92	55,022	250	205,685	342	261,707

CLEARED.

Nationality.	Sailing. Number of Vessels.	Sailing. Tons.	Steam. Number of Vessels.	Steam. Tons.	Total Number of Vessels.	Total Tons.
British	21	36,085	8	13,264	29	49,349
American	65	7,505	125	122,750	190	130,255
Other countries	2	2,065	70	7,763	72	9,828
Total	88	45,655	203	143,777	291	189,432
,, for the year preceding	96	59,394	248	202,910	344	262,304

UNITED STATES.

Pacific mail steamers.

I am indebted to Mr. A. Higgins, Deputy Collector of Customs, for the information given in the preceding tables.

The steamers of the Pacific Mail Company have ceased to call at San Diego, and direct communication with the south is thus cut off for the present. It is stated that a new company formed in Mexico is about to put on some steamers, which will call at this port.

Population and Industries.

County.

San Diego County comprises the southern end of the State of California, and has an area of about 9,000 square miles. The population is over 34,000, the census of 1890 showing an increase of about 305 per cent. over 1880. The assessed valuation is about 5,800,000*l*.

City.

The city of San Diego has a population of about 18,000, and the lowest death rate of any city in California, and has a most equable climate. It has 5 miles of paved streets, 15 hotels, 23 churches, 14 public schools, 5 banks, 10 miles of electric street car line, two steamship lines, one trans-continental railroad.

Signal service record.

One of the great attractions of San Diego is its climate. According to the official records of the United Sates Signal Service, during 22 years (from 1872 to 1894), out of 8,035 days 7,445 were clear or fair, and there were only 935 days in which rain fell to the amount of ·01 of an inch, or over. During 19 years (from 1875 to 1894), out of 6,936 days there were 6,723 days in which the temperature fell to 32. There have been but two years, 1878 and 1885, in which the temperature has reached 100 degrees on any day. The mean temperature of each month for the past 19 years has been as follows :—

Month.	Degrees.
January	54·0
February	54·6
March	56·2
April	58·2
May	61·1
June	64·4
July	68·2
August	70·0
September	67·0
October	63·4
November	59·7
December	54·2

Country settling up.

Although there is not much of interest to report as regards the city of San Diego, it is different with regard to the surrounding country. There has been much tree planting during the past 2 years; over 2,500 acres were planted last year; and settlers continue to arrive in increasing numbers.

Notwithstanding the general depression, building has gone on with energy, an indication of growth and progress not to be overlooked. Many good business structures and good private residences attest this fact. *Building interest.*

Several water companies are making offers to the city of San Diego for further supplying the city and surrounding country with water for irrigation and domestic purposes, and it is probable that one or more of the propositions will be accepted, and will, no doubt, lead to a great development of the county and city. *Water companies.*

The mineral products of the country consist of gold, silver, tin, copper, lead, gypsum, asbestos, mica, ochre, salt, alum, borax, limestone, iron, quicksilver, and sulphur. There are also a number of granite and marble quarries in operation. *Mineral products.*

Agriculture.

Among the dairies of this region the largest is the Santa Ysabel, which milks 800 cows, and ships the butter to San Diego, where it finds a ready market at an average of 10d. per lb. the year round. The skim milk fattens many hogs, selling readily at from 2½d. to 3½d. per lb. *Dairies.*

San Diego County has for a number of years been one of the leading counties in the United States in the production of honey. The annual product varies from 1,000,000 lbs. to 2,000,000 lbs. Formerly it exceeded the latter figure, but new settlers are making inroads on the bee pasture. Bees do well up to 4,500 feet above sea-level, and the large varieties of wild flowers on the mountain sides are particularly favourable to bee raising. White sage grows in abundance, and produces a fine grade of honey. *Honey.*

Among the fruits which may be gathered fresh from the trees the year round are the orange, lemon, and lime. Strawberries and guaras are gathered nearly all the year; figs from July to Christmas; apples and pears July to November; grapes, watermelons, and mulberries, July to December; loquats and currants, May and June; raspberries, from June to January; olives, December and January; pomegranates, September to December; almonds, October; quinces, October to December. Several kinds of vegetables are ready for market every day in the year. *Fruits.*

It has been estimated that there are upwards of 3,000,000 fruit trees in the county, of which about 300,000 are orange and 400,000 are lemon trees. The lemons grown in this county are very fine. *Citrus trees.*

The area suitable to the production of the lemon is so small in proportion to the vast extent of countries where it cannot be grown, and where the demand as a necessity and not a luxury is daily growing very rapidly, that the price is always high and the demand good. Then, unlike many other products, the lemon can be cured and kept in the storehouse for several months, rendering it unnecessary to hurry the marketing at any given *Lemons.*

time. The advantages of climate and soil obtainable in these parts for lemon culture should render it safe and profitable.

In the San Diego Bay region are 100,000 acres of choice Mesa lands, practically frostless, that cannot be excelled anywhere for lemon growing.

Olives. — The acreage in olives is yet small, perhaps because growers of fruit prefer quicker returns upon their investments. The olive is propagated from cuttings, and grows rapidly even on poor soil, with little care, but, like any other tree, repays culture. Land that is very rich makes the tree run to wood. The tree begins to bear in from 3 to 5 years from the planting of 1-year-old rooted cuttings. Pure oil is scarce, and is sold by druggists at 6s. per quart bottle. Pickled olives are sold at 2s. to 4s. per gallon. The machinery for extracting the oil is simple and inexpensive.

Peaches. — Peach growing is yet on the threshold of the great future in store for it, although some of the finest peaches have been produced here.

Canaigre root. — The canaigre root is attracting some attention, as there is a good deal of land suitable to its cultivation. Should it be grown to any extent, it would probably lead to the erection of a tanning establishment in the vicinity. The canaigre root appears to make as good a tanning medium as oak bark, and is far superior to hemlock.

Land values. — The prices of land in this county have a wide range, owing to location and quality, the average being about 50 per cent. of the prevailing prices in Los Angeles and other southern California counties to the north.

Good citrus fruit land can be had, with water privileges, at from 12*l.* to 70*l.* per acre, while good farming land, adapted to the culture of cereals and deciduous fruits, and to stock raising, can be had in the cereal or mountain region at prices ranging from 1*l.* to 10*l.* per acre. There are over 2,000,000 acres of arable land in the county, of which, up to the present, 20,000 acres is irrigated land.

Round National City, on the Chula Vista tract, and in the Sweetwater Valley, all under the Sweetwater irrigation system, lands bring all the way from 20*l.* to 70*l.* per acre.

Land values in suburbs. — This is the most thickly settled portion of the county outside San Diego. People have bought and are buying these lands because of their proximity to San Diego, their intrinsic productive value, the railroad facilities, and the absolute certainty of a permanent water supply.

Public Works.

Jetty. — The harbour is subjected to conflicting currents, caused by the Zuninga Shoals, lying south of North Island and east of the bar. To prevent further shoaling, and to maintain the present depth of water over the bar and entrance, the Government is building a jetty along the Zuninga Shoals, so as to form a solid wall for the eastern side of the harbour mouth, parallel with Point Loma. The tides will then flow straight in and out over the bar, and scour the channel in so doing. The depth at the bar will remain the same, or will possibly be increased. The jetty will be about 7,200 feet in length, 22 feet wide at bottom, and reaching to a height above the highest tides.

Efforts are being made to build a new railway to the east, Railways. viâ Yuma and Phœnix, Arizona. The San Diego, Cuyamaca, and Eastern Railway is in operation from San Diego to Fosters', 25 miles north-east. An independent trans-continental line, if completed, would bring prosperity with it, as it would utilise San Diego's splendid harbour.

Dollars have been converted into sterling at the rate of 5 dol. to 1*l*.

(1984)

LONDON:
Printed for Her Majesty's Stationery Office,
By HARRISON AND SONS,
Printers in Ordinary to Her Majesty.
(75 7 | 95—H & S   1984)

FOREIGN OFFICE.
1895.
ANNUAL SERIES.

Nº· 1590.

DIPLOMATIC AND CONSULAR REPORTS ON TRADE AND FINANCE.

UNITED STATES.

REPORT FOR THE YEAR 1894

ON THE

AGRICULTURE OF THE STATES OF NEW YORK, NEW JERSEY, CONNECTICUT, DELAWARE, AND RHODE ISLAND.

REFERENCE TO PREVIOUS REPORT, Annual Series No. 1319.

Issued during the Recess and Presented to both Houses of Parliament by Command of Her Majesty.

LONDON:
PRINTED FOR HER MAJESTY'S STATIONERY OFFICE,
BY HARRISON AND SONS, ST. MARTIN'S LANE,
PRINTERS IN ORDINARY TO HER MAJESTY.

And to be purchased, either directly or through any Bookseller, from
EYRE & SPOTTISWOODE, EAST HARDING STREET, FLEET STREET, E.C., and
32, ABINGDON STREET, WESTMINSTER, S.W.; or
JOHN MENZIES & Co., 12, HANOVER STREET, EDINBURGH, and
90, WEST NILE STREET, GLASGOW; or
HODGES, FIGGIS, & Co., Limited. 104, GRAFTON STREET, DUBLIN.

1895.

[C. 7828—7.] *Price One Penny.*

New Series of Reports.

Reports of the Annual Series have been issued from Her Majesty's Diplomatic and Consular Officers at the following places, and may be obtained from the sources indicated on the title-page:—

No.		Price.	No.		Price.
1470.	Dantzig	5d.	1530.	Wuhu	1½d.
1471.	Guayaquil	1d.	1531.	Rio de Janeiro	2½d.
1472.	Canton	1½d.	1532.	Trieste	2d.
1473.	Dar-al-Baida	3d.	1533.	Brest	1½d.
1474.	Teheran	2d.	1534.	Stockholm	2d.
1475.	Bushire	2d.	1535.	Warsaw	1d.
1476.	Tangier	2d.	1536.	Boston	1½d.
1477.	Rome	2d.	1537.	Mozambique	2½d.
1478.	Hamburg	4d.	1538.	Callao	1d.
1479.	The Hague	1½d.	1539.	Aleppo	1½d.
1480.	Belgrade	2d.	1540.	Jaffa	½d.
1481.	Batoum	1½d.	1541.	Boston	1d.
1482.	Teneriffe	½d.	1542.	New Orleans	1½d.
1483.	Lisbon	2½d.	1543.	Chicago	3d.
1484.	Buda-Pesth	½d.	1544.	Palermo	2½d.
1485.	Rome	5½d.	1545.	Bengazi	1½d.
1486.	Para	1d.	1546.	Cagliari	1d.
1487.	Odessa	1d.	1547.	Pernambuco	7½d.
1488.	Hakodate	1d.	1548.	Madrid	1½d.
1489.	Beira	1½d.	1549.	Corunna	5d.
1490.	Berne	1½d.	1550.	Leghorn	2d.
1491.	Copenhagen	1d.	1551.	New Orleans	2½d.
1492.	Stettin	2½d.	1552.	Syra	1½d.
1493.	Rio Grande do Sul	1½d.	1553.	Genoa	9d.
1494.	Serajevo	1d.	1554.	Berlin	2½d.
1495.	Buenos Ayres	9d.	1555.	Tainan	1d.
1496.	Florence	2d.	1556.	Zanzibar	4d.
1497.	Lisbon	1½d.	1557.	Dunkirk	1d.
1498.	Paris	2d.	1558.	Ningpo	1d.
1499.	Bolivia	1½d.	1559.	Pakhoi	1d.
1500.	Patras	1½d.	1560.	Chinkiang	1d.
1501.	Bordeaux	3d.	1561.	New York	2d.
1502.	Madrid	2d.	1562.	Batoum	11½d.
1503.	Amsterdam	1d.	1563.	Naples	2d.
1504.	Suakin	1d.	1564.	Resht	4½d.
1505.	Angora	1d.	1565.	Copenhagen	1½d.
1506.	Havre	2½d.	1566.	Porto Rico	1½d.
1507.	Algiers	11d.	1567.	Malaga	3d.
1508.	La Rochelle	3d.	1568.	Galveston	7½d.
1509.	Vera Cruz	2d.	1569.	Tabreez	½d.
1510.	Puerto Cortes	1d.	1570.	Fiji	½d.
1511.	Taganrog	1d.	1571.	Athens	2½d.
1512.	Baltimore	1½d.	1572.	Bilbao	3½d.
1513.	Mexico	1½d.	1573.	Barcelona	3d.
1514.	Zaila	1d.	1574.	Fiume	2d.
1515.	Zomba	3½d.	1575.	Tahiti	1d.
1516.	Valparaiso	2½d.	1576.	San Francisco	6d.
1517.	Charleston	2½d.	1577.	Ichang	1½d.
1518.	Serajevo	1d.	1578.	Amoy	1½d.
1519.	Saigon	1d.	1579.	Wênchow	1d.
1520.	Bangkok	2d.	1580.	Smyrna	2½d.
1521.	Tripoli	1d.	1581.	Nice	1½d.
1522.	Batavia	1½d.	1582.	Sôul	1½d.
1523.	Dakar	½d.	1583.	Rio Grande do Sul	4d.
1524.	Havana	2d.	1584.	Nagasaki	1d.
1525.	Riga	2d.	1585.	Hakodate	1d.
1526.	Trebizond	1½d.	1586.	Frankfort	3d.
1527.	Piræus	2½d.	1587.	Samoa	1d.
1528.	Guayaquil	1½d.	1588.	Cherbourg	1¼d.
1529.	Marseilles	1½d.	1589.	Damascus	1d.

No. 1590.

Reference to previous Report, Annual Series No. 1319.

UNITED STATES.

NEW YORK.

Consul-General Sanderson to the Earl of Kimberley.

My Lord,　　　　　　　　　　New York, June 18, 1895.

I HAVE the honour to enclose my Annual Report on the Agricultural Condition of this Consular District.

I have, &c.
(Signed)　　PERCY SANDERSON.

Report on the Agricultural Condition of the Consular District of New York.

ABSTRACT of Contents.

	PAGE
New York—	
General depression	2
Cereals	2
Dairy industry	3
Milch cows	3
Butter and cheese	4
Cows	6
Live stock	6
Wool clip	8
Hay	8
Potatoes	9
Hops	9
Apples	10
Tobacco	10
Onions	10
Vegetables and fruit	10
New Jersey—	
Labourers' wages	11
Farming	11
Farms in New Jersey	12

(2019)

UNITED STATES.

General depression.

The agricultural interests in the five States which constitute this Consular District, suffered severely in the year 1894, in common with all other branches of trade and industry.

It is true that the production of cereals is not, and has not been for many years past, of any great importance as compared with that of other States (hence, perhaps, in a certain measure the great difficulty which is experienced in obtaining reliable statistics), but all prices ruled exceptionally low for livestock as well as for the different kinds of farm produce.

Cereals.

The following tables give the production in bushels of the different States in 1894 as compared with 1893:—

NEW YORK.

	Quantity 1894.	Quantity 1893.
	Bushels.	Bushels.
Wheat	6,297,000	6,389,000
Maize	13,854,000	15,255,000
Oats	30,320,000	30,208,000
Rye	3,610,000	3,424,000
Barley	4,546,000	5,493,000
Buckwheat	4,513,000	4,111,000

NEW JERSEY.

	Quantity 1894.	Quantity 1893.
	Bushels.	Bushels.
Wheat	1,779,000	1,794,000
Maize	8,991,000	7,179,000
Oats	3,085,000	2,622,000
Rye	1,120,000	1,024,000
Buckwheat	196,000	196,000

CONNECTICUT.

	Quantity 1894.	Quantity 1893.
	Bushels.	Bushels.
Maize	1,404,000	1,228,000
Oats	606,352	593,000
Rye	207,664	256,000
Buckwheat	65,000	66,000

NEW YORK.

DELAWARE.

	Quantity.	
	1894.	1893.
	Bushels.	Bushels.
Wheat	1,331,000	1,413,000
Maize	4,397,000	4,917,000
Oats	427,823	534,000
Buckwheat	6,500	6,000

RHODE ISLAND.

	Quantity.	
	1894.	1893.
	Bushels.	Bushels.
Maize	281,000	218,000
Oats	112,950	116,000
Barley	11,100	9,000

The total production of the United States in 1894 is estimated as follows:—

	Quantity.	
	1894.	1893.
	Bushels.	Bushels.
Wheat	460,267,416	396,131,725
Maize	1,212,770,052	1,619,496,131
Oats	662,036,928	638,854,850
Rye	26,727,615	26,555,000
Barley	61,400,465	69,869,000
Buckwheat	12,668,200	12,132,000

A very large amount of capital is invested in dairies, and the following figures give the number and value of the milch cows on January 1, 1895, and 1894 respectively:— *Dairy Industry. Milch cows.*

(2019.)

UNITED STATES.

	1895.		1894.	
	Number.	Value.	Number.	Value.
		£		£
New York	1,588,167	8,757,153	1,572,443	8,107,516
New Jersey	192,461	1,211,326	190,734	1,342,600
Connecticut	137,582	808,400	137,582	796,325
Delaware	38,836	169,180	33,836	165,796
Rhode Island	25,013	145,000	24,765	131,750
Total for United States	16,504,629	72,520,386	16,487,450	71,800,000

Butter and cheese. As regards the production of butter and cheese there is great difficulty in obtaining reliable statistics. The following figures are taken from the census of 1890, and appear to be the latest available for the purposes of comparison; even these, however, are unsatisfactory, inasmuch as it appeared on investigation that they referred only to farms, to the exclusion of creameries and factories:—

STATE of New Jersey, 1894.

	Quantity.		
	Butter.	Cheese.	Milk.
	Lbs.	Lbs.	Gallons.
New York	98,241,813	4,324,028	663,917,000
New Jersey	8,367,218	23,613	64,003,950
Connecticut	7,196,000	112,566	54,413,000
Delaware	2,026,490	359	10,699,362
Rhode Island	965,456	24,631	10,610,547
Total	116,796,985	4,485,197	803,643,859
,, United States	1,023,821,770	18,725,218	5,207,121,309

Thus, so far as the farms are concerned, these five States would seem to produce about 11 per cent. of the butter, 24 per cent. of the cheese, and 15 per cent. of the milk of the United States.

The latest obtainable figures respecting the production of butter and cheese in factories and creameries in the State of New York are those furnished by the Commissioner of Agriculture in his report for the year ending September 30, 1893; this report shows that in 12 counties there were no factories of this nature, and that in the remaining 48 counties there were 255 butter factories and 1,156 cheese factories, also 213 factories making both butter and cheese. The whole number of factories was 1,624, and their product for the year 1892 was 19,497,357 lbs. of butter and 131,148,310 lbs. of cheese.

NEW YORK.

The receipts of butter, cheese, and eggs at New York during the last 3 years are given as follows:—

Year.	Quantity.		
	Butter.	Cheese.	Eggs.
	Lbs.	Lbs.	Dozens.
1892	99,850,640	100,112,400	64,867,490
1893	97,632,300	78,388,950	67,429,230
1894	103,062,600	79,731,250	71,751,270

The following report was recently received from Utica, one of the largest dairy markets in the State of New York.

"The prices of dairy products are the lowest since 1879, the best butter being sold at $16\frac{1}{2}$ c. to 17 c. per lb., cheese from 5 c. to $5\frac{1}{4}$ c. (quotation of May 15), and milk is being sold to the factories at $4\frac{1}{2}$ c. to $4\frac{3}{4}$ c. for each 10 lbs."

All cheese and butter, so far this spring, has been sold on commission, none of the jobbers buying outright. These prices represent about $8\frac{1}{2}d.$ a lb. for butter, rather over $2\frac{1}{2}d.$ for cheese, and a little over $2\frac{1}{4}d.$ per 10 lbs. of milk.

They apply to fodder butter and cheese; when grass butter and cheese come on the market better prices are expected.

The following statistics of the two great interior cheese markets of the State of New York, namely, Utica and Little Falls, in the Mohawk Valley, give the receipts and prices for the past 3 years:—

UTICA.

Year.	Boxes Sold.	Highest Price.		Lowest Price.	
		Currency.	Sterling.	Currency.	Sterling.
		Cents.	d.	Cents.	d.
1892	248,470	$10\frac{3}{4}$	$5\frac{3}{8}$	$8\frac{1}{4}$	$4\frac{1}{8}$
1893	217,762	$12\frac{1}{2}$	$6\frac{1}{4}$	$8\frac{1}{8}$	$4\frac{1}{16}$
1894	273,896	$11\frac{1}{4}$	$5\frac{5}{8}$	$7\frac{3}{4}$	$3\frac{7}{8}$

VALUE.

Year.	Currency.	Sterling.
	Dollars.	£
1892	1,390,935	278,187
1893	1,260,484	252,097
1894	1,555,455	311,091

(2019)

UNITED STATES.

LITTLE FALLS.

Year.	Boxes Sold, Including Dairy.	Highest Price. Currency.	Highest Price. Sterling.	Lowest Price. Currency.	Lowest Price. Sterling.
		Cents.	d.	Cents.	d.
1892	219,939	10¾	5⅜	7	3½
1893	197,865	11¼	5⅝	8	4
1894	202,028	11	5½	7½	3¾

VALUE.

Year.	Currency.	Sterling.
	Dollars.	£
1892	1,218,662	243,732
1893	1,106,337	221,267
1894	1,088,475	217,695

Cows. From statistics which have been compiled it would appear that between the years 1880 and 1890 the number of cows increased by 33 per cent., and the class of stock was much improved; many creameries sprang up and there was a tendency towards over-production; the fall in prices and the late general depression has checked production and discouraged breeding. The high price of beef which has ruled lately led to the slaughter of certain number of cows, and it is stated that the number of milch cows in proportion to the population is lower now than it has been for years.

With a probable diminution in the production and an improvement in general business, butter and cheese seem likely to command higher prices, and the restrictions on the sale of oleomargarine which have been adopted in several States would also tend in this direction.

Live stock. The following tables show the number and estimated value of the livestock on the farms on January 1 of the past 2 years:—

HORSES.

State.	1895. Number.	1895. Value. Currency.	1895. Value. Sterling.	1894. Number.	1894. Value. Currency.	1894. Value. Sterling.
		Dollars.	£		Dollars.	£
New York	695,793	40,802,649	8,160,530	702,840	50,466,294	10,093,200
New Jersey	84,987	5,608,180	1,121,636	83,821	7,105,037	1,421,007
Connecticut	43,478	2,660,000	532,000	45,776	4,116,471	823,294
Delaware	29,386	1,203,345	240,669	29,386	1,484,924	296,985
Rhode Island	10,234	831,121	166,224	10,443	996,565	199,313
Total	863,878	51,105,295	10,221,059	871,737	64,169,291	12,835,860
" for United States	15,893,318	576,730,580	115,346,116	16,081,139	769,224,799	153,844,960

NEW YORK.

Cattle and Oxen.

State.	1895. Number.	1895. Value. Currency.	1895. Value. Sterling.	1894. Number.	1894. Value. Currency.	1894. Value. Sterling.
		Dollars.	£		Dollars.	£
New York	671,267	15,697,187	3,139,438	706,597	18,434,989	3,696,998
New Jersey	48,956	1,174,323	234,865	52,641	1,532,272	306,454
Connecticut	73,042	2,085,891	417,178	76,886	2,125,980	425,196
Delaware	26,544	410,898	82,180	26,544	462,924	82,585
Rhode Island	11,596	275,982	55,198	11,713	247,451	49,490
Total	831,495	19,644,281	3,928,856	874,341	22,853,616	4,570,723
,, for United States	34,364,216	482,999,129	96,599,826	36,608,168	536,789,747	107,357,949

Sheep.

State.	1895. Number.	1895. Value. Currency.	1895. Value. Sterling.	1894. Number.	1894. Value. Currency.	1894. Value. Sterling.
		Dollars.	£		Dollars.	£
New York	1,096,560	2,486,449	497,289	1,388,051	3,962,885	792,577
New Jersey	50,662	172,849	34,569	57,571	235,177	47,035
Connecticut	37,934	123,234	24,647	39,930	138,014	27,603
Delaware	12,873	33,921	6,784	12,873	40,968	8,193
Rhode Island	11,279	31,468	6,293	11,279	41,168	8,233
Total	1,209,309	2,847,921	569,584	1,509,704	4,416,212	883,242
,, for United States	42,294,064	66,685,767	13,337,153	45,048,017	89,186,110	17,837,222

Hogs.

State.	1895. Number.	1895. Value. Currency.	1895. Value. Sterling.	1894. Number.	1894. Value. Currency.	1894. Value. Sterling.
		Dollars.	£		Dollars.	£
New York	658,605	5,041,487	1,008,297	658,005	5,940,680	1,188,136
New Jersey	175,515	1,316,729	263,346	182,830	1,981,880	376,376
Connecticut	52,172	603,940	120,788	53,785	579,596	115,919
Delaware	52,167	271,268	54,253	52,167	198,234	39,647
Rhode Island	13,616	137,030	27,406	13,481	152,664	30,533
Total	952,075	7,370,454	1,474,091	960,268	8,853,054	1,770,611
,, for United States	44,165,716	219,501,267	43,900,253	45,206,498	270,384,626	54,076,925

The following table gives the value per head of live-stock as estimated at the beginning of 1894 and 1895:—

UNITED STATES.

	1894.		1895.	
	Currency.	Sterling.	Currency.	Sterling.
	Dol. c.	£ s. d.	Dol. c.	£ s. d.
Horses	47 83	9 11 5	36 29	7 5 2
Mules	62 17	12 8 8	47 55	9 10 3
Milch cows	21 77	4 7 3	21 97	4 8 0
Cattle	14 66	2 18 8	14 6	2 16 3
Sheep	1 98	0 8 0	1 58	0 6 4
Swine	5 98	1 5 0	4 97	0 19 11

From these figures it will be seen that there has been a fall in values in every case except that of milch cows, and this, notwithstanding the low prices ruling at the beginning of 1894. The fall is most noticeable in the value of horses and mules, and seems to be due to the general introduction of electric and cable cars in the streets and to the very extensive adoption of the bicycle.

While the prices of hogs and beef cattle have risen since the beginning of the year, there has been no corresponding rise in the values of horses and mules.

Wool clip.

The return of the number of sheep in connection with the wool clip are given as under:—

States.	Number of Sheep.		Average Weight of Fleece.	Wool Clip, Washed and Unwashed.	Shrinkage.	Scoured Wool.
	January 1, 1894.	April 1, 1894.				
			Bales.	Bales.	Per cwt.	Bales.
New York	1,388,051	1,349,186	6¼	8,432,413	53	3,963,234
New Jersey	57,571	54,980	5	274,900	48	142,948
Connecticut	39,930	38,692	6	232,152	44	130,005
Delaware	12,873	12,525	5½	68,888	46	37,200
Rhode Island	11,279	10,704	6	64,224	43	36,608

Hay.

The production of hay was as follows:—

States.	1894.				Value, 1895.
	Acres.	Quantity.	Value.		
			Currency.	Sterling.	
		Tons.	Dollars.	£	£
New York	5,297,087	6,197,592	59,868,739	11,973,748	16,537,740
New Jersey	505,554	586,443	8,262,982	1,652,596	1,836,564
Connecticut	517,699	450,398	7,008,193	1,401,639	1,793,800
Delaware	61,524	79,981	1,199,715	239,949	146,600
Rhode Island	81,543	64,907	1,059,931	211,986	281,400

The hay crop of the United States is given as 54,874,000 tons, of the value of 468,578,000 dol. (93,715,600*l.*) in 1894, as compared with 65,766,000 tons, valued at 570,883,000 dol. (114,176,600*l.*) in 1893.

NEW YORK.

The crop of 1894 was a short one, having been affected by the dry weather. A large area has been planted in hay this year, and as moisture has been abundant, a heavy yield is anticipated; this may possibly have an effect on prices, which have risen since the beginning of the year.

Potatoes.

The figures of the potato crop are given as follows:—

	1894.				Value, 1895.
States.	Acres.	Quantity.	Value.		
			Currency.	Sterling.	
		Bushels.	Dollars.	£	£
New York	378,728	29,162,056	13,997,787	2,799,558	2,751,000
New Jersey	46,611	2,796,660	1,733,929	346,786	537,200
Connecticut	26,012	2,054,948	1,397,365	279,473	317,200
Delaware	4,521	226,050	113,025	22,605	29,400
Rhode Island	6,481	861,973	620,661	124,134	105,200

The total crop of the United States was estimated at 170,787,000 bushels, of the value of 91,526,000 dols. (18,305,200*l.*) in 1894, as compared with 183,034,000 bushels, valued at 108,662,000 dol. (21,732,400*l.*) in 1893. New York is the State which produces the largest quantity of potatoes, prices did not quite come up to the expectations, but the return was considered satisfactory on the whole, and a large area has been planted this year.

Hops.

New York is the only State in the East which produces any large quantity of hops, and the area planted is steadily decreasing from year to year owing to the competition from Pacific States, and to the poor financial returns in consequence. The decrease in the acreage planted this year in the State of New York is estimated at about 10 per cent.

The following figures show the progressive decrease of production in the Eastern States, and increase in the Pacific States during the last 3 years:—

PRODUCTION of Hops.

	Quantity.		
	1894.	1893.	1892.
	Bales.	Bales.	Bales.
Oregon	42,000	28,467	13,330
Washington	40,000	41,487	32,707
California	58,000	50,892	43,816
Total Pacific	140,000	120,846	89,853
New York	90,000	97,575	118,212
Wisconsin, &c.	5,000	5,889	4,876
Total, United States	235,000	224,310	217,941

UNITED STATES.

Apples

The apple crop of 1893 was a failure, and that of 1894 was below an average; the yield this year is however likely to be considerably in excess of that of 1894, with a corresponding increase in the exports.

Tobacco.

The production of cigar leaf tobacco was at one time an important industry in the States of New York and Connecticut, but it has fallen off of late years owing to large importations from Sumatra of a leaf of more elastic properties.

The following are the returns given in the statistical abstract of the United States for 1894:—

1894.

	Acres.	Quantity.	Value. Currency.	Value. Sterling.
		Lbs.	Dollars.	£
New York	5,530	6,934,620	554,770	110,954
Connecticut	6,731	10,176,908	1,628,305	325,661

1893.

	Acres.	Quantity.	Value. Currency.	Value. Sterling.
		Lbs.	Dollars.	£
New York	8,133	7,360,365	1,118,775	223,775
Connecticut	7,450	10,658,911	1,492,248	298,450

The unsatisfactory returns of the past 2 years are likely to lead to a further decrease of the area under this crop, which is placed as high as 25 per cent. for this year.

Onions.

The crop of onions was cut short by drought, blight, and insects, it was the smallest for many years past, and the quality was poor. High prices have stimulated planting, and the acreage this year will exceed that planted in 1894 by about 15 per cent.

Vegetables and fruit.

The unsatisfactory prices obtained for most of the minor agricultural products for some years past has tended to discourage large planting. Peas, beans, sweet corn, tomatoes, and cabbage show more or less reduction in acreage. The prospect was favourable for all crops up to the early part of May, when much damage was done by a sudden change in the weather to frost and snow. Grapes are said to have suffered very heavily, the loss in Chatangua country being estimated at fully 1,000 dol. (200*l.*).

In New England all the vegetable crops above ground were reported to have been killed, and the vegetable gardens in New Jersey were badly damaged.

NEW YORK.

The larger fruit, such as apples, peaches, and pears, do not appear to have been materially injured, however, and grain and grass crops escaped damage.

In the report of the State Board of Agriculture for the State of New Jersey, the wages of farm labourers in 1894 are compared with those ruling in former years:—

Labourer's wages.

| | Monthly. || Daily. ||
Year.	With Board.	Without Board.	With Board.	Without Board.
	Dol. c.	Dol. c.	Dol. c.	Dol. c.
1866	18 98	32 27	1 20	1 68
1885	14 10	23 30	0 83	1 17
1894	15 0	27 22	0 90	1 25

These figures show that wages have increased slightly since 1885. Without board, men employed by the month or year, usually have a house afforded by their employer in addition to the money consideration. Labourers on the farms are said to have been more plentiful in 1894, in consequence of the want of employment in cities and factories.

Farming.

Speaking of farming as a business, the secretary in his report points out that against the lower prices ruling for cereals must be put the reduced prices of farms to the buyer, they being only about half what they were in 1866, the fall in the value of horses owing to the adoption of electricity in towns, and the lower price of machinery together with its greater adaptability to agricultural purposes.

The following table and remarks are extracted from this report:—

STATE of New Jersey, 1894.

Product.	Acres.	Quantity.	Value. Currency.	Value. Sterling.
		Bushels.	Dollars.	£
Corn	271,639	8,991,251	4,855,276	971,055
Wheat	116,279	1,779,069	1,085,232	217,046
Oats	108,647	3,085,575	1,172,519	234,504
Rye	75,708	1,120,478	616,268	123,253
Buckwheat	13,647	196,517	127,736	25,587
Potatoes	46,611	2,796,660	1,733,929	346,786
		Tons.		
Hay	505,554	586,443	8,262,982	1,652,596
Total value	..	..	17,853,937	3,570,787

Farms in New Jersey.

Adding to this the dairy products, the fruits, the horticultural and greenhouse and the poultry, leaving out the lumber, will give 11,143,412 dol. (2,228,683*l.*) additional, or a total of 28,997,349 dol. (5,799,470*l.*), a value per acre of 10 dol. 89 c. (2*l.* 3*s.* 7*d.*), being higher in New Jersey than in any State of the Union, and an average value per acre of the improved land of 14 dol. 51 c. (2*l.* 18*s.*). The improved land constitutes 75·1 per cent. of the total area in the State. The average size of farms in New Jersey is 86 acres; average value of land, fences, and buildings, 5,166 dol. (1,034*l.*); of implements and machinery per farm, 239 dol. (48*l.*); of live-stock, 513 dol. (103*l.*). Total average value per farm, 5,918 dol. (1,184*l.*).

Rate of gross earnings on capital invested, 15·9 per cent. Of the 30,828 farms in New Jersey 22,422 are worked by their owners, 3,449 are rented for money, and 4,937 are worked for a share of the products.

FOREIGN OFFICE.
1896.
ANNUAL SERIES.

No. 1687.

DIPLOMATIC AND CONSULAR REPORTS ON TRADE AND FINANCE.

UNITED STATES.

REPORT FOR THE YEAR 1895
ON THE
TRADE OF THE CONSULAR DISTRICT OF GALVESTON.

REFERENCE TO PREVIOUS REPORT, Annual Series No. 1568.

Presented to both Houses of Parliament by Command of Her Majesty,
APRIL, 1896.

LONDON:
PRINTED FOR HER MAJESTY'S STATIONERY OFFICE,
BY HARRISON AND SONS, ST. MARTIN'S LANE,
PRINTERS IN ORDINARY TO HER MAJESTY.

And to be purchased, either directly or through any Bookseller, from
EYRE & SPOTTISWOODE, EAST HARDING STREET, FLEET STREET, E.C., and
32, ABINGDON STREET, WESTMINSTER, S.W.; or
JOHN MENZIES & Co., 12, HANOVER STREET, EDINBURGH, and
90, WEST NILE STREET, GLASGOW; or
HODGES, FIGGIS, & Co., Limited, 104, GRAFTON STREET, DUBLIN.

1896.

[C. 7919—55.] *Price Twopence Halfpenny.*

New Series of Reports.

Reports of the Annual Series have been issued from Her Majesty's Diplomatic and Consular Officers at the following places, and may be obtained from the sources indicated on the title-page:—

No.		Price.	No.		Price.
1565.	Copenhagen	1½d.	1626.	Beyrout	1d.
1566.	Porto Rico	1½d.	1627.	Bushire	2d.
1567.	Malaga	3d.	1628.	Stettin	2½d.
1568.	Galveston	7½d.	1629.	Porto Rico	1d.
1569.	Tabreez	½d.	1630.	Rotterdam	½d.
1570.	Fiji	½d.	1631.	Alexandria	1½d.
1571.	Athens	2½d.	1632.	Tokio	2½d.
1572.	Bilbao	3½d.	1633.	Tangier	1½d.
1573.	Barcelona	3d.	1634.	Oporto	1½d.
1574.	Fiume	2d.	1635.	St. Petersburg	4d.
1575.	Tahiti	1d.	1636.	Dantzig	2d.
1576.	San Francisco	6d.	1637.	Macao	1d.
1577.	Ichang	1½d.	1638.	Hiogo and Osaka	6d.
1578.	Amoy	1½d.	1639.	Naples	1½d.
1579.	Wênchow	1d.	1640.	Kiungchow	½d.
1580.	Smyrna	2½d.	1641.	Rome	1½d.
1581.	Nice	1½d.	1642.	Beira	½d.
1582.	Söul	1½d.	1643.	St. Jago de Cuba	4½d.
1583.	Rio Grande do Sul	4d.	1644.	Christiania	6d.
1584.	Nagasaki	1d.	1645.	Lisbon	1½d.
1585.	Hakodate	1d.	1646.	Brussels	½d.
1586.	Frankfort	3d.	1647.	Vera Cruz	½d.
1587.	Samoa	1d.	1648.	Tunis	1d.
1588.	Cherbourg	1½d.	1649.	Antwerp	1d.
1589.	Damascus	1d.	1650.	Tokio	1d.
1590.	New York	1d.	1651.	Honolulu	½d.
1591.	Athens	2d.	1652.	Stettin	1½d.
1592.	Baghdad	1d.	1653.	Bangkok	1d.
1593.	Vienna	1½d.	1654.	Batoum	1½d.
1594.	Montevideo	2½d.	1655.	Mexico	9½d.
1595.	Swatow	1½d.	1656.	Odessa	1½d.
1596.	Foochow	1d.	1657.	Réunion	1d.
1597.	Tamsui	1d.	1658.	Tokio	1½d.
1598.	Chungking	1d.	1659.	Maranham	1d.
1599.	Chefoo	1d.	1660.	Copenhagen	1d.
1600.	Tokio	1½d.	1661.	Berlin	1½d.
1601.	Bangkok	1d.	1662.	Teheran	2½d.
1602.	Caracas	1½d.	1663.	Salonica	1½d.
1603.	Sofia	2½d.	1664.	Manila	½d.
1604.	Belgrade	2½d.	1665.	Florence	5½d.
1605.	Shanghai	2½d.	1666.	Dakar	½d.
1606.	Canton	1½d.	1667.	Havre	2d.
1607.	Meshed	1½d.	1668.	Rouen	2d.
1608.	Erzeroum	1d.	1669.	Corfu	½d.
1609.	Galatz	2d.	1670.	Calais	1d.
1610.	Port Said	1½d.	1671.	Tehran	1½d.
1611.	The Hague	1½d.	1672.	Barcelona	2d.
1612.	Calais	1d.	1673.	Amsterdam	1d.
1613.	Newchwang	1d.	1674.	Bordeaux	2½d.
1614.	Copenhagen	1d.	1675.	Warsaw	1d.
1615.	Odessa	2d.	1676.	Havana	1½d.
1616.	Gothenburg	2d.	1677.	Berlin	½d.
1617.	Mannheim	1½d.	1678.	Beira	1½d.
1618.	Old Calabar	5d.	1679.	Saigon	1d.
1619.	Pekin	2½d.	1680.	Trebizond	1d.
1620.	Taganrog	2d.	1681.	Vera Cruz	1½d.
1621.	Brindisi	2½d.	1682.	Patras	1d.
1622.	Jeddah	1½d.	1683.	La Rochelle	1½d.
1623.	Hamburg	3d.	1684.	Madrid	1½d.
1624.	Angora	1½d.	1685.	Belgrade	2d.
1625.	Buda-Pesth	1½d.	1686.	Algiers	5d.

No. 1687.

Reference to previous Report, Annual Series No. 1568.

UNITED STATES.

GALVESTON.

Consul Nugent to the Marquis of Salisbury.

My Lord,   *Galveston, February* 29, 1896.

I HAVE the honour to forward, herewith enclosed, my Annual Report on the Trade and Commerce of this Consular District for the year 1895.

         I have, &c.
         (Signed)   HORACE D. NUGENT.

Report on the Trade and Commerce of the Consular District of Galveston for the Year 1895.

ABSTRACT of Contents.

	PAGE
Introductory remarks—	
Notable year for Galveston	3
Imports required	3
General foreign trade—	
Total value of trade	4
Value of imports	4
„ exports	4
Imports—	
Value of direct imports	4
Imports free of duty	4
Dutiable imports	4
Remarks on import trade	4
Imports from Great Britain	5
„ Germany	6
„ France	6
„ Belgium	6
Exports—	
Total value of exports	6
Exports from Galveston	6
„ Velasco	6
„ Sabine Pass	6
Cotton	6
Cottonseed oilcake	7
„ oil	7

(2123)

UNITED STATES.

Abstract of Contents—continued.

	Page
Exports—continued—	
Maize	7
Wheat flour	7
Logs	7
Lumber	7
Exports to Great Britain	7
„ Germany	8
„ France	8
„ other countries	8
Shipping—	
Coastwise shipping	9
British shipping	9
Values of cargoes of British ships	10
New lines of British shipping	10
Freights	10
Railroads—	
New line constructed	10
Merchandise conveyed by Texas lines	11
Discrimination in rates against Galveston	12
Grain Trade—	
Only maize exported	13
Good prospect for Galveston as a grain port	13
Facilities for loading grain at Galveston	13
Charges	13
Exports of maize	13
Improvements—	
Action of Wharf Company	14
Good standing of Galveston	14
Facilities for loading and unloading cargo	15
Cotton Crop of 1894-95—	
Gain in Texas	15
Average price of the crop	15
„ commercial value of the crop	16
Total value of crop	16
Texas crop	16
Percentage of deliveries from various groups of cotton-growing States	17
Receipts of cotton at various United States ports	17
Exports „ „	18
Cotton Crop of 1895-96—	
Short crop expected	18
Estimated Texas crop	18
Receipts at Galveston	18
Exports from Galveston	19
Foreign exports	19
Coastwise „	19
Standing of Galveston this season	20
Exports to date	21
Cotton prices	21
Harbour works at Galveston—	
Good progress made	22
6½ feet added to depth of water	22
Monthly depths of water in 1895	22
Work of the dredge boats	22
„ done on the jetties	23
Expected advantage to be gained by Galveston now that she has deep water	23
New Mexico—	
Review of 1895	24
Land titles	25
Taxable property	26
Territorial debt	27
Railways	28
Stock raising	28
Irrigation	28
Mining	29
Tables	30-34

GALVESTON.

Introductory Remarks.

The year 1895 cannot be considered on the whole as having been a particulary prosperous one in the State of Texas.

At the commencement of the year people were confronted with the low prices attendant on the largest crop of cotton ever grown in the State, and this condition was especially hard on the farmer.

At the end of the year the position was entirely reversed, as the cotton crop grown in 1895 was one of the smallest ever known. Whilst this did not so particularly affect the farmer, as he obtained better prices for his cotton, yet it militated against the general prosperity of the State.

Fewer men were employed in the cotton fields, and by railroads and cotton gins. Much less cotton was conveyed by rail, and naturally far fewer men employed by stevedores and those handling cotton.

It is often asserted, especially by the farmer, that a large cotton crop brings him much less prosperity than a short one, owing to the lowering of prices; but, as regards the towns, and especially railroad centres and ports like Galveston, it is undoubtedly better for the general labouring population to have a large crop than a small one.

Despite the poor business done by Galveston in the latter part of 1895, the past year has been a notable one in many ways for this port. *Notable year for Galveston.*

In the first place a deep-water channel of over 20 feet has been obtained direct to the sea. This alone is expected to prove of incalculable benefit to Galveston.

Secondly, Galveston has begun to take her place as one of the large grain-importing points of the south-west, thus evidencing the value of the new deep water.

Thirdly, good progress has been made in the way of providing sheds and other wharf facilities for the handling of ship's cargoes.

Fourthly, the railroads running into Galveston, on which the port is largely dependent for the commodities forming her export trade, have increased in number, and others are on the point of coming here.

Hitherto, as I have remarked in former reports, Galveston has been almost purely an export point, the imports having fallen off of late years, and are ridiculously out of proportion to the exports.

Now that the bar no longer forms an obstacle to the ingress of fully laden vessels, and that the railways which terminate in this point are anxious to obtain return freights, there is no reason why Galveston should not become the port of entry for the great south-west.

It may be appropriate to mention a few of the leading commodities which would be especially useful if imported directly here, and for which there is always a market. I quote the *Imports required.*

(2123)

following from a list recently drawn up by a practical merchant here:—

"From Europe cement, earthenware, crockery, tinplate, salt, glassware, patented goods of every kind, beer, ale, porter, wines, and other goods of a similar character can be imported with profit; bottled goods, and especially the bottled waters of the famous springs of Europe, tinned goods not put up in this country, firebrick, anthracite coal, potash, lemons (from Italy), and fabrics of every kind in the textile department, especially the cheaper goods of Germany and Irish linens, hosiery, &c.

"From the West Indies and South and Central America could be obtained coffee, sugar, hardwoods, and all kinds of tropical fruits, including bananas, cocoanuts, pineapples, oranges, lemons, limes, &c.

"In addition to these commodities, hides and alligator skins, leaf tobacco, sisal, Trinidad asphalt, vanilla, cocoa, &c., could with advantage also be imported through this port, as well as every other product of the tropics."

I give the above list for the information of the chambers of commerce and merchants in general.

General Foreign Trade.

Total value of trade. The total value of trade to and from Galveston and district during the year 1895 amounted to 36,270,411 dol. (7,480,000*l*.), compared with 36,840,000 dol. (7,590,000*l*.) in 1894, a very slight decrease.

Value of imports. Value of exports. Of this amount, 337,178 dol. represented the amount of imports, and 35,933,233 dol. that of exports.

Taken on the whole, despite the short cotton crop of the present season, the volume of trade was well up to the average of the past four years.

Imports.

Value of direct imports. The total value of the direct imports into Galveston during 1895 amounted to 337,178 dol., a great falling-off compared with 1894, when they amounted to 677,636 dol.

It must be noted, however, that in 1894 sugar to the value of 349,206 dol. was imported from Cuba, and such importation has naturally ceased during the year just closed, owing to the disturbed state of the island, and when this is taken into consideration it will be seen that the imports are in reality, with this exception, not behind those of 1894.

Imports free of duty. Of this amount of 337,178 dol., 133,254 dol. represents the value of goods imported free of duty, and 203,924 dol. that of merchandise paying duty.

Remarks on import trade. It may be here remarked that whilst no doubt it would be extremely advantageous for the port of Galveston to encourage direct importation of merchandise from foreign countries, yet, as long as New York continues, as it is now, the one great port of entry in the United States, it will be extremely difficult to contend with and overcome the vested interests there, so as to build up a large import trade in this port.

By far the greater proportion of foreign products used in the State of Texas arrives, indirectly, either by rail or by the bi-weekly boats of the Mallory line.

As regards Great Britain, efforts have been made during the past year to arrange for direct importation into Galveston of various commodities needed here, and there is no doubt that, with the present realisation of a deep-water channel into the harbour, such direct importations will increase. At present, however, they are a " mere drop of a bucket."

The imports from Great Britain and colonies show a satisfactory increase in 1895 over 1894. The total value of such imports was 228,118 dol., as against 156,411 dol. The figures show direct importation from Great Britain to the value of 186,334 dol., as against 152,231 dol. in 1894; whilst from the colonies imports to the value of 41,784 dol. arrived, compared with 4,180 dol. in 1894.

Imports from Great Britain.

TABLES showing Increase or Decrease of Dutiable Imports from Great Britain and Colonies.

INCREASE.

Articles.	Value. 1894.	Value. 1895.
	Dollars.	Dollars.
Sheep dip	3,080	18,250
Manufactures of jute	8,121	13,611
Tin plates	11,298	19,519
Malt liquors	9,325	9,925
Fruits in spirit	..	3,757
Fish in oil	..	1,646

DECREASE.

Articles.	Value. 1894.	Value. 1895.
	Dollars.	Dollars.
Cement	10,390	..
Coal	8,427	4,722
Dead oil creosote	7,513	4,623
Crockery	14,519	13,275
Manufactures of iron and steel (including machinery)	6,692	3,599
Preserved vegetables	3,126	2,812
Burlaps	10,414	29

As regards goods free of duty, the chief items from Great Britain were anthracite coal, value 3,957 dol., as against 7,668 dol. in 1894, and salt, 49,650 dol., as against 14,172 dol. in 1894.

New importations worthy of remark are, paper stock (old bagging), value 6,234 dol., and cotton ties (iron and steel), value 19,529 dol.

Jute butts to the value 28,749 dol. were imported from British India, and asphalte to the amount of 9,735 dol. from the British West Indies.

Imports from Germany. The imports from Germany show a surprising increase, being 50,772 dol., as against 7,909 dol. in 1894.

The chief items were cement, value 19,231 dol.; rice, 9,772 dol.; and beetroot-sugar, 12,289 dol.

Imports from France. The imports from France were 10,982 dol., chiefly preserved fruits and vegetables.

Imports from Belgium. Cement to the value of 34,874 dol. was imported from Belgium.

Tables showing the imports in detail are annexed.

Exports.

Total value of exports. The total value of exports from the customs district of Galveston, *i.e.*, the ports of Galveston, Velasco, and Sabine Pass was, in 1895, 35,933,233 dol., as compared with 36,162,455 dol. in 1894.

Although this shows a very slight decrease from 1894, the values in reality were up to the average of the last 5 years.

Exports from Galveston. Of the total estimated value of exports by far the greater proportion left the port of Galveston, the figures showing 35,532,123 dol., as against 35,205,837 dol. in 1894.

Exports from Velasco. **Exports from Sabine Pass.** Those leaving Velasco in 1895 were valued at 212,571 dol., as against 885,949 in 1894; whilst the figures for Sabine Pass show exports to the value of 188,539 dol. for 1895, as against 70,669 dol. in 1894.

From this it will be seen that the business of the port of Velasco has greatly decreased, and Galveston has benefited in proportion by absorbing trade that formerly belonged to that port.

Thus, whilst the total export business of the whole customs district was in 1895 slightly below that of 1894 in value, the port of Galveston shows an increase of values over 1894 at the expense of Velasco.

Sabine Pass shows a steady increase in export trade, owing, undoubtedly, to the success of the Government work in doing away with the bar at that place.

The exports rose to 188,539 dol. in 1895, as compared with 70,889 dol. in 1894, and 22,757 dol. in 1893.

Cotton. Of the exports from the district, cotton, as usual, was the leading commodity.

During the year 1895, 931,259 bales of cotton, valued at 32,672,746 dol. left Galveston for foreign ports.

This, although much beyond the average, shows a falling-off from 1894, a year with a phenomenal cotton crop.

In that year the figures were 1,073,976 bales, valued at 33,520,164 dol.

The average estimated value per bale was 35 dol. in 1895, as compared with 31 dol. 20 c. in 1894.

All the cotton, except 92 bales, left the port of Galveston.

Cottonseed oilcake. The next export in importance to cotton was cottonseed oil-cake and meal, which was exported from this district to the amount of 105,736 tons, valued at 2,117,218 dol., as compared with 95,128 tons, valued at 2,131,543 dol. in 1894. Of this amount of 105,736 tons, 97,752 tons left the port of Galveston, and 7,984 tons Velasco.

The exports of this commodity from Galveston itself in 1895 show a large increase over 1894, when only 60,513 tons left this port, and those from Velasco a corresponding decrease.

Cottonseed oil. Cottonseed oil was exported from the district to the amount of 637,766 gallons, valued at 236,208 dol.

Here again a large increase is shown; the figures for 1894 being 218,362 gallons, value 78,665 dol.

The exports of cottonseed oil from Galveston in 1895 were 411,268 gallons, valued at 187,217 dol., and from Velasco 226,498 gallons, valued at 48,991 dol.

Maize. An increased business has recently sprung up in the exportation of maize (Indian corn) from Galveston.

From November to December, 1895, 1,233,477 bushels, value 390,760 dol., were exported from Galveston.

Small quantities of maize have been exported in previous years, but never on such a large scale as during 1895, as will be seen when it is mentioned that the largest total exportation in previous years was only 144,755 bushels in 1892.

Wheat flour. No wheat itself was exported, but 53,244 barrels of wheat flour, value 187,682 dol., left this port in 1895, as compared with 59,859 barrels, value 214,792 dol., in 1894, thus showing a slight decrease.

Logs. The value of logs exported from the district was 77,209 dol. in 1895, as against 34,885 dol. in 1894, a material gain in this branch of trade.

Lumber. The lumber trade shows a decided gain over the last four years.

The value of lumber exported in 1895 was 231,072 dol., as compared with 70,154 dol. in 1894. All of the lumber exported, except some 49,000 dol. worth, left the port of Sabine Pass, where there are several British vessels regularly engaged in this trade.

Exports to Great Britain. The export trade to Great Britain was, as usual, the largest and most important from this port.

The total value of the goods exported to Great Britain in 1895 was 20,470,179 dol., as compared with 20,776,012 dol. in 1894, thus showing a slight falling-off.

Cotton to the amount of 579,596 bales, valued at 20,009,589 dol., was exported to Great Britain in 1895, as against 647,372 bales, valued at 20,255,300 dol., in 1894, thus showing a considerable decrease in actual quantity, but only a slight diminution in value.

Cottonseed oilcake and meal to the amount of 16,453 tons, valued at 336,241 dol., was also sent to Great Britain.

The figures in 1894 were 21,803 tons, valued at 477,840 dol., and a decided falling-off in this branch of export trade to Great Britain has taken place in recent years.

The only other item of importance, as regards export trade to Great Britain, was maize, of which 337,613 bushels, valued at 110,062 dol., left this port.

Exports to Germany.

Germany occupies the second place as regards values of exports from Galveston, the total amount of the exports being 8,692,268 dol. during 1895, as compared with 8,132,298 dol. in 1894, thus showing a material increase.

It is worthy of remark that the export trade to Germany from Galveston has steadily increased during the last five years, it having been only 2,417,382 dol. in 1891.

Nearly all the exports to Germany left the port of Galveston, commodities to the amount of 115,660 dol. alone going by way of Velasco, as compared with 708,992 dol. in 1894.

The exports of cotton to Germany in 1895, whilst showing a slight decrease in number of bales as compared with 1894—the figures being 191,028 as against 214,971—show an increase in value, 6,796,684 dol. against 6,650,976 dol.

Cottonseed oilcake and meal were exported to Germany in 1895 from Galveston to the amount of 74,572 tons, value 1,551,353 dol., and from Velasco 5,374 tons, value 102,020 dol. The total was 79,946 tons, value 1,653,373 dol., showing a considerable gain over 1894, when the figures were 61,361 tons, value 1,376,135 dol.

Cottonseed oil to the amount of 48,785 gallons, value 10,860 dol., was also exported to Germany—considerable falling-off from 1894, when the figures showed 164,138 gallons, value 60,000 dol.

Other important exports to Germany from this district in 1895 were 313,679 bushels of corn, valued at 97,507 dol., and logs to the value of 76,154 dol.

Exports to France.

The exports to France show a falling-off in 1895 from 1894, being 4,974,755 dol., as against 5,732,851 dol. in 1894.

As usual, cotton formed the bulk of the exports to France, 134,063 bales, value 4,893,463 dol., leaving Galveston, as against 182,832 bales, value 5,722,551 dol., in 1894.

The only other item of importance exported to France was 235,713 bushels of corn, value 73,485 dol.

Exports to other countries.

The exports from Galveston to other countries were of minor importance as compared with those to Great Britain, Germany, and France, the largest being 498,138 dol. to Belgium.

Tables showing the exports in detail are annexed.

Shipping.

Owing to the short cotton crop of the season of 1895–96, the foreign-going shipping of Galveston shows a considerable falling-off in 1895 as compared with 1894, but was, nevertheless, nearly up to the average of the last few years.

If, however, the domestic shipping entering Galveston in 1895 be taken into consideration, it will be found that there was an advance, on the whole, in point of numbers over 1894.

From returns furnished by the United States customs-house here it was shown that 537 vessels entered the port of Galveston during 1895, as against 516 in 1894. This return does not include foreign shipping coming from any other United States port, and in consequence some 30 or 35 vessels may be added to the above, and the total number of vessels entering the port of Galveston during 1895 may be set down as about 550, or very nearly the same as in 1894.

Coastwise shipping. Of the above estimated number of vessels 325 were American coasting craft, tonnage 333,370, as compared with 309, tonnage 306,388, in 1894.

These figures include the bi-weekly service of the Mallory line from New York. Of the remaining number of vessels 145 were British and 63 foreign, including 24 Norwegian (mostly small sailing craft) and 24 Spanish (chiefly the vessels of the "Sena" line).

British shipping. The movement of British shipping shows a considerable decrease in 1895 from 1894. From the tables annexed to this report it will be seen that the total number of British vessels that entered the port of Galveston during 1895 was 145, their total registered tonnage being 223,519 tons, and the numbers of their crews 3,819. This shows a considerable decrease from 1894, when the vessels numbered 187, their combined registered tonnage being 292,382 tons, and the numbers of the crews 4,391.

Of the above 145 vessels, 25 brought full or partial cargoes, as against 17 in 1894.

54 British vessels arrived directly from either Great Britain or a British colony, 20 from other United States ports, 15 from the Cape Verde Islands, 12 from Mexico, 9 from the Canary Islands, 8 from Brazil, 5 from Belgium, and 5 from Cuba, the remaining 17 coming from various other points.

The number of British vessels cleared from Galveston during 1895 was 163, tonnage 253,202 tons, as compared with 169, tonnage 259,586 tons in 1894.

The crews of vessels clearing numbered 4,000, as against 3,959 in 1894.

Of these 163 vessels, 69 went direct to English ports, as against 90 in 1894; 55 to Germany, as compared with 43 in 1894; 21 to France, as against 26 in 1894; and the remaining 18 to various other destinations.

All except 5 vessels carried cargoes, these 5 proceeding hence to other United States ports in ballast.

Values of cargoes of British ships.

The total value of cargoes conveyed from Galveston in British vessels during the year 1895 was 30,085,499 dol. (6,203,193*l*.). Of this, 15,553,318 dol. (3,206,870*l*.) went to Great Britain, 8,532,710 dol. (1,759,321*l*.) to Germany, and 4,895,666 dol. (1,009,415*l*.) to France.

The average registered tonnage per vessel was higher than ever before recorded, viz., 1,540 tons.

The largest vessel was the steamship "Kintuck," 2,880 tons register; the smallest the steamship "Pioneer" 287 tons register.

New lines of British shipping.

Two facts are worthy of notice as regards British shipping here in 1895; first, that, owing to deep water having been obtained, regular lines, such as the West Indian Pacific and Harrison lines are now likely to come regularly to Galveston, vessels of both these lines having entered Galveston during the past season; secondly, that direct importations from Great Britain and the Continent are likely to largely increase, the number of vessels bringing cargoes having augmented sensibly during the last few months.

The large increase of British vessels clearing for Germany will also be noticed from the table, there having been 55 in 1895, as against 43 in 1894 and 30 in 1893.

Freights.

The year 1895 opened with cotton freights at $\frac{9}{32}d.$ and 5 per cent., and oilcake 1*l*. 1*s*., declining at the end of January to $\frac{17}{64}d.$ and 5 per cent. for cotton. February saw a further decline to $\frac{1}{4}d.$ and 5 per cent., and March to $\frac{15}{64}d.$ and 5 per cent., oilcake then being 1*l*., at which point they remained till the close of the season in April.

At the opening of the season 1895–96 in September, rates were $\frac{15}{64}d.$ and 5 per cent. for cotton, and 17*s*. 6*d*. per ton for oilcake, &c.

Owing to the small cotton crop, these rates declined in October and November, varying from above to as low as $\frac{11}{64}d.$ and 5 per cent. for cotton, and 15*s*. for oilcake, lower than ever experienced.

During December, however, they rose to $\frac{1}{4}d.$ and 5 per cent. for the former, and 17*s*. 6*d*. for oilcake.

The increased depth of water on the bar this year enabled full cargoes of grain to be taken, and owing to the huge corn crop in Texas, the Indian Territory, and Kansas, a large business was done in this line after the month of October, rates varying from 3*s*. for parcels to the United Kingdom, and the Continent to 3*s*. 3*d*. and 3*s*. 6*d*. per quarter.

This trade has proved a complete success, and a large tonnage in shipping may consequently be expected at this port in the future.

Railroads.

New line constructed.

Although comparatively speaking little was accomplished in

1895 in the way of new railway construction in Texas, yet the length of new line laid down was greater than in any other State in the Union.

The length of this new line constructed was 224 miles, making a total of 10,585 miles at present being worked in this State. This includes construction on several new lines, two or three of which are expected to add greatly to the trade of Galveston.

There are at present three lines directly running into this port, one of which, the Missouri, Kansas, and Texas, has only lately resumed its direct connection with Galveston. Every additional line entering the port will, of course, be calculated to add to the business of the place.

The following table issued by the Railroad Commission of Texas shows the amount of tonnage conveyed by the railways of the State for the years ending respectively June 30, 1894, and June 30, 1895. It shows a considerable increase in business done :— *Merchandise conveyed by Texas lines.*

UNITED STATES.

Tonnage of Texas Railroads.

Articles.	Year ending June 30, 1894.	Year ending June 30, 1895.
	Tons.	Tons.
Grain	760,065	683,110
Flour	363,442	408,930
Other mill products	79,485	87,405
Hay	105,841	93,478
Tobacco	16,858	15,745
Cotton	1,649,304	1,860,132
Cotton-seed meal and cake	572,051	787,013
Rice	12,555	11,696
Fruits and vegetables	351,017	379,825
Other agricultural products	217,128	231,582
Live stock	1,239,988	1,300,211
Dressed meats, poultry, game, and fish	37,551	37,421
Other packing-house products	71,524	82,778
Wool	68,887	73,170
Hides, leather	39,388	39,423
Other annual products	8,718	9,626
Coal and coke	1,435,270	1,742,134
Ores	149,504	107,442
Salt	54,564	52,546
Stone, sand, and like articles	894,095	1,140,109
Other mineral products	24,054	743
Limber	2,149,669	2,273,582
Shingles	80,868	81,551
Other forest products	441,298	552,012
Petroleum and other oils	160,800	212,351
Sugar and molasses	186,672	204,160
Pig and bloom iron	11,162	10,683
Iron and steel rails	61,443	56,446
Other castings and machinery	141,970	170,246
Bar and sheet metal	94,714	85,459
Cement, bricks, and lime	146,122	152,795
Agricultural implements	29,382	32,157
Wagons, carriages, tools, &c.	32,005	43,362
Wines, liquors, and beers	216,172	231,444
Household goods and furniture	59,893	60,765
Other manufactures	245,173	393,620
Merchandise	1,109,053	1,223,182
Railroad materials not specified	114,303	210,970
Miscellaneous	453,509	452,558
Total	13,885,497	15,591,862

Discrimination in rates against Galveston. The alleged discrimination in railroad rates against the port of Galveston, which was alluded to at some length in my last annual report, remains still unsettled and has again given rise to numerous complaints on the part of Galveston shippers. The matter has been extensively discussed by numerous commercial bodies and individual merchants affected by these rates, and is now the subject of a thorough investigation on the part of the Railroad Commissioners. It is to be hoped that it will shortly receive a permanent and equitable settlement, and one that will do away with the complaints of alleged discrimination against Galveston and in favour of other ports; and until this question of rates receives

GALVESTON.

such settlement the cotton export business of this port will continue to suffer.

Grain Trade.

As predicted in my last yearly report, owing to the recently-acquired deep-water outlet from Galveston, it has been found possible to load vessels with dead-weight cargoes, and the result has been a great impetus to the export of grain from here.

The grain exported has been almost entirely maize, consequent on there having been a large surplus crop in the States tributary to this port. *Only maize exported.*

It has been found possible for the farmers of Kansas and Texas to ship their corn viâ Galveston with a profit to themselves of 5 c. per bushel over and above shipments through other ports.

The result has been that since November last maize has been steadily coming into Galveston, and the grain elevator on the wharves, with a capacity of over 1,000,000 bushels, has been kept hard at work.

Recently, owing to the railway rates to Galveston on corn having been slightly raised, the quantity arriving here has been decreasing; but, in spite of this, there is no doubt that Galveston will continue to be the outlet for the surplus of the annual crop of cereals of the territory tributary to this port, and the prospects of a large and permanent grain-exporting business appear very favourable. *Good prospect for Galveston as a grain port.*

As a specimen of the facilities for loading grain here, the following instances may be given:— *Facilities for loading grain at Galveston.*

1. The Norwegian steamship "Blaamanden" loaded 139,108 bushels of corn in the actual time of 13 hours, and was in port only 64 hours.

2. The "Eugenie," another Norwegian steamer, loaded 107,000 bushels of corn in 4 hours.

3. The British steamship "Helen" received in 8 hours 128,000 bushels of corn in bulk, 3 hours of the time being consumed in trimming; the actual time, therefore, being only 5 hours.

The elevator also sacked 30,000 bushels for this ship in 15 hours, and could have reduced the time one-half.

The total cargo of the "Helen"—158,000 bushels—is said to be the largest cargo of grain ever shipped from the south.

The charges for handling grain at Galveston, it may not be out of place to mention, are but 1 c. per bushel from the car to the ship, including wharfage and the use of the elevator, with 30 days' storage. *Charges.*

The following table shows the quantity of corn exported from this port up to the date of writing, and its destination:— *Exports of maize.*

To—	This Season.
Germany	995,043
France	283,985
Mexico and Gulf Ports	25,112
Denmark	798,108
Great Britain and Ireland	718,472
Holland and Belgium	396,001
Total	3,216,721

The amount of corn received to date (February 21) is 6,714 car-loads (3,997,687 bushels).

Improvements.

As mentioned in my last report, steady improvement has been made of late years in the terminal and wharf facilities in the port of Galveston.

Action of Wharf Company. These have been largely due to the action of the Wharf Company, a large corporation owning a great part of the water-front of this town, and whose action has been based on their confidence of the final success of the jetty system now being carried out by the United States Government.

To-day the results of the jetty system are a proved success, and the improvements instituted by the Wharf Company, during the past 3 or 4 years have placed the port of Galveston in a position to take immediate advantage of the increased trade and shipping that will doubtless at once follow the successful efforts to do away with the bar at the mouth of Galveston harbour.

Good standing of Galveston. Taking it all in all, it can be said without fear of contradiction that no port in the United States is at present better equipped for commerce than Galveston.

The total length of wharfage in the port for ocean-going vessels is about 15,000 feet; allowing 300 feet for each vessel, 50 vessels can be berthed at one and the same time, and by placing vessels side by side, as is sometimes done, a large addition can be made to the number of vessels loading.

It is not likely, however, that the commerce of this port will so greatly increase in the near future as to require more than 50 vessels to be loaded at one time. Of course, cotton is still, and will probably be, always the chief export from Galveston.

This port receives, as a rule, about 50 per cent. at least of the cotton crop of the State.

In 1894–95 the Texas crop was the largest ever known, 1,660,000 bales passing through Galveston.

When it is considered that a vessel under ordinary circumstances can load 1,000 bales of cotton per day, and that there is accommodation for 50 vessels to load at one time, thus giving the total loading capacity of 50,000 bales per day, it will be seen that the whole amount of the cotton received here could have been shipped in 35 days, or the entire Texas crop—supposing it to pass through Galveston—in 70 days.

From the above statement it will be seen how fully prepared Galveston is, as far as wharf accommodation is concerned, to meet an indefinitely large expansion of her commerce.

It must be also noticed that of late years the wharves have been covered with excellent shed accommodation, thus affording ample protection to merchandise of all classes during the process of loading or unloading. *Facilities for loading and unloading cargo.*

Three new large sheds are now under construction, and when these are completed the wharves will be entirely covered.

To give some idea of the extent of these sheds it may be mentioned that the three in question are 1,600 feet by 200 feet, 875 feet by 200 feet, and 600 feet by 200 feet respectively.

All sheds are to be furnished with water mains and hydrants, and the protection against fire and weather is nearly perfect.

It may here be remarked that the good effect of this protection of cotton by sheds has been amply shown during the last year by the fact that not one single fire has occurred.

In conclusion it may be appropriate to quote the following extract from a report of the Chairman of the Committee on Harbour of the Galveston Cotton Exchange, recently made to that body:—"Some facts you are not familiar with, and to these your committee desires to call your attention, not in a boastful spirit, but merely to let you and the outside world know that it is not an idle and baseless assertion to say that Galveston is one of the cheapest and best-equipped ports in this country; that greater care is taken to protect goods and merchandise against weather and fire, and that more care is expended to secure the rapid and economical handling of such goods and merchandise than at any other port with which your committee is familiar."

Cotton Crop of 1894–95.

According to the annual report of the Secretary of the New Orleans Cotton Exchange, the cotton crop of the United States for the year ended August 31, 1895, amounted to 9,901,251 bales, showing an increase over the crop of 1893–94 of 2,351,434 bales, and over the largest previous commercial crop (that of 1891–92, when the total was 9,035,379 bales) of 865,872 bales.

The largest gain over 1893–94 was 1,216,798 bales, in Texas, where the production was phenomenal. *Gain in Texas.*

The Atlantic States increased 350,949 bales, and the Gulf States 784,587 bales, over the crop of 1893–94.

The average price of the entire crop was estimated at 5·92 c. per lb. for middling cotton, or about 8 dol. per bale less than the crop of 1893–94. *Average price of the crop.*

(2123)

UNITED STATES.

Average commercial value of the crop. The average commercial value of the crop of 1894-95 was 30 dol. per bale of 509 lbs., as against 37 dol. 50 c. in 1893-94, and 42 dol. 50 c. in 1892-93. The bales, however, in the latter 2 years were about 9 lbs. lighter.

Total value of crop. The total value of the crop of 1894-95 was estimated at 297,037,530 dol., as against 283,118,137 dol. in 1893-94.

The following table shows the commercial crop and its value for the four seasons from 1891-92 to 1894-95:—

Commercial Crop.

Year.	Quantity.	Value.
	Bales.	Dollars.
1894-95	9,901,251	297,037,530
1893-94	7,549,817	283,118,137
1892-93	6,700,365	284,765,512
1891-92	9,035,379	338,826,712

It may be remarked that, owing to the increased average weight per bale, the crop of 1894-95 was in reality equal to 10,099,000 bales of the growth of 1891-92, thus showing an increase of 1,064,000 bales over the largest previous crop on record.

Texas Crop.

This is usually held by compilers of statistics to include the cotton grown on Indian territory.

Texas crop. The Texas crop of 1894-95, as was above remarked, was a phenomenal one, exceeding that of 1893-94 by 1,216,978 bales, and that of 1891-92 by 875,000 bales.

The following figures give in detail the Texas commercial crops of 1894-95 and 1893-94:—

	Quantity.	
	1894-95.	1893-94.
	Bales.	Bales.
Receipts at Texas seaboard	1,660,591	1,029,766
Shipped inland to Mexico and points west of Mississippi River	86,749	44,988
Shipped by rail viâ St. Louis and Cairo	460,014	316,652
Receipts at New Orleans (exclusive of Galveston)	1,025,334	633,688
Receipts at points on Mississippi River north of St. Louis, bound eastward	43,270	33,966
Total	3,275,958	2,059,060

GALVESTON.

During the last five seasons the proportion of deliveries from the various groups of the cotton-growing States was as follows:—

Percentage of deliveries from various groups of cotton-growing States.

DELIVERIES from the Cotton States.

In Thousands of Bales.

	1894-95.	1893-94.	1892-93.	1891-92.	1890-91.
Texas and Indian territory	3,276	2,059	2,108	2,400	2,100
Other Gulf States	3,000	2,216	1,865	3,035	2,666
Atlantic States	3,625	3,275	2,727	3,600	3,887
Total	9,901	7,550	6,700	9,035	8,653

The following tables show the net receipts of cotton at different United States ports during the seasons of 1894-95 and 1893-94, together with exports for these seasons from the same ports, and by which it will be seen that the Galveston receipts increased in the former year by more than 638,000 bales; whilst her exports for the same year exceeded those of 1893-94 by the substantial quantity of 574,637 bales:—

Receipts of cotton at various United States ports.

TABLE showing Net Receipts of Cotton at United States Ports (as per Form in use by the Cotton Exchanges).

	Quantity.	
	1894-95.	1893-94.
	Bales.	Bales.
New Orleans	2,584,115	1,893,094
Galveston	1,659,999	1,021,724
Mobile and Pensacola	253,187	215,616
Savannah	944,410	969,430
Charleston	425,487	340,603
Wilmington	234,621	189,840
Norfolk	472,540	502,194
Baltimore	118,872	63,673
New York	187,794	108,387
Boston	335,453	101,854
Philadelphia	121,573	50,702
West Point	285,937	239,352
Newport News	33,685	45,668
Brunswick	102,013	67,058
Port Royal	159,150	77,867
El Paso, Texas	9,166	1,650
Laredo, Texas	32,833	20,261
Eagle Pass, Texas	14,985	9,075
Velasco	592	8,042
Other minor points	29,765	14,002
Total	8,006,177	5,940,092

UNITED STATES.

TABLE showing Exports from United States Ports for 1894–95.

From—	Great Britain.	France.	Continent and Channel.	Total.	Total in 1893–94.
	Bales.	Bales.	Bales.	Bales.	Bales.
New Orleans	917,026	463,774	673,031	2,053,831	1,636,811
Galveston	810,469	212,413	325,679	1,348,561	773,924
Mobile and Pensacola	92,175	...	30,820	122,995	35,160
Savannah	63,132	27,160	455,335	545,627	516,322
Charleston	122,967	1,200	215,686	339,853	324,368
Wilmington	63,371	4,160	134,739	202,270	167,404
Norfolk	143,899	...	44,425	188,324	174,010
Baltimore	108,708	7,155	158,643	274,506	206,816
New York	457,003	41,923	310,493	809,419	786,506
Boston	290,137	...	...	290,137	231,071
Philadelphia	59,330	...	4,799	64,129	31,163
West Point	71,021	...	36,287	107,308	96,011
Newport News	33,363	...	...	33,363	47,166
Brunswick	75,014	...	28,794	103,808	71,310
Port Royal	135,959	16,691	6,500	159,150	77,867
El Paso, &c.	...	...	11,176	11,176	1,981
Laredo	...	...	32,833	32,833	20,261
Eagle Pass	...	...	14,985	14,985	9,075
Velasco	...	...	592	592	8,042
San Francisco	...	...	16,094	16,094	6,929
Total	3,443,574	774,476	2,500,911	6,718,961	5,222,197
Last year	2,859,114	587,299	1,775,784	5,222,197	...
Year before	2,307,489	555,239	1,523,639	4,386,367	...

Cotton Crop of 1895–96.

Short crop expected.

During the summer of 1895 the weather was such as to lead experts to predict a very short cotton crop for the present season. These predictions have been more than verified, and it is doubtful whether the total crop of the United States for 1895–96 will reach 7,000,000 bales. A conservative estimate places the crop at from 6,750,000 to 7,000,000 bales.

Whilst the crop was short all over the United States, Texas, in particular, shows a large decrease. This State, as a rule, produces to-day about 30 per cent. of the total crop, and therefore taking that crop at 7,000,000, Texas production should be, under ordinary circumstances, 2,100,000 bales.

Estimated Texas crop.

From present appearances, however, it is doubtful if Texas has produced this season more than 1,750,000 bales.

The shortness of the crop has of course greatly affected the receipts and exports at Galveston, and a glance at the annexed tables will show a great falling-off from late years, and more especially from last year, when the business done here was phenomenal.

In spite of this, Galveston has held her own as second cotton port in the United States, though the difference between the amount of cotton handled here and at New Orleans is more marked this season than it was last.

Receipts at Galveston.

The following table, giving the receipts during the past seven seasons up to February 22, shows the receipts at this port this season have been the smallest since 1889–90:—

GALVESTON.

Year.	Receipts to Date.	Receipts, Season.	Texas Crop.
	Bales.	Bales.	Bales.
1889-90	795,404	860,112	1,748,320
1890-91	881,286	1,023,599	2,111,090
1891-92	1,024,465	1,154,208	2,406,108
1892-93	947,253	1,047,910	2,025,060
1893-94	930,233	1,021,724	1,824,922
1894-95	1,500,672	1,659,999	3,275,938
1895-96	807,760	..	..

The receipts at Galveston thus far this season, and those for the same period for 1894-95, are compared in the following table, with the receipts for the same periods at New Orleans, Savannah, and Charleston, with a percentage of decrease this year, as shown below:—

	Galveston.	New Orleans.	Savannah.	Charleston.
	Bales.	Bales.	Bales	Bales.
Receipts to February 21, 1895	1,497,294	2,127,424	811,653	377,084
Receipts to February 21, 1896	804,901	1,481,097	627,424	251,161
Percentage decrease	46	30	22	33

The following table gives the receipts, exports (foreign and coastwise), and stocks from the beginning of the cotton season on September 1 up to and including February 22 of each year for the last 7 years. **Exports from Galveston.**

The marked decrease of foreign exports is particularly noticeable, these being less than in any year within the period covered by the table. **Foreign exports.**

Coastwise exports, on the contrary, have held their own very well, and whilst the total receipts have fallen off some 50 per cent., the coastwise shipments are only some 12 per cent. less than last year:— **Coastwise exports.**

Year.	Receipts, Net.	Exports. Foreign.	Exports. Coastwise.	Stock, February 22.
	Bales.	Bales.	Bales.	Bales.
1889-90	795,404	726,945	343,031	39,337
1890-91	881,286	552,198	285,990	61,427
1891-92	1,024,465	710,042	244,881	85,594
1892-93	947,253	681,230	201,227	87,783
1893-94	930,233	710,061	148,544	85,958
1894-95	1,500,972	1,165,168	196,653	145,067
1895-96	804,901	546,845	172,515	95,994

(2123)

UNITED STATES.

Standing of Galveston this season.

The following tables show the standing of Galveston this season, as compared with the other cotton-exporting ports of the United States, up to the date of writing, February 21, and, further, the exports of cotton in detail up to the same date:—

Receipts at all United States Ports.

Ports.	This Season.	Last Season.
	Bales.	Bales.
Galveston	804,901	1,497,254
New Orleans	1,481,097	2,127,424
Mobile	184,443	220,042
Savannah	627,474	811,653
Charleston	251,161	377,084
Wilmington	155,534	223,923
Norfolk	264,634	388,823
Baltimore	35,293	93,937
New York	82,452	152,406
Boston	94,414	51,938
Philadelphia	28,913	79,322
West Point	136,833	284,496
Newport News	9,917	30,786
Brunswick	66,774	92,317
Laredo	..	8,970
Eagle Pass	..	4,824
Texas City	49,205	..
Port Royal	51,764	129,423
Velasco	..	592
Other ports	9,414	1,150
Total	4,334,223	6,576,364
Last year	6,576,364	..
Difference	2,242,141	..

Table of Receipts and Exports at Galveston, 1895–96, up to February 21, 1896.

Receipts.

	This Season.	Last Season.
	Bales.	Bales.
Net	804,901	1,497,254
Other ports in district	1,510	..
Gross	806,411	1,497,254

GALVESTON.

EXPORTS.

	This Season.	Last Season.
	Bales.	Bales.
Great Britain	324,211	701,364
France	90,916	185,694
Continent	129,108	285,418
Channel	2,610	..
Total foreign	546,845	1,172,476
New York	153,685	191,999
Morgan City	2,215	846
Other domestic ports	15,812	7,041
North, by rail	803	52
Total coastwise	172,515	199,938
Local consumption	2,908	2,604

RECAPITULATION OF EXPORTS.

	This Season.	Last Season.
	Bales.	Bales.
Foreign	546,845	1,172,476
Coastwise	172,515	199,938
Local consumption	2,908	2,604
Total exports	722,268	1,375,018

Cotton Prices.

The following table shows the range of prices for spot middling cotton at Galveston during the year 1895, by months. The great rise in prices up to October will be noticed:—

Month.	First Day.	High.	Low.	Last Day.
January	$5\frac{1}{16}$	$5\frac{3}{16}$	$5\frac{1}{16}$	$5\frac{1}{8}$
February	$5\frac{1}{8}$	$5\frac{3}{16}$	$5\frac{1}{16}$	$5\frac{1}{8}$
March	$5\frac{1}{8}$	$5\frac{7}{8}$	$5\frac{3}{16}$	$5\frac{3}{4}$
April	$5\frac{3}{4}$	$6\frac{7}{16}$	$5\frac{3}{4}$	$6\frac{3}{8}$
May	$6\frac{3}{8}$	$6\frac{7}{8}$	$6\frac{1}{4}$	$6\frac{7}{8}$
June	$6\frac{7}{8}$	$6\frac{13}{16}$	$6\frac{5}{8}$	$6\frac{5}{8}$
July	$6\frac{5}{8}$	$6\frac{11}{16}$	$6\frac{5}{8}$	$6\frac{5}{8}$
August	$6\frac{5}{8}$	$7\frac{3}{4}$	$6\frac{5}{8}$	$7\frac{3}{4}$
September	$7\frac{7}{8}$	$8\frac{3}{4}$	$7\frac{7}{8}$	$8\frac{3}{4}$
October	$8\frac{3}{4}$	$9\frac{1}{16}$	$8\frac{1}{4}$	$8\frac{9}{16}$
November	$8\frac{9}{16}$	$8\frac{9}{16}$	$8\frac{1}{16}$	$8\frac{5}{16}$
December	$8\frac{1}{4}$	$8\frac{1}{4}$	$7\frac{13}{16}$	$7\frac{15}{16}$

(2123)

UNITED STATES.

Harbour Works at Galveston.

Good progress made.

In the report from the Consulate, as well as in the Supplementary Report forwarded in May last, allusion was made to the extremely satisfactory progress shown as regards the great jetty works being carried out here by the United States Government, under the able superintendence of Major Miller, United States Corps of Engineers. This progress has been uninterruptedly kept up during the year 1895, and the faith which has always been expressed by competent judges as to the ultimate success of the jetty system has been amply justified.

During the year 1895 nearly $6\frac{1}{2}$ feet have been added to the depth of the channel over the Galveston bar. The channel itself has changed from an irregular to a straight course. In January, 1895, the greatest depth of water according to the official survey was $14\frac{1}{2}$ feet over the bar. In December of the same year the survey showed 21 feet on the bar, a gain for the year, as before remarked, of $6\frac{1}{2}$ feet.

$6\frac{1}{2}$ feet added to depth of water.

Monthly depths of water.

The following table shows the monthly depths of the channel in 1895, and the gradual deepening of water over the bar:—

Months.	Depth.
	Feet.
January	$14\frac{1}{2}$
February	15
March	$16\frac{3}{4}$
April	17
May	$18\frac{1}{4}$
June	$17\frac{3}{4}$
July	$17\frac{3}{4}$
August	$18\frac{1}{2}$
September	$19\frac{3}{4}$
October	20
November	$20\frac{3}{4}$
December	21

Work of the dredge-boats.

The attainment of this depth of water has been largely aided in 1895 by the use of dredgers. The dredge-boat "Jumbo" was set at work on April 11, and continued working until September, when she was relieved by the dredge-boat "General Comstock."

The actual work done by these boats was as follows:—

	Cubic Yards.
"Jumbo," April to September	213,596
"General Comstock," September to December	74,391
Total	287,987

One result of the use of these dredgers is that the entire covering of sand at the bottom of the channel has been removed and a firm clay bottom found, which it is expected when excavated will form a permanent channel, and one needing far less attention in the way of dredging than a channel with a sand bottom. It may be further remarked that the channel ought to be kept free from filling in owing to the force of the current, which, when conditions are normal, and the tide ebbs and flows, runs at about 4 knots per hour.

As regards the actual work done on the jetties themselves during the year 1895, work was continued on the north jetty during the whole of the year, and the jetty was pushed out from 13,000 feet to 21,200 feet, complete, a total advance of 8,125 feet, whilst the incomplete portion was advanced from the 22,000 foot mark to the 23,774 foot mark, a gain of 1,774 feet. Work done on the jetties.

The work on the south jetty was only resumed in August. From then to the end of the year the trestle work was pushed forward 1,766 feet further to sea, and the rip-rap apron completed for an additional 1,061 feet; but the actual completed portion of the south jetty remains as it was in January, 1895, viz., 32,000 feet.

The amount of rip-rap stone placed in position in the north jetty during the year 1895 was 126,049 tons, and on the south jetty 35,674 tons. Granite blocks to the amount of 107,963 tons were used in 1895 on the north jetty, and 2,134 tons on the south jetty.

It is believed to be shortly the intention of the engineers to simultaneously advance both jetties until a channel of 30 feet in depth is obtained. It is estimated that another 14 months will be required to completely finish the work at the present rate of progress.

In my last report I alluded at some length to the advantages which it was thought would undoubtedly accrue to the port of Galveston in the event of deep water being obtained, and I see no reason to in any way alter the conclusions that I then drew. In my opinion it is undoubtedly certain that Galveston, now that she has obtained a deep-water outlet to the sea, will eventually become a port of the first importance. Expected advantage to be gained by Galveston now that she has deep water.

Whilst the town itself may never grow to be a very populous city, I am still of opinion that the port of Galveston is destined in the near future, provided the proper steps are taken to turn to good account the facilities for trade and shipping now at command here, to become one of the leading if not the leading "entrepôts" for the outgoing and incoming commerce of the great south-west.

Already every indication points to this conclusion, and it needs but the active co-operation of the commercial men of this and the neighbouring states, in conjunction with additional railroad facilities, to amply justify in increased business the labour and money that have been expended by the Federal Government in providing this port with a system of jetties that has successfully done away with the long existing impediment to direct communication with the sea.

This, the year just ended, has hardly proved a fit one in which to test the value of the new position of Galveston. The export trade here is largely dependent on the Texas crop of cotton, and as this has been a phenomenally short one this season, and there has been nothing really to take its place, a full trial of the new conditions has yet to be made.

When it is known to the world, however, that every facility for exporting and importing cargoes of any nature, including those known as "dead weight" cargoes, exists here, that a permanent and deep channel of over 20 feet leading directly to the open sea is now in use, that there is no longer any danger of vessels being delayed or damaged through striking the bar, that vessels can now load their entire cargoes at the wharf, thus obviating the expense formerly attendant on lightering, which no longer is necessary, that wharfage rates are as low as in any other port in the United States, and the facilities for loading and storing cargo of essentially modern character, it cannot be doubted that the trade and shipping of this port will receive a great impetus.

The commercial bodies of this and neighbouring south-western States are already moving in the matter, and a Deep Water Utilization Committee, consisting of delegates from the various States tributary to this port, has been formed with the object, as the name implies, of securing for Galveston all that portion of the trade of the south-west that looks to this port as its natural outlet.

Of course, Galveston must expect to meet with vigorous competition and commercial rivalry on the part of other competing ports, but despite this it is the calm opinion of practical business men that in the long run she will hold her own, and even more than this, gain on her rivals.

In this opinion I, for my part, fully concur, and I should not be surprised, given good cotton and grain crops this year, to see a material increase in the trade of this port, and such increase become permanent.

NEW MEXICO.

Review of 1895.

The following appears in the report of the Governor of New Mexico to the United States secretary, of June 30, 1895, and which speaks for itself:—

"There has been no material increase in the population of New Mexico during the last fiscal year, although a healthy immigration has been coming into all parts of the territory of a most excellent class of farmers, and several of the mining camps that had been temporarily abandoned during the depression are again filling up with miners.

"The financial depression and business stagnation that affected this territory, in common with all parts of the Union, so disastrously last year has in a great measure passed away, and upon every hand may be seen the evidence of renewed business activity and coming prosperity.

"New Mexico has never been so wonderfully blessed with

copious rains, and all that tends to the production of a bounteous harvest, as during the present season.

"Everywhere across the broad plains, and over mountains and valleys, we find a most luxurious growth of native grasses such as has seldom been seen before, and the extensive herds of sheep, cattle, and horses pasturing thereon are in an excellent condition.

"The farmers and orchardists have harvested a most abundant crop of grain, alfalfa, wheat, oats, and other cereals, while the orchards and vineyards are filled with the most delicious fruits and grapes. This is the news from every portion of the territory. Those best informed pronounce the present crop of fruit, grapes, grasses and grains to be the largest in the history of New Mexico.

"This, together with an advance of fully 25 per cent. in the value of range cattle and sheep, and an advance of 35 per cent. in the value of wool, has given new life and impetus to the ranchmen and agriculturists, relieved them largely from their financial embarrassments, and greatly added to the material prosperity of the territory.

"The healthful immigration which had set in in the Pecos Valley, in the counties of Eddy and Chaves, referred to in my last annual report to the Secretary of the Interior, has continued and somewhat increased during the past year. Especially is this the case in the county of Chaves, where the immigration has been very large.

"This is due largely to the completion of the works of the Pecos Valley Irrigating and Improvement Company, to which reference will hereafter be made. The same may be said of the counties of San Juan, Valencia, Bernalillo, and Colfax, where like enterprises are in progress, the completion of such enterprises being the attraction of these localities, bringing as they do into the market large bodies to most excellent farming land, which, by means of ditches and reservoirs, are made available for this purpose.

"The mining camps of the counties of Santa Fé, Grant, Socono, Sierra, Lincoln, and Bernalillo, where business was at a standstill 12 months ago, are again filling with throngs of miners whose year's labour has resulted in a large increase of the production of the precious minerals.

"No census of the population has been taken during the year, but a careful estimate, made by well-informed persons from the different counties, places, the immigration to the territory during the year at about 6,000, mostly adult farmers or miners."

Land Titles.

Considerable progress has been made by the Court of Private Land Claims in respect of settling titles to vast areas of land in New Mexico.

The Court apparently fulfils the intention with which it was organised, and its work has hitherto been rapid and excellent.

The uncertainty of title has done much to retard the settlement of New Mexico, and until this uncertainty has been removed by the action of such courts as the one under notice no great development or immigration can be expected.

Up to now the Court, in its existence of two years, has disposed of suits affecting 6,800,667 acres of land. 108 cases have been tried by the Court, of which 35 were heard between August, 1894, and July, 1895.

Taxable Property.

Taxable property.

The total assessed value of the real estate, live stock, merchandise, and miscellaneous property for the year ending June 30, 1895, was 41,128,620 dol., as against 43,620,244 dol. in 1894. Only lands, houses, and live stock are taxable.

The following are the rates of assessment:—

For—	Mills on the Dollar.
Territorial purposes	6
Casual deficit bonds	0·25
Territorial institutions	1·50
Total	7·75

The following table shows the value of real and personal property subject to tax for 1894–5:

Counties.	Value.			
	1894.		1895.	
	Dol.	c.	Dol.	c.
Bernalillo	6,377,277	0	6,993,569	64
Chaves	1,446,002	0	1,671,008	0
Colfax	3,834,620	0	2,902,670	0
Donna Ana	2,733,563	0	2,755,285	0
Eddy	1,992,095	70	1,549,775	0
Grant	4,129,168	34	3,677,835	0
Guadaloupe	1,166,120	0	705,724	0
Lincoln	1,546,588	67	1,583,840	0
Mora	1,427,476	94	1,101,474	0
Rio Arriba	1,027,277	0	869,334	0
San Juan	520,844	69	656,799	85
Santa Fé	2,631,898	0	2,436,457	0
San Miguel	5,954,079	0	5,232,305	0
Sierra	1,380,097	52	1,427,162	81
Socorro	2,935,968	0	2,730,110	0
Taos	618,335	0	1,157,210	16
Valencia	1,783,133	95	2,127,723	49
Union	..		1,550,338	0
	41,574,844	81	41,128,620	95
Deduct exemptions to heads of family, under Sec. 1 cap. 6, laws of 1893, on total valuation	2,055,400	0	2,038,119	31
Total balance, subject to taxation	39,519,444	81	39,090,501	64

Territorial Debt.

The following is a statement of the territorial indebtedness, as it appeared on July 25, 1895:—

STATEMENT of Debt of New Mexico.

	Title of Bond.	Date.	Amount. Outstanding.
			Dollars.
I.	Capitol Building Bonds	1884-85	200,000
II.	„ Contingent Fund Bonds	1887	50,000
III.	Current Expense Bonds	1887-88	150,000
IV.	Provisional Indebtedness Bonds	1889	200,000
V.	Insane Asylum Bonds	1891	25,000
VI.	Casual Deficit „	1893	100,800
VII.	Refunding „	„	101,000
VIII.	Penitentiary Refunding Bonds	1894	81,000
	Total		907,800

All of this debt, excepting the Casual Deficit Bonds, which are 5 per cent. bonds, and the Capitol Building Bonds, which are 7 per cent. bonds, bears interest at 6 per cent.

There was a cash balance of 115,802 dol. in the Treasury on January 25, 1895.

Railways.

There was no new railroad building in New Mexico during 1895; but there are indications that the Pecos Valley Railroad, which was built in 1894 as far as Roswell, will, in the near future, be extended in a north-easterly direction to connect with the Atchison, Topeka, and Santa Fé at some point in Texas or the Indian territory. There are also prospects of railways being built from El Paso to Roswell, and from Santa Fé westerly across the Rio Grande into the Cochiti mining district.

Stock Raising.

An impetus was given to the stock-raising interests of North Mexico during 1895 owing to the advance in the price of cotton and sheep, and the excellent season for fodder.

New Mexico is largely interested in both cattle and sheep, and stands fifth among the states in the number of her sheep, and seventh in the value of her wool.

During the year ending June 30, 1895, there were sent to market from New Mexico about 150,000 head, mostly steer cattle, and about 15,000 were slaughtered during that period for home consumption. About 300,000 head of sheep were also exported, and about 14,700,000 lbs. of wool.

Irrigation.

This is always an important subject as regards New Mexico, where the greater portion of the land, to be productive, needs irrigation. In every part of the territory people are alive to the necessity of these methods, and new systems are being rapidly undertaken, and those already in existence completed.

In the extreme north-west, in the county of San Juan, four extensive enterprises are in course of completion. Four hundred miles of ditches have already been completed, and it is estimated that they will cover 225,000 acres of land, of which from 60,000 to 80,000 acres are already under cultivation.

This is given as an example of these irrigation enterprises:—

In the Pecos Valley the system of irrigation is said to be one of the most complete in the world. It has been in use some six years.

During the year ended July, 1895, the length of the canals has been increased by 100 miles, bringing the total up to 1,300 miles.

The whole of the Pecos Valley is an example of the successful employment of irrigation.

Mining.

During the year ended June 30, 1895, the mining industry in New Mexico revived greatly, owing to the better prices for silver and lead, the two minerals chiefly found there. The gold camps in particular received much impetus, and there were engaged almost as many miners as at any time in the previous history of New Mexico.

Return of British Shipping at the Port of Galveston in the Year 1895

Direct Trade in British Vessels from and to Great Britain and British Colonies.

Entered.

Total Number of Vessels.			Total Tonnage.			Total Number of Crews.	Total Value of Cargoes.
With Cargoes.	In Ballast.	Total.	With Cargoes.	In Ballast.	Total.		£
12	42	54	19,740	69,790	89,530	1,367	...

Cleared.

Total Number of Vessels.			Total Tonnage.			Total Number of Crews.	Total Value of Cargoes.
With Cargoes.	In Ballast.	Total.	With Cargoes.	In Ballast.	Total.		£
69	...	69	113,411	...	113,411	1,758	3,206,870

Indirect or Carrying Trade in British Vessels from and to other Countries.

Entered.

Countries whence Arrived.	Number of Vessels.			Tonnage.			Number of Crews.	Value of Cargoes.
	With Cargoes.	In Ballast.	Total.	With Cargoes.	In Ballast.	Total.		£
United States of America	3	17	20	4,293	24,390	28,683	487	...
Cape Verde Islands	...	15	15	...	22,406	22,406	343	...
Mexico	2	10	12	2,914	14,109	17,023	285	...
Canary Islands	...	9	9	...	15,685	15,685	227	...
Brazil	...	8	8	...	9,959	9,959	149	...
Belgium	3	2	5	4,996	3,261	8,257	123	...
Cuba	...	5	5	...	7,702	7,702	134	...
West Indies	1	3	4	949	4,617	5,566	84	...
Germany	3	...	3	4,106	...	4,106	69	...
Argentine Republic	...	2	2	...	3,340	3,340	53	...
Azores	...	2	2	...	2,947	2,947	46	...
Central America	...	1	1	...	1,792	1,792	30	...
Guatemala	...	1	1	...	1,319	1,319	23	...
United States of Colombia	1	...	1	1,211	...	1,211	25	...
Madeira	...	1	1	...	1,584	1,584	24	...
Portugal	...	1	1	...	1,247	1,247	20	...
Venezuela	...	1	1	...	1,132	1,132	25	...
Total	13	78	91	18,469	115,520	133,989	2,152	...

Cleared.

Countries to which Departed.	Number of Vessels.			Tonnage.			Number of Crews.	Value of Cargoes.
	With Cargoes.	In Ballast.	Total.	With Cargoes.	In Ballast.	Total.		£
Germany	55	...	55	81,484	...	81,484	1,301	1,759,321
France	21	...	21	32,080	...	32,080	508	1,009,415
United States of America	3	5	8	3,853	9,933	13,786	202	22,234
Belgium	6	...	6	8,765	...	8,765	144	156,542
Denmark	1	...	1	818	...	818	28	5,113
Italy	1	...	1	1,477	...	1,477	26	34,833
Mexico	1	...	1	1,094	...	1,094	21	6,103
West Indies	1	...	1	287	...	287	17	2,762
Total	89	5	94	129,858	9,933	139,791	2,247	2,996,323

STATEMENT of Vessels Entered and Cleared Coastwise, District of Galveston, for Years stated below.

ENTERED.

Year.	Domestic Vessels.		Foreign Vessels.	
	Number of Vessels.	Tons.	Number of Vessels.	Tons.
1895	325	333,370	28	28,834
1894	309	306,388	27	37,776
1893	257	287,071	36	50,176
1892	240	302,325	22	34,928

CLEARED.

Year.	Domestic Vessels.		Foreign Vessels.	
	Number of Vessels.	Tons.	Number of Vessels.	Tons.
1895	272	289,577	10	12,463
1894	267	282,752	6	2,886
1893	196	252,055	6	8,205
1892	147	250,358	6	6,429

(2123)

UNITED STATES.

STATEMENT of Exports of Commodities of Domestic Manufacture and Growth from the Customs District of Galveston for the Year ending December 31, 1895.

Destination.	Cotton. Quantity. Bales.	Cotton. Value. Dollars.	Cottonseed Oilcake and Meal. Quantity. Tons.	Cottonseed Oilcake and Meal. Value. Dollars.	Wheat. Quantity. Bushels.	Wheat. Value. Dollars.	Corn. Quantity. Bushels.	Corn. Value. Dollars.
Belgium— From Port of Galveston	12,966	468,034	400	10,304	..	..	55,715	19,800
Denmark— From Port of Galveston	..	..	423	10,902	..	..	80,000	24,800
,, ,, Velasco	..	..	2,610	57,420	..	..	..	..
France— From Port of Galveston	134,063	4,893,463	..	..	..	..	285,713	73,485
Germany— From Port of Galveston	190,936	6,795,204	74,572	1,551,353	..	..	313,679	97,507
,, ,, Velasco	92	1,480	5,374	102,020	..	..	..	..
Italy— From Port of Galveston	7,309	297,034	..	..	..	..	25,714	6,942
Netherlands— From Port of Galveston	1,250	39,712	5,904	48,978	..	..	163,014	50,517
Russia— From Port of Galveston	3,947	115,630	..	..	..	..	..	..
Great Britain— From Port of Galveston	579,596	20,009,589	16,458	336,241	..	..	387,613	110,062
Mexico— From Port of Galveston	1,100	52,600	..	..	..	..	22,029	7,647
,, ,, Velasco	..	..	..	..	..	..	..	..
,, ,, Sabine Pass	..	..	..	..	..	..	..	..

GALVESTON.

Statement of Exports of Commodities of Domestic Manufacture and Growth from the Customs District of Galveston for the Year ending December 31, 1895—continued.

Destination.	Cotton. Quantity. Bales.	Cotton. Value. Dollars.	Cottonseed Oilcake and Meal. Quantity. Tons.	Cottonseed Oilcake and Meal. Value. Dollars.	Wheat. Quantity. Bushels.	Wheat. Value. Dollars.	Corn. Quantity. Bushels.	Corn. Value. Dollars.
West Indies— From Port of Galveston	..	..	..	..	..	..	..	..
,, ,, Sabine Pass	..	..	..	..	..	..	..	..
Cuba— From Port of Galveston	..	..	..	..	..	..	..	..
Argentine— From Port of Sabine Pass	..	..	..	..	..	..	..	..
Brazil— From Port of Sabine Pass	..	..	..	..	..	..	..	..
British Guiana— From Port of Galveston	..	..	..	..	..	..	..	..
Uruguay— From Port of Sabine Pass	..	..	..	..	..	..	..	..
Totals for 1895	931,259	32,672,746	105,736	2,117,218	..	..	1,233,477	390,760
,, 1894	1,073,976	33,520,164	95,128	2,131,543	135,137	77,459	5,412	2,597
,, 1893	757,593	31,534,595	118,230	2,942,914	1,308,950	934,269	98,509	50,710
,, 1892	808,628	32,610,901	79,088	1,867,441	377,985	335,240	144,775	95,925
,, 1891	774,826	34,217,492	43,196	1,008,541	587,395	588,058	12,741	7,251
,, 1890	499,189	26,303,400	53,484	1,202,779	..	..	35,246	11,989

(2123)

UNITED STATES.

STATEMENT of Exports of Commodities of Domestic Manufacture and Growth from the Customs District of Galveston for the Year ending December 31, 1895—continued.

Destination.	Wheat Flour. Quantity. Barrels.	Wheat Flour. Value. Dollars.	Lumber. Quantity. M. feet.	Lumber. Value. Dollars.	Cottonseed Oil. Quantity. Gallons.	Cottonseed Oil. Value. Dollars.	Logs. Value. Dollars.	Sundries. Value. Dollars.	Total. Value. Dollars.
Belgium—									
From Port of Galveston	..	..	..	..	..	..	..	..	498,138
Denmark—									
From Port of Galveston	..	..	..	..	..	..	..	..	35,702
,, ,, Velasco	..	..	..	..	..	..	..	..	57,420
France—									
From Port of Galveston	..	..	..	..	20,500	7,509	..	298	4,974,755
Germany—									
From Port of Galveston	6	28	1,048	49,283	22,225	6,860	73,994	2,379	8,576,608
,, ,, Velasco	..	..	..	..	26,560	10,000	2,160	..	115,660
Italy—									
From Port of Galveston	..	..	..	..	5,000	1,375	..	..	305,351
Netherlands—									
From Port of Galveston	..	..	..	..	391,750	169,980	..	..	309,187
Russia—									
From Port of Galveston	..	..	..	..	..	..	..	..	115,630
Great Britain—									
From Port of Galveston	3,360	5,936	..	..	70	10	..	8,341	20,470,179
Mexico—									
From Port of Galveston	300	1,280	..	..	12,723	1,483	..	26	63,036
,, ,, Velasco	..	..	..	..	199,938	38,991	..	500	39,491
,, ,, Sabine Pass	..	..	10,481	107,968	..	..	..	2,290	110,258
West Indies—									
From Port of Galveston	..	..	..	..	..	..	1,055	..	1,055
,, ,, Sabine Pass	..	..	2,765	38,512	..	..	..	4,460	37,972

GALVESTON.

Statement of Exports of Commodities of Domestic Manufacture and Growth from the Customs District of Galveston for the Year ending December 31, 1895—continued.

Destination.	Wheat Flour. Quantity.	Wheat Flour. Value.	Lumber. Quantity.	Lumber. Value.	Cottonseed Oil. Quantity.	Cottonseed Oil. Value.	Logs. Value.	Sundries. Value.	Total. Value.
	Barrels.	Dollars.	M. feet.	Dollars.	Gallons.	Dollars.	Dollars.	Dollars.	Dollars.
Cuba— From Port of Galveston	45,578	168,438	..	..	..	..	..	847	169,285
Argentine— From Port of Sabine Pass	..	..	1,409	14,467	..	..	..	..	14,467
Brazil— From Port of Sabine Pass	..	..	1,111	11,740	..	..	..	..	11,740
British Guiana— From Port of Galveston	4,000	12,000	..	..	..	..	..	1,197	13,197
Uruguay— From Port of Sabine Pass	..	..	1,271	14,102	..	..	..	..	14,102
Totals for 1895	53,244	187,682	18,085	231,072	678,766	236,208	77,209	20,338	35,933,233
,, 1894	59,859	214,792	5,909	70,154	218,362	78,665	34,885	32,196	36,162,455
,, 1893	49,057	198,925	1,477	17,689	303,170	116,040	74,694	25,359	35,895,195
,, 1892	21,296	98,226	1,334	16,726	41,263	15,639	47,000	9,904	35,097,002
,, 1891	11,929	51,320	..	16,893	..	2,250	..	72,655	35,964,460
,, 1890	19,481	30,511	..	200,600	..	..	..	104,210	27,853,489

UNITED STATES.

STATEMENT of Imports Free of Duty at the Port of Galveston, Texas, for the Year ending December 31, 1895.

Commodities.		Quantity.	Germany.	Great Britain.	France.	Netherlands.	Mexico.	Porto Rico.	Turkey.	Spain.
			Dollars.	Dollars.	Dollars.	Dollars.	Dollars.	Dollars.	Dollars.	Dollars.
American manufactures re-imported	...	...	2,999	4,401	...	...	...	...	...	...
Art works	...	...	66	...	...	...	...	...	...	...
Asphaltum (crude)	Tons	240	...	...	...	...	...	...	...	...
Books and printed matter	...	...	...	235	39	...	...	...	...	...
Coal, anthracite	Tons	1,300	...	3,957	...	...	...	...	...	...
Coffee	Lbs.	39,914	...	...	...	...	632	6,286	...	...
Cotton ties (iron and steel)	,,	1,494,924	...	19,529	...	...	...	...	...	...
Fruits and nuts (green and ripe)	...	...	...	814	...	...	18	...	...	...
Household and personal effects	...	...	2,096	...	...	...	...	...	...	...
Mineral waters, natural	Gallons	3,625	686	...	...	...	...	...	...	...
Paper stock (old bagging)	Lbs.	534,072	...	6,234	...	...	...	...	...	...
Salt	,,	35,674,639	...	49,650	...	...	...	...	...	...
Scientific apparatus	...	...	1,026	...	...	...	...	...	...	...
Vegetable fibres, jute and jute butts	Tons	1,784	...	35	...	...	...	...	...	...
Miscellaneous articles (all other)	...	...	...	...	...	...	...	...	...	...
Totals free for 1895			6,873	84,885	39	...	650	6,286	...	...
,, 1894			3,626	42,486	281	631	3,369	2,981	673*	...
,, 1893			1,616	26,349	100	522	6,055	3,180	...	...
,, 1892			2,003	52,875	725	4,730	3,477	10,857	...	...
,, 1891			...	...	...	...	...	...	...	...

* Japan.

GALVESTON.

Statement of Imports Free of Duty at the Port of Galveston, Texas, for the Year ending December 31, 1895—continued.

Commodities.		Quantity.	Italy.	Honduras.	British West Indies.	Cuba.	British East Indies.	Belgium.	Austria-Hungary.	Total, 1895.	Total, 1894.
			Dollars.	Dollars.	Dollars.	Dollars.	Dollars.	Dollars.	Dollars.	Dollars.	Dollars.
American manufactures re-imported		...	...	...	...	...	...	...	...	7,400	17,407
Art works		...	455	...	...	...	...	...	...	521	...
Asphaltum (crude)	Tons	240	...	...	883	1,851	...	...	...	2,734	...
Books and printed matter	...	...	...	...	...	...	...	...	...	274	...
Coal, anthracite	Tons	1,330	...	...	...	...	...	...	...	3,957	7,668
Coffee	Lbs.	39,914	...	...	...	...	...	...	...	6,918	4,030
Cotton ties (iron and steel)	,,	1,494,924	...	...	...	...	...	...	...	19,529	...
Fruits and nuts (green and ripe)	...	...	...	395	1,539	...	...	...	...	1,952	21,426
Household and personal effects	...	...	...	...	...	...	...	...	...	2,940	5,347
Mineral waters, natural	Gallons	3,625	...	...	...	...	...	...	...	686	631
Paper stock (old bagging)	Lbs.	534,072	...	...	...	...	...	...	...	6,234	...
Salt	,,	35,674,639	...	...	...	...	...	...	...	49,650	14,172
Scientific apparatus	...	...	...	...	...	...	...	...	584	1,610	...
Vegetable fibres, jute and jute butts	Tons	1,784	...	...	...	...	28,749	...	...	28,749	...
Miscellaneous articles (all other)	...	...	60	5	...	...	...	...	...	*100	2,506
Totals free for 1895		...	515	400	2,422	1,851	28,749	...	584	133,254	...
,, 1894		...	...	769	3,695	364,592	...	2,325†	...	425,428	...
,, 1893		...	158	439,723*	...	621,186	41,903	227	...	701,138	...
,, 1892		...	...	...	2,578	45,743	...	...	...	562,869	...
,, 1891		...	...	...	...	...	...	...	...	557,981	...

* Brazil. † British Columbia.

STATEMENT of Imports Subject to Duty at Port of Galveston, Texas, for the Year ending December 31, 1895.

Commodities.		Quantity.	Germany.	Great Britain.	France.	Netherlands.	Mexico.	Porto Rico.	Turkey.	Spain.
			Dollars.	Dollars.	Dollars.	Dollars.	Dollars.	Dollars.	Dollars.	Dollars.
Asphaltum, treated	...	...	...	506	...	...	...	...	...	...
Books and printed matter	...	...	...	215	188	...	...	...	...	...
Breadstuffs, macaroni, cakes, and biscuits	...	...	19,231	...	...	...	...	...	...	...
Cement, Portland, barrels, 400 lbs. gross, each	Lbs.	20,563,919	...	4,722	...	...	...	...	...	...
Coal, bituminous, and coke	Tons	1,789	...	...	...	...	...	...	...	...
Chemicals—										
Sheep dip	...	...	...	18,250	...	...	...	...	...	...
Dead oil, creosote	Gallons	160,000	...	4,623	...	...	...	...	...	...
Other compounds	...	...	568	1,097	...	...	13	...	...	...
Cotton manufactures, and laces and embroideries	...	...	...	21	...	...	...	...	...	...
Earthenware—										
Plain and decorative crockery	...	...	260	13,275	34	...	...	...	...	...
Firebrick and tiles	...	...	...	1,492	...	...	...	...	...	...
Flax and hemp, manufactures of—										
Jute	...	...	...	13,611	...	...	7	...	...	...
Other manufactures of	...	...	...	29	...	...	493	...	...	...
Fruits and nuts, green and ripe	...	...	...	...	...	...	...	49	...	...
Fruits—										
Preserved and prepared	...	...	...	484	190	...	...	...	...	...
In spirits	...	...	...	3,757	6,043	...	...	...	...	...
Fish—										
Sardines in oil	...	...	...	...	1,606	...	...	...	...	...
All other	...	...	...	1,646	394	...	...	...	...	...
Glass, all kinds	...	...	631	177	113	...	...	...	...	...

GALVESTON.

STATEMENT of Imports Subject to Duty at the Port of Galveston, Texas, for the Year ending December 31, 1895—continued.

Commodities		Quantity.	Germany.	Great Britain.	France.	Netherlands.	Mexico.	Porto Rico.	Turkey.	Spain.
			Dollars.	Dollars.	Dollars.	Dollars.	Dollars.	Dollars.	Dollars.	Dollars.
Iron and steel—			...	1,014	...	...	...	...	35	...
Manufactures of and machinery	...	...	...	19,519	...	...	...	...	...	...
Tin and terne plate	...	...	48	2,585	...	...	110	...	...	...
Metals, manufactures of	...	...	...	9,925	...	...	...	...	...	...
Malt liquors, ale and porter in bottles	Gallons	8,955	...	...	5	...	...	...	...	...
Oils, vegetable and olive	...	724	...	...	...	...	...	...	...	...
Provisions, cheese	Lbs.	381	...	3	...	...	...	...	...	...
Rice	,,	556,778	9,772	...	...	...	...	...	...	...
Sugar, beet (above No. 16 D.S.)	,,	448,229	12,289	528	...	...	...	...	...	...
Spirits, distilled	Gallons	340	...	2,812	1,275	...	...	...	...	...
Vegetables, preserved and prepared	...	...	678	81	993	...	...	...	...	...
Wines, sparkling and still	...	...	209	5	...	...	...	...	...	...
Wood, manufactures of	...	...	27	113	...	...	...	...	...	...
Wool, manufactures of	...	...	186	959	12	...	...	...	316	...
Miscellaneous, all other dutiable articles	...	...								
Subject to duty for 1895	...	...	43,899	101,449	10,853	...	623	49	351	...
Free of duty for 1895	...	...	6,873	84,885	39	...	650	6,286	...	...
Grand total for 1895	...	...	50,772	186,334	10,892	...	1,273	6,335	351	...
,, 1894	...	...	7,909	152,231	11,292	631	7,257	3,668	673*	487
,, 1893	...	...	9,023	201,961	7,093	4,072	6,599	3,180	...	...
,, 1892	...	...	11,318	304,314	13,144	27,304	5,604	11,629	355	...

* Japan.

(2123)

UNITED STATES.

STATEMENT of Imports Subject to Duty at the Port of Galveston, Texas, for the Year ending December 31, 1895—continued.

Commodities.		Quantity.	Italy.	Honduras.	British West Indies.	Cuba.	British East Indies.	Belgium.	Austria-Hungary.	Total, 1895.	Total, 1894.
			Dollars.	Dollars.	Dollars. 9,735	Dollars.	Dollars.	Dollars.	Dollars.	Dollars. 9,735	Dollars. ...
Asphaltum, treate l...		...	...	...	...	...	...	...	...	506	...
Books and printed matter...		...	...	...	...	...	...	...	...	403	248
Breadstuffs, macaroni, cakes and biscuits											
Cement, Portland, barrels, 400 lbs. gross, each	Lbs.	20,563,919	...	...	...	...	...	34,874	...	54,105	30,624
Coal, bituminous, and coke	Tons	1,789	...	...	...	...	...	...	...	4,722	8,427
Chemicals—											
Sheep dip		...	...	...	...	...	...	...	...	18,250	3,080
Dead oil, creosote	Gallons	160,000	...	...	...	...	...	...	...	4,623	7,513
Other compounds		...	...	...	...	...	...	...	...	1,665	6,416
Cotton manufactures, and laces and embroideries		...	...	...	...	...	762	...	8	804	612
Earthenware—											
Plain and decorated crockery		...	...	...	...	...	...	...	...	13,569	14,519
Firebrick and tiles		...	...	...	...	...	...	...	...	1,492	496
Flax and hemp, manufactures of—											
Jute		...	...	...	...	...	...	...	...	13,611	8,121
Other manufactures of		...	...	16	48	...	...	...	...	36	10,414
Fruits and nuts, green and ripe		...	...	...	...	...	...	...	...	606	1,230
Fruits—											
Preserved and prepared		...	...	...	...	...	...	...	...	674	6,529
In spirits		...	...	...	...	...	...	...	...	9,800	...
Fish—											
Sardines in oil		...	45	...	...	...	...	...	...	1,606	1,624
All other		...	...	...	...	...	...	...	...	2,085	...
Glass, all kinds		...	...	...	...	...	...	...	...	921	1,567

GALVESTON.

STATEMENT of Imports Subject to Duty at the Port of Galveston, Texas, for the Year ending December 31, 1895—continued.

Commodities.		Quantity.	Italy.	Honduras.	British West Indies.	Cuba.	British East Indies.	Belgium.	Austria-Hungary.	Total, 1895.	Total, 1894.
			Dollars.	Dollars.	Dollars.	Dollars.	Dollars.	Dollars.	Dollars.	Dollars.	Dollars.
Iron and steel—		...	...	...	...	...	...	...	...	1,049	6,692
Manufactures of and machinery	...	...	...	...	...	...	...	...	...	19,519	11,298
Tin and terne plate	Lbs.	765,460	...	...	...	...	...	...	...	2,743	...
Metals, manufactures of	...	...	...	...	...	...	...	...	...	9,925	9,825
Malt liquors, ale and porter in bottles	Gallons	8,955	540	...	...	...	...	...	65	610	689
Oils, vegetable and olive	...	724	54	...	...	...	...	...	...	57	150
Provisions, cheese	Lbs.	381	...	...	...	...	...	...	...	9,772	...
Rice	"	556,788	...	...	...	...	...	...	...	12,289	3,738
Sugar, beet (above No. 16 D S.)	"	448,229	...	...	...	...	...	...	...	528	521
Spirits, distilled	Gallons	340	48	...	...	...	...	...	...	4,135	3,717
Vegetables, preserved and prepared	...	...	199	...	...	...	...	...	...	1,951	1,781
Wines, sparkling and still	...	...	...	...	...	...	...	...	...	214	178
Wood, and manufactures of	...	...	...	...	...	...	5	...	...	145	213
Wool, manufactures of	...	...	...	...	...	...	...	...	...		
Miscellaneous, all other dutiable articles	...	...	136	...	...	...	63	...	102	1,774	1,984
Subject to duty for 1895	...	...	1,022	16	9,783	...	830	34,874	175	203,924	...
Free of duty for 1895	...	...	515	400	2,422	1,851	28,749	...	584	133,254	...
Grand total for 1895	...	...	1,537	416	12,205	1,851	29,579	34,874	759	337,178	...
,, 1894	...	...	1,319	769	3,808	364,592	272	20,353	50† 2,325‡	577,636	...
,, 1893	...	...	968	...	...	621,186	42,315	31,823	123	928,343	...
,, 1892	...	...	1,218	439,723*	3,097	46,275	...	...	...	863,981	...

* Brazil. † Austria. ‡ British Columbia.

42 UNITED STATES.

STATEMENT of Vessels engaged in the Foreign Trade in the District of Galveston during the Year ending December 31, 1895.

ENTERED.

Nationality.	Galveston.					Velasco.				Sabine Pass.			
	In Ballast.		With Cargo.		In Ballast.		With Cargo.		In Ballast.		With Cargo.	
	Number of Vessels.	Tons.	Number of Vessels.	Tons.	Number of Vessels.	Tons.	Number of Vessels.	Tons.	Number of Vessels.	Tons.	Number of Vessels.	Tons.
American	..	..	4	646	..	..	..	..	13	6,477	..	..
British	96	145,984	27	45,186	5	6,791	..	..	4	2,719	..	..
German	..	..	..	..	..	..	..	..	..	..	..	..
Greek	..	..	..	..	..	..	..	..	..	..	..	..
Mexican	6	1,062	..	..	2	354	..	..	..	..	..	..
Norwegian	20	11,253	4	2,186	..	..	..	..	8	3,599	..	..
Spanish	24	37,728	..	..	..	..	..	..	..	..	..	..
Swedish	2	771	..	..	..	..	..	..	1	336	..	..
Russian	1	279	..	..	..	..	..	..	..	..	..	..
Totals for 1895	149	197,077	35	48,020	7	7,145	..	..	26	13,131	..	..
,, 1894	148	264,257	32	38,683	12	16,655	..	..	15	6,217	..	..
,, 1893	133	188,366	38	31,518	19	24,543	..	..	3	841	..	..
,, 1892	117	167,090	41	42,595	9	11,497	1	116	2	645	..	..
,, 1891	148	169,010	75	63,892	..	..	..	..	..	..	..	..

STATEMENT of Vessels engaged in the Foreign Trade in the District of Galveston during the Year ending December 31, 1895—continued.

CLEARED.

| Nationality. | Galveston. |||| Velasco. |||| Sabine Pass. ||||
| | In Ballast. || With Cargo. || In Ballast. || With Cargo. || In Ballast. || With Cargo. ||
	Number of Vessels.	Tons.	Number of Vessels.	Tons.	Number of Vessels.	Tons.	Number of Vessels.	Tons.	Number of Vessels.	Tons.	Number of Vessels.	Tons.
American	..	..	..	..	..	..	..	..	..	..	29	10,197
British	..	..	163	256,177	..	..	2	2,709	..	..	6	3,687
German	..	..	..	..	..	..	..	..	..	..	..	..
Greek	..	..	1	1,743	..	..	..	..	..	..	..	..
Mexican	..	..	2	354	..	..	4	708	..	..	..	..
Norwegian	..	..	13	8,346	..	..	1	1,350	..	..	13	5,170
Spanish	..	..	25	39,634	..	..	..	..	..	..	..	..
Swedish	..	..	1	357	..	..	..	..	..	..	2	770
Russian	..	..	1	279	..	..	..	..	..	..	..	..
Totals for 1895	..	..	206	306,890	..	..	7	4,767	..	..	50	19,824
,, 1894	7	9,447	199	300,528	..	..	13	18,112	..	..	23	7,700
,, 1893	2	477	194	268,354	..	..	25	33,138	..	..	17	3,710
,, 1892	7	3,493	182	246,517	..	..	10	11,355	3	1,078	2	801
,, 1891	12	4,432	232	250,671	..	..	..	..	..	..	..	..

(2123)

LONDON:
Printed for Her Majesty's Stationery Office.
BY HARRISON AND SONS,
Printers in Ordinary to Her Majesty.
(75   4 | 96—H & S   2123)

FOREIGN OFFICE.
1896.
ANNUAL SERIES.

No. 1688.

DIPLOMATIC AND CONSULAR REPORTS ON TRADE AND FINANCE.

UNITED STATES.

REPORT FOR THE YEAR 1895
ON THE
TRADE OF NEW ORLEANS.

REFERENCE TO PREVIOUS REPORT, Annual Series No. 1551.

Presented to both Houses of Parliament by Command of Her Majesty,
APRIL, 1896.

LONDON:
PRINTED FOR HER MAJESTY'S STATIONERY OFFICE,
BY HARRISON AND SONS, ST. MARTIN'S LANE,
PRINTERS IN ORDINARY TO HER MAJESTY.

And to be purchased, either directly or through any Bookseller, from
EYRE & SPOTTISWOODE, EAST HARDING STREET, FLEET STREET, E.C., and
32, ABINGDON STREET, WESTMINSTER, S.W.; or
JOHN MENZIES & Co., 12, HANOVER STREET, EDINBURGH, and
90, WEST NILE STREET, GLASGOW; or
HODGES, FIGGIS, & Co., Limited, 104, GRAFTON STREET, DUBLIN.

1896.

[C. 7919—56.]   *Price Twopence.*

New Series of Reports.

Reports of the Annual Series have been issued from Her Majesty's Diplomatic and Consular Officers at the following places, and may be obtained from the sources indicated on the title-page:—

No.		Price.	No.		Price.
1570.	Fiji	½d.	1629.	Porto Rico	1d.
1571.	Athens	2½d.	1630.	Rotterdam	½d.
1572.	Bilbao	3½d.	1631.	Alexandria	1½d.
1573.	Barcelona	3d.	1632.	Tokio	2½d.
1574.	Fiume	2d.	1633.	Tangier	1½d.
1575.	Tahiti	1d.	1634.	Oporto	1½d.
1576.	San Francisco	6d.	1635.	St. Petersburg	4d.
1577.	Ichang	1½d.	1636.	Dantzig	2d.
1578.	Amoy	1½d.	1637.	Macao	1d.
1579.	Wênchow	1d.	1638.	Hiogo and Osaka	6d.
1580.	Smyrna	2½d.	1639.	Naples	1½d.
1581.	Nice	1½d.	1640.	Kiungchow	½d.
1582.	Sôul	1½d.	1641.	Rome	1½d.
1583.	Rio Grande do Sul	4d.	1642.	Beira	½d.
1584.	Nagasaki	1d.	1643.	St. Jago de Cuba	4½d.
1585.	Hakodate	1d.	1644.	Christiania	6d.
1586.	Frankfort	3d.	1645.	Lisbon	1½d.
1587.	Samoa	1d.	1646.	Brussels	½d.
1588.	Cherbourg	1½d.	1647.	Vera Cruz	½d.
1589.	Damascus	1d.	1648.	Tunis	1d.
1590.	New York	1d.	1649.	Antwerp	1d.
1591.	Athens	2d.	1650.	Tokio	1d.
1592.	Baghdad	1d.	1651.	Honolulu	½d.
1593.	Vienna	1½d.	1652.	Stettin	1½d.
1594.	Montevideo	2½d.	1653.	Bangkok	1d.
1595.	Swatow	1½d.	1654.	Batoum	1½d.
1596.	Foochow	1d.	1655.	Mexico	9½d.
1597.	Tamsui	1d.	1656.	Odessa	1½d.
1598.	Chungking	1d.	1657.	Réunion	1d.
1599.	Chefoo	1d.	1658.	Tokio	1½d.
1600.	Tokio	1½d.	1659.	Maranham	1d.
1601.	Bangkok	1d.	1660.	Copenhagen	1d.
1602.	Caracas	1½d.	1661.	Berlin	1½d.
1603.	Sofia	2½d.	1662.	Teheran	2½d.
1604.	Belgrade	2½d.	1663.	Salonica	1½d.
1605.	Shanghai	2½d.	1664.	Manila	½d.
1606.	Canton	1½d.	1665.	Florence	5½d.
1607.	Meshed	1½d.	1666.	Dakar	½d.
1608.	Erzeroum	1d.	1667.	Havre	2d.
1609.	Galatz	2d.	1668.	Rouen	2d.
1610.	Port Said	1½d.	1669.	Corfu	½d.
1611.	The Hague	1½d.	1670.	Calais	1d.
1612.	Calais	1d.	1671.	Tehran	1½d.
1613.	Newchwang	1d.	1672.	Barcelona	2d.
1614.	Copenhagen	1d.	1673.	Amsterdam	1d.
1615.	Odessa	2d.	1674.	Bordeaux	2½d.
1616.	Gothenburg	2d.	1675.	Warsaw	1d.
1617.	Mannheim	1½d.	1676.	Havana	1½d.
1618.	Old Calabar	5d.	1677.	Berlin	1d.
1619.	Pekin	2½d.	1678.	Beira	1½d.
1620.	Taganrog	2d.	1679.	Saigon	1d.
1621.	Brindisi	2½d.	1680.	Trebizond	1d.
1622.	Jeddah	1½d.	1681.	Vera Cruz	1½d.
1623.	Hamburg	3d.	1682.	Patras	1d.
1624.	Angora	1½d.	1683.	La Rochelle	1½d.
1625.	Buda-Pesth	1½d.	1684.	Madrid	1½d.
1626.	Beyrout	1d.	1685.	Belgrade	2d.
1627.	Bushire	2d.	1686.	Algiers	5d.
1628.	Stettin	2½d.	1687.	Galveston	2½d.

No. 1688.

Reference to previous Report, Annual Series No. 1551.

UNITED STATES.

NEW ORLEANS.

Consul St. John to the Marquis of Salisbury.

My Lord,   New Orleans, March 11, 1896.

I HAVE the honour to transmit herewith my Annual Trade Report for 1895, as well as those from Mr. Howe, Her Majesty's Vice-Consul at Pensacola, and Mr. Barnewall, British Vice-Consul at Mobile.

I have &c.
(Signed)   C. L. ST. JOHN.

Report on the Trade and Commerce of the Consular District of New Orleans for the Year 1895.

ABSTRACT of Contents.

	PAGE
New Orleans—	
Commerce	3
Finance	4
Cotton	4
,, prices	5
,, shipments	5
,, mills	5
,, spindles	5
,, looms	5
,, baling	6
,, seed	6
Breadstuffs and grain	6
Flour	6
Sugar	7
Rice	7
Wool	7
Hides	7
Tallow	8
Furs	8
Fruit	8

(2125)

UNITED STATES.

Abstract of Contents—continued.

	PAGE
New Orleans—continued.	
Wines	8
Beer	8
Whisky	8
Horses and mules	8
Livestock	9
Oak staves	9
Liverpool salt	9
Baling stuffs	9
Cotton ties	9
Ocean freights	10
Free wharves	10
Port Chalmette, description of	10
Labour troubles	12
City drainage	12
Health statistics	12
Electric street cars	13
Principal exports	14
British shipping returns	15
Annex A	15
Pensacola—	
Trade	16
New line of steamers	16
Imports, principal articles of	16
Exports, timber	16
Shipping	17
British tonnage keeps up	17
Strandings on Pensacola bar; channel being deepened	17
Coal, exports	17
Pensacola a coaling port	17
Business with Cuba	17
General remarks	18
Agricultural notes	18
Annexes—	
A.—Return of imports	18
B.— ,, exports	19
C.— ,, imports and exports by countries	20
D.— ,, shipping	20
Mobile—	
Cotton receipts and prices	21
,, exports	21
Lumber, prices and exports	22
,, shipments	22
Staves	24
Wool	24
Naval stores	25
Coal trade	25
Coke	25
Fruit trade	27
Vegetables	28
Mobile Bay and Harbour	28
Rivers	28
Harbourmaster's report	28
Returns of shipping	30

Commerce.

The commerce of New Orleans has seen many fluctuations and changes during the last 10 years, changes that have diverted some of the business that formerly came here, but at the same time New Orleans has extended its commercial influence in other directions. The river business has been very materially affected. What formerly was handled by steamboats is now done by railroads. A point to be observed is the shrinkage in values, running up to 30 per cent. in many cases. Thus, New Orleans the past season received 691,000 bales of cotton in excess of the season 1893-94, yet the exports of the 2 seasons differ only by a few thousand dollars in value.

Owing to the building of the jetties at the mouth of the river the inconveniences of 1870 have been avoided. At that time the river was frequently closed for weeks, and generally at the busiest season of the year, for all vessels over 1,200 tons. There is no doubt that New Orleans enjoys exceptional advantages for a manufacturing town; an abundance of raw material, particularly cotton, wool, leather, lumber, iron and coal, cheap cost of living as compared with the north, and a climate allowing work to be done throughout the year, The State constitution exempts from taxation all capital engaged in manufactures.

The average yearly wages paid to the factory hands in New Orleans was 442 dol. (90*l*. about), but a slight decrease has lately taken place, and there is at the present moment a great demand for employment. I would warn British subjects not to be induced by prospects of what appear to be high wages, for living, though less costly than in the north, is anything but cheap—especially house rent—and the population is more than sufficient to fill up every kind of employment.

Compared with the other cities of the United States New Orleans holds, this year, the third place in exports, and the sixth in imports, which are as follows:—

	Value. Currency.	Value. Sterling.
	Dollars.	£
Exports	71,327,601	14,706,700
Imports	15,185,356	3,156,330

Compared with 1894 the imports show an increase in value of 32,100*l*., and the exports a decrease of 234,780*l*.

Annexed will be found a return of the principal articles of export carried in British ships during the year.

The total arrivals of vessels during the year were (not counting coastwise American) 868 vessels of all nationalities, equalling 975,939 tons, as shown in Table A annexed.

(2125)

Finance.

The local money market has shown no special feature during the past commercial year, except an abnormally abundant supply and lowness of rates, attributed to the depression of business generally in all lines.

The unusually high rates for foreign exchange that have prevailed during the past season can be traced to several causes. First, the prices at which the bulk of products sold were the lowest known for the past 50 years; then, the exports of grain were remarkably small, due to the good crops made in Europe. But the most important factor in the case was the selling out by European holders of enormous amounts of American investments, their confidence in several large railroad companies in this country having been shaken.

Since January 1 the rates for sight exchange on New York in this market were lower than usual, owing to the fact that southern banks and large commercial houses had borrowed comparatively little from their northern correspondents, and the engagements they had to meet were much less than in former years. As a rule these loans were made in the late summer, or early in the autumn, when the crops began to move, and did not fall due until after January 1, 1895.

Silver, though not fluctuating so widely as last year, has, at times, been quite depressed.

Cotton.

The cotton industry of the United States, according to the "Times-Democrat," has received another set back during the past 12 months. Some other industries may have fared as badly, but scarcely worse. The year opened with idle spindles in all parts of the country; idle, not because of insolvency, or any approach to insolvency, but simply because financial and commercial affairs in the United States were greatly deranged. Hence, with the advent of the new year, the future of the cotton industry assumed the position of the most important matter before the people of the Southern States. Such being the case the policy with respect to the next crop became a serious problem. The result was a determination to reduce the cotton acreage by 25 per cent.

In December and January of the present cotton year (1894-95) it became obvious that America would not, and could not, plant another big crop at such low prices. As the depression lasted until near the middle of March, it became evident that there were prospects of a reduced acreage. Then came several very pronounced influences, all moving in the same direction, namely, a continual rise in silver; a further strengthened conviction of a largely reduced acreage in America; the feeling that the war in the far East was drawing to a conclusion; and the weather conditions were still unfavourable, with a marked want of rain in Texas. The present crop had been estimated from 9,000,000 to 11,000,000 bales; the actual crop was 9,901,251 bales.

Prices of cotton. The prices during the past season (1894-95) reached the lowest figures on record: Middling, $4\frac{7}{8}$ c. in November (1894), at New Orleans; middling Gulf, $5\frac{3}{4}$ c. in November, February, and March, at New York; and middling Americans, $2\frac{31}{32}d.$ in November, January, and February at Liverpool.

The present crop (1895-96) showed here in September, prices advancing, middling, $7\frac{9}{16}$ c. spot, reaching, on October 16, as high as $9\frac{3}{16}$ c.; the rate now is $7\frac{3}{8}$ c.

While production has been growing consumption of cotton has also made considerable progress, the quantity absorbed year by year having risen from 6,080,000 bales in 1866-67 to 6,312,000 bales in 1871-72; 7,270,000 bales in 1877-78; 9,290,000 bales in 1883-84; 11,055,000 bales in 1889-90; and 11,714,000 in 1893-94. Cotton prices have, however, not by any means been maintained during the last 30 years. They have been, in fact, especially recently, phenomenally low, a state of things which would appear to show that production has really out-stripped consumption. It is noticeable that while the consumption of cotton in Great Britain has increased on the whole during the past 30 years, it has made much more rapid advances in other quarters. When we come to deal with Continental Europe we find that the consumption rose from 1,700,000 bales in 1866-67 to 2,032,000 in 1872-73; from 2,596,000 bales in 1878-79 to 3,255,000 bales in 1884-85; and from 4,538,000 bales in 1890-91 to 4,784,000 in 1893-94.

Shipments of cotton. The cotton shipments during the late year (1894-95) increased nearly 1,500,000 bales, and reached the enormous and unprecedented total of 6,718,961 bales—almost 7,000,000 bales.

Cotton mills. According to the latest available statistics (1894-95) the number of cotton mills in the south is, as follows:—Alabama 30, Arkansas 3, Georgia 70, Kentucky 11, Louisiana 5, Mississippi 11, North Carolina 161, South Carolina 80, Texas 10, Virginia 15, Tennessee 34, Missouri 4. Total completed mills, and in course of erection 435, of which 44 are new, not yet finished—a total of 435, as against 180 in 1880 and 264 in 1890.

Spindles. The total number of spindles in mills now erected and in operation in the south is 3,177,310 in 1894-95, as against 1,699,082 in 1890, showing an increase of 1,478,228 in the last 5 years.

Looms. With regard to looms, there are at the present moment 70,874, against 38,865 in 1890, showing an increase during the last 5 years of 32,009.

(2125)

UNITED STATES.

RETURN showing Weight of Bales during the Year 1894–95.

State.	Number of Bales.	Average Weight.	Quantity.
			Lbs.
Louisiana	2,584,115	511·19	1,320,973,747
Alabama	240,220	507·85	121,995,727
Florida and Georgia	1,108,661	491·63	545,051,007

Cotton baling. The Cotton Baling Convention of Steamship Agents, Railroad, and Steamboat Men, held in February, was well attended. Its objects were the consideration of the methods in baling and shipping, and to take some action tending to increase the density of the bales by better compression, which would at once tend to reduce the cost of transportation, and at the same time to lessen the risks from fire.

In March the "International City Press" valued at about 10,000*l*. was burnt, and 17,000 bales of cotton valued at 100,000*l*. were also destroyed.

Cotton seed. In 1889 there were a few small mills making cotton seed products, worth, perhaps, 1,000,000*l*. Now the trade uses a capital of near 8,000,000*l*., and makes a product worth over 14,000,000*l*. The material consumed was regarded as worthless in 1861. In 1892–93 the price was 3*l*. 10*s*. per ton, but fell to about 3*l*. per ton or under. In 1894–95, owing to the largeness of the cotton crop, the price fell to less than 2*l*. a ton. There are some 300 mills manufacturing cotton oil from the seed. The value of the foreign business (1895) amounted to over 1,000,000*l*. The greatest demand comes from the United Kingdom.

It is estimated that the total crush of cotton-seed by the mills of New Orleans from September 1, 1894, to August 31, 1895, was about 115,000 tons, yielding in round figures about 4,600,000 gallons crude oil, say 92,000 barrels, 43,125 tons of cake and meal.

Breadstuffs and grain. With the wheat crop small, it was inevitable that the wheat exports should show a further reduction in 1894–95 after a very considerable reduction in both 1893–94 and 1892–93. But nevertheless the total of exports is yet considerable, being about 145,000,000 bushels (though in 1891–92 they amounted to 225,000 bushels). On the year's exports the average price has been under 58 c. (2*s*. 5*d*.) per bushel.

Flour. The reduction in flour has been equally striking. For 1894–95 the average is only a little over $3\frac{1}{3}$ dol. (13*s*. 7*d*.) per barrel; whereas in 1891–92 it was almost 5 dol. (about 20*s*.) per barrel.

An important increase, however, is observable in flour in barrels; but there has been a falling-off in receipts of Indian corn and wheat as compared with last year. A larger foreign exporting business is expected at this port for the coming season of 1895-96. The shipping facilities are abundant and first class, principally by English steamers.

Sugar. The total consumption of sugar in the entire United States in 1894 was 2,024,668 tons, against 1,905,862 tons in 1893, and 1,853,370 tons in 1892. The increase for 1894 is 118,786 tons, or 6·23 per cent., against 54,492 tons, or 2·8 per cent. increase on 1893. The consumption of 1894 consisted of 265,500 tons of domestic cane-sugar, 20,000 tons of domestic beet sugar, 300 tons of sorghum sugar, 5,000 tons of maple sugar, 15,000 tons of domestic manufactured molasses sugar; making a total of 305,800 tons of United States production, and 1,554,528 tons of foreign cane and other sugar, making a total of 1,718,868 tons of foreign production.

When the consumption of sugar was 1,000,000 tons the cost of centrifugals was 7·79 c. per lb., and of granulated 9·23 c. per lb., a difference of 1·44 c. per lb. When the consumption was 2,000,000 tons, the centrifugals cost 3·24 c. per lb., and the granulated 4·12 c. per lb., a difference of 0·88 c. per lb., a lowering of the cost of sugar to the people of 5·11 c. per lb., or 55 per cent. This great saving, it is said, has been brought about by European countries, especially Germany, in promoting and protecting their beet sugar industries under a system of bounties, and it is stated that there is no good reason why the last increase of 1,000,000 tons consumption should not have been provided by local planters under exactly the same stimulus as that given by Germany.

At the opening of the past sugar season, and for some time after, several causes depressed sugar in this country, the principal of which was the large stock accumulated last summer (1894) in anticipation of a tariff duty on sugar. The accumulation, however, was gradually worked off. The great damage done to the fruit crop by the severe weather in February, 1895, greatly curtailed the usual large demand for refined sugar for preserving fruit.

Rice. The past rice crop was short. This combined with the Chinese-Japanese war, which practically stopped the importation of foreign rice from across the Pacific, tended to stiffen prices somewhat. With regard to the present crop, a high average quality is expected. Reports show that the coming crop is in excess of local requirements.

Wool. The wool season opened about May 1, with rather an uncertain feeling, but as the season progressed the market commenced to advance, and continued to do so until a point $3\frac{1}{2}$ c. above the opening figure was reached on Lake, and $2\frac{1}{2}$ c. to 3 c. on Lousiana clear, Burry was rather neglected during the season, and did not share the same advance as clear wools. The London sales stimulated this market very much. Prices ranged from $12\frac{1}{2}$ to 16 c. for Lake; 11 to 13 c. for Louisiana clear; Burry $6\frac{1}{2}$ to 8 c.

Hides. The market for hides was very dull and lifeless up to March, after that date occurred one of the most remarkable advances known

Tallow.

to the trade. Heavy steer hides used for sole leather advanced from 3½ c. in March to 8 c. Calf skins have been in good demand, and advanced in price 40 to 50 c. (1s. 8d. to 2s.) each; but the season for that class of goods being over, prices are likely to decline 15 to 20 per cent.

The tallow market was very quiet during the whole year. At the opening the figure was about 4¾ c., and at the close of the year 4¼ c. There is no probability of an advance in the near future. The production was about the same as usual.

Furs.

The business in furs was very limited. Prices declined 25 to 40 per cent. Large accumulations were held, and it did not pay hunters for their trouble.

Fruit.

The fruit trade of the city of New Orleans for the past commercial year was no exception to the general sluggishness that prevailed in all other lines of business.

The almost total loss of the marketable orange crop, as was mentioned in last year's report, was caused by a severe frost. The prospects are that it will be some years before the business will be on the same footing. English growers, of whom there are many in Florida, have sustained large losses. The autumn and winter crop of apples of 1894-95 was again below the average. The tropical and Mediterranean fruit trade here has had about the same unsatisfactory results attending operations in other lines of the fruit trade. The excessive port and wharfage charges have driven the fruit trade to other ports on the coast.

Wines.

The importation of Bordeaux wines, as well as liquor, has materially fallen off during the past year. This is due as much to the financial condition of the country as to the competition of the California products. Champagne, as was stated in last year's report, has suffered most; but it is one of the articles most likely to recover with prosperous times. The consumption of California wine has considerably increased at New Orleans, the prices being very low. Consumers are able to buy from their grocers, if not a high flavoured wine, at all events a tolerable but pure table claret at 1s. a gallon.

Beer.

At New Orleans, during the year ended June 30, 1895, laager beer to the amount of 333,276 barrels was manufactured. There are now seven breweries, with a capital estimated at about 1,600,000*l.* The demand for British malt liquor is so insignificant as not to be worth mentioning. It is considered too heavy for this climate.

Whisky.

The same may be said of whisky. A little is imported by English merchants for private consumption.

Horses and mules.

The past season proved an unprofitable one for the sale of horses and mules. As there was a small demand there were not many on the market. The following is an average of the prices fetched:—

Description.	Prices. From—	To—
	£	£
Town mules	30	40
For sugar plantations	30	35
rice "	10	16
cotton "	10	16
Saddle and harness horses	30	50
Heavy draught horses	20	30
Common horses	10	20

Live-stock. The total of all descriptions of live-stock handled at this market shows a falling-off, except in milch cows. Common to ordinary cows bought from 1*l.* 16*s.* to 2*l.* 4*s.* per head, the lowest. The highest from 2*l.* 8*s.* to 3*l.* for medium butcher cows. Choice Texas beef fetched about 2½*d.* per lb.

Oak staves. The total export of oak staves from the port of New Orleans, August, 1894, to August, 1895, amounted to 8,119,570, of which 722,515 went to the United Kingdom, 4,128,804 to Spain, and 1,572,560 to Portugal. In addition to the above, about 4,000,000 dressed staves were exported to European ports, the value being estimated at nearly 500,000*l.*

Liverpool salt. Owing to the reduction of duties on some salt, there was an increase in the importation to this port of certain grades. The receipts of Liverpool salt for the year closed in August, 1895, were 180,000 sacks, an increase of 35 per cent. on 1894. The trade would have been more satisfactory here but for the large receipts, far in excess of their capacity in consumption by neighbouring ports. Prices were more unsteady than for many years, tendency being downward, and now very low.

Baling stuffs. The consumption of jute bagging from this port for the season of 1894–95 equalled about 9,000,000 yards, at an average price of about 6 c. per yard for 2 lbs., the market having opened at 6⅛ c. Under heavy demand, owing to the large crop of cotton, it was advanced to 7 c., and finally closed at 5¼ c., the present quotation for 2-lb. bagging.

The demand this season is principally for 2-lb. and 2¼-lb., the planting interest having at last concluded to abandon the use of 1½-lb. and 1¾-lb. covering for cotton bales. It is said the American mills are able to hold the trade on this class of goods against foreign mills, and that the latter are not able to compete in price, notwithstanding the Wilson Tariff Bill placing jute-bagging on the free list, heretofore protected to the extent of about ⅝ c. per yard.

Cotton ties. The consumption of cotton ties at this port this season amounted to about 150,000 bundles of 45 lbs. each, containing 30 steel bands 11½ feet long. This market opened at 60 c. (2*s.* 5*d.*) for 45-lb. ties, but has since advanced to 70 c. (2*s.* 11*d.*). The advance was caused by the recent rise in the price of iron.

UNITED STATES.

Ocean freights.

The season of 1894-95 showed no improvement in freights, notwithstanding the fact that the cotton exports were much larger than the preceding year. The almost total absence of grain made itself seriously felt. Had the shipments of this article been as large as usual, cotton and other freights would have been much higher. The prospects are very favourable for the present season, as the outlook is most promising for a very large Indian corn crop in the country contiguous to this port.

The lowest and highest ocean freights for the undernamed articles were as follows:—

Articles.	Port.		Ocean Freights.	
			Lowest.	Highest.
			d.	d.
Cotton	Liverpool	Per lb.	3/32	17/64
	Havre	,,	5/16	17/32
	Bremen	,,	5/32	17/64
	Antwerp	,,	5/32	17/64
	Hamburg	,,	5/32	17/64
	Genoa	,,	7/32	19/64
	Barcelona	,,	¼	21/64
	Baltic, viâ Hamburg	,,	15/64	23/64
Grain	Liverpool	Per bushel	1½	4
	Continent	,,	2	4½
			£ s. d.	£ s. d.
Oilcake and oilmeal	Liverpool	Per ton	0 8 0	0 18 0
Oilcake	Continent	,,	0 10 0	1 0 0
Oil	Continent	Per barrel	0 4 6	0 5 6
Flour	United Kingdom and Continent	Per ton	0 12 0	1 0 0
Staves	Spain	Per M.	13 0 0	16 0 0

Free wharves.

The question of free wharves is one of paramount importance to British shipping. There are free wharves above and below the city, but the greater portion at New Orleans are, until 1901, under lease to a company able to make themselves obnoxious in many ways to the shipping community. Attempts were made some time since to buy out the lessees, but the amount charged was so unreasonable that the lease in all probability will run out before any change can be effected. There is no doubt that the commerce of New Orleans is injured by its high wharfage dues and port charges, and that trade, to some extent, has been driven elsewhere.

The matter was again taken up last August, and is said to be progressing. New Orleans is one of the few cities owning its wharfage front, and, therefore, when again in full possession, will be in a position to exercise full control.

Port Chalmette.

Besides Southport, situated within the custom-house city limits, there is Port Westwego above New Orleans, and on the opposite side of the river. Also Port Chalmette, some 2 to 3 miles below New Orleans and on the same side. This port, which has just been opened, has as yet no custom-house; consequently, for the present and until a bill has passed Congress admitting it within the city custom-house limits, all vessels have first to come to New Orleans to be entered, after which, if they so desire it, permission can be obtained at Washington to take in cargo at Port Chalmette.

When the bill is passed, the conveniences offered to British shipping will be very great; and, therefore, a description of this new enterprise will not be out of place.

Port Chalmette is the terminal of the N.O. and W. Railroad which forms a belt line around the city of New Orleans, connecting with the various railway systems entering the city. The N.O. and W. is also lessee of the N.O. and S. Railway Company, which extends from New Orleans, south of the east bank of the river, some 59 miles.

The port of Chalmette has been built with a view of centralising and facilitating the export and import trade of New Orleans. With that purpose in view, extensive railway yards have been established there, comprising 15 miles of tracks, capable of holding about 3,000 railway freight cars. The principal feature of Port Chalmette is its extensive warehouse system. Eighty warehouses, each covering 6,000 square feet of ground, built in substantial, and as nearly as possible fire-proof manner, are located on about 40 acres of land, with sufficient space between to have proper fire protection, and connected with each other by a series of double railroad tracks, all leading to the wharves of the company. Those wharves will be capable of accommodating 10 steamships at one time, and covered with substantial sheds to keep out the rain and sun. Connected with these wharves by a long conveyor is the grain elevator of 500,000 bushels capacity.

The entire space between warehouses, wharves, and elevator is well supplied with a large waterworks plant, and thoroughly lit up at night by an ample supply of arc and incandescent lights.

A novel feature introduced in this connection, for the first time in America, is the use of compressed air as a motive power, to haul and handle cars loaded with cotton or other products on these premises. The pneumatic locomotives used are supplied with compressed air at a density of 600 pounds per inch, and they are capable of hauling a load of 80 tons over the yards for a period of 1 hour without recharging. The cost of handling bulky freight from warehouses to ship's side has thus been materially reduced, and the great danger of fire, so dangerous to cotton yards, eliminated.

Another important feature is the location of powerful cotton compresses in close proximity to the wharves and ships. Two of the most modern hydraulic compresses are employed, capable of compressing cotton to a density of 40 pounds per cubic foot. The result of this superior compressing can best be shown by the recent example, where the ship "Stalwart," a British sailing vessel, was loaded with 6,400 bales of cotton, whereas the same ship had, at its previous maximum load, or cargo, on 4,300 bales.

Nearly 2,000,000 dol. (about 400,000*l.*) has been expended in the construction of these new terminals, and the result of the new facilities appears to be equally gratifying to the new company and to the exporters using the same.

Labour troubles. As stated in my last year's report the labour troubles continued through January and February; in March several riots took place, to quell which and to preserve peace and order the Governor of the State was appealed to; he found it necessary to call out several companies of the militia who were placed in charge of the levees for 10 or 12 days until order was restored. During one of these riots the purser of a British steamship was shot in the head and wounded very severely.

City drainage. In July the drainage plan of the city, as recommended by the committee, was adopted.

The Mayor of the city has just vetoed the ordinance which invited bids to do the drainage work under the specifications already proposed by the city engineer. One of the principal reasons for this veto was the public feeling that a contract of this magnitude (about 8,000,000 dol.) should be advertised for a much longer period than this ordinance called for (only 30 days) in order that the very bids might be secured, as it is believed that contractors would require several months to carefully study before making their calculations.

Health statistics. Taking the estimated population of the city at 275,000, the average death-rate was much higher in 1895 than in 1894, 29·25 against 24·88 per cent., or 1,202 persons, the increase, contrary to the usual showing, being chiefly among the whites. There is no doubt that defective drainage and a lack of pure water are very formidable factors in producing this result. The percentage of deaths is as follows:—

Description.	Estimated Population.	Number of Deaths.	Rate per 1,000.
			Per cent.
Whites	195,000	4,951	25·39
Coloured	80,000	3,094	38·68

NEW ORLEANS.

The principal causes of death were—

Description.	Number of Deaths.
Phthisis pulmonalis	871
Pneumonia (nearly double 1894)	618
Bright's disease	368
Malarial fevers	340
Senile debility	327
Old age	34
Cholera infantum	299
Enteritis	224
Cancer	180
Bronchitis	166
Typhoid	113
Diarrhœa	184
Dysentery	95
Meningitis	38
Influenza	35
Diphtheria	80
Infantile debility	95
Apoplexy	207
Accidents	272
Small-pox (2 only in 1894)	56
Measles (4 only in 1894)	57
All other causes	3,386
Total, 1895	8,045
,, 1894	6,843

The ages were—

From—	Number of Deaths.
1 to 5	2,411*
5 10	177
10 25	854
25 40	1,318
40 60	1,626
60 100	1,649
Centenarians	10
Total	8,045

* 1,750 were infants, 1 year and under.

1,789 deaths occurred in hospitals, asylums, and other public institutions.

There were 600 still-births—not recorded amongst deaths.

The highest mortality was in May (799), and the lowest in September (506).

The question of electric street-cars is so important that it would not be out of place to enter on the subject. *Electric street-cars.*

I believe no town anywhere has made more progress, and is more perfect in this respect, than New Orleans. A year or two ago the mule-car system was in force, by which much time was lost, only 5 miles per hour could be made; now that the transit

UNITED STATES.

is by electric car a speed of 12 miles an hour is obtained. In New Orleans with an average saving to each passenger of 12 minutes there is an economy of 10,000,000 hours a year, equivalent to 1,250,000 days' labour of 8 hours. If time is money, and 1 day's labour is worth 4s., which it certainly is at New Orleans, the electric cars are saving the city 250,000l. a year in time.

In 1880 New Orleans boasted of 140 miles of tramways, 373 cars, 671 employés, and of carrying 23,716,327 passengers during the year. To-day she has 180 miles of lines carrying 47,250,000 passengers, at a uniform rate of 5 c. (about $2\frac{1}{2}d.$), some of the distances being 4 to 5 miles. There is a project before the town council for 79 additional miles, bringing the total up to 260 miles.

A quick transit not only saves time but also reduces rent, as less expensive districts can be reached by the working classes.

It is only a question of time when such a system will be adopted in London and other European capitals, where at the present moment the streets are so encumbered by carriages as to convey the impression that there is no room for electric tramways; whereas it must be borne in mind that the introduction of such a system would relieve traffic by very much reducing the number of vehicles drawn by horses. At New Orleans, where in one street, the principal thoroughfare, there are no less than five lines, and the safety of the walking public is in no way protected by the police, there are few accidents. In London, where police protection is so admirably carried out, there would be far less danger than at present from innumerable vehicles driving in all directions and when least expected.

RETURN of Principal Exports Carried in British Ships during the Year 1895.

Articles		Quantity
Cotton	Bales	1 409,295
,, seed	Sacks	60,591
,, ,, oil	Barrels	50,336
,, ,, cake	Sacks	397 383
,, ,, meal	,,	623,097
,, ,, soap stock	Barrels	15,882
Corn	Bushels	6 018,782
Wheat	,,	608,338
Flour	Sacks	22 743
Staves	Pieces	4,531,425
Timber	,,	57,013
Lumber	Feet	1,800,100
Molasses	Barrels	8,082

NEW ORLEANS.

Compared with 1894 British shipping returns for 1895 show a decrease in entrances and an increase in clearances from this port:—

ENTERED.

Year.	Steam. Number of Vessels.	Tons.	Sailing. Number of Vessels.	Tons.	Total. Number of Vessels.	Tons.
1895	291	541,000	2	1,514	293	542,514
1894	329	601,449	6	3,445	335	604,894

CLEARED.

Year.	Steam. Number of Vessels.	Tons.	Sailing. Number of Vessels.	Tons.	Total. Number of Vessels.	Tons.
1895	310	580,559	3	3,075	313	583,634
1894	309	558,319	5	1,874	314	560,193

Annex A.—RETURN of all Shipping at the Port of New Orleans during the Year 1895.

ENTERED.

Nationality.	Steam. Number of Vessels.	Tons.	Sailing. Number of Vessels.	Tons.	Total. Number of Vessels.	Tons.
British	291	541,000	2	1,514	293	542,514
American	216	127,087	23	6,617	239	133,704
Norwegian, &c.	204	85,132	...	...	204	85,132
Spanish	51	107,220	8	5,096	59	113,316
German	25	43,112	9	10,138	34	53,250
Italian	6	9,476	5	3,185	11	12,661
French	8	15,855	...	...	8	15,855
Danish	...	...	1	334	1	334
Mexican	4	1,268	...	...	4	1,268
Dutch	4	9,185	...	...	4	9,185
Portuguese	1	1,645	9	5,868	10	7,513
Austrian	1	1,207	...	...	1	1,207
Total	...	...	...	...	868	975,939
,, for the year preceding	...	...	...	...	919	1,059,239

NOTE.—The above figures do not include American coastwise tonnage.

UNITED STATES.

CLEARED.

Nationality.	Steam. Number of Vessels.	Steam. Tons.	Sailing. Number of Vessels.	Sailing. Tons.	Total. Number of Vessels.	Total. Tons.
British	310	580,559	3	3,075	313	583,634
American	177	100,114	1	661	178	100,775
Norwegian, &c.	203	91,446	...	..	203	91,446
Spanish	59	118,298	3	2,702	62	121,000
German	26	47,718	6	7,621	32	55,339
Italian	5	7,615	5	3,251	10	10,866
French	9	18,867	...	...	9	18,867
Danish	2	2,570	1	334	3	2,904
Mexican	4	1,268	...	...	4	1,268
Dutch	4	9,190	...	...	4	9,190
Portuguese	1	1,645	8	5,971	9	7,616
Austrian	1	1,647	...	...	1	1,647
Total	...	...	...	...	828	1,004,552
,, for the year preceding	...	...	...	...	859	991,413

NOTE.—The above figures do not include American coastwise tonnage.

PENSACOLA.

Mr. Vice-Consul Howe reports as follows:—

Trade. There is no new feature in the trade of Pensacola to report upon which would be of interest to the British business public at home or abroad; except that British shipowners may in future place a few more steamers yearly at this port, as a new steamship line has recently been inaugurated here for monthly sailings, between Pensacola and Liverpool, to load with southern and western products, such as cotton, grain, and other things. A British steamer made the initial voyage in this trade, and the same vessel returned to Pensacola for a similar loading.

Imports. Under the head of imports, I must repeat that principal articles of supply for the Pensacola general consumption are received here for the large markets at the western and northern States of this country. And among these supplies it is safe to believe that some British manufactures find a place, if even limited, owing to the restrictions surrounding their importations to the northern markets, and in turn the supply thence to this market with the additional outlay on their first cost at home. Some few things still continue to come direct from the United Kingdom and Continental ports, such as salt from Liverpool, fertilizers from Germany, iron ore from ports in Spain and Portugal—this latter article going forward to smelting iron works in Birmingham, Alabama—and oranges and bananas from the British and other islands not far off, and, occasionally, sugar from Cuba.

Exports. The large export timber trade from Pensacola continues without apparent diminution. Last year's shipments (1895), although not quite up to the year preceding, were still quite large, and, with the tonnage required to move the cargoes, may be considered as a fair average business of former years.

As regards British tonnage during the year at Pensacola, not only did it hold its own, but went beyond the year preceding and some years before, as will be observed in the table on shipping hereto annexed.

Shipping.

British vessels loaded at Pensacola during the year represented over one-third of all clearances at this port in foreign tonnage; and the cargoes taken out by British vessels amounted to about one-half of the whole quantity of cargoes taken out by vessels of flags other than American; inasmuch as the British steamers carried much more cargo to their tonnage, as is always the case, than the loads taken by sailing vessels in comparison with the tonnage of the latter.

British tonnage largest. Took largest quantity.

Several British steamers and sailing vessels, as well as other vessels, grounded on the Pensacola bar during the year, when outward bound, loaded with cargoes of pitch-pine timber. These strandings, when cargo has to be discharged, as sometimes is necessary to float the stranded vessel, cause an immense outlay of money, particularly where steamers are concerned. These strandings are invariably attributed to deficiency of water in the bar channel; but it sometimes appears that other causes contribute to the groundings of the vessels. The channel is now being deepened by the general Government, and it is to be hoped that when this work is finished there will be no more strandings on the bar. Before this last dredging commenced—there have been dredgings of the bar before—23 feet of water could be found in the bar channel with very full tides.

Strandings on Pensacola bar.

Cause large outlay of money.

Channel being deepened.

In coal shipments from Pensacola—an important branch of Pensacola's export trade—the business continues active, although last year's shipments show a decrease when compared with the exports of coal the year preceding. As before stated in these reports, this coal is brought to Pensacola by railroad from the extensive coal mines of Alabama. Large quantities of this article go forward from Pensacola to the port of Galveston in this country; and some shipments are yearly made to ports in Mexico. British steamers are sometimes employed in this coal trade to Mexico, but the principal mode of transit is in barges towed by powerful steam tugs, which vessels—barges and tugs—are owned by the Company operating this coal trade, in connection with the Louisville and Nashville Railroad. A wrecked and condemned British steamer, of about 1,000 tons net register, was lately bought by this coal company, refitted, and put under the American flag; and now plies regularly between Pensacola and Galveston with cargoes of coal. In this connection it may be said that Pensacola may become quite a coaling place for vessels. Six British steamers, bound from Gulf ports to Europe, called at Pensacola during the year to coal. Among the tables following will be found the quantity of coal shipped from Pensacola during the year 1895.

Coal.

To Galveston and Mexico. British steamers.

Principal mode of transit.

Coaling port.

The business between Pensacola and Cuba in western products and general merchandise, which has sprung up within the last few years, independently of the hitherto and continued

Business with Cuba.

(2125)

General remarks. yearly shipments of pitch-pine lumber to that island, still goes on, but has been very much reduced in volume by reason of the unsettled state of things in that island, owing to the insurrection there. A British steamer, however, still continues to ply between Pensacola and Cuba in this trade.

As regards the condition of the people generally of this community, it may be said that no unusual incidents arose during the past year to interfere with their accustomed quiet and prosperity. The timber shippers—the leading business houses here—go steadily on. The large number of workers in ships of these timber cargoes—the main employment here—find their usual work. And skilled labour in all branches of employment for mechanics keeps to about the usual yearly demand. There are no public works here to add to the employment of the people. I take pleasure in repeating, as stated in some of my former annual reports, that Pensacola's timber trade, her staple business, on which all prosperity here mostly depends, appears to continue to provide yearly towards meeting all requirements for the continued happiness of this community.

Health. The city of Pensacola and its surroundings have been healthy and free from epidemics during the past year.

Agriculture. I take the opportunity of mentioning here that I have not on this occasion anything of sufficient note on agriculture to report on which would be of interest in England or the British dominions. The usual productions of the well-equipped and largely-productive farms at Pensacola and suburbs of fruit, vegetables, and poultry, &c., have continued in full supply, mostly for consumption here.

Tables. The tables connected with this report now follow:—

Annex A.—RETURN of Principal Articles of Import to Pensacola during the Years 1895–94.

Articles.	Value.	
	1895.	1894.
	£	£
Chief articles	..	..
Other articles	9,276	6,950

NOTE.—The value of chief articles brought to Pensacola yearly amounts to several millions of dollars

Annex B.—RETURN of Principal Articles of Export from Pensacola during the Years 1895-94.

Articles.		1895.		1894.	
		Quantity.	Value.	Quantity.	Value.
			£ s. d.		£ s. d.
Pitch pine lumber	Super. feet	152,851,000	382,127 9 8	148,310,000	370,775 0 0
Sawn pitch pine timber	Cubic feet	11,078,165	276,954 3 4	11,080,277	277,006 18 6
Hewn ,, ,,	,,	323,701	7,417 16 0	325,912	7,468 16 4
Cypress	,,	81,062	5,910 16 4	...	...
Oak	,,	16,840	1,578 14 0	...	...
Cotton	Bales	6,915	72,031 5 0	300	2,500 0 0
Coal	Tons	87,428	72,856 14 0	116,591	97,159 3 4
Coke	,,	2,200	2,062 10 0	...	...
Pig-iron	,,	4,082	8,504 3 4	3,718	7,745 16 8
Flour	Sacks	47,407	39,505 16 0	98,425	82,020 16 8
Corn	Bushels	80,505	8,385 16 0	408,798	42,583 2 6
Rosin	Barrels	2,093	1,308 0 0	2,176	1,360 0 0
Turpentine	,,	30	75 0 0	...	...
Tobacco	Hogsheads	103	1,596 18 0	...	...
Lard	Tierces	724	4,826 12 0	1,341	8,982 1 8
Other articles	...	...	607 5 3	...	29,116 6 2
Total	...	...	885,748 18 11	...	926,718 1 10

NOTE.—The following as regards the foregoing table of exports is descriptive of the quantities, values, weights, and measures, the conversion of money into sterling being at the rate of 4 dol. 80 c. per 1*l*.; lumber at average of 2*l*. 10*s*. per 1,000 superficial feet, board measure; sawn timber at an average of 6*d*. per cubic foot, basis 40 feet average; hewn timber at an average of 5½*d*. per cubic foot, basis 100 feet average; cotton at an average of 5*d*. per lb., in bales of 500 lbs., average weight each bale; coal, 16*s*. 8*d*. per ton; cypress at 1*s*. 5½*d*. per cubic foot; flour at 16*s*. 8*d*. per sack of 200 lbs.; corn at 2*s*. 1*d*. per bushel; rosin at 12*s*. 6*d*. per barrel; pig-iron at 2*l*. 1*s*. 8*d*. per ton; oak at 1*s*. 10½*d*. per cubic foot; coke at 18*s*. 9*d*. per ton; lard, 6*l*. 13*s*. 4*d*. per tierce.

(2125)

Annex C.—TABLE showing Total Value of all Articles Exported from and Imported to Pensacola from and to Foreign Countries during the Years 1895-94.

	Exports.		Imports.	
Countries.	1895.	1894.	1895.	1894.
	£ s. d.	£ s. d.	£	£
United Kingdom	312,870 0 0	252,090 11 8	4,696	1,650
British possessions	10,507 16 0	4,257 0 0	200	300
Spain and colonies	70,099 11 6	197,076 2 8	2,000	58,980
France	62,814 10 0	52,351 0 0	...	...
Argentine Republic	59,186 4 0	42,870 0 0	...	...
Brazil	55,579 3 6	33,842 0 0	...	...
Italy	55,379 3 5	47,786 0 0	...	...
Netherlands	53,259 7 7	54,913 0 0	...	...
Belgium	25,502 0 0	26,544 0 0	...	...
Germany	17,947 18 0	17,899 0 0	2,380	5,000
Egypt	8,129 3 5	5,476 0 0	...	...
Austria	7,699 0 0	7,590 0 0	...	...
Uruguay	7,545 0 0	14,320 0 0	...	...
Portugal	6,493 10 0	10,578 0 0	...	...
Mexico	1,833 6 0	28,071 17 6	...	...
Russia	1,088 10 0	...	...	...
Turkey	806 13 6	835 0 0	...	...
Venezuela	786 0 0	...	...	...
Denmark	589 12 0	...	...	...
Central America	...	4,644 10 0	...	...
Total to foreign countries	759,116 8 11	801,144 1 10	...	...
„ to ports in the United States	126,632 10 0	125,574 0 0	...	...
Grand total	885,748 18 11	926,718 1 10	9,276	65,930

Annex D.—RETURN of all Shipping in the Port of Pensacola during the Year 1895.

ENTERED.

	Sailing.		Steam.		Total.	
Nationality.	Number of Vessels.	Tons.	Number of Vessels.	Tons.	Number of Vessels.	Tons.
British	36	28,800	70	106,119	106	134,919
American	187	83,258	6	4,708	193	87,966
Swedish and Norwegian	118	104,666	5	4,000	123	108,666
Italian	74	49,840	...	...	74	49,840
Russian	33	22,274	...	...	33	22,274
Spanish	3	2,171	5	8,701	8	10,872
Austrian	13	8,890	...	...	13	8,890
German	3	1,759	2	3,304	5	5,063
Netherlands	7	5,045	...	...	7	5,045
Danish	3	2,231	...	...	3	2,231
French	2	1,679	...	...	2	1,679
Argentine Republic	1	893	...	...	1	893
Portugal	1	601	...	...	1	601
Total	481	312,107	88	126,832	569	438,939
„ for the year preceding	491	349,610	97	129,118	588	468,728

NEW ORLEANS.

Cleared.

Nationality.	Sailing. Number of Vessels.	Sailing. Tons.	Steam. Number of Vessels.	Steam. Tons.	Total. Number of Vessels.	Total. Tons.
British	31	24,791	70	106,119	101	130,910
American	174	81,376	6	4,708	180	86,084
Swedish and Norwegian	128	113,628	4	3,999	132	117,627
Italian	73	50,316	...	...	73	50,316
Russian	30	21,228	...	...	30	21,228
Spanish	3	2,171	5	8,701	8	10,872
Austrian	16	10,539	...	...	16	10,539
German	3	1,759	2	3,304	5	5,063
Netherlands	7	5,045	...	...	7	5,045
Danish	3	2,231	...	...	3	2,231
French	2	1,679	...	...	2	1,679
Argentine Republic	1	893	...	...	1	893
Portugal	1	601	...	...	1	601
Total	472	316,257	87	126,831	559	443,088
,, for the year preceding	510	369,880	97	129,117	607	497,997

MOBILE, ALABAMA.

Mr. Vice-Consul Barnewall reports as follows:—

The commercial year commences on September 1, 1894, and ends on August 31, 1895.

Cotton receipts were 253,187 bales, valued at 7,150,000 dol., against 215,116 bales, valued at 7,982,955 dol. of the year previous; average price per lb. 5·56 c., against 7·41 c. the previous year. *Cotton receipts and prices.*

There has been an increase in the direct exports to Liverpool of 58,601 bales, and to other foreign ports an increase of 29,734 bales. *Exports.*

Lumber.

The season commenced with prices higher than at present, but still low as compared with the prices that ruled last season, and as the season advanced prices continued to decline, until at the close of the season they reached the lowest point ever recorded in this city before. *Prices.*

By reference to the tabulated statements below, it will be seen that in our lumber exports, foreign and coastwise, we are, in round numbers, 10,000,000 feet behind the exports of last season, and this decrease is accounted for from the fact that there has been just that amount of falling-off in the shipments to Cuba, due to the unsettled state of affairs in that country. As the season has drawn to a close, there has sprung up a decided revival in the South American trade, and there are now in hand orders for South America which have not yet been filled.

There has been an increase in the exports to the United Kingdom of 2,000,000 feet, and while there has been a slight falling-off in exports to Mexico, there has been an increase to *Exports.*

UNITED STATES.

Germany and British West Indies. In both branches of the timber exports there has been an increase over the past season, the totals showing that in hewn the increase has been 184,303 cubic feet, and in sawn 149,574 cubic feet.

The local consumption in lumber has increased 7,000,000 feet during the past year, owing to the erection of some 200 or 300 houses, mostly dwellings, and to the building of new wharves and extensive improvements to others. The following is in detail the amount shipped and destination:—

Shipments.

Destination.	Quantity. 1894-95. Super. feet.	Quantity. 1893-94. Super. feet.
FOREIGN.		
United Kingdom	10,438,245	8,260,390
France	754,648	833,270
Spain	..	308,571
Germany	1,010,891	476,459
Belgium	..	903,571
Holland	461,298	1,627,137
Nicaragua and U.S. Colombia	2,608,173	1,682,546
British West Indies	1,403,002	..
Mexico	3,536,652	4,896,437
Cuba	9,806,797	19,577,218
Jamaica	2,552,924	2,199,683
Trinidad	1,593,259	833,787
Africa	888,403	939,276
Hayti	1,825,840	1,211,195
River Plate	1,053,821	..
Argentine Republic	8,402,932	..
Uruguay	967,899	..
Austria	62,967	..
Denmark	216,841	..
Italy	628,168	..
Paraguay	360,000	..
Costa Rica	213,038	..
Various	4,271,487	..
Total	53,057,305	58,146,327
COASTWISE.		
New York	1,799,023	5,862,024
Boston	1,434,000	3,201,846
Philadelphia	997,709	..
Portland, Me.	300,000	..
Total	4,530,732	9,063,870
Grand total	57,588,037	67,150,197

NEW ORLEANS.

Timber.

Country.	Hewn. Quantity.	Hewn. Value.	Sawn. Quantity.	Sawn. Value.
	Cub. feet.	Dollars.	Cub. feet.	Dollars.
United Kingdom	1,069,142	..	2,026,904	..
France	42,089	..	153,644	..
Holland	64,918	..	190,970	..
Africa	..	..	172,170	..
Germany	13,561	..	277,147	..
Denmark	16,916	..	46,775	..
Austria	49,703	..	28,108	..
Coastwise	..	..	60,070	..
Various	63,048	..	..	..
Total	1,319,377	15,172,835	3,062,325	36,366,738

Comparative Table.

Year.	Quantity. Hewn.	Quantity. Sawn.
	Cub. feet.	Cub. feet.
1893-94	1,135,074	3,012,751
1894-95	1,319,377	3,162,325

Summary.

The following summary of lumber and timber business done in this port shows the standing of 1894-95 as compared with 1893-94. The timber is reduced to superficial feet for the sake of comparison:—

Description.	Quantity. 1894-95.	Quantity. 1893-94.
	Super. feet.	Super. feet.
Lumber, total foreign and coastwise	57,588,037	67,150,197
,, railroads	3,650,900	5,650,800
,, towed to Ship Island	500,000	..
,, local or river	12,000,000	5,000,000
Timber, direct in vessels—		
Hewn	15,832,524	13,620,888
Sawn	37,947,900	34,953,012
Towed to Ship Island	450,000	100,000
Sawn	650,000	150,000
Total	128,619,361	126,624,897
Increase	..	1,994,464

Hardwoods.

Shipments.

Shipments of hardwoods the past season show a heavy increase as compared to the previous season.

Articles.	Quantity.	
	1894–95.	1893–94.
	Cub. feet.	Cub. feet.
Oak, hewn	162,145	64,597
Cedar „	2,873	59,889
Poplar „	252,797	61,455
Ash „	5,504	37,251
Assorted, hewn	44,547	..
Total	467,866	223,192
Increase	244,674	..

Article.	1894–95.		1893–94.	
	Quantity.	Value.	Quantity.	Value.
		Dollars.		Dol. c.
Staves	335,000	41,900	319,262	33,673 12

Wool.

Prices.

Wool opened at very low prices owing to the enormous importation from all quarters since the passage of the Free Wool Bill, however when dealers realised that the clip would be short a speculative movement set in which forced the market beyond its value; prices have since been restored to normal value, ranging from 12½ c. to 16 c., the average price paid being about 14½ c.

Receipts.

The receipts show a heavy falling-off the past season, this is due in a measure to the heavy losses of sheep during the winter's heavy snow and severe weather, and to a probable over-estimate of receipts for 1893–94.

Year.	Quantity.	Value.
	Barrels.	Dollars.
1894–95	410,000	60,000
1893–94	1,534,625	184,155

NEW ORLEANS.

Naval Stores.

Year.	Quantity.	
	Rosin.	Turpentine.
	Barrels.	Barrels.
1893-94	85,619	24,091
1894-95	85,842	32,697
Increase	223	8,606

Mobile's Coal Trade.

The coal deposits of Alabama, which are a continuation of the great Apalachian coal-field, are situated in the northern part of the State, and underlie the counties of Bibb, Jefferson, St. Clair, Shilby, Tuskaloosa, and Walker, extending with small deposits into Blount, Cherokee, Cullman, and Etowah. These measures are divided into three separate regions or fields, the aggregate area of which is estimated at about 8,600 square miles.

Production. The coal-mining industry of Alabama has made rapid progress within a few years, rising from a total product of 13,200 tons for 1870 to 5,529,312 tons in 1892, which was the largest production as yet in this State. In the last year, owing to labour troubles and closing of mines, the total tonnage taken from the mines amounted to 4,381,195 tons, a decrease of 788,847 tons from the product of 1893.

Prices. The average price at the mines for the total product of 1894 was 99 c. per ton. *Coke.* The total amount of coke manufactured in Alabama in the year 1894 was 924,002 tons, a decrease of 140,850 tons. The largest producing county was Jefferson with 2,776,302 tons, and the smallest Blount with 8,000 tons.

The coal business of Mobile is yearly improving, especially in steam coal.

The large increase in the number of steamers which have entered this port in 1894, and the establishment of the Liverpool line, have tended to develop more activity in the sale of steam coal.

The fruit steamers use 2,500 tons a month, or about 30,000 tons a year. The home consumption in Mobile is about 7,000 tons.

Range of prices. The range of prices in Mobile for retail lots has been as follows:—Alabama, 4 dol. to 6 dol. 50 c.; anthracite, 6 dol. 50 c. to 7 dol. per ton; export coal, cargo lots, 2 dol. to 2 dol. 10 c. per ton of 2,000 lbs. f.o.b. vessels at dock; tug coal, 2 dol. 50 c. in bunkers; bunker coal for steamers, 2 dol. 25 c. placed in vessel's bunkers trimmed. Coke, carload lots on cars, 4 dol. 50 c. per ton.

Receipts. The total receipts during the year 1894-95 were 156,996 tons, as compared with 104,340 tons during 1893–94, this applies to Alabama coal alone. The importation of foreign coal was barely 2,200 tons.

The United States Government last winter directed the Secretary of the Navy to make an analysis of the various coals, and to ascertain those that were suitable for use in the Navy. Under date of February 15, 1895, the Secretary of the Navy transmitted to the Senate his report, showing analyses of various coals that had been shipped to Washington direct from the coal mines to be analysed. The fixed carbon in the coal is the element that gives it its value as a steam coal. It is the element that produces the heat in burning, and burns longer, and will fairly determine its value, unless the coal contains foreign substance interfering with its burning or producing clinker. The amount of ashes the coal makes shows of course that much less combustible material. The carbon and ash shown in the analyses is as follows :—

	Pearson.	Sloss.	Pratt.	Milldale.	Blocton.
Fixed carbon	72,030	70,311	69,327	69,236	64,329
Ash	1,261	2,737	2,321	1,770	6,695

The product of the State by counties for 1894 is given as follows compared with 1892 and 1893. The figures are those of Messrs. Alder and Ruley of Philadelphia, obtained from official sources :—

Coal Production.

County.	Quantity.		
	1892.	1893.	1894.
	Tons.	Tons.	Tons.
Bibb	793,469	806,214	401,061
Blount	..	..	8,000
Jefferson	3,399,274	3,133,538	2,776,302
Shilby	27,968	58,339	76,619
Tuskaloosa	163,039	167,506	190,981
Walker	1,103,612	919,205	871,770
St. Clair	24,905	72,000	43,517
Other counties (small mines)	12,000	13,240	13,045
Total	5,529,312	5,170,042	4,381,195

NEW ORLEANS.

Coke Production.

County.	Quantity.		
	1892.	1893.	1894.
	Tons.	Tons.	Tons.
Bibb	65,237	43,227	4,218
Jefferson	1,439,630	935,047	870 71
St. Clair	3,200	6,000	,034
Tuskaloosa	26,795	29,364	29,899
Walker	96,381	51,214	13,780
Total	1,631,246	1,064,852	924,002

Our Fruit Trade.

Taken all round we have to record a gratifying increase in our fruit trade, indicating that it has come to stay and that it is not, as alleged by ports possessing inferior facilities for handling it, a momentary commercial inflation consequent on speculation. Judging from the increased importation annually recorded, and observing the energy with which the existing process is carried on, the assertion can safely be made that a long period will elapse before it reaches its zenith.

Fruit trade.

Receipts of Bananas and Cocoanuts.

Articles.	Quantity.	
	1894–5.	1893–4.
Bananas	2,261,088	1,539,344
Cocoanuts	4,921,832	5,018,150

Imports of Miscellaneous Fruit.

Articles.		Quantity.	
		1894–5.	1893–4.
Pineapples	Bunches	20,244	104,810
"	Barrels	4,000	1,652
Oranges	Bulk	653,100	613,385
"	Boxes	22,701	32,718
"	Barrels	659	819
Lemons	Boxes	2,620	27,500
Limes	"	45,700	..
Plantains	"	173,925	169,172
Mangoes	Barrels	70	..

UNITED STATES.

Vegetables.

Owing to unfavourable weather there has been a large falling-off in the production of cabbages, while in potatoes there has been a large increase as compared with the previous year.

Year.	Cabbages. Quantity.	Cabbages. Value.	Potatoes. Quantity.	Potatoes. Value.
	Crates.	Dollars.	Barrels.	Dollars.
1894	71,218	89,022	25,079	43,890
1895	34,439	60,268	108,528	162,795

Mobile Bay and Harbour.

The channel excavated is 33·09 miles long, with a channel depth of 23 feet 2 inches from the Chickasaboque to the lower anchorage, there has been excavated from between the channel lines the enormous quantity of 15,500,000 cubic yards of material, of which 6,500,000 yards were taken out during the past year. On the bar the water is also deepening by a natural process of scouring, which is caused by the discharge accumulated from the drainage of 40,000 square miles. From 21·5 feet in 1856 the depth has increased constantly and steadily, until to-day the lead shows 24 feet over the bar at mean high water. The eastern and western walls of this natural jetty are contracting from Fort Morgan to the bar, giving additional scouring force to the water discharging into the Gulf. In regard to the time of transit in the channel, any steamer can cover the distance in 4 or 5 hours ordinary speed.

Rivers. The improvements on the Warrior River, extending 14¾ miles, from Tuskaloosa to Daniels Creek, in the heart of the Warrior coal-fields, are progressing very rapidly. The locks are completed as well as the abutments for the dam, the gates are in position, and practically the entire work at Tuskaloosa is finished, and everything will be ready for operation during the coming winter. This will enable barges to be floated down from the coal-fields to Mobile at mean high water, even prior to the completion of the improvements on the lower Tambigbee, for there the plans are completed, and land has been purchased for the lowest lock about 100 miles from Mobile.

Harbourmaster's Report.

Annexed is a statement showing the number of large sea-going vessels of different rig that have arrived and departed from this port, commencing September 1, 1894, and ending August 31, 1895; also showing the maximum

NEW ORLEANS.

draft of water they draw coming up and going down the channel and over Mobile bar, and the corresponding number and draft for the previous year:—

Description.	Number of Vessels.
Steamships, up channel, drawing up to and including 17 feet	336
Steamships, down channel, drawing up to and including 23 feet..	334
Ships and barks, up channel, drawing up to and including 16 feet 6 inches	125
Ships and barks, down channel, drawing up to and including 23 feet 7 inches	120
Brigs, up channel, drawing up to and including 11 feet	9
Brigs, down channel, drawing up to and including 16 feet 6 inches	9
Schooners, four, three, and two-masters, up channel, drawing up to and including 17 feet	134
Schooners, four, three, and two-masters, down channel, drawing up to and including 19 feet	130
Total vessels up channel	604
,, down channel	593
,, up and down channel	1,197
,, up channel, 1893-94	484
,, down channel, 1893-94	497
,, up and down channel, 1893-94	981
Increase over 1893-94	216

From the above it will be noted that the deepest draft that has passed through the channel this year was 23 feet 7 inches, while the deepest draft for the corresponding previous year was 22 feet 7 inches, a gain of 12 inches.

Referring to the above report, these vessels, with their respective drafts, have without material detention passed safely up and down the channel.

If Mobile bar continues from natural causes (as in the past) to increase in depth, it will have the deepest bar in the Gulf barring none. The channel has been for the last several months lighted from one end to the other. Two gas buoys at the extreme south and the remainder with large lamps. These lights have been only experimental and temporary, but have been of considerable assistance in navigating the channel at night. The Lighthouse Board has concluded to light the channel throughout permanently with gas lights, and these temporary lights will be replaced with the Pintsch gas lights, which will give us a brilliantly lighted channel, and our tides in the winter season being better at night will enable us to work the channel to better advantage.

Annex A.—Return of all Shipping at the Port of Mobile during the Year 1895.

Entered.

Nationality.	Sailing. Number of Vessels.	Sailing. Tons.	Steam. Number of Vessels.	Steam. Tons.	Total. Number of Vessels.	Total. Tons.
British	64	26,057	59	72,135	123	98,192
Norwegian	116	83,387	129	51,586	245	134,973
American	42	14,577	1	401	43	14,978
German	...	...	15	8,693	15	8,693
Italian	15	10,405	...	...	15	10,405
Austrian	3	2,053	1	951	4	3,004
Swedish	5	3,741	...	...	5	3,741
Russian	9	6,337	...	...	9	6,337
Danish	2	1,530	1	1,260	6	2,790
Dutch	1	660	...	...	1	660
Colombian	3	198	...	...	3	198
Total	260	148,945	209	135,026	469	283,971
Coastwise	...	...	...	...	73	55,427
Grand total	...	...	...	...	542	339,398
Total for the year preceding	...	...	...	...	565	293,204

Cleared.

Nationality.	Sailing. Number of Vessels.	Sailing. Tons.	Steam. Number of Vessels.	Steam. Tons.	Total. Number of Vessels.	Total. Tons.
British	60	27,134	60	73,763	120	100,897
Norwegian	62	60,983	180	71,275	242	132,258
American	48	15,818	2	994	50	16,812
German	...	...	17	9,855	17	9,855
Italian	15	10,109	...	...	15	10,109
Austrian	3	2,053	1	951	4	3,004
Swedish	5	3,177	...	...	5	3,177
Russian	12	8,197	...	...	12	8,197
Danish	1	765	4	1,260	5	2,025
Dutch	1	660	...	...	1	660
Colombian	3	198	1	1,773	3	198
Spanish	...	...	...	...	1	1,773
Total	210	129,094	265	159,871	475	288,965
Coastwise	...	...	...	...	52	22,326
Grand total	...	...	...	...	527	311,291
Total for the year preceding	...	...	...	...	564	285,269

LONDON:
Printed for Her Majesty's Stationery Office,
By HARRISON AND SONS,
Printers in Ordinary to Her Majesty.
(75 4 | 96—H & S 2125)

FOREIGN OFFICE.
1896.
ANNUAL SERIES.

Nº. 1701.

DIPLOMATIC AND CONSULAR REPORTS ON TRADE AND FINANCE.

UNITED STATES.

REPORT FOR THE YEAR 1895
ON THE
TRADE OF THE BOSTON CONSULAR DISTRICT.

REFERENCE TO PREVIOUS REPORT, Annual Series No. 1536.

Presented to both Houses of Parliament by Command of Her Majesty,
MAY, 1896.

LONDON:
PRINTED FOR HER MAJESTY'S STATIONERY OFFICE,
BY HARRISON AND SONS, ST. MARTIN'S LANE,
PRINTERS IN ORDINARY TO HER MAJESTY.

And to be purchased, either directly or through any Bookseller, from
EYRE & SPOTTISWOODE, EAST HARDING STREET, FLEET STREET, E.C., and
32, ABINGDON STREET, WESTMINSTER, S.W.; or
JOHN MENZIES & Co., 12, HANOVER STREET, EDINBURGH, and
90, WEST NILE STREET, GLASGOW; or
HODGES, FIGGIS, & Co., Limited, 104, GRAFTON STREET, DUBLIN.

1896.

[C. 7919—69.] *Price Three Halfpence.*

New Series of Reports.

Reports of the Annual Series have been issued from Her Majesty's Diplomatic and Consular Officers at the following places, and may be obtained from the sources indicated on the title-page:—

No.		Price.	No.		Price.
1579.	Wênchow	1d.	1640.	Kiungchow	½d.
1580.	Smyrna	2½d.	1641.	Rome	1½d.
1581.	Nice	1½d.	1642.	Beira	½d.
1582.	Sŏul	1½d.	1643.	St. Jago de Cuba	4½d.
1583.	Rio Grande do Sul	4d.	1644.	Christiania	6d.
1584.	Nagasaki	1d.	1645.	Lisbon	1½d.
1585.	Hakodate	1d.	1646.	Brussels	½d.
1586.	Frankfort	3d.	1647.	Vera Cruz	½d.
1587.	Samoa	1d.	1648.	Tunis	1d.
1588.	Cherbourg	1½d.	1649.	Antwerp	1d.
1589.	Damascus	1d.	1650.	Tokio	1d.
590.	New York	1d.	1651.	Honolulu	½d.
1591.	Athens	2d.	1652.	Stettin	1½d.
1592.	Baghdad	1d.	1653.	Bangkok	1d.
1593.	Vienna	1½d.	1654.	Batoum	1½d.
1594.	Montevideo	2½d.	1655.	Mexico	9½d.
1595.	Swatow	1½d.	1656.	Odessa	1½d.
1596.	Foochow	1d.	1657.	Réunion	1d.
1597.	Tamsui	1d.	1658.	Tokio	1½d.
1598.	Chungking	1d.	1659.	Maranham	1d.
1599.	Chefoo	1d.	1660.	Copenhagen	1d.
1600.	Tokio	1½d.	1661.	Berlin	1½d.
1601.	Bangkok	1d.	1662.	Teheran	2½d.
1602.	Caracas	1½d.	1663.	Salonica	1½d.
1603.	Sofia	2½d.	1664.	Manila	½d.
1604.	Belgrade	2½d.	1665.	Florence	5½d.
1605.	Shanghai	2½d.	1666.	Dakar	½d.
1606.	Canton	1½d.	1667.	Havre	2d.
1607.	Meshed	1½d.	1668.	Rouen	2d.
1608.	Erzeroum	1d.	1669.	Corfu	½d.
1609.	Galatz	2d.	1670.	Calais	1d.
1610.	Port Said	1½d.	1671.	Tehran	1½d.
1611.	The Hague	1½d.	1672.	Barcelona	2d.
1612.	Calais	1d.	1673.	Amsterdam	1d.
1613.	Newchwang	1d.	1674.	Bordeaux	2½d.
1614.	Copenhagen	1d.	1675.	Warsaw	1d.
1615.	Odessa	2d.	1676.	Havana	1½d.
1616.	Gothenburg	2d.	1677.	Berlin	1d.
1617.	Mannheim	1½d.	1678.	Beira	1½d.
1618.	Old Calabar	5d.	1679.	Saigon	1d.
1619.	Pekin	2½d.	1680.	Trebizond	1d.
1620.	Taganrog	2d.	1681.	Vera Cruz	1½d.
1621.	Brindisi	2½d.	1682.	Patras	1d.
1622.	Jeddah	1½d.	1683.	La Rochelle	1½d.
1623.	Hamburg	3d.	1684.	Madrid	1½d.
1624.	Angora	1½d.	1685.	Belgrade	2d.
1625.	Buda-Pesth	1½d.	1686.	Algiers	5d.
1626.	Beyrout	1d.	1687.	Galveston	2½d.
1627.	Bushire	2d.	1688.	New Orleans	2d.
1628.	Stettin	2½d.	1689.	Suakin	1d.
1629.	Porto Rico	1d.	1690.	Pernambuco	1d.
1630.	Rotterdam	½d.	1691.	Guatemala	1½d.
1631.	Alexandria	1½d.	1692.	Guayaquil	1d.
1632.	Tokio	2½d.	1693.	Wênchow	1d.
1633.	Tangier	1½d.	1694.	Piræus	3d.
1634.	Oporto	1½d.	1695.	Tokio	3d.
1635.	St. Petersburg	4d.	1696.	Marseilles	1d.
1636.	Dantzig	2d.	1697.	Manila	1d.
1637.	Macao	1d.	1698.	Jerusalem	1d.
1638.	Hiogo and Osaka	6d.	1699.	Cherbourg	2d.
1639.	Naples	1½d.	1700.	Leghorn	1½d.

No. 1701.

Reference to previous Report, Annual Series No. 1536.

UNITED STATES.

BOSTON.

Acting-Consul Stuart to the Marquis of Salisbury.

My Lord,   Boston, March 20, 1896.
 I HAVE the honour to enclose my Annual Report on the Trade and Commerce of Boston and its Consular District for the year 1895.

            I have, &c.
    (Signed)   W. H. STUART.

Report on the Trade and Commerce of Boston and its Consular District for the Year 1895.

ABSTRACT of Contents.

	PAGE
General conditions of trade	2
Failures and street railways	2
Boston as a shipping port	3
Foreign and maritime trade	4
Cattle, &c.	5
Grain, cotton, &c.	5
Provisions	6
Wool	7
Metals	7
Hides and leather	8
Fish	8
Money and sterling rates	10
Freights	11
Exports	12
Growth of cereals	13
Concluding remarks	13
Tables	14–22

NOTE.—Sterling amounts in this report are given at 5 dol. = 1*l.*

(2128)

UNITED STATES.

General Conditions of Trade.

Looking backwards to January of last year, and reviewing the commercial features for the 12 months generally, we cannot regard them with entire satisfaction.

It followed a 2 years' period of industrial inactivity and stagnation. Consumptive demand during this time remained small, still it exceeded production to such an extent that it made heavy inroads upon accumulated stocks.

The year began with few signs of any immediate resumption of commercial or industrial activity, but the hope was always expressed that business would be better before the year was ended. For the summer months, moreover, matters certainly looked far better, the financial world was hopeful, the stock exchange buoyant, and talk of returning confidence was generally heard.

The promise of recovery, however, has not been fully realised, although some industries have shown a marked improvement, but many more, while making a steady growth, have made it but slowly.

Improvement there has been, and fair profits have been made, but normal conditions have not returned, and it is evident that the disturbing influences of the year 1893 have not been eradicated and are still felt, the fear and distrust created by such an upheaval having proved to be more far-reaching and prolonged than could possibly have been imagined. In these New England States, in which the leading men, as also the best of the population, are for "sound money," the conspicuous influence which retards recovery and progress in business in all branches is the currency question.

While, however, the slow recovery to normal trade conditions is disappointing in one sense, on the other hand it probably indicates more conservative action in all lines of business, thereby placing affairs on a sounder and more lasting basis.

Labour apparently has benefitted, there having been a marked freedom from labour and social troubles. Fewer strikes of any magnitude occurring in 1895, more opportunities for employing labour were offered, and in many cases an advance of wages given, many manufacturing establishments giving this advance voluntarily.

While regretting that the return to prosperous trade conditions has not been more rapid, the retrospect shows us that we are another 12 months removed from the dark cloud of 1893, and that, though slowly, business is surely improving; and this is certainly proved by the enormous increase in the business, both local and through, shown by the railroads.

In the measure of improvement obtained throughout the country, Boston and Massachusetts have obtained a full share, and the year ends with a general belief that in 1896 the merchandise markets will go on improving, and that there will be a greater progress than was noted in 1895.

Failures. The total number of individuals, firms, and corporations reported by Bradstreet as having an established place of business in the United States in the year 1895 is shown to have been 1,053,633, while the number failing was 12,958, the proportion of the Eastern States being respectively 105,458 in business, and 1,680 failing, with assets of 1,802,188*l.* and liabilities of 3,985,000*l.*

The total length of the streets and roads of Massachusetts in 1895 used for electric and horse-car purposes was 1,155 miles, the average cost per mile being for construction 4,797*l.*; for equipment, 2,096*l.*; and for land, buildings, and other permanent property, 2,853*l.*; making a total average cost of 9,746*l.* per mile. This 1,155 miles is held by 75 companies, out of which 33 alone paid dividends, running from 9 to 2 per cent. on the capital stock, being an average of 6·63 per cent., as against 7 per cent. in 1894. The whole of the street railways in the State are now electric, minus about 62 miles of the original horse railway.

Street railways.

The yearly Report of the Boston Chamber of Commerce states that: "The statistics of the commerce of the port of Boston for the past year are most gratifying. Not only does Boston continue to rank as the second port in the United States in volume of foreign commerce, but it occupies the unique position of being the only one among the five principal ports on the Eastern seaboard and the Gulf to increase the volume of its exports during the past year.

Boston as a shipping port.

The figures for 1895, from January to December, with the percentages of increase or decrease as compared with the previous year, are as follows:—

Port.	Exports.	Increase and Decrease.	Imports.	Increase and Decrease.	Total Imports and Exports.	Increase and Decrease.
	£		£		£	
Boston	16,003,975	+ 5·15	15,989,555	+ 49·7	31,993,530	+ 22·4
New York	66,470,064	− 2·41	103,257,355	+ 17·8	169,727,419	+ 8·9
Philadelphia	7,366,757	− 2·11	9,454,287	− 8·3	16,821,044	− 5·7
Baltimore	14,265,520	− 1·92	3,037,071	+ ·02	17,302,591	− 1·5
New Orleans	12,036,019	− 9·20	2,801,906	+ 17·4	14,837,925	− 5·2

From the foregoing table it will be observed that the total foreign commerce of Boston increased 22 per cent., while that of its principal competitors, with the single exception of the port of New York, decreased. The character of the commerce of the port of Boston differs somewhat from that of the country as a whole.

For example, while the products of agriculture represent 58 per cent. of the entire exports of the United States, they form 85 per cent. of the total exports of Boston. The products of manufacture form but 14 per cent. of the exports of this port, while they represent 31 per cent. of the exports of the country as a whole.

The following table shows that the change which has taken place in the last 25 years in the relative volume of the principal

(2128)

classes of merchandise exported from the United States has been reversed so far as the exports from Boston are concerned:—

TABLE showing Comparison by Percentages of Exports Classified according to Sources of Production.

Sources of Production.	Entire United States. 1870.*	Entire United States. 1895.†	Boston. 1870.*	Boston. 1895.*
	Per cent.	Per cent.	Per cent.	Per cent.
Production of agriculture	80·06	69·68	51·22	84·70
Manufactures	14·41	23·14	33·76	13·86
Mining	1·06	2·35	0·14	0·08
Forest	3·21	3·62	6·08	0·94
Fisheries	0·61	0·68	5·74	0·06
Miscellaneous	0·65	0·53	3·06	0·36
Total for the fiscal year ending June 30	100·00	100·00	100·00	100·00

* Increase. † Decrease.

Foreign and maritime trade.

The total number of vessels of all nationalities which entered the port of Boston in 1895 from foreign ports was, according to the custom-house returns, 2,216 vessels, measuring 1,723,089 tons, as against 2,078 vessels measuring 1,749,058 tons. Of these, 734, of 1,337,806 tons, were British steamers, and 1,138, of 171,668 tons, British sailing vessels, as follows:—

Nationality.	Number of Vessels.	Tons.
British	1,872	150,947
American	226	115,809
Other foreign nations	118	97,806

The totals show an increase in the number of vessels, but a decrease in the aggregate tonnage. This is probably due to a law which came into force on March 2, 1895, allowing an increase in deductions from the gross tonnage, to conform with the measurement laws of the other principal maritime nations. The reduction in the net tonnage of vessels under the new regulations for measurement varies from $2\frac{1}{2}$ to 10 per cent.

The number of British vessels from all ports, including United States ports, entered at the Consulate during the year 1895 was 1,925 vessels of 1,493,506 net tons, the total increase being 205 vessels of 13,063 tons.

These figures show the continued preponderance of the carrying trade under the British flag.

The increasing size, speed, and conveniences in steamers for carrying passengers, as also freight, and (at Boston especially) cattle must be particularly mentioned.

American shippers and travellers prefer and are willing to pay more for room, great speed, and comforts, and for the British to hold the carrying trade from this country it will be necessary to keep in the front rank and not fear competition, but if necessary build vessels of such speed and size that one new steamer will be competent to do the work of two of the old type.

Cattle. The exports of cattle from Boston during the year exceeded those of any other United States port, being 115,000 head to Liverpool and London, the relatively light mortality on shipboard showing the superior facilities given at Boston to the exporters of cattle and sheep.

Statistics show the losses, from all causes, of cattle shipped from Boston to Great Britain in 1895, including the loss of the "Venetian" and the accident to the "Angloman," when 288 cattle were jettisoned, to have been ·44 per cent., or only two-thirds of the percentage of loss incurred from all United States ports, whilst the losses on sheep were 1·55 per cent., or about nine-sixteenths of the percentage for the whole of the United States ports. These figures are of great interest to shippers of cattle and sheep, and especially so to the underwriters.

Real estate. The improvement and increase in real estate during 1895 has been very great. The cost of buildings completed during the year is above 3,634,300*l.*, as compared with 1,272,346*l.* in 1894, part of this large increase being due to the completion of the new court house and the handsome new public library, the cost of these two buildings being about 1,164,000*l.*

Wheat, corn, &c. Wheat prices have covered a wide range, sudden and marked fluctuations having occurred several times during the year, the downward prices of 1894 giving place for a time to a strength that almost promised 4s. wheat; this promise, however, was not realised, and during the last half of the year prices dropped to the modern low level. The year opened with cash wheat at 2s. 2½d., but it made a low record on January 29 at 2s. 0¼d. After this prices improved by 1s. 2d. until July, through reports of a small crop and good foreign demand, but grew gradually less until September, when the market recovered slightly, and continued better until the end of the year. The exports were 7,216,709 bushels, against 6,011,826 bushels in 1894.

Corn. The tremendous corn crop was the cause of the lowest prices ever known in Boston, steamer yellow corn ranging from 1s. 7¼d. to 2s. 7¾d., the exports being nearly 2,000,000 bushels more than in 1894.

Oats. There was an exceedingly large crop, but not up to the average quality, owing to an admixture of injurious seeds. The receipts were nearly 500,000 bushels less than in 1894. Prices ruled low, the year closing with number two white oats quoted in the Boston market at 1s. 0¾d.

Flour. In April a very sharp advance in price occurred, but it did not last, all flours experiencing a marked decline, excepting winter wheat flour, owing to a shortage in the crop. The foreign demand was much less than usual. It is understood that, with the improved roller mills in use in England, the millers there can produce a better flour from mixed wheat of various qualities than the American millers can when using more than a single grade of wheat, which does not allow the American producer to compete with the English in point of price. Prices have ranged from 6s., the highest price of spring patents being 1l. per barrel.

Exports for the year were over 1,575,962 barrels, against 2,210,364 barrels in 1894.

Cotton and cotton goods. The low prices reached in November, 1894, came again in March, 1895, middling uplands selling at 5·23 c., but prices rose again, till in September, 1895, the price on spot cotton was $8\frac{3}{16}$ c. for middling uplands, but in October the lowest prices for 50 years was reached, $4\frac{7}{8}$ c. per lb., or a fraction under $2\frac{1}{2}d.$ per lb. being quoted.

The year closed with the price at 8 c. per lb. The total imports of foreign cotton into this port were 56,094 bales, of which 43,780 bales were Egyptian cotton, for which, at the end of 1895, the current quotation was $12\frac{3}{4}$ c., as compared with $9\frac{3}{4}$ c. in December, 1894. In cotton goods, staple ginghams are 15 to 20 per cent. higher than a year ago. Prints from 7 to 10 per cent. better, extras now being quoted at $1\frac{1}{2}d.$

Goods are now being made from the low-cost cotton bought early last year, and when this low-cost cotton has all been used, the printing cloth market will undoubtedly respond with better figures.

Lumber. Spruce lumber ends the year at 4s. a thousand better than in December, 1894. Late in the summer spruce lumber became quite short in supply, prices began to rise, and orders gave the mills work for several months ahead. This winter, there being not any snow to date in Maine, has been against lumber operations, and if relief does not come soon the mills will not have logs to cut. Spruce for pulp is becoming more of a feature than ever. The demand for southern pine has equalled the supply, and building orders are booked with leading firms, for hard pine, for many million feet to be delivered in early spring of 1896. Western pine has been in fair supply and moderate demand, as also is hardwood lumber, except black walnut and cherry, which are scarce and high.

Pine clapboards are in small supply and also demand, but spruce clapboards have been firm during the last 6 months, and are likely to go much higher.

Provisions, &c. The provision market for the year has not been satisfactory; while demand and exports have been good, the prices have fallen in a most discouraging manner for producers.

The number of hogs packed in Boston were 1,430,971 in 1895, as against 1,743,659 in 1894. The hay crop was about one-eighth less than the crop in 1894, and came to little better than 1 ton to the acre, at a value of 1*l*. 13*s*. 6d. per ton on the farm.

Oleomargarine was in reduced receipts, owing to a decision of the Supreme Court of Massachusetts prohibiting colouring to imitate butter. Of 28,949 packages received in Boston, 23,160 packages were exported, whereas in the year 1894, out of 180,370 packages received, 174,070 were consumed in Boston. With butter the year opened quiet, western extra being quoted at 1*s*. to 1*s*. 1*d*., per 1 lb., but poor quality dropped values to 10*d*. per 1 lb. in March, fell to 8½*d*. per 1 lb. in May, but, through light receipts, rose again to 1*s*. 1½*d*. per 1 lb. in December.

The exports of butter in 1895 from Boston amounted to 2,102,504 lbs. Prices in the cheese market have ruled lower than for many years, and the receipts were the largest, as also the exports; but this was owing to the Canadian cheese being sent abroad viâ Boston.

Wool, &c.

The year has been remarkable, having broken all previous records in the volume of wool sales. In the 3 principal markets of the United States, up to December 12, 1895, the sales amounted to 347,060,105 lbs., out of which large amount the sales in Boston alone amounted to 135,137,347 lbs., or over one-third of the whole amount sold in the 3 principal markets of the United States. It has also been remarkable for the great development in the worsted industry, and for the lead which combed yarn fabrics have held in the woollen dry goods trade. The end of the year came with 41,014,928 lbs. of domestic wool on hand. The imports of foreign wool entered at Boston to June 30, 1895 (the end of the fiscal year), were 325,900 bales, at a value of 2,720,685*l*., making nearly nine-twentieths of the whole of the imports into the United States. There was left on hand, December 31, 1895, 10,076,500 lbs. The year began with Australian combing wools quoted at 8½*d*. to 11*d*.; clothing, 8½*d*. to 10*d*.; and cross-breds, 10*d*. Fine Ohio delaine selling at 9½*d*. to 10*d*., and domestic ½, ⅜, and ¼ unwashed combing at 7½*d*. to 8½*d*. The year ended with prices about 1*d*. per 1 lb. lower than prices at the end of 1894.

Domestic woollen goods have suffered from competition with foreign importations. While some of the large manufacturers have been and are busy, having orders 3 months ahead, the others, especially all the small concerns, complain that they cannot compete with the markets abroad, and the owners of mills making those classes of goods are hoping that legislation soon may, by raising the duty on foreign goods sufficiently high, bar them out of the American markets.

Metals.

The iron market is the barometer of other markets, and the record of 1895 shows the barometer to have been a true prophet, as during the year, while improving slowly in demand and prices obtained, still the improvement has been steady and sure. Twelve months past pig-iron from Alabama brought 2*l*. 9*s*., while at the end of the year the same grade was nominally quoted at 2l. 18s., and in Bessemer iron the improvement is even greater, with a good promise for 1896.

Manufactured iron improved greatly in the spring and summer of 1895, beams from mill and plate-iron being quoted at the end of the year at 6s. 6d. each, and steel rails quoted a year ago at 4l. 8s. at mill closed the year with quotations up to 5l. 15s. at mill.

The increasing use of iron in buildings, together with bridge, railway, and shipbuilding demands, makes the market bright with promise for 1896. Copper is in a much stronger position than a year ago. Lake ingot began the year 1895 at $4\frac{3}{4}d.$ per 1 lb., speedily rising to $6\frac{1}{2}d.$ per 1 lb., but declined again, till at the end of the year prices reached 5d. per 1 lb., offered, with consumption ahead of supply. Tin has been low compared with former years, owing to the removal of the tariff. Lead began the year low, and has remained so throughout, there being an improvement of $\frac{1}{4}d.$ per 1 lb. only.

Hides and leather.

Hides began the year at about 3d., but advanced till in the summer they were quoted at $5\frac{1}{4}d.$

Leather was higher also. These prices frightened manufacturers, and jobbers refused to place orders for shoes for the spring season. When No. 1 leather was quoted by every one at 1s. 6d., a prominent house suddenly offered a large quantity at 1s. 5d., and the decline continued till the end of the year, when No. 1 was quoted at 1s. 2d.

Domestic hides also went down, being quoted in November at $2\frac{3}{4}d.$, but closed the year at $3\frac{3}{4}d.$ During the year a foreign demand for American leather arose, and Boston exported 1,687,364l. worth, double that of any former year.

Fish.

The year opened with a good demand and stocks light, and while prices ruled high, it was expected the stock on hand would be entirely sold before the new fish began to arrive, but the catches as a rule were not good, as rough weather and the prevailing fog caused them to be poor and that, on the south shore, to be almost a failure, being little more than one-third of the catch in 1894. The large bodies of mackerel seen at different points were wild, did not school, and could not be taken, and while prices ruled high the catches were so small that few vessels paid expenses.

Owing to bad conditions of weather the catches of mackerel off the Canadian shore were also reported poor.

The curers of Irish mackerel as recommended by me some years past have evidently profited by past mistakes with the result that the fish are better handled and reach this market in much better condition than formerly, and a large percentage of those received from the best packers now compare favourably with the best fish here.

The mackerel put up on the English coast have evidently, through inexperience, been poorly handled, cured, and packed, therefore the values netted were not remunerative.

The imports of salt mackerel into Boston during 1895, were

27,980 barrels, against 45,919 barrels in 1894. In July some 30 barrels from Ireland, the first of the season, arrived and brought about 2l. 16s., counting 250 fish, of a good white colour, to the barrel, and in September and October they were good enough in quality to bring as high as 3l. 14s. per barrel.

Salt mackerel from Magdalen Islands brought from 3l. 5s. to 4l. 5s. per barrel, Nova Scotia mackerel bringing from 2l. 13s. to 5l. 2s. per barrel, according to quality. The year closes with stock well cleared up, with some Irish mackerel still on hand, and on which the market is firm.

It cannot be too strongly impressed on the catchers and curers of salt mackerel that to obtain good prices and a ready sale for their fish in this market they must be careful in handling the mackerel after being caught and not bruise them; also, they must not let the fish lie too long before splitting, salting, and putting them into pickle, for if they do, especially if the weather be warm or muggy, the fish become soft; also in packing they must use good barrels with strong heads, so that they will not leak and let the pickle run out, which causes the fish to become rusty, and consequently unmarketable except at low prices. Taking these precautions and selecting good fish is sure to obtain a good market here, and prices perhaps as high as 5l. a barrel. The catches of codfish off the coast have shown a decrease, but the fish were remarkably plentiful on the grand banks. Prices ruled low because stock left over was large and the new catches abundant.

The catch of herring has been the best for years, both in quantity, size, and fatness, but prices have ruled so low that they barely paid expenses of catching. The receipts of smoked herring amounted to 800,936 boxes. The receipts of smelts during the season which ended March 15 were 28,311 boxes, mostly from foreign ports, as against 40,813 boxes in 1894.

The pack of canned sardines and mackerel was small, but canning lobsters paid well, the demand being large and prices high. 12 vessels were lost during the past year, representing a capital of 16,500l., and 107 seamen were drowned; therefore, taken as a whole, the catch of 1895 may be considered as a failure.

In connection with the fisheries, it may be interesting to know that at Woods Hall, near Boston, the United States Fish Commission have facilities for the incubation of 65,000,000 cod and 95,000,000 lobster eggs at one time. Last year the Commission planted 40,000,000 embryo in the waters of Buzzards Bay and Vineyard Sound, and the present season it is contemplated planting 175,000,000 lobster and cod eggs.

One of the Commissioners reports that he placed some lobster eggs in water in the autumn and kept them through the winter, taking the temperature of the water each day, and twice a week sending some of the eggs to Cambridge, Massachusetts, for microscopical examination. It was found that no trace of development in the eggs could be found until spring, when the water had risen to the temperature of 55° F., showing that the eggs will not hatch under colder conditions.

The hatchery for cod at Gloucester was first established in 1888, and, allowing sufficient time for the fish to attain to a catchable size, it is generally admitted that there has been a steady and even improvement in the shore fishing for cod since that date. It is this branch of the industry that the fish commission was designed especially to help—that is, the shore sea fishing which is done for market, the fish being caught within 20 miles of the shore, and brought in at once and sold fresh. 10 to 12 years ago the inshore fishing industry was in its last stages, so far as cod-fishing went, but now the fishermen, one and all, will tell you that it is improving every year, and that, especially round Ipswich Bay and other places not far removed from the station, it has not been so plentiful for many years.

It is possible that this increase in the fish may be due to other causes, but, under all the circumstances, it is only reasonable to believe that the increase is due to the hatchery. It is hoped that the experiment in hatching lobsters may bring an improvement in the lobster fishing in the course of a few years. At present the Boston market is supplied with lobsters from Nova Scotia, &c.

Money and sterling exchange. Money ruled fairly easy throughout the year on both call and time loans. The Boston Bank clearings showed total exchanges of 951,536,919*l.*, and total balances of 109,896,066*l.* The total sales for the year 1895 at the Boston Stock Exchange amounted to 6,515,674 listed shares, and 2,478,393 unlisted shares of stocks, also of 13,289,225*l.* of bonds. Bankers' sight bills of exchange on London were, in January, 4 dol. 88½ c. to 4 dol. 89½ c. per 1*l.* sterling; in April the same; in June, 4 dol. 88 c. to 4 dol. 89½ c. to the 1*l.* sterling, and in October, 4 dol. 87 c. to 4 dol. 88½ c. to the 1*l.* sterling.

TABLE showing Freights ruling during 1895 from Boston to Liverpool.

Month.	Grain.		Flour.		Provisions.		Cotton.		Cattle.		Apples.	Leather, Finished.		Sole Leather.		Hay.
	Per Bushel.		Per Ton.		Per Ton.		Per Lb.		Per Head.		Per Barrel.			Per Ton.		Per Ton.
	d.	d.	s. d.	s. d.	s. d.	s. d.	d.	d.	s.	s.	s. d.	s. d.	s. d.	s. d.	s. d.	s. d.
January ..	$1\frac{5}{8}$ to	$2\frac{3}{4}$	5 0 to	10 0	8 9 to	17 6	$\frac{3}{32}$ to	$\frac{9}{64}$	30 to	50	1 6	16 3 to	17 6	25 0 to	30 0	..
February ..	$1\frac{1}{4}$	2	6 0	10 0	7 0	10 0	$\frac{5}{64}$		30	35	..	15 0		17 6	25 0	20 0
March	$1\frac{1}{4}$	$1\frac{3}{4}$	5 6	7 6	7 6	10 0	$\frac{1}{16}$		30		..	15 0		..		..
April	..		7 0	7 6	8 3	10 0		$\frac{7}{64}$	25	30	..	12 6	15 0	..		10 0
May	1		5 0	12 6	7 6	8 9	$\frac{3}{64}$	$\frac{5}{64}$	..		..	10 0	12 6	11 3		..
June	$\frac{1}{2}$	1	3 10	7 6	5 0	7 0	$\frac{3}{64}$	$\frac{7}{64}$	..		..	7 6	8 9	8 6	15 0	9 to 10s.
July	$\frac{3}{8}$	$1\frac{5}{8}$	4 0	5 0	4 6	7 6	$\frac{1}{32}$	$\frac{5}{64}$	..		..	..		8 9		..
August.. ..	$\frac{1}{2}$	$1\frac{1}{8}$	4 0	5 6	4 6	7 0		$\frac{1}{16}$	..		..		10 0		10 0	10 9
September ..	$\frac{3}{4}$	$1\frac{1}{2}$	4 6	6 0	7 0	8 6	$\frac{1}{16}$	$\frac{9}{64}$	..		..	..		..		..
October ..	$1\frac{3}{4}$	$3\frac{1}{4}$	5 0	7 3	7 0	7 6		$\frac{5}{64}$	20	25	1 6	..		15 0		10 0
November ..		$2\frac{3}{4}$	6 0	7 3	7 6	15 0	..		25	30	..		12 6	12 6	20 0	..
December ..	$1\frac{5}{8}$		5 0	10 0	11 3	15 0	..			30	..	17 6		15 0	17 6	..

Exports. The principal articles of export from Boston and the quantities exported were as follows:—

Articles.		Quantity.	
		1895.	1894.
Cotton to Great Britain	Bales..	290,137	231,071
Flour	Sacks..	1,824,988	2,569,143
,,	Barrels	298,471	411,964
Wheat	Bushels	7,216,704	6,011,826
Corn	,,	5,664,192	3,894,159
Oats	,,	83,000	57,126
Peas	,,	14,996	16,083
Cornmeal	Barrels	66,189	42,425
Oatmeal	,,	21,358	17,070
,,	Sacks..	56,948	30,204
Mill-feed	Tons ..	4,844	4,952
Barley	Bushels	30,207	7,238
Oilcake	Sacks..	60,270	27,251
Butter	Lbs. ..	2,102,504	1,072,190
Cheese	,,	20,756,422	12,924,472
Olive oil	,,	1,618,605	2,694,880
Apples	Barrels	140,927	459,154
Pork	,,	16,010	16,103
,,	Tierces	9,417	9,475
Beef	Barrels	9,615	11,964
,,	Tierces	9,378	12,374
Bacon	Boxes	400,945	376,679
Lard	Lbs. ..	89,456,444	76,677,826
Tallow	Barrels	254	3,223
,,	Tierces	1,557	3,568
Grease	Barrels	8,435	4,665
Hams	,,	360	787
,,	Tierces	1,106	1,320
Fresh beef	Quarters	417,583	425,922
Cattle	Head..	114,884	133,711
Sheep	Carcase	500	12,374
,,	Head..	181,620	86,127
Petroleum	Cases..	3,4538	62,309
,,	Barrels	3,732	7,641
Hay	Bales..	210,205	690,476
Onions	Bags ..	440	7,307

and leather, 108,381 rolls, 50,914 bales, 499,500 bags, 10,252 cases, 11,391 packages, and 1,084,560 staves and pieces.

During the year, 146,271*l.* of foreign merchandise was re-exported from Boston.

The growth of Cereals in this Consular District for the year 1895 was as follows:—

Growth of cereals.

Articles.	State.		Quantity.	Value.
				£
Wheat	Maine	Bushels	83,808	13,744
	Massachusetts	,,	..	..
	New Hampshire	,,	48,134	7,316
	Vermont	,,	185,078	25,541
Corn	Maine	,,	596,904	64,465
	Massachusetts	,,	1,847,224	192,111
	New Hampshire	,,	1,079,531	110,112
	Vermont	,,	2,153,464	206,732
Oats	Maine	,,	5,551,484	377,501
	Massachusetts	,,	549,864	37,391
	New Hampshire	,,	1,094,122	76,589
	Vermont	,,	5,100,598	336,639
Hay	Maine	Tons	1,127,031	2,181,932
	Massachusetts	,,	649,838	2,274,433
	New Hampshire	,,	590,527	1,476,317
	Vermont	,,	893,959	2,190,199
Potatoes	Maine	Bushels	10,139,089	689,458
	Massachusetts	,,	4,303,082	413,096
	United States	,,	3,134,930	200,636
	Vermont	,,	5,134,052	266,971

Concluding Remarks.

Reviewing these conditions, we find that, although the feeling of satisfaction at the results of the year's business is not so great as might have been wished, because of the tardiness of general recovery of business conditions, still the year ends with a universal belief that affairs in all branches are in a healthier condition; and, given a fair promise of quietness in international matters, combined with a united movement and a strong pressure from every influential quarter to urge a speedy solving of the currency question, fear and distrust will be displaced by confidence, and the promise of a general improvement and a large expansion of trade and commerce for the year 1896 becomes not only hopeful but a certainty.

UNITED STATES.

Immigrants.

Arrivals of immigrants at the port of Boston.

Annex A.—STATEMENT showing the Number of British Immigrants, &c., who Arrived at the Port of Boston during the year ending December 31, 1895.

Country.	Number. 1895.	Number. 1894.
Ireland	10,995	6,750
England	5,007	3,395
Scotland	1,161	686
Wales	60	34
All other countries	6,414	4,403
Total	23,637	15,268

In addition to the above there arrived at the port of Massachusetts from the Dominion of Canada by water during 1895 20,806 aliens, against 17,893 in 1894.

The existing laws of the United States now exclude certain classes of immigrants, who, it is univerally agreed, would be most undesirable additions to the population. These laws have been strictly enforced with beneficial results. The chief executive of Massachusetts and others, however, do not consider the law as far-reaching enough, and propose getting Washington to legislate, so that any and all immigrants, of whatever nationality, should not be allowed entry at any port of the United States unless they can prove to the proper officers appointed to regulate such entries that they can, to a reasonable degree, both read and write.

Annex B.—TABLE showing Vessels of all Nationalities Entered at the Port of Boston from Foreign Countries during the Year 1895.

BOSTON.

Nationality.	Steam.					Sailing.					Total.	
	With Cargo.		In Ballast.		With Cargo.		In Ballast.			
	Number of Vessels.	Tons.	Number of Vessels.	Tons.	Number of Vessels.	Tons.	Number of Vessels.	Tons.	Number of Vessels.	Tons.
Great Britain and Dependencies	734	1,337,806	..	..	1,137	17,221	1	447	1,872	1,385,474
Belgium	2	4,122	..	..	..	..	..	..	2	4,122
Denmark	1	315	..	..	2	296	..	..	3	611
France	12	4,068	..	..	3	279	..	..	15	4,347
Germany	20	40,343	..	..	1	1,424	..	..	21	41,767
Haiti	..	..	..	..	1	142	..	..	1	142
Holland	..	..	..	..	1	111	..	..	1	111
Italy	..	..	..	..	9	6,257	..	..	9	6,257
Norway	56	32,999	..	..	5	3,013	..	..	61	36,012
Russia	1	649	..	..	..	..	..	..	1	649
Spain	2	3,182	..	..	..	..	..	..	2	3,182
Sweden	..	..	..	..	2	606	..	..	2	606
Total, foreign	828	1,423,484	..	..	1,161	29,349	1	447	1,990	1,453,280
,, United States	29	30,624	1	78	196	85,107	..	..	226	115,809
Grand total	857	1,454,108	1	78	1,357	114,456	1	447	2,216	1,569,089

(2128)

UNITED STATES.

Annex C.—Table showing Vessels of all Nationalities Cleared from the Port of Boston for Foreign Countries during the Year 1895.

Nationality.	Steam. With Cargo. Number of Vessels.	Steam. With Cargo. Tons.	Steam. In Ballast. Number of Vessels.	Steam. In Ballast. Tons.	Sailing. With Cargo. Number of Vessels.	Sailing. With Cargo. Tons.	Sailing. In Ballast. Number of Vessels.	Sailing. In Ballast. Tons.	Total. Number of Vessels.	Total. Tons.
Great Britain and Dependencies	555	1,059,569	42	40,800	595	72,225	575	87,688	1,767	1,260,282
France	12	4,068	..	..	4	475	..	..	16	4,543
Germany	2	3,538	..	..	..	..	..	..	2	3,538
Holland	..	..	..	..	..	..	1	111	1	111
Italy	..	..	..	..	1	1,019	2	1,673	3	2,692
Norway	3	1,506	45	25,281	1	886	3	1,745	52	29,418
Sweden	..	..	..	..	..	..	1	247	1	247
Total, foreign	572	1,068,681	87	66,081	601	74,605	582	91,464	1,842	1,300,831
„ United States	24	26,041	7	4,647	84	29,091	190	62,617	305	122,396
Grand total	596	1,094,722	94	70,728	685	103,696	772	154,081	2,147	1,423,227

BOSTON.

Annex D.—RETURN of British Shipping at the Port of Boston in the Year 1895.

Direct Trade from and to Great Britain and British Colonies.

Entered.

Number of Vessels.			Total Tonnage.			Total Number of Crews.	Total Value of Cargoes.
With Cargoes.	In Ballast.	Total.	With Cargoes.	In Ballast.	Total.		£
1,659	3	1,662	1,283,167	2,763	1,285,930	...	...

Cleared.

Number of Vessels.			Total Tonnage.			Total Number of Crews.	Total Value of Cargoes.
With Cargoes.	In Ballast.	Total.	With Cargoes.	In Ballast.	Total.		£
1,452	313	1,765	1,171,952	73,008	1,244,960	...	...

Indirect or Carrying Trade in British Vessels from and to all Foreign Countries.

Entered.

Number of Vessels.			Total Tonnage.			Total Number of Crews.	Total Value of Cargoes.
With Cargoes.	In Ballast.	Total.	With Cargoes.	In Ballast.	Total.		£
225	38	263	200,306	7,270	207,576	...	...

Cleared.

Number of Vessels.			Total Tonnage.			Total Number of Crews.	Total Value of Cargoes.
With Cargoes.	In Ballast.	Total.	With Cargoes.	In Ballast.	Total.		£
19	152	171	15,413	237,874	253,287	...	...

(2128)

UNITED STATES.

Annex E.—Table showing Steamship Sailings from Boston to European Ports during the Year 1895.

Month.	To Liverpool.	To London.	To Glasgow.	To Hamburg.	To Bristol.	To Hull, England.	To Antwerp, viâ Baltimore.	To Hamburg, viâ Baltimore.	To Hull, England, viâ New York.	Total.
January	16	7	3	1	1	..	2	1	2	33
February	13	5	3	1	1	..	2	1	1	27
March	14	5	3	..	..	..	1	..	1	24
April	14	6	3	1	1	..	1	..	3	29
May	19	5	2	..	1	..	2	..	1	30
June	18	5	3	..	1	..	1	..	2	30
July	15	4	2	..	..	..	2	..	2	25
August	13	4	2	..	..	..	2	..	2	23
September	13	4	2	..	..	..	2	..	2	23
October	17	7	2	..	..	..	1	1	2	30
November	15	4	2	1	..	1	2	..	1	25
December	16	6	2	..	..	1	1	..	..	27
Total	183	62	29	4	5	2	19	3	19	326

Annex F.—TABLE showing Exports and Imports at Boston in Detail for the Fiscal Year ending June 30, 1895.

EXPORTS.

Articles.	Value.
	£
Provisions	7,160,485
,, live animals	2,384,069
Breadstuffs	2,429,389
Cotton	1,902,933
,, manufactures of	160,382
Leather	1,197,854
,, manufactures of	34,594
Fruit and nuts	228,412
Rum	225,404
Wood, and manufactures of	213,552
Iron, and manufactures of	202,929
Tobacco, and manufactures of	64,972
Agricultural implements	46,807
Paper, and manufactures of	42,669
Flax, hemp, and jute, manufactures of	42,545
Chemicals, dyes, and medicines	41,545
Hay	40,472
Blacking	40,154
Oilcake	37,141
Musical instruments	34,391
Glucose	26,068
Oils, mineral	22,904
,, all other	9,042
Books, &c.	16,133
Copper, and manufactures of	17,766
Soap stock	16,642
Seeds	15,691
Fertilisers	15,413
Cider	14,938
Sugar and molasses	14,494
Hops	13,741
Paints	12,764
Naval stores	12,611
Wool, and manufactures of	12,495
Hides and skins	11,274
Brass, and manufactures of	9,875
Fish	9,865
Hair, and manufactures of	7,251
All other articles	113,166
Furs and fur skins	52,268
Rubber, and manufactures of	50,139
Total	17,005,239

UNITED STATES.

TABLE showing Exports and Imports at Boston in Detail for the Fiscal Year ending June 30, 1895.—continued.

IMPORTS.

Articles.	Value.
	£
Wool	2,720,685
„ manufactures of	372,530
Sugar and molasses	1,732,875
Chemicals, drugs, and dyes	1,017,774
Hides and skins	805,214
Leather	739,472
„ manufactures of	80,373
Vegetable fibres	737,676
„ „ manufactures of	324,581
Cotton	671,508
„ manufactures of	264,431
Iron, and manufactures of	573,062
Fruit and nuts	344,561
Wood, and manufactures of	284,599
Paper stock	268,697
Fish	261,042
Crockery	200,978
India-rubber, and manufactures of	183,153
Tobacco, and manufactures of	137,365
Cocoa and coffee	131,405
Oils, vegetable	91,235
Silk and manufactures of	87,785
Wines	72,686
Glass and glassware	71,858
Cement	70,758
Clay	68,025
Hair, and manufactures of	66,836
Vegetables	61,087
Grease	53,119
Stone, and manufactures of	44,915
Books, &c.	39,339
Metal compositions	33,515
Furs and fur skins	32,159
Tin	32,139
Art works	30,455
Toys	23,286
Lead and manufactures of	23,400
Spices	22,327
Coal	20,257
Tea	18,188
All other articles	434,308
Malt liquors	41,283
Spirits	41,431
Paper, and manufactures of	39,607
Total	13,371,979

These figures do not tally with the figures in Annex G, the above being for the fiscal year ending June, 1895, and Annex G being from January to December.

The Boston custom-house returns for 1895 (from January to December) show import of goods to the value of 15,976,312*l*., gold and silver coin and bullion, 7,051*l*.; and exports to the value of 17,803,974*l*., and gold and silver coin and bullion, 3,840*l*. The value of free goods imported was 9,370,196*l*., and the value of goods subject to duty was 6,606,115*l*. The increase of exports over those in the year 1894 amounted to 892,647*l*., and the increase in imports over 50 per cent., viz., 5,296,785*l*. The smallness of the amount in 1894 must be placed entirely to the disturbing influences of the financial crisis the year before, 1893.

From this table it will be seen that the trade of the United States with Great Britain amounts to 35 per cent. of the total foreign commerce. These figures show that 70 per cent. of Boston's total foreign commerce is with Great Britain, and that of exports she absorbs 92 per cent.

UNITED STATES.

Annex G.—TABLE showing the Amount of the Trade of the United States with the Principal Foreign Nations during the Past Year (January 1 to December 31), with Similar Comparisons as regards the Business of Boston.

Country.	Boston.				United States.	
	Imports.	Percentage of Total.	Exports.	Percentage of Total.	Percentage of Total Imports and Exports.	Imports and Exports.	Percentage of Total.

Country.	Imports. (£)	Percentage of Total.	Exports. (£)	Percentage of Total.	Percentage of Total Imports and Exports.	Imports and Exports. (£)	Percentage of Total.
United Kingdom	7,354,781	46·0	16,382,562	92·0	70·3	114,852,718	35·3
United Kingdom and dependencies—							
Nova Scotia, &c.	443,137		293,975			2,176,433	
All other Canada	18,467		47,826			17,660,856	
East Indies	913,827		3,780			5,294,999	
West Indies	131,613	12·3	27,539	3·5	7·7	3,569,069	11·3
Australasia	358,849		17,445			3,042,007	
Africa	51,211		224,491			1,643,840	
All other	46,832		..			3,267,815	
France	877,900	5·5	3,663	..	2·6	22,993,965	7·1
Germany	728,096	4·6	216,117	1·2	2·8	36,450,434	11·2
Belgium	394,733	2·5	149,724	0·8	1·6	7,668,860	2·4
Cuba	1,096,162	6·9	549	..	3·2	12,230,036	3·8
Argentine Republic	801,986	5·0	41,423	0·2	2·5	3,020,199	0·9
Egypt	630,886	3·9	..	..	1·8	795,582	0·2
Netherlands	154,145	1·0	174,548	1·0	1·0	9,083,280	2·8
Italy	272,044	1·7	..	..	0·8	7,954,489	2·4
Mexico	263,836	1·6	..	..	0·8	6,991,465	2·1
All other	1,438,807	9·0	220,328	1·3	4·9	66,609,144	20·5
Total	15,976,312	100·0	17,803,974	100·0	100·0	325,305,191	100·0

FOREIGN OFFICE.
1896.
ANNUAL SERIES.

No. 1711.

DIPLOMATIC AND CONSULAR REPORTS ON TRADE AND FINANCE.

UNITED STATES.

REPORT FOR THE YEAR 1895
ON THE
TRADE OF THE CHARLESTON CONSULAR DISTRICT.

REFERENCE TO PREVIOUS REPORT, Annual Series No. 1517.

Presented to both Houses of Parliament by Command of Her Majesty,
MAY, 1896.

LONDON:
PRINTED FOR HER MAJESTY'S STATIONERY OFFICE,
BY HARRISON AND SONS, ST. MARTIN'S LANE,
PRINTERS IN ORDINARY TO HER MAJESTY.

And to be purchased, either directly or through any Bookseller, from
EYRE & SPOTTISWOODE, EAST HARDING STREET, FLEET STREET, E.C., and
32, ABINGDON STREET, WESTMINSTER, S.W.; or
JOHN MENZIES & Co., 12, HANOVER STREET, EDINBURGH, and
90, WEST NILE STREET, GLASGOW; or
HODGES, FIGGIS, & Co., Limited, 104, GRAFTON STREET, DUBLIN.

1896.

[C. 7919—79.] *Price Twopence Halfpenny.*

New Series of Reports.

Reports of the Annual Series have been issued from Her Majesty's Diplomatic and Consular Officers at the following places, and may be obtained from the sources indicated on the title-page:—

No.		Price.	No.		Price.
1591.	Athens	2d.	1651.	Honolulu	½d.
1592.	Baghdad	1d.	1652.	Stettin	1½d.
1593.	Vienna	1½d.	1653.	Bangkok	1d.
1594.	Montevideo	2½d.	1654.	Batoum	1½d.
1595.	Swatow	1½d.	1655.	Mexico	9½d.
1596.	Foochow	1d.	1656.	Odessa	1½d.
1597.	Tamsui	1d.	1657.	Réunion	1d.
1598.	Chungking	1d.	1658.	Tokio	1½d.
1599.	Chefoo	1d.	1659.	Maranham	1d.
1600.	Tokio	1½d.	1660.	Copenhagen	1d.
1601.	Bangkok	1d.	1661.	Berlin	1½d.
1602.	Caracas	1½d.	1662.	Teheran	2½d.
1603.	Sofia	2½d.	1663.	Salonica	1½d.
1604.	Belgrade	2½d.	1664.	Manila	½d.
1605.	Shanghai	2½d.	1665.	Florence	5½d.
1606.	Canton	1½d.	1666.	Dakar	½d.
1607.	Meshed	1½d.	1667.	Havre	2d.
1608.	Erzeroum	1d.	1668.	Rouen	2d.
1609.	Galatz	2d.	1669.	Corfu	½d.
1610.	Port Said	1½d.	1670.	Calais	1d.
1611.	The Hague	1½d.	1671.	Tehran	1½d.
1612.	Calais	1d.	1672.	Barcelona	2d.
1613.	Newchwang	1d.	1673.	Amsterdam	1d.
1614.	Copenhagen	1d.	1674.	Bordeaux	2½d.
1615.	Odessa	2d.	1675.	Warsaw	1d.
1616.	Gothenburg	2d.	1676.	Havana	1½d.
1617.	Mannheim	1½d.	1677.	Berlin	1d.
1618.	Old Calabar	5d.	1678.	Beira	1½d.
1619.	Pekin	2½d.	1679.	Saigon	1d.
1620.	Taganrog	2d.	1680.	Trebizond	1d.
1621.	Brindisi	2½d.	1681.	Vera Cruz	1½d.
1622.	Jeddah	1½d.	1682.	Patras	1d.
1623.	Hamburg	3d.	1683.	La Rochelle	1½d.
1624.	Angora	1½d.	1684.	Madrid	1½d.
1625.	Buda-Pesth	1½d.	1685.	Belgrade	2d.
1626.	Beyrout	1d.	1686.	Algiers	5d.
1627.	Bushire	2d.	1687.	Galveston	2½d.
1628.	Stettin	2½d.	1688.	New Orleans	2d.
1629.	Porto Rico	1d.	1689.	Suakin	1d.
1630.	Rotterdam	½d.	1690.	Pernambuco	1d.
1631.	Alexandria	1½d.	1691.	Guatemala	1½d.
1632.	Tokio	2½d.	1692.	Guayaquil	1d.
1633.	Tangier	1½d.	1693.	Wênchow	1d.
1634.	Oporto	1½d.	1694.	Piræus	3d.
1635.	St. Petersburg	4d.	1695.	Tokio	3d.
1636.	Dantzig	2d.	1696.	Marseilles	1d.
1637.	Macao	1d.	1697.	Manila	1d.
1638.	Hiogo and Osaka	6d.	1698.	Jerusalem	1d.
1639.	Naples	1½d.	1699.	Cherbourg	2d.
1640.	Kiungchow	½d.	1700.	Leghorn	1½d.
1641.	Rome	1½d.	1701.	Boston	1½d.
1642.	Beira	½d.	1702.	Kiungchow	1d.
1643.	St. Jago de Cuba	4½d.	1703.	Naples	2½d.
1644.	Christiania	6d.	1704.	Stockholm	2d.
1645.	Lisbon	1½d.	1705.	Corunna	2d.
1646.	Brussels	½d.	1706.	Rio de Janeiro	2½d.
1647.	Vera Cruz	½d.	1707.	San José	1d.
1648.	Tunis	1d.	1708.	Paramaribo	2d.
1649.	Antwerp	1d.	1709.	Brest	1½d.
1650.	Tokio	1d.	1710.	Montevideo	½d.

No. 1711.

Reference to previous Report, Annual Series No. 1517.

UNITED STATES.

CHARLESTON.

Consul Coëtlogon to the Marquis of Salisbury.

My Lord,   Charleston, March 25, 1896.

I HAVE the honour to transmit, herewith enclosed, Annual Trade Report for the Consular District of Charleston for the past year of 1895.

I have, &c.
(Signed)   H. DE COËTLOGON.

Report on the Trade and Commerce of the Consular District of Charleston for the Year 1895.

ABSTRACT of Contents.

	PAGE
General trade	2
Cotton	10
Phosphates and fertilisers	16
Naval stores and lumber	17–19
Rice	21
Shipping and navigation	22
Miscellaneous	25
Savannah Vice-Consulate	27
Brunswick „ „	32
Port Royal „ „	34
Wilmington „ „	37

(2152)

Generl Trade.

Total trade.

The total trade of Charleston for the past season shows that for the commercial year of 1894-95, which ended on August 31 last, there was a falling off in the volume of business at this port of about 4,000,000 dol. currency, equal in sterling to say 800,000*l*., the total trade last year amounting to 67,000,000 dol. (13,400,000*l*.), compared with 71,000,000 dol. (14,200,000*l*.) for the year before; these figures being in round numbers, the exact amounts for the two years under comparison were 71,319,702 dols. for 1893-94, and 67,246,348 dol. for last season. The decrease

Decrease.

thus shown, although less than the proportionate decline reported a year ago, is, nevertheless, sufficient to show the serious nature of the principal causes to which last year's falling-off is principally

Causes.

attributable, namely, unusual depression in the phosphate and fertiliser business, and low prices prevailing in the cotton market. There was also a moderate decrease in the turpentine trade, the receipts showing about 2,000 casks less than for the previous year; this, however, is hardly more than may perhaps be fairly considered a normal decline in this branch of industry, which has been a steadily declining one at Charleston for many years past, owing to the gradual exhaustion of the pine forests of South and North Carolina and the other sections of country naturally tributary to this port. There was, however, a moderate increase in the receipts of resin last year, which partly made up for the deficit in the turpentine business. On the other hand, the detailed figures given later on in this report show a gratifying and substantial increase in several important branches of trade, among

Cotton receipts. Increase.

which may be mentioned cotton, which shows an increase in receipts of 17,686 bales last year, as compared with the year before; rice, increased receipts of 31,787 barrels; lumber, an increase of 9,408,589 feet; cotton goods, an increase of 13,573 bales in the shipments; and a gain of 1,268,165 dol. in the value of the manufacturing business. But these figures, encouraging as they are in themselves, were more than outbalanced, as already

Low prices.

intimated, by the unusually low prices of cotton during the greater part of the year, and the falling off in the phosphate and fertiliser business, which taken altogether shows the extraordinary decline for the year in crude and ground rock and fertilisers of

Phosphates.

214,504 tons, the total product last season being only 441,778 tons, compared with 656,282 tons for the year before. Indeed, so serious has become the condition of the Carolina phosphate business that, at the close of the year, one or two of the largest mining companies, in which much English capital is invested, in Beaufort county have closed down their plants, and indefinitely

Suspended operations.

suspended operations owing to the impossibility of mining rock profitably any longer at present prices and under existing conditions; and the Coosaw Company, the largest in the State, has made considerable reductions in the extent of its operations.

The year has been on the whole a hard one, not only at Charleston, but throughout the commercial world; the country at large has not entirely recovered from the effects of the financial troubles of 1893-94, and low prices and general depression were the prevailing characteristics during the greater part of the year under review. Under these adverse conditions it is perhaps only natural that Charleston has not been able to make much progress last season, and, under the circumstances, it is perhaps a matter of congratulation that she has lost so little ground, and that as the year closes, it is possible to state that her credit is not impaired, and her resources are well in hand. The capital of the banks has been maintained, there have been few failures of importance among business men, the management of the city's financial affairs has been excellent, and there has been a marked advance in the value of both city and State securities. *General depression. Credit unimpaired.*

Reports received from the principal places throughout the State at the end of the year go to show that the people in the agricultural districts are in a very much better position financially than they have been for many years past, that they are now well supplied with home-produced bread and meat, and that cotton, the great money crop of this section, now commands over 2 c. a pound more than it did twelve months ago, quotations then being about 5 c. having advanced now to over 7 c. per pound for this staple. *Agricultural condition.*

The improvement in the harbour has also been constant and steady, notwithstanding some uneasiness occasioned last spring by a reported shoaling of the entrance to the new jetty channel, which, however, proved to be only a temporary difficulty, partly the result of continuous off-shore winds, and easily remedied with proper dredging. The special reports of United States engineers in charge of the jetty works for January 1, 1896, show that deep water has been obtained on the bar, and that the channels are of sufficient depth (a fraction over 23 feet) to accommodate vessels of from 2,000 to 3,000 tons, and drawing 20 to 22 feet of water, at high tide. The jetties are now practically completed, the last stone having been deposited on them about the middle of July, 1895; but dredging operations will be necessary for some time longer, that is to say, until the channel has become permanently adjusted to the new conditions. The north and south jetties, now forming the entrance to Charleston harbour, contain about 1,000,000 tons of rock resting upon 500,000 square yards of sunken log mattresses, which are the foundations of these structures. At the time they were first projected they were longer than any known jetties built for harbour improvement, but since they have been undertaken, even larger work of the same kind has been designed, as at Galveston, Texas. The new entrance to Charleston harbour lies between Fort Sumpter and Fort Moultrie. The first-named fort is situated on an artificial island, practically connected with James Island by a flat sand shoal, bare at low water; and Fort Moultrie, which is on Sullivan's Island, just opposite to Sumpter, may be considered as the northern mainland, when studying the discharge of water from the main tidal basin of the harbour as it flows *Harbour improvements. Jetties completed. Harbour entrance.*

(2152)

outward, with accelerated force, through the narrowing jetty walls into deep water beyond the entrance.

Deep water.

In view of the satisfactory depth of water now on the bar, and the successful completion of the jetty system, it is a matter of regret to have to report fewer arrivals of British vessels at Charleston last year than for any year during the past six seasons, only 46 British ships having entered in 1895, compared with 60 arrivals for the year before. This result, however, was in no way owing to lack of enterprise on the part of British or local shipping interests, but was brought about almost solely by the before-mentioned general trade depression prevailing throughout the country, and which has more or less affected shipping business at all of the cotton ports. The present condition of affairs also furnishes an additional illustration of the fact that something more than deep water and good harbour facilities are necessary in order to build up a large foreign shipping business at a port.

Shipping decrease.

Causes general.

Freights.

Freight to put in the ships and cheap port charges are as essentially necessary as deep water and good harbour facilities. In respect to the matter of securing freights for ships Charleston has, for a number of years, been seriously handicapped by the want of proper railway arrangements, existing lines having to a considerable extent been operated by their managers so as to divert much cotton and other produce to the rival ports of Norfolk, Wilmington, Savannah, and Port Royal, instead of bringing it to this port, where, apparently, it should under ordinary conditions naturally come. No great change has taken place in the general status of the railway situation since last year, but it may be mentioned that the South Carolina and Georgia Railway, which is the main business feeder of the port, has obtained right of way and secured permission from the city authorities to build a track through the town from their main station to the new docks, now being built just above the Union wharves, which will enable the said railway company to be in a position of comparative independence hereafter of the transfer charges now exacted by the East Shore Terminal Railway, which charges have occasioned much complaint, being onerous and burdensome to commerce, and hurtful to the interests of the port. The effect of this on next year's business it is believed will be a material reduction, or possibly a practical abolition of transfer port charges at Charleston, increased terminal facilities, and, as a natural consequence, it is hoped a larger volume of business than was handled last year. The railway authorities will be able to offer shippers better terms for freights sent here, and can compete more advantageously than heretofore with inducements offered by rival ports for business.

Railway discrimination.

Terminal improvements.

Terminal charges.

Better crop prospects.

In addition to these things it is almost sure that, unless unforeseen contingencies should arise, the next American cotton crop will be very much larger than last year's. Indeed, from present indications, cotton experts are of opinion that the next crop of this staple will likely be as large a one as the planters can produce, so that with more cotton grown and better opportunities for securing freights from interior shippers it seems only reasonable to expect that an increased number of British vessels will be able to obtain more profitable cargoes next season than during the past one which is generally regarded as the low-water trade mark in the history of this port.

British shipping.

With reference to the matter of port charges it may be of interest to the shipping world to know that, during the past year, pilotage rates on vessels coming here for coal have been reduced about one-half, pilot rates only being charged now for one way in all such cases. There has also been a material reduction in prices for steam coal, a number of ships having been supplied with the same quality of coal furnished at Newport News and Norfolk, namely New River and Pochahontas coal, at contract prices of 3 dol. 80 c. to 4 dol. per ton, at which rates the dealers claim it is cheaper for vessels to coal at Charleston than at Norfolk, when the 2 days' time lost putting into Norfolk for coal is taken into due consideration. The above-mentioned reductions in coal and pilot rates now places this port more on a parity in this respect with her two principal competitors, Port Royal and Norfolk, than was the case a year ago, and marks a distinct step forward in port charge reductions.

Reduction of coal and pilot charges.

It may also be remarked that the abolition of charges for fumigation and disinfection of vessels at quarantine here, which went into effect about a year and a half ago, has not only worked a reduction of importance in port expenses to foreign shipping, but it has also resulted in a significant cessation of complaints from masters of ships in regard to alleged useless detentions and loss of time at the station, vessels only being detained and fumigated now where a proper regard for the public health makes it absolutely necessary. In former years quarantine charges and detentions were a source of great hardship to foreign shipping, and frequent protests and complaints were made from time to time by shipmasters to H.M. Embassy at Washington as well as to this Consulate, and the relief afforded by the changed conditions seems to be of great advantage to shipping interests.

Quarantine detentions fewer.

In view, therefore, of the reductions as above stated that have been made in port charges, and the prospective lowering or abolition of transfer terminal charges, it is to be regretted that no modification has yet been made in the quarantine inspection fee of 15 dol. levied from every foreign or American vessel from foreign or infected ports arriving at the Charleston quarantine station. A special enactment in the State quarantine law authorises a levy of 15 dol. inspection fee at those ports in South Carolina having what is known as the "Holt System of Marine Sanitation," whereas the general State law fixes the fee at 3 dol. for each ship. As Charleston is the only port in the State where the "Holt System" is in operation, the result has been that, for many years past, the inspection fee at Charleston has been 15. dol., and at all other South Carolina ports, including Port Royal, only 3 dol.—an apparent discrimination in the law

Inspection fee discrimination.

as it stands of 12 dol. in this particular port charge against vessels inspected at Charleston as compared with other South Carolina ports. In these days of keen competition between rival cotton ports, the above charge, on its face, seems to be not only inequitable to shipping coming to different ports of this State, making as the law now does flesh of one and fowl of another, but it would appear at the same time to be harmful to the true business interests of Charleston, by reason of the disadvantage in which she is placed for securing business on account of this discriminating charge.

Injurious to port.

Up to 2 years ago it was estimated that British shipowners spent annually about 20,000*l.* at American cotton ports for quarantine charges, levied under authority of State or local laws, which charges there seemed good ground for believing were unconstitutional, inasmuch as that part of the State law authorising charges for quarantine fumigations and disinfections appeared to be clearly in conflict with the provisions of the American Constitution and decisions of the United States Supreme Court on the subject, the said National Constitution expressly ordaining that no State shall lay any tonnage tax on foreign shipping, and the United States Supreme Court having decided in well-known cases on record that the collection of fumigation charges from foreign ships was in the nature of a tonnage tax; and further, as the Constitution above-mentioned is the Supreme law of the land in this country, over-riding and rendering null and void all laws and parts of laws passed by States or municipalities that can be shown to be in conflict with its provisions; and as the Supreme Court is the highest tribunal for determining the interpretation of these provisions, from whose decisions there is no appeal, it was at one time seriously thought that the validity of the quarantine charges could most likely be successfully assailed if the matter were carried to the court of highest resort and the question tested. Fortunately, however, expensive and protracted litigation of this nature was avoided, and the desired result obtained through the enlightened self interest of the citizens of the port, who have voluntarily relieved shipping of all quarantine charges heretofore levied at Charleston, with the exception of the 15 dol. inspection fee.

Quarantine rules and expenses.

Doubtful constitutionality.

Conflicting national laws.

Fumigation fees, &c., abolished.

It is not sought to show that the inspection fee is probably unconstitutional as well as the fumigation and disinfection charges, although at first this was thought to be the case, as the latest Supreme Court decisions give colour to the theory that a reasonable inspection fee is a charge for a necessary service rendered, that it cannot be fairly considered in the nature of a tonnage tax, and is not, consequently, inhibited by the provisions of the National Constitution. It is only the inequality and discriminating nature of the charge that appears to be objectionable, and it is to be hoped that the same enlightened self interest that inspired the doing away with fumigation and disinfection expenses as being conducive to the best interests of

Inspection fee constitutional.

Inequitable fees.

the port will also result eventually in a satisfactory modification of both the quarantine inspection and transfer terminal charges.

Tobacco crop. A noteworthy development took place last year in the South Carolina tobacco-growing industry. A few years ago there was little or no tobacco grown in this State, and last year mention was made of some successful experimental tobacco growing that had been made in what is known as the Pee Dee section, embracing the counties of Darlington, Florence, Sumpter, Clarendon, and Williamsburg. What was only an experiment a year ago now appears to bid fair to become one of the staple agricultural products of the State. **Established industry.** From recently published statistics it is reported that 11,865 acres of land in South Carolina were under cultivation in tobacco during last season, and that the total product was about 10,000,000 lbs. The actual sales up to January 15, 1896, were within a fraction of 4,000,000*l*. lbs., which at current price realised for the planters the sum of 400,000 dol., equal to, say, 80,000*l*. sterling, for tobacco marketed up to the above-mentioned date, which had been grown upon light land. **Product.** In addition to the tobacco sold in the local markets much of it was shipped away by planters direct to other States from the various railway stations in their districts, and it is also stated that at the close of the year 1895 at least one-third of the entire crop still remains in the hands of planters. **Infancy stage.** This industry, however, is still only in its infancy as a State crop, being but one year old, and it is probable that next season the article will be grown in a number of sections of the State situated in other counties than those already named, and that many more acres will be added to those now cultivated in the established tobacco-growing regions. A few years ago not an acre of land was cultiin tobacco in South Carolina, and not a dollar's worth was raised or sold so far as the obtainable records show, while to-day the large and rapidly increasing figures given speak for themselves. Tobacco farms, barns, pack-houses, factories, and warehouses have been established on a considerable scale, and the industry, **Probable increase.** already an important one, promises to increase rapidly in the future, and to become a prominent feature in the general trade of the State. The most reliable and best-posted tobacco men estimate that the total crop of tobacco made in South Carolina last year, 10,000,000 lbs. in quantity, was worth 1,000,000 dol. (200,000*l*.). **Value.**

Manufactures. Attention is also called to the growth of general manufactures here, and particularly of cotton manufacturing enterprises, throughout the State. It is reported that, on December 31, 1895, there were 293 manufacturing establishments situated in Charleston, giving employment to 6,747 hands, and representing an invested capital of about 10,000,000 dol. (2,100,000*l*.), and that the product of these various enterprises amounted in value to 14,800,000 dol. (2,960,000*l*.), the principal item of the manu- **Value.** factures here being phosphate fertilisers, cotton goods, and yellow pine products, all, however, only local industries, embracing but one cotton mill immediately at this port.

8 UNITED STATES.

Cotton manufacturing. Of infinitely greater importance, however, is the growth of the cotton spinning and weaving industry, and the establishment of many new enterprises on a large scale for cotton manufacturing in the upper part of South Carolina, North Carolina, and Georgia, these States containing the principal Southern cotton mills, and are situated in this consular district. Most of the mills are run by water power, of which there are vast undeveloped quantities available in the belt of land 30 to 60 miles wide forming the eastern watershed of the Blue Ridge mountain range, and extending from Virginia southward through the three States above named to Alabama.

Growth of industry. The American cotton States can no longer be regarded as merely cotton-raising States, as they are yearly increasing the extent of their facilities for manufacturing the staple, and, besides, in climatic and other natural advantages for that work, in completeness of plant, and in provision for the comfort of the operatives, there are now, among the Southern mills, many establishments which rival similar mills and mill villages in the Northern States.

Prospects. With reference to the future of the cotton manufacturing industry in South Carolina, it appears to be the inevitable tendency of the times for mills to come to the cotton fields, but as yet, however, the Northern operatives are able to turn out more product than the Southerners, as they have had longer experience at the work, and are more skilful. The cost of labour in the South, however, is cheaper than in the North, and, more-

Advantages. over, the Southern mills enjoy the further advantages of cheaper lands, closeness to building materials, and proximity to the cotton fields, as is illustrated in the case of one of the most typical Southern mills, the Courtenay Manufacturing Company, located at Newry, South Carolina, operated by Charleston capital, and controlled by Charleston men. The site of this mill was primeval forest a little over 2 years ago. It contains 16,500 spindles and 540 looms, and its annual consumption of 3,500 bales of cotton is raised within a radius of 20 miles of the mill, farmers bringing the cotton direct to the mill in their own wagons, this being the only step from the cotton fields to the spindles, with no middleman handling the raw material between producer and manufacturer.

Profits. Under these circumstances it is, perhaps, not surprising that South Carolina's cotton mills should yield average dividends of 7 to 12 per cent. yearly, after allowing a reasonable surplus for improvements, new mill buildings, &c. The growth of cotton weaving and spinning in this State is largely owing to her splendid water power, nine-tenths of which is, as yet, still undeveloped. All of the cotton mills in the New England States combined have not as much water power as is available in South

Possible development. Carolina. There are in the Piedmont region of the State three great water powers, with many smaller ones still undeveloped, one of which, that at Landsford on the Catawba River, is susceptible of developing power sufficient to work 10,000 to

15,000 looms, and hundreds of thousands of spindles, it being simply a question of the height of the dam, there being an abundant supply of water, with no ice or other interference either summer or winter.

There are altogether about 50 different water powers existing in the State, both large and small. Some of them, representing from 20,000 to 100,000 spindles, which it is estimated could be improved for 1 dol. 50 c. (6s.) per spindle, equal in all to about 150,000 dol. (30,000*l*.) for large powers, and an average of 2 dol. to 2 dol. 50 c. (8 to 10s.) for smaller powers. A thousand horse-power in South Carolina will turn 30,000 spindles, at a yearly cost of 2,500 dol. (500*l*.), while the same horse-power developed in New England by steam would cost 15,000 dol. (3,000*l*.) which would be 15 dol., or 3*l*. per horse-power. *[Water power. Cost of power.]*

Large amounts of money have been invested by British capitalists in the phosphate industries of Carolina and Florida, and in former years many of these investments have been very profitable, but keen competition, trade depression, and other adverse influences have so reduced profits in this business that it is no longer as inviting a field for the investment of capital as formerly, and it might be worth while, under the changed conditions, for investors to turn their attention to cotton manufacturing in the South, and the inducements it offers for the safe and profitable employment of idle capital. *[Investment of capital.]*

No serious fires on board of cotton-loaded vessels of either British or other nationality have occurred at Charleston for the last 5 years, and during the past season the record has been equally good at all the ports in this district with the exception of Savannah, where three or four British steamers took fire almost simultaneously in the early part of the season while taking in cotton, during the labour troubles then existing between the longshoremen and stevedores. These fires, which were undoubtedly of incendiary origin, did not do a great deal of damage, and they furnish the only exceptions, so far as known, to the good record of the year. Six or seven years ago fires on British cotton ships at Charleston and Savannah were of alarming frequency and occasioned much loss to insurers and ship interests, and the comparative immunity that now seems to be enjoyed from casualties of this nature is all the more gratifying owing to the fact that the exemption from fire has not been confined merely to ships loading at their docks; as very few—one or two instances only—have been reported for several years in which British ships with cotton cargoes loaded at Carolina or Georgia ports have had this particularly dangerous kind kind of fire to break out after going to sea and on the way to their destinations. *[Cotton fires rare. Formerly frequent. Fires at Savannah.]*

Mention was made in last year's report from this consulate of the growing importance of Port Royal, South Carolina, as a cotton and trading point for British shipping and the business done during the past year appears to show that she is maintaining her position very well as a progressive cotton port; over 50 British steamers took cargoes at Port Royal, Beaufort, Coosaw, *[Port Royal.]*

UNITED STATES.

British shipping increased.

&c., all situated in the Beaufort custom-house district, many of the vessels being of larger tonnage and draft than can enter any of the other South Atlantic ports. Indeed more British ships (59 in number) came to Port Royal during the year than to Charleston, but, as already stated, Charleston's shipping business was unusually light last season. Up to about 2 years ago the yearly cotton receipts at Port Royal had been almost "nil," but in the last two seasons her receipts of the staple have grown from nothing to 159,144 bales received during the last cotton year. In addition to the cotton now exported from Port Royal, considerable quantities of western flour and grain are also sent to Europe.

Exports.

A noticeable feature of the cotton received and exported from Port Royal is that much of it is drawn from comparatively remote territory, such for instance as Memphis, in Tennessee, and other places not immediately contiguous to the rival Atlantic ports of Charleston, Savannah, Brunswick, and Wilmington. For the last 15 or 20 years almost the sole item of foreign export was crude and dried phosphate rock, with small quantities of yellow pine lumber, and the recent development of cotton and grain business has resulted from the action of the United States Courts, under whose decisions the control of the Port Royal and Augusta Railway passed from the hands of the Central Railway system of Georgia, that had throttled and repressed, as far as possible, the business of the place in order to divert trade away in the interests of the rival port of Savannah.

Causes of development.

Railway and steamers interested.

Since the emancipation of Port Royal from the adverse controlling influence of Savannah, much energy and enterprise has been displayed by the newly established English shipping firm of William Johnston and Co., Limited, who, in connection with the new management of the Port Royal and Augusta Railway, have been mainly instrumental in bringing up the general trade of the port to its present proportions.

Details of business.

Fuller details as to the principal divisions of business at Charleston and throughout the district last year are given herewith, unnecessary tabulations of figures and verbiage being eliminated as far as seems consistent with a proper understanding of important facts in regard to the year's trade.

Cotton.

Increased receipts.

The total receipts of all classes of cotton at this port during the commercial year ending August 31, 1895, were 425,529 bales compared with 407,843 bales received the previous year, showing an increase last year of 17,686 bales. This increase was not as large as was expected by cotton men, but it was made, nevertheless, in the face of many difficulties and railway combinations discriminating against Charleston. Cotton, as well as all the great staple products of this section, suffered greatly owing to the general depression throughout the country, and, at their lowest point, prices closely approximated the cheapest figures

Low prices.

CHARLESTON.

ever quoted in this market. At the opening of the Charleston market for the business season of 1894–95, which was on September 1, 1894, upland middling cotton was offered 6¾ c. per 1 lb., but, under the accumulation of stocks at the ports, depressed trade, and the marketing of the largest crop of American cotton ever made (about 10,000,000 bales), quotations were gradually but steadily lowered, until the latter part of November following, when the quotations ruled at 4¾ c.; a decline of 2 c. per 1 lb. which would be equivalent to a loss of say 10 dol. per bale, or about 100,000,000 dol. (20,000,000l.) on the total crop. *Loss to planters.*

There was a slight improvement in prices by January 1, 1895, when middlings were worth 5⅛ c. per 1 lb., values fluctuating at various fractions between 5 c. and 6 c., until the middle of April when they had advanced to a trifle over 6 c. During the summer months there was a small but steady improvement, and by September 1, 1895, when the new cotton season of 1895–96 commences, quotations were 7½ c. per 1 lb. for middling grades. From this time until the end of the year there were occasional moderate advances and recessions in values that occurred from time to time, but on the whole, prices were fairly well maintained, and on the last day of December, 1895 the following were the ruling prices in the Charleston cotton market, namely: for middling upland cotton, 7¾ c.; good middling, 8 c.; and middling fair, 8½ c. per 1 lb. *Improved quotations.* *Closing prices.*

The total receipts of cotton at Charleston from September 1, 1895 to December 31, 1895 amounted to 203,907 bales, in comparison with 314,378 bales received during the same period of the previous year, showing a falling-off in last year's receipts for the 4 months under comparison of 110,471 bales, or about 33 per cent. *Later receipts.*

It will be observed, however, that while the actual decrease in receipts here was 33 per cent., the total cotton crops of the United States for the 2 years will, from present indications, probably show about the same same relative proportionate decline; that is, a 10,000,000 bale crop for the season of 1894–95, compared with perhaps 7,000,000 bales for 1895–96. *Relative decrease.*

Export of cotton uplands from this port during the year ending September 1, 1895 compared with the same period of the previous year were as follows:— *Exports.*

Comparative Exports.

Foreign Exports.

To—	Quantity.	
	1894–95.	1893–94.
	Bales.	Bales.
Liverpool	119,663	151,907
Havre	2,100	16,206
Other Continental ports	215,633	155,964
Total	337,376	324,077

UNITED STATES.

COASTWISE EXPORTS.

To—	Quantity.	
	1894–95.	1893–94.
	Bales.	Bales.
New York	59,735	70,206
Philadelphia	5,748	..
Interior, by rail	1,300	900
Total	66,783	71,106

GRAND TOTAL.

	Quantity.	
	1894–95.	1893–94.
	Bales.	Bales.
Grand total, foreign and coastwise	404,179	395,183

Receipts, &c. The receipts, exports, and consumption by city mills, together with the stock of upland cotton on hand for the year ending August 31, 1895, were—

	Quantity.
	Bales.
Stock on hand, September 1, 1894	11,277
Received during the year	420,169
Total	431,446

	Quantity.
	Bales.
Exports, foreign and domestic	404,179
Taken by city mill	12,879
Stock on hand, August 31, 1895	14,370
Total	431,428

COMPARATIVE Exports of Upland and Sea Island Cotton from Charleston from September 1, 1895, to January 3, 1896.

FOREIGN.

To—	1895-96.		1894-95.	
	Sea Islands.	Uplands.	Sea Islands.	Uplands.
	Bales.	Bales.	Bales.	Bales.
Liverpool	2,719	19,015	1,627	85,170
Havre	..	..	53	2,100
Continental ports	64	107,127	..	114,894
Total	2,783	126,142	1,680	202,164

COASTWISE.

To—	1895-96.		1894-95.	
	Sea Islands.	Uplands.	Sea Islands.	Uplands.
	Bales.	Bales.	Bales.	Bales.
New York	3,413	41,805	1,939	36,546
Interior, by rail	20	100	..	..
Philadelphia	..	..	..	642
Total	3,433	41,905	1,939	37,188

GRAND TOTAL.

	1895-96.		1894-95.	
	Sea Islands.	Uplands.	Sea Islands.	Uplands.
	Bales.	Bales.	Bales.	Bales.
Grand total, foreign and coastwise	6,216	168,047	3,619	239,352

Sea Island Cotton.

The prices for medium fine Carolinas at the opening of the past cotton season, were 18 c. per 1 lb., but a decline soon took place to 17 c. Later on, however, the market reacted, and towards the close of the season 24 c. was quoted for this grade of cotton, while extra fine sea islands sold at 32 to 35 c., with a good demand. {Prices.}

Florida and Georgia Sea Islands opened in this market at 14 c. for fine, declining to 12 c., and advancing to about the opening prices again later on in the season. The choice and finer grades of Sea Islands were in such small supply, notwithstanding the

UNITED STATES.

Crop.

large general crop produced, that there was only a very small decline in these qualities, and they soon advanced to 16½ to 17 c. per 1 lb. There was very little fancy Georgia or choice East Florida Sea Island cotton offered in this market, but the limited sales made commanded full prices.

Last year's Carolina crop was a very good one, and was in marked contrast with that of the previous season of 1893-94, which was almost a failure, owing to the hurricane which had destroyed or injured most of the crops on the Sea Islands of Carolina and Georgia in the early part of that year.

The total crop of Sea Islands is produced in a comparatively narrow strip of country skirting along the sea coast of South Carolina, Georgia, and Florida, and for the year ending September 1st, 1895, it amounted altogether to 74,628 bags, compared with 61,650 for the previous year. Of last year's crop, South Carolina produced 5,871 bags, compared with 2,623 the year before.

The total receipts, exports and stock, of all grades of Sea Islands at Charlestown last season, in comparison with the year before, were as follows :—

RECEIPTS.

Receipts.

	Quantity.	
	1894-95.	1893-94.
	Bags.	Bags.
South Carolinas	5,383	2,556
Georgias and Floridas	61	15
Stock on hand, Sept. 1, 1894 ..	463	422
Total	5,907	2,993

EXPORTS.

Exports.

To—	Quantity.	
	1894-95.	1893-94.
	Bags.	Bags.
Liverpool	3,407	1,019
Havre	1,021	267
Continental ports	53	17
Total foreign	4,481	1,303
Total coastwise to New York ..	1,424	1,227
Grand total of foreign and coastwise	5,905	2,530

CHARLESTON.

Phosphates and Fertilisers.

Last year's business in the mining of phosphate rock and manufacture of fertilisers, having this article as a basis, was the worst ever experienced in this State. The depression has been long and steady, and low prices appear to have had no effect to increase the volume of trade. Matters also seem to have been equally bad here and abroad, and the business has had to contend with such a limited demand, as well as low prices, that it has been exceedingly difficult for some of the companies that were very active in manufacturing and shipping the year before to get through last season without actual loss. Notwithstanding this, however, there was considerable activity shown, and some of the companies managed to make moderate dividends. Miners of rock met many times during the year, harmony existed, and measures were adopted for regulating a hurtful system that prevailed by which Florida agents had been enabled to almost control prices for phosphate rock by a method agents of foreign houses had of first buying small cargoes, then advancing money on rock mined and not shipped; and also by buying rock for future shipment, merely paying down sufficient cash to make contracts binding. All of this, however, is now done away with, and it is expected that next season, miners will regulate prices by combination among themselves, no matter where the demand comes from. *Trade depression.* *Little demand.* *Phosphate combinations.*

The shipments of phosphate rock from South Carolina last year, from her two principal ports, Charleston and Beaufort (Port Royal included), in comparison with the previous season, were as follows:— *Shipments.*

TABLE showing Shipment of Rock to Foreign and Domestic Ports for the Years ending September 1, 1895–94.

FOREIGN.

From—	Quantity.	
	1893–94.	1894–95.
	Tons.	Tons.
Charleston	12,417	7 940
Beaufort	82,448	117 445
Total	94,875	125,385

(2152)

UNITED STATES.

Domestic.

From—	Quantity.	
	1893–94.	1894–95.
	Tons.	Tons.
Charleston	187,374	148,810
Beaufort	53,950	37 152
Total	241,324	185,962

Exports.

The export of crude and ground phosphate rock from Charleston from September 1st, 1895, to December 31st, 1895, were, to coastwise ports 43,619 tons, compared with 29,294 tons for the same period of the year before, there being no exports during this time to foreign countries, these figures showing a falling-off for the last four months of the year 1895 of 14,325 tons, or about 33 per cent., a decline practically in the same ratio as in the cotton trade for the same time.

The phosphate trade is, to a considerable extent, the handmaid of cotton, prospering when cotton business is good, and falling off when adversity overtakes the great leading staple of the south.

Quotations.

The market was very quiet up to the end of the year, with very little demand, closing quotations being, for crude rock 2 dol. 75 c. per ton, delivered at the mines; for Ashley river hot air-dried rock, alongside vessel, 3 dol. 10 c. per ton; and for ground rock, in bulk, 5 dol. per ton.

Fertilisers.

For many years past Charleston's principal manufacturing industry has been the making of commercial manures from phosphate rock as a basis, with the admixture of such imported ingredients as kainit, nitrate, muriate, potash, dried blood, &c., the different products being generally known as phosphate fertilisers. During the past year a number of new features were brought into the trade from various causes, mostly, however, resulting from low prices.

Trade conditions.

Sales were only of a nominal character, and grave fears were felt throughout this industry owing to a want of confidence existing in nearly all branches of commercial, manufacturing, and agricultural pursuits. Many good companies experienced much annoyance from having produced larger quantities of fertilisers than they were able to sell. Meetings were held during the active season in order to regulate prices and to maintain or improve the standard grades of fertilisers, and some of the stronger companies were consolidated together with the double object of reducing expenses, and, at the same time, enlarging their capital,

CHARLESTON.

capacities, and business. It is estimated that only about 75 per cent. of the usual quantity of commercial manures was used by planters in the production of last year's crop, and in several other respects also the year was a hard one for the trade; notwithstanding, however, some of the city mills, and a few of the interior ones, were fortunate enough to do a tolerably good business. *Decreased consumption.*

Shipments of fertilisers from Charleston last year for the season ending September 1, 1895, were, to coastwise ports and interior points by railway, 159,526 tons, compared with 316,611 tons for the previous year, a decline of 157,085 tons; there were no shipments of manufactured fertilisers to foreign countries, crude and dried rock being the only form in which phosphates are exported foreign from South Carolina. *Shipments.*

The sales of manufactured fertilisers at this port for the year ending September 1, 1895, amounted to 159,526 tons, in comparison with 316,611 tons, showing the same decline of 157,085 tons as in the shipments. *Sales.*

The imports of chemicals used in the manufacture of fertilisers at Charleston during the past commercial year, showing in detail the quantities and values of the different articles, as compared with the previous season, were as follows:— *Chemical imports.*

IMPORTS OF CHEMICALS.

Articles.	1893–94. Quantity.	1893–94. Value.	1894–95. Quantity.	1894–95. Value.
	Tons.	Dollars.	Tons.	Dollars.
Kainit	19,483	140 019	22,128	120,572
Sulphur	14,605	53,306	10,3 0	37,667
Muriate of potash	4,214	157,194	4,097	152,572
Pyrites	12,064	29,083	6,562	17,428
Nitrate of soda	876	26,575	3,141	106,514
Manure salt	50	1,164	..	..
Brimstone	9,136	130,305	11,526	143,832
Sulphate potash	51	2,363	62	2,495
Total	60,479	540,009	57,836	581,080

Naval Stores and Lumber.

There was no very material change in the naval stores business last season; receipts of resin and turpentine were light owing to the decrease in the yellow pine timber territory, from which shipments are made to Charleston, and the gradual but steady exhaustion of the pine forests in sections still tributary to this port. The receipts and stock on hand of resin and spirits of turpentine for the year ending September 1, 1895, as compared with the year before, were as follows:— *Resin and turpentine.*

UNITED STATES.

	1894–95.		1893–94.	
	Spirits.	Resin.	Spirits.	Resin.
	Casks.	Barrels.	Casks.	Barrels.
Stock on hand	2,685	10,289	2,941	9,497
Receipts	11,939	74,492	14,415	71,392
Total	14,624	84,781	17,356	80,889

The exports of resin and turpentine during the same periods to coastwise and foreign ports were:—

COASTWISE EXPORTS.

To—	1894–95.		1893–94.	
	Spirits.	Resin.	Spirits.	Resin.
	Casks.	Barrels.	Casks.	Barrels.
New York	6,337	28,572	9,785	19,755
Philadelphia	1	223	..	..
Interior, by railway	1,932	3,576	..	..
Total	8,270	32,371	9,785	19,755

Foreign. The total exports to foreign countries from September 1, 1894, to September 1, 1895, in comparison with the previous year, were:—

FOREIGN EXPORTS.

To—	1894–95.		1893–94.	
	Spirits.	Resin.	Spirits.	Resin.
	Casks.	Barrels.	Casks.	Barrels.
Rotterdam	..	3,000	..	..
Hamburg	..	..	..	12,044
Trieste	..	2,692	..	..
Genoa	..	..	402	5,445
London	..	..	3,664	3,583
Liverpool	..	4,816	..	1,000
Harburg	..	3,656	..	2,921
Newcastle	275	7,169	..	3,728
Bremen	..	1,500	..	2,767
Venice	..	..	..	2,725
Nordkopping	..	..	..	200
Europe, viâ Savannah	..	9,619	..	900
Falmouth	..	..	..	1,000
Belfast	..	..	100	5,322
Riga	..	..	..	3,231
Uddevalla	..	..	..	400
Bristol	809	4,463	700	1,919
Middlesboro'	..	3,400	..	..
Glasgow	3,300	2,640	..	..
Total	4,384	42,955	4,866	47,185

CHARLESTON.

There are no available statistics of naval stores from September 1 of last year, as the business year begins April 1, but the following figures include the period from April 1, 1895, to December 31, 1895, and give a fair idea of the trade in this industry up to the close of the year just ended. *Later statistics.*

The total receipts of naval stores at Charleston from April 1, 1895, to December 31, 1895, were 10,296 casks of spirits of turpentine and 57,269 barrels of resin, compared with 12,578 casks of turpentine and 52,613 barrels of resin for the same period during the preceding year. *Receipts.*

The exports from April 1, 1895, to December 31, 1895, were 9,618 casks turpentine and 48,045 barrels resin, in comparison with 12,988 casks turpentine and 52,034 barrels resin for the previous year; the stock on hand and on shipboard on last day of the year 1895 being 1,321 casks of turpentine and 15,845 barrels resin, compared with 565 casks of turpentine and 4,540 barrels resin on the corresponding day of the year before. Of the exports last year, 5,822 casks of turpentine and 29,431 barrels resin were shipped coastwise to American ports, the remainder going to foreign countries, Great Britain taking 3,196 casks of turpentine and 10,616 barrels resin, most of the other foreign shipments going to Northern Europe or other Continental ports for orders. *Exports.*

Lumber and Timber.

The lumber trade at Charleston held out moderately well last year, as compared with other branches of business at this port, and also of rival lumber shipping points. It is to be noted, however, that there was a radical change during the year both in regard to the sources of supply and character of the material, which has resulted in largely doing away with the necessity of the city lumber mills, most of the lumber now coming to this market by water, and also, but to a less extent, by railway. The city mills did not suspend operations, but they continued to run mostly to supplement orders or to fill unusual or small orders for quick delivery. Orders secured last year were promptly filled, and the creditable local business done, and the regularity of shipments, showed the ability of the lumber men to compete with other markets, notwithstanding the generally depressed trade conditions of the year. *Changed conditions.*

Exports.

The comparative exports of lumber, timber, and railway cross-ties (sleepers) from this port from September 1, 1894, to September 1, 1895, and for the same period of the previous year, will be found in the following tables:—

(2152)

UNITED STATES.

Coastwise Exports.

To—	Quantity.	
	1894-95.	1893-94.
	Feet.	Feet.
New York	60,262,138	45,356,453
Boston	1,586,600	2,170,000
Philadelphia	6,475,168	4,337,000
Baltimore	1,816,000	941,000
Other ports of the United States	3,890,000	4,775,000
Total	74,029,906	57,619,453

Foreign Exports.

To—	Quantity.	
	1894-95.	1893-94.
	Feet.	Feet.
West Indies	878,623	2,570,000
Other foreign ports	..	725,000
Total	878,623	3,295,000

Grand Total.

	Quantity.	
	1894-95.	1893-94.
	Feet.	Feet.
Grand total of coastwise and foreign	74,908,529	60,914,453

The exports from Charleston of lumber from September 1, 1895, to December 31, 1895, compared with the same period of the year before, were altogether, including foreign and coastwise, 22,587,564 feet for 1895, and 21,264,872 feet for 1894. The only foreign shipments during this time were 668,000 feet to the West Indies last year, and 419,523 feet to the same islands in 1894.

Quotations.

The lumber market closed at the end of the year with a light demand for well-manufactured stock and a fair export trade, quotations being 14 to 16 dol. per 1,000 feet for merchantable city sawed:—

12 to 14 dol. for railroad lumber, square and sound; 9 to 12 dol. for ordinary railroad lumber; 8 to 11 dol. for raft; 4 dol. 50 c. to 6 dol. 50 c. for dock timber, and 5 to 7 dol. for shingles per 1,000.

CHARLESTON.

Rice.

It is estimated that there was a reduction of 25 per cent. in the Carolina rice acreage planted last year, owing to damage done the plantations by the hurricane of 1893, which almost ruined many planters, some of whom could not cultivate their lands at all, while others were forced to curtail the extent of their operations. The crop, therefore, of last season falls considerably below the average of several years previous to the storm-blighted crop of 1893-94. *Reduced acreage.*

There were no serious disasters to last year's growth, but frequent rains during September retarded plantation work, did some damage to the quality of the rice, and caused a reduction in the yield per acre; the harvest was, therefore, only a good one in comparison with the preceding crop, which had been exceptionally bad. *Decreased yield.*

The total rice crop of the Atlantic Coast States, produced almost entirely in the two Carolinas and Georgia, amounted to 1,169,244 bushels of rough rice for the year ended September 1, 1895, as compared with 868,489 bushels for the year before. Of the total crop South Carolina mills received last season 790,484 bushels, compared with 426,629 bushels the year before. The total rice crop of the United States last year, which includes the Atlantic Coast and Gulf crops, was 4,578,800 bushels, in comparison with 4,754,749 bushels for the previous year. *Total crop.*

The first arrivals of Carolina rice came to this market September 8, 1894, from Georgetown county; 3 days later 2 barges were received from Pon Pon River, and these were soon followed by others. Opening prices at the beginning of the season were $5\frac{1}{2}$ to $5\frac{3}{4}$ c. per 1 lb. for cleaned rice; but these figures soon declined to $4\frac{3}{4}$ to $4\frac{7}{8}$ c., and, as the supply increased, there was a gradual downward tendency until 4 to $4\frac{1}{4}$ c. were the ruling quotations for good grades, which prices were fairly well sustained during the remainder of the winter and spring of 1895. By June, however, there was a further decrease in values of a fraction per 1 lb., but the stock in the mills was by that time exceedingly light. The supply of high grades was very limited, with a good demand throughout the year. *Prices.*

The rice crop for the Atlantic Coast States of North and South Carolina and Georgia for the year ending September 1, 1895, was as follows:—

22 UNITED STATES.

TABLE showing Rice Milled and Packed in Barrels averaging 200 Lbs. net Weight each during the Year 1894–95.

Rice Crop of—	Quantity.
	Barrels.
SOUTH CAROLINA.	
Milled at Charleston	48,470
„ Georgetown	21,420
NORTH CAROLINA.	
Milled at Wilmington, Washington, and Newberne	12,500
GEORGIA.	
Milled at Savannah	20,800
Total coast crop	103,190

Exports.

Comparative exports. There were no foreign exports of rice from this port during the past year, but the shipments to domestic ports and towns by steamer and railway amounted to 47,390 barrels of milled rice during the year ending September 1, 1895, compared with 25,603 barrels for the year before; the city consumption during the same periods being 20,000 barrels last season and 10,000 barrels the previous one, with no stock remaining on hand to be carried forward into the current year.

Statistics. Rice statistics from September 1, 1895, to December 1, 1895, were as follows:—Receipts, 31,592 barrels, compared with 25,156 barrels for the corresponding period of the year before; exports, to domestic points only, 20,285 barrels last year and 14,711 barrels for the year before; stock on hand and on shipboard December 31, 1895, 6,607 barrels, in comparison with 7,745 barrels on the same date of the year before; there being no direct shipments of rice from Charleston to foreign countries during either of the last 2 seasons, any Carolina rice going abroad having been reshipped from New York or Philadelphia, to which places most of the Charleston shipments now go.

Closing prices The closing quotations in this market at the end of the past year were:—For prime rice, $4\frac{1}{2}$ to $4\frac{3}{4}$ c. per 1 lb.; for good, $3\frac{3}{4}$ to $4\frac{1}{4}$ c.; for fair, $3\frac{1}{4}$ to $3\frac{1}{2}$ c.; and for common grades, $2\frac{1}{2}$ to 3 c.; the market closing with a steady tone, and sales of 400 barrels reported for the last week of the year.

Shipping and Navigation.

Arrivals. From a special report prepared by the harbour-master, it appears that the total number of vessels arriving at Charleston during the year 1895, of all nationalities, was 785, with a net registered tonnage of 850,484 tons; these figures being exclusive of vessels under 100 tons, or steamers running to South Carolina ports. Of the above-named arrivals the total number of each nationality and tonnage was as follows, viz.:—

Nationality.	Number of Vessels.	Tons.
American	707	850,484
British	46	63,670
Norwegian	11	6,768
Spanish	8	8,981
Italian	5	2,906
Swedish	4	7,041
German	2	2,289
Danish	1	862
Russian	1	315

Comparative tonnage. By way of comparison it may be mentioned that the total of arrivals here in 1894 was 753 vessels, with a total tonnage of 808,174 tons, of which 60 were British with a tonnage of 88,493 tons.

Freights. Cotton freights to foreign ports ruled very low during the greater part of the year, but this was the prevailing condition almost everywhere in this part of the world. Naval store freights remained about the same as during the previous season. Coastwise freights were only fairly good, having been low early in the year, but advancing later on.

During the early part of the autumn tonnage was plentiful, and freight rates, under a lessened demand, rather inclined to the interests of shippers; freights coming this way were small in volume, many vessels coming in ballast to carry away lumber, cotton, &c., the shipments of lumber and railway cross-ties last year having been the largest in the history of the port.

Pilotage. The pilotage service at Charleston is performed by 30 skilled full branch pilots and 1 12-foot branch pilot, with 3 well-appointed pilot boats, 1 of which is kept constantly on duty cruising near the harbour entrance for the accommodation of incoming vessels.

Coastwise steamers. The tri-weekly steamer service between this port, New York, and Jacksonville continues to be performed by the American Clyde Line steamships, who added a new ship to their fleet during the past fall, named the "Comanche," somewhat larger and faster than the other vessels of the line. These ships have been especially built for this port, and are able to enter and depart at any stage of the tide.

British and other foreign vessels are unable to share in the large and important coastwise trade, owing to the American Shipping Laws, which prohibit any but vessels of the United States from engaging in this business.

RETURN of British Shipping at the Port of Charleston, S.C., in the Year 1895.

Direct Trade in British Vessels from and to Great Britain and British Colonies.

Entered.

Total Number of Vessels.			Total Tonnage.			Total Number of Crews.	Total Value of Cargoes.
With Cargoes.	In Ballast.	Total.	With Cargoes.	In Ballast.	Total.		
1	5	6	1,049	6,759	8,408	129	£ 13,000

Cleared.

Total Number of Vessels.			Total Tonnage.			Total Number of Crews.	Total Value of Cargoes.
With Cargoes.	In Ballast.	Total.	With Cargoes.	In Ballast.	Total.		
9	...	9	11,608	...	11,608	192	£ 351,190

Indirect or Carrying Trade in British Vessels from and to other Countries.

Entered.

Countries whence Arrived.	Number of Vessels.			Tonnage.			Number of Crews.	Value of Cargoes.
	With Cargoes.	In Ballast.	Total.	With Cargoes.	In Ballast.	Total.		
Germany	6	...	6	9,965	...	9,965	142	£ 45,930
Italy	2	...	2	2,093	...	2,093	42	5,000
Chili	1	...	1	514	...	514	17	14,000
Mexico	...	1	1	...	88	88	13	...
Portugal	4	1	5	5,260	1,571	6,881	109	37,000
Spain	5	1	6	6,171	466	6,637	126	16,000
United States	3	16	19	5,827	23,307	29,134	425	14,700
Total	21	19	40	29,830	25,432	55,262	874	132,630

Cleared.

Countries to which Departed.	Number of Vessels.			Tonnage.			Number of Crews.	Value of Cargoes.
	With Cargoes.	In Ballast.	Total.	With Cargoes.	In Ballast.	Total.		
Germany	14	...	14	24,224	...	24,224	338	£ 744,000
Mexico	...	1	1	...	1,389	1,389	21	...
Russia	1	...	1	1,457	...	1,457	22	468,000
Spain	8	...	8	10,522	...	10,522	175	256,150
United States	...	11	11	...	13,527	13,527	228	...
Total	23	12	35	36,203	14,916	51,119	784	1,046,950

Miscellaneous.

An important feature of Charleston's trade for a number of years past has been the shipments of early fruits and vegetables to northern and western markets, competing in some branches of this business with the products of British growers in the Bermudas and several of the other West India islands. *Early fruits and vegetables.*

The unprecedented severity, however, of the winter and early spring of 1895, at one time threatened the entire destruction of the early vegetable and fruit crops in the neighbourhood of this place, but the disaster was not quite so bad eventually as was expected.

The unusual cold spells that occurred in the last part of December, 1894, and also in February, 1895, practically ruined for the time all early vegetables from Norfolk, in Virginia, down to the southern part of Florida, and at the same time retarded, but did not destroy, the early berry crop. When the blizzard was over the planters managed to replant and harvest a fairly good crop of vegetables, for which they obtained average prices in the northern markets, although the season in which shipments could be profitably made was necessarily a short one. *Unusual cold.*

In spite of all drawbacks, however, Charleston shipped last year 372,668 quarts of strawberries, in comparison with 253,672 quarts the year before, an increase last season of 118,996 quarts. *Shipments.*

She also marketed 58,153 barrels of potatoes last season, compared with 37,467 barrels the year before, an increase of 20,686 barrels in potatoe shipments, the loss of trade resulting from the severe cold falling mainly upon the cabbage growers, whose shipments, taken together with other miscellaneous vegetable-producers, amounted last year to only 283,134 crates, as compared with 331,316 crates the previous year, showing a decrease last season of 48,172 crates.

The total value of last year's shipments were 2,200,000 dol. (440,000*l.*), compared with 2,000,000 dol. (400,000*l.*) the previous year, a falling-off the past season of 200,000*l.* (40,000*l.*). *Value.*

The wholesale trade of last season was about the same as for the year before; and jobbing business, though by no means brilliantly successful, was nevertheless tolerably satisfactory, and in some respects even encouraging. The adverse political conditions which prevailed throughout the State a year ago have, fortunately, undergone an appreciable abatement, and the hurtful effects on business of bitter political party feelings and class animosities, as pointed out in last year's report, is, perhaps, a trifle less apparent now than then. *Wholesale trade.*

The wholesome effects on trade of changes made in national legislation during the year has been marked, and expectations of beneficial results to business following the repeal of the well-known McKinley Tariff Acts, and the Sherman Silver Purchase Act, has been more than fulfilled; the only question now appears *Beneficial legislation.*

to be as to what extent South Carolina will be able to share in the generally returning prosperity of the country at large.

Few failures. There were very few failures in the wholesale trade of this State last season, notwithstanding the universal lowering of values and settling down to new business conditions. There was also a partial recovery of old territory that had been lost in recent years, and an acquisition of new territory took place in some cases. Taken altogether, however, while profits were probably not so good as the previous season, the volume of trade was larger, and even measured by their money value, the past two seasons were nearly equal. Merchants generally regard last year's trade as a sort of slack-water period in the wholesale business, and seem to think that there are now good reasons to expect that during the **Prospects.** next season an increasing and more profitable business will be done.

Manufactures. Manufactures, excluding the fertiliser industry, had a hard year, but there was a very apparent improvement in almost every **Cotton.** direction during the early part of the autumn. The Charleston cotton factory did well, and, almost for the first time in the history of the mill, made money. The product for the year was about the same as the previous season, but better prices were obtained, and raw material was cheap, cloths and yarns bringing more satisfactory figures than were realised for the output of the year before.

Bagging. The bagging factory did a fairly satisfactory year's work, the product turned out being about the same as in 1894, but prices commanded were somewhat lower, reducing the value of the last annual product about 50,000 dol. (10,000*l*.), as compared with the season before.

Ice, &c. The two ice factories and the envelope and box manufacturing company also did a fairly good business at remunerative prices. The barrel manufacturing trade shows no material change.

Brewery. The Charleston Brewery was a good deal handicapped, owing to the royalty it has to pay to the State under the Dispensary Law contract, which permits it to dispose of its beer to private parties; but it is cut off from the large profits it formerly derived from the numerous liquor saloons, when they were allowed to operate. The quality of the beer made was considerably improved last year, and the business was not confined to Charleston, shipments of its products being made throughout this and several adjoining States.

Royalty. The amount of the royalty paid to the State by the brewery on account of sales for the year ending September 1, 1895, was in the neighbourhood of 25,000 dol. (5,000*l*.). Towards the end of the year the brewery became involved in financial difficulties, and it is now in the hands of the courts, and is being operated by a receiver, pending litigation and the final decree of the court in the matter.

SAVANNAH.

Mr. Vice-Consul Robertson reports as follows:—

Introductory. The trade and commerce of Savannah for the year 1895 has, on the whole, been generally good. While the total amount of business done is not so great as in the preceding year, a much better feeling has prevailed, and the entire trade of the port has been conducted on a more solid and substantial basis.

The falling-off in the total amount of business done during the year was principally in cotton. This is readily accounted for by the very low prices realised during the early part of the season.

The bankruptcy of the Central Railroad of Georgia had a very depressing effect on the general trade of Savannah. Vast amounts of our local capital was so locked up that it was utterly useless for business purposes. With the re-organisation a better effect is already felt. People now know where they stand financially, and the quick recovery goes to show the greatness of Savannah's resources.

If no more such misfortunes come to the city, and the next few years are prosperous ones, the progress of the port will be far greater than in any previous period of her history. We now have deep water in our harbour, 26 feet from the wharves to the sea, which makes our port available to most all classes of mercantile vessels. With the completion of the work now in hand, and the improvements now before Congress carried out, the commerce of the port will become greater each year, and the growth in business, industries, population, and wealth keep pace with that of her commerce.

Cotton. Savannah still holds her own as the third cotton market in the United States. The total receipts for the season were: Uplands, 884,101 bales; Sea Island, 64,727 bales.

The value of the cotton per bale was considerably less than in previous years. This, however, has proved rather a benefit than otherwise. Farmers have made their crops more economically than ever before, and, as a result, are better off financially than they have been for several years. With crops in keeping with reasonable trade demands, and diversified farming, there is no reason why the Southern agriculturists should not always be the most self-contained and successful part of the rural population of this country.

Naval stores. In naval stores, as in other products, an anticipated consumptive demand was not realised, and prices stood close upon cost of production. The fluctuations and low range in prices is hard to account for. Some deeper cause than the increase in receipts is evident.

Lumber. The lumber business for the year under review was more satisfactory than the past few years in so far as volume was concerned. As to the prices, there was little or no improvement.

Owing to the unsatisfactory financial conditions of the South

American Republics, but little business has been done with those ports, the principal shipments being to northern ports.

Rice. Some few plantations were again planted during the year, and as the planters had a year of immunity from any serious disaster, there is every disposition to increase the acreage for 1896. The planters have been able to bring about an appreciable reduction in the cost of production, and at the end of the year were well satisfied with the season's result.

Fertilisers. The recent business depression affected this commodity as it did every other. Yet, in spite of the curtailment in the demand during the season, Savannah merchants held their own. There are few brands of fertilisers more popular with planters than those made by the Savannah companies. This enviable reputation is well earned, as it is known they use only the best crude material.

Shipping. The shipping at this port during 1895 was not up to the average of former years. The total number of foreign-going vessels entered during the year was 310, with a tonnage of 275,144 tons. Of this number 74 were British, with a tonnage of 82,252 tons, against 112 vessels and 146,698 tons during 1894.

The falling-off is accounted for by the reasons of short cotton crop and over-abundance of freight-room on the coastwise steamers. Owing to the fact that there have been no oranges for shipment during this cotton season, caused through the heavy freeze, by which most of the trees were killed. The local lines of steamers have been glad to obtain cotton at freights far less than foreign steamers could be chartered for. Exporters have therefore sent their cotton by these vessels to northern ports, to be carried by direct steamers to the ports of destination.

Port charges. The charges for loading vessels at this port have remained as low as at any port, and everything has worked well and smoothly, there having been no labour or other troubles.

The Quarantine Fees, which were abolished in 1894, were again put in force this year, the cost of the station being more than the city could afford to run free of charge.

Casualties. It is gratifying to report that the year was free from all cotton fires and other casualties.

Railroads. But little headway has been made in increasing the railroads coming into Savannah; the cause of this is undoubtedly the very depressed state of the world at large. The South to-day offers more inducements for increased railroads than any other part of the country, and with the return of more settled and prosperous times one or more of the projected lines will enter Savannah.

The Southern Railway Company—now the owners of the old Central, of Georgia—are already looking to make this port an outlet for grain shipments from the West. The grain elevator built many years ago, but never used, is at the present time being overhauled and put into working condition.

CHARLESTON.

Annex A.—RETURN of Principal Articles of Import to Savannah during the Year 1895.

Articles.		Quantity.	Value.
			£
Kainit			6,200
Muriate of potash	Lbs.	995,162	3,119
Brimstone	Tons	4,964	14,165
Cement	Lbs.	16,950,748	9,359
Salt	,,	30,029,440	7,510
Tin-plates	,,	1,295,236	6,000
Bagging			2,173
Dyes			1,878
All other articles			4,430
Total			54,834

Annex B.—RETURN of Principal Articles of Export from Savannah during the Year 1895.

Articles.		Quantity.	Value.
			£
Cotton	Lbs.	212,964,799	3,175,413
,, seed	,,	1,037,930	1,167
Resin	Barrels	1,166,769	378,206
Spirits of turpentine	Gallons	11,148,976	591,742
Phosphate rock	Tons	80,682	155,005
Lumber	Feet	17,039,876	25,942
Iron	Tons	2,392	5,975
Stoves			14,203
All other articles			3,637
Total			4,351,290

Annex C.—RETURN of all Shipping at the Port of Savannah during the Year 1895.

ENTERED.

Nationality.	Sailing.		Steam.		Total.	
	Number of Vessels.	Tons.	Number of Vessels.	Tons.	Number of Vessels.	Tons.
American	8	5,052	...	...	8	5,052
British	8	5,288	66	76,964	74	82,252
Norwegian	119	87,509	...	...	119	87,509
German	25	23,703	2	3,665	27	27,368
Spanish	1	348	8	11,908	9	12,256
Other countries	60	36,463	13	24,244	73	60,707
Total	221	158,363	89	116,781	310	275,144

UNITED STATES.

Cleared.

Nationality.	Sailing. Number of Vessels.	Sailing. Tons.	Steam. Number of Vessels.	Steam. Tons.	Total. Number of Vessels.	Total. Tons.
American	2	718	...	...	2	718
British	7	5,170	67	82,508	74	87,678
Norwegian	115	83,717	1	1,981	116	85,698
German	28	27,187	5	8,824	33	36,011
Spanish	2	1,517	11	16,841	13	18,358
Other countries	61	35,531	12	20,420	73	55,951
Total	215	153,840	96	130,574	311	284,414

CHARLESTON.

Annex D.—RETURN of British Shipping at the Port of Savannah in the Year 1895.

Direct Trade in British Vessels from and to Great Britain and British Colonies.

Entered.

Total Number of Vessels.			Total Tonnage.			Total Number of Crews.	Total Value of Cargoes.
With Cargoes.	In Ballast.	Total.	With Cargoes.	In Ballast.	Total.		£
4	12	16	6,299	12,266	18,565	336	8,781

Cleared.

Total Number of Vessels.			Total Tonnage.			Total Number of Crews.	Total Value of Cargoes.
With Cargoes.	In Ballast.	Total.	With Cargoes.	In Ballast.	Total.		
26	...	26	29,165	...	29,165	623	855,134

Indirect or Carrying Trade in British Vessels from and to other Countries.

Entered.

Countries whence Arrived.	Number of Vessels.			Total Tonnage.			Number of Crews.	Value of Cargoes.
	With Cargoes.	In Ballast.	Total.	With Cargoes.	In Ballast.	Total.		£
United States of America	1	28	29	1,204	32,950	34,154	650	10,000
Argentine Republic	...	4	4	...	2,203	2,203	52	...
Brazil	...	6	6	...	5,245	5,245	102	...
Germany	3	1	4	4,509	1,526	6,035	103	15,127
Portugal	...	6	6	...	8,019	8,019	129	...
Spain	...	7	7	...	5,868	5,868	109	...
Uruguay	...	2	2	...	2,163	2,163	32	...
Total	4	54	58	5,713	57,974	63,687	1,177	25,127

Cleared.

Countries to which Departed.	Number of Vessels.			Total Tonnage.			Number of Crews.	Value of Cargoes.
	With Cargoes.	In Ballast.	Total.	With Cargoes.	In Ballast.	Total.		£
United States of America	...	4	4	...	6,047	6,047	87	...
Brazil	2	...	2	1,346	...	1,346	29	26,147
Belgium	3	...	3	5,024	...	5,024	69	185,843
France	6	...	6	6,046	...	6,046	127	247,326
Germany	10	...	10	12,743	...	12,743	297	402,465
Italy	6	...	6	5,997	...	5,997	132	307,892
Russia	5	...	5	5,949	...	5,949	119	269,864
Sweden	2	...	2	3,042	...	3,042	45	26,420
Spain	10	...	10	12,319	...	12,319	267	429,369
Total	44	4	48	52,466	6,047	58,513	1,172	1,895,326

(2152)

BRUNSWICK.

Mr. Vice-Consul Torras reported as follows:—

During this year the business of this port has improved to some extent in the amount of business done compared with last year; but the prices of the most important products of this section of the country for export have been remarkably low, thus causing depression and discontent in all classes of business.

Work on St. Simon's Bar. — The contractor for deepening the water on the St. Simon's Bar has been at work on every occasion when the sea on the bar was not too rough, and now claims to have a depth of 24 feet at mean high water. This work has been watched with keen interest by the engineers of the country, who as a general rule do not believe he will be successful, though the indications are in his favour.

Health. — This is now one of the healthiest cities in the country, due probably to the new system of sewerage, which seems to be as near perfect as possible, and to the strict health ordinances now in force.

RETURN of Exports to Great Britain and British Possessions from the Port of Brunswick during the Year 1895.

To—	Value.
	Dollars.
Great Britain	2,078,553
British Possessions	18,932
Total	2,097,485

RETURN of all Shipping Entered at the Port of Brunswick during the Year 1895.

Nationality.	Number of Vessels.	Tons.
American	349	231,059
British	28	36,605
Norwegian	38	26,039
Spanish	35	19,040
German	9	7,359
Russian	7	3,535
Swedish	4	2,225
Dutch	3	1,909
Italian	3	1,732
Portuguese	2	575
Brazilian	1	537
French	1	469
Total	480	334,084

CHARLESTON.

RETURN of Exports at the Port of Brunswick, Georgia, for the Year 1895.

Month.	Number of Vessels.	Tonnage.	Cotton. Bales.	Cotton Seed. Tons.	Phosphate. Tons.	Turpentine. Barrels.	Resin. Barrels.	Timber. Feet.	Lumber. Feet.	Crossties. Pieces.	Shingles. Pieces.	Value. Dollars.
January	45	34,196	27,849	486	4,200	3,475	11,864	386,000	8,349,000	93,024	2,447	1,033,676
February	39	29,172	11,364	...	6,785	720	18,496	1,295,000	7,435,000	88,395	8,335	562,780
March	32	25,576	7,635	...	4,300	1,345	26,595	511,000	5,475,000	67,310	14,100	452,378
April	32	22,566	4,243	...	4,046	2,068	14,316	383,000	6,736,000	51,195	...	370,070
May	33	23,173	8,365	...	2,722	5,292	15,064	143,000	8,640,000	25,582	217,875	502,602
June	36	22,404	1,240	...	...	7,688	16,689	1,127,000	7,622,000	45,758	405,000	344,989
July	37	23,556	1,652	...	...	4,906	18,216	132,000	8,132,000	79,971	37,260	334,881
August	41	26,992	1,835	...	...	7,225	20,059	1,092,000	8,276,000	67,587	1,615,000	306,804
September	32	21,762	3,802	...	...	5,775	21,806	...	7,756,000	29,815	650,000	393,150
October	38	28,609	26,878	180	2,892	4,849	16,705	...	8,658,000	40,906	150,000	1,426,246
November	35	29,961	23,092	360	...	2,758	14,419	214,000	9,186,000	57,494	...	1,188,539
December	39	31,975	25,806	495	2,737	6,912	20,120	268,000	8,034,000	41,309	545,000	1,424,029
Total	439	349,942	143,771	1,521	27,682	52,979	214,349	6,251,000	94,299,000	688,946	3,645,007	8,340,144

(2152)

UNITED STATES.

Port Royal.

Mr. Vice-Consul Kessler reports as follows:—

Port Royal is situated about 18 miles from the sea, and has a depth of water on the bar of 21 feet at mean low tides. Vessels of any draught can cross the bar, and can proceed to the docks and load a full and complete cargo.

The total tonnage of vessels arriving at this port amounted to about 129,500 tons, of which 91,500 tons were British ships.

Cotton. The cotton exports for the past year has been very favourable.

Phosphate rock. Phosphate rock, one of our principal exports, has been quiet owing to the low prices paid for the rock, but must say that the prices are again advancing, and expect to do a larger business this year.

Port charges. The charges of this port are as reasonable as any port on the coast.

There is also a first-class coaling station, and ships calling here for coal are coaled with quick dispatch day or night. The prices of coal are as cheap as any coaling station on the Atlantic coast.

There is also a direct line of steamers (British) plying between Port Royal and Liverpool. There are being large quantities of grain shipped this season to England.

Table showing Quantity and Value of Exports to and Imports from England in British Ships.

Exports.

Articles.		Quantity.
Cotton	Bales..	118,590
Cotton-seed	Sacks..	12,475
,, meal	,,	11,520
Phosphate rock..	Tons ..	118,771
Flour	Sacks..	69,897
Grain	Bushels	115,165
Moss	Bales .	14
Pig-iron..	Tons ..	100
Lumber ..	,,	1 648
Oil	Barrels	1,000
Furniture	Cases ..	6
Oil paintings	,,	1
Canned goods	,,	500
Ochre	Barrels	35
Sea Island cotton	Bales ..	46
Resin	Barrels	2,750

CHARLESTON.

Imports.

Articles.		Quantity.
Sugar	Bags	1,000
Salt	Tons	9,685
Dried blood	,,	500
Kainitt	,,	2,000
Pyrites	,,	3,900
Sulphur	,,	900

UNITED STATES.

RETURN of British Shipping at the Port of Port Royal in the Year 1895.

Direct Trade in British Vessels from and to Great Britain and British Colonies.

Entered.

Total Number of Vessels.			Total Tonnage.			Total Number of Crews.	Total Value of Cargoes.
With Cargoes.	In Ballast.	Total.	With Cargoes.	In Ballast.	Total.		£
11	7	18	22,000	12,600	34,600	540	...

Cleared.

Total Number of Vessels.			Total Tonnage.			Total Number of Crews.	Total Value of Cargoes.
With Cargoes.	In Ballast.	Total.	With Cargoes.	In Ballast.	Total.		£
44	...	44	123,945	...	123,945	1,114	...

Indirect or Carrying Trade in British Vessels from and to other Countries.

Entered.

Countries whence Arrived.	Number of Vessels.			Tonnage.			Number of Crews.	Value of Cargoes.
	With Cargoes.	In Ballast.	Total.	With Cargoes.	In Ballast.	Total.		£
France	...	...	...	...	...	...	...	...
Germany	...	...	...	...	...	...	...	...
Holland	...	...	...	...	...	...	...	...
Portugal	...	8	8	...	12,000	12,000	192	...
Phillipine Islands	1	...	1	1,920	...	1,920	23	...
American	...	32	32	...	44,800	44,800	736	...
Total	1	40	41	1,920	56,800	58,720	951	...

Cleared.

Countries to which Departed.	Number of Vessels.			Tonnage.			Number of Crews.	Value of Cargoes.
	With Cargoes.	In Ballast.	Total.	With Cargoes.	In Ballast.	Total.		£
France	9	...	9	24,665	...	24,665	216	...
Germany	4	...	4	8,000	...	8,000	87	...
Holland	1	...	1	1,600	...	1,600	22	...
Portugal	...	...	...	...	...	...	...	...
American	...	2	2	...	3,600	3,600	47	...
Denmark	1	...	1	1,900	...	1,900	24	...
Total	15	2	17	36,165	3,600	39,765	376	...

WILMINGTON (North Carolina).

Mr. Vice-Consul Sprunt reports as follows:—

Wilmington, North Carolina, is situated on the west bank of the Cape Fear River, in latitude 34° 14′ and in longitude 77° 56′. Cape Fear River was known in the early history of North Carolina as the River Clarendon. The first settlement on its banks was made in the year 1659 or 1660, and abandoned in 1663. In 1665 Sir John Yeamans, with colonists from Barbadoes made a second settlement; a few years thereafter Sir John and most of the colonists removed to Port Royal. The earliest reliable information of the town of Brunswick does not go further back than 1720. In 1725 quite a colony settled at the town of Brunswick, but in 1730 they removed to the present site of Wilmington. The town was called New Liverpool until about 1732 when the name was changed to Newton, and in 1739 this name was changed to that of Wilmington. The city limits extend from north to south 2¾ miles, and from east to west 1⅛ miles, comprising a total area of about 2,400 acres. The general contour of the city is that of an elevated sand ridge, running parallel with the river, intersected with dunes and rivulets emptying into the river and adjacent streams.

Sanitary. Artificial drainage has in recent years carried the storm water from the city into the tributary streams of the Cape Fear. As a result, malarial fever has greatly decreased, and it may be truly said that the city has become exceptionally healthy. Drainage has not and cannot, it is true, alter the malarial influence upon crews of vessels sleeping on the river in the months of July, August, September, and October, yet it has been demonstrated that these fevers are preventable, in a marked degree. There is a home for seamen in which they can find a safe retreat from the effluvia of the river, ample provision being made for more sailors than ever visit this port at one time.

Improvement of Cape Fear River. The United States began to improve the river between the bar and Wilmington in 1829 and the channel on the bar in 1853. In 1829 the river was so obstructed that vessels drawing more than 10 feet were obliged to anchor 14 miles below Wilmington and discharge a part of their cargoes into lighters. In 1853 at low water on the bar the least mid channel depth was 7 feet in the western channel, 7½ feet in the eastern channel, and 8 feet at New Inlet, 7 miles above the mouth. The original project of 1827 was to deepen the channel through the shoals in the 8 miles next below Wilmington by contracting it by jetties, and by diverting into it water from Brunswick River and from Fishing and Rodman's Creeks. The project of 1853 was to straighten and deepen the channel on the bar by building jetties and a wing dam by dredging, by diverting water through it from New Inlet, by building a jetty at Federal Point, and by closing two small breaches in Zeke's Island. The project of 1870 was to deepen the bar channel by closing the breaches between Smith's and Zeke's islands, with the ultimate closure of New Inlet in view. The project of 1873 was to deepen the channel through the bar, added to that of 1870, to dredge in the Baldhead (eastern) channel, to extend across Zeke's Island and beyond it into the river, the dam being built to close the breaches between Smith's and Zeke's islands and to close New Inlet, commencing with the building of a jetty from Federal Point. The project of 1874 was to get 12 feet at low water as high as the city of Wilmington, by dredging a channel, 100 feet wide, through Horseshoe Shoal below New Inlet and through three other shoals near Wilmington. The project of 1881 was to dredge a channel, $2\frac{3}{4}$ miles in length, through Horseshoe Shoal and through eight other shoals above it 270 feet wide and 16 feet deep at mean low water from deep water at Southport to Wilmington. On February 28, 1889, pursuant to a requirement of the River and Harbour Act of August 11, 1888, the cost of obtaining a channel 20 feet deep at mean low water from Wilmington to the ocean was reported to be 1,800,000 dol. In the annual report for 1889 it was reported that an additional appropriation of 25,000 dol. would be required to complete the project of 1881, and obtain a channel, 16 feet deep, from Wilmington to the ocean. By the River and Harbour Act of September 19, 1890, congress appropriated 170,000 dol. for improving the Cape Fear River at and below Wilmington, and dredging to the depth of 20 feet, commenced at Wilmington, January 19, 1891, and ceased at Brunswick River Shoal, $4\frac{1}{2}$ miles below Wilmington, September 7, 1892. Since September 7, 1892, work has been in progress to obtain a channel through the shoals between Wilmington and the bar, and on the latter 18 feet deep at mean low water. To June 30, 1894, 2,427,584 dol. 46 c. (including outstanding liabilities) had been expended upon this improvement. At that date the depth of the channel at mean low water was as follows:—From Wilmington, 20 miles, to Snows Marsh Shoal, 18 feet, except where shoaling had occurred at the lower extremity of Lilliput Shoal, where the depth was $16\frac{1}{2}$ feet and the bottom of very soft sludge; at Snows Marsh Shoal, 14 feet; on the inner shoals at the bar 16 feet by a crooked channel and 14·3 feet by a straight course, and on the outer bar, 16·6 feet. With the amount applied during the fiscal year ending June 30, 1895, a channel has been obtained 18 feet deep at mean low water of variable widths, but nowhere less than 148 feet through all the shoals except at Snows Marsh where the depth is 16·7 feet; a training dyke, 5,692 feet in length has been built at the latter locality; a suction dredging steamer has been built under contract and placed in operation on the bar and at Snows Marsh Shoal, and a breach made by the sea in the east bank of the river around the end of New Inlet dam was closed by the deposit of 1,353 tons of granite. Twenty-four square miles of hydrography and 27 miles of shore line have been surveyed. There is now $18\frac{1}{2}$ to 19 feet water from Wilmington to sea on an average tide.

CHARLESTON.

Commerce.

There are few changes from year to year in the general conditions of trade, and yet by a comparison at intervals of a few years, it is plain that the naval stores trade is slowly decreasing.

The trade has been constantly developed, and there has been a large and steady increase in receipts when compared with quantity produced. The receipts for 1895 were 154,152 bales: the exports were 166,958 bales. — Cotton.

Naval stores for years were the staple productions of this section, and the chief exports of this port, but ever year there is a falling-off in this trade on account of decreased production. Receipts for the year 1895: spirits of turpentine, 44,620 barrels; resin, 193,112 barrels; tar, 66,920 barrels; and crude turpentine, 13,045 barrels. Exports: spirits of turpentine, 44,129 barrels; resin, 199,704 barrels; tar, 63,640 barrels; and crude turpentine, 13,908 barrels. — Naval stores.

This article produces a large movement in the commercial affairs of Wilmington, and feeds considerably the maritime traffic. The topographical situation of the port through its waterways and railroads makes it almost an emporium for this merchandise. The exportation of lumber for the year 1895 shows an increase over 1894 of 534,619 feet, the domestic shipments being 20,329,678 feet, and the foreign exports 15,023,734 feet, making a total of 35,353,412 feet. — Lumber.

During the last few years the reclamation of old rice lands on the Cape Fear, many of which have been restored to a high and profitable state of cultivation, has been one of the principal industries. The mills here have made a market for all grades, and planters are not obliged to ship their goods elsewhere. The clean rice from this port is chiefly shipped to eastern and northern cities, where it receives an appreciative market, and is well known as the best rice milled in this country. — Rice.

The North Carolina peanut is mostly marketed here, the annual production being about 150,000 bushels. The nuts are received in a very crude condition, and are put in mercantile order by the dealers, and dealt out to the trade, the markets being mostly North-western and Southern cities. — Peanuts.

Truck farming is increasing every year in this section. Vegetables and fruits of almost every description are grown under the highest cultivation and best results. The continued widerspreading cultivation of the soil and agriculture is now forming one of the principal sources of wealth, and in some of its branches is surpassed by no other country. Farmers who have long resided in the North and West are being attracted to this locality on account of climate, adaptability of soil to the growth of tuck, and unsurpassed transportatian facilities. This immigration is increasing the value of lands, and largely augmenting the population in rural districts. — Truck farming.

The fisheries of the rivers and sounds are by no means — Fisheries.

(2152)

insignificant. The waters furnish nearly every variety of fish, among which are shad, mullets, blue fish or skip jack, speckled trout, pig fish, red and black drum, black fish, rock or bass, Spanish mackerel, sunfish, spots, croakers, sheep's-head, whiting, &c., and also various kinds of freshwater fish, trout, perch, &c. The extent of the oyster business is also worthy of consideration. The best oysters come from New River. The beds are said to be inexhaustible, and there are no better oysters in the country. Myrtle Grove oysters are smaller than the New River, yet compare favourably in flavour with the bulk of those grown elsewhere. Several boats, both sail and steam, are engaged in the clam business, and large shipments are made daily during the season, which are easily disposed of in the large cities of the east and north.

Industrial establishments. New industrial establishments are increasing, and there prevails a tendency to extend the several branches of industry in the manufacture of barrels, boxes, crates, and baskets for the packing of fish, vegetables, and fruits. Several new sawmills have recently been erected, and are working to their full capacity. A large fertilising plant has been built, and is now in successful operation. An entirely new enterprise for removing lint from the seed of cotton is being developed. The Standard Oil Company has increased its facilities, and made this the distributing point for its trade in several Southern States, which will increase our shipping and add very much to the traffic of our railways.

British vessels. During 1895 there were 45 arrivals of British vessels, 17 steamers and 28 sailing vessels, the tonnage aggregating 33,678 tons. Most of the smaller sailing vessels came laden with fruits, while but a few of the larger sailing vessels, and only two of the steamers, brought in cargoes. All these vessels had outward cargoes of cotton, naval stores, and lumber.

LONDON:
Printed for Her Majesty's Stationery Office,
By HARRISON AND SONS,
Printers in Ordinary to Her Majesty.
(75 5 | 96—H & S 2152)

FOREIGN OFFICE.
1896.
ANNUAL SERIES.

No. 1712.

DIPLOMATIC AND CONSULAR REPORTS ON TRADE AND FINANCE.

UNITED STATES.

REPORT FOR THE YEAR 1895

ON THE

TRADE OF THE BALTIMORE CONSULAR DISTRICT.

REFERENCE TO PREVIOUS REPORT, Annual Series No. 1512.

Presented to both Houses of Parliament by Command of Her Majesty,
MAY, 1896.

LONDON:
PRINTED FOR HER MAJESTY'S STATIONERY OFFICE,
BY HARRISON AND SONS, ST. MARTIN'S LANE,
PRINTERS IN ORDINARY TO HER MAJESTY.

And to be purchased, either directly or through any Bookseller, from
EYRE & SPOTTISWOODE, East Harding Street, Fleet Street, E.C., and
32, Abingdon Street, Westminster, S.W.; or
JOHN MENZIES & Co., 12, Hanover Street, Edinburgh, and
90, West Nile Street, Glasgow; or
HODGES, FIGGIS, & Co., Limited, 104, Grafton Street, Dublin.

1896.

[C. 7919—80.] *Price One Penny.*

New Series of Reports.

Reports of the Annual Series have been issued from Her Majesty's Diplomatic and Consular Officers at the following places, and may be obtained from the sources indicated on the title-page:—

No.		Price.
1592. Baghdad		1d.
1593. Vienna		1½d.
1594. Montevideo		2½d.
1595. Swatow		1½d.
1596. Foochow		1d.
1597. Tamsui		1d.
1598. Chungking		1d.
1599. Chefoo		1d.
1600. Tokio		1½d.
1601. Bangkok		1d.
1602. Caracas		1½d.
1603. Sofia		2½d.
1604. Belgrade		2½d.
1605. Shanghai		2½d.
1606. Canton		1½d.
1607. Meshed		1½d.
1608. Erzeroum		1d.
1609. Galatz		2d.
1610. Port Said		1½d.
1611. The Hague		1½d.
1612. Calais		1d.
1613. Newchwang		1d.
1614. Copenhagen		1d.
1615. Odessa		2d.
1616. Gothenburg		2d.
1617. Mannheim		1½d.
1618. Old Calabar		5d.
1619. Pekin		2½d.
1620. Taganrog		2d.
1621. Brindisi		2½d.
1622. Jeddah		1½d.
1623. Hamburg		3d.
1624. Angora		1½d.
1625. Buda-Pesth		1½d.
1626. Beyrout		1d.
1627. Bushire		2d.
1628. Stettin		2½d.
1629. Porto Rico		1d.
1630. Rotterdam		½d.
1631. Alexandria		1½d.
1632. Tokio		2½d.
1633. Tangier		1½d.
1634. Oporto		1½d.
1635. St. Petersburg		4d.
1636. Dantzig		2d.
1637. Macao		1d.
1638. Hiogo and Osaka		6d.
1639. Naples		1½d.
1640. Kiungchow		½d.
1641. Rome		1½d.
1642. Beira		½d.
1643. St. Jago de Cuba		4½d.
1644. Christiania		6d.
1645. Lisbon		1½d.
1646. Brussels		½d.
1647. Vera Cruz		½d.
1648. Tunis		1d.
1649. Antwerp		1d.
1650. Tokio		1d.
1651. Honolulu		½d.
1652. Stettin		1½d.
1653. Bangkok		1d.
1654. Batoum		1½d.
1655. Mexico		9½d.
1656. Odessa		1½d.
1657. Réunion		1d.
1658. Tokio		1½d.
1659. Maranham		1d.
1660. Copenhagen		1d.
1661. Berlin		1½d.
1662. Teheran		2½d.
1663. Salonica		1½d.
1664. Manila		½d.
1665. Florence		5½d.
1666. Dakar		½d.
1667. Havre		2d.
1668. Rouen		2d.
1669. Corfu		½d.
1670. Calais		1d.
1671. Tehran		1½d.
1672. Barcelona		2d.
1673. Amsterdam		1d.
1674. Bordeaux		2½d.
1675. Warsaw		1d.
1676. Havana		1½d.
1677. Berlin		1d.
1678. Beira		1½d.
1679. Saigon		1d.
1680. Trebizond		1d.
1681. Vera Cruz		1½d.
1682. Patras		1d.
1683. La Rochelle		1½d.
1684. Madrid		1½d.
1685. Belgrade		2d.
1686. Algiers		5d.
1687. Galveston		2½d.
1688. New Orleans		2d.
1689. Suakin		1d.
1690. Pernambuco		1d.
1691. Guatemala		1½d.
1692. Guayaquil		1d.
1693. Wênchow		1d.
1694. Piræus		3d.
1695. Tokio		3d.
1696. Marseilles		1d.
1697. Manila		1d.
1698. Jerusalem		1d.
1699. Cherbourg		2d.
1700. Leghorn		1½d.
1701. Boston		1½d.
1702. Kiungchow		1d.
1703. Naples		2½d.
1704. Stockholm		2d.
1705. Corunna		2d.
1706. Rio de Janeiro		2½d.
1707. San José		1d.
1708. Paramaribo		2d.
1709. Brest		1½d.
1710. Montevideo		½d.
1711. Charleston		2½d.

No. 1712.

Reference to previous Report, Annual Series No. 1512.

UNITED STATES.

BALTIMORE.

Vice-Consul Coates to the Marquis of Salisbury.

My Lord,   *Baltimore, April* 4, 1896.

I HAVE the honour to transmit herewith to your Lordship a Report, drawn up by me, on the Trade and Commerce of Baltimore during the year 1895, together with similar Reports from the Vice-Consuls at Norfolk, Va., and Richmond, Va.

I have, &c.
(Signed)   A. G. COATES.

Report on the Trade and Commerce of the Consular District of Baltimore for the Year 1895.

Abstract of Contents.

	Page
Finance	2
Shipping	2
Cereals	2
Fruit	2
Oysters	3
Coffee	3
Cotton	3
Tobacco	3
Immigration	3
Shipping returns	4
Exports	5
Imports	6
Trade Report of Norfolk Vice-Consulate	7
" Richmond Vice-Consulate	9

(2151)

UNITED STATES.

Trade of Baltimore. The trade and volume of business at Baltimore show an increase during 1895, as compared with 1894. The city, however, has not yet recovered from the depression of the last few years.

The early part of the year was marked by many of the unfavourable conditions of 1894. Values were on a low basis and easily susceptible to a change in the status of affairs. By the second half of the year more confidence was shown in the outlook, and values began to advance.

Local finance. The bank clearances of the year were 695,707,281 dol., showing an increase of 22,263,679 dol., as compared with 1894, and a further improvement is anticipated in 1896.

Shipping. A fewer number of ships of all nationalities entered and cleared here than in 1894 (though the number of British vessels was the same). The tonnage, however, of those which entered show a slight increase, but there was a decrease in that of the vessels which cleared.

Ship-building. During the year 9 vessels were built in the district of Baltimore. They consisted of 5 steamships and 4 sailing ships, having a net tonnage of $459\frac{34}{100}$, and valued at 95,800 dol.

Marine disasters. Reports of 59 marine disasters were received at the customhouse, showing a loss of 28 lives, and 104,140 dol. in shipping, and 134,640 in cargo property.

Pilotage. A recent change in the law of Maryland releases from compulsory pilotage American vessels wholly or partially laden with coke or coal mined in the United States.

There is a considerable trade in coal from this port to Mexico, which is at present chiefly carried in British ships. The change of law gives American ships an advantage in that trade over British ships, which latter must still employ a pilot if he offers his services, or pay pilotage fees if the master does not accept them.

Carrying trade. The carrying trade was unsatisfactory, owing to the small foreign demand for wheat; but the coal trade has shown favourable symptoms.

It is to be regretted that a large carrying trade in fruit from the West Indies, especially bananas from Jamaica, is now done by Norwegian ships instead of by British ships as formerly. Importers explain this change by asserting that they can charter Norwegian ships suitable to this trade at a far cheaper rate.

Grain. There has been great depression in the grain trade during the year, and there are no good grounds for expecting any material improvement in 1896.

Wheat. The condition of the wheat trade was unsatisfactory. The price of that staple fell off and had a depressing effect upon other industries.

Dry goods, &c. Dry goods, hides, and leather, and their manufactures have been prosperous.

Canned goods. The canned goods trade fell off, and there were several failures in that industry and others dependent on it.

Peaches. The crop of peaches was short, and the quantity packed less than that of 1894.

Owing to over-production large stocks of tomatoes and corn were on hand at the end of the year, and this served to keep down prices. *Tomatoes and corn.*

Oyster packing was limited owing to the high prices of raw stock; and unless the spring pack is unusually good, a scarcity of canned goods is anticipated for next summer. *Oysters.*

The coffee trade of the year compares favourably with that of 1894, though merchants are still dissatisfied. Prices advanced steadily until March, when the highest quotations were noted. No. 7 Rio was then sold at $16\frac{3}{4}$ c. per lb. and 17 c. per lb. From March the market gradually declined until the end of the year, when $14\frac{1}{2}$ c. per lb. to $14\frac{5}{8}$ c. per lb. was quoted for No. 7 Rio. *Coffee.*

The total receipts of coffee, which is chiefly imported from Rio, were for the past 3 years as follows:—

Year.	Quantity.
	Bags.
1895	245,532
1894	213,842
1893	237,454

The crop of Maryland tobacco amounted to 28,085 hogsheads. The general quality was lighter and better, but the quantity was 25 per cent. less than the crop of 1894. *Tobacco.*

The demand for the lower grades was unusually small, and the prices fell for good sound tobacco to $1\frac{1}{2}$ c. per lb. and occasionally to $1\frac{1}{4}$ c. per lb. The latter price is said to have been the lowest quoted since the civil war.

The French Government contracted for about 12,000 hogsheads of the Maryland crop.

The Eastern Ohio crop, which finds an exclusive market in Baltimore, amounted to 7,000 hogsheads. It was not so ripe or of so good a quality as the crop of the previous year.

The total stock of tobacco on hand here from all sources at the end of the year was 17,546 hogsheads.

The cotton trade improved, as compared with 1894, and prices advanced $2\frac{1}{2}$ c. per lb. This improvement was especially marked from April to October. From that month to the close of the year prices gradually fell to $8\frac{1}{4}$ c. per lb. *Cotton.*

About 65,000 bales were used in the mills in the neighbourhood of Baltimore, and 79,000 bales were sent coastwise, against 75,300 in 1894.

The foreign exports of cotton amounted to 229,796 bales, against 207,684 in 1894.

The number of immigrants arriving at this port continues to be restricted, owing to the rigid enforcement of the immigration laws. *Immigration.*

During the year 9,321 immigrants arrived, showing the slight increase of 625 as compared with 1894. They were of the following nationalities:—

	Number.
Scotland	25
England	3
Ireland	2
Wales	1
Colonies (British)	24
Austria-Hungary	2,743
Germany	3,737
Russia	2,751
Denmark	8
Sweden	8
Roumania	11
Various	8
Total	9,321

Of which there were—

	Number.
Males	5,040
Females	4,281
Total	9,321

Annex A.—RETURN of all Shipping at the Port of Baltimore during the Year 1895.

ENTERED.

Nationality.	Sailing.		Steam.		Total.	
	Number of Vessels.	Tons.	Number of Vessels.	Tons.	Number of Vessels.	Tons.
British	26	4,370	362	701,854	388	706,224
American, foreign	110	37,285	10	4,085	120	41,370
German	...	...	106	384,703	106	384,703
Italian	11	8,793	...	...	11	8,793
Norwegian	1	285	44	23,152	45	23,437

CLEARED.

Nationality.	Sailing.		Steam.		Total.	
	Number of Vessels.	Tons.	Number of Vessels.	Tons.	Number of Vessels.	Tons.
British	26	4,370	351	700,097	377	704,467
American, foreign	132	60,469	15	7,336	147	67,805
German	...	...	105	380,983	105	380,983
Italian	9	7,144	...	...	9	7,144
Norwegian	1	285	43	22,652	44	22,937

Annex B.—RETURN of all Principal Articles of Export from Baltimore during the Years 1894–95.

Articles.		Quantity.	
		1895.	1894.
Wheat	Bushels	4,033,922	8,448,448
Flour	Barrels	2,485,360	2,943,562
Maize	Bushels	9,515,021	7,758,377
Oats	,,	134,318	46
Clover seed	,,	51,424	146,454
Timothy	,,	23,579	22,666
Cattle	Head	40,111	61,089
Sheep	,,	107,325	107,325
Canned goods	Cases	321,619	244,961
Lard	Lbs.	69,257,241	68,464,601
Petroleum, refined	Gallons	45,689,227	41,975,180
Coal	Tons	80,880	122,094
Lumber	Feet	26,488,000	30,979,000
Staves		2,087,000	1,512,000
Logs		89,003	68,392
Tobacco	Hogsheads	60,929	65,126
Oil-seed cakes	Tons	25,562	18,657
Cotton	Bales	223,581	205,994
Rosin	Barrels	115,355	111,834
Hay	Tons	823	3,265
Horses	Head	961	195

VALUE OF EXPORTS FROM BALTIMORE.

Year.	Value.	
	Currency.	Sterling.
	Dollars.	£
1895	60,154,904	12,326,824
1894	63,961,279	13,166,819

(2151)

Annex C.—RETURN of Principal Articles of Import into Baltimore during the Years 1894–95.

Articles.		Quantity.	
		1895.	1894.
Iron ore..	Tons..	249,163	88,078
Salt	,, ..	10,945	4,220
,,	Sacks..	76,118	24,790
,,	Bushels	128,082	135,226
Chemicals	Packages	257,306	219,783
Manure salt	Tons..	34,246	37,064
Brimstone	,, ..	9,526	15,612
Phosphate	Bags..	18,890	49,815
Nitrate of soda..	,, ..	23,804	11,955
Cement..	Casks..	331,916	247,106
Whisky..	Barrels	7,481	13,891
Bananas..	Bunches	899,458	1,004,339
Cocoanuts		1,945,000	2,315,000
Coffee	Bags..	262,011	214,030
Rice	,, ..	82,546	45,532
Sugar	,, ..	196,462	21,709
Matting..	Rolls..	13,753	16,601

VALUE OF IMPORTS INTO BALTIMORE.

Year.	Value.	
	Currency.	Sterling.
	Dollars.	£
1895	19,934,369	4,084,911
1894	11,749,927	2,407,771

Annex D.—TABLE showing Total Value of all Articles Exported from or Imported into Baltimore during the Years 1894–95.

Country.	Exports.		Imports.	
	1895.	1894.	1895.	1894.
	Dollars.	Dollars.	Dollars.	Dollars.
Great Britain	30,644,356	30,640,863	4,927,113	4,346,472
Belgium	3,934,335	2,578,708	120,562	71,122
Brazil	2,852,144	3,580,879	4,579,526	4,127,814
Cuba and Spain	105,109	166,144	414,94	266,019
France	3,166,127	3,410,630	122,516	100,586
Germany	10,322,494	16,015,750	1,953,694	1,313,391
Netherlands	8,385,045	9,014,646	217,267	171,081
Mexico	398,046	138,484	7,945	844
Italy	3,865	..	443,987	336,636
Other countries	360,070	373,918	1,212,827	1,202,050

NORFOLK.

The report of trade for the port of Norfolk for the year 1895 emphasises the fact that increasing transportation facilities, represented by about 18,000 miles of tributary railroads, and by steamship lines to Atlantic ports and Europe, pointed to this becoming one of the most important seaports on the Atlantic. During the year 1895 the various railways centering here have added either to their connections or to their terminal properties, but the most important event of the year has been the transfer of the deep water terminus of the Southern Railway Company from West Point, Virginia, to Norfolk.

This is the largest railway system in the South, having about 6,000 miles of road, and extending to all important points south and west.

In transportation facilities Norfolk is now placed in the forefront of Southern ports, and great increase may be expected in her trade and manufactures.

The following comparative statement of receipts of merchandise at the port during the years 1888 and 1895, will give the best evidence of the development of the port during the last 7 years.

Attention is also called to the statements herewith enclosed, showing the number and tonnage of vessels entered and cleared at this port for the past year; also the principal articles of import and export, and the value thereof.

TABLE showing the Movement of all Shipping at the Port of Norfolk during the Year 1895.

ENTERED.

Nationality.	Sailing. Number of Vessels.	Sailing. Tons.	Steam. Number of Vessels.	Steam. Tons.	Total. Number of Vessels.	Total. Tons.
British	6	6,282	271	427,548	277	433,830
Spanish	...	...	41	68,793	41	68,793
German	...	...	9	18,053	9	18,053
Norwegian	1	382	2	782	3	1,164
American	42	18,529	...	...	42	18,529
Italian	7	3,982	...	...	7	3,982
All others	1	2,416	1	2,245	2	4,661
Total	57	31,591	324	517,421	381	549,012

UNITED STATES.

CLEARED.

Nationality.	Sailing. Number of Vessels.	Sailing. Tons.	Steam. Number of Vessels.	Steam. Tons.	Total. Number of Vessels.	Total. Tons.
British	6	7,303	284	438,535	290	445,838
Spanish	...	...	38	64,489	38	64,489
German	...	...	9	18,053	9	18,053
Norwegian	...	...	2	782	2	782
American	47	26,902	...	...	47	26,902
Italian	8	4,506	...	...	8	4,506
All others	1	2,416	1	2,245	2	4,661
Total	62	41,127	334	524,104	396	565,231

COMPARATIVE Statement of the Receipts of Merchandise at the Port of Norfolk for the Years 1888 and 1895.

Articles.		Quantity. 1888.	Quantity. 1895.
Lumber	Feet	138,625,263	324,869,264
Logs	,,	105,637 554	115,026,631
Staves	Mille	..	3,552,779
Shingles	,,	30,714,540	38,575,659
R.R. ties	,,	..	115,791
Hay	Tons	7 709	19,873
Corn	Bushels	736,858	4,266,493
Oats	,,	247,970	330,152
Rough rice	,,	6,168	7,352
Bran	,,	103,442	146,824
Wheat	,,	138 338	330,005
Peanut	Bags	289,162	419,394
Coffee	,,	10,024	13,269
Sugar	Barrels	30,154	54,007
Cheese	Boxes	14,168	29,463
Butter	Tubs	20,185	21,322
Flour	Bags	2,300	104,443
,,	Barrels	181,798	324,732
Fish	Packages	23,989	41,389
Meat	Lbs.	13,819,075	20,893,668
Cotton-seed oil	Barrels	5,799	52,789
,, meal	Bushels	61,539	119,918
Naval stores	Barrels	14,198	20,421
Horses	Head	922	8,703
Cattle	,,	2,949	11,651
Best coal	Tons	938,369	1,704,680
Pig-iron	,,	168	4,005

BALTIMORE.

TABLE showing Principal Articles of Export and Import at the Port of Norfolk during the Past Year.

EXPORTS.

Articles.		Quantity.	Value.
			Dollars.
Corn and wheat..	Bushels	3,412,915	1,626,953
Cotton	Bales..	124,241	3,387,718
Leaf tobacco	Lbs.	2,997,136	290,547
Coal	Tons..	116,943	362,563
Logs and lumber			326,928
Staves and headings			184,665
Cotton-seed oil	Gallons	206,080	70,250
Flour	Barrels	34,435	102,769
Cotton-seed meal	Bags..	54,792	43,843
Lard	Gallons	129,500	7,770
,,	Lbs.	137,800	9,646
Gunpowder	,,	100,000	12,000
Sheep	Head..	2,270	13,335
Feathers..	Lbs.		25,878
Cotton-waste			52,537
Bark and chemicals			19,119
Corn meal	Bushels	80,000	5,000
Dried apples	Lbs.	25,000	1,000
Coke	Tons..	1,145	3,222
Clover seed	Lbs.	3,000	1,860
Phosphate rock..	Tons..	600	3,330
,,	Bags..	325	712
Oats	Bushels	860	325
Total			6,551,960

IMPORTS.

Articles.		Quantity.	Value.
			Dollars.
Sulphate of ammonia	Bags..	5,496	23,558
Tinplate..	Boxes..	4,205	16,430
Coffee	Bags..	2,753	53,401
Sperm oil	Gallons	19,600	7,840
Brimstone	Tons..	700	8,368
Salt	,,	700	2,046
Nitrate of soda..			80,018
Miscellaneous			17,308
Total			208,969

RICHMOND.

Mr. Vice-Consul Brine report as follows:—

The reaction after severe business depression of 1893, which General trade. proved so disastrous to many portions of the country, the extreme conservatism of the year 1894, during which invest-

UNITED STATES.

ments were close and deliberate, the immense exportations of gold to foreign markets, the uncertain condition of the money market, and various other influences that characterised the past 2 years as one of the severest tests to which our business men have been subjected for years. The low price of cotton in the South, where the bulk of the wholesale business of this city is transacted, had a strong influence upon the condition of trade. Collections were slow, and retail houses were not at all disposed to purchase large stocks on account of the business conditions prevailing.

Despite all these influences, however, Richmond has held her own remarkably well.

Manufacturing. There was a considerable increase in the manufacturing business. In 1894 there were 867 manufacturing plants in the city, which employed 17,590 hands, and in which the amount of 15,445,800 dol. was invested, while the sales for the year amounted to 31,684,000 dol. In 1895 the number of manufacturing plants was 889, employing 181,333, and in which was invested the amount of 16,163,000 dol. The sales for 1895 amounted to 32,026,000 dol.

Jobbing trade. The result for the jobbing trade for the year may be analysed as follows:—

The total annual sales for the year 1895 amounted to 30,189,524 dol., while the sales for the year 1894 amounted to 29,213,880 dol.

The failures for the year 1895 were comparatively heavy. Two or three of these, however, covered the greater part of the amount involved, and when the number of failures is considered, the figures do not appear discouraging.

For the year 1895 the number of failures in the city was sixty-nine, representing assets to the amount of 1,356,340 dol., and liabilities amounting to 1,751,710 dol. In 1894 the number of failures was forty-five, with assets to the amount of 82,800 dol., and liabilities amounting to 169,000 dol. In 1893 there were fifty-seven failures, with assets amounting to 525,850 dol., and liabilities amounting to 799,100 dol.

Banks. The banks' clearings show a decided increase. In 1893 the clearings were 114,957,212 dol.; 1894 the amount was 113,327,889 dol.; while in 1895 the amount reached 121,545,780 dol., an increase over last year of 8,217,891 dol.

Tobacco. It is gratifying to state that the Richmond market this year has more buyers of loose tobacco than it has had at any time during the past 3 or 4 years. There are several large export buyers for foreign markets who have bought freely this season.

The new bright tobacco crop is thought to be up to an average in colour, but deficient in wrappers and good body fillers, and will probably fall short in actual weight in pounds at least one-fourth as compared with last year's crop.

The dark tobacco crop has unfortunately been damaged about 40 per cent. in quality by frost, and will fall short in weight at least 30 per cent., as compared with the crop of last year, and the loss would be much greater than it is, but for the fact that the farmers are selling a good deal of their frosted tobacco, which is almost completely worthless for export or for manufacturing purposes.

The work on the James River being carried on by the United States Government, has been steadily prosecuted during the year. *James River improvement.*

The export trade from Richmond which should be accredited to this port for the year past is practically nothing, the Southern Railways having sent its export trade to shipping points other than its terminal at West Point, which heretofore handled this business. *Export trade.*

The port of West Point is now altogether abandoned by the Southern Railways as an export terminal, that company having established extensive wharves and shipping facilities at Norfolk (Pinners Point).

Only three vessels (steam) entered and cleared for foreign ports from West Point (sub-port of Richmond), and their cargoes consisted of cotton, valued at 382,637 dol.

Specifications of Articles Imported into Richmond, Va., during the Year 1895.

Articles.	Value.
	Dollars.
Tin-plate	33,012
Farm and garden seeds	26,936
China and earthenware	10,746
Guano	10,200
Tobacco and cigars	7,260
Wines and spirits	5,401
Miscellaneous	11,559
Total	105,114

Return showing Value of Articles Imported into Richmond, Va., during the Year 1895.

Country.	Value.
	Dollars.
Great Britain	48,006
France	21,715
Orchilla, W.I.	10,200
Germany	7,781
Canada	4,124
Cuba	3,145
Other European countries	10,143
Total	105,114

LONDON:
Printed for Her Majesty's Stationery Office,
By HARRISON AND SONS,
Printers in Ordinary to Her Majesty.
(75 5 | 96—H & S 2151)

FOREIGN OFFICE.
1896.
ANNUAL SERIES.

No. 1725.

DIPLOMATIC AND CONSULAR REPORTS ON TRADE AND FINANCE.

UNITED STATES.

REPORT FOR THE YEAR 1895

ON THE

TRADE OF THE CONSULAR DISTRICT OF CHICAGO.

REFERENCE TO PREVIOUS REPORT, Annual Series No. 1543.

Presented to both Houses of Parliament by Command of Her Majesty,
MAY, 1896.

LONDON:
PRINTED FOR HER MAJESTY'S STATIONERY OFFICE,
BY HARRISON AND SONS, ST. MARTIN'S LANE,
PRINTERS IN ORDINARY TO HER MAJESTY.

And to be purchased, either directly or through any Bookseller, from
EYRE & SPOTTISWOODE, East Harding Street, Fleet Street, E.C., and
32, Abingdon Street, Westminster, S.W.; or
JOHN MENZIES & Co., 12, Hanover Street, Edinburgh, and
90, West Nile Street, Glasgow; or
HODGES, FIGGIS, & Co., Limited, 104, Grafton Street, Dublin.

1896.

[C. 7919—93.]   *Price Sevenpence Halfpenny.*

New Series of Reports.

Reports of the Annual Series have been issued from Her Majesty's Diplomatic and Consular Officers at the following places, and may be obtained from the sources indicated on the title-page:—

No.		Price.	No.		Price.
1603.	Sofia	2½d.	1664.	Manila	½d.
1604.	Belgrade	2½d.	1665.	Florence	5¼d.
1605.	Shanghai	2½d.	1666.	Dakar	½d.
1606.	Canton	1½d.	1667.	Havre	2d.
1607.	Meshed	1¼d.	1668.	Rouen	2d.
1608.	Erzeroum	1d.	1669.	Corfu	½d.
1609.	Galatz	2d.	1670.	Calais	1d.
1610.	Port Said	1½d.	1671.	Tehran	1½d.
1611.	The Hague	1½d.	1672.	Barcelona	2d.
1612.	Calais	1d.	1673.	Amsterdam	1d.
1613.	Newchwang	1d.	1674.	Bordeaux	2½d.
1614.	Copenhagen	1d.	1675.	Warsaw	1d.
1615.	Odessa	2d.	1676.	Havana	1½d.
1616.	Gothenburg	2d.	1677.	Berlin	1d.
1617.	Mannheim	1½d.	1678.	Beira	1½d.
1618.	Old Calabar	5d.	1679.	Saigon	1d.
1619.	Pekin	2½d.	1680.	Trebizond	1d.
1620.	Taganrog	2d.	1681.	Vera Cruz	1½d.
1621.	Brindisi	2½d.	1682.	Patras	1d.
1622.	Jeddah	1½d.	1683.	La Rochelle	1½d.
1623.	Hamburg	3d.	1684.	Madrid	1½d.
1624.	Angora	1½d.	1685.	Belgrade	2d.
1625.	Buda-Pesth	1½d.	1686.	Algiers	5d.
1626.	Beyrout	1d.	1687.	Galveston	2½d.
1627.	Bushire	2d.	1688.	New Orleans	2d.
1628.	Stettin	2½d.	1689.	Suakin	1d.
1629.	Porto Rico	1d.	1690.	Pernambuco	1d.
1630.	Rotterdam	½d.	1691.	Guatemala	1½d.
1631.	Alexandria	1½d.	1692.	Guayaquil	1d.
1632.	Tokio	2½d.	1693.	Wênchow	1d.
1633.	Tangier	1½d.	1694.	Piræus	3d.
1634.	Oporto	1½d.	1695.	Tokio	3d.
1635.	St. Petersburg	4d.	1696.	Marseilles	1d.
1636.	Dantzig	2d.	1697.	Manila	1d.
1637.	Macao	1d.	1698.	Jerusalem	1d.
1638.	Hiogo and Osaka	6d.	1699.	Cherbourg	2d.
1639.	Naples	1½d.	1700.	Leghorn	1½d.
1640.	Kiungchow	½d.	1701.	Boston	1½d.
1641.	Rome	1½d.	1702.	Kiungchow	1d.
1642.	Beira	½d.	1703.	Naples	2½d.
1643.	St. Jago de Cuba	4½d.	1704.	Stockholm	2d.
1644.	Christiania	6d.	1705.	Corunna	2d.
1645.	Lisbon	1½d.	1706.	Rio de Janeiro	2½d.
1646.	Brussels	½d.	1707.	San José	1d.
1647.	Vera Cruz	½d.	1708.	Paramaribo	2d.
1648.	Tunis	1d.	1709.	Brest	1½d.
1649.	Antwerp	1d.	1710.	Montevideo	½d.
1650.	Tokio	1d.	1711.	Charleston	2½d.
1651.	Honolulu	½d.	1712.	Baltimore	1d.
1652.	Stettin	1½d.	1713.	Tripoli	1d.
1653.	Bangkok	1d.	1714.	Callao	½d.
1654.	Batoum	1½d.	1715.	Ningpo	1d.
1655.	Mexico	9½d.	1716.	Dunkirk	1½d.
1656.	Odessa	1½d.	1717.	Batoum	2d.
1657.	Réunion	1d.	1718.	Hankow	1½d.
1658.	Tokio	1½d.	1719.	Foochow	3½d.
1659.	Maranham	1d.	1720.	Syra	½d.
1660.	Copenhagen	1d.	1721.	Panama	1d.
1661.	Berlin	1½d.	1722.	Batavia	1½d.
1662.	Teheran	2½d.	1723.	Genoa	3d.
1663.	Salonica	1½d.	1724.	Cagliari	2½d.

No. 1725

Reference to previous Report, Annual Series No. 1543.

UNITED STATES.

CHICAGO.

Mr. Vansittart to the Marquis of Salisbury.

My Lord,   Chicago, March 27, 1896.

I HAVE the honour to transmit herewith my Report on the Trade and Commerce of Chicago during the year 1895, together with the Reports of the British Vice-Consuls at Denver, Kansas City, St. Louis, and St. Paul.

Mr. P. E. Burrough has drawn up an exceedingly complete and interesting Report, and many of the subjects treated by him in full, viz. Oklahoma and Indian Territories, &c., have never yet been reported upon. All manner of subjects which can interest the British importer or exporter in the western parts of the United States, as well as valuable suggestions, have been carefully gone into, and I would venture to call special attention to the following matters in his Report, viz., the livestock and packing house industry; grain situation; railroads and transportation; and also the building of the Kansas City, Pittsburg and Gulf Railroad from Kansas City, Missouri, to Port Arthur, Texas.

Kansas City is situated in the centre of a vast agricultural region where crops of such magnitude, and livestock in such numbers are produced yearly, that that district is entitled to one of the foremost places of interest and importance in the United States.

Perhaps the most important item is the transportation of produce from the west to British and European markets viâ the Gulf of Mexico ports, instead of viâ the Atlantic coast ports.

I have, &c.
(Signed)   A. G. VANSITTART.

(2148)

UNITED STATES.

Report on the Trade and Commerce of the Consular District of Chicago for the Year 1895.

Abstract of Contents.

	PAGE
Chicago Trade Report—	
Introductory and general review	5
Trade of Chicago	7
Produce trade	8
Wholesale trade	14
Manufacturing trade	16
Shipping and freights	18
Drainage canal	22
Miscellaneous	23
Denver Trade Report	27
Kansas Trade Report—	
Introductory	32
Statistics	33
Increase business, 7 years	34
Internal revenue receipts, 5 years	34
Name of Kansas City	34
Street improvements	35
Consular post	35
Death rate	35
Retail trade	35
Butter and eggs	35
Department stores	35
Business failures	35
Caustic soda, saltpetre, essential oils	35
Oatmeal	36
Sterilised air	36
Hints to British merchants	36
Customs receipts	36
Swedish iron	36
Tinplate	36
Furs	37
Salt	37
Straw matting	38
Earthenware, crockery, china, glassware	38
Knit stockings	38
Rice	38
Miscellaneous importation	38
Agricultural implements	38
Binding twine	39
Apples, cold storage	39
Plate glass	40
Fuller's earth	40
Enamel ware	40
Wholesale trade	40
Silicate of aluminum	41
Street railway	41
Bank clearings	41
Labour complaints	42
Labour condition	42
Labour for women	43
Labour for children	43
Strikes	43
Potatoes	43
Russian thistle	43
Fraudulent employment agencies	43
Investment warning	43
Sub-soiling	44

NOTE.—Exchange is taken at 4 dol. 86 c. to the 1*l*.

CHICAGO.

ABSTRACT of Contents—continued.

	PAGE
Kansas Trade Report—continued—	
Divorce laws	44
Gold discoveries	44
United States Bond deal	44
Smelter at Kansas City	44
Smelter statistics	44
United States mine report	46
Silver ore imported	46
Metal production of United States, 1895	47
Flax-seed and oil	47
Tanning by electricity	48
Tanning by canaigre	48
Investments	48
Game and poultry	48
Centre of population	48
Navigation injured by irrigation	41
Cement	48
Waterworks	48
Boulevards	49
Gas	49
Mail	49
New custom-house	49
Bicycles	49
Hides, horn, hoof, and hair	49
Tallow, stearine, bristles, bones, &c.	49
Milling	49
Overcrowded cities	49
Military forts	49
United States Government Penitentiary	50
Soldiers' Home	50
Lottery companies	50
Tariff issue	50
Small-pox	50
Horseless mail wagons	50
Electricity	50
Zinc and lead	50
Mineral deposits	51
Walnut, cherry lumber	51
Oak, ash lumber	51
Steamship lines	51
Savings banks	51
Building loan associations	51
Warning, bogus mining stocks	51
Shipbuilding lumber	51
Stockyards	51
Texas live-stock	52
Export of cattle from Republic of Mexico	68
McKinley Tariff, effects on cattle	68
Wilson Bill, effects on cattle	68
Texas fever	69
Dehorning of cattle	70
Armour Packing Company	71
Packing of hogs, western point	73
Fertilizer	75
Export of hog product for 1895 to all foreign countries	75
Oleomargarine	77
Horses and mules	78
Grain	79
Grain, viâ Gulf of Mexico	93
Distances	94
Rumoured steamship line	96
Railways, City	96

(2148)

UNITED STATES.

Abstract of Contents—continued.

	PAGE
Kansas Trade Report—continued—	
Proposed new docks	102
New dredge and construction company	102
Kansas—	
Size, population	102
Droughts	103
Alfalfa	103
Kaffir and Jerusalem corn	103
General information	103
Natural gas	103
Lead and zinc	104
Broom corn	104
Agricultural products	104
Quantities, values	105
Live-stock	105
Labour statistics	106
Strikes	106
Statistics	106
Prohibition	106
Salt	106
Fruit	107
Milling industry	107
Population statistics	108
Immigration	108
Importation of young women from Ireland by Catholics	109
Report of Railroad Commissioners	109
Mines, lead and zinc	110
Gold discovery	110
Cotton	110
Oil discovery	111
Nebraska—	
Crops	111
Manufacturing	111
Livestock shipments	111
Sugar, beet	111
,, products	112
,, bounties	113
Railroads	114
Proposed new railways	114
Irrigation	114
Omaha City—	
Trans-Mississippi Exposition, 1897	115
Custom-house receipts	116
Death rate	116
Smelter products	116
Bank clearings	116
Packing-houses	117
Livestock	117
Missouri—	
Resources	118
Lead and zinc	118
Mining improvements	119
Mineral statistics	119
Livestock	120
Poultry, melons	121
Butter, canned goods	121
Proposed new railways	121
Finances	121
Apples	121
Population	121
Capital, investments	122

Abstract of Contents—continued.

CHICAGO.

ABSTRACT of Contents—continued.

	PAGE
Missouri—continued—	
Banks	122
Missouri productions	123
Saint Joseph—	
Textile manufactories	123
Packing houses	124
Internal revenue	124
Custom-house receipts	124
Oklahoma—	
Resources	124
Five civilised tribes	124
Timber	124
Grain products	124
Bill in Congress for Statehood	125
Desperadoes	125
Railways	125
Educational notes	125
Population	125
Banks	125
Livestock	126
Cotton	126
Cotton-oil mill	126
Gold discovered	126
Indian territory—	
Resources	126
Population	126
Five civilised tribes, Indians	126
Livestock items	127
Cotton	127
Cotton-oil mill	127
Strikes	127
Bill to Congress for Statehood	127
Railways	128
St. Louis	128
St. Paul	135

CHICAGO.

Introductory and General Review.

The commercial and manufacturing record of Chicago for 1895 shows a decided improvement over that for the preceding year, though the totals are smaller in value, and do not average much greater in volume than those of 1892. But this was to be expected. The year 1895 was only the third of the series, and it would perhaps be out of accord with the teachings of history, if this city, and the country at large, had thus early recovered from the effects of the panic which swept the United States in the early part of 1893. There was, however, a noteworthy improvement in conditions over those of 1894. A greater number of toilers found employment, most of them at higher wages than it had been necessary to insist on 2 years ago, and the city was spared the repetition of almost overwhelming disaster from strikes such as paralysed American railroads, tied up numerous other departments of activity, for want of material or ability to

(2148)

supply the market, and caused the destruction of many millions worth of property in 1894.

Produce is the one great department which shows a decrease, and this is mostly due to smaller crops (corn in 1894), in the sections which chiefly directly supply the markets of Chicago. The total gain of 2·9 per cent. is a gratifying one, mostly by contrast with the great decadence noted for 1894, which was all the greater as it followed on the closing of the World's Fair; 1894 being a season of reaction from the exhilarating experiences of 1893.

Corn was very heavy, though in such short supplies through the summer, the three preceding crops having been small ones, that it was seriously doubted if there would be enough for the consumer's use till the new crop was available. On a big yield being assured it dropped to the lowest prices known for the third part of a century, and oats followed the example. Hog products, too, were unusually low in price, and that fact failed to bring out the active English demand for meats which has been the rule in other seasons of cheapness. Speculative trading on the Board of Trade was dull most of the year.

The first decided rise in the prices of merchandise last year was in dry goods, this being stimulated by fears that the cotton crop would be short in yield. Then leather boomed on rumours that the supply of cattle was much smaller than usual. The iron and steel interests soon responded to a sharp demand which kept the mills active, and enabled the manufacturers to make large profits, as they mostly worked on ore, the supplies of which had been contracted for while trade was dull. The demand for material chiefly came from parties who had suspended buying early in 1893.

There was not much construction of new railroad lines, but old rails had to be replaced by new ones, and there was a good demand for buildings iron and steel, with more wanted for vessels, work on which was exceedingly active. Undoubtedly much more iron and steel would have been consumed last year but for the fact that the manufacturers pushed up prices too high. One notable result of this was the making of a contract for 10,000 tons of rails to go to the Pacific coast, and a more general one was a sharp falling-off in the demand late in the autumn.

There was but little advance in the demand for luxuries, and it is stated on all hands that the average buyer has been notably conservative during the last 12 months, as if he had not forgotten the experiences of 1893, and was more disposed to caution in holding back a reserve for another possibly "rainy day"; but payments were prompt and collections easy, and responsibilities at banks met with little trouble.

There was a noticeable falling-off in wheat and flour receipts which is partly due to the fact that the crop of winter wheat was short last year. Receipts of corn were also smaller last year than in 1894, though the crop of 1895 is understood to be the biggest ever grown in the United States.

CHICAGO.

It is pleasing to note one important reform, viz., the Civil Service Act. The commencement of the present year sees it in full, fair working order. Policemen, firemen, clerks, and other city employés have been appointed under it, and are now at work.

Finally, it may be stated that the changes of conditions in the last 12 months include a decrease of, perhaps, 5 per cent. in the average cost of living, though rents are somewhat higher on account of a partial filling up of room that had been left vacant after the closing of the World's Fair. As regards labour, the tendency has been to obtain larger results by the employment of about the same number of workers as before. The public health was good throughout the year, and there are distinct signs of a steady, though perhaps slow, revival of trade and prosperity in the future.

Trade of Chicago.

The following table tells in a concise and general way the story of the year for all the commercial interests of the city:—

		1895.		1894.	
		Quantity.	Amount.	Quantity.	Amount.
			£		£
Bank clearings	...	...	951,542,103	...	889,782,420
Board of Trade clearings	...	...	16,109,937	...	11,558,824
Grain, cars inspected	Number ...	223,077	...	204,556	...
Flour and grain received	Bushels ...	189,432,919	...	187,553,470	...
Flour and grain shipped	,, ...	171,464,137	...	148,638,821	...
Live-stock received	Head ...	13,921,927	...	13,557,316	...

An increase in the bank clearings of 61,760,412*l*., nearly 7 per cent., means that the business of the entire community increased about that much over last year.

The Board of Trade clearings indicate for the great grain exchange what the bank clearings do for the whole community. Last year they increased, about 40 per cent. improvement as compared with 1894. There was an enormous swell in speculation in the spring, when wheat advanced suddenly 1*s*. 2¾*d*. a bushel; but those days, when commission firms turned away business because overwhelmed by it, have since been followed by days of excessive dulness.

The total of actual grain received and shipped shows that the swell in the Board of Trade's transactions was not entirely in its speculative departments. The grain receipts exceeded those of 1894 by almost 2,000,000 bushels, the shipments by nearly 23,000,000 bushels.

The stockyard interests had the same kind of experience, the live-stock receipts exceeding those of 1894 by 364,611 head.

The total surplus of the 22 State banks was 1,702,144*l*., as against 1,580,420*l*. in 1894, an increase of 121,724*l*., showing a net gain of 4·8 per cent. on the capital stock of 2,531,340*l*. Dividends

State banks.

paid by the State banks in 1895 were 16,896,257*l*., an increase of 1,306,511*l*., and total loans were 14,068,620*l*., an increase of 2,275,528*l*. against the previous year. The relative financial strength of State and national banks does not differ greatly, the State banks having had at the beginning of 1895 a surplus of 57·5 per cent., and national banks of 66·1 per cent. of their respective capitalisations. The percentage of dividends paid by each class of banks was about the same.

Real estate. The sales were somewhat less in number, but considerations were higher. Thus there were 15,802 sales, consideration 23,628,396*l*. in 1895, as against 16,606 sales, and consideration 20,496,576*l*. in 1894. The average number of sales daily in 1895 was 52, as against 55 in previous year. The average consideration for each sale in 1895 was 1,495*l*., as against 1,232*l*. in 1894.

Building trade. Although the year was not in all respects a satisfactory one from a business point of view, yet something like 7,216,494*l*. were invested in new buildings, or nearly 309,278*l*. more than in 1894. There were not as many structures put up by 1,200 as there were in 1894, and the frontage was 14,000 feet less. The expenditure was greater, partly because there were a number of costly buildings erected in the business district, and partly because materials and labour were lower in 1894 than in 1895. The amount invested in buildings last year was very much less than in 1891 and 1892. But those were World's Fair years, into which was crowded much building, which, but for the Exposition, would have been postponed for some time. Then, too, the cost of construction was much greater than it is now.

The total number of building permits granted during the year was 8,633, with 218,360 feet frontage, and cost 7,218,566*l*. The year was also notable for a development of new electrical street enterprises, and great activity in the building of new street railroad lines.

Produce Trade of Chicago.

The movement of produce, compared with that of the preceding year, will be seen by the following table, which gives the receipts and shipments of the principal articles compiled by the Board of Trade:—

CHICAGO.

Principal Articles.		Receipts. 1895.	Receipts. 1894.	Shipments. 1895.	Shipments. 1894.
Flour	Barrels	3,005,460	4,223,182	2,532,000	3,714,007
Wheat	Bushels	20,637,642	25,665,902	22,775,780	18,213,443
Corn	,,	59,527,718	64,951,815	59,964,265	54,528,482
Oats	,,	79,890,792	63,144,885	66,839,596	50,376,089
Rye	,,	1,657,216	1,368,157	1,168,252	1,100,558
Barley	,,	14,194,981	13,418,391	9,322,244	7,707,218
Grass seeds	Lbs.	63,868,526	47,524,961	65,566,528	66,207,092
Flax seeds	Bushels	8,525,237	5,102,668	4,726,818	2,353,757
Cured meats	Lbs.	172,203,523	139,003,374	698,210.341	570,276,662
Dressed beef	,,	109,351,714	136,476,783	910,339,175	1,080,053,993
Canned meats	Cases	7,584	64,636	1,143,131	1,159,748
Lard	Lbs.	53,936,324	63,177,799	387,437,689	409,211,462
Pork	Barrels	9,672	5,999	300,026	272,878
Cheese	Lbs.	59,012,937	60,424,190	52,226,141	56,062,563
Butter	,,	185,453,997	144,868,216	176,846,168	155,062,053
Live hogs	Number	7,901,883	7,483,228	2,103,244	2,465,058
Cattle	,,	2,599,422	2,974,363	789,925	950,738
Sheep	,,	3,420,622	3,099,725	476,587	333,398
Hides	Lbs.	90,822,102	91,640,992	174,807,918	200,652,329
Wool	,,	51,371,694	51,544,381	63,441,329	69,101,205
Coal	Tons	6,092,284	5,336,124	985,158	810,417
Lumber	Met. feet	1,638,130	1,562,527	773,983	632,069
Salt	Barrels	1,994,053	1,287,521	806,144	688,820
Potatoes	Bushels	4,934,391	4,114,899	1,123,556	1,051,594
Eggs	Cases	2,146,040	2,106,680	1,207,373	1,221,355

Wheat and flour. For the 11 months of the year, January to November, the average margin for milling was less than in any of the previous 9 years. On the whole the action of the wheat market during the past year was similar in many respects to that of the two preceding years. It has been a year of over-production of all kinds of grain. The average price of No. 2 wheat during the year was 2s. 7d. a bushel, against 2s. 4d. in 1894. The highest price reached was in the month of May, viz., 3s. 7½d., and the lowest in February, viz., 2s. 0½d. per bushel.

Corn. The average price of No. 2 corn throughout the year was 1s. 7½d. a bushel against 1s. 9d. in 1894. The highest price reached was in May, viz., 2s. 4d., and the lowest in December, viz., 1s. per bushel. The low prices during the latter part of the year stimulated the export demand, but the new England and interior demand was never allowed to become very urgent. The movement of corn during the last month of navigation was so erratic that the range in vessel rates was unusually wide.

Oats. The interesting features in the oats market were confined mainly to the first half of the year. A sharp cut in all-rail rates eastward to about the lowest point on record led shipping houses to get the grain into New York, although there was no sensational demand in that quarter. Over 600,000 bushels were taken out of store in a few days, and No. 2 cash oats touched 1s. 3d. The average price of No. 2 oats throughout the year was low, viz., 1s. 0½d., against 1s. 3½d. in 1894. The highest price reached was only 1s. 3½d. in June. The lowest in the months of November and December, viz., 8d. a bushel.

Rye and barley. Distillers and millers bought in a conservative way, and not so as to stimulate prices at any period. The average price of No. 2 rye throughout the year was only 1d. higher than preceding year, viz., 1s. 8½d.

Barley prices averaged fully 40 per cent. lower on the latest crop than on that of 1894, due to the much larger proportion of light weight grain. The choicest came from Minnesota, containing the largest proportion of saccharine matter, and commanded a premium. Wisconsin barley stood second. Owing to the low prices prevailing, a big shipping business was done to Eastern markets, and the amount shipped was over 25 per cent. more than in 1894. The average price of barley, considering sales of 1894 barley, made during the early part of the year was 1s. 5½d.

Flax seed.

The average price of No. 1 flax-seed in the market during the year was about 4s. 11½d., as against 5s. 7½d. in 1894. Large crops were reported almost without exception, as the weather conditions were favourable in most of the lands where this industry is carried on. At the close of the year there was a visible supply in storage at the Western lake ports of fully 2,700,000 bushels.

Provisions.

Trade in provisions was quiet and uneventful. It was a year of low prices in all lines, heavy supplies at all times, and indifferent demand most of the year. The cholera scare of the early autumn was the occasion of numerous speculators, taking the long side, in the expectation that receipts of hogs would fall off. Prices were low, mess pork selling at an average price of 2l. 2s. 8d., against 2l. 11s. 6d. in 1894.

Packing.

The packing industry in the Union stockyards for the first 11 months of 1895, while perhaps not as satisfactory to the packers as it was 2 years ago, was larger in volume than in the corresponding period in 1894, excepting in cattle. Although the prices during the earlier months were higher than for many years, particularly on light or cutting cattle, the ranches did not send their usual quota of this grade. The prices on hogs and hog products steadily declined from the beginning of the year until in December they were lower than for some years. Collections were better than last year, and things seem to be shaping themselves for a large and satisfactory business in 1896. Chicago still stands perhaps unrivalled as the market which at all times can use the live-stock of the country with the best results to the producer, and supply the consumers of this country, and the world, with the highest class of finished product, always at competing prices.

Live-stock.

Native beef steers averaged about 1s. 3d. higher than in 1894. Native cows advanced 1s. 5½d. on smaller supplies. Texas cattle averaged 1s. 3d. higher. Top range cattle sold at 2s. 0½d. The highest realised on fed Texas cattle was 1l. 3s. 8½d.

The number of Texas cattle was the smallest since 1886, but included a larger number of cotton-seed meal fed cattle than ever before. Total receipts of all kinds of cattle at Chicago for the year were 2,595,000, the smallest year's total since 1887, nearly 400,000 less than arrived in 1894, and nearly 1,000,000 less than arrived in 1892.

Hogs.

The hog business was anything but satisfactory to country dealers. Chicago was the only market of the leading Western States that received more hogs than in 1894. Receipts in 1895 increased about 420,000, while Omaha decreased 750,000, Kansas City 105,000, and St. Louis over 60,000. Com-

CHICAGO.

bined receipts at the four markets for 1895 were about 12,600,000, which total has been surpassed 3 out of the previous 5 years. It was 440,000 smaller than in 1894; 2,460,000 larger than in 1893; almost 1,000,000 smaller than in 1891; and 500,000 smaller than in 1890.

The prevalence of hog cholera, or swine plague, carried away numbers of little pigs, and forced a very large number of young hogs to market from infected localities. Average price of all grades of hogs for 1895 was 18s. 1d., or 3s. 1d. lower than in 1894. The average weight of hogs for 1895 was about 230 lbs., against 233 lbs. for 1894, and 240 lbs. for 1893. Early in the year hogs were comparatively light, because corn was so scarce and high, and hogs relatively low. About 7,900,000 arrived at Chicago for the 12 months of 1895.

Supplies of sheep were the heaviest ever recorded at the Union stockyards, and foot up a grand total of 3,400,000 head, which shows an increase over 1894 of nearly 400,000 head. There was a great demand for export sheep during the whole year. Over 200,000 sheep were exported from Chicago during the year, nearly all of which went to England, with a few to France and Belgium. The feeding demand has also been better than usual, and fully 250,000 light sheep were shipped to the country during the year for that purpose. The top price of the year was 1l. 2s. 8d. in May, and the best sheep at the close of the year were selling at 14s. 5d. The average price of the year was 13s. 7d., against 11s. 6d. in 1894. *Sheep.*

During 1895 Chicago received in round numbers 113,300 horses, or 16,000 more than arrived in 1894, and 12,000 more than the previous largest receipts on record. Trade was generally active throughout the year, and prices for drafters, drivers, coachers, and carriage horses averaged about 3l. 1s. 10½d. per head higher than in 1894, while streeters averaged 2l. 1s. 3d., and saddlers about 4l. 2s. 6d. per head lower. *Horses.*

The following table gives combined receipts of cattle, hogs, and sheep at Chicago, Kansas City, Omaha, and St. Louis for the last 7 years:—

Year.	Cattle.	Hogs.	Sheep.
1895	5,537,844	12,660,091	4,933,532
1894	6,148,725	13,099,807	4,225,348
1893	6,403,154	10,197,533	4,203,005
1892	6,459,270	12,572,999	3,070,407
1891	5,752,634	13,578,228	3,057,735
1890	6,094,846	13,160,826	3,156,297
1889	5,107,059	10,051,820	2,641,271

Prices of all kinds of meat, with the exception of veal, were reduced from 10 to 15 per cent. The best steer beef sold from 7d. to 11d.; choice mutton from 5d. to 7d.; pork roasts, 3d.; and other kinds proportionately low. Buyers practised economy and *Price of meat.*

bought sparingly. The consumption of beef-tea has increased so largely that 50 per cent. more was made by the firms engaged in its manufacture than in the preceding year. The quality of the animals received at the stockyards was good. Hogs were exceptionally good, cattle likewise, and the same can be said of sheep. These facts were due to the abundance of grain in all sections, and the prevailing low price. Owing to the Government having instituted local inspection of live-stock to be used by the packers, every animal slaughtered is at the present time inspected.

Hides, pelt, and tallow.

There were some sensational advances in hides. Native steers, which are the leading selection of packer hides, were quoted at 4d. per lb. in January and December, but during the year touched 7d.; the highest point in the history of the trade. The advance was caused by the heavy purchases of the United States Leather Company. They bought all the hides available in this country, as well as sent their purchasing representatives to all the principal European and South American cities. The year in hides closed with small stocks, and a feeling that the trade in 1896 will be steadier and less adventurous.

The pelt market was not changed materially as compared with 1894. The slaughter of sheep was large, and this fact, coupled with the stagnant condition of the wool market, kept pelts from rallying from the unprecedently low prices of the last 2 years. Dealers ascribe this weakness to the liberality of the Government in admitting, practically free of duty, the wool product of the world.

Tallow was more depressed than for any year during the last 5, caused by the remission of the tariff, and the admission of the Australian product in large quantities. The average price for the year was from $1\frac{3}{4}d.$ to $2\frac{1}{4}d.$ There were practically no exports during the year, and home consumption was all that dealers had to depend on for a market.

Wool.

The year 1895 was an unsatisfactory one to most of those engaged in the wool business. But the receipts in the Chicago market increased over those of 1894 fully 25 per cent. Most of the mills were running late in the year, and the consumption was about normal. Immense shipments of wool were received from the territories of Montana, Idaho, and Utah which averaged $5\frac{1}{2}d.$; domestic, all grades, averaging 7d. Dealers and shippers are encouraged by a prospect of a regulation of freight rates to Boston from all Western points, former rates having done much to retard shipments.

Salt.

The movement of salt was fully 15 per cent. larger than that of the preceding year, while prices ruled from 8 to 10 per cent. lower. A decided gain in the Southern trade was experienced, and Michigan salt more than held its own in connection with the imported article, the relative merits of the two deciding the controversy. The quality of the salt was good, and the average price during the year was $2s. 10\frac{3}{4}d.$ On the whole, dealers pronounce the trade satisfactory, and are encouraged at the outlook for future business.

CHICAGO.

Coal.
The tonnage in coal was heavy. In anthracite coal both dock and all-rail showed almost an even tonnage, as compared with preceding year. A satisfactory feature of the trade is the fact that prices have ruled higher than for the corresponding period of 1894, the advance being from 2s. 0¾d. to 3s. 1d. The major portion of the soft coal received here comes from Indiana and Illinois; the shipments from the latter showing a vastly increased tonnage for 1895 over any previous year. The northern and central districts show the largest gains. There has also been a large increase in the receipts of Hocking coal, and for this grade the city has become a large distributing centre. West Virginia and Kentucky are also extensive shippers, and the Southern cannel finds a ready market here. Despite the fact that Iowa is in possession of extensive coalfields, none of its products reach Chicago —home consumption and western shipments taking the entire tonnage mined. The important feature of the year was the formation of a number of combinations, dealers associating themselves for the purpose of cutting down the individual expenses and regulating an even price for certain products, thereby benefiting the general public. A nominal price at retail for the last sales of the year was 1l. 6s. 9d. Wilmington and La Salle coal sold at 6s. 7d. f.o.b. (goods delivered) at the mines. Hocking at 12s. 4½d. f.o.b., Chicago and Brazil block at 9s. 5¾d.

Lumber.
The cargo market of 1895 for lumber, as a rule, was steady. The trade of the year in white pine was fairly good. Business in hard woods was much improved, manufacturing interests constantly increasing, and the use of this grade being more popular it now constitutes about 20 per cent. out of the total lumber trade of the city. A comparison of shipments made during the last 2 years shows an increase in favour of 1895 of 16,000,000 feet, or almost 20 per cent. A like comparison of city comsumption favours last year by 31,000,000 feet, or a gain of about 4 per cent.

Common inch sold at 2l. 5s. 4½d. to 2l. 7s. 4½d. up to nearly the middle of August, when a decline set it.

Butter and cheese.
Dairy products, on the whole, proved profitable to the farmer, prices being steady to firm, as compared with the previous year. The Butter and Egg Board of the Produce Exchange has been largely instrumental in bringing about good results by the establishment and maintenance of legitimate prices, on which buyers and sellers alike throughout the west have learned to place confidence, as a basis for their contract sales. Chicago receipts, during the early summer months, show an increase for that period of over 34 per cent. over those of last year, while the Eastern markets do not show over 9 per cent. increase for the same period. The business in cold-storage was large. The amount being estimated at 180,000 packages of an average weight of 60 lbs., and the goods, contrary to expectation, were put away at very good prices.

The supply of fresh country stock cheese was ample throughout the year, and prices ruled steady, with little fluctuations. The lowest point of the year was in April, when 5d. to 5½d. was

Potatoes and vegetables.

touched, and the highest prices were in December, when 10½d. was the quotation. Cooler stock was heavy at the end of the year, 120,000 cases being in storage.

Receipts of potatoes ran as high as 100 cars per day, and as many as 275 cars, 130,000 bushels, were on track at one time. The average daily consumption for all purposes is only 30 cars. Consumers have been especially favoured, the charge for transfer from car to commission dealer being 1½d., and an added 2½d. constituting his profit. Thus the best varieties have been placed in the retailer's hands at from 1s. 0¼d. to 1s. 2¾d. per bushel. Staple vegetables sold fully 40 per cent. cheaper than in 1894. The market gardening industry has increased rapidly within the last few years, and supplies were bountiful throughout the entire season. Green peas were 50 per cent. cheaper than in 1894; onions the same; cauliflower, 60 per cent.; cabbage, the same; tomatoes, 75 per cent.; string beans, 80 per cent., and sweet corn the same.

Fruit.

The total crop of apples in 1895 is estimated at 24,000,000 barrels, that of Illinois being 1,375,000. The crop in the belt of country extending from the Missouri River in the west to the mountains of Virginia and Pennsylvania on the east, and from about the 40th parallel of latitude extending about 200 miles south, was so great that prices were kept on a very low basis, viz., 7s. 2d. to 8s. 3d. for standard stock December 1.

Receipts of peaches from Michigan were very heavy, as many as 250,000 baskets of fruit arriving in a single day. Cities like Kansas City, St. Louis, St. Paul, and Minneapolis were supplied from this point by the train-load, and hundreds of smaller places had regular daily car shipments. A fair estimate of the Michigan crop places the total at some 4,000,000 bushels in all. Prices were relatively low, good qualities selling at 4s. 1½d. per bushel.

The Illinois crop of melons was good, this State having developed a capacity for producing large quantities within recent years. Alton and vicinity has become a large producer. The Osage retained its place as a favourite, selling at 1s. 0¼d. to 1s. 5¼d. per crate.

Wholesale Trade.

The following table gives the totals for last year, with corresponding figures for 1894, of the business done in the wholesale trade:—

CHICAGO.

Articles.	Value. 1895.	Value. 1894.
	£	£
Dry goods and carpets	18,556,700	15,464,000
Groceries	13,608,247	12,783,505
Lumber	7,216,494	7,113,402
Manufactured iron	3,298,969	2,474,226
Clothing	4,020,618	3,917,525
Boots and shoes	7,422,680	6,185,566
Drugs and chemicals	1,701,033	1,546,391
Crockery and glassware	1,206,185	1,237,113
Hats and caps	1,649,484	1,597,938
Millinery	927,835	1,030,927
Tobacco and cigars	3,092,783	2,783,504
Fresh and salt fish and oysters	1,443,298	1,391,752
Oil	876,288	1,000,000
Dried fruits	876,288	979,382
Building material	824,742	824,742
Furs	721,649	752,577
Carriages	371,134	360,824
Pianos, organs, and instruments	1,701,033	1,670,103
Music books and sheet music	123,711	103,092
Books, stationery, and wall-paper	5,061,855	5,051,546
Paper	5,412,370	5,154,638
Paper stock	927,835	876,288
Pig-iron	3,453,607	2,628,865
Coal	3,628,865	3,298,969
Hardware and cutlery	4,432,989	4,123,712
Wooden and willow ware	1,144,329	804,123
Liquors	3,402,061	3,092,783
Jewellery, watches, and diamonds	4,226,803	4,123,712
Leather and findings	773,195	721,650
Pig-lead and copper	1,113,402	927,835
Iron ore	515,463	412,371
Miscellaneous	1,237,113	1,237,113
Totals	104,969,058	95,670,174

Increase for the year, a little over 8 per cent.

Wholesale dry goods. Everything considered, it is believed that the results of the years have been most satisfactory to all concerned, and especially to those doing business in Chicago and the tributory territories. There have been comparatively few failures, and, generally speaking, the condition of all dry goods merchants is better than it has been for some years.

Retail dry goods. The retail dry goods business of the country, as a whole, showed an increase over 1894 of from 20 to 35 per cent. during the first six months of the year, and during the last six months quite considerable gains in business were realised. During the year there was an added decrease in the selling price of many of the leading lines of dry goods, silks being especially low, as were dress goods, men's furnishing goods, and hosiery. Carpets reached a very low point, linens remained firm, while cotton goods, as a single exception, were slightly advanced.

Groceries. Considerably more business was done by the wholesale grocery

(2148)

establishments during the year than in 1894, but by reason of a shrinkage in values of from 10 to 15 per cent. on the average, the monetary returns of trade show only a trifle increase in favour of 1895. Sugars declined fully 10 per cent., dried fruits 25 per cent., farinaceous goods 25 per cent., coffees 5 per cent.; flour is 10 per cent. higher; tea and salt fish remained steady.

The increase in the consumption of coffee causes a corresponding falling-off in the market for teas, particularly China sorts. But Indian, Ceylon, and Japan teas are annually becoming more popular in this country. There was a good market for spices throughout the year. Canned goods are constantly growing in popularity, and there was a disposition upon the part of the packers to put up a good quality of goods the past season.

Manufacturing Trade.

Iron and steel. The year 1895 was a remarkable one in the iron and steel industry, not only of Chicago, but of the entire country. The production was enormous. The advance from minimum condition and prices to October was as follows:—On pig-iron, from 1*l*. 4*s*. 8½*d*. to 1*l*. 12*s*. 11¾*d*. per ton, or 60 to 80 per cent.; on steel billets, 1*l*. 12*s*. 11¾*d*. to 2*l*. 1*s*. 3*d*. per ton, or 50 to 66 per cent.; on other of the open hearth and Bessemer products, 40 to 80 per cent. Iron ore did not to any great degree benefit by these advances, because the bulk of iron ore product is sold for deliveries covering periods of twelve months. The increase of the year over 1894 was fully 35 per cent. in tonnage, in some branches going as high as 50 per cent. In car wheel, and other heavy castings, there was an improvement of fully 25 per cent. Coke iron advanced to 2*l*. 13*s*. 7¼*d*., almost 100 per cent., when the boom came, while other irons took flights of about 1*l*. 0*s*. 7½*d*. on the ton.

Shipbuilding. The principal shipbuilding concern of the city states that, at the close of 1894, it had three ships under contract, while at the end of 1895 eight were ordered for as early completion as possible. The business of the two years has been on about the basis represented by these figures, 3 to 8.

Agricultural implements. The agricultural machinery trade in the west and north-west was fairly good in 1895. In the central States, such as Indiana, Illinois, Eastern Iowa, Missouri, and parts of Kansas and Wisconsin, the extreme drought prevailing during July greatly injured the small grain crop, causing a great many orders, particularly for thrashers and engines, to be countermanded. The great drawback which dealers had to contend with was slow collections. These were poorer than for a number of years past. In the last two years the farmer has been a scant buyer of tools on account of the prevailing conditions. His implements have been wearing out, and if crop prospects are at all good there will be an unusually brisk trade in 1896.

On the whole, export trade was fairly good, and manufactories were active throughout the year. Wrought-iron goods advanced 60 per cent., cast-iron 40 per cent., brass goods 20 per cent., and earthenware 20 per cent.

Copper. The tonnage of copper received was fully 20 per cent. greater than for the year preceding, and prices advanced 10 per cent. Total receipts are estimated at 4,000,000 lbs., at an average price of 5d. One cause of increased use is the fact that copper is much cheaper than 2 or 3 years ago. The great bulk of the copper used here comes from Montana, but little Lake Superior copper being received. New electrical processes, now in use, separates the gold and silver from the copper ore to the extent that the sheet grades 99 99–100 per cent. pure copper.

Pianos and organs. Chicago has had a steady growth in the manufacture of pianos and organs, each year becoming more a manufacturing centre and gradually encroaching on the business of the east. The number of instruments turned out was never so great, but the decline in prices prevented the otherwise excellent showing. Musical instruments sold well. Music books and sheet music had an increase of 20 per cent. in value of sales.

Hardware and cutlery. Hardware and cutlery trade presented a large increase in volume. The prices in staple goods, particularly nails and barbed wire, advanced; and the great bulk of manufactured goods, in which labour forms a large part of the cost, as a rule held firmly to the advances made during the year.

Oysters and fish. Trade in oysters and fish for 1895 was considerably increased. The use of these articles of diet has of late years become much extended, and Chicago is now in possession of an enormous business in both lines. Lake fish have been abundant, frozen stocks coming in at any time the supply ran at all short. In salt water varieties the market was well stocked at all times, and prices were comparatively low during the entire year.

From Newfoundland to the Gulf of Mexico the choicest fish, shrimps, scallops, turtle, and lobsters were received in immense quantities.

Boots and shoes. As a distributing point for shoes and rubbers Chicago stands first after Boston. Manufacturing is increasing, but the factories operated by Chicago capital are mainly in contiguous towns. In the number of pairs sold 1895 was equal to 1894, considerably in advance of 1893, but below the record of 1892. Shoes are 20 per cent. higher, owing to the advance in leather, but jobbers say the old prices will prevail in 1896. Tans sold well and bid fair to continue in favour. In this line Chicago is constantly adding to the territory for sales, and making inroads on sections of the country that formerly bought in the east exclusively.

Linseed oil mills. The business done by the linseed oil mills during last year was fully 20 per cent. greater than in 1894. The production almost equalled that of a normal year, a material gain, when it is considered that the panic brought a decline the first year of its existence of 11,000,000 gallons. The price of oil decreased by reason of the immense production of flax-seed, opening at 2s. 3d.,

UNITED STATES.

going in March to 2s. 4d., in June to 2s. 5d., and closing at 1s. 6¼d., or 9d. less than at the end of 1894. Formerly all cake was exported, but in 1895 scarcely 20 per cent. went abroad. The total production for the year is not far from 33,000,000 gallons.

Bicycles.

In the various branches of the bicycle business the year was one of unusual prosperity. Early in the spring the leading manufacturers reduced the price of wheels from 25l. 15s. 7d. to 20l. 12s. 6d. This, together with a rapid increase in the number of riders, caused an almost unprecedented demand, so great, in fact, that dealers had difficulty in meeting it. The stocks, especially of ladies' wheels, gave out, and purchasers were frequently obliged to wait for months before their orders were filled. The outlook for next season is equally bright, and many cheap wheels will be put on the market, but the prices of standard wheels will probably remain the same as they were this season. New factories have opened up all over the country, and all kinds and modes are on the market. An estimate of the number manufactured during the last year is a round million, and that the demand is not abating is shown by one single firm having made preparations to finish 100,000 machines during 1896.

Shipping and Freights.

General remarks.

The commerce of the lakes had a great revival during the season of 1895. The depression in the lake-carrying business caused by the panic of the two preceding years gave place to a state of business activity and prosperity which bids fair to continue far into the future.

During the season of 1894 and the early months of 1895, freight rates were at the lowest figure ever reached in the history of the lake marine, but when the reaction came the prices for moving cargoes advanced with unprecedented rapidity. In the latter part of the season rates were nearly double those of 1894, and in place of vesselmen begging for loads, in many cases it was the shipper who ran after the agent who had a boat to charter. The volume of business done was never before equalled. The only drawback was that the stage of water throughout the great lakes was extremely low. All former "low-water marks" being exceeded. This limited the carrying capacity of every large craft, and caused numerous strandings, involving delay, damage, and expense. These strandings also caused the insurance companies to lose heavily, especially on steel steamers, as the damage done them by grounding is always greater than it is in the case of a wooden boat. Although the losses of property were large, the loss of life in storms was unusually small, the fatalities aggregating a much smaller total than for many years past. The small loss of life is due principally to the increasing size and power of lake vessels. The winter work in the big shipyards around the lakes denotes the tendency of the lake business. While the number of craft is not large, the total of tonnage on the stocks is exceptionally so. The day of the small steamer or sailing vessel seems to have passed for ever, and the business boat of the lakes now carries from 3,000 to 5,000 tons of cargo.

The port of Chicago has more vessels entering and departing in a year than the combined ports of New York and San Francisco, the chief shipping ports on the Atlantic and Pacific coasts. I append the following official reports of the collectors of the three ports for the fiscal year ending June 3, 1895, for comparison :— *Port of Chicago.*

Port.	Number of Vessels. Entered.	Number of Vessels. Cleared.	Total.
New York	7,248	6,605	13,852
San Francisco	1,099	1,416	2,515
Total for the two ports	8,347	8,021	16,368
Chicago	8,515	8,476	16,991
Excess of Chicago over	168	455	623

The total number of entries and clearances for the ports of Baltimore, Boston, New York, Philadelphia, New Orleans, and San Francisco is 32,439, less than twice the amount of shipping for Chicago alone.

The following two tables give the arrivals and clearances of vessels in the Chicago district during 1895, showing the coastwise and foreign trade by ports. The table includes the two ports of South Chicago and Michigan City.

(2148)

TABLE showing the Arrivals and Clearances of Vessels in the Chicago District during the Year 1895.

ARRIVALS.

Port.	Coastwise Trade. American Vessels. Number of Vessels.	Tons.	Foreign Trade. American Vessels. Number of Vessels.	Tons.	Foreign Vessels. Number of Vessels.	Tons.	Total. Number of Vessels.	Tons.
Chicago..	7,593	4,588,954	41	12,239	3	1,315	7,637	4,602,508
South Chicago..	1,403	1,681,742	1	261	..	..	1,404	1,682,003
Michigan City..	171	45,191	..	..	..	..	171	45,191
Total..	9,167	6,315,887	42	12,500	3	1,315	9,212	6,329,702

CLEARANCES.

Port.	Coastwise Trade. American Vessels. Number of Vessels.	Tons.	Foreign Trade. American Vessels. Number of Vessels.	Tons.	Foreign Vessels. Number of Vessels.	Tons.	Total. Number of Vessels.	Tons.
Chicago..	7,577	4,521,419	107	63,100	3	1,315	7,687	4,585,834
South Chicago..	1,495	1,751,665	9	9,173	..	..	1,504	1,760,838
Michigan City..	172	45,825	..	..	..	..	172	45,825
Total..	9,244	6,318,909	116	72,273	3	1,315	9,363	6,392,497

CHICAGO.

The following table exhibits the quantities of various articles of domestic produce shipped from Chicago during 1895, consigned to European ports on through bills of lading issued in Chicago:—

TABLE showing Exports of Domestic Produce during the Year 1895.

Articles.	Quantities.
	Kilos.
Flour	11,554,909
Oatmeal	6,399,000
Cornmeal	1,122,636
Wheat	2,968,753
Corn	55,997,473
Oats	334,182
Clover seed	970,964
Other seeds	1,275,561
Cured meats	68,152,000
Canned meats	8,479,886
Tongue	1,159,773
Beef, fresh	9,320,688
Pork	4,025,955
Lard	72,041,181
Tallow	2,470,636
Butter	750
Cheese	40,630
Hides	783,088
Leather	144,754
Tobacco	612,255
Oil	1,198,545
Oil, oleo	8,994,000
Oil-cake	8,119,889
Miscellaneous	8,604,782

The coastwise trade of the great lakes from the port of Chicago was exceedingly large during the year. The chief articles of shipment were the cereals and their products.

The average rate through the season of navigation for carrying a bushel of corn from Chicago to Buffalo was 6s. 11½d., against 4s. 10½d. the previous year, the latter rate being the lowest average on record. The total inspection in and out for the fiscal year ending November 1, 1895, was 265,737,585 bushels, as against 252,081,997 bushels for preceding period. 17,077 more cars of grain were received.

Growth of South Chicago shipping. The phenomenal growth of the shipping of South Chicago is a constant surprise to the business public of the city. Business has grown so rapidly that South threatens to ultimately rival the receipts and discharges of the Chicago River. Owing to the deeper water at that point, much of the heavy business is drifting that way, and the great freighters that cannot enter the Chicago River on account of the 16-feet draught over the La Salle Street tunnel, discharge and load at the deeper waters of South Chicago. The question of an outer harbour has been discussed amongst experts, but the general opinion is that the plan is not practical.

The principal points adduced in favour of a South Chicago harbour are, that it is removed from the congested portion of the city; that it possesses a large area of dockage land, which is comparatively cheap; and that its geographical relation to the roads running east and west is such as to afford them the best facilities for reaching the harbour and contiguous manufactories.

The future waterway between the Mississippi and Lake Michigan would, it is supposed, probably be made to connect at South Chicago, and Lake Calumet would then become an inner harbour, when the area of the river is exhausted. At present the Lehigh Company has secured there dockage rights to the value of 41,237*l*. Three large modern elevators were erected last year, and five more are under weigh this year.

The lake passenger boats of the city carry about 400,000 passengers a year. Of these, the Graham and Morton, and the Goodrich lines handle 125,000 each. It is this traffic which it is hoped will be concentrated on the lake front. The Graham and Morton Line is the only company owning its own dock land in the city, but it appears they claim that they would welcome the change.

The city suffers from long delay in the river, expensive towage bills, &c., and the number of boats passing through bridges at present on week days is only the equivalent of what used to be done on Sudays. Milwaukee has received more coal this year by lake than Chicago, and has, moreover, a lake coal rate of 5*d*. in her favour.

Finally, the opinion of experts is that, owing to the enormous expense in connection with lowering the tunnels and construction of modern bridges, &c., the commerce of the Chicago River is bound to die away gradually, and that the docks and railroad yards will eventually go to South Chicago.

Drainage Canal.

The annual report of Clerk Judge, of the sanitary district in Chicago, shows, with the end of 1895, nearly 80 per cent. of the work of the great drainage channel completed between Robey Street and Lockport, Illinois. The sum of 3,892,658*l*. has been expended to date, of which 1,525,920*l*. was spent this year, the largest amount so far.

The work may be summed up as follows:—The first contracts, Sections 1 to 14, were let in June, 1892, and bids for the last work on the main channel, the regulating works on Section 15, were opened November 20, 1895. The first shovel of earth was lifted September 3, 1892, the official inauguration of the work. The total amount of the contract work on the entire channel, not including bridges and masonry for the same, is nearly 3,917,520*l*.

During August, September, and October last, there were 8,700 men at work on the canal. The lowest wages ever paid were 7½*d*. per hour, and from that up to 1*s*. 8*d*. per hour.

The main channel, which may be looked upon as the main trunk line, will cost not less than 5,773,195*l*., and, as the city grows, the system must be further extended.

The sanitary district is in a favourable position to develop and control from 10,000 to 20,000 horse-power.

The total value of the work done to January 1, on regular and collateral contracts, is 3,047,500*l*., or 77·83 per cent. of the entire work done upon a basis of existing contracts. The percentage of work done, January 1, 1895, is 44·38. So the percentage done in 1895 amounts to 33·45.

It is expected that the balance of the work will be done by December, 1896.

Miscellaneous.

Health of Chicago. The annual report of the city health department shows the death rate in Chicago to be lower than that of any other city in the world having a population of 200,000 or more, and lower than Chicago's own rate of 1894, which was below all previous records. A computation, based on the unrevised figures, gives the death rate for 1895 at 15·11 in 1,000, against 15·24 for the year before. It is shown that the improved sanitary condition of the city is due to the crusade made by the department against unpure milk, unclean ice, and the treatment of diphtheria, as well as the reports made of the condition of the water supply. The warnings sent out by the health department, when the lake was contaminated by sewage, have induced the inhabitants to boil their drinking water, and thus avoid typhoid and other fevers to a great extent. As regards the milk trade, in August last 60 to 65 per cent. of the samples taken from the dealers were found to be impure. Constant prosecution and other means taken have repressed the practice of adulteration to such an extent that only 5 samples in 100 are now found to be below the required standard.

The results obtained by the use of antitoxin in treating diphtheria are cited as the most conclusive proofs of its value. It is shown that out of 629 cases treated, 591 recovered, only 38, or 6 per cent. of the whole number, died, and there were no deaths in the cases treated within 24 hours after the disease had made its appearance. Of 437 persons exposed to contagion and immunised, not one contracted the disease.

Dealing with smoke, the report says 11,252 violations of the Ordnance have been reported, 259 suits prosecuted and 179 convictions secured, but the results obtained by the year's work have not been satisfactory.

Population. The rapid growth of Chicago is nothing less than phenomenal. The best and most reliable data obtainable show the rate of increase 106½ per cent. If this continues for about 4 decades, Chicago will pass all other cities, even London, and will be the largest city in the world. At present the population is put down at over 1,700,000 inhabitants, but it is fully expected that the next census will show 2,000,000. The total area of the city is 186,138 square miles.

Gains in the population of Iowa and Wisconsin.

From the last census materials the population of Iowa is placed at 2,035,000, as against 1,911,894 in 1890. The greatest gain in Iowa has been in the cities of the newer counties, the cities and towns of the older counties remaining practically at a standstill. The new counties are all being settled by farmers who are securing homesteads of their own. The greatest gains in the State have been in towns from 3,000 to 8,000 population. Towns under 1,000 show only an infinitesimal gain.

Statistics in Wisconsin.

The last census, just published, places the total population of Wisconsin for 1895 at 1,937,915, as against 1,686,880 in 1890. An increase of 14·9 per cent. from 1890-95. The increase in population at different periods can be directly traced to the extension of railway systems through the length and breadth of the State.

The number of acres of wheat in Wisconsin has considerably decreased since 1885. In that year there were 1,221,313 acres, but in 1895 only 471,163 acres were reported.

The number of horses and mules have likewise diminished, whereas in tobacco, wool industry, and corn crop, there has been a great falling-off; in all the branches of dairy industry there has been a substantial increase. The number of pounds of butter has increased 38,413,299 over 1885, the number of pounds of cheese, 19,001,915. The increase in the growing and value of oats is quite large—as compared with 1885 there has been an increase of 18,936,901 bushels. In the manufacturing industries there has been a large increase in nearly every branch. On the whole there is a material development of the resources and wealth of the State.

Nebraska.

The condition of Nebraska is prosperous, and the State now appears to have recovered from the results of the drought of 1894. Much of the surplus grain supply will be used this year within the State for feeding purposes.

The total acreage of corn was 6,564,112 acres; the total yield was 123,740,984 bushels. This is an increase of 110,000,000 bushels over last year. The total wheat acreage was 1,460,540; the yield was 17,756 bushels. There is an especially large number of sheep being fed along the line of the Union Pacific. There are 75,000 head of sheep at Shelton, and fully 200,000 between Schuyler, and Wood River, on the Union Pacific lines. Most of these sheep have been shipped in from Mexico and Colorado, and will be ready for the market during the winter months. The population of Nebraska numbers 1,000,000.

The dairy products of the State are rapidly gaining in importance, and its production of sugar beets is of excellent quality. Although the manufacturing and mechanical industries of this State are still in their infancy, yet the exhibits in the recent Atlanta Exhibition of the products of Nebraskan factories, mills, and workshops appear to have created a favourable impression.

Dakota.

The country, on the whole, is prosperous. Many new mines have been opened the last few years, and large and expensive works have been erected. More are needed to meet the wants of the increasing output of ore. The unlimited resources of South Dakota are being developed, and, in the coming years, the Black Hills region should be relied upon to contribute a largely increased ratio to the supremacy of the gold standard of the world.

According to the statistics of the Director of the United States Mint for the calendar year 1894, the Black Hills produced 680,200*l*. in gold, ranking fourth in the gold-producing States and territories.

In 1895 the output reached 1,030,925*l*. in round numbers, and for 1896 the State mine inspector estimates the yield at 1,443,295*l*.

The last season has been the most active period known in this State in prospecting, developing, and marketing Wyoming oil. Many large enterprises have recently been inaugurated with Eastern and European capital for practical operations in iron, oil, and gold at various points. Great interest exists in the opening up of the Bessemer iron ore deposits of the Hartville district, 100 miles north of Cheyenne. The belt covers an area of over 25 square miles, and experts estimate 20,000,000 tons of the purest iron ore as now in sight. Arrangements are being made to build a railroad to the mines and take out the ore for shipment to furnaces and smelters in Colorado, and in connection with an iron enterprise at Cheyenne. Casper, in the central part of the State, is the centre of the largest petroleum development in the State, as well as being a geographical centre of the oil belt. Gold prospecting all over the country was one of the features of last season, and a large gold output is being predicted for the next season.

Wyoming

The beer war, which had continued during the past year, has now been settled. All the brewing companies doing business in Chicago have perfected a mutual agreement by which the price of beer will be advanced in January to 1*l*. 0*s*. 7½*d*. a barrel, the present price being 16*s*. 10*d*., or less. It is estimated that this will result in the closing of some 2,000 saloons in this city during the first 3 months of 1896.

Brewing.

The effect of the new compact will probably be far reaching. The past year has been most disastrous to the brewing business in the west. When the old Brewers' Association disbanded, beer was selling at 1*l*. 4*s*. 9*d*. a barrel. In many cases brewers paid the license fee of saloon keepers to hold their trade, and the result was that they lost heavily; syndicates were compelled to pass their dividends, and the industrial concerns made no profits. Under the new circumstances, all those extraneous expenses will now be done away with, and the consequence will be that the price to the saloon keepers will be increased, and it is expected that the public will get a better article than hitherto.

The production in Illinois for the year ending June 30, 1895, was 20,816,627 gallons, as compared with 30,803,660 gallons for the year ending June 30, 1894. Even with this heavy decrease, viz., 10,000,000 gallons, Illinois maintains her position as the second

Whisky.

greatest producer of whisky and spirits in the United States. The only other State that exceeded this production was Kentucky. The third State in the amount produced this year is Indiana, which made 6,979,576 gallons; then comes Wisconsin with 1,356,000, Minnesota with 817,340, and Nebraska with 288,384 gallons.

Illinois withdrew more spirits for consumption this year than any State in the Union. The amount up to June 30, 1895, was 24,837,886 gallons, a decrease from the figures for the year ending June 30, 1894, when 29,371,218 gallons were withdrawn, of about 5,000,000 gallons.

The stock of spirits remaining in bond in the State has been decreased during the year by more than 4,000,000 gallons. On June 30, 1894, it was 10,757,400 gallons, and on June 30, 1895, it was 6,310,449 gallons.

City and country. Among the social and industrial movements of the time, the drift of population toward the cities is reckoned a great evil. The startling statement is made on good authority that in the four great agricultural States of Ohio, Indiana, Illinois, and Iowa, half the townships were less populous in 1890 than in 1880, while the large cities had greatly increased in size. There was a corresponding diminution of the number of productive enterprises carried on in rural districts. The result is, abandoned farms on the one hand, and overcrowded trades in the cities on the other; and also an increase in the cost of food through diminished production, and a lowering of wages through over competition. Various causes are assigned. Railroads and their discriminating freight rates are blamed. Others say it is because farming means harder work and poorer pay than city businesses. Some think it is because of the superior social and educational advantages of the city. Others, on the other hand, admit that American haste to get rich is responsible.

The Trans-Mississippi Exposition. A movement is on foot to hold a trans-Mississippi exposition at Omaha in 1898, to be open 6 months. The purpose is to make a grand display of the resources of the whole country, but especially of the 24 States and territories west of the Mississippi River. It is the intention to let the world see what a magnificent region west of Chicago there is still to be developed. It is hoped to make the exhibit, as a whole, second only in splendour to the World's Fair which was held in this city in 1893, and no effort will be spared to make it take that rank in history. The population of the States and territories west of the Mississippi River increased from 5,665,683 in 1870, to 14,215,490 in 1890, the proportion for the extremes of the 20-year period being about 100 to 250. The gain in wealth was far greater, and the increase since 1890 is a large one. 25 years since Nebraska, on the eastern edge of which the Exposition of 1898 will be held, was thinly settled, with little or nothing beyond the distance of 150 miles west from the Missouri River; and west of that was a wilderness.

Nebraska now contains more than 1,000,000 people, with 1,000,000 acres of land under irrigation, and barns and farmhouses

CHICAGO.

extend all the way from the Missouri to Cheyenne. The then territories are now States, though not all of them merit that distinction, perhaps.

A local company has been organised at Omaha for preliminary work, but each State will be asked to recognise and co-operate.

Denver.

Mr. Vice-Consul Pearce reports as follows:—

It will be seen from the following report that the State of Colorado and its varied industries have been fairly prosperous during the year 1895.

The value of new buildings erected in Denver during the year was 227,020*l.*, an increase of 74,424*l.* over 1894. One of the principal buildings was a Home for Consumptives, which was built at a cost of 16,000*l.*, and is very complete in every detail. *Value of new buildings.*

The transactions in real estate for the year were 2,436,100*l.*, a decrease of 507,916*l.* from 1894. Denver ranked twelfth among the cities of the United States in real estate transactions for the year. *Real estate.*

The records of the Bank Clearing House of Denver for 1895 show a total of 27,768,392*l.*, an increase of 406,288*l.* over 1894. *Clearing house records.*

During the year the Union National Bank of Denver went into liquidation, and there are now 6 national banks in the city. The following table shows the condition of these banks for the past 2 years:— *Banks.*

Year.	Resources.	Loans.	Deposits.
	£	£	£
1894	4,769,008	2,657,709	3,510,280
1895	4,820,478	2,451,328	3,817,222

The manufacturing trade of Denver for 1895 shows a marked improvement over the previous year, the increase in value being 2,062,770*l.* The total value, which includes the products of the smelting establishments, was 8,059,472*l.* The number of men employed was 12,866, an increase of 3,997, and the amount of wages paid was 1,201,263*l.*, an increase of 126,551*l.* *Manufacturing.*

The rates of wages were generally lower, and the year was remarkably free from labour disturbances.

The records of the Health Department show the mortality to be the lowest in the history of the city, being 11·04 per 1,000 in a population estimated at 145,000. *Health.*

The total valuation of assessed property in Colorado, for the year, was 40,313,733*l.*, a decrease of 1,467,323*l.* from 1894. The decrease in values is principally in agricultural and grazing lands, and horses and mules. Mining property shows an increase of nearly 200,000*l.* *Value of taxable property.*

UNITED STATES.

Agriculture. During the year the price of farm products of all kinds, with the exception of wheat, was at least one-third lower than in previous years, and although the crops harvested were larger, the total value shows a decrease of 337,300*l.* as compared with 1894. The value of the product from the 2,000,000 acres of land under cultivation, principally by irrigation, is estimated as follows:—

Articles.	Value.
	£
Wheat	816,000
Alfalfa	700,000
Clover and timothy	140,000
Native grass	250,000
Corn, oats, barley, &c.	800,000
Potatoes	194,000
Garden products	650,000
Fruit	521,300
Total	4,071,300

Live-stock. The number and value of the live-stock of the State for the year is given by the State Veterinary Surgeon, as follows:—

Description.	Number.	Value.
		£
Cattle	750,000	2,400,000
Horses	250,000	1,400,000
Sheep	1,000,000	300,000
Swine	50,000	30,000
Mules	25,000	70,000
Total	2,075,000	4,200,000

This shows an increase in value of 560,000*l.* over 1894.

Poultry. The value of the poultry industry of the State shows an increase over the previous year of 10 per cent. The total value is estimated at 400,000*l.*

Railroads. According to the report of the State Board of Equalisation for 1895, the total assessed valuation of railroad property in Colorado is 6,150,367*l.*, which is 103,348*l.* in excess of 1894.

From a careful estimate it is seen that the business of the various railroads in the State increased 25 per cent. over the previous year.

Iron industry. The following detailed statement of production and value of the iron industry in the State for the year is furnished by the Colorado Fuel and Iron Company, the only company in the State which produces and manufactures iron from Colorado ores:—

Articles.	Quantity.	Value.
	Lbs.	£
Pig iron	118,988,720	190,381
Spiegel	6,772,210	20,116
Castings	6,940,861	34,700
Cast-iron pipe	8,714,230	25,270
Steel rails	83,967,724	268,691
Spikes	5,348,706	24,333
Steel angle bars	3,259,718	10,751
Merchant iron	31,808,122	127,232
Iron ore	203,049,150	117,219
Total	..	818,693

The production of coal and coke for the year shows an increase of 373,869 tons. There has been an increased demand for coal for local purposes in the State, together with a large export trade to neighbouring States and territories.

Coal and coke.

TABLE showing the Output of Coal by Counties for the Year 1894-95.

Counties.	Quantity.	
	1894.	1895.
	Tons of 2,000 lbs.	Tons of 2,000 lbs.
Arapahoe	604	540
Boulder	335,807	421,013
Dolores		2,500
El Paso	64,588	49,929
Fremont	275,033	387,533
Gunnison	193,650	231,096
Garfield	82,226	218,634
Huerfano	414,884	412,704
Jefferson	39,359	38,460
Las Animas	1,181,005	1,220,433
La Plata	92,822	101,254
Mesa	35,990	19,236
Montezuma	..	2,000
Park	97,118	41,881
Pitkin	43,486	123,928
Weld	39,456	56,377
Small mines	125,000	..
Total	3,021,028	3,327,518

UNITED STATES.

TABLE showing Coke Production for the Year 1894-95.

Counties.	Quantity. 1894.	Quantity. 1895.
	Tons of 2,000 lbs.	Tons of 2,000 lbs.
Gunnison	37,570	35,168
Las Animas	191,762	254,666
La Plata	5,000	1,900
Pitkin	49,213	59,190
Total	283,545	350,924

Building stone. The year's production of building stone is estimated at a value of 107,240*l*.

Oil. The total product of the oil fields of the State for the year was 15,000,000 gallons, valued at 300,000*l*. 32,000*l*. were paid out in wages in this industry.

Mining.

TABLE showing the Value of the Output from the Mines in Colorado for the Year 1895.

Articles.	Value.
	£
Gold	3,000,000
Silver	2,851,800
Lead	600,000
Copper	180,000
Total	6,631,800

Gold increase, 876,707*l*.; silver decrease, 140,448*l*.; lead decrease, 53,723*l*.; copper increase, 26,516*l*.; net increase, 709,052*l*. The average price of silver for the year was $65\frac{2}{10}$ c. (2s. 8d.) per ounce, as against 63 c. (2s. 7d.) in 1894.

Gold mining throughout the State has received fresh impetus during the year, due in a great measure to the large increased production of gold from the Cripple Creek Mines. The output from this district for the year is said to amount to the sum of 1,600,000*l*., as against 580,000*l*. for 1894, or nearly 3 times as much more. A few of the older camps, notably Lake, Clear Creek, Ouray, and San Miguel Counties, also show a marked increase in the gold returns for the year.

There has been a further falling-off in the yield of silver from Colorado mines, notwithstanding that the average price per ounce was $2\frac{2}{10}$ c. higher than in 1894.

The State records show that 632 mining companies were incorporated and registered during the year, representing a total capital of nearly 108,000,000*l*. These figures are of little value, except to show the extent of the speculative fever which has started since the discoveries in Cripple Creek; this district alone being credited with at least two-thirds of the above total companies registered. I need scarcely add that by far the largest proportion of these companies, representing such an enormous capital, have at present no value whatever. The number of mines in the Cripple Creek district which at this time are actually producing gold ore in paying quantities is probably less than 20.

Prospectors are at work all through the State where conditions are favourable for the occurrence of gold, and this will undoubtedly lead to fresh discoveries, and will add materially to the gold output.

The cheapening of transportation, and the low charges for reduction of ores which now prevail both tend to make the mining industry of the State profitable, and will help in a measure, to compensate for the failure in the silver mining industry brought about by the depreciation of silver.

In some of the larger silver mines, which suffered greatly from the decline in silver in 1893, the tribute system has been adopted with great success. It has so far cheapened production that many of the mines can be worked at a small profit even at the present low price of silver.

STATEMENT of Values of Imports from Great Britain, Entered at the Port of Denver, during the Year 1895.

Articles.	Value.
	£ *s.*
Garden and other seeds	107 16
Tea	331 16
Iron bedsteads	334 8
Tin and terne plates	2,267 12
Still wines	239 4
Whisky	184 8
Brandy	44 8
Clocks	10 0
Carpets	6 16
Books and printed matter	120 0
Firearms (shot guns)	324 8
Woollen cloths	413 12
Cotton ,,	577 4
Medicinal preparations	5 12
Bonnets and hats	13 8
Paintings (water-colours)	4 16
Wearing apparel	224 0
Assay scales	108 12
Chinaware	281 16
Precious stones (cut, not set)	52 12
Ale and stout	273 0
Personal effects	51 16
Photographic goods	41 8
Manufactures of flax	129 0
Salad oil	89 0
Gelatine	185 0
Tobacco	59 8
Total	6,481 4

(2148)

RECORDS of Imports from Great Britain for the Past Nine Years.

Year.	Value.
	£ s.
1887	5,053 12
1888	8,109 12
1889	17,585 7
1890	32,512 4
1891	26,008 16
1892	9,357 4
1893	6,603 16
1894	4,984 4
1895	6,481 4

KANSAS.

Mr. Vice-Consul P. E. Burrough reports as follows:—

Introductory.

As this is the first general report of this Vice-Consulate, I desire to say that I have compiled what I consider the most important points; at the same time I have reduced the same as much as possible. It will be seen by the report that the foreign trade, as a whole, to and from this Vice-Consulate, is greater than any other section in North America. I have made mention of facts whereby the importer and exporter of Great Britain may profit.

I have, at the kind suggestion of Mr. Consul Vansittart, given a report regarding Kansas, Nebraska, Indiana, and Oklahoma Teritories, because Kansas City is their nearest and natural wholesale market. I have touched upon Missouri for the reason that Kansas City is located within that State and does a share of its business in its products. I trust the report will meet with approval.

TABLE showing General Statistics for Kansas City for the last Five Years.

Year.	Assessed Valuation. £	City Expenditure. £	Municipal Indebtedness. £	Bank Capital. £	Bank Clearings. £	Real Estate Transfers. £	Building Permits. Number.	Building Permits. Cost. £	Pieces of Mail Handled.	Post Office Receipts. £
1891	15,231,657	193,181	228,009	2,084,710	95,572,933	4,551,011	2,566	642,656	78,275,467	93,062
1892	13,387,000	168,491	219,062	148,595	156,663,163	3,850,972	1,147	225,778	87,478,960	99,871
1893	12,706,770	158,403	294,628	142,148	98,072,870	3,634,927	1,504	308,939	89,567,482	96,250
1894	11,927,020	151,427	262,789	134,307	99,910,580	2,554,419	1,363	206,350	91,488,212	97,751
1895	11,892,039	175,062	847,314*	114,256	107,617,899	2,500,009	1,737	293,119	99,550,548	101,146

* 640,400 waterworks bonds.

(2148)

UNITED STATES.

Increase in business.

To show the rapid increase of business at Kansas City, I give below comparisons for seven years:—

Year.	Amount.
	£
1870	1,786,920
1880	9,475,396
1890	30,399,332
1892	32,399,545
1893	34,808,941
1894	36,461,911
1895	37,948,490

Internal revenue for five years.

The internal revenue receipts for past five years show a good increase for this point:—

Year.	Amount.
	£
1890	88,936
1892	84,106
1893	88,362
1894	90,721
1895	89,037

Name.

Kansas City was called by such a name on account of its being founded at the mouth of the Kansas River, where it empties into the Missouri River. It was a trading point in early years for the Indians; was also the most important steamboat landing for many years. The river is used but little now, on account of the government not making appropriations to keep it dredged. It is said by experts that the Missouri River has the most deceptive and changeable course of any river in the world, and on this account navigation is not profitable, and railroad competition is too severe. In olden times the "Santa Fé Trail" started from here, viâ Kansas City, the overland routes of mail, with goods for all western territory, accepting even California. It must not be forgotten that Kansas City covers territory within the State of Kansas and Missouri, and has two separate and distinct governments, but in reality one city. The transition from a population of 4,000 in 1865 to 32,000 in 1870, 55,000 in 1880, and 132,000 in 1890, all United States census figures, to 175,000 at the present time, while Kansas City, Kansas, has a population of over 50,000 (total 225,000), seems like a dream; but it is a stern reality. The foundation has merely been laid for one of the grandest cities in the United States.

With the greatest railroad centre in the world, and with such an unlimited territory for trade to the north, west, and south, extending for many hundreds and thousands of miles, and which is being settled so fast, Kansas City cannot but become one of the greatest commercial cities of this continent. It is probable that no city on this continent is surrounded by a country possessing such vast natural advantages tending to make a great commercial city. Kansas City is directly in the centre of the great corn belt, which is one of the foundation stones of the packing house industry, and is also one of the greatest agricultural country cities in the world, and is the natural market of the greatest grazing and live stock producing country in the world.

Street improvements. Vast improvements in the streets took place in 1895, costing 110,000*l.*, consisting of asphalt, brick, macadam, and stone block pavements; wooden block paving has proven a failure in the west.

Consular post. Kansas City is the only Consular post on the Missouri River and in the Mississippi Valley; seven foreign countries have Consular officers here, namely, Great Britain, France, Spain, Mexico, Italy, Denmark, and Bolivia.

Death rate. Kansas City is believed to be the healthiest city of its size in the world; the death rate for 1894, per thousand, was 10·59, and for 1895, 11·49. Only one epidemic prevailed during 1895, which was diphtheria; 275 cases were reported to the Board of Health, of which 71 cases were fatal. Estimated population, 225,000.

Retail trade. The retail trade of Kansas City was 20 per cent. larger for 1895 than for 1894, sales amounting to 9,000,009*l.*

Butter, eggs. The butter, egg, and produce trade of Kansas City for 1895 was about 487,000*l.*, and this trade is in a very healthy condition, for the eastern States are always good market for these goods.

Kansas City is the centre of the greatest egg country of the west. Missouri last year produced 23,765,835 dozen eggs; Kansas, 21,418,203 dozen, and Iowa about the same, or a total of 70,000,000 dozen. All are shipped to eastern cities.

Department stores. Kansas City has its large retail department stores, and they certainly work a great hardship against the legitimate exclusive retailers of goods. The third largest department house in the United States is located here.

Failures. The business failures of 1895, for these western States, of which Kansas City is the centre, showed a decline, the abundant crops giving new life and health to trade.

Year.	Number of Failures.	Liabilities.
		£
1894	1,464	3,493,876
1895	1,425	2,890,914

Chemicals. Large quantities of essential oils, caustic soda, and saltpetre are used in this western country, and some is bought from eastern cities; large quantities are of British production, and home merchants should ship and sell direct to the western consumer.

The manufacture of oatmeal is becoming an important feature in this Vice-Consulate. No less than five very large oatmeal mills are running full capacity; they are just preparing to engage in

Oatmeal.

shipping oatmeal abroad. Some few orders have already been filled, and give satisfaction. The oats this year are very fine, and produce the finest grade of oatmeal, which is prepared in such a manner that ten minutes' cooking prepares it for breakfast. The oatmeal is so cheap it can be put on the British and Continental trade with good profits and results.

Sterilised air.

Great interest is manifested by all the exporters of perishables in this western country in the report that sterilised air will take the place of ice. It is reported that patents have been secured all over the world; the first patent was secured in this country, and was perfected by an American. The plans patented cover a process of preserving meats, fruits, and all perishable products during transportation by the use of sterilised air. The first shipments are to be made soon on fruits. Should sterilised air become a success, it will enable the Australian meat companies to compete against the American meat companies. Should it become a success, it will no doubt assist the foreign exporters of fruit of the world to compete for the foreign trade, where at present those at the greatest distance are at a disadvantage.

Hints to British merchants.

British importers and exporters can further their trade in this western country if they will note mention made in this report on the following articles; I am confident they will profit thereby: Earthenware, crockery, plate glass, enamelled ware, oilcake, quicksilver, caustic soda, tallow, flax seed, binding twine, tin plate salt, saltpetre, Fuller's earth, furs, Swedish iron, carpets, woollen goods, and knit goods. Merchants when figuring freight should not forget that rates can frequently be obtained lower, viâ the Gulf of Mexico ports than Atlantic coast ports.

Customs receipts.

I am pleased to report that the Custom House returns of Kansas City show a good increase for 1895. Both import and export trade outlook is good, for the west, and bids fair for the Custom House of Kansas City to become a very important post in this country. It must be remembered that St. Joseph, Missouri, and Omaha, Nebraska, both have Custom Houses, as well as Kansas City, but both combined do not handle as much business as Kansas City. Below find receipts for the past three years:—

Year.	Amount.
	£
1893	30,191
1894	36,247
1895	79,197

Swedish iron.

I am very desirous of calling attention to some of the articles imported, that the British merchants may profit thereby.

During 1895 the first shipment of Swedish iron (charcoal bars) was received, consisting of 75,321 lbs. and valued at 208*l*. More of them are expected to be ordered during the coming year.

Tin plate.

Much has been said of tin plate, but by personal observation and enquiry it has been demonstrated that for household or hard usage the British tin outlasts the American product; it is true the British tin is not so bright, but it is more durable, has more body, and does not rust so quickly. Kansas City uses more tin than any other city in the United States on account of the large production of packing house products that are put up in tin packages of all descriptions. The American tin is just as good for this purpose as British tin. Merchants should bear in mind that the imported British tin is but a small part of what is used at Kansas City, the bulk of tin used being American; at the same time, large quantities of British tin are being used here, and more would be used if the trade were pushed more by the British merchants. Following shows quantities of British tin imported during the past three years :—

Year.	Quantity.	Import Duty.
	Lbs.	£
1893	4,127,065	10,917
1894	4,823,919	11,011
1895	6,774,851	16,795

Tin is an article that is increasing in use, and many new plants for the production of tin have been opened in the eastern States, and there is a prospect of a hard competition for the tin trade.

The amount of tin plate in the United States is about 890,000 tons per year; last year the United States produced 820,000 tons, and with the new plants the capacity for 1896 will be about 30,000 tons more; even then tin must be imported to supply the demand.

Another point to remember is that the new tariff has reduced the profits of American manufacturers, and also brought the British tin-plate manufacturers into this country as competitors. Its only effect on prices, if any, has been to lower them to consumers. The American tin mines do not amount to anything, so most of the pig tin has to be imported from Great Britain, Australia, and elsewhere. The present duty is about $\frac{1}{2}d.$ per pound. One firm in Kansas City uses about 7,000,000 lbs. of tin annually.

Furs. Furs in the rough (not made up) were imported to Kansas City during 1895 amounting to 2,136*l.* All came from various parts of Europe, and this is the first year of importation here of furs.

Salt. 3,395,992 lbs. of Ashton (English) salt were received through the Kansas City custom-house during 1895. Although this country abounds with salt (see Kansas report, same edition), at the same time a certain amount of salt must be imported from England for special use by beef and pork packers. There is no duty on salt here, but a certain amount of salt will always be imported by packers, no matter what the duty may be. Certain brands of meat, intended for foreign markets, must positively be cured with English salt to be marketable in certain climates; but the free salt clause of the Wilson Bill benefited no one but the English

(2148)

producer, his market being enlarged, and that of the American salt producer being correspondingly curtailed. Salt is brought to this country free from freight charges, being utilised as ballast for steamers, and is, therefore, landed on American soil at exactly the cost of production, which is less than American salt can be produced for by well-paid American labour, and the American can only sit by and see the English salt go on the market at a wholesale price he cannot meet, and then see it retailed at exactly the price his salt would have brought.

Straw matting. During 1895 one shipment of 1,600 square yards of straw matting from England was an experiment, and proved profitable.

Earthenware, &c. The importation of earthenware, crockery, china, glassware, &c., to Kansas City was three times larger for 1895 than 1894; the larger part was from Great Britain. The value of importation in 1895 was 15,871*l*. This trade could easily be doubled if handled properly. I know of no branch of business that has such a future as this for the British merchants in this western country.

Stockings. Two shipments of knit stockings, consisting of 5,569 dozen pair, were also an experiment; they were also from England.

Rice. The first rice imported here arrived in 1895; it consisted of 150,000 lbs., and came from Japan.

Custom-house records show also importations from Europe, of cutlery, lithographs, books, silks, laces, embroideries, tobaccos, wines, musical instruments, paints and oils.

Very large quantities of products of wool, including Brussels, tapestry, and other grades of carpets, very fine cloth, dress-goods, &c., were received from Great Britain and Europe to the extent of 59,369 square yards. At one time 420*l*. duty was paid on one lot of carpet from Manchester, England. This trade can be increased by British merchants if handled prudently.

Agricultural implements. Kansas City is the largest wholesale agricultural implement market in the world; quite a number of implements are exported to foreign countries from here. The practical failure of the wheat crop in the Great West this year caused sales to be much lighter than was expected. Manufacturers and jobbers were, indeed, more careful in making sales and limited their orders, which caused the retailer to be restricted somewhat in his sales. It must be understood that none of the agricultural implements sold are made here, but all are shipped to this point from eastern States, except hay presses; they are manufactured here by three large factories, and this is the largest hay press market in the world, and they are shipped from here into several foreign countries.

The sales of agricultural implements at Kansas City were:—

	Amount.
	£
1892	4,000,000
1893	3,572,000
1894 .. ..·	3,272,000
1895	3,285,273
Capital invested	1,999,386
Persons employed .. (Number)	1,186
Annual salaries paid	176,391

Binding twine. Binding twine for harvesting machines, for binding wheat when reaped, is a staple article in this market; many millions of pounds are sold in Kansas City annually. To-day standard is worth 4d. per lb., and sisal 3d. per lb. here. The demand is rapidly increasing, and British merchants can secure a share of this trade by looking after it. Cheaper freights from Great Britain can be obtained to this point by way of New Orleans or Galveston than by the Eastern seaports.

Apples, storage. Early last autumn the Armour Packing Company offered a limited space in their cold storage beef coolers for the storage of apples, and accepted some 15,000 barrels, the greater part of which are still there (February 15, 1896) and in perfect condition. The Armours are storing, and will also furnish refrigerator cars for the safe shipment of stock during winter. Referring to the new department, constituting one of the big buildings of the Armour Company plant, is what is called the "new beef house." This building is the largest and best equipped cold storage plant in the world. It was built to hold an enormous surplus of beef, in case emergency required; within the eight big storage compartments more than 20,000 beef carcases can be hung in any desired temperature. Every scientific device applicable to artificial refrigeration is in use in this plant, and improvements are being added constantly.

When the building was finished about two years ago, it was the intention of the Armour Packing Company to keep the unoccupied refrigerating rooms simply as reserve space. Last summer, however, when there was so much talk of Kansas City being unable to furnish cold storage for fruit and vegetables to the growers of Kansas and Missouri, Armour decided to utilise the storage facilities of the new beef house for general refrigerating purposes. They therefore agreed to take a consignment of 8,000 barrels of apples, as an experiment; the apples were put in cold storage about October 1; since then the temperature about them has not varied from 33°. The room is 135 feet wide by 175 feet long, and contains about 275,000 cubic feet of refrigeration space. The 8,000 barrels of apples occupy only about half this space, so it will be seen that the entire capacity of the building is something like 16,000 barrels. Several barrels of the apples were opened, and all were found to be in perfect conditon.

For the preservation of fruit and vegetables in cold storage, it is absolutely necessary that the temperature shall be maintained as nearly stationary as possible, and that the air shall be dry; ventilation is also a matter of great importance. The Armour cold storage warehouse is cooled by large pipes, through which a a constant stream of freezing cold brine is kept flowing. The brine is made cold by a process of ammonia evaporation. In the basement are two engines and machinery for producing cold sufficient to freeze 600 tons of ice every 24 hours. The engines are each of 200 horse-power.

In all parts of the house are thermometers; there are 96 reports of the registration of the thermometers every day; in this way the temperature is closely watched and kept even; the system of ventilation is so perfect that in one room 100 barrels of onions could not be detected by their odour, although a person pass within a few feet of them.

Economy of time and labour being the chief ideas upon which a packing house is operated, the cold storage warehouse is fitted up with all manner of mechanical conveniences for handling the barrels, boxes, and crates that may be consigned to it: at one end of the building is a big elevator that reaches a covered platform below, and along this platform runs a railroad switch. It is the intention of the Armour Packing Company to open their cold storage warehouse for business at once. The immense quantities of butter and eggs from Kansas and Missouri, which have heretofore been stored in St. Louis and Chicago, will now be sought by Kansas City. This would add much to Kansas City's business as a distributing centre. The 186,000 square feet, or nearly 5 acres of floor space, will amply accommodate almost any demand that shippers may make upon it.

Plate glass. Plate glass amounting to the value of 5,723*l*. was imported to Kansas City during 1895 from France and Germany. There is a great field here for the importation of plate-glass by British merchants if they will look to it. If France and Germany export, why not Great Britain?

Fuller's earth. Large deposits of Fuller's earth have recently been discovered in this eastern country; one deposit is said to be of 5,000 acres magnitude, and a company is to be formed at once to open up same. Extensive quantities of this earth is used by the packing houses of this country, but nearly all comes from the eastern States, but originally from England. During 1895 135 tons were imported here direct from England. This is another trade that can be enlarged if the merchants will look after it; lower rates can be obtained viâ the Gulf of Mexico ports than viâ the eastern ports.

Enamel ware. There is a demand in this western country for all kinds of household enamel ware; many enquiries for same have been made during the past year, and it finds ready sale.

The wholesale and jobbing trade of Kansas City for 1895 was larger than that of 1894, and amounted to 21,000,000*l*. Below find principal classes of goods sold:—

CHICAGO.

Articles.	Value.
	£
Agricultural implements	3,285,273
Groceries	3,000,009
Dry goods	6,115,470
Coal	1,140,000
Lumber	1,215,242
Fruits	1,110,714
Drugs	410,000
Hardware	700,000
Tobacco	471,090
Jewellery	429,000
Tea, coffee, spices	359,060
Boots and shoes	401,210
Harness, saddlery	272,040
Hats, caps, gloves	170,000
Notions	109,940
Miscellaneous	1,810,900
Total	20,999,948

Aluminium. A new product has been discovered in this vicinity, which is called silicate of aluminium; it is a soft stone that can be cut with a pen-knife. When placed in cold water for about four hours, it expands about three times its size, and becomes a natural paste; this paste is put on horses' feet that have become sore from over travel on hard roads, and it has proven a speedy and effective cure in many cities in this country. Foreign cities are now trying it, and one china house has made some goods out of, and is pleased with the results, and contemplates manufacturing chinaware goods out of same. It has been used for bunions, sprains, and also for tooth powder, with good results.

Street railway. During 1895 all the cable, electric, and one steam railway company have been consolidated under one name and company; the steam, all the street, and part of the cable railways have since been changed into electric railways, and are proving a vast improvement. The combined mileage of this system is about 150 miles. Ordinances are being prepared for the building of two or three new electric lines, which if constructed, will add much to the welfare of the city and the accommodation of people in some of the suburbs. Many miles of old lines are to be rebuilt with heavier steel rails during 1896.

The capital stock of this company is 1,157,700*l.*; it owns 147 grip cars, 249 cable trailers, 109 combination cable cars, 54 electric motors, 15 electric trailers and 47 horse cars. To furnish power to all the lines of this immense system of street railways, the company has an engine and boiler capacity of over 6,000 horse power, distributed through the eight power houses of the company. The engine is the same one used at the World's Fair, Chicago, in 1893.

Bank clearings. Bank clearings for 1895 show a wonderful increase over 1894 and with the rapid strides that this young giant city is making, it is bound to become the ninth city in the United States for volume of business and amount of bank clearings. During the year 1895 bank clearings were 97,870,675*l.*; 1894, 99,910,580*l.*; and 1895, 107,617,899*l.*, showing a good increase for the last year.

There are nine national and ten state and private banks, with a capital of 2,350,000*l.*

The export trade of this western country being large and rapidly increasing, the exporters are very much interested in the matter of preventing dishonest goods being sent out of the country.

The United States Government has taken another means to protect the export trade. This consists in denying the right of exportation of all horses, mules, live cattle and preserved meats, not accompanied by a certificate from the inspector of the department of agriculture of the absence of all epizootic in the first cases, and of everything hurtful to the health, in the latter. This measure seems to be important in a double sense; it is, first, a bold official initiative for putting an end to the export of a food product capable of injuring American commerce in the great foreign markets; then, it is taking a stand for reducing to nought a certain number, at least, of the complaints which prompted the prohibition in Europe of certain American food products. Both of these things may have important consequences. The first is, perhaps, the beginning of this movement so desirable, not only in the United States, but in the other great countries, and which will end by hindering the exportation of every indigenous or other product of a nature to compromise the interests of exportation. Whoever has resided awhile abroad knows the immense injury done to honest trade, by dishonest trade, and will be happy to see the custom houses of the different countries organize a kind of international commercial gendarmerie, and prevent the exportation of everything that is bad.

Labour.

Great complaint is made by the printing fraternity against the introduction of the "Margenthaler" type-setting machines now being used in all the large newspaper offices; they claim it is ruining the printing profession, and reducing greatly the number of men required. The machines cannot be used to set display advertisements. The cost of hand composition was, on morning papers, 12·9*d.* per 1,000 ens, and on afternoon papers 12·7*d.*; by machines it is 5½*d.* and 5*d.* respectively. These figures represent the amount paid to compositors, without taking into consideration any other expense. The cost of the "Margenthaler" machine (the kind used) when sold outright, is 630*l.* Royalty on machines, when not purchased, 5*l.* 0*s.* 8*d.* per week (108*l.* per year). Cost of operation of machine, per day, without royalty or operator's salary, 1*s.* 9*d.*; cost of operation of machine per day, including royalty but not operator's salary, 7*s.* 6*d.*

Condition of labour in this city does not show any improvement, the supply is far ahead of the demand. Owing to the large number of unions existing it is hard for non-union and unskilled labourers to get work. The same trouble prevails here as elsewhere; that is, that every idle person insists in flocking to the city for work, and the city becomes badly over-done. Owing to the despotic character of the numerous labour organisations, which have not carried their pretentions to a successful issue without violence, a working man has little chance of employment at the rate paid by the trade, unless he first becomes affiliated to some union. The bulk of employment given here is by the live stock, packing house and railway industry.

The class of employment for women still continues to offer the best chance of saving in domestic service—this class of work is performed nearly altogether by foreign women, for it is not a popular service with the native, from a feeling of independence; wages for this class of work are very high compared with other labour. *Female labour.*

Women stenographers, typewriters and office helps are much more plentiful and increasing; for 1895 the wages for this class of work have decreased 5 per cent. The salaries of the girls and women employed at the great department stores, laundries, and factories of all descriptions remains the same as last year, and no material change can be noticed.

The employment of children in this city is allowed. In some of the large department stores they can be seen working as cash boys and girls between the ages of 9 and 15 years. *Child labour.*

Only one strike took place in this city in 1895, that was about 300 granite-stone cutters who wanted an increase of 10 per cent. in their wages, and demanded their salary paid twice per month. The work was being done on the new custom-house, and the government only paid once per month; after several weeks strike and absence from work the men returned to their work, but did not gain the point for which they struck. *Strikes.*

The last report of the United States Commissioner of Labour places the loss to working men, during the past 13 years through strikes and lockouts at 39,256,193*l*.

Large quantities of potatoes are raised in this western country and shipped to all parts of the United States; the soil is well adapted to this industry. *Potatoes.*

The Russian thistle is fast spreading over this western country; one reason is because of so much prairie land and so much wind that the seed is carried much quicker. In some States the authorities have been compelled to devise ways and means for the destruction of the weed. *Russian thistle.*

During 1895 over 60 young men were sent into this Vice-Consular district under false pretences from Great Britain; in every case they came through unreliable employment agencies in London; they were sent here under the pretext of their being apprenticed on large stock farms, for which they paid money in advance; after arrival here they were placed on small farms, and in some cases not provided with work, but left to the mercy of strangers, which forced them to seek assistance and advice from the Vice-Consul. Such employment agencies should be investigated and suppressed. *Employment agencies.*

British people should be very careful about placing investments in this western country; there are so many illegitimate and bogus mining, real estate, manufacturing and railroad schemes *Warning to investors.*

Sub-soiling.

whose main object is to get foreign capital to buy stock. My advice is "hands off" until you have proof as to the party or firm with whom you are dealing.

Sub-soiling is being tried all over this western country, and so far, is proving a great success, especially on cultivated prairie land.

Divorce.

The divorce laws in this western country are indeed very loose. People from many foreign countries go into Oklahoma Territory (including British subjects) and remain 90 days, then make application for divorce; in 30 days divorce is granted, and the plaintiff returns to his foreign home, with papers. In divorce cases, citizenship was never questioned; the law does not require it. Several foreign judges claim that such a divorce is illegally obtained, for foreign countries cannot legally divorce subjects of another country.

Gold at Cripple Creek.

At the present time (February) great excitement prevails among the people over the alleged wonderful discoveries of gold at Cripple Creek, Colorado; many are flocking there from this district; it is quite a craze; but caution should be observed by intending investors.

During 1894 and 1895 the cry was for free silver throughout this western country, but as the people by this time have studied its advantages and disadvantages to commercial trade, and the latter in the greater portion, the free silver agitation has become very quiet. Another great blow to free silver is the alleged discovery of such vast quantities of gold in the Rocky Mountains.

Bond deal.

Referring to the recent United States bond deal (February), one must notice that practically no bids were sent out from this western country; money out here can be loaned or invested in smaller lots and pay much higher rates of interest; the effect of the issuance of the bonds is not going to stimulate the trade as some people have predicted.

Smelters.

At Kansas City is located one of the largest smelters in this country. It was opened in 1881 and employed 150 workmen, to-day it employs about 800 men, paying annually the sum of 258,249*l*. for wages. The capacity of the smelter, per annum, is as follows:—

Articles.		Quantity.
Lead	Tons	50,000
Copper	”	500
Silver	Ounces	1,500,000
Gold		Unlimited.

Following are the amounts of the various refined metals shipped during 1895:—

Articles.		Quantity.
Gold	Ounces	133,470
Silver	,,	11,533,000
Lead	Lbs.	66,791,000
Copper	,,	4,609,000

To give the reader a better idea of the vast amount of these products, below find them at their money value for the products of 1895:—

	Value.
	£
Gold, at coinage rate	57,009
Silver, at coinage rate	3,080,807
Lead, at New York price	441,597
Copper, at New York price	95,226
Total	3,674,639

Refined products at Kansas City smelter for past 5 years:—

Year.	Silver.	Gold.	Lead.	Copper.
	Ounces.	Ounces.	Ounces.	Lbs.
1891	7,771,963	29,718	55,789,193	..
1892	8,901,353	27,158	59,162,542	2,663,545
1893	9,237,106	29,398	52,918,297	1,544,168
1894	9,498,386	93,438	57,743,361	2,031,294
1895	11,533,000	133,470	66,791,000	4,609,000

The total freight business of this company for 1895 shows by its books that it amounts to over 2,000 trains of 14 cars each, or 84 cars per day.

Following is a list of number of cars of products shipped from Kansas City smelter for the past 5 years:—

Year.	Number.
1891	23,393
1892	23,850
1893	20,978
1894	24,071
1895	25,050

The decrease in 1893 is accounted for by the fact that it was the year of the panic, when every kind of business suffered, and when the production of the different mines was curtailed greatly

UNITED STATES.

by the rapid fall in the price of metals, especially silver. Bear in mind that ore is shipped from all the western states to this point, and large quantities from the Republic of Mexico.

The production of gold and silver in the United States in 1895 as reported to the Director of the Mint by those employed to collect these statistics, is as follows:—

State.	Value of Gold.	Silver, Fine.
	£	Ounces.
Alaska	309,917	..
Arizona	427,087	1,000,000
California	3,223,140	154,700
Colorado	3,104,147	2,000,000
Idaho	576,591	4,000,000
Michigan	8,297	35,000
Montana	907,642	14,500,000
Nevada	351,239	622,600
New Mexico	222,107	154,700
Oregon	454,545	7,700
South Appalachian States	65,330	1,200
South Dakota	879,132	82,200
Texas	..	206,000
Utah	279,388	8,223,800
Washington	61,983	11,600
All others	5,165	500
Total	10,875,710	51,000,000

The Director of the Mint is of the opinion that the estimate of the gold product of Oregon is 123,967*l.* too high; of Montana, 51,642*l.* too high; of South Dakota, 83,834*l.* too high; and that when the final figures are compiled, the production of gold by the mines of the United States in 1895 will be found to be about 9,607,644*l.*, and the silver product, about 46,000,000 fine ounces. The product last year was about 8,161,157*l.* of gold, and 49,500,000 fine ounces of silver.

Silver production. The above estimates of silver production do not agree with the movement of silver, and that has been true of the official estimates of silver production for some years past. The net exports of silver in 1895 were 8,383,409*l.* The average price was about 2*s.* 8*d.*, so that over 60,000,000 ounces were exported. The domestic consumption amounts to fully 10,000,000 ounces, so that the total production must have been 70,000,000 ounces instead of 51,000,000 ounces. The exports in 1894 were about 57,000,000 ounces, and about 10,000,000 ounces were used in this country, so the 1894 production must have been about 67,000,000 ounces, instead of 49,500,000 ounces. The imports of silver in 1895 were about 18,000,000 ounces.

Silver ore was imported into Kansas city during 1895 from the Republic of Mexico and British Columbia, and was for the big Kansas City smelter. This is a new feature, and it is expected that if the mining industry develops in both named countries, as expected, it will certainly increase. For 1895 Kansas City received through its custom-house 26,487,885 lbs. of ore; the duty upon it was 41,019*l.*

The value of metals produced from domestic ore in the United States for 1895 amounted to 49,792,776*l.*, as compared with 40,102,409*l.*, he value of same metal in 1894; increase, 24·2 per cent. The value of coal output increased 16·6 per cent., or 5,635,975*l.* Iron ore increased 112·1 per cent., or 3,409,090*l.*

TABLE showing Metal Production in the United States during the Year 1895.

Metals.		Quantity.	Value at Place of Production.
			£
Aluminium	Lbs.	850,000	96,591
Antimony	Short tons	425	13,960
Copper	Lbs.	386,000,000	7,994,938
Gold	Troy oz.	2,152,877	9,270,865
Iron (pig)	Long tons	9,346,906	23,173,403
Lead (value New York)	Short tons	159,245	2,125,460
Quicksilver	Flask, 76½ lbs.	33,978	271,402
Silver (com. val.)	Troy oz.	41,238,764	5,563,784
Zinc (spelter)	Short tons	85,491	1,282,365
Total metals			49,792,768
Coal	Tons	195,000,000	43,801,625
Iron ore	Long tons	18,000,000	6,508,264
Zinc oxide	Short tons	22,690	328,161
Total value			50,638,077

It seems probable that the total mineral production, including iron ore, of the United States in 1895 amounted to 144,282,024*l.*, as compared with 117,398,038*l.* for 1894. The production of gold in the United States from domestic ore in 1895 was 2,170,827 fine ounces, or 9,270,867*l.*; of silver, 41,238,764 fine ounces, valued at 5,563,783*l.* A large amount of gold and silver has been refined here from British Columbia and Republic of Mexico; in fact the gold amounted to 202,715 fine ounces, or 864,487*l.*; and silver, 29,323,446 fine ounces, valued at 3,956,242*l.* The total production of refined gold and silver in the United States was therefore 2,373,542 ounces gold, and 70,562,210 ounces silver.

Flax seed. Extensive quantities of flax-seed are produced in this western country; quite a large number of oil mills are in operation, and large quantities of oils, flax seed, and oilcake are exported annually.

Tanning by electricity. Tanning by electricity is a new thing in the world, and is being experimented upon here at present, and looks favourable; should it prove so, it is rumoured that a tannery will be established, controlled by the packers, for the tanning of hides from their houses. In the test, oak, bark, and canaigre are used, and a current of electricity through the tanning liquor prevents fermentation, and tanning can be accomplished in about one-eighth of the usual time used. The experiment is being tried by an Englishman, formerly in the British service.

Tanning with canaigre is also being tried at this point; this is a new discovery. Canaigre is produced from trees, same as oak-bark, and is in abundance in the west. Tanning in the United States is all done in the east; but a few small tanneries exist in the west.

Investments. There is considerable British and other foreign capital invested in this western country; some are good investments, and others are not. There are at times good opportunities for good investments, but one must be confident of the parties through whom he is transacting his business.

Game and poultry. A large trade is done at this point in frozen game and poultry; some of the packing houses buy up large quantities when same is cheap in winter, and in summer it is sold at fabulous prices. The game is kept by refrigeration, and is a success.

Centre of population. During the past 15 years the centre of population of the United States has left the east, and is now in the trans-Missouri States. This can readily be seen by the vast amount of produce raised and exported, and the railway facilities for transporting same. One can hardly realise it unless living here; such a change has taken place. Merchants who used to go to New York for everything now buy nearer home, and just as satisfactorily; hence the building up of the wholesale trade here is marvellous.

It may be said that values in everything are gradually declining in the west. Fictitious prices are no more.

Irrigation. Several years ago, during the season, quite a number of steamboats landed here; but, owing partly to droughts in the west, and to thousands of miles of ditches opened up in the Platte and Missouri River valleys, so much water has been taken from the rivers that it has practically stopped navigation. Should irrigation be furthered, as predicted, it is a question if there will be enough water to supply the needs.

Cement. In this territory the British merchants are fast losing their trade in Portland cements. The reason given is on account of its being more or less adulterated of late years. But such is not the case with German and Belgian Portland cement; they keep up their standard grade, and have now secured the bulk of the trade in the west. Of this imported cement used in the west, about 10 per cent. is English, 20 per cent. Belgian, and 70 per cent. German. Considerable cement is produced locally, but it is not a grade that takes the place of imported cement.

Waterworks. The city purchased during 1895, at an expense of 650,000*l*., the waterworks from a local company; the water used is entirely from the Missouri River.

Boulevards. During 1895 work on a boulevard was begun, to encircle the city and to connect twelve small public parks, making a vast improvement for the city. Owing to a new State law in Missouri, it gives the city government power to condemn property and rights-of-way for parks and boulevards.

Kansas City enjoys the competition of two gas companies; the price of gas is 2s. 1d. per 1,000, and it is of good quality.

Gas.

Kansas City is one of the most important points in this country regarding mail matters, owing to the vast number of railways centreing here; and it is obtained from valuable information that four-fifths of the mails passing between the Atlantic and Pacific coasts passes through here.

Mails.

The United States is now building a new custom-house here, at an expense of 625,000l.; it has been necessary on account of the large growth of western business.

Custom-house.

Bicycle transportation has had a serious effect upon cables and electric transportation; also on the market for the sale of cheap riding horses and ponies. It was estimated that in 1894 there were in use in Kansas City 3,000 bicycles, and now there are at least 8,000 in use. There are quite a number of English bicycles in use here; but the use of them is somewhat hindered, as they are made a little too heavy; and in case of breaking any of the parts, it is hard to procure repairing supplies. 795,000 bicycles were in use in the United States in 1895.

Bicycles.

A large trade is done here in hides, horns, hoofs, hair, shank bones, tallow, bristles, and stearine. One can imagine the volume of this trade when the packers of Kansas City alone killed 940,974 cattle, 2,170,827 hogs, 575,806 sheep. Besides this, Kansas City handles all such products for this western country, which is a vast amount. The hides are shipped east for tanning, no tanneries being located here; horns are shipped east for combs; some hoofs are made into glue here, and some shipped east; the hair is shipped east for stuffing mattresses and some for glue; shank bones are used in eastern cities for special purposes; bristles are shipped east and used in the manufacture of brushes; stearine is used for making soap in this country—some of it finds its way to Holland for oleomargarine purposes. Tallow is here in abundance and accumulating, and if merchants can use it, they can buy at a low figure, for there is more than the demand can possibly use.

Hides, &c.

The milling industry is quite a business in and near Kansas City; so much flour is made from Kansas hard wheat, which is almost entirely used abroad. The finest and largest private mill in the world is the new Rex Mill, at Kansas City; it is built to make flour only for foreign trade. There is located in Kansas City, and within 30 miles of it, 20 mills, with daily output of 21,000 barrels.

Milling.

All the western cities are over-crowded. It seems to be a fad that as soon as a person desires they have an idea that to go to a city insures work. It is a sad mistake; parents should keep their children at home, as they are far better in the country or small towns than coming to cities and being compelled to undergo severe hardships.

Overcrowding of towns.

Two of the most important military forts in the United States are located near here: one at Fort Leavenworth, Kansas (Foot), 30 miles north of Kansas City; the other at Fort Riley, Kansas, 130

Military forts.

(2148)

miles west of Kansas City, and is the largest cavalry post in the United States. There are many small forts and posts all over this western country, especially in the Indian districts.

At Fort Leavenworth, Kansas, is also located the United States Government Penitentiary, containing at present 380 prisoners; this is the only exclusive government prison in the United States, and was made such in July, 1895.

Soldiers' homes. There are two soldiers' homes in this district: one at Grand Island, Nebraska, containing about 1,800 men, and the other at Leavenworth, Kansas, caring for about 2,800 men. They are kept in good shape, and everything is done for the comfort and enjoyment of the inmates.

Lotteries. Several years ago Kansas City was headquarters for dozens of bogus lotteries, but new laws were made and enforced, which has driven them away. It is not uncommon at present for complaints to come from all parts of the world of people being swindled by agents claiming that their lottery company is reliable, and their home office at Kansas City, I beg to warn all against buying such tickets, for lotteries are not allowed to operate anywhere in this country.

The unsettled condition of the tariff question in this country seriously hampers business; merchants will not buy more than actual needs, hence it forces them to carry much smaller stock than they would do otherwise.

Sanitary. At the time of writing (March 1, 1896) a great many cases of small-pox exist within 100 miles of here. Owing to the mildness of the weather is the only reason given that it has not caused more trouble in spreading; deaths from small-pox are comparately few.

Horseless mail wagons will soon be put in use in all the large cities of this country, but it is understood they will not be tried in Kansas City, on account of the large and excessive inclines and hills.

Electricity. Great improvements in electricity have been made in this city; the large office buildings, stock yards, packing houses, and railroad shops are all equipped with dynamos, and make their own light; a great many freight and passenger elevators are operated by electricity here, and cost less than by water or steam. There are four companies here furnishing arc and incandescent lights for business purposes, and many residences are equipped with incandescent lights.

Zinc and lead ore. It is stated from good authority that very extensive quantities of zinc and lead exists in Marion and Boone counties, Arkansas; but to develop same a railway of about 140 miles in length would have to be constructed, at a cost of about 450,000*l.* Several surveys have been made, but no selection has been made.

I beg to state that along the line of the Kansas City, Pittsburg, and Gulf Railway, between Kansas City and Port Arthur, I am reliably informed that there are vast deposits of copper, lead, zinc, and semi-anthracite coal; the opening of this territory will develop these properties, and provide some product for export. There is also a vast amount of short and long leaf yellow pine, which grows to an enormous height. It has been used in a small way for shipbuilding, and gives satisfaction. Hardwood, for furnishing purposes, grows in abundance, consisting of walnut, beech, oak, ash, cherry, also cypress and hickory. From enquiries now being made, some of it will, no doubt, be exported as soon as the railway opens up.

Two Dutch steamship lines are figuring to operate ships between Port Arthur and Holland in connection with said railroad. All such matters are consummated here. I would suggest that British shipowners bear this in mind. It may be of service to them.

There are very few savings banks in this western country; so many have failed through mismanagement that the people will not put their savings into them.

A large number of loan and building associations are in existence here, and thriving. They are all under the supervision of the State, and the laws governing same are rigidly enforced.

Owing to the great gold-mining craze of Cripple Creek, Colorado, there are hundreds and thousands of companies being formed. Some of them are valueless, and efforts are being made to establish agencies in Europe to sell stock and defraud people. I beg to warn the British people not to buy such stock, unless they are positively doing so from reliable firms.

The foundation of Kansas City is the stockyards, and it is the *Stockyards.* corner stone upon which the city was built, and in the branch of commercial industry it has made more rapid strides than any other industry in this country. No other city in the world can show such a marvellous gain of trade in any one line of commerce, as the following figures will indicate.

The stockyards of Kansas City were commenced in 1870, and occupied 5 acres of ground, and to-day they occupy 191 acres of land, of which some 40 acres are covered with elaborate sheep and hog pens, doubling the yardage room of the said 40 acres. In the yards is located the exchange building, of about 400 office rooms. In the building are several telegraph and telephone offices and banks, and also representatives of every railroad entering the city.

This is the greatest railroad centre in the world, and every railroad has its connections direct with the stockyards. It is surprising to see the volume of trade handled daily at these yards, and at some times with much rapidity.

The new addition of the exchange building of 140 office rooms and many other improvements, including the building of a separate waterworks system, buying land, fencing, paving, constructing overhead drive ways, new fire engine houses, and many other things, caused an outlay of 400,000*l.*, and more improvements will have to be made shortly to keep up with the growing demand.

Located, as is Kansas City, in the very centre of the great Indian corn belt and the natural market, and adjacent to the greatest grazing and live stock producing territory in the world, Kansas City is bound to become the leading live stock and packing meat mart in the world. The eastern part of this continent is

(2148)

gradually declining in the raising of live stock, farms are being divided and becoming more valuable for other uses, while the great natural territory for live-stock west of Kansas City is capable of producing 10 times more annually than it has ever produced.

The great railway lines of this western country all penetrate the great cattle ranges; all of them lead to, and some of them through, Kansas City, which naturally brings the live stock to this market.

I have compiled a table for the reader to see where the cattle come from, and in what numbers, and have also compiled many tables showing comparisons, which, no doubt, will be very interesting to many.

Nearly 200 firms are located in the stockyards, and many foreign buyers are located here.

Texas sends a vast amount of live stock to Kansas City. The Texas assessments, January 1, 1896, show that there is within the borders 4,873,898 cattle, 2,386,822 sheep, 1,494,981 hogs, 206,071 goats, and 1,500,923 horses and mules. A large amount of this stock will find its way here.

With the beginning of 1896 the live stock industry at Kansas City is on a firmer basis than at any previous time since its inception. Within 5 years the cattle trade has metamorphosed into a first-class market, instead of a combined market and feeding point. Everything in the way of cattle sells upon arrival, which is saying no small thing, since over 1,500,000 cattle are annually received.

There has been less change in the status of the hog trade than in any other branch of this industry. For many years the capacity to handle hogs by the local houses has been far in excess of the supply, so that there is no development to report along the line of pork packing. As the sparsely-peopled territory to the south-west is dotted with small farms, however, more hogs will be raised, and Kansas City will be supplied with many thousand more. More rapidity has been shown in the growth of the sheep trade than in any other branch of industry. Western and south-western holders during the past two years have been acquainted with the advantages attendant on the establishment of a robust sheep market at this point, being closer to the south-western and western source of supply than any other market. An increase in sheep business of about 100 per cent. since 1892 tells the marvellous tale.

The horse and mule market has also had an impetus during the past two years. The immense barns erected to accommodate this trade are the finest, as well as the largest in this country. The main barns will accommodate 1,000 horses comfortably. The sales pavilion is roomy, well lighted and heated, and it is a novel sight to see a horse sold every minute, which has been done at several auctions.

Over 9,300 horses were handled and sold in December, 1895, an average of 357 for each commercial day.

So rapidly has the stock industry grown at Kansas City that for many years the Stockyards Company has been devoting much time and millions of money in caring for the increasing business. The business has augmented as fast as more room could be secured. Even during 1895 radical changes were necessary in the general plan of the yards. In the first place, the exchange building was inadequate to the needs of an ever-increasing army of commission men, so that the space in the old buildings was nearly doubled; a four-storey building has just been added, making the present accommodations the most ample of any live-stock exchange in the world. The new building is 246 feet long and 60 feet wide. It contains 112 offices, and cost 15,000*l*. There are now five wings to the exchange building, containing floor space to the amount of 152,000 square feet, or $3\frac{1}{2}$ acres.

The most gigantic deal of the year was the acquisition of four blocks of ground, the removal of scores of residences therefrom, and the erection on the vacated ground of pens capable of holding 5,000 cattle. The great portion of the yards has been paved with vitrified brick, an electric light plant erected to supply the whole of the yards with light, and other improvements too numerous to mention. The expense account of the yard company for improvements alone will run into millions for the year 1895. Eastern stockmen, who are familiar with all the stockyards of the United States, pronounce the Kansas City yards the most nearly perfect in their appointments of any in the country. At present the yards will store away 25,000 cattle, 40,000 hogs, and 15,000 sheep.

UNITED STATES.

TABLE showing Origin of Receipts of Cattle at Kansas City for the Years 1894–95, with Gain or Loss, from the different States and Territories tributary.

State.	1894.	1895.	Gain.	Loss.
Arkansas	3,173	2,099	..	1,074
Arizona	6,321	2,131	..	4,189
Colorado	39,843	62,770	22,927	..
California	332	556	224	..
Indiana	22	..	..	22
Illinois	218	468	250	..
Iowa	8,307	15,588	7,281	..
Indian Territory	228,283	191,314	..	36,969
Idaho	822	5,565	4,743	..
Kansas	959,305	762,205	..	197,100
Louisiana	..	25	25	..
Michigan	..	106	106	..
Mississippi	23	..	..	23
Minnesota	882	8,274	7,392	..
Montana	201	235	34	..
Missouri	200,889	215,388	14,499	..
Nebraska	86,485	86,971	486	..
New Mexico	35,582	22,682	..	12,900
Nevada	1,424	4,372	2,948	..
Ohio	..	33	33	..
Oregon	749	685	..	91
Oklahoma	40,260	61,515	21,255	..
South Dakota	137	977	840	..
Tennessee	120	..	..	120
Texas	153,871	231,986	78,115	..
Utah	3,925	7,724	4,699	..
Washington	206	89	..	117
Wyoming	2,011	5,103	3,092	..
Mexico	54	536	482	..
Total	1,772,545	1,689,652	..	..

TABLE showing Receipts of Hogs at Kansas City in the Year 1895 Shipped from the undermentioned States and Territories.

State.	1894.	1895.	Gain.	Loss.
Arkansas	7,761	3,218	..	4,543
Colorado	292	742	450	..
Iowa	68	287	219	..
Indian Territory	35,796	39,518	3,722	..
Idaho	162	..	..	162
Illinois	..	6	6	..
Kansas	1,698,795	1,528,002	..	170,793
Missouri	601,681	693,211	91,530	..
Minnesota	..	178	178	..
Nebraska	149,307	129,627	..	19,680
New Mexico	..	14	14	..
Oklahoma	46,655	56,587	9,932	..
Texas	6,560	6,060	..	500
Washington	..	247	247	..
Total	2,547,077	2,457,697	..	..

CHICAGO.

Export of live hogs from the United States to Great Britain is not a success, owing to the great distance. In 1894 1,919 hogs were exported, and in 1895 2,678 hogs were exported.

Mexican duty on live hogs is $3\frac{1}{2}d.$ per kilo., and on lard 5d., hence the reason that live hogs are exported from here in lieu of lard.

At this time (February) some heavy contracts are about to be consummated for several large orders of live hogs to the city of Mexico, and as hogs are cheaper no doubt many will be shipped to that country.

TABLE showing Sheep Receipts at Kansas City in 1895, Shipped from the undermentioned States and Territories.

State.	1894.	1895.	Gain.	Loss.
Arkansas	1,512	1,542	36	..
Arizona	23,794	44,852	21,058	..
Colorado	72,661	145,892	33,231	..
California	602	1,016	414	..
Illinois	..	914	914	..
Iowa	646	773	127	..
Indian territory	933	1,352	419	..
Idaho	4,787	12,606	7,819	..
Kansas	216,233	191,038	..	25,195
Missouri	98,201	132,877	34,676	..
Mexico	..	1,628	1,628	..
Nevada	1,395	8,513	7,118	..
Nebraska	15,478	12,011	..	3,467
New Mexico	39,934	71,462	31,528	..
Oklahoma	893	3,168	2,275	..
Oregon	..	854	854	..
Texas	38,787	166,570	127,783	..
Utah	68,766	102,555	33,789	..
Wyoming	4,932	5,083	151	..
Total	589,555	864,713	275,148	..

The following shows the average weight of hogs marketed at Kansas City for 1895, by months; also corresponding period of 1894:—

Month.	1895.	1894.
	Lbs.	Lbs.
January	216	226
February	213	220
March	213	216
April	213	211
May	211	212
June	212	209
July	213	215
August	209	199
September	212	203
October	220	208
November	227	223
December	235	221

Average weight of hogs for 1895, 216 lbs., and for 1894 215 lbs.

The largest receipts at Kansas City stockyards was as follows :—

LARGEST RECEIPTS IN ONE DAY.

	Date.	Quantity.
Cattle	October 16, 1894	17,030
Calves	August 31, 1893	1,747
Hogs	July 30, 1890	26,408
Sheep	May 27, 1895	11,504
Horses and mules	December 17, 1895	797

LARGEST RECEIPTS IN ONE WEEK.

	Date.	Quantity.
Cattle	August 31, 1894	78,005
Calves	August 31, 1892	7,022
Hogs	July 31, 1890	155,044
Sheep	May 31, 1890	38,912
Horses and mules	October 31, 1895	2,959

LARGEST RECEIPTS IN ONE MONTH.

	Date.	Quantity.
Cattle	October, 1893	226,248
Calves	August, 1892	19,848
Hogs	July, 1890	347,469
Sheep	October, 1895	105,915
Horses and mules	December, 1895	9,340

LARGEST RECEIPTS IN ONE YEAR.

	Date.	Quantity.
Cattle	1894	1,689,193
Calves	1892	92,077
Hogs	1890	2,865,171
Sheep	1895	864,713
Horses and mules	1895	52,607

The Fall Cattle Feeder's Movement.

The heavy trade in cattle for feeding and fattening usually begins in September, and is over by the last of November. This business at Kansas City during these 3 months of 1895 far exceeded that of any similar period. Car lot shipments were as follows :—

CHICAGO.

Month.	Number of Cars.		
	1895.	1894.	1893.
September	1,630	999	1,267
October	1,902	1,792	1,716
November	1,518	1,644	1,450
Total	5,051	4,434	4,433

The increase was pretty evenly divided between Kansas and Missouri, each having more to its credit than ever before. The heavy corn crop in Missouri, the large supply of such cattle at Kansas City, and the smaller supply at Chicago and Omaha, sent many Missouri feeder buyers to Kansas City market, that were accustomed to buy elsewhere. As a consequence, Missouri got more feeder cattle here than did Kansas ; the first time such a thing has happened since 1891, when Kansas was experiencing the after-effects of a drought.

Shipments to Kansas during the three months of the various years were as follows :—

Month.	Number of Cars.		
	1995.	1894.	1893.
September	536	331	596
October	941	937	765
November	770	916	765
Total	2,247	2,184	2,126

And to Missouri :—

Month.	Number of Cars.		
	1895.	1894.	1893.
September	988	648	573
October	836	774	830
November	633	671	572
Total	2,457	2,093	1,975

NOTE.—Estimate 25 feeders to a car.

The following shows the total yearly receipts of cattle, hogs, sheep, horses, and mules since the opening of the stockyards at Kansas City for business in June, 1871 :—

Year.	Cattle.	Calves.	Hogs.	Sheep.	Mules and Horses.
1871	120,827	...	41,036	4,527	809
1872	236,802	...	104,639	6,071	2,648
1873	227,689	...	221,815	5,975	4,202
1874	207,080	...	212,532	8,855	3,679
1875	174,754	...	63,350	25,327	2,646
1876	183,378	...	153,777	55,045	5,339
1877	215,768	...	192,645	42,190	4,279
1878	175,344	...	427,777	36,700	10,796
1879	211,415	...	588,908	61,684	15,829
1880	244,709	...	676,477	50,611	14,086
1881	285,863	...	1,014,304	79,924	12,592
1882	439,671	...	963,036	80,724	11,716
1883	460,780	...	1,379,401	119,665	19,860
1884	533,526	...	1,723,586	237,964	27,163
1885	506,627	...	2,358,718	221,801	24,506
1886	490,971	...	2,264,484	172,659	33,188
1887	669,224	...	2,423,262	209,956	29,690
1888	1,056,086	...	2,008,984	351,050	27,650
1889	1,239,343	...	2,073,910	370,772	34,553
1890	1,472,229	76,568	2,865,171	535,869	37,118
1891	1,270,917	76,570	2,599,109	386,760	31,740
1892	1,479,078	92,077	2,397,477	438,268	32,505
1893	1,660,807	86,021	1,948,373	569,517	35,097
1894	1,689,193	83,352	2,547,077	589,555	44,237
1895	1,613,454	76,198	2,457,697	864,713	52,607
Total	16,846,535	490,786	33,707,545	5,526,182	518,545

Valuation of the stock handled at the Kansas City stockyards in 1895, 93,200,329 dol., against 98,577,164 dol. in 1894, or equal to 19,216,563*l.* for 1895, and 20,325,190*l.* for 1894. Although the value is less for 1895, it must be remembered that prices are much lower.

TABLE showing Total Number of Head and Valuation of Stock handled at Kansas City Yards for past 25 Years.

Year.	Number.	Valuation.
	Head.	£
1871	167,199	868,700
1872	350,160	1,630,060
1873	459,681	1,423,050
1874	432,146	1,402,210
1875	266,077	1,217,320
1876	397,539	1,483,610
1877	454,882	1,621,070
1878	650,617	1,517,820
1879	877,836	2,198,910
1880	985,883	2,949,030
1881	1,392,683	4,842,710
1882	1,495,147	6,748,200
1883	1,979,706	7,400,173
1884	2,522,239	8,542,411
1885	3,111,652	8,095,510
1886	2,961,302	7,400,071
1887	3,332,132	9,000,007
1888	3,443,770	11,559,774
1889	3,699,588	12,304,657
1890	4,986,955	15,600,091
1891	4,365,096	13,236,307
1892	4,439,405	15,104,009
1893	4,299,815	18,963,627
1894	4,953,414	20,367,098
1895	5,064,669	19,264,591
Total	57,089,593	194,741,016

CHICAGO.

TABLE showing Number of Swine in the Western States, of all Ages, in January.

State.	Number. 1895.	1894.	1893.
Illinois	3,148,658	3,422,454	3,720,059
Iowa	5,516,485	5,996,179	6,181,628
Missouri	3,561,136	3,709,517	4,076,392
Kansas	1,822,268	2,249,714	2,445,341
Nebraska	1,316,047	2,088,964	2,198,909
Minnesota	578,306	566,967	550,453
Wisconsin	911,623	930,228	921,018
Texas	2,734,341	2,555,459	2,344,548
Arkansas	1,547,689	1,547,689	1,563,322
California	487,943	435,663	399,691
Oregon	229,714	210,747	204,609
Nevada	11,590	11,596	11,363
Colorado	26,021	26,021	25,511
Arizona	20,904	19,536	19,536
Dakota	282,193	340,918	329,500
Idaho	64,598	58,725	57,015
Montano	45,690	39,388	38,616
New Mexico	28,897	27,521	24,355
Utah	54,443	51,850	47,136
Washington	211,870	162,977	158,230
Wyoming	15,834	15,834	15,834
Oklahoma	48,318	24,158	..

The Department of Agriculture reports that the actual value of food animals exported to Great Britain in 1895 was 5,089,200*l.* worth of cattle; Canada ranks next, her contributions in cattle being valued at 1,583,880*l.* The United States sent live sheep, valued at 795,313*l.* The Argentine Republic ranked next, with sheep valued at 522,231*l.*; Canada was third, having sent 400,000*l.* worth of sheep. Of fresh beef, the United States exported to Great Britain in 1895, the value is placed at 3,564,400*l.*, and 2,786,709*l.* worth of hams. Out of a total of 8,198,139*l.* paid by the Britons for imported bacon, 4,748,011*l.* were paid to the United States, and 2,587,404*l.* to Denmark, which ranks next.

TABLE showing the number of Cattle, Hogs, and Sheep killed by Packers at Kansas City, by Years, since 1868.

Year.	Cattle.	Hogs.	Sheep.
1868	4,200	13,000	..
1869	4,420	23,000	..
1870	21,000	36,700	..
1871	20,313	38,705	644
1872	30,332	95,806	660
1873	45,421	186,964	1,668
1874	40,550	98,145	1,901
1875	47,940	47,306	7,568
1876	62,916	126,916	32,369
1877	89,201	177,231	14,004
1878	43,788	334,684	6,529
1879	55,530	380,943	13,375
1880	49,860	523,928	14,719
1881	62,145	819,923	18,770
1882	80,509	770,518	28,056
1883	73,000	1,065,126	57,201
1884	90,991	1,134,154	131,241
1885	104,196	1,557,865	107,333
1886	120,556	1,726,318	89,163
1887	185,690	1,899,054	106,365
1888	372,925	1,595,313	181,864
1889	474,885	1,741,850	195,027
1890	570,163	2,305,127	199,000
1891	570,761	1,995,652	209,641
1892	727,981	1,805,114	218,909
1893	956,792	1,427,763	372,385
1894	972,808	2,050,784	393,298
1895	940,974	2,170,827	575,806

Below is a statement of receipts of cattle, hogs, and sheep at Kansas City, Chicago, Omaha, and St. Louis.

Chicago is the oldest of the four markets, the commencement of the period when it could be regarded as such having been December 27, 1865. In June, 1871, the Kansas City stockyards were opened for business. In 1874 the National stockyards at St. Louis were opened for business. In August, 1884, the stockyards at Omaha were opened for business. Thus is briefly stated the period when the four leading western live stock markets were started, which will give an idea of the time they have been competitors for trade, and the wonderful progress made.

In the 30 years Chicago has been a live stock market there were received there:—

	Number.
Cattle	49,214,663
Hogs	152,779,500
Sheep	30,080,121

CHICAGO.

In the 24 years and 7 months that Kansas City has been a live-stock market, there have been received:—

	Number.
Cattle	16,846,535
Hogs	33,807,545
Sheep	5,526,182

In the 21 years that the National Stock Yards have been the market for St. Louis, there were received:—

	Number.
Cattle	9,313,052
Hogs	13,416,297
Sheep	5,129,008

From August, 1884, to December 31, 1895, 11 years and 4 months, the receipts at Omaha were:—

	Number.
Cattle	5,654,944
Hogs	13,546,539
Sheep	1,681,968

As Omaha is the youngest of the four markets, in order to give an idea of the comparative receipts by years, 1884, the year that stock was first marketed there, should be selected as a period from which to commence comparison.

COMPARATIVE Yearly Receipts of Cattle at Kansas City, Omaha, Chicago, and St. Louis, from 1884-95.

Year.	Kansas City.	Chicago.	Omaha.	St. Louis.
1884	535,526	1,817,697	88,603	390,569
1885	506,627	1,905,518	116,963	311,702
1886	490,971	1,963,900	148,515	307,244
1887	669,224	2,382,008	239,337	387,709
1888	1,056,086	2,611,543	355,923	453,918
1889	1,220,343	3,023,281	473,094	396,095
1890	1,472,229	3,484,280	615,337	510,755
1891	1,270,917	3,290,359	602,002	630,356
1892	1,479,078	3,571,796	755,059	653,337
1893	1,660,807	3,133,406	852,456	756,485
1894	1,699,193	2,974,363	821,512	663,657
1895	1,613,454	2,588,558	586,103	733,526

UNITED STATES.

From the above it appears that the high water mark in Chicago in the matter of cattle receipts was reached in 1892, when they numbered 3,571,796, and since that year there has been a steady falling-off, the supplies of cattle marketed there in 1895 having been 985,238 less than in 1892. The decrease in the cattle receipts at Chicago for 1895 from what they were in 1892 is, therefore, larger than the total receipts of cattle at either Omaha or St. Louis in 1895.

COMPARATIVE Yearly Receipts of Hogs at Kansas City, Chicago, Omaha, and St. Louis, from 1884–95.

Year.	Number.			
	Kansas City.	Chicago.	Omaha.	St. Louis.
1884	1,723,586	5,351,967	3,686	1,079,827
1885	2,358,718	6,937,535	152,524	1,145,546
1886	2,246,484	6,718,791	477,119	935,995
1887	2,423,262	5,470,852	1,056,242	772,171
1888	2,008,984	4,921,712	1,224,691	652,127
1889	2,073,910	5,998,526	1,262,647	772,579
1890	2,865,171	7,663,829	1,702,723	925,480
1891	2,599,109	8,600,805	1,537,387	840,927
1892	2,397,477	7,714,435	1,633,384	847,703
1893	1,948,373	6,057,278	1,406,451	777,433
1894	2,537,077	7,483,228	1,932,677	1,146,925
1895	2,457,697	7,885,283	1,186,726	1,084,574

TABLE showing Receipts of Cattle, Hogs, and Sheep, at the Four Leading Western Markets, in 1895, compared with previous Years, in the United States.

	Number.		
	Cattle.	Hogs.	Sheep.
Kansas City	1,613,454	2,457,697	864,713
Chicago	2,588,558	7,885,283	3,406,739
Omaha	586,103	1,186,726	204,870
St. Louis	733,526	1,084,574	454,852
Total, 1895	5,521,641	12,614,280	4,931,174
„ 1894	6,148,724	13,099,907	4,225,348
„ 1893	6,403,154	10,197,535	4,203,005
„ 1892	6,459,370	12,572,999	3,070,407
„ 1891	5,752,634	13,578,228	3,057,735
„ 1890	6,094,846	13,160,826	3,156,297
„ 1889	5,107,059	10,051,820	2,641,271
„ 1888	4,462,016	8,866,423	2,393,415
„ 1887	3,674,664	9,677,991	1,962,378
„ 1886	2,906,572	10,309,727	1,433,745
„ 1885	2,808,010	10,572,666	1,490,777
„ 1884	2,778,690	8,157,243	1,331,460

CHICAGO.

Mr. Washington C. Ford, of the Bureau of Statistics, Treasury Department, furnishes the following report of exports of provisions and their value from the United States for January, 1896 and 1895:—

Articles.	January, 1896. Quantity.	January, 1896. Value.	January, 1895. Quantity.	January, 1895. Value.
	Lbs.	£	Lbs.	£
Canned beef	10,032,160	189,949	5,464,223	99,235
Fresh beef	17,690,058	307,749	16,990,058	308,435
Salted beef	6,363,425	76,277	6,628,530	81,282
Tallow	4,337,163	44,690	1,160,427	12,400
Bacon	46,931,901	752,412	40,208,147	677,845
Hams	13,658,398	276,828	7,876,312	102,262
Pork	7,526,152	88,280	5,223,339	77,080
Lard	55,434,515	760,544	3,803,019	785,748

In the matter of receipts of hogs at Chicago, the year 1891 was the banner one, when the hogs marketed there reached 8,600,805 head, while in 1895 the receipts were 7,885,283 head, or 715,522 less than in 1891.

Comparative yearly receipts of sheep at Kansas City, Chicago, Omaha, and St. Louis from 1884 to 1895, were:—

Year.	Kansas City.	Chicago.	Omaha.	St. Louis.
1884	237,964	801,630	5,503	277,678
1885	221,801	1,003,588	19,484	245,793
1886	172,659	1,008,790	41,490	212,101
1887	209,956	1,360,862	79,422	315,546
1888	351,050	1,515,014	172,138	368,848
1889	370,772	1,832,469	152,517	278,977
1890	535,869	2,182,667	153,873	282,206
1891	386,760	2,153,537	169,865	347,573
1892	438,268	2,145,079	185,588	298,432
1893	569,517	3,031,174	252,273	350,041
1894	589,555	3,099,725	234,945	292,223
1895	864,713	3,406,739	204,870	454,852

Omaha was the only one of the four markets at which sheep receipts showed a falling-off in 1895, when compared with previous years, but it was the banner year at Kansas City, Chicago, and St. Louis. The increased marketing of sheep at the four markets in 1895 amounted to 705,826.

One of the new industries of the Kansas City Stock Yards is the exportation of live hogs to the Republic of Mexico; during 1895, 6,111 hogs, average weight of 305 lbs., and valued at 15,139*l*. The Mexican people will not use American lard on account of its being adulterated with tallow and cotton seed oil.

(2148)

UNITED STATES.

As this is the first exportation of hogs to Mexico, and same has proven successful, it looks very much as though it will continue and increase.

In the official report of Mr. Washington C. Ford, the Chief of the Bureau, showing the exports of provisions in 1895, and corresponding time in 1894, these figures appear :—

		Quantity.	
Articles.		1895.	1894.
		Lbs.	Lbs.
Pork	.. ..	68,862,817	63,164,725
Lard	.. ..	501,880,718	471,811,107
Hams	.. ..	109,737,776	95,078,552
Bacon	.. ..	439,529,132	439,012,690
Fresh beef	.. ..	184,316,122	204,042,746
Salted beef	.. ..	64,332,430	64,456,731
Canned beef	.. ..	60,935,753	58,661,435
Tallow	.. ..	23,581,902	33,661,435

In the report for 1895 it will be observed that the export of pork, lard, hams, bacon, and canned beef, show an increase, while those of fresh beefs, salted beefs, and tallow, show a falling-off.

The exports of lard to Germany were large, but not so very far behind those of Great Britain, while those of boxed meats were small, and the same may be said in regard to the exports of France.

Cattle, Sheep, and Swine in the United States.

From reports of the Department of Agriculture showing number of cattle, sheep, and swine in the United States for January of the years indicated :—

Year.		Total.			Aggregate Number.
		Cattle.	Sheep.	Swine.	
		Number.	Number.	Number.	
1879	.. ..	33,234,500	38,123,800	34,766,200	106,124,500
1880	.. ..	33,258,000	40,765,900	34,765,100	108,057,000
1881	.. ..	33,306,385	43,576,899	36,227,603	113,110,887
1882	.. ..	35,891,870	45,016,224	44,122,300	125,030,294
1883	.. ..	41,171,762	49,237,291	43,270,086	133,679,139
1884	.. ..	42,547,307	50,626,626	44,200,893	137,374,826
1885	.. ..	43,771,295	50,360,243	45,142,657	139,274,195
1886	.. ..	45,510,630	48,322,331	46,092,043	139,925,004
1887	.. ..	48,033,833	44,759,314	44,612,836	137,405,983
1888	.. ..	49,234,777	43,544,755	44,346,525	137,126,057
1889	.. ..	50,331,042	42,599,079	50,301,592	143,231,713
1890	.. ..	52,801,907	44,336,072	51,602,780	148,740,759
1891	.. ..	52,895,239	43,431,136	50,625,106	146,951,481
1892	.. ..	54,067,590	44,938,365	52,398,019	151,403,974
1893	.. ..	52,378,283	47,273,553	46,094,807	145,746,643
1894	.. ..	53,095,568	45,048,017	45,206,498	143,350,083
1895	.. ..	50,868,845	42,294,064	44,164,716	137,328,625

CHICAGO.

The report of the Secretary of Agriculture begins with a review of the work of the Bureau of Animal Industry. The total number of animals inspected at the slaughter-houses was considerably over 18,000,000, an increase of more than 5,000,000 over the previous year. During the year 1895 ante-mortem inspection was also made of 5,000,000 animals; the cost of inspection was reduced to $\frac{1}{2}d.$ per animal. In 1893 inspection cost $4\frac{1}{2}d.$ per animal, and in 1894 it cost $1\frac{1}{2}d.$ Over 1,360,000 animals, cattle and sheep, were inspected for foreign markets, of which 675,000 were shipped abroad. Over 45,000,000 lbs. of pork were inspected microscopically and exported in 1895; 35,000,000 lbs. in 1894, and 23,000,000 lbs. in 1893. Of the amount exported in 1895, nearly 23,000,000 went to Germany, and over 9,000,000 to France. The inspection involved the placing of over 1,900,000 specimens under the microscope; the cost of each examination was less than $2\frac{1}{2}d.$ per carcass, a considerable reduction over the previous year.

Losses of cattle in transit to Europe were greater in 1895 than in 1894, being respectively for 1895 and 1894, 0·62 and 0·37 per cent.

Over 30,000 cars, carrying over 820,000 animals, were inspected for Texas fever at quarantine pens during the quarantine season; nearly 9,000 carloads of cattle being inspected also in transit, and over 28,000 cars were cleaned and disinfected. Besides over 156,000 cattle from the non-infected districts of Texas were inspected for shipment to the Northern States. The Secretary urges their importation free of duty as advantageous to feeders having a surplus of feed, and to the consumers who outnumber the producers.

From 1878 to 1894, from statistics compiled by the Treasury Department, it appears that the largest exports of fresh beef were in 1892, when the number of lbs. reached 232,983,369; the next largest was last year, when the quantity was 204,314,960 lbs. Of salted beef, the largest quantity exported in any one year was 110,797,355 lbs. in 1860, when canned beef also led with 104,913,390 lbs. The largest total exports of beef were 398,216,561 lbs. in 1890, and the smallest, 133,297,610 lbs. in 1882. The lowest valuation of the exports was 2,602,259*l.* in 1887, and the highest 6,413,581*l.* in 1892.

Of the exports of hog product from 1882 to 1894, the largest was 1,205,814,413 lbs. in 1890, and the smallest, 651,169,020 lbs. in 1882. In 1895 the exports amounted to 1,078,997,153 lbs., and in 1894, 821,323,280 lbs.

The exports of cattle reached the top notch in 1894, when the number is reported to have been 420,835 head, the value of which was placed at 8,050,321*l.* To show comparison with previous years the table below will be found of interest:—

(2148)

UNITED STATES.

Year.	Number.	Value.
		£
1890	416,777	6,882,162
1891	330,558	5,860,319
1892	290,945	7,313,230
1893	248,284	4,748,877
1894	420,835	8,050,321

The Department of Agriculture returns for January, 1896, show the total number of cattle in the United States as follows:—

States and Territories.	Number. 1895.	1894.
Maine ..	306,932	308,130
New Hampshire	207,593	205,483
Vermont	207,593	398,703
Massachusetts	261,100	264,557
Rhode Island ..	36,609	36,478
Connecticut	210,623	214,468
New York	2,259,434	2,279,040
Pennsylvania ..	1,624,647	1,676,301
New Jersey	241,597	243,375
Delaware	60,380	60,380
Maryland	261,296	260,170
Virginia	668,417	687,623
North Carolina	653,528	661,257
South Carolina	289,439	287,287
Georgia	867,260	870,387
Florida	486,553	490,313
Alabama	863,112	856,877
Mississippi	819,656	858,547
Louisiana	549,116	566,915
Texas ..	6,881,044	7,400,302
Arkansas	943,810	983,073
Tennessee	943,810	983,073
West Virginia	510,012	536,641
Kentucky	870,749	928,556
Ohio ..	1,554,197	1,570,971
Michigan	936,310	941,108
Indiana	1,518,253	1,500,983
Illinois	2,551,045	2,592,504
Wisconsin	1,559,067	1,566,614
Minnesota	1,343,437	1,355,234
Iowa ..	3,767,290	4,009,616
Missouri	2,548,117	2,635,016
Kansas	2,481,996	2,647,236
California	1,225,358	1,254,739
Nebraska	1,756,098	2,148,759
Oregon	917,149	914,941
Nevada	277,274	277,274
Colorado	1,004,206	1,072,425
Arizona	664,380	664,380
Dakotas	1,108,673	1,149,216
Idaho ..	429,253	460,366
Montana	1,117,424	1,093,371
New Mexico ..	998,589	1,242,946
Utah ..	415,320	407,727
Washington ..	542,670	507,828
Wyoming	785,899	870,252
Oklahoma	173,240	141,494
Total ..	50,868,845	53,095,568

CHICAGO.

The Department of Agriculture returns for January, 1896, show the number of sheep in the Western States as follows:—

State.	Number. 1895.	1894.	1893.
Ohio	3,577,419	3,765,701	4,378,725
Illinois	857,370	1,032,976	1,187,329
Wisconsin	895,756	1,066,376	1,198,175
Minnesota	489,192	514,939	499,941
Iowa	627,930	775,220	791,043
Missouri	860,820	1,000,953	1,099,948
Kansas	274,883	323,392	389,629
Nebraska	183,448	277,952	272,502
Dakotas	690,653	707,840	714,400
Montana	2,808,717	2,780,908	2,528,098
Wyoming	1,222,538	1,198,567	1,198,567
Colorado	1,305,989	1,293,058	1,231,484
New Mexico	3,008,824	2,921,188	2,730,082
Arizona	746,546	691,246	580,879
Utah	2,039,226	1,905,819	2,117,577
Nevada	544,077	544,077	555,181
Idaho	919,865	779,547	764,262
Washington	847,807	832,063	832,825
Oregon	2,529,759	2,529,759	2,456,077
California	3,526,341	3,918,157	4,124,376
Oklahoma	22,778	18,222	..
Texas	3,738,116	3,814,405	4,334,551
Arkansas	212,328	228,310	240,326

The Agricultural Department returns for the United States for January, 1896, show the following table:—

	Total Number.	Price per Head. £ s.	Aggregate Value. £
Horses	15,124,057	8 3	103,334,749
Mules	2,278,946	9 7	21,323,233
Milch cows	16,137,586	4 13	75,155,649
Oxen and other cattle	32,085,409	3 5	105,109,176
Sheep	38,298,783	0 7	13,464,408
Swine	42,842,759	0 18	38,549,059
Total	..	..	356,936,247

In number, decreases have been as follows:—

	Per Cent.
Horses	4·8
Mules	2·3
Milch cows	2·2
Oxen and other cattle	6·6
Sheep	9·4
Swine	3

(2148)

The cotton States and the Rocky Mountain States show an increase in horses and mules, otherwise the decrease is general. Milch cows are more numerous in the north-eastern or city supply States, also in Minnesota and Dakotas and westward, but fewer elsewhere. Decrease in other cattle and sheep is generally distributed, except in the mountain regions. Swine have increased generally throughout the east, west, and south, with a falling-off in the great central States. In the report of the price per head, horses, mules, and swine are lower than in January, 1895, while milch cows, other cattle and sheep are higher. In aggregate value horses have decreased 13·3 per cent.; mules, 7 per cent.; sheep, 2.3 per cent.; and swine, 15 per cent. during 1895, while milch cows have increased 4 per cent., and other cattle, 5·4 per cent. The grand total of live-stock has fallen off 18,909,090*l.*, or 5 per cent., from January, 1895.

Under the McKinley Tariff Law, the duty of cattle imported from the Republic of Mexico was 2*l.* 1*s.* per head, which was changed, by the passage of the Wilson Tariff Bill, in 1894, to 20 per cent. ad valorem. In other words, a Mexican steer, valued at 1*l.* 13*s.*, under the McKinley Law would have cost 3*l.* 14*s.* by the time he crossed the Mexican border, whereas under the Wilson Law he will cost 2*l.*, the 2*l.* 1*s.* tax having been reduced to 6*s.* 6*d.*, by the change of a 2*l.* 1*s.* per capita tax to a 20 per cent. ad valorem tax. This reduction has naturally caused large numbers of cattle to be imported into the United States from Mexico; in fact, under the McKinley tariff there were no importations of any consequence. The figures below show the importation of cattle which commenced with the Wilson Bill, which took effect, August 15, 1894:—

Year.	Number.		
	Cattle.	Sheep.	Hogs.
1894	44,690	..	..
1895	239,575	1,322	78

It is stated on good authority that there are at present 1,200,000 cattle in the State of Chihuahua, Mexico, and 300,000 in the State of Sonora, Mexico, of which the bulk of them will eventually be imported to the United States. The cattle, when brought into this country are only good for grazing and fattening, and are not fit for market until they are first put upon a range, and then brought into the corn belt and fattened for market. It is more profitable for feeders to use corn in this manner than to sell it. If the Wilson Bill continues in force, the cattle importation in the future will be very large, and it will be as great a help to the feeder in this country as to the breeder in Mexico, for they do not have the grain in Mexico to fatten the cattle, and if they did they have no market.

CHICAGO.

There are a number of sheep on feed, a much larger number than in 1895, and sellers expect higher prices for them than they realised last year, but the question to be decided when they are offered for sale will be their quality; this is a matter which raisers of sheep are paying more attention to. For many years the sheep raisers of the United States paid more attention to wool than to mutton, but now that it is being demonstrated that the tastes of the American people have been educated up to the point that they are becoming mutton-eaters, as well as beef and pork-eaters, it is much to the interest of those engaged in raising sheep that they do not neglect the mutton grades. In the matter of improving the mutton grades of sheep, not only will it have the effect of increasing the consumptive demand in this country, but will also be advantageous to exporters, for the Briton who takes most of the mutton exported is really more of a connoisseur than the American, inasmuch as it has been a favourite in Great Britain for years.

There was practically no Texas fever in this western country during 1895. The officers of the United States Board of Agriculture have been very active in looking after same, and keeping the cattle within the quarantine lines defined by law, and great precaution is taken at all stockyards to keep cattle from within the quarantine limits coming in contact with those from without, so that there is no danger of the fever being carried should it break out. Diseases of all kinds are really obscure from live-stock except cholera among the hogs, which has been prevalent throughout the year, and for which there seems to be no preventative; it destroys a herd quickly.

Texas fever.

The United States officials are rigidly enforcing the laws of inspection of live-stock and dressed meats; no greater care can be taken. The writer has examined, personally, the methods prescribed, and is always on the alert to report to Her Majesty's Government any matter that should come before his notice that would be to the detriment of, or injure the British people of their trade. Below find points in the regulation of inspections at the Kansas City stockyards :—

The dockage or shrinkage for each sow in pig is 40 lbs.; for each stag, 80 lbs.; when under 150 lbs. weight, the former, 20 lbs., and the latter, 40 lbs. When cows show, beyond a doubt, that they are pregnant, they cannot be sold for killing purposes, but for the purpose of increase of cattle. All cattle, hogs, and sheep that are very thin, skinny, badly frozen, boily or cut, scored or gored, broken legs, diseased, badly ruptured (or castrated and not healed), are unmerchantable and are killed and sold to the desiccating companies for what they are worth for such purposes.

A great many sheep are handled at Kansas City from Texas. From the following, it can be readily seen that the sheep industry in Texas has had its ups and downs in the last 15 years. The official reports of the Comptroller of the State shows that in 1870 there were 924,749 sheep, valued at an average of 4s. 7d. per head; this number increased annually up to 1885, when there were 4,749,625 sheep, of an average value per head of 5s. 4d. From then until 1892 the annual number did not fall below 4,000,000, and the average price per head for those years ranged from 5s. 4d. to 8s. 6d. In 1892 and 1893 the number of sheep was respectively 3,564,490 and 3,366,257, and the valuation was 5s. 8d. and 5s. 10d. In 1894 the number decreased to 2,859,269, and in 1895 to 2,386,822, and the valuation to 4s. in the former year, and 4s. 5d. in the latter. The aggregate of the clip increased from 5,068,119 lbs. in 1870, to 29,534,472 lbs. in 1886; since then there has been a gradual decrease, the clip in 1895 amounting to only 16,707,754 lbs.

A great many sheep, at times, are shipped to Nebraska, from Arizona, New Mexico, Utah, Colorada, and Wyoming; from good authority it is stated that at least 400,000 sheep will be fed in Nebraska during 1896; the sheep are hardy and healthy, and with plenty of good feed good results must follow.

Dehorning. Dehorning in cattle is fast becoming popular in this western country, and it certainly has many advantages that persons cannot appreciate unless in the trade. It is unwise to dehorn old cattle, as it sets them back, and it takes some time for them to regain their strength; besides, after they are dehorned, only poor results are obtained. The proper time to dehorn is when the calf is but a few weeks old, by nipping the bud with an instrument made for the purpose; it is not very painful, and heals in a few days; the work is then over, and the horns never grow. There are many excellent reasons for dehorning, as follows:—The cattle are more contented, gentle and docile, and if a person could visit the stockyards at this point, and see the pens filled separately with horned and dehorned cattle, they would see the wonderful advantage of dehorning; the dehorned cattle stand perfectly still and contented; at the same time, the horned cattle are restless and prodding each other with their horns. When dehorned, it takes a little less to fatten cattle, and when shipping, 2 more cattle can be put into a car, and thus saving freight, for cattle are shipped by carloads and not by weight, although shipping by weight is to be tried here by all railways at an early date. When selling, dehorned cattle bring from 2d. to 4d. per 100 more than horned cattle, for there is the weight of the horns less, and when killed the hides are not scored, gored and cut by their being crowded into cars and their fighting with horns.

I consider it a humane act to dehorn cattle in this western country, for it is surprising to see the number of cattle unloaded at this point, with their horns broken off and other damages caused by horns; besides, many cattle are shipped hundreds and thousands of miles, and when in transit are standing up, if a horned beef gets down it is almost impossible to get it up, but if a dehorned one gets down it is easily assisted to its feet.

The exportation of live cattle is much larger for 1895 than was expected, and it looks as though it will be experimented to a very great extent in the future. Two or three of the largest feeders are talking of establishing a steamship line for the handling of live-stock to ply between the Atlantic coast and Great Britain.

CHICAGO.

In 1894 the United States exported to Great Britain, 271,629 head of cattle, and in 1895, 390,391, showing a healthy increase.

The first shipment of live cattle for export to England, viâ the Gulf of Mexico, will be made this month (February), viâ New Orleans, Louisiana. The cattle are now being fed in Oklahoma, and every effort and much care will be taken to make the first shipment a success ; if it proves successful, then more shipments will follow at an early date. (See Transportation to Europe, viâ the Gulf of Mexico ports, this issue.)

Despite the fact that the financial depression of the land and the consequent interruption to trade in all its branches, the year just closed has been a satisfactory one to the packers of this city. During the year they have not only maintained the great volume of business done in former years, but have extended their territory and opened up new avenues and gradually widened the circle of trade. So great has the spread of the business become, that the products of the Kansas City packing houses are sold in every land beneath the sun. The tin cans that have contained the packing-house products prepared here, lie not only in the alleys of every city, village, and hamlet of this country, but are seen in the sands of Sahara, are buried in the mud along the banks of the Nile, and are carried in the haversack of many soldiers in foreign lands and by the hardy explorer along the Congo, and furnish sustenance and comfort to the diamond hunters in South Africa. In all these places the merits of the great packing-houses of Kansas City are tested every day, and the fame of her excellent products continues to spread.

The past year has witnessed several extensions and improvements to the packing-houses of this city.

Armour Packing Company. The Armour Packing Company of Kansas City has the most complete and largest house of its kind in the world ; they make a fine line (in connection with packing-house business) of beef tea, soups, consommé, canned beef, tripe, pig's feet, and numerous other articles of that class ; the latest and most potent article is canned bacon ; it is sliced bacon ready for the frying pan ; it is put in cans ranging from 7 ozs. each to any size required. This canned bacon is subjected to a test of 280 degrees for 5 minutes ; this is done to kill any disease or trichina in the meat, should any appear. The goods are being pushed into several foreign countries for army and navy use. It can also be said that this firm makes and sells many goods for military and Government purposes, and the trade is destined to increase. To their plant they have also added a large game and poultry department to all its branches. To give an idea of the size of this plant, below find the illustration :—

UNITED STATES.

General Statistics of Armour's Kansas City Plant.

	Quantity. Lbs.	Acreage.
Ground acreage covered by buildings, and used for other purposes	..	30
Floor acreage in buildings	..	90
Cold-air rooms	..	30
Storage capacity	200,000,000	..

There is an ice capacity of 14 ice machines producing a refrigeration equal to the melting of 1,350 tons of ice every 24 hours, an electric light capacity equal to that used in a well lighted city of 25,000 inhabitants, and a daily killing capacity as follows:—Hogs, 12,000; cattle, 4,000; sheep, 5,000. Total shipments for 1895, 400,500,000 lbs.

The Armour beef house in Kansas City is alone the largest in the world, being seven stories high, with a cold storage capacity of 15,000 dressed beef, and covering an area of 300 by 500 feet.

The Armour Packing Company killed during 1895:—

	Number.
Cattle	326,982
Hogs	810,963
Sheep	177,113
Calves	12,235

Located here are four other packing-houses, namely:—Fowler Packing Company (Limited), Swift and Company, J. Dold Packing Company, Schwartzchild and Sulzberger.

The last-named is really an export beef house, and its foreign trade is increasing rapidly. All of the five packing-houses improved and increased their plants in 1895. The five houses combined killed during 1895:—

	Number.
Cattle	895,512
Calves	47,640
Hogs	2,164,604
Sheep	575,601

The five houses named give employment to 10,600 men; this gives an idea of the immensity of this industry.

There has been considerable comment regarding horse flesh being substituted for beef in packing-houses in this western country; the writer is always on the look-out for such canards, and upon investigation, reports that so far as the packing-houses in this Vice-Consulate are concerned there is no truth in such stories. The packing industry could not and would not permit such to take place, for it would injure their local business far more seriously than their foreign trade. Every precaution is taken to put out goods as pure and wholesome as possible.

Packing of Hogs at Western Points.

The packing of hogs at the leading western markets in various years, and the percentage of the total receipts killed, are as follows:—

UNITED STATES.

Table showing the Packing of Hogs at the leading Western Markets in Various Years, and the Percentage of the Total Receipts Killed.

	1891.		1892.		1893.		1894.		1895.	
	Number.	Percentage of Receipts.	Number.	Percentage of Receipts.	Number.	Percentage of Receipts.	Number.	Percentage of Receipts.	Number.	Percentage of Receipts.
Kansas City	2,001,900	77·4	1,754,121	73·1	1,400,205	72·0	2,013,295	79·2	2,145,131	87·2
Chicago	5,638,291	65·5	4,788,290	62·0	3,908,868	64·5	5,018,170	67·0	5,784,670	73·3
Omaha	1,293,649	84·0	1,229,075	76·1	1,031,180	73·3	1,531,446	79·2	1,136,557	95·7
St. Louis	347,685	41·3	285,570	33·6	277,210	35·6	601,444	52·4	566,221	52·2
Total	9,291,525	61·0	8,057,056	64·0	6,616,463	64·9	9,164,345	69·9	9,632,570	76·3

CHICAGO.

The packing houses of Kansas City and Omaha manufacture from their offal a very superior article of fertiliser; the bulk of it is used in this country and the balance goes abroad, some of it into Canada and Nova Scotia.

In 1890 the capital invested in the United States in the manufacture of commercial fertilisers was 9,787,103*l*.; 10,000 men were employed, and the output was 1,250,000 tons. In 1894 the output was 2,000,000 tons, and the capital still greater in proportion. It is now conceded that the artificial fertilisers produced in this country are fully equal in all desirable points to the Peruvian guano or the old style manure, and they possess, besides, the merits of cleanliness and wholesomeness.

Fertilizers.

TABLES showing the Export of Hog Products during the 12 months ending June 30, 1895, as compared with the Exports of the previous 12 months, and the Countries to which Exported.

BACON.

Country.	1894-95.	1893-94.
	Lbs.	Lbs.
United Kingdom	351,294,279	334,985,389
Germany	13,160,325	12,537,849
France	9,296,962	666,049
Other countries in Europe	44,180,025	37,767,698
British North America	5,380,492	10,311,030
Mexico	86,451	38,516
Central American States and British Honduras	197,412	112,642
Cuba	5,137,535	6,154,077
Porto Rico	399,222	230,976
San Domingo	112,210	126,471
Other—West Indies and Bermuda	412,130	467,974
Brazil	22,564,112	12,935,681
Colombia	6,097	12,970
Other countries in South America	219,461	233,839
China	15,800	14,767
Asia and Oceania	75,698	58,024
Africa	5,781	6,000
Other countries	5,984	625
Total	452,549,976	416,657,577

UNITED STATES.

Hams.

Country.	Quantity. 1894-95.	1893-94.
	Lbs.	Lbs.
United Kingdom	89,800,462	73,994,248
Germany	1,977,212	1,293,735
France	545,086	129,442
Other countries in Europe	3,567,735	1,605,582
British North America	2,013,960	951,944
Mexico	211,148	229,734
Central American States and British Honduras	213,606	151,843
Cuba	3,929,994	5,272,640
Porto Rico	680,411	799,812
San Domingo	63,576	96,274
Other—West Indies and Burmuda	1,072,685	1,036,268
Brazil	18,470	20,739
Colombia	90,805	77,521
Other countries in South America	967,500	1,023,836
China	46,918	36,850
British Australia	20,170	41,683
Asia and Oceania	337,825	181,683
Africa	20,176	14,975
Other countries	14,384	5,660
Total	105,494,123	86,970,571

Pork, Fish, and Pickles.

Country.	Quantity. 1894-95.	1893-94.
	Lbs.	Lbs.
United Kingdom	15,020,502	14,272,957
Germany	2,149,850	2,431,325
France	236,600	150,250
Other countries in Europe	927,882	1,196,700
British North America	8,052,652	10,521,427
Central American States and British Honduras	967,141	1,095,607
Cuba	462,640	626,033
Porto Rico	3,285,200	4,480,400
San Domingo	271,322	411,505
Other—West Indies and Bermuda	22,283,239	23,520,940
Brazil	1,123,292	109,150
Colombia	83,314	103,170
Other countries in South America	3,821,960	5,477,600
Asia and Oceania	148,590	165,595
Africa	59,737	75,184
Other countries	191,553	106,385
Total	59,085,474	64,744,528

CHICAGO.

LARD.

Country.	Quantity.	
	1894–95.	1893–94.
	Lbs.	Lbs.
United Kingdom	184,251,911	149,691,959
Germany	104,121,137	96,010,508
France	34,665,860	29,841,320
Other countries in Europe	77,630,616	85,611,859
British North America	2,397,933	2,753,524
Mexico	1,908,076	1,414,209
Central American States and British Honduras	2,202,687	1,858,315
Cuba	30,672,512	42,340,578
Porto Rico	3,414,798	3,979,784
San Domingo	459,460	574,914
Other West Indies and Bermuda	7,161,407	7,193,960
Argentine Republic	12,724	60,274
Brazil	12,556,461	11,886,364
Columbia	1,928,255	1,760,795
Other countries in South America	10,670,217	11,697,238
Asia and Oceania	365,635	382,379
Africa	432,663	478,611
Other countries	42,912	30,193
Total	474,895,274	447,566,867

Oleo-margarine.

A new law was passed in Missouri in 1891 making it a misdemeanour to put colouring of any kind into oleomargarine, making it look like butter, and fraudulently selling it as such. The new law has been rigidly enforced, and the sale of oleomargarine (or artificial butter) has almost stopped. The new law was passed because colouring of an injurious character was being used, injuring the health of the people.

The adverse legislation in many of the thickly settled States has had a depressing effect upon the manufacture of oleomargarine by the packers of this city and other cities, and the showing of the year will be very bad compared with the business done in former years. Minnesota legislators decreed that the "oleo" sold there should be coloured pink; Kansas tried to have it coloured blue; Missouri decided it must be left colourless, while Wisconsin, Massachusetts, New York, and other places where large quantities have been sold in former years, have prevented its sale absolutely, or else hedged it about with such conditions as to make it impracticable to sell it. The consequence is that the trade is now small and altogether unsatisfactory to the producers. The crusade against "bull butter," as it has been derisively termed, appears to be something of a contagion, and the "oleo" people in this city and elsewhere expect to be shut out from many other States shortly. They argue that when it is once out of the market there will be a shortage of choice butter, and the consumers will be forced to pay heavy prices for what they may be able to get. The packing houses who are oleomargarine makers do not export this article only in very small quantities, but they do export vast quantities of what is termed "oleo oil"; it is a mixture of cattle fats and cotton-seed oil, prepared to be mixed with pure butter. The largest market for "oleo oil" is Rotterdam and Amsterdam, Holland.

Horses and mules.

Viewing the horse situation in the light of prophecy, there will no doubt be a great improvement in the breeding of horses in the future. One of the greatest reasons for low prices of horses is due to the fact that owners have neglected to keep up the standard of breeds. 87 per cent. of horses received at Kansas City are not fit to work, but as the foreign demand continues, it will stimulate the horse trade and force the breeders to raise a better class of horses. Bicycles and electric and cable railways have reduced the demand for horses, and have, of course, assisted in lowering their prices. During the past 10 years the number of horse dealers in this country has quadrupled.

One must not forget that Texas supplies Kansas City with a great many horses; on January 1, 1896, there were in Texas 1,500,923 horses and mules, and 14,189 jacks and jennets.

On January 1, 1896, there were, in Kansas, 864,000 horses and a great many mules; the whole western country is preparing to breed horses for foreign trade; the foreign trade, as a whole, calls for round, good colour, clean, sound horses ranging from 975 to 1,025 lbs. each for cab purposes in cities; or the same animals ranging from 1,250 to 1,900 lbs. each. From foreign information gleaned, the American horse, as a whole, gives universal satisfaction.

The horse and mule trade of Kansas City is becoming a very important industry: they are shipped here from all over the western country, and on account of their quality it has caused many buyers, who contract horses and mules for foreign Governments and countries to make their headquarters at this point. Over forty large foreign contracts were filled at this point during 1895, and several orders are waiting to be filled at this writing. The largest horse and mule firm in the world is located at this point. Horses and mules can be raised cheaper and more successfully in this western country than any other territory in the world. Following are receipts of horses and mules at Kansas City for 1893, 35,097; 1894, 44,237; and 1895, 52,384, showing an increase every year.

Exportation of horses and mules is a new industry for this country, and will, from all appearances, increase. In going from this country, it takes but a short time for them to become acclimated in foreign climates. Exports for foreign countries from the United States are as follows:—1893, 14,212; 1894, 22,714. For the first 6 months of 1895, 22,755 American horses were landed and sold in the United Kingdom, and it is predicted that fully 40,000 American horses and mules will be landed and sold during 1895.

A trial shipment was made recently of horses from Kansas City to Mexico, and same proved a success, and surely will increase

CHICAGO.

in the future. At present the Mexican duty is 8*l*. per head on good costly horses, but thoroughbreds for breeding are admitted free.

TABLE showing Number and Value of Horses, Cattle, Hogs, and Sheep Exported and Imported between the United States and the United Kingdom for the Years ending June 30, 1894, and 1895.

EXPORTS.

	1894.		1895.	
	Number.	Value.	Number.	Value.
		£		£
Horses	1,355	63,507	5,834	192,675
Cattle	345,734	6,682,899	305,068	5,886,864
Hogs	..	..	60	111
Sheep	79,786	134,739	335,882	485,292

IMPORTS.

	1894.		1895.	
	Number.	Value.	Number.	Value.
		£		£
Horses—				
Free	291	130,299	161	62,959
Dutiable	28	1,576	58	2,579
Cattle—				
Free	3	96	98	3,077
Dutiable	..	..	17	128
Hogs	..	..	..	..
Sheep—				
Free	721	2,658	149	1,173
Dutiable	2	25	..	..

Kansas City is located in the centre of the great Indian maize country, and does an enormous trade, not only in this country, but abroad. Maize has been sold by Kansas City merchants, to merchants in Germany, Spain, France, and United Kingdom; four cargoes were sold and shipped from here for Copenhagen free port. The leading maize-growing States are the following:— *Grain.*

UNITED STATES.

States.	Acreage, 1895.	Quantity. Estimated.	1894.
		Bushels.	Bushels.
Iowa	8,504,400	298,504,000	81,334,110
Illinois	6,821,800	255,125,000	169,121,491
Missouri	6,613,100	238,072,000	116,011,654
Kansas	8,426,300	204,759,000	41,797,728
Nebraska	7,880,100	176,034,600	13,855,524

Of these States, Missouri, Kansas, and Nebraska, which are directly tributary to Kansas City, show the largest increase in the production of corn this year over 1894.

Here it will prove of interest to give the figures showing the exports of corn from the United States, also the crop, in bushels, in the United States since 1888:—

Year.	Quantity. Exports.	Crop.
	Bushels.	Bushels.
1888	24,278,417	1,987,790,000
1889	69,592,929	2,111,892,000
1890	101,973,717	1,489,970,000
1891	39,768,213	2,060,154,000
1892	75,451,849	1,628,464,000
1893	46,037,274	1,619,496,000
1894	65,324,841	1,212,770,000

TABLE showing Stocks of Grain in Store and on Track at Kansas City, January 1, 1895. Receipts and Shipments during the year, Mill Products, City Consumption and Stock in Store and on Track, January 1, 1896.

RECEIPTS.

	Wheat.	Corn.	Oats.	Rye.	Barley.
In store, January 1, 1895	1,602,986	179,545	315,066	7,522	...
On track, January 1, 1895	5,400	30,000	20,000	600	...
Received by railroads	8,230,800	8,395,500	3,410,000	127,200	29,400
Teams in street	23,700	150,150	98,700	...	...
Total, 1895	9,862,886	8,755,195	3,843,766	135,322	29,400

SHIPMENTS.

	Wheat.	Corn.	Oats.	Rye.	Barley.
Handled and reshipped	6,738,980	6,982,757	1,175,240	103,089	20,200
Mill products (bushels)	1,541,326	1,230,000	1,300,000	2,509	...
In store, January 1, 1896	1,552,580	6,688	56,972	29,133	...
On track, January 1, 1896	30,000	75,000	22,000	600	...
City consumption, 1895	...	460,750	1,289,554	...	9,200
Total, 1895	9,862,886	8,755,195	3,289,766	135,322	29,400

CHICAGO.

Manufactured in 1895.

Articles.	Quantity.
	Barrels.
Flour	342,617
Corn meal	307,500

TABLE showing Receipts of Grain, Flax, Bran, Hay, in Carloads, for the Year 1895.

Articles.	Cars.		Quantity.
	Number.		
Wheat	13,718	Bushels	8,230,800
Corn	11,194	,,	8,395,500
Oats	3,410	,,	3,410,000
Rye	212	,,	127,200
Barley	49	,,	29,400
Flax	805	,,	483,000
Bran	198	Tons	3,960
Hay	12,258	,,	122,580

Kansas City's hay market has increased in importance, year by year, with phenomenal strides, until it is now one of the richest sources of the city's wealth and prosperity. In 1894 the hay crop of the United States amounted to 65,000,000 tons, valued at 121,901,632*l.*, twice as much as the wheat crop, and 15 times as much as the tobacco crop. During that year the hay crop in Kansas City's territory was as follows:—

State.	Quantity.
	Tons.
Kansas	2,545,535
Missouri	2,152,469
Nebraska	1,152,535
Iowa	3,426,115
Colorado	1,786,045
Texas	618,095
Arkansas	248,247
Total	11,901,041
Valuation £	9,843,835

The Oklahoma and Indian territories both began producing some fine hay during 1895, and promise rich harvests of hay in the future.

(2148)

STATEMENT showing Annual Product of Wheat, Corn, and Oats of Kansas for the past Four Years.

Articles.	1892.	1893.	1894.	1895.
	Acres.	Acres.	Acres.	Acres.
Wheat	4,129,829	2,651,299	3,965,689	4,171,971
Corn	5,603,588	6,172,462	3,731,940	8,394,871
Oats	1,559,049	1,758,127	1,436,088	1,606,343
	Bushels.	Bushels.	Bushels.	Bushels.
Wheat	74,538,906	24,827,523	35,315,259	16,001,396
Corn	138,658,621	118,624,369	41,797,728	201,457,296
Oats	43,722,484	28,194,717	25,705,975	31,664,748
	£	£	£	£
Wheat	8,407,388	2,301,692	3,210,478	1,336,529
Corn	8,987,380	6,740,033	3,713,434	3,701,019
Oats	2,301,700	1,340,557	1,647,519	1,184,782

The statement below gives the quantities of potatoes and hay produced in these Western States for 1895:—

State.	Potatoes.	Hay.
	Bushels.	Tons.
Iowa	21,340,980	4,612,583
Missouri	10,765,276	2,725,785
Kansas	7,869,240	4,181,289
Nebraska	7,998,373	1,811,454
Colorado	3,491,820	1,961,187

The area sown in winter wheat exceeds that of 1895 by 4·6 per cent.; there is a general increase in the Eastern Mississippi Valley and Lake States; the increase in Kansas is 20 per cent. There is a slight decrease along the Atlantic and Gulf coasts, while Idaho, Washington, and California show an increase of 8, 12, and 3 per cent. respectively, to last year's area. The general average of condition (February 22, 1896) was 81·4 per cent. against 89 per cent. in 1894, and 91·5 per cent. in 1893. If a large crop of wheat should be harvested in these Western States, it would result in a large exportation of flour to Great Britain and the Continent.

Owing to such large crops of grain throughout the United States in 1895, causes it to be so cheap, the foreign demand is very light, and the outlook for higher prices is indeed very poor. The figures attached show that 22,000,000 bushels of grain were handled at Kansas City; this amount was actually received in Kansas City, but over 50,000,000 bushels were handled by Kansas City merchants in 1895; the majority of the grain was loaded and shipped direct from the country stations to port of sailing, and there was no need of its being brought to Kansas City, as it would cause extra expense.

The statement below shows the wheat yield in the States and Territories named in 1895 and 1894:—

State.	Quantity.	
	1895.	1894.
	Bushels.	Bushels.
Missouri	18,499,688	23,353,920
Kansas	22,919,566	35,315,259
Nebraska	14,787,024	8,754,900
Iowa	13,654,778	10,737,400
Colorado	2,808,250	2,144,009
New Mexico	809,248	691,668
Oklahoma	2,592,655	2,315,234

The following table shows the aggregate wheat crop of the United States for 6 years:—

Year.	Quantity.
	Bushels.
1895	467,102,947
1894	460,267,416
1893	396,131,725
1892	515,949,000
1891	611,780,000
1890	399,262,000

The corn crop of the States is finally estimated by the Department of Ariculture's report, as follows:—

State.	Quantity.	
	1895.	1894.
	Bushels.	Bushels.
Missouri	238,072,248	116,011,654
Kansas	204,759,746	41,797,728
Nebraska	125,685,069	13,855,524
Iowa	298,502,650	81,344,010
Colorado	3,690,976	2,743,709
New Mexico	733,203	451,639

(2148)

84   UNITED STATES.

The corn crop of the United States for the past 6 years has been as follows:—

Year.	Quantity.
	Bushels.
1895	2,151,138,580
1894	1,212,770,032
1893	1,619,496,431
1892	1,628,464,000
1891	2,060,154,000
1890	1,489,970,000

The following table represents the crops of grain and potatoes in the United States for the past 6 years, as presented by the Agricultural Department at Washington (in bushels).

TABLE showing the Crops of Grain and Potatoes in the United States for the past Six Years.

Year.	Quantity.						
	Wheat.	Corn.	Oats.	Rye.	Barley.	Buckwheat.	Potatoes.
	Bushels.	Bushels.	Bushels.	Bushels.	Bushels.	Bushels.	Bushels.
1890	399,262,000	1,489,970,000	533,621,000	28,000,000	63,000,000	11,000,000	140,000,000
1891	611,780,000	2,060,154,000	738,394,000	33,000,000	75,000,000	12,000,000	225,700,000
1892	515,949,000	1,628,464,000	661,035,000	30,000,000	70,000,000	11,000,000	150,000,000
1893	396,131,000	1,619,496,000	638,854,000	26,555,000	69,869,000	12,668,000	183,000,000
1894	460,267,000	1,212,770,000	662,087,000	26,727,000	61,400,000	12,668,000	170,787,000
1895	467,103,000	2,151,139,000	824,444,000	27,210,000	87,000,000	15,341,000	297,237,000

UNITED STATES.

The estimated production of flax seed in the United States, in bushels, for the past 6 years is shown in the following table:—

Year.	Quantity.
	Bushels.
1890	3,000,000
1891	19,000,000
1892	11,000,000
1893	10,000,000
1894	7,500,000
1895	15,000,000

Many million bushels of Indian corn have been cribbed in each of the Western States; the export orders for all foreign countries are not as large as one would imagine; all are slow to buy. Judging from past movement, it would take 2 years to get rid of the 1895 crops; thousands of people are cribbing it at low prices, expecting to get fabulous prices for it later on, but in this great producing country it is a risky thing to do; but the grain speculation is very great, in fact, all Americans are speculators, more or less. There is no way to get rid of this corn only to export it.

The final estimates of the crops of 1895, as compiled by the statistician of the Department of Agriculture for the United States, are as follows:—

TABLE showing the Final Estimates of the Crops of 1895.

		Quantity.
CORN.		
Area	Acres..	82,075,830
Product	Bushels	2,151,139,000
Yield per acre	,,	26·2
Farm price per bushel	Value	1s. 1d.
Value of products		117,253,925l.
WINTER WHEAT.		
Area	Acres..	22,609,322
Product	Bushels	261,242,000
Yield per acre	,,	11·55
SPRING WHEAT.		
Area	Acres..	11,438,010
Product	Bushels	205,861,000
Yield per acre	,,	18·00
Total wheat area	Acres..	34,047,332
Product	Bushels	467,103,000
Value		49,160,950l.
Yield per acre	Bushels	13·7
Farm price per bushel	Value..	2s. 0½d.

CHICAGO.

TABLE showing the Final Estimates of the Crops of 1895 —continued.

		Quantity.
OATS.		
Area	Acres..	27,818,406
Product	Bushels	824,444,000
Value	..	33,813,016*l*.
Yield per acre	Bushels	29·6
Farm price per bushel	Value..	10*d*.
RYE.		
Area	Acres..	1,890,345
Product	Bushels	27,210,000
Value	..	2,286,157*l*.
Yield per acre	Bushels	14·4
Farm price per bushel	Value..	1*s*. 10*d*.
BARLEY.		
Area	Acres..	3,299,973
Product	Bushels	87,073,000
Value	..	6,056,198*l*.
Yield per acre	Bushels	26·4
Farm price per bushel	Value..	1*s*. 5*d*.
BUCKWHEAT.		
Area	Acres..	963,277
Product	Bushels	15,341,000
Value	..	1,435,124*l*.
Yield per acre	Bushels	21·1
Farm price per bushel	Value..	1*s*. 11*d*.
POTATOES.		
Area	Acres..	2,954,952
Product	Bushels	297,237,000
Value	..	16,319,215*l*.
Yield per acre	Bushels	100·6
Farm price per bushel	Value..	1*s*. 1½*d*.
HAY.		
Area	Acres..	44,206,453
Product	Tons ..	47,078,541
Value	..	81,235,537*l*.
Yield per acre	Tons ..	1·06
Farm price per ton	Value..	1*l*. 14*s*. 8*d*.

According to the Government Bureau of Statistics, the export of breadstuffs from the United States, for 12 months ending December 31, 1895, with comparisons, were as follows:—

Articles.		Quantity.	
		1895.	1894.
Wheat	Bushels	66,398,166	72,256,221
Flour	Barrels	14,061,152	15,740,246
Wheat and flour	Bushels	129,673,350	143,087,328
Corn	,,	57,924,886	40,210,348
Oats	,,	2,019,278	581,973
Rye	,,	838	8,654
Barley	,,	3,535,068	2,212,278
Corn meal	Barrels	260,232	255,579
Oatmeal	Lbs.	35,047,649	11,886,371
Total value of above items	Value £	24,569,000	25,061,403

The following table, furnished by the Treasury Department at Washington, shows the distribution of wheat, flour, and corn exported from the United States during the year ending June 30, 1895, as compared with 1893–94.

FLOUR.

Country.	Quantity.	
	1894–95.	1893–94.
	Barrels.	Barrels.
United Kingdom	8,857,529	9,987,179
Germany	256,650	286,129
France	1,102	1,963
Other countries in Europe	1,050,310	1,565,064
British North America	916,995	550,740
Mexico	52,065	51,700
Central American States and British Honduras	282,323	258,235
Cuba	379,856	662,248
Porto Rico	118,617	200,813
San Domingo	41,836	44,173
Other West Indies and Bermuda	951,492	937,556
Brazil	775,425	920,869
Columbia	113,020	108,465
Other countries in South America	446,811	486,677
China	36,144	23,717
British India and East Indies	8,165	3,600
Oriental countries, Asia and Oceania	951,732	736,809
Africa	14,757	19,015
Other countries	14,063	14,581
Total	15,268,892	16,859,533

CHICAGO.

Wheat.

Country.	Quantity. 1894-95.	1893-94.
	Bushels.	Bushels.
United Kingdom	54,373,341	50,868,680
Germany	2,526,930	1,760,779
France	1,596,791	8,701,100
Other countries in Europe	13,296,961	22,657,145
British North America	4,110,255	4,260,805
Mexico	7,938	6,130
Central American States and British Honduras	90,991	40,572
West Indies and Bermuda	9,518	15,614
Other countries in South America	2,950	5,239
Asia and Oceania	38,760	12,117
Africa and other countries	48,269	87,049
Total	76,102,704	88,415,230

Corn.

Country.	Quantity. 1894-95.	1893-94.
	Bushels.	Bushels.
United Kingdom	15,363,975	26,849,826
Germany	3,217,837	11,438,349
France	621,101	2,316,428
Other countries in Europe	4,022,629	11,553,976
British North America	3,013,178	10,468,588
Mexico	179,614	431,516
Central American States and British Honduras	142,021	337,229
Cuba	392,204	1,136,657
Porto Rico	1,200	17,449
San Domingo	615,530	625,464
South America	103,356	125,103
Asia and Oceania	10,567	16,840
Other countries	4,269	5,449
Total	27,691,137	65,324,841

In the past, owing to the bulk of the export business being shipped from Atlantic ports, grain prices for the United States were made on basis of Chicago prices, but present indications point to the fact that if as much grain is shipped from the Gulf of Mexico ports as predicted, Chicago prices will not govern, as a rule, in the future.

UNITED STATES.

The following shows the lowest and highest prices for No. 2 Contract wheat in the Chicago market for the past 6 years, and the month in which extreme prices were reached:—

Prices of Wheat for Six Years.

Year.	Month the Lowest Prices were Reached.	Yearly Range.	Month the Highest Prices were Reached.
1890	February	·74¼ to 1·08¼	August
1891	July	·85 1·16	April
1892	October	·69⅛ ·91¾	February
1893	July	·54 ·88	April
1894	September	·50 ·65¼	April
1895	January	·48¾ ·85⅜	May

Prices of Corn for Six Years.

Year.	Month the Lowest Prices were Reached.	Yearly Range.	Month the Highest Prices were Reached.
1890	February	·27½ to ·53⅞	November
1891	December	·39⅜ ·75½	April
1892	March	·36½ 1·00	May
1893	December	·34¼ ·44¾	January
1894	January, February	·34 ·59½	August
1895	December	·25 ·55½	May

Prices of Oats for Six Years.

Year.	Month the Lowest Prices were Reached.	Yearly Range.	Month the Highest Prices were Reached.
1890	February	·19¼ to ·45	November
1891	October	·26¼ ·57¾	April
1892	March	·27 ·35½	June
1893	August	·22 ·32	January, February, May
1894	January	·27 ·50	June
1895	December	·16⅞ ·31½	June

The increasing shipping interests of the Gulf of Mexico ports, and the shorter haul from the grain fields of the West to those ports, explain the future trend of the south-western export grain trade. St. Louis has an important advantage over all other markets bidding for gulf trade in that, during a large period of the year, the Mississippi River offers very low freight rates.

Another argument for the Gulf of Mexico ports is that the

ports are never blocked by snow in winter, but can always arrive and depart; ofttimes the eastern railroads are snowbound, and the lakes and eastern ports frozen up by winter, and exports are of course delayed. It is a down-hill grade from the Western States to the Gulf of Mexico ports, so that very large trains can be handled. The first shipment of live cattle from the Gulf of Mexico ports goes forward this month, and it is watched with intense interest, for if it is successful more will certainly follow. The Kansas City, Pittsburg, and Gulf Railway Company, it is rumoured, will shortly complete arrangements with a Dutch line of steamers to commence running from Port Arthur, Texas, their southern terminus, to Great Britain; the service to commence in the autumn of 1896. No meat products have ever been exported from Gulf of Mexico ports until this year; in January, 1896, over 200 carloads were shipped viâ New Orleans from Kansas City.

This season grain has been exported to foreign countries viâ Port Royal, South Carolina, Savannah, Georgia, Charleston, Pensacola, Florida, New Orleans, Louisiana, and Galveston, Texas.

To give an idea of the export trade of Kansas City proper for 1895, I beg to make a few items:—

From—	Destination.	Articles.	Quantity.
			Lbs.
A packing house	Liverpool, England	Meat and lard	40,000,000
,,	Liverpool and London	,,	5,000,000
,,	,, ,,	,,	60,000,000
,,	Rotterdam and Hamburg	,,	10,000,000
,,	London, Liverpool, and Hull	,,	10,000,000
,,	,, ,,	Dressed beef	25,000,000
,,	Bremen and Hamburg	Oleo oil	7,500,000
,,	England	Canned meat	5,000,000
	Total		162,500,000

This is a partial list of the exports from Kansas City only. Omaha, Nebraska, in 1895 exported 625,000,000 lbs. of meat and lard to foreign countries, and there is no question but what the railroads will arrange tariff and rates to apply as far north as Minneapolis and St. Paul, Minnesota, whose products can be handled cheaper viâ the Gulf of Mexico ports than the Atlantic coast points. During 1895, which was a very small year, Minneapolis alone exported flour amounting to 2,370,756 barrels.

There are also many export flour mills all over the West who will, if they can secure lower rates, viâ the Gulf of Mexico, be enabled to ship flour to Europe where they are now shut out. During 1895 many millions of bushels of grain have been shipped by Kansas City merchants to Europe, viâ the Gulf of Mexico; the grain came from Kansas City territory, and it will increase as fast as the service becomes better and more satisfactory.

British merchants should bear in mind that there is a good

field here for their products. In the past they have dwelt too much upon selling only to the eastern cities upon this continent; they should pay attention to the western cities also, for they would find safe customers at a better profit.

Kansas City is at present exporting more grain and packing-house products through the Gulf of Mexico ports than at any time before, and if the Eastern Railroad managers continue to ignore the Gulf of Mexico ports, and maintain the present high basis, the percentages will not be so favourable to Atlantic coast ports in the future. Grain, through New Orleans alone, for the month of December, 1895, was 3,135,291 bushels, practically all of which was produced in Kansas City territory; most of it, however, was handled by Kansas City merchants. Galveston also handled more export grain in the month of December, 1895, than ever before in the history of Galveston.

The four great grain-producing States tributary to Kansas City in an average year produce 25 per cent. of the wheat, 40 per cent. of the corn, and over 30 per cent. of the oats produced in the United States; the States and territories tributary to Kansas City produce 40 per cent. of the cattle, 60 per cent. of the sheep of the United States, and more of the packing-house and livestock products of Kansas City are exported than of any other city in the United States, except Chicago; so you can readily see the importance of the Gulf of Mexico ports to Kansas City and territory tributary.

Exports and imports for 1890 for the United States were handled at the following ports of entry, showing the percentage:—

Port.	Percentage.
New York	52·55
Boston	8·14
Philadelphia	5·55
Baltimore	5·29
New Orleans	7·45
San Francisco	5·20
All other points	15·72

Men of recognised commercial ability have spent time and money in the study and investigation of the relative position of the food-producing sections of the United States to the millions of consumers in foreign countries. These men have demonstrated with irrefutable figures that deepwater ports in the Gulf of Mexico coast, with direct railroad connections with the north and north-west, would bring about an unprecedented era of commercial, industrial, and agricultural development throughout these sections of the country. Many schemes have been projected, gigantic railroads have been constructed, but not until the past year has an effort to accomplish the desired results been made that plainly evidences all elements of success.

Six railways of Kansas City, namely the Atchison, Topeka,

and Santa Fé Railway; the Chicago, Rock Island, and Pacific Railway; the Missouri, Kansas and Texas Railway; Missouri Pacific Railway; Kansas City, Springfield, and Memphis Railway; Kansas City, Pittsburg and Gulf Railway, are now accepting and transporting extensive quantities of grain and grain products, and packing house products, from Kansas City and territory tributary to the Gulf of Mexico ports for shipment to European, South American and Cuban ports, that heretofore were routed viâ Atlantic coast ports. There is no question but what the bulk of the exports and imports in territory west of the Mississippi River will in the future be handled by Gulf of Mexico ports. It will be seen by distances given in table attached, that British merchants, when exporting or importing goods, should not fail to look into the rates viâ the Gulf of Mexico, as it may be the means, by lower rates, of securing orders that may be lost by higher rates.

The growing export trade at Gulf of Mexico ports is a subject that is at this time causing the grain merchants of St. Louis, Chicago, and eastern markets considerable uneasiness. The low freight rates made to Gulf ports by western and southern lines has diverted an immense amount of corn for export from central primary markets and eastern ports to the Gulf of Mexico. As regards Chicago and eastern ports, however, there is no likelihood that any change at all probable in the situation could restore to those markets their former interest in that portion of the western crops exported. The Gulf export business that was predicted for years has become a reality. It is the natural result of a business trend that long ago was inevitable to the people of the south and west, but it is even now hardly appreciated by the lake region and east coast markets. Kansas City will gain by this change, although at times, as a market, it will suffer from rate manipulation. It will, however, grow in importance, and the value of the grain trade will increase in proportion to the expansion of imports and exports viâ the Gulf of Mexico ports. Kansas City is a natural and commanding primary market of the grain grown in Nebraska, Missouri, Kansas, Iowa, Arkansas, Oklahoma territory and Indian territory, besides being a dangerous competitor for grain grown in a much wider area. St. Louis will also contribute more business to Gulf of Mexico ports in years to come than she has in the past, the business from that city, viâ the Gulf, as from Kansas City, depending more on the harvest outturn and the export demand than any competition likely to come from the north and east.

TABLE showing Distance from Kansas City to the undermentioned Cities.

City.	Number of Miles.
New York, N.Y.	1,303
Philadelphia, Pennsylvania	1,228
Baltimore, Maryland	1,197
Newport News, Virginia	1,208
Charleston, South Carolina	1,194
Port Royal, South Carolina	1,104
Savannah, Georgia	1,168
Pensacola, Florida	996
Mobile, Alabama	869
New Orleans, Louisiana	878
Galveston, Texas	799
Port Arthur, Texas	767

TABLE showing Distance from Kansas City to the undermentioned Cities.

City.	Viâ Newport News, Va.			Viâ New Orleans, La.			Viâ Port Arthur, Texas.			Viâ Galveston, Texas.		
	Land.	Water.	Total.	Land.	Water.	Total.	Land.	Water.	Total.	Land.	Water.	Total.
	Miles.	Miles.	Miles.	Miles.	Miles.	Miles.	Miles.	Miles.	Miles.	Miles.	Miles.	Miles.
Liverpool	1,208	3,160	4,368	878	4,700	5,578	767	4,800	5,567	799	4,850	5,649
London	..	3,420	4,628	..	4,960	5,838	..	5,060	5,827	..	5,110	5,909
Glasgow	..	3,000	4,208	..	4,700	5,578	..	4,800	5,567	..	4,850	5,640
Bremen	..	3,710	4,918	..	5,030	5,908	..	5,130	5,897	..	5,180	5,979
Havre	..	3,160	4,368	..	4,570	5,448	..	4,670	5,437	..	4,720	5,510
Hamburg	..	3,160	5,008	..	5,030	5,908	..	5,130	5,897	..	5,180	5,978

(2148)

UNITED STATES.

Table showing Distance to Havana, Cuba, from Kansas City, Missouri.

	Land.	Water.	Total.
	Miles.	Miles.	Miles.
Viâ New York, N.Y. ..	1,303	1,190	2,493
Viâ New Orleans, La...	878	575	1,453
Viâ Port Arthur	767	675	1,442
Viâ Galveston, Texas ..	799	725	1,524

It is rumoured that a Dutch Steamship line will shortly be operated between Rotterdam, Liverpool, and Port Arthur, Texas; the ships are at present plying to South American ports, but they will be diverted one by one as trade increases.

Railways. Kansas City has 18 systems of railways, but some of them enter the city from more than one direction; hence there are running into Kansas City at present 30 lines of railroad, with a total mileage of 47,013 miles, which radiate in every direction, and give better facilities for reaching tributary territory than any city west of Chicago. Kansas City railroads traverse 32 States and territories. Kansas City has as many railroads as any city in the world, and before the expiration of 1896 will have more than any other city in the world.

Railroad terminal facilities in Kansas City consist of 326 miles track, with 1,436 switches within Kansas City manufacturing district. 346,211 loaded cars were switched for account of other railroads, from and to local industries, in 1895. There were 97,037 freight trains in and out of Kansas City in 1895; passenger trains in, 43,062; out, 43,003; total, 86,065. Total passenger and freight trains in and out in 1895, 183,102.

A new railroad company known as the "Missouri Midland Railway, has been organised for the purpose of constructing a new railway from Marshall, Missouri, to Galveston, Texas; the line will be built through the States of Missouri, Arkansas, Louisiana, and Texas. The line is designed as a single track standard gauge railway, with a Kansas City connection.

The Missouri Pacific Railway during 1896 will build a new line from Atchison, Kansas, to St. Joseph, Missouri, distance 21 miles.

Following is a list of 18 railroads entering Kansas City, with their lines coming into the city from 30 different directions, making it the greatest railway centre of the world:—

Name of Road.	Miles in System.
Atchison, Topeka and Sante Fé Railway	10,346
Chicago, Rock Island and Pacific Railway	3,931
Union Pacific Railway	4,469
Missouri Pacific Railway	5,533
The Wabash Railroad	2,123
Chicago and Alton Railway	917
Chicago, Burlington and Quincy Railway	7,743
Chicago and Great Western Railway	906
Kansas City, St. Joseph and Council Bluffs Railway	309
Kansas City, Pittsburg and Gulf Railway	767
(Now in construction; 400 miles in operation.)	
Kansas City, Osceola and Southern Railway	112
Kansas City, Fort Scott and Memphis Railway	1,187
Kansas City Air Line Railway	11
Chicago, Milwaukee and St. Paul Railway	6,169
Kansas City and Atlantic Railway	21
Missouri, Kansas and Texas Railway	2,370
Kansas City Suburban Belt Railway	40
Kansas City Belt Railway	59
Total	47,013

The St. Louis and San Francisco Railway propose to build a branch from Sapulpa, Indian territory, to Oklahoma City, Oklahoma, during the coming year. It will be about 100 miles long.

A new line of railroad is expected to be built during 1896 from Ft. Smith, Arkansas, to Atoka, Choctaw Nation, Indian territory, distance 107 miles.

During 1896 will be many changes in railways north of Kansas City. The sale of the Des Moines and Kansas Railway to the Keokuk and Western Railway recently, and the sale of the Omaha and St. Louis Railway to a party who represents the stockholders will, it is rumoured, develop into a large company in connection with the Kansas City and Atlantic Railway, who will construct the great Kansas City and Atlantic Bridge across the Missouri River at Kansas City. Should this be done it is thought that perhaps the Illinois Central Railway, Chicago and North-Western Railway, and the Baltimore and Ohio Railways, three large lines representing a total of 11,131 miles, will perfect arrangements to run into Kansas City over this system. If such should be done it would be of vast importance to Kansas City.

Negotiations are pending at present for the building of a railroad to be known as Kansas, Oklahoma, and South-Western Railway. The road will be constructed from Cherryvale, Kansas, viâ Guthrie and El Reno, Oklahoma, to some point in Northern Texas not yet determined; a branch will also be built into the coalfields in the Indian territory.

A charter has been issued for the new Santa Fé, Oklahoma, and Western Railway, capital 400,000*l*. This is to be from Sapulpa, Indian territory, through the Oklahoma territory, to Vernon, Texas.

(2148)

A Bill has passed in Congress authorising the Kansas City, Fort Scott, and Memphis Railway to construct a line about 30 miles in length from Baxter Springs, Kansas, to Miami, Indian territory.

Plans have just been drawn for a railroad, wagon, and foot bridge across the Missouri River at Kansas City. Owing to its now being the greatest railway centre of the world, and becoming more so by the intention of other lines to build into this city, it has been determined to build a bridge (there are two railroad bridges now across the Missouri River at this point) that will accommodate several lines of railroad. The bridge proper will be 2,000 feet long without approaches, and will have two distinct floors; on the first floor in the centre will be two railway tracks; outside of each track will be space for wagonway, two drays side by side; outside of each wagonway a footpath, 8 feet wide, for passengers. Fifty feet above the first floor will be constructed a second floor with two railway tracks only, so that four railway trains can cross the bridge at one and the same time. In the centre of the bridge is the lift or draw span, which is to be constructed on an entirely new plan, by means of an electric motor of sufficient power erected in a tower in the centre and above the said lift span; the first floor of the bridge will be lifted up bodily and folded into the second floor above it, thus leaving a space of 65 feet from the bottom of the first floor (when lifted) to water, at high-water mark. The United States Government only require 55 feet at this point owing to little or no navigation. The same gentleman who perfected these plans also drew plans and built the Halstead Street Lift Bridge at Chicago, Illinois, and it has proven a success. If it were not for the great expense would furnish sketches which would be more explanatory. This style of bridge would indeed be very beneficial to any city where navigation is very great, for the first floor can be lifted in less than 30 seconds.

Experiments have recently been made with steel freight cars, which, it is designed, shall take the place of the cumbersome wooden freight cars now in use on all railroads. The railroad men are watching the trial with interest, as it means a decreased cost and weight of cars, and vastly increased carrying capacity. Not a piece of wood is used in the construction of the new cars, and their lightness and durability will enable them to stand any amount of hard usage and heavy loading. A detailed description of the new cars says that the most radical departure from present methods of construction is in the floor and sills, which are practically one series of channels $14\frac{1}{2}$ inches wide, with 8-inch flanges, placed side by side, with the flanges downward, the flanges forming the sills of the car, and the back of the web making the floor of the car. The channels are secured together by tie rods passing through the flanges near the web. Each rod also passes through struts of malleable castings fitted between the flanges of each channel, which supports the webs of channels at short intervals, so that the stiffness of the plate is not alone depended upon to sustain the floor. The car is virtually constructed in the form of a truss, of which the floor itself forms the top or compression member. This keeps the body square without braces or gusset plates, thus making a much lighter construction possible than where an independent floor is used. In a test made the car easily sustained 5·2 lbs. of load to 1 lb. of the car, and, taking the body alone, which weighs 11,780 lbs., the load was over 10 to 1. In this test the car, loaded with 118,000 lbs., was coupled to a locomotive and rapidly shifted back and forth over a four-track crossing which was in a badly worn condition, and this without any perceptible vibration of the car body. The weight of this car is from 2,000 to 4,000 lbs. less than that of the wooden cars, usually constructed for and rated at 60,000 lbs. capacity, which rating is sometimes in excess of their elastic limit. It is claimed by the builders that the cost of maintenance of this car, leaving out of account the wheels, axles, journal bearings, and couplers, will be less than 25 per cent. of the average cost of wood cars now in service, and that ten times the number can be kept in repair with the same ground and shop capacity that is now required, with proportionately less investment in material for repairs.

The extension, equipping, and furtherance of facilities for the better transportation of passengers and freight is taking place on all roads in this western country. During the past 2 years new railroad bridges have been completed across the Missouri River, one at Sioux City, Iowa, costing 300,000*l.*, connecting Iowa and Nebraska; one at Jefferson City, Missouri, costing 276,000*l.*, connecting the north and south sides of the State; and one at Leavenworth, Kansas, costing 247,000*l.*, connecting Missouri and Kansas. All of the bridges are iron and are supplied with foot and wagon facilities, as well as railroad tracks.

Surveyors are now in the field laying plans for route for new line of railroad from Grant City, Missouri, to Rula, Nebraska.

Railway building in the United States in 1895 reached a lower point than in any of the last 20 years, and in only 2 years since 1865 has so small a mileage been built. The record for 1895 shows only 1,782 miles of track laid. In the 8 years since that time the decrease in construction has been great and continuous, and this year the total built was only about 100 miles more than in the year 1855, 40 years ago. The greatest amount of track laid was in Texas where 224 miles were put down. In fifteen States no increase whatever was made. The railroads of the United States on December 31 will aggregate a little over 181,000 miles.

Referring to railways of 1895, the receiverships numbered 31 roads, having an aggregate mileage of 4,089, a funded debt of 45,663,430*l.*, capital stock of 30,545,000*l.*, and an aggregate capitalisation of 76,252,066*l.* About 150 roads are now being operated by receivers; the foreclosures were the largest in 20 years, with the exception of two, 1879 and 1877. The sales numbered 52, representing 12,831 miles of road, 67,403,098*l.* of bonded debt and 89,933,884*l.* of capital stock, and a total capitalisation of 156,956,404*l.*

(2148)

During the year 1895 the Missouri, Kansas, and Eastern Railway was built by the Missouri, Kansas, and Texas Railway Company; they also built a connection from Holden, Missouri, to Green Ridge, Missouri, which now gives Kansas City another St. Louis and eastern outlet. This line of traffic will be initiated early in 1896.

The Baldwin Locomotive Works have shipped to the Westinghouse Electric Works in Alleghany, Pennsylvania, a new electric locomotive for use on a steam railroad. The Baldwin Works made everything about the engine except the electric mechanism, which will be supplied by the Westinghouse Company. The locomotive is about 30 feet long and mounted upon two four-wheel trucks; completed it will weigh 60 tons; it is geared for 800 horse-power, which will pull a loaded freight train 40 miles an hour. By a single change of the gearing this engine can be run up to 1,600 horse-power, and can pull a train 80 miles an hour. The new electric locomotive is intended to haul freight trains; the passenger ones will attain a far greater speed; the wheels are 42 inches in diameter. Only a space 8 feet square is needed in the locomotive for the electric motor; one man will operate the locomotive by means of a controller similar to that on a common trolley car, only much larger and stronger. The locomotive is built to be operated by either overhead or underground trolley wires; it carries no coal fire-box, smoke-stack, or water tank; in front is a powerful electric search-light for use at night to light the track. The cost of the new electric locomotive is about equal to that of a steam locomotive, or 2,160*l*.

One railroad in Kansas City is now using electric headlights on all engines, and same is satisfactory.

The Kansas railroads are much interested in the discovery of oil in that State, and should it be in such volumes as predicted they will buy engines and burn crude oil instead of other fuel; it would be cheaper and cleaner, for it has been tried here and in Russia. The Baldwin Locomotive Works has contracted to build 32 additional locomotives to go to Russia; these engines will burn oil.

Kansas City being such an important railroad point all matters of railway construction are of importance.

All of the 13 locomotive building companies of the United States, except one, built more locomotives in 1895 than in 1894; the total number of engines built was 1,109 against 695 in 1894; this is something of an increase, but that it does not represent a normal increase seems evident from the number of engines built in the five previous years, when never less than 2,000 were built in any one year. That this is a safe deduction the large orders for locomotives have been placed in recent weeks give additional evidence. Two of the companies reported building locomotives in 1895 did not build any in 1894, and one other company did not report in the latter year. The larger locomotive works seem to have been in a better position to profit by the large increase of orders, and several of such works built more than twice their output in 1894. Reports from the car building companies show that car building also has taken an upward turn, the output of the contracting shops in 1895 being 31,893 freight cars, this is in comparison with 17,029 freight cars built in 1894. The total number of cars built in 1895 is not a large record by any means, and makes the number built in years previous (51,000 in 1893 and 93,000 in 1892) appear extraordinarily large.

The most important railway improvements in this western country is the building of the Kansas City, Pittsburg and Gulf Railroad from Kansas City, Missouri, to Port Arthur, Texas; the distance being 767 miles, of which 463 miles are now in operation; the remainder will be completed during 1896. This line opens a new field for Kansas City trade of many kinds and in many different directions. The connections of the Kansas City, Pittsburg and Gulf Railway are very great, and although the line will be constructed through to Port Arthur, it will by no means be dependent on Port Arthur for the bulk of the business, for it can be seen at a glance that the connections are so great that success, as a business enterprise, is assured. The connections will be as follows:—

At Gulfton, Missouri, with Saint Louis and San Francisco Railway, for St. Louis business on the east and Kansas City on the west; at Neosho, Missouri, with Saint Louis and San Franciso Railway for the great live-stock district of the famous Indian territory; at Katy, Missouri, with Missouri, Kansas and Texas Railway, for all points in Missouri, Kansas, Indian territory and Texas; at Salisaw, Indian territory, with Missouri Pacific Railway, for Little Rock, Memphis, Tennessee, and all southern and eastern points; at Porteau, Indian territory, with Saint Louis and San Francisco Railway, for points in Texas, Mexico and Pacific coast; at Texarkana, Texas, with the Texas Pacific, Saint Louis and Iron Mountain, and Cotton Belt Railways. At Shreveport, Louisiana, with Texas Pacific; Houston, East and West Texas, and Queen and Crescent Railways, where connections will be made for New Orleans, Galveston and Houston, Texas, at the same time giving these cities and country the shortest line to Kansas City.

At Beaumont, Texas, it will connect with the Southern Pacific Railway, for New Orleans, Houston and all points on the Southern Pacific system, including the Pacific coast; hence it will be seen that the connection will be invaluable to this line. The road will be a main line and will not have any branches. Located on this are extensive quantities of coal, railway ties, lumber, hardwood, long leaf and short leaf pine, lead and zinc; this alone will insure a vast amount of freight. Besides, freight can be shipped viâ this line as readily for New Orleans, Memphis, Galveston, or Houston, as for Port Arthur, Texas.

The main object of this line is to build up the export and import business from the West, viâ Gulf of Mexico ports. By looking into this report one will see that the bulk of produce raised in these western States are exported to European countries;

hence the chance of business for this line is marvellous, for this section of the United States is rapidly developing.

This Company has acquired a large tract of land at Port Arthur, Texas, for railway facilities; new docks will be built, and great efforts for the handling of imports and exports to and from Kansas City and the entire western and northern country.

The Kansas City, Pittsburg and Gulf Railway have secured the right of way, and also for a spur, to be built from a point on the main line, to Fort Smith, Arkansas; distance, 16 miles.

A company has been formed here, 200,000*l.* capital, for dredging Port Arthur Harbour, 16 feet of water is now there, but 24 feet is the depth required; also to erect grain elevators, cotton compresses, docks, wharves, and other facilities necessary to conduct and transmit heavy export business.

This road will have great weight in diverting heavy export business from the West to the Gulf of Mexico Ports, for Europe. Several years ago the situation became plain to the people of this western country, and the subject of deep water ports on the Gulf of Mexico was agitated; conventions were held, and the Government appealed to for an outlet. Galveston was selected; about one and one-third million pounds have been expended, and Galveston has a harbour of about 22 feet of water. Galveston, anticipating the grain trade through that port, has built an elevator of 1,000,000 bushels capacity, for loading and unloading about 250 cars grain per day. This season the bulk of corn shipped from Kansas, Missouri, Nebraska, Oklahoma and Indian territory for export, has gone to Galveston and New Orleans, owing to a shorter haul, and at prices which have been about 9*d.* per bushel net to the interior dealer. Before the Gulf of Mexico ports were opened, this grain was forced viâ Atlantic coast ports, and the low price of $5\frac{1}{2}d.$ per bushel has been the common price, notwithstanding 1895 crop has been the largest in the world's record. If direct competition with Europe, viâ the south, brings about a result of this kind in corn, it necessarily will do so in other classes of trade, and at the same time give the British merchant a chance to import his wares direct to this western country.

It is reported that from September 1, 1895, to January 1, 1896, about 150 ships cleared from Galveston, of which about one-half were British. With such a vast change of export trade from the western States, perhaps it would be well for the British shipowner to keep this matter before him.

The State of Kansas contains 820,809 square miles, and is a prairie country—no trees or timber whatever grows within its limits; population in 1890, 1,427,096.

Though but little over a generation old, and subjected to the profligate agricultural treatment usually given to low-priced lands, the State at large—including the so-called "arid region" in the western part—has produced as high as $48\frac{4}{5}$ bushels of corn per acre, 22·29 bushels of wheat per acre and 44·61 bushels of oats per acre. She has raised a wheat crop of 74,538,906 bushels and an oat crop of 54,665,055 bushels, while this year's (1895) crop of corn has amounted to a quarter billion bushels. 1893 and 1894 were the most disastrous years, agriculturally, in the history of the western States, and yet in those years the value of the field crops and live-stock products of Kansas reached a total of 4,876,090*l*., or 35*l*. 11*s*. for each man, woman and child in the entire State.

In Kansas, where droughts so often seriously affect the crops, many farmers of late years have learned to plant alfalfa, as an experiment, and it has been very successful; in 1890 only 34,384 acres were planted; in 1894, 90,825 acres, and in 1895, 125,000 acres, or an increase of 38 per cent. More of it will be planted during 1896 than ever before. Large quantities of Kaffir and Jerusalem corn were raised during 1895, and the same was a grand success, and in 1896 a very large acreage will be planted for the purpose of feeding cattle. The majority will be planted in the dry prairies of Kansas.

When the territory of Kansas was organised in 1854, not a white man, except a few Indian agencies and Indian missionaries, had a home on its soil; when the State was admitted in 1861 it had but 107,000 inhabitants. In 1861 it had no State institutions; now it has a fine State house, a State university, an elegant agricultural college, a normal school, institutions for the blind, deaf and dumb, and insane, a soldiers' home, and a home for their orphans; it has its penitentiary, reform school and reformatory. These institutions, owned and controlled by the State, have cost 1,446,280*l*., only 113,636*l*. of which is represented by State indebtedness. The entire State debt is but 168,181*l*., of which 89,463*l*. are held in the State treasurer's hands for school funds, to meet this debt they have a wealth of 3,719,000*l*., and the population of the State has increased during that period to 1,341,000. Money has been expended with a lavish hand in establishing and maintaining an excellent system of common schools; also in the building up of colleges and academies; the expenditures for this purpose have increased more rapidly than the population. The total value of school property, 35 years ago, was but little more than 2,420*l*., and to-day it exceeds 2,066,242*l*. Then the entire State had enrolled 6,600 children of school age, employing 319 teachers; to-day there are nearly 400,000 children enrolled, with 12,000 teachers; then the total amount raised for schools for the year was scarcely 1,426*l*., now they pay 1,104,000*l*. for the support of the school system; there are 9,000 school-houses owned by the district; also 40 colleges, academies and private schools. The endowment for the school system has been wisely managed, and they have interest-bearing securities amounting to 1,232,000*l*., and State educational institutions have a separate endowment of 217,000*l*.

Natural gas has been discovered in large amounts in South-eastern Kansas, one well at a depth of 809 feet shows a pressure of 310 lbs. when harnessed. Several towns use natural gas for boilers, instead of furnishing power for water-works, electric light plants, &c. Natural gas is also used in many hotels and residences for heating and lighting. In the very same locality as is found natural gas, can also be found crude petroleum in large quantities, and one railroad is experimenting in burning crude petroleum instead of coal; the cost would be less, with much less labour and dirt, and the heat provided would be much more even.

One of the industries of Kansas is the wonderful amount of lead and zinc ore produced; 40 per cent. of the ore produced in the United States is produced by Kansas. In 1895 Kansas produced 25,000,000 lbs. of lead ore and 82,500,000 lbs. of zinc ore; the wages for producing the same was 7,800*l.* per week. Mining this class of ore is but in its infancy, and in a few years will grow to enormous proportions.

Kansas raises immense quantities of broom corn, and some of it is exported to foreign countries to be made up into brooms. In 1885 Kansas grew 28,942 acres; in 1890, 67,222 acres, and in 1895, 135,000 acres, raising about 20,000 tons.

I have prepared an advance summary, showing the acreage, quantities and values of Kansas agricultural products, also numbers and values of live-stock for the year 1895. Compared with those of 1894, the figures show an increase this year of 1,910,421 acres, or 9·7 per cent. The farm and live-stock products combined show an increase in value over the preceding year of 3,407,050*l.*, or 13·3 per cent. A complete summary is as follows:—

		Quantity.	Value.
Crops—			£
Winter wheat	Bushels	15,512,241	1,629,902
Spring ,,	,,	488,819	59,961
Corn	,,	201,457,396	10,907,972
Oats	,,	31,664,748	1,203,794
Rye	,,	1,655,713	174,623
Barley	,,	1,690,545	871,615
Buckwheat	,,	6,598	694
Irish potatoes	,,	7,635,866	579,811
Sweet potatoes	,,	372,429	269,943
Sorghum		..	587,904
Castor beans	Bushels	22,857	4,997
Cotton	Lbs.	286,400	3,981
Flax	Bushels	1,639,530	298,615
Hemp	Lbs.	145,600	1,491
Tobacco	,,	282,800	6,917
Broom corn	,,	60,511,360	294,973
Millet and Hungarian	Tons	611,160	479,261
Milo maize	,,	53,491	29,607
Kaffir corn	,,	639,993	378,911
Jerusalem corn		99,670	67,174
Tame grasses	Tons	464,234	492,003
Prairie grass, fenced	,,	1,153,757	688,741
Total			19,031,890
Animals slaughtered or sold for slaughter			8,994,671
Poultry and eggs sold			784,961
Wool clip	Lbs.	828,778	16,992
Cheese	,,	729,489	17,194
Butter	,,	31,154,220	907,064
Milk sold			87,049
Garden products marketed			197,841
Horticultural products marketed			195,762
Wine manufactured	Gallons	205,895	37,057
Honey and beeswax	Lbs.	268,778	8,964
Wood marketed			39,909
Total			11,287,464
Grand total			30,319,354

TABLE showing Number and Value of Live Stock in Kansas, March 1, 1895.

	Number.	Value.
		£
Horses	852,789	5,070,923
Mules and asses	65,169	794,060
Milch cows	517,254	2,569,921
Other cattle	1,258,919	5,072,073
Sheep	136,520	66,701
Swine	1,666,221	2,007,992
Total		15,581,670

UNITED STATES.

The labour situation in Kansas is critical; while there is not enough work for the idle masses, at the same time those who are working are formed into Unions, and seem to do all in their power against companies and corporations making a success of their enterprises. Strikes are frequent and the majority uncalled for; as a whole, the strikes in Kansas for 1895 were unsuccessful; there were 31 strikes; the nine largest involved 3,225 men.

Kansas consists of 81,700 square miles of land, and has a population of about 1,600,000.

	Number.	Value.
		£
Value of church property in Kansas	..	1,424,862
Number of organisations	5,357	..
Aggregate membership	311,422	..
Value of school property	..	2,020,957
Number of school houses	8,235	..
Number of public libraries	458	..
Number of volumes	162,985	..
Number of private libraries	12,037	..
Number of volumes	1,235,616	..
Number of newspapers	560	..
Aggregate circulation	712,423	..
Number of persons supported at public expense, in whole or part	5,212	..
Cost of annual support	..	24,355
Number of persons convicted of any crime	4,788	..
Misdemeanors	4,214	..
Homicides	106	..
Felonies, other than homicides	468	..
Number of persons in county jail or other prisons	314	..

Prohibition in Kansas, as a whole, is not a success; in some small towns it no doubt does good, but in towns of any size, large quantities of all kinds of liquors, beer, and extracts under fictitious names are disposed of by irresponsible proprietors of hotels, drug shops, and other business houses. In quite a number of towns joints are running (a joint is a renegade beer shop), and are occasionally closed, but they soon re-open. The law, owing to flaws in it, is weak, and the authorities weaker in attempting to crush out the liquor traffic. By travelling through Kansas one can readily see that its claim as a prohibition State is very absurd.

Within a few years a large deposit of salt has been discovered in the State of Kansas and rapidly developed, until now it can be safely said that the salt deposit of Kansas ranks among the largest in the world. It extends across the State for over 200 miles northerly, and southerly in a belt of solid salt about 50 miles wide, cropping out at the surface at the south line of the State, and dipping towards the north several hundred feet, being at Hutchison, where the largest plants are located, 400 feet below the surface, and the vein is 300 feet thick. The supply is simply inexhaustible, and the quality is most excellent. Large plants have been established and are successfully worked at Hutchison, Kingman, Lyons, and Kanopolis. Already more than 3,000,000 dol. of capital is invested in the business. It can be safely asserted that no country on earth has a larger deposit of salt of any better quality than that of Kansas.

Year.	Quantity produced.	Rock Salt.
	Barrels.	Tons.
1893	650,000	7,000
1894	800,000	11,240
1895	1,100,000	17,110

Kansas is fast pressing to the front as the great fruit State of the Union. Apples, plums, cherries, and grapes are easily raised with ordinary care and proper labour. 35 years ago there was not a bearing orchard in the State; in all the eastern part of the State the prairies are dotted over with fine orchards, producing an abundance of choice fruit. There are at present 7,000,000 apple trees, while 5,000,000 more have been planted, and soon will be affording rich returns.

Kansas is peculiarly well adapted for the fostering of milling; this is due to the superiority of hard wheats and the condition of the climate, which causes flour to stand transportation across the ocean and gives it great keeping qualities, especially desirable in warm and damp climates.

Kansas ranks tenth in the United States in the magnitude of its milling, and contained in 1895, 385 mills, employing 2,349 men. The output of these, as given by the United States census in 1890, when there were only 348 mills, amounted to 3,615,700*l*. Kansas hard wheat flours have within the past 10 years attained the foremost rank in quality in the eastern and European markets; they command the highest price in Belgium, Holland, England, and France; they are peculiarly well adapted for bread baking, being rich in gluten and other nutritive elements, and keep the moisture in the bread better than those made of spring wheat or the soft winter varieties.

In amount of capital invested and value of output, milling exceeds all other industries in Kansas; in fact it represents over 15 per cent. of all industries combined, and is capable of indefinite extension, provided favourable conditions are obtained. The financial depression of late has seriously affected the milling industry, and especially in Kansas, so that the increase in the number of mills during the past 10 years has been but 10 per cent., or about 3 mills per annum. Not but what more mills have been built, but many have been abandoned or have been destroyed by fire.

Mr. F. D. Coburn, Secretary of the Department of Agriculture, has issued a statement presenting deductions and summaries from the Kansas State census returns, made to the State Board of Agriculture by township assessors. The total population of Kansas is 1,334,734, and the number of families, 279,816, which makes an average number of persons in each family of 4·77. The male population is 51·99 per cent., or 693,928; the female population, 48·01 per cent., or 640,806.

Other figures in the summary follow:—

	Per Cent.	Number.
Native population	90·38	1,206,332
Native male population	46·54	621,185
Native female population	43·84	585,402
Foreign population	9·62	128,402
Foreign male population	5·45	72,744
Foreign female population	4·17	55,658
White population	96·33	1,285,749
White male population	50·15	644,804
White female population	49·85	540,945
Coloured population (including Chinese and Indians)	3·67	48,985
Coloured males	1·84	24,559
Coloured females	1·83	24,426
Persons of school age	37·41	499,323
Males of school age	18·90	252,264
Females of school age	18·51	247,059
Persons under and over school age	..	835,411
Males of military age (18 to 44 years)	..	280,693

Males of voting age (21 years and over), 51·83 per cent. of the male population, or 359,663.

Persons 21 years and over, 50·09 per cent., or 668,568.

Persons engaged in occupation, 25·07 per cent., or 342,626.

Per cent. of persons 21 years and over engaged in occupation, 51·25.

Persons engaged in agriculture, 13·89 per cent. of the total population, or 185,394.

Proportion of persons engaged in agriculture, compared with those in all classes of occupations, 54·10 per cent.

Proportion of persons engaged in professional or personal services, compared with those in all other occupations, 18·59 per cent., or 63,694.

Proportion of persons engaged in trade and transportation, compared with those in all occupations, 12·45 per cent., or 42,574.

Proportion of persons engaged in mechanical and manufacturing industries, compared with those in all other occupations, 12·76 per cent., or 43,719.

Proportions of persons engaged in mining, compared with those in all occupations, 2·10 per cent., or 7,195.

Immigration continues to come steadily to Kansas, Nebraska, and Oklahoma, and the Indian territories, the majority being British and Swedish persons, and some Germans. As a rule, they come with an idea of rural life; it is not wise for married people to come to this country, for they never, as a rule, do as well as single people, for the simple reason that they cannot get accustomed to the ways and manners as quickly; or, in other words, the foreigner must practically be transplanted in this western country, to make a success. No encouragement should be given to those contemplating coming west, for this is a very hard country for a man to make a start; reverses are many, and change of climate and water affects all for the best part of a year. Do not encourage immigration to the west.

During 1895 there were imported from Ireland 46 young women at one time, by St. Mary's Academy (Roman Catholic), Leavenworth, Kansas, for the purpose of their entering the Sisterhood. This is the first case of this kind in this western country.

Report of Railroad Commissioners of Kansas for the year ending December, 1895, shows that there are 73 railroad companies interested, by some form of ownership, in the roads which are operated wholly in Kansas, or which lying in Kansas and other States form systems which are operated partly in the State of Kansas. The mileage represented by these 73 companies is operated by 26 companies, the remaining 47 being subsidiary. In railway companies, the subsidiary companies are variously related to the main companies; some by lease, others by contract, and still others as proprietary companies; all, or at least more than a majority of the stock of the proprietary companies, and perhaps a portion of their funded debt, being owned by the main companies. This relationship is oftentimes quite complex, and is perplexing when the attempt is made to present clearly the exact situation. The mileage reported for 1895, as owned in Kansas, exceeds that reported for 1894 by 92·19 miles. Of the 8,888·13 miles owned in Kansas, 8,855·23 miles are reported as operated, leaving 32·90 miles not operated. During the year the Chicago, Burlington, and Quincy Railroad Company and the Chicago, Rock Island, and Pacific Railroad Company paid dividends of the 26 operating roads which reported; none others paid dividends. The total number of railroad employés in Kansas is 19,631, including officers; their salaries last year aggregated 2,175,128*l*. The total mileage of lines or systems operated in Kansas is 26,555·71—greater than the earth's circumference; more than one-third of this vast mileage, or 8,888·13 miles—exceeding the diameter of the earth—is in Kansas; they require, in their operation, 81,054 men, and carried 19,000,000 passengers during the year ending June 30, 1895, and transported nearly 27,000,000 tons of freight, and yet, notwithstanding this almost incomprehensible traffic in human freight and in commodities, there were killed by accident on the entire system, for the year, of passengers, employés, and trespassers, 502, and injured, 1,617. Of the killed, 19 were passengers, 161 employés, and 267 trespassers, and 55 other than passengers and employés; of the injured, 174 were passengers, 1,097 employés and 228 trespassers, and 118 not classed with any of the above.

In Kansas, with more than one-third of the operated mileage and carrying by reasonable approximation one-third of the gross number of passengers, the per. cent. of the injured was 25·7, and the killed, 21·4. Of the passengers killed, none were killed by collision, and but one by derailment, two at stations, and 14 from all other causes. In Kansas, of the total passengers, employés, trespassers, and others, 102 were killed, none by collision or derailment, and 406 injured. Compared with the previous year, the total number of deaths in Kansas from accident increased by 22, yet the total number injured from all causes was reduced 247. Total number of deaths and injured reduced, as compared with previous year, 225. Not a railroad strike occurred in Kansas during 1895.

The mining industries of the State of Kansas, though in their infancy, are fast assuming proportions of great importance. The deposits of coal are distributed over a considerable area. There are being worked in the State, 226 drift, slope, and shaft mines, with a large number of strip mines. In 1891 the output of coal exceeded 58,000,000 bushels, nearly reaching that of Missouri, which stands first among the coal producing States west of the Mississippi River; more than 10,000 miners are given employment in this industry alone. In the counties of Crawford and Cherokee, large and rich deposits of lead and zinc have been found, and are being rapidly developed. Around Galena and Empire City are the richest lead and zinc producing mines in the world, and yet so little has been said that their value to Kansas is but little appreciated outside of the State. It is difficult to obtain reliable data and authentic statistics in regard to these mines, but those afforded show something of the magnitude of these industries. For 1886 the output of lead in the Galena district was nearly 6,000,000 lbs., of the value of 21,486*l*. During the same year nearly 32,000 tons of zinc ore were mined. The same products for 1890 were 8,000,000 lbs. of lead ore, and nearly 22,000 tons of zinc ore, valued at 123,966*l*. The production for the first 11 months of 1895 was largely in excess of those years, and has a value of 309,917*l*. More than 2,479,338*l*. worth of lead and zinc ore have been mined and marketed within a radius of 2½ miles of Galena, Kansas. The future development of these mines will only be limited by the demand for these metals; thousands of acres of rich mineral land in this section of the State are as yet undeveloped.

Gold has been discovered in the northern part of Kansas during the past month (January, 1896). Prospecting is going on at several places, and the result of the assayers shows that gold exists in the locality, but so far it is not on a paying basis, but it may develop later.

During the past few years a small amount of cotton has been raised in the southern part of Kansas; during the coming year an effort will be made to increase same.

During 1895 oil was discovered in several places in eastern Kansas, close to Kansas City; several large companies are being organised to fully develop and equip wells. Railroads would use vast quantities of it, crude, if it could be obtained, and railroad engines would be arranged for burning same.

Nebraska is a very fine agricultural State, one of the best in the United States; it is comprised of 77,510 square miles and is very level, being composed entirely of prairie land; it is well watered, and for that reason, makes it very valuable for agricultural and live-stock pursuits. From the following table can be seen what progress has been made:—

TABLE showing Corn, Oats, and Wheat produced in Nebraska from 1871 to 1895.

Year.	Corn. Bushels.	Corn. Acres.	Oats. Bushels.	Oats. Acres.	Wheat. Bushels.	Wheat. Acres.
1871	7,288,000	174,168	1,226,000	38,553	1,829,000	177,527
1876	25,500,000	850,000	3,500,000	138,339	4,330,000	3,776,521
1881	58,913,000	2,149,200	6,976,000	325,300	13,840,000	1,958,500
1886	106,129,000	3,879,128	21,865,000	742,051	17,449,000	1,579,727
1891	167,652,000	4,762,840	48,599,000	1,308,977	18,080,000	1,205,350
1895	176,034,600	5,026,600	35,342,400	1,178,000	13,017,600	1,084,800

TABLE showing Manufacturing Establishments in Nebraska in 1895.

	Number.	Amount. £
Number	3,014	..
,, employed	23,876	..
Wages paid	..	2,992,094
Amount invested	..	8,170,643
Cost of material..	..	15,921,062
Value of finished products	..	19,787,611

In 1895 Nebraska shipped to Kansas City 86,485 cattle, 15,478 sheep, and 149,307 hogs, and on January 1, 1896, there were in Nebraska 1,756,098 cattle, 1,316,047 hogs, 183,448 sheep, and about 460,000 horses and mules. Shipments of live-stock for 1895 were light, because of failure of crops of 1894.

The history of the sugar beet industry in Nebraska is that in 1888 and 1889 some preliminary experiments in beet culture were made near Grand Island, Nebraska, and in 1889 a Bill was passed giving a bounty of 1 c. per 1 lb. to the manufacturers. In 1890 the Oxnards put their first factory into operation at Grand Island, Nebraska, but it was a drought year, and the yield obtained by farmers was very small, in addition to which they paid only 12s. per ton for beets, although they had a bounty of 2 c. from the

United States, and 1 c. from the State of Nebraska. This crop was very discouraging to beet growers.

In the session of the State Legislature in 1891 the Nebraska Bounty Law was repealed, and under it the Oxnards obtained, in the shape of a bounty, 1,543*l.* The Oxnard factory at Norfolk, Nebraska, was by this time already designed, and I think in process of construction. I do not know anything as to the volume of the crops of 1890, 1891, and 1892 in Nebraska, but very little headway was made in the introduction of the culture to farmers, and the total tonnage of beets worked by the 2 factories was inconsiderable, compared to their capacity. In 1893 and 1894 the Ames, Nebraska, crops were very successful, and contributed in 1893 about 30 per cent., and in 1894 about 25 per cent. of all the beets worked in Nebraska.

It had been supposed that beet-growing was rather too difficult to become firmly established in Nebraska, until the Ames, Nebraska, crops were harvested with such conspicuous success, that in 1894, in the face of the worst drought ever known in Nebraska, and in 1895, the Oxnards were easily able to secure contracts for all the acreage they wanted, something they had never been able to do before.

Future plans have been delayed and made uncertain by the repeal of the McKinley Law and present uncertainty of the future, and it is not now known what will be the next step forward in Nebraska. A test was recently made of a new evaporator, by the use of which it is claimed that a great economy can be made in the treatment of the clarified juices, and just now this seems a reasonable expectation to some reliable people.

I do not know the total products of sugar in Nebraska for each year, but it was about as follows, for refined, granulated sugar:—

Year.	Quantity.
	Lbs.
1890	750,000
1891	2,000,000
1892	2,000,000
1893	4,000,000
1894	4,000,000
1895	11,000,000

The production of sugar will keep its footing in Nebraska and continue to grow; if it has proper attention it will grow rapidly. The price of other farm products is so low that people are now ready to grow beets, and it is really only a question of raising the money to build factories, just now this is a very difficult thing to do, but this may change. I think the natural conditions for sugar production are very good.

In October, 1890, a law was enacted by the general Government providing for a bounty of 1*d.* per 1 lb. to the producer of sugar from beets, sorghum or sugar-cane grown in the United

States, the same to continue in force until 1905; this law was repealed in July, 1894. Under the provision of this law there has been paid, in Nebraska, as follows:—

Year.	Sugar.	Amount.
	Lbs.	£
1892..	2,734,700	11,300
1893..	3,808,500	15,737
1894..	5,934,200	26,625
Total paid by general Government	..	53,662
Bounty paid by the State of Nebraska ..	..	12,617
Grand total ..	..	66,279

If we take into account the total beet sugar product of Nebraska for the past 5 years, and the total bounty paid, both State and National, during that time, we find the average to be a trifle over $\frac{1}{2}d.$ per 1 lb.

Without question, the payment of a small bounty upon sugar manufactured from plants grown in Nebraska would greatly stimulate the growth of the sugar beet, and doubtless such was the intention of the Law, both State and National; but when we consider the promises made when such laws are enacted, and then the greatly changed conditions when, after a brief time, such laws were repealed, it is extremely doubtful if the 66,279l. which has been received as a bounty for beet sugar grown and manufactured in Nebraska has been of any material benefit to the growth and development of the industry as a whole. From various sources is gleaned the number of pounds of sugar manufactured from a ton of beets:—

Year.	Source.	Quantity. Beets.	Quantity. Sugar.	Lbs. of Sugar per Ton.
		Tons.	Lbs.	
1891 ..	Norfolk factory ..	8,183	1,318,700	161
1892 ..	Norfolk factory ..	10,725	1,698,400	157
1893 ..	Norfolk factory ..	22,625	4,107,300	181·5
1893 ..	Grand Island factory ..	11,149	1,835,900	164·7
1894 ..	Norfolk factory ..	25,633	6,000,000	218
1895 ..	Norfolk factory ..	27,204	4,991,300	183·4
1895 ..	Grand Island factory ..	15,475	2,539,500	164·1
	Total for Nebraska ..	120,949	22,491,100	182

Below is a comparison for 3 crops of beets at Ames, Nebraska:—

1893.

Total cost per acre	11*l.*
Number of acres	500
Number of tons produced	8,733·57
Average tons per acre	17·46
Net tons delivered to Grand Island, Nebraska factory	7,514
Or, tons per acre	15·02
Per cent. of shrink in transit	13·43
Tons of beets grown in shade and fed to cattle (these are deducted from gross tonnage in computing per cent. of shrink)	52·97

1894.

Total cost per acre	7*l.*
Number of acres	569
Gross tons	6,165·04
Net tons	5,803·10
Average tons per acre	10·10
„ tare for entire acreage, per cent.	5·80
„ sugar content, per cent.	14·95
„ purity, per cent.	79·28
Highest purity, per cent.	85·90

1895.

Total cost per acre	6*l.* 10*s.*
Number of acres	164
Gross tons	4,326
Net tons	4,062

The State of Nebraska has 25 main lines and branches of railway, with a total of 4,687 miles. The facilities for conveying the immense crops of live-stock and grain out of the State are very good and fully ample.

A new line of railway is projected from North Platte, Nebraska, to Grand Junction, Wyoming. This line will be a feeder to the Union Pacific Railway, and will open up a vast and successful irrigated country, and will pass through the North Platte River Valley.

Owing to the drought in Nebraska for the past 3 years, great improvements have been made in irrigation, and, so far, results have been wonderful and more than successful. Plans for increase of ditches are of great magnitude, and will, no doubt, be of immeasurable value to the State and people. The majority of the irrigation ditches are constructed in the Platte River Valley; the cheapness of construction is attributed to the fact that this valley ranges from 10 to 50 miles in width, and for over 300 miles the Platte River has a fall of less than 6 feet to the mile; this is one of the most beautiful, level, and richest valleys in the United States. All the water used for irrigation is drawn from the Platte River, and the question in the future will be, if irrigation is extended as intended, will there be water enough in the said river to meet the requirements?

The following figures may be of interest:—

	Number.	Amount.
		£
Miles of canal completed	1,121·78	..
,, ,, uncompleted	811·22	..
Total miles	1,933·00	..
Estimated cost of work	..	419,994
Cost to date	..	257,387
Number of acres covered	863,221	..
,, ,, under survey	1,422,000	..
Estimated increase in land values	..	1,583,279

Omaha is the largest city in Nebraska, and has a population of 140,452, and is quite a wholesale market for territory north of it. The post office receipts of Omaha for 5 years ending December 31, 1895, was 300,000*l*., not including money order business. Omaha collects all internal revenue for Nebraska, South Dakota, and North Dakota. From January 1, 1895, to December 31, 1895, it amounted to 50,114*l*.

British merchants should endeavour to do business in Omaha, as well as Saint Joseph, Missouri, and Kansas City, Missouri. There is an opening at all points to transact business in below-named imports:—Tin-plate, earthenware, clothing, tea, rice, liquor, tobacco, plate-glass, Fuller's earth, enamelled ware, caustic soda, binding twine, saltpetre, furs, carpets, woollen goods, &c.; and merchants, when importing, should endeavour to secure rates viâ the Gulf of Mexico ports, for rates can often be obtained lower than viâ other routes.

Omaha will hold a Trans-Mississippi Exposition during 1897. The object is to build up and develop the territory west of the Mississippi River in agricultural, financial, and mineral ways.

A large union station is proposed for Omaha, length 668 feet; width, with train shed, 368 feet; to cost about 425,000*l*. Eight railways centre in Omaha-Nebraska.

Large quantities of ore are shipped to Omaha smelter, from the Republic of Mexico and British Columbia, and it looks as though British Columbia will send much more ore this year than heretofore.

The custom-house and port of Omaha, Nebraska, maintains its importance. In the one item of salt there was a decrease, owing to the development of western salt fields. In the articles not produced in this country, but imported and distributed by Omaha jobbers, there was a decided increase.

As compared with 1894, the imports, all from Great Britain, increased as follows:—

(2148)

Articles.		Quantity.	
		From—	To—
Tea .. Lbs. ..		485,000	793,000
Tin-plate .. ,, ..		4,500,000	4,980,000
Rice .. ,, ..		313,000	412,000
Tobacco ,, ..		10,280	52,300
Lead ore ,, ..		1,600,000	3,200,000
Earthenware.. Crates ..		422	612

There were 313,000 ozs. of silver passed through the custom-house to be refined at Omaha's big smelter and refinery.

The import duties collected amounted to 30,462*l*., as compared with 28,753*l*. during 1894. In 1890 the duty collected amounted to only 13,889*l*.

Omaha, Nebraska, still retains the right to the title of the healthiest city of the world of its size. During the past year there were but 1,130 deaths in the city, which, based on a population of 140,000, gives a rate of 8·01 to the thousand. The following figures are furnished by the Board of Health from its official records:—

Year.	Births.	Deaths.	Rate.
	Number.	Number.	
1892 ..	1,856	1,199	8·91
1893 ..	1,960	1,204	8·06
1894 ..	1,887	1,149	8·04
1895 ..	1,875	1,130	8·01

The Omaha Grant Smelting Company is located at Omaha, Nebraska, and operates one of the largest smelters and refineries in the world, and reports an increase of business during the last year of about 30 per cent. over 1894. The company, during 1895, expended about 18,000*l*. in additions and improvements to its big plant, and has furnished employment to about 700 men. Its product was, for 1895:—

	Quantities.	Value.
	Ounces.	£
Silver	12,000,000	1,694,215
Gold	260,000	1,074,379
Lead	..	629,030
Copper	..	62,094
Total	..	3,459,718

The following statement shows the bank clearings for Omaha, Nebraska, for the past 5 years. The decrease for 1894-95 is due to the failure of crops by drought, and were the first two crop failures for Nebraska for over 25 years:—

Date.	Amount.
	£
October 1, 1890, to September 30, 1891 ..	45,687,600
October 1, 1891, to September 30, 1892 ..	56,390,495
October 1, 1892, to September 30, 1893 ..	65,380,092
January 1, 1894, to December 31, 1894 ..	49,945,454
January 1, 1895, to December 31, 1895 ..	39,389,098

Omaha, Nebraska, has four packing-houses, with a daily killing capacity of 6,000 cattle; hogs, 18,000; and 4,000 sheep. Omaha is the youngest of the four large packing points in the United States. The four establishments cover about 30 acres of ground, and give employment to about 4,900 men. The four houses killed during 1895:—

	Number.
Cattle	318,146
Hogs	1,082,859
Sheep	87,310

The Omaha plant does more general home trade and a much less export trade in proportion than the other packing points.

TABLE showing Total Receipts of Live Stock at Omaha, Nebraska, for Twelve Years.

Year.	Number.			
	Cattle.	Hogs.	Sheep.	Horses and Mules.
1884	86,898	1,863	4,188	466
1885	114,163	130,867	18,985	1,959
1886	144,457	390,487	40,195	3,028
1887	235,723	1,011,706	76,014	3,202
1888	340,469	1,283,600	158,503	5,035
1889	467,340	1,206,605	159,053	7,595
1890	606,699	1,673,314	156,186	5,318
1891	593,044	1,462,423	170,849	8,592
1892	738,186	1,705,687	185,457	14,183
1893	852,642	1,435,271	242,581	12,269
1894	829,171	1,904,238	252,218	8,122
1895	602,222	1,188,421	208,633	6,789
Total ..	5,611,014	13,394,482	1,672,862	76,558

UNITED STATES.

Table showing Live Stock Receipts at Omaha, Nebraska.

Largest Receipts in One Day.

	Date.	Number.
Cattle	October 4, 1894	8,647
Hogs	July 31, 1894	20,684
Sheep	October 8, 1894	10,222
Horses and mules	June 6, 1889	718
Cars	July 10, 1894	490

Largest Receipts in One Week.

	Date.	Number.
Cattle	Week ending October 31, 1891	37,190
Hogs	,, ,, July 31, 1894	103,837
Sheep	,, ,, October 8, 1894	20,256
Horses and mules	,, ,, September 14, 1892	1,083
Cars	,, ,, July 31, 1894	2,032

Largest Receipts in One Month.

	Date.	Number.
Cattle	October, 1894	112,927
Hogs	August, 1890	250,322
Sheep	October, 1894	45,426
Horses and mules	June, 1889	2,073
Cars	October, 1893	6,042

Largest Receipts in One Year.

	Date.	Number.
Cattle	1893	852,642
Hogs	1894	1,904,238
Sheep	1894	252,218
Horses and mules	1892	14,183
Cars	1894	61,784

Missouri is one of the best States in this country, and is abundantly rich with minerals, timber and coal. The land is fertile and rich, and the State is not only a good agricultural State, but also a good fruit, tobacco, and live-stock State. Missouri contains 69,415 square miles of land; the Mississippi River runs along the east side of it, and the Missouri River through its centre, and, with numerous other streams, makes it a well watered State. 26,900 square miles of the land are underlaid with coal. It produces more zinc ore than any other State in this country, it is second in the production of lead, and it also produces some copper.

There has been an increase in the production of both lead and zinc, of a decided character, as compared with the previous year.

The output of lead ore for 1895 was 61,618 tons, an increase of 9,615 tons. The average price of lead, embracing all grades, was 6*l.* 4*s.* per ton, amounting to 382,794*l.* The zinc ore produced was 101,294 tons, an increase of 12,144 tons. The average per ton received for the zinc was 3*l.* 9*s.*, making the output amount to 352,809*l.*, and a total of 735,537*l.* While there is an increased production of lead, there was a marked decrease in the price of the ore, and in consequence many large operators closed their mines rather than exhaust them at prices which are not remunerative. This condition of affairs shows the productiveness and richness of the mines that are operated. With zinc ore the experience was the reverse of lead in the matter of prices. Zinc ore not only shows a larger output, but increase in the price per ton.

The advance in this metal did not occur until late in the year covered by the report, but it is largely responsible for the great activity in zinc mining, so noticeable of late in the State. Many mines which were closed as a result of the low price in zinc ore have been opened up again, and a number of new mines have been developed, many of which have grown to be good producers.

Many new and valuable discoveries have recently been made east and west of Joplin and Carterville, and each are experiencing many new developments, the prospects in many instances indicating paying mines. There are several points where good lead and zinc mines have been developed, and, in fact, a much larger area is under the test of the churn drill than ever before witnessed. If one is to judge from the prospects, which are so flattering, and the numerous new shafts sunk in altogether new mining territories, that there is every reason to anticipate a much larger yield than ever before known.

Many new plants for dressing the ore were erected during the year, and many others are in process of erection, which have connected with them many new devices superior to the old methods in general use throughout the district. In South-eastern Missouri, where the enormous deposits of disseminated lead ores are found, gigantic strides have been made, not only in the development of ore bodies, but in the application of machinery to reduce the cost of mining and milling these large bodies of low grade ores.

Great quantities of these ores are brought to Kansas City to be smelted.

Missouri's Mineral Statistics.

Coal Production.

	1893.	1894.
	Number.	Number.
Number of mines	404	365
Tons of coal mined	3,190,442	2,383,322
	£ s. d.	£ s. d.
Average price per ton	0 5 2	0 5 3
Amount received for total output	826,380 0 0	622,536 0 0

UNITED STATES.

Lead Production.

	1893.	1894.
Tons mined	Number. 49,626	Number. 52,003
Amount received for output	£ s. d. 453,311 0 0	£ s. d. 403,803 0 0
Average price per ton	9 2 7	7 15 0

Zinc Production.

	1893.	1894.
Tons of ore mined..	Number. 131,487	Number. 89,150
Value of zinc production	£ s. d. 591,373 0 0	£ s. d. 276,444 0 0
Average price per ton—		
Silicate of zinc ore	..	1 18 6
Zinc blende	4 10 0	3 8 4

Table showing Number of Men Employed in Coal, Lead, and Zinc Mines in 1894.

	Miners.	Others Employed.	Total.
Coal mines	6,125	1,518	7,643
Lead and zinc mines	3,421	1,644	5,065
Total ..	9,546	3,162	12,708

Missouri produced in 1895 288,974,640 lbs. of zinc, and 92,587,470 lbs. of lead; total value, 820,644*l*.

Missouri has 52 lines of railway penetrating it, with a total mileage of 6,487 miles. Every mile is being operated.

Missouri is prominent as a live-stock State. Below find shipments direct to Kansas City, which is part of what the State produces:—

	1894.	1895.
Cattle	200,889	215,388
Sheep	98,201	132,877
Hogs	601,681	693,211
Horses and mules	3,007	4,912

To give the reader an idea of the magnitude of the cattle industry in Missouri on January 1, 1896, there were in the State:—

	Number.
Cattle	2,548,117
Sheep	860,820
Hogs	3,561,136
Horses and mules .. (about)	137,000

Taking Missouri as a State, we find it one of the best in this country. For example, Missouri does not claim to be a lumber State like Michigan or Wisconsin, at the same time it marketed in 1894, 296,130,430 feet of lumber; 2,186,144 ties, and about 40,000,000 feet of logs. In 1895 Misssouri shipped 44,160,662 lbs. of poultry, 1,939 cars of melons, 2,810,880 lbs. of butter, and 33,461,155 lbs. of canned goods.

The Chicago and Alton Railway has a surveying party now making surveys from Jefferson City, Missouri, to Fort Smith, Arkansas. The line, if built, will fairly intersect the great coal, lead, zinc, and lumber regions between the two points named.

The finances of Missouri are in a highly satisfactory condition:—

	Amount.
	£
Balance January 1, 1895 ..	148,709
Receipts in 1895 ..	786,358
Disbursements ..	866,051
Balance January 1, 1896 ..	69,011

Of the 567,453*l.* appropriated from the revenue fund for the general expenses of the State in 1895-96, 347,785*l.* was drawn in 1895, leaving only 219,254*l.* to be paid out in 1896.

Bonded debt, January 1, 1895, 1,242,975*l.*; paid in 1895, 108,887*l.*; outstanding January 1, 1896, 1,134,008*l.* The bonded debt now consists of 1,050,826*l.*, in 3½ per cent. bonds, redeemable at the pleasure of the State at any time before 1907, and of 83,256*l.* in 6 per cent. bonds. On July 1 of this year 69,227*l.* of the 6 per cent. bonds will fall due and be paid, leaving only 2,272*l.* to be met in 1897.

A great many apples were raised in Missouri in 1895. One man shipped 18,375 barrels, which brought him about 6,420*l.* Over 1,000,000 barrels of apples were shipped in 1895 from Missouri.

The population of Missouri (1890), 2,679,184. On December 31, 1894, there were confined in the penitentiary 2,178 convicts; December 31, 1895, 2,196 convicts. This is said to be the largest State prison in the world.

Following are statistics showing the amount of capital invested, the number of wage-earners employed, value of goods made, &c., by 864 of Missouri's principal establishments. The invested capital of these concerns reached the snug sum of 15,623,430*l*., to which amount there should be added 9,632,293*l*., that sum representing the cost of the buildings and grounds and machinery necessary to carry on the operations of the 864 manufactories. The value of the goods manufactured was 23,522,533*l*.; 4,236 and 43,006 wage-earners were required in the production of the goods made by the 864 concerns; 1,094,902*l*. were paid to clerks, and 3,688,848*l*. were paid out in wages, an average wage of 85*l*. 5*s*. during the year to each workman. More goods were manufactured in the tobacco than any other one industry, the selling value of the tobacco manufactured being 2,990,690*l*., not including 243,848*l*. worth of cigars. The next largest item of manufacture is 2,575,027*l*. worth of pork and beef. Brewers come third, with a total of 2,133,713 barrels of beer, worth 2,274,473*l*. In St. Louis more capital seems to be invested in breweries than in any other industry, the buildings and grounds of the city's 22 breweries being valued at 1,511,400*l*., their machinery at 317,487*l*., and their capital at 3,022,520*l*. The capital of the nine tobacco factories, which rank second among the 67 industries, in point of amount of capital invested, is 1,129,194*l*. Although the tobacco factories have not as much capital, the product of their factories sell for a great deal more than the product of the breweries. The 51,156,420 lbs. of tobacco manufactured in St. Louis sold for 2,762,923*l*., whereas the beer of the 22 breweries sold for only 2,080,000*l*. With beer and tobacco out of the way, the figures take an enormous drop, the next industry being pork and beef, with only 1,035,817*l*. worth of goods made in the year, or less than one-half the amount for which the beer was sold.

The clothing establishments are a close fourth in the list, the 27 factories having sold their products for 1,009,487*l*. The 109 Kansas City establishments which reported to the bureau have an invested capital of 1,009,359*l*., and ground and buildings valued at 595,519*l*., with machinery costing 265,579*l*. 728*l*. 7*s*. worth of goods were made by each of the 4,144 employés in the 109 Kansas City establishments. The average yearly wages of each employé was 85*l*. 5*s*.

More capital is invested in the pork and beef business in Kansas City than in any other one industry; the figures in that business are about 220,000*l*. The three Kansas City breweries which made a report have a capital of 143,549*l*.

Sash, door, and blind factories have a capital of 109,549*l*. Kansas City manufactured 15,000 tons of ice, valued at 122,809*l*.

The consolidated statement of the condition of State and private banks in Missouri in December 31, 1895, compiled by the Secretary of State, shows the resources of the State banks to be 10,389,518*l*., and the private banks 14,772*l*. These banks are located in places other than Kansas City and St. Louis. The resources of the Kansas City State banks are given at 530,507*l*., and those of St. Louis at 10,300,752*l*. Most of the banking business of Kansas City, in fact more than nine-tenths, is done through national banks.

The State of Missouri produced and shipped out during 1894 the following articles. Attention is called to cotton, tobacco, wool, poultry, fruits, and their products.

Articles.		Quantity.
Apples	Bushels	1,406,048
Butter	Lbs.	2,810,880
Cattle	Head	864,823
Cotton	Bales	11,865
Canned fruit	Lbs.	33,461,155
Copper ore	Tons	20
Coal	,,	1,495,622
Eggs	Dozen	23,765,835
Flax	Lbs.	20,136,336
Fruit, small	Crates	65,187
Fruit and vegetables	Lbs.	8,483,930
Fire-clay	Cars	2,525
Fire-brick	,,	1,796
Fertiliser	Lbs.	4,659,000
Game	,,	1,083,897
Gravel	Cars	7,739
Granite	,,	2,218
Horses and mules	Head	66,567
Hogs	,,	2,896,077
Hay	Bales	1,644,485
Hides	Lbs.	6,755,177
Honey	,,	10,228
Iron ore and pig-iron	,,	2,932
Lead	Tons	60,972
Lime	Barrels	1,477,714
Logs	Feet	39,042,000
Logs, walnut	,,	160,000
Lumber	,,	296,130,430
Poultry	Lbs.	44,160,662
Piling	Feet	3,989,500
Sheep	Head	294,109
Sewer pipe and tile	Cars	1,920
Sand	,,	2,721
Stone	,,	3,664
Tobacco	Lbs.	3,291,618
Terra-cotta	Cars	76
Tripoli	Lbs.	2,068,000
Wool	,,	2,503,660
Zinc	Tons	76,410

St. Joseph, Missouri, is located 70 miles north of Kansas City and has a population of about 60,000 people. It is an old steady wealthy city, and is really a jobbing and manufacturing city. For 1895 the jobbers sold about 10,000,000*l.* worth of goods, and the manufacturers about 12,500,000*l.* In the manufacture of shirts, overalls, trousers, jackets, &c., St. Joseph manufactures more than any other city in the United States. The sale for 1895 in this line amounted to about 2,200,000*l.*, and gave employment to about 4,000 men and women. The British merchants can do business here as well as at Omaha and Kansas City, if they will seek it

Two packing-houses and a stockyard are located at St. Joseph, and they do more or less of an exporting business.

The internal revenue of St. Joseph for 1894 was 10,040*l.*, for 1895, 11,607*l.* Customs collected for 1894, 11,424*l.*, and for 1895, 13,731*l.* The customs are not large, considering the volume of business done; that is because so many imported goods are cleared at eastern ports, and rehandled by foreign agents. At the same time, goods should be sold direct by British merchants, and they should reap better prices, doing away with the middle man.

It may be said that one of the finest pieces of land in this western country is that part known as the Oklahoma territory, which was organised in 1890, and which contains 39,030 square miles, 18,699 miles of which is not yet open for settlement. This territory transacts the bulk of its business at Kansas City, on account of its being the nearest large and wholesale city, but more particularly on account of the vast live-stock industry. The growth of the Oklahoma territory in the past 6 years has been, in many respects, wonderful. Where once the deer bounded in freedom over the plains and through the timber, now are found farm-houses and wheat-fields, not differing materially from the older States. In it are located many beautiful and modern towns, fully equipped with electric lights, waterworks, and charitable institutions. There are within the Oklahoma territory a great many Indians; all are civilised, and are of the following tribes: —Iowas, Sac, Foxes, Pottawatomies, Absentees, Shawnees, Cheyennes, Arapahoes, Pawnees, Cherokees, and Tankawas. The United States is doing good work in the school and religious training, and which must, in course of time, bring forth good results. All business is carried on by white people.

There is an abundance of fine timber in the territory, and the soil is very productive. The principal products are Indian maize, wheat, oats, cotton, sorghum, millet, broom corn, rye, flax, and vegetables, and rapid strides are being taken in horticulture.

It may be said that no territory in this country has ever been developed as rapidly as this. The live-stock industry is increasing, and in a few years will become the leading occupation.

A Bill has been introduced in Congress for the purpose of compelling those who have cattle grazing on the Wichita, Ponca, Kiowa, Comanche, Apache, Otoe, and Missouri reservations, to pay taxes on the same to the territory of Oklahoma. The value of the cattle now on these reservations is estimated at 2,200,000*l.* The question of taxation has been pending in the courts of Oklahoma for some time, and is now being contested. The Wichita, Kiowa, Comanche, and Apache country is added to Canadian county, Oklahoma, for judicial purposes; but the contention on the part of the cattlemen has been that they should not be compelled to pay taxes. The Bill, as presented, legalises the assessment and levy of taxes on personal property on the various Indian reservations in the territory of Oklahoma, and provides that the assessment and levy of all taxes heretofore made of personal property located on Indian reservations, by the local and proper authorities in Oklahoma be ratified, confirmed, and validated. The proper authorities in Oklahoma are authorised to assess, levy, and collect a tax in harmony with the provisions of the territorial statutes, upon all personal property located, kept, and owned by citizens of the United States upon any Indian reservation within Oklahoma to the same extent and under the same rule that the property of other citizens of the territory is assessed. The Act is to take effect and be enforced upon its passage.

In the past many noted desperadoes and criminals have held sway in this territory, but such is not the case now; all have been driven out by the laws being strictly enforced, and whenever they now do make a raid upon the settlers, it is generally to their sorrow.

Three railways have laid many miles of steel rails through the territory, namely:—Atchison, Topeka, and Santa Fé Railway; Chicago, Rock Island, and Pacific Railway; and Choctaw, Oklahoma and Gulf Railway. The two first named run direct to Kansas City. Two or three new lines are contemplated for the coming year, and the lines already established will build some branches.

It can be readily seen that for such a new country rapid headway is being made. During 1895 many public schools—the University of Oklahoma, Territorial Normal School, Oklahoma Agricultural and Mechanical College, and the Oklahoma Insane Asylum have been erected. Owing to the very few criminals, it has been deemed wise not to expend money for a penitentiary but confine them in the Kansas State Penitentiary.

Effort is now being made to present a Bill to Congress, to admit Oklahoma territory to Statehood. If same object is accomplished, it will assist advancement of the country.

A few statistics are given below:—

	1893.	1894.	1895.
	Number.	Number.	Number.
Population, of all classes	151,213	212,635	275,065
Number of private banks	24	50	52
Number of national banks	6	6	5
Atchison, Topeka, and Santa Fé Railway Company, miles operated	97	251	279
Chicago, Rock Island, and Pacific Railway Company, miles operated	61	124	163
Choctaw, Oklahoma, and Gulf Railway Company	32	34	74
Number of churches built, Protestant	..	61	79
Number of churches built, Catholic	..	60	77
Taxable property	..	4,262,000*l*.	8,910,000*l*.

The Kansas, Oklahoma, and Southern Railway contemplate building during 1896; this line will be constructed from Cherryvale, Kansas, viâ Guthrie, Oklahoma, to a point in Northern Texas not determined; a branch will also be built into the immense coal fields of the Indian territory.

A charter has been issued for the Santa Fé, Oklahoma, and Western Railway, capital 400,000*l.* This line will be constructed from Sapulpa, Indian territory, to Vernon, Texas, and will no doubt be good property, for it will pass through a wonderful fine cattle country.

On January 1, 1896, there were 22,778 sheep, 48,318 hogs, and 173,240 cattle in Oklahoma, which goes to show that it is a wonderful live stock country. In 1895 Oklahoma shipped to Kansas City alone, 61,515 cattle, 3,168 sheep, and 48,210 hogs, and also shipped quite a number of horses and mules.

Cotton raising in Oklahoma was commenced in 1893, and promises soon to make a showing in the production for this country; rapid headway is being made, as will be seen by the following figures :—

Year.	Quantity.
	Bales.*
1893..	6,000
1894..	9,000
1895..	15,000

* Bales averaging 500 lbs. each.

There is only one cotton-seed oil mill in the Oklahoma territory, but it is positive that other mills will be erected shortly, in order to keep up with the increase of the production of cotton.

Gold has been discovered in many places in Oklahoma, but it has never been discovered in paying quantities; a great deal of prospecting is now in progress.

The Indian territory is one of the finest pieces of land in the western country; it consists of 31,400 square miles, of which 20,000 square miles are underlaid with rich coal, of which some has tested 98 per cent. carbon, which establishes its quality, and in a short time it will supply a large per cent. of the country tributory to it. Large quantities of this coal are now being used in Kansas City; in 1890, 869,229 tons of coal, valued at 327,000*l.* were shipped, but fully ten times as much was shipped during 1895.

The population, in 1890, was 66,289, the majority of which are Indians; they are known as the Five Civilised Tribes, each tribe is a nation, and are named Chickasaw nation, Cherokee nation, Creek nation, Choctaw nation, and Seminole nation; each nation has a governor, who controls all matters for his tribe. There are not many whites in the Indian territory, on account of its lawlessness; there is more crime in it than in any other State or territory in the United States. From March 5, 1895, to October 25, 1895, 186 murders were reported, and no doubt many were committed and not reported; the whites who are there are not the best, as a whole; a number of them are renegades and outlaws, and they marry into Indian families, and their offspring do not make good citizens.

In 1890 only 390,000 acres were under cultivation, and in 1895, 2,000,000 acres. The Indian territory, strictly speaking, is a cattle country, and has produced great numbers of cattle to the Kansas City market, and will produce greater numbers in the future. In 1894 Indian territory shipped to Kansas City, 228,283 cattle; in 1895, 191,314. Sheep: 1894, 4,016; 1895, 7,042. Hogs: 1894, 27,046; 1895, 35,769. Horses: 1894, 1,070; 1895, 2,090. On January 1, 1896, there were in the Indian territory:—

	Number.
Cattle	200,075
Hogs	50,642
Sheep	19,036
Horses and mules (about)	11,000

Hence it can readily be seen that the Indian territory must become an important factor in the live stock industry.

I beg to report that cotton raising in the Indian territory is yet in its infancy, it produced in—

	Quantity.
	Bales.*
1893	4,000
1894	6,240
1895	17,807

* Estimating 500 lbs. per bale.

So far there is only one cotton-seed oil mill in the Indian territory, but others will soon be built.

Only one strike prevailed, and was unsuccessful, during 1895; that existed among the coal miners at the numerous mining points, involving about 2,000 men; they struck for an advance of 10d. per ton for screened coal, and 7½d. per ton for mine run; the company agreed not to grant any advance, and after several weeks loss of time the miners returned to work at the old wages.

Owing to location, the bulk of the business of the Indian territory is transacted at Kansas City, it being the natural market.

A Bill has been presented to Congress to make the Indian territory a State. Should the Bill be granted, it will be of great value developing same, and assisting materially in the suppression of crime.

Six railways penetrate the Indian territory, namely:—

(2148)

	Number of Miles.
Atchison, Topeka, and Santa Fé Railway	164
Chicago, Rock Island, and Pacific Railway	103
Choctaw and Gulf Railway	40
Missouri, Kansas, and Texas Railway	274
St. Louis and Santa Fé Railway	260
Kansas City, Pittsburg, and Gulf Railway	70
Total	911

The St. Louis and San Francisco Railway Company will build, in 1896, a railway line from Sapulpa, Indian territory, to Oklahoma City. Oklahoma; it will be about 100 miles long.

A new line of railway will be built in 1896 from Fort Smith, Arkansas, to Atoka, Choctaw nation, Indian territory; distance, 107 miles.

A new line of railway will shortly be built, to be known as the Kansas, Oklahoma, and Southern Railway; the line will be constructed from Cherryvale, Kansas, viâ Guthrie and El Reno, Oklahoma, into Northern Texas; a branch will also be constructed into the coal fields of the Indian territory.

The Santa Fé, Oklahoma, and Western Railway Company, capital 400,000*l.*, will build from Sapulpa, Indian territory, through the Oklahoma territory, to Vernon, Texas; a charter has been issued for same.

The Kansas City, Pittsburg, and Gulf Railway, will build, during 1896, a branch from a point on their line in the Indian territory to Fort Smith, Arkansas.

The Kansas City, Fort Scot, and Memphis Railway will build, in 1896, a line from Baxter Springs, Kansas, to Miami, Indian territory; distance, 40 miles.

St. Louis.

Mr. Vice-Consul Western Bascome reports as follows:—

Reviewing the business of the year 1895 as a whole, it will be found to be more satisfactory than for the previous year.

In many lines an increase in volume is reported, while in no commodity, except perhaps grain, has there been a falling off.

In the receipts of grain there is a large decrease, but only in the one cereal, corn.

The same condition, however, prevails in other markets, the cause being the unusually low price of that cereal and the consequent unwillingness of holders, both farmers and shippers, to market the crop.

The detailed statements of the various lines of business to be found in subsequent pages will show a gradual improvement over the past 2 years; but has not yet recovered the high-water mark of 1892, as a whole, though some commodities exceed that year's marketing, in volume at least.

There was an increase in the amount of flour manufactured, but a loss on the amount handled in this market.

Grain. The total receipt of wheat was 11,275,885 bushels in 1895, a slight gain over the previous year, but not half the amount handled in 1892.

There was also an increase in oats, rye, and barley, but corn fell off from 23,546,945 bushels in 1894 to only 8,779,290 bushels in 1895, or only about one-third of the receipts of 1894.

Increase. Hay, tobacco, cattle, sheep, lumber, coffee, rice, lead, coal, potatoes, salt, and butter show an increase in volume over 1894.

Decrease. Cotton, bagging, hog products, shingles, lath, wool, hides, sugar, molasses, and nails show a decrease from the previous year.

Tonnage. The total tonnage for 1895 was 16,650,856, against 15,239,765 for 1894, an increase of 1,411,091, or nearly 10 per cent. increase.

Saddlery. The saddlery trade has been injuriously affected by the popularity of bicycles, and some of our largest houses have opened cycling departments.

Brick. The brick manufacturing and other trades connected with it, report a poor year as far as prices are concerned. It is not claimed that the volume of business was less than in previous years, but outside competition has come in, and prices have been exceptionally unsatisfactory from the manufacturers and wholesalers' standpoint. There have been very few failures, and none of any magnitude.

Banking. There have been no bank failures here in 10 years. The beginning of 1895 found them in a very strong and healthy condition, having a ratio of $44\frac{1}{4}$ per cent. of cash on hand to deposits; this has been drawn down at the end of the year to $33\frac{1}{2}$ per cent., indicating great activity as well as confidence in the future stability of credits.

These improved conditions are reflected in unparalled increased clearings, being for 1895, 248,864,730*l.*, an increase of 10 per cent. on 1894. The largest annual total prior to this was 246,314,392*l.* in 1892, which year has always since been referred to as the banner year for new building and new enterprises, marking the zenith of St. Louis prosperity.

New buildings. The value of new buildings commenced or completed in 1895 was exceedingly large, and is another indication of the improved financial condition and confidence in the city's future.

The building permits issued in 1895 aggregated 3,000,000*l.*, against 2,400,000*l.* in 1894, an increase of 600,000*l.*, but it did not equal that of 1892 by about 400,000*l.*

Municipal Finances.

Municipal finances. The balance in the city Treasury at the close of the fiscal year April, 1895, was 467,760*l.* Adding this to the unexpended appropriations of 63,421*l.* make the total resources 531,181*l.* The bonded debt is composed of 1,222,200*l.*, formerly county bonds assumed by the city; 1,161,600*l*., waterworks bonds; and 1,821,142*l*. issued by the city; a total of 4,204,942*l*. The bonds matured during the year 1894 were 434,500*l*., and were redeemed as they fell due by 14,032*l*. out of the revenue from the sinking fund and the proceeds of the sale of 400,000*l*. renewal bonds. These bonds bear 4 per cent. interest payable in gold, and brought an average of 105,092*l*. flat.

The bonds matured in 1895 amounted to 270,500*l*. Of this amount, 197,000*l*. was provided by sale of renewal bonds, and 75,500*l*. out of the revenue of the sinking fund. The renewal bonds are dated May 1, 1895, due May 1, 1915, and bear interest at the rate of 3·65 per cent. per annum, principal payable in gold coin of present standard and fineness. They were offered at public letting and brought 103·15 flat, the best price this city has ever obtained for its bonds, and is gratifyingly low.

The annual interest charges on the outstanding debt amounts to 187,292*l*., the average ratio of interest being 4·454 per cent.

The city owns its waterworks, hospitals, insane asylums, poor-houses, city hall, court-house, jail, house of refuge, workhouse fire-engine houses, police-station, and public parks. The waterworks are valued at 3,000,000*l*., and all other property belonging to the city at 3,200,000*l*., an aggregate of 6,200,000*l*.

Taxation. The assessed valuation of taxable property for the taxes of 1895 amounted to 65,292,720*l*., an increase of 3,224,350*l*. over the preceding year.

The rate of taxation in the old limits is 1·40 per cent., and for the new limits or suburban property 1·00 per cent., and for State and school purposes added it amounted to 2·05 in old limits, and 1·67 in new limits.

Fire insurance losses. The losses by fire during 1895 amounted to 155,935*l*., against 238,821*l*. in 1894, a decrease of 82,886*l* in 1895, making a very prosperous year for the insurance companies.

Population. The population by the directory estimate was 603,837 in 1895, against 596,157 in 1894, an ancrease of only 7,680 in 1895.

Post office department. The Post Office Department shows an increased business in volume of over 10 per cent., and about the same (10 per cent.) in the money order business.

Internal revenue. The internal revenue shows a falling-off in 1895 from 1894 of about 12 per cent., this being in spirit stamps alone, consequent upon the closing of several distilleries in 1895.

Wholesale and Jobbing Trade.

Boots and shoes. The "Shoe and Leather Gazette" reports the boot and shoe trade of St. Louis for 1895 as amounting to 6,453,255*l*., a jobbing business of 4,379,655*l*., and manufacturing 2,073,600*l*.

This beats her unparallelled record of 1894, and lessens the distance between her second place and that of first place held by the City of Boston; the total receipts being 875,931 cases in 1895, against 783,793 cases in 1894. There was much greater

CHICAGO.

activity in the factories in 1895, the increased output being 510,000 pairs. Owing to the advance in leather, the average per pair value in 1895 was not less than 1 dol. 80 c.—materially greater than in 1894.

Groceries.

The trade in groceries in 1895 is estimated to be about the same in value under an increased volume, but low prices have prevailed to prevent its augmentation.

Coffee. The receipts of coffee were 259,289 sacks, or about 5 per cent. increase over 1894. Prices have been steady, closing about 1 c. lower per pound than at the opening of the year 1895.

Rice. The receipts of rice were 93,039 packages in 1895, against 66,576 in 1894.

Teas. The trade in teas has not varied much from previous seasons.

Sugar. The trade in sugar declined in 1895 to 419,703 barrels, 351,842 bags and 3,127 hogsheads, from 453,439 barrels 377,840 bags and 1,979 hogsheads in 1894; prices ruling very low in the early season, and in the face of a large fruit crop, which usually consumes a large quantity for preserving, the price stiffened up at the close of the year in view of the depleted crops of Cuban plantations.

Hardware. The wholesale hardware trade in 1895 is reported to have been increased about 20 per cent., partly in increased volume and partly in increased values.

This covers bicycles, sporting goods, wire and nails, sheet metals, stoves, ranges and furnaces, steam and hot-water apparatus.

Tobacco. Leaf tobacco shows an increase in 1895 of nearly 5,000 hogsheads, most of which has been brought from other States; the crop of Missouri being 2,000 hogsheads. All the receipts were taken by local manufactories. St. Louis still maintains its first position as the leading manufacturing tobacco city in the country, the output being 59,347,555 lbs. in 1895, an increase of 23·90 per cent. over 1894.

Cattle.

Cattle. The receipts of cattle in 1895 show a gratifying increase, prices having also increased.

Hogs. The receipts of hogs in 1895 show a net decrease of 49,514 head as compared with 1894, and sold at an average of about 1 dol. (4s. 1½d.) per 100 lbs. less than in 1894.

Sheep. St. Louis made a wonderful advance in handling sheep in 1895, aggregating 510,660 sheep, an increase of 150,762 over 1894, and prices did not fluctuate much during the year.

Horses and mules. Notwithstanding the decreased local demand for horses and mules for street car purposes, all lines now being run by cable or electricity, the receipts reached 77,820 head, the south, as usual,

Cotton.

The gross receipts of cotton were 926,285 bales larger than any previous year, the gain being in through shipments for St. Louis account. There was a falling-off in the net receipts for local account of at least 10 per cent. The shipments as reported aggregated 999,919 bales; of this amount 296,455 bales were exported to Europe, 44,415 bales to Canada, and the balance to eastern points.

The year ending August 31, 1895, marked the lowest prices ever obtained, being $4\frac{7}{8}$ c. (2d.) per pound, while in St. Louis the minimum price was 5 c. (2$\frac{1}{2}d$.) per pound in December, 1894. There seems to be a discrepancy between receipts and shipments for the year of 63,406 bales, but diligent enquiry has failed to locate the error. Prices have ranged from 5 c. (2$\frac{1}{2}d$.), the lowest, to $7\frac{1}{2}$ c. ($3\frac{3}{4}d$.), the highest, during the year for middlings.

Grain.

The grain trade for the year 1895 was disappointing, the aggregate receipts of all cereals being the smallest in 10 years. The St. Louis receipts for 1895 were 32,850,282 bushels, against 45,970,515 bushels in 1894, a falling-off of about 30 per cent., this being wholly in corn. Prices of No. 2 red wheat ranged from $48\frac{3}{4}$ in January, to $66\frac{1}{2}$ in December last. The lowest price for corn was $23\frac{1}{2}$ c. in December last.

The receipts of oats were about the average.

The receipts of rye were 224,821 bushels, and shipments 173,296 bushels.

The receipts of barley were 2,104,126 bushels, nearly all of which were consumed here by the large brewing interests, there being 60,823,844 gallons of beer manufactured in this city in 1895, an increase of about 1,000,000 gallons over 1894.

Foreign grain trade. The export grain trade of St. Louis for the year 1895 was satisfactory under conditions quite unusual. Heretofore the movement has been principally by river viâ New Orleans, that being the cheaper route, but on account of the low stage of water in the Mississippi River, which practically suspended all movement by that route, shippers had to look to other points to fill their engagements and ship by railroads to tidewater.

The failure of the corn crop of 1894 west of the Mississippi River made prices in the early months above export value, the States east of the river being able to supply the eastern market at lower prices.

The immense crop of corn in 1895 resulted in such low prices that it did not move with any freedom from the west, farmers and dealers preferring to store in cribs rather than accept prevailing prices.

The amount of corn exported viâ New Orleans was 8,795,708 bushels, the largest since 1890. A large portion of this was for St. Louis account, being purchased in the States of Illinois, Indiana, Kansas and Nebraska, and forwarded to New Orleans by rail. The movement viâ the Atlantic seaboard was as usual considerable, amounting to 455,923 bushels of wheat and 2,005,404 bushels of corn, most of which was for European account. A shipment of 23,573 bushels of corn went to Cuba, and 19,000 bushels to Mexico.

The export demand for corn has been good, and will doubtless continue at present low prices.

Flour. The foreign shipments of flour on through bills of lading from St. Louis by railroad and river for the year 1895 was 983,322 barrels to England, 3,600 barrels to Germany, 71,345 barrels to Scotland, 58,265 barrels to Ireland, 320 barrels to Denmark, 32,735 barrels to Norway, 5,185 to Holland, 9,500 to Belgium, 495 to Finland, 35,555 to Newfoundland, 2,740 to Canada, 91,310 to Cuba, and 13,304 to Central and South American ports.

Importations.

The principal commodities imported into St. Louis are ale and beer, anvils, barley, brushes, carpets, chemicals and drugs, china and earthenware, corks and manufactures of cork, cutlery, fish, guns and firearms, hops, manufactures of cotton, linen, iron, leather, paper, silk and wool, granulated rice, sugar, steel wire, tin and tern plate, wines and liquors, tobacco and cigars, and window glass. These articles are brought here viâ Atlantic ports and do not furnish a complete list of foreign importations. The larger portion of such goods coming here are bought of foreign importers in the Atlantic cities and are freed from bond in those cities, consequently it is impossible to ascertain the aggregate of foreign commodities handled in St. Louis.

The natural gateway for heavy and bulky articles, not very valuable, is viâ New Orleans and Waterborn to this city by river to save freight; but little comes that route now, the bulk coming from Atlantic ports.

This mode of importation makes it difficult to suggest openings for British trade. Portland cement, which ought to be imported viâ New Orleans, is not imported at all, but is purchased of importers in the Atlantic cities.

It has been my opinion, from close observation over many years, that, given a fair stage of water in the river, say 6 to 9 feet, all heavy and bulky freight can be imported much cheaper by river; and the exportation of cereals by that route would be greatly cheapened. With the present unsatisfactory condition of the river, the average difference in grain freights viâ New Orleans to Liverpool is 3*d.* and over per bushel.

Thirteen States bordering on the Mississippi River produced in 1895 1,785,000,000 bushels of corn, three-fourths of the entire production of the country, a large portion of which should seek this natural gateway.

(2148)

The high-water rate from St. Louis is 1 dol. 60 c. (6s. 7d.) per ton, or 1·33 mills per ton per mile, while the Inter-State Commission gives the rail rate for the whole country as 8·32 mills per ton per mile.

There is an effort being made in Congress to get a bill through upon the basis of that under which Eads succeeded in deepening the jetties at New Orleans, and the best river authorities are sanguine of success; if the authority is obtained, the compensation to be determined by the depth of water obtained and maintained annually. If this project succeeds there will be a large opening for British trade of the character suggested, both by importation and the exportation of heavy and bulky products of both countries.

TABLE showing Comparative Business in Leading Articles at St. Louis during the Years 1894–95.

Articles.		Quantity. 1894.	1895.
Flour, amount, manufactured	Barrels	1,656,645	1,740,026
” handled	”	4,717,954	3,753,370
Wheat, total receipts	Bushels	10,003,242	11,275,885
Corn ”	”	23,546,945	8,779,290
Oats ”	”	10,196,605	10,466,160
Rye ”	”	140,285	224,821
Barley ”	”	2,083,438	2,104,126
All grain received (including flour reduced to wheat)	”	51,646,405	37,410,330
Cotton, receipts	Bales	812,705	699,798
Bagging, manufactured	Yards	13,000,000	11,700,000
Hay, receipts	Tons	159,969	195,582
Tobacco, receipts	Hogsheads	43,264	48,642
Lead, receipts	In 80 lbs. pigs	1,463,229	1,500,923
Hog products, total shipments	Lbs.	345,481,499	339,340,499
Cattle, receipts	Head	773,571	851,275
Sheep ”	”	359,895	510,660
Hogs ”	”	1,489,856	1,440,342
Horses and mules, receipts	”	59,882	77,820
Lumber and logs ”	Feet	694,395,856	826,175,742
Shingles, receipts	Pieces	106,782,000	64,185,937
Lath ”	”	31,354,350	18,033,570
Wool, total receipts	Lbs.	24,861,455	21,593,780
Hides ”	”	46,456,970	44,169,790
Sugar, received	”	198,869,450	185,832,650
Molasses (including glucose) received	”	5,765,901	4,310,327
Coffee, received	Bags	246,612	259,289
Rice, receipts	Packages	66,576	93,039
Coal ”	Bushels	74,644,375	88,589,935
Nails ,	Kegs	522,673	428,042
Potatoes, receipts	Bushels	1,392,522	2,469,371
Salt, receipts	Barrels	248,830	304,204
”	Bushels in bulk	620,500	804,980
Butter	Lbs.	14,138,544	15,812,095
Tons of freight of all kinds received and shipped		15,239,765	16,650,856

CHICAGO.

CUSTOM-HOUSE Transactions for 1895.—Condensed Classification Imported into St. Louis, Mo., showing Value and Duty Paid.

Commodities.	Value.	Duty.
	£ s. d.	£ s. d.
Ale and beer	6,358 0 0	1,784 6 6
Anvils	3,422 16 0	889 4 0
Barley	883 4 0	264 19 0
Brushes	1,872 8 0	655 6 6
Carpets and carpeting	5,354 16 0	1,937 12 6
Chemicals	40,741 0 0	11,122 1 6
China and earthenware	36,466 4 0	11,658 14 6
Cork and manufactures of cork	7,321 12 0	1,430 5 0
Cutlery	19,792 4 0	9,160 4 6
Fancy goods	4,716 16 0	1,215 6 6
Fish	10,687 4 0	1,287 1 6
Free goods	69,353 8 0	..
Guns and firearms	19,442 4 0	6,028 17 6
Hops	5,208 4 0	1,751 13 0
Manufactured cotton	67,406 16 0	11,498 2 6
,, linen	24,943 16 0	8,814 15 6
,, iron	8,710 12 0	3,403 15 6
,, leather	2,084 8 0	491 1 0
,, metal	7,885 12 0	2,737 9 6
,, paper	5,237 8 0	1,373 10 6
,, silk	5,332 4 0	2,683 14 6
,, wood	2,665 4 0	663 12 6
,, wool	59,351 8 0	18,857 19 6
Granulated rice	28,688 8 0	5,226 7 6
Sugar	8,967 8 0	3,599 12 0
Steel wire	31,333 8 0	12,713 17 0
Tin-plate and tern plate	9,556 8 6	5,268 8 6
Spirituous liquors	5,286 16 0	5,848 2 0
Tobacco and cigars	62,032 0 0	70,157 5 0
Wine, sparkling, &c.	15,445 0 0	6,147 5 0
Window glass	28,651 12 0	6,563 10 0
Miscellaneous merchandise	27,226 12 0	7,677 12 0
Collections from other sources	..	19,022 9 0
Total	632,425 4 0	241,934 1 6

ST. PAUL.

Mr. Vice-Consul Murphy reports as follows:—

A rapid sketch of the State of Minnesota, of which St. Paul is the capital and chief business centre would not be amiss.

Minnesota lies in the geographical centre of North America equi-distant from the Atlantic on the east and the Pacific on the west, and from Hudson's Bay on the north and the Gulf of Mexico on the south. Its western boundary is regular, its eastern very irregular, having an average breadth of 250 miles, and measuring 381 miles from Manitoba to the Iowa boundary. Its area is 83,531 square miles, or 53,459,840 acres—exceeding the whole of New England, and nearly equal to that of Ohio and Pennsylvania combined. Of this more than 3,000,000 acres are water surface. In the northern part of the State are the head waters of three

Geographical position of Minnesota.

Area.

UNITED STATES.

Rainfall. great rivers—the Mississippi, flowing south; the Red River of the North, flowing north; and St. Louis River, flowing east. There are nearly 3,000 miles of navigable water in the State. The climate of Minnesota gives the State a position second only to Colorado, as a natural sanitarium. Miasma or malaria does not exist here. The annual rainfall is about 25 inches, while New England has 43 inches, and the Pacific coast over 60 inches. The annual mean temperature of the State is about 44 degrees.

Soil. The fertile soil of Minnesota is unsurpassed for quantity and quality of its cereal productions, vegetables and small fruits. **Products.** Stock raising and dairying, on account of the natural nutritive grasses, pure air and water, has taken a recognised position in the front.

Lumber and mining are rapidly adding wealth to the State. The latter is still undeveloped, except as an index of the future.

Minnesota's location is unique for water and rail transportation. It is without possible parallel that an interior State, lying midway between the oceans, should find within itself the starting point and commercial focus of two trans-continental lines. It is the witness of that unique advantage of situation at the head of the great waterways of the continent which gives to Minnesota, for all practical purposes, the position of a seaboard state, in addition to the advantages of a central location.

St. Paul. The City of St. Paul, as I have said, is the capital of the State and the chief business centre. A glance at the map will show that this city is situated in the very centre of North America, " equi-distant from the waters of Hudson's Bay and the Gulf of Mexico—from the Atlantic Ocean to the ocean in which the sun sets."

Early settlement. The first settlement on the site of St. Paul was in 1838, when an unimportant trading post was established by adventurers. In 1841 a Jesuit missionary built a log chapel and dedicated it to St. Paul, whence the name of the hamlet. The site of the future city was surveyed and laid out in 1849, the same year that the territory of Minnesota was organised. Minnesota was admitted into the Union in 1858 and St. Paul designated as the capital. **Area.** The city now contains 35,482 acres, or a little over 55 square miles. The distance east and west is about 10 miles, and 5 miles from the northern to the southern boundaries.

St. Paul is a very healthy city, and one of the most beautiful in America. The ground on which the city is built rises from the Mississippi River to a series of terraces, the elevated plateaus furnishing superior locations for residences.

Population of State and city. The population of the State in 1890, official report, was 1,300,017; in 1895, 1,574,619. Of these 1,057,084 were native born, and 517,535 of foreign birth. Of the foreign born there are 49,213 Canadians; 26,106 Irish; 12,941 English; 5,344 Scotch; 1,246 Welsh, a total of 94,850 from the British Empire. The other foreign-born population is made up of Germans, Swedish, Bohemians, Poles, Russians, Finns and Icelanders.

St. Paul had a population in 1890 of 133,158; in 1895, 140,292

There are 21 incorporated banks doing business in the city. The bank clearings for 1894 and 1895 were as follows:—

Year.	Amount. Currency.	Sterling.
	Dol. c.	£
1894..	183,856,875 90	37,908,600
1895..	222,332,186 41	45,841,600

Gross income of the St Paul post-office:—

Year.	Amount. Currency.	Sterling.
	Dol. c.	£
1894..	363,674 39	74,900
1895..	422,046 07	87,000

St. Paul is by far the most important wholesale mercantile centre in the north-west. In the early days of the settlement of Minnesota, the towns standing at the head of navigation on the Mississippi River had a natural advantage for selling goods to the frontier trading posts and farming settlements. That advantage already gave St. Paul its first start. When railways were built, the importance it had acquired made it the focus of activity for the new transportation system. To-day, St. Paul is the commanding trade centre of the north-west, for two reasons; first, because it is the chief railway centre, and second, because of its proximity to the head of Lake Superior, which gives it the great advantage of cheap water communication with the east. In fact, the water way of the great lakes is the key to the commercial position of St. Paul. The lake route is a regulator of freight rates by rail. It enables the St. Paul wholesaler to compete with Chicago on equal terms in a large part of the territory in which he operates, and on better terms in a still larger part. The distance from St. Paul to Duluth and Superior is only 150 miles. The competition of three railways secures as low freight rates as the roads can possibly afford. When the goods are put down in St. Paul, they have not lost any distance by reason of this 150 miles of rail carriage, but are just so much nearer to the points of consumption in most of Minnesota, in the two Dakotas, and the country further west.

The territory in which the St. Paul jobbers operate comprises North-Western Wisconsin, Northern Iowa, the whole of Minnesota, North and South Dakota, Montana, Northern Idaho, Washington, and, to some extent, Oregon. Some business is also done with Manitoba and the rest of the Canadian North-West, and much more will be done if Canada is brought into close relations with the United States. The enterprise and the favourable position of the St. Paul jobbing houses have enabled them to promptly establish trade relations with new territory when opened.

All of the territory embraced in the scope of St. Paul's trade relations is comparatively new and will easily support four or five times its present population. No new jobbing city is likely to spring up at a point further west. St. Paul has no apprehension that any part of its trade east of the Rocky Mountains will ever be taken from it by the growth of new commercial cities.

The tendency with all our St. Paul houses is to enlarge their premises to accommodate their growing trade, to carry heavier stocks, and to increase their force of employés. Several of the principal firms have already been forced to move into more spacious quarters, and in some cases very large and handsome buildings have been erected by jobbing concerns for their own use. The news of our enormous crops in the north-west has spread over the whole world, and a large immigration movement is confidently expected for 1896.

Jobbing and manufacturing business done, 1885, 1890, 1895.

The amount of jobbing and manufacturing done in St. Paul for 1885, 1890, and 1895 is given to show the progress made each 5 years:—

	1885.		1890.		1895.	
	Currency.	Sterling.	Currency.	Sterling.	Currency.	Sterling.
	Dollars.	£	Dollars.	£	Dollars.	£
Jobbing	81,596,000	16,823,900	122,223,048	25,200,600	146,464,000	30,198,700
Manufactures	29,437,000	6,069,400	61,720,595	12,725,800	74,280,000	15,315,200

TABLE showing Number of Manufacturing Concerns Operating in St. Paul.

	Number.
Agricultural implements	3
Architectural works	4
Awnings, tents, &c.	6
Babbitt metal	1
Badges and medals	3
Bags, cotton, and paper	1
Baggage checks	1
Baking powder	3
Baskets	1
Bed springs	1
Bedding materials	2
Bird cages	1
Blacking, shoe	1
Blank books	5
Blueing	1
Boats	2
Boilers, steam power	3
Bolts and nuts	3
Boots and shoes	6
Boot and shoe uppers	2
Boxes, wood	4
,, cigars	3
,, paper	2
Brass goods foundry	2
Brewers	9
Brickmakers	14
Brooms	7
Brushes	3
Carpet weavers	10
Carriages and waggons	16
Chewing gum	1
Chemicals	1
Cigars	8
Clothing	6
Coffee and spices	4
Crackers	4
Cut stone	4
Cooperage	7
Candy	5
Cordage	1
Cornices	4
Corsets	1
Creameries	3
Derricks	1
Desks and office furniture	6
Dies and punches	2
Distilleries	1
Electrical goods	4
Electrine	1
Electrotype founders	3
Elevators	3
Fire-engines	1
Fireproof doors	4
Fireworks	1
Flags	2
Flour	3
Furnaces	1
Furniture	5
Fur goods	8
Gas and coke	1

UNITED STATES.

TABLE showing Number of Manufacturing Concerns Operating in St. Paul—continued.

	Number.
Harness	6
Ink	1
Iron foundries	4
Jewellery	4
Law books	2
Lumber mill companies	22
Maccaroni	1
Malsters	1
Mantels, wood	6
Maps	2
Marble and granite	6
Matresses	2
Meat packers	8
Medicines	10
Mineral waters	4
Models	6
Mustard	1
Oils	3
Paints	3
Photo engravers	3
Pickles	3
Ploughs	1
Ranges, steel	1
Roofing	2
Sash, doors, and blinds	15
Sash weights	1
Sausages	1
School furniture	1
Shirts	7
Show cases	2
Soap	2
Stairs	4
Stone, artificial	4
Stoves	1
Terra-cotta works	1
Tobacco	1
Trunks	4
Type	1
Willow ware	2
Window shades	1
Wagon woodwork	1
Total	363

CHICAGO.

INTERNAL REVENUE.—Collections for the Years ending December 31, 1892–95.

	1892. Currency.	1892. Sterling.	1893. Currency.	1893. Sterling.	1894. Currency.	1894. Sterling.	1895. Currency.	1895. Sterling.
	Dol. c.	£	Dol. c.	£	Dol. c.	£	Dol. c.	£
Playing cards	..	..	..	..	6,982 50	1,236	224 42	46
Spirits	1,979,080 30	408,000	1,604,499 80	330,000	1,493,812 90	307,000	1,491,329 84	307,000
Tobacco, snuff, and cigars	163,145 76	33,000	132,923 24	27,000	126,956 85	25,700	129,032 94	26,000
Fermented liquors	373,797 85	77,000	371,664 32	76,000	374,885 86	77,000	402,057 08	82,000
Penalties	2,199 56	450	2,400 68	495	3,671 53	750	9,575 52	1,850
Special taxes	116,557 95	24,000	124,791 52	25,000	123,460 23	25,000	128,581 28	26,000
Total	2,634,781 42	542,450	2,236,279 56	458,495	2,129,719 87	436,686	2,160,801 08	442,916

142   UNITED STATES.

Custom House.

Contains the offices of the United States officials, post office, and United States Courts. Built in 1870, of grey stone, and cost 600,000 dol. (123,700*l*.). St. Paul is a port of entry for direct importations, and the receipt of goods through the custom-house for 1892, 1893, 1894, and 1895 were as follows :—

CHICAGO.

RECEIPT of Goods through the Customs-house for 1892-95.

	1892.		1893.		1894.		1895.	
	Currency. Dol. c.	Sterling. £	Currency. Dol. c.	Sterling. £	Currency. Dol. c.	Sterling. £	Currency. Dol. c.	Sterling. £
Value of dutiable goods	902,305 0	185,567	813,339 0	167,000	503,281 0	103,000	751,462 0	154,000
Total duties collected..	424,177 40	87,600	400,501 88	82,000	241,302 0	49,000	320,760 20	66,000
Value of free goods	321,458 0	66,000	323,452 0	66,000	398,945 0	82,000	866,394 0	178,000
Value of domestic exports	221,585 0	45,000	241,195 0	49,000	386,582 0	79,000	172,968 0	35,500

(2148)

144 UNITED STATES.

Immigration association. In November, 1895, the Minnesota State Immigration Association was organised for the purpose of encouraging immigration to the State, and for giving information in regard to lands, timber, minerals, manufacturing, merchandising, and other trades. Mr. T. L. Schurmeier, one of the leading merchants of St. Paul, is president, and Mr. P. B. Groat, secretary.

LONDON:
Printed for Her Majesty's Stationery Office,
By HARRISON AND SONS,
Printers in Ordinary to Her Majesty.
(75 5 | 96—H & S 2148)

FOREIGN OFFICE.
1896.
ANNUAL SERIES.

No. 1734.

DIPLOMATIC AND CONSULAR REPORTS ON TRADE AND FINANCE.

UNITED STATES.

REPORT FOR THE YEAR 1895
ON THE
TRADE OF THE CONSULAR DISTRICT OF PORTLAND (OREGON).

REFERENCE TO PREVIOUS REPORT, Annual Series No. 1576.

Presented to both Houses of Parliament by Command of Her Majesty,
JUNE, 1896.

LONDON:
PRINTED FOR HER MAJESTY'S STATIONERY OFFICE,
BY HARRISON AND SONS, ST. MARTIN'S LANE,
PRINTERS IN ORDINARY TO HER MAJESTY.

And to be purchased, either directly or through any Bookseller, from
EYRE & SPOTTISWOODE, EAST HARDING STREET, FLEET STREET, E.C., and
32, ABINGDON STREET, WESTMINSTER, S.W.; or
JOHN MENZIES & Co., 12, HANOVER STREET, EDINBURGH, and
90, WEST NILE STREET, GLASGOW; or
HODGES, FIGGIS, & Co., Limited, 104, GRAFTON STREET, DUBLIN.

1896.

[C. 7919—102.]   *Price Threepence.*

New Series of Reports.

Reports of the Annual Series have been issued from Her Majesty's Diplomatic and Consular Officers at the following places, and may be obtained from the sources indicated on the title-page:—

No.		Price.	No.		Price.
1616.	Gothenburg	2d.	1675.	Warsaw	1d.
1617.	Mannheim	1½d.	1676.	Havana	1½d.
1618.	Old Calabar	5d.	1677.	Berlin	1d.
1619.	Pekin	2½d.	1678.	Beira	1½d.
1620.	Taganrog	2d.	1679.	Saigon	1d.
1621.	Brindisi	2½d.	1680.	Trebizond	1d.
1622.	Jeddah	1¼d.	1681.	Vera Cruz	1½d.
1623.	Hamburg	3d.	1682.	Patras	1d.
1624.	Angora	1½d.	1683.	La Rochelle	1½d.
1625.	Buda-Pesth	1½d.	1684.	Madrid	1½d.
1626.	Beyrout	1d.	1685.	Belgrade	2d.
1627.	Bushire	2d.	1686.	Algiers	5d.
1628.	Stettin	2½d.	1687.	Galveston	2½d.
1629.	Porto Rico	1d.	1688.	New Orleans	2d.
1630.	Rotterdam	½d.	1689.	Suakin	1d.
1631.	Alexandria	1½d.	1690.	Pernambuco	1d.
1632.	Tokio	2½d.	1691.	Guatemala	1½d.
1633.	Tangier	1½d.	1692.	Guayaquil	1d.
1634.	Oporto	1½d.	1693.	Wênchow	1d.
1635.	St. Petersburg	4d.	1694.	Piræus	3d.
1636.	Dantzig	2d.	1695.	Tokio	3d.
1637.	Macao	1d.	1696.	Marseilles	1d.
1638.	Hiogo and Osaka	6d.	1697.	Manila	1d.
1639.	Naples	1½d.	1698.	Jerusalem	1d.
1640.	Kiungchow	½d.	1699.	Cherbourg	2d
1641.	Rome	1½d.	1700.	Leghorn	1½d.
1642.	Beira	½d.	1701.	Boston	1½d.
1643.	St. Jago de Cuba	4½d.	1702.	Kiungchow	1d.
1644.	Christiania	6d.	1703.	Naples	2½d.
1645.	Lisbon	1½d.	1704.	Stockholm	2d.
1646.	Brussels	½d.	1705.	Corunna	2d.
1647.	Vera Cruz	½d.	1706.	Rio de Janeiro	2½d.
1648.	Tunis	1d.	1707.	San José	1d.
1649.	Antwerp	1d.	1708.	Paramaribo	2d.
1650.	Tokio	1d.	1709.	Brest	1½d.
1651.	Honolulu	½d.	1710.	Montevideo	½d.
1652.	Stettin	1½d.	1711.	Charleston	2½d.
1653.	Bangkok	1d.	1712.	Baltimore	1d.
1654.	Batoum	1½d.	1713.	Tripoli	1d.
1655.	Mexico	9½d.	1714.	Callao	½d.
1656.	Odessa	1½d.	1715.	Ningpo	1d.
1657.	Réunion	1d.	1716.	Dunkirk	1½d.
1658.	Tokio	1½d.	1717.	Batoum	2d.
1659.	Maranham	1d	1718.	Hankow	1½d.
1660.	Copenhagen	1d.	1719.	Foochow	3½d.
1661.	Berlin	1½d	1720.	Syra	½d.
1662.	Teheran	2½d.	1721.	Panama	1d.
1663.	Salonica	1½d.	1722.	Batavia	1½d.
1664.	Manila	½d.	1723.	Genoa	3d.
1665.	Florence	5½d.	1724.	Cagliari	2½d.
1666.	Dakar	½d.	1725.	Chicago	7½d.
1667.	Havre	2d.	1726.	Trieste	1d.
1668.	Rouen	2d.	1727.	Hakodate	1d.
1669.	Corfu	½d.	1728.	Mannheim	1d.
1670.	Calais	1d.	1729.	Panama	1d.
1671.	Tehran	1½d.	1730.	Caracas	1d.
1672.	Barcelona	2d.	1731.	Riga	6½d.
1673.	Amsterdam	1d.	1732.	Tokio	1½d.
1674.	Bordeaux	2½d.	1733.	Tainan	1d.

No. 1734.

Reference to previous Report, Annual Series No. 1576.

UNITED STATES.

PORTLAND.

Consul Laidlaw to the Marquis of Salisbury.

My Lord,   Portland, *April* 29, 1896.

I HAVE the honour to inclose Annual Commercial Report on the Trade and Commerce of Portland for the year 1895, with some Agricultural and other information with regard to other parts of my Consular District. I have annexed Annual Reports from the Vice-Consuls at Astoria, Tacoma, and Port Townsend. Mr. Alexander's able Report embraces a large amount of matter and detail which can only be indirectly of interest in Great Britain, but I venture to transmit it in its entirety as a special Report on the State of Washington, which might be useful to intending immigrants, and if re-written would cause undue delay in forwarding the complete Report of this District, already somewhat delayed by an unusual difficulty in procuring statistical matter.

I have, &c.
(Signed)   JAMES LAIDLAW.

Report on the Trade, Commerce, and Agriculture of the Consular District of Portland for the Year 1895.

ABSTRACT of Contents.

	PAGE
Portland Consulate—	
Introductory remarks; general review	3
Trade and commerce; British trade	3
Wheat; flour; barley; other grain; hop trade	4
Fruit trade; wool trade; timber	4
Fisheries; salmon; market prices	5
Import trade; glass; cement	6
Coal; bags and bagging; tinplates	6
Financial failures; banks	6
Clearing house; exchange	7
Shipping and navigation; British tonnage	8

(2178)

UNITED STATES.

ABSTRACT of Contents—continued.

	PAGE
Portland—continued—	
Freights; steamers; lights; projected lights	8
Fog signals; life-saving stations	9
Sailors; mariners' home; seamen's institute	9
Population and industries; census	10
Health; diseases; mining	11
Gold and silver production; coal	11
Iron; factories; horse meat	12
Labour; warning to clerks, &c.	13
Public works; jetty; river bars	13
Agriculture; census returns	15
Wheat; cost of production; oats; barley, &c.	16
Orchards and fruits; cattle and sheep	16
Cost of sheep raising in Oregon; swine	17
General remarks; taxation and assessment	18
City finances; bonded debt; real estate	18
Annexes—	
A.—Table of entrances and clearances of vessels	19
B.— „ exports and imports, by articles	19
C.— „ total value of exports and imports, by countries	20
Astoria Vice-Consulate—	
General remarks	21
Shipping and navigation; pilot service	21
Trade and commerce; industries	21
Salmon fishing and canning; other fishing	21
Logging; box-making; can-making	22
Public works; waterworks; railways	23
Government works; range lights	23
Population and health	23
Annexes—	
A.—Table of entrances and clearances of vessels	24
B.— „ exports and imports, by articles	24
C.— „ value of exports and imports, by countries	25
Tacoma Vice-Consulate—	
General remarks on State; health; births; deaths	25
Cattle diseases; weather and climate	25
Industries; timber; railways; mining	26
Fisheries; artificial propagation of salmon	27
Agriculture; general remarks; grain	29
Average prices; grain inspection and grading	30
Agricultural shows; dairying; horticulture	33
Market gardening; hops; flax; seeds	37
Road making; population and assessment	38
General outlook; commercial relations	39
China and Japan; South Africa; Central America	39
General remarks on Tacoma	40
Shipping and navigation; entrances and clearances	40
Exports and imports; timber; dry dock	41
Smelter; trade with China and Japan	42
Population; births; deaths; diseases	44
Financial condition	44
Annexes—	
A.—Table of entrances and clearances of vessels	45
B.— „ exports and imports by articles	45
C.— „ value of exports and imports by countries	46
Seattle—	
General remarks; shipping and navigation	47
Trade and commerce; timber	47
Relations with other countries	48
Population; births; deaths; diseases	48
Climate; industries; fisheries	48
Shipbuilding; post office	49
Financial; business failures; land office	49
Harbourmaster's report	49

PORTLAND.

Abstract of Contents—continued.

	PAGE
Seattle—continued—	
Annexes—	
A.—Table of entrances and clearances of vessels	50
B.— ,, exports and imports by articles	50
C.— ,, value of exports and imports by countries	51
Port Townsend Vice-Consulate—	
Lumber trade; prices advance	52
Shipping and freight; shipbuilding	52
Steamship lines; hydrographic office	53
Dry dock; lightship and lighthouses	53
Marine hospital; cement	53
Manufactures; paper; nails; fur-sealing	53
Fishing; disasters	54
Import trade; export trade; health	54
Annexes—	
A.—Table of entrances and clearances of vessels	54
B.— ,, exports and imports by articles	55
C.— ,, ,, countries	56

Introductory Remarks.

General review. Statistics show quite an improvement in business at this port during 1895, and generally throughout this consular district. Although prices for all produce were very low they were as a rule higher than last year, and towards the close of the year prices of wheat were fairly profitable, which has not been the case for some time past. The value of imports and exports was much higher than last year, and rates of freight averaged about the same. The production of gold has largely increased and a great impetus has been given to gold mining. Silver mining has been carried on to some extent, but it is claimed that the Cœur d'Alene Mines generally cannot be worked to a profit under existing conditions. The state of the labour market is not satisfactory; the supply, skilled and unskilled, being largely in excess of the demand.

A line of British steamers between Japanese and Chinese ports and Portland has been in successful operation during the year. I look for a slow and steady improvement in business affairs throughout this consular district, but as, at present, the State of Oregon is to a great extent dependent upon agriculture, a quick recovery from the depression existing during the past 3 years is largely contingent upon the state of markets for such produce.

Trade and Commerce.

Increase in exports and imports. The comparison of exports and imports as given in Annex B, attached to this report, shows over 40 per cent. increase in value of exports and 9 per cent. increase in value of imports, the latter not including the transit trade in bond, the value of which is given in these tables. Annex C shows a very gratifying increase in British trade and also in direct trade with India and Australia. **Increased British trade** The value of principal articles of produce shipped by sea to domestic ports was 310,000*l*.

UNITED STATES.

Wheat. The average quality of Walla Walla wheat was not equal to that of 1894, but the Valley was fully so. Market prices advanced slowly; 15s. per quarter was paid in January for Walla Walla, as high as 18s. 4d. in June, consequent on a demand for shipment by rail to Middle Western States, closing in December at 17s. per quarter. Valley 18s. per quarter, against 14s. and 15s. 6d. respectively in 1894. **Total shipments.** The shipments coastwise and to San Francisco were only 33,591 quarters, and the total shipments, including cargoes cleared, but not sailed from the Columbia River, were 1,102,291 quarters, value 893,946l. being an average of 16s. 3d. The average last year was 15s. 4d. and 19s. 11d. in 1893. The total shipments, foreign, from this consular district, inclusive of clearances, were 1,461,470 quarters.

Flour. Exports of flour were larger than for years past. Shipments to China and Japan from Portland were equal to 164,702 sacks, while in 1894 shipments were 81,773 sacks. **Total shipments.** Total shipments foreign and coastwise 467,141 sacks, valued at 323,100l. Average export value per sack 13s. 10d. In January patent roller extras sold at 13s. 1d., and superfines at 10s. 4d. per sack. In July prices had advanced to 16s. 3d. and 12s. 10d., dropping after September, and in December quotations were 14s. 10d. for extras and 11s. 3d. for superfines. The total shipments from this consular district to foreign countries were 645,403 sacks.

Barley. Three ships partially loaded with 74,148 centals of barley were cleared for Bristol, valued at 12,620l., an average of 3s. 5d. per cental. Shipments coastwise were 265,856 centals.

Other grains. There were considerable shipments coastwise of oats and flax-seed.

Hop trade. Yeild enormous. The year has been a disastrous one for the hop-growers in this consular district, the yield being enormous and there being practically no market for the product. Quality in Oregon was below **Quality below average.** average, but freer from mould and lice than in 1894.

Some choice hops were contracted for early at $6\frac{1}{2}$ c. ($3\frac{1}{4}d$.), but the tendency was continually downwards, and at the close of the year there was a heavy stock of mixed qualities, choice selling at 4 c. (2d.), and likely to go much lower. All accounts agree that the yield in Oregon was about 100,000 bales, of which about half was choice and prime, and the rest mediums and low grade, all qualities being inferior to last year. A large proportion of the Washington hops were not harvested. Quality was very inferior, selling at not over 4 c. (2d.) for best quality. Dealers' statements of crop vary materially. Probably it was about 20,000 bales of 185 lbs.

Fruit trade. There is a continually-increasing trade in green fruit, with an improving home consumption and a good demand for the Middle Western States. The yield was not as large as in 1894, but 15,000,000 lbs. of fresh fruit, apples, pears, peaches, prunes, plums, apricots, cherries, raspberries and strawberries were sent East by rail. Some 4,000,000 lbs. of dried fruit, principally prunes, were also shipped. Good prices were realised for fresh fruit, but dried sold nearly 50 per cent. lower than last year. The total yield of this consular district was not less than 53,000,000 lbs. of green fruit.

PORTLAND.

It is difficult to give fairly correct statistics of the clip of this district, the wool being shipped from so many different points, generally to the Eastern States, but as nearly as can be estimated Eastern Oregon produced 17,000,000 lbs. of wool, shrinkage 64 to 78 per cent., which sold at from 6 c. (3d.) to 10 c. (5d.), according to quality. The Willamette and Umpqua Valleys produced about 1,700,000 lbs., shrinkage 45 to 62 per cent. The market prices of this quality might be given at from 10 c. (5d.) to 14 c. (7d.). These prices are better than those of 1894, but this trade is in a very unsatisfactory condition. The clip of Washington is given as 9,000,000 lbs., and that of Idaho at 8,000,000 lbs., but I am inclined to believe these figures are very much too high.

The consumption of local woollen mills was between 1,750,000 and 2,000,000 lbs., shipments coastwise 1,237,800 lbs.

There has been a decided improvement in the demand for lumber this year and prices have improved. The exports to coastwise points by Portland mills were about 25,302,000 feet of sawn timber, valued at 45,000l. The foreign trade was not quite 3,000,000 feet. The total of the lumber trade of this district is enormous, as will be seen by reference to the reports of the vice-consuls at Tacoma, Port Townsend and Astoria. Puget Sound District exported over 130,000,000 feet.

Astoria is the centre of the fishing business, but the trade on Puget Sound is increasing. Very interesting and exhaustive reports were published by the Oregon Fish and Game Protector and the Washington State Fish Commissioner, and I regret that the limits of this report preclude any extended extracts from these documents. The following is a pretty correct summary of this business for the district:—

	Quantity.	Value.
	Cases.	£
Columbia River (spring), Oregon side	317,094	372,900
„ (fall) „	116,084	83,580
„ (spring), Washington side	173,282	204,180
„ (fall) „	11,000	7,920
Rogue River (spring), Oregon	11,000	13,200
Other rivers and bays in Oregon (fall)	51,640	37,160
Grays Harbour and Shoalwater, Washington	32,644	18,680
Puget Sound, Washington	105,500	..
Point Roberts „	53,118	91,400
Total	871,362	829,020

Each case represents 48 lbs. of salmon. The prices paid for raw salmon, 5 c. or 2½d. per lb., with rather lower prices than last year for the manufactured article, do not leave very much profit to the factories for the great risk run in loss of nets, gear, &c., and the uncertainty of the supply.

Market prices were, as nearly as can be given—spring catch: flat 1-lb. tins 5s. 6d. to 6s., talls 5s. to 5s. 6d., ovals 7s. 2d.;

UNITED STATES.

½-lb. flats 3s. 2d. per dozen. Fall catch sold at 3s. 2d. to 3s. 7d. per dozen 1-lb. talls.

A larger proportion of the pack was shipped direct to the United Kingdom than last year, and some proportion of the spring pack was put up in oval tins and in ½-lb. flats, 8 dozen in a case.

Import trade. A large proportion of the import trade is always done by sail and rail from the Eastern States and San Francisco, of which there can be no correct record.

The custom house records, as noted in Annex B, show a large increase in imports of coal, tinplate, salt, hemp and jute, and bags and bagging.

Window glass. For some time back the window glass trade has been monopolised by Belgian manufacturers.

Cement. Smaller imports. Better prices. Imports were not much over one-fifth of that of 1894. Of these, 18,000 barrels were from Great Britain, 9,632 barrels from Hamburg, and 21,838 barrels from Belgium. British manufacturers seem to be steadily losing trade. Market prices averaged about 10s. per barrel, which is higher than last year, though as high as 13s. was paid during a temporary scarcity.

Coal. Larger imports. Consumption of foreign coal was greater than last year, and imports increased 47 per cent., Australian sold at an average of about 18s. 6d. duty paid. Receipts were: From Australia 13,719 tons, British Columbia 581 tons, Great Britain 562 tons. From coast mines by sail and rail about 8,500 tons; from Atlantic ports by sea 6,018 tons.

Bags and bagging. A much larger proportion of bags and bagging was imported direct from Calcutta, now the principal source of supply, by sail and steamer. The consumption was not so great as expected, and while standards sold early in the year at 2¼d. and over, prices fell after August below 2d.

Tinplates. Imports of tinplates were more than double those of 1894. Standard weight B.V. grades of coke sold at an average of about 16s. 6d. per box. The consumption in this district is quite heavy, principally for the tinned salmon trade. A large proportion of the tinplate used is now of lighter weight, about 100 lbs. net to the box.

Raw hemp and jute. Of the imports of hemp and jute about 2,522 tons were jute and jute butts for the Washington Penitentiary bag factory, the rope manufactory here importing 619 tons of higher grade hemp.

Flax twine. There has been some importation of flax bagging twine in competition with that of American manufacture, and nearly all the twine for net making has been imported from the United Kingdom.

Other articles. Salt. Chemicals. Earthenware. Of other articles of importation from Great Britain the heaviest increase was in salt, which has been carried at almost nominal freights, and the imports of soda ash, caustic soda, chloride of lime and earthenware have also been greater.

The value of all imports and exports by countries is given in Annex C to this report.

Financial failures. The following is a comparison of commercial failures in this district during the last 3 years:—

PORTLAND.

States.	1895. Number of Failures.	1895. Liabilities.	1894. Number of Failures.	1894. Liabilities.	1893. Number of Failures.	1893. Liabilities.
		£		£		£
Oregon	216	351,714	207	508,498	221	391,420
Washington	160	315,815	180	414,736	272	793,600
Idaho	85	77,205	124	92,323	76	166,865
Total	461	744,734	511	1,015,557	569	1,351,885

The condition of the six National Banks in Portland, Oregon, on December 13, 1895, was as under:— *Banks.*

RESOURCES.

	Amount. 1895.	Amount. 1894.
	£	£
Loans and discounts	753,073	925,860
United States bonds	250,000	250,000
Other stocks and bonds..	298,338	203,070
Premium on bonds	16,538	22,188
Real estate, furniture and fixtures	49,776	34,424
Redemption fund, United States treasurer	2,250	2,250
Due from other banks	79,592	101,480
,, reserve agents	102,380	199,710
Cash on hand	188,549	190,350
Total	1,740,496	1,929,332

LIABILITIES.

	Amount. 1895.	Amount. 1894.
	£	£
Capital paid in	340,000	390,000
Surplus and profits, less expenses	172,828	191,594
Dividends unpaid	500	500
Circulation	41,310	41,750
Deposits and bank balances	1,186,358	1,305,488
Total	1,740,496	1,929,332

Besides these, there are two British and eight savings and private banks with deposits of over 800,000*l.*, and capital and surplus of 1,568,900*l.*

Transactions of the Portland Clearing House during the last 3 years were as under:— *Clearing house.*

	Amount.		
	1895.	1894.	1893.
	£	£	£
Exchanges	11,768,457	11,316,504	15,312,951
Balances	2,319,994	2,534,606	3,031,088

Exchange. Exchange was very steady during the greater portion of the year, and averaged 4 dol. 88 c. per 1*l.* for bank, and 4 dol. 85 c. per 1*l.* for commercial. The rate was lowest in May, when commercial bills ran as low as 4 dol. 83 c. per 1*l.*

Shipping and Navigation.

British tonnage. The British tonnage employed in the foreign trade was 85 per cent. of the whole, last year it was 91 per cent. Details are given in Annex A attached to this report.

Freights. The average rate of freight during the year for iron and steel vessels was 1*l.* 13*s.* 10*d.* for the United Kingdom for orders, including Havre, Antwerp, or Dunkirk, and in some cases Hamburg, at the same rate. Highest rate paid was 1*l.* 19*s.*, and lowest 1*l.* 7*s.* 6*d.*

Tonnage engagements. Exclusive of coasting voyages, the following were the tonnage engagements at Portland for sailing vessels:—

Cargoes.	Tons Register.	
	1895.	1894.
Grain and flour	138 356	129,055
Timber	8,419	1,764
Miscellaneous	843	5,808
Total	147 618	136,627

Steamers. A new line of steamers running in connection with the Oregon Railway and Navigation Company, has been doing a good business. The steamers are under the British flag, and touch at Victoria, Honolulu, Hong Kong, and Japanese ports. Cargoes inwards principally tea, and outwards flour.

Lights. The following are the points at which lighthouses are now established in this district, on the coasts of Oregon and Washington, and on the Sound: Cape Blanco, Cape Arago, Umpqua, Heceta Head, Yaquina Head, Cape Meares, Tillamook Rock, Point Adams, Columbia River light-vessel No 50, Cape Disappointment, Willapa Bay, Destruction Island, Cape Flattery, Ediz Hook, New Dungeness, Smith Island, Point Wilson, Admiralty Head, Marrowstone Point, Point No Point, West Point, Robinson Point,

Turn Point, Patos Island, and there are also numerous post, range, and harbour lights in the various harbours on Columbia River and Puget Sound.

New light, Coquille. A light of the fourth order will be established about February 29, 1896, showing fixed white for 28 seconds, followed by an eclipse of 2 seconds. On the westerly part of Rackliff Rock, light may be seen $12\frac{1}{3}$ miles in clear weather, but can be seen from seaward only between Cape Arago to the northward, and the outlying rocks to the southward.

The approximate geographical position of the light as taken from chart No. 6900 of the United States Coast and Geodetic Survey is:—

Latitude North 43° 07′ (13″).
Longtitude West 124° 25′ (40″).

Fog trumpet. During thick or foggy weather a Daboll trumpet will sound blasts of 5 seconds duration, separated by silent intervals of 25 seconds. There is a life-saving station at this point.

Projected lights. Appropriations have been made for lights on North Head, Cape Disappointment, and a light and fog-signal at Grays Harbour, Washington. A light-vessel is being built for Umatilla Reef, off the Strait of Juan de Fuca.

Fog signals. There are fog signals operated at the following stations:— Tillamook Rock, Columbia River light-vessel, Destruction Island, Cape Flattery, Ediz Hook, New Dungeness, Point Wilson, Marrowstone Point, Point No Point, West Point, Robinson Point, Turn Point, Patos Island.

Life-saving stations. There are life-saving stations at Coquille, Coos Bay, Umpqua, Yaquina, inside of jetty Columbia River, Fort Canby and Ilwaco Beach, Cape Shoalwater.

Sailors. Wages of A.B. seamen out of this port have been uniformly 4*l*. There is no real necessity for ship-masters paying any bonus for crews, as crimps in these ports are now well under control, nevertheless, as a general rule, ship-masters have paid about 2*l*. per man, and I must say a preference is given to men from crimps' houses, who are compelled to demand 8*l*. advance whether they require it or not. It is not creditable that a seaman who keeps clear of the boarding houses does not as a rule get a fair chance of employment from the average ship-master.

Mariners' home. Owing to lack of support, I fear the Mariners' Home will be closed before long. The Portland Seamen's Friend Society have striven for a long time against the passive, if not open, hostility of ship-masters, and the preference given to crimps when men are required to fill up a crew.

Seamen's institute. A seamen's institute was established by the Portland Seamen's Friend Society, and I believe has been productive of much good amongst the sailors and apprentices. It needs and deserves support from the British ship-owner to make it more effective.

Changes in crews. The number and changes in crews of British ships entering this port have been as follows:—

UNITED STATES.

	Number.
Total number of crews	2,280
Deserted	252
Discharged	96
Engaged	323
Reported dead	2
Sent to hospital	15

Population and Industries—Health.

Census.

The official census taken last year, as compiled by the State Department of Oregon, shows an increase of nearly 100 per cent. in population of the State during the last 10 years..

Population.

The following is a comparison:—

	Number of Persons.
Population in 1865	65,090
,, 1875	104,908
,, 1885	187,096
,, 1895	362,513

City population.

According to the census taken of Portland during the year, the population is 81,342, a gain of over 6,300 since the United States census of 1890. The number of marriages during the year was 763, and the births registered 1,333.

The Health Officer's report for 1895 gives the following classification of the deaths in this city:—

Diseases.

Description.	Number of Deaths.
Miasmatic	115
Enthetic and diatetic	9
Constitutional diseases	43
Tubercular	126
Local diseases	68
Circulatory system	63
Respiratory ,,	73
Digestive ,,	77
Other zymotic diseases	58
Developmental ,,	145
Violent deaths	57
Unascertained	13
Total	847

There has been no epidemic disease throughout this district, and the percentage of deaths from contagious diseases has been very small. The death rate, excluding 55 stillborn and premature births, and deducting deaths of 93 non-residents brought here for treatment, is only 8·60 per 1,000. The large percentage of tubercular disease is amongst the Chinese, and consequent upon their living in large numbers in unsanitary quarters.

Sanitary. The sanitary state of the city is much improved and the ample supply of purest water will tend to keep down the death rate materially.

Mining. There has been much more activity in mining, and an increased production of gold throughout this district, but silver mining has been in a depressed condition, and many good low grade mines closed. **Oregon.** The mining districts of Oregon are in Jackson and Josephine counties in the southern end of the State, on the west slope of the Cascades, near the Santiam River, in Grant, Union and Baker counties along the Blue Mountains in Eastern Oregon.

Washington. Idaho. In Washington, in Stevens and Okanogan counties, and in Idaho, in the Cœur D'Alene Mountains, and throughout Southern Idaho.

Gold and silver. The Director of the Mint gives the following as approximate estimates of the product of gold and silver in this district:—

	Gold Value.	Silver.
	£	Ounces.
Oregon	440,000	7,700
Washington	60,000	11,600
Idaho	558,140	4,000,000
Total	1,058,140	4,019,300

Wells, Fargo, and Co.'s annual report gives the value of shipments of the precious metals during the year as—

	Gold.	Silver.	Ores and Base Bullion.
	£	£	£
Oregon	349,957	20,529	..
Washington	67,963	40,630	..
Idaho	504,200	544,729	434,450
Total	922,120	605,788	434,450

Coal. The coal mined in this district is of a lignite character, and is largely used for steam purposes. The following is given as the product of the principal mines, but is probably somewhat over-estimated:—

	Quantity.
	Tons.
Newcastle mines, Washington	180,000
Franklin „ „	80,000
Gilman „ „	100,000
South Prairie „ „	..*
Wilkeson „ „	..*
Roslyn „ „	300,000
Black Diamond mines, Washington ..	150,000
Coos Bay mines, Oregon	56,800

* Not given.

Iron. Very little was done in iron mining; the deposits at various points are quite extensive.

Ironworks. The Oregon Iron and Steel Company's furnaces at Oswego were blown out during the year, but the Company produced 3,134 tons of cast-iron water pipe.

Flour mills. The flouring mills were running to capacity most of the year.

Pulp and paper mills. The pulp and paper mills at Oregon City and La Camas, employ a large number of hands, and were running steadily during the year on straw manilla papers and pulp from cottonwood and spruce.

Meat packing. A new establishment went into operation during the year. The principal factory near Portland slaughtered 11,000 cattle, 6,000 calves, 48,000 sheep, and 28,000 hogs, and the value of its product was 182,000*l*.

Horse meat, &c. A horse-killing establishment was put in operation during the year, and 7,000 horses were brought from the ranges to Portland and slaughtered. The Company had a fair demand for the hides and for the oil for lubricating purposes. The offal was manufactured into a fertilizer, and some of the meat was packed and shipped to Belgium, which seems to have been the best market for horse meat. I am told, however, that an absolute interdict has been laid on the importation of American horse-flesh, so that this enterprise is likely to come to an end. The horses brought from the ranges were generally scrub-ponies, and cost about 1*l*. a head.

Saw mills. The demand for lumber was so much better that several of the mills closed last year re-opened, and prospects are now better.

Foundries. Foundry and repair shops were very slack all the year.

Woollen mills. Several hundred hands are employed regularly in the three woollen mills, which did a steady business.

Cordage works. The cordage works here did a good and steady business, though the field is as yet somewhat limited.

Linseed oil. The linseed oil mill was not in operation. Trade was supplied by tank cars from the Eastern States.

Fisheries. There are 25 salmon factories in Oregon alone, and during the season 1,236 boats were employed with 1,331 gill nets besides traps and seines. The number of hands employed in the fisheries of Oregon, and allied industries, during the season, is given in the Fish and Game Protector's Report as 5,349. Similar statistics are not given in the Washington Commissioner's Report.

Furniture factories and workshops generally are still very slack, but prospects are for a slow improvement. *Other workshops.*

Very few buildings are going up and there is a very slack demand for labour in the building trade. *Buildings.*

I cannot report a great demand for labour, either skilled or unskilled, and as the Government works now in progress are nearly completed, there is not much chance of improvement at present, If the construction of the Astoria Railroad should be pushed during the coming year, there will be an outlet for common labourers and also for railway carpenters. *Labour.*

I have again to repeat my annual warning to clerks, salesmen, and persons who have no particular trade, against coming here with the expectation of securing prompt employment. For every vacant position there are numerous applicants, and I could give many very distressing instances of well-deserving persons, who, after exhausting every means to procure employment, have had to seek charity. This would not be the case in this wide district were it not for the prevailing agricultural depression. *Warning to clerks.*

Public Works.

Under supervision of United States engineer, Major James C. Post, improvements of the Columbia and Willamette Rivers have been continued. *Government works.*

The great jetty at the mouth of the Columbia has been completed during the year, and operations have ceased. The work has been a pronounced success in its object, and the channel is now 30 feet in depth at low water, and seven-eighths of a mile wide. Within this channel there is a depth of at least 31 feet at low water over a width of one half-mile. During the fiscal year ended June 30, 1895, 136,900 tons of rock were dumped on the jetty. *Mouth of Columbia jetty.*

The operations on the various bars between Portland and Astoria were confined to dredging, and the channels were kept open, so that with the aid of the tides, vessels drawing 23 feet of water could pass to Portland with little or no detention, according to stage of water. The channel is now 20 feet at dead low water, and it is proposed to continue until a depth of 25 feet at low water can be secured. *River bars.*

I extract the following from the report of Captain Thomas W. Symons, United States engineer in charge, for the fiscal year ended June 30, 1895:— *Minor harbours in Oregon.*

The present project of improvement at Coos Bay is to build two high tide stone jetties, one from Coos Head, and one from the south end of the north spit, extending out toward the bar and leaving an entrance about 1,500 feet wide. It also includes the protection of the north spit by plantations to prevent sand from blowing into the harbour. The estimated cost is 493,280*l*. The amount expended to end of fiscal year is 127,877*l*. in all. The north jetty tramway was built to its full length of 10,368 feet and its enrockment well advanced. Expended during the *Coos Bay.*

year, 19,718*l*., and a bar depth of from 18 to 20 feet at low water has been maintained. Considerable dredging is also to be done in this harbour, which is quite an important one.

Yaquina Bay, Oregon.

Yaquina Bay has been improved by jetties at a cost of about 132,630*l*., and the work has been successful, there being a permanent channel through the bar of 12 to 15 feet depth where there formerly existed an uncertain shifting channel of 6 to 7 feet. The engineers report that in their opinion no further improvement should be attempted, as the harbour cannot be made available for foreign commerce by large vessels.

Willapa Harbour, Washington.

Willapa Harbour, formerly known as Shoalwater Bay, has quite a large lumber trade, and while the generality of ships landing here are of small draught, some have been loaded to 20 feet. The United States Government has been improving the harbour by a system of dykes and dredging.

Grays Harbour, Washington.

This harbour has some foreign trade, but has a large coasting trade, principally in lumber. The average draught is small, the maximum being 17 feet loaded. The plan of improvement is to close the middle channel and contract the south channel, so as to give a greater depth on the north or principal channel. A plan for further improvement by jetties at the mouth, estimated to cost 472,660*l*., has been submitted by the engineers, which they believe would give a draught over the bar at the mean of the lower low waters of 24 feet.

Other rivers and harbours.

Considerable improvements have been made or are in progress on Coquille, Umpqua, and Siuslaw Rivers, which are only valuable for coasting trade, and also on the upper reaches of the Snake and Columbia Rivers.

Railways.

The only railroad in progress in this consular district is between Portland and Astoria.

Boat railway.

Supplementary to the improvement of navigation of the upper Columbia River by the canal and locks at the Cascades, now nearly completed, it is proposed to build a boat railway about 9 miles long around the rapids above the Dalles. As located by the United States engineers, it has but four curves, each of one-half degree, lifts at the upper and lower terminals are 62 feet and 77 feet respectively. By this means some river steamboats will be passed up and down the river without moving cargo. The estimated cost is 452,900*l*.

Canals. Cascades Canal.

Lock gates largest in the world.

Under charge of Lieutenant Harry Taylor, United States engineer, the great canal at the Cascades, Columbia River, Oregon, which has been in progress since 1877, is nearing completion. During the year a large amount of excavation was done and masonry laid, and the lower guard and lock gates and upper guard gates have been put in place. These gates are the largest in the world. They are of steel, of the single skin type, and swing freely on pivots without the aid of rollers or flotation chambers. Each leaf has a developed length exposed to pressure of 53½ feet. The length of the lower guard gate above the mitre sill is 36 feet; of the lower lock gate, 46 feet; of the upper lock gate, 40 feet; and of the upper guard gate, 54 feet. The gates when closed form a segment of a circle, the rise of mitre still being one-fifth of the span.

Some modifications of the original plan, suggested by the extraordinary high flood of 1894, have been adopted. The work has cost 688,700*l*., and over 80,000*l*. will still be required to complete it as modified. Cost.

Congress has appropriated money to begin preliminary work on a ship canal to connect deep water of Puget Sound with Lakes Washington and Union at Seattle. Its length will be 7·86 miles. Estimated cost, according to route selected, 580,000*l*. or 700,000*l*. Lake Washington Canal.

Agriculture.

The following is the enumeration of agricultural products of Oregon, according to State census of 1895:— Census returns.

		Quantity.
Acres under cultivation	Number	1,764,728
Wheat raised preceding year	Bushels	12,517,158
Oats " "	"	6,375,016
Barley " "	"	1,530,661
Corn " "	"	338,821
Hay	Tons	732,073
Butter and cheese	Lbs.	5,734,182
Flax-seed	Bushels	17,890
Tobacco	Lbs.	12,952
Hops	"	15,626,882
Potatoes	Bushels	3,365,243
Apples	"	1,102,673
Prunes and plums	"	289,204
Wool	Lbs.	12,038,091
Sheep	Number	2,267,626
Hogs	"	367,496
Horses	"	191,059
Mules	"	5,056
Cattle	"	403,718

The variety of agricultural products of Oregon, Washington, and Idaho is considerable, but wheat is the staple grain, and being the most readily marketed is on the whole most profitable. Agriculture depressed.

Agriculture in all its branches has, however, been in a depressed condition though there has been some improvement over the year 1894.

The grain harvests of this consular district during 1895 are said to have been about as given below, but as there are no reliable statistics kept, these figures are only approximate:— Cereals.

Articles.	Quantity.
	Bushels.
Wheat	25,000,000
Oats	15,000,000
Barley	2,000,000
Corn	500,000
Rye	200,000

Cost of production.

In view of the ruinously low prices of wheat in 1894 there was considerable less acreage sown to wheat in Eastern Oregon and Washington, and a further deficiency was caused by loss from hot weather during May and June. The crop did not exceed 70 per cent. of that of 1894, but better prices were obtained. Statistics are given under another head in this report, but the following estimate of the cost of production, made by an experienced farmer in the Walla Walla Valley, may be of interest. The figures are made on the basis of 400 acres yielding 10,000 bushels of blue-stem wheat. The land was summer fallowed in 1894, and valued at 6*l.* per acre. The locality is one where water and material are reasonably convenient and the land not very hilly and easy to work:—

	Amount.	
	Dol.	c.
Ploughing, twice, at 90 c. per acre each time	720	0
Harrowing, thrice, at 11 c.	132	0
500 bushels of seed wheat, at 50 c.	250	0
Cleaning and vitriolising seed	24	50
Sowing, at 15 c. per acre	60	0
Cutting, at 1 dol. per acre	400	0
Threshing 10,000 bushels, at 4½ c.	450	0
4,400 sacks, at 49 dol. per 1,000	215	60
30 lbs. twine, at 33⅓ c.	10	0
Hauling to railroad, at 2½ c. per sack	110	0
Interest on payments	181	90
Warehouse charges for season	120	0
Total	2,674	0

or, say, 26¾ c. (1*s.* 0·83*d.*) per bushel.

Oats. Oats were a full crop of fair average quality. Prices were very low and unprofitable. After harvest good oats sold at an average of 62½ c. (2*s.* 6*d.*) per cental, but the average for the year was about 2*s.* 10*d.* Shipments coastwise were 163,000 centals.

Barley. Prices of barley were very low throughout the year.

Flax seed. Flax seed was not grown to such an extent as last year.

Potatoes. There was a full crop of potatoes of good average quality, but prices were so low that they hardly paid more than cost of marketing. Farmer's prices did not average much over 15 c. (7½*d*). per 100 lbs

Hops. It costs the hopgrowers from 2*d.* to 2¼*d.* per 1 lb. to get their produce to market, and as they could not generally sell to cover cost the season was unfortunate for them, and prospects are very depressing.

Orchards and fruits. I think there is very little doubt that horticulturists fared better than others engaged in agriculture. There was a fair crop of fruit and a good market at paying prices. The markets are not likely, however, to keep pace with the new orchards as they come into bearing, and lower prices may be expected.

PORTLAND.

Cattle and Sheep.

The winter of 1894 was an open one and losses of cattle and sheep on the ranges were light. The following is a comparison of numbers of animals in this district at the end of 1893, according to the report of the United States Department of Agriculture with a recently published return:— **Numbrs.**

	Year.	Horses.	Mules.	Cows.	Other Cattle.	Sheep.	Swine.
		Number.	Number.	Number.	Number.	Number.	Number.
Oregon	1893	235,607	6,182	110,398	804,543	2,529,759	210,747
,,	1895	222,000	5,000	124,000	520,000	2,006,000	270,000
Washington	1893	193,076	1,392	108,535	408,293	832,663	162,977
,,	1895	182,000	1,000	109,000	260,000	384,000	204,000
Idaho	1893	144,688	900	30,419	429,947	779,547	58,725
,,	1895*	...	...	...	...	...	...

* Not given separately.

From the above figures it will be seen that there has been a decrease in the numbers of all domestic animals except swine.

The demand for horses has not improved during the year. **Horses.**

Cattle have been in demand at somewhat higher prices than last year; the average price for fat steers on the ranges is said to have been about 26½ dol. (5l. 6s.). **Cattle.**

There is said to have been little profit on sheep, though the price paid here was about 8s., or about 6s. on the range. The following figures give the actual results from a flock of sheep last year:— **Sheep.**

	Amount.
	£ s. d.
3,320 acres of land, at 1l. per acre	3,320 0 0
1,200 breeding yews, at 5s.	300 0 0
3,380 yearlings, at 4s.	676 0 0
Capital invested	4,296 0 0

Sales.

	Amount.
	£ s. d
2,110 sheep, at 6s.	633 0 0
Wool sales	556 0 0
1,200, increase 100 per cent.	240 0 0
Gross income	1,429 0
Less expenses	778 0 4
15·15 per cent. net profit..	650 19 8

(2178)

UNITED STATES.

Expenses.

	Amount.
	£ s. d.
Two herders, at 6*l.* per month, 1 year	144 0 0
One camp tender, 4 months	24 0 0
Feed, actual cost	80 0 0
Shearing, at 5½ c. = 246 dol. 90 c.	49 7 7
115 sacks, at 28 c. = 32 dol. 20 c.	6 8 9
Hauling wool	5 0 0
1 ton salt	3 12 0
Taxes	20 0 0
	332 8 4
Interest on land, at 5 per cent.	166 0 0
„ sheep, at 10 „	97 12 0
910 yearlings to keep up number in old stock	182 0 0
Total	778 0 4

Swine. A large number of swine were fed on the wheat of 1893, and there has been more money in these. The butchers and packers here paid on an average 1*l.* 16*s.* per head.

General Remarks.

Taxation. Assessed value of all property within the State was 31,908,000*l.* in 1894, and 28,889,085*l.* in 1895. Within this city the valuation in 1894 was 9,537,850*l.*, and in 1895 was 9,271,410*l.*

Taxes were levied at the rate of 2·40 per cent., payable in 1896, including State, County, and City taxes

City finances. The total revenue of this city, including balances carried over from 1894, was 187,281*l.*, and the total expenditure 153,074*l.*, which includes Street and Sewer Assessments.

Bonded debt. The bonded indebtedness of the City of Portland is now 976,794*l.* During the year, 40,000*l.* in Water Bonds sold at 114, and 40,000*l.* Bridge Bonds at 115·65.

Real estate. But little business has been done in real estate. The total transfers and sales recorded in the county of Multnomah only amounted to 913,510*l.*

PORTLAND.

Annex A.—Return of all Shipping at the Port of Portland, Oregon, during the Year 1895.

Entered.

Nationality.	Sailing. Number of Vessels.	Sailing. Tons.	Steam. Number of Vessels.	Steam. Tons.	Total. Number of Vessels.	Total. Tons.
British	79	131,576	7	10,425	86	142,001
American, from foreign countries	2	826	19	8,752	21	9,578
American, from Atlantic ports	6	9,167	...	...	6	9,167
American, coasting	54	16,229	156	134,940	210	151,169
German	6	9,434	...	...	6	9,434
Russian	1	2,153	...	...	1	2,153
Danish	1	1,456	...	...	1	1,456
French	1	1,148	...	...	1	1,148
Chilian	1	634	...	...	1	634
Total	151	172,623	182	154,117	333	326,740
,, for the year preceding	125	148,507	164	162,480	289	310,987

Cleared.

Nationality.	Sailing. Number of Vessels.	Sailing. Tons.	Steam. Number of Vessels.	Steam. Tons.	Total Number of Vessels.	Total Tons.
British	84	141,881	7	10,425	91	152,306
American, to foreign countries	7	9,525	15	5,880	12	15,405
American, coasting	60	18,137	154	139,031	214	157,168
German	3	5,733	...	...	3	5,733
Norwegian	2	3,801	...	...	2	3,801
Danish	1	1,288	...	...	1	1,288
French	1	1,148	...	...	1	1,148
Chilian	1	634	...	...	1	634
Total	159	182,147	176	155,336	335	337,483
,, for the year preceding	126	141,225	169	173,453	295	314,678

Annex B.—Return of Principal Articles of Export from Portland, Oregon, during the Years 1895–94.

Articles.		1895. Quantity.	1895. Value. £	1894. Quantity.	1894. Value. £
Wheat	Quarters	988,553	832,790	752,039	596,810
,, flour	Sacks	342,812	230,753	212,721	144,731
Timber	Feet	2,937,700	4,193	502,000	891
Barley	Bushels	121,018	11,115	90,838	9,045
Other articles	...	...	7,820	...	6,343
Tinned salmon	Lbs.	96,000	2,380	...	...
Total		...	1,089,051	...	757,820

(2178)

Return of Principal Articles of Import to Portland, Oregon, during the Years 1895-94.

Articles.		1895. Quantity.	1895. Value.	1894. Quantity.	1894. Value.
			£		£
Coals and coke	Tons	14,587	6,621	9,903	4,628
Tin and tin-plate	Lbs.	1,909,913	9,297	849,423	4,441
Rice	,,	1,666,569	4,931	2,437,086	15,765
Earthenware and glass	...	...	6,825	...	4,685
Salt	Lbs.	12,797,630	6,374	5,541,709	3,261
Cement	Barrels	49,470	12,136	228,762	34,551
Tea	Lbs.	424,185	10.969	345,930	9,559
Coffee	,,	180,707	6,414	206,127	7,346
Hemp and jute	Tons	3,141	14,666	833	13,265
Window glass	Lbs.	287,421	887	357,400	1,203
Bags and bagging	...	...	40,015	...	6,703
Sugar	Lbs.	503,258	2,808	1,830,994	13,483
Caustic soda	,,	388,592	1,393	...	...
Manufactures of flax and hemp, including fishing twine	...	...	8,121	...	...
Soda ash	Lbs.	312,630	460	..	...
Chloride of lime	,,	140,036	584	...	...
Soda	,,	360,398	408	...	...
Sulphur	Tons	885	1,884	...	...
All other articles	...	...	30,966	...	33,171
Total	...	...	165,759	...	152,061
Entered for transportation to other districts—					
Tin	Lbs.	5,134,122	123,537	...	...
Other articles	...	...	92,073	...	...
Grand total	...	...	381,369	...	...

NOTE.—The above returns do not include coastwise trade.

Annex C.—TABLE showing Total Value of all Articles Exported from and Imported to Portland, Oregon, from and to Foreign Countries during the Years 1895-94.

Country.	Exports. 1895.	Exports. 1894.	Imports. 1895.	Imports. 1894.
	£	£	£	£
Great Britain	959,032	679,783	49,875	35,476
Belgium	..	10,000	8,029	27,032
British Columbia	2,318	10,020	1,980	2,157
China and Japan	114,202	51,997	30,550	39,480
China and Japan in transit	..	..	215,610	..
Australia	2,348	.	7,405	3,178
France	..	..	898	1,177
Cuba	..	..	896	532
Philippine Islands	..	2,250	2,500	8,178
India	..	..	56,512	19,817
Germany	..	..	5,634	1,954
Hawaiian Islands	6,088	..	630	12,645
All other countries	5,063	3,770	850	435
Total	1,089,051	757,820	381,369	152,061

ASTORIA.

Mr. Vice-Consul Cherry reports as follows:—

<small>General remarks.</small>

The trade, commerce, and prosperity of the district shows a marked improvement over that of last year and is, in fact, better than for a number of years back, and is again owing to the pack of salmon being the largest that has been put up since 1886.

The town has shown the results in the improvements in its streets and buildings, and banks report an improvement in their deposit accounts.

Commercial travellers all unite in giving this town the credit of being the town least in debt of the whole Pacific coast. The position may be condensed as one of uneventful prosperity.

<small>Shipping and navigation.</small>

An increase of over 27 per cent. in the number and 36 per cent. in tonnage of the vessels that entered the Columbia River in the foreign commerce is to be noted over that of 1894. Of this total the British flag has $84\frac{1}{2}$ per cent. of vessels and 89 per cent. of tonnage, as against 81 per cent. and 86 per cent. respectively in 1894.

<small>Pilot service.</small>

The regular boat of the Oregon Board was in service for most of the year, being off for two months during the summer. An opposition boat was put on but was drawn off as the lateness of the season and her small size was against her in earning her keep.

There is some talk of putting another boat under the State of Washington pilots as an opposition.

<small>Trade and commerce.</small>

The effect of the increased pack of preserved salmon shows very well in the increased imports of tin-plate from the British Islands, as it has more than doubled. The import of steam coals from Australia has increased by three times.

In exports the quantity and values have all increased, mostly in preserved salmon which shows an increase of nearly eleven times over the shipments of 1894. All of this went to the British Islands, and this does not represent the full amount of shipments to the United Kingdom, for quite a large number of cases of preserved salmon have gone by the various railroads to New York and New Orleans for trans-shipment from thence to the United Kingdom by steamer.

<small>Industries, salmon fishing.</small>

This industry in connection with salmon-canning still keeps its position prominently to the front as the leading occupation, the price remained the same, viz., $2\frac{1}{2}d.$ per lb., equal on the average to at least 5s. 6d. per fish for Chinook salmon, and $1\frac{1}{2}d.$ per lb. or 3s. per fish for fall fish and steel heads.

<small>Salmon canning.</small>

Was unusually successful, the total pack was well ahead of 1894 both for the river and coast, viz.:—

	Quantity.
	Cases.
Columbia River, spring catch	548.000
,, fall catch	137,000
Coast canneries	92,200
Total	777,200

Of the spring or Chinook salmon Great Britain took a far greater proportion than for a number of years back, mounting up to over 150,000 cases all of the choicest brands and shapes, again the fishing interests gained by the fact that the upper river canneries were handicapped by a very low stage of water in the river keeping a number of fish wheels from catching fish.

Sturgeon fishing. This industry has attracted the attention of the State Fish Commissioner who advocates protective measures, also hatcheries; however the fact that the river is owned in common by the three States of Oregon, Washington, and Idaho, each of which can legislate adversely to the interest of the others makes it evident that for their mutual benefit the United States Government be asked to intervene. I understand that application has been made in this direction by some of the chambers of commerce interested.

Smaller river fish. Continue to be caught. The market here is extremely limited, and the greater part are used in Portland.

Deep-sea fishing. None of the ventures have proved remunerative, solely on account of want of market.

Logging. There is some revival in this industry owing to the increased demand for sawn lumber from this coast, both for the foreign and domestic markets, though I can find but two vessels clearing foreign from Astoria, both for South America.

The two years of mishaps in attempting to take down rafts of logs to San Francisco did not deter the same parties from making another attempt this year, and this time with great success. A raft of 450 feet in length by 52 feet beam and over 30 feet deep, drawing 22 feet of water, contained 75 miles linear of spars and piles measuring 4,500,000 feet board measure, was taken down to San Francisco the past summer. Most of the contents of the raft are intended to be used for driving piles for wharves and for bridges, and are not suitable for sawing.

Gray's Harbour reports a large increase in its foreign shipments.

Box-making. Is still struggling for a more extended market, but the freight rates so far have been found prohibitory. An attempt to build up a trade by the newly-organised line of British steamers to Japan and Hong-Kong fell through by reason of high freights asked.

I feel sure that in the course of a few years there will be a great deal done in shipments both of rough lumber and finished wood for boxes, &c.

The local can-making factory did a very much larger business both locally with the salmon canneries and further afield with fruit cans.	Can-making.
This factory now imports all of its tin-plates mostly direct from Liverpool.	
The out-put from the local tannery keeps up its high-class leather, its reputation for making a high grade of saddle leather is known now as far away as Chicago.	Leather tanning.
Still keeps up with an increasing output, California as before still taking the product.	Paper-pulp.
Waterworks for the town was practically finished at the end of the year, and is considered, for its cost, 40,000*l.*, to be one of the best and most cheaply constructed water supplies of any on the Pacific Coast, and has a capacity for supplying a town of 40,000 inhabitants. The water-power at the upper reservoir is estimated to afford sufficient power to light the streets of the town, and when the present contract with a local electrical company expires, it is the intention of the City Water Commission to bid for the lighting of the city.	Public works and improvements.
After a great deal of negotiating a contract was finally entered into with a large railroad contractor to complete the existing railroad (that turns off 50 miles up the river) down the river bank to Astoria, the time specified for the completion of the work was April 1, 1898.	Railways.
Construction was commenced most energetically and the clearing of two vessels with steel rails from England and the lading of two others promises the completion of the road before the end of 1896.	
This will stimulate the trade of the town considerably, doing away with the re-shipment of goods which was so detrimental to the moving of low price articles like lumber and box material.	
The work on the jetty at the mouth of the river was finally finished last November, the total cost being under the estimates.	Government works.
The work has stood uninjured a great deal of stormy weather and its success is shown by a constantly increasing depth in the channel, and also has increased the line of bare land now making to the south of the jetty, making a great protection to the river from the effects of the south-west swells.	
This matter is agitated and is no doubt a much-needed want, as it is the pilots refuse to bring in any vessel after dark unless it is an exceptionally clear night; as the larger part of the foreign commerce is done during the winter months its usefulness will be readily appreciated.	Range lights.
The new lighthouse on the north head of Cape Disappointment has not been commenced as yet.	
A steadily increasing addition to the population of Astoria and its vicinity is to be noted, brought here by the rumours of its railway building and general prosperity. The great majority of them, I am sorry to say, are in the position of waiting till something turns up. I am informed that every house in the town is occupied and in some cases to overcrowding.	Population and health.

UNITED STATES.

The health of the district has remained good, no diseases have shown themselves.

Annex A.—RETURN of all Shipping at the Port of Astoria, Oregon, during the Year 1895.

ENTERED.

Nationality.	Sailing. Number of Vessels.	Sailing. Tons.	Steam. Number of Vessels.	Steam. Tons.	Total. Number of Vessels.	Total. Tons.
British	95	173,475	6	9,443	104	182,918
American, coasting	115	43,770	344	288,736	459	332,506
,, foreign	4	2,252	2	1,255	7	3,507
Danish	1	1,336	...	...	1	1,336
Russian	1	2,154	...	...	1	2,154
German	9	15,265	...	...	9	15,265
French	1	1,125	...	...	1	1,125
Total	230	239,377	352	299,434	582	538,811
,, for the year preceding	143	177,255	408	334,238	551	511,493

CLEARED.

Nationality.	Sailing. Number of Vessels.	Sailing. Tons.	Steam. Number of Vessels.	Steam. Tons.	Total. Number of Vessels.	Total. Tons.
British	93	164,446	3	5,177	96	169,623
American, coasting	111	39,755	286	285,341	397	325,096
,, foreign	4	5,241	12	4,704	16	9,945
Danish	1	1,288	...	...	1	1,288
German	6	9,532	...	...	6	9,532
Total	215	220,262	301	295,222	516	515,484
,, for the year preceding	152	173,957	360	331,169	512	515,231

Annex B.—RETURN of Principal Articles of Export from Astoria, Oregon, during the Years 1895-94.

Articles.		1895. Quantity.	1895. Value.	1894. Quantity.	1894. Value.
			£		£
Salmon	Cases	81,583	105,882	7,800	10,033
Wheat	Bushels	263,171	27,868	58,575	5,589
Flour	Barrels	...	...	...	...
Lumber	M. feet	1,344	1,918	739	1,363
Sundries		...	951	...	340
Total		346,098	136,619	67,114	17,325

PORTLAND.

RETURN of Principal Articles of Import to Astoria, Oregon, during the Years 1895-94.

Articles.		1895.		1894.	
		Quantity.	Value.	Quantity.	Value.
			£		£
Tin-plates	Boxes	49,365	25,659	20,755	12,257
Salt	Lbs.	...	...	112,000	66
Coal	Tons	2,866	1,566	910	593
Sundries	...	...	1,366	...	3,142
Total	...	52,231	28,591	133,665	16,058

Annex C.—TABLE showing Total Value of all Articles Exported from and Imported to the Port of Astoria, Oregon, from and to Foreign Countries during the Years 1895-94.

Country.	Exports.		Imports.	
	1895.	1894.	1895.	1894.
	£	£	£	£
Great Britain	130,294	15,713	25,708	12,272
British colonies	2,105	21	2,883	591
Other countries	3,425	1,565	21	3,109
Total	135,824	17,299	28,612	15,972

TACOMA.

Mr. Vice-Consul Alexander reports as follows:—

General remarks relative to the State. The State of Washington has experienced very little, if any, improvement from a financial and business point of view. Low prices have continued to prevail, and land in particular has shrunk in value causing many failures.

Health births, and deaths. It has been impossible to procure any data relative to the number of births, marriages, and deaths in the State, no report being called for from the State officials. Generally speaking, the health of the country has been good; no epidemic diseases have made their appearance during the year, either among human beings or cattle. Instances have, of course, occurred of some infectious and contagious diseases, but these have been of a slight nature, and the precautions taken and methods adopted have prevented their spreading. Reports of tuberculosis among cattle were circulated, but on investigation by the proper authorities were found to be erroneous. *Cattle disease.*

Weather and climate. The weather conditions which prevailed in the State during 1895 were furnished to the central office at Seattle by the monthly reports from 28 stations. The mean temperature for the year, as deduced from the reports of 50 stations, was 48·7 degrees, and the mean monthly precipitation 2·96 inches. During the year 1895 the total rainfall was 35·56 inches. The year was an unusually dry one, the rainfall being 3·50 inches below normal. The months during which the rainfall was in excess were January, May, and December; the driest month was August. The warmest day of the year was July 23, when the thermometer reached 109 degrees at Connell. The coldest days were January 11 and 12, when the thermometer went down to 6 degrees below zero at Ellensburg.

Industries. Timber. It is estimated that there are 11,971,700 acres of timber land in Western Washington, containing some 303,355,000,000 feet of standing timber; and in Eastern Washington 11,616,000 acres, with 106,978,000,000 feet, thus giving an average for Western Washington of about 25,000 feet to the acre, and for Eastern Washington 9,000 feet. There are in the State about 270 saw mills, 275 shingle mills, and nearly 100 other establishments in which wood forms the staple of manufacture. These turned out articles of various descriptions, valued at about 3,000,000*l.*, and gave direct employment to almost 12,000 persons. The railway shipments to eastern points, viâ the Northern Pacific, Great Northern and Canadian Pacific Railroads, amounted during the year to 5,662 truckloads of timber, and 13,776 truckloads of shingles, as compared with 4,279 truckloads of timber, and 12,295 of shingles in 1894. These shipments consisted of 90,984,000 feet of timber, as compared with 77,590,000 in the preceding year, and 2,181,240,000 shingles, as against 1,764,320,000; thus showing an increase in the shipment of both products as compared with the year 1894. It is estimated that the cargo shipments for 1895 from the State were 152,294,000 feet foreign, and 259,299,000 feet coastwise, making a total of 411,593,900 feet. These figures represent the amount shipped by ten of the largest cargo mills in the State. The price of shingles was still low, ranging from 3*s.* 6*d.* to 4*s.* 6*d.* per thousand. Railroad freights have fluctuated more or less during the year. The average cargo freight to United Kingdom has been about 3*l.* 5*s.*

Railways. No marked extension has been made by the railway companies operating in the State, so far as can be learned, in the way of mileage, with the exception of about 3 miles of new line laid by one company; but extensive improvements have been made in the rolling-stock and permanent road bed, which all tend to augment the efficiency of the service. It is expected that these improvements will still further shorten the time from the Atlantic to the Pacific seaboard, and thus draw a greater volume of trade to the shores of Puget Sound.

Mining. During the year very little, if anything, has been done in the way of developing coal-mining. The mines have been kept in operation, but the quantity mined will probably be less than last year. The test of the various coals of the State, ordered by the United States Navy Department, and made on some of its vessels sent here for that purpose, have not proved, perhaps, quite so satisfactory as the mine-owners could have wished, the general impression being that as yet the coal is taken from too near the surface to be satisfactory. It is expected that further developments may yield a quality better suited for steam purposes.

In regard to the mining of the precious metals very little has been accomplished. Improvements have been made, and some extensions undertaken in and around the Monte Cristo district, where new machinery has been installed. The mining country, which is probably attracting the greatest attention amongst prospectors, has been that on the border between Canada and the United States, the Canadian territory receiving the most attention.

From information kindly furnished by the State Fish Commissioner, who reports on each district in the State separately, it appears that the spring pack of salmon in the Columbia River district amounted to 490,376 cases, at a valuation of 542,371*l*. (2,711,854 dol.), the amount paid for the fish being 355,309*l*. (1,776,547 dol.). The autumn pack amounted to 137,086 cases, at a valuation of 91,122*l*. (456,509 dol.); besides which, fresh and salted salmon were sold to the value of 32,933*l*. (164,664 dol.). The above figures are for both Oregon and Washington, but the Commissioner says that Washington must be credited with considerably over one-half of the whole amount. Washington must also be credited with half of the sturgeon catch in this district, which was valued at 10,040*l*. (50,202 dol.), exclusive of 2,931*l*. (14,655 dol.) received from the sale of caviare made from the roe of this fish. The value of smelt taken in the Columbia River amounted to 1,336*l*. (9,682 dol.), and trout, carp, and other smaller fish taken there will make a total of 1,600*l*. (8,000 dol.) more for this district. The fishing industry in the Willapa and Gray's Harbour districts has increased during the past year, and a new cannery has been erected and operated. The salmon pack at Gray's Harbour amounted to 10,600 cases, valued at 4,760*l*. (23,800 dol.), and about 1,031,512 lbs. of fresh salmon were shipped, amounting to 4,555*l*. (22,785 dol.). Willapa Harbour put up salmon to the value of about 14,000*l*. (69,000 dol.), and shipped also 100*l*. worth of fresh salmon. In the Puget Sound district the salmon fishing industry has increased marvellously, mainly due to the fact that means have been discovered for catching the sockeye salmon, a species identical with the blueback of the Columbia River, which it has heretofore been impossible to take in Puget Sound waters. The spawning grounds of this fish are at the headwaters of the Fraser River in British Columbia, and it is the principal variety of salmon packed by the canneries on that river. These fish are now taken in the waters surrounding the San Juan Islands, and in the Gulf of Georgia, where efforts are being made to secure locations for traps, the means by which they are captured, and new canneries are being erected. The total cases of the Puget Sound pack were 147,118, valued at 91,408*l*. (457,000 dol.). There were, in addition, 7,357,500 lbs. of fresh salmon sold, valued at 34,787*l*. (173,937 dol.); 60,000 lbs. of smoked salmon, valued at 1,200*l*.

Fisheries.

(6,000 dol.); and 1,000 barrels of salted salmon, valued at 800*l*. (4,000 dol.), selling at about 16*s*. (4 dol.) per barrel. There were taken 1,700,000 lbs. of halibut, valued at 7,000*l*. (34,000 dol.); 645,750 lbs. of codfish, valued at 3,534*l*. (17,672 dol.); and small fish—trout, herring, soles, &c.—to the value of 2,400*l*. (12,000 dol.). During the past year a small sardine cannery has been opened at Port Townsend with fair prospects of success. A demand has arisen lately for shrimps, and about 8,000 lbs. have been caught, valued at 160*l*. (800 dol.), which seem to be of unusual size and excellent flavour. These shrimps are taken with a drag-net amongst the islands and bays of the Upper Sound, in a depth of from 5 to 6 fathoms of water. The oyster catch for the year in the Willapa Harbour district amounted to 44,000 sacks, valued at 13,300*l*. (66,500 dol.), in addition to 200*l*. worth of clams and crabs. From the Puget Sound district 12,632 sacks of oysters were sold, at a valuation of 6,316*l*. (31,580 dol.), besides 2,650*l*. (14,250 dol.) worth of clams and other shellfish. It has been noticed that the eastern oysters which were planted in Willapa Harbour by the United States Fish Commission in the autumn of 1894, as an experiment for seed purposes, had lived and grown, but had shown as yet no signs of propagating.

In regard to the important matter of the artificial propagation of fish, much has already been done with eminently satisfactory results. At the last session of the Legislature an appropriation of 4,000*l*. (20,000 dol.) was made for the purpose of the artificial propagation of salmon. The Act also created a Board of Fish Commissioners, to consist of the Governor, State Treasurer, and State Fish Commissioner, whose duties are the selection of sites for and establishment of salmon hatcheries. The management of the hatcheries, after their erection, is placed in the hands of the State Fish Commissioner. The first hatchery was constructed on the Kalama River, in Cowlitz County, about four miles from the Columbia River, and is fully equipped with every modern appliance for successfully operating an artificial hatchery. Although the contract for the building was not let until July 19 last, the entire work was completed in sufficient time to obtain and save over 4,000,000 salmon eggs during the spawning season, and it is expected that a like number of young salmon will be turned into the Kalama River during the coming spring.

This hatchery has a capacity for turning out 6,000,000 young salmon annually. An experimental station for taking and eyeing spawn has also been built on the Chinook River, in Pacific County. The total amount expended from the Fish Hatchery Fund up to November 1, 1895, including the construction of the buildings on the Kalama and Chinook Rivers, was only 1,415*l*. (7,077 dol.). The money received from licenses issued to the owners of stationary salmon-catching appliances on the Columbia River and Puget Sound, amounting during the past year to 1,102*l*. (5,610 dol.), and paid into what is known as the Fish Commissioner's Fund has also been applied to the experiments in artificial propagation Owing to a decision rendered by the Superior Court of Whatcom

County, that the Gulf of Georgia does not form a part of Puget Sound, the State has been deprived of considerable revenue which it would otherwise have derived from fishing licenses. This decision has also caused much annoyance to persons desirous of fishing in these waters, and to the Fish Commissioner. The statutes of the State are wholly deficient in legislation bearing upon the gathering of statistics pertinent to the fishing industry by the State Fish Commissioner, and it is hoped that the next Legislature may enact laws which may remedy this defect and make it obligatory on owners or managers of canneries to furnish the Commissioner with such statistics as may be at their command. In connection with this subject the Joint Fish Commission, appointed in 1894 by Great Britain and the United States, has almost completed its labours, having made a thorough examination of the waters of the Fraser River, and the fishing grounds of Puget Sound and the Columbia River. Its report, which is to be published by June, 1896, will be awaited with special interest by all in any way connected with the fishing industry in this State. The money invested in the fishing industry on Puget Sound, for schooners, boats, traps, seines, fish-wheels, &c., aggregated over 200,000*l*. Many thousands of pounds are also invested in canneries, and for these latter this has been one of the most successful seasons on record. The catch of fish in the waters of Puget Sound comprises salmon, halibut, sturgeon, smelt, herring, perch, flounder, sole, black bass, sea trout, shad, carp, cod, catfish, black cod, turbot, plaice, shrimps, crabs, oysters, and clams.

Agriculture.

For agricultural purposes the State may be divided into three sections, differing widely in climate, soil, and agricultural products. The first, or Western Washington, is characterised by a moist climate. The second, or Central Washington, is an irrigated region, and contains some of the best agricultural lands. In the Yakima Valley alone there are 140,000 acres of irrigated lands, of which 60,000 are under cultivation. These have been fully described in previous reports. The third, or Eastern Washington, is a region of rolling hills, having a soil tending rather to a stiff clay, and a rainfall which just suffices for crop production. The character of the soil is such that it retains the moisture to a remarkable degree, and, although the summers are excessively dry, the moisture in the soil from the winter rains is sufficient to mature all crops adapted to the rather short seasons. This section is distinctly a grain-growing country, wheat, barley, oats, rye, and flax being the principal products. Maize is grown to some extent for fodder, and all of the root crops, except white turnips, are produced in abundance. In the irrigated district of Central Washington alfalfa (lucerne) is the one great agricultural product, and in Western Washington the most important farm crop is red clover, which thrives there in great luxuriance. In the grain-growing

General remarks

section of Eastern Washington the most serious hindrance to agriculture is the squirrel. On account of the dry and mild winter preceding, these squirrels have been more numerous and more destructive than in any former year since the settlement of the country. In the drier parts of Whitman and the adjacent counties many wheat fields were totally destroyed by these pests. The crop season of 1895 opened very auspiciously. The month of February and the first part of March were dry and warm, and favourable for the beginning of farm work. March was cool during its middle part and wet at the close. The ground seemed to be of the right degree of moisture, and rains, though copious enough, were not excessive. Some ploughing and seeding were done in the opening days of February and March, but in April the seeding in the eastern section seemed to drag along, owing to the cold and showery weather. The closing week of April and first week of May were warm and sunny. and fine growing weeks. Grain, grass, fruit, and vegetables all progressed favourably. During the next week there was a severe frost in the eastern section, and a light one in the western. Considerable fruit was destroyed, and there was much damage to winter and spring wheat by the late frost in May. The last two weeks of May were warm and genial, and followed by needed showers, causing much grain to germinate which would otherwise not have done so. Throughout June a dry period, with parching winds, prevailed in the eastern section, which was unfavourable to grain. In the west there were a few gentle showers, and it was fine haying weather. The drought was broken on July 4 and 5 by a heavy general rainstorm. Fine haying weather followed in the western section, which was also favourable to the oat crop in the Skagit Valley, but a drought began which was general over Washington until the first week in September, and which was considered unfavourable to grain in Eastern Washington, and to vegetables in the western part. The weather in the harvest season was very favourable for the purpose, though the dense smoke which prevailed from forest fires was somewhat disagreeable. Showers occurred during the middle weeks of September, and a warm, sunny period at its close. Though a dry September the soil was left in a good condition for autumn ploughing. The drought of July and August is regarded as one of the most severe and prolonged that ever occurred in the State.

Grain. The following table gives the estimated acreage and yield of the different crops for the whole State during the year 1895:—

Crop.	Acreage.		Average Yield per Acre.	Total Yield.
Wheat	475,000	Bushels	15	7,125,000
Oats	95,000	,,	42	3,990,000
Barley	75,000	,,	38	2,850,000
Rye	25,000	,,	27	67,000
Maize	5,450	,,	17	93,000
Potatoes	16,190	,,	149	2,412,750
Hops	7,000	Bales	..	40,000
Hay (1 ton = 2,000 lbs.)	324,470	Tons	1·85	600,270

The average net price of wheat to the farmers was 1s. 8d. (40 c.) per bushel; of oats, 1s. 10½d. (45 c.) per cental; of rye, 3s. (75 c.) per bushel; of barley, 1s. 9½d. (43 c.) per cental; hops, 1½d. per lb.; hay, 16s. (4 dol.) per ton. The average freight from the grain districts to tidewater was 18s. (4 dol. 60 c.) per ton. Farmers are very much encouraged by the prices in wheat towards the end of the year, and a very large increase in the acreage is expected. The average in 1895 was 30 per cent. short, owing to the low prices and a desire to summer fallow. This summer fallowing has been found the most advantageous and inexpensive method of destroying the wild oats which abound in many places to the detriment of the crops. The wheat crop was a fair average one, both in quantity and in quality; 75 per cent. of the crop would grade as No. 1.

Grain inspection and grading. So much dissatisfaction and difference of opinion between the farmers and the buyers of grain having occurred, it was deemed advisable for the best interests of all parties that the Legislature should enact a law creating a chief State Grain Inspector and a State Grain Commission, the latter to consist of the chief State Grain Inspector and a grain dealer from the sea coast, the third member to be elected from amongst the large grain producers of the State. Three years' experience in the grain trade of Washington, Oregon, and Idaho was to be an indispensable qualification for the office of chief State Grain Inspector, and all the members of the Commission were further placed under heavy bonds for the faithful performance of their duties. These duties consist in determining a fair and fixed standard of grades at the beginning of each grain season, and the classification of all grain received for milling or export in truck-load lots. The three towns of Tacoma, Seattle, and Spokane have been designated as stations for the State inspection of grain. This system has been found to work admirably, giving great satisfaction; so much so that San Francisco buyers have adopted the practice of making their purchases of Washington grain on the State grades, and about 10,000 tons of grain have been shipped since the beginning of the grain season from Seattle and Tacoma to San Francisco, and no appeal has yet been taken from the grade fixed by the State Inspector. Four cargoes at the request of the parties interested have been inspected as the grain went aboard the ships for foreign shipment, the cost being 2s. (50 c.) per hour during the time the inspector is engaged. The inspection thus given is very thorough, each sack being examined as it goes from the warehouse into the trucks, and then again, just as carefully, by another inspector as it goes aboard the ships. The amount of grain received at the three places named above, September 10, 1895, to December 31, 1895, was as follows:—

	Quantity.		
	Tacoma.	Seattle.	Spokane.
	Bushels.	Bushels.	Bushels.
Wheat	1,605,000	419,400	433,800
Oats	73,200	220,800	..
Barley	30,600	55,200	..

The following are a few of the regulations provided by the law for State grain weighing and grading, together with the requirements for the different grades to be known as "Washington grades." Wheat is classed under two heads, blue-stem and club, and each of these classes is subdivided into three grades, to be known as No. 1, No. 2, and No. 3. No. 1 blue-stem wheat must be sound, dry, reasonably plump, of good colour, reasonably free from smut, reasonably well cleaned; and must not have mixed with it over 15 per cent. of any other varieties of wheat than blue-stem. Where blue-stem wheat has mixed with it over 15 per cent. and less than 30 per cent. of any other variety of wheat than blue-stem, it is to be regarded as No. 2 blue-stem, unless for other reasons it is graded lower. No. 2 blue-stem wheat must be sound, of fairly good colour, but little shrivelled, reasonably clean, and a good milling quality of blue-stem. No. 3 blue-stem wheat shall be any blue-stem which is so badly shrivelled, or from any cause too poor to be graded as No. 2, but still fit for milling purposes. A similar standard is required for the various grades of club wheat. Rejected wheat shall be any which is very badly shrivelled, badly bleached, badly smutted, wet, the least musty, or from any cause unfit for milling purpose. Fair average quality Washington wheat shall be a mixture of the different varieties of club wheat suitable for milling purposes grown in the different parts of the State of Washington. Oats are to be classed as milling and feed. There is only one grade of milling oats, but two of feed. Barley is also divided into two classes, to be known as brewing and feed; there being one grade of brewing and two of feed. No. 1 brewing barley shall be plump, dry, sound, of good colour, clean and substantially free from broken and skinned grains and from the other varieties of grain, and testing not less than 46 lbs. per measured bushel. No. 1 feed barley may be slightly stained and slightly shrunken, and contain a small admixture of other grains. Rejected barley shall include all barley which is badly damaged, in a heating condition, or from any cause unfit for No. 2 feed. If, in inspecting the grain, it shall be found that any of it has not been properly cleaned, the inspector shall place upon it the grade it is entitled to if properly cleaned, and state upon his inspection report the grade if properly cleaned. No inspector shall in any case make the grade of any lot of grain above that of the poorest quality found in the lot, when it clearly bears evidence of having been plugged or doctored for the purpose of deception.

The export of wheat by sea has amounted to about 90,000 tons during the year, and of flour 30,000 tons. The average cargo freight on wheat to United Kingdom has been about 1*l*. 11*s*. 3*d*.

Agricultural shows.

The Annual State Agricultural Show was again held at North Yakima. There were fine exhibits of the various kinds of grain, grasses, and agricultural products, in addition to vegetables and fruits, together with a small but very creditable collection of dairy manufactures. It is to be regretted that there was no apparent improvement in the live-stock, very little interest being displayed in this direction. Greater inducements should be offered to farmers to show their animals. The Horticultural Show at Spokane in the autumn was probably the most attractive of those held in the State, every county in Eastern Washington being admirably represented. The collection of fruit, vegetables, and garden produce of every description was excellent and very tastefully arranged, doing great credit to the officers of the show. There was a very fine Show of Roses and Strawberries held at Tacoma, and, later in the year, both at this town and at Whatcom Poultry Shows attracted considerable attention, some 500 birds being placed on exhibition.

Dairying.

Dairying in the State of Washington is advancing rapidly to a position amongst the leading industries. The climate, on the whole, is adapted to this business, and each of the sections of the State is suited to it in its own peculiar way. The luxuriant growth of the clovers in Western Washington and the ease with which grasses are grown eminently adapted that section to dairying. The wonderful growth of alfalfa (lucerne) in Central Washington and the cheapness of grain makes it possible to feed a dairy cow on an ideal ration for less than 5*d*. a day. In this district dairying is already the leading industry. In Eastern Washington the various root crops, especially carrots, mangolds, sugar-beets, ruta-bagas, and potatoes, are produced in great abundance. The grains grow there to perfection, and the one thing lacking, so far, is leguminous crops, without which no system of agriculture, and particularly dairying, can long be successful. There are indications, however, that some of the less common leguminous crops may be grown here advantageously. Among these are sweet melilot and the hairy vetch. It is hoped that others may be found to do equally well. Red clover thrives fairly in many places. There were in the State, during the year 1895, 52 creameries and cheese factories in successful operation, the daily output of which was 7,000 lbs. of butter and 2,400 lbs.

(2178)

of cheese, making an annual production for the State of 2,190,000 lbs. of butter and 547,000 lbs. of cheese. The State consumed during the year 2,920,000 lbs. of butter and 730,000 lbs. of cheese. In the face of the depression in all kinds of business in the country, the products of the dairy maintained their price. In 1891 there were shipped into the State butter and cheese to the value of 500,000*l.*, and up to the end of this year, 1895, less than 60,000*l.*, showing an increase in the home product of about 400,000*l.* With the increased attention directed to dairying, it is fully expected that this State will be exporting these products within the next 2 or 3 years, instead of importing them. The Act regulating the manufacture of dairy products and to prevent deception or fraud in the sale of the same or imitations thereof, passed by the Legislature of 1895, had, as its main object, to make it unlawful to dispose of any impure dairy products or any imitations of the same. It also provided that milk, in order to comply with the standard, shall contain not less than 3 per cent. of pure butter fat, when subjected to chemical analysis; that all dairy herds shall be free from any disease; and further, that all dairy products shall be stamped so as to show their exact nature. In the case of cheese, it was provided that there shall be three grades, to be known as Washington full cream, skimmed, and half skimmed, respectively. The first grade to contain the whole portion of the butter fat and other solids, the second to be made from pure skimmed milk, and the third to contain not less than 15 per cent. of pure butter fat. The sale of oleomargarine is not prohibited, provided it be in a separate package distinctly marked, so as to indicate clearly its real nature. In June of this year a Dairy Commissioner was appointed by the State, who is to devote his entire time to the dairy interests of the State, more especially the enforcement of the laws relating to the manufacture and sale of dairy products. He is to make personal inspections of any articles believed to be impure or adulterated, and to prosecute the manufacturers of such articles, and has authority to call on the chemists of any State institution to furnish analyses of such articles as he may submit to them for analysis without compensation, as well as to enter any creameries, manufactories, or shops and to seize any articles which he may have reason to suspect of being adulterated. The prosecuting attorneys of the different counties are also required to render him any legal assistance he may require in carrying out his duties. The State Agricultural College and Experiment Station, at Pullman, in Eastern Washington, is doing its share in addition to its other work, in encouraging the farmers to take a special interest in dairying, and with that object in view will open a model dairy school in the early part of 1896, where a course of lectures, as well as practical instruction, extending over 2 months, will be given free of all charge to residents of the State, both men and women, in all phases of milk-testing, butter-making, cheese-making, and the management of cows and of the machinery of the dairy, including both the theoretical and practical sides of the business.

The institution is fully equipped for this purpose, having the most improved modern machinery and appliances, as well as a fine herd of selected dairy cattle.

There are now about 60,000 acres in this State planted with fruit trees. The varieties of fruits mostly planted up to the present time are apples, prunes, peaches, pears, cherries, and apricots. Many of the young orchards are now commencing to bear fruit with gratifying results. There has been a great demand for winter apple trees for planting, the favourite varieties in Western Washington being the Baldwin, Newtown Pippin, Jonathan, Northern Spy, and English Russet. In Eastern Washington, in addition to the above varieties, the White Pearmain, Spitzenburg, King of Tomkins County, Waxen and Rhode Island Greening have been in request. These late varieties are in favour on account of their good keeping and shipping qualities, the supply from California spoiling the market for the earlier varieties. The crop this year was a little below the average, but prices were fairly high, ranging from 2s. 6d. (60 c.) to 8s. (2 dol.) per box of 50 lbs. The highest price (8s.) was paid for extra fine specimens of the Spitzenburg, but the average price of this variety has been from 5s. 6d. (1 dol. 35 c.) to 6s. (1 dol. 50 c.) per box; the Baldwin commanding the next highest price, 3s. 6d. (85 c.) to 4s. (1 dol.), and the cheapest variety being the Waxens at 2s. 3d. (60 c.) to 2s. 6d. (65 c.) per box. It has been noticed that in Western Washington the Baldwin hardly attains its characteristic high colour. There has also been a large acreage planted to prunes, chiefly the Italian variety, which for flavour and quality cannot be equalled. In Clarke County alone about 1,000 acres were in bearing. This county enjoys the reputation of being the leading prune district of the State, having produced nearly 2,000,000 lbs. of evaporated fruit during the past season. There are 50 prune driers in operation in this county which have been erected at a cost of about 160l. a-piece. In quality the prunes grade mostly "No. 1," which quality requires from 40 to 50 of the dried fruits to the 1 lb. A large proportion of the crop, if assorted, would grade from 30 to 40 to the 1 lb., known by the brand "finest," for which the very highest prices are obtained. In spite of the good results, the lack of experience of the driers and packers in some districts has caused an inferior article to be placed on the market and the product in general to be, consequently, under-rated. The "No. 1" grade has sold at about 3d. per lb., with an upward tendency toward the close of the year, and prospects are that prices will not depreciate. There has been some demand for sample packages for shipment to England and other foreign parts, while the domestic shipments included many truck loads to New York, St. Louis, and other points. The cherry crop was excellent; besides supplying all the local markets several truck loads were sent to the Eastern States. The price remained steady at 2d. per lb. in the orchards. This fruit is one of the most profitable in Western Washington, and it is probable that it will be largely planted during the coming year. The varieties which have been

(2178)

found most suited to this State are the Bigarreaus and Morellas, among which the Poland Bigarreau or Royal Ann, the Black Republican and the Black Tartarian may be specially mentioned. The Bing, a new, large, dark variety is also highly spoken of for its excellent shipping qualities. In regard to apricots, it has been found that the temperature of Western Washington, although the annual mean by day is higher than in the eastern part of the State, is yet too cold at night for the successful growing and maturing of this fruit. In Eastern Washington, in the Yakima, Snake River and Walla Walla districts the apricot does remarkably well producing enormous crops of fine flavour and quality. While the greater portion of the crop, during the past year, has been marketed as green or fresh fruit, large quantities have been evaporated, and greater attention should be paid to this particular branch. Almost the same conditions apply to peaches, although in some favoured localities along the shores of Puget Sound, some excellent peaches have been grown, equal in all respects to those of Eastern Washington. The crop in the State during the year has been good and prices fairly high. The western part of the State is especially suited to the growing of all small fruits such as strawberries, red raspberries, currants, and gooseberries; the moist, cool climate and the valley soils being admirably adapted to this class of fruit. The best of the small fruits are probably the strawberry and the red raspberry. Large shipments of these have been made during the year. The red raspberry is of the very finest quality for jams and jellies, and although there was an over-supply last year—much of the fruit going to waste—this was, in many instances, due to the growers either not knowing or not utilising the best methods of preserving the fruit. As mentioned in previous reports, there is no doubt but that the preserving of all small fruits in the form of jams, jellies, &c., offers a profitable investment, and there is the additional advantage of being able to obtain the shipments to the factories by water, thus avoiding the high freight rates by rail. Another field for investment should be the establishment of canneries, for putting up tinned fruits and vegetables, especially peaches, apricots, peas, and beans, as well as tomatoes and cucumbers, of which latter vast quantities are grown in the irrigated districts of South-Eastern Washington. Very stringent measures against the importation of fruit trees affected with disease have been enacted during the last session of the Legislature, and strenuous efforts are being made to stamp out the insect pests, including scale, aphis, and codlin moth or scab, from the orchards of the State, by means of intelligent spraying. At an average cost of 6d. per tree for the season it has been found that the orchards can be kept free from many of these diseases, and the yield of fruit increased about 88 per cent. At the Annual Convention of Fruit-growers, held in Walla Walla at the close of the year, the question of the adoption of a uniform schedule of weights for the various standard fruit packages received considerable attention, and it was strongly recommended that it be made the subject of legislation. The weights proposed were as follows: 4 basket crates, 25 lbs.; standard peach box, 20 lbs.; pear box, 45 lbs.; apple box, 50 lbs.; cherry box, 10 lbs.; crate of 24 boxes for small fruits, 25 lbs. The remark that "if the fruit-growers in Western America will ever learn that there is more in packing fruit than in raising it, then, and not till then, will there be profit in the crop," is truly applicable to the fruit-growers in this State, and cannot be too highly emphasised.

Market gardening has commanded a great deal of attention during the past year, and many tracts of land, ranging from 5 to 20 acres, are being put into a high state of cultivation, vegetables of almost every kind being grown. Some persons are making a very profitable investment by growing the early and more tender vegetables under glass, a ready market for these being found in the larger towns, and good prices obtained, thus allowing of successful competition with the imported products from Oregon and California. Many acres have been planted to asparagus and celery. *Market gardening.*

The hop season was almost a complete failure, owing to the appearance of lice in some of the yards; and the low prices offered so discouraged the growers that many yards remained unpicked. *Hops.*

Regarding the flax culture in this State, the experiments carried on in Western Washington, and for which an appropriation of 160*l.* was made by the legislature, have proved very satisfactory. At the North-west Agricultural and Industrial Fair held at Whatcom in September, special prizes were offered for flax exhibits. One part of the exhibition was a factory on a small scale, where flax straw, by scutching, hackling, and spinning, was converted into thread. There were numerous exhibits of flax products from the straw as pulled in the field to the finished cloth from the loom. After the "fair" samples of the hackled line were sent to many factories in the country, with the result that requests for larger consignments have been received, for which market prices will be paid, the manufacturers stating that the quality is quite equal to that of imported flax. These favourable results have attracted the attention not only of eastern manufacturers, but a representative of one of the largest cloth-weaving and spinning concerns in Ireland has spent some time on Puget Sound during the year, investigating the possibilities of this industry. In Whatcom County $2\frac{3}{4}$ to 4 tons of straw per acre yield 1,375 to 2,000 lbs. of clean fibre. Fibre is worth, at the factory, from $3\frac{1}{2}d.$ to 1*s.* per lb., and the finest quality even higher. At a price below the average, say 5*d.* per lb., 3,000 lbs. of fibre will bring 40*l.* Seed is worth, on an average, 7*s.* per bushel for sowing purposes, and for the oil mill about 4*s.* The first year's crop from imported seed is good for sowing, the second not. Putting the seed at 3*s.* 6*d.* per bushel, which means 5*l.* 10*s.* (27 dol. 72 c.) per acre, makes a total of 45*l.* 10*s.* (227 dol. 72 c.) for fibre and seed. In Whatcom County the cost is given as 13*l.* (65 dol. 25 c.) per acre; freight from Whatcom to factory, 4*l.* (20 dol The total expenses being 17*l.* (85 dol. 25 c.), leaving a net profit *Flax.*

of 28*l.* (142 dol. 47 c.) per acre. There are in Whatcom County 200,000 acres well fitted to produce flax. In Eastern Washington flax has never been grown for fibre, but is grown to a considerable extent for seed, the yield being from 6 to 18 bushels per acre. Experiments are to be made during the coming year, 1896, in growing flax for fibre at the State Agricultural Experiment Farm, near Pullman, in Eastern Washington.

Seeds for planting.
In parts of Eastern and Western Washington vegetable seeds of all kinds and of the best quality can be produced in abundance, the favourable conditions of soil and climate tending to develop seeds of good germinating power. Seed houses in the Eastern States are contracting for large quantities of seeds from these districts, regarding them as of peculiar value. In the Puget Sound region the cabbage and cauliflower seeds are particularly fine, and great quantities are being placed on the market; while, although the increase in the dried peas product has been almost 400 per cent., the crop grown is entirely insufficient for the demand. In Eastern Washington the acreage sown to peas for seed purposes could be increased to great advantage and profit. Around Waterville, over 600 acres have been devoted to growing seeds, chiefly peas, of which 15 to 20 bushels were produced to the acre, the net price being 4s. 6d. (1 dol. 10 c.) to 10s. (2 dol. 50 c.) per bushel, the buyers furnishing the seed and sacks to growers.

Road making.
The value of good roads for the opening up and development of the country is becoming appreciated. There are 17 road laws, covering the needs of villages, townships, and counties, in force in this State, with 7 auxiliary Acts partly in force, and a town organisation law. The Act of 1895, passed by the last Legislature, makes it compulsory on every road district to levy a special tax annually of not less than one mill or more than ten mills on every dollar's worth of property in said district. One county alone in Western Washington, within the last 3 years, has spent 37,427*l.* (187,337 dol.) in constructing 50 miles of main roads and substantial bridges, thus opening up many acres of rich agricultural lands; with 50 miles of extensions and cross-roads, which will be practically completed two years hence.

Population and Assessment.

The population of the State in 1895 is estimated at 450,000. The total value of real and personal property and railway lines in the State, as assessed by the State Board of Equalisation is as follows:—real property, 33,026,400*l.* (165,132,000 dol.); personal property, 5,227,940*l.* (26,139,700 dol.); railway lines, 2,583,700*l.* (12,918,500 dol.); making a total of 40,838,060*l.* (204,190,300 dol.). The total amount of State taxes to be paid for the year 1896 is fixed at 122,514*l.* (612,570 dol.), and the total amount of school tax at 129,200*l.* (646,000 dol.).

PORTLAND. 39

General Outlook.

The prospects for trade for the State generally are somewhat improved, although no very material change can be expected for some little time. Improvement will visit this coast possibly last of all, working from the Atlantic seaboard, and until business improves in the Eastern States the West cannot look for any marked change. The crop prospects for the coming season are pretty good, so far as can be told, although the winter, which has been very severe in the eastern part of the State may cause a little re-seeding. There has been no material loss in stock; farmers now paying greater attention to providing winter feed. The country has been free from labour troubles and other strikes, which so disturbed the condition of affairs last year.

The trade with other countries appears to be improving. That with China and Japan takes the lead, of which a fuller account is given later in this Report.

Commercial relations. China and Japan.

That with South Africa has been carried on chiefly by sailing vessels, although two or three steamship cargoes have been sent off, and has consisted mainly of timber. This trade began to decline towards the autumn on account of the unsettled state of affairs, but revived again from another source, in a most unexpected form, due to the following circumstances. The unlooked for shortage of wheat in the Australian colonies during the year has led merchants to seek another source of supply. This was found in Puget Sound; with the result that, during the last 3 months of this year, large quantities of wheat, flour, and other bread-stuffs have left for this country, causing the prices in these commodities to rise very perceptibly, much to the gratification of the farmer, who had kept his wheat. It is hardly expected that this trade will long maintain its present conditions, and it will, in all probability, decline in a few months. The average freight rate for breadstuffs is about 30*s.* per ton, and for timber, 75*s.* per 1,000 feet.

South Africa.

About a year and a half ago some Seattle merchants chartered a small sailing vessel and loaded her for San José, Guatemala, with products from the State of Washington, and meeting with success in the disposal of the first shipment, chartered other vessels, eventually leading to the formation of the Puget Sound and Central American Steamship Company, which is now operating a line of steamers between Puget Sound ports and the ports of San Salvador and Guatemala, Central America. This trade, started in a small way, shows good prospects for business between these countries and this section, increasing as the line becomes known, shipments coming from many eastern points. The Company now contemplates extending its business to other Central American ports, and will then operate more steamers and give better facilities to shippers, Seattle being the terminal point on Puget Sound. The freight rates on the principal commodities to Central American ports range about as follows:—flour, 30*s.* (7 dol. 50 c.) per ton; wheat, 35*s.* (8 dol.) per ton; other breadstuffs

Central America.

UNITED STATES.

from 35s. (8 dol.) to 65s. (18 dol.); timber, 60s. (15 dol.) per 1,000 feet; general merchandise, 40s. (10 dol.) to 48s. (12 dol.).

The following is a more detailed report of the trade, commerce, and other matters of interest of Tacoma and Seattle separately.

Valuable information and assistance for this report have been afforded by Professor W. J. Spillman, of the State Agricultural Experiment Station at Pullman; Mr. G. N. Salisbury, Observer of the State Weather Bureau; Mr. C. A. Tonneson, Secretary of the State Board of Horticulture; and by several other officials and gentlemen of these two towns.

General Remarks.

Tacoma has maintained its position during the year 1895 as the chief shipping centre of the foreign trade of the State. While the exports have shown a rather marked falling-off, this is more than counterbalanced by the remarkable expansion in the amount of imports. The wheat crop turned out fairly well, but the low prices for grain and almost every other commodity which had previously prevailed found no material improvement until the last of the year, when a better feeling existed. These conditions may, in a large measure, account for the decline in exports; farmers holding back their grain, hoping for better prices, which, quite unexpectedly, came in the demand for bread-stuffs and other commodities for South Africa and Central America. The imports show an increase of 680 per cent., mainly on account of the oriental trade.

Shipping and Navigation.

The Annexes A, B, and C at the end of this report have been obtained from the custom-house records at this sub-port, through the courtesy of J. C. Saunders, Esq., Collector of Customs for this Puget Sound District, and represent distinctly the foreign business only, no domestic trade being taken account of.

Entrances and clearances. By referring to Annex A, it will be seen that the number of vessels entering the port was 33 more than in 1894, the increase being in the number of steamships. In British vessels there was an increase of 11. The clearances show two vessels less than in that year; in British vessels also there was a decrease of two. It will be noticed that, in the entrances of vessels, there is an increase in the registered tonnage of about one-third, while the clearances show a slight decrease.

Imports and exports. The harbour-master reports that during the year 1895, 417 vessels, with a total of 601,707 registered tons, entered the sub-port of Tacoma. The inward cargo tonnage was 102,516 tons. The registered tonnage of vessels leaving the port amounted to 551,506, and the cargo tonnage is reported as 652,187. This does not include the local vessels which ply up and down Puget Sound.

Trade and Commerce.

By referring to Annex B the exports and imports for the past two years will be seen. Among the other articles in the export table are included chiefly the articles to Chinese and Japanese ports, consisting of tinned meats and fruits, butterine, beer, ginseng, oil and machinery, a large part of the latter being electrical appliances.

The bulk of the merchandise landed here from oriental ports comes through in bond for immediate shipment to eastern points, this port receiving no credit for such shipments, and consequently no estimate can be made of them, as the duty on such merchandise is paid at the port of destination.

Exports and imports.

The exports show a decrease of 178,735*l*., as compared with 1894, while the imports show the exceedingly large increase of 893,738*l*. The chief decline in exports has been in the wheat and tinned fish shipments which have fallen off about one-half; while there has been an increase in the flour, timber and cotton, the timber shipments having more than doubled. In regard to the wheat shipments there should be, in reality, a further deduction made, as several of the vessels clearing from this port loaded a portion of their cargoes at the sub-port of Seattle : probably about 400,000 bushels being taken on board there. The markets for timber in Cape Colony and the settlements in South Africa, particularly in British and Portuguese territory, are rapidly increasing, six cargoes having gone to that country during the year. Two cargoes of flour have left during this period for Europe, one going to London direct: the remaining shipments have been made to oriental ports.

Commenting on the imports it may be remarked that the increase is largely due to large shipments of non-dutiable articles from oriental ports, the principal being tea, of which the quantity imported has almost doubled, and silk. The amount of ore landed here has increased very largely, as have also the imports of grain bags. Among the articles paying duty there appears to be no very large increase over the year 1894, with the possible exception of fresh fish, very large consignments of which have been landed for trans-shipment to eastern markets—chiefly as a result of the favourable arrangements made between the shippers and the Northern Pacific Railroad. The fish, after being re-packed in boxes filled with ice, are placed in refrigerator vans, attached to the passenger trains, and thus reach their destination in the Eastern States on passenger time. No account is taken in Annex B of the articles landed in bond, nor of the domestic trade, the foreign trade alone being represented.

The harbour-master's statement shows that during the year 1895 there was 3,385,292 bushels of wheat shipped from this port of the approximate value of 301,590*l*. (1,507,953 dol.); there were 295,938 barrels of flour, valued approximately at 141,601*l*. (708,008 dol.); the timber shipped was over 94,000,000 feet, with a value of about 174,040*l*. (870,200 dol.); the coal shipments amounted to

319,015 tons, having an estimated value of 194,785*l.* (973,928 dol.). The value of the merchandise to China and Japan, exclusive of flour, is estimated at 88,314*l.* (441,574 dol.), and that to British Columbia at 26,345*l.* (131,725 dol.); making a total of 926,675*l.* (4,633,389 dol.). His statement further shows that there were 23 cargoes of oriental merchandise imported hither, to which is assigned a value of 3,542,326*l.* (17,711,631 dol.). This value is entirely too high; a very liberal estimate would make an average of 200,000*l.* (1,000,000 dol.) a month. Large quantities of local merchandise pass over the wharves, of which no account is taken.

Timber. The timber trade tributary to Tacoma is represented by 11 saw and shingle mills, which were in operation during the year 1895. The two largest mills are those of the St. Paul and Tacoma Lumber Company and the Tacoma Mill Company. These mills have employed night shifts also during a part of this time. The output of these mills was 122,280,800 feet of timber, 24,986,300 feet of lath, and 120,250,000 shingles. 140 cargoes to various points, of which 37 were foreign, carried away of this amount 91,082,000 feet of timber and 21,899,000 feet of lath, the estimated value being 172,364*l.* (861,820 dol.). Comparing these figures with those of 1894, there is a marked improvement in the cargo shipments over those of that year, which were valued at 106,978*l.* The rail shipments during 1895 amounted to 1,077 trucks of timber and 474 trucks of lath, as compared with 1,180 trucks of timber and 895 trucks of shingles in the preceding year.

Dry dock. The Puget Sound Dry Dock Company, with its floating dock at Quartermaster Harbour, has had 48 vessels, aggregating 36,973 tons, in dock during the year; being 27 steamships, with 17,662 tons gross register, and 21 sailing vessels, with 19,311 tons net register. This dock shows an increase in business over the past year, the company having undertaken several large contracts, not only for the United States Government, which has had five of its steamers docked for extensive repairs, but also for our own and the Norwegian Governments. The company has employed an average of 30 men all the year round, including the artisans working in its foundry and machine shops in this town.

Tacoma smelter. The Tacoma Smelting and Refining Company produced during the year 38,300 bars of bullion, weighing 4,000,000 lbs. Of this, 17,700 ozs. were gold, 38,600 ozs. were silver, 3,994,000 lbs. lead, and about 200,000 lbs. copper; the total value being 150,000*l.* (750,000 dol.). The average silver quotation for the year was 2*s.* 6*d.* (65⅓ c.). The gross weight of ore received during the year was over 34,000,000 lbs., of which about 20,000 ozs. were gold, 350,000 ozs. silver, and 5,000,000 lbs. lead. The ore purchased during the year by the company from territory within the United States, including Alaska, was over 16,000,000 lbs., of which over 10,000 ozs. were gold, 20,000 ozs. silver, and 3,000,000 lbs. lead. From territory outside of the United States over 16,000,000 lbs. were purchased, of which about 7,000 ozs. were gold, 17,000 ozs. silver, and 1,500,000 lbs. lead. Of these amounts the State of Washington produced over 2,000,000 lbs., consisting of about 400 ozs. of gold, 30,000 ozs. of silver, and almost 400,000 lbs. of lead. This is a very gratifying return for the State of Washington. The company has employed an average of 65 men, with a pay roll of over 1,000*l.* a month.

By referring to Annex C it will be noticed that the exports to Queenstown for orders are shown by themselves, Great Britain being credited with the amount actually due her. A large decrease in exports will be noticed in the cases of Great Britain, Hong-Kong, and Mexico, while the trade with China, Australia, and Chile has increased very materially. Europe still claims the bulk of the wheat trade, while Australia imports the largest amount of timber, closely followed, however, by Portuguese South Africa and Chile. The increase in the trade with China is noticeable chiefly in flour, machinery, and iron manufactures. Turning to the imports, the greater portion of the trade appears to have been with China, Japan, and Canada, and it must be assumed that the imports from Canada are also mainly oriental goods brought over by the Canadian Pacific steamships and re-shipped to this port. The import trade with Europe and other countries is quite insignificant, showing perhaps a decrease rather than an increase. The imports from India have consisted mostly in jute for the manufacture of grain bags.

Commercial relations with other countries.

The Northern Pacific Steamship Company, which operates a line of British ships between Tacoma, Japan, and Hong-Kong, has increased its number of sailings, the total arrivals being 18 in 1895, as against 15 during the previous year. Its fleet consisted of four steamships, while others of large tonnage were chartered for the eastward voyage only, bringing full cargoes from the Orient and taking timber hence to South African ports. Besides these steamers the general agents, Messrs. Dodwell, Carlill, and Co., loaded in connection with the Northern Pacific Railroad four large British sailing vessels, which brought, all told, 11,865,387 lbs. of Japan tea, besides a large quantity of matting, curios, and other cargo for United States and Canadian towns. This company has now four regular steamships in service, the "Tacoma," "Victoria," "Olympia," and "Columbia," all of which have first-class accommodation for saloon and steerage passengers. In addition to these it is quite likely that there will be some extra steamships this coming year, as the service the company is instituting will have a sailing every 18 days. The low rates of freight on merchandise from the Orient that prevailed during the summer induced increased tonnage across the Pacific, and the same conditions will probably prevail during 1896. There has been a steady increase in the cotton and timber shipments by these steamships, the cotton coming from Alabama, Mississippi, and Texas is brought to this port by the Northern Pacific Railway; timber, on the contrary, being sawn at the mills here. The principal demand is for matched (tongued and grooved) flooring, but orders from Japan for long lengths of large dimensions have recently been received by the mills, and it is quite likely that business in this material will increase. There has been an increase also in the

Trade with China and Japan.

export of electrical and other machinery, as well as of condensed milk and other sundries. In the past year flour shows a slight decrease owing, in a great measure, to the heavy stocks held in Hong-Kong and the lessened demand in Japan consequent upon the closing of the Chino-Japanese war.

Population and Industries.

Population. Tacoma has an estimated population of about 45,000, and at the last registration there were 6,400 names recorded having legal votes, still showing a decrease from the previous year.

Births. There were 585 births reported, 295 being males and 290 females.

Deaths. The total number of deaths, including 13 premature births, occurring during the past year was 318, 170 males and 148 females. Of these, 151 were single persons, 106 married, 51 widowers or widows, and 10 unknown; 192 were natives of the United States, 91 foreign born, and 35 of unknown nationality.

Diseases. The diseases which caused the greatest number of deaths were:—Heart disease 28, Bright's disease 15, consumption 10, bronchitis 9, meningitis 8. The Health Officer states that there were no cases of diphtheria or croup, but he received 95 reports of other contagious or infectious diseases, in such form, however, that no satisfactory data can be furnished. There were no instances of epidemic diseases during the year.

Financial condition. During the year the financial conditions of affairs have remained about the same. The inability to realise securities, and the generally depressed state of affairs caused three or four banks to close their doors, thus reducing the number now doing business in the town. This may have a beneficial effect, as the large number trying to do business was quite in excess of commercial requirements. Some business houses have failed entirely, while others have been placed in the hands of receivers to try to pull through, with more or less prospect of success. It is expected that the financial condition of the town and its municipal affairs, which have been lately investigated by a body of business men, will now be established on a firmer basis, and good men, qualified for their offices, will receive appointments.

Shipping and Navigation.

The following table shows the number and nationalities of vessels which entered and cleared during the last year:—

PORTLAND.

Annex A.—RETURN of all Shipping at the Port of Tacoma during the Year 1895.

ENTERED.

Nationality.	Sailing. Number of Vessels.	Sailing. Tons.	Steam. Number of Vessels.	Steam. Tons.	Total. Number of Vessels.	Total. Tons.
British	25	46,421	35	40,963	60	87,384
American	5	5,061	25	19,492	30	24,553
German	2	3,489	...	...	2	3,489
Chilian	1	528	...	...	1	528
Total	33	55,499	60	60,455	93	115,954
,, for the year preceding	30	58,673	30	31,146	60	89,819

CLEARED.

Nationality.	Sailing. Number of Vessels.	Sailing. Tons.	Steam. Number of Vessels.	Steam. Tons.	Total. Number of Vessels.	Total. Tons.
British	24	45,207	32	36,903	56	82,110
American	20	19,712	12	14,405	32	34,117
German	2	3,090	...	...	2	3,090
Chilian	2	1,457	...	...	2	1,457
Norwegian	...	...	1	1,988	1	1,988
Total	48	69,446	45	55,303	93	124,769
,, for the year preceding	58	93,345	37	45,784	95	139,129

Trade and Commerce.

The following tables show the exports and imports for the past two years:—

Annex B.—RETURN of Principal Articles of Export from Tacoma during the Years 1895-94.

Articles.		1895. Quantity.	1895. Value.	1894. Quantity.	1894. Value.
			£		£
Wheat	Bushels	2,045,627	197,078	4,083,045	390,457
Flour	Barrels	301,657	143,786	285,496	139,466
Timber	M. feet	34,574	62,688	15,713	27,974
Cotton	...	...	34,564	...	...
Milk, condensed	...	...	8,915	...	...
Fish, tinned	Lbs.	40,800	500	...	52,950
Other articles	...	...	41,354	...	66,793
Total	...	...	488,885	...	667,640

UNITED STATES.

RETURN of Principal Articles of Import to Tacoma during the Years 1895-94.

Articles.		1895.		1894.	
		Quantity.	Value.	Quantity.	Value.
			£		£
Free—					
Tea	Lbs.	1,000,308	18,734	509,818	11,030
Silk, raw	,,	2,188,430	874,917	...	...
Jute	,,	411,500	2,631	1,484,000	9,151
Ore	...	...	15,027	...	1,538
Grain bags	M. lbs.	1,228	798	...	...
Household effects	...	...	765	...	1,143
Other articles	...	...	16,441	...	9,872
Total	...	...	930,078	...	32,734
Dutiable—					
Sugar	M. lbs.	10,290	44,537	6,309	41,345
Rice	,,	1,105	3,386	602	2.092
Cement	,,	6,178	3,882	10,557	5,401
Fish, fresh	,,	602	3,435	...	...
Coal	Tons	1,090	768	1,140	653
Ore	...	...	13,897	...	...
Other articles	...	...	24,619	...	48,639
Total	...	...	94,524	...	98,130
,, free and dutiable	...	...	1,024,602	...	130,864

NOTE.—Exchange has been figured at 5 dol. to the 1*l*.

The following table shows the value of all exports and imports:—

Annex C.—TABLE showing Total Value of all Articles Exported from and Imported to Tacoma to and from Foreign Countries during the Years 1895-94.

Country.	Exports.		Imports.	
	1895.	1894.	1895.	1894.
	£	£	£	£
Great Britain	36,508	375,439	4,478	5,657
Queenstown, for orders	191,276	..	..	..
Hong-Kong	97,683	105,611	..	..
Japan	76,126	74,508	688,780	14,468
China	24,269	2,629	285,421	99,119
Australia	21,601	11,642	..	..
Africa, Portuguese	16,815	3,901	..	..
Africa, British	3,086	..	..	..
Chile	10,235	..	..	..
Mexico	4,281	7,955	..	..
Canada	3,451	2,257	37,125	7,262
Peru	1,784	..	..	..
Hawaiian Islands	1,497	..	..	733
India	..	..	8,599	3,114
Other countries	273	93,698	199	511
Total	488,885	677,640	1,024,602	130,864

NOTE.—The domestic trade and goods for immediate transportation are not included in this table.

SEATTLE.

Mr. Vice-Consul Alexander reports as follows:—

This town, which maintains its position as the business town of the State, is admirably situated in King County, on the east side of Puget Sound, having connection with three transcontinental railway lines, one of which, the Great Northern, makes its tidewater terminus here. In addition there are other smaller local railways. The town has made no very perceptible growth during the year 1895, although several new industries have commenced operations and improvements for the benefit of the public, which have long been in contemplation, are now in progress.

General remarks.

Shipping and Navigation.

By referring to Annex A at the end of this report it will be seen that there was an increase by 2 in the total number of vessels which entered this port over the year 1894, the registered tonnage remaining almost the same. This annex also shows an increase by 4 in the number of British vessels entering, and in their tonnage of 4,000 tons. In turning to the clearances for the same period there is found a falling-off of 12 vessels, the tonnage remaining comparatively unchanged. A marked improvement is shown in the number of British vessels clearing, which has increased by 12, and their tonnage by 15,227 tons.

Trade and Commerce.

By referring to Annex B the exports and imports for the last 2 years will be seen, from which it may be noticed that the exports are many times larger than in 1894, showing an increase of 107,876*l*., while the imports have declined 9,737*l*. The increase in the exports is due to grain cargoes, representing a valuation of 87,887*l*. over those of the preceding year. A large quantity of tinned salmon was also exported. Referring to the imports, the most noticeable feature is the great decline in oriental merchandise, more especially in sugar. This is to be accounted for by the fact that the oriental steamships land the bulk of the sugar at Tacoma. The Northern Pacific Steamship Company giving a through rate from oriental ports to Tacoma, Seattle, and Portland at the same figure, and the sugar being consequently billed for the most part to Tacoma, as the terminus of their steamship line, pays duty there and is distributed from that point to its destination. The imports from European countries have been chiefly tin-plates, cement (both Portland and German), and soda-ash.

While the town has no very large cargo mills, there are, tributary to this port, the saw-mill situated at Ballard and other mills, the principal of which is the mill belonging to the Port

Timber.

Blakeley Mill Company situated at this place. This mill has sawn up during the past year a larger amount of timber than any mill in the State, the total amount being aggregated at 102,426,000 feet, of which 68,740,800 feet were carried to foreign ports, and 37,685,000 feet to domestic ports. The outlook for business during the coming year is very favourable, large orders having already been received.

Relations with other countries. By referring to Annex C, and comparing the years 1895 and 1894, it will be seen that the bulk of the export trade, consisting of wheat, still goes to Great Britain. The trade with Australia, mostly consisting of timber, has declined, but the shipments to Portuguese South Africa show an encouraging extension. A new field has, towards the latter part of the year, appeared in San Salvador, and a steamship is now making monthly trips to the Central American countries carrying general merchandise, chiefly breadstuffs and timber. While the total amount of imports has appreciably diminished it is gratifying to observe that there has been a large increase in the trade with Great Britain and Canada, the countries mainly suffering from the decline being China and Japan. These tables take no account of the domestic trade which is carried on at this port, and of which it is impossible to give an estimate, vessels leaving here not only for the Puget Sound Country but also for Alaska.

Population and Industry.

Population. The population of Seattle has probably decreased somewhat since last year, being between 50,000 and 55,000.

Health. Births and deaths. There were 462 birth reports, of which 205 were males and 257 females. There were 50 still-births reported. The total number of deaths from all causes during the year was 425, as against 467 in 1894. Of these 265 were males and 160 females.

Diseases. The causes of death are classified as follows:—Zymotic, 85; constitutional, 74; developmental, 46; local, 163; accidental, 50; unclassed, 7. There were no cases of small-pox, but 264 of scarlatina, with 7 deaths. 110 of measles, with no deaths. 12 of diphtheria, with 1 death. 7 of membranous croup, with 4 deaths. And 147 of typhoid fever, with 24 deaths.

Climate. The mean annual temperature for the Seattle station has been 51·2 degrees, the highest being 90 degrees on June 27, and the lowest 27 degrees on December 17. The total precipitation for the year was 29·69 inches. The mean maximum temperature for the year was 58·1, and the mean minimum 44·3. For the same period the mean monthly rainfall was 2·47. There was during the year 18 inches of snow.

Industry. Fisheries. This town may be considered the headquarters of the fishing industry on Puget Sound, in the neighbourhood, 30 vessels being employed in the halibut fishing alone during the season. The Deputy State Fish Commissioner reports that there was shipped from Seattle in 1895 the following:—Salmon, fresh,

5,210,000 lbs., smoked 60,000 lbs., salted in barrels 10,000 lbs.; halibut fresh, 15,100,000 lbs., smoked 100,000 lbs.; small fish, soles, cod, smelt, trout, &c., 244,000 lbs.; oysters, 4,975 sacks; shrimps, 2,890 lbs.; with large quantities of other shell fish. In addition to this there were put up at the Seattle cannery 60,000 case of tinned salmon, aggregating almost 3,000,000 lbs., which were all shipped to one house in the east.

Iron and steel manufactures. The various industries mentioned in previous reports have been carrying on operations with more or less success during the year; though it is doubtful if any marked progress has been made. The greatest improvement has been in shipbuilding, due, in a measure, to the impetus given by the United States Government having awarded a contract for the construction of a torpedo boat to a Seattle firm, the contract price being 33,400*l*. (671,000 dol.). This firm has also done extensive repairs for several other Government vessels during the same period.

Post-office. The post-office receipts during the year amounted to 16,845*l*. (84,230 dol.), of which 16,005*l*. (80,027 dol.) was derived from the sale of stamps, and 840*l*. (4,200 dol.) from box rents. The salaries paid amounted to 9,866*l*. (49,329 dol.), and the rent of office and incidentals to 983*l*. (4,814 dol.).

Financial condition. The bank clearings during the year 1895, amounting to 5,136,231*l*. (25,691,156 dol.), show a decrease from those of the preceding year of 257,754*l*. (1,289,769 dol.). The last 6 months of the year, however, present a decided improvement as compared with 1894, the increase being 186,523*l*. (932,627 dol.).

Business failures. There are reported 34 business failures during the year, and 1 bank failure. The year has been, from a business point of view, most depressed, and no fixed improvement in the condition of affairs can be looked for in under 2 years.

United States Land Office. The United States Land Office for the Seattle district, comprising the nine north-westerly counties of the State, reports the total purchase price received for lands during the year as 2,661*l*. (13,306 dol.); 2,327·79 acres in 18 timber land entries realising 1,163*l*. (5,818 dol.); 3,142·04 acres in 27 commuted homesteads realising 805*l*. (4,008 dol.); 1,179·84 acres in 9 pre-emptions realising 299*l*. (1,488 dol.); private and special land sales realising 324*l*. (1,622 dol.); and 118,33 acres in 3 mineral land entries realising 70*l*. (350 dol.). In addition to these amounts 2,046*l*. (10,203 dol.) were received for fees, commissions, &c.

Harbour master's report. The harbour-master reports that, during the year 1895, 302 vessels, of which 187 were steam and 115 sailing, and having a registered tonnage of 314,242 tons, visited the sub-port of Seattle. The merchandise received from Puget Sound ports amounted to 44,980 tons, and from outside ports to 42,884 tons; that shipped coastwise to 24,637 tons, to local ports 51,716 tons, and to foreign ports 41,000 tons. Of coal, 181,501 tons were shipped coastwise, and of timber, 18,948,000 feet, while 11,241 tons of wheat, and 17,323 cases of salmon went to foreign ports. Of fresh fish, 4,808,000 lbs. were landed, not including that used at the cannery, besides 6,775 seal skins. The dues at this port amounted to 262*l*. (1,306 dol.), and the expenses to 184*l*. (917 dol.).

(2178)

UNITED STATES.

Shipping and Navigation.

The following table shows the number and nationalities of vessels which entered and cleared during the past year:—

Annex A.—RETURN of all Shipping at the Port of Seattle during the Year 1895.

ENTERED.

Nationality.	Sailing. Number of Vessels.	Sailing. Tons.	Steam. Number of Vessels.	Steam. Tons.	Total. Number of Vessels.	Total. Tons.
British	8	12,631	6	2,013	14	14,644
American	22	4,299	81	97,486	103	101,785
German	1	1,437	...	...	1	1,437
Norwegian	...	...	1	840	1	840
Total	31	18,367	88	100,339	119	118,706
,, for the year preceding	26	13,472	91	105,256	117	118,728

CLEARED.

Nationality.	Sailing. Number of Vessels.	Sailing. Tons.	Steam. Number of Vessels.	Steam. Tons.	Total. Number of Vessels.	Total. Tons.
British	10	18,899	7	2,075	17	20,974
American	36	12,012	55	19,808	91	31,820
German	1	1,836	...	...	1	1,836
Norwegian	...	...	2	1,680	2	1,680
Chilian	1	915	...	...	1	915
Total	48	33,662	64	23,563	112	57,225
,, for the year preceding	37	23,397	87	33,984	124	57,381

NOTE.—The entrances and clearances of American vessels do not include the domestic trade.

Trade and Commerce.

The following tables show the exports and imports for the past two years:—

Annex B.—RETURN of Principal Articles of Export from Seattle during the Years 1895–94.

Articles.		1895. Quantity.	1895. Value.	1894. Quantity.	1894. Value.
			£		£
Timber	Feet	9,644,600	19,822	12,763,600	22,900
Wheat	Bushels	1,050,096	106,887	178,330	19,000
Fish (salmon)	Cases	17,323	11,870	...	...
Other articles	...	...	12,897	...	1,700
Total	...	...	151,476	...	43,600

PORTLAND.

RETURN of Principal Articles of Import to Seattle during the Years 1895–94.

Articles.		1895. Quantity.	1895. Value.	1894. Quantity.	1894. Value.
			£		£
Free—					
Tin-plates	Lbs.	112,000	227	...	...
Salt	,,	1,594,000	975	...	...
Other articles		...	2,978	...	1,205
Total		...	4,180	...	1,205
Dutiable—					
Rice	Lbs.	739,000	1,693	1,378,400	3,956
Sugar	,,	425,000	2,907	2,118,000	14,974
Tin-plates	,,	212,000	986	...	...
Cement		...	1,989	...	1,843
Coal	Tons	624	416	686	492
Liquors		...	2,790	...	1,300
Fish		...	377	...	...
Other articles		...	3,971	...	2,301
Total		...	15,129	...	24,866
,, free and dutiable		...	19,309	...	26,071

NOTE.—Exchange has been figured at 5 dol. to the 1*l*.

The following table shows the value of all exports and imports:—

Annex C.—TABLE showing Total Value of all Articles Exported from and Imported to Seattle from and to Foreign Countries during the Years 1895–94.

Country.	Exports. 1895.	Exports. 1894.	Imports. 1895.	Imports. 1894.
	£	£	£	£
Great Britain	120,468	22,130	7,297	2,359
Canada	3,522	..	7,030	2,027
Australia	4,612	8,333	..	..
China	4,268	4,633	..	..
Chile	974	2,594	..	..
Africa (Portuguese)	3,865	1,689	..	..
Mexico	731	..	..	..
Hawaiian Islands	1,752	1,067	..	..
San Salvador	9,835	..	..	..
Guatemala	1,449	..	..	..
Viâ oriental steamships	..	..	4,165	18,273
Other countries	..	3,154	817	13,412
Total	151,476	43,600	19,309	26,071

UNITED STATES.

Port Townsend.

Mr. Vice-Consul Klöcker reports as follows:—

Lumber trade. The improvement indicated in last report has been fully maintained both in domestic and foreign trades, the extent of which can be seen by following figures:—

	Quantity.	
	Domestic.	Foreign.
	Feet.	Feet.
1895	246,929,909	147,140,924
1894	197,640,000	86,147,790
Increase	48,289,909	60,993,134

This increase in foreign shipments was materially assisted by building of railways and development of gold-mining in South Africa, also the improved demand in Australia and West Coast of South America. China has also become an active buyer of Puget Sound lumber, principally large-sized lumber, and it is reported that orders are in the market for large quantities of lumber required for railroad and bridge building in that country. The general outlook for lumber business is considered brighter than it has been at any time during the past 5 years.

Prices advanced. The prices for lumber have been advanced, which is mainly due to the fact that all the mills on the Pacific coast, as well as in British Columbia, are reported to have formed a combine to uphold prices and limit the output. This year has seen an innovation in the lumber-carrying business, *i.e.*, employment of steamers. It has always been claimed that facilities at various mills for giving requisite dispatch in loading steamers with lumber precluded them from the trade, but experience with steamers loaded seems to have been fairly satisfactory.

Steamers loaded were for the following destinations:—South Africa, 11 cargoes; South America, 1 cargo; Buenos Ayres, 1 cargo.

Shipping and freight. Lumber freights have been improved all round as will be seen from annexed list of rates:—

	Per 1,000 feet.	
	Highest.	Lowest.
	£ s. d.	£ s. d.
Sydney, N.S.W...	1 18 6	1 10 0
Melbourne, Port Pirie, and Adelaide	2 3 6	1 18 9
Brisbane, Freemantle	2 5 0	2 2 6
China, Shanghai	2 10 0	2 5 0
Africa, Delagoa Bay	3 15 0	3 2 6
West Coast South America	2 7 6	1 17 6
United Kingdom	3 10 0	3 3 9

The rates as quoted above are for sailing ships, and steamers have received from 5s. to 7s. 6d. in addition per 1,000 feet.

The iron shipbuilding plant at Everett is still closed down. A foundry and engineering company in Seattle are erecting a plant for the construction of small steam vessels, and have secured contract to build for United States Government a torpedo-boat and steam-tug for revenue service. *Shipbuilding.*

As a result of improved lumber freights there is considerable activity in building of large 4-masted schooners; 3 vessels, each of 1,000,000 feet capacity, were launched during the year, and a similar number are now being built. Two small wooden revenue steamers, with speed of 16 knots, are building at this port, and are to be used in suppressing of smuggling of opium and Chinamen from British Columbia.

It is reported that another steamship line for China and Japan will be organised during the summer, having Seattle as headquarters, and running in conjunction with the Great Northern Railroad. *Steamship lines.*

Steamer service with Puget Sound, Mexican, and Central American ports has been established by a corporation of Seattle merchants and shippers. The indications are favourable for the success of this venture, which it is intended to conduct with foreign-built and operated steamers.

The rush to the gold fields of Yukon, Alaska, still continues, steamers having repeatedly to refuse freight and passengers. The opposition line is still maintained, and additional boats are being prepared for this season's service.

A pilot chart of the North Pacific Ocean is issued monthly, and the attention of shipmasters is earnestly called to the desirability of their furnishing all the data possible of any obstructions, floating logs, derelicts, &c., in order that its efficiency may be maintained. *Hydrographic Office.*

An accident in fitting caisson delayed completion of the United States naval dry dock at Port Orchard last year, but it is now reported to be ready for use. *Dry dock.*

The contract for the lightship to be placed on Umatilla Reef has been let to a firm at Portland, Oregon, and the vessel is to be on station by September next. *Lightship and lighthouses.*

A lighthouse with large fog-bell has also been built and taken in use on Marrowstone Point.

The new hospital for the United States Marine Hospital Service has been finished, and is a great improvement over the old building, being fitted with all modern conveniences and very pleasantly situated. *Marine Hospital.*

Importations for the year were very light. Two cargoes are listed from Hamburg which will be the first shipments made direct from Hamburg to Puget Sound. Prices are low, owing to limited demand and extensive stocks held, both by dealers and importers. *Cement.*

The nail works and paper mills at Everett are reported to be running full time, the latter shipping large quantities of paper to *Manufactures.*

54 UNITED STATES.

Paper. Australia, which is sent viâ Canadian Pacific Australian steamers, running from Vancouver, B.C.

Nails. The nail works at this place have again resumed operations, and it is claimed are making nails to be shipped to China.

Fur sealing. The sealing business last year was rather less than in 1894, the sealers claiming that they are at a disadvantage without the use of firearms, the new regulations stipulating that all seals must be speared.

Fishing. The fishing industry is increasing every year, and several new canneries have been established at different points on Puget Sound. Large quantities of fresh fish have also been imported from Alaska for the Puget Sound market as well as to be sent east, even as far as New York and Boston, special cars for that purpose going, with the fast passenger trains from Puget Sound, to New York, in 5 days.

Disasters. The year has been a very fatal one for British shipping, several vessels having been lost bound for this port, as follows:—

British ship "Janet Cowan," 2,498 tons, official No. 93,219, stranded on Vancouver Island and became a total wreck.

British ship "Nineveh," 1,174 tons, official No. 48,854, bound from British Columbia to Australia with lumber, sprung a leak, was abandoned, and became a total wreck.

British steamer "Strathnevis," 2,303 tons, official No. 102,672, was disabled in Pacific Ocean, bound to China, from Puget Sound, was towed into Port Townsend with loss of propeller after drifting around for about a month and a half.

Import. The import trade shows a decrease of 73,286*l.* as compared with last year.

Export. The export trade shows an increase of 171,457*l.* as compared with last year.

Health. The health of the city has been good, with no infectious or contagious diseases.

I append the several annexes, marked A, B, and C, to show the commerce and trade in this district.

Annex A.—RETURN of all Shipping at the Port of Port Townsend during the Year 1895.

ENTERED.

Nationality.	Sailing. Number of Vessels.	Sailing. Tons.	Steam. Number of Vessels.	Steam. Tons.	Total. Number of Vessels.	Total. Tons.
British	25	39,472	25	13,077	50	52,549
American	75	40,177	1,368	666,195	1,443	706,372
Norwegian	3	3,302	3	6,181	6	9,483
Chilian	14	13,694	...	...	14	13,694
German	2	3,125	...	...	2	3,125
Nicaraguan	2	1,132	...	...	2	1,132
Italian	1	1,354	...	...	1	1,354
Hawaiian	4	6,373	...	...	4	6,373
Total	126	108,629	1,396	685,453	1,522	794,082
,, for the year preceding	83	76,780	860	499,565	943	576,345

PORTLAND.

CLEARED.

Nationality.	Sailing. Number of Vessels.	Sailing. Tons.	Steam. Number of Vessels.	Steam. Tons.	Total. Number of Vessels.	Total. Tons.
British	18	23,473	24	10,621	42	34,094
American	89	68,924	1,416	760,805	1,505	829,729
Norwegian	3	3,302	2	4,193	5	7,495
Chilian	14	13,694	...	...	14	13,694
German	1	1,702	...	...	1	1,702
Nicaraguan	3	2,387	...	...	3	2,387
Italian	1	1,354	...	...	1	1,354
Hawaiian	5	7,152	...	...	5	7,152
Total	134	121,988	1,442	775,619	1,576	897,607
,, for the year preceding	96	76,222	845	480,114	941	556,336

Annex B.—RETURN of Principal Articles of Export from Port Townsend during the Years 1895-94.

Articles.	1895. Quantity.	1895. Value.	1894. Quantity.	1894. Value.
	Feet.	£	Feet.	£
Flour	..	..	..	1,516
Timber	144,409,000	180,731	55,035,234	113,426
Iron and manufactures of iron	..	40,640	..	12,300
Oils	..	7,634	..	8,200
Furs and hides	..	41,620	..	43,350
Provisions, meats	..	28,124	..	25,100
Cattle	..	24,060	..	19,100
Liquors and wines	..	4,165	..	2,275
Wool and manufactures of wool	..	11,553	..	6,660
Cotton	..	..	..	24,300
Fish	..	5,013	..	400
Tinned fruits and vegetables	..	7,312	..	2,900
Other articles	..	125,626	..	45,491
Total	..	476,478	..	305,021

UNITED STATES.

RETURN of Principal Articles of Import to Port Townsend during the Years 1895-94.

Articles.	Value. 1895.	Value. 1894.
	£	£
Cement	554	1,238
Coal	3,117	216
Iron and manufactures of iron	412	3,153
Steel wire rods	941	5,892
Tin-plates	115	2,495
Lead and ore	17,405	2,100
Zinc	..	150
Jute	..	1,470
Sugar	1,724	1,870
Rice	5,041	22,800
Tea	5,498	4,969
Silk, raw	1,532	2,490
Fish	16,630	78,000
Other articles	10,167	9,579
Total	63,136	136,422

Annex C.—TABLE showing Total Value of all Articles Exported from and Imported to Port Townsend from and to Foreign Countries during the Years 1895-94.

Country.	Export 1895.	Export 1894.	Import 1895.	Import 1894.
	£	£	£	£
Great Britain	12,136	1,567	248	3,846
British colonies and Canada	300,674	166,723	47,490	103,785
Australia	44,580	37,055	..	..
Belgium	..	1,005	..	5,300
Hawaiian Islands	26,480	24,161	499	4,870
Chile	31,510	29,680	..	..
China	4,612	12,837	5,633	11,132
Peru	4,517	9,100	..	..
Mexico	1,651	1,325	..	..
Japan	..	900	1,898	2,156
Africa	35,454	8,311	..	..
Germany	..	3,020	1,099	280
India	134	..	4,102	2,484
Netherlands	1,430	2,133	..	..
Guatemala	2,660	2,723	..	..
New Caledonia	6,610	..	..	..
Argentine Republic	..	2,100	..	..
Fiji Islands	3,510	2,320	..	480
Other countries	520	61	2,167	2,089
Total	476,478	305,021	63,136	136,422

(75 5 | 96—H & S 2178)

FOREIGN OFFICE.
1896.
ANNUAL SERIES.

No. 1750.

DIPLOMATIC AND CONSULAR REPORTS ON TRADE AND FINANCE.

UNITED STATES.

REPORT FOR THE YEAR 1895

ON THE

TRADE AND AGRICULTURE OF THE CONSULAR DISTRICT OF SAN FRANCISCO.

REFERENCE TO PREVIOUS REPORT, Annual Series No. 1576.

Presented to both Houses of Parliament by Command of Her Majesty,
JUNE, 1896.

LONDON:
PRINTED FOR HER MAJESTY'S STATIONERY OFFICE,
BY HARRISON AND SONS, ST. MARTIN'S LANE,
PRINTERS IN ORDINARY TO HER MAJESTY.

And to be purchased, either directly or through any Bookseller, from
EYRE & SPOTTISWOODE, EAST HARDING STREET, FLEET STREET, E.C., and
32, ABINGDON STREET, WESTMINSTER, S.W.; or
JOHN MENZIES & Co., 12, HANOVER STREET, EDINBURGH, and
90, WEST NILE STREET, GLASGOW; or
HODGES, FIGGIS, & Co., Limited, 104, GRAFTON STREET, DUBLIN.

1896.

[C. 7919—118.] *Price Threepence.*

New Series of Reports.

Reports of the Annual Series have been issued from Her Majesty's Diplomatic and Consular Officers at the following places, and may be obtained from the sources indicated on the title-page:—

No.		Price.	No.		Price.
1628.	Stettin	2½d.	1689.	Suakin	1d.
1629.	Porto Rico	1d.	1690.	Pernambuco	1d.
1630.	Rotterdam	½d.	1691.	Guatemala	1½d.
1631.	Alexandria	1½d.	1692.	Guayaquil	1d.
1632.	Tokio	2½d.	1693.	Wenchow	1d.
1633.	Tangier	1½d.	1694.	Piræus	3d.
1634.	Oporto	1½d.	1695.	Tokio	3d.
1635.	St. Petersburg	4d.	1696.	Marseilles	1d.
1636.	Dantzig	2d.	1697.	Manila	1d.
1637.	Macao	1d.	1698.	Jerusalem	1d.
1638.	Hiogo and Osaka	6d.	1699.	Cherbourg	2d.
1639.	Naples	1½d.	1700.	Leghorn	1½d.
1640.	Kiungchow	½d.	1701.	Boston	1½d.
1641.	Rome	1½d.	1702.	Kiungchow	1d.
1642.	Beira	½d.	1703.	Naples	2½d.
1643.	St. Jago de Cuba	4½d.	1704.	Stockholm	2d.
1644.	Christiania	6d.	1705.	Corunna	2d.
1645.	Lisbon	1½d.	1706.	Rio de Janeiro	2½d.
1646.	Brussels	½d.	1707.	San José	1d.
1647.	Vera Cruz	½d.	1708.	Paramaribo	2d.
1648.	Tunis	1d.	1709.	Brest	1½d.
1649.	Antwerp	1d.	1710.	Montevideo	½d.
1650.	Tokio	1d.	1711.	Charleston	2½d.
1651.	Honolulu	½d.	1712.	Baltimore	1d.
1652.	Stettin	1½d.	1713.	Tripoli	1d.
1653.	Bangkok	1d.	1714.	Callao	½d.
1654.	Batoum	1½d.	1715.	Ningpo	1d.
1655.	Mexico	9½d.	1716.	Dunkirk	1½d.
1656.	Odessa	1½d.	1717.	Batoum	2d.
1657.	Réunion	1d.	1718.	Hankow	1½d.
1658.	Tokio	1½d.	1719.	Foochow	3½d.
1659.	Maranham	1d.	1720.	Syra	½d.
1660.	Copenhagen	1d.	1721.	Panama	1d.
1661.	Berlin	1½d.	1722.	Batavia	1½d.
1662.	Teheran	2½d.	1723.	Genoa	3d.
1663.	Salonica	1½d.	1724.	Cagliari	2½d.
1664.	Manila	½d.	1725.	Chicago	7½d.
1665.	Florence	5½d.	1726.	Trieste	1d.
1666.	Dakar	½d.	1727.	Hakodate	1d.
1667.	Havre	2d.	1728.	Mannheim	1d.
1668.	Rouen	2d.	1729.	Panama	1d.
1669.	Corfu	½d.	1730.	Caracas	1d.
1670.	Calais	1d.	1731.	Riga	6½d.
1671.	Tehran	1½d.	1732.	Tokio	1½d.
1672.	Barcelona	2d.	1733.	Tainan	1d.
1673.	Amsterdam	1d.	1734.	Portland	3d.
1674.	Bordeaux	2½d.	1735.	Fiume	1½d.
1675.	Warsaw	1d.	1736.	Taganrog	2d.
1676.	Havana	1½d.	1737.	Swatow	1d.
1677.	Berlin	1d.	1738.	Chungking	1½d.
1678.	Beira	1½d.	1739.	Angora	1½d.
1679.	Saigon	1d.	1740.	Shanghai	2½d.
1680.	Trebizond	1d.	1741.	Bilbao	3½d.
1681.	Vera Cruz	1½d.	1742.	Tahiti	1½d.
1682.	Patras	1d.	1743.	New Caledonia	1½d.
1683.	La Rochelle	1½d.	1744.	Amoy	1½d.
1684.	Madrid	1½d.	1745.	Ichang	1d.
1685.	Belgrade	2d.	1746.	Berlin	½d.
1686.	Algiers	5d.	1747.	Rio de Janeiro	5½d.
1687.	Galveston	2½d.	1748.	Porto Rico	1½d.
1688.	New Orleans	2d.	1749.	Montevideo	1½d.

No. 1750.

Reference to previous Report, Annual Series No. 1576.

UNITED STATES.

SAN FRANCISCO.

Consul-General Warburton to the Marquis of Salisbury.

My Lord,   *San Francisco, May* 1, 1896.

I HAVE the honour to enclose my Annual Report on the Trade, Commerce, and Agriculture of this Consular District, together with Reports from the British Vice-Consuls at Los Angeles and San Diego.

I have, &c.
(Signed)   J. W. WARBURTON.

Report on the Trade, Commerce, and Agriculture of the Consular District of San Francisco for the Year 1895.

ABSTRACT of Contents.

	PAGE
San Francisco—	
General remarks	2
Clearing-house returns	3
Failures	3
Insurance	3
Shipping and navigation	5
Freights	5
Seamen's wages	5
Steamer lines	5
New port of entry	6
Port charges	6–22
Shipbuilding	6
Whaling season, results of	6
Seamen's institute	6
Trade and commerce	7
Exports	7
Imports	10
Manufactures	11
Railway construction	11
Mining	12
Hydraulic process, injury done by	12
Precious and other metals	12–24
Other mining produce	13

(2158)

UNITED STATES.

Abstract of Contents—continued.

	PAGE
San Francisco—continued—	
Nitrate deposits	13
Coal supply and consumption	14–15
Prices of foreign and other coals	14
Mineral oil	15
Agriculture; cereal and fruit growing, &c.; wool	15
Labour market	18
Rights of aliens	18
Advice to intending emigrants	18
Health; death rate	19
Los Angeles—	
Introductory remarks	25
Information for British capitalists	26
Property sales	27
Advice to emigrants	27
Rights of aliens	29
Shipping and navigation	30
Port facilities and charges	30
Mistakes of English manufacturers	31
Produce; wines, fruit, &c.	33
Exports and imports	35
Vital statistics and social matters	36
New buildings, public schools, &c.	37
Industries; mining; sugar; oil, &c.	37
Public works; railways	39
Agriculture	41
Fruit tree pests and vine diseases	42
Irrigation act and works	43
San Diego—	
Trade depression	44
Exports and imports	44
Shipping and navigation	46
Harbour facilities	47
Population and industries	48
Mining	48
Irrigation laws	49
Agriculture	49
Public works	50

Note.—Calculations are made throughout this report at 5 dol. to the 1*l*.

General Remarks.

At the commencement of the year 1895 hopes were entertained that there would be a recovery from the great business depression of the previous year, and that the new year would prove to be an active one. But a careful study of the operations of the year shows that these hopes have not to any great extent been fulfilled. Still there has been an undoubted if not a very considerable improvement.

The cereal and fruit crops showed a reduction, but in the case of wheat the reduction in quantity was to a great extent, though not altogether, made up by better prices.

The lumber, iron and hardware business showed a considerable increase over that of 1894, and prices in the iron trade also showed an advance in sympathy with those in the East. In most other goods prices were low, though in some cases, such as cottons and woollens, they improved towards the close of the year. Profits were, however, small in most classes of goods.

The Clearing House exchanges in this city for 1895 were 138,415,848*l*., against 131,705,361*l*. in 1894, showing an increase of 6,710,486*l*., or somewhat less than 6 per cent. The improvement manifested itself chiefly in the latter part of the year, the figures being for the last quarter of each year—1894, 35,303,665*l*.; 1895, 39,341,093*l*.

The principal banks added largely to their stocks of gold, and this strengthened the financial situation, and their condition in general was satisfactory.

There were few failures of any importance. The principal one was that of the Grangers' bank, which was compelled to suspend operations in consequence of losses resulting from the continued low prices in the wheat business. But it is said that every depositor will be paid in full.

Insurance.

The past year was, as far as profits go, one of the worst ever experienced on the West coast. This was not so much owing to a falling-off in the amount of business, or to exceptionally heavy payments for losses, as to the war of rates, which so reduced premiums that in many instances there were no profits left. There was, however, in spite of lower rates, less written than in other years, and marine losses were very serious.

The Insurance Commissioner in his report says that there are no marked general changes in the business of the level premium companies, the amount in force being about the same as last year, while the amount written is a little less. The marine insurance companies increased the amount written over 1894 by about 20,000,000 dol., with a corresponding increase in receipts of 135,000 dol. The year, however, was a very disastrous one, the losses increasing from 418,106 dol. 22 c. in 1894 to 887,761 dol. 60 c. in 1895. The loss ratio in consequence jumped from 37·5 to 71·1. The fire tables will furnish a field for study to insurance men for many months. It is a well-known fact that rates have been sadly demoralised during the entire year; that much business expiring beyond 1895 has been cancelled and re-written at the lower rates; and that many persons are carrying larger lines than formerly. Naturally every one thought that the amount of business written would be greatly increased. On the contrary, about 20,000,000 dol. less was written than last year, 30,000,000*l*. dol. less than in 1893, and 40,000,000 dol. less than in 1892, while the amount in force was slightly increased. The student of rates will find sufficient employment for the balance of the year. Some of the most conservative companies in the matter of rates average no higher than those that have been condemned as violent rate-cutters. Others report a higher average rate for the business written during the year than on the amount in force, an anomaly no one spoken to is able to clearly explain. The incomes

UNITED STATES.

of the companies have suffered greatly, and the insured are now carrying about as much insurance as usual, at a saving to them of at least 1,500,000 dol. This has naturally made a very high loss ratio for California, and for purposes of comparison (at least during the time of the compact) a false one. The average percentage of losses to premiums on fire risks for 1895 is 60·6. The average percentage of losses to premiums on marine risks for 1895 is 71·1. The ratio of losses to premiums on fire risks for the 5 years have been:—

Year.	Percentage.
1891	36·1
1892	38·9
1893	39·4
1894	44·4
1895	60·6

Fire Insurance.

	Amount.
	Dollars c.
Amount written	358,738,159 0
Premiums on same	4,704,584 11
Losses paid	2,850,672 07
	Percentage.
Ratio of losses to premiums..	60·60

Marine Insurance.

	Amount.
	Dollars c.
Amount written	127,937,123 0
Premiums on same	1,249,317 11
Losses paid	887,761 60
	Percentage.
Ratio of losses to premiums..	71·1

The companies of this State have only written 31,514,873 dol., or about one-eleventh of the whole, in fire insurance, and only about one-tenth, or 12,223,255 dol., in marine, companies of other States having done 135,405,607 dol. in fire, and 8,353,710 dol. in marine, while companies of foreign countries have written 191,818,679 dol. in fire, and 107,360,158 dol. in marine. The rates on fire have been only a little over 1 per cent. The Sun sold out to the Fireman's Fund during the year.

SAN FRANCISCO.

Shipping and Navigation.

The accompanying table shows the number and nationality of vessels which entered and cleared at this port during the past year.

British shipping shows an increase over 1894. 29 more vessels, with 76,167 more tons, entered, and 33 more vessels, with 138,033 more tons, cleared. American shipping to and from foreign countries fell off, 35 vessels less than in 1894 having entered, and 55 less having cleared. The shipping of other countries shows a slight decrease also.

<small>Annex A. Shipping.</small>

For a considerable portion of the year the wheat rates were below what was regarded as paying rates, and several times vessels declined freights at the rates prevailing. It was not until the Syndicate wheat began to be shipped and the owners wanted vessels that the market showed any activity. Rates then went up high, and it was thought that they would keep up, but no sooner was it known that iron ships were getting good rates here than there was a rush from all quarters to participate in them, and they soon began to fall, and towards the close of the year they were pretty low. Since the close of the year they have dropped down to as low as 1*l*. 1*s*. 3*d*. for iron United Kingdom orders, with the usual difference in favour of a direct port of 16*s*.

<small>Charters. Freights.</small>

The rates for the year were as follows:—

Month.	Prices. From— £ s. d.	Prices. To— £ s. d.
January	..	1 7 6
February	1 3 9	1 6 3
March	1 3 9	1 6 3
April	1 3 9	1 10 0
May	1 10 0	1 13 0
June	..	1 15 0
July	1 15 0	1 17 6
August	1 15 0	1 7 6
September	1 7 6	1 4 6
October	1 7 6	1 10 0
November	..	1 7 6
December	1 7 6	1 6 3

These ruled 3*l*. 10*s*. per month for the greater part of the year, but for a short period went down to 3*l*. At the close of the year they advanced to 4*l*.

<small>Seamen's wages.</small>

Up to the end of last year the Pacific Mail Company and the Panama Railway Company ran steamers between this port and Panama, and between Colon and New York, but at the beginning of the present year, under an agreement concluded between the two companies, the Pacific Line withdrew its steamers from the Atlantic side, and the Railway Company theirs from the

<small>Steam lines to New York viâ Panama.</small>

(2158)

Pacific side of the Isthmus. This arrangement leaves the Pacific Mail Company without a competitor between San Francisco and Panama.

New port of entry. The town of Oakland, situated on the eastern side of the bay opposite to San Francisco, has been created a sub-port of entry, and a custom house has been established there. Foreign vessels can now make entry at or clear from there.

Port charges. San Francisco has long enjoyed the unenviable reputation of being one of the most expensive ports in the world, and an organized effort is now being made to obtain a reduction of the port charges. A meeting of delegates from the different trade organisations more or less interested in the matter has been held, and committees have been formed to make inquiries into the different charges on shipping, with a view to getting them reduced. A table of the various rates and tolls is annexed.

Shipbuilding.

Shipbuilding. This industry was insignificant, and even so continues to show a falling-off. The tonnage for the bay being as follows for the last 2 years:—

Year.		Gross Tonnage.	Net Tonnage.
1894	.. ..	2,577	2,095
1895	.. .. (about)	1,580	1,349

Most of the vessels built were small schooners, the two largest being respectively of 536 and 146 gross tonnage. All the rest but two were under 50 tons. There were a few steamers built, the two largest being respectively of 200 and 197 gross tonnage.

Catch of the Whaling Fleet.

Whaling. The catch of the Arctic whaling fleet for the past year was less than for 1894. The figures are:—

Year.	Quantity.		
	Oil.	Bone.	Ivory.
	Barrels.	Lbs.	Lbs.
1894	8,119	274,579	7,367
1895	4,390	104,595	4 160

Seamen's institute. This establishment is doing good work, and is well worthy of support by British shipowners. The records of the Consulate show that in the 2 years previous to its opening 122 apprentices deserted from British vessels in port, while during the 2 years and 10 months since it was established only 32 apprentices have deserted.

Trade and Commerce.

The following tables show the exports and imports for 1894 and 1895:—

There was a considerable increase in exports by sea, amounting to about 25 per cent. over those of 1894. This increase was owing to larger shipments of cereals, salmon, and canned goods to Europe and to the East by Panama, also to a great increase in the trade with countries on the Pacific coasts, especially Central America and Japan. On the other hand exports by rail showed a reduction, chiefly in fruit and sugar. Annex B. Exports.

The exports of wheat and flour by sea during 1895 were: wheat, 11,051,002 centals; flour, 948,762 barrels, of a total value of 2,636,102*l*., or an increase of 3,850,186 centals of wheat and 161,305 barrels of flour over 1894. Of this the United Kingdom took 10,786,735 centals of wheat and 48,580 barrels of flour, and Australia 128,109 centals of wheat and 20,912 barrels of flour. Wheat and flour.

Of barley and oats there were exported in 1895: barley, 1,631,916 centals; oats, 16,898 centals, showing an increase in barley of 571,466 centals, and a decrease in oats of 5,239 centals as compared with 1894. Barley and oats.

The export of hops was for the 2 years as follows:— Hops.

	Quantity.	
	1894.	1895.
	Lbs.	Lbs.
From San Francisco, by sea	406,198	804,115
" by rail	500,000	784,000
From the interior of California, by rail	8,764,000	6,554,000
Total	9,670,198	8,142,115

showing a falling-off in 1895 of 1,528,083 lbs.

The shipments of fruit and canned goods to the East by rail were as follows:— Fruit and canned goods.

Articles.	Quantity.	
	1894.	1895.
	Lbs.	Lbs.
Canned goods	97,106,000	59,142,000
Dried fruit	88,232,000	102,686,000
Green fruit	164,402,000	119,734,000
Raisins	83,134,000	85,352,000
Total	432,874,000	366,914,000

These shipments, however, do not represent the total movement, as the Southern Pacific Railway Company declined to give any returns for the southern section of the State represented by the terminals Los Angeles and Colton.

Citrus and green fruits. Shipments of green and citrus fruits were made from the following terminal points:—

	Quantity.	
	1894.	1895.
	Lbs.	Lbs.
Sacramento	106,304,000	73,082,000
San José	25,530,000	20,186,000
Stockton	12,844,000	15,382,000
San Francisco	202,000	176,000
Marysville	8,950,000	5,496,000
Oakland	101,572,000	5,412,000
Total	166,402,000	119,734,000

Canned goods and dried fruits. The shipments of canned goods, dried fruits, and raisins in 1895 from the same terminals were:—

	Quantity.		
	Canned Goods.	Dried Fruits.	Raisins.
	Lbs.	Lbs.	Lbs.
Sacramento	10,424,000	16,266,000	1,578,000
San José	11,662,000	48,444,000	22,000
Stockton	652,000	16,764,000	82,432,000
San Francisco	23,468,000	11,596,000	908,000
Marysville	7,302,000	7,338,000	412,000
Oakland	5,634,000	2,278,000	..
Total	59,142,000	102,686,000	85,352,000

SAN FRANCISCO.

The exports of tinned salmon by sea for the 2 years were:— Salmon.

Year.	Quantity.		Value.
	Cases.	Packages.	£
1894	640,163	7,735	540,945
1895	902,089	11,072	744,337

Of this the United Kingdom took 507,163 cases and 10 packages. Australia took 43,304 cases and 4,285 packages, and New Zealand 4,796 cases and 110 packages.

The shipments by rail from San Francisco and the interior of the State were in 1895:—

	Quantity.
	Lbs.
San Francisco, canned	13,534,000
„ pickled	2,636,000
Interior, canned	1,226,000

The exports of wine and brandy for 1895 were:— Wine and brandy.

	Quantity.	
	Wine.	Brandy.
	Gallons.	Gallons.
By sea, from San Francisco ..	4,054,608	93,008
By rail, from the State	10,796,200	476,000
Total	14,850,808	569,008

Wines show an increase of 287,816 gallons, and brandy a decrease of 222,673 gallons in 1895, as compared with 1894.

The exports of lumber by sea for the 2 years were: 1894, Lumber. 18,428,272 feet; 1895, 17,671,082 feet, showing a decrease in 1895 of 757,190 feet. Of this article the United Kingdom took (for Dunnage) in 1894, 7,280,563 feet; 1895, 3,758,600 feet, and Australia took, in 1894, 1,744,958 feet; 1895, 2,511,615 feet.

The exports of quicksilver by sea and rail were, in 1895, Quicksilver. 30,687 flasks, being an excess of 1,803 flasks over those of 1894. Of this article, 13,000 flasks went to New York and 3,897 flasks to Mexico.

The export of wool in 1895 was 26,356,000 lbs., of the Wool. value of 700,000l., being a reduction in 1895 of 284,444 lbs.

The total value of all exports excepting treasure, shipped by Total exports. sea from San Francisco for 1894 and 1895 were: 1894, 5,282,134l.;

1895, 6,652,972*l*., showing an increase in 1895 of 1,370,838*l*. Of this the United Kingdom took 2,907,845*l*. in 1895, as compared with 1,931,332*l*. in 1894; Australia took 230,206 in 1895, as against 144,105*l*. in 1894.

Imports. There was a slight falling-off in imports from foreign countries by rail, but the total value of all imports in 1895 was 7,785,121*l*., showing an increase on 1894 of 82,184*l*.

The value of free goods amounted to 5,436,022*l*., or a falling-off of 375,074. Dutiable goods amounted to 2,349,098*l*., or an increase of 457,258*l*. over 1894. The increase in dutiable goods represents principally imports from European States.

Silk. Of the free goods, raw silks for Eastern factories represent a value of 2,280,108*l*., so that the imports of free goods for home consumption in the State were considerably less than they appear to be.

Of the imports, goods to the value of 517,625*l*. were imported by rail in bond from New York to New Orleans, and 7,267,496*l*. direct from foreign countries.

Of the imports by sea, goods to the value of 3,754,416*l*. were imported in American ships, and of 4,030,236*l*. in foreign ships, showing a decrease of over 500,000*l*. in goods carried in American ships as compared with 1894, and an increase of over 640,000*l*. imported in foreign ships.

Goods entered for consumption amounted to a value of 7,143,397*l*., and those warehoused to 641,724*l*. This represents an increase of over 350,000*l*. in goods entered for consumption, and a corresponding decrease in those warehoused, as compared with 1894, resulting chiefly from the anticipation of an increase in import duties.

Sugar. The imports of sugar for 1894 and 1895 were respectively 333,327,082 lbs. and 275,510,840 lbs., or a decrease of 57,816,242 lbs. in 1895. Of this article 246,553,204 lbs. came from the Hawaiian Islands, 26,213,095 lbs. from China, and 1,379,977 from Mexico.

Coffee. The quantity of coffee imported in 1895 was 21,981,168 lbs., or a decrease of 5,158,041 as against 1894; of this the British East Indies contributed in 1895 366,450 lbs. and Australia 90,803 lbs., as compared with 230,213 lbs. and 100 lbs. respectively in 1894. The increase from Australia is worthy of notice.

Tea. The amount of tea imported in 1895 was 5,984,910 lbs., of which 139,139 lbs. came from British East Indies.

Rice. Of rice 49,208,550 lbs. were imported in 1895, an increase of 3,302,537 lbs. over 1894. The British East Indies contributed 3,019,955 lbs. of this total.

Silk. Of the imports of raw silk in 1895, 2,674,404 lbs. came from Japan and 1,108,494 lbs. from China.

Coal. The imports of coal from the United Kingdom and British possessions for the 2 years were:—

Country.	Quantity.	
	1894.	1895.
	Tons.	Tons.
United Kingdom	174,000	203,800
Australia	177,200	220,800
British Columbia	487,600	507,300

Showing an increase in each case in 1895.

Of coke 24,688 tons were imported in 1895, mainly from England and Belgium. **Coke.**

There was imported from the United Kingdon in 1895 152,735 barrels of cement. **Cement.**

The following were the chief importations in heavy iron goods from the United Kingdom in 1895:— **Iron goods. Tin-plates.**

Articles.		Quantity.
Tin-plates	Lbs.	45,755,609
Iron-bars	,,	354,505
Scrap-iron	Tons	12
Pig-iron	,,	1,722
Sheet, plate, &c.	Lbs.	355,790
Wire and wire rope	,,	1,242,438
R. R. bars	Tons	671

Industries.

There was a slight increase in manufactures. In refined sugars, flour and mill stuffs, and malt liquors there has been little change. There was an increase in the production of beet sugar, fresh and packed meats, biscuits (crackers), grain, spirits, textiles and clothing, in iron and steel manufactures, and in the cut and manufacture of lumber. Also in the manufacture of leather and of boots and shoes. **Manufactures.**

The quantity of canned goods packed has been less than in 1894. Wine and brandy have remained about the same. On the whole it is estimated that the improvement in manufactures has been about 2 per cent.

Railway Construction.

Of the San Joaquin Valley Railroad referred to in Mr. Moore's report for 1894, about 31 miles have been completed. The Southern Pacific opened a number of branch lines and the Alameda and San Joaquin Railway built 26 miles. **Railways.**

Mining.

Gold. Silver.

There was a great increase in the production of gold during 1895 in almost every State and territory. The production of silver remained about the same. The great improvements in the means of winning gold have been the cause of the re-opening of many old workings, and there is every prospect that California will soon rival its old fame as a gold-producing country.

Copper.

Copper-mining in California promises a considerable advance during the present year, and the production of the coast will, it is estimated, amount to about 25,000,000 dol.

Damage caused by hydraulic mining.

The hydraulic process of mining is causing serious damage. The California Debris Commission, in their report for the 12 months ended June 30 last, say:—

"The rapid washing of the large deposits of auriferous gravel on the western slope of the Sierra Nevada Mountains by the so-called hydraulic process resulted in the discharging into the cañyons of large quantities of gravel, sand, and other detritus, which the floods subsequently carried down, to be at first deposited largely where the streams emerged from the foothills into the level plains of the Sacramento Valley, afterwards to be moved farther down to the navigable streams, and the finer portions even to tide water. The result was that near the foothills the beds of some of the streams filled up much more rapidly than their banks rose, so that their channels largely disappeared, and at flood time the streams spread over the valley lands, frequently destroying their value by covering the rich alluvium with gravel, sand, &c., often several feet deep. Long and high levees were built by the landowners to prevent as much as possible such damage. The finer particles brought down by the streams were carried into the navigable rivers, filling up the deep pools, and in general changing the character of the bed from a succession of pools and shoals to a continuous shoal. The capacities of the streams to discharge their flood waters without overflowing their banks were reduced. Legal action brought against the mine operators by persons owning damaged lands, and by the United States in the interests of navigation, resulted in injunctions against the principal mines and ultimately in the practical suppression of hydraulic mining in the region under consideration. Subsequently Congress created the Commission with the duties as heretofore outlined. (For a detailed history of the effects of hydraulic mining reference is made to House Ex. Doc. No. 98, Forty-seventh Congress, first session; also House Ex. Doc. No. 267, Fifty-first Congress, second session; and to the last annual report of the Commission.)"

Precious metals, production of.

Messrs. Wells, Fargo, and Co. give the following as the approximate returns of precious and base metals produced in the States and territories which are comprised within the jurisdiction of this consulate general,* and carried by rail and otherwise.

---

* In comparing these figures with those of last year it must be remembered that the States of Oregon, Washington, and Idaho are no longer within this consular district, but under that of Portland, which has been raised to a consulate.

States and Territories.	Gold Dust and Bullion by Express.	Gold Dust and Bullion by other Conveyances.	Silver Bullion by Express.	Ores and Base Bullion by Express.	Total.
	Dollars.	Dollars.	Dollars.	Dollars.	Dollars.
California	10,940,491	3,063,617	157,229	286,575	14,447,912
Nevada	1,239,735	319,581	662,647	359,950	2,581,913
Utah	647,405	704,785	1,116,767	6,753,095	9,222,052
Arizona	1,206,503	1,230,069	160,019	4,756,185	7,352,776
Total	14,034,134	5,318,052	2,096,662	12,155,805	33,604,653
Eq. in sterling £	2,806,826	1,063,610	419,332	2,431,161	6,720,931

Messrs. Wells, Fargo, and Co., however, point out that allowance must be made for possible variations from reported figures by reason of the constantly increasing facilities for transporting bullion, ores, and base metal outside of the express, and the difficulty of getting entirely reliable data from private sources. The above figures, therefore, while only approximately correct, may be accepted as the closest estimate possible under the circumstances.

Copper and lead. The value of copper and lead produced in all the States and territories west of the Missouri, including British Columbia (the amount for each individual State and territory is not given) was approximately, copper 27,052,115 dol., about 5,410,421l.; lead, 7,170,367, about 1,434,075l. The values at which the three inferior metals are estimated are, silver, 65 c. per oz.; copper, 11 c. per lb.; lead, 3·23 dol. per cwt.

Silver. The exports of silver during 1895 to China, Japan, the Straits Settlements., &c., from San Francisco amounted to 12,933,307 dol., or about 2,586,661l.

Produce of coal, borax, quicksilver, petroleum, asphalt, and bituminous rock. The value of coal produced in California was about 50,000l. in 1895.; of borax, 180,000l.; of quicksilver, 225,000l.; of petroleum, 500,000l.; of asphalt and bituminous rock, 69,798l.

Nitrate.

Two gentlemen called on me recently to ask for information respecting the nitrate industry in Chile, which I gave them. They told me that there were valuable deposits of nitrate at Lovelock, near Humboldt Lake, Nevada, for the working of which endeavours would be made to form a company. This company it was proposed to bring out in London. They showed me the draft prospectus, and promised me a copy of it.

It has been well known for many years that nitrate exists in small quantities in many places in the great alkali deserts of Nevada and this State, but though much search has been made, and particularly in the district referred to, it has never been found in quantities sufficient to be of any commercial value. I am making inquiries into the matter, and will report further. Meanwhile I should recommend British capitalists to be very cautious about embarking in any such enterprise until they have satisfied themselves of the commercial value of the deposits.

UNITED STATES.

Coal Supply and Consumption.

Coal.   The quantity of coal consumed in 1895 was greater than any year since 1891. This is mainly attributed to the low prices which have ruled, and which are said to be the lowest known, and in part also to the somewhat greater activity of manufactures. It is thought that these low prices will prevail for some time to come. The best grades of steam coal in Australia were quoted at 1·75 per ton, and freights from there were much reduced. Swansea anthracite coal is becoming popular as a steam producer, and 65,000 more tons were imported in the past year than in 1894. This class of coal is admitted duty free, while bituminous coal pays 40 c. a ton. Crude oil is being used at several factories for reasons of economy, but with coal at present prices the saving is said to be slight. Gas companies are liberal consumers of this oil, which, combined with anthracite, is an economical gas producer. Very little bituminous coal is used in making gas. It is feared in some quarters that the low prices of Australian and English coals will materially interfere with the Northern collieries of the State, and cause a diminished output. At the same time the developments of the Corral Hollow mines have been progressing rapidly. A railway will soon connect them with Stockton, and it is expected that they will supply an abundance of cheap fuel to this city and neighbourhood.

The following table will will show the monthly fluctuations of foreign coals for "spot" cargoes. The average price is given for each month:—

Month.	Australian (Gas).	English Steam.	Scotch Splint.	West Hartley.
	Dol. c.	Dol. c.	Dol. c.	Dol. c.
January..	5 75	6 25	7 0	6 25
February	5 75	6 25	7 0	6 25
March ..	6 0	6 25	7 0	6 25
April ..	6 0	6 25	7 0	6 50
May ..	5 75	6 0	6 50	6 25
June ..	5 75	6 0	6 50	6 25
July ..	5 75	6 0	6 50	6 25
August..	5 40	5 75	7 0	6 25
September	5 40	5 75	7 0	6 25
October..	5 40	5 75	7 0	6 25
November	5 30	6 0	6 75	6 0
December	5 20	6 0	6 50	6 0

The retail prices to householders of various qualities per ton of 20 cwt., as fixed on July 1, 1895, and which have been in force since then are as follows:—

		Prices.
		Dol. c.
Scotch .. .. .. (about)		10 0
Cannel		10 50
Welsh "egg"		11 50
Australian		9 50

Americans ranged from 14 dol. 50 c. for Pennsylvanian "egg" down to 7 dol. 25 c. for Beaver Hill, the average being about 9 dol. 20 c.

The following table shows the sources from which for the last four years the coal supply has been derived. The table includes all arrivals by water at San Pedro, Los Angeles, San Diego, and Santa Barbara, amounting to 199,130 tons.

Source of coal supply.

	Quantity.			
	1892.	1893.	1894.	1895.
	Tons.	Tons.	Tons.	Tons.
British Columbia ..	554,600	588,527	647,110	651,295
Australia	314,280	202,017	211,733	268,960
English and Welsh ..	210,660	151,269	157,562	201,180
Scotch	24,900	18,809	18,636	4,098
Eastern (Cumberland and Anthracite) ..	35,720	18,960	16,640	26,863
Seattle (Franklin and Green River) ..	164,930	167,550	153,199	150,888
Carbon Hill and South Prairie ..	218,390	261,435	241,974	256,267
Mount Diablo and Coos Bay	66,150	63,460	65,263	84,954
Japan, &c.	4,220	7,758	15,637	9,015
Total	1,593,850	1,479,785	1,527,754	1,653,520

Ovens on a large scale are being erected at the Union Mine at Comoa, British Columbia, with a view to supplying the Californian market with coke. The coal is said to be well adapted for coke producing.

Petroleum.

Considerable activity has of late taken place in the development of the petroleum industry in this State. New wells are being sunk near Los Angeles, Whittier, St. Gabriel, Huron, and other places, and a great increase in the production may shortly be expected.

Petroleum.

Agriculture.

The Report of the State Board of Agriculture for 1895 has

Agriculture.

not yet been issued to the public, but the "Chronicle" and "Call" newspapers give very good abstracts of and quotations from it.

The report begins with a review of the season of 1895, of which it says:—"With the exception of a slight improvement in prices for cereals occasioned to a certain extent by a reaction from the bottom prices of 1894, this season was the most unsatisfactory in the history of grain growing in this State." "Our estimate of the entire yield of wheat for 1895 was 20,779,832 bushels, as against 26,071,510 bushels in 1894, while the quality showed the lowest average of any grown for many years."

"The yield of barley shows a marked increase over 1894. Good barley is selling at 75 c., with a fairly good demand for export grades. There is an increased demand in the English market for bright grain California barley; it is rated as second to the best grade barleys of Smyrna, and is regarded among the best malting barley in the market."

Wheat raising for export no longer pays.
The report says in discussing wheat growing:—"There is in this State a confirmed feeling that the growing of wheat as a staple cereal product for export is an industry of the past, and that its production must be confined to home consumption. In 1854 our total export of wheat was 214,610 centals, or 360,000 bushels. From that time forth, with the exception of one or two seasons of drought, there was a steady and healthy increase, until the season of 1882 showed the total amount to be 25,320,316 centals, or 42,200,526 bushels. That season the wheat industry was in its zenith in California, for the export price obtained was 1 dol. 70 c. per cental, or 1 dol. 2 c. per bushel, which figure, although maintained through the next year, has never again been reached. It will be observed that the value of wheat exported from California in 1882 was 42,000,000 dol. in round numbers. In 1893–94 the total amount was but 18,000,000 bushels, at tide-water price of 46·8 c. per bushel."

The report declares that Argentina, Russia, and Australia, are surely crowding America from the European market. The first-named alone, it is stated, can ship over 35,000,000 bushels annually. But the outlook for barley is much better, and there is a steadily growing demand for the California product.

As the result of over 1,600 inquiries sent out by the Board, reaching every township in the State, it is shown that the wages of farm-hands have steadily declined, but land values have not shown a corresponding decrease. The report then says:—"There is no disguising the fact that thorough reorganisation of farming methods is needed. The cities, through their property-owners, their merchants, their capitalists, must, sooner or later, take hold of the question of agriculture. The depression in this noble following will not be fully felt by the cities until it is too late to apply a remedy."

Other produce recommended.
It goes on to say that "One thing that farmers must certainly do is to get out of the old wheat-raising rut," and it suggests other productions such as poultry, dairy produce, sugar beet, &c.

As to the fruit industry it says that, "The condition of this **Fruit** industry is much more encouraging. The falling-off in grain **growing.** shipments was in a large measure made good by the development of the fruit business. In 1882 the total value of this product was less than 2,000,000 dol., while in 1894 it was a little more than 15,000,000 dol."

The following significant comment is made as a warning to orchardists:—"At this time we have about met the demand for fruit, and we deem it inadvisable to further extend the planting of new orchards until an increased market is assured, as the trees now in full bearing and those that will come into bearing within the next few years will supply all ordinary demand. We consider it better to extend other agricultural possibilities than to cripple those now on a paying basis. In this report we have mentioned other products that will bear extension, and thereby overcome a condition that would tend to reduce farming to a struggle for existence. A preventive is to direct our attention to such products as will warrant stimulation and consequent extension. The cultivation of sugar beets and tobacco, truck-farming, the raising of poultry, and dairying, offer better inducements at this time than does the further extension of the fruit industry."

The report says, however, that the conditions last year were not altogether favourable to fruit growers. In the spring an unusual frost seriously damaged apricots, cherries and peaches. Later there was a disagreement between the growers and shippers which interfered with business. The shipments (per rail) were 80 per cent. less than in 1894, but the prices were materially higher.

The report urges upon the farmers the importance of fostering our dairy interests, and declares that the oriental markets are open to us, but we must be prepared to compete with the great North west. It favours the organisation of dairymen.

The possibilities in the culture of tobacco are pointed out and the report declares that many portions of the State are well adapted to its culture. The development of the sugar beet industry is also urged. The estimated sugar crop of 1895 is placed at 48,000,000 lbs.

Fruit-growers are urged to pay more attention to the packing of the dried product. This class of fruit should be graded and sold in boxes of from 5 to 50 lbs.

The following estimate of the clip of Californian wool is pub- **Wool.** lished by the San Francisco Chamber of Commerce.

(2158)

UNITED STATES.

Estimate of the Clip.

	Quantity.	
	Bales.	Lbs.
Receipts of California wool at San Francisco—		
Spring	58,467	19,294,110
Fall	25,742	9,257,120
California wool shipped from the interior—		
Spring	..	4,724,000
Fall	..	823,460
Pulled (and San Francisco)	..	1,758,000
Total California clip	..	35,856,690
On hand, December 31, 1894	..	6,000,000
Received from Oregon	6,963	2,088,900
„ Nevada and territories	..	2,000,000
Foreign	..	2,273,600
Total stock	..	48,219,190

The clip for 1894 was 36,968,400 lbs. and the decrease in 1895 was therefore 1,111,700 lbs., but last year's clip was the largest since 1886 with the exception of that of 1894.

State of the Labour Market.

Labour market. This continues in a very depressed state. Numbers of labourers are without employment. Many clerks, who have been dismissed from business houses which are compelled to reduce their expenses, are in the same position. The insurance offices, especially owing to the causes stated above, have been obliged to part with many of their employés.

Rights of aliens The question as to the rights of aliens to acquire, inherit, possess, enjoy and transmit real and other estate in California, in view of the amendment in the constitution to which attention was called by Mr. Moore in his report for 1894 remains in the same position of uncertainty. No case has yet been decided by the courts.

Advice to intending emigrants. Repeated warnings have been given in previous reports from this Consulate—and notably by Mr. Donohoe in his report for 1893 and by Mr. Moore and Mr. Vice-Consul Mortimer in the report for 1894—to British subjects not to invest in land in this State until they have been here sufficiently long to enable them to acquire some knowledge of the conditions of the country, and to form an opinion as to the prospects of success.

The question appears to me of great importance in view of the sad fate of many who, relying on the specious prospectuses published by certain unscrupulous owners of land and the delusive promises of success held out, have invested their capital and labour in fruit and other farms, and have found themselves involved in ruin. I cannot too strongly endorse the warnings and advice given to intending settlers by Mr. Donohoe, Mr. Moore, and Mr. Mortimer.

Health and Mortality.

The deaths for the 12 months ended June 30, 1895, amounted in San Francisco to 6,059 or about 18·36 per 1,000. The causes of death were:—

Diseases.
Death rate.

	Number of Deaths.
Zymotic diseases	539
Constitutional diseases	1,477
Local diseases	3,129
Developmental diseases	574
Violent deaths	339
Unascertained causes	1

Annex A.—RETURN of all Shipping at the Port of San Francisco during the Year 1895.

ENTERED.

Nationality.	Sailing.		Steam.		Total.	
	Number of Vessels.	Tons.	Number of Vessels.	Tons.	Number of Vessels.	Tons.
British	180	333,675	54	111,407	234	445,082
American, from foreign countries	299	259,173	214	381,922	513	641,095
American, from Atlantic ports of Union	24	70,805	1	2,004	25	72,809
Hawaiian	15	15,134	14	17,298	29	32,432
Nicaraguan	5	3,441	22	28,028	27	31,469
Norwegian	3	4,285	11	22,098	14	26,383
Italian	9	19,055	...	...	9	19,055
German	11	17,246	...	...	11	17,246
Others	5	5,532	1	272	6	5,804
Total	551	728,346	317	563,029	868	1,291,375
,, for the year preceding	558	655,012	316	534,130	874	1,189,142

(2158)

UNITED STATES.

Cleared.

Nationality.	Sailing. Number of Vessels.	Sailing. Tons.	Steam. Number of Vessels.	Steam. Tons.	Total. Number of Vessels.	Total. Tons.
British	175	326,208	54	113,408	229	439,616
American, to foreign countries	279	246,764	207	369,489	486	616,253
American, to Atlantic ports of Union	6	12,818	...	...	6	12,818
Hawaiian	15	13,544	15	17,352	30	30,896
Nicaraguan	3	1,966	21	26,754	24	28,720
Norwegian	3	3,097	12	24,083	15	27,180
Italian	9	14,666	...	...	9	14,666
German	6	9,796	...	...	6	9,796
Others	7	3,668	2	671	9	4,339
Total	503	632,527	311	551,757	814	1,184,284
,, for the year preceding	517	545,006	315	538,765	832	1,083,771

Note.—The entrances and clearances of American ships do not include the coasting trade, whaling, or fishing voyages.

Annex B.—Return of Principal Articles of Export from San Francisco during the Years 1895-94.

Articles.		1895. Quantity.	1895. Value.	1894. Quantity.	1894. Value.
			£		£
Wheat and flour	Centals	13,897,288	2,636,103	9,563,187	1,804,021
Tinned salmon	Cases	581,423	480,133	388,207	352,717
Barley	Centals	1,605,285	256,846	1,012,926	201,980
Tinned fruit and vegetables	Cases	330,409	225,026	164,955	122,567
Wine	Gallons	707,129	70,517	561,348	56,267
Timber	Feet	17,121,866	57,538	17,530,939	66,784
Quicksilver	Flasks	4,265	32,627	7,228	52,042
Hops	Lbs.	804,115	11,201	406,198	11,074
Brandy	Gallons	37,294	5,959	300,193	60,563
Other articles	...	...	2,096,143	...	1,800,610
Total merchandise	...	...	5,872,093	...	4,528,625
Treasure	...	...	3,759,934	...	2,795,774
Grand total	...	...	9,632,027	...	7,324,399

Return of Principal Articles of Import to San Francisco during the Years 1895-94.

Articles.		1895. Quantity.	1895. Value.	1894. Quantity.	1894. Value.
			£		£
Raw silk	Lbs.	3,782,898	2,280,108	4,194,038	2,203,967
Sugar	Tons	122,996	1,465,949	148,807	1,841,286
Coal	,,	983,600	1,032,780	894,900	984,390
Coffee	Lbs.	21,981,168	676,896	27,139,209	823,833
Tin-plates	Boxes	435,768	233,288	124,659	134,319
Tea	Lbs.	5,822,061	160,150	5,419,466	142,040
Rice	Tons	21,968	148,212	20,494	155,573
Cement	Barrels	289,624	78,262	306,824	80,656
Pig-iron	Tons	1,847	4,693	1,422	3,764
Other articles	...	...	1,704,783	...	1,333,109
Total merchandise	...	...	7,785,121	...	7,702,937
Treasure	...	...	686,859	...	714,484
Grand total	...	...	8,471,980	...	8,417,421

Annex C.—TABLE showing Total Value of all Articles Exported from and Imported to San Francisco from and to Foreign Countries during the Years 1895-94.

Country.	Exports. 1895.	Exports. 1894.	Imports. 1895.	Imports. 1894.
	£	£	£	£
Great Britain	2,907,846	1,931,332	774,315	534,433
Hawaiian Islands	691,099	602,839	1,396,574	1,774,489
Central America	637,745	498,694	564,582	692,227
China	465,664	481,801	1,198,022	1,205,438
Japan	361,099	264,438	2,086,944	1,854,237
Australasia	271,471	175,007	176,416	117,535
Mexico	246,570	226,176	49,913	174,155
Canada	73,715	90,710	436,568	414,856
Pacific Islands	65,068	76,855	40,374	63,309
Asiatic Russia	49,384	32,165	69,227	88,202
South America	23,072	22,786	141,669	78,260
Germany	17,480	65,700	188,362	123,156
East Indies	11,983	9,370	258,211	249,490
France	2,777	20,085	162,112	133,402
Belgium	..	788	124,403	96,868
Italy	..	..	27,298	34,048
Other countries	47,120	29,879	90,131	68,832
Total merchandise	5,872,093	4,528,625	7,785,121	7,702,937
Treasure	3,759,934	2,795,774	686,859	714,484
Grand total	9,632,027	7,324,399	8,471,980	8,417,421

NOTE.—The imports by rail, included in the above totals of merchandise, amounted to 517,625*l.* in 1895, as against 360,596*l.* in 1894.

(2158)

UNITED STATES.

Rates and Tolls in force in the Harbour and Docks of San Francisco.

Stevedore Rates.

	Amount.
	Dol. c.
General merchandise, weight and measurement, per ton	0 35
Coal, pig iron and ballast, per ton	0 32½
Steel blooms, glass, sheet and bar iron	0 40
Sulphur and shale, in quantities over 50 tons, per ton	0 55
Railroad iron, coke and bricks, per ton	0 60
Loading—	
Wheat, flour, borax in bags, ton of 2,240 lbs.	0 30
Barley, per ton of 2,000 lbs.	0 30
Salmon and fruit in cases, per ton of 2,240 lbs.	0 45
Orchilla, cotton, pulu, in small lots of 2,240 lbs., per ton	0 45
Lumber, per M., according to size, from	0 90 to 1 15
Charges for entering—	
Survey	3 0
Entry	2 50
Official certificate and oath	0 20
Charges for clearance—	
Clearance	2 50
Official certificate and oath	0 20
Post entry, if any	2 00

Rates of Pilotage into or out of the Harbour of San Francisco.

All vessels under 500 tons, 5 dol. per foot draught; all vessels over 500 tons, 5 dol. per foot draught and 4 c. per ton for each and every ton registered measurement; when a vessel is spoken, inward or outward bound, and the services of a pilot are declined, one-half of the above rates shall be paid. In all cases where inward-bound vessels are not spoken until inside the bar, the rates of pilotage and one-half pilotage above provided shall be reduced 50 per cent. Vessels engaged in the whaling or fishing trade shall be exempt from all pilotage, except where a pilot is actually employed.

Rates of Dockage for the Port of San Francisco.

Each rate is for a day of 24 hours, or any part thereof.

1. For all ocean vessels, steam or sail, and all sail vessels, navigating the bay of San Francisco, and the rivers and other water flowing into it, of 200 net registered tons or under, 2 c. per ton; for all such vessels of over 200 net registered tons, 4 dol. for the first 200 tons, and ¾ c. for each additional ton.

2. For steamboats navigating the Bay of San Francisco and the waters flowing into it, and used for carrying freight or passengers, of 200 tons or under, gross hull measurement, 2 c. per ton on such measurement, for such boats of over 200 tons, gross hull

measurement, 4 dol. for the first 200 tons of such measurement, and ¾ c. for each additional ton.

3. For barges of 200 tons or under, 2 c. per ton; for barges over 200 tons, 4 dol. for first 200 tons, and ¾ c. for each additional ton.

4. Vessels while taking in cargo, or receiving or discharging ballast, or lying idle, or occupying outside berths, or moored in docks, slips, basins, or canals, are subject only to half rates of dockage; provided, that vessels not used for carrying freight or passengers shall not be entitled to such half rates.

5. When the per diem dockage of a vessel, as above prescribed, is not a multiple of five, it must be reduced or increased, as the case may be, to the nearest such multiple; provided, that if it be equally near to two such multiples, it must be increased to the first such multiple above.

Tolls.

A ton is, by weight, 2,000 lbs., unless otherwise specified; by measurement, 40 cubic feet.

Merchandise for the purpose of tolls and wharfage, must be estimated by weight or measurement as the one mode or the other will give the greater number of tons.

Tolls on loads hauled on, or off, a wharf are as follows:—On single loads (except where the article hauled is charged for, otherwise than by the ton), of a ton or less, 5 c.; of more than a ton, for each additional ton, or part of a ton, an additional 5 c. *Tolls per load.*

Of the following articles, 2,240 lbs. constitute a ton:—

Coal, railroad iron, pig iron, gypsum, asphaltum, ores, paving stones, sand and ballast.

Agricultural implements, to wit: reapers, mowers, headers, separators, horse rakes, hay presses, ploughs, cultivators and wheeled vehicles, when knocked down, will be taken by measurement.

On wheat or flour shipped from any wharf, no tolls will be collected for such shipment.

P.S.—Since this report was written the statistics of the bullion product of California for the years 1894 and 1895 have been prepared by the U.S. Mint in this city, and forwarded to the Director of the Mint at Washington for publication in his Annual Report. The Report is not yet in print, but Mr. Yale, the statistician of the Mint here, has very courteously furnished me with copies of the tables included therein, showing the yield of the State by counties.

From these tables, which are annexed, it will be seen that the gold yield in 1895 exceeded that of 1894 by 1,411,035 dol. 80 c. and the silver product exceeded that of 1894 by 302,458 dol. 15 c., making a total increase in the produce of the precious metals of 1,713,493 dol. 95 c. The report states that the yield of gold in 1892 and 1893 was: 1892, 12,571,900 dol. 57 c.; 1893, 12,422,811 dol. 60 c.

TABLES showing Production of Gold and Silver in 1895-94.

1895.

County.	Gold. Dol.	c.	Silver. Dol.	c.	Total. Dol.	c.
Amador*	1,391,929	40	1,089	00	1,393,018	40
Butte	697,260	85	8,935	53	706,196	38
Calaveras	1,717,916	14	77	00	1,717,993	14
Del Norte	8,250	00			8,250	00
El Dorado	700,101	31	447	68	700,548	99
Fresno	47,249	00			47,249	00
Humboldt	92,635	20			92,635	20
Inyo	92,142	28	188,329	23	280,471	51
Kern	231,433	31	46,064	28	277,497	59
Lassen	25,000	00			25,000	00
Los Angeles	23,330	00			23,330	00
Madera	162,323	74			162,323	74
Mariposa	216,622	39	7	07	216,629	46
Merced	1,500	00			1,500	00
Mono	552,690	54	84,910	37	637,600	91
Nevada	1,789,815	66	400	00	1,790,215	66
Orange	144	00			144	00
Placer	1,599,634	79	5,272	53	1,604,907	32
Plumas	602,951	05	271	52	603,222	57
Riverside	285,106	00	2,550	00	287,656	00
Sacramento	145,872	75			145,872	75
San Bernardino	131,360	00	219,410	30	350,770	30
San Diego	344,307	57	600	00	344,907	57
S. Luis Obispo	3,000	00			3,000	00
Santa Barbara	4,000	00			4,000	00
Shasta	781,696	32	28,417	20	810,113	52
Sierra	694,469	67	106	96	694,576	63
Siskiyou	950,006	43	177	30	950,183	73
Stanislaus	26,481	50			26,481	50
Trinity	1,166,745	13	1,257	28	1,168,002	41
Tulare	16,320	00			16,320	00
Tuolumne	666,754	15	312	62	667,066	77
Yuba	111,482	34			111,482	34
Unapportioned†	53,786	17	11,153	83	64,940	00
Total	15,334,317	69	599,789	70	15,934,107	39

* Based on returns at San Francisco Mint.
† "Unapportioned" includes product of single mines, &c., in counties, so as to conceal their identity; and also includes estimates of product of properties known to be working, but from which no returns were obtained.
Counties not mentioned in this list made no returns for 1895.

SAN FRANCISCO.

TABLES showing Production of Gold and Silver—continued.

1894.

County.	Gold.		Silver.		Total.	
	Dol.	c.	Dol.	c.	Dol.	c.
Amador	1,331,916	54	280	27	1,332,196	81
Butte	473,672	65			473,672	65
Calaveras	2,119,365	67	5,182	80	2,124,548	47
Del Norte	8,000	00			8,000	00
El Dorado	366,707	67	356	00	367,063	67
Fresno	8,202	00			8,202	00
Humboldt	41,326	00	13	86	41,339	86
Inyo	52,638	91	83,640	00	136,278	91
Kern	310,706	91	39,700	00	350,406	91
Lassen	35,283	00			35,283	00
Los Angeles	34,500	00			34,500	00
Madera	167,791	60	180	00	167,971	60
Mariposa	153,707	51	38	75	153,746	26
Merced	762	50			762	50
Mono	358,824	46	11,549	12	370,373	58
Monterey	8,000	00			8,000	00
Nevada	1,830,154	80	475	51	1,830,630	31
Placer	1,851,214	52	664	37	1,851,878	89
Plumas	499,358	83			499,358	83
Riverside	93,322	50			93,322	50
Sacramento	70,326	00			70,326	00
San Bernardino	130,419	78	148,242	89	278,662	67
San Diego	266,408	73	189	60	266,598	33
San Luis Obispo	1,200	00			1,200	00
Shasta	617,436	68	5,032	31	672,468	99
Sierra	604,721	54			604,721	54
Siskiyou	760,781	83			760,781	83
Stanislaus	26,368	50			26,368	50
Trinity	1,012,665	84	325	00	1,012,990	84
Tuolumne	547,448	06	1,072	16	548,520	22
Yuba	107,480	20			107,480	20
Unapportioned	32,568	66	388	91	32,957	57
Total	13,923,281	89	297,331	55	14,220,613	44

LOS ANGELES.

For some time prior to the "boom" of 1887, and for a short time thereafter, this district experienced a remarkable increase in wealth and population; depression and inactivity in business followed for several years, terminating about 3 years ago. A period of development and comparative prosperity then commenced, which, owing to the depression in business complained of so generally throughout the country, was somewhat remarkable. The following figures show a steady increase in the past 3 years.

The Superintendent of Buildings reports the issuance of building permits in this city as follows:—

Year.	Amount.
	£
1893	328,000
1894	465,000
1895	841,000

The Los Angeles Clearing-house (which, however, does not include all the banks) reports clearings (in round numbers) as follows:—

Year.	Amount.
	£
1893	8,900,000
1894	9,400,000
1895	12,400,000

Towards the close of 1895 war rumours had an unfavourable effect on the business revival, and insufficient rainfall this winter to insure good crops, with other causes, now render it probable that the progress of this district will be temporarily arrested. The "other causes" to which I refer are summarised by the editor of the "Commercial Bulletin" of this city, as follows:—"No doubt the causes which have made business dull in all parts of the country affect us here. The continual agitation maintained at Washington for 3 years over the tariff schedule, our finances and foreign relations, is the chief reason why business is stagnant. This, too, is a presidential year, and one promising a radical change in the national administration, and this is a factor which always unsettles business."

The fact that Southern California has been advancing steadily in manufacturing and agriculture, and has enjoyed general prosperity, notwithstanding the "hard times" elsewhere in the United States, makes it probable that the present depression will last but a short time.

The considerations named in all deeds filed in the office of the Recorder here, in 1895, aggregated 3,500,000*l*. The corresponding figures for the city and county of San Francisco were 2,725,000*l*. In view of the fact that San Francisco has quite three times as large a population, this is a very good showing for Los Angeles.

The completion of the extensive improvements in the National Tehuantepec Isthmus Railroad, and of its terminal ports on the Gulf of Mexico and the Pacific Coast, may possibly afford some relief to the fruit growers here in opening the European markets to them; in any case I should think it probable that a line of steamers could build up a good trade between this district and Mexican ports, having for their southernmost port the Pacific end of the Tehuantepec Railway.

General Remarks.

Information for British capitalists. Bonds. The bonded indebtedness of this county amounts to 172,100*l*., bearing interest at from 4½ to 6 per cent., the lower rate being on the later issues. From time to time, school, municipal and other good gold bonds, bearing about 5 per cent., can be purchased here.

In 1890 city school bonds, to the amount of 40,000*l.*, were issued, bearing 5 per cent., of this issue 12,000*l.* has been redeemed. In July last a new issue of 61,000*l.* was made, bearing 4½ per cent. The interest and one-fortieth of the principal is paid annually. These bonds are largely held by the banks here, and can be purchased to pay 4¼ per cent. They are guaranteed by the State, are a first lien on the school property, referred to elsewhere in this report, and in my opinion are absolutely safe.

Elsewhere in this report I comment on the "Wright Act," and the irrigation bonds issued under the authority of that Act. *Irrigation bonds.*

It is stated in the "Investor," a financial paper published in this city, that during 1895 the sum of 2,128,000*l.* was advanced on mortgage on the security of real property in this city and county of Los Angeles, and that releases of mortgages to the amount of 1,462,000*l.* were recorded. 7 per cent. net can be obtained on the best first mortgage security. First mortgages on good real property, and the bonds of legitimate enterprises are the safest investments for English investors. *Mortgages.*

It was stated in the Los Angeles "Times" recently, that Messrs. Easton and Eldrige, real estate agents of this city, obtained an option on 39,000 acres of the Chino ranch in August last, the price of the land being fixed in the option at 320,000*l.*; and that they had negotiated a sale to an English syndicate at an advance of 180,000*l.*, the price to the syndicate being 500,000*l.* Mr. Holabird, the general manager of the ranch, writes me under date March 18, as follows:— *Sale of Chino Ranch.*

"Regarding the sale to the English syndicate, it is not yet completed. We hope it will not fall through. The account appearing in the 'Times' was substantially correct."

It is unnecessary for me to comment on this.

The San Jacinto Estate, Limited, an English tin mining company, purchased 45,000 acres of land in this vicinity for 300,000*l.* about 6 years ago, and spent about 100,000*l.*, in ascertaining that it would not pay to work the tin mines on the property. It was recently stated in the Press here that valuable gold mines had been discovered at Gavilan, on the estate, and in reply to an enquiry, Mr. Pedley, the general manager, writes me as follows:— *The San Jacinto Estate, Ltd.*

"The developments at Gavilan are as yet too young to say anything definite; there is some extremely rich ore, but it is only a very thin ledge; probably a stringer; there are several large ledges of low grade ore which are likely to be much more valuable.

"We have some 1,500 acres watered, and of this we have sold about 100 acres; much of the rest is planted, and we have gone in for diversified agriculture; we expect to turn out about 5,000 hogs a year when we breed up to our full capacity."

So much of the land is suitable for horticulture and agriculture that it is not improbable that the company will be very successful.

I have received a pamphlet entitled "California, a handbook of useful and reliable information, gained by fruit farmers of many *Advice to emigrants.*

years standing:" issued by a London firm from their office in Piccadilly. It is stated in this pamphlet that the "expenses on a 10-acre orange orchard to the end of the fourth year, exclusive of loss of interest, amount to 506*l*.; that the returns will pay the expenses (50*l*.) for the fifth year, and the following statement is then made :—

"The sixth year's crop being no better than the average of young orchards in the vicinity, should pay back more than the total of all the expenses on the land from the start, with 6 per cent. interest added in addition to the expenses of the sixth year. This has not failed to be accomplished in by far the majority of instances."

The following paragraph is also taken from the same pamphlet :—

Farm pupils. "From time to time openings occur on fruit ranches for pupils at a premium of from 100*l*. to 150*l*. inclusive. They are treated as one of the family, thoroughly taught the business of fruit farming, have short hours of work, and share in all the advantages of the club, athletic associations, and sport in the locality."

There is no royal road to success in fruit farming. "Clubs," "athletic associations," and "sport" must be eschewed, and "for short hours of work," short hours of rest must be the rule. "Farm pupils" who have paid large premiums in London to be taught farming in California constantly apply to me for advice and assistance, stating that they have been swindled, and although this particular swindle has been exposed in the London press over and over again the crop of fools appears to be perennial. In my report for 1891 I commented on the matter as follows :—

"Complaint has been made to me that a London firm of emigration agents is sending young English lads here to be taught farming, and is charging a fee of 50*l*., for which the pupils receive little value. As a rule the employment obtained for these lads is not any better than that which they could obtain without the aid of the introduction afforded by the agent of the firm in question, and in all cases they would be 50*l*. better off if, to use a colloquialism, they came on their own hook. The qualities which will insure success here are conspicuously absent in young men who will pay 50*l*. for the kind of employment which they suppose they are to obtain here. In one case, reported to me a few days ago by the person to whose house one of the pupils was sent, the 'pupil' was led to believe in London that the rough work on the farm he was to be sent to would be done by Chinamen. After 10 days' experience, this 'pupil' resigned and left this State."

The belief prevalent in England that fruit farming is a species of pastime is a very erroneous one. Fruit farming is much more laborious than general farming, and taken as a whole (excluding some exceptional years) it has not been profitable. It is still very largely in the experimental stage, and as the more unprofitable branches are dropped and more experience is gained in production and marketing, it is probable that success will yet crown the efforts of the fruit farmers. The question is fairly and ably discussed in an article in the August number of "The National Review," London. Persons who think of engaging in the industry here should read this article.

The labour unions of this city issued an address in the early part of 1895, advising mechanics not to come to Southern California; a part of this address is as follows:—

"We wish again to warn the people in the East against the published misstatements gross exaggerations and beautiful pictures that are strewn broadcast with a lavish hand. Southern California is indeed a paradise for those who are not compelled to toil, or those who have that happy faculty of living off the labour of others, but for the mechanic and labourer, and those whose sole capital is their labour, Southern California is as poor as the poorest. This is the land where the Chinaman is preferred to the white man; a land where thousands of honest and willing toilers lay down at night not knowing where the substance to maintain life the following day is to come from. A land where a society of men and women are working for their food and clothing alone, and who are grateful for the privilege."

Commenting on this address, the Los Angeles "Express" remarks in part as follows:—

"We heartily agree with the circular that all the mechanical help needed is here now, and we would encourage no wage earner to come here seeking work, although we believe this community will compare favourably with any section of the country in point of prosperity.

"Until we get more manufactures, a larger country population, and a more extensive trade, clerks, mechanics, and labouring men will find this market as overstocked as the rest of the country."

Alien ownership of land.

In my report for 1894, I stated that by a recent amendment to the Constitution (of this State) the right of aliens to own real property in California had been taken away. I was probably in error in making this statement. The facts are briefly as follows:— In November, 1894, an amendment to the Constitution was submitted to the people, providing that thereafter aliens would not be allowed to purchase land in this State; I was informed by several members of the legislature that it was the intention of that body that the amendment, if adopted by the people, should be self-enacting. It was voted on and adopted, and for some time it was generally believed that it was in operation. The best lawyers in this State now hold that this amendment was not so framed as to be self-enacting, and that it is not, and will not be in force, until the legislature passes an Act putting it in force, and providing penalties for its infringement. If this view be correct, the only effect of the affirmative vote of the people has been to give the legislature power to pass an Exclusion Act.

Public Library.

The Public Library in this city now contains 41,600 volumes, and is free to all residents of the city, who can also borrow books for home use without charge. It is maintained by an annual tax levy on all taxable property in the city (not to exceed 1s. on each 100l.). The income last year amounted to 4,600l. The record of books borrowed in 1893 and 1895 shows the following results:—

| | Volumes. ||
	1893.	1895.
Fiction and periodicals	294,516	410,637
All other books	92,743	79,604
Total	387,259	490,241

The registered borrowers, that is persons who take books for home use, numbered 13,495 in 1893, and now number 22,223.

Despite the care of the librarian, improper books are sometimes purchased. The press having drawn attention to the purchase of an immoral book, a dissenting minister publicly prayed for the librarian by name, and she responded by a suit for damages. The case did not come to trial, so the legal right of a minister to offer public prayers for officials who are not members of his congregation has not been determined.

Shipping and Navigation.

Congress has not yet made an appropriation for the construction of a good harbour for this district, and owing to the rival claims of Port Los Angeles (18 miles west of this city) and San Pedro (22 miles south), it is not probable that an appropriation will be secured at the present session. The Southern Pacific Company's wharf at Port Los Angeles, which is nearly a mile long, is safe for the largest vessels, except for a few days in the year, and the expense of discharging and receiving cargo is so much less than at San Pedro, that the foreign-going vessels have abandoned the latter port. United States army engineers have reported in favour of San Pedro, and should a breakwater be constructed, then wharves will be built, and the shipping will again go to that port. The following are prices for ballast and water:—

| | | Prices ||
| | | Port Los Angeles. | San Pedro. |
		£ s. d.	£ s. d.
Ballast delivered on board	Per ton	0 2 6	0 7 0
Water ,, ,,	Per 1,000 gallons	0 2 0	0 4 0

The difference in expense is due to the fact that at San Pedro cargo is received and discharged into lighters, as foreign-going vessels cannot get to the wharves in the inner harbour.

The rates for dockage at Port Los Angeles, for all vessels

'over 200 tons, are 16s. a day for the first 200 tons, and three-quarters of ½d. for each additional ton.

Since writing the foregoing, I see it stated in the press that the House Committee on Rivers and Harbours have agreed to place San Pedro on the continuing contract system. This means that the work of improvement will be commenced and carried on till completed. The engineer-in-charge estimating each year how much money can be profitably expended on the improvements. It is not stated whether the improvements will consist in the construction of a breakwater in the outer harbour, or deepening the channel to admit foreign-going ships to the inner harbour.

It is also stated that a large appropriation for Port Los Angeles has been included in the River and Harbour Bill. It is not probable, however, that appropriations will be made for both harbours.

I am indebted to the Collector of Customs for the following return of shipping. It does not include the coast trade:—

Annex A.—RETURN of all Shipping at the Port of Los Angeles, California, during the Year 1895.

ENTERED.

Nationality.	Sailing. Number of Vessels.	Tons.	Steam. Number of Vessels.	Tons.	Total. Number of Vessels.	Tons.
British	10	15,551	1	1,267	11	16,818
American	20	10,030	8	15,136	28	25,166
Other countries	...	...	19	38,526	19	38,526
Total	30	25,581	28	54,929	58	80,510
,, for the year preceding	16	24,324	30	54,080	46	78,404

NOTE.—This return does not include the sailing and steam coasting vessels.

CLEARED.

Nationality.	Sailing. Number of Vessels.	Tons.	Steam. Number of Vessels.	Tons.	Total. Number of Vessels.	Tons.
British	10	15,551	1	1,267	11	16,818
American	6	4,241	8	15,136	14	19,377
Other countries	...	...	19	38,526	19	38,526
Total	16	19,792	28	54,929	44	74,721
,, for the year preceding	16	24,324	30	54,080	46	78,404

Trade and Commerce.

Mistakes of English manufacturers.

English manufacturers have been accused more than once of not adapting themselves to the methods of business prevailing in foreign countries, and it has been asserted that, in consequence, Continental manufacturers are supplanting them. The following seems to be a case in point. I wrote to Messrs. M. A. Newmark and Co., wholesale grocers in this city, enquiring generally as to the increase or decrease in amount and value of English goods handled by them. In reply, I have received the following letter:—

"We acknowledge the receipt of your favour of the 19th inst., and, replying to the same, beg to state that, as a rule, our consumption of English goods has materially decreased during the past few years. This is due to several causes, principal among which are the following:—

"Times have naturally been exceedingly hard for the people at large who are the consumers, and as a matter of course their requirements have been rather for cheap than expensive articles under the circumstances.

"Aside from this fact, however, we believe that the large English manufacturers who sell their products to some extent on this coast, are responsible for a portion of this loss of business. Their agents, as a rule, are wholesalers like ourselves, and go to the retail trade and sell at about the same prices that they do to us, thus antagonising the wholesaler, who will handle anything in preference to the brands sold in this manner.

"We believe that our sales of Liverpool salt keep up, but for the reasons above mentioned English goods generally have lost some of their prestige."

Upon receipt of this reply, I wrote to a number of firms in other lines, enquiring whether the agents of British manufacturers on this coast antagonise the wholesale dealers in the way indicated by Messrs. Newmark and Co., and I have received replies, from which I select the following as specimens:—

Messrs. Crane Company, importers of tin plate, and manufacturers of iron pipe, iron fittings, steam and gas fitters' tools, &c., state:—

"It is only too true that the representatives of English manufacturers make but a slight difference in price between that given the jobber and the retailer."

Messrs. Aylesworth, Haskell, and Co., jobbers in fancy goods, stationery, &c., write me as follows:—

"We buy but few goods from the agents on this coast, on account of the fact that they make prices to small buyers the same as the largest quantity buyers. Hence we go to New York importers and agents direct for all English goods. Our best purchases are made through agencies in New York."

Harper, Reynolds, and Co., wholesale hardware merchants, write me as follows:—

"In answer to yours of the 24th inst., will say that we handle very few English goods, and the percentage is on the decrease rather than on the increase.

"We have handled considerable English tin plate during the past year, but at the present prices of English and American tin, the American tin would be as cheap if not cheaper.

"As far as we know, it is a fact that English manufacturers sell to the retail trade at the same, or about the same, price as to the wholesale, thus antagonising them (the wholesalers)."

SAN FRANCISCO.

It is apparent that there must be something radically wrong in the handling of English goods on this coast when the wholesale dealers here find it to their advantage to buy in New York, and pay the heavy railway charges for a 3,000 mile haul.

Messrs. Haas, Baruch, and Co., wholesale grocers, write me as follows:—

"We really have nothing to report as to any increase in English products handled by us during last year, with the exception of salt, which has probably been the only commodity on which we could note an increase of perhaps 10 per cent. over previous years, prices being about the same as we have always paid on former importations."

Messrs. W. P. Fuller and Co., manufacturers and importers of paints, oils, window-glass, &c., write me as follows:—

"The only English goods we have imported for the past year have been 500 barrels of earth paint. The value of same is about 500*l*. Our cement and glass was imported direct from Belgium." **Paint and Portland cement.**

Messrs. F. W. Braun & Co., importers and wholesale druggists, write me as follows:—

"We do sell English goods to a very considerable extent. We are not prepared to say whether our sales of English commodities have increased during the year 1895, for the reason that we do not keep a separate tabulated record of individual items, but as our general business has increased somewhat, we assume that our sales of English goods have likewise increased in proportion."

Messrs. Hayden, Lewis, and Company, saddlery, hardware, harness, shoe leather, findings, &c., write me:—"We sell very few imported goods, and them we buy from the importers in the Eastern States."

Messrs. Blake, Moffit, and Towne, importers and dealers in paper of every description, write me that they do not handle any English goods. I am surprised at this, as I am satisfied that there are various grades of English paper which, after paying duty, would undersell corresponding grades sold here.

The sweet wines and brandies produced in this district are pure and wholesome, and are marketed principally in the Eastern States, little, if any, being shipped to England. Mr. Bichowski, the manager of L. J. Rose and Company, Limited (an English Company), writes me that the price of wine grapes has ranged from 1*l*. to 2*l*. per ton in the last two years. He adds, "The prices now obtained for South California wines are fairly remunerative to producers owing to the formation of the Sweet Wine Association of California. Without the existence of this combination the prices of sweet wines would have been considerably lower than the cost of production." **Wines.**

The manager of the Southern California Packing Company writes me that his company packed 1,440,000 cans of 2 lbs. 1 oz. each in 1895, and that his pack in 1894 was 2,160,000 cans. He states that "the output for 1895 was purposely curtailed on account of the exceedingly low prices prevailing." A great deal **Canned fruit.**

(2158)

Oranges.

of fruit was allowed to rot on the trees, entailing heavy loss to the farmers.

The shipment of oranges from this district for the past two years has been as follows:—

Year.	Quantity.
	Tons.
1894	49,770
1895	77,000

Owing to heavy losses by frost at Riverside, and other causes, the shipment for 1896 will probably not exceed that of 1895. Very early and very late varieties of oranges have been planted in this district in recent years, the result being that in 1895 oranges were shipped East during every month of the year, the latest varieties overlapping the fruit of the earliest ones.

Raisins.

Raisin growers are again demanding increased duties on foreign raisins. The price, owing to foreign competition, is now so low that unless it increases it is probable that many raisin vineyards will be dug up and the land used for other purposes.

Vegetables.

The transcontinental railways write me that 16,700 tons of vegetables were shipped from this district in 1894, and 18,440 tons in 1895.

California fruit in England.

A representative of the Department of Agriculture at Washington attended the California fruit sales at Covent Garden in 1895, and reports that only the finest quality of fruit can be remuneratively sent to England, and that it must arrive during July and August to avoid competition with Continental fruit. The sales referred to were principally of peaches and pears. Shipments on a large scale will probably not be attempted until the Nicaragua Canal be opened.

R. G. Dun and Co.'s report.

R. G. Dun & Co.'s mercantile agency has offices in all the large cities in the United States and Canada, and some in England. Mr. Burnham, the manager for this district, has kindly sent me a copy of his last report, from which I make the following extracts:—

"During the year 14 new manufacturing enterprises have been put into operation. While this multiplying of workshops is encouraging, it is not satisfying. When we consider our existing advantages for producing cheaply, it becomes a matter of legitimate surprise that greater attention is not given by our capitalists to the opportunities offered for the manufacture here of articles which to import relieves us of much of our gain through other avenues of industry. Now that we have the cheap fuel in abundance, the lack of which for manufacturing purposes has been so deplored in the past, our zeal seems to be directed mainly to efforts for disposing of it to northern manufacturers at low figures. Los Angeles is well placed as a distributing point. Our transportation facilities, both by land and sea, are abundant for our present needs, and the building and projection of roads con-

SAN FRANCISCO.

tinues to an extent that promises to meet all possible demands of our extending trade."

"General trade for the year has been good, exceeding in volume all previous records. Our statistics show a falling-off in small dealers throughout the country, but this has strengthened rather than weakened the district commercially."

Mr. Burnham further informs me that the failures in this district for 1894 and 1895 were as follows:—

| Year. | Amount. ||
	Liabilities.	Assets.
	£	£
1894	252 200	80,000
1895	93 530	48 000

The report concludes as follows:—"The business outlook for the new year is excellent. Indications point to a period of substantial prosperity. The only ground for apprehension now lies in the fact that the rainfall of the season has not been up to the average at this date."

Mr. Burnham further writes me as follows:—

"As to our business in England, we have on our list only 13 houses on whom we are asked to send reports to London, and I am satisfied that among them are very few who import direct."

I am indebted to Mr. Gaffey, collector of customs for this district, for the following statistics:—

Annex B.—RETURN of Principal Articles of Export from Los Angeles, California, during the Years 1894-95.

| Articles. | 1894. || 1895. ||
	Quantity.	Value.	Quantity.	Value.
Nil	..	..	..	..

RETURN of Principal Articles of Import to Los Angeles, California, during the Years 1894-95.

| Articles. | 1894. || 1895. ||
	Quantity.	Value.	Quantity.	Value.
	Tons.	£	Tons.	£
Coal	131,655	91,568	128,249	84,620
Cement	..	3,594	5,933	9,060
Other articles	..	..	3,236	7,577
Total	131,655	95,162	137,418	101,257

(2158)

UNITED STATES.

Annex C.—TABLE showing the Total Value of all Articles Exported from and Imported to Los Angeles from and to Foreign Countries during the Years 1894–95.

Country.	Exports. 1894.	Exports. 1895.	Imports. 1894.	Imports. 1895.
Total	£ Nil	£ Nil	£ 101,408	£ 101,257

Industries and Population.

Vital statistics.

The city health officer has kindly given me the following statistics:—

Year.	Total Number of Deaths.	Total Number of Births.
1894	1,176	1,249
1895	1,181	1,588

In round numbers, about one-fourth of the deaths were caused by consumption, contracted elsewhere.

The population of this city has increased very rapidly in the past 2 years. The following are the figures given me by the city health officer:—

	Estimated Population.
January, 1894	65,000
June, 1894	75,000
January, 1895	80,000
December, 1895	100,000

Divorce.

Decrees of divorce were granted by the Superior Court of Los Angeles County in the past 3 years as follows:—

Year.	Number.
1893	209
1894	285
1895	312

In commenting on this subject last year, I pointed out that but few divorces were obtained for adultery, and I hazarded the opinion that the increase in divorce was not due to immorality, but rather to the fact that the Legislature, in its desire to protect women, has rendered it too easy for them to obtain divorces from husbands who treat them with less consideration than they think they are entitled to.

I make the following extracts from the annual report of the superintendent of buildings:— **New buildings.**

"The building operations for the past year have increased in volume and cost from those of the preceding year, or any year in the history of the city. This, in connection with the fact of the business depression throughout the country, is very gratifying .... another feature of the building activity which should not be overlooked is the fact that the mortgages recorded are less than one-half the amount of real estate sales and building construction."

The total loss from fire in 1895 was about 10,000*l*.

The county assessor's valuation of the taxable property in this county for the past 2 years is as follows:—

Year.	Value.
	£
1894	15,900,000
1895	17,000 000

There are 38 free schools in this city, and eight more are in course of construction. Upwards of 11,000 pupils attend these schools, for whose instruction there are 290 teachers. **Public schools.**

The estimated value of the school property, exclusive of new schools now being built at a cost of about 40,000*l*., is 154,100*l*. The annual revenue for the maintenance of the schools, which is derived from direct taxation, is 71,000*l*. From the foregoing figure it appears that the cost per pupil is 6*l*. 10*s*., per annum, without taking into account the loss of interest on the money invested in school property.

Interest in gold mining in this district has steadily increased for the past 2 years, and many mines containing low grade ore, which it was formerly thought were not worth working, are now being operated. The profits on many of these mines are quite small, and it is only on account of the decrease in the price of fuel, and transportation, that it is possible to work them. The work of prospecting for gold is being carried on very briskly, new mines are constantly being discovered, and from time to time valuable mines can be purchased for a small sum from discoverers who are unable to operate them. **Mining.**

Three copper mines were recently discovered in this vicinity, and will be worked as soon as the machinery can be placed on the ground.

The product of beet sugar is increasing very rapidly in this district. A large factory is in operation at Chino, a town 40 miles east of this city, and I am informed that other factories will shortly be completed and opened. **Beet-sugar.**

I am indebted to Mr. Cottman, manager of the Chino Valley Beet Sugar Company, for the following statistics:—

	Quantity.
	Tons.
Product of sugar at Chino, 1894	4,736
,, 1895	10,393

To show the relative importance of the product here, I give the following figures, supplied to me by Mr. Cottman:—

	Quantity.
	Tons.
Product of sugar in California, 1895	25,000
,, United States, 1895	405,000
Consumption of sugar in United States, 1895	1,949,744

It appears from the foregoing that the imports last year exceeded 1,500,000 tons. The percentage of sugar in the beets here is larger than elsewhere in the United States, and the climate admits of a succession of crops. On the other hand, labour, insurance, and interest on money are so much higher here than in the Eastern States, that it is alleged that the beet sugar factories in this State will have to close, unless the sugar bounty be continued.

Oil. In February, 1894, oil suitable for fuel was discovered about three-quarters of a mile from the centre of this city, and upwards of 400 wells have been sunk. Many of these wells produce upwards of 60 barrels of oil per day. Owing to the low price of oil, however, some of the wells are not being worked. The output is so much in excess of the demand that the price, which 2 years ago was 7s. per barrel (42 gallons), dropped to 1s. 3d. per barrel.

The output in this district in the last 2 years has been approximately as follows:—

Year.	Quantity.
	Barrels.
1894	450,000
1895	720,000

The manager of the Los Angeles branch of the Union Oil Company writes me that the average cost of production is about 2s. 5d. per barrel; that prices have ranged in 1895 from 5s. down to 1s. 5d. per barrel; that his company produced about 240,000 barrels of oil in 1895; and that "under treatment intelligently applied to produce best results, 3 to 3½ barrels of oil equal 1 ton of the best Australian coal."

The general manager of the Southern Pacific Company writes me as follows:—

"The use of crude oil as fuel on our locomotives can thus far be regarded as but in the experimental stage. We have at present but one engine equipped with the oil-burning apparatus, and it is yet too early to announce any definite conclusions as to the use of this fuel for locomotive steam purposes."

The railway from Los Angeles to Redondo (20 miles), the Los Angeles Electric Railway, and other local railways, use oil only for fuel.

The horseless carriage contest in France appears to have demonstrated that, although the vehicle propelled by gasoline won the prize in the race from Paris to Bordeaux and back, yet petroleum proved to be the most serviceable fuel. This use for petroleum will doubtless help to increase the demand for the article in this district.

Public Works.

This city is connected with San Francisco (487 miles north- Railways. west) by the Southern Pacific Railway, the line running through the central counties. For some years past the Southern Pacific has been constructing a line along the coast, and this new line is now completed and in operation as far south as Someo, and as far north as Ellwood, stations in Santa Barbara county about 35 miles apart. In addition to the work on the coast line (35 miles of mountain road), the same company has constructed three short branch lines, near Los Angeles, aggregating 15 miles in length. A number of other short lines have been built in this district in 1895. I have not received the exact figures from other companies. I may say, however, that more work has been done than for some years past, and, from present indications, the activity in railroad construction will be kept up for some time. The general manager of the Southern Pacific Company writes me as follows:—

"The population of Southern California in 1880 was double that of 1870, and in 1890 was nearly six times that of 1870. Notwithstanding this extraordinary increase in population, the building of railroad lines has more than kept pace with it. While in 1870 there were practically no railroads in Southern California, in the year 1890 there were more than 1,700 miles, or an average of 75 miles for each 10,000 of population. The amount of railroad facilities this provided in proportion to the population will perhaps be better appreciated when it is considered that the average for the whole United States, as shown by the last report of the Interstate Commerce Commission, was but 26 miles to each 10,000 people, or about one-third as much as Southern California."

The proposed railway from Los Angeles to Salt Lake City, Railway to Utah, is of the last importance to this district, and will, in a Salt Lake. variety of ways, directly affect important British interests.

The line has been constructed from Salt Lake City to Pioche, Nevada (350 miles), and from Los Angeles to Blake (150 miles). This leaves a gap of about 300 miles to complete the line. The

Secretary of the Salt Lake Chamber of Commerce writes me, under date March 16, 1896, as follows:—

"The line is certain to be built. The best men in Utah are behind it. For the first time, we are confident that the long-desired connection with the Pacific Coast, viâ Los Angeles, will soon be an accomplished fact."

The Los Angeles end of the line is known as the Nevada Southern Railway, and is in process of foreclosure, that company having failed to sell its bonds on the London market. A gentleman who was acting for the company in its negotiations with English capitalists writes me as follows:—

"Nothing can be done effectively until all chance of redemption under foreclosure expires. This does not occur until April next. I had people ready to take it up, but the possibility of war put a stop to anything American being placed in England, and I fear nothing can be done until the Venezuela matter be finally settled."

The 500 miles completed is in the hands of different companies. Were it in the hands of one company, with a debt of not more than one-third its cost, the whole line would be fair security for the 2,000,000 required to build the 300 mile gap between the present termini.

I have reliable reports of the extraordinary mineral wealth of the district to be traversed (coal, iron, and the precious metals), and, apart from this source of revenue, the line would shorten the distance from Los Angeles to Chicago by nearly a day's journey. English people who think of purchasing the bonds must see that they are well secured, as the building of American railways by English bond-holders (the American stock-holders only contributing "experience") is, to use a colloquialism, "played out."

Electric railways. Los Angeles is now connected with the mountains (20 miles) by an electric railway, and another line will be opened in a few days connecting Los Angeles with the sea (16 miles). In this city the cable roads have been converted into electric roads. The manager of the Los Angeles Railway Company writes me as follows:—

"This company is operating about 90 miles of road. As to its original cost, I cannot advise you very definitely, as it was built up at various and sundry times.

"It has a bond issue of 600,000*l*. As to whether any of the bonds are held in England or not I do not know, but my impression is that they are exclusively held in this country.

"The property will eventually much more than pay interest on this amount. As you know, within the last year we have been changing our cable lines to electric, and remodelling our power-house. This change is still in progress, and will be consummated shortly; there are certain additions which we will make in the near future, but which are improper at this time to discuss."

The Los Angeles Traction Company constructed during the 1895, about 6 miles of double track electric road. In all there are about 130 miles of street railways in this city.

Agriculture.

I am indebted to Mr. Cayley, an Englishman who is engaged in orange growing at Riverside, for the following information as to the damage sustained there this season from frost.

Orange growing.

"I have had some difficulty in obtaining the real facts as to the damage done by the late frost here. The estimates of damage have been very varied, and we are only now able to know how much fruit cannot be shipped. The Riverside crop to be marketed this season promised to be about 30,000 tons. Of this amount, probably only 15,000 tons will be shipped. Therefore the loss may be said to represent 15,000 tons. I think that a fair estimate of the money loss may be said to be about 100,000*l*. Many packers, however, claim that 150,000*l*. is nearer the mark. Of this amount probably 66 per cent. is directly attributable to frost, the remainder being due to a hot electrical north wind at the beginning of the season, which scorched many trees and dried up the stems of the fruit, causing it to fall to the ground. The damage done by the frost was chiefly in the lower parts of the valley, many orchards on higher ground escaping altogether. Frost appears to run along the hollows and depressions in the land, and an orchard planted on a slightly higher level than the adjoining land will probably escape damage. This season growers whose crops escaped the frost are realising high prices for their fruit, though not so high as in some former years."

In my report for 1894, I embodied a long letter from Mr. Cayley on orange growing, from which I make the following extract:—

"I have not gone much into figures, as they are very deceptive, and two ranches close together often receive very different returns. The whole question seems to be frost and no frost, and the only way to invest profitably is to make sure of buying a ranch practically free from frost, as some of them are." Persons who think of engaging in orange culture should purchase my report for 1894.

The orange growers in Southern California have sustained heavy losses from frost in the past 3 years. The eastern portion of Los Angeles County and some other places have escaped, the loss falling principally on the Riverside growers. Various expedients, such as flooding the orchards, and building fires around them when the indications pointed to frost, have been tried with little success. The following is taken from a recently published letter, written by Mr. Fleming of Visalia, to Mr. Hammond, of the United States weather bureau:—

"In endeavouring to carry out your idea of evaporating as much water as possible with the least amount of rising heat, we used several plans. We could not spray water on our fires, as, in order to make evaporation continuous, it required a man to attend each fire. We burned brush beforehand on our avenues and open spaces, and the beds of live coals formed were smudged with wet straw and manure several hours before sunrise and kept wet.

This could not be done among the trees without danger of burning them. We, therefore, heaped wet straw on a wire network 4 feet square stretched from four stakes driven into the ground, the straw being about 1½ feet from the ground. Small fires were built under them, and a man could attend to several, occasionally replenishing the fire and wetting the straw.

"But we finally hit on a still better scheme. We built similar wire frames on our low truck wagons, stretching them from four wagon stakes and heaping wet manure over them. Dirt was thrown on the wagon beds to protect them, and pots of burning tar were set underneath the straw roof. A barrel of water on the wagon was used to keep the straw wet. These wagons were driven about and did the best work, as they could go wherever most needed. The smoke and vapour were carried to the rear as the wagon moved, and, being at once out of the rising heat, fell close to the ground in a long white trail. At daylight our whole 400 acres of orchard was covered with a white fog extending from the ground about 20 feet high.

"It looks now as if one could absolutely protect against any ordinary frost, and if so you will have earned our everlasting gratitude."

Mr. Scott, horticultural commissioner for this county, writes me as follows:—

Fruit tree pests.

"The general condition of the fruit trees in Southern California is good; a great deal of spraying and fumigation has been done during the past year, and consequently the damage done by insect pests has been greatly reduced.

"In some of the old seedling orchards red scale is still doing damage, in the choice orange growing sections planted to budded fruit it is almost stamped out. It is certainly the worst pest citrus fruit growers have to contend with in Southern California.

"The report on frost lately published in the Los Angeles 'Times' gives a very fair estimate of the damage done; it certainly did not exaggerate."

In the report Mr. Scott refers to, the loss by frost is estimated at 20 per cent. of the entire orange crop, and it is recommended that the orange groves in the lowlands at Riverside be cut down and alfalfa planted.

Vine diseases.

A recent report made by Professor Newton B. Pierce, and issued by the Agricultural Department at Washington, shows that the California vine disease, which I have referred to in previous reports, has destroyed more than 30,000 acres of vines. The disease originated in this district, and practically all the damage has been done in Southern California. Professor Pierce writes me as to this disease and as to the phylloxera as follows:—

"The California vine disease is still observable in several of the counties of Southern California, although, as a whole, it is probably growing less both in the number of affected vineyards and diseased vines. There is one section of Northern California, however, where this disease is doing considerable damage, and is rather on the increase. This is the upper end of the Sacramento Valley on the east side of the Sacramento River.

"So far as I am able to state, phylloxera has been stamped out in the small vineyard where it was first detected in Southern California. The vines were destroyed some two or three years ago and no signs of the insects have been seen since, so far as I am aware. The pest continues to increase in the northern part of the State, and some new points of infection have been reported within the past year.

"The general health of the vineyards in the great unaffected districts of the San Joaquim Valley and much of Southern California, as well as vines on resistant roots in the phylloxera-infested districts of Northern California, is good."

Olives. As far as I am able to judge, the prospects of the olive-growers in this district are better than in any other branch of horticulture. The price for pure olive oil is good, the demand is steady, and, judging by the amount imported into this country, the demand will keep up. Messrs. Howland Bros., of Pomona, who have a large olive grove, write me that the production of olives and olive oil increased in 1895 over the figures of 1894 by about 50 per cent., that the demand for the olive oil is greater than the supply, and that the price continues to be 1*l*. per gallon.

Canaigre. The cultivation of canaigre is extending in this district. The United States Department of Agriculture reports that the roots grown here contain from 4 to 7 per cent. more tannic acid, the percentage running as high as 41·79 in the small air dried roots. It is stated that the tanning from canaigre tans leather quickly, making it soft and tough. I am not aware that it has been used here as yet in the manufacture of ink. The root is easily cultivated, and will, I think, be a very important crop in the near future.

Irrigation Act. In previous years I have commented at some length on an irrigation law of this State, known as the "Wright Act," under which two-thirds of the freeholders in any district capable of irrigation from a common source may form an irrigation district, vote bonds, and use the money in supplying their lands with water, and I have advised English people not to purchase these bonds until the United States Courts have passed on the constitutionality of the Act under which the bonds were issued. Judge Ross, of the United States Circuit Court, has now held that the Act is unconstitutional. The case has been appealed to the Supreme Court of the United States, and should Judge Ross's decision be affirmed, the holders of the bonds sold will suffer heavy loss. Bonds to the amount of about 2,000,000*l*. have been issued in this district, and it is estimated that bonds to the amount of 3,800,000*l*. have been sold, of which about 1,400,000*l*. have been purchased by English people.

Irrigation works. The most successful irrigation schemes in this State have been carried on by private companies not working under the Irrigation Law. The canals of the Kern County Land Company aggregate nearly 700 miles in length, and the Bear Valley Irrigation Works are nearly as extensive. The Columbian Irrigation Company has now been incorporated to carry out an irrigation project of much greater magnitude than anything heretofore attempted. This company controls the waters of the Mojave River, and at Victor, a station on the Southern California Railway, about 60 miles northeast of Los Angeles, the company is about to construct a dam at a point where the river flows through a gorge 300 feet deep and 200 feet wide. A dam at this point 150 feet high will create an artificial lake 10 miles long, and several miles in width. The reservoir thus created will irrigate a tract of 400,000 acres of dry land, now practically valueless. The Company also propose to build a city, to be called Columbia, which will be amply supplied with electric light and power from the 30,000 horse-power which can be developed at the dam. As much of the power as is not needed at Columbia can be carried to adjacent towns, in the form of an electric current. The land to be irrigated is desert-land owned by the United States Government, and can be purchased from the Government in tracts of 320 acres, provided the purchaser can, within 3 years from the date of his application, satisfy the Government that he has reclaimed it by conducting water to it. If the affairs of the Company be honestly administered, the bonds they now offer for sale ought to be good security

San Diego.

Mr. Vice-Consul Allen reports as follows :—

Trade and Commerce.

Trade depression. The past year has again to be noted as one of depression in all lines of business, and I may add, as I did in my report of last year, that there is little prospect of improvement in the near future—as the year of a Presidential election is always dull as regards business.

Grain. Two grain cargoes left for the United Kingdom during the year—one in an English vessel, the other in a German, valued at 20,132*l*. 16*s*.

Imports. Most of the imports, with the exception of coal and cement, were received by sail and rail from the Eastern States.

Exports. A list of the exports of the San Diego Bay region as received from the various transportation companies for the year 1895, including exports from the Escondido district, and honey from the back country, and figured entirely in car loads (about 10 tons): Oranges 107 cars, lemons 135, raisins 75, wool 23, wine 4, preserves 1, leather 1, hay 52, hogs 5, oats 56, wheat 44, barley 9, corn 11, fish 31, beeswax 1, dried fruit 19, honey 58, hides 31, green fruit 15, granite 52, mineral water 10, ore 1, brick 1, wood 6, olives 1, miscellaneous 6, Total 755 car loads.

Coal. Since the opening of the oil wells at Los Angeles, coal importations have fallen off considerably. The decrease for last year is given as about one-third less than in 1894. The Santa Fé railway has taken to burning oil in its locomotives, and many private firms who used large quantities of coal have now taken to the oil.

The ever-increasing population of the city and county will, however, gradually bring this loss up again to its former figures, I fancy, as nothing can be used as a substitute for coal for domestic purposes.

Cement continues to hold its own as building goes on briskly, notwithstanding the business depression. The whole of the sidewalks of San Diego are cemented, and a good deal is expended in this way during each year, not to mention the large quantities used in foundations and other building purposes. *Cement.*

The consumption of tin plates here is next to nothing, as cans for fruit preserving are purchased ready-made in San Francisco. *Tin-plate.*

The following tables show the imports and exports for the past two years.

RETURN of Principal Articles of Import to San Diego, California, during the Years 1894–95.

Articles.		1894. Quantity.	1894. Value.	1895. Quantity.	1895. Value.
			£ s.		£ s.
Coals	Tons	86,594	49,435 8	70,809	36,264 12
Cement	Casks	55,925	14,750 16	52,100	13,712 8
Other articles	...	...	24,294 0	...	7,277 0
Stock	Number	...	...	3,455	7,968 0
Guano	Tons	...	...	1,405	3,505 12
Bullion	Gold	...	...	...	15,495 16
Total	...	...	88,430 4	...	84,223 8
Lumber received from domestic ports	Feet	17,758,000	...	20,612,000	...

RETURN of Principal Articles of Export from San Diego, California, during the Years 1894–95.

Articles.		1894. Quantity.	1894. Value.	1895. Quantity.	1895. Value.
			£ s.		£ s.
Barley	Bushels	150,382	10,614 16	1,316	128 8
Wheat	,,	138,792	17,114 16	179,709	20,132 16
Agricultural implements	...	...	145 8	...	323 12
Fruit and nuts	...	...	124 16	...	194 12
Manufactured iron and steel	...	...	1,682 0	...	2,873 0
Wine	...	...	50 16	...	82 4
Powder and explosives	...	...	188 4	...	227 12
Lumber	...	...	1,075 12	...	1,099 4
Lime and cement	...	...	48 12	...	74 0
Coals	Tons	...	3 4	873	633 16
Other articles	...	...	8,064 12	...	7,843 16
Total	...	...	39,112 16	...	33,613 0

UNITED STATES.

TABLE showing Total Value of all Articles Exported from and Imported to San Diego from and to Foreign Countries during the Years 1894-95.

Country.	Exports. 1894. £ s.	Exports. 1895. £ s.	Imports. 1894. £ s.	Imports. 1895. £ s.
Great Britain and British possessions	27,326 16	20,398 16	65,392 8	53,613 4
Mexico	11,786 0	13,214 4	23,028 12	34,346 8
Not classified	..	..	59 0	29 16
Total	39,112 16	33,613 0	88,480 0	87,989 8

CUSTOMS Return for Port of San Diego, California, for the Year ending June 30, 1895.

	Value. £ s. d.
Value of dutiable imports	59,058 2 0
„ free „	27,008 13 6
„ coal „	40,026 16 6
„ cement „	12,255 2 0
„ grain exports	700 4 0

The revenue collected for the fiscal year ending June 30, 1895, was 11,940*l.* 12*s.*

Shipping and Navigation.

Shipping.

The following official figures have been furnished me by the United States Customs for 1894-95.

The number of vessels arriving was 375, classified as follows:—

Nationality.	Number of Vessels.	Total Net Tonnage.
American	278	157,054
British	30	50,980
Nicaraguan	63	6,552
Mexican	1	587
Norwegian	3	6,218
Total (for fiscal year ending June 30, 1895)	375	221,391

British vessels.

The number of entries and clearings of British vessels has diminished during the past year. This is partly owing to the wreck of the British steamer, "Crown of England," which came to this port eight or nine times annually, carrying coal from

Nanaimo, British Columbia. Her place has now been taken in the business by the Norwegian steamer, "Peter Gebsen." The value of the coal imported from British Columbia during the past year amounted to 18,808*l*. It is, however, quite likely that these cargoes may again fall to a British vessel at any time. One British cement cargo was also carried by a German vessel, value 5,074*l*. 16*s*. 8*d*.

The port of San Diego is situated 450 miles south-west of San Francisco, and is the only completely land-locked harbour south of that city. The dimensions of the bay are as follows:— Length, 13 miles; available anchorage, 6 square miles; average width of channel, 800 yards; total area of bay, 22 square miles; area at a depth of 18 feet, 2·83 square miles; area at a depth of 30 feet, 1·36 square miles; rise and fall of tides, 5 feet; depth of water over bar at low tide, 22 feet; at high tide, 28 feet. *Harbour facilities.*

Some idea of the wharf accommodation may be had from a partial description of Spreckles Bros., which is 3,500 feet long, and was built at a cost of over 18,000*l*. The coal bunkers on the wharf have a capacity of over 15,000 gross tons. The machinery is of the most modern and best improved type. *Coal bunkers.*

The wharf has a track connecting it with the Southern California Railway. Ships are unloaded directly into the bunkers, from which a train may be loaded in 15 minutes.

In addition to the Spreckles Bros. wharf there are the Santa Fé's, the Pacific Coast Steamship Company, the Dock Company, and the Russ Lumber and Mill Company's wharfs.

The following table shows the number and nationalities of vessels which entered and cleared during the year:—

RETURN of all Shipping at the Port of San Diego, California, United States of America, during the Year 1895.

ENTERED.

Nationality.	Sailing. Number of Vessels.	Sailing. Tons.	Steam. Number of Vessels.	Steam. Tons.	Total. Number of Vessels.	Total. Tons.
British	21	37,904	3	5,138	24	43,042
American	145	18,667	171	141,573	316	160,240
Other countries	3	2,781	75	15,591	78	18,372
Total	169	59,352	249	162,302	418	221,654
,, for the year preceding	93	49,807	206	145,064	299	194,871

UNITED STATES.

CLEARED.

Nationality.	Sailing. Number of Vessels.	Tons.	Steam. Number of Vessels.	Tons.	Total. Number of Vessels.	Tons.
British	23	41,884	3	5,138	26	47,022
American	143	18,240	170	141,208	313	159,448
Other countries	3	2,781	75	15,591	78	18,372
Total	169	62,905	248	161,937	417	224,842
,, for the year preceding	88	45,655	203	143,777	291	189,432

I am indebted to Mr. A. Higgins, Deputy Collector of Customs, for the information given in the preceding tables.

Population and Industries.

Immigration has been steadily on the increase in this locality; a good deal of British among it.

Building. For the past two years the building record in this city has been unusually large, and there is every probability that the activity in this line will be continued in the future. San Diego is far ahead of the average city, so far as handsome buildings are concerned. The indications are that the year 1896 will be even more prosperous in this way than last season.

Fish. The fishing industry has not yet gained the prominence the facilities would warrant. More than 100 varieties of good food fish are caught in the bay and ocean. At certain periods of the year large schools of sardines are found in the waters of the bay. As the output of olive oil increases there will be an excellent opportunity to establish a sardine cannery, whose goods could compete with the foreign article. Besides large exports of fresh fish, much is cured and shipped to Honolulu, San Francisco, and Eastern points. Totals, fresh, 12,500*l.*; dried and pickled, 5,872*l.*; crayfish, 1,000*l.*; clams, &c., 350*l.*; abalone shells, 400*l.*; abalone meat, 600*l.* Total, 20,722*l.*

Game. There is still a considerable amount of game upon the slopes and among the hills such as rabbit, quail, &c., not unfrequently deer and mountain lion. Wild ducks and water fowls abound in the lagoons and upon the bay.

Mining. Gold, silver, iron, cement, and asbestos are mined in varying quantities. During the past year there has been a revival of interest and renewed activity in mining circles. Some old mines have been re-opened and many rich strikes recorded, and considerable stock has changed hands. Some of the richest mines are located in the Julian and Banner Section, though much valuable ore is turned out in the Excondido Valley.

The gold mines at Gold Rock and Picacho, on the desert, have become among the best known in the State. The first-named camp produces 30,000*l.* gold per month, and a company has lately taken charge of the Picacho mines for immediate development.

Brooms have recently become an important branch of local manufacture. A flour mill is in successful operation, and supplies the country tributary to San Diego city. A soap factory meets the local demand and ships its product abroad. Baking powder is a San Diego manufacture recently presented to the public. From a small beginning a good trade has been established at home, and large quantities shipped to Mexico. *Minor industries.*

No decision has as yet been handed down by the Supreme Court of the United States as regards the legality of the Wright Irrigation Law; but it is expected to be given shortly. *Irrigation laws.*

Although several water companies have made propositions for further supplies of water for the city and the surrounding country, none have as yet been accepted. This year will no doubt see some decisive action taken in the matter. *Water companies.*

Agriculture.

Fruit ranches generally have not made very high returns to their owners of late years, though lemons, walnuts, almonds, nuts, olives, and, this season again, oranges have made good money. A large acreage is still being planted with lemons, as this region is very free from frosts, and in many other ways peculiarly adapted to their growth. Oranges have commanded a much better price this season owing to the heavy frosts suffered in Florida last year. Orange exports from the bay region and with Excondido and the intervening country will probably aggregate 200 cars for 1896. The output of lemons for 1895 was 135 carloads. This will probably be doubled this year and perhaps more, as it is difficult to tell exactly the acreage of trees coming into bearing for 1896. The apple crop of San Diego county in 1895 was 50 per cent. greater than ever before. It amounts, according to the Horticultural Commissioner, to about 80,000 boxes, or 250 carloads. The value of this product is not far from 15,000*l*. *Fruit generally.*

Olive growing is attracting as much attention in Southern California to-day as any other industry. Many new groves are being planted. Near Fulerton, in Orange county, a tract of 400 acres is being prepared for the trees, the number to be planted being 40,000. *Olives.*

Near Whittier 240 acres are being planted with olives. In the vicinity of Colton a tract of 340 acres is being transformed into an olive grove as fast as the work can be done. These are only a few instances. All through the southern counties olive orchards are being set out, and lands adapted to them are in special demand. There has been money for California growers both in olives and oil. The product of this State is steadily growing in popularity in the east. The oil especially is gaining in favour. It is very difficult to obtain pure imported olive oil. Even when high prices are paid, the purchaser, unless he chances to be an expert, will get cottonseed oil or even not so harmless an adulterant.

Now that the superiority of California pure oil is becoming known there is no danger of any lack of demand. Pure oil is scarce, and is sold at 6s. per quart bottle. Pickled olives are sold at 2s. to 4s. per gallon.

Public Works.

The only Government work under way in connection with the harbour of San Diego, and with the exception of a little money appropriation for building a levee to divert the San Diego River into False Bay, the only money ever expended by the Government on this valuable harbour is the jetty at Zuninga Shoals. The jetty will extend 7,200 feet due south from the western point of North Island, parallel with Point Loma and directly east of it. The entire cost of the work is estimated at 80,000*l.* to 90,000*l.* Congress has made three appropriations of 10,000*l.* each for this work. As the regular River and Harbour Bill is passed every other year, the work is not likely to be completed for a number of years.

Dollars have been converted into sterling at the rate of 5 dol. to the 1*l.*

LONDON:
Printed for Her Majesty's Stationery Office,
By HARRISON AND SONS,
Printers in Ordinary to Her Majesty.
(75 6 | 96 —H & S 2158)

FOREIGN OFFICE.
1896.
ANNUAL SERIES.

No. 1767.

DIPLOMATIC AND CONSULAR REPORTS ON TRADE AND FINANCE.

UNITED STATES.

REPORT FOR THE YEAR 1895
ON THE
TRADE OF THE DISTRICT OF THE NEW YORK CONSULATE GENERAL.

REFERENCE TO PREVIOUS REPORT, Annual Series No. 1561.

Presented to both Houses of Parliament by Command of Her Majesty,
JULY, 1896.

LONDON:
PRINTED FOR HER MAJESTY'S STATIONERY OFFICE,
BY HARRISON AND SONS, ST. MARTIN'S LANE,
PRINTERS IN ORDINARY TO HER MAJESTY.

And to be purchased, either directly or through any Bookseller, from
EYRE & SPOTTISWOODE, EAST HARDING STREET, FLEET STREET, E.C., and
32, ABINGDON STREET, WESTMINSTER, S.W.; or
JOHN MENZIES & Co., 12, HANOVER STREET, EDINBURGH, and
90, WEST NILE STREET, GLASGOW; or
HODGES, FIGGIS, & Co., Limited, 104, GRAFTON STREET, DUBLIN.

1896.

[C. 7919—135.] *Price Twopence.*

New Series of Reports.

Reports of the Annual Series have been issued from Her Majesty's Diplomatic and Consular Officers at the following places, and may be obtained from the sources indicated on the title-page:—

No.		Price.	No.		Price.
1645. Lisbon	.. ..	1½d.	1706. Rio de Janeiro	.. ..	2½d.
1646. Brussels	.. ..	½d.	1707. San José	.. ..	1d.
1647. Vera Cruz	.. ..	½d.	1708. Paramaribo	.. ..	2d.
1648. Tunis	.. ..	1d.	1709. Brest	.. ..	1½d.
1649. Antwerp	.. ..	1d.	1710. Montevideo	.. ..	½d.
1650. Tokio	.. ..	1d.	1711. Charleston	.. ..	2½d.
1651. Honolulu	.. ..	½d.	1712. Baltimore	.. ..	1d.
1652. Stettin	.. ..	1½d.	1713. Tripoli	.. ..	1d.
1653. Bangkok	.. ..	1d.	1714. Callao	.. ..	½d.
1654. Batoum	.. ..	1½d.	1715. Ningpo	.. ..	1d.
1655. Mexico	.. ..	9½d.	1716. Dunkirk	.. ..	1½d.
1656. Odessa	.. ..	1½d.	1717. Batoum	.. ..	2d.
1657. Réunion	.. ..	1d.	1718. Hankow	.. ..	1½d.
1658. Tokio	.. ..	1½d.	1719. Foochow	.. ..	3½d.
1659. Maranham	.. ..	1d.	1720. Syra	.. ..	½d.
1660. Copenhagen	.. ..	1d.	1721. Panama	.. ..	1d.
1661. Berlin	.. ..	1½d.	1722. Batavia	.. ..	1½d.
1662. Teheran	.. ..	2½d.	1723. Genoa	.. ..	3d.
1663. Salonica	.. ..	1½d.	1724. Cagliari	.. ..	2½d.
1664. Manila	.. ..	½d.	1725. Chicago	.. ..	7½d.
1665. Florence	.. ..	5½d.	1726. Trieste	.. ..	1d.
1666. Dakar	.. ..	½d.	1727. Hakodate	.. ..	1d.
1667. Havre	.. ..	2d.	1728. Mannheim	.. ..	1d.
1668. Rouen	.. ..	2d.	1729. Panama	.. ..	1d.
1669. Corfu	.. ..	½d.	1730. Caracas	.. ..	1d.
1670. Calais	.. ..	1d.	1731. Riga	.. ..	6½d.
1671. Tehran	.. ..	1½d.	1732. Tokio	.. ..	1½d.
1672. Barcelona	.. ..	2d.	1733. Tainan	.. ..	1d.
1673. Amsterdam	.. ..	1d.	1734. Portland	.. ..	3d.
1674. Bordeaux	.. ..	2½d.	1735. Fiume	.. ..	1½d.
1675. Warsaw	.. ..	1d.	1736. Taganrog	.. ..	2d.
1676. Havana	.. ..	1½d.	1737. Swatow	.. ..	1d.
1677. Berlin	.. ..	1d.	1738. Chungking	.. ..	1½d.
1678. Beira	.. ..	1½d.	1739. Angora	.. ..	1½d.
1679. Saigon	.. ..	1d.	1740. Shanghai	.. ..	2½d.
1680. Trebizond	.. ..	1d.	1741. Bilbao	.. ..	3½d.
1681. Vera Cruz	.. ..	1½d.	1742. Tahiti	.. ..	1½d.
1682. Patras	.. ..	1d.	1743. New Caledonia	.. ..	1½d.
1683. La Rochelle	.. ..	1½d.	1744. Amoy	.. ..	1½d.
1684. Madrid	.. ..	1½d.	1745. Ichang	.. ..	1d.
1685. Belgrade	.. ..	2d.	1746. Berlin	.. ..	½d.
1686. Algiers	.. ..	5d.	1747. Rio de Janeiro	.. ..	5½d.
1687. Galveston	.. ..	2½d.	1748. Porto Rico	.. ..	1½d.
1688. New Orleans	.. ..	2d.	1749. Montevideo	.. ..	1½d.
1689. Suakin	.. ..	1d.	1750. San Francisco	.. ..	3d.
1690. Pernambuco	.. ..	1d.	1751. Cayenne	.. ..	½d.
1691. Guatemala	.. ..	1½d.	1752. Frankfort	.. ..	3d.
1692. Guayaquil	.. ..	1d.	1753. Malaga	.. ..	8½d.
1693. Wênchow	.. ..	1d.	1754. Söul	.. ..	1d.
1694. Piræus	.. ..	3d.	1755. Copenhagen	.. ..	3d.
1695. Tokio	.. ..	3d.	1756. Nice	.. ..	1d.
1696. Marseilles	.. ..	1d.	1757. Lisbon	.. ..	1½d.
1697. Manila	.. ..	1d.	1758. Nagasaki	.. ..	1d.
1698. Jerusalem	.. ..	1d.	1759. Hamburg	.. ..	2½d.
1699. Cherbourg	.. ..	2d.	1760. Mozambique	.. ..	2d.
1700. Leghorn	.. ..	1½d.	1761. Cettinjé	.. ..	1½d.
1701. Boston	.. ..	1½d.	1762. The Hague	.. ..	1½d.
1702. Kiungchow	.. ..	1d.	1763. Cephalonia	.. ..	1d.
1703. Naples	.. ..	2½d.	1764. Bahia	.. ..	1d.
1704. Stockholm	.. ..	2d.	1765. Zanzibar	.. ..	1½d.
1705. Corunna	.. ..	2d.	1766. Pakhoi	.. ..	1d.

No. 1767.

Reference to previous Report, Annual Series No. 1561.

UNITED STATES.

NEW YORK.

Consul-General Sanderson to the Marquis of Salisbury.

My Lord,   New York, May 26, 1896.

I HAVE the honour to forward my Annual Report on the Trade and Commerce of the Consular District of New York, together with a Report of a similar character which I have received from Mr. Vice-Consul Stockwell respecting Providence, Rhode Island.

I have, &c.
(Signed)   PERCY SANDERSON.

Report on the Trade and Commerce of the Consular District of New York for the Year 1895.

ABSTRACT of Contents.

	PAGE
New York—	
General review of trade	3
Improvement on 1894	3
Situation of Treasury	3
Contract with syndicate for gold	3
Agricultural produce	4
Railways	4
Imports and exports	4
New York money market	4
New York banks	5
New York clearing-house returns	5
Clearings outside New York	6
Sterling exchange	6
Rate adopted in this report	7
Stock Exchange	7
Cotton Exchange	7
Produce Exchange	7
Failures	7
State banks of deposit and discount	7

(2204)

UNITED STATES.

ABSTRACT of Contents—continued.

	PAGE
New York—continued—	
Legislation	8
Number	8
Capital	8
Resources and liabilities	8
Debt of State of New York	9
New York City debt	9
Valuation	9
Trade and commerce—	
Coal	9
Iron and steel	9
Comparative prices of staple commodities	10
Silk	10
Textile manufactures	10
Effects of the new tariff	10
Leather	10
Optical goods	10
Musical instruments	10
Fancy goods	10
China and glass	10
Paintings	10
Books, &c.	10
Silk	11
Woollen dress goods	11
Hosiery	11
Linen	11
Bicycles	11
Metal parts of umbrellas	11
Customs tariff	11
"Ad valorem duties"	11
Review of the freight market	12
Business in general	12
Grain freights	12
Cotton	13
Petroleum	13
Timber	13
Sugar	13
Cattle	13
Public works —	
Canal improvements	13
„ transport between New York and Cleveland	14
Harlem River Ship Canal	14
Proposed canal across New Jersey	14
Railroads—	
Railroad traffic	15
Vital statistics	16
Immigration	17
Strikes	17
Report of Board of Mediation and Arbitration	17
Return of shipping	18
Principal articles of export	19
„ import	20
Total value of imports and exports	21
Specie	22
Grain shipments	23
Return of number of seamen engaged and discharged at New York	24
Providence, Rhode Island—	
Money	25
Tonnage	25
Duties	25
Cotton manufactures	25
Wool and woollens	25
Jewellery	25
Wages	26

NEW YORK.

Abstract of Contents—continued.

	PAGE
Providence, Rhode Island—continued—	
New buildings	26
Fire loss	26
Terminal facilities	26
Public improvements	26
Census	26
Return of shipping	28
Principal articles of export	28
" import	29
Total value of imports and exports	29

General Review of Trade.

The year 1894 had been one of extraordinary depression in trade and industry, owing in a large measure to exceptional causes, such as general strikes, heavy floods, extensive forest fires, and the unsettled state of business consequent on the prolonged discussion of the tariff. *[Improvement on 1894.]*

In 1895 the labour troubles were few and of a minor character, the other special causes tending to depression did not recur and there was a steady and general improvement, making the year compare very favourably with its predecessor although it cannot be ranked among those of full business activity.

The recovery in trade is also attributed in a large measure to the restoration of confidence in the ability of the country to maintain gold payments. *[Situation of Treasury contract with syndicate for gold.]*

In 1894 two sales of bonds had been made with the view of replenishing the gold reserve of the Treasury, gold, however, seemed to flow out almost as fast as it flowed in. At the close of the year there was a feeling of insecurity as to whether the policy of paying in gold might not be altered at some future time, and during December there were heavy withdrawals of gold.

The demand was less heavy during the first few days of January, 1895, but as the public became apprehensive as to the situation of the Treasury, withdrawals increased, and at the end of the month gold was being withdrawn in large quantities, both for export and for domestic account. Negotiations were opened by the Government with a syndicate for the purchase of gold and the sale of United States bonds, and a contract was signed in February providing for the sale to the Government of 3,500,000 ozs. of gold for 4 per cent. bonds with 30 years to run, the price obtained for the bonds being 104·49.

At least half of the gold was to come from Europe, but the shipments were not required to exceed 300,000 ozs. a month. The syndicate also agreed to exert all financial influence and make all legitimate efforts to protect the Treasury against withdrawals of gold pending the complete performance of the contract. The results of this contract were at once apparent, the withdrawals of gold stopped, exports ceased, and some of the gold which had been taken out of the Treasury was returned.

(2204)

When it was found that the reserve of gold in the Treasury was being maintained, confidence revived and business activity began to spread.

The production of iron and steel increased enormously, prices rose in almost every branch of trade, and voluntary advances in the rate of wages were of frequent occurrence. At the close of the year the reserve of gold in the Treasury was again impaired, and a fresh loan was in prospect, the message of the President and the action of Congress on the question of the boundary between British Guiana and Venezuela created a panic on the Stock Exchange and had a disturbing effect on trade in general, but came too late in the year to affect the results considered as a whole.

Agricultural produce.

The crops were very good, that of Indian corn throughout the United States being given as 2,151,000,000 bushels as compared with 1,212,000,000 in 1894. Wheat 467,000,000 bushels as compared with 460,000,000, and oats 824,000,000 bushels, as against 662,000,000 in 1894. The price of Indian corn was much lower in consequence of the very heavy crop, and it stood at about $34\frac{1}{2}$ c. ($17\frac{1}{4}d.$) a bushel on December 31, 1895, against $51\frac{3}{4}$ c. ($25\frac{7}{8}d.$) at the same date in 1894. Winter wheat was seriously damaged and the price advanced early in the year, but the spring crop was very large and later in the year the greater part of this advance was lost, the closing price being only a trifle above that of last year, viz., $66\frac{1}{4}$ c. ($33\frac{1}{8}d.$), as compared with $60\frac{5}{8}$ c. ($30\frac{5}{16}d.$) per bushel.

The cotton crop was a short one and the price at one time reached 9 c. ($4\frac{1}{2}d.$) per 1 lb., it closed, however, at about 8 c. ($4d.$), as compared with $5\frac{1}{4}$ c. or $2\frac{5}{8}d.$ in 1894.

Railways.

The earnings of the railways showed considerable improvement on the whole; some suffered from exceptional causes, such as the short cotton crops and the damage done by the frost to the orange crop in Florida, but on the whole there was a marked recovery in 1895, as compared with 1894, although not sufficient to bring the earnings up to what might be considered a normal point prior to that year.

Imports and Exports.

Imports and exports.

The value of the total imports of merchandise into the United States showed an increase of about 125,000,000 dol. (or 25,000,000*l.*) in 1895, as compared with 1894, while the value of the exports seems to have been as nearly as possible the same in those 2 years.

The excess of silver exports over the imports of the same metal is given as about 30,000,000 dol., and of gold as about 70,500,000 dol., or 10,000,000 dol. less than in 1894.

Money Market.

New York money market.

During the year 1895 there was no such accumulation of currency in the banks as had been the case in 1894.

NEW YORK.

The surplus reserve was at its highest point on January 26 and at the lowest on March 30, the figures being respectively 45,880,450 dol. (about 9,200,000*l.*) and 13,413,450 dol. (about 2,700,000*l.*).

The rates for loans on the Stock Exchange were higher than in 1894, reaching 3 per cent., and on one occasion 5 per cent. at the beginning of March. In the last few days of December there was a panic on the Stock Exchange and loans were quoted at any figure up to 50 and even 100 per cent. The discount rates for good commercial bills having 60 to 90 days to run varied between 2½ and 5 per cent. reaching 6 per cent. at the end of December.

The following table shows the position of the New York Clearing House Banks at different periods of the year, the rate of conversion being 5 dol. to the 1*l*.

New York banks.

TABLE showing the Position of the New York Clearing House Banks during the Year 1895.

Week ending—	Loans.	Deposits.	Specie.	Legal Tenders.	Reserve to Deposits.	Surplus Reserve.
	£	£	£	£	Per cent.	£
January 5 ...	98,678,000	110,569,600	15,173,400	19,641,000	31·48	7,172,400
February 2 ...	98,069,100	109,393,000	16,311,000	18,387,500	31·71	7,350,300
March 2 ...	96,841,000	105,688,100	13,918,500	18,114,400	30·30	5,610,900
April 6 ...	96,087,700	100,164,500	12,894,300	14,932,900	27·78	2,786,000
May 4 ...	96,982,500	105,399,600	13,945,600	17,851,000	30·16	5,446,700
June 1 ...	100,509,400	113,246,000	14,128,200	22,427,500	32·28	8,244,200
July 6 ...	102,720,900	113,974,700	12,899,300	22,029,100	30·65	6,434,800
August 3 ...	101,865,400	114,861,000	13,095,000	23,803,700	32·13	8,183,400
September 7 ...	103,673,100	115,371,100	12,885,400	22,926,700	31·04	6,969,400
October 5 ...	102,040,500	108,099,900	12,187,600	18,111,700	28·04	3,294,300
November 2 ...	100,138,400	105,972,500	12,841,700	17,170,300	28·32	3,519,000
December 7 ...	97,964,000	104,337,300	13,474,400	16,668,800	28·88	4,058,800
,, 28 ...	95,693,300	100,218,000	13,422,800	14,819,600	28·18	3,188,000

The surplus reserve represents the excess over 25 per cent. of the deposits, and the returns give the averages of each week, not the actual figures for the day mentioned.

In 1894 the maximum of deposits was 119,021,000*l.*, and the minimum 103,704,000*l.*; the maximum of the surplus reserve 22,324,600*l.*, and the minimum 7,153,800*l.*

The New York Clearing House returns show an increase of 22·3 per cent. as compared with 1894, but, with the exception of that year, the total is the smallest for 10 years; the figures are 29,841,796,924 dol., or about 5,968,359,385*l.*, in 1895; and 24,387,807,020 dol., or about 4,877,561,404*l.*, in 1894.

New York Clearing House returns.

The following table shows that the increase is most marked in the three last quarters of the year, that is to say after the contract made by the Government with a syndicate for the supply of gold to the Treasury:—

(2204)

UNITED STATES.

Year.	1st Quarter.	2nd Quarter.	3rd Quarter.	4th Quarter.	Total.
	\multicolumn{5}{c}{In Thousands.}
1895	Dollars. 6,499,855 / £ 1,299,971	Dollars. 7,688,165 / £ 1,537,633	Dollars. 7,217,060 / £ 1,443,412	Dollars. 8,436,717 / £ 1,687,343	Dollars. 29,841,797 / £ 5,968,359
1894	Dollars. 5,938,415 / £ 1,187,683	Dollars. 6,010,034 / £ 1,202,007	Dollars. 5,580,060 / £ 1,116,012	Dollars. 6,859,298 / £ 1,371,860	Dollars. 24,387,807 / £ 4,877,562

Clearings outside New York. The clearings outside of New York amounted to a little over 23,506,000,000 dol., or about 4,701,500,000*l.*, and while these figures only show an increase of about 10½ per cent. the total is the largest on record except that for the year 1892. Here, again, the increase for the first quarter of the year was a little over 5 per cent., and 11½, 12½, and 11½ per cent. in the other three quarters.

Sterling exchange. Sterling exchange in London was higher than in 1894. The following table gives the posted rates, highest and lowest, for each month in the year, these being, however, as a rule, fractionally higher than the rates at which the bulk of business is done:—

TABLE showing the Posted Rates of Sterling Exchange for the Year 1895.

Month.		At 60 Days.	At Sight.
January	lowest	4·88½	4·89½
	highest	4·89½	4·90½
February	lowest	4·87½	4·89
	highest	4·89	4·90
March	lowest	4·88	4·89¼
	highest	4·89	4·90½
April	lowest	4·88½	4·90
	highest	4·89½	4·90½
May	lowest	4·86½	4·87½
	highest	4·89	4·90½
June	lowest	4·88	4·89
	highest	4·89½	4·90½
July	lowest	4·89	4·90
	highest	4·90	4·91
August	lowest	4·89	4·90
	highest	4·90	4·91
September	lowest	4·88	4·89
	highest	4·90	4·91
October	lowest	4·87	4·88
	highest	4·88½	4·89½
November	lowest	4·88	4·90
	highest	4·88½	4·90
December	lowest	4·88	4·89½
	highest	4·89½	4·91

NEW YORK

Under ordinary circumstances the rate for bills payable on demand, which admits of the export of gold from New York to London, is about 4 dol. 88 c. for bars and 4 dol. 89 c. for coin, and the rate at which gold can be imported without loss is about 4 dol. 83½ c.

The rate of exchange adopted in this report is the London Stock Exchange rate of 5 dol. to the 1*l*. {Rate adopted in this report.}

On the Stock Exchange the sales amounted to 66,583,232 shares, as compared with 49,075,032 shares in 1894, and thus showed a considerable improvement, although the volume of business was still considerably below the average of the former 10 years. The most active months were May and September, and, as noted above, a panic occurred at the latter end of December. {Stock Exchange.}

On the Cotton Exchange there was increased activity and a good deal of speculation for the rise consequent on reports of a short crop. {Cotton Exchange.}

The transactions on the Produce Exchange also showed a considerable increase, which occurred mainly in the second quarter of the year, when a rise occurred in the price of wheat owing to the damage suffered by the winter crop. {Produce Exchange.}

The following taken from tables prepared by Messrs. R. G. Dun and Co. show the number of commercial failures in this Consular district in 1895 as compared with 1894:— {Failures.}

	Number of Failures.		Amount of Liabilities.	
	1895.	1894.	1895.	1894.
			£	£
New York	1,940	1,976	9,045,107	7,371,645
Connecticut	254	253	488,596	364,230
New Jersey	182	212	722,500	670,350
Rhode Island	202	187	754,280	296,120
Delaware	68	61	92,020	187,360
Whole of United States	13,197	13,885	34,639,212	34,598,600

The largest proportion of these failures occurred in the last quarter of the year, and the considerable increase in the liabilities shown in the State of New York cannot be attributed to the failure of banking concerns in consequence of the panic, inasmuch as the total liabilities for the whole year in respect of banks which failed were only 529,436*l*. in New York and 233,305*l*. in Rhode Island. Taking the whole of the United States there is remarkably little difference between the two years as regards the number of failures, the amount of liabilities, or the amount of assets, which were 24,204,307*l*. in 1895 and 24,250,227*l*. in 1894, or about 70 per cent. in each case.

In his report for the fiscal year ended September 30, 1895, the Superintendent of Banks of the State of New York shows that the Banking Department of the State has the absolute supervision of banks of discount and deposit, individual bankers, {State banks of deposit and discount.}

UNITED STATES.

Legislation.

saving banks, trust companies, savings and loan associations, foreign mortgage companies, and safe deposit companies, in fact that the jurisdiction of the Banking Department is now extended by law to all moneyed corporations except insurance companies.

He enumerates the more recent amendments to the Banking Law as follows :—Conferring on the Superintendent of Banks the power to take possession of a bank whenever in his judgment and from an examination made it appeared to be unsafe and inexpedient for it to continue business; requiring banks of deposit and discount to keep a reserve of at least 15 per cent. in cities of 800,000 inhabitants or over, and 10 per cent. in other cities or villages; limiting loans to any person, company, &c., to one-fifth part of the capital stock and surplus; requiring directors to own at least 1,000 dol. in value of the stock of a bank with a capital of 50,000 dol. or over, and 500 dol. worth in a bank with a capital of less than that amount; requiring all unclaimed dividends and deposits amounting to 50 dol. or over, and which have remained unclaimed for 5 years, to be published in an official paper at Albany at least once a week for 6 weeks.

The following amendments to the banking law were adopted in 1895. Prohibiting any officer, director, clerk, or agent of a bank from borrowing of the corporation any sum of money without the consent and approval of a majority of the board of directors or trustees; prohibiting banks from lending or discounting on the security of the shares of their own capital stock, or from purchasing or holding any such shares, unless this be necessary to prevent loss upon a debt previously contracted in good faith.

Requiring that before a dividend can be declared, one-tenth part of the profits earned since the last dividend shall be credited to surplus funds until the same shall amount to 20 per cent. of the bank's capital; requiring that all the capital stock of a bank shall be paid up before it commences business. The legislature also prohibited any savings bank being located in the same room, or in any room communicating with any bank of discount and deposit or national banking association, and provided that it should not be lawful for a majority of the board of trustees of savings banks to belong to the board of directors of any one bank or national banking association. In another part of his report the superintendent mentions that eleven new banks with a total capital of 188,000*l.* were organised, and four with a capital of about 61,300*l.* were closed, one for insolvency, and the other three by means of voluntary liquidation.

Number.

Capital.

Resources and liabilities.

The total capital employed by the banking establishments in the State on October 1, 1895, was about 6,624,000*l.*, showing an increase for the year of a little over 120,000*l.*, and the resources and liabilities about 60,650,000*l.*, showing an increase of about 6,350,000*l.* The report concludes with a repetition of the recommendation made last year that the legal tender and Treasury notes be retired by the issue of long term bonds at a low rate of interest.

NEW YORK.

The only indebtedness of the State of New York is the loan recently authorised for the enlargement of the canals. The amount for which authority has been given is 9,000,000 dol., but only about 2,000,000 dol. (400,000*l*.) has been negotiated at present. The tax rate for the present fiscal year 1895–6 is 3 dol. 24 c. per 1,000, as compared with 2 dol. 18 c. in 1894–95.

Debt of State of New York.

The position of the funded and temporary debt of the City of New York on December 31, 1895, as compared with December 31, 1894, is shown below:—

New York City debt.

	December 31, 1895.		December 31, 1894.	
	Currency.	Sterling.	Currency.	Sterling.
	Dollars.	£	Dollars.	£
Funded debt	185,588,597	..	173,991,081	..
Sinking fund	75,703,087	..	69,912,260	..
Net funded debt	109,885,510	21,977,102	104,078,820	20,815,764
Temporary debt	2,564,511	512,902	1,699,034	339,807

The valuations for the year 1895 were, real estate, 1,646,028,655 dol.; personal estate residents, 250,620,354 dol.; non-residents, 37,955,233 dol.; shareholders of banks, 82,343,420 dol.; a total of 2,016,947,662 dol., equal to about 403,389,533*l*., as compared with about 400,670,000*l*. in 1894. The total taxes were 38,403,761 dol. (7,680,752*l*.), as compared with 35,659,000 dol. (7,132,000*l*.) in 1894, and the rate of taxation 1·91 per cent. on the assessed valuations of real and personal estate, and 1·7278 per cent. on the assessed valuation of the personal estate of such corporations, &c., as are subject to local taxation thereon; the rates for 1894 were 1·79 and 1·585 per cent. respectively.

Valuation.

Trade and Commerce.

The coal companies no longer publish official statistics of the output, but it is understood that it amounted to about 43,000,000 tons in 1895 as compared with about 41,400,000 tons in 1894 and about 43,100,000 tons in 1893.

Coal trade.

The average prices were lower than in 1894, and in consequence of the inactivity of the market, stocks tended to increase.

At the beginning of 1895 the prices of iron and steel were extremely low, they commenced to show maintained improvement in April, and from May up to the middle of September the advance was rapid and continuous, then a decline set in which, however, did not carry prices down to the low level at which they had started.

Iron and steel.

Bessemer pig-iron and Bessemer steel billets, which are the largest factors in this trade, showed the greatest fluctuations.

Bessemer pig-iron, January 3, per ton, 9 dol. 85 c.;

September 12, highest, 17 dol. 25 c.; December 26, 11 dol. 25 c. Bessemer steel billets, January 3, per ton, 14 dol. 80 c.; September 12, highest, 25 dol.; December 26, 16 dol.

Comparative prices of staple commodities.

The prices of staple commodities advanced sharply in many instances during 1895, and then to a considerable extent fell off again, the highest quotations being about the middle four months of the year.

Comparing the quotations of 104 staple commodities on January 2, 1896, with those ruling about January 1, 1895, it is found that 59 are higher, compared with April 1, 1895, only 56 are higher, with July 1, 1895, only 48 are higher, but compared with October 1, 1895, there are 51 higher.

From a table published in Bradstreets, giving quarterly quotations of these 104 articles for the past 5 years, it appears that comparing prices with what they were 5 years ago 24 out of these 104 are higher and 78 lower, compared with January, 1892, there are 34 articles higher and 68 lower as compared with January, 1893, there are 22 articles higher and 38 lower when the comparison is made with January, 1894.

Silk.

The value of the imports of silk manufactures at the port of New York in 1895 was about 5,464,600*l.*, as compared with about 4,457,000*l.* in 1894 and 6,500,000*l.* in 1893. The imports of silk piece-goods amounted to about 3,020,000*l.*, a considerable increase on 1894, and much about the same as in 1893; that of velvets also increased and was nearly equal to the average of former years, but as regards other articles, although the values, as a rule, are above those of 1894 they are below the average of former years. The imports of raw material, viz., raw silk, waste silk, noils, and pierced cocoons at all parts of the United States again increased, the total being 11,070,941 lbs., valued at about 6,240,000*l.*, compared with 9,088,389 lbs., valued at about 5,040,000*l.* in 1894.

Textile manufactures.

The year 1895 was a prosperous one for the majority of the firms engaged in the manufacture of textile fabrics.

Several of the cotton mills have been making extensions or repairs, and in the woollen manufacturing industry the number of new mills constructed was larger in 1895 than in 1894, and a large quantity of antiquated and worn out machinery was replaced by that of the newest and most approved construction.

Effects of the new tariff.

The new tariff came into force in August, 1894, and its effects upon importation up to June 30, 1895, were summed up by the appraiser of the port of New York in the following sense:—

Leather.

Importations of leather show a decrease, probably in consequence of the development and improvement of American production.

Optical goods. Musical instruments. Fancy goods. China and glass. Paintings. Books, &c.

Optical goods, musical instruments, and fancy goods show an increase of from 10 to 15 per cent.; china and glass show only a moderate increase. The importations of paintings increased largely after they were placed on the free list, and there was a sensible increase in the importation of books, lithographs, and stationery, which might be attributable to renewed business activity as well as to the reduction in duty. The increase in silk goods was very large, and there was a considerable increase in woollen dress goods, cotton and woollen hosiery, and heavy woollens. Linen and cotton showed an increase of 75 per cent., principally in linens, cotton, and yarn; on the other hand burlaps and grain bags showed no perceptible increase although they are admitted free. Parts of bicycles, such as lamps and saddles, were largely imported, but there were very few finished bicycles imported, the manufacture in America being extremely large.

Silk. Woollen dress goods. Hosiery. Linen. Bicycles.

Metal parts of umbrellas such as ribs showed a falling-off caused partly by the increase in duty and partly by the increased manufacture in the United States.

Metal parts of umbrellas.

The custom-house tariff of the United States is for the most part an ad valorem tariff, comparatively few articles being liable to a specific duty, and in the Act of Congress of June 10, 1890, which came into force on August 1, 1890, and which is still the law on the subject, provision is made for declarations as to "market value" by the consignee, importer, or agent; or by the owner in cases where the merchandise has been actually purchased; or by the manufacturer or owner in cases where the merchandise has not been actually purchased. Section 10 provides that it shall be the duty of the appraisers of the United States to ascertain or estimate by all reasonable ways and means in their power the actual market value and wholesale price of the merchandise at the time of exportation to the United States in the principal markets of the country from which it has been exported, and this irrespective of any invoice, or affidavit, or statement of cost, or cost of production.

Customs tariff. Ad valorem duties.

Importers should bear in mind that, although they may export to this country parcels of goods which they may have bought cheap, as being out of fashion, or for one reason or another, and may declare the actual price they paid for them, that price will not be accepted by the appraisers as a basis for taxation. Further than this, where a contract has been made for the supply of a certain class of goods by instalments over a certain term at a fixed rate irrespective of the fluctuations of the market, the price agreed upon furnishes, as it were, the irreducible minimum, but should the value rise, such increased value must be declared as the basis of taxation for each consignment received while the higher price rules. Section 11 of the Law lays down that when the actual market value of any article cannot be ascertained to the satisfaction of the appraising officer: "The appraiser or appraisers shall use all available means to ascertain the cost of production at the time of exportation to the United States and at the place of manufacture, such cost of production to include cost of materials and of fabrication, all general expenses covering each and every outlay of whatsoever nature incident to such production; together with the expense of preparing and putting up such merchandise ready for shipment, and an addition of 8 per cent. upon the total cost as thus ascertained." At first sight it would appear that articles manufactured solely for the

American market would come under this rule for valuation, such, however, is not the case if competing firms manufacture similar goods for their home market as well as for the United States and other countries. The Supreme Court of the United States decided (in the Cliquot champagne case) that the market value for goods not sold in the open markets abroad could be established by comparison with the value of similar goods which were so sold. The principle is that the requirements of Section 11 of the Customs Administrative Act of June 10, 1890, can only be resorted to in cases where it is impossible to establish the market value for such merchandise as sold in wholesale quantities in the country from whence exported.

If the appraised value of goods imported exceeds the value declared on entry by more than 10 per cent., then in addition to the duty a fine is levied of 2 per cent. of the appraised value for every 1 per cent. by which the appraised value exceeds the declared value; if the appraised value exceeds the value declared on entry by more than 40 per cent. the entry may be held to be fraudulent and the goods may be confiscated.

The whole question of market value has been a good deal agitated of late in consequence of the action of the Customs Textile Association, who have been carrying on a campaign against undervaluations where, in their opinion, the invoices did not reflect the rise in raw materials. On the one hand, it is stated that domestic manufacturers and the people they employ have suffered from the undervaluation of imported goods, but on the other side, statistics are quoted to show that imports of wool and the consumption of native raw material in 1895 exceeded those of 1894, and in addition woollen mills have for the most part been running up to their full capacity, and wages have been voluntarily increased. It would appear that in disputed cases the customs officials take the opinions of reputable importers of the same class of goods who do not know on whose invoice they are pronouncing. The Supreme Court holds the general appraiser to be the expert arbitrator between the Government and the importer. There has been some talk of forming an Importers' Protective Association.

Review of the Freight Market.

Business in general.

Taking the business in general which has offered for vessels from America, the year 1895 can scarcely be said to have shown much improvement on 1894.

Grain freights.

The year commenced with extremely low rates of freight in consequence of a short crop of maize and an absence of demand for American wheat, and continued in the same way till the autumn when the very heavy crop of maize harvested caused a good demand for tonnage, and rates hardened. At the close of the year they stood at 3s. to 3s. 3d. per quarter. Wheat contributed but little to this advance as the demand fell off in consequence of the high price asked. There was a large surplus stock of grain at the end of the year, and a prospect of better rates of freight after the re-opening of navigation on the canals.

There has been a very large increase of shipments, not of maize alone, but also of general merchandise from Newport News and Norfolk, which ports have profited mainly at the expense of New York. This diversion has been caused, to a great extent, by the difference in the railway rates amounting to 2 to 3 c. per 100 lbs. in favour of Philadelphia, Baltimore, and the two ports mentioned as compared with New York; provisions and flour have also been diverted in this way to ports which had not received shipments of this nature before, and the regular lines of vessels in New York have been the principal sufferers.

Cotton freights ruled at about the same rates as in 1894, but less cotton than usual was shipped owing to the small and late crops. *Cotton.*

Cotton and grain have been carried by steamer only.

The shipments of petroleum in tank steamers has taken almost all the European business away from sailing vessels, they maintain, however, some of the export business of petroleum in boxes for the East Indies, China, and Japan at gradually declining rates in competition with Russian oil from Batoum. *Petroleum.*

The Standard Oil Company ships all the petroleum it controls to the exclusion of independent shippers. Rates of freight have ruled low, and there does not seem much prospect of an advance.

Timber has been largely carried by steamers, although sailing vessels have had a share in this business. The rates of freight for timber, as well as for naval stores, have remained practically the same as last year. *Timber.*

There has been a fair business in deals from the British Colonies and sailing vessels have had a slight preference over steamers in consequence of their taking smaller cargoes, and giving more favourable terms as regards lay days.

During the sugar season the principal amount of the sugar produced in Cuba was carried in steamers which obtained fairly remunerative rates, but owing to the troubles on that island there is likely to be very little export this year. *Sugar.*

Cattle shipments were comparatively small during 1895 owing to the high prices prevailing in the West in the spring. All the cattle exported were carried by vessels of the regular lines, but it seems probable that during the present year more freight of this class will be offering, and that vessels of the regular lines will not be able to provide all the room that will be required. *Cattle.*

Public Works.

The report of the Superintendent of Public Works has not yet been published.

At the election held in November, 1894, in the State of New York there was a considerable majority of votes in favour of im- *Canal improvements.*

proving the canals in such a manner as the legislature should provide by law, and in his Message at the beginning of 1895 the Governor strongly advocated canal improvement. He pointed out that the Erie Canal was begun more than three-quarters of a century ago, and had been a prime feature in the establishment and maintenance of the commercial eminence of the port of New York; that when it was first constructed it had no competition, but that it now had to compete with five of the most perfect trunk line systems of railroad in the world, and that whereas these had made steady and rapid progress with improved methods and inventions, the system of the canal had scarcely been changed, and as a consequence tonnage had shown a marked decrease during the last few years.

A bill for deepening and widening the Erie, Champlain, and Oswego was prepared, approved by the Executive Canal Committee and passed by the legislature. This again had to be submitted to the popular vote in November, and at one of the meetings held in favour of the measure, it was recalled that by a vote taken in 1882, all tolls on the canals had been abolished, but that up to 1883 the total cost of the Erie, Champlain, and Oswego Canals had been under 98,000,000 dol., and the receipts during the same period had been nearly 132,000,000 dol. The law was accepted by a large majority of the voters, it provides for an appropriation of 9,000,000 dol. (1,800,000*l*.), of which 4,000,000 dol. (800,000*l*.) would be immediately available, and the money is to be furnished to the State Department of Public Works at such times and in such amounts as may be required for construction purposes.

Canal transport between New York and Cleveland.

A system of transportation between New York and Cleveland, Ohio, was introduced last year with a view to equalising rates as between Cleveland and Buffalo. The difference in the railway charges from Buffalo and from Cleveland to New York was 16 c., and the difference to Chicago only 6 c., the railroads saying that they were forced to this by the competition of the Erie Canal. Hence came the idea of using the Erie Canal for Cleveland as well as for Buffalo, and operations are likely to be carried on during the present year on a larger scale than in 1895. The West bound freight will be general merchandise, and in these trips the boats will come into competition with the railways, but East bound they will carry almost entirely grain that has heretofore been sent to Montreal and ports other than New York.

Harlem River Ship Canal.

The Harlem River Ship Canal was opened on June 17, 1895. It is a cutting which connects Long Island Sound with the Hudson River, and it had been under consideration and in progress since 1873. The new channel, which at the time of opening was 10 feet deep, is intended to be 18 feet in depth at mean low water when completed, and will have a breadth varying from 350 to 400 feet. The distance in transit from the North River to the Sound will be reduced by from 10 to 12 miles.

Proposed canal across New Jersey.

In 1892 the New York Board of Trade and Transportation

passed a resolution that the members from the State should urge upon Congress the appropriation of a sum of not less than 25,000 dol. for an examination, survey and report upon a 20 foot navigable channel between Raritan Bay and the Delaware River, in view of the national importance that the Atlantic and Gulf Coast waterway should be developed to its fullest extent as a strategic and defensive measure, and for commercial purposes. Similar resolutions were adopted by the Trades League of Philadelphia, the Boards of Trade of Trenton, Camden, New Brunswick, Long Branch, and Asbury Park, all in New Jersey, as well as by the Franklin Institute and Manufacturers' Club of Philadelphia. Eventually the matter was taken up by the city Councils of Philadelphia, who appointed a Canal Commission, and appropriated 10,000 dol. for the purpose of collecting the necessary data upon which to base a reliable estimate of the cost of such a canal. The reports of the engineers employed contains estimates for two sizes of canal, one 96 feet wide at the bottom, 150 feet at the water surface, and 20 feet deep in the centre for vessels not exceeding 18 feet draught, the cost being a trifle over 14,500,000 dol., or nearly 3,000,000*l.* sterling; the other would be 100 feet wide at the bottom, 184 feet at the water surface, and 28 feet deep for vessels not exceeding 26 feet draught, the cost of which is estimated at over 24,000,000 dol., or not far from 5,000,000*l.* sterling. The distance saved would be about 184 miles, or 67 per cent. of the whole distance. The consulting engineer in his report states that the water supply of the Delaware is undoubtedly sufficient; he estimates that the probable traffic would be 5,000,000 tons per annum, and that to cover operating expenses and pay 5 per cent. would require tolls of 20 c. per ton for the 20 foot canal, and 30 c. for the 28 foot canal; he is in favour of the wider canal, but points out that before any canal can be put in operation, the approaches to it will require improvement; these consist of about 27 miles on the Delaware River, and from 7 to 15 miles on the Raritan River and Bay, the distance depending on the depth adopted for the canal.

The consulting engineer remarks that it has been impossible as yet to make the necessary systematic studies in connection with these approaches, and that the improvements must necessarily be carried out by the National Government, who would only undertake the work on plans and estimates made by their own engineer.

The Canal Commission reported in June, 1895, that they were not prepared at present to offer any recommendation on the reports of the experts, but they suggested that they be authorised to continue the study of the subject.

Railroads.

During the year 1895 the total tonnage of all classes of merchandise sent westward from New York City by rail was 1,446,495 tons of 2,000 lbs.; that received from or west of

Railroad traffic.

UNITED STATES.

Buffalo, Salamanca, Pittsburg, Bellaire, &c., amounted to 4,585,745 tons. The railroads carrying these goods are the New York Central and Hudson River; Erie; Pennsylvania; Baltimore and Ohio; West Shore: Delaware, Lackawanna, and Western; Lehigh Valley; and New York, Ontario, and Western.

The amounts show an increase, as compared with the figures in 1894, namely, 1,335,926 tons sent, and 3,571,318 tons received; they are also higher than those of 1893, but below the amount carried in 1892.

Vital statistics. Vital statistics of New York City for the years 1895–94 are as follows:—

	Number. 1895.	Number. 1894.
Births*	53,731	55,636
Still-births*	3,372	
Marriages*	20,612	17,388
Deaths	43,420	41,175

*· Returns for 1895 incomplete.

Of the deaths reported, 18,221 were of children under 5 years of age.

Cause of Death.	Number. 1895.	Number. 1894.
Small-pox	10	154
Measles	793	584
Scarlet fever	468	541
Diphtheria	1,634	2,359
Croup	342	511
Whooping cough	496	..
Typhoid fever	322	326
Diarrhœal diseases	6,047	2,996
Puerperal fever	218	..
Cancer	1,030	..
Phthisis	5,205	4,658
Congenital debility	2,670	..
Diseases of nervous system	3,429	..
Heart diseases	2,297	2,170
Bronchitis	1,636	1,329
Pneumonia	5,751	4,725
Diseases of digestive organs	3,181	..
Bright's disease	2,019	2,479
Acute nephritis	678	..
Accident	2,045	
Homicide	76	1,780
Suicide	376	

The estimated population on July 1, 1895, was 1,879,195, and the death-rate for the year is given as 23·11, as compared with 21·05 in 1894.

Immigration.

The immigration returns show a decided increase in the numbers, as compared with 1894, but they are considerably lower than in 1893, the numbers being 229,370 in 1895, 167,665 in 1894, and 352,885 in 1893. The countries from which they came and their destination are noted below:—

Country.	Male.	Female.	Total 1895.	Total 1894.
	Number.	Number.	Number.	Number.
Great Britain	10,329	6,263	16,592	13,339
Ireland	11,254	15,735	26,989	20,476
Austria-Hungary	26,046	16,139	42,185	19,054
Belgium	546	353	899	640
Denmark	1,913	1,564	3,477	3,661
France	1,503	1,084	2,587	2,074
Germany	13,324	11,221	24,545	25,818
Greece	1,077	36	1,113	1,035
Italy	29,744	12,527	42,271	36,723
Netherlands	724	505	1,229	1,135
Norway	4,229	2,766	6,995	5,424
Portugal	637	713	1,350	1,173
Roumania	384	249	633	382
Russia	21,078	15,269	36,347	21,559
Spain	121	33	154	148
Sweden	7,465	7,794	15,259	10,367
Switzerland	1,476	968	2,444	2,207
Turkey	2,874	1,150	4,024	2,162
Other countries	238	39	277	288
Total	134,962	94,408	229,370	167,665

Destination.	Number.
North Atlantic States	182,042
South " "	2,550
North Central "	36,730
South " "	2,461
Western and Pacific States	5,587
Total	229,370

In addition to the above, 2,055 immigrants were refused—four as being insane, 1,287 as being paupers, or likely to become a public charge, and 764 as contract labourers.

Strikes.

The report of the Board of Mediation and Arbitration mentions that over 400 strikes and lock-outs occurred in the State of New York during the year ended October 31, 1895, but these

(2204)

include several of the same trade ordered successively in different workshops. Eighty only lasted a few hours, and over 200 were settled within a few days.

The number is about the same as that of the preceding year. The most serious strike was that of the men, to the number of about 6,000, employed on the 48 different lines of tramway-cars, worked by the electric trolley system in Brooklyn.

The demands of the men comprised an advance of 25 c. (or a little over 1s.) on the then existing rate of pay, viz., 2 dol. (over 8s.) a-day; and a reduction in the number of the men employed only during the busy hours of the day, and paid by the trip.

Satisfactory arrangements were made on the first day with some few of the lines, but about 4,500 men employed on 43 lines left work on January 14; on the 19th of the same month so much violence was being resorted to that the Brooklyn Militia was called out, and on the morning of the 21st they were reinforced by the 1st Brigade of the National Guard of New York. At an early period of the strike the men showed a disposition to abandon the demand for increased pay, and partial settlements were made from time to time, but it was not till February 16 that the strike was declared off.

In the report of the Board of Mediation and Arbitration, issued early in February, the strike is said to be the direct consequence of the inability of the officers of the roads on the one hand, and of the executive officers of the men employed, and belonging to District Assembly No. 75, Knights of Labour, on the other hand, to renew for 1895 the contract they had made for 1894, with certain amendments proposed by the men.

The Board recommended legislation, with a view to making strikes of this nature impossible in the future, by regulating the relations between corporations created by the State to serve the public and the men employed by them.

RETURN of all Shipping at the Port of New York during the Year 1895.

ENTERED.

Countries.	Steam. Number of Vessels.	Steam. Tons.	Sailing. Number of Vessels.	Sailing. Tons.	Total. Number of Vessels.	Total. Tons.
Great Britain and colonies	1,437	2,816,052	726	381,495	2,163	3,197,547
United States	360	825,296	708	359,355	1,068	1,184,651
Germany	404	1,209,088	57	66,250	461	1,275,338
France	94	299,143	6	4,540	100	303,683
Sweden and Norway	176	96,795	49	43,240	225	140,035
Belgium	72	226,937	...	...	72	226,937
Italy	5	5,891	47	37,956	52	43,847
Netherlands	127	280,078	11	14,534	138	294,612
Austria	1	1,849	3	2,423	4	4,272
Spain	45	72,190	4	1,600	49	73,790
Denmark	25	45,820	10	7,640	35	53,460
Other European countries	22	30,575	5	3,477	27	34,052
South America	...	...	7	3,422	7	3,422
Other countries	...	...	5	3,021	5	3,021

NEW YORK.

CLEARED.

Countries.	Steam. Number of Vessels.	Steam. Tons.	Sailing. Number of Vessels.	Sailing. Tons.	Total. Number of Vessels.	Total. Tons.
Great Britain and colonies	1,345	2,708,434	822	422,604	2,167	3,131,038
United States	360	836,255	455	247,651	815	1,083,906
Germany	355	1,047,966	42	51,331	397	1,099,297
France	94	291,772	3	1,251	97	293,023
Sweden and Norway	179	97,440	57	47,751	236	145,191
Belgium	68	219,677	...	...	68	219,677
Italy	2	3,262	48	35,990	50	39,252
Netherlands	125	276,736	9	11,533	134	288,269
Austria	1	1,848	3	2,323	4	4,171
Spain	43	70,637	3	814	46	71,451
Denmark	125	276,736	9	11,533	134	288,269
Other European countries	23	31,054	7	5,777	30	36,831
South America	...	...	4	2,119	4	2,119
Other countries	...	...	4	2,757	4	2,757

RETURN of Principal Articles of Export from New York during the Years 1895-94.

Articles.		1895. Quantity.	1895. Value. £	1894. Quantity.	1894. Value. £
Agricultural implements	...	...	877,041	...	869,498
Bacon and ham	Tons	119,850	4,566,484	107,469	4,273,145
Beef—					
Fresh	,,	42,712	1,650,758	4,858	1,785,518
Canned	,,	15,612	566,911	14,658	494,889
Salted and cured	,,	17,004	441,513	18,157	471,756
Butter	,,	4,970	335,996	3,548	266,213
Cattle (live)	Number	98,288	1,935,860	160,694	3,129,404
Cheese	Tons	13,702	505,929	23,431	1,009,404
Copper	,,	48,142	1,898,633	57,542	2,395,474
Cotton—					
Raw	,,	162,349	5,249,070	179,057	5,917,275
Cloths	Yards	156,707,244	1,744,233	172,705,834	2,039,147
Flour	Barrels	4,516,145	3,325,648	6,292,106	4,629,909
Hops	Tons	7,186	313,585	5,724	377,743
Indian corn	Bushels	19,626,817	1,843,687	4,912	1,081,229
Lard	Tons	136,476	4,248,043	134,458	4,868,600
Leather	,,	15,337	1,163,226	16,540	1,100,092
Machinery	...	...	1,545,441	...	1,511,189
Oil—					
Illuminating	Gallons	421,988,543	5,398,822	475,094,530	4,206,985
Lubricating	,,	33,762,469	950,582	28,320,462	834,594
Oilcake and meal	Tons	92,473	419,605	70,732	397,730
Pork	,,	20,774	588,406	21,019	717,140
Sewing machines	...	...	554,747	...	366,292
Specie and bullion	...	...	27,990,391	...	3,142,162
The oil	Tons	28,512	1,050,537	38,666	1,630,087
Tobacco (leaf)	,,	72,522	2,776,516	69,449	2,694,618
Wheat	Bushels (of 60 lbs.)	20,339,263	2,739,782	22,913,945	2,930,037

(2204)

UNITED STATES.

Return of Principal Articles of Import into New York during the Years 1895-94.

Articles.		1895. Quantity.	1895. Value. £	1894. Quantity.	1894. Value. £
Free.					
Art works	...	...	686,037	...	...
Argols	Tons	12,760	438,224	...	...
Books	...	...	285,227	...	...
Chemicals	...	...	1,338,206	...	...
Cocoa, and shells of	Tons	11,567	554,350	...	...
Coffee	,,	236,553	15,934,519	215,996	14,861,377
Cotton (unmanufactured)	,,	5,199	255,365	...	...
Feathers and downs (crude)	...	...	413,053	...	...
Fruits	...	...	317,723	...	604,079
Gum	...	...	1,101,612	...	...
Indiarubber	Tons	17,299	3,602,982	14,755	3,041,721
Jute, manilla, and sisal grass	,,	118,069	903,487	...	...
Liquorice root	,,	32,619	238,968	...	...
Nitrate of soda	,,	75,391	488,779	...	...
Oils	...	...	531,571	...	...
Skins	...	...	5,656,595	...	2,671,223
Silk (raw)	Tons	1,456	1,703,452	1,612	1,853,071
Tea	,,	22,151	1,664,001	30,153	1,859,222
Tin, bars or pigs	,,	21,638	1,321,134	...	...
Wool	,,	38,114	1,784,630	1,409	600,000
Dutiable.					
Cheese	Tons	3,973	251,322	...	...
Chemicals	...	...	923,509	...	...
China	...	...	1,085,058	...	...
Coal-tar colours	...	...	506,984	...	...
Dry goods—					
Cotton (manufactured)	...	...	5,317,336	...	3,894,942
Silk ,,	...	...	5,578,847	...	4,655,671
Woollen ,,	...	...	9,634,406	...	3,192,262
Fish	...	...	454,774	...	415,143
Flax and hemp manufactures	...	...	3,205,712	...	...
Fruits and nuts	...	...	1,812,747	...	1,463,416
Furs (manufactured)	...	...	1,432,188	...	1,091,915
Glass	...	...	1,223,830	...	944,592
Gloves and manufactured leather	...	...	1,726,466	...	1,329,814
Jewellery and precious stones	...	...	1,401,132	...	1,305,574
Lead (pigs)	Tons	34,753	228,322	...	691,489
Linseed	Bushels	2,588,562	499,984	...	...
Metals, N.Y.S.	...	...	637,003	...	...
Paper, and manufactures of	...	...	448,189	...	...
Specie and bullion	...	...	6,571,225	...	4,134,247
Sugar	...	...	7,272,873	...	...
Tobacco (leaf)	...	...	2,257,017	7,314	2,205,708
Tin-plates	Tons	83,112	848,153	86,473	949,866
Wines and spirits	...	...	1,301,659	...	1,321,034

TABLE showing Total Value of all Articles Exported from and Imported to New York from and to Foreign Countries during the Year 1895.

Country.	Exports.	Imports.
	£	£
Great Britain and Ireland	27,185,412	21,449,669
British possessions	5,774,200	6,170,033
Germany	6,722,372	13,998,920
France and possessions	3,136,685	11,708,881
Belgium	2,933,269	1,738,623
Spain and possessions	2,023,987	7,006,184
Netherlands	3,360,146	3,465,897
United States of Colombia	432,975	839,670
Central American States	581,433	1,268,952
Italy	1,612,489	3,692,230
Brazil	2,100,613	13,800,768
China	653,640	2,099,112
Denmark and possessions	549,675	114,899
Venezuela	737,444	2,096,094
Portugal	642,545	370,238
Argentine Republic	803,871	1,189,529
Mexico	721,647	1,774,692
Hayti	934,816	471,716
Sweden and Norway	615,817	350,937
Japan	295,417	1,723,374
Chile	624,296	588,683
San Domingo	186,452	352,605
Uruguay	215,875	604,976
Austria	254,993	1,193,288
Russia	325,435	433,624
Peru	145,137	102,288
Other countries	1,107,759	16,357,483
Total	64,680,400	115,257,355

(2204)

UNITED STATES.

Port of New York.

TABLE showing Countries to and from which Specie was Imported and Exported during the Year 1895.

Country.	1895. Imports. Currency. Dollars.	1895. Imports. Sterling. £	1895. Exports. Currency. Dollars.	1895. Exports. Sterling. £	1894. Imports. Currency. Dollars.	1894. Imports. Sterling. £	1894. Exports. Currency. Dollars.	1894. Exports. Sterling. £
Great Britain	13,389,193	2,677,839	97,760,123	19,552,025	2,726,027	545,205	1,258,075	251,615
France	8,498,889	1,699,778	13,999,173	2,799,834	6,333,127	1,266,626	1,978,500	395,700
Germany	1,319,297	263,860	13,113,704	2,622,741	1,591,739	318,348	7,000	1,400
Cuba	1,505,789	301,158	9,322,955	1,864,591	4,127,937	825,587	11,766,596	2,353,319
Mexico	5,309,482	1,061,896	399	80	2,989,775	597,955	49,155	9,831
Other countries	2,833,472	566,694	5,755,603	1,151,120	2,902,631	580,526	651,485	130,297
Total	32,856,122	6,571,225	139,951,957	27,990,391	20,671,236	4,134,247	15,710,811	3,142,162

TABLE showing Shipments of Grain from the Port of New York to Great Britain and the Continent of Europe, with the Nationality of the Vessels, for the Years 1895-94.

	Steam Vessels.	Sailing Vessels.	1895. Total Number of Vessels.	1895. Total Number of Bushels.	1894. Number of Vessels.	1894. Number of Bushels.
Great Britain	492	7	499	28,509,783	494	21,007,461
Belgium	48	...	48	2,466,669	40	2,620,121
Netherlands	66	...	66	2,274,708	83	3,272,307
Germany	143	...	143	5,695,932	95	2,678,221
France	15	...	15	424,313	22	1,200,269
Portugal	16	...	16	1,266,141	22	1,530,196
Denmark	20	...	20	743,824	13	494,326
Italy	1	1	2	94,118	8	416,758
Spain	2	...	2	369,538	4	122,323
Norway	...	...	...	...	...	...
Russia	...	...	...	...	1	42,970
America	1	...	1	48,000	...	...
Austria	1	1	2	77,272	...	...
Total	805	9	814	41;970,298	782	33,384,952

The grain shipments for 1895 were as follow:—

Name of Grain.	In— Steam Vessels.	In— Sailing Vessels.	Total Quantity. 1895.	Total Quantity. 1894.
	Bushels.	Bushels.	Bushels.	Bushels.
Wheat	22,207,765	774,205	22,981,970	24,085,167
Maize	17,966,126	..	17,966,126	8,959,959
Rye	..	..	..	20,625
Oats	878,377	..	878,377	1,060
Barley	11,200	..	11,200	23,237
Buckwheat	96,723	..	96,723	173,057
Flax-seed	..	..	..	6,185
Peas	35,902	..	35,902	115,662

UNITED STATES.

Return of the Number of Seamen who have been Engaged, Discharged, Left Behind, Reported Dead, or Deserted, or who have been Relieved at the British Consulate-General, New York, and showing the Total Number of British and Foreign Sailors who were Engaged, Discharged, &c., from British Ships, with the Amount of Wages paid at the Consulate to Seamen on discharge from their Ships, and from Hospital or Jail; and also showing the Number of New Agreements entered into during the Year 1895.

		Seamen.									Wages.			Agreements.
Engaged.	Discharged.	Left Behind.			Dead.			Deserted.	Relieved.	Nationality.		Total Number of Seamen.	Paid on Discharge from Vessels.	Paid on Discharge from Hospital or Jail.	Total Wages Paid.	Number Opened.
		In Hospital.	In Jail.	Total.	At Sea.	On Shore.	Total.			British.	Foreign.					
10,433	8,873	173	5	178	48	27	75	1,797	182	10,491	11,047	21,538	Dol. c. 409,326 90	Dol. c. 3,777 8	Dol. c. 413,103 98	165

Providence, R.I.

Mr. Vice-Consul Stockwell reports as follows:—

The year 1895 has brought prosperity generally to both capital and labour however invested or directed, and to all dependent upon either. In any year before the active campaign that may result in a change of Government officials, and of administration of public affairs, there is less political disturbance, each party holding the dogs of controversy that affects legislation and business in leash till after election.

There was an exception in 1895 when the cry of war was heard in the land, but the reaction to sense and reason came quickly, and the tide of business set in even more strongly than before.

The snug commonwealth of Rhode Island has applied herself rigidly during the year to mending home interests, and has her reward in the increase of capital, employed and well-paid labour, and in general prosperity and contentment. Industries, generally, have been prosecuted throughout all working days, and in some cases the night has been encroached upon that the supply might keep pace with the demand.

Money. The lowest rate of discount at the banks at the beginning of the year was $3\frac{1}{2}$ per cent., but after April the rate was 6 per cent., and so continued till the end of the year. The bank clearings in 1894 amounted to 224,445,400 dol., and in 1895 the amount was 280,809,700 dol. The clearings in 1895 were higher than in any year since 1882, with the exception of 1885, when they amounted to 290,908,500 dol.

Tonnage. Duties. Total number of vessels hailing from this port: Sailing, 82, tonnage, 10,299·98; steam, 48, tonnage, 21,983·21. Total amount of duties collected during the year, 272,337 dol. 13 c.

Cotton manufactures. The cotton manufacturer has nothing to complain of in a review of the business of 1895. Rhode Island has 93 cotton mills, and during the year all have been in operation full time, and some of them have been driven overtime. The price of cotton has ranged from $5\frac{35}{100}$ c. to $9\frac{63}{100}$ c., closing at $7\frac{39}{100}$ c. During October and November about 6,000,000 dol. went south to exchange for cotton.

Wool and woollens. The woollen manufacturer has returned to a state of cheerfulness and satisfaction. For two years or longer the woollen business was discouraging. During the year all woollen establishments in the State, 34 in number, have been in continuous operation, and some of them have kept their machinery going 20 hours a day. The price of wool closed 1 to 3 c. higher than at the opening of the year. The business of the year has shown a great development of the manufacture of worsteds. Worsteds make the popular woollen fabric now demanded by the people.

Jewellery. The jewellery business has been limping along on one leg for several years, but during the year 1895 it may be said that it has used the other leg, carefully, perhaps, and made satisfactory progress. In the City of Providence there are about 200 jewellery establishments, and most of them have had more orders than usual. The usual period of activity covers only about six months of the year, but in 1895 the time was extended.

Wages. Wages have not changed during the year, and no strikes of any importance have occurred. As noted elsewhere, the cotton and woollen operatives have had steady employment, and have not attempted to quarrel with their bread and butter. In the building trades, wages remain unchanged, and employment has kept all industrious mechanics busy.

New buildings. During the year 861 new buildings were erected in the City of Providence at a cost of 4,876,995 dol., and improvements in old buildings were made at a cost of 335,450 dol., making a total of 5,212,445 dol. as the cost of new structures and parts of structures.

Fire loss. The loss by fire in the City of Providence during the year 1895 amounted to 139,441 dol., and the insurance paid amounted to 105,327 dol.

Terminal facilities. The plan of terminal facilities for railways, mentioned in this report every year for five years or more, has not yet been fully carried out, but it is in progress, and in another year the City of Providence may have a railway station and approaches second to none in the United States.

Public improvements. The new State House in the Providence capital (Rhode Island has another capital at Newport), to cost 2,000,000 dol., and to be built of marble, has not yet arisen above the foundation, but in five years it is expected that the structure will be completed. A new normal school building, a new high-school building, in addition to the one now in use, and a new grammar school building are in process of erection.

Census. A census of the State is taken every five years alternately by the United States Government and by the State authorities. The last census by the United States was made in 1890; the last census by the State, for 1895, is not yet complete. Statistics of population, however, are obtainable, while those of agriculture, the mechanic arts and industries are still in progress of compilation.

The total population of the State is 384,758, an increase of 80,474, or 26·45 per cent. since the last State census in 1885. The increase between 1875 and 1885 was 46,045, or 17·83 per cent. The population of the city of Providence is 145,472, an increase of 27,402, or 23·21 per cent. since 1885. The population of Providence county is 286,776, an increase of 66,170, or 29·99 per cent. since 1885. The population of the city of Newport is 21,537, an increase of 1,971, or 10·07 per cent. in ten years.

On June 1, 1895, there were in the State 112,860 adult males, of whom 90,556 were citizens, and 22,304 were aliens. The number of voters in the State is 86,709; of these 62,094 are native born, and 24,615 are foreign born. Since 1885 the native born have increased 11,320, and the foreign born 17,190. The number of males of military age (18 to 44) is 51,143 native born, and 34,731 foreign born. Compared with the census of 1885 there has been an increase of 9,777, or 23·64 per cent., in the native born, and 12,132, or 53·68 per cent., in the foreign born, a total increase of 21,909, or 34·25 per cent.

Since 1885 the native born population has increased 43,260, or 19·78 per cent., while the foreign born population has increased 37,214, or 43·49 per cent. The native born population represents 68·09 per cent. of the total population. In one town the native population is 97·65 per cent. In 1875 the native population of the State was 72·26 per cent., and in 1885, 71·85 per cent.

Miscellaneous Facts and Figures.

William Blackstone, first white settler in Rhode Island, 1634.
Roger Williams settled in Providence, 1636.
Area of the State, 1,054 square miles.
  „   Narragansett Bay, 246 square miles.
Greatest length of the State, 48 miles; greatest width, 37 miles.
Coast line, 400 miles.
Cities, 5.
Towns, 32.
Highest elevation above the sea, 805 feet.
  „   rate of taxation in towns, 1 dol. 20 c. per 100 dol.
Lowest   „   „   50 c. per 100 dol.
Highest   „   „ cities, 1 dol. 60 c. per 100 dol.
Lowest   „   „   92 c. per 100 dol.
Post offices in the State, 144.
Representation in Congress, 4.
Schools, 1,051.
Teachers, 1,718.
Pupils, 38,005.
Public libraries, 45.
Volumes, 186,180.
Latitude of Providence, 41° 49′ 26″.
Longitude, 71° 24′ 20″.
National banks, 59.
Capital, 20,184,000 dol.
State banks, 10.
Capital, 1,566,685 dol.
Savings banks, 38.
Depositors, 131,652.
Deposits, 63,719,419 dol. 57 c.

During the year 1895, 556 persons came to the British Vice-Consulate on business connected therewith.

UNITED STATES.

Annex A.—RETURN of Shipping at the Port of Providence during the Year 1895.

ENTERED.

Nationality.	Sailing. Number of Vessels.	Tons.
British	83	10,110
American	21	6,476
Austrian	1	526
Italian	1	539
Total	106	17,651
„ 1894	74	11,477

CLEARED.

Nationality.	Sailing. Number of Vessels.	Tons.
British	75	7,973
American	6	3,475
Total	81	11,448
„ 1894	50	6,373

Annex B.—RETURN of Principal Articles of Export from Providence during the Years 1895–94.

Articles.	Value. 1895.	1894.
	£	£
Coal	..	32
Iron	958	1,313
Provisions	..	548
Miscellaneous	..	4
Total	958	1,897

RETURN of Principal Articles of Import into Providence during the Years 1895-94.

Articles.	Value.	
	1895.	1894.
	£	£
Dry goods	48,922	29,702
Chemicals	26,506	19,313
Metals	45,220	13,545
Wool	31,628	..
Liquors	3,293	..
All others	79,726	48,748
Total	235,295	111,308

Annex C.—TABLE showing Total Value of all Articles Exported from and Imported into Providence from and to all Countries during the Years 1895-94.

Country.	Exports.		Imports.	
	1895.	1894.	1895.	1894.
	£	£	£	£
Austria	..	..	2,336	..
Belgium	..	..	1,678	4,565
British East Indies	..	..	48	..
British India	..	..	25	..
British West Indies	..	548	14,312	7,123
Canada	958	1,349	27,118	8,731
Cuba	..	..	2,813	2,723
Dutch West Indies	..	..	791	542
Egypt	..	..	35	..
England	..	..	102,729	47,215
Germany	..	..	32,781	8,241
France	..	..	19,071	11,476
Hayti	..	..	659	5,241
Ireland	..	..	123	..
Italy	..	..	4,506	7,269
Japan	..	..	924	134
Netherlands	..	..	339	4,975
Portugal	..	..	271	72
Scotland	..	..	3,536	1,860
Spain	..	..	588	..
Sweden	..	..	7,815	..
Switzerland	..	..	4,306	..
Turkey in Asia	..	..	30	..
Turkey in Europe	..	..	19	..
All others	..	..	8,441	..
Total	958	1,897	235,295	110,167

LONDON:
Printed for Her Majesty's Stationery Office,
By HARRISON AND SONS,
Printers in Ordinary to Her Majesty.
(75 7 | 96—H & S 2204)